P9-DGQ-203

INTERNATIONAL ENCYCLOPEDIA OF DANCE

INTERNATIONAL ENCYCLOPEDIA OF

DANCE

A project of Dance Perspectives Foundation, Inc.

FOUNDING EDITOR

Selma Jeanne Cohen

AREA EDITORS

George Dorris   Nancy Goldner   Beate Gordon
Nancy Reynolds   David Vaughan
Suzanne Youngerman

CONSULTANTS

Thomas F. Kelly   Horst Koegler   Richard Ralph
Elizabeth Souritz

VOLUME 6

OXFORD UNIVERSITY PRESS

New York   1998   Oxford

OXFORD UNIVERSITY PRESS

Oxford New York
Athens Auckland Bangkok Bogotá Bombay
Buenos Aires Calcutta Cape Town Dar es Salaam
Delhi Florence Hong Kong Istanbul Karachi
Kuala Lumpur Madras Madrid Melbourne
Mexico City Nairobi Paris Singapore
Taipei Tokyo Toronto Warsaw
and associated companies in
Berlin Ibadan

Published by Oxford University Press, Inc.,
198 Madison Avenue, New York, New York 10016

This work was initiated with funds granted by the
National Endowment for the Humanities,
a federal agency

Library of Congress Cataloging-in-Publication Data
International encyclopedia of dance : a project of Dance
Perspectives Foundation, Inc. / founding editor, Selma Jeanne Cohen;
area editors, George Dorris et al.; consultants, Thomas F. Kelly et al.
p. cm.
Includes bibliographical references and index.
1. Dance—Encyclopedias. 2. Ballet—Encyclopedias. I. Cohen,
Selma Jeanne, 1920-. II. Dance Perspectives Foundation.
GV1585.I586 1998 97-36562 792.6′2′03—dc21 CIP
ISBN 0-19-509462-X (set)
ISBN 0-19-512310-7 (vol. 6)

Printing (last digit): 9 8 7 6 5 4 3 2

Printed in the United States of America
on acid-free paper

S

CONTINUED

STRATE, GRANT (born 7 December 1927 in Cardston, Alberta), Canadian dancer, choreographer, and educator. Strate had just embarked on a law career when, with only rudimentary dance training, he was invited by Celia Franca to join the newly established National Ballet of Canada in 1951. Continuing his training with Franca and with Betty Oliphant, ballet mistress of the company, he was promoted to soloist rank in 1953 and soon achieved public notice as a talented character dancer. He also displayed a marked gift for administration, which enabled him to assist Franca in her responsibilities as artistic director of the company.

Strate's primary interest and primary talent, however, lay neither in performing nor in administration but in choreography. Appointed resident choreographer for the National Ballet in 1958, he served the company in that capacity for eleven years, until 1969. During his tenure he created numerous original works, some of them overtly modernistic. Among the most successful were three works set to the music of Canadian composer Harry Somers: *The Fisherman and His Soul* (1956), *Ballad* (1958), and, best known of all, *The House of Atreus* (1964). Other works that entered the National Ballet repertory included *The Willow* (1957), to music by Arthur Foote; *Antic Spring* (1960), to music by Jacques Ibert; *Triptych* (1965), to music by Mozart; *Pulcinella* (1966), to the Stravinsky score; *Studies in White* (1967), to music by Telemann; *The Arena* (1968), to music by Benjamin Britten; and *Phases* (1969), to music by Eric Satie. He also created or restaged ballets for the Studio Ballet of Antwerp, the Royal Swedish Ballet, and several Canadian modern dance companies and solo dancers, often employing Canadian composers and designers.

In 1970 Strate left the National Ballet of Canada to become founding chairman of the Dance Department at York University, Toronto, where he remained as professor until his appointment in 1978 as director of the Centre for the Arts at Simon Fraser University, Burnaby, British Columbia. During his years at York, he also played a crucial role, as founding chairman and board member of the

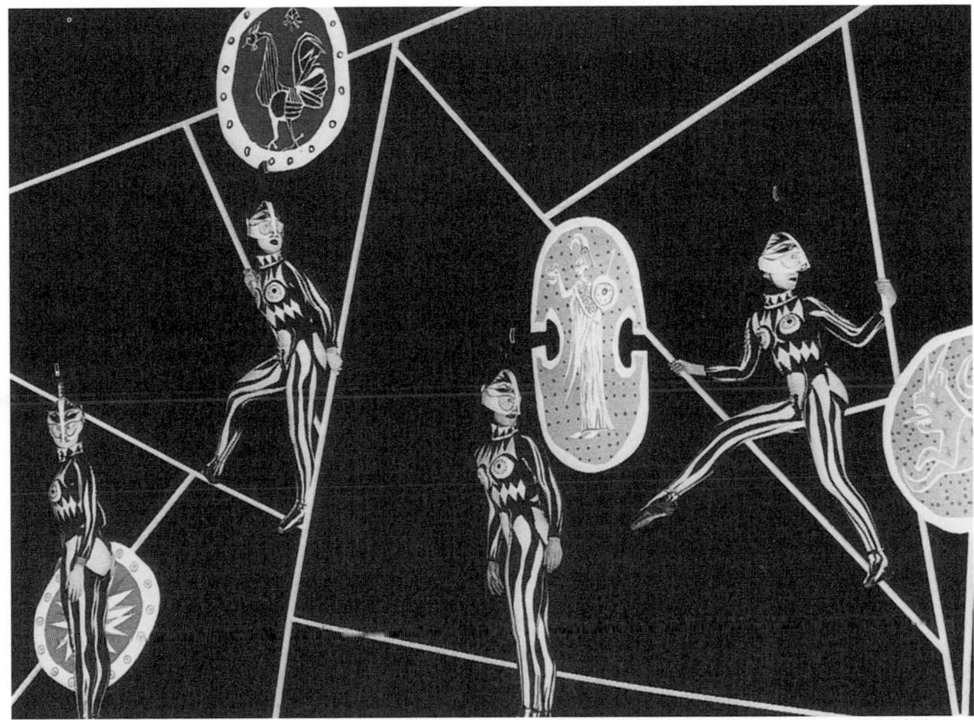

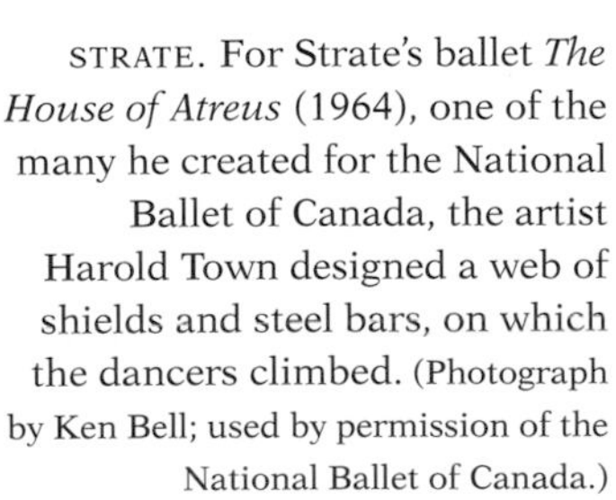

STRATE. For Strate's ballet *The House of Atreus* (1964), one of the many he created for the National Ballet of Canada, the artist Harold Town designed a web of shields and steel bars, on which the dancers climbed. (Photograph by Ken Bell; used by permission of the National Ballet of Canada.)

Dance in Canada Association from 1973 to 1978, in establishing the organization as a national service agency for the dance community. Since his retirement from his university post in 1993, Strate has remained active as an adviser to several Canadian dance companies and cultural organizations, as a guest teacher, and as an organizer of choreographic seminars. His influence on the development of the recent generation of Canadian dancers and choreographers has been profound. He was appointed to the Order of Canada in 1995 and was the recipient of the Governor General's Performing Arts Award in 1996.

BIBLIOGRAPHY

Bell, Ken, and Celia Franca. *The National Ballet of Canada: A Celebration.* Toronto, 1978.

Crabb, Michael. "Prime Mover Number One: Grant Strate and Dance in Canada." *Dance in Canada,* no. 38 (Winter 1983–1984): 15–19.

Neufeld, James. *Power to Rise: The Story of the National Ballet of Canada.* Toronto, 1996.

MICHAEL CRABB

STRAUSS FAMILY, a Viennese family of bandleaders and composers who flourished during the nineteenth century and whose name became synonymous with the popular Viennese waltz. Notable members include the father, Johann Strauss the elder, and his children, Johann Strauss the younger, Josef Strauss, and Eduard Strauss.

Johann Strauss the elder (Johann Baptist Strauss [I]; born 14 March 1804 in Vienna, died 25 September 1849 in Vienna), conductor and composer. Johann Strauss began his career as a violist in dance ensembles playing in the inns and public dance halls of Vienna. In the 1820s he and Joseph Lanner (1801–1843), who both led their ensembles on the violin, became established as the foremost dance bandleaders in Vienna when the waltz became a popular craze. They built orchestras of twenty to thirty string and wind instrumentalists—sometimes even more for special functions such as the Habsburg court balls of the 1830s and 1840s. Their compositions included not only waltzes but also galops and later quadrilles and polkas; it was the waltz, however, that spread their fame. Strauss was more ebullient in both temperament and musical style than Lanner and built on the popularity of his compositions, even taking his orchestra abroad. He performed at concerts and balls throughout Britain in 1838, Queen Victoria's coronation year, and returned there in 1849 just a few weeks before his death.

In the early nineteenth century the waltz dance program typically consisted of an ad hoc sequence of short, simple melodies. Under Lanner and Strauss, the classical waltz form became established as a set sequence of perhaps five two-part waltz sections (making ten waltz melodies in all), preceded by a short introduction and ended by a coda that recapitulated the main theme. When the introductory section became a mood-setting passage and the whole program was given a picturesque title, each waltz composition acquired an individual identity.

These traditions, established by Lanner and Strauss and practiced by others such as the Bohemian Joseph Labitzky (1802–1881) in Carlsbad and the Hungarian Joseph Gungl (1809–1889) in Berlin, were developed further by Johann Strauss's three sons. The eldest, **Johann Strauss the younger** (Johann Baptist Strauss [II], also known as the Waltz King; born 25 October 1825 in Vienna, died 3 June 1899 in Vienna), composer and conductor, is the most famous of the three sons. **Josef Strauss** (born 20 August 1827 in Vienna, died 22 July 1870 in Vienna), engineer, conductor, and composer. Josef is considered by connoisseurs of the family's music to have had the more profound talent. His introverted nature is reflected in harmonically adventurous introductions and a great emotional range in his waltz melodies. Considered to be less inspired was the youngest son, **Eduard Strauss** (born 15 March 1835 in Vienna, died 28 December 1916 in Vienna), conductor and composer.

Johann the younger and Josef produced dance music that is exceptional in transcending the constraints of dance rhythms. To the polka's regular beat they added a unique range of picturesque invention, often discreetly using special effects to give each piece individuality. No other practitioners could match their melodic invention or their abilities to tug at the heart with yearning waltz themes and to string together melodies varied in shape and mood—alternately bold, reflective, teasing, or caressing, each melody reestablishing the listener's attention with its originality. The introduction of each waltz became a miniature tone poem, giving the whole composition an elegant orchestral context that was as worthy of the concert hall as of the dance hall. It has been Johann's waltzes that have most readily captured the popular imagination. His music gained a place in the orchestral repertory unlike that of any other composer with origins in the dance hall.

Particularly celebrated are the younger Johann's waltz classics of the 1860s: "Accelerations" (1860), "Morning Papers" (1864), "By the Beautiful Blue Danube" (1867), "Artist's Life" (1867), "Tales from the Vienna Woods" (1868), and "Wine, Woman, and Song" (1869). His most famous polkas include the "Anna Polka" (1852), "Chit-Chat Polka" (1858), "In Thunder and Lightning" (1868), and the "Pizzicato Polka" (1869), which was composed with Josef.

After 1870, Johann the younger concentrated on composing operettas, establishing the distinctively Viennese operetta style built around the waltz. Other waltz composers became prominent, such as the Frenchman Émile Waldteufel (1837–1915) and the Viennese Carl Michael Ziehrer (1843–1922), but Strauss still matched them with the occasional outstanding waltz, such as "Vienna Blood" (1873), "Voices of Spring" (1883), devised as a coloratura soprano showpiece, and the majestic "Emperor Waltz" (1889). In addition, he successfully arranged waltzes on themes from his operettas, such as "1001 Nights" from *Indigo* (1871) and "Roses from the South" from *The Queen's Lace Handkerchief* (1880).

In all, the younger Johann composed some 180 waltzes, 130 polkas, 30 quick polkas or galops, 30 polka mazurkas, 80 quadrilles, and 50 marches. Besides his 15 operettas, he composed one opera, *Ritter Pázmán* (best known for its ballet music), and one full-length ballet, *Cinderella.* In the years since his death, many stage works have been created using his melodies, including the ballet scores for Léonide Massine's *Le Beau Danube* and David Lichine's *Graduation Ball.* Publication of a complete edition of the younger Johann Strauss's works in full score was begun under the imprint of Doblinger and Universal Edition of Vienna, but it has made limited progress.

[*For related discussion, see* Music for Dance, *article on* Western Music, 1800–1900.]

BIBLIOGRAPHY

Carner, Mosco. *The Waltz.* New York, 1948.

Carner, Mosco, and Max Schönherr. "Strauss." In *The New Grove Dictionary of Music and Musicians.* London, 1980.

Decsey, Ernst. *Johann Strauss.* Stuttgart, 1922.

Eisenberg, L. *Johann Strauss: Ein Lebensbild.* Leipzig, 1894.

Jacob, Heinrich E. *Johann Strauss und das Neunzehnte Jahrhundert.* Amsterdam, 1937.

Kemp, Peter. *The Strauss Family: Portrait of a Musical Dynasty.* Tunbridge Wells, Kent, 1985.

Lamb, Andrew. "Waltz." In *The New Grove Dictionary of Music and Musicians.* London, 1980.

Mailer, Franz. *Joseph Strauss: Genie wider Willen.* Vienna, 1977.

Mailer, Franz, ed. *Johann Strauss (Sohn): Leben und Werk in Briefen und Dokumenten.* Tutzing, 1983–.

Pastene, Jerome. *Three-Quarter Time: The Life and Music of the Strauss Family of Vienna.* New York, 1951.

Prawy, Marcel. *Johann Strauss: Weltgeschichte im Waltzertakt.* Vienna, 1975.

Schönherr, Max, and Karl Reinöhl. *Johann Strauss Vater: Ein Werkverzeichnis.* London, 1954.

Schönherr, Max. "Ästhetik des Walzers." *Österreichische Musikzeitschrift* 31 (February 1976): 57–120.

Wechsberg, Joseph. *The Waltz Emperors: The Life and Times and Music of the Strauss Family.* London, 1973.

ANDREW LAMB

STRAVINSKY, IGOR (Igor' Fedorovich Stravinskii; born 5 [17] June 1882 in Oranienbaum, Russia, died 6 April 1971 in New York City), composer. Stravinsky was one of the most important composers of the twentieth century and its most significant composer of ballet music. Stravinsky's father was a leading bass singer at the Maryinsky Theater in Saint Petersburg. The third of four children, the young Igor was frequently exposed to music and theater in the city and to folk music during summers spent at relatives' country estates. He began piano lessons at the age of nine and later received private instruction in harmony and counterpoint. Although his family insisted that he read law at the university, his attention to these studies was desultory. Long before his graduation in 1906, his interest in musical composition had led him to seek the advice of Nikolai Rimsky-Korsakov, whose son Vladimir was a fellow student; his private lessons in composition with Rimsky-Korsakov continued from 1902 until the master's death in 1908. In January 1906 Stravinsky married his first cousin, Katerina Nossenko; they had four children.

Early Career. Although some of Stravinsky's works from these years, including a dirge on his teacher's death, are lost, a piano sonata (1904) and a symphony (1907) composed under Rimsky-Korsakov's tutelage document Stravinsky's absorption of the Russian cosmopolitan, or Western, style, epitomized by Petr Ilich Tchaikovsky and Aleksandr Glazunov and the antithesis of the folkloric style of which Rimsky-Korsakov was a leading proponent. Two orchestral scores, the *Scherzo Fantastique* and *Feu d'Artifice,* both completed in 1908, also show the influence of the modern French school, exemplified by Paul Dukas and Claude Debussy. Performed at a concert in Saint Petersburg on 6 February 1909, these two works attracted the attention of Serge Diaghilev, who commissioned some orchestrations from Stravinsky for his 1909 Paris season. Diaghilev also turned to Stravinsky to compose *The Firebird,* a Michel Fokine ballet intended for the 1910 Ballets Russes season in Paris, when Anatoly Lyadov required too much time to do so.

Russian and Western influences are constructively juxtaposed in *The Firebird* (1910), a brilliantly colorful and pictorial score based on folkloric material; as in Rimsky-Korsakov's opera *Le Coq d'Or,* chromatic writing for the supernatural creatures is contrasted with modal-diatonic music for the human figures. Its success launched Stravinsky's international career, centered in Paris, where he soon became a figure in the musical world and a friend of Debussy and Maurice Ravel. Two further ballets for Diaghilev followed, also on Russian subjects. An opera, *Le Rossignol,* based on a Hans Christian Andersen tale, begun before *The Firebird,* was not completed until 1914; in 1917 Stravinsky arranged from it a symphonic poem, *Le Chant du Rossignol,* which was staged by Diaghilev in 1920, with sets by Henri Matisse and choreography by Léonide Massine.

Stravinsky's *Petrouchka* (1911), described as a "burlesque," is a tale of a puppet hero, set in the milieu of the Saint Petersburg Shrovetide fair. Devised in collaboration with the designer Alexandre Benois, it was also choreographed by Fokine. As in *The Firebird,* Stravinsky drew on folk and popular material, this time in an increasingly dissonant and rhythmically irregular context; a *concertante* piano soloist represents Petrouchka in the orchestra, and the material of the central scenes, based on the superimposed chords of C major and F-sharp major, was in fact first conceived as a concert piece for piano and orchestra. The out-of-doors scenes vividly evoke the milieu and the sounds of the street fair.

Le Sacre du Printemps (1913), enacting a ritual of human sacrifice, was developed in collaboration with Nikolai Roerich (who also designed it) and choreographed by Vaslav Nijinsky. In this score Stravinsky elevated to a constructive principle the metrical irregularities prominent in the preceding works: rhythm in *Le Sacre* is no longer a matter of subdividing a regular pulse but of cumulating groups of beats in ever-changing numbers. Equally revolutionary (and profoundly antithetical to traditional Western modes of symphonic development) are the formal techniques of montage: sequential crosscutting between, and simultaneous layering of, musical materials. These had been employed representationally in the fair scenes of *Petrouchka* but were now used structurally in their own right. They continued to be a basic stylistic feature of Stravinsky's music throughout his life. The speeds of the montaged materials are always carefully coordinated, and Stravinsky assigns such metrical relationships a role often as significant as that of tonal relationships in earlier music.

Research by Lawrence Morton and Richard Taruskin has demonstrated the importance of Russian folk music as a source for the melodic material of *Le Sacre,* despite Stravinsky's subsequent emphatic denials of such origins; from the standpoint of his later aesthetic preoccupations, he preferred to regard it as concert music without ethnological purport. The work's harmony centers on the superimposed chords of E-flat major and F-flat major, which make up the famous "chugging" sonority in the "Dance of the Adolescents"; although highly dissonant, these harmonies are essentially static in nature and function. Pieter van den Toorn has demonstrated Stravinsky's extensive reliance throughout his career on the octatonic scale, a pattern of alternating half and whole steps. Although *Le Sacre* is a work of explicit primitivism, its monumental orchestration marks it as still very much a part of the post-Wagnerian European high culture that Stravinsky, and many others, were soon to reject violently. Its premiere on 29 May 1913 in Paris was the occasion of one of the most famous theatrical demonstrations of modern times, inspired equally by the brutalism of the music and the unconventionality of Nijinsky's choreography.

Cut off from Russia and the revenues from his German publishers and his Russian estate by the beginning of World War I, Stravinsky settled in neutral Switzerland. Working from various collections of Russian folk poetry, some of which he had hastily retrieved on a brief trip home in July 1914, he composed a number of small works, mostly vocal, developing musical ideas related to the language of *Le Sacre* but in a less violent expressive framework. By this time Stravinsky's internalization of his native musical folklore was as complete as Béla Bartók's. Inspired by traditional Russian theatrical genres, he turned from the grandiose scale of Diaghilev, whose operations had in any case been curtailed by the war, to novel and economical combinations of music, dance, speech, and pantomime. Thus began a series of theater works—continuing through *Perséphone* in 1934—that, because they call for singers, actors, or special instrumentations, fall outside, or between, the resources of most institutional repertory companies.

Le Renard (1916) is a "burlesque in song and dance," with a text assembled by Stravinsky from Russian folk material. *The Soldier's Tale* (1918), a collaboration with the Swiss writer C. F. Ramuz, after a Russian folk transmutation of the Faust legend, is "to be read, played, and danced" as a traveling theater piece, in the tradition of the oral folk theater of Russian soldiers and convicts. At this time Stravinsky became fascinated by the cimbalom, a Hungarian stringed instrument played with mallets, which he used in *Le Renard* and in the instrumental piece *Rag-time* (1918). Like many European composers at the end of the war, Stravinsky was interested in American jazz although at this point Stravinsky knew only printed music, not performed and improvised jazz.

However, the principal project of these years was *Les Noces,* intended for the Ballets Russes. Although he began the work in 1914 and substantially completed the score by 1917, Stravinsky experimented with several novel orchestrations. It was not until 1923 that he completed the final version, in which vocal soloists and chorus are accompanied by the "black and white" ensemble of four pianos and percussion. Stravinsky had wanted the instruments on stage with the dancers, but this was not achieved in Bronislava Nijinska's original production. The stylized, ritualistic character of *Les Noces* and *Le Renard* is underlined by the vocal layout, as the solo singers have no specific identities in the action.

Exile in France. With the success of the Bolshevik Revolution in Russia, the exile of Stravinsky and of Diaghilev became permanent. The impresario turned primarily to France and to French composers and, following the lead of Jean Cocteau, espoused a more conservative, "objective" aesthetic in preference to his prewar avant-gardism. In the aftermath of the war, this explicitly involved rejection of any traces of Wagnerianism and of the German Romantic sensibility. Stravinsky followed in this path, but the composer, cut off not only from his Russian roots but from a Russian audience, also faced the problem of a language for vocal music. His only subsequent major work in Russian would be the opera *Mavra* (1922)—dedicated, significantly, to the great cosmopolitan Westernizers of Russian culture, Aleksandr Pushkin, Mikhail Glinka, and Tchaikovsky. Although he took up residence in France in 1920, Stravinsky's next major vocal works would be in Latin: *Oedipus Rex* (1927) and the Symphony of Psalms (1930).

With the abandonment of the Russian language, Stravinsky also stopped drawing on the Russian folk material that had stimulated much of his music for more than a decade. As early as the dance episodes of *The Soldier's Tale,* stylistic parody of Western materials had begun to play a role in his music. The decisive experience for his reorientation came with *Pulcinella* (1920), a "ballet with song" for Diaghilev based on eighteenth-century pieces (attributed to Giambattista Pergolesi, but now known to be the work of other composers), with sets by Pablo Picasso and choreography by Massine. Diaghilev presumably expected something along the lines of *Les Femmes de Bonne Humeur,* Vincenzo Tommasini's slick modern orchestrations of Domenico Scarlatti keyboard sonatas, but *Pulcinella* turned out to be something quite different: "art about art," in which by subtle adjustments the eighteenth-century surface was made to embrace Stravinskian asymmetry and nondirectional harmony. The ostensibly eighteenth-century orchestration, incorporating the Baroque contrast of small and larger ensembles, nonetheless yielded a characteristic sonority. Stravinsky even found ways to elicit percussive sounds without percussion instruments. *Pulcinella* showed Stravinsky a direction in which he could move away from Russia without becoming entirely rootless, and it inaugurated his so-called neoclassical period, which would last about twenty-five years.

The Symphonies of Wind Instruments (1920), dedicated to the memory of Debussy, and especially the Octet (1923) confirmed the new direction. In part because of financial pressures, Stravinsky began in 1924 to be active as a touring pianist and composed several works for his own use: Concerto for Piano and Winds (1924), Piano Sonata (1924), Serenade in A (1925), Capriccio for Piano and Orchestra (1929), and the Concerto for Two Solo Pianos (1935). He had also begun to conduct his own music. After a period during which he made piano-roll recordings of most of his music, Stravinsky in 1925 turned his attention to the phonograph, regularly recording his own performances of his new works and rerecording his older ones to new technical standards. Even if they failed in their professed purpose of fixing his interpretation as an inviolate standard—and indeed they differ significantly among themselves and are variously flawed in detail and execution—Stravinsky's recordings played an important role in propagating his music.

Although Stravinsky's works of the neoclassical period have their definable stimuli in earlier music, they always are wholly Stravinskian; each work establishes its own world of harmonic and rhythmic tensions, its own characteristic sonority. What to early listeners often seemed willful defacement of classical styles has with time established a stylistic identity of its own.

Although no further dance works for the Ballets Russes followed *Les Noces,* the opera-oratorio *Oedipus Rex* (1927) was composed to celebrate Diaghilev's twentieth anniversary as an impresario. However, relations with Diaghilev became strained by Stravinsky's acceptance of patronage from other quarters. *Apollon Musagète* (1928) was commissioned by the American Elizabeth Sprague Coolidge and first performed at the Library of Congress with choreography by Adolph Bolm; six weeks later George Balanchine made his classic version for Diaghilev. The allegorical ballet *Le Baiser de la Fée* (1928), based on music by Tchaikovsky, thereby affirming Stravinsky's new preference for the cosmopolitan rather than the nationalistic tradition of Russian music, was written for Ida Rubinstein. After Diaghilev's death in 1929, Rubinstein also commissioned the melodrama *Perséphone* (1934), with a text by André Gide, in which she recited as well as danced. Completed the year he became a French citizen, this was Stravinsky's only setting of French words since a pair of Verlaine songs in 1910.

In the early 1930s Stravinsky and American violinist Samuel Dushkin undertook a series of concert tours, for which new works were specially made: the Violin Concerto in D (1931), the Duo Concertante for Violin and Piano (1932), and a variety of transcriptions of earlier works. Perhaps as a result of such tours, additional commissions came from the United States. Lincoln Kirstein and Edward Warburg commissioned *Jeu de Cartes,* a "ballet in three deals" (1936) for Balanchine's American Ballet; Mr. and Mrs. Robert Woods Bliss, the Concerto in E-flat for Chamber Orchestra (*Dumbarton Oaks,* 1938); and the Chicago Symphony, the Symphony in C (1940).

Immigration to the United States. In March 1939 Stravinsky's wife died of tuberculosis; their eldest child had died the year before, and the composer himself suffered with tuberculosis at this time. In September 1939, with the onset of war in Europe, he moved to the United States, where he had been invited to deliver the Charles Eliot Norton lectures at Harvard University. His lectures, published under the title *Poetics of Music* (1947), were actually written by the French critic Alexis Roland-Manuel; earlier his *Autobiography* (1936) had been ghosted by Diaghilev's associate Walter Nouvel. On 9 March 1940 Stravinsky married Vera de Bosset, regularizing a long-standing liaison. The Stravinskys, who would become naturalized American citizens in 1945, settled in Beverly Hills, California, which remained their home until the fall of 1969.

During World War II, commissions were hard to come by. Besides continuing his conducting and playing activities, Stravinsky worked for some improbable patrons: the *Circus Polka,* "for a young elephant" (1942), was written for Ringling Brothers and Barnum & Bailey circus; the bandleaders Paul Whiteman and Woody Herman commissioned, respectively, *Scherzo à la Russe* (1944) and *Ebony Concerto* (1945); the Broadway producer Billy Rose ordered *Scènes de Ballet* for the revue *The Seven Lively Arts* (1944). Ostensibly a concert work, *Danses Concertantes* (1942), commissioned by the conductor Werner Janssen, has the structure of a ballet score and was choreographed by Balanchine in 1944. In 1945 Stravinsky completed a major orchestral work, the Symphony in Three Movements.

After the war, a new publishing arrangement with the firm of Boosey and Hawkes placed the composer on a sounder financial basis. Because Russia and the United States had not been adherents of the Berne copyright convention, Stravinsky's earlier works were in the public domain in the United States; Stravinsky now sought to reestablish control over them by preparing revised editions. The most radical alteration among the theater scores was the rescoring of *Petrouchka* for a smaller orchestra, and many errors in this and other scores were corrected.

Stravinsky's major ballet of this period was *Orpheus* (1947), commissioned by Kirstein for Balanchine and Ballet Society. The following years were devoted principally to the composition of the three-act opera *The Rake's Progress* (1951), with a libretto by W. H. Auden and Chester Kallman suggested by William Hogarth's famous series of paintings. Stravinsky's only full-evening theater work and an homage to the eighteenth-century number opera (made up of separate arias and ensembles rather than through-composed in the Wagnerian manner), it culminated Stravinsky's neoclassical period.

In the early 1950s, encouraged by Robert Craft, a young musician who had joined his household in 1948 as a secretary and assistant, Stravinsky interested himself in the music and compositional technique of Arnold Schoenberg and his disciples, Alban Berg and Anton Webern. At first in songs and chamber works, Stravinsky began cautious experiments with aspects of Schoenberg's twelve-tone method. These discoveries were gradually absorbed into his style during the composition of the ballet *Agon,* begun in 1953 but not completed until 1957. For this plotless work, another Kirstein commission for Balanchine's company, now the New York City Ballet, Stravinsky was stimulated by the French court dances described in François de Lauze's *Apologie de la Danse* and by music examples in the writings of French mathematician Marin Mersenne.

Craft, a man of wide interests in literature and philosophy as well as music, vastly stimulated the Stravinskys' intellectual life, introducing them to new music, new books, and new friends; by forcing them to speak English, he brought them into closer contact with American culture. Craft also functioned as Stravinsky's assistant conductor, rehearsing orchestras for concerts and recordings; as the composer grew older and his new music became more difficult to conduct, Craft also acted as co-conductor. Beginning in 1959, he collaborated with Stravinsky on a series of books that take the form of conversations. The exact nature of the collaboration, especially during Stravinsky's final years, has been a subject of some controversy.

Agon was Stravinsky's final ballet score, although *The Flood* (1962), composed for CBS television, also included dance episodes choreographed by Balanchine and has been performed theatrically. In his later years, Stravinsky composed a number of religious vocal pieces: *Canticum Sacrum* (1955), *Threni* (1958), *A Sermon, a Narrative, and a Prayer* (1961), *Abraham and Isaac* (1963), and *Requiem Canticles* (1966). These continued a strain in his work dating back to the mid-1920s, when he had rejoined the Russian Orthodox Church, and also manifest in the Symphony of Psalms and the Mass, completed in 1948. Another preoccupation of the 1950s and 1960s was writing memorial pieces for, among others, Dylan Thomas, Raoul Dufy, John F. Kennedy, and T. S. Eliot. He also composed two substantial orchestral works: *Movements* (1959), for piano and orchestra, and *Variations* (1964), which was dedicated to the memory of Aldous Huxley. With their dense and often contrapuntal textures, angular melodies, and somber colors, the works of Stravinsky's seventies and eighties have not yet found a wide audience.

In 1962, at the invitation of the Soviet government in honor of his eightieth birthday, Stravinsky made a much-publicized return to Russia—his first trip there in forty-eight years. After this journey, Stravinsky's public appearances and the range of his compositional activity were gradually curtailed by ill health. His last completed work was a setting for voice and piano of Edward Lear's "The Owl and the Pussycat," one of his wife's favorite poems (1966); subsequently, he made instrumentations of two songs by Hugo Wolf and worked at scoring some pieces from Johann Sebastian Bach's *Well-Tempered Clavier.* In the fall of 1969 the Stravinskys moved to New York and remained there until the composer's death, some fourteen months short of his ninetieth birthday.

Contributions. Thanks to what Jeremy Noble has described as Stravinsky's "ability to express physical gestures and movements (and the psychological states that prompt them) in purely musical terms—a gift in which he has had no rival since Wagner," and to the inexhaustible fertility of his rhythmic invention, his music has consistently commanded the interest of choreographers. Few (if any) of his scores, whatever their initial purpose, have failed to find their way into theatrical use. The weight of his major works and their central concerns—rituals of purification and regeneration *(Le Sacre du Printemps, Les Noces, Oedipus Rex, Perséphone, The Rake's Progress)* and myths of artistic creation *(Apollon Musagète, Orpheus)*—have ensured their prominence in twentieth-century theatrical experience.

Stravinsky's connection with Diaghilev fixed a lifelong relationship to ballet and accustomed Stravinsky to a culture of novelty and avant-gardism and to the uses of publicity. His unpredictable stylistic transformations, variously stimulated by geography, patronage, and economic circumstances, were major events in the artistic world. If his early scores remained the most popular with the general public, the neoclassical style was long the most influential with composers, in both France and the United States, through the example of the music itself and through the teaching of Nadia Boulanger, the formidable French pedagogue and Stravinsky disciple. In the 1950s Stravinsky's conversion to serialism lent enormous prestige to the worldwide movement to use such techniques. At his death, he was widely recognized as the last representative of a long tradition of great composers of international stature.

[*See also* Agon; Apollo; Firebird, The; Noces, Les; Petrouchka; *and* Sacre du Printemps, Le.]

BIBLIOGRAPHY

Balanchine, George. "The Dance Elements in Stravinsky's Music." *Ballet Review* 10 (Summer 1982): 14–18.

Boucourechliev, André. *Stravinsky.* Translated by Martin Cooper. New York, 1987.

Garafola, Lynn. *Diaghilev's Ballets Russes.* New York, 1989.

Harris, Dale. "Balanchine: Working with Stravinsky." *Ballet Review* 10 (Summer 1982): 19–24.

Karlinsky, Simon. "Stravinsky and Russian Pre-Literate Theater." *Nineteenth-Century Music* 6 (Spring 1983): 232–240.

Kirstein, Lincoln. "Working with Stravinsky." In Kirstein's *By With To and From.* New York, 1991.

Lederman, Minna, ed. *Stravinsky in the Theatre.* New York, 1949.

Pasler, Jann C. "Debussy, Stravinsky, and the Ballets Russes." Ph.D. diss., University of Chicago, 1981.

Schouvaloff, Alexander, and Victor Borovsky. *Stravinsky on Stage.* London, 1982.

Stravinsky, Igor. *Stravinsky: Autobiography.* New York, 1936.

Stravinsky, Igor. *Poetics of Music.* Translated by Arthur Knodel and Ingolf Dahl. New York, 1947.

Stravinsky, Igor, and Robert Craft. *Conversations with Igor Stravinsky.* Garden City, N.Y., 1959.

Stravinsky, Igor, and Robert Craft. *Memories and Commentaries.* Berkeley, 1960.

Stravinsky, Igor, and Robert Craft. *Expositions and Developments.* Garden City, N.Y., 1962.

Stravinsky, Igor, and Robert Craft. *Dialogues and a Diary.* Garden City, N.Y., 1963.

Stravinsky, Igor, and Robert Craft. *Themes and Episodes.* New York, 1966.

Stravinsky, Igor, and Robert Craft. *Retrospectives and Conclusions.* New York, 1969.

Stravinsky, Igor. *Selected Correspondence.* 3 vols. Translated and edited by Robert Craft. New York, 1982–1985.

Stravinsky, Vera, and Robert Craft. *Stravinsky in Pictures and Documents.* New York, 1978.

Taruskin, Richard. *Stravinsky and the Russian Traditions: A Biography of the Works through Mavra.* 2 vols. Berkeley, 1996.

Toorn, Pieter C. van den. *The Music of Igor Stravinsky.* New Haven, 1983.

White, Eric W. *Stravinsky: The Composer and His Works.* 2d ed. Berkeley, 1979.

White, Eric W., and Jeremy Noble. "Stravinsky, Igor." In *The New Grove Dictionary of Music and Musicians.* London, 1980.

DAVID HAMILTON

STRIPTEASE. *See* Fan Dancing.

STRUCHKOVA, RAISA (Raisa Stepanovna Struchkova; born 5 October 1925 in Moscow), Russian dancer and teacher. Struchkova graduated from the Moscow School of Choreography in 1944. Her teacher and coach was Elisaveta Gerdt, who brought the classicism of the Saint Petersburg school to Moscow. From 1944 to 1978 Struchkova was the leading ballerina of the Bolshoi Ballet. After leaving the stage she continued to coach the

STRUCHKOVA. With Yuri Zhdanov as Albrecht in act 1 of *Giselle,* c.1955. Struchkova's interpretation was marked by a sweetness and simplicity that set her apart from other famous performers of the role at the Bolshoi Theater. (Photograph by Fritz Peyer; from a private collection.)

company, and in 1968 she began teaching also at the Lunacharsky Institute of Theatrical Art. In 1981, she became editor in chief of *Sovietskii balet* (Soviet Ballet) magazine.

A classical ballerina in the grand style and a talented actress, Struchkova was famous for the musicality of her dance in a broad range of roles, including lyrical, dramatic, and comic characters. She danced more than thirty roles in the classical and modern repertory, creating, among others, Leili in *Leili and Medzhnun* (1964), choreographed by Kasyan Goleizovsky, and the Maid of Honor in *Lieutenant Kijé* (1963), by Aleksandr Lapauri and Olga Tarasova, set to music by Sergei Prokofiev. She starred in the ballet feature films *The Crystal Shoe (Cinderella), Lieutenant Kijé,* and *I Am Your Name* (music by Francis Poulenc, choreography by Lapauri and Tarasova to poetry of Paul Éluard). She danced in a broad concert repertory and performed with her partner and husband Lapauri in *Moszkowski Waltz* and Reinhold Glière's *Étude* with great success, demonstrating a nearly acrobatic virtuosity.

STRUCHKOVA. With Aleksandr Lapauri in their most celebrated concert number, sometimes billed as *Moszkowski Waltz* and sometimes simply as *Waltz,* c.1960. Choreographed by Vasily Vainonen to a rousing waltz by Moritz Moszkowski, it is arguably the most exciting number ever performed on a ballet stage. Dancing with joyous abandon, Struchkova was the embodiment of reckless happiness. As she gleefully soared through the air, with complete trust in her partner and complete disregard of danger, audiences were invariably thrilled. (Photograph reprinted from a Bolshoi Ballet souvenir program, 1962.)

Struchkova's distinctive talents lay particularly in the improvisational playfulness of her dancing. Her dancing was fresh and original; in the established roles she found her own interpretations rather than copying others' performances. It is customary to consider Struchkova a fundamentally lyrical dancer. However, she was fascinating as the temperamental Kitri in Rostislav Zakharov's version of *Don Quixote,* as the clambering Bacchante in Leonid Lavrovsky's *Walpurgis Night,* and as the sparkling title character in Vasily Vainonen's *Mirandolina,* based on motifs from the plays of Carlo Goldoni. The contemporary comedy-satire *Lieutenant Kijé* revealed still another facet of her talent as an actress. Marina Semenova wrote of her, "I do not recall Struchkova ever making a mistake in dancing her role or feigning sincerity on the stage. This is perhaps what matters most in Struchkova as an actress; her genuine sincerity. This is the essence of her art." Struchkova's guest performances in more than thirty-five countries evoked the admiration of her audiences. The fame of the Bolshoi Ballet in the West was for many years associated with her name as a prime representative of Soviet ballet theater, with its traditions of realism, psychological penetration, and philosophical profundity.

Struchkova won First Prize at the World Festival of Youth and Students in Prague (1947), Budapest (1949), and Berlin (1951). She was named People's Artist of the USSR in 1959 and professor of the chair of choreography at the Lunacharsky Institute of Theatrical Art in 1978. She has served as a member of the jury of ballet competitions at home and abroad.

BIBLIOGRAPHY

Dolgopolov, Mikhail. "Raisa Struchkova." *The Dancing Times* (September 1949): 689–690.

Fradkin, Herman. *Raisa Struchkova* (in English). Moscow, 1956.

Greskovic, Robert. "The Bolshoi: The Picture Changes." *Ballet Review* 4.5 (1973): 35–49.

Moore, Lillian. "The Bolshoi Ballet Arrives on Film." *Dance Magazine* (January 1958): 36–43.

Poesio, Giannandrea. "Raissa Struchkova." *The Dancing Times* (July 1993): 971–972.

Semenova, Marina. "V osobom mire baleta." *Ogonek* 42 (1975).

Sinclair, Janet. "Raissa Struchkova: An Appreciation." *Ballet Today* (November 1963): 14–15.

Sluzhenie iskusstvu. Moscow, 1979. Booklet of the Moscow Bolshoi on the thirty-fifth anniversary of the stage activities of Struchkova.

Zakharov, Rostislav. "V ee tantsakh—sama zhizn." *Sovetskaia Kul'tura* (27 April 1973).

GALINA V. BELYAYEVA-CHELOMBITKO
Translated from Russian

STUTTGART BALLET, formerly known as the Ballet of the Württemberg State Theater (Ballett der Württembergischen Staatstheater Stuttgart). Until 1759 the

Stuttgart court opera ballet was a company like many others in Germany: patronized by petty princes and largely directed by French ballet masters. In that year, Duke Karl Eugen of Württemberg, an absolutist ruler but a lavish patron of the arts, appointed the young French choreographer Jean-Georges Noverre as his court ballet master. For the next seven years Stuttgart became the capital of the burgeoning fashion for *ballets d'action*, with Noverre creating a large number of works, often in collaboration with Niccolò Jommelli, the internationally famous Stuttgart court *Kapellmeister*.

Thus, at the nearby Ludwigsburg court theater, many historic works had their premieres, including *Renaud et Armide* (c.1760), *Admète et Alceste* (1761), *Médée et Jason* (1763), *Der Sieg des Neptun* (The Triumph of Neptune; 1763), *Hypernestra* (also known as *Les Danaïdes*, 1764), and *Der Raub der Proserpina* (The Abduction of Persephone; 1766). These works were performed by a company that listed seven male and seven female solo dancers and forty-four other dancers, evenly divided by sex; they were augmented occasionally by guest stars such as Gaëtan Vestris, Maximilien Gardel, Jean Dauberval, Anna Friedrike Heinel, and Nicolas Sauveur.

The duke's extravagance, however, created ever-mounting debt problems, and one of the court's first economic remedies was the drastic reduction of the ballet company, which led Noverre to leave for Vienna in 1767. Ballet in Stuttgart returned to its former inconspicuous state although a ballet school attached to the court theater lasted from 1771 until 1794. Stuttgart regained some of its former splendor when Filippo Taglioni was engaged as court ballet master at the end of 1824; he stayed through March 1828. Taglioni replaced Noverre's heroic approach with Romantic idylls in productions featuring his ballerina daughter Marie, partnered principally by Anton Stuhlmüller. This brief association saw the premier of *Jocko, the Brazilian Ape* (1826), which soon left Stuttgart for the international circuit.

After the Taglionis, Stuttgart returned to its ballet provincialism. The next date of historic significance was not until 1922, with the first performance of Oskar Schlemmer's *Triadic Ballet*. This, however, had no lasting consequences for the repertory of the company, which favored such classics as *The Fairy Doll*. Even after World War II there was no marked change in the role of ballet when the Stuttgart State Opera resumed operation.

Not until the 1958 arrival of Nicholas Beriozoff did the company, now known as the Ballet of the Württemberg State Theater, assume a stronger identity. Beriozoff insisted on strengthening the company's classical base, concentrating on a repertory of classics from the nineteenth century as well as from his own years with the Ballets Russes and on improving the teaching standards at the attached opera ballet school. He also collaborated with the local Noverre Society, established in 1958 to further the cause of ballet and to assist young dancers and aspiring choreographers through the awarding of scholarhips and creation of a platform on which they might demonstrate their gifts. Beriozoff was succeeded in 1961 by John Cranko, and under the latter's guidance, which lasted until his death in 1973, the Stuttgart Ballet acquired its present international reputation.

STUTTGART BALLET. Marcia Haydée and Richard Cragun in John Cranko's comic masterpiece *The Taming of the Shrew*, created for the company in 1969. (Photograph from the Dance Collection, New York Public Library for the Performing Arts.)

Drawing from his experiences with the British Sadler's Wells Ballet and the Royal Ballet, and collaborating with Anne Woolliams and Peter Wright, Cranko built a company that soon drew international attention. Basing its repertory on highly individual productions of the classics and on British revivals, the Stuttgart Ballet was especially strong in such full-length works as Cranko's *Romeo and Juliet*, *Onegin*, and *The Taming of the Shrew*. These were supplemented by a few Balanchine imports and occasional contributions from Kenneth MacMillan, who created *Las Hermanas*, *Das Lied von der Erde*, and, after Cranko's death, *Requiem* and *My Brother, My Sisters*. Em-

STUTTGART BALLET. Using music by Aleksandr Scriabin, Cranko created *Poème de l'Extase* for guest artist Margot Fonteyn in 1970. She is seen here with Richard Cragun (left) and Egon Madsen (center). (Photograph from the Dance Collection, New York Public Library for the Performing Arts.)

phasizing the dramatic potential of ballet, Cranko carefully nurtured the dancers to express his ideas. Early on he found his ideal ballerina in Marcia Haydée, whom he surrounded with an ensemble of individualistic artists such as Ray Barra, Richard Cragun, Birgit Keil, Egon Madsen, and Heinz Clauss.

One of Cranko's special concerns was the school's consolidation, which included the addition of a boarding wing. He also was active as a lecturer at the matinees of the Noverre Society, which increasingly developed into a forum for the promotion of new choreographers such as Ashley Killar, Gray Veredon, John Neumeier, and Jiří Kylián. Thus Cranko created new ballet awareness not only in Stuttgart but also in other German cities (both Berlin and Munich tried to lure him away); this appreciation increased when the company returned from its first successful tours abroad. The company and city were shocked when Cranko died suddenly in 1973.

STUTTGART BALLET. Heinz Spoerli's *Sackgasse* (Dead End), set to music by Igor Stravinsky, was created for the company in 1982, with leading roles for Birgit Keil and Vladimir Klos. Keil is pictured here with Christopher Boatwright in a later performance. (Photograph © by Hannes Kilian; used by permission.)

After a leaderless season, Glen Tetley was appointed as Cranko's successor from 1974 to 1976, but he never truly took control of the company, which survived because of its solid Cranko repertory. In 1976 Marcia Haydée became artistic director of the company, maintaining its by now rather obsolete Cranko orientation but infusing new blood by encouraging younger dancer-choreographers such as Patrice Montagnon, William Forsythe, and Uwe Scholz. This honest effort, however, was slow to pay dividends. Haydée was more successful in inviting John Neumeier to create *The Lady of the Camellias* and *A Streetcar Named Desire* for the company and relied mostly on works by Hans van Manen and Maurice Béjart.

Although most of the company's present dancers never worked with Cranko, the company's international status in the 1980s rested largely on his repertory, performed by such Cranko stalwarts as Keil, Cragun, Susanne Hanke, and Haydée herself. Until Haydée's resignation in the summer of 1996, the repertory consisted mainly of works by Cranko, van Manen, Neumeier, and Béjart, along with Haydée's highly successful production of *The Sleeping Beauty*. There were also contributions from such young choreographers as Nacho Duato, Renato Zanella, Stefan Thoss, and Roberto de Oliveira. For the 1996/97 season,

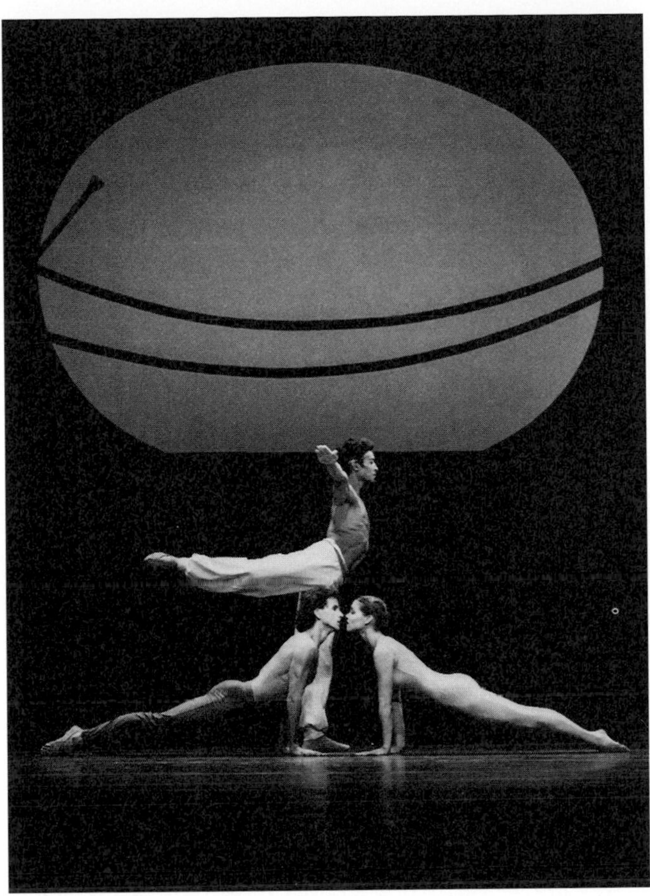

STUTTGART BALLET. Maurice Béjart mounted his production of *Die Zauberflöte* (The Magic Flute) for the company in 1994. The dancers in this beautifully geometric grouping are Benito Marcelino (in arabesque), Tamas Detrich, and Marion Jäger. The striking scenic design was made by Béjart. (Photograph © by Gundel Kilian; used by permission.)

Reid Anderson was appointed artistic director, with a three-year contract.

[*See also the entries on Noverre, Cranko, and other principal figures mentioned herein.*]

BIBLIOGRAPHY

Ballett Annual. Stuttgart, 1978–. Published by the John Cranko Gesellschaft und Württembergische Staatstheater Stuttgart.

Kilian, Gundel. *Stuttgarter Ballett.* New ed. Weingarten, 1991.

Koegler, Horst. *Stuttgart Ballet.* London, 1978.

Schmidt, Jochen. "The Guardians of Cranko's Legacy." *Ballett International* 9 (October 1986): 18–23.

HORST KOEGLER

SUBLIGNY, MARIE-THÉRÈSE (Marie-Thérèse Perdou [Perdoult] de Subligny; born July 1666 in Paris, death date unknown), French dancer. According to the *Dictionnaire critique de biographie et d'histoire* (Paris, 1878): "On 18 July 1666, was baptized Marie-Thérèse, daughter of Adrien-Thomas Pardoult [*sic*], *escuyer,* Sieur de Subligny, and dlle. Claude Bourgoin, the mother, living at rue de Richelieu. The godfather: Martin Ducas [Lucas], *conseiller aumonier* of the King; the godmother: Dame Elisabeth de Villaret (Villares), mother of the Sieur de Subligny." Her paternal grandparents were Adrien Perdou and Elisabeth de Villars; her maternal grandparents were Jean Bourgoin, seigneur d'Ailly, one of the king's secretaries, and Claude de Saucort. Marie-Thérèse Subligny belonged to a somewhat noble lineage, or at least to one with pretensions to some nobility. At the time of her parents' marriage, on 5 September 1667, she was already "thirteen months old or about" and her "legalization" had to be completed. Her father was a writer and a journalist, author of *Fausse Clélie* (1677) and of *Muze Dauphine,* a gazette written in verse, in imitation of the renowned *Muze historique* (1650) by Jean Loret.

Almost nothing personal is known about this famous dancer, whose career can be traced through ballet programs only. She appeared in the last court ballets given by Louis XIV. In *Ballet de Flore* (January 1689), she danced with Mesdemoiselles de La Fontaine, Lesueur, and Durieux. At the Paris Opera, her name is first seen in the cast of *Cadmus et Hermione* (1690) and appeared regularly in all the ballets until her retirement in 1705. Many of Subligny's dances have survived, thanks to the Feuillet notation system. Her famous partnership with Claude Ballon brought them an invitation to perform in England in 1699, where they scored a popular success. In 1703, the *London Stage* was still advertising a "new dance by the Devonshire girl [Mrs. Campion] in imitation of Mademoiselle Subligny." Her name made its last appearance on Opera programs in 1705, for the ballets *Roland, La Fêtes Vénitiennes,* and *Le Triomphe de l'Amour.*

Two racy anecdotes found in a police report indicate that Marie-Thérèse de Subligny was still living in 1735. She was said to be sharing an apartment in rue Saint Honoré with a woman friend named Madeleine Bailleul, without servants (Archives Nationales y. 10.750).

BIBLIOGRAPHY

Hilton, Wendy. *Dance of Court and Theatre: The French Noble Style, 1690–1725.* Princeton, 1981.

Lajarte, Théodore de. *Bibliothèque musicale du Théâtre de l'Opéra* (1878). 2 vols. Geneva, 1969.

Maurepas, Jean. *Recueil de chansons.* N.p., 1696. Manuscript located in Paris, Bibliothèque Nationale, fr.12644.

Migel, Parmenia. *The Ballerinas: From the Court of Louis XIV to Pavlova.* New York, 1972.

Parfaict, François, and Claude Parfaict. *Histoire manuscrite de l'Académie Royale de Musique.* Paris, n.d. Manuscript located in Paris, Bibliothèque Nationale, fr.12355.

Winter, Marian Hannah. *The Pre-Romantic Ballet.* London, 1974.

RÉGINE ASTIER

SUB-SAHARAN AFRICA. [*To survey the diverse dance traditions found in sub-Saharan Africa, this entry comprises three articles:*

An Overview
Popular Dance
Dance Research and Publication

The first article presents the importance of dance in African societies, the variety of dance styles, and the evolution of theatrical styles based on traditional dances; the second explores recreational forms of social dancing; the third focuses on dance scholarship and writing. For related discussion, see Central and East Africa; Southern Africa; *and* West Africa. *For more general discussion, see* Aesthetics, *article on* African Aesthetics; Costume in African Traditions; Mask and Makeup; Music for Dance, *article on* African Music; *and* Ritual Dance.]

An Overview

In indigenous sub-Saharan African societies, dance serves diverse functions as an integral part of communal life, in which people share language, religious belief, and social organization. Although functionally similar, the dances of Africa's diverse cultures display radically different styles.

Social Function. Within an indigenous traditional society, a dance usually has a principal overt function and several related subsidiary associations that may be conscious expressions or implicit reflections of the society's organization and its people's traditional values. This multiplicity of intentions is exemplified in the dance performed in the Yoruba town of Ijio, Nigeria, by the Efe masquerader at the Gelede ceremonies. A dramatic midnight appearance of this key figure is designed at a ritual level to appease the Great Earth Mother and the women on whom she bestows mystic powers. The Efe masquerade enters the market dancing to the Bembe drum rhythms with an aggressive display of stamping feet and rapid turns that awe the spectators. The Ososo drums take over as he moves around the square, pausing to sing and dance in honor of the ritual and political leaders present. He thus reaffirms the social hierarchy within the community. As night wears on, the Efe dancer relaxes into informal songs and dances. Using mimetic gestures, he ridicules improper behavior by selected individuals over the past year, thus exercising social control while entertaining his audience.

In sub-Saharan African cultures, dance is used as an expression of social organization. It differentiates and defines the roles of individuals and groups. Members related by status, age, sex, or work express their identity and cohesion in dances appropriate to the occasion, which emphasize the qualities proper to the performers. In the hierarchical society of the Yoruba, dance is used as a validation of leadership. A ruler is expected to state his authority in formal dances, and failure to meet the required standard may be a serious threat to his prestige. His wives and lesser chiefs also have dances through which they express their dignity and status. In Ghana, the Asantehene, ruler of the Akan, dances the *kete* in his palace, with gestures conveying that "apart from the Gods and the Earth, there is no one greater than the Asantehene." Other chiefs honor their leader in dance, each with his own formalized gestures that express his allegiance and position.

For priests and priestesses, dance is a statement of their spiritual leadership. When they are possessed by the powers they serve, their gestures give mimetic expression to the nature of the deity or spirit. Initiates have their own styles of dance in which they act as supporting choruses for the ritual leaders. For example, Yoruba priests in Benin who serve Shango, the god of thunder, express his wrath in the lightning speed of their arm gestures and the "thunderous" roll of their shoulders in the highly formalized rhythms of their *lanku* dance. At the same time, women praise-singers dance in honor of the god by forming a circle and raising their headdresses when they mention his name. In Zimbabwe, the Mhondora spirit mediums connect the Shona people with the guardian spirits of the dead. They move into a state of trance as they sing and perform a characteristic dance of rhythmic foot patterns to the music of the *mbira* (a hand piano).

Masquerade dancers are a feature of religious societies in most African cultures. Four main types, with different roles, can be identified: those who embody deities or spirits; those who embody the ancestral spirits returning to guide their descendants; those who placate the spirits; and those who perform principally as entertainers.

In Mali, the animal-spirit masqueraders of the Bambara carry stylized carvings of bush animals and dance in imitation of their movements to ensure fertility in their community. *Bedu* masquerade dancers of the Nafana in Côte d'Ivoire make their night appearance wearing abstract animal masks that are the central feature of their purification rites. The heavier the mask, the less freedom for dance: *Epa* masqueraders of the Ekiti Yoruba wear complex head masks, whose weight allows them to perform only stately processional dances. Costume can also facilitate dance: the voluminous cloth costumes of the ancestral *ikhien-ani-mhin* masquerades of the Ishan permit leaping turns that demand virtuosic skill.

Secular masqueraders who perform as entertainers have emerged from the ritual societies. The Egúngún entertainers of the Nigerian Yoruba appear at the Egúngún festival but may also be invited to perform for a fee and travel abroad to earn money, although they are bound to offer sacrifice to their ancestors before performing. The company usually starts its performance with simple acrobatic dances and then displays its magic powers by changing into a series of costumes and masks that represent gods, heroes, and animals or that satirically impersonate politicians, wrongdoers, and strangers, such as visiting Europeans.

In societies that stress stratification by age people born around the same date belong to an age set and move together through several life stages with prescribed roles and rites of passage. The qualities proper to a particular phase of life are expressed in its dances. For example, certain dances are intended to keep young men physically fit and teach them the discipline necessary for warfare. The dances of young Zulu and Ndebele (Matabele) men in southern Africa, as well as the *takai* dance of the male aristocrats of the Barabra in western Africa recall the victories of past warriors. Among the Owo Yoruba, male adolescents perform the lively *ajabure* with ceremonial swords, while the stately *totorigi* dance is for older men and women. The transition from one life stage to the next may be marked by ritual ceremonies, as in initiation rites for adolescents, when dances stress sexual fertility and customary behavior between the sexes. In the *otufo* initiation rites for girls among the Ga of Accra in Ghana, dance is part of preparation for womanhood and enables them to display their charms to suitors. The *sikyi* dance of the Akan allows formalized flirtation between the sexes. The mixed-sex dances of the Ika people in Nigeria are openly erotic, and this is unusual; in most traditional sub-Saharan African dances, men and women do not perform the same style of dance or dance in direct relation to each other. This is becoming more frequent, however, in areas where the original context of the dance has been disrupted by external influences. As a rule, idealized male and female qualities are expressed in the movements of each gender's dances. Even if both join a circle or share a dance rhythm, their movement patterns are usually quite distinct. The erotic is expressed with humor.

Men of an age set often work together and celebrate a successful project with beer-drinking and vigorous dances that express their occupational skills. For example, Nupe fishermen are renowned for their net-throwing, which they have formalized in dance patterns; young Irigwe men at agricultural festivals on the Jos Plateau in Nigeria leap to encourage symbolically the growth of crops.

Professional organizations or guilds of experts such as blacksmiths, hunters, and woodcarvers also have their own expressive dances in sub-Saharan Africa. Hunters may reenact their exploits or mime the movements of animals as a ritual means of controlling both wild beasts and their own fears. The *abofour* dance of the Akan is a mime dance staged after the killing of a dangerous animal. It placates the spirit of the beast and informs the community of the manner in which it was killed.

In many cultures, established dance groups are invited to perform as part of the celebration of important social occasions, such as marriages and funerals, as well as to entertain visitors at the bidding of the elders. Dance is a particularly important part of the funeral service, where it may be performed during or after burial ceremonies or at a later anniversary celebration honoring the dead. Some dances are specifically designed for the occasion; in the *igogo* dance of the Owo Yoruba, young men use stamping movements to pack the earth of the grave into place. Others are social dances that can be performed on various occasions, including honoring the dead and comforting the bereaved.

Dance clubs have become popular in Africa's urban centers. They allow people of the same culture to perpetuate their heritage in a multicultural environment. People of both sexes and various ages meet to perfect their skill in traditional dances, which are tailored for performance in

SUB-SAHARAN AFRICA: An Overview. Among the Baga people of Guinea, the dance of the female mask Sörsörne is performed by a male dancer. The expandable costume is seen here extended to its full height; the carved mask at top is characterized by curved horns and prominent breasts. (Photograph © 1987 by Frederick Lamp; used by permission.)

a new setting. Dance teams are formed, and as their reputations grow, they are invited to perform on social occasions.

Dance is also important as an educational medium. Repetitive dance patterns teach children physical control and stress traditional behavior patterns and standards of conduct. Children may form their own dance and masquerade groups, as among the Kalabari of Nigeria; they may join adults at the end of a dance line, as in the dances of the Gungawa (Reshe) in Borgu Division, Nigeria; or they may simply have a space allocated to them in a performing area at the time of a festival.

Ritual dance is used as therapy in many cultures, particularly in West Africa. Cults commonly known as *bori* (or *ajun* among the Jukun) have female elders who treat women with mental disturbances, by exorcising the evil spirits thought to be responsible, in ceremonies that initiate the sufferers into the cult. During a three-month preparation period in a house shrine, a patient is taught songs and dances that play a therapeutic role. The period culminates in a ceremony in which the initiate publicly joins the members of the society to perform the *ajun-kpa* dance.

Throughout Africa, dance is the most popular form of recreation. In towns, members of different age groups meet informally on occasions when men and women may dance together. In villages, informal dancing may take place in the evenings, but relations between the sexes are more tightly overseen and controlled.

Dancing Style. The variety of sub-Saharan African dancing styles arises in part from the physical contexts of cultures. Differing musical styles are interrelated with dance, as well. A third factor determining style is the history of a society and its external relations.

Influence of environment and material culture. Africa has extensive areas of both open savanna and dense forest, tropical and subtropical; and the continent displays extremes of barren desert and moist temperate lands. The physical environment has influenced the way in which people conceive space and time, two of the cultural constructs on which they have patterned their movements; so undoubtedly the environment has affected their styles of dance.

The Lopawa farmers of Nigeria live on the solid earth of the savanna, surrounded by open spaces extending to the far horizon. When dancing, they place their feet firmly on the sun-baked earth as they follow their team leader through the clearly defined circular pattern; with upright carriage they perform simple foot patterns to a steady tempo. This is a basic style of dance for many of the savanna farmers. The various cultures have, however, devised a wide variety of movements on the basic pattern.

The Ijo-speaking people live in the mangrove swamps of the Niger Delta, where their villages are regularly flooded. Canoes provide their transport and fishing their livelihood; the women's dances reflect this. They use light, precise foot beats, moving their weight rapidly from heel to toe and side to side in a variety of rhythmic patterns as they lean forward from the hips, with their arms extended to the sides as though balancing in an unsteady canoe or wading. Similarly, the Nembe women of mime paddling as they dance. These are common patterns of dance in riverine cultures.

Like many of Africa's desert peoples, the Kanuri of the

SUB-SAHARAN AFRICA: An Overview. The Wè (or Guéré) people live in the southwestern region of the Côte d'Ivoire. At a village festival at Zilebli, Canton Bo, this woman danced as an *oudhué*-spirit, wearing a warrior's headdress and brandishing hair whisks. Behind her are two supporting women dancers and an audience of appreciative villagers. (Photograph © 1985 by Monni Adams; used by permission.)

desert fringes conserve their energy by performing stately, measured dances with economical movements, extending their gestures into manipulation of their flowing robes. In contrast, the dances of forest-dwellers, such as the southern Yoruba, are freer and faster. Their foot patterns and sequences of body movements are performed in time to drums. The leading drummer may unexpectedly change the tempo and rhythm of the dance. Such alterations and their movement patterns suggest movement through forest undergrowth and alert reactions to the unexpected.

Environmental conditions are basic to a society's subsistence patterns. The movements used in such work, in turn, contribute to styles of dance. The knee-bend accompanying the farmer's swing of his machete can be recognized in the heightened elaboration of a dance gesture. Architecture, furniture, and dress are other cultural elements that influence posture, gesture, and the use of energy. For example, the Kambari of Nigeria must bend forward to enter the low doors of their houses, and their dance posture reflects this. The Nigerian Nupe, like most other Africans, sit on low stools or on the floor with their legs crossed or extended. Their flexible knees and strong leg tendons allow them to perform continuous deep kneebends in their dance movements. Igbo boys in Nigeria wear short dance skirts that allow them a variety of rapid dance patterns with minimal expenditure of energy (in contrast to dancers in flowing robes, who use their energy in gestures away from the body center).

These basic influences in the development of African dance styles have been obscured by historical events—such as migrations—for example, the movement of Bantu-speaking peoples to the east and south, of Kwa speakers down the western coast, or of many populations along trade routes. For centuries, intertribal wars, and more recently religious persecution by Muslims and Christians, have also displaced people.

The boundaries that were established by colonial regimes to demarcate modern states often cut through traditional territories of homogeneous peoples, while bringing together entirely disparate cultures in a single new state. In some areas, neighbors now share a basic style of dance; in others, they perform in radically different styles. Thus, groups in widely separated locations in East, West, Central, and southern Africa may have dance styles that share features not present in the dance of their immediate neighbors. Nigeria, the largest nation in sub-Saharan Africa, has more than four hundred distinct ethnic groups, with elements of the dance styles that exist in most of sub-Saharan Africa. Yet dances in some regions may differ markedly in detail, and a few—such as the high-kicking dance of Zulu men and the leaping dances of the East African Masai—are not present in Nigeria.

Rhythmic patterns. African dances are based on a wide variety of rhythmic arrangements, many of which give the

SUB-SAHARAN AFRICA: An Overview. Women of the royal court of Dahomey (present-day Benin) dancing in homage to the family of King Justin Hao, at Abomey in the late 1950s. The black-and-white dresses and elaborate hair styles were mandatory for court dress. Each hair style, sculpted with the aid of oil and wire, could take an entire day to create. This undulating dance around the court was the beginning of a fetishistic ritual. (Photograph by Dominique Darbois; reprinted from *African Dance*, Prague, 1962, p. 26.)

dances their names. The most elementary is the continuous repetition of a simple rhythmic pattern throughout a dance. The Kambari of Nigeria use this technique in their *maranji* dance. A team of men moves in a circle around two drummers playing a two-beat rhythm on large *kagbandari* (snare drums). The dancers progress by sliding one foot forward while the other stamps out the rhythmic beat, which is emphasized by iron leg rattles. Each forward-inclined dancer turns slowly on his own axis. The dance continues for hours. At the end of the circle, standing upright, women dancers sing and step to the beats of the same rhythm.

By contrast, Urhobo women in Nigeria dance with strong contractions of the torso, thrusting their arms back and forth to a repetitive drum rhythm. As the dance progresses, the tempo accelerates to encourage ecstatic individuals to emerge from the group and dance in a state of trancelike possession.

The *ikhien-ani-mhin* masqueraders of the Ishan (Esan) are improvisational soloists. Each starts his acrobatic

SUB-SAHARAN AFRICA: An Overview. This festive group of Ijo people in Nigeria left their homes and went out on a highway to welcome home a local man who had just received a university degree. Their celebratory dance of greeting incorporated movements from traditional dances of the region. (Photograph © 1990 by Judith Gleason; used by permission.)

dance to the rhythms of the Okpodu drummers. They in turn conform to his rhythm as he begins to accelerate his movements. These include leaping turns in which the dancer begins in an upright position and then abruptly leans over at an angle. The turn speeds increase, reaching a climax in which the dancer's body revolves parallel to the ground while he maintains his rotation by touching the earth, in passing, with a foot or a hand. The dance displays amazing skill—the drummer and dancer are one in a repetitive, steadily mounting crescendo of rhythm.

Many cultures have team dances involving the repetition of a rhythmic phrase at a steady tempo. For example, in the *lwele le dag chun* dance of Birom girls in northern Nigeria, the girls take four running steps along a circle line, ending in a half turn with their feet spread. They then bend forward and mime the cutting of the vegetable *accha* using three arm-beats and ending in a half turn to the starting position.

The Afo men of Nassarrawa, Nigeria, perform the *goro goro,* a ritual dance to awaken their oracle in which a simple rhythmic phrase is extended during the performance. The dance begins with eleven men in a circle, each carrying a large metal *kokpo* gong on a handle of buffalo horn. Seven times they run, stopping to stamp in the center. The seventh time, they strike their gongs three times. This new pattern is repeated; then they add three kicks to the gong; this elongated pattern is also repeated. The tempo increases until the rhythm and movement phase ends with the dancers swinging the gongs around their bodies and striking them vigorously.

Many savanna farmers dance in teams and play instruments simultaneously to establish the rhythm. The Nga in Shiwer village blow fourteen large buffalo horns as they perform the repetitive step pattern of the *rumada* dance, in which they move along a circle or in and out of its center. Neighboring Chip men, playing flutes of four different pitches that blend to form a rhythmic melody, perform a dance in which they run lightly; at the end of each phrase, the dancers turn to the center and execute a series of light hopping movements. The close-knit relationship between music and dance limits innovation in choreography.

The Igbo of eastern Nigeria dance to a range of sophisticated rhythms. A dance performed by a boys' team with an adult leader, the *ubi-ogazu* (guinea fowl), is a version of the popular *etilogwu* dance and a good example of the most elaborate style of team dancing. The lead dancer plays an *oga* (flute) to set the rhythm, supported by an *igba* (drum), an *ududu* (pot drum), two *igedegwa* (xylophones), and an *ekwe* (bamboo gong). The dance consists of thirteen variations, each with a distinct rhythm and pattern of movement. Each variation is danced for five minutes, while the rhythm repeats with a rising tempo. The beat is light and rapid, and the boys dance in unison, with rhythmic precision, moving from one variation to the next with strong attack.

In contrast to the precision and teamwork required for the *ubi-ogazu,* the *apala* dance of the Yoruba allows a solo dancer to move freely among his fellow dancers in a pattern of his own devising. He relates directly to the rhythm of the leading drum and chooses his own sequence of movements within the recognized style of the dance. He competes with fellow dancers in interpretation of the rhythm and swift response to changes or unexpected nuances within it. The dancers are accompanied by an ensemble of Bata drummers. At a certain point in the dance, the leading drummer joins an outstanding dancer in a rhythmic exchange, urging him to yet greater feats of invention. These may include a variety of subtle foot patterns leading into turns, kicks, or small neat jumps accompanied by flourishes with a horse tail and a range of restrained and expansive dance movements.

Tradition and creativity. An Igbo dance performance presents a series of rehearsed dances of calculated variety, developed in rehearsal by the leader, who introduces new themes and creates movements to interpret them. Months of practice are required before a dance group is permitted by the elders to perform on a public occasion. The Yoruba dancer, by contrast, learns his skill as a child and uses his creativity to interpret the drum rhythm. African dance tradition is not static but a vital expression of immediate experience, skillfully ordered and formalized into various styles by generations of master dancers. The hierarchical Yoruba allow their dancers great personal freedom of interpretation and invention, albeit based on years of disciplined training. The more democratic Igbos place emphasis on team discipline under the strict control of a leader, who is responsible for innovations. The Igbo tradition has grown out of a horizontal social structure organized by age group, while the status-conscious Yoruba are highly competitive individualists in dance as well as in every other aspect of their lives.

Common Elements. Throughout sub-Saharan Africa, dance has common and basic formal features. Rhythm is the central element from which the dance form emerges. This rhythm is provided by musicians playing percussion instruments or by singers. Dancers may wear rattles that emphasize rhythms as they move. Normally the musicians lead the dancers, but in some cultures the dancer takes the initiative in establishing a dialogue of rhythmic exchange. The musicians initiate the performance by playing the basic pulse of the rhythm, the dancer warms up by shifting his weight from one part of the body to another—feet, knees, hips, or shoulders—until the rhythm is established by the musicians accenting and eliminating pulses to form the required pattern.

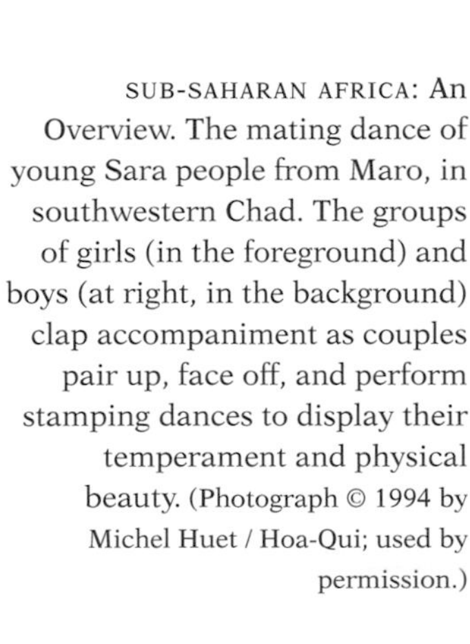

SUB-SAHARAN AFRICA: An Overview. The mating dance of young Sara people from Maro, in southwestern Chad. The groups of girls (in the foreground) and boys (at right, in the background) clap accompaniment as couples pair up, face off, and perform stamping dances to display their temperament and physical beauty. (Photograph © 1994 by Michel Huet / Hoa-Qui; used by permission.)

To dance rhythmically, the dancer uses relaxed knees as springs to transfer weight from one foot or one hip to the other. The back is held straight, with the center of control in the lower spine; the head is lightly poised. The shoulders are relaxed and move independently of the torso.

The dancer's weight is usually directed toward the ground. The performer does not resist gravity but rather emphasizes the body's weight in response to the rhythmic beats of the dance. The Earth Mother, a key figure in many African religions, controls the fertility of the earth and of people. Guardian ancestral spirits live within her domain, and dancers celebrate this deep-rooted relationship.

African dancers employ three characteristic dance postures. The first is an upright position with the back straight, typically used in the dance of chiefs, expressing their authority. The second posture requires a forward inclination from the hips, which directs the dancer's attention and gestures toward the earth. This posture may be maintained throughout a dance, as the Kambari do, or the dancer may move from the upright to the inclined position, as in the Yoruba *apala* dance. In the third posture, the dancer inclines the back parallel to the ground, bearing the body weight on the balls of the feet. Many riverine people use this posture in their dances, either throughout the performance or in alternation with the inclined and upright postures.

The fact that dancers are weighted toward the earth does not necessarily mean that they are heavy-footed. In some cultures, the dancers use the full foot to stamp out the rhythms; in others, they leap while performing light foot movements. Whatever the style of movement, however, the weight is pulled toward the earth, and leaps accent the return to the earth.

SUB-SAHARAN AFRICA: An Overview. This historic photograph, taken sometime between 1909 and 1915 near Rungu, in the Belgian Congo, shows an entire village of Bangba people engaged in a circle dance. An American explorer, a member of the expeditionary team, can be seen standing in the background, wearing a white shirt and a pith helmet. (Photograph by Herbert Lang; from the Department of Library Services, American Museum of Natural History, New York [no. 224585]; used by permission.)

Formal Elements: A Basis for Analysis. Any analysis of African dance must emphasize the time element of rhythm, which is experienced in the performance of rhythmic dance patterns and which forms an inseparable bond between dancers and musicians, as well as between a dance leader and the members of his team. A dancer is evaluated according to ability to follow the percussive musical rhythm—"to play the drums with one's feet" or with whatever part of the body that articulates the rhythm. This rhythmic skill underlies the abilities to hold the correct posture with the essential straight back and to use the means of progression and the gestures required by the dance style at the correct tempo. The dancer allows the rhythm to move through the body in accordance with the norms of the tradition.

Each dance has a characteristic movement pattern by which it is immediately identified. Some dance styles are exemplified by foot patterns, others by contraction of the torso, strong shoulder beats, or rapid vibrations or twists of the buttocks. The duration of a movement may be limited or unlimited, depending on how much physical exertion the dance requires and its context.

In addition to patterns of bodily movements, dances are characterized by the patterns of progression traced on the ground or floor surface—either formal or free-flowing, or a combination of these. Among the formal patterns used by teams are circles or circling lines, in which dancers usually move counterclockwise. Some linear patterns suggest the influence of drill routines from the West, but they are in fact traditional in the dances of warriors. Free-flowing patterns allow the members of a group to dance freely among themselves. A loosely organized linear or half-circle formation allows a soloist to emerge and interpret the music personally, rather than through a leader.

Spatial movements grow out of the rhythm; the dancer moves through rather than to each position, creating sculptural rather than geometric shapes. Precision is rhythmic rather than spatial, in contrast to dances traditional to most Western cultures. This characteristic does not imply simplicity; in fact, body rhythms are percussive and far more complex than those in most Western dance forms. A dancer may sustain two or three distinct rhythms simultaneously with different body parts.

The arts of Africa are united in performance. From childhood, specialist musicians, singers, dancers, sculptors, and costume-makers have learned family skills. The dance masquerader, in elaborate costume carrying a carved mask, embodies all the arts of Africa.

From Tradition to Theater. Dance in Africa may be divided into three interrelated categories—traditional, neotraditional, and theatrical. In African societies, the year revolves around a series of festivals at which traditional arts may be seen in the contexts for which they were created, performed by leading artists in a form of village theater. Five main types of festival are distinguished by their functions: (1) ritual festivals in honor of the guardian spirits, such as the Kpledzo festival of the Ga; (2) festivals in honor of ancestors, such as the Ade festival of the Akan; (3) those that reinvest a divinely appointed king with power, such as the royal festivals of the Bini; (4) those that commemorate historical events, such as the Dumba festival in Ghana, at which Muslims celebrate the birth of the prophet Muḥammad; (5) and those that mark the annual work cycle, such as the Kundum festival of the Nzema and Ahanta. Placatory sacrificial rites at a shrine are followed by processions of key figures through the town or village, featuring music and dance and culminating in the market square, where the theme of the festival is stated in artistic terms.

In a village community, the spectators at a ceremony or social celebration are familiar with the style and intention of the dance. They are present to participate in artistic reaffirmation of the customs and values that sustain their communal life. A close-knit relationship is established between the performers and the audience who surround them, creating their dance space and supporting them by clapping or singing if the occasion allows. Audiences also assess the performances and decide whether innovations accord with tradition. Only highly skilled dancers are selected by the elders to perform at important public events. Master dancers hold a position of prestige which they must work to maintain, because spectators are fiercely critical of errors or mishaps. For example, a stilt dancer who falls is ordered out of the area in disgrace by the organizer, who may discipline audience and performers alike.

Within the various traditions, gradual changes in dance styles usually occur under the guidance of dance leaders. But when a sudden or major cultural change—such as invasion, religious conversion, or the introduction of universal primary education—occurs in a country or community, the pattern of life alters radically, as are attitudes toward dance. Conversion to Christianity banned or minimized dances in the past; now Muslims too often forbid converts to attend traditional festivals or perform their dances. Today some Christian churches attempt to Africanize their liturgies with music and dance, bringing familiar styles into new contexts, so gestures and tempos have to be rethought.

The introduction of long-term formal education to Africa since World War II has meant that many children had no time to learn traditional dancing skills. Ghana's Ministry of Education introduced dance and music into the school syllabus in the 1960s. This has affected dance styles in the towns and villages to which the pupils return. Dances in schools are performed in a different environment and with different intentions than those that are part of a village tradition. When the two coincide, the

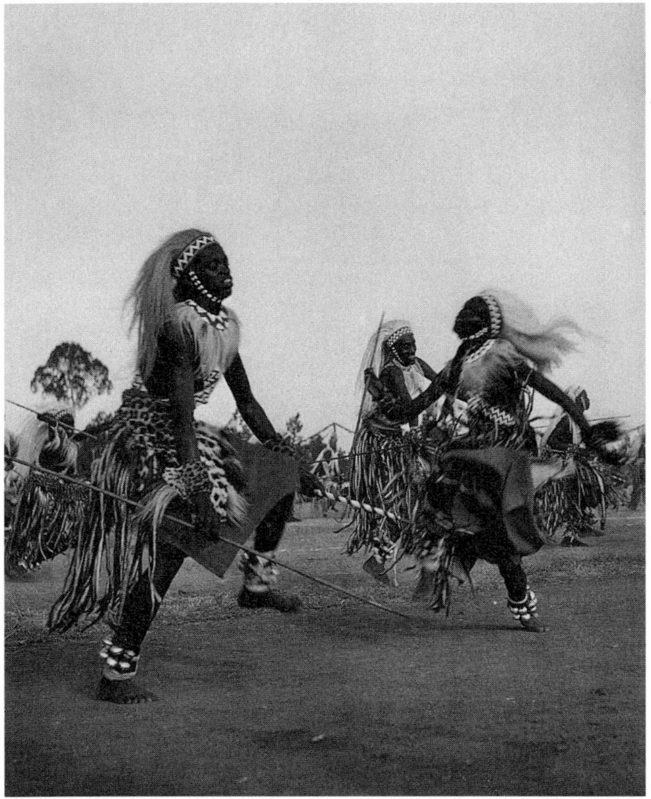

SUB-SAHARAN AFRICA: An Overview. Men of the Tutsi tribe in Rwanda performing the dance of the *intore,* the warrior elite of the kingdom. Wearing their typical headdresses with long raffia manes and richly bedecked with bead necklaces and leopard skins, the *intore* perform a vigorous, leaping dance while brandishing bows and spears. Accompaniment is provided by horn players and by the jangling of bells strapped to the dancers' ankles. (Photograph © 1994 by Michel Huet / Hoa-Qui; used by permission.)

dance styles are affected by changes in organization, duration, and dress; the resulting performances successfully met a new need, so the altered dance styles became accepted.

Modern transport has affected dance styles by bringing together people from diverse cultures, at times with spectacular results. The introduction of modern media, such as transistor radios played in villages, has led the young to turn to new styles of dance, with emphasis on entertainment and recreation. When a master dancer dies nowadays, he may have no replacement; however, the changing pattern of village life stimulates creative individuals to build new dance patterns that reflect modern interests. More radical changes occur as dancers move to urban centers where westernized lifestyles, films, and television are common.

A major catalyst for change has been governmental organization of civic arts festivals to promote traditional arts. Cultural officials, with varying knowledge of the arts, hold village competitions, selecting the best dancers to compete in a series of elimination events from town to national levels.

When a traditional dance is taken out of its village context and performed for a diverse audience unfamiliar with its original intention or style, the dance may be regarded as pure entertainment, and the motivation and intention of the performers may change as well. The performers may restructure traditional dances to emphasize spectacular elements in attempts to please the audience or gain prizes, fees, or prestige. Cultural officials often rearrange performances on the basis of audience reaction, limiting duration and encouraging a concentration of spectacular movements from several dances into a single performance. Costumes may be changed to suit occasions or to express national sentiments. Movement patterns may be altered to suit modern stages or to please important donors. When traditional dance forms are thus disrupted, a neotraditional style emerges.

The highly organized teams of the Igbo, however, perform in a number of contexts within their village tradition. Their discipline and rehearsal technique allow them to make the transition to a modern stage with spectacular results, especially if the master dancers are allowed to alter the dance patterns in creative response to the stimulation of fresh venues and foreign audiences. Nonetheless, with continuous repetition for purely commercial motives even such lively dances as the *etilogwu* or the Zulu war dance can become hackneyed and faded.

Neotraditional dance styles may imitate the externals of traditional styles yet lose the vital motivation that gives the dance meaning for performer and audience. Master dancers may become or give way to theatrical choreographers who can create works for the contemporary theater that are meaningful specifically in performance terms, not merely compromised versions of traditional dances. At the University of Ife in Nigeria, at the Mudra Centre in Dakar, Senegal, and in Guinea, contemporary training for African dance theater has been established. The technique taught at Ife has been based purely on dance patterns drawn from a wide range of African traditions; the Mudra Centre, established in 1977, has imported theatrical techniques from the West.

Dance drama has become a popular form in African theaters, but the most common role for theatrical dance is in conjunction with other performing arts in theater productions, preserving the essence of the traditional interrelation of artists in different performance media. The first professional theaters in West Africa were companies created by actor-managers, most of whom had been schoolteachers experienced in dramatizing Bible stories in Christian churches. They set up traveling companies that performed in native languages, utilizing full ranges of theater arts to reach both urban and rural audiences. Programs, readily adaptable, could be toured to halls, open spaces, or theaters.

The Yoruba opera companies are examples of this popular form of theater in Nigeria. Each company works under the artistic direction of the actor-manager, who plays leading parts. In productions based on musical ensembles, the performers move fluidly from the use of words in song, poetry, and dialogue to the use of movement in mime and dance. Dialogue is initially improvised and finally scripted. The dance, music, poetry, and costumes are drawn from Yoruba traditions and used creatively in a dramatic setting.

The themes in the works of the leading companies' dramatists indicate their range of material. Duro Lapido based his work on Yoruba mythology. Actor and mime Kola Ogunmola created domestic comedies focused on his brilliant use of mime, while Herbert Ogunde staged social narratives and political satires, using music and dance influenced by the British concert-hall performances in vogue when he began his career in Lagos in the 1930s. Ladipo died in 1973, hailed in Nigeria as a leading theatrical innovator for his use of African traditions as a basis of contemporary theater.

In Ghana, since the 1920s the popular Bob Cole worked, through improvisation, to produce theatrical comedies that combined music and dance with dialogue. These are known in Africa as the Trios, and their influence as indigenous theater is apparent in the works of contemporary choreographic directors.

In many African states, government ministries have set up national dance schools that feed dance companies promoted to tour in Africa and abroad. Some companies, such as the National Ballet of Senegal, are neotraditional rather than theatrical and offer sophisticated adaptations

SUB-SAHARAN AFRICA: An Overview. The *ngodo*, the elaborate orchestral dance of the Chopi people of Mozambique, is an ancient tradition, having been documented by Portuguese explorers in the sixteenth century. The orchestra is composed of xylophones made in five pitches (treble, alto, tenor, bass, and double bass), seen here in the foreground. In front of the seated xylophone players stand four rattle players. The dancers have just made their entrance into the performing area and have turned to face the orchestra. A complete dance may have as many as nine to fifteen sections and take up to an hour to perform. The complexities of the dance, the poetry of the lyrics, and the beauty of the music place the Chopi *ngodo* in a class by itself among the performing arts of sub-Saharan Africa. (Photograph by Merlyn Severn; reprinted by permission from Hugh Tracey, *African Dances of the Witwatersrand Gold Mines*, Johannesburg, 1952, p. 131.)

SUB-SAHARAN AFRICA: An Overview. A troupe of Zulu youths performing a gumboot dance at the Robinson Deep Mine dance arena, near Johannesburg. To the accompaniment of a guitar, the dancers perform in unison, slapping their boots and stamping their feet to create elaborate rhythmic patterns. The percussive effects achieved with heavy rubber Wellington boots are not unlike those in tap dancing. The dome-shaped straw hut is typically Zulu. (Photograph by Merlyn Severn; reprinted by permission from Hugh Tracey, *African Dances of the Witwatersrand Gold Mines*, Johannesburg, 1952, p. 52.)

of traditional dance styles in fast-moving productions. Others, such as Les Ballets Africains, use these traditions to create contemporary African styles. [*See* Ballets Africains, Les; *and* National Ballet of Senegal.] National theater companies may be static, promoting conservative works, or inventive, aiming to appeal to all strata of society. For example, the National Theatre of Kenya was established in the 1960s under the directorship of Ngugi Wa'Thiongo, who was later banished to his village. There, he set up a cooperative theater in which villagers worked together, using the full range of performing arts in productions that spoke of their lives and problems. At the other extreme are the musical extravaganzas on stereotyped African themes that were sponsored by South Africa's government to support its former doctrine of *apartheid*, such as the stage musical *Ipo-Tombi*, presented in London and New York. An effective response was the refreshing simplicity and artistic excellence of the musical *Poppie Nongena*, in which a small cast of black South Africans based their performance on song and used dance as an integral part of the drama.

Contemporary theater in Africa is at its most successful when a creative director works with talented artists who have not lost the strength and vigor of the traditional arts. Other twentieth-century phenomena are the growth of popular dance forms, such as highlife and juju, and the counterinfluence of African-American and Caribbean music and dance on new African styles and genres.

BIBLIOGRAPHY

Åkesson, Birgit. *Källvattnets mask: Om dans i Afrika*. Stockholm, 1983.

Briginshaw, Valerie A. "African Dance Bibliography." *Africana Journal* 10.1 (1979).

Hanna, Judith Lynne. "African Dance Research: Past, Present, and Future." *Africana Journal* 11.1–2 (1980): 33–51.

Harper, Peggy. "Dance in a Changing Society." *African Arts* 1 (Fall 1967): 10–13, 76–80.

Harper, Peggy. "Dance in Nigeria." In *Dance in Africa, Asia, and the Pacific*, edited by Judy Van Zile. New York, 1976.

Harper, Peggy. "The Arts of Theatre and Ritual." *Theoria of Theory* 2.3 (1977).

Harper, Peggy. "Dance." In *The Cambridge Encyclopedia of Africa*. Cambridge, 1981.

Huet, Michel. *The Dance, Art, and Ritual of Africa*. New York, 1978.

Huet, Michel, and Claude Savary. *Africa Dances*. London, 1995.

Kubik, Gerhard. *Maskentraditionen im bantu-sprachigen Afrika*. Munich, 1993.

Nketia, J. H. Kwabena. *The Music of Africa*. New York, 1974.

Opoku, Albert M. "The Presentation of Traditional Music and Dance in the Theatre." *World of Music* 18.4 (1976): 58–67.

Schaeffner, André. *Le sistre et le hochet: Musique, théâtre et danse dans les sociétés africaines*. Paris, 1990.

Thompson, Robert Farris. *African Art in Motion: Icon and Act*. 2d ed. Los Angeles, 1979.

Thompson-Drewal, Margaret, and Glorianne Jackson, comps. *Sources on African and African-Related Dance*. New York, 1974.

Tiérou, Alphonse. *Dooplé: The Eternal Law of African Dance*. Translated by Deirdre McMahon. Chur, 1992.

PEGGY HARPER

Popular Dance

In the context of sub-Saharan Africa, the term *popular dance* refers to purely recreational forms of social dancing that developed in the growing urban centers of the colonial period (sixteenth to twentieth centuries). These dances rapidly diffused into the countryside, where they have thrived as irrepressibly as in urban settings. During the twentieth century, large towns have served as centers of invention and dissemination for popular dance. In rural areas, precolonial or traditional recreational dances and older styles of popular dance still flourish. Rural areas not only provide a constant source of enrichment for urban dance culture but also are continually reinvigorated by new influences from the cities.

African popular music and dance emerged from the confrontation and confluence of indigenous and foreign cultures around 1900. Their development and performance represent a creative response to the demands of a challenging and rapidly changing environment. African popular dances exemplify the process of syncretism, in which stylistic elements drawn from two or more cultures in contact not only blend but also cross-fertilize in response to new social needs. The actual forms these dances take depend on the social experiences, cognitive cultural models, and expressive resources of their creators.

Widely distributed throughout English-speaking West Africa is highlife, a popular dance style and an example of syncretism. The term *highlife* seems first to have attained popularity during the 1920s, although the creative origins of the dance may go back another century to the beginning of a significant British presence in Ghana (the former Gold Coast). The British employed Africans throughout the lower levels of their colonial administration. To succeed within the system, Africans had to learn the cultural forms of their employers. This they did in the mission churches and schools, the colonial service, and the enterprises of the colonial economy. Adopting European forms of social dancing was a creative and enjoyable aspect of acceding to cultural imperialism.

Both the British expatriates and the African colonial elite needed dance music, so before recordings became available African musicians were trained on Western in-

SUB-SAHARAN AFRICA: Popular Dance. The famous New Year's Carnival in Cape Town, South Africa, draws visitors from far and near. These youngsters, wearing matching outfits and carrying yellow parasols, are typical of the numerous groups organized to go dancing in the streets of the city. (Photograph by Doug Pithey; used by permission of the Cape Newspaper Picture Service.)

struments in the mission schools and in the military bands of the West African Frontier Force. Soon these musicians came together in dance bands to play for the social events of the colonial elite, both white and black. Obliged to perform while fellow Africans in formal dress disported themselves in the manner of the British, these musicians named this music "highlife," a satirical reference to the social ambitions of their patrons. Specifically, the term denoted indigenous African melodies that were orchestrated for dance bands, as well as to European hymns and march tunes that were transformed into dance music by the influence of African intonations, harmonies, and rhythms. West Indian, Latin American, and African-American music entered the mix via Europe and the dance craze of the 1920s.

As a dance, highlife displayed the same complex syncretism as the music, using a relatively uncomplicated set of steps. Unlike traditional African dances, highlife was performed by couples in the European fashion; rather than holding onto each other, however, partners moved individually, smoothly orchestrating simultaneous movements of head, shoulders, hips, and feet in a graceful alternating two-step, to the multiple accents of an easy calypso-like rhythm.

During the same period, another form of highlife was also developing out of a different colonial experience. African artisans from the Gold Goast, who had been sent to work in the coastal towns of Sierra Leone, Nigeria, and Cameroon, learned and brought back new dances and musical influences. In such ports as Sekondi-Takoradi (in Ghana), they met Liberian, West Indian, and African-American sailors, who were introducing the guitar into West African urban folk music. Soon a tradition of guitar band or "palm wine" highlife developed among the new urban African working class. Among its most famous innovators was Yao Amponsah, after whom the most common highlife rhythm is named. Amponsah claimed to have learned guitar in the 1920s from a Liberian Kru sailor at Takoradi.

Unlike dance-band highlife, guitar-band highlife emphasized lengthy narrative songs of social commentary and satire that were similar to the traditional ballads of the Akan-speaking peoples of Ghana. They were performed to the accompaniment of guitar and traditional percussion instruments, often for casual listeners and dancers at the palm wine bars found throughout Ghana's urban working-class neighborhoods. In the countryside, and in precolonial towns such as the Ashanti capital, Kumasi, guitar highlife was strongly influenced by traditional dances such as *adowa*, which led to the emergence of new virtuosic styles of solo dancing—traditional highlife and highlife *adowa*.

Following Ghanaian independence in 1957, dance-band and guitar-band highlife gradually converged, becoming part of the emerging cultural nationalism of postcolonial Africa. Well before this, highlife had spread to Nigeria and other West African countries, and bands from several countries toured throughout the region. In Congo (formerly Zaïre), a popular guitar-band style—based on Afro-Latin rhythms and Mediterranean, African, and West Indian melodies—emerged and spread throughout East and Francophone Africa. Called "Congo Beat," it is still sub-Saharan Africa's most widely played and popular style of music and dance. In Nigeria, *juju* music has become the most popular form; its exponents perform regularly in Britain and the United States as well as in West Africa. In southern Africa, the blending of African dance with African-American soul and jazz has produced the energetic jive style.

At nightclubs and social gatherings throughout sub-Saharan Africa today, styles of homegrown popular dance flourish side by side with the latest imported recordings and African-American dances. Together, all these factors nourish the continuing vitality of African dance and provide a means of cultural expression, representation, and reorientation.

BIBLIOGRAPHY

African Urban Notes 5.4 (1970).

African Urban Studies 6 (Winter 1979–1980).

Coplan, David. "Go to My Town, Cape Coast! The Social History of Ghanaian Highlife." In *Eight Urban Musical Cultures: Tradition and Change,* edited by Bruno Nettl. Urbana, Ill., 1978.

Coplan, David. *In Township Tonight! South Africa's Black City Music and Theatre.* Johannesburg, 1985.

Roberts, John Storm. *Black Music of Two Worlds.* New York, 1972.

RECORDINGS. King Sunny Ade and His African Beats, *Juju Music* (Mango Records, MLPS 9712). African Brothers Dance Band, *African Brothers Dance Band (International)* (Afribros, PAB 110). Eric Agyeman, *Highlife Safari* (Apogee Records, BEBLOP 013). Dollar Brand, *Mannenburg—Is Where It's Happening* (The Sun, SRK 786134). Franco et le T.P. O.K. Jazz, *Disque d'or et maracas d'or 1982,* vol. 6 (Disco Stock Makossa, DM 5004). Fela Ransome Kuti and the Africa 70, *Shakara* (Editions Makossa International, EM 23.05). Tabu Ley et l'Afrisa International, *Rochereau,* vol. 6 (Star Musique, SMP 6006). Prince Nico Mbarga & Rocafil Jazz, *Sweet Mother* (Rounder Records, 5007). Ebenezer Obey, *Chief Commander Ebenezer Obey and His International Brothers* (Decca [West Africa], WAP 38). Oboade, *Kpanlogo Party with Oboade* (Lyrichord, LLST7251). Soul Brothers, *Dumela* (Masterpiece, LMS 528). *Sound d'Afrique* (Mango Records, MLPS 9697).

DAVID COPLAN

Dance Research and Publication

Few Western scholars who have done sustained field-work in Africa have had specific training in observing, describing, documenting, and analyzing dance. Among the few who have such training are Odette Blum, Margaret Thompson-Drewal, Judith Lynne Hanna, and Peggy Harper.

Blum (1973) characterized certain dance styles in four Ghanaian cultures. Margaret Thompson-Drewal, Hanna, and Harper studied dance primarily in Nigeria. Hanna's

1963 fieldwork among the Ubakala Igbo (1976, 1977a, 1977b, 1979) considered the functions of dance as a communicative system. Harper worked with filmmaker Francis Speed and used effort-shape theory to establish a relationship between dance styles and work movements (1968a, 1968b, 1969, 1970a, 1970b, 1972). Margaret Thompson-Drewal, both alone (1975, 1978, 1984) and with Henry John Drewal (1987) investigated indigenous concepts of performance, their bases in philosophies, and the ways in which dance articulates those philosophies and concepts. A semiological approach is of particular interest to Céline Baduel-Mathon (1969).

Since 1970, much of the available information on African dance has come from the writings of anthropologists, art historians, and musicologists; dance performance, however, is only incidental to their primary interests. The art historian Robert Farris Thompson, for example, wrote *African Art in Motion* (1974; 2d ed., 1979). Two of Thompson's former students, Frederick Lamp (1978) and Judith Bettelheim (1976), also explored dance. Lamp studied with Irmgard Bartenieff in preparation for fieldwork among the Temne people of Sierra Leone, and Bettelheim concentrated on documenting African influences in Caribbean performance genres.

Perhaps the best contributions of art historians to dance scholarship come from their studies of masked performances, a genre that combines their interests in costumes and sculpted masks with the context of dance. Works by Jean Borgatti (1976, 1979), Henry John Drewal (1977, 1979), Wilson Perkins Foss (1973), and René Bravmann (1977) are of particular note.

Ethnomusicologists—including Paul Berliner (1975–1976), John Blacking (1977), Gerhard Kubik (1977), and J. H. Kwabena Nketia (1974, pp. 206–230)—and the art historians Thompson (1966) and Borgatti have also been interested in dance styles and performances. Films, too, provide rich glimpses of African dance styles; see Margaret Thompson-Drewal and Glorianne Jackson (1974), also Ruth M. Stone (1982).

Anthropological information on African dance has often come as a byproduct of research on ritual, especially its functional and symbolic dimensions. Anthropologists who have concentrated specifically on dance include Jacques Binet (1972), James W. Fernandez (1975–1976), T. O. Ranger (1975), and Victor Turner (1968). Their work reveals how dance functions as a part of social processes, but not how dancers actually perform or how such performance relates to those social processes or to a culture's total symbolic system. Exceptions are found in works by Walter H. Sangree (1976) and by Judith Lynne Hanna. Hanna's studies consider formal and stylistic elements of Ubakala Igbo dance plays within a functionalist interpretation.

Possession trance is one important area of research that has been explored by both anthropologists and ethnomusicologists (see Walker 1972; Zaretsky and Shambaugh, 1978). The literature on possession in Africa, however, concentrates on neurological and psycho-physiological explanations of trance. Dance scholars can provide fresh insights into this phenomenon by examining it as performance—because trance in Africa is frequently expressed in dance that varies greatly even within cultures (as among the Yoruba) and requires a certain level of technical mastery. Dance scholars can analyze and compare the formal aspects of possession trance, the training of performers, and their movement styles and techniques.

The issue of gender should also be an important consideration in dance research in Africa. Earlier scholars tended either to accept men's and women's dances as cultural givens or to explain them in terms of corresponding social roles, without accounting for dance roles and categories as cultural constructions. Questions arise, then, about how gender concepts shape dance, and vice versa.

Poststructuralist trends in anthropology suggest new directions in African dance research. A view has developed that holds traditional African dance to be unfixed, fluid, always emerging through interpretive processes, and thus simultaneously created anew and re-presented at each performance.

BIBLIOGRAPHY

Baduel-Mathon, Céline. "Pour une semiologie du geste en Afrique occidentale." *Semiotica* 1 (1969).

Berliner, Paul. "Music and Spirit Possession at a Shona Bira." *African Music Society Journal* 5 (1975–1976).

Bettelheim, Judith. "The Jonkonnu Festival: Its Relation to Caribbean and African Masquerades." *Jamaica Journal* 10 (1976).

Binet, Jacques. *Sociétés de danse chez les Fang du Gabon*. Paris, 1972.

Blacking, John. "An Introduction to Venda Traditional Dances." *Dance Studies* 2 (1977): 34–56.

Blum, Odette. "Dance in Ghana." *Dance Perspectives*, no. 56 (Winter 1973).

Borgatti, Jean. "The Festival as Art Event: Form and Iconography." Ph.D.diss., University of California, Los Angeles, 1976.

Borgatti, Jean. *From the Hands of Lawrence Ajanaku*. Los Angeles, 1979.

Bravmann, René A. "Gyinna-Gyinna: Making the Djinn Manifest." *African Arts* 10 (April 1977).

Drewal, Henry John. "Art and the Perception of Women in Yoruba Culture." *Cahiers d'études africaines* 17 (1977).

Drewal, Henry John. "Pageantry and Power in Yoruba Costuming." In *The Fabrics of Culture*, edited by Justine M. Cordwell and Ronald A. Schwarz. The Hague, 1979.

Fernandez, James W. "Dance Exchange in Western Equatorial Africa." *Dance Research Journal* 8 (Fall–Winter 1975–1976): 1–7.

Foss, Wilson Perkins. "Festival of Ohworu at Evwreni." *African Arts* 6 (1973).

Hanna, Judith Lynne. "The Anthropology of Dance Ritual: Nigeria's Ubakala Nkwa di Iche Iche." Ph.D.diss., Columbia University, 1976.

Hanna, Judith Lynne. "Ubakala Dance Movement: Aesthetics, Sex, and Other Sociocultural Patterns." *African Studies Papers* (1977).

Hanna, Judith Lynne. "Dance and Social Structure: The Ubakala of Nigeria." *Journal of Communication* 29 (Autumn 1979): 184–191.

Harper, Peggy. *The Irigwe Dancers of Miango Village on the Jos Plateau.* Studies in Nigerian Dance, no. 2. Ibadan, 1968a.

Harper, Peggy. *Tiv Women: The Icough Dance.* Studies in Nigerian Dance, no. 1. Ibadan, 1968b.

Harper, Peggy. "Dance in Nigeria." *Ethnomusicology* 13.2 (1969): 280–295.

Harper, Peggy. "Icough: A Tiv Dance." *African Notes* 6 (1970a).

Harper, Peggy. "The Role of Dance in the Gelede Ceremonies of the Village of Ijio." *Odu,* n.s. 4 (1970b).

Harper, Peggy. "The Kambari People and Their Dances." *Odu,* n.s. 7 (April 1972).

Kubik, Gerhard. "Patterns of Body Movement in the Music of Boys' Initiation in South-East Angola." In *The Anthropology of the Body,* edited by John Blacking. London, 1977.

Lamp, Frederick. "Frogs into Princes: The Temne Rabai Initiation." *African Arts* 11 (January 1978).

Nketia, J. H. Kwabena. *The Music of Africa.* New York, 1974.

Ranger, T. O. *Dance and Society in Eastern Africa, 1890–1970: The Beni Ngoma.* London, 1975.

Sangree, Walter H. "Dancers as Emissaries in Irigwe, Nigeria." *Dance Research Journal* 8 (Spring-Summer 1976): 31–35.

Stone, Ruth M. "Twenty-Five Years of Selected Films in Ethnomusicology: Africa." *Ethnomusicology* 26 (1982).

Thompson, Robert Farris. "An Aesthetic of the Cool: West African Dance." *African Forum* 2.2 (1966): 85–102.

Thompson, Robert Farris. *African Art in Motion: Icon and Act.* 2d ed. Los Angeles, 1979.

Thompson-Drewal, Margaret, and Glorianne Jackson, comps. *Sources on African and African-Related Dance.* New York, 1974.

Thompson-Drewal, Margaret. "Symbols of Possession: A Study of Movement and Regalia in an Anago-Yoruba Ceremony." *Dance Research Journal* 7 (Spring–Summer 1975): 15–24.

Thompson-Drewal, Margaret, and Henry John Drewal. "More Powerful Than Each Other: An Egbado Classification of Egungun." *African Arts* 11 (Spring 1978).

Thompson-Drewal, Margaret. "Appendix B (Dance)." In *From the Hands of Lawrence Ajanaku,* by Jean Borgatti. Los Angeles, 1979.

Thompson-Drewal, Margaret, and Henry John Drewal. "Composing Time and Space in Yoruba Art." In *The Relationship of the Verbal and Visual Arts among the Yoruba,* edited by Rowland Abiodun. 1987.

Thompson-Drewal, Margaret. "Dancing for Ogun in Yorubaland and in Brazil." In *Africa's Ogun: Old World and New,* edited by Sandra T. Barnes. Bloomington, 1989.

Turner, Victor. *The Drums of Affliction: A Study of Religious Processes among the Ndembu of Zambia.* Oxford, 1968.

Walker, Sheila S. *Ceremonial Spirit Possession in Africa and Afro-America.* Leiden, 1972.

Zaretsky, Irving I., and Cynthia Shambaugh. *Spirit Possession and Spirit Mediumship in Africa and Afro-America: An Annotated Bibliography.* New York, 1978.

MARGARET THOMPSON-DREWAL

SUDAN. *See* Nuba Dance; *and* Zār. *For discussion of Sudanese influence on Egyptian traditional dance, see* Egypt, *article on* Traditional Dance.

SUFI DANCE. *See* Dance and Islam. *See also* Turkey.

SUITE FOR FIVE. Original title: *Suite for Five in Space and Time.* Choreography: Merce Cunningham. Music: *Music for Piano* 8–84, John Cage. Costumes: Robert Rauschenberg. First performance: 18 May 1956, University of Notre Dame, South Bend, Indiana, Merce Cunningham Dance Company. Dancers: Merce Cunningham, Carolyn Brown, Viola Farber, Marianne Preger, Remy Charlip.

Suite for Five is an expanded version of Merce Cunningham's 1953 *Solo Suite in Space and Time.* To the original five solos, Cunningham added a trio (for Farber, Preger, and Charlip), a duet (for Cunningham and Brown), and a quintet. In the first performance the order was solo ("At Random"), trio ("Transition"), solo ("Stillness"), duet ("Extended Moment"), solo ("Repetition"), solo ("Excursion"), quintet ("Meetings"), solo ("For the Air"). Subsequently the solos "Repetition" and "For the Air" were omitted. In 1958, for a duet version titled *Suite for Two,* Cunningham choreographed "A Meander," a solo for Carolyn Brown. It was interpolated between the opening solo and the trio in the group version and this became the definitive *Suite for Five.* From 1953 until 1973 the solo, duet, and quintet versions were in the Cunningham company repertory, seen throughout the United States, Europe, and Asia.

Cunningham and Cage used chance operation in the choreography and music composition. A detailed explanation of Cage's process may be found in his *Silence.* Cunningham used Cage's process to determine the space, spatial relationships, and durations of phrases. Each dance has a designated time length. "This was one of the first dances where meter was completely abandoned," according to Cunningham, "and [the] dancers had to rely on [their] own dance timing to guard the length of any phrase, and the timing of a complete dance" (*A John Cage Reader,* p. 111). The following note appeared in the program: "The events and sounds of this dance revolve around a quiet center, which, though silent and unmoving, is the source from which it happens." *Suite for Five* is a seminal work that explores movement in time and space, and one might describe it as Cunningham's earliest choreographic realization of the hypothesis that time and space cannot be defined independently of motion.

BIBLIOGRAPHY

Cunningham, Merce. *Changes: Notes on Choreography.* Edited by Frances Starr. New York, 1968.

Cage, John. *Silence.* Middletown, Connecticut, 1961.

A John Cage Reader. New York, 1982.

CAROLYN BROWN

SULAWESI. *See* Indonesia, *article on* Dance Traditions of the Outlying Islands.

SUMATRA. *See* Indonesia, *article on* Sumatran Dance Traditions.

SUMMERSPACE. Full title: *Summerspace—A Lyric Dance.* Choreography: Merce Cunningham. Music: *Xion,* Morton Feldman. Scenery and costumes: Robert Rauschenberg. First performance: 17 August 1958, Connecticut College, New London, Connecticut, Merce Cunningham Dance Company. Dancers: Merce Cunningham, Carolyn Brown, Viola Farber, Cynthia Stone, Marilyn Wood, Remy Charlip.

Summerspace is the second in a series of dances by Merce Cunningham named for the four seasons. *Springweather and People* (1955), *Rune* (originally *Autumn Rune*; 1959), and *Winterbranch* (1964) complete the cycle. *Time* Magazine (29 February 1960) described *Summerspace* as "an impressionistic work evoking the shimmering heat of summer, the play of light and shade . . . danced before a pointillistic back drop. . . . The dancers wore similarly dappled costumes which permitted them to disappear into and emerge from the scenery as if they were passing through a wall."

"With *Summerspace* (the summer part of the title came after the dance was finished, but the notion of space was always present), the principal momentum was a concern for steps that carry one through space, and not only into it," wrote Cunningham in 1968. "Like the passage of birds, stopping for moments on the ground and then going on, or automobiles more relentlessly throbbing along turnpikes and under and over cloverleaves. This led to the idea of using kinds of movement that would be continuous, and would carry the dancer into the playing area, and out of it." In his notes, Cunningham explains his use of chance procedures applied to a gamut of movement to determine such things as direction, speed, shape of the space, number of dancers involved in a particular action, and so on.

Summerspace is one of the best known of Cunningham's dances for two reasons: its unusual and striking pointillist decor by Robert Rauschenberg and the fact that it is one of the few works Cunningham choreographed for his own company that has been performed by other companies, namely the New York City Ballet, the Cullberg Ballet, the Boston Ballet, and the Théâtre du Silence in La Rochelle, France. In both the New York City Ballet and the Boston Ballet productions the womens' roles were danced in pointe shoes.

The first performance of *Summerspace* at Connecticut College in 1958 was virtually ignored by the dance press. On the Cunningham company's 1964 six-month world tour, *Summerspace* was seen by audiences in London, Paris, Brussels, Venice, New Delhi, and Tokyo, among other cities, and received considerable press coverage. But in 1965, when the company gave two performances at the New York State Theater the dance once again received little attention from American critics. However, the same work on the same stage performed by the New York City Ballet only one year later was greeted with reviews in six New York City daily newspapers and much preperformance publicity, and yet many agreed with Walter Terry that it was Cunningham's dancers rather than Balanchine's who communicated a sense of alertness, of responsiveness to stillness as well as to sound.

BIBLIOGRAPHY

Cunningham, Merce. "*Summerspace* Story." *Dance Magazine* (June 1966): 52–54.

Cunningham, Merce. *Changes: Notes on Choreography.* Edited by Frances Starr. New York, 1968.

Reynold, Nance, and Susan Reimer-Torn. *Dance Classics.* Pennington, N.J., 1991.

Terry, Walter. Review. *New York Herald Tribune* (15 April 1966).

CAROLYN BROWN

SUNDA. *See* Indonesia, *article on* Sundanese Dance Traditions.

SUSANA (Susana Janssen-Audeoud; born 10 October 1916 in Köniz, Switzerland), performer, teacher, and choreographer of Spanish dance. Although dance was not cultivated in her childhood home, Susana Janssen-Audeoud expressed herself even as a little girl in dances of her own invention. She danced in response to an inner need and without any urging from her parents. Later, when she began formal studies of classical and modern dance, she discovered Spanish dancing and recognized it as her true métier. Because Spanish dancing sought a connection with the earth as intensely as it sought passion and an opening upward, it corresponded closely to her own nature, and it became the medium through which she developed as an artist.

Despite her Swiss birth, Susana became an embodiment of Spanish dance. Juan Estampio and Cojo de Sevilla had the most decisive artistic impact upon her during her formative years. Beginning in 1948, she spent twenty years touring with José Udaeta as the dance team of Susana y José. They toured the world with a repertory that included theatricalized folk dances and their own creations in the spirit of Spanish dance.

In 1970, Susana became intensively involved in dance education and was soon a much sought-after teacher of Spanish dance, giving courses of instruction at the National Ballet School of Canada, in Toronto; at Mudra, Maurice Béjart's name for the École de Danse et d'Interpretation Artistique, in Brussels; and at the international summer Academy of Dance in Cologne. As vivacious and intuitive a teacher as a performer, Susana developed a precisely structured course of instruction based on a variety of forms of Spanish dance in a sequence of exercises comparable to those taught in a classical ballet class.

In developing this material, Susana became increasingly aware of the rich and genuine vocabulary of movement that Spanish dance offered, and she began to wonder if it could be used in developing theatrical works, as was the classical vocabulary. In addition to bringing explicitly Spanish dances to the stage, Susana used Spanish material in independent choreographic figurations of dance themes. Toward these ends, she was greatly helped by her collaboration with the composer Antonio Robledo, who willingly included the rhythmic and melodic material of flamenco in his ballet scores, which closely followed her own creative ideas. The results of their collaboration were a merging of music and choreography virtually unseen since the days of Serge Diaghilev.

Two notable works from their repertory are *Ronda de Toros* (1977) and *Los Siete Puñales* (1981), Susana's version of Federico García Lorca's *Blood Wedding*. In *Los Siete Puñales* (The Seven Daggers), the story is told in pantomime enriched by Spanish dance, and the situation and characters are expressed through elements of Spanish dance used in innovative ways. This choreographic approach was particularly successful in the depiction of the seducer Leonardo and in the duel, where dramatic tension is expressed chiefly by the *zapateado* heelwork of the onlookers.

In 1985, Susana and Robledo formed their own small company, which they called Flamencos en Route. In the following five years the two artists created for it their two masterpieces, *Soledad* and *A Juan*. In both these works, Spanish folklore is transformed into a language of high art, combining the power and energy of dance with the expressive sensibility of music.

BIBLIOGRAPHY

Merz, Richard. "En Route: Susana." *Ballet-Info* 4 (June 1981): 15–18.

Merz, Richard. "What Is a Dance Event?" *Ballett International* 11 (March 1988): 10–15.

Pastori, Jean-Pierre. *Dance and Ballet in Switzerland*. Translated by Jacqueline Gartmann. 2d ed., rev. and enl. Zurich, 1989.

Zacharias, Gerhard. *Susana y José*. Vienna, 1970.

RICHARD MERZ
Translated from German

SVETLOV, VALERIAN (Valerian Iakovlevich Ivchenko; born 1860 in Saint Petersburg, died 1934 in Paris), Russian critic, writer, and editor. Svetlov was an associate of Serge Diaghilev, a founding member of the Association for the Organization of the Russian Seasons Abroad, and an ardent champion of Michel Fokine's innovations in choreography. He was a prolific writer both in Russia and in France following his 1917 emigration there. Svetlov was the third husband of the dancer Vera Trefilova.

Editor of the popular literary journal *Niva*, Svetlov also wrote numerous full-length works as well as articles that appeared in such periodicals as *Peterburgskaia gazeta, Birzhevye vedomosti, Slovo, Le temps russe, Vozrozhdenie, Dancing Times, Archives internationales de la danse*, and *American Dancer*. He contributed extensive accounts of Diaghilev's Paris seasons to the Russian press and always enthusiastically supported Fokine's work. In 1910, for instance, Svetlov summarized the season by noting that "Diaghilev not only organized this mighty and serious artistic enterprise but served as its inspiration, breathing new life into an art that had frozen in a state of senility. He provided a broad arena for Fokine's outstanding talents." Svetlov's accounts of Diaghilev productions were not always full of praise, however. In 1912 Svetlov wrote two lengthy articles about *L'Après-midi d'un Faune* in which he argued that although Léon Bakst's decor was "beautiful and striking in its use of color, creating a Bacchanalia of all possible spots, like a multicolored, attractive rug," it was completely out of keeping with the ballet's bas-relief theme. In Svetlov's view, the ballet's illustrious creators had simply made a *faux pas*, and he predicted that the *Faune* failure would simply go unnoticed.

In addition to being Fokine's chief supporter among the critics, Svetlov collaborated with Fokine on the production of *Eros* in 1915. His story "The Fiesole Angel" provided the scenario for the ballet.

Svetlov is perhaps best remembered for his 1911 book *Sovremennyi balet*, published the following year in French as *Le ballet contemporain*. Among the first expositions of the new ballet and its influence on western Europe, the book also served as a compilation and summary of Svetlov's own views about the new ballet. The book includes a chapter on the Petipa legacy, Svetlov's accounts of the first Russian season in Paris, a discussion of French critical reaction to the Diaghilev enterprise, and an article on Isadora Duncan. Duncan, Svetlov wrote, "arrived in the dead of winter, nude, like an ancient goddess, and transported us back to that faraway land of blue skies and golden sunshine where the plastic arts were born."

[*For related discussion, see the entries on Koni, Levinson, Volynsky, and Zotov.*]

BIBLIOGRAPHY

Karsavina, Tamara. *Theatre Street*. Rev. and enl. ed. London, 1948.

Scholl, Tim. "From Apollon to Apollo." *Ballet Review* 21 (Winter 1993): 82–96.

Svetlov, Valerian. *Terpsikhora: Stati, ocherki, zamietki*. St. Petersburg, 1906.

Svetlov, Valerian. *Sovremennyi balet*. St. Petersburg, 1911.

Svetlov, Valerian. *Le ballet contemporain*. St. Petersburg, 1912.

Svetlov, Valerian. *Anna Pavlova*. Translated by A. Grey. Paris, 1922.

Svetlov, Valerian. *Thamar Karsavina*. London, 1922.

Svetlov, Valerian. *Bakst*. New York, 1927.

Svetlov, Valerian. "The Diaghileff Ballet in Paris." *The Dancing Times* (December 1929): 263–274; (January 1930): 460–463; (February 1930): 569–574.

SUSAN COOK SUMMER

SWAINE, ALEXANDER VON (Alexander Freiherr von Swaine; born 28 December 1905 in Munich), German dancer and teacher. Swaine was one of the most versatile and technically brilliant dancers of his time. The peaks of his artistic career in Europe were in the 1930s and the 1950s. The most striking feature of his dance style was his ability to fascinate with his expressive power in both classical and modern dance.

From 1924 to 1928 Swaine studied classical dance in Berlin with Evgenia Eduardova, a veteran of Pavlova's company. At the same time he worked with Max Reinhardt in Berlin and Salzburg, appearing as Puck in *A Midsummer Night's Dream.* In 1928 he went on tour with his own dance evening; its program bore the strong imprint of interpretive dance, but its classical background was also recognizable. In 1932 he continued his studies with Margaret Craske in London. In 1933 he was hired as a solo dancer with the Berlin City Opera, but in 1935 he left this position and joined the Berlin State Opera as soloist.

Swaine quickly made a name for himself as a dancer of tremendous dramatic power. His tension-filled characterizations, reinforced by mime and physical endowments as well as dance technique, fitted him for both classical roles and for interpretive dance on the concert stage. Numerous tours, some of them with Darja Collin and Rosalia Chladek, won him high esteem in other countries. During World War II, he lived and taught in Java and India. In 1947, after being interned by the British, he returned to Germany.

With the Hungarian dancer Lisa Czobel, whose repertory similarly included both classical and modern dance, Swaine appeared in joint programs for almost twenty years thereafter, making numerous tours throughout Europe and overseas. In 1960 Swaine was hired as a teacher of classical and modern dance at the School of Fine Arts in Mexico City. In 1965 he appeared in a final dance evening with Czobel. Thereafter he concentrated on teaching, an activity that also led to guest assignments outside Mexico, including some in the United States.

BIBLIOGRAPHY

Ballett in Berlin, 1945–1978. Berlin, 1978.

Haskell, Arnold L. "The Art of Alexander von Swaine." *The Dancing Times* (January 1938): 508–509.

Huwe, Gisela, ed. *Der Deutsche Oper Berlin.* Berlin, 1984.

Peters, Kurt. "Alexander von Swaine." *Das Tanzarchiv* 28 (December 1980): 717–720.

Regitz, Hartmut, ed. *Tanz in Deutschland: Ballett seit 1945.* Berlin, 1984.

HEDWIG MÜLLER
Translated from German

SWAN, THE. *See* Dying Swan, The.

SWAN LAKE. [*This entry comprises of two articles on ballets choreographed to the score for "Swan Lake," written by Petr Ilich Tchaikovsky: the first describes the original Russian production choreographed by Wentzel Reisinger, the later version choreographed by Marius Petipa and Lev Ivanov, and subsequent productions by other choreographers in Russia; the second is a survey of productions outside Russia.*]

Productions in Russia

There is no extant draft of the original score of *Swan Lake,* and neither the librettist nor his sources are identified on the announcements or programs of the premiere. The plot was in essence similar to the one that is familiar today, telling of the maiden-turned-swan and the prince who swears he loves her but is tricked by an evil magician into betraying her. Asked by the directorate of the Bolshoi Theater to compose a ballet, Tchaikovsky requested a chivalrous theme. Given only six months to create the four-act score (in the end it took two years), he evidently planned to use material from his unfinished opera *Ondine* and needed a similar theme. (A comparison of the finished scores shows that the final duet of *Ondine* is identical to the second-act adagio of *Swan Lake.*)

Tchaikovsky began working on the score late in May 1875. He had previously used dance music in his operas, instrumental works, and even symphonies, making them more accessible to the public by introducing elements of popular music. In composing *Swan Lake* he pursued no reformist objectives, but his penchant for innovation was nevertheless at work. He did not use the method of sustained symphonic development that he would later apply in *The Sleeping Beauty* and *The Nutcracker,* but even here the music served the dance as more than an elementary rhythmic pattern by conveying its own dramatic message and complex characterizations. The integrity of the score was ensured not only by the leitmotifs that occurred throughout but also by the tonal interdependence of the episodes, which constituted an intricate system of layered associations based on the thematic material.

Original Production. Russian title: *Lebedinoe Ozero.* Ballet in four acts. Choreography: Julius (Wentzel) Reisinger. Music: Petr Ilich Tchaikovsky. Libretto: Vladimir Begichev and Vasily Geltser. Scenery: Karl Valz, Ivan Shanguine, and Karl Gropius. First performance: 20 February [4 March] 1877, Bolshoi Theater, Moscow. Principals: Polina Karpakova (Odette), Arnold Gillert (Siegfried).

In writing his score, Tchaikovsky had acted as a ballet dramatist, laying down new principles of organization that, in turn, required innovative choreographic thinking. The ballet dramaturgy of the day failed to realize this and consequently the first production of *Swan Lake* did not

SWAN LAKE: Productions in Russia. Anyone naming the great Swan Queens in Russian ballet history could not fail to mention Maya Plisetskaya. She first danced the dual role of Odette-Odile in 1947, and after the retirement of Galina Ulanova in 1962 she became the undisputed owner of the role at the Bolshoi Theater. She is pictured here in act 2, with Nikolai Fadeyechev as Siegfried and members of the female ensemble as the enchanted swan-maidens. (Photograph from the Dance Collection, New York Public Library for the Performing Arts.)

succeed. The critics found Reisinger's dances weak and gymnastic; the swan scenes were monotonous and poor in fantasy. The choreographer had failed to penetrate the complex world of Tchaikovsky's musical-psychological drama and seemingly had no feeling for its inherent lyricism. For the fourth performance on 25 April 1877 Anna Sobeshchanskaya replaced Polina Karpakova in the role of Odette, performing a new pas de deux she had commissioned from Marius Petipa.

Further alterations followed. On 13 January 1880 Joseph Hansen choreographed a new *Swan Lake* with Evdokia Kalmykova as Odette and Alfred Bekefi as Siegfried. Before it was dropped from the repertory in 1883 the ballet had been given forty-one performances. In 1888 the second act, choreographed by Augustin Berger, was shown at a concert given in honor of Tchaikovsky in Prague. In response the composer wrote in a letter to his family that he had experienced a moment of blissful happiness.

In 1894 the same act, this time choreographed by Lev Ivanov, was shown in a program at the Maryinsky Theater in Saint Petersburg commemorating Tchaikovsky, who had died the year before. After this successful showing, the decision was made to restage the entire ballet.

Petipa-Ivanov Version. Fantastic ballet in three acts and four scenes. Choreography: Marius Petipa and Lev Ivanov. Music: Petr Ilich Tchaikovsky. Libretto: Vladimir Begichev and Vasily Geltser. Scenery by Colonel Andreyev, Mikhail Bocharov, and Heinrich Levogt. Costumes by Evgeny Ponomaryov. First performance: 15 [27] January 1895, Maryinsky Theater, Saint Petersburg. Principals: Pierina Legnani (Odette-Odile), Pavel Gerdt (Prince Siegfried). Supporting cast: Sergei Bulgakov (Von Rothbart, the Evil Genie), Giuseppina Cecchetti (A Sovereign Princess, Siegfried's Mother), Aleksandr Oblakov (Benno).

For the new version of *Swan Lake,* Tchaikovsky's brother, Modest, considerably revised the original score and edited the libretto newly written by Vladimir Begichev and Vasily Geltser. Many details were altered that clarified the action and made Prince Siegfried more serious and sympathetic. The score was reworked to accommodate the revised libretto: some of the composer's piano pieces were added and some numbers were deleted or altered, while others were repositioned. Riccardo Drigo prepared a new orchestration. The first and third scenes were choreographed by Petipa; the second and fourth by Ivanov, who also staged the Hungarian and Venetian dances in the third scene.

In this version the psychological drama that Tchaikovsky had conceived gave way to magic and fairy tale. Petipa misunderstood the musical logic of the first act, regarding it as an insignificant prelude to the main events, rather than the portrait of Siegfried that Tchaikovsky had intended. (It was no accident that in later productions of the ballet it was the first scene that was most often revised.) Petipa staged the third scene (act 2) after the stereotypical model of a "ball *divertissement,*" creating the impressive pas de deux for the black swan, Odile, and Siegfried as a *pas d'action* that echoed the adagio for Siegfried and the white swan, Odette, in the second scene of act 1. Nevertheless, the production owed its success to Ivanov, whose profound understanding of the music enabled him to devise scenes of intense lyricism, in which the geometry of lines was often sharpened by the asymmetric positions of the corps de ballet and all the movement configurations reflected the image of captive, enchanted beauty. Despite the mixture of styles, the ballet was a success.

Subsequent Productions. Following the success of the Petipa-Ivanov version, numerous choreographers mounted productions of *Swan Lake* at various theaters in Russia. Notable among them are those of Aleksandr Gorsky, Agrippina Vaganova, Fedor Lopukhov, Vladimir Burmeister, and Yuri Grigorovich.

Gorsky production. In 1901 Aleksandr Gorsky introduced the Petipa-Ivanov version to the Moscow stage, but with a number of changes. In the first and third scenes he sought to intensify the dramatic elements and to clarify the psychological motivation. Later revivals of Gorsky's staging tended to present the tale as a straightforward conflict between good and evil, the good Prince Siegfried opposed to the evil sorcerer Rothbart.

Vaganova production. Attempts to depart from the Petipa-Ivanov version were also undertaken in Leningrad. In 1933 Agrippina Vaganova—collaborating with the artist Vladimir Dmitriev, who also wrote the new libretto, and the musicologist Boris Asafiev—offered her own interpretation. This staging was of fundamental significance and influenced all later Soviet productions. Previously deleted musical pieces were restored, while the mystical and fantastic elements of the plot were intensified. The action was transferred from the Middle Ages to the Romantic period of the early nineteenth century. The lake scenes emerged as if in the imagination of Siegfried, danced elegiacally by Konstantin Sergeyev. The roles of the Swan (Odette) and Odile (reimagined as the daughter of a ruined landlord rather than an evil magician) were now danced by different ballerinas, Galina Ulanova and Olga Jordan, respectively. Vaganova replaced the pantomime episodes with danced scenes that have been retained in contemporary stagings. She also accentuated the imitative movements of the swan corps de ballet.

Lopukhov and Burmeister productions. Fedor Lopukhov gave *Swan Lake* a more classical appearance in Leningrad in 1945. He restored the plot of the Petipa-Ivanov version but strengthened the role of Siegfried. His interpretation was the starting point for Vladimir Burmeister, who produced the ballet for the Stanislavsky and Nemirovich-Danchenko Musical Theater in Moscow in 1956. Burmeister used the original sequence of musical numbers but provided crudely literal explanations for the actions.

Grigorovich production. In 1969 Yuri Grigorovich produced the ballet at the Bolshoi Theater in Moscow, making extensive revisions in all but the second act. Adhering to the original conception of the plot, he avoided modernization. The first act was an extended exposition that contrasted the worlds of Siegfried and Rothbart. The latter, now with more dancing than mime, became Siegfried's alter ego, a symbol of the dark, subconscious forces dormant in the human soul. This opposition also reflected the conflict between the white and black swans. In his final version Grigorovich preserved the happy ending that became common in Russian productions.

Swan Lake's role of Odette-Odile has been an important vehicle for many ballerinas over time, including Tamara Karsavina, Olga Spessivtseva, Marina Semenova, Maya Plisetskaya, and Natalia Bessmertnova. The ballet has been staged in all the republics of the former Soviet Union.

[*See also the entries on the principal figures mentioned herein.*]

BIBLIOGRAPHY

Beaumont, Cyril W. *Complete Book of Ballets.* Rev. ed. London, 1951.

Brown, David. "Tchaikovsky's Ballets: Swan Lake." *Dance Now* 2 (Spring 1993): 26–34.

Demidov, Alexander P. *Lebedinoe Ozero.* Moscow, 1985.

Grigorovich, Yuri, and Alexander Demidov. *The Official Bolshoi Ballet Book of Swan Lake.* Translated by Yuri S. Shirokov. Neptune, N.J., 1986.

Krasovskaya, Vera. *Russkii baletnyi teatr vtoroi poloviny deviatnadtsatogo veka.* Leningrad, 1963.

Macaulay, Alastair. "Why a Swan?" *Dance Ink* 3 (Summer 1992): 16–20.

Ross, Janice, ed. *Why a Swan?* San Francisco, 1989.

Slonimsky, Yuri. *P. I. Chaikovskii i baletnyi teatr ego vremeni.* Moscow, 1956.

Souritz, Elizabeth. *Soviet Choreographers in the 1920s.* Translated by Lynn Visson. Durham, N.C., 1990.

Vanslov, Victor V. *Balety Grigorovicha i problemy khoreografii.* 2d ed. Moscow, 1971.

Wiley, Roland John. *Tchaikovsky's Ballets: "Swan Lake," "Sleeping Beauty," "Nutcracker."* Oxford, 1985.

Wiley, Roland John. *The Life and Ballets of Lev Ivanov.* Oxford, 1997.

ALEXANDER P. DEMIDOV
Translated from Russian

Productions outside Russia

There is a succession of phases in the history of the ballet *Swan Lake* in the West: exports of the scenario, nearly always with the original score by Petr Ilich Tchaikovsky;

tours of the 1895 Saint Petersburg production by companies of Russian dancers; re-creations of the 1895 Saint Petersburg production by companies in the West; and revisions of the ballet and its score according to the many choreographers' experimentations with its characterizations and themes. These phases are continuous for more than one hundred years, beginning within several years of the ballet's 1877 premiere in Moscow.

The 1877 choreography by Julius Reisinger for the Bolshoi was revised by Joseph Hansen in 1880 and 1882. Soon afterward, Hansen left Russia and became ballet master at the Alhambra Theatre in London where he mounted a ballet called *The Swans,* to music by Georges Jacobi, the Alhambra's music director. Although a December 1884 announcement in London's *Daily Telegraph* referred to an 1813 Christmas pantomime produced at Covent Garden as its antecedent, the action of the one-act ballet at the Alhambra resembled the Bolshoi version: a Swan Queen falls in love with Roland, leader of the hunters; it takes place in a forest where the swans transform themselves into "pretty feminine shapes"; at the end, the Swan Queen and Roland are united in a boat drawn by the swans across the water.

The first production set to Tchaikovsky's music outside Russia was mounted at the Prague National Theater on 21 February 1888, during a visit by the composer. The ballet master August Berger, who also took the role of the Prince, choreographed act 2 for the second of two concerts in which Tchaikovsky conducted some of his own works. Adolph Cech conducted for the ballet performances, and Giulietta Paltrinieri-Bergrova appeared as the Swan Queen. Eight performances were given of Berger's version.

Despite these early versions of *Swan Lake,* only the transmission of the choreography by Marius Petipa and Lev Ivanov for the Maryinsky Theater production in Saint Petersburg has inspired subsequent generations. The Petipa-Ivanov *Swan Lake,* which remained in the Saint Petersburg repertory, became one of the most renowned artistic exports from Russia. In 1908, Anna Pavlova and Adolph Bolm, who led the first tour of wholly trained Russian dancers to the West, presented the middle two acts of *Swan Lake* in Scandinavia and Germany. In 1909, the czar's dancers visited a wider circuit of European cities, including Vienna. Pavlova, with Nicholas Legat as partner, danced *Swan Lake's* leading role in a three-act version. The ballet was seen in London on 16 May 1910 in a production at the London Hippodrome starring Olga Preobrajenska and a group of twenty performers; it was in New York at the Metropolitan Opera House on 20 December 1911 in a production staged by Mikhail Mordkin for fourteen solo dancers and a corps de ballet—Ekaterina Geltser appeared as the Swan Queen, with Mordkin as the Prince.

Although an early production of *Swan Lake* was choreographed in 1907 by Archille Viscusi in Prague, the version for Diaghilev's Ballets Russes, which premiered in London on 30 November 1911, is generally considered the first major production outside Russia.

Accounts by Diaghilev inner-circle members Serge Grigoriev and Alexandre Benois suggest that Diaghilev included *Swan Lake* in the repertory to entice Matilda Kshessinska, *prima ballerina assoluta* of the Maryinsky company, into appearing with the troupe. Diaghilev shortened *Swan Lake* to two acts and three scenes, because, in Grigoriev's words, "he considered some of the choreography dull and repetitive" (Grigoriev, 1953, p. 59). The first scene of the Saint Petersburg original was deleted. The second scene and second act were retained with revisions. The last act was shortened into a brief scene by the lake and amended without a break to the ballroom act. The choreography was attributed to Petipa, except for the waltz and the dance of the Prince in the second scene, by Michel Fokine. A new role, the Fiancée of the Prince, was created. Tchaikovsky's score was shortened and amended with the "Dance of the Sugarplum Fairy" from *The Nutcracker* added for the Prince and an interpretation of music by Andrei Kadlets for Kshessinska's solo. Vaslav Nijinsky and Kshessinska led the cast on opening night, with Enrico Cecchetti as Master of Ceremonies, Bronislava Nijinska and Ludmilla Schollar as the leading Swan Maidens, and Adolph Bolm and Sofia Fedorova in the ballroom *divertissements* in the "Spanish Dance." Mischa Elman played the violin solos at the opening.

Some changes in the libretto were made for the performances at Monte Carlo in 1912, but the two-act *Swan Lake* remained in Diaghilev's Ballets Russes repertory from 1911 to 1914 and was revived after World War I, from 1923 to 1926. For the last four years of the company's existence, a one-act version was performed, starring Alexandra Danilova and Olga Spessivtseva. George Balanchine made minor alterations in the one-act version while he was ballet master, deleting part of the Swan Queen's mime and rearranging ensemble movements for a corps de ballet decreased in size.

After Diaghilev's death and the dispersal of the Ballets Russes in 1929, one-act reductions of *Swan Lake* were presented at the Chicago Civic Opera House in 1930 with choreography by Laurent Novikoff, by Colonel W. de Basil's Ballets Russes in 1934, and by the Ballet Russe de Monte Carlo in 1938.

One of the Russian ballet émigrés to the West had more than just memories of *Swan Lake's* complete production as it was performed in Saint Petersburg before the Russian Revolution. Nicholas Sergeyev, former dancer and regisseur for the Maryinsky Theater, had used the Stepanov system of notation to record the classic repertory; he had brought his notebooks, scores, and memorabilia out of Russia in 1918. In London, Ninette de Valois, director of the Sadler's Wells Ballet, hired Sergeyev to stage the full-length *Swan Lake* for her company in 1934. Alicia Markova and Anton Dolin had already mounted act 2 for her in 1932, based on their memories of the Diaghilev production.

Sergeyev's notebooks contained directions for twenty-three dances from the original, with steps and floor plans. The notations were a compendium of the various changes that had been made in the production from 1895 to the end of the Imperial period. The only omission in Sergeyev's production for Sadler's Wells was the Venetian Dance in act 3. The Sadler's Wells premiere took place on 20 November 1934, with Alicia Markova and Robert Helpmann leading the cast.

Margot Fonteyn danced her first *Swan Lake* for Sadler's Wells as Odette, with Ruth French as Odile, on 16 December 1935. Fonteyn danced the dual role for the first time on 15 November 1938. The production was redressed with new sets and costumes by Leslie Hurry on 7 September 1943, and it was first performed in the United States on 10 October 1949. Additions by Frederick Ashton were made in 1952—the *valse pas de six* in act 2 and the pas de deux Neapolitan tarantella made on the unused "Venetian Dance." In 1963, Ashton added a prologue that was dropped in 1967; a new pas de six; a pas de quatre in act 2, later moved to act 3; a "Spanish Dance" for act 3; and a new choreography for the last act. In the 1973/74 season, after forty years of revisions to Sergeyev's production, his setting of the original Petipa-Ivanov version was restored.

Sergeyev also produced the complete work for Mona Inglesby's International Ballet, with decor and costumes by Hugh Stevenson, which premiered 18 March 1947, at the Adelphi Theatre in London, with Nana Gollner and Paul Petroff. It was virtually identical to the 1934 Sadler's Wells version but included the "Venetian Dance." After Sergeyev's death, in an appreciation written by Inglesby, she remembered that Sergeyev's mission was to "preserve the spirit

SWAN LAKE: Productions outside Russia. In 1963, Robert Helpmann staged a new production of the Petipa-Ivanov classic for Britain's Royal Ballet, with additional choreography by Frederick Ashton and designs by Carl Toms. Pictured here in act 2 are Georgina Parkinson as Odette and Anthony Dowell as Siegfried, c.1968. (Photograph by Houston Rogers; used by permission of the Board of Trustees of the Theatre Museum, London.)

SWAN LAKE: Productions outside Russia. In London in 1996, Matthew Bourne created an all-male version of *Swan Lake* for his company, Adventures in Motion Pictures, to critical acclaim. Adam Cooper is pictured here in the starring role, as the Swan. (Photograph © by Andrew Cockrill; used by permission.)

and atmosphere of the original rendering" of the ballets (Inglesby, 1951, p. 655).

The first full-length American production of *Swan Lake* was produced by the San Francisco Ballet within two years of the company's founding. Artistic director William Christensen provided the choreography "after Petipa and Ivanov," with the help of the large colony of Russian émigrés living in the city. Jacqueline Martin danced Odette, Janet Reed danced Odile, and Lew Christensen appeared as Prince Siegfried at the ballet's premiere at the War Memorial Opera House on 25 September 1940. The company included the production in its 1941/42 winter tour of the Midwest and Pacific Northwest.

By the 1940s, the story and music of *Swan Lake* were widely recognized in the United States as the paradigm for ballet. Balanchine had choreographed a capsule version for the 1940 Twentieth Century–Fox film *I Was an Adventuress,* with Vera Zorina as the Swan Queen and Lew Christensen as the Prince. Balanchine was seen in the film as the orchestra leader conducting the ballet. Catherine Littlefield produced a *Swan Lake* on ice skates for the extravaganza called *It Happens on Ice* at the Center Theater in New York on 10 October 1940. A *Swan Lake* in East Indian idiom was choreographed and performed by the American ethnic dancer La Meri on 20 February 1944.

In 1951, Balanchine choreographed a shortened *Swan Lake,* the first traditional ballet to enter the New York City Ballet repertory. The thirty-five-minute work was a composite of acts 2 and 4 of Ivanov's portions of the ballet. Balanchine kept only the central adagio, the Swan Queen's variation and coda, and the pas de quatre of the cygnets. Balanchine's new choreography of the group passages and his elimination of all mime passages resulted in a greatly enlarged role for the corps de ballet. Balanchine cast twenty-four women as swans and eight men as hunters; Maria Tallchief was Swan Queen and André Eglevsky was the Prince at the New York premiere at the City Center of Music and Drama on 20 November 1951. The scenery and costumes had been designed by Cecil Beaton. Balanchine's version has remained in the repertory since then, but he continued to tinker with the choreography. New productions were mounted by the New York City Ballet in 1964 (scenery and costumes by Rouben Ter-Arutunian) and in 1986 (designed by Alain Vaes); in the 1986 production, the swans were clad in black, except for the Swan Queen.

The British dancer David Blair went to Atlanta, Georgia, in 1965 to stage a full-length production of *Swan Lake* and star as Prince Siegfried for the Municipal Theater. A company of fifty-eight dancers was recruited from companies in New York and Chicago and from regional ballet companies in Georgia, Florida, Alabama, North Carolina, Virginia, and Tennessee. As a member of Sadler's Wells Ballet (and the Royal Ballet), Blair was able to restage the traditional Petipa-Ivanov choreography, assisted by his wife Maryon Lane. Lupe Serrano of American Ballet Theatre danced the Swan Queen at the premiere. Blair also mounted the first full-length *Swan Lake* for American Ballet Theatre. It premiered on 16 February 1967 at the Civic Opera House, Chicago, and was similar to the Sadler's Wells production. Nadia Nerina and Royes Fernandez danced the leading roles in Chicago, while Toni Lander and Bruce Marks danced the leads at the New York premiere on 9 May 1967. Lucia Chase, director of the company, appeared as the Queen Mother. In 1981, American Ballet Theatre mounted a new production, staged by Mikhail Baryshnikov.

Inspiration for revisionist thinking on *Swan Lake* came partially from Soviet ballet master Vladimir Burmeister's staging of the work for the ballet company of Moscow's Stanislavsky and Nemirovich-Danchenko Musical Theater. Burmeister used Tchaikovsky's autograph score and added a prologue to the main "swan theme" for the production, which the Russian company brought to the Paris Opera in 1956. He made the Prince a character in his own right, not merely a partner for the Swan Queen. Erik Bruhn claims to have been influenced by his memories of the 1956 visit, and Rudolf Nureyev danced in the Burmeister version choreographed at the Paris Opera in 1960. The Soviet choreographer also staged act 2 for the London Festival Ballet in 1961 and a version for the same company in 1965, co-choreographed by Vaslav Orlikovsky.

John Cranko, Nureyev, and Bruhn created full-length versions of *Swan Lake* that focused on the Prince as the major character. Cranko's Siegfried, in his version for the

Stuttgart Ballet (premiere 14 November 1963), was a tragic hero, doomed to death in the waves that flooded the stage in act 4. Prince Siegfried, as choreographed and performed by Nureyev for the Vienna State Opera Ballet with Margot Fonteyn as the Swan Queen (premiere 15 October 1964), was a suffering hero, described by the critic Clive Barnes as "manic-depressive"; he not only failed to win Odette but was killed by Von Rothbart. In Bruhn's Freudian version for the National Ballet of Canada (premiere 27 March 1967 at O'Keefe Centre, Toronto), the magician Von Rothbart opposes Prince Siegfried and is changed to a Black Queen, the alter ego of the Prince's mother. At the end of the ballet, Siegfried is killed by the corps of swan maidens.

Two more recent productions of *Swan Lake* have framed the ballet as a dream. John Neumeier's production for the Hamburg Ballet (1976) made Prince Ludwig of Bavaria the protagonist who recalls his past obsession with *Swan Lake*. His identification with Siegfried accounts for the recollections that follow. Nureyev's 1986 production for the Paris Opera revised the scenario so that the Prince's tutor and Von Rothbart were combined into one character (danced by Nureyev). Siegfried, asleep on a throne, sees the action as a dream, which then follows the standard scenario. At the end, when Siegfried is dying of despair over the loss of his idealized love, the image returns of the hero with his dream.

In March 1987, Anthony Dowell staged a "new" production of *Swan Lake* for the Royal Ballet. Dowell enlisted a team of collaborators that included Professor Roland John Wiley, an expert on the Stepanov notations that Sergeyev had used to mount the 1934 Vic-Wells production. The notations are now housed in the Harvard Theater Collection. Dowell's intention was to strip away the accretions of the many revivals of *Swan Lake* so as to restore the Petipa choreography. The critical reviews were mixed. The settings were designed by Yolanda Sonnabend, who set the court scenes in Imperial Russia. Cynthia Harvey and Jonathan Cape were the first-cast leads, with Deanne Bergsma as Siegfried's mother and Derek Rencher as Rothbart.

The Boston Ballet produced an American-Soviet *Swan Lake* during May 1990. The company imported Konstantin Sergeyev and his wife, the former ballerina Natalia Dudinskaya, from Leningrad to teach Sergeyev's version of the traditional ballet to the Boston dancers. John Conklin designed the sets. Anna-Marie Holmes assisted in the staging, and Bruce Marks brought in Soviet dancers to partner members of the Boston Ballet in the leads. The first-cast leads were Nina Ananiashvili partnered by Fernando Bujones, with Daniel Meja as the Jester, a Soviet interpolation, and Simon Dow as Von Rothbart. Other guest Soviet dancers were Tatiana Terekhova and Konstantin Zaklinsky of the Kirov Ballet. The production was highly praised for its flowing performance, with Sergeyev omitting much of the mime. The production was revived in 1992 and 1994.

Perhaps Professor Wiley is correct in calling *Swan Lake* a "work in progress," since there seems to be no end to variations on the theme.

BIBLIOGRAPHY

Barnes, Clive. "Swan Lake" (parts 1–2). *Dance and Dancers* (December 1963–January 1964).

Beaumont, Cyril W. *The Ballet Called Swan Lake*. London, 1952.

Briginshaw, Valerie A. "Analysis of Variation in Choreography and Performance: *Swan Lake* Act II Pas de Deux." In *Dance Analysis: Theory and Practice*, by Janet Adshead et al. London, 1988.

Cook, Michael. *Swan Lake: The Making of a Ballet*. Sydney, 1978.

Dorris, George. "Once More to the Lake." *Ballet Review* 6.4 (1977–1978): 99–108.

Grigoriev, S. L. *The Diaghilev Ballet 1909–1929*. Translated and edited by Vera Bowen. London, 1953.

Guest, Ivor. *"Swan Lake." About the House* 1 (December 1963): 24–28.

Hellman, Eric. "The *Swan* That Got Away." *Ballet Review* 20 (Fall 1992): 47–53.

Kirstein, Lincoln. *Movement and Metaphor: Four Centuries of Ballet*. New York, 1970.

Maynard, Olga. "*Swan Lake:* USA, USSR." *Dance Magazine* (May 1990): 39–43.

Pudełek, Janina. "*Swan Lake* in Warsaw, 1900." *Dance Chronicle* 13 (Winter 1990–1991): 359–367.

Ross, Janice. "High Tide on *Swan Lake*." *Dance Magazine* (August 1988): 36–41.

Ross, Janice, and Stephan Cobbett Steinberg, comps. *Why a Swan? Essays, Interviews, and Conversations on "Swan Lake."* San Francisco, 1989.

Wiley, Roland John. "The Revival of *Swan Lake*." *The Dancing Times* (March 1987): 492.

ARCHIVE. The Sergeyev Collection, consisting of choreographic notations and memorabilia, is housed at the Harvard Theatre Collection, Pusey Library, Cambridge, Massachusetts.

IRIS M. FANGER

SWEDEN. [*To survey the dance traditions of Sweden, this entry comprises seven articles:*

Traditional Dance
Theatrical Dance before 1771
Theatrical Dance, 1771–1900
Theatrical Dance since 1900
Court Theaters
Dance Education
Dance Research and Publication

For further discussion of theatrical dance, see the entries on individual companies, choreographers, and dancers.]

Traditional Dance

Swedish culture, including dance and dance music, is in many ways similar to that of the neighboring countries. In western Sweden, along the border with Norway, much of the dance and music is very like the Norwegian. In the eastern counties of Sweden, indigenous Swedish characteristics are more pronounced than those shared with neighboring countries. In the far north of Sweden live Finnish-speaking and Saami (Lapp) minorities; in the southernmost region, Scania, it is possible to see cultural similarities with Denmark and Germany.

Traditional dances and dancing, usually called folk dance or old-time dance, have a rather low status and profile in contemporary Swedish culture and the education system. There is no obligatory folk dance taught in schools, and at the National College of Dance (Danshögskolan) the folk dance department is new and small compared with those for other dance genres. When dance is spoken of in official cultural and political discussion, it is above all ballet and modern dance that are meant, never folk dance or ballroom dance.

For most Swedes, folk dances are those done in folk dance clubs. There are associations for folk costume and for dance performances at Midsummer's Eve. Today there is little if any interaction between folk dance and court, social, or popular dances. Folk dance is restricted to dance clubs.

Interactions between folk dance and stage genres are also rare today. Choreographers have occasionally incorporated folkloric images into ballets, and in a few cases they have actually used folk dance movement motifs. Ivo Cramér used folk dance movements in some of his dance creations. The Swedish Folk Dance Ensemble (Svensk Folkdansensamble), a semiprofessional group that existed between 1976 and 1994, performed a dance drama based on August Strindberg's *Kronbruden*. Theatrical productions have also used folk dance as a basic movement repertory; an example is Västanå Teater's version of Selma Lagerlöf's *Gösta Berlings Saga*.

The majority of Swedish folk dances used today were documented, reconstructed, or composed between the end of the nineteenth century and the first half of the twentieth. Older sources are rare and difficult to interpret in isolation. The Swedish bishop Olaus Magnus, who immigrated to Rome during the Reformation, wrote in 1555 in his *Historia de gentibus septentrionalibus* (History of Nordic People), our oldest source, about the Sword Dance *(svärdsdans)* and the Bow Dance *(bågdans)*, but they are not really described, just mentioned. From the mid-eighteenth century there are some dance descriptions made by Carl von Linné (Linnaeus), the famous Swedish botanist, who traveled extensively in Sweden and wrote on many topics other than botany. He mentions, for example, the Weaving Dance *(väva vadmal)* and the longdance from Mora *(Mora långdans)*.

It was in the twentieth century, however, that the greater part of Swedish folk dances were first documented, mainly by members of the Swedish folk dance movement, such as Gustav Karlsson, Johan Larsson, Ingvar Norman, Göran Karlholm, and Börje Wallin. In the 1970s and 1980s Henry Sjöberg, who played a vital role in establishing the Archive for Folk Dance, was an important inspiration for many young researchers, teachers, and performers of folk dance.

In the academic field, the most important folk dance researchers have been Tobias Norlind, Ernst Klein, and Mats Rehnberg. As early as the 1920s Klein used film for dance documentation, a technique that unfortunately was not continued. Not until around 1970 were film and video once again used regularly in field documentation, in the work of Henry Sjöberg. All dance descriptions have been made with words rather than with any notation system.

The collection of dances during the nineteenth and twentieth centuries was carried out in the name of nationalism, but it reflected more a spirit of provincialism and local patriotism. At the end of the nineteenth century, Artur Hazelius founded the Nordic Museum (Nordiska Museet), the national museum for folk culture, and Skansen, an outdoor museum with buildings brought from throughout Sweden. At Skansen, folk dance and music performances are held in summer.

Although sources are scarce, it is still possible to construct a fairly valid Swedish dance history. In addition to the dances mentioned by Olaus Magnus and Linné, sources from the Middle Ages mention circle dances, line dances, and chain dances of the branle and farandole type, danced both to ballad singing and to instrumental accompaniment. During the seventeenth century couple dances appeared, often referred to as *polska,* which appear under many local names, such as *springlek, bleking, slängpolska, trinning,* or *hamburska*.

Group dances, often called *engelska* ("English"), became common during the eighteenth century, along with the quadrille *(kadrilj)* and minuet *(menuett)*. During the second half of the nineteenth century, first the waltz *(vals)* and then the polka, schottische, and mazurka became the most popular social dances. Today these couple dances from the nineteenth century are collectively termed *gammaldanser* ("old-time dances"). The *hambo,* the best-known Swedish folk dance, is probably a local variation of the mazurka danced to *polska* music; it became very popular throughout Sweden around 1900.

After about 1910 American dances such as the two-step, one-step, and fox trot became popular among young Swedes. Older dances such as the waltz, polka and schottische, as well as folk dances such as the *engelska* and quadrille, gradually disappeared from general social use and became limited to clubs of enthusiasts.

Swedish folk dances are nearly always couple dances or group dances based on couples. There are a few gender-specific dances, such as the *björndans* ("bear dance"), and a few solo dances, such as the *halling,* for men, and the *sjuskevilappen* ("messy fool") for women.

There is no evidence for ritual dance in Swedish culture since the Middle Ages. Swedish dancing has been and is still a social event for amusement. There are, however, some competition dances in which it is possible to show dance and balance skill, such as the "Dansa på Strå" (Dance on a Straw) and "Skinnkompass" (from French, *cinque pas*).

The basic repertory of folk dance clubs in the twentieth century is made up not of rural dances but of dances choreographed for stage use during the Romantic era. For example, the ballet master at the Royal Opera, Anders Selinder, composed and stylized folk dances for *Värmländingarna* (People of Varmland) in 1846. Among these "Selinder dances" are "Fryksdalspolska", "Vingåkersdans", "Skrälåt", and "Daldans", dances that still are an important part of the folk dance club repertory.

When the first Swedish folk dance club, Philochoros, started in 1880, it was the Selinder dances and dances stylized by club members that largely formed its repertory. In 1920 several folk dance clubs formed a national organization, which a year later took the name Svenska Ungdomsringen för Bygdekultur (Swedish Youth Clubs for Country Culture). As the name indicates, there was a great interest in all forms of folk art and folk culture, including dance.

The repertory of the folk dance organizations continued to be the dances of Selinder and Philochoros, augmented with rediscovered, reconstructed, and newly choreographed dances, such as "Västgötapolska" and "Fjällnäspolska". Many of these new compositions were of the quadrille type, as were the dances of Selinder and Philochoros.

In Sweden, dancers and musicians do not interact much during the dancing; the music merely provides the meter and rhythm. Dance music may be in even measure, 2/4 and 4/4 (schottische, polka, quadrille, and *engelska*), or in uneven measure, 3/4 *(polska,* waltz, mazurka, *hambo)*. Throughout the nineteenth and twentieth centuries, the most important instruments for making dance music were the fiddle and accordion *(fiol, dragspel)*. From the Middle Ages onward, and in a few places today, dance music was played on the key harp, bagpipe, clarinet, and drum *(nyckelharpa, säckpipa, klarinett,* and *trumma)*.

Today folk dance is performed nearly exclusively at festivals and in dance clubs. There are approximately four hundred clubs with about thirty thousand members in the largest organization, Svenska Ungdomsringen för Bygdekultur. A smaller number of clubs are grouped in other nationwide organizations; for example, old-time dancers have their own national network, and revival groups from the 1970s form Riksföreingen för Folkmusik och Dans (Swedish Folk Music and Folk Dance Association).

It is possible to join clubs and to dance just for fun. A common goal, however, is to prepare programs for performance at festivals or on tours abroad. At Midsummer's Eve nearly all clubs give performances around the maypole. The public usually does not participate in these performances, but after the display there is communal song and dancing in which everyone, especially children, takes part.

The summer Rättvik Folklore Festival is the most important folk dance festival in Sweden. There are also a number of smaller local festivals and *spelmansstämmor* (dance musicians' gatherings), with dancing throughout the country. Also in the summer is the Hälsingehambon, the world championship in *hambo* dancing, in which about fifteen hundred couples compete for titles.

In Swedish schools, folk dance, if it is taught at all, is an optional subject. If dance is on the curriculum, it is usually a part of athletics—or occasionally of music or other aesthetic or cultural subjects.

There are a few professional Swedish folk dance teachers educated at the National College of Dance (Danshögskolan), but there is no professional dance ensemble or theater group that has folk dance as basic repertory. Education in practical folk dancing is offered at the National College of Dance and at some *folkhögskolor* (schools for continuing education). Folk dance as a theoretical subject is offered, together with folk song, only in a five-week course at the Department of Ethnology of Gothenburg University. Sometimes folk dance is included in basic anthropology and ethnology courses, and it is possible to choose folk dance as a subject of individual interest at higher levels in these fields.

[*For related discussion, see* European Traditional Dance.]

BIBLIOGRAPHY

Dąbrowska, Grażyna, et al. *International Monograph on Folk Dance*, vol. 2, *Poland, Portugal, Sweden*. Budapest, 1987.

Klein, Ernst. *Om folkdans*. Stockholm, 1978.

Norlind, Tobias. *Studier i svensk folklore*. Lund, 1911.

Norlind, Tobias. *Dansens historia med särskild hänsyn till dansen i Sverige*. Stockholm, 1941.

Olaus Magnus. *Historia om de nordiska folken* (1555). Edited by John Granlund. Stockholm, 1976.

Rehnberg, Mats. *Klackarna i taket: Om halling och jösseháradspolska*. Stockholm, 1966.

Salvén, Erik. *Dances of Sweden*. Translated by Veronica Wright. London, 1949.

Sjöberg, Henry, and Anita Etzler. *Folklig dans*. 3 vols. Stockholm, 1970–1976.

Svenska folkdanser. 2 vols. 5th ed. Stockholm, 1964–1971.

ARCHIVES. Arkivet för Folklig Dans, Dansmuseet, Stockholm, which holds the largest public collection of videotapes and films on Swedish folk dances. Danshögskolan, Stockholm. Department of Ethnology, Gothenburg University. Riksföreingen för Folkmusik och Dans. Svenska Ungdomsringen för Bygdekultur, Stockholm.

MATS NILSSON

Theatrical Dance before 1771

The art of ballet reached Sweden in 1637, when the Swedish Royal Council imported Antoine de Beaulieu to polish the nobility's courtly behavior. In less than a year, the courtiers were so accomplished in dance that Beaulieu produced the first court ballet in Sweden on 28 January 1638. The *Ballet des Plaisirs de la Vie des Enfans sans Soucy* (Pleasures of Carefree Childhood) was a typical French *ballet à entrées,* with thirteen *entrées* (or *divertissements*) and a grand ballet for twelve nobles in a style that was simultaneously burlesque and pompous.

In 1645, Beaulieu mounted his fourth ballet, *Le Monde Reiovi* (Rejoicing Worlds), which introduced Italian stage machinery, three settings (Heaven, the Sea, and Earth), twenty-four *entrées,* and fifty roles. The entertainment's style had become distinguished and heroic. In 1646, the dance master Monsieur Daniel presented *L'Amour Constant,* which offered a legitimate plot about Ulysses and Penelope; all previous presentations had been little more than pleas for Queen Christina to marry.

In 1649, Christina expressed her own ideas about marriage in *Den Fångne Cupido* (Cupid Out of His Humor), which had a text by the Parisian poet Hélie Poirier; Christina herself danced as Diana in her conquest of Cupid. This was the first ballet to be published in three languages—French, German, and Swedish (in a more elaborate translation by George Stiernhielm)—and to include both women and men. It was revived by Mary Skeaping for the court theater in 1956.

Soon after, *La Naissance de la Paix* (The Birth of Peace) was presented to the court. This ballet is remarkable not only because it was written by the mathematician and philosopher René Descartes but also because it showed the inglorious side of warfare. What had been burlesque in earlier ballets now became a sinister *danse macabre* of mutilated soldiers and peasants. Christina danced this time as Pallas, the goddess of temperance who arranges for peace—just as Christina herself had mediated peace at Westphalia in 1648. Several entertainments were presented in 1650, with and without dance; the culmination was the New Year's Day 1651 presentation of the ballet *Parnassus Triumphans* by George Stiernhielm. The performance included more than one hundred ten roles for sixty-eight participants, all male except for the lone woman who played Aurora; there were thirty *entrées* in different settings, and magnificent stage machinery by Antonio Brunati.

These three ballets—*Den Fångne Cupido, La Naissance de la Paix,* and *Parnassus Triumphans*—constituted a high point in form and ideas and were judged the equal of contemporary French works. Beaulieu was then succeeded by his assistant, Des Aunez (also written Desaunai and de Sonnes), and Stiernhielm retired to the country.

Urban Chevreau's *Les Liberalités des Dieux* (The Bounties of the Gods; 1652) was written for twenty-two couples and had only fifteen *entrées.* One concerned three Swedish ghosts, evidence of a growing interest in native folklore. Christina made a last appearance in the 1653 ballet *Gudarnas Högtid* (The Feast of the Gods), a *bergerette* or pastoral. All Christina's guests appeared as gods, she was the shepherdess Amaranta, and her courtiers were shepherds and shepherdesses. At the conclusion she presented jewels from her dress to guests she chose to honor; thus was inaugurated the Swedish Order of Amarant.

After Christina's abdication in 1654, few occasions arose for true court ballets. Still, for the 1654 wedding of Charles X Gustav, Christina's successor, Chevreau arranged *Ballet de la Félicité* in three parts. His subjects included the five senses, happiness, and the gifts of nature and the noble soul. In 1669 the Swedish poet Erik Lindesköld wrote *Den stora genius* (The Great Genius), which was performed by sixty noble couples in twenty *entrées* and a grand ballet. The young Charles XI appeared as a Turk in a rather solemn allegory of evil and good genius. In 1689, the last true Baroque court ballet, *Lycko-Priis* (The Price of Happiness), was danced; however, it used as much speech and singing as it did dance, and of the seventy-one roles, only eighteen were solely danced.

In 1699, a troupe of professional French dancers under a Monsieur Rosidor was invited to Sweden. It introduced in 1701 the new French comedy and Italian *commedia dell'arte* in the farcical *Ballet Mêlé de Chants Héroïques.* The music by Andreas Düben is the earliest preserved example of this type of ballet. The company soon left Sweden, however, because it could not find a regular audience.

During the first half of the eighteenth century, comedies were danced and played primarily by enthusiastic court amateurs. Such was the case with *Feste Royal* (1706), whose four intermezzi were sandwiched between three comedies in the Medici style of the fifteenth century.

In the 1720s a new royal dance master, Jean-Baptiste Landé, introduced the court to the new French style with such dances as the *rigaudon, loure, gigue,* and *menuet.* Professional dancers returned to Sweden in 1753 with a royal invitation to another French company. The twelve Italian and French dancers were led by Louis Frossard.

In 1758 Frossard left for Paris and Vienna, and Louis Gallodier took his place. The following year an Italian opera company under Francesco Uttini arrived for a ten-year stay to perform complete operas with ballet in the Paris style. In addition, the 1750s saw operas by Charles-Simon Favart and Jean-Jacques Rousseau, with choreography by Gallodier.

BIBLIOGRAPHY

Gustafsson, Lars. "Amor et Mars vaincu." In *Queen Christina of Sweden: Documents and Studies.* Analecta Reginensia, 1. Stockholm, 1966.

Skeaping, Mary. "Ballet under the Three Crowns." *Dance Perspectives*, no. 32 (1967).

MAGNUS BLOMKVIST

Theatrical Dance, 1771–1900

The pre-Romantic style in the Swedish theater is associated with King Gustav III. He looked upon theater not only as a courtly entertainment (among others), but as a vehicle for his political ambition. He wished to be an absolute ruler, looked to as a father by the people, and to lead a national cultural revival. The theater was to help to cultivate the Swedish language and, above all, in dramatic form, to give a picture of Sweden's glorious history. As a child, the theater had been Gustav's favorite occupation. His fantasy had fed on the repertory of the French troupe imported by his mother, Queen Lovisa Ulrika, sister of Frederick II of Prussia. Gustav was to be a skilled actor, a playwright, and a stage director. When he came to the throne in 1771 he dismissed his mother's French company to build up a national Swedish theater. The lack of skilled Swedish actors and playwrights compelled him to concentrate his ingenuity and economic resources on creating a Swedish opera.

Count Ehrenswärd, who was to be the first director of the Royal Opera, wrote,

> An opera which consists of pleasing and catchy music, a properly trained ballet, attractive costumes, and beautiful, well-painted scenery is so captivating that ear, eye, and all the other senses are satisfied at the same time. In this way one gets accustomed to the language, whose harshness is minimized by absorption in the music.

The old Tennis Court Theater in Stockholm was restored and equipped with new stage machinery. There were some first-class singers and musicians in Stockholm, as well as the conductor and composer Francesco Antonio Uttini, who had been part of the Italian opera company in Lovisa Ulrika's day. The dancers from the dismissed French company were also still in Stockholm and became the nucleus of the opera-ballet.

Gustav III's efforts were brought to fruition in the 1780s: plays and operas were given at the new (1782) opera house in Stockholm. The company even performed for the court at theaters in palaces outside Stockholm—at Ulriksdal and Gripsholm and in the Drottningholm Theater (that had been built in 1766), which was still in its original state, its scenery and stage machinery untouched. In 1781 a new French acting company, under the leadership of Boutet de Monvel, was imported. In 1787 the king at last initiated his much longed-for national dramatic theater company. The repertory consisted of original compositions based mostly on French prototypes and foreign operas translated into Swedish. Christoph Willbald Gluck's opera *Orfeo ed Euridice* was presented even before its Paris premiere. Most Gustavian operas were influenced by Gluck, both their music (by the German composers Joseph Martin Kraus, Johann Gottlieb Naumann, and Johann Christian Friedrich Haeffner) and libretti (by the Swedish poets Kellgren and Adlerbeth among others). More original were the historical-romantic operas with the king's own text. His greatest success was *Gustav Wasa* (1786).

Gustav III even added music and dance to plays, the first attempt being *Birger Jarl* (1774). With these and many other works, the king succeeded in bringing Swedish history to life and arousing enthusiasm for some of his royal predecessors. The people were portrayed as true-hearted peasants, loyal to the king. A certain amount of realism was reflected in costumes, dance, and music—an early instance of genuine folklore in the theater. The choreography was integrated in the dramatic plot, following the ideas of Jean-Georges Noverre.

The most important figure in establishing Gustav III's opera-ballet was Louis Gallodier, who arrived in Sweden in 1758 to join Lovisa Ulrika's French troupe and was to become the first ballet master of the Swedish Royal Opera (1773–1795). Gallodier obtained dancers for the new compagny—Louis Frossand and his wife Ninon Bubois, and Le Clerc, and Madame Soligny from the dismissed French company. Others were imported from France, most of them trained by Jean Dauberval: Didelot the elder, Madame Du Tillet from the Royal Theater in Copenhagen, Giovanna Bassi, Antoine Bournonville, Julie Bournonville-Alix, and Jean Marcadet, who was also a gifted choreographer. The dancers were generously paid—better paid than the singers and actors. The Swedish dancers in the company first had to be trained. At the start, there were only about thirty dancers, but by the 1780s there were about seventy-two. Unfortunately, Sweden lost two of its dancers who became outstanding choreographers—Charles-Louis Didelot and Antoine Bournonville (who, in 1792, settled in Copenhagen). Despite Noverre's influence on ballet in Sweden, the king did not take Noverre into his service, even though Noverre, in 1791, had requested the post of ballet master to the Swedish court. Political disturbances at the time had left Gustav III with no energy for or interest in the theater. In March 1792, he was assassinated at a masked ball in the opera house. A glorious period came to an end, and the Swedish ballet was left out of the mainstream of dance for more than a century.

The history of the Romantic ballet in Sweden is the story of decline. The theater was no longer sufficiently supported by the court and the government, either economically or artistically. The directors of the Royal Theater had to consider the audience's taste and the repertory had to have box-office appeal. For ballet, this meant giving *divertissements* and ballet-pantomimes in the comic and sentimental genres, most of them remnants of the Gustavian era, which endured into the 1830s. Although ballet had declined to a mere entertainment in Sweden, technical skills, it seems, were kept to a tolerable level by members of the old Gustavian company.

After the death of Gustav III, Marcadet left Sweden. Gallodier remained ballet master until his death in 1803. From 1795 onward, he was assisted by Federico Nadi Terrade, then newly arrived from Italy. Terrade was responsible for most of the dances in the operas. Meanwhile, the young Louis Joseph Deland, sent by Gustav III to be a student of Pierre Gardel's in Paris from 1783 to 1788, returned to Stockholm and followed the French style, so that the repertory was dominated by such Parisian pantomime ballets as *Le Jugement de Pâris* (1793) and *La Dansomanie* (1800). The decade that bridged the centuries witnessed the most intense dance activity yet seen in Stockholm, with nine new ballets a year and several new choreographies for the favorite operas, which sometimes included up to thirty-five separate numbers.

All this activity was silenced in 1806 when war with Russia and shortage of funds caused the young king, Gustav IV Adolph, to close the opera house and dismiss the entire ballet company. The French tradition endured because of Sophie Daguin, who had been trained by Didelot in Paris. She was a dancer at the Stockholm Royal Theater in 1815, and from 1830 to 1856 she trained students at the ballet school.

More important to Swedish ballet was the first native-born ballet master, Ander Selinder. He entered the ballet school of the Royal Theater as a boy and was nominated premier danseur in 1829 and ballet master in 1833. After his retirement from the Royal Theater in 1856, he started a company with talented children that gave ballet and vaudeville performances at various boulevard theaters until 1871. He composed about eighteen ballets for the Royal Theater company, most of them *divertissements* and small pantomine ballets. In addition, he arranged the dances for the Romantic operas of Giacomo Meyerbeer and Vincento Bellini.

Of importance to Swedish dance history are the folk dances Selinder arranged for some Swedish Romantic plays from the middle of the 1840s onward. As dramatic texts these plays are weak but, in performance, together with the dances, songs, music, costumes, and scenery, they evoked Swedish peasant life. They were genuinely Romantic in spirit, unlike the picturesque peasantry of the Gustavian era, and the dances were authentic folk dances arranged for the stage. One of these plays, *Värmlänningarna* (1846), remains popular. Selinder also continued to arrange folk dances for his children's company.

The most talented dancer of the period was Christian Johansson. Born in Stockholm in 1817, he entered the Royal Theater's ballet school in 1829. In the 1830s he was sent to August Bournonville in Copenhagen for advanced studies. He returned to Stockholm in 1837 and was nominated premier danseur. Selinder did not make use of Johansson's talent, and in 1840 Johansson went to Saint Petersburg, where he became one of the founders of the Russian school of dancing. He only returned to Sweden once, in 1841, when he partnered Marie Taglioni in her guest performances in Stockholm. [*See the entry on Johansson.*] Her repertory contained the pas de deux and ballet from act 3 of *Robert of Normandie,* scenes from *La Sylphide, Le Lac des Fées,* and *L'Élève de L'Amour,* and some *divertissements.* Her success was enormous—spectators became almost hysterical. It may not be without significance that she was part Swedish. Her father, Filippo Taglioni, had worked at the Royal Opera in 1803 and 1804, where he met and married Sofia Karsten, the daughter of the great Swedish singer C. C. Karsten. In 1818 Filippo returned to Stockholm for three months as ballet master. In 1843 Paul Taglioni visited to mount *La Sylphide,* with Marie in the title role. [*See the entry on the Taglioni family.*]

The visits of August Bournonville had a more lasting influence. He came from Copenhagen with some of his dancers in 1839 for a brief guest performance. In 1847 he paid another visit, as choreographer, and mounted his ballets *The Toreador, Faust,* and *Bellman* with great success. In 1857 he returned once more to stage *Festival in Albano, The Dancing School,* and *The Wedding Festival in Hardanger.* This time the criticism was somewhat sour: dance was no longer regarded as fitting for the Royal Theater. His most important and lasting influence on the Swedish theater was as superintendent and stage director, from 1861 to 1864, at the Royal Theater. He was responsible for opera and drama but not for ballet. According to him, at that time the quality of the dance and choreography had hit bottom.

BIBLIOGRAPHY

Beijer, Agne. *Drottningholms slottsteater på Lovisa Ulrikas och Gustaf III:s tid.* Stockholm, 1981.

Bournonville, August. *My Theatre Life* (1848–1978). 3 vols. Translated and edited by Patricia McAndrew. Middletown, Conn., 1979.

Dahlgren, F. A. *Förteckning öfver svenska skådespel uppförda på Stockholms teatrar, 1737–1863.* Stockholm, 1866.

Dahms, Sibylle. "The 'Ballet d'Action' in Theory and Practice." In *Proceedings of the Stockholm Symposium on Opera and Dance in the Gustavian Era, 1711–1809.* Stockholm, 1986.

Koegler, Horst. "From the Early Days of Ballet." *Ballett International* 9 (October 1986): 24–27.

Koegler, Horst. "The Swedes and Their Theatre King." *Dance Chronicle* 10.2 (1987): 223–229.

Mattson, Inger, ed. *Gustavian Opera: An Interdisciplinary Reader in Swedish Opera, Dance, and Theatre, 1771–1809.* Translated by Paul B. Austin. Stockholm, 1991.

Proceedings of the Stockholm Symposium on Opera and Dance in the Gustavian Era, 1771–1809. Stockholm, 1986.

Skeaping, Mary. "Ballet under the Three Crowns." *Dance Perspectives,* no. 32 (1967).

Stribolt, Barbro, ed. *The Drottningholm Theatre Museum.* Drottningholm, 1984.

Strömbeck, K. G., et al. *Kungliga Teatern i Stockholm repertoar 1773–1973.* Stockholm, 1974.

Winter, Marian Hannah. *The Pre-Romantic Ballet.* London, 1974.

KIRSTEN GRAM HOLMSTRÖM

Theatrical Dance since 1900

At the beginning of the twentieth century two guest performances made the Stockholm public aware of new trends in dance: Isadora Duncan danced in 1906 and made a lasting impression; Anna Pavlova arrived in 1908 with her ensemble and performed ballets from the repertory of the Maryinsky Theater. It was Pavlova's first venture abroad, and her overwhelming reception in Stockholm encouraged her to start an international career. Duncan and Pavlova paved the way for a dance revival.

Michel Fokine had fallen out with Serge Diaghilev in 1912, so was free from the Ballets Russes. The Royal Theater in Stockholm approached him, and Fokine accepted a position as guest choreographer. He spent working periods in Stockholm in 1913 and 1914 and staged five of the ballets with which the Diaghilev Ballets Russes had recently conquered Paris. He and his wife, Vera Fokina, danced the main roles and then turned them over to Swedish dancers. *Cléopâtra, Les Sylphides, Le Spectre de la Rose, Carnaval,* and *Schéhérazade* offered new and exciting possibilities. Fokine also discovered and encouraged young talent.

Fokine brought the painter Boris Anisfeld to Stockholm from Saint Petersburg. He painted decor based on sketches by Léon Bakst and created a romantic setting for *Les Sylphides,* which has been used for this ballet's frequent revivals. The Royal Theater has also preserved Anisfeld's decor for *Schéhérazade,* based on Bakst. Its colorful splendor was used by Ulf Gadd for his 1933 version of *Schéhérazade.*

Fokine and his ballets were enthusiastically received. Newspapers and literary magazines were filled with articles about the "new" ballet. Fokine influenced not only dance in Sweden but also art, design, and theater. There were negotiations with Fokine to take over the leadership of the Royal Swedish Ballet, but World War I intervened and he returned to Paris. After the Russian Revolution Fokine lived in Denmark. Swedish dancers journeyed there to study with him, and some of them—Jean Börlin, Jenny Hasselquist, and Carina Ari—joined Les Ballets Suédois in Paris in 1920. Sven Tropp, Lisa Steier, and others returned to Stockholm and assumed responsibility for the company, not an easy task since Les Ballets Suédois had robbed the ensemble of one third of its dancers. Lisa Steier introduced her own choreographies for Igor Stravinsky's *The Firebird* and *Pulcinella* at the Royal Theater in 1927. She died young, a short time later.

SWEDEN: Theatrical Dance since 1900. Elsa-Marianne von Rosen and Julius Mengarelli, as the original Julie and Jean in *Miss Julie* (1950), Birgit Cullberg's ballet based on the 1888 play by August Strindberg. (Photograph © by Enar Merkel Rydberg; used by permission.)

In Sweden during the 1930s and 1940s ballet was again overshadowed by opera. Very few ballets were staged to Swedish music and with Swedish themes. The repertory reflected to some extent the legacy of Diaghilev's Ballets Russes; attempts were made to stage classics or parts of them, and new works of varied value were introduced. The economic depression was felt, and World War II broke out, limiting cultural exchange.

Renaissance of the Royal Swedish Ballet. The postwar ballet renaissance in Europe and the United States also reached Sweden, through visits by excellent ballet companies. The Royal Theater decided to encourage its own ballet. Antony Tudor came as ballet director for the 1949/50 season, followed by Mary Skeaping in 1953; she remained with the company until 1962. In these very fruitful years, she gave it a classical repertory. Between the wars the ballet world had been hostile to modern dancers, but now the Royal Swedish Ballet was ready to

SWEDEN: Theatrical Dance since 1900. Antony Tudor created his *Ekon av Trumpeter* (Echoing of Trumpets), for the Royal Swedish Ballet in 1963. In this scene, Gerd Andersson reaches for the body of her executed lover and is restrained by Mario Mengarelli, as the leading Nazi soldier. Sets and costumes were designed by Birger Bergling. (Photograph © by Enar Merkel Rydberg; used by permission.)

try new dance styles and invited three Swedish choreographers to work with the dancers. Birgit Cullberg, Birgit Åkesson, and Ivo Cramér created dance dramas in different styles. The influence of Kurt Jooss was felt in Cullberg's dramatic ballets. Åkesson belonged to the avant-garde and collaborated with contemporary composers and painters, often using texts by the poet Erik Lindegren. Cramér took his themes from folklore and history. Tudor returned on several occasions, staged his old ballets, and created a new one, *Echoing of Trumpets* (1963). George Balanchine's beautiful, musical ballets were much admired when performed on tour by New York City Ballet. He generously shared the best of his productions, and the Royal Swedish Ballet was happy to get five of them. During this decade the company toured Europe and China.

In the 1950s Mary Skeaping began to revive ballets from Swedish dance history for the Drottningholm Court Theater. Her dancers learned early steps and techniques and mastered old styles. Ivo Cramér joined her as co-choreographer, and Regina Beck-Friis became her assistant and successor. The Royal Swedish Ballet was now able to perform dance from four centuries.

During its formative years the company could rely on soloists with distinctive personalities and dramatic talent. Important roles were performed by Ellen Rasch, Teddy Rhodin, Bjørn Holmgren, Elsa-Marianne von Rosen, Julius Mengarelli, and Gunnel Lindgren; they were supplemented in time by Mariane Orlando, Gerd Andersson, Caj Selling, Verner Klavsen, Kari Sylwan, Conny Borg, Mario Mengarelli, and Berit Sköld.

In 1962 Yuri Grigorovich staged *The Stone Flower* for the Swedes, their first exposure to the virtuoso Soviet style. He had just been named ballet master of the Bolshoi Theater in Moscow, and this was his first assignment outside the Soviet Union. More guests arrived from the USSR, some to dance and Nathalie Conus to stage a new version of *Swan Lake.* The Canadian Brian Macdonald led the ballet between 1964 and 1967 and was house choreographer, stimulating the public with a spring ballet festival. He was succeeded in 1967 by Erik Bruhn, who strengthened the modern repertory with some masterpieces.

Jerome Robbins staged his version of *Les Noces,* and Kenneth MacMillan his *Romeo and Juliet;* both ballets have been carefully preserved in the repertory. An important period in the history of modern dance was illuminated when José Limón visited Stockholm in 1970 and introduced *There Is a Time, The Exiles,* and *Missa Brevis;* in 1972 he brought *The Moor's Pavane.* A younger generation of American choreographers was represented by Glen Tetley with *Ricercare* and *Embrace Tiger and Return to Mountain,* and by Eliot Feld with *At Midnight* and *The Consort.*

New dancers came to the fore: Kerstin Lidström, Annette av Paul, Jonas Kåge, Maria Lang, Ulf Gadd, Nils-Åke Häggbom, Istvan Kisch, and Jens Graff. Marianne Orlando remained *prima ballerina* throughout her stage career.

The Royal Swedish Ballet had for many years been oriented toward the Anglo-Saxon dance world. It was a special occasion when Frederick Ashton came in 1972 to stage *La Fille Mal Gardée* with Kerstin Lidström as Lise, Imre Dózsa as Colas, and Istvan Kisch as Mother Simone.

When Ivo Cramér became ballet director in 1975, he found that it was high time to explore continental Europe. From Stuttgart he acquired John Cranko's *Onegin* and *The Taming of the Shrew,* both giving ballerina Astrid Strüwer roles that suited her temperament and virtuosity. Cramér also contacted Jiří Kylián, whose first assignment outside the Netherlands Dance Theater was at Stockholm in 1977 with *Blue Skin.* Since then four of Kylián's works have been staged at the Royal Theater; his *Intimate Letters* was staged for Swedish television.

In 1980 Gunilla Roempke assumed the post of ballet director, and the company began to make room for more Swedish choreography. Birgit Cullberg had returned in 1976 to do a ballet on a large scale. She used Allan Pettersson's Seventh Symphony to make her choreographic

SWEDEN: Theatrical Dance since 1900. *(above)* Scene from the Royal Swedish Ballet's 1969 production of Kenneth MacMillan's *Romeo and Juliet,* with Annette av Paul and Nils-Åke Häggbom as the young lovers. *(right)* Kerstin Lidström and Imre Dózsa in Frederick Ashton's *La Fille Mal Gardée,* first staged for the Royal Swedish Ballet in 1972. (Photograph above © by Enar Merkel Rydberg; used by permission. Photograph at right from the Dance Collection, New York Public Library for the Performing Arts.)

Report on the condition of the world and the gap between rich and poor. Her son Niklas Ek, former soloist with Maurice Béjart's Ballet du XXe Siècle and the Cullberg Ballet, danced the leading role and then joined the Royal Swedish Ballet as a principal dancer. Roempke invited three young choreographers to work with the company: Ulf Gadd presented *Orpheus;* Mats Ek created *Cain and Abel;* and the modern dancer Per Jonsson was introduced to the public in 1984 with his first work, *Shaft.* Jonsson, a farmer's son from the north, was recognized as an unusual talent with his own approach to movement and form. A welcome addition to the repertory of classics and large-scale dance dramas was Kenneth MacMillan's *Manon* in 1980. *The Sleeping Beauty,* staged by Beryl Grey, was an appreciated classic. Principal dancers during the 1980s were Anneli Alkhanko, Per-Arthur Segerström, Johanna Björnson, Madeleine Onne, Weit Carlson, Pär Isbert, Hans Nilsson, and Mats Wegmann.

After a short spell with Egon Madsen as ballet director, Nils-Åke Häggbom, a former principal dancer, took over in 1987. The first new ballet he offered the public was by Ulf Gadd, who based his dance drama on the novel *Gösta Berling's Saga* by the Nobel Prize winner Selma Lagerlöf. Next season brought an old classic, Petipa's *La Bayadère,* staged by Natalia Makarova; it was succeeded by Frederick Ashton's *Cinderella.* Häggbom then approached John Neumeier in Hamburg, regarded as the last master of the type of European dance drama that had for decades dominated theaters in Russia, England, Germany, and Scandinavia. Neumeier staged his masterpieces *A Midsummer Night's Dream* in 1990 and his *Peer Gynt* in 1992.

SWEDEN: Theatrical Dance since 1900. Mats Ek staged his *Våroffer* (Rite of Spring) in Japanese style for the Cullberg Ballet. The dancers seen here are Ana Laguna and Yvan Auzely. (Photograph by Lesley Leslie-Spinks; from the Dance Collection, New York Public Library for the Performing Arts.)

Häggbom also made room for other contemporary choreographers. Maurice Béjart was represented by *Lieder eines Fahrenden Gesellen* and *Le Sacre du Printemps;* Nils Christe by *Before Nightfall;* and, in 1993, Ulysses Dove with his remarkable *Dancing on the Front Porch of Heaven.* Glen Tetley's *The Tempest* was also added to the repertory in 1993.

Regular workshops were fruitful. Several dancers were asked to do choreography for operas, as well as short ballets. Most active among them was the principal dancer Pär Isbert, who created television ballets and works for the theater. During the 1995 Christmas season he presented a new version of *The Nutcracker,* inspiried by pictures in popular Swedish children's books by Elsa Beskow.

The Swedish Ballet School produced many male dancers of quality. In the 1990s the company had such leading male dancers as Göran Svalberg, Jan-Erik Wikström and Anders Nordström. There was also Maria Lindqvist, a talented ballerina.

Since the foundation of the Royal Theater in 1773, outstanding singers have been given the title of court singer. In 1990 King Charles XVI Gustav decided to honor dance, and the first court dancers named were Anneli Alhanko and Per-Arthur Segerström, followed by Johanna Björnson, Madeleine Onne, and Hans Nilsson.

The Royal Swedish Ballet with its ensemble of seventy-five dancers often went abroad on tour during the 1980s and 1990s. The company danced in Spain, England, Finland, Norway, Japan, and Brazil.

Other Companies. There are other dance companies in Sweden besides the Royal Swedish Ballet. In Göteborg, Ballet at Teatern (Great Theater) flourished under Conny Borg and Elsa-Marianne von Rosen, but especially since Ulf Gadd became ballet director in 1979. Gadd gave his ensemble a distinctive profile in a series of strong dance dramas. He retired in 1988 and spent seven years in Bali studying and dancing, but he was recalled in 1995 to replace Robert North and became director of the ballet, now resident in the new opera house.

Malmö had a ballet attached to the Stadsteatern; its directors included Teddy Rhodin, Conny Borg, Elsa-Marianne von Rosen, and Jonas Kåge. Here full-length classics were favored. Because of a reorganization of the theater

SWEDEN: Theatrical Dance since 1900. Per Jonsson, one of Sweden's foremost modern dance choreographers, staged his *Mellan Två Trädgårdar* (Between Two Gardens), for the Cullberg Ballet in 1985. (Photograph by Lesley Leslie-Spinks; courtesy of Anna Greta Ståhle.)

in 1994, the ballet was moved to the university town of Lund to work independently.

The umbrella organization Riksteatern administered two touring companies: the Cullberg Ballet, founded in 1967, and the Cramér Ballet, active from 1968 to 1986. In 1971 a small company was formed at the regional theater Östgötateatern. This company has specialized in contemporary works by young choreographers. Since the early 1970s independent companies of dancers of modern, ethnic, or historical styles have been active in Sweden; their organization Danscentrum gives support.

Modern dance has a long tradition in Sweden, and interest in new dance styles is growing fast. Some of the modern groups became internationally known: L'Étoile du Nord, Wind Witches, and the Pyramides, whose choreographers were Susanne Valentin, Eva Lundqvist, and Margaretha Åsberg, respectively. Lundqvist and Åsberg opened the first theaters devoted to modern dance in Stockholm, Glashuset and Moderna Dansteatern. An experimental avant-garde group called Rubicon was founded in Göteborg in 1978 by Gun Lund, Evan Ingemarsson, and Gunilla Witt; in 1987 Rubicon moved into a theater of its own. In the 1990s young modern choreographers such as Per Jonsson and Jens Östberg came to the fore, attracted many followers, and founded their own groups.

[*For further discussion, see the entries on Åkesson, Ari, Åsberg, Beck-Friis, Behle, Cramér, Cullberg, Ek, Gadd, Johansson, Orlando, Rosen, and Skeaping.*]

BIBLIOGRAPHY

Baer, Nancy Van Norman, ed. *Paris Modern: The Swedish Ballet, 1920–1925.* San Francisco, 1995. Exhibition catalog.

Beijer, Agne. *Drottningholms slottsteater på Lovisa Ulrikas och Gustaf III:s tid.* Stockholm, 1981.

Dahlgren, F. A. *Förteckning öfver svenska skådespel uppförda på Stockholms teatrar, 1737–1863.* Stockholm, 1866.

Engdahl, Horace. *Swedish Ballet and Dance: A Critic's View.* Translated by Paul Kessel and Erika Svedberg. Stockholm, 1992.

Gustafsson, Lars. "Amor et Mars vaincu." In *Queen Christina of Sweden: Documents and Studies.* Analecta Reginensia, 1. Stockholm, 1966.

Hood, Robin [Idestam-Almqvist, Bengt]. *Svensk balett.* Malmö, 1951.

Palmqvist, Bertil. *Malmöbaletten.* Malmö, 1985.

Riwkin-Brick, Anna. *Svensk danskonst på scen och i skola.* Stockholm, 1932.

Rootzén, Kajsa. *Den svenska baletten.* Stockholm, 1945.

Sjögren, Margareta. *Biljett till balett.* Stockholm, 1957.

Sjögren, Margareta. *Skandinavisk balett.* Stockholm, 1988.

Skeaping, Mary. "Ballet under the Three Crowns." *Dance Perspectives,* no. 32 (1967).

Skeaping, Mary, and Anna Greta Ståhle. *Balett på Stockholmsoperan.* Stockholm, 1979.

Strömbeck, K. G., et al. *Kungliga Teatern i Stockholm repertoar 1773–1973.* Stockholm, 1974.

Winter, Marian Hannah. *The Pre-Romantic Ballet.* London, 1974.

ANNA GRETA STÅHLE

Court Theaters

The royal palace of Drottningholm, three miles (ten kilometers) west of Stockholm, is best known now for its theater, where seventeenth- and eighteenth-century ballets and opera are staged in authentic surroundings. The palace was built from 1661 to 1681 but gained its final form in 1750. In 1756 Carl Fredrik Adelcrantz designed and constructed a theater at the palace, to replace an ear-

SWEDEN: Court Theaters. In 1956, Mary Skeaping staged *Cupid Out of His Humor* in the style of the seventeenth-century court ballets, for the Drottningholm Court Theater. In this scene, the four continents (Istvan Kisch, Per Arthur Segerström, Verner Klavsen, and Nils-Åke Häggbom) pay their respects to the god of love (Nisse Winqvist, center). (Photograph © by Enar Merkel Rydberg; used by permission.)

lier theater. Although it caught fire during a performance in 1762 and was destroyed, Queen Lovisa Ulrika immediately ordered Adelcrantz to have a new theater built on the same site; it opened in 1766 and is still in use.

If outwardly rather modest in appearance, the theater possesses one of the world's most beautiful eighteenth-century interiors. The stage is a reflection of the auditorium, which was decorated by Adrien Masreliez; it is almost sixty feet (nineteen meters) in depth, with a proscenium almost thirty feet (nine meters) wide and about twenty-one feet (seven meters) high. Ingenious stage machinery, constructed by Donato Stopani, permits as many as four rapid changes of scene.

After King Gustav III received the palace in 1777 from his mother, Lovisa Ulrika, most of Sweden's important theatrical productions were staged at Drottningholm until the new royal opera house in Stockholm opened in 1782. After the king was assassinated in 1792, however, Drottningholm was considered old-fashioned; with the advance of more realistic staging, the theater was closed.

In 1921 the historian Agne Beijer rediscovered the theater. He realized that it constituted a treasure, with its thirty complete sets from the end of the eighteenth century and its still functional stage machinery. After careful restoration the theatre was opened to the public in 1922. A demonstration of all the stage effects was given, and members of the Ballet School performed minuets arranged by Lisa Steier.

No general performances were scheduled until 1935, however—merely the occasional show for a visiting congress or society. These entertainments often included dances by members of the Ballet School, and Valborg Franchi, director of the school from 1924 through 1949, was principally responsible for arranging them. She introduced dances from Uttini's *Thetis och Pelée,* along with minuets by Mozart and Haydn. In 1935 plans were laid for more ambitious performances, and three short ballad-operas, by Höpken, Kraus, and Bellman, were presented that fall. They included dances choreographed by Franchi and continued to be given during the 1940s.

On the twentieth anniversary of the theater's resurrection, 1941/42, the Royal Swedish Ballet appeared at Drottningholm in a mixed program of dances arranged by George Gé. These were criticized as being too far from eighteenth-century style to be suited to that stage, as were the dances by Sven Tropp that were introduced into Mozart's opera *Bastien und Bastienne,* written in 1768 when he was only twelve.

In 1947, Cissi Olsson-Åhrberg, a former *prima ballerina*, first choreographed at Drottningholm. She returned in 1949 with an evening of dances from the Baroque era to the Romantic era, after studying the work of the eighteenth-century theorist Gennaro Magri in Paris (where she also acquired an old version of *Giselle* from Alexandre Volinine, once Pavlova's partner). The program included highlights from André Campra's *L'Europe Galante* of 1697; they suited the theater perfectly and remained in the repertory for three years.

In 1951 the Royal Swedish Opera agreed to stage performances at Drottningholm each summer, which allowed it to present complete operas. When Mary Skeaping became director of the Royal Swedish Ballet in 1953, she realized what opportunities the Drottningholm theater offered for research into seventeenth- and eighteenth-century ballet, which the company developed under her guidance.

Skeaping's first production, *Den Fångne Cupido* (Cupid Out of His Humor), in 1956, was in the style of seventeenth-century court ballet, to music by Henry Purcell. It was followed in 1957 by Christoph Willibald Gluck's *Orfeo ed Euridice* (1762), with all the dances included. This enjoyed such success that an entire cycle of Gluck operas was produced in the 1960s—*Iphigénie en Tauride* in 1960, *Alcestes* in 1962, and *Iphigénie en Aulide* in 1963—all three had been in the original repertory at Drottningholm.

In 1964 Skeaping staged *Atis och Camilla,* a ballet based on an eighteenth-century poem by the Swedish poet Gustav Philip Creutz, set to music by Johan Helmich Roman. The choreography was her own, but the steps derived from authentic eighteenth-century sources. In 1966, she staged a reconstruction of Filippo Taglioni's *Le Retour du Printemps* (The Return of Spring), which evoked a pre-Romantic sensibility; in 1968 her staging of act 2 of *Giselle* revived the true Romantic-era's style.

That same year Skeaping's assistant, Regina Beck-Friis, showed the same accuracy of style in the dances she arranged for operas by Scarlatti and Grétry. In 1969, the company staged George Frideric Handel's *Il Pastor Fido* (1712), with a large portion of the dances by Skeaping, and it introduced to Sweden Vincenzo Galeotti's *Amors og Balletmesterens Luner* (The Whims of Cupid and the Ballet Master), given in the 1786 version from Copenhagen, revived by Elsa-Marianne von Rosen. *Orfeo ed Euridice* was restaged in 1971, this time with choreography by Beck-Friis on the pattern of a 1774 production. She revived with splendid success such Baroque period French *opéra-ballets* as Lully's *Le Carnaval* in 1975 and Rameau's *Platée* in 1978.

Skeaping joined Ivo Cramér in 1971 in a fruitful collaboration that led to re-creations of Antoine Bournonville's eighteenth-century ballet *Fiskarena* (The Fishermen), to the original music by Joseph Martin Kraus, and in 1976 a presentation of Pierre Gardel's *La Dansomanie* (1800).

SWEDEN: Court Theaters. Pierre Gardel's *La Dansomanie,* first performed at Stockholm's Royal Opera in 1804, was revived by Ivo Cramér, with assistance from Mary Skeaping, for the Drottningholm Court Theater in 1976. (Photograph © by Enar Merkel Rydberg; used by permission.)

Cramér subsequently did further research on ballets of the Gustavian period. He restaged *La Mort d'Arlequin* (1796), originally by Terrade, and *Arlequin, Magicien par Amour* (1793), originally by Marcadet; both of them fully exploit the fabulous stage machinery of the Drottningholm theater.

In 1985 Beck-Friis created a new version of Gasparo Angiolini's *Don Juan* of 1761, to the original music by Gluck, using the technique of Gennaro Magri according to Mary Skeaping's translation of his *Trattato teorico-prattica di ballo* (1779). This successful ballet stimulated a new interest in Angiolini, his predecessor Franz Hilverding, and their style of *ballet d'action.*

The Stockholm vicinity is blessed with two more eighteenth-century theaters, the Ulriksdal Court Theater and the Gripsholm Court Theater. The Ulriksdal Court Theater, originally built as a riding school, was transformed by Carl Fredrik Adelcrantz to a small theater in 1753 for Queen Lovisa Ulrika. During her reign and that of her son Gustav III, it was used exclusively for the court's amusement, with a repertory mostly of French plays, *opéra-comique,* and *divertissements.* In the nineteenth century it was damaged and turned into a royal hunting lodge; later, like Drottningholm, it was forgotten.

In 1976 it was decided to reconstruct the theater, and the next year a *divertissement* was given in the theater, still decorated with hunting motifs. During the 1980s all the audience area was restored, but the stage was newly built. Under the artistic direction of Kjerstin Dellert the theater, now called Confidencen, grew more and more authentic in style, with a repertory of ballets and musical theater of the eighteenth century and later epochs, choreographed by Beck-Friis and Cramér.

The Gripsholm Court Theater was originally designed in 1772 by Carl Fredrik Adelcrantz in the upper floor of one of the towers of the medieval castle, after a suggestion of Gustave III himself. It was a very small theater, for the frequent dramatic activities of the royal court during the winters of 1775 to 1779. In 1782 the young architect Eric Palmstedt was asked to build a new, larger theater in the same tower, which resulted in a real architectual jewel of the neoclassical style. The audience area is rounded like the tower, while the small stage, equipped with full stage machinery, extends into the queen's wing and is raised to the same level as the tower.

Like the other court theaters the Gripsholm was forgotten in the nineteenth century but restored to functional order in the twentieth by Agne Beijer. Now it is primarily a museum; from time to time *divertissements,* plays, and concerts are given for small audiences in connection with the visits of dignitaries.

BIBLIOGRAPHY

Beijer, Agne. *Drottningholms slottsteater på Lovisa Ulrikas och Gustaf III:s tid.* Stockholm, 1981.

MAGNUS BLOMKVIST

Dance Education

The Royal Swedish Ballet School was founded in 1773, together with the Royal Opera, by King Gustav III. After an unbroken tradition of 210 years the school moved out of the Royal Opera House in 1983 to become the Swedish Ballet School, a communal and state-supported school integrated into the communal school of Högalid in Stockholm. From 1983 to 1992 the school expanded greatly and now has about two hundred fifty pupils in a basic school of six grades and a high school of three year-levels. The school belongs to the largest and best known in Europe and has a reputation for producing fine male dancers. In the basic school classical ballet, modern dance, jazz, and character dance are taught, as well as pas de deux and repertory. In the high school two alternative programs exist, one with a focus on traditional classical ballet and repertory, and the other (since 1989) for modern dance, jazz, and creativity.

Aside from the Swedish Ballet School in Stockholm, similar professional schools have been integrated into school systems in the towns of Göteborg and Malmö (1992 and 1993), where the pupils also complete their ordinary schoolwork. The high school attached to the Swedish Ballet School in Stockholm is available after entrance examination to students from throughout Sweden, and offers a high school diploma.

The Choreographic Institute of the Royal Academy of Music, now University College of Dance, was founded in 1963. An independent college under the Department of Education, the college offers four full-time courses: two, dance education and choreography (three years), lead to the equivalent of a bachelor of fine arts degree; two others, folk dance and further education for dancers in modern and contemporary dance (two years), lead to a university diploma. The college also organizes single-subject courses on a regular basis in historical dance and dance therapy. The college aims to educate students for careers in dance and to provide an environment for research and artistic experimentation.

In recent years several communities in Sweden have started to include dance education in the preschools and elementary schools. The upper secondary school curriculum has added a program for practical and artistic subjects, with a special option in dance and theater.

Private dance schools flourished in Sweden earlier in the twentieth century, but few survive today. Their courses in dance for adults and children have been integrated into ten organizations that promote adult education. The largest and most popular of these is Balettakademien, a part of Folkuniversitetet, the extramural department of Stockholm University, which has eleven thousand pupils in dance, thirty-six hundred of them in Stockholm. Of these students, seventy of age sixteen to twenty-one attend a full-time professional school. Balettakademien arranges annual summer courses in ballet, modern dance, and jazz dance. Internationally famous teachers from Europe and the United States are invited to Stockholm for stints of five weeks.

BIBLIOGRAPHY

Cullberg, Birgit, and Lilian Karina Vasarhelyi. *Balettskolan.* Vastaras, 1960.

Cullberg, Birgit. "Why Study Ballet?" *Dance Magazine* (May 1961): 27–28.

Feinberg, Gunilla. *Lår dig dansa: 200 års danslåroböcker.* Malmö, 1989.

Hood, Robin [Idestam-Almqvist, Bengt]. *Svensk balett/The Ballet in Sweden.* Malmö, 1951.

Palmqvist, Bertil. *Malmöbaletten.* Malmö, 1985.

Riwkin-Brick, Anna. *Svensk danskonst på scen och i skola.* Stockholm, 1932.

LULLI SVEDIN

Dance Research and Publication

The study of Swedish folk dance began during the late 1800s and early 1900s and was a consequence of romantic nationalism and a general interest in folklore during that period. Ernst Klein, curator of the Nordiska Museet in Stockholm, was a pioneer in this field; Mats Rehnberg pursued the study of folk dance in the next generation. The Dance Museum (Dansmuseet) in Stockholm opened a special section for folk dance, with Henry Sjöberg as curator. Sjöberg established an archive of all existing literature on folk and social dancing in Sweden, both collecting original books and obtaining photocopies of material in other libraries. Contributors to the Dance Museum's folk dance section have studied and preserved folk dances by embarking on expeditions to the countryside, where traditions still live, and filming authentic folk dances. Contributors to Svenska Visarkivet, the archive for Swedish songs and ballads, have undertaken similar expeditions; however, they emphasize the musical aspect of song dance.

The first ballet criticism published in Sweden was written by Johan Henrik Kellgren, a major poet and writer representative of the Enlightenment. When King Gustav III founded the Swedish Academy in 1786, Kellgren was chosen to be one of the first thirteen members. He was a regular contributor to the *Stockholmsposten* from its inception in 1778. One of his first articles is a review of an opera performance, Uttini's *Aline, Queen of Golconda.* He gave the newly-engaged dancer Jean Marcadet credit for a joyful shepherd's dance but adds that the ballets need more vitality and that most of the time there are only poses to look at. He wrote, "All theatrical dance should be an imitation of human actions and passions. The steps are only the mechanism, but the pantomime the very soul."

In subsequent articles Kellgren championed Jean-Georges Noverre's ideas of the new *ballet d'action.* He kept Noverre's *Lettres sur la danse* in his private library; not surprisingly, two of Noverre's letters were translated and published in the *Stockholmsposten* in 1781. Since the *Stockholmsposten* exerted a strong influence on intellectual and artistic circles in Stockholm, Kellgren's pressure was effective. In 1782 the Royal Theater engaged Noverre's pupil Antoine Bournonville as *premier danseur* and choreographer; consequently, the repertory of *ballets d'action* grew and the dancing improved.

Kellgren was familiar with the writings of C. J. Dorat and used his "Notions sur la danse ancienne et moderne" (an addition in prose to his cycle of poems *La déclamation théâtrale: La danse*) to publish in the *Stockholmsposten* in 1779 the first dance history written in Swedish. The piece is not a strict translation of Dorat; rather, Kellgren enlarged and commented on it in his own elegant, witty style. In 1782 he wrote a short piece in the *Stockholmsposten* that provided the French recipe for saving boring, wooden operas: lengthen the ballets and shorten the skirts.

Ballet criticism in the modern sense, written by dance experts, is a recent phenomenon in Sweden, beginning in the 1940s. Before that time, during the early decades of the twentieth century, music critics and authorities on arts and crafts covered dance events in daily newspapers and literary magazines.

A special category of writers to emerge was the first generation of newspaperwomen, all of them suffragettes, who gave modern dance their support. Isadora Duncan's guest appearance in Stockholm in 1906 had a great impact on the young generation. When the Swede Anna Behle, a pupil of Duncan and Émile Jaques-Dalcroze, returned from abroad and started to perform and teach, the press filled many columns with articles about the new dance and the ideals behind it.

One music critic, Kajsa Rootzén of the conservative *Svenska dagbladet,* explored the history of dance more thoroughly than her contemporaries. In 1945 she wrote the first history of Swedish ballet, *Den svenska baletten,* covering the development of the Royal Swedish Ballet from 1773 until her own time.

In the 1940s new dance critics appeared in the daily newspapers. Bengt Idestam-Almquist was a supporter of pure classical ballet and author of *Svensk balett* (1951). Bengt Häger wrote criticism and the book *Balett klassisk og fri* (Ballet Classical and Modern, first published in Denmark in 1945) and *Les Ballets Suédois* (1989); he became active as curator of the Dance Museum at its foundation in 1953. Anna Greta Ståhle, critic and editor of the entertainment pages of the *Dagens nyheter,* was later a lecturer at Stockholm University and the State Dance College. Margareta Sjögren succeeded Rootzén and wrote *Biljett till balett* (1957), which included chapters about Swedish dancers and choreographers in the 1950s; she published

Skandinavisk balett in 1988. Madeleine Katz, who wrote for the *Expressen,* was a former dancer writing about dance and literature, especially psychology. Erik Näslund, author of monographs on Birgit Cullberg and Carina Ari, editor of the magazine *Dans* from 1973 to 1981, and dance critic of the *Svenska dagbladet,* became director of the Dansmuseet in Stockholm. Other writers on dance include Gunilla Jensen, a playwright working for Swedish television, and Brit Svedbert from Göteborg, an artist and writer who has published and exhibited her drawings of dancers. Horace Engdahl is critic of the *Dagens nyheter* and contributor to the cultural section of articles on literature and philosophy; his knowledge and support of modern dance has been of great value. Engdal is the author of *Swedish Ballet and Dance* (1992).

With five ballet companies and a growing number of modern dance groups, more coverage is needed. New writers in the 1990s are Bodil Persson, Anna Ångström, and Margareta Sörenson. *Dans tidningen,* a magazine devoted to dance, has been published regularly since 1991. Photographers have contributed to preserving dance history by their records of performances. Important photographic pioneers in Sweden were Beata Bergström and Enar Merkel Rydberg, later followed by Leslie Leslie-Spinks and Tomas Gidén.

Research in Swedish archives, conducted by Mary Skeaping and continued by Ivo Cramér and Regina Beck-Friis, resulted in the reconstruction of ballets depicting the period of Gustav III. Another specialist is Gunilla Roempke. Her research led to an exhibition of Gustavian ballet at the Dansmuseet and to a book about the lives of some Gustavian ballerinas. Magnus Blomkvist produced the articles "Public Entertainment in Stockholm 1773–1806" and "Ballet Music at the Royal Academy of Music 1773–1806" in 1972 and 1973. A symposium held in Stockholm in 1987 centered on theatrical dance and opera at the Drottningholm Court Theater.

Dance has also entered the curricula of Swedish universities. Since 1988 it has been possible to study the history and aesthetics of dance at Stockholm University. Students have prepared papers on specific dance subjects, for example, "Fokine in Sweden." Others have written about Birgit Cullberg, Ivo Cramér, Birgit Åkesson, and Ronny Johansson. In the early 1990s several doctoral dissertations were completed. Lena Hammergren wrote "Form och mening i Dansen" (Form and Meaning in Dance); and Cecilia Olsson wrote "Dansföreställningar" (Dance Performances), centering on George Balanchine and Antony Tudor. In the field of ethnic dance Owe Ronström studied the dances of Yugoslav immigrants and their evolution. In 1995 Erik Näslund presented "Birgit Cullberg's Fröken Julie, en svensk Balettklassiker" (Birgit Cullberg's *Miss Julia,* a Swedish Ballet Classic).

The State Dance College has encouraged research and university studies. Several teachers have prepared papers on children's dances for the university's departments of pedagogy and psychology; Erna Grönlund of the State Dance College presented a 1994 dissertation, "Barns känslor bearbetade i dans: Dansterapi för barn med tidiga störningar" (Dance Therapy as a Treatment for Children with Early Emotional Disturbances). Peter Rajka, also at the State Dance College, is experimenting with a new form of dance notation.

ANNA GRETA STÅHLE

SWEIGARD, LULU. *See* Body Therapies, *overview article.*

SWING DANCE. *See* Lindy Hop.

SWISS MILKMAID, THE. Originally titled *Das Schweizer Milchmädchen;* also known as *Nathalie, ou La Laitière Suisse.* Ballet in two acts. Choreography: Filippo Taglioni. Music: Adalbert Gyrowetz. Scenery: Janitz, Gail, and Pran. Costumes: Philipp Stubenrauch. First performance: 8 October 1821, Kärntnertor Theater, Vienna. Principals: Johanna Bretel (Henriette), Théodore Rozier (Nathalie), Therese Heberle (Nannette), Filippo Taglioni (Alexis).

Inspired by Gaetano Gioja's ballet *I Minatori Valacchi,* which had its premiere on 9 February 1814, Filippo Taglioni used French-speaking Switzerland as the scene of the story for *The Swiss Milkmaid.* Alexis, an army officer, is in love with Henriette and has her abducted to the castle. In a series of pantomime scenes, the peasant girl expresses her amazement at her lordly surroundings while standing in front of a statue of Alexis. Unknown to her, Alexis has substituted himself for the statue at a moment when she was not looking. Enraptured with Henriette, Alexis falls at her feet and declares his love. After she recovers from the shock of her discovery, she agrees to marry him. Other principal characters include Henriette's father and two sisters, and the lord of the castle.

The ballet was a sensation in Europe. It offered the principal dancer an opportunity to show off her qualities as a mime—qualities that Fanny Elssler possessed to a greater degree than any other ballerina of the Romantic era. Antoine Titus produced the ballet for the Berlin debut of the Elssler sisters on 8 October 1830. On 4 February 1831, Elssler danced the role for the first time in Vienna. The dancers added two pas de deux, which she danced partnered by her sisters.

On 25 September 1823, Titus (who had worked in Vienna in 1822) produced the ballet at the Théâtre de la

Porte-Saint-Martin in Paris. In 1832, Filippo Taglioni did the ballet under the title *Nathalie, ou La Laitière Suisse,* with additional music by Michele Carafa, and with his daughter Marie in the title role. For this Paris version of the ballet, Taglioni changed both the characters' names and the story. Although Marie Taglioni was successful in this role, which she also danced in a London production at the King's Theatre, the role nevertheless remained linked with the name of her rival Elssler.

In August 1840 Elssler danced the ballet for the first time in New York, where it had been performed the previous year in a production by Paul Taglioni, who also produced his father's ballet in 1841 in Copenhagen. Elssler danced the milkmaid for the last time on 16 December 1849, at the Bolshoi Theater in Saint Petersburg, where Titus had already produced the ballet in 1832. This version, by Marius Petipa jointly with Jules Perrot, was Petipa's first work for Saint Petersburg. The ballet now went under the title *Lida, oder Das Schweizer Milchmädchen.*

In 1980 Pierre Lacotte created a reconstruction of the ballet for the Classical Ballet of Moscow, with Ekaterina Maximova in the title role.

[*See also the entries on the principal figures mentioned herein.*]

BIBLIOGRAPHY

Beaumont, Cyril W. *Complete Book of Ballets.* London, 1937.
Guest, Ivor. *The Romantic Ballet in England.* London, 1972.
Guest, Ivor. *The Romantic Ballet in Paris.* 2d rev. ed. London, 1980.

ARCHIVE. Riki Raab Archives, Vienna.

GUNHILD OBERZAUCHER-SCHÜLLER
Translated from German

SWITZERLAND. In the late 1960s, Alfonso Catà added a number of works by George Balanchine to the repertory of the Ballet du Grand Théâtre de Genève. This trio of dancers in a 1971 performance of *Donizetti Variations* is made up of Liane Schween, Heinz Spoerli, and Colette Jeschke. (Photograph courtesy of Claude Conyers. Choreography by George Balanchine © The George Balanchine Trust.)

SWITZERLAND. To reflect the current state of dance in Switzerland, any survey must take account not only of the historical mainstream of dance in municipal theaters and opera houses, including the "ballet boom" following World War II, but also of the "dance explosion," a phenomenon of extratheatrical dance activity, that has occurred in the later decades of the twentieth century.

Early History. Although the eighteenth-century Swiss elite followed the French example and on occasion staged dance spectacles, it was not until the nineteenth century, when municipal theaters were founded for opera and drama, that the theatrical arts were established in Switzerland on an ongoing basis. During the first decades of the century, many artists employed in theaters were amateurs. It is known, for instance, that many well-trained but nonprofessional musicians played in theater orchestras. Very little, however, is known about stage dance at the time. While it might be assumed that amateur dancers were as common as amateur musicians, the parallel could be misleading, for, although high-caliber musical instruction was common among the Swiss middle class, dance instruction beyond the level of social dance was comparatively rare.

Throughout the nineteenth century and well into the twentieth, most stage dancing took the form of operatic interludes. Some independent performances were staged, but they remained peripheral to the overall concerns of theater artists and audiences. One notable exception was *The Fairy Doll,* Joseph Hassreiter's perennially popular pantomime ballet, which enjoyed a number of performances in various Swiss theaters around the turn of the century. More typical were the statistics associated with the Zurich municipal theater: during its first fifty years (1891–1941), productions on its stage included only twenty-five ballets, most of which were performed a mere five or six times.

In the first half of the twentieth century, German modern dance, called *Ausdruckstanz* ("expressive dance"), had a far greater impact in Switzerland that did classical ballet. Émile Jaques-Dalcroze, whose theories of eurhythmics formed the basis of much of early modern dance, began his teaching career in 1892 at the Conservatoire de Musique in Geneva. In 1910 he left to work at Hellerau in Germany, but from 1915 until his death in 1950 he continued his work in Geneva at the institute that still bears his name. In the years surrounding World War I, Rudolf Laban and Mary Wigman, the originators of German modern dance, worked in Ascona, an artists' colony on the shore of Lake Maggiore in the Swiss Alps, near the Italian

SWITZERLAND. In Basel in 1978, Heinz Spoerli created what is perhaps the quintessential Swiss ballet. Based on Swiss folklore, it is entitled *Chäs* (Cheese). Seen here are Martin Schläpfer (kicking his heel over his head) and members of the ensemble in a typically frolicsome moment. The ballet was set to music by André Bauer and Edi Baer and was danced in front of a backdrop created by Hannes Meyer. The costumes, in bright yellow and red, relieved by black and white, were designed by Anuschka Meyer-Riehl. (Photograph © by Gundel Kilian; used by permission.)

border. Their circle of dancers included Sophie Täuber, who performed at the Dada Gallery in Zurich. The intensive experimental work of these German artists laid the groundwork for later developments throughout central Europe.

After World War I, modern dance reached a larger public. Charlotte Bara, a German dancer who took Berlin by storm in the 1920s, settled near Ascona and in 1927–1928 opened her Teatro San Materno. Designed specifically for dance, it was considered to be the first truly modern theater in Switzerland. There, Bara presented not only her own productions but also those of other modernists on tour, including Valeska Gert, Rosalia Chladek, and Trudi Schoop. Schoop, a Swiss-born dancer who had studied in Germany and who had opened a school in Zurich in 1926, trained a company that toured at home and abroad from 1930 to 1947. During the same period, the frequent tours of Clothilde and Alexander Sakharoff popularized modern dance for a broad theatergoing public.

From 1939 to 1957, Mara Jovanovits, a dancer trained by Gret Palucca, directed the dance ensemble at the small theater in Sankt Gallen (Saint Gall). In the isolation of the war years, Jovanovits's choreographic style became increasingly classical. In this way her work showed a natural evolution away from *Ausdruckstanz* and anticipated the postwar turn toward ballet. Unlike the state theaters in Germany, where the performing arts were brought to a virtual standstill during World War II, Swiss theaters continued to function more or less normally, yet after the war Swiss artists and audiences, like those in Germany, found ballet far more compelling than modern dance. To postwar audiences in both Switzerland and Germany, ballet was considered a novelty, whereas, ironically, "modern" dance was considered old-fashioned.

The Ballet Boom. The postwar ballet boom centered on the six government-subsidized ballet ensembles at theaters in Basel, Bern, Geneva, Lucerne, Saint Gall, and Zurich. The status of these companies has depended largely on the support, or lack thereof, offered by the general director of the theater and by the strength of personality projected by the resident choreographer or ballet master. Not surprisingly, each of the six companies has experienced high and low points.

Basel. In the late 1950s and early 1960s Vaslav Orlikovsky guided the Basel Ballet to renown as a "Swiss ballet miracle" comparable to John Cranko's "Stuttgart ballet miracle." In 1973, Heinz Spoerli began a long and distinguished tenure that brought the company to a second peak of international fame. In 1991, when Spoerli left for Düsseldorf, he was replaced by Youri Vámos, and in 1996 the Basel Ballet was disbanded and replaced by a *Tanztheater* directed by Joachim Schlömer. [*See* Basel Ballet.]

Geneva. Regular ballet performances in Geneva began only in the early 1960s, following the opening of the rebuilt Grand Théâtre. The first directors of the Geneva Ballet were Janine Charrat (1962–1964) and Serge Golovine (1964–1969), who presented a conventional repertory. The arrival of Alfonso Catà in 1969 signaled a major change. Catà, a Cuban-American who had danced with the New York City Ballet, persuaded George Balanchine to become an artistic adviser to the company and to help build a repertory featuring his ballets. Patricia Neary continued this policy during her tenure as director of the company from 1973 to 1978. She was succeeded by Peter van Dyk (1978–1980) and Oscar Araiz (1980–1988), who replaced the neoclassical repertory with his own scenic works. From 1988 to 1996 the Geneva Ballet was directed by Gradimir Pankov. At the center of his repertory were works by Jiří Kylián, Ohad Naharin, and Christopher Bruce.

Zurich. Nicholas Beriozoff built a strong ballet audience in Zurich during the 1960s, but in the 1970s the company was plagued by frequent changes in artistic directorship. In the early 1980s, Patricia Neary built up a broad-based repertory, starting with the works by Balanchine that she had mounted earlier at the Grand Théâtre de Genève and then proving the versatility and strength of the Zurich company with performances of works ranging from such Romantic classics as *Giselle,* as staged by Heinz Spoerli, to the violently contemporary *Love Songs* by William Forsythe. In 1985, Neary was replaced as head of the Zurich Ballet by Uwe Scholz, who had the company concentrate on his own choreography. In 1991 Scholz was succeeded by Bernd Roger Biernert, who held the directorship for five confused years before being replaced, in 1996, by Spoerli, who was persuaded to return to Switzerland from Germany. [*See* Zurich Ballet.]

Lucerne. As ballet master at the municipal theater in Lucerne, the Swiss dancer and choreographer Riccardo Duse built a versatile and imaginative repertory in the early 1970s. Taking over from Duse in 1976, Dieter Ammann creatively guided the ballet company in the late 1970s and the 1980s. Then, in 1990, the Lucerne company created a small sensation by obtaining star dancer Ben van Cauwenberg as director and former Kirov ballerina Galina Panova as soloist and ballet mistress. Their tenure was relatively brief, and they were followed in 1992 by the young choreographer and director Thorsten Kreissig, whose free and easy works met with huge success, arousing the spirited approval of Lucerne audiences. In 1996, Kreissig was replaced by Richard Wherlock, who introduced instead of ballet the currently fashionable style of *Tanztheater.*

Bern and Saint Gall. The relatively small cities of Bern and Saint Gall have not been widely known as centers of theatrical dance. Riccardo Duse worked at the municipal theater in Bern in the early 1980s, and in 1991 the French dancer François Klaus took over the ballet company there. His story ballets, such as *Peer Gynt,* were highly successful. Since 1994, the company has been directed by Martin Schläpfer, formerly a soloist with Spoerli's Basel Ballet, who has given it a level of quality and a range of style almost unprecedented for such a small company performing on such a small stage. With even more restricted means, Marianne Fuchs has since 1990 built for the small company in Saint Gall an interesting repertory, including works by such well-known choreographers as Tom Schilling. Considering that the company directors in Bern and Saint Gall, like their colleague in Lucerne, work with troupes of fewer than twenty members and are frequently called upon to stage dances in operas and operettas, their achievements are especially impressive.

Lausanne. In addition to the six cities that support municipal ballet companies, Lausanne, at the eastern end of Lake Geneva, has played a prominent part in the dance history of Switzerland. Thanks to the Festival de Lausanne, the city's Théâtre Beaulieu has been the principal Swiss venue for ballet and modern dance companies from abroad. In 1973, the Prix de Lausanne was established by a group of culturally minded industrialists to provide a

SWITZERLAND. Thorsten Kreissig's *Dornröschen—Die Schlafende Schönheit* was presented at the Municipal Theater in Lucerne in 1993. Audiences expecting to see a production of *The Sleeping Beauty* were, however, in for a surprise. Although set to the familiar Tchaikovsky score, the ballet told a completely different story. Critics admitted that it was entertaining but complained about misuse of a classic musical score. (Photograph by Peter Schnetz; reprinted from *World Ballet and Dance, 1993–1994,* Oxford, 1994, p. 136).

scholarship to a talented teenage ballet dancer who has not yet begun a professional career. It is awarded each year by a international jury of about ten prominent teachers and choreographers to the winner of a four-day competition.

In 1987, the noted French choreographer and company director Maurice Béjart disbanded his famed Ballet du XXe Siècle in Brussels, relocated to Lausanne, and founded a new company, which he named the Ballet Béjart Lausanne. In 1992, following the model of his Brussels school, Mudra, he founded in Lausanne the École-Atelier Rudra Béjart Lausanne. He has continued to be a prolific choreographer and a master of theatrical spectacle.

The Dance Explosion. Since the 1960s, Switzerland has been the site of explosive growth in all types of dance. It is difficult to determine whether the increased esteem for theater dance has encouraged and facilitated the extratheatrical activities or whether the extratheatrical activities have themselves attracted larger audiences for performances of theater dance. Perhaps the influence is reciprocal.

Opera houses and municipal theaters often sponsor studio demonstrations and experimental workshop performances in addition to ballet evenings. The number of professional dancers working outside the subsidized theater has increased exponentially, while small, nonsubsidized groups have proliferated, although many have been short-lived. It is impossible to assess or even survey all of the performances taking place on small stages and in improvised theaters throughout the country.

It is clear, however, that these performances exhibit a wide range of styles and types of musical accompaniment. Although scores by Swiss composers written specifically for dance constitute only a small fraction of the repertory, a quiet explosion has occurred even in this domain. Since 1900, more than one hundred composers have written more than two hundred and fifty scores specifically for dance. Still, composers of music for dance receive little direct support or official encouragement.

In contrast, the needs of other dance professionals and related institutions are well supported. The Migros training scholarship, for example, and the Prix de Lausanne both aim to encourage talented young dancers. The Schweizerischer Dachverband, a kind of umbrella organization, coordinates activities in a wide range of areas, while local associations have focused their support on specific institutions. Several different organizations look after the interests of teachers. In 1996, there were more than five hundred ballet schools in Switzerland, of which more than fifty provided professional training.

Perhaps most surprising is the widespread participation in extratheatrical dance. In dance studios all over the country, amateurs study ballet, modern dance, and jazz. Even small towns boast popular discothèques and dance clubs, and American fads such as break dancing and hip-hop are imported immediately. In recent years, residents of Zurich have even cultivated a Carnival tradition, taking Basel's famous Fasnacht as their model. For three consecutive nights every year, a dense crowd dances in the squares of the Old City, stamping their feet and whirling about to the rhythms of traditional tunes as well as modern music. In just a few decades, attitudes toward dance have changed decisively in Switzerland, enabling it to become an integral part of theatrical and extratheatrical life.

[*See also the entries on the principal figures mentioned herein.*]

BIBLIOGRAPHY

Baumann, Dorothea, ed. *Théâtre musical: L'oeuvre de compositeurs suisses du vingtième siècle.* Bonstetten, 1983.

Buffat, Serge. *Oscar Araiz: Carnets de danse, Genève 1980–1988.* Lausanne, 1988.

Cunha, Antonio. "Le Béjart Ballet de Lausanne et les enjeux de la politique culturelle." In *La danse, art du XXe siècle.* Lausanne, 1990.

Flury, Phillip, and Peter Kaufmann. *Heinz Spoerli: Ballett-Fazination.* 2d ed. Zurich, 1996.

Levieux, Francette. *Prix de Lausanne: Un tremplin pour les jeunes danseurs de talents.* Lausanne, 1989.

Merz, Richard. "Von zweitrangiger Bedeutung zu unerwarteter Popularität: Ballett in der Schweiz." In *Tanz in Deutschland: Ballett seit 1945,* edited by Hartmut Regitz. Berlin, 1984.

Muriset, Yvan, and Jean-Pierre Pastori. *Béjart, le tournant.* New ed. Lausanne, 1988.

Pastori, Jean-Pierre. "The Emancipation of Dance in the Municipal Theatres." *Ballett International* 10 (June 1987): 12–18.

Pastori, Jean-Pierre. *Dance and Ballet in Switzerland.* Translated by Jacqueline Gartmann. 2d ed., rev. and enl. Zurich, 1989.

Pastori, Jean-Pierre. *De Diaghilev à Béjart: Lausanne danse, 1915–1993.* Lausanne, 1993.

Schouvaloff, Alexander. *Set and Costume Designs for Ballet and Theatre.* London, 1987.

Vollmer, Horst. "Direktorenkarussell." *Tanz und Gymnastik* 51.3 (1995): 42–46.

Weber, Conrad G. *Brauchtum in der Schweiz.* Zurich, 1985.

RICHARD MERZ
Translated from German

SWORD DANCE. The linked, closed-circle, hilt-and-point sword dance is known throughout Europe but is especially concentrated in the Germanic countries and in the northeast of England. The dance has considerable regional variety, but the core choreographic principle is to weave a number of figures without releasing the swords, culminating in the tying and display of a polygonal braid of the swords. Dancers hold the hilt of their swords in their right hand and the point of their neighbor's in their left hand, to form a closed circle. In England there are two types of sword dance—the long-sword and the rapper, the latter an outgrowth of the former.

The sword dance proper, especially in the long-sword

traditions, is only part of a much larger seasonal ceremonial. The performance begins with the captain of the team singing a "calling-on" song, the signal that allows him to clear a space for the dance and to introduce the dancers one by one. Each of the dancers is mythologized as a hero or a villain, and the song concludes with an exhortation to dance. The closed, hilt-and-point circle is formed and a few figures are danced. One of the performers is (mock) slain, then a play, recited in doggerel, is enacted, ending in the appearance of a quack doctor who through general horseplay resurrects the dead man. The dancers complete their stock of figures and finish by tying a lock.

Traditionally, the sword dance is performed at Christmastime. Each team takes its performance on a tour of important points around the village or group of neighboring villages. The overt function of the dance is to entertain and to earn some pocket money by passing the hat. Implicitly, though, the dance serves to maintain and strengthen social solidarity by providing a locally recognizable and significant aesthetic focus to general festival activity.

The long-sword dance is performed in and around Yorkshire by six or eight men wearing quasi-military or uniform costumes decked with rosettes and ribbons; each man carries a dancing sword, a thirty- to forty-inch (about one meter) lath of steel with a fixed, wooden handle. The stepping is a rhythmic, slightly dotted, running step using any 4/4, 2/2, or 6/8 tune that can be played at a moderate pace. The basic figure from which the others start is a wide, closed ring circling clockwise. Each of the figures is performed with all possible combinations of dancers; for example, if the first dancer raises his sword and the rest file under it ("single under"), then the second through the sixth (or eighth) dancers will do likewise in turn. Other figures include "over your own sword" (each dancer hops over his sword in turn), "over your neighbor's sword," and "single over" (the dancers file over a sword held as a hurdle). The overall aesthetic effect is of a hypnotic, mathematical certainty.

The rapper dance almost certainly developed out of the long-sword tradition in the eighteenth century, although it did not reach its present form until the early part of the twentieth century. It is performed almost exclusively by coal miners from Northumbria. There are five central dancers dressed in white shirts decorated with rosettes, dark open-knee breeches, and white stockings. They are accompanied by two characters, Tommy and Bessy, who serve as clowns, occasionally joining in the main dance. One of the characters sings the calling-on song. Plays are no longer performed, although two are known from the mid-nineteenth century. The dance is performed to double jigs played very fast, with the dancers alternating a running step with a 6/8 shuffle-tap step. Each dancer carries a rapper, a twenty-eight-inch (about 0.75 meter) lath of flexible spring steel, with a swivel handle at one end and a fixed one at the other. The characteristics of this strange implement (of unknown origin or function outside the dance) make the dance unique. In the long-sword dance the lock is the final figure because strength and precision timing are required to tie it and because it is virtually impossible to untie it without breaking the circle. With the flexible rappers, however, the lock, called a *nut*, can be easily tied and untied by turning the circle inside out without the dancers releasing the rappers. This has made the aesthetic of the rapper dance a display of the different ways that the nut can be tied.

The speed of the rapper dance does not allow for the wide circles and generous motions of the long-sword dance. The set is always tightly packed, and all movement is carried out shoulder to shoulder. The characteristic rapper figure is two counterrotating circles with various possibilities for crossing from one circle to the opposite, tangling the rappers in a seemingly hopeless mess. At the end of the dance Tommy and Bessy may enter the set, making the counterrotating circles and the resultant jumble of rappers even more amazing and the final nut more complex.

Early folklorists speculated that the sword dance, with its death-and-resurrection motif, is a remnant of a pre-Christian ritual cycle designed to propitiate the forces of nature in midwinter and to ensure the return of the sun. Apart from imputing to early Europeans a naïveté that contemporary anthropology has shown to be unwarranted, the historical evidence for such a theory does not exist. The earliest reference to the sword dance in Europe is in Nuremberg in 1350, and the earliest in England is 1638. Because the great majority of sword dances are native to areas with old mining sites, there has been theoretical speculation that the earliest dancers were members of a sacral brotherhood of metal workers that performed essential rituals during the annual cycle. The more mundane explanation is that it was easiest to have special swords for dancing made at mining sites, which were also centers for metal working. There is as yet no sound theory of the origin and evolution of hilt-and-point sword dancing in Europe.

[*See also* Great Britain, *article on* English Traditional Dance; Jig; Matachins; *and* Morris Dance.]

BIBLIOGRAPHY

Alford, Violet. *Sword Dance and Drama.* London, 1962.

Cawte, E. C. "A History of the Rapper Dance." *Folk Music Journal* 4.2 (1981): 79–116.

Corrsin, Stephen D. *Sword Dancing: A History.* Enfield Lock, 1996.

Sharp, Cecil J. *The Sword Dances of Northern England.* 3 vols. London, 1912–1913. 2d ed. London, 1951.

JOHN FORREST

SYDNEY DANCE COMPANY. Acclaimed for its large and varied repertory of contemporary and theatrically innovative works, Sydney Dance Company has mostly Australian choreographers. From the beginning of their association with the company, current artistic director Graeme Murphy and his assistant artistic director Janet Vernon have aimed to develop a repertory that is relevant to contemporary Australians, with a style that reflects contemporary Australian society.

The company was called the Dance Company (NSW) when Murphy took over its direction at the end of 1976. The Dance Company (NSW) had been founded by Suzanne Musitz in 1965 as a dance-in-education group, but it developed as a full-fledged performing company that was led first by Musitz and then in 1975 and 1976 by Jaap Flier. Murphy changed its name to Sydney Dance Company in 1979, hoping to give the company a stronger image and a recognizable sense of place. The company survived financial difficulties that had it on the brink of receivership in 1983, and is now the only major dance company, classical or modern, whose permanent base is in Sydney. It is often regarded as one of Sydney's cultural icons, although its frequent national and overseas tours have ensured that it is now widely known outside the city that gave it birth.

SYDNEY DANCE COMPANY. Carl Morrow and Victoria Taylor in *Daphnis and Chloe,* choreographed by the company's longtime director Graeme Murphy to the score by Maurice Ravel. (Photograph by Branco Gaica; used by permission.)

The company's repertory consists largely of works choreographed by Murphy. They range from full-length works, his first being *Poppy* (1978) inspired by the life and art of French author Jean Cocteau, to shorter one-act pieces. They are sometimes clearly narrative-based, although Murphy frequently manipulates or reworks a given narrative. Thus *After Venice* (1984) was based on the Thomas Mann novella *Death in Venice,* but it focused on the character of Tadzio and presented a psychological exploration of his relations with the other characters in the novella. Some works have Australian themes, such as *Rumours* (1978/79), *Homelands* (1982), *Wilderness* (1982) and *Nearly Beloved* (1986), although in recent years Murphy has rarely chosen an overtly Australian subject. At other times Murphy's works for Sydney Dance Company are strongly nonnarrative. *Kraanerg* (1988) and *Piano Sonata* (1992), for example, were influenced in their choreographic structure by the music Murphy chose, a score by Iannis Xenakis for *Kraanerg* and a sonata by Carl Vine for *Piano Sonata.* The works are often also multimedia creations, making use of film, slide projections, and complex stage machinery and lighting.

Murphy has always seen Sydney Dance Company as a vehicle for the showing of work by Australian visual artists and composers and the company has a strong history of commissioning music and design. In recent years the company has worked with live performance ensembles who appear on stage and who have become an intrinsic part of the dance work, as in *Synergy with Synergy* (1992) made with the Australian percussion group Synergy. *Free Radicals* (1996) took this process one step further when both the music, by four percussionists, and the choreography were created side by side in the rehearsal process.

The repertory of Sydney Dance Company includes works by choreographers other than Murphy, such as Louis Falco, Ralph Lemon, Ohad Naharin, and Douglas Wright; the several Australians include Paul Mercurio, Gideon Obarzanek, Stephen Page, Garth Welch, and Kim Walker. Many company dancers have contributed to the repertory over the years, often in workshop seasons, and the company has also nurtured some dancers who have gone on to start their own or direct other companies, including Mercurio (Australian Choreographic Ensemble), Obarzanek (Chunky Move), and Page (Bangarra Dance Theatre).

In the mid-1990s, Sydney Dance Company took on an

entrepreneurial role in order, Murphy says, to expand the choices available to Australian dance audiences. The company has brought a number of French and American companies to Australia often to perform as part of a Sydney Dance Company season. Companies that have come to Australia under this arrangement include those led by Maguy Marin and Angelin Preljocaj as well as Momix and the Parsons Dance Company.

Sydney Dance Company dancers all have a strong classical training, although not all have the perfectly proportioned classical body. Although it does not promote a hierarchical system of star dancers, certain dancers have come to be closely identified with the company, especially Janet Vernon, who, as well as assisting Murphy with artistic direction, has danced with it since 1976. Vernon and Murphy had a notable dancing partnership in early Sydney Dance Company seasons and Vernon's performance skills as a dancer and actor are strongly individualistic. She is also often described as Murphy's muse, and Murphy has created many of the leading roles in his works on her, including those in some of his most recent works like *The Protecting Veil* (1994) and *Fornicon* (1995).

The company's first international opportunity came in 1980 when it visited Italy. In 1981 it went to New York where its novelty, originality, and sheer theatrical quality received favorable notice. *New York Times* critic Clive Barnes wrote:

> Murphy is the kind of choreographer you will want to tell your grandchildren about. The man is a major find—and so is his company.

In the same year recitals were given at the Spoleto Festival in Charleston, South Carolina, and in Washington, D.C. In 1985, it returned to New York and soon became the first contemporary dance company to perform in China. In 1988, after a long tour to Europe, the company shared a program with the Australian Ballet at the Royal Opera House in London. Since then Sydney Dance Company has continued to tour internationally, visiting the United States, Europe, China, and South America.

[*See also* Australia, *article on* Modern Dance; *and the entry on Murphy.*]

BIBLIOGRAPHY

Pask, Edward H. *Ballet in Australia: The Second Act, 1940–1980.* Melbourne, 1982.

Sydney Dance Company: Repertoire and Touring History. Sydney, 1995.

Ulzen, Karen van. "'Kraanerg' and the Rest." *Dance Australia,* no. 39 (December 1988–January 1989): 18–20.

INTERVIEWS. Graeme Murphy, by Hazel de Berg (April 1981), National Library of Australia, Canberra (de B 1222/3). Graeme Murphy, by Shirley McKechnie (May 1990), National Library of Australia, Canberra (TRC 2680). Graeme Murphy, by Michelle Potter (August 1996), National Library of Australia, Canberra (TRC 3478).

MICHELLE POTTER

SYLPHIDE, LA. Ballet in two acts. Choreography: Filippo Taglioni. Music: Jean Schneitzhoeffer. Libretto: Adolphe Nourrit. Scenery: Pierre Ciceri. Costumes: Eugène Lami. First performance: 12 March 1832, Académie Royale de Musique, Paris. Principals: Marie Taglioni (The Sylphide), Joseph Mazilier (James), Lise Noblet (Effie).

Although *La Sylphide* has earned the title of the first Romantic ballet, none of the components for which it is famed (pointe work, the white muslin ballet skirt, gas lighting, and the use of supernatural beings as characters) was literally new in ballet in 1832. *La Sylphide,* however, united these components and made them serve a powerful and evocative Romantic theme, that of a mortal torn between two realms—the material and the spiritual. The Sylphide of the title, personified as a beautiful young woman dressed in white, symbolized a transcendental world that a mortal may perceive and aspire to, yet never attain. The popularity of this ballet led to a host of imitations centering on white-clad supernatural heroines (hence the term *ballet blanc*); few of these ballets, however, could match the poetry of *La Sylphide.*

LA SYLPHIDE. A lithograph of Marie Taglioni in the title role of *La Sylphide.* This famous image was first published as a plate in *Les danseuses de l'Opéra,* issued in Paris in 1865. (Dance Collection, New York Public Library for the Performing Arts.)

The mysterious and unreal world represented in act 2 of *La Sylphide* was foreshadowed by Jean Coralli's sylphides ballet in a melodramatic version of *Faust* (1828) and the "Ballet of the Nuns" in Giacomo Meyerbeer's opera *Robert le Diable* (1831). The "Ballet of the Nuns," the direct predecessor of *La Sylphide,* was choreographed by Filippo Taglioni for his daughter Marie, who, dressed in a white habit, led the ensemble of seductive ghosts. The ballet was set in a medieval cloister spectrally illuminated by gas lighting. During the opera's rehearsals, the tenor Adolphe Nourrit, who sang the role of Robert, wrote a ballet libretto loosely based on Charles Nodier's story *Trilby, ou Le Lutin d'Argaïl* (1822), a tale of a male sprite who falls in love with the wife of a Scottish fisherman. Marie and Filippo Taglioni approved of the libretto but reversed the male and female roles—thus *La Sylphide* was born.

Set in Scotland, the ballet opens on the wedding day of James Reuben, who is discovered asleep in an armchair, watched over by the Sylphide. Waking him with a kiss, she vanishes up the chimney. As James and his kinsfolk prepare for the wedding, the Sylphide appears again and again, distracting him from his fiancée Effie. Madge, a hideous witch whom James tries to eject from the house, reads Effie's palm and tells her that it is Gurn, James's rival, and not James, who truly loves her. The wedding festivities begin, but as James is about to place his ring on Effie's finger, the Sylphide snatches it away and flies from the house, with James in hot pursuit.

In the forest, Madge and her coven cast spells around a cauldron. James enters in search of the Sylphide, who eludes all his efforts to retain her. In desperation he accepts Madge's aid: an enchanted scarf that will compel the Sylphide to remain beside him. He wraps it around the Sylphide; her wings fall off; she sinks to the ground, dying. As her sister sylphs bear her aloft, James sees in the distance the bridal procession of Effie and Gurn.

Taglioni's dancing, polished by her father, reached a zenith of perfection in the role of the Sylphide. Abjuring the mannerisms and technical displays of the *danse noble,* she danced in a more natural style, rising to her pointes not as an acrobatic stunt but as a means of depicting the Sylphide's insubstantiality. Her lightness and fluidity of movement were enhanced by her gauzy white skirts, which became the uniform of the ballet, the Romantic tutu. [*See* Tutu.]

Taglioni's success in *La Sylphide* not only ensured her personal fame but also paved the way for the nineteenth-century reign of the ballerina. Paradoxically, many writers view James, not the Sylphide, as the focal point of the story. Although the ballet is superficially a love story, the characters are most significant as symbols. James represents the Romantic artist, restless, discontent with the world as it is, and filled with inchoate longings. The Sylphide is a symbol of his longings given feminine form, like Liberty in Eugène Delacroix's painting *The 28th July* (1830).

LA SYLPHIDE. Ghislaine Thesmar in the title role in Pierre Lacotte's "reconstitution" of Taglioni's *La Sylphide,* broadcast on French television in April 1971. (Photograph by Colette Masson; used by permission of Agence Enguerand/Iliade, Paris.)

The ballet soon became an international sensation. Taglioni danced it in London and Berlin in the year of its premiere; in 1837 she danced it in Russia, where Antoine Titus had already staged it in 1835. Madame Celeste danced an excerpt of it in New York in 1835, but it was not until 1839 that a complete and authentic version was presented in the United States by Paul and Amalia Taglioni. Upon Marie Taglioni's return to Paris in 1840, she added a pas de trois for James, Effie, and the Sylphide, using choreography that she had danced first in Vienna in 1839 (Guest, 1980) and probably in her father's ballet *L'Ombre* in Saint Petersburg later that year. The Paris Opera last revived it in 1858 for the ill-fated Emma Livry.

Filippo Taglioni's choreography survived longer in Russia but was revised in 1892 by Marius Petipa. In 1946 Victor Gsovsky, Boris Kochno, and Roland Petit attempted to reconstruct Taglioni's work, on the basis of contemporary prints and writings, for the Ballets des Champs-Élysées; a similar attempt was made by Richard Adama for the Bremen Ballet in 1965. Pierre Lacotte's "reconstitution," filmed in 1971 and presented at the Paris Opera in 1972, is the best-known reconstruction of Taglioni's choreography. In addition to the materials used previously, he also consulted Filippo's annotated musical scores, sketches, performance notes, and class notebooks.

Most revivals have been based on the version choreographed by August Bournonville in Copenhagen in 1836 to a new score by Herman Løvenskjold. Lucile Grahn danced the Sylphide, while James was danced by Bournonville himself. His version is noted for a stronger sense of drama than Taglioni's, a greater emphasis on male dancing, and a heightened contrast between the folk dances in act 1 and the more academic choreography for the sylphides. It has formed the basis of revivals by Harald Lander, Elsa-Marianne von Rosen, Erik Bruhn, Hans Brenaa, Peter Schaufuss, Peter Martins, and others.

The use of pointe work has caused controversy in many revivals. Following Bournonville's lead, pointe work is often limited to the sylphides, thus preserving the distinction between mortals and supernaturals. Lacotte, however, contends that Taglioni placed the Scottish girls on pointe and also gave the ballerina more demanding pointe work than was previously thought possible for the period. In Adama's version, only the Sylphide dances on pointe.

LA SYLPHIDE. August Bournonville's version of *La Sylphide* has rarely been absent from the repertory of the Royal Danish Ballet since he mounted it in 1836. Firmly in the tradition of the great Danish interpreters of the roles of James Reuben and the Sylphide are Erik Bruhn and Margrethe Schanne, pictured here in 1952. (Photograph © by Rigmor Mydstkov; used by permission.)

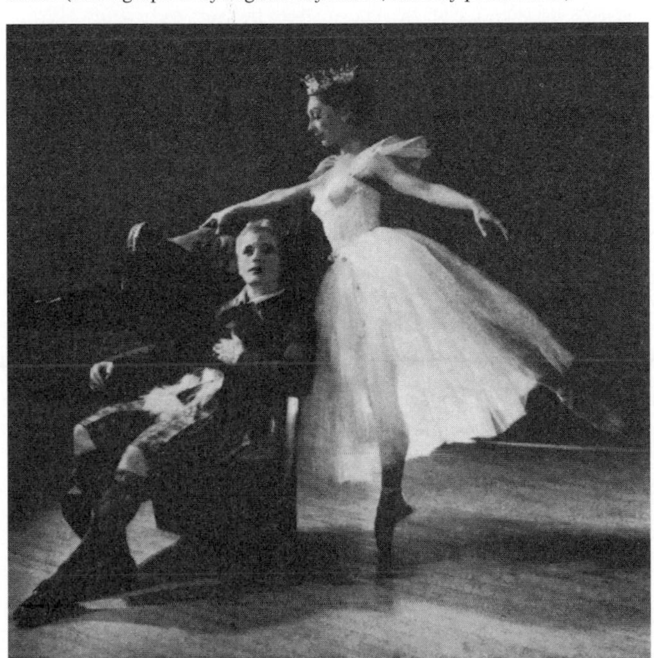

Over the years both versions of the ballet have been subjected to cuts and additions. James, Gurn, and Effie are often given new solos; some revivals also add a pas de deux for James and Effie. Lacotte added to act 1 a pas de deux comparable to the peasant pas de deux in *Giselle;* Schaufuss added a pas de huit for the wedding guests. Lander and Schaufuss elaborated the witches' scene, strengthening Madge's motive of revenge. In act 2, the dances of the Sylphide, James, and the ensemble of sylphides have frequently been revised.

[*Many of the figures herein are the subjects of independent entries.*]

BIBLIOGRAPHY

Aschengreen, Erik. "The Beautiful Danger: Facets of the Romantic Ballet." Translated by Patricia McAndrew. *Dance Perspectives,* no. 58 (Summer 1974).

Beaumont, Cyril W. "La Sylphide." In Beaumont's *Complete Book of Ballets.* London, 1937.

Bournonville, August. "La Sylphide." Translated by Patricia McAndrew in *Dance as a Theatre Art,* edited by Selma Jeanne Cohen. New York, 1974.

Guest, Ivor. *The Ballet of the Second Empire.* London, 1974.

Guest, Ivor. *The Romantic Ballet in Paris.* 2d rev. ed. London, 1980.

Hallar, Marianne, and Alette Scavenius, eds. *Bournonvilleana.* Translated by Gaye Kynoch. Copenhagen, 1992.

Lacotte, Pierre. "Looking for *La Sylphide.*" *Dance and Dancers* (October 1982): 14–16.

Levinson, André. *Marie Taglioni* (1929). Translated by Cyril W. Beaumont. London, 1977.

Macaulay, Alastair. "The Author of *La Sylphide,* Adolphe Nourrit." *The Dancing Times* (November 1989): 140–143.

Maynard, Olga. "The Ballet of La Sylphide." In Maynard's *The Ballet Companion.* Philadelphia, 1957.

Moore, Lillian. "*La Sylphide:* Epitome of the Romantic Ballet." *Dance Magazine* (March 1965): 42–47.

Sowell, Debra Hickenlooper. "'Virtue (almost) Triumphant' Revisited: Of Sylphs and Silfidi." *Dance Chronicle* 18.2 (1995): 293–301.

SUSAN AU

SYLPHIDES, LES. [*To document the origins and development of Michel Fokine's seminal ballet, this entry comprises two articles. The first gives details of the versions presented in Saint Petersburg in 1907–1909; the second discusses the historic production by Diaghilev's Ballets Russes in Paris in June 1909.*]

Russian Origins

The ballet that was to become widely known as Michel Fokine's masterpiece, *Les Sylphides,* took shape gradually, as Fokine reworked it and reshaped it over the course of some two years. The first version, entitled *Chopiniana,* was presented to the public on 10 February 1907, at a charity performance at the Maryinsky Theater, Saint Petersburg, for the Society for the Prevention of Cruelty to Children. It consisted of five scenes set to a suite of piano pieces by Frédéric Chopin orchestrated by Aleksandr Glazunov: a polonaise, a nocturne, a mazurka, a waltz, and a tarantella. The scenery and costumes were selected from the wardrobes and costume rooms of the Imperial Theaters, with the exception of the ballerina's costume for the waltz, which was designed especially for the occasion by Léon Bakst.

The opening Polonaise in A Major (op. 40, no. 1) was staged as "a ballroom in Warsaw" and was danced by a group of couples in colorful Polish costumes. Then, to the music of the Nocturne in F Major (op. 15, no. 1), the second scene depicted Chopin (Aleksei Bulgakov), in his music room in Majorca. In his feverish dreams, the ominous shadows of monks were superseded by the radiant vision of his muse, danced by A. P. Urakova. The third scene, set to the Mazurka in C-sharp Minor (op. 50, no. 3), was staged as "A Peasant Wedding in a Polish Village," where, at the height of the ceremonies, the young bride (Julia Sedova) threw her engagement ring to the elderly bridegroom and eloped with her lover. Then came the Waltz in C-sharp Minor (op. 64, no. 2), and the scene called "Moonlight Vision," a pas de deux for a sylphide and a youth, danced by Anna Pavlova and Mikhail Obukov in a Romantic style reminiscent of Marie Taglioni and Jules Perrot. The final scene was "A Square in Naples," where the lively Tarantella in A-flat Major (op. 43) was performed by a group of dancers led by Vera Fokina and Aleksandr Shiriaev. Fokine later wrote that each scene of *Chopiniana* was designed to illustrate the diversity of the paths open to ballet.

For the February charity performance the following year, 1908, Fokine was obliged to mount a work on short notice, owing to the last-minute cancelation of plans for a series of *divertissements*. He had been working on a new ballet based on the Romantic motifs of the *Chopiniana* waltz and set to an expanded score orchestrated by Maurice Keller. As neither the ballet nor the orchestrations were yet complete, he decided to present excerpts from this work danced to piano accompaniment. Thus at the charity performance at the Maryinsky Theater on 16 February 1908 a work entitled *Danses sur la Musique de Chopin* featured a solo mazurka by Anna Pavlova, the *Chopiniana* waltz danced by Pavlova and Fokine himself, and a nocturne and a waltz performed by twenty members of the female corps de ballet wearing long white dresses copied from the one designed by Bakst for Pavlova the previous year.

Only a few weeks later, Keller's orchestrations were completed, and Fokin's new ballet was given at a benefit performance at the Maryinsky on 8 March 1908 under the title *Rêverie Romantique: Ballet sur la Musique de Chopin*. It included a nocturne, a waltz, a mazurka, a second waltz, a prelude, a second mazurka, and a concluding *grande valse brillante,* and it was danced by Anna Pavlova, Olga Preobrajenska, Tamara Karsavina, Vaslav Nijinsky, and a corps de ballet of sixteen women. The female soloists and the corps de ballet all wore long white tutus. Nijinsky, only recently graduated from the Imperial Theater School but already recognized as a phenomenal dancer, wore a costume designed for him by Bakst for his appearances with Matilda Kshessinska in a pas de deux called *Nocturnes*: a black velvet tunic over a filmy white shirt, a blond wig, and white tights. Fokine had choreographed a mazurka solo for Nijinsky only the day before the performance, and he continued to make changes in the groupings with the corps de ballet even during the intermission on the day of performance. When the curtain rose, the scene was revealed as a moonlit glade, with the dancers posed before an improvised backdrop, a section of the forest panorama designed for *The Sleeping Beauty*.

Only three weeks later, on 6 April 1908, this version of the work was again performed at the Maryinsky Theater, this time by ballet students in Fokine's class at the Imperial Theater School. The choreography remained essentially the same as in the March performance, but the title of the work was once again changed: at the student performance the work was billed as *Grand Pas sur la Musique de Chopin*.

At the February charity performance the following year, which took place on 19 February 1909, the work was once again entitled *Chopiniana* and was once again danced by artists of the Imperial Ballet: Pavlova, Preobrajenska, Karsavina, and Nijinsky. At this performance, for which a polonaise was played as an overture, the corps de ballet included Nijinsky's younger sister, Bronislava, who later vividly recalled the performance in her memoirs (Nijinska, 1981, pp. 251–252). Thereafter, the ballet became a part of the permanent repertory of the Maryinsky Theater.

As performed in Saint Petersburg today, *Chopiniana* is danced by three female soloists, a male soloist, and a corps de ballet of sixteen. It opens with the Polonaise in A Major (op. 40, no. 1), played as the overture. Then comes the Nocturne in A-flat Major (op. 32, no. 2), performed by the corps de ballet, two female soloists, and the lone male dancer. This is followed by the Waltz in G-flat Major (op. 70, no. 1), performed by three female soloists; the Mazurka in C Major (op. 33, no. 3), danced by the male soloist; the Mazurka in D Major (op. 33, no. 2), performed by the first female soloists; the Prelude in A Major (op. 28, no. 7), performed by the second female soloist; the Waltz in C-sharp Minor (op. 64, no. 2), danced by the first female soloist and the male soloist; and the final Grand Waltz in E-flat Major (op. 18, no. 1), for the entire ensemble.

The final version of *Chopiniana* has the sylphides and the youth dancing against the backdrop of a poetic, bosky landscape. By combining the image of the ethereal sylphide created by Marie Taglioni with the music of Chopin, Fokine sought to resurrect the concept of Romantic ballet. The various miniatures that comprise *Chopiniana* exhibit the utmost subtleties of choreographic art, as Fokine used a new, freer vocabulary of movement to suggest the Romantic moods of languor, anticipation, sorrow, and joy that characterize the dances of the three principal sylphides and the young man. Abandoning the episodic and narrative elements of Romantic ballet, he was able to suggest, purely through dance, the inner world of his characters' imagination, a world of poetic fantasy and dreams. In the final version of his *Grand Pas,* Fokine created the first plotless ballet of the twentieth century.

BIBLIOGRAPHY

Dobrovolskaya, Galina N. "*Chopiniana* M. Fokina i puti zarubezhnogo baleta." In *Zapiski o teatre,* edited by L. A. Levbarg. Leningrad, 1968.

Fokine, Michel. *Memoirs of a Ballet Master.* Translated by Vitale Fokine. Edited by Anatole Chujoy. London, 1961.

Horwitz, Dawn Lille. *Michel Fokine.* Boston, 1985.

Karsavina, Tamara. *Theatre Street.* Rev. and enl. ed. London, 1948.

Krasovskaya, Vera. *Russkii baletnyi teatr nachala dvadtatogo veka.* 2 vols. Leningrad, 1971–1972.

Krasovskaya, Vera. *Nijinsky.* Translated by John E. Bowlt. New York, 1979.

Lazzarini, John, and Roberta Lazzarini. *Pavlova: Repertoire of a Legend.* New York, 1980.

Nijinska, Bronislava. *Early Memoirs.* Translated and edited by Irina Nijinska and Jean Rawlinson. New York, 1981.

GALINA N. DOBROVOLSKAYA
Translated from Russian

LES SYLPHIDES: Diaghilev Production. The poster designed by Valentin Serov for Diaghilev's first season in Paris featured a drawing of Anna Pavlova in *Les Sylphides.* (Photograph from the Dance Collection, New York Public Library for the Performing Arts.)

Diaghilev Production

Title: *Les Sylphides.* Ballet in one act. Choreography: Michel Fokine. Music: Frédéric Chopin, orchestrated by Aleksandr Glazunov, Igor Stravinsky, Nikolai Tcherepnin, and Anatol Liadov. Scenery and costumes: Alexandre Benois. First performance: 2 June 1909, Théâtre du Châtelet, Paris, Ballets Russes de Serge Diaghilev. Principals: Anna Pavlova, Tamara Karsavina, Alexandra Baldina, Vaslav Nijinsky.

Les Sylphides, Fokine's one-act abstract ballet to music by Chopin, may be the most widely and consistently performed ballet of this century, surviving as a popular example of Fokine's contributions to the development of modern ballet choreography. The ballet originated in two distinct versions presented in Saint Petersburg in 1907 and 1908, but it took its final form only when Fokine staged it for Serge Diaghilev's Saison Russe in Paris in June 1909. Several minor but significant changes were made from the second version Fokine had staged in Russia: the title was changed, at Diaghilev's suggestion, from *Chopiniana* to *Les Sylphides;* new scenery and costumes were designed by Alexandre Benois; the Prelude in A Major (op. 28, no. 7) replaced the Polonaise in A Major (op. 40, no. 1) as the overture; and Stravinsky (in his first commission for Diaghilev) reorchestrated the Nocturne in A-flat Major (op. 32, no. 2) and the Grand Waltz in E-flat Major (op. 18, no. 1). Fokine's choreography, however, remained essentially the same as in his second Russian version.

Although the ballet's Western premiere attracted little attention in the press, the work has since accumulated abundant critical literature. Through repeated performances, Diaghilev established *Les Sylphides* as a signature piece in his company's repertory. For the European public nurtured on Ballets Russes productions between 1909 and 1929, *Les Sylphides* epitomized the essence of ballet: purity of line, expressiveness, and soft, flowing movements executed by clusters of women dressed in long white skirts.

The Prelude overture sets a quiet, contemplative mood. The curtain rises on a moonlit glade near an ancient ruin. The opening tableau shows three ballerinas surrounding the *danseur,* one on each arm, another reclined at his feet, while the corps pose symmetrically around them. In the

Nocturne, the corps undulate their arms, echoing the music's pulse while the soloists dance the melody, weaving in and among the corps's ever-shifting patterns. The Waltz soloist marks the music's joyous rhythms with each *enchaînement,* ending suddenly with her back to the audience. The Mazurka soloist soars diagonally across stage doing *grands jetés,* while the corps trace her flight with softly waving arms. Sustained jumps and balances characterize the male variation, where the movements match the curved line of melody. The Prelude soloist sweeps noiselessly about the stage, pauses, and seems to listen to a distant call. In the pas de deux, the ballerina appears descending from her partner's arms, the dance marked by evanescent poses and swift, fluttering movements that correspond to the contrasting moods of the melody. The final Grand Waltz is the livliest section: the whole cast sprints about before calmly reforming the opening tableau.

The structure and technique of *Les Sylphides* identify Fokine's choreographic innovations. These include the expansion of flowing port de bras and an extended use of *épaulement,* the liberation of the ensemble from the hierarchial groupings employed in nineteenth-century ballets, and the emphasis on the more subtle qualities of controlled balances, the seemingly effortless flow of the dancers' movements, and their ability to create and sustain a mood. In contrast to Petipa ballets, there is no announcement of solos, no virtuoso steps to show off the dancer's prowess, and each variation ends differently. *Les Sylphides* employs an arabesque motif that unifies the choreography. The corps move in silence in between each section to give added continuity to the string of dances and allowing no breaks for applause. The ballet includes turning the back to the audience as a direct reference to Romantic ballets such as *Giselle.* The work's abstract nature introduces the idea of introspection to twentieth-century ballet. In his *Memoirs,* Fokine tells how he implored his dancers not to project their movements toward the audience but to dance for themselves.

Les Sylphides is the twentieth century's first successful abstract ballet and remains a classic in international repertory. Fokine staged the work for the Royal Swedish Ballet in 1913, the Royal Danish Ballet in 1925, René Blum's Ballet Russe de Monte Carlo in 1936; Ballet Russe de Monte Carlo (Massine) in 1939; and Ballet Theatre (later American Ballet Theatre) in 1940. Other companies received the ballet from ballerinas who worked directly under Fokine, and a surprising consistency in steps and performance style has been maintained in the West. Karsavina staged the work for Marie Rambert's Dancers (later Ballet Rambert) in 1930, and the Royal Ballet's staging is by Alicia Markova, originally set for the Vic-Wells Ballet in 1932. A slightly different version is danced in Russia as *Chopiniana,* where the Polonaise in A Major (op. 40, no. 1) is still played as the overture and an alternate male variation is performed to the Mazurka in C Major (op. 33, no. 3). The production as a whole is faster paced and more extroverted than its Western counterpart.

An experiment in separating *Les Sylphides* from its Romantic trappings was given by the New York City Ballet in 1972. Alexandra Danilova restaged the work and dressed the dancers in plain practice clothes. This performance showed the purity and strength of the choreography but raised questions concerning the importance of scenery and costumes in the work. The ballet in this form had only a brief existence.

BIBLIOGRAPHY

Balanchine, George, and Francis Mason. *One Hundred and One Stories of the Great Ballets.* New York, 1989.

Benois, Alexandre. *Reminiscences of the Russian Ballet.* Translated by Mary Britnieva. London, 1941.

Fokine, Michel. *Memoirs of a Ballet Master.* Translated by Vitale Fokine. Edited by Anatole Chujoy. London, 1961.

Garafola, Lynn. *Diaghilev's Ballets Russes.* New York, 1989.

Goodwin, Noël. "Fokine and Chopin." *Dance and Dancers* (November 1991): 15–17.

Gregory, John. *Les Sylphides—Chopiniana.* Croesor, Wales, 1989.

Horwitz, Dawn Lille. *Michel Fokine.* Boston, 1985.

Lomax, Sondra. "Fokine's Manifesto and *Les Sylphides.*" In *New Directions in Dance,* edited by Diana Theodores Taplin. Toronto, 1979.

Maynard, Olga. *"Les Sylphides." Dance Magazine* (December 1971): 44–63.

Vaughan, David. "Fokine in the Contemporary Repertory." *Ballet Review* 7.2–3 (1978–1979): 19–27.

INTERVIEWS: Alexandra Danilova and Nathalie Krassovska, by Sondra Lomax.

SONDRA LOMAX

SYLVIA. Full French title: *Sylvia, ou La Nymphe de Diane.* Ballet in three acts and four scenes. Choreography: Louis Mérante. Music: Léo Delibes. Libretto: Jules Barbier and Baron de Reinach, based on the pastoral play *Aminta* by Torquato Tasso. Scenery and costumes: Jules Cheret, August Rubé, Philippe Chaperon, and Eugène Lacoste. First performance: 14 June 1876, Théâtre de l'Opéra, Paris. Principals: Rita Sangalli (Sylvia), Louis Mérante (Aminta), Louise Marquet (Diana), Marie Sanlaville (Eros), and Francesco Magri (Orion).

Synopsis. The nymph Sylvia and her companions discover the sleeping shepherd Aminta while they are slaking their thirst at a stream. The shepherd falls in love with Sylvia. She feels that the love of a mere mortal is unworthy of a nymph, and she aims an arrow at a statue of Eros, god of love, erected near the site. The arrow wounds Aminta, who is trying to protect the god. The statue comes to life and shoots an arrow of his own, wounding Sylvia in turn. Disturbed, she remains alone while her companions go off. Orion, the Dark Hunter, who has desired Sylvia for a long time, arrives at that moment, surprises her, and carries her off. Meanwhile, an old witch has been taking care of Aminta, who is able to set out in pursuit of the nymph, thanks to instructions given him by Eros.

In the second act, Sylvia is a prisoner in Orion's cave. She gets Orion drunk, then tries unsuccessfully to flee. She prays to Eros to come to her assistance. The grotto disappears, and the discouraged shepherd is seen sitting on a rock. In the third act, thanks to the efforts of Eros, Sylvia is restored to Aminta. But Orion comes looking for her. In despair, the lovers beg the protection of Diana. Orion is then killed by the goddess, who remains unbending when the young couple try to obtain her forgiveness. Diana softens, however, when Eros pleads for them, invoking the memory of Diana and Endymion. She pardons them, and there is general rejoicing.

History. In 1876 the Théâtre de l'Opéra was relatively new, and Olivier Halanzier, the director, was eager to mount new productions. The authors of the book for *Sylvia* contacted Léo Delibes, who prepared an outline of the score in collaboration with the choreographer and the star dancer. Some pieces were written several times, as for *Coppélia,* which is why the score follows the scenic action so closely. The best-known sections include the *valse lente* in the first act; the grotto scene, in which violincellos and bassoons evoke the passion of the hunter; the brilliant bacchanal at the beginning of the third act; the famous pizzicato, to which the veiled Sylvia reveals her identity to Aminta; the *pas* of the slaves, in which the drum punctuates the melody of the woodwinds; Sylvia's waltz variation; and the somber passage expressing Diana's anger. The score of *Sylvia* is one of the most homogeneous and complete in the repertory. Petr Ilich Tchaikovsky was fond of saying that if he had known the music of *Sylvia,* he

SYLVIA. Frederick Ashton mounted his version of *Sylvia* for the Sadler's Wells Ballet in 1952, with Margot Fonteyn in the title role and Michael Somes as Aminta. Robin and Christopher Ironside designed the elaborate scenery and costumes. (Photograph from the Dance Collection, New York Public Library for the Performing Arts.)

would never have dared to compose *Swan Lake* (Mannoni, 1982, p. 112). Delibes used it as the source for a very graceful orchestral suite. [*See the entry on Delibes.*]

Sylvia remained in the repertory of the Paris Opera until 1893. Although less gifted than his predecessor Arthur Saint-Léon, Louis Mérante was nevertheless a competent partner for Rita Sangalli, and as a soloist he was fully able to perform variations of a high degree of virtuosity. Rosita Mauri succeeded Sangalli in 1892, but her physique was not very suitable for the character. A fire destroyed the sets in 1894, and the ballet disappeared from the repertory for more than twenty years. It was restaged in 1919 under Léo Staats, with Carlotta Zambelli as Sylvia, Albert Aveline as Aminta, and Staats himself in the expanded role of Orion. Zambelli was an ideal Sylvia, and her name remains permanently connected with the role, which she danced until 1929. A new and shorter version was created in 1941 by Serge Lifar and was danced by Suzanne Lorcia, Solange Schwarz, and Lycette Darsonval.

In 1946, Albert Aveline, a teacher at the Paris Opera Ballet School, restaged the ballet following Mérante's original choreography. He sought Zambelli's help in refreshing his memory of the version they had danced in 1919. Zambelli herself passed on the pizzicato variation to her students. At the premiere in November 1946, Lycette Darsonval again danced the title role and again showed the brilliant pointe work for which she was famous. More than thirty years later, in November 1979, with the help of Violette Verdy, then dance director of the Opera, Darsonval reconstructed Aveline's staging and mounted *Sylvia* with sets and costumes by Bernard Daydé and with Noëlla Pointois, Jean-Yves Lormeau, and Cyril Atanassoff in the principal roles. [*See the entry on Darsonval.*]

Outside France, *Sylvia* has been mounted by numerous choreographers. It was produced in Vienna in 1877 and in Berlin in 1884. In 1886, Giorgio Saracco mounted it at the Teatro alla Scala in Milan, with Carlotta Brianza in the title role. In Saint Petersburg the production mounted by Lev Ivanov in 1901 at the Maryinsky Theater was notable not only for the performance of Olga Preobrajenska as Sylvia but for the dispute that led to Serge Diaghilev's resignation from the theater staff. In London an abridged version was presented in 1911 at the Empire Theatre with choreography by Fred Farren and with Lydia Kyasht in the principal role.

In the United States, George Balanchine, who was very fond of the music, created his *Sylvia: Pas de Deux* for the New York City Ballet in 1950, using the *valse lente* from act 1 and the pas de deux from act 3. In costumes designed by Barbara Karinska, the original performers were Maria Tallchief and Nicholas Magallanes. This showpiece was frequently televised and was later staged, sometimes with the choreography credited to André Eglevsky, for numerous companies in the United States and Canada.

In England, Frederick Ashton staged a complete version of *Sylvia* for the Sadler's Wells Ballet in September 1952, with sets and costumes by Robin and Christopher Ironside. The original cast featured Margot Fonteyn as Sylvia, Michael Somes as Aminta, John Hart as Orion, and Alexander Grant as Eros. The noted historian and critic Cyril Beaumont disliked this production but acknowledged that Fonteyn's performance of "the well-known Polka Pizzicato, concluding with a series of accelerated *coupés jetés posés sur la pointe* travelled on a straight line, is theatrically effective" (Beaumont, 1954, p. 36).

In later years *Sylvia* continued to be mounted by various choreographers around the globe. László Seregi's version, originally staged at the Budapest Opera in 1972, was mounted for the Zurich Ballet in 1976. Lycette Darsonval's version was mounted for the National Ballet of China in Beijing in 1980, and Balanchine's pas de deux was staged for the Matsuyama Ballet in Tokyo in 1981.

BIBLIOGRAPHY

Balanchine, George, with Francis Mason. *Balanchine's Complete Stories of the Great Ballets.* Rev. and enl. ed. Garden City, N.Y., 1977.

Beaumont, Cyril W. *Complete Book of Ballets.* Rev. ed. London, 1951.

Beaumont, Cyril W. *Ballets of Today: Being a Second Supplement to the Complete Book of Ballets.* London, 1954.

Guest, Ivor. "*Sylvia,* from Mérante to Ashton." *Ballet Annual* 8 (1954): 67–72.

Macdonald, Nesta. "Hijacked." *Dance and Dancers* (January–February 1992): 19–22.

Mannoni, Gérard. *Grands ballets de l'Opéra de Paris.* Paris, 1982.

Vaughan, David. *Frederick Ashton and His Ballets.* London, 1977.

MONIQUE BABSKY
Translated from French

SYMPHONIC BALLET. *See the entry on Léonide Massine.*

SYMPHONIC VARIATIONS. Ballet in one act. Choreography: Frederick Ashton. Music: César Franck, Symphonic Variations for Piano and Orchestra (1885). Scenery and costumes: Sophie Fedorovitch. First performance: 24 April 1946, Royal Opera House, Covent Garden, London, Sadler's Wells Ballet. Principals: Margot Fonteyn, Pamela May, Moira Shearer, Michael Somes, Brian Shaw, Henry Danton.

Ashton's original scheme for *Symphonic Variations* included a blend of spiritual ideas—divine love, a mystical marriage, and the cycle of the seasons. As he began the choreography, however, he became anxious to eliminate all traces of such material. In reaction against the literary or symbolic content of much British choreography of the day, he wished to demonstrate that "the subject of ballet is dancing." For him, therefore, *Symphonic Variations* became a testament, emphasizing dance values, formal organization, harmonious coordination, and musicality.

The six dancers never leave the stage, although some or all of them often stand on its borders. The ground patterns complement the linear geometries of Sophie Fedorovitch's backdrop. The six dancers begin spaced about the perimeters of the stage, with one foot crossed over the other and resting on *pointe tendue*. This stance and some *ports de bras* in the opening dance for the women become choreographic motifs. Further elaborations build up in a sequence of quartets, duets, sextets, and solos. The ballet's musicality also moves from ritualistic simplicity to subtle counterpoint.

To its early audiences, sequences involving the three women and leading danseur evoked memories of *Les Sylphides* and *Apollo;* the critic A. V. Coton considered *Symphonic Variations* to be, after those two, the century's third masterpiece of plotless ballet. Its refinement of English style was emphasized by the casting of three ballerinas of the utmost accomplishment; all three danced Aurora in *The Sleeping Beauty* at that time. The avoidance of hierarchy, the concern with stage geometries, and the incorporation of both academic ballet and simple movements such as running, were typical Ashton characteristics.

Symphonic Variations was also a test of stamina and stylistic purity that made new demands, especially on the male dancers. The original cast was greatly admired, particularly Margot Fonteyn for her radiance and tranquility within the harmonious ensemble. The ballet was widely considered the Royal Ballet's signature work for many years.

BIBLIOGRAPHY

Ashton, Frederick. "A Conversation with Clement Crisp." In *Dance as a Theatre Art,* edited by Selma Jeanne Cohen. New York, 1974.

Buckle, Richard. Interview with Ashton. *Ballet* 4.5 (1947).

Fonteyn, Margot. *Margot Fonteyn: Autobiography.* London, 1975.

Rigby, Cormac. "A Ballet of Perfect Englishness." *Dance Now* 1 (Winter 1992–1993): 22–27.

Vaughan, David. *Frederick Ashton and His Ballets.* London, 1977.

ALASTAIR MACAULAY

SYMPHONY IN C. Original title: *Le Palais de Cristal.* Ballet in four movements. Choreography: George Balanchine. Music: Georges Bizet; Symphony no. 1 in C Major. Scenery and costumes: Léonor Fini. First performance: 28 July 1947, Théâtre National de l'Opéra, Paris Opera Ballet. Principals: Lycette Darsonval, Alexandre Kalioujny; Tamara Toumanova, Roger Ritz; Micheline Bardin, Michel Renault; Madeleine Lafon, Max Bozzoni. Restaged as *Symphony in C:* 22 March 1948, City Center of Music and Drama, New York, Ballet Society. Lighting: Jean Rosenthal. Principals: Maria Tallchief, Nicholas Magallanes; Tanaquil Le Clercq, Francisco Moncion; Beatrice Tompkins, Herbert Bliss; Elise Reiman, John Taras.

The original title of Balanchine's opulent ballet to Bizet's first symphony, *Le Palais de Cristal,* was singularly apt, for this work is indeed a palatial construction, exhibiting a crystalline purity of design and an unashamedly ornate ballet vocabulary. Mounted on the Paris Opera Ballet, it paid tribute to the grandeur of the Opera's heritage while forging ahead by fully exploiting the resources of classical technique. Léonor Fini's scenery included a staircase, balconies, galleries, and gargoyles, creating the kind of elaborate setting to which Parisian audiences had been long accustomed. Somewhat unexpected, however, were Fini's costumes for the women, which were not classical tutus but flowing dresses in jewel tones of red, brown, green, and yellow. The cast was huge, consisting of the eight principals, two demi-soloist couples in each movement, and a corps de ballet of six women in each movement, for a total of forty-eight. Lycette Darsonval danced the sparkling first movement, and Tamara Toumanova, a woman of almost unearthly beauty, performed the pivotal adagio in the second movement.

When Balanchine transferred the work to Ballet Society, his own company in New York, he staged a streamlined version, dispensing with the elaborate setting and using fewer dancers, who doubled in the corps from movement to movement. At the premiere of this production, in March 1948, the featured ballerinas in the first and second movements were Maria Tallchief and Tanaquil Le Clercq. On 11 October 1948, *Symphony in C,* as the work was then called, was performed on the first program of the New York City Ballet, along with *Concerto Barocco* and *Orpheus,* at New York's City Center of Music and Drama. A new production was mounted in 1950 with spectacular women's costumes designed by Barbara Karinska: shimmering tutus of ivory satin and tulle, accented by headpieces of jewels and flowers. By 1971 the growth of the company had allowed expansion of the cast to a total of fifty-two.

Symphony in C is as elegant and as grandly proportioned as its score, written when its prodigiously talented composer was only seventeen years old, in 1855. The first two movements are designed to present the talents of two quite different ballerinas, the first commanding, the second ethereal and expansive. The demanding "Scottish" folk dance in the third movement calls for parallel unison dancing by the principal couple. All cast members join forces in the fourth movement, a recapitulative climactic finale. The corps de ballet forms a three-sided frame around the soloists and demi-soloists, whose unison dancing builds to a powerful crescendo of movement, as the music rises in key and as row upon row of dancers enters into the joyous conclusion of the work.

Over the years, *Symphony in C* has wielded a strong influence on dancers and has been a significant work in the history of New York City Ballet. Jerome Robbins, for instance, was so impressed by a performance of it in 1949 that he asked to join the company. Other dancers found in it roles perfectly suited to their particular talents. Patricia McBride and Merrill Ashley both gave memorable bravura performances in the dizzying sequences of the first movement; Edward Villella, John Clifford, Ethan Stiefel, and Peter Boal have been outstanding among many male dancers who have bounded happily through the exuberant third movement.

It is, however, in the renowned adagio of the second movement that a number of ballerinas made an indelible impression, among them Allegra Kent, Mimi Paul, and Suzanne Farrell, who danced it in her first performance upon returning to the company in 1975 after a five-year absence, and again, as a memorial to Balanchine, on the day of his death, 30 April 1983. Others who have shone in the role include the Danish dancer Mona Vangsaae, who was partnered by Erik Bruhn in the 1953 production in Copenhagen; the French ballerina Sylvie Guillem, who danced in a revival of *Le Palais de Cristal* by the Paris Opera Ballet in 1986; and the Georgian dancer Nina Ananiashvili, who appeared as a guest artist with New York City Ballet in 1988.

Symphony in C remains a part of the permanent repertory of New York City Ballet. It has also been mounted for La Scala Ballet, the Royal Swedish Ballet, the Dutch National Ballet, the Hamburg Ballet, the German Opera Ballet (Berlin), the Rome Opera Ballet, the Stuttgart Ballet, the Hungarian State Opera Ballet, the Zurich Ballet, the Royal Ballet (London), and numerous regional companies in the United States.

BIBLIOGRAPHY

Balanchine, George, with Francis Mason. *Balanchine's Complete Stories of the Great Ballets.* Rev. and enl. ed. Garden City, N.Y., 1977.

Barnes, Clive. "Balanchine: Mercilessly Inquisitive." *New York Times* (23 November 1975).

Barnes, Clive. "The Danish Festival." *Dance and Dancers* 5 (July 1954): 13–15.

Barzel, Ann, et al. "A Symposium." *Ballet Annual* 7 (1953): 63–75.

Choreography by George Balanchine: A Catalogue of Works. New York, 1984.

Kaplan, Larry. "Corps Choreography by Balanchine." *Ballet Review* 15 (Winter 1988): 64–75.

Kirstein, Lincoln. *Thirty Years: The New York City Ballet.* New York, 1978.

Reynolds, Nancy. *Repertory in Review: Forty Years of the New York City Ballet.* New York, 1977.

Scholl, Tim. *From Petipa to Balanchine: Classical Revival and the Modernization of Ballet.* New York, 1994.

Terry, Walter. Review. *New York Herald Tribune* (23 March 1948).

NOTATED SCORES. *Symphony in C,* Benesh notation documented by Jürg Lanzrein (1973). *Symphony in C,* Labanotation documented by Ann Hutchinson Guest (1948), held in the Dance Notation Bureau.

FILM. *Lincoln Center Day* (1963) presents the second and fourth movements of the ballet, available in the Dance Collection, New York Public Library for the Performing Arts.

REBA ANN ADLER

SZEGED CONTEMPORARY BALLET. The youngest of the four full-time companies of Hungary, the Szeged Contemporary Ballet adopted its present name in 1993. Its history goes back to 1946, however, when Károly Zsedényi, solo dancer of the Budapest Opera, staged *Schéhérazade;* the following year he staged *Coppélia* and Gyula Harangozó's *Scene in the Inn.* Full-evening ballets could also be staged since many of the dancers came from the Kolozsvár (today Cluj) Opera. The company functioned under ballet director György Lőrinc until 1949, when he staged Belá Bartók's *The Miraculous Mandarin.*

In 1958, classically trained dancers formed the company of the Szeged National Theater with compositions by guest choreographers in styles that deviated somewhat from the academic. Zoltán Imre started his dancing and creative career with his 1966 *Metamorphosis,* to music by Endre Szervánszky, and his 1968 *Combat of Forms,* to music by Johann Sebastian Bach. For economic reasons, the staff slowly departed and Imre left the country.

In 1986, after the reconstruction of the theater, writer and manager Roland Bokor re-launched the company with dancers trained in a variety of styles; he then called Imre back from abroad to supervise the repertory. Imre conveyed his knowledge of such contemporary techniques as Martha Graham's and José Limón's to his dancers and, in 1987, organized a "Night of Hungarian Choreographers Working Abroad." He staged György Vámos's *Rhapsody,* to music by Sergei Rachmaninov; Ferenc Barbay's *Firebird—A Pas de Deux,* to music by Igor Stravinsky and Tomita; Zoltán Imre's *Woman's Love—Woman's Fate,* to music by Robert Schumann; and Imre's *The Demon,* to music by Robert Wittinger. The multifaceted stylistic training of the dancers even made them suitable for performing dances in musicals such as Eva Reinthaller's *Jesus Christ Superstar* and Gyula Harangozó's *Polovtsian Dances* from *Prince Igor* in 1988. Their first important tour was to the Babylon Festival, and their repertory was enlarged with Saad Munir Bashir's piece *Ishtar,* to his own music. László Seregi taught them Leonard Bernstein's musical *On the Town,* and there were two premieres—György Krámer's *The Wind Is Rising,* to music by István Márta, and Imre's ballet to Giovanni Pergolesi's *Stabat Mater.*

Imre staged his *Infernal Games* in memory of Jean Cocteau to a montage of Claudio Monteverdi and Aleksandr Scriabin, the hit of the season in December 1989, which gave young Tamás Juronics the chance of scoring a great success as the principal (he is now head of the company). At the end of the same season, the chamber theater gave its stage to a triple bill with Matthew Hawkins' *The Fruits of Labour,* the music consisting of Scottish folk songs; Imre's *The Medium,* an Alban Berg and Arnold Schoenberg montage; and Krámer's *Exodus,* to music by

W. Kylar. This essentially constituted a second stage for ballet.

In 1990 Imre created the Szeged Studio Ballet, which functioned until 1993 and produced contemporary ballets like Tamás Juronics's 1990 *Dances Born from Need,* set to folk music and 1991's *The Reminiscences of a Hardly Used Clothes Line,* to a musical montage. Both hits were incorporated in the repertory of the big theatre. The other premieres of the 1990/91 season included Katalin Lőrinc's *Tatyana and the Others,* to music by Tchaikovsky, and Jorma Uotinen's *Beyond Dreams,* to a musical montage. Open to foreign influences and exposed to the creative impetus of Juronics, the Studio Ballet closed its 1992/93 season with ballets, including Imre's *Dream about Kafka,* to music by Alban Berg; Yvette Bozsik's *Expectation,* to music by Erik Satie; Juronics's *Our Cell,* to music by Maurice Jarre; Bertrand d'At's *The Night,* to a modern montage; and Roberto Galvan's *Concerto for Piano, Accordion and Orchestra,* to music by Astor Piazzola.

The company started the 1993/94 season under the name of Szeged Contemporary Ballet, headed by Tamás Juronics but under the dominating choreographic personality of Roberto Galvan. Their first night in November 1993 included Juronics's *Croquis,* to music by Arvo Pärt and Galvan's *Requiem,* to music by Mozart. Since then, mainly foreign guest artists have choreographed for the company.

BIBLIOGRAPHY

Dienes, Gedeon. "Balett vidéken 1945 és 1985 között." In *A szinpadi tánc története Magyarországon,* edited by Gedeon Dienes and L. Fuchs, Budapest.

Körtvélyes, Géza. "Korszerű tendenciák a magyar táncmű́észetben 1957 ésö 1977 köztt. In *Tánctudányi tanulmányck 1978–1979,* edited by Gedeon Dienes and E. Pesovár. Budapest, 1979.

Kővágó, Zsuzsa. "Szegedi Balett 1987–1993." In *Fordulatok. Hungarian Theatres 1994.* Jászberény, 1994.

Lőrinc, Katalin. "Szegedi Kortárs Balett 1993–1995." In *Magyar táncművészet 1990 és 1995 között.* Budapest, 1996.

Vitáni, Iván. "Uj törekvések a magyar balettművészetben." In *Tánctudományi tanulmányok 1969–1970,* edited by Gedeon Dienes and L. Maácz. Budapest, 1970.

Zsuzsa Kővágó

T

TAGLIONI FAMILY, family of Italian dancers, choreographers, and ballet masters of the late eighteenth and nineteenth centuries. One of the great dancing dynasties, their lives were closely intertwined with those of other leading dancers and choreographers of the day. Most of the family were well traveled, though the men eventually settled down to establish their own spheres of influence: Carlo and Salvatore in Italy (the later particularly in Naples), Filippo in Warsaw, and Paul in Berlin. All the men choreographed original ballets, as did at least one of the women, the elder Marie. The most notable members were Carlo Taglioni; his children Filippo, Salvatore, Giuseppa, and Louise; Filippo's children Marie and Paul; Salvatore's daughter Louise; and Paul's daughter Marie.

Carlo Taglioni (born c.1750 in Turin), dancer and choreographer. Little is known about the early life of Carlo Taglioni. He began to dance, usually in the grotesque genre, in various Italian cities during the 1770s. In 1774 and 1775 he appeared in his native Turin in dances arranged by Innocenzo Gambuzzi for the operas *Merope* and *Alcina e Ruggiero;* he also danced in Gambuzzi's works in Milan in 1778. He performed in the serious or noble genre in Venice in 1782, where he danced in the ballets of Gaspero Angiolini. He worked in Rome in 1785–1786, at the same time as Salvatore Viganò.

Although Carlo Taglioni may have started to choreograph in the 1770s, his early works have fallen into obscurity. He created *Il Villano Rincivilito, ossia Il Barone Molletta di Rocca Antica,* a comic ballet, in Florence in 1790, following it with *Li Due Sindaci, ossia La Vendemmia* (The Two Mayors, or The Grape Harvest) in Lucca during the same year. In Venice, where he worked as a choreographer from 1796 to 1798, he mounted *La Scuola Olandese, ossia L'Amante in Statua* (The Dutch School, or The Statue of the Lover), *La Sposa Rapita* (The Abducted Bride), *La Recluta con Ingano* (The Deceived Recruit), and other ballets.

Carlo Taglioni made several trips to Paris to recruit French dancers for Italian companies. There he choreographed ballets for the Gaîté and Porte-Saint-Martin theaters in the early 1800s. According to Lillian Moore (1938), he had Bonapartist connections: he taught dancing to Joachim Murat's corps of pages in Naples, then went to Paris at the request of Lucien Bonaparte "to infuse new life into the ballet of the Italian opera."

Carlo Taglioni married Maria Petracchi, who may have danced under her married name, Maria Taglioni, thus becoming the first bearer of an exalted name in dance history. Of their five children, two sons (Filippo and Salvatore) and both daughters (Giuseppa and Louise) became dancers.

Giuseppa Taglioni (born c.1780 in Turin), dancer and choreographer. Beyond the fact that she made her debut at the Teatro La Fenice in Venice in 1797 and probably toured with her father and brothers in Italy, little is known about Giuseppa. A renowned beauty, she retired early to marry the Venetian count Antonio Contarini.

Louise Taglioni (also known as Luisa or Luigia; born c.1785), dancer. The first of two dancers of that name, she studied with Jean-François Coulon in Paris and is said to have made her debut at the Opera with her brother Filippo in 1799 in the opera *La Caravane.* Her roles at the Opera included Terpsichore in *Psyché* and Eucharis in *Télémaque,* both choreographed by Pierre Gardel; she also danced a featured role in Louis-Jacques Milon's *Les Noces de Gamache* (1801). In 1827, when her niece Marie made her Opera debut, the journal *Le réunion* published a letter that affectionately recalled Louise as "fresh, affable, and as light as a sylphide" (quoted by Guest, 1980).

Louise Taglioni resigned from the Opera in 1806 when her brother Salvatore's exorbitant contractual demands (which had included a promotion and raise in salary for Louise) were turned down by the administration. She accompanied him to Lyon, where she met and married Count Aimé Dubourg and consequently retired from the stage.

Salvatore Taglioni (born 1789 in Palermo, died 1868 in Naples), dancer, choreographer, and teacher. Carlo's son Salvatore also studied with Coulon in Paris, where he made his Opera debut in 1806. Vaillat (1942) stated that he was of medium height and very well made, and would have been handsome if not for a turned-up nose and chin. He was not engaged by the Opera because of his inflated demands, which included three months' vacation and the right to dance what he chose and to choreograph his own steps. He and Louise went to Lyon, where he married the dancer Adélaïde Perrault (or Perraud), who appeared in his ballets.

TAGLIONI FAMILY. Louise Taglioni the younger (1823–1893), depicted in a *divertissement* from Halévy's opera *Le Juif Errant* (1852). Arthur Saint-Léon choreographed it for her to a *grande valse brillante* by Friedrich Burgmüller. (Courtesy of Madison U. Sowell and Debra H. Sowell, Brigham Young University, Provo, Utah.)

A prolific choreographer, Salvatore Taglioni did most of his work in Naples, with some at the Teatro alla Scala in Milan and in Turin. In 1812 he and Louis Henry founded the school of ballet at the Teatro San Carlo in Naples at the order of Joachim Murat, then king of Naples. Salvatore taught the *classe de perfectionnement,* a position he held for most of his life. As his first choreographic assignment, Salvatore restaged Jean Dauberval's *La Fille Mal Gardée* in Naples. Many of his early works were in the fashionable mythological or historical mode. *La Conquista di Malacca, ossia I Portoghesi nell'Indie* (The Conquest of Malacca, or The Portuguese in the Indies; 1819), *Castore e Polluce* (1820), *Sesostri* (1823), and *Tippoo-Saeb* (1823).

In 1826 Fanny and Thérèse Elssler danced in Salvatore's ballets in Naples. Fanny played Briseis in his mythological ballet *L'Ira di Achille* (The Wrath of Achilles) and also appeared in *Alcibiade.* Both sisters performed in *Acbar Gran Mogul,* which Salvatore completed after the death of its original choreographer, Gaetano Gioja.

In 1832 Salvatore choreographed one of his best-known ballets, *Romanow.* This historical ballet was noted for its use of horses on stage, particularly in a scene where a young Russian girl on horseback jumped from a bridge.

The Neapolitan ballerina Fanny Cerrito probably studied with Salvatore and gained performing experience in his works of the 1830s, among them the Chinese ballet *L'Ombra di Tsi-Ven, ossia La Costanza Premiata* (The Shade of Tsi-Ven, or Loyalty Rewarded). She and Carlotta Grisi respectively played the roles of Iris and Amor in Salvatore's *Amore e Psiche.* Jules Perrot, soon to become Grisi's mentor and lover, partnered Amalia Brugnoli in Salvatore's *Il Ritorno di Ulisse* in 1836; Grisi was also a member of the cast.

Salvatore's ballet *Faust* (1838) earned acclaim in Naples ten years before Perrot's treatment of the same theme at La Scala. Brugnoli returned to dance in his fantasy-ballet *Nadan, o L'Orgoglio Punito* (Nadan, or Pride Punished, 1839), in which Salvatore's daughter Louise also appeared. The historical ballet *Marco Visconti* and the romantic *La Foresta d'Hermanstadt* (both 1841), were also admired. Gustave Carey, a member of another famous dancing dynasty, choreographed sequences in both ballets. One of Perrot's earliest choreographic efforts, a pas de deux for himself and Grisi, was inserted into Salvatore's *Il Rajah de Benares* (1841).

In the first volume of *My Theatre Life,* published in 1848, August Bournonville called Salvatore Taglioni "the finest living ballet composer in Italy." He singled out for praise *Romanow, Ettore Fieramosca,* and *Marco Visconti.*

In 1854 Salvatore choreographed *Hulda,* with a libretto by his son-in-law Alexandre Fuchs and a pas de deux by Louis Mérante, a future ballet master at the Paris Opera. He continued his association with Carey, who collaborated with him on restagings of Giovanni Casati's *Shakespeare* (1855) and Perrot's *La Filleule des Fées,* which they retitled *Isaura* (1856).

Salvatore continued to choreograph until the early 1860s. Among his last ballets were *Rita* and *Il Figlio dello Shak,* both produced in Naples.

Louise Taglioni (born 13 March 1823 in Naples, died April 1893 in Cufrofiano [Lecce]), dancer and choreographer. Salvatore's daughter Louise became the second Louise Taglioni to dance at the Paris Opera. She probably began her career in Naples, where she danced in her father's ballet *Nadan, o L'Orgoglio Punito* in 1839. In 1841 she danced with Bournonville in two excerpts from his ballets, the *grand pas de deux* from *Waldemar* and the *bolero* from *The Toreador.*

By 1846 Louise the younger had traveled north to London, where she appeared in Perrot's ballets at Her Majesty's Theatre. Reviews of her London debut as Venus in the *pas de modèles* of *Catarina* noted her "grace, distinction and modesty of manner" and her "poetry of motion" (quoted by Guest, 1984). She danced in the pas de neuf in *Lalla Rookh* and played one of the three Graces in *Le Jugement de Pâris,* in which her renowned cousin, the elder Marie, took a leading role. Louise also played Giannina, the hero's mortal sweetheart, in a revival of Perrot's *Ondine*, and took the leading female role in Perrot's *Un Bal sous Louis XIV*, with Lucile Grahn, *en travesti*, as her cavalier.

Louise Taglioni the younger was engaged by the Paris Opera in 1848, making her debut in a solo in Auguste Mabille's *Nisida;* however, she returned to London for guest engagements at Covent Garden every year between 1849 and 1851. Among the roles she created at the Opera were the benevolent Pink Fairy in Perrot's *La Filleule des Fées;* Louiselle, who ultimately relinquishes her fiancé to the eponymous heroine of Arthur Saint-Léon's *Stella* (1850); one of the Graces in Joseph Mazilier's *Aelia et Mysis* (1853); and the bride Marietta in Cerrito's *Gemma* (1854). With Nadezdha Bogdanova, she led Saint-Léon's *divertissement Les Abeilles* in Fromenthal Halévy's opera *Le Juif Errant* (1852), and she played Effie when Saint-Léon revived *La Sylphide* in 1852. Around 1850 she married Alexandre Fuchs, also a dancer at the Opera, and she occasionally danced under the name Taglioni-Fuschs.

In 1855 the younger Louise appeared at the National Theater in New York City, performing Irish and Scottish character dances, including a solo to "Comin' through the Rye." After leaving the Paris Opera with her husband in 1857, she became the director of a school of theatrical dancing in Naples. She retired from this position after her husband's death.

Filippo Taglioni (also known as Philippe; born 5 November 1777 in Milan, died 11 September 1871 in Como), dancer and choreographer. Filippo was Carlo's eldest son and, after his own daughter Marie, the best-known member of the clan. He may have appeared on stage as early as 1783, playing a cupid; by the mid-1790s he was playing female roles *en travesti* in various Italian cities. In 1799 he went to Paris to study with Coulon, and he is said to have made his Opera debut with his sister Louise in the opera *La Caravane.* According to Léandre Vaillat (1942), however, his debut came about by chance, much as Marie Camargo's had in an earlier day: he went on at the last minute to replace an indisposed *premier danseur.* During his engagement at the Opera he danced in Milon's *Les Noces de Gamache* and in Gardel's *La Dansomanie* and *Le Retour de Zéphire.* Despite his popularity, however, he left the Opera in 1802 to assume the position of *premier danseur* and ballet master in Stockholm.

This decision had historic consequences for ballet, for in Stockholm Filippo Taglioni met and married Edwige Sofia Karsten, the daughter of a Swedish opera singer. The couple moved to Vienna when their daughter Marie was barely a year old, and Filippo first tried his hand at choreography there, restaging Gardel's *La Dansomanie.*

Although Filippo's family accompanied him to Kassel, where he served as *premier danseur* and ballet master under King Jerome of Westphalia, he left them behind when he went to Italy in 1816, and they subsequently settled in Paris. During the late 1810s Filippo worked in Munich, Stockholm, Copenhagen, Hamburg, and Berlin, as well as in various Italian cities. Bournonville saw him dance during this period and praised his virtuosity. By 1819 Filippo had established himself in Vienna, where he assumed the post of ballet master at the Hoftheater (Court Theater) after the departure of Jean-Louis Aumer in 1821. That year he choreographed *Das Schweizer Milchmädchen* (The Swiss Milkmaid), a ballet that he revived repeatedly under several different names in the 1830s.

Filippo's family joined him in Vienna in 1821, and he began to prepare Marie for her debut. Filippo's wife had misled him as to the extent of Marie's progress under Coulon in Paris, and when Marie arrived in Vienna Filippo discovered that she was far from ready to dance on stage. He immediately set her to work for six hours a day, concentrating on different aspects of ballet technique. In later life Marie attributed her success to her father's rigorous teaching. The style he instilled in her emphasized elevation, effortlessness, fluidity, and suppleness. In addition, he demanded of his daughter a modest and well-bred demeanor that Louis Véron, the director of the Paris Opera, later contrasted favorably with the coquettish behavior encouraged by the teaching of Auguste Vestris.

By June 1822 Filippo deemed Marie ready to dance in public and choreographed the ballet in which she made her debut, *La Réception d'une Jeune Nymphe à la Cour de Terpsichore.* He appeared in it himself in a pas de trois with her and Therese Heberle.

From that time until 1843 Filippo's fortunes were symbiotically linked with those of Marie. He had refined her technique and shaped her unique style. He traveled throughout Europe with her, advised her, negotiated her contracts, and used his insight as father and teacher to create ballets that would best display her special gifts.

Despite his preoccupation with his daughter, Filippo had other concerns. His own career as a dancer continued until the late 1820s or early 1830s. He sometimes danced with Marie: in Louis Henry's *Les Amazones,* which they performed in Vienna in 1823, she took him captive and dragged him off by his hair, to the great delight of the audience. Both of them were engaged as dancers in Stuttgart from 1824 to 1828, in a company that included Louise Pierson, Anton Stuhlmüller, Angelica Saint-Romain, and Filippo's son Paul. In 1831 father and daughter danced a minuet and gavotte at the King's Theatre in London.

Filippo also had to create works for other ballerinas. Fanny Elssler was a junior member of the Viennese company and danced in Filippo's *Lodoïska* in 1823. Amalia Brugnoli and Elise Vaque-Moulin, early exponents of the pointe technique, appeared as guest artists in Vienna. According to Winter (1974), iconographic evidence suggests that many of the female dancers in Filippo's Stuttgart company danced on pointe. Despite his use of this innovation, Winter continues, his choreography preserved an equality between male and female dancing.

Filippo took his family to Paris in 1824 in an attempt to obtain an engagement for Marie at the Opera, but he was unsuccessful. Although some sources state that Marie danced at the Théâtre de la Porte-Saint-Martin at this time, no evidence of this has been found (Guest, 1980). Filippo had to content himself with an engagement in Stuttgart, where in 1826 he choreographed the very popular *Danina, oder Jocko der Brasilianische Affe* (Danina, or Jocko the Brazilian Ape), inspired by Charles Mazurier's success in the similarly titled *Jocko, ou Le Singe du Brésil* at the Porte-Saint-Martin in 1825.

A personal friend of Filippo, Baron Laflèche, smoothed the way for a second attempt on the Opera in 1827. Filippo choreographed the dance, inserted into the ballet *Le Sicilien,* in which Marie first appeared before the Parisian public. She was awarded a contract, and Filippo was able to insist on the condition that she would dance only in his choreography.

TAGLIONI FAMILY. Marie Taglioni's performance in *La Sylphide* (1832) is legendary for its ascendency on both the physical and spiritual planes. In this mezzotint, after an 1834 painting by Gabriel Lépaulle, Taglioni is pictured as the weightless Sylphide, gently resting beside the sleeping James. (Courtesy of Madison U. Sowell and Debra H. Sowell, Brigham Young University, Provo, Utah.)

After a final season in Stuttgart, Filippo's family moved to Paris in the spring of 1828 to take up Marie's new engagement. In 1830 Filippo choreographed her first great role, Zoloë in Daniel Auber's opera *Le Dieu et la Bayadère.* Marie had to mime as well as dance, and Filippo created an affecting dance of supplication before the god Brahmā. His *pas de shalls,* a formula much used by himself and others, proved to be surprisingly effective, particularly in the moment when the scarves of the dancing girls were arranged to make Marie resemble a Botticellian Venus standing on her scallop shell.

Filippo's and Marie's next triumph was the "Ballet of the Nuns" in Giacomo Meyerbeer's opera *Robert le Diable* (1831). Aided by the ghostly ambience of gas-lighting (introduced at the Opera less than a decade before), and by the opera's tale of supernatural beings and sensational events, Filippo wove a dance that blended fear and seduction. The dead nuns, led by Marie as their abbess Helena, rose from their tombs to abandon themselves to unholy revels in their ruined cloister.

This performance made such an impression on Adolphe Nourrit, the tenor who sang the role of Robert, that he conceived a ballet scenario for Marie. Filippo was the natural choice to choreograph this new ballet, *La Sylphide* (1832). In it he took Marie's greatest gifts—elevation, ease, and pointe work—and presented them within an otherworldly framework suggested by the "Ballet of the Nuns." For the first time, pointe work was justified as a means of poetic expression, and Filippo's choreography ensured that his daughter made the most of the opportunity. [*See* Sylphide, La.]

La Sylphide was the high point of Filippo's career; none of his other ballets would achieve its lasting fame. He continued, however, to choreograph new vehicles for Marie. *Nathalie,* presented at the Opera in November 1832, was a revival of *Das Schweizer Milchmädchen,* which Filippo had resurrected earlier that year as *Divertissement Suisse* in Berlin and *La Ressemblance* in London. Its simple story involved a farmer's daughter who is abducted by a lord and who expresses her love for him before his statue without noticing that the real lord has taken its place. All ends happily when he offers her honorable marriage.

Filippo's much-lauded dances in the ballroom scene of Auber's opera *Gustave* (1833) did not include Marie. He created amusing dances for ingeniously costumed couples, and an intoxicating galop for one hundred and twenty-two performers ended the scene. Louis Henry, however, accused Filippo of plagiarizing it from a ballet Henry had produced in Milan in 1830.

Henry's accusations followed Filippo to his next ballet, *La Révolte au Sérail* (1833), allegedly taken from Henry's *Les Amazones,* which Filippo and Marie had danced in Vienna. As Zulma in her father's ballet, Marie incited a harem to revolt against its master and led the women in military drills. One of the highlights was a pas de deux for her and the high-leaping Perrot.

Filippo's last ballet for the Opera, *La Fille du Danube* (1836), was considered a rehash of his earlier successes. Its complicated fairy-tale plot revolved around Fleur-des-Champs (Marie) and her lover Rudolph (Joseph Mazilier), who successfully identifies her among the water sprites of the Danube. The critics agreed that Marie's performance alone saved the ballet.

Filippo left the Opera in 1837 to accompany Marie to Saint Petersburg, where they played five seasons between 1837 and 1842. Some of the new ballets he choreographed for her there were subsequently restaged in the West. In *Miranda,* loosely based on Shakespeare's *The Tempest,* the daughter of the Good Genius wins the love of a shipwrecked Spaniard. *La Gitana,* the story of a girl abducted as a child by Gypsies, gave Marie the opportunity to perform the type of balleticized Spanish dances that had made Fanny Elssler's name. *L'Ombre* was a ghost story about a murdered girl who is ultimately reunited with her lover in death. Filippo's Russian works also included the pirate tale *L'Écumeur de Mer; Le Lac des Fées,* which was suggested by Tsar Nicholas I; and *Herta, la Reine des Elfrides.* In *Aglaë, ou L'Élève d'Amour,* which bore the same title as a ballet Filippo had first presented in Munich in the 1820s, Marie took a dancing lesson with Cupid, awakening the love of a youth and a faun.

The Russian seasons were interspersed with engagements in London and Milan. In 1843, however, Filippo and Marie apparently parted company. Filippo went to Warsaw, where he became the ballet master and director of the ballet company and school. He was also named a member of the directorate of government theaters in Warsaw. According to Janina Pudełek, he staged nine new ballets before his retirement in 1853, among them *Indian Morning, A Day at the Carnival in Venice, The Isle of the Amazons, The Lame Little Devil,* and *A Panorama of Naples.*

Filippo spent his final years in a villa on Lake Como. During a visit to Paris in 1860 he watched a rehearsal of Marie's ballet *Le Papillon,* which he criticized for not being in time, though he conceded that the dances were "well arranged and very pretty" (quoted by Guest, 1953–1955).

Marie Taglioni (born 23 April 1804 in Stockholm, died 22 April 1884 in Marseille), dancer and choreographer. Even though Marie may not have satisfied her father as a choreographer, she was matchless as a dancer. During her lifetime she became the standard by which other ballerinas were measured, and her name is still invoked today as an exemplar of the art.

Her 1822 debut in *La Réception d'une Jeune Nymphe à la Cour de Terpsichore,* which took the form of a dancing lesson given by Terpsichore and her nymphs, required Marie to display her proficiency in all styles of dance—noble, *demi-caractère,* and comic. Fanny Elssler, who was destined to become her greatest rival, may have been among the corps at Marie's debut; she is listed as a Bacchante in the ballet's second performance.

TAGLIONI FAMILY. Marie Taglioni dancing the mazurka from Filippo Taglioni's *La Gitana* (1838). (Courtesy of Madison U. Sowell and Debra H. Sowell, Brigham Young University, Provo, Utah.)

In Vienna, Marie had the opportunity to observe the pointe technique of Brugnoli and Vaque-Moulin, and it is recorded that she rather waspishly remarked on the efforts Brugnoli made with her arms in order to stay on pointe. She probably learned to dance on pointe at this stage of her career, but the technique still held an odor of the circus; not until Filippo's *La Sylphide* would it be transformed into poetry.

During the 1820s Marie performed in Vienna, Munich, and Stuttgart in ballets by her father and other choreographers. She played Venus in Armand Vestris's *Psyché* and the eponymous heroine in her father's popular *Danina, oder Jocko der Brasilianische Affe.* For Filippo's *Aglaë, ou L'Élève d'Amour,* her mother made her a costume that was a prototype of her Sylphide tutu, white and diaphanous, with a ribbon girdle and a wreath of flowers in her hair.

Although her father failed in his first attempt in 1824 to get her an engagement at the Paris Opera, Marie was granted permission in 1827 to make the six debut performances required before a contract could be negotiated. She first appeared on 23 July in a pas de deux with her brother. It contained a considerable amount of pointe work, which was not entirely new to Paris, having been introduced in the 1810s by Geneviève Gosselin; however, combined with Marie's other qualities—lightness, fluidity, ease, and modesty—it made an indelible impression. She was hailed as the progenitor of a new style; her example inspired the other dancers to "taglionize," and the Opera awarded her a three-year contract.

Despite the public favor she had won at her debut, Marie was not always given principal roles during her first years at the Opera. Also, by the terms of her contract she was limited to her father's choreography. She pleased the audience, however, in dances such as "La Naïade" in Aumer's *Sleeping Beauty* and the "Tyrolienne" in Gioacchino Rossini's opera *Guillaume Tell,* both of which she performed throughout her career. In 1830 she danced in a revival of Charles-Louis Didelot's *Flore et Zéphire* in London and repeated her triumph in Paris the following year, with Perrot "the aerial" as her partner.

Marie's performance as Zoloë in *Le Dieu et la Bayadère* sealed her position as a leading ballerina of the Opera. Although she was considered disappointing in the mimed portions of the role, her father's choreography highlighted her special gifts as a dancer, presenting her as ethereal rather than sensual. The Opera awarded her a six-year contract, from 1831 to 1837. Between seasons she danced in London and Berlin, often in revivals of Parisian triumphs.

The crucial year of 1831 brought Marie the role of the ghostly yet enticing abbess Helena in *Robert le Diable,* which in turn led to the creation of *La Sylphide* (1832). Although this ballet is generally associated today with the use of the pointe technique, and Marie's name has come down in history as the dancer who gave artistic legitimacy to toe-dancing, Marie never regarded pointe work as an end in itself. It was simply part of an arsenal that included her supernal lightness and elasticity in steps of elevation (a quality that led critics to speak of her *ballonné* style); the ease and fluidity of her arm movements, which showed none of the strain for which she had criticized Brugnoli; and the effortlessness that characterized her dancing as a whole, earning her the sobriquet "Marie full of grace." These qualities made Marie's Sylphide the prototype of the ethereal, otherworldly heroines who began to take over the Opera in the 1830s, their pale and diaphanous costumes providing the name of a new genre, the "white ballet."

The fact that Marie's performances often salvaged her father's undistinguished choreography, such as that of *La Révolte au Sérail* and *La Fille du Danube,* did not go unnoticed by the critics. Charles de Boigne remarked, "All Father Taglioni's ballets are alike: a complete absence of ideas, second-hand stuff, always the same. . . . But the ballerina is there to rescue the choreographer, the daughter to rescue the father" (quoted by Guest, 1980). This working relationship continued when Marie left the Opera in 1837 on the expiration of her contract and went to dance in Saint Petersburg. There Filippo choreographed for her the ballet that enabled her to meet Elssler on her own ground, *La Gitana* (1838).

The rivalry between Marie and Elssler, who was six years younger, had developed gradually. Prior to Elssler's debut at the Opera in 1834, the two had shared stages in Vienna and London. By 1836, however, Elssler had perfected a style that many viewers considered antithetical to Marie's. Théophile Gautier's often-quoted comparison of the two as the "pagan" dancer (Elssler) and the "Christian" (Marie) succinctly describes the difference in their stage personalities, just as the opposition of the terms *taqueté* (Elssler) and *ballonné* (Marie) contrasts their technical styles: one exploited brilliant but earthbound steps, while the other emphasized lightness and elevation. The Opera's director, Véron, considered the rivalry good for business and encouraged the factionalism of the "Taglionists" and the "Elsslerists."

Marie, however, was no stranger to Elssler's specialty, character dancing, as her repeated performances of the "Tyrolienne" indicate. *La Gitana* gave her a mazurka and a Spanish dance in the style of Elssler's signature dance, the *cachucha.* She impressed her own qualities on the Spanish dance, which one observer described as "a succession of flying movements expressive of alarm" (quoted by Beaumont, 1937). *La Gitana* was a great success and long remained in her repertory.

Marie traveled widely in the late 1830s and the 1840s, appearing in Britain, Italy, Austria, Poland, France, Belgium, and her native Sweden. In 1841 she danced for the first time at La Scala, where she became embroiled in a rivalry with Fanny Cerrito in 1843. In the final years of her career she enjoyed a second spring of adulation at Her Majesty's Theatre in London, where she appeared in Perrot's *Pas de Quatre* (1845) and *Le Jugement de Pâris* (1846). She was undeniably the cynosure of these star-studded *divertissements,* and the other ballerinas (Grisi, Cerrito, and Grahn) unquestioningly deferred to her. Her performances in Perrot's one-act version of *La Sylphide* inspired the famous series of lithographs by Alfred Chalon, *La Sylphide: Souvenir d'adieu de Marie Taglioni* (1845). She gave her farewell performance in London on 21 August 1847, dancing in *Le Jugement de Pâris.*

Although her performing career had ended, Marie returned to the world of dance in 1858, soon after the debut of Emma Livry in *La Sylphide.* Livry, who reincarnated

Marie's own qualities as a dancer, became her protégée, and in 1860 Marie choreographed for her *Le Papillon,* a fairy tale of a girl who is magically transformed into a butterfly. Despite its complicated plot, the ballet was well received, and Marie had begun to rehearse a second work for Livry, *Zara,* when Livry's costume caught fire during a rehearsal, burning her severely. After her death some months later, a few attempts were made to produce *Zara* with other ballerinas, but this ballet was never realized.

In the meantime Marie had been appointed as *inspectrice de la danse* at the Opera and later as *professeur de la classe de perfectionnement.* These positions allowed her to institute certain reforms at the Opera, including a system of examinations (she sat on the first jury) for promotions within the ranks of the corps de ballet.

During the 1860s Marie lost her fortune (according to some sources, through Filippo's speculations). In 1870 she opened a school of ballroom dancing and deportment in London, where, as a former pupil recalled, she paid particular attention to graceful movements of the arms, curtsying, and the pointing of the toes. In 1880 she retired to Marseille to live with her son Georges. She was survived by him and by her daughter Eugénie-Marie-Edwige.

Paul Taglioni (born 12 January 1800 in Vienna, died 6 January 1884 in Berlin), dancer and choreographer. Paul studied dancing with his father Filippo and with Coulon, making his debut in Stuttgart in 1824 or 1825. He was engaged as a soloist in Vienna from 1826 to 1829, although in 1827 he partnered his sister Marie in her debut appearances at the Paris Opera. In 1829 he married the German ballerina Amalia Galster (c.1808–1881), who became his regular partner.

Although Paul danced in Paris and London in the early 1830s, by 1835 he had settled in Berlin, which became his home base. Some of his earliest ballets were choreographed there, among them *Amors Triumph* and *Der Arme Fischer* (both 1835), as well as his first major work, *Undine* (1836), which was based on Friedrich de La Motte-Fouqué's romance about a water nymph who falls in love with a knight.

Paul and Amalia accepted an engagement in the United States in 1839, appearing in New York, Baltimore, Philadelphia, Boston, and Providence. They made their American debut in New York's Park Theater on 22 May in the first full-length version of *La Sylphide* presented in the United States; their repertory also included *Undine* and Filippo's *Nathalie* and *Le Dieu et la Bayadère.* They were very well received; Paul's virtuosity was particularly admired, for good male dancers were rare in the United States at the time.

The *Spirit of the Times* (New York) described Paul as "Italian in appearance, wondrously well formed—limbs clean and sinewy like those of a race-horse, with a face which reminds you of the pictures of his famous sister, particularly about the mouth" (quoted by Moore, 1942). The same journal later commented upon "his remarkable activity, and his muscular power," though it faulted him for lack of grace.

In 1841 Paul was asked to replace August Bournonville temporarily in Copenhagen, an engagement that ended in disaster when his restaging of *Nathalie* was hissed at its second performance, causing him to break his contract and leave. He remained on friendly terms, however, with Bournonville, who used Paul's choreography for the final *seguidillas* in his ballet *La Ventana* (1853).

In 1844 and 1845 Paul and Amalia made guest appearances in Warsaw, where Filippo was ballet master. According to Pudełek, Paul's ballets *Les Plaisirs de l'Hiver* and *La Prima Ballerina, ou L'Embuscade* were first produced here in 1845 rather than in London in 1849, as was formerly believed. The ice-skating scene of *Les Plaisirs de l'Hiver* anticipated Frederick Ashton's twentieth-century *Les Patineurs. La Prima Ballerina* was purportedly based on an actual experience of Marie's, in which bandits stopped her carriage on a deserted road but let her go free after she danced for them.

Paul served as ballet master at Her Majesty's Theatre in London from 1847 to 1851, sharing the post with Perrot in his first two years. He restaged *Undine* (retitled *Coralia* to avoid confusion with Perrot's *Ondine*), as well several new ballets. In the rather sugary *Théa, ou La Fée aux Fleurs,* the heroine (Carolina Rosati) wins her prince's love only after she has been transformed into a rosebush. *Electra,* which was famous for its use of electric lighting on stage, featured Grisi as a star that comes to earth. As the protean heroine of *Les Métamorphoses* (later restaged in Berlin as *Santanella*), Grisi played both male and female roles, among them a coquette and the cavalier who woos her. Paul himself danced the male leads in many of his ballets. His choreography tended to emphasize dancing at the expense of dramatic action, but this evidently accorded with contemporary taste; the *Times* praised *Théa* as "so much better than those long pieces of action in which the public is worn out with processions and non-dancing magnificence. It is, in fact, one blaze of brilliant dancing from the beginning to the end" (quoted by Beaumont, 1937).

Beginning in the 1850s Paul worked as ballet master in Naples and Vienna as well as London and Berlin. He also began to stage ballets at La Scala during the 1860s. His most popular and frequently revived ballet, *Flick und Flocks Abenteuer* (Berlin, 1858), depicted the magical adventures of two friends who visit the kingdom of the gnomes and the undersea palace of Amphitrite. Arthur Saint-Léon, who saw the ballet some years after its premiere, criticized it as "a sort of faery with every known trick—out of date rococo groups, no delicacy, not a witty idea—and, if only one could forget it, the cocking-the-snook dance." He conceded, however, that "there is much precision in the general dances" (Guest, 1981).

Paul's penchant for extravagant fantasies enlivened with much dancing and elaborate scenery evidently persisted into the next decade, when Bournonville noted these characteristics in *Fantasca* (Berlin, 1869). "I admire his skill in choreographic arrangement, which, regardless of dramatic worth or poetic inspiration, must enrapture the avid spectator," confessed the Danish choreographer. Although the full range of Paul's works has yet to be studied, he appears to have been a skillful purveyor of the type of spectacular ballets favored in the late nineteenth century. He remained active as a choreographer in Berlin until 1883, a year before his death.

Marie Taglioni (born 27 October 1830 in Berlin, died 27 April 1891 in Neu-Aigen, near Vienna), dancer. Paul's daughter Marie was called "the second," "the younger," or "Marie Paul" in order to distinguish her from her illustrious aunt. She made her debut in 1847 at Her Majesty's Theatre in London, where her father was ballet master. In a review of her solo *pas de la rosière* in Paul's *Coralia,* the *Times* described her as "light, agile, graceful, and, at the same time, possessed of remarkable power of muscle" (quoted by Beaumont, 1937). She also created the role of the Flower Fairy in her father's *Théa.* Her strength, also an attribute of Paul, was again noted the following year when she played Hertha in Paul's *Fiorita.*

TAGLIONI FAMILY. Marie Taglioni the younger (1830–1891) in the title role of *Saltanella.* This lithograph, by Louis Veit after a photograph, was printed in Eduard Bloch's *Album der Bühnen-Costüme,* Berlin, 1859. (Courtesy of Madison U. Sowell and Debra H. Sowell, Brigham Young University, Provo, Utah.)

During the same year Marie also created the role of Winter in Perrot's *Les Quatre Saisons,* dancing alongside Cerrito, Grisi, and Rosati. She played one of the rival goddesses, with Cerrito and Rosati, in a revival of Perrot's *Le Jugement de Pâris.* Marie also assumed the title role of *Théa* in Berlin that year. After seeing her in this role, her aunt Marie wrote, "I find her charming, very suited to the stage: she has much aplomb and ease, and sufficient elevation; she is graceful in pantomime. She will bring honor to the name of Taglioni" (quoted by Vaillat, 1942).

Along with her father, Marie returned repeatedly to Her Majesty's Theatre. In the role of Edda in Paul's *Electra* (1849), she danced the pas de deux "Le Lutte" with Grisi, in which the two vied for the love of Ehrick, played by Paul. She also appeared that year as Myrtha in *Giselle.* In 1850 she danced in Paul's ballets *Les Grâces* and *Les Métamorphoses;* she later took the title role in the latter ballet when it was restaged in Berlin as *Santanella.* She danced her aunt's famous role of the Sylphide in London in 1851.

In 1851 Marie also paid a visit to Warsaw, where her grandfather Filippo was ballet master, and danced before the court and at the Wielki Theater. She spent the years 1853 to 1856 in Vienna, then joined her father at the Berlin Court Opera from 1856 to 1866, with a few guest appearances in London, dancing in Paul's ballets *Flick und Flocks Abenteur, Des Malers Traumbild,* and *Sardanapal.* She retired from the stage in 1866 after her marriage to Prince Josef von Windisch-Graetz.

[*See also entries on the principal figures mentioned herein.*]

BIBLIOGRAPHY

Beaumont, Cyril W. *Complete Book of Ballets.* Rev. ed. London, 1951.

Binney, Edward, 3rd. *Longing for the Ideal: Images of Marie Taglioni in the Romantic Ballet.* Cambridge, Mass., 1984.

Bournonville, August. *My Theatre Life* (1848–1878). Translated by Patricia McAndrew. Middletown, Conn., 1979.

Cavalletti, Lavinia. "Salvatore Taglioni re di Napoli." *La Danza Italiana* 8–9 (Winter 1990): 109–134.

Celi, Claudia, and Andrea Toschi. "Alla ricerca dell'anello mancante: 'Flik e Flok' e l'Unità d'Italia." *Chorégraphie* 1 (Autumn 1993): 58–72.

Chazin-Bennahum, Judith. *Dance in the Shadow of the Guillotine.* Carbondale, Ill., 1988.

Guest, Ivor. *Fanny Elssler.* London, 1970.

Guest, Ivor. *The Romantic Ballet in England.* London, 1972.

Guest, Ivor. *The Ballet of the Second Empire.* London, 1974.

Guest, Ivor. *Fanny Cerrito.* 2d rev. ed. London, 1974.

Guest, Ivor. *The Romantic Ballet in Paris.* 2d rev. ed. London, 1980.

Guest, Ivor. *Jules Perrot.* London, 1984.

Guest, Ivor. "L'Italia e il balletto romantico." *La Danza Italiana* 8–9 (Winter 1990): 7–25.

Heiberg, Johanne L. "Memories of Taglioni and Elssler." Translated by Patricia McAndrew. *Dance Chronicle* 4.1 (1981): 14–18.
Hill, Lorna. *La Sylphide: The Life of Marie Taglioni.* London, 1967.
Lecomte, Nathalie. "Marie Taglioni alla Scala." *La Danza Italiana* 8–9 (Winter 1990): 47–71.
Levinson, André. *Marie Taglioni* (1929). Translated by Cyril W. Beaumont. London, 1977.
Lifar, Serge. *A History of Russian Ballet.* Translated by Arnold L. Haskell. New York, 1954.
Migel, Parmenia. *The Ballerinas: From the Court of Louis XIV to Pavlova.* New York, 1972.
Moore, Lillian. *Artists of the Dance.* New York, 1938.
Moore, Lillian. "A Dancer's Odyssey: Paul and Amelie Taglioni" (1942). In Moore's *Echoes of American Ballet.* Brooklyn, 1976.
Pudełek, Janina. "The Warsaw Ballet under the Directorships of Maurice Pion and Filippo Taglioni, 1832–1853." *Dance Chronicle* 11.2 (1988): 219–273.
Roslavleva, Natalia. *Era of the Russian Ballet* (1966). New York, 1979.
Saint-Léon, Arthur. *Letters from a Ballet Master: The Correspondence of Arthur Saint-Léon.* Edited by Ivor Guest. New York, 1981.
Sasportes, José. "La danza, 1737–1900." In *Il Teatro di San Carlo,* edited by Bruno Cagli and Agostino Ziino. Naples, 1987.
Tani, Gino. "Taglioni." In *Enciclopedia dello spettacolo.* Rome, 1954–.
Testa, Alberto. "Duecentocinquanta anni di balletto al Teatro oli San Carlo." In *Il Teatro di San Carlo 1737–1987.* 2 vols., Naples (1987): 333–344.
Testa, Alberto. "Taglioni." In *Storia della Danzae del Balletto.* Rome, 1994.
Vaillat, Léandre. *La Taglioni, ou, La vie d'une danseuse.* Paris, 1942.
Véron, Louis Désiré. "Behind the Scenes at the Opéra in Marie Taglioni's Day." Translated by Cyril W. Beaumont. *The Dancing Times* (January 1924): 403–407.
Wiley, Roland John, trans. and ed. *A Century of Russian Ballet: Documents and Accounts, 1810–1910.* Oxford, 1990. Includes Filippo Taglioni's libretto of *La Fille du Danube* and an account of the Taglionis in Russia.
Wiley, Roland John. "Images of *La Sylphide:* Two Accounts by a Contemporary Witness of Marie Taglioni's Appearances in St. Petersburg." *Dance Research* 13 (Summer 1995): 21–32.
Winter, Marian Hannah. *The Pre-Romantic Ballet.* London, 1974.
Woodcock, Sarah C. "Margaret Rolfe's Memoirs of Marie Taglioni" (parts 1–2). *Dance Research* 7 (Spring 1989): 3–19; 7 (Autumn 1989): 55–69.

ARCHIVE. Dance Collection, New York Public Library for the Performing Arts, in particular the files of unpublished research notes by Lillian Moore and the Walter Toscanini collection of research materials in dance.

ALBERTO TESTA
Translated from Italian

TAHITI. The largest and most populous of the Society Islands, Tahiti is the capital and administrative center for French Polynesia, an overseas territory of France comprising five culturally differentiated island groups in the southern Pacific Ocean. Because Tahiti is also the best-known island in the Society chain and enjoys a central position in the economic, political, and cultural life of the archipelago, the term *Tahitian* generally designates the language, people, and culture shared throughout the nine islands of that archipelago. In its larger sense, it may also refer to French Polynesia as a whole.

TAHITI. Female dancers posing for a photograph, c.1910. (Photograph from the Department of Library Services, American Museum of Natural History, New York [no. 33110]; used by permission.)

History. Early European visitors to Tahiti (the first was the English navigator Samuel Wallis in 1767) described a society in which dance was a favorite source of entertainment, beauty, and excitement. It was moreover an integral part of daily life, included in such varied activities as community projects and celebrations, certain rites of passage, war, politics, and religion. Europeans wrote about the elegant and beautiful motions of the hands and fingers, of a rapid circular hip movement employed by the women, of dances that incorporated various "lascivious postures," and of the fact that facial distortion was highly admired by the Tahitians. They noted that most dances were accompanied by the drum *(pahu)* and the nose flute *(vivo),* and that costuming varied widely, from nudity to elaborate costumes made of prized bark cloth.

Western influence and the missionaries' suppression of native dance—forbidden by law as early as the 1820s—have left a dance culture that today is considerably different from the original. In 1928 the Tahitian chronicler Teuira Henry lamented that "the ancient dancers would not recognize the modern form." Most contemporary Tahitians, however, do not focus on the past, but view their dance as part of a vibrant artistic life woven from many threads of change. The years since the 1950s have brought a proliferation of both amateur and professional dance groups, an increased respect for traditional dance in the eyes of modern Tahitians, and substantial government support of dance groups and folklore research. Influences from other Polynesian islands have also left their mark on the performing arts as Tahitians turned to neighboring cultures for ideas to fuel their creativity and desire for innovative material. In the 1990s, choreographers have added movements and techniques to the basic core of Tahitian dance, ushering in a new era of artistic transformation and prompting new definitions of traditional dance.

Dance in Contemporary Tahiti. The popular Western partner dances are the norm for social dancing at parties, celebrations, and evenings in night spots. Western classical dance is not widely known and is represented by only one ballet school in the capital, Papeete. Traditional Tahitian dance, however, can be viewed regularly in tourist hotels and at school, church, tourist-related, and official events throughout the year. The Heiva dance competitions in summer are considered the highlight of the dance year.

A notable feature of Tahitian dance in the 1990s is the emergence and growth of dance schools, a development representing a conspicuous change in the way Tahitians transmit dance knowledge. Whereas earlier generations learned dance through observation and repetition in informal group rehearsals, young dancers in the 1990s prefer to enroll in classes at the government-sponsored Conservatoire Artistique Territorial or at private dance schools established by Tahiti's well-known dancers. Such classes stress the acquisition and perfection of technique, thereby encouraging both increased virtuosity in dance and the codification of dance technique and vocabulary.

Tahitian dance is a group activity (competition groups in 1995 and 1996 had as many as 120 dancers; hotel performances may have only ten), choreographed and directed by a group leader and accompanied by a minimum of five musicians. Costumes may feature the simple *pareu*, the wraparound cloth, or finely worked natural materials (such as the inner bark of the purau tree, dried or fresh leaves, shells, seeds, and flowers) made into dance skirts with elaborately decorated belts, headdresses or head garlands, breast coverings, and neck ornaments.

Most dances call for gender-specific movements, revolving hip movements for women (*fa'arapu*) and a vigorous opening and closing of the knees for men (*pa'oti*). These movements, properly known as *'ori tahiti* (Tahitian dance), are also popularly referred to as the *tāmūrē*. The following are genres of Tahitian dance found today.

TAHITI. Men dancing in Papeete, c.1925. The vigorous knee-flapping, caught mid-motion here, is a characteristic feature of many Tahitian men's dances. (Photograph by R. H. Beck; from the Department of Library Services, American Museum of Natural History, New York [no. 122415]; used by permission.)

Once a men's dance, the *'ōte'a* today is performed by all-male, all-female, or mixed groups. The best known of all Tahitian dances, it is marked by a fast pace, the strong rhythmic drive of accompanying drums (slit drums and membranophones), the use of *'ori tahiti* movements, and predominantly abstract arm gestures. The dancers stand in columns facing the front of the performing area and use changing configurations to provide choreographic variety or to express the overall theme of the dance.

The *pā'ō'ā* is said by many Tahitians to have originated in the work of making bark cloth. Today it is a dance in which a group leader joins the drummers in the middle of a full or partial circle formed by a seated, mixed group. As the group members slap their thighs in rhythm with the basic pulse, one or two dancers rise and improvise a dance based on *'ori tahiti* movements. Accounts from the turn of the twentieth century describe the *pā'ō'ā* as having a solo female dancer; today the dance may be performed by a male-female couple.

The *hivinau* ("heave, now!") takes its name from the shouts of sailors lifting anchor on the nineteenth-century schooners that traveled between the islands. Used as a social mixer in the early years of the twentieth century, the *hivinau* now occurs within the context of presentational dance. It is performed in a double concentric circle formation (one circle male, one female) enclosing the group leader and the drummers. The men and women move in opposite directions using a stylized walking step, then stop momentarily to share a brief *'ori tahiti* dance with the person opposite.

The *'aparima* is a storytelling dance in which the gestures of the arms and hands play an important role. Two basic types of *'aparima* are found. Both may be performed by a mixed or same-sex group. The *'aparima vāvā* (mute *'aparima*) is a mimed dance accompanied by a drumming ensemble. Its gestures represent activities of daily life (fishing, canoe-paddling, or making coconut milk). It is performed in a seated or kneeling position.

The *'aparima hīmene* ("sung" *'aparima*) tells a story by means of a song text and accompanying hand and arm gestures. Gestures are predominantly symbolic or mimetic in nature and relate to the text of the song, highlighting important words or amplifying underlying meanings in the text. Choreographers also employ ornamental, nontext-related gestures to provide visual interest and fill the visual space between highlighted words.

'Aparima hīmene dances are accompanied by stringed instruments (guitars and locally made ukuleles) and bass drum; they may be performed seated, kneeling, or standing. In the 1980s standing dances began to exhibit increasing variety in foot and lower torso movements. Whereas the older *'aparima* used a simple sideways step (similar to the Hawaiian *kāholo*) or were performed in place with dancers marking the basic pulse of the music by tapping one heel or foot, dances in the 1990s incorporate level changes, locomotion, and a wide assortment of foot and hip movements (including many from Hawaiian hula).

Tahitian dance in the mid-1990s is clearly an art form molded by a global culture, interweaving elements from other artistic traditions with local motifs and yet remaining a recognizable symbol of Tahitian cultural identity for both islanders and visitors. As the dance becomes more virtuosic and institutionalized, increasingly complex and sophisticated performances will become the norm in urban areas, even as rural communities continue to feature amateur dance based on older models and older definitions of what it means to be Tahitian—both styles contributing to the richness and viability of Tahitian dance culture.

[*See also* Oceanic Dance Traditions *and* Polynesia.]

BIBLIOGRAPHY

Henry, Teuira. *Ancient Tahiti.* Bishop Museum Bulletin, no. 48. Honolulu, 1928.

Moulin, Jane Freeman. *The Dance of Tahiti.* Papeete, Tahiti, 1979.

Oliver, Douglas L. *Ancient Tahitian Society.* Honolulu, 1974.

JANE FREEMAN MOULIN

TAIWAN. An island in the western Pacific Ocean, Taiwan (formerly called Formosa) lies between the East and the South China seas, some ninety miles (145 kilometers) from the coast of the Chinese mainland. Taiwan and thirteen small islands of the Taiwan group constitute 12,847 square miles (35,860 square kilometers); since 1949, when the People's Republic of China (PRC) was established, the government of the Republic of China (ROC) and millions of Chinese moved to Taiwan, with their capital at Taipei. Some twenty million people now live on Taiwan, including the pre-Chinese indigenous peoples, collectively called Kaoshan. The Chinese began arriving in the seventeenth century; before 1945 they were rice farmers and fisherfolk from Fujian and Guangdong provinces, speaking Cantonese, Hakka, or Min dialects (they are known as Taiwanese). From 1945 to 1950, some three million anti-Communist Chinese from every province arrived, many from Shanghai. Today, both Taiwanese and Chinese constitute 98.5 percent of the population and speak Mandarin Chinese (the official dialect of both the ROC and PRC governments).

Dance in Taiwan has a long and rich cultural legacy. Some traditional dance genres include Kaoshan indigenous dance, the ancient Confucian ritual dance *(yayue)* of the Han people of China, the banquet music and dance *(yanyue)* dating from the Tang dynasty (618–906), as well as other types of Kaoshan, Taiwanese, and Chinese folk dance. Dancers stage numerous performances as part of traditional ritual ceremonies, appearing in theaters and even in the streets of Taiwan. In the 1940s, Western ballet and modern dance came to Taiwan.

Indigenous Dance. There are nine aboriginal peoples in Taiwan—the Ami, Atayal, Bunun, Paiwan, Puyuma, Rukai, Saisiyat, Tsou, and Yami. Their religious beliefs are based on ancestor worship and animism, a polytheism of nature gods and spirits. The Yami experience an intense awe of the dead, and many believe in and practice shamanism. [*See* Shamanism.] The indigenous dance of all the peoples of Taiwan is intimately related to traditional religious beliefs; the dances and songs are an intrinsic part of ceremonies, which include the worship of the ancestors and the souls of the dead. Song and dance also accompany rituals that celebrate sexual maturity and marriage, the harvesting of food, and the hunt—they express respect and gratitude to the ancestors and reenactment of heroic deeds and historic events. Less formally, singing and dancing also provide them with a source of pleasure and amusement in their daily lives.

Aboriginal dance is not accompanied by musical instruments. After the lead singer provides the first line, the dancers join in, singing and dancing. The rhythms are usually 4/4, 2/4, 6/4, 8/4, and 3/4. Some steps can be used with a variety of songs. Songs are sung spontaneously to welcome guests or for simple pleasure and amusement, and some degree of improvisation often occurs. Such dancing is often joyful and relaxing.

Aboriginal dance formations include the closed circle, the open semicircle, the spiral, and the lateral row. A variety of steps include walking, running, stamping, pointing, hopping, jumping, and zig-zaging in circular patterns, both clockwise and counterclockwise. Another step, the gallop, is found in the Paiwan people's hunting dance. Aboriginal dance does not place much emphasis on arm movements; most often, dancers join hands and move their arms up and down to the rhythm of the dance. They employ a movement with their hands swung back and forth and from left to right; occasionally they simply clap their hands. They use their torsos to sway from side to side, often bending forward in a deep bow, to mime the waves of the ocean. One very famous dance performed by Yami women is called the Hair Dance. Women with long, loose tresses line up side by side and take hands, kicking rhythmically, bending forward and back, and tossing their hair in the air, again, as if communing with the ocean.

Traditional aboriginal costumes are very colorful, and each people has its own distinctive ones. Costumes and accessories may include pants for men, blouses, skirts, leggings, headpieces, garlands, necklaces, bells, and bags of betel nuts. Yami men often wear simple T-pants for casual dancing but don embroidered shirts and silver hats for formal rituals. Paiwanese noblemen dance in blouses embroidered in patterns of poisonous snakes. Tsou male dancers engage in singing and dancing to honor their ancestors and the nature deities, but there is a taboo against women and children taking part or appearing at the altar.

Traditional Chinese Dance. Confucian ritual dance *(yayue)* is the oldest traditional dance of the Han people of

TAIWAN. Performers of the Formosa Aboriginal Dance Troupe of Taiwan in a dance of the Tsou people from the village of Tufuya. (Photograph © 1993 by Linda Vartoogian; used by permission.)

China. This dance was an important part of the scholarly curriculum in ancient China, and its performance was obligatory in rituals. After 1911, the Republic of China was founded, and many of China's traditions underwent changes; with the overthrow of the emperor and traditional absolutism, the rituals for sacrifices to heaven and earth, the mountains, the rivers, and the ancestors were generally abandoned. Thus, Confucian ritual music and dance lost its high status in Chinese society. Today, only four kinds of ancient Confucian dances are performed in Taiwan. (1) The ancient Yi Dance has been performed over the centuries in rituals of ancestor worship. Five variations, with a description and figures, are recorded in historical documents. The Yi Dance is performed annually in the Temple of Confucius on 28 September, his birthday. The reconstruction used has been taken from figure drawings and illustrations dating from the Qing dynasty (1644–1912). (2) The World Completely Reformed is a civil dance. (3) Majesty Invests the Four Seas, a martial dance, were composed by Ye Fang in December of 1089. Their movements/meaning were recorded at the time, and both pieces were performed during the Emperor's court gatherings and rituals. (In 1984, Liu Feng-Shueh reconstructed and staged them; both are now recorded in Labanotation.) (4) Dance of the People, choreographed by Chu Tsai-yü (1536–c.1610), served as an educational dance for children and is imbued with a strong moral sense.

Some characteristics of Confucian ritual dance may now be discussed. Dance formations as well as the number of dancers are strictly limited. Rituals devoted to ancestor worship, sacrifices to heaven and earth, and those in honor of the grain harvest were often hosted by the emperor. On such an occasion the dance consisted of sixty-four dancers—eight dancers arranged in eight rows. If the host and high priest were feudal lords, the required number of dancers was reduced to thirty-six—six dancers in six rows (sometimes a row had eight dancers, making forty-eight dancers in all). If the host and high priest were merely high ranking officers, the number of dancers would be sixteen, with four dancers in four rows (or eight dancers in four rows, making thirty-two dancers in all). If the host and high priest were but common civilians, then there would be two dancers in two rows (or eight dancers in two rows, sixteen in all). The significance of such arrangements was based on numerical symbolism and a striving for harmony and social order as expressed in music, dance, and rituals.

The patterns of movement in Confucian ritual dance were not intended to explore the expressive aspect of dance, since the beauty of the dance lies in its spirit. The purpose of life was to arrive at moral fulfillment and to attain the ideal sphere in which humans become an integral part of nature. These and other related ideas are ex-

TAIWAN. *Chun Ying Chuan* (Oriole's Chirping) is a Tang-dynasty court dance. Upon hearing orioles singing one morning, Emperor Tang Gaozong (650–683) ordered his court musician Bai Mingda to compose the music and dance. Preserved by the Japanese court, the dance also symbolizes ancient Chinese women's beauty and spirituality. Liu Feng-Shueh staged the reconstruction pictured here with dancers Liu Jen-ying, Chao Huey-ren, Chen Chuen-mey, Shih Show-tseng, Cheng Guey-mei, Cheng Ten-shiang, and Lin Shou-shiang. (Photograph courtesy of the Neo-Classical Dance Company, Taiwan.)

pressed in Confucian ritual dance. Many movements are thematic; for example, in The World Completely Reformed, saluting, declining, and modesty are types of comportment that follow strict rules of social etiquette. In the Dance of the People, eight traditional Confucian moral virtues are revealed—loyalty, filial piety, love, benevolence, righteousness, wisdom, propriety, and faithfulness—through eight different movements. In Majesty Invests the Four Seas, the dance extols the achievements of the imperial army. In general, Confucian ritual dances are performed for the sake of increasing one's self-discipline and devotion to others.

Singing and music accompany the dance. Three of the dances—the Yi Dance, The World Completely Reformed, and Majesty Invests the Four Seas—have three song parts, with eight lines in each part, four words in each line. Each word corresponds to one note and one movement. During the first wine offering of the rituals, the first part is performed. The second part is performed during the middle wine offering, and the third part during the final wine offering. The costumes for these three Confucian ritual dances consisted of the ceremonial dress of the period. At performances of the civil dance, the dancer typically holds a flute in his left hand and a feather in his right hand. The dancer in the martial dance bears a shield in his left hand and a pike in his right hand. The dancer in the Dance of the People does not have anything in his hands; he waves his sleeves in a token of respect.

Banquet music and dance. This dance genre, called *yanyue,* was performed during major court ceremonies and national banquets of the Tang dynasty (618–906). According to Tang-era records, more than three hundred of such dances were performed at the court. Most came from India, Iran, and the northwestern part of China, while others were created by the Han people. The musical scores for most of them are no longer extant, but some fragments exist. Of these, "The Scores of Dunhuang" has been examined by the scholar Peng Song and has been recorded in Labanotation. Liu Feng-Shueh initiated his study of Tang banquet dance in 1957 and in 1983 completed his reconstruction of a major work, entitled "The Emperor Destroys the Formations." This dance, martial in nature, was originally created in 634 and was brought to Japan in 701. Liu Feng-Shueh reconstructed the work based on a Japanese description, then recorded it in Labanotation (the music has been reproduced by L. E. R. Picken of Cambridge University). The dance includes a prelude and a broaching; it is twenty-five minutes long. Four dancers form a square, and their steps range from walking and stamping to pointing and sliding. Arm gestures include forward and sideward motions, swaying sideways, hitting, and cutting. Body movements include turns, forward tilts, and diagonal forward and backward tilts, accompanied by the fanning out of wide sleeves. The movements represent a typical Chinese martial manner and attitude. The color of

TAIWAN. Liu Feng-Shueh's *The Seance* (1974), a modern dance work inspired by a poem from *Chu Tsu,* incorporates elements of witchcraft, folk dance practices from northern China and Taiwan, and narrative exploring the self-searching process of the artist. The dancer seen here is Shih Kun-cheng. (Photograph by Li Ming-hsun; courtesy of the Neo-Classical Dance Company, Taiwan.)

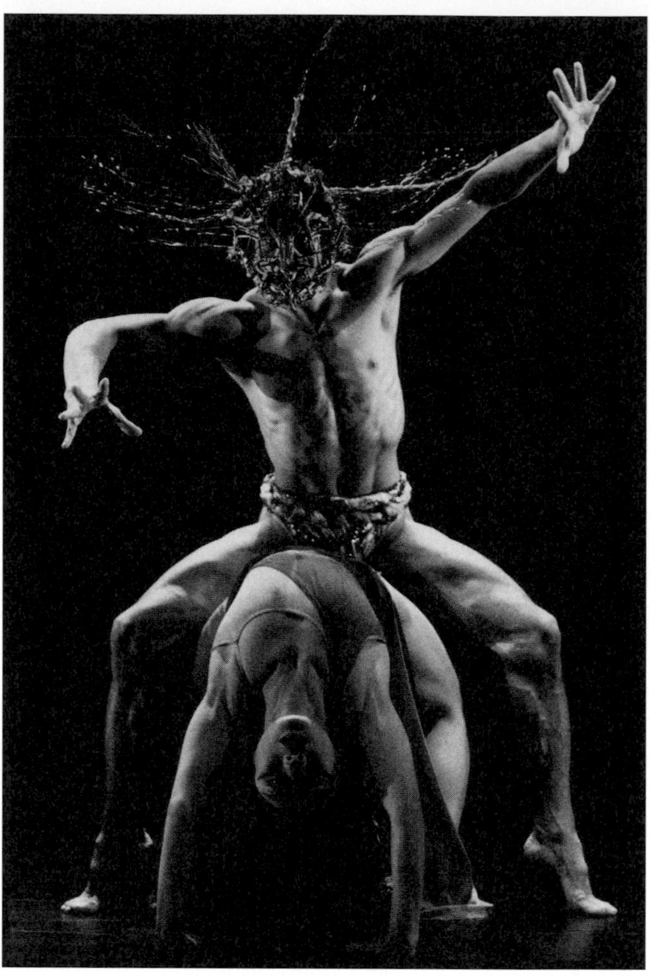

TAIWAN. A scene from the Cloud Gate Dance Theater's production of *Nine Songs,* chorographed by Lin Hwai-min. Pictured here are Lee Ching-chun as the Shaman and Deng Kei-fu as the Sun God in a 1993 performance at the National Theater, Taipei. (Photograph © 1993 by Deng Yu-lin; used by permission.)

the costumes is primarily red; costumes include blouses, pants, short skirts, long tails, belts, headpieces, and boots. Although "The Emperor Destroys the Formations" is a martial dance, the four dancers are not armed for the performance.

Theatrical Dance. Since the 1940s, ballet has become increasingly popular in Taiwan. Many children began studying ballet in private studios after regular school hours. Since the 1960s, ballet has become a required course in college dance departments. In the 1970s, small semiprofessional ballet troupes began making their appearance. Occasionally they have attempted creative works characterized and inspired by local events, but the general public prefers to attend the classical grand ballets, such as *Swan Lake*.

In Taiwan, modern dance started to develop along with ballet in the 1940s. For fifty years, however, these two dance genres have gone in different directions. Early local development was based on the theory and approaches to modern dance of Rudolf Laban and Mary Wigman. Thereafter, the approaches of Doris Humphrey, Martha Graham, and Jośe Limón were widely adopted by dance professionals in Taiwan. In the 1990s, because of the enlightened government policy, national support for dance groups has increased substantially. Moreover, with the cross-fertilization between Eastern and Western schools, the world of dance has begun flourishing. Dance education has become innovative and creative, with an emphasis placed on individual talent and development. A growing number of excellent dancers exist and their skill has earned them a glowing reputation.

Since the 1980s, numerous theaters have been built in Taiwan with the support of both local and national governments. This has resulted in more opportunities and sites for Taiwan's wide range of modern dance groups and choreographers, rich in personal expression and creativity. The most well-known dance companies in Taiwan are the Cloud Gate Dance Theater, the Henry Yu Dance Company, and the Neo-Classic Dance Company.

[*See also* China.]

BIBLIOGRAPHY

Ch'ên Yang. *Yüeh Shu* (1101). Reprinted, Kuang Chou, 1987.

Chu Ts'ai-yü. *Lü-Lü Ching–i* (1596). Reprinted by Shang-wu Yin-shu-kuan, Taipei, 1967.

Li Chih-tso. *P'an Kung Li yüeh shu* (1615). Reprinted by Wei-wên t'u-shu ch'u-pan-shê, Taipei, 1970.

Liu Feng-Shueh. "A Documented Historical and Analytical Study of Chinese Ritual and Ceremonial Dance from the Second Millennium BC to the Thirteenth Century." Ph.D. diss., Laban Centre for Movement and Dance at the University of London, Goldsmiths' College, 1986.

Picken, L. E. R. *Music from the T'ang Court*. 2 vols. Oxford, 1981. Reprinted, Cambridge, 1985.

Sung Shih (1345). In *Ssŭ-pu t'sung-k'an*. 128 vols. Reprinted, Shang-wu Yin-shu-kuan, Shanghai, 1936.

LIU FENG-SHUEH

TAJIKISTAN. Inhabited by Persians from the sixth century BCE onward, Tajikistan in Central Asia was subject throughout its history to a series of invasions by its neighbors—China on the east, Afghanistan on the south, Uzbekistan and Kyrgyzstan on the west and north—and by Arabs who in the seventh and eighth centuries converted the nation to Islam. Part of Tajikistan belonged to the emirate of Bukhara, under despotic Uzbek rule, until Russian suzerainty was imposed in the late nineteenth century; then Tajikistan was incorporated into Russian Turkistan. In 1924 Tajikistan became a Soviet autonomous republic within the Uzbek domain and in 1929 a constituent republic of the USSR. Tajikistan achieved independence in 1991 with the Soviet Union's dissolution.

After becoming a dominated region—by Islamic law, by tsarist repression, and later by Soviet conformism—cultural development in Tajikistan was circumscribed. The lives of women, in particular, were severely restricted: hidden from strangers under the *yashmak,* women were allowed to sing and dance only in the half of the home reserved for them; exception was made for harem dancers in wealthier households, who had been introduced by foreign conquerors. Despite the successive invasions of the country, Tajiki dance did manage to survive, so some traditions are known, but much was irretrievably lost.

Not until 1935 was the Tajiki musical theater founded. Teachers from Russia introduced regular classes in acting and classical dance. The first national musical, staged in 1939, was *Lola* (Tulip), choreographed by A. Islamova and Gafur Balamat-zade to music by Sergei Balasanian and S. Urbach. Conforming to Socialist Realism, it shows neighboring farmers who, having completed their plan of spring work, assemble for a traditional tulip festival. A competition of skill among singers, dancers, and jesters takes place on a lawn in front of a teahouse; modern social and round dances are also represented. The production thus combined contemporary motifs with traditional folk dance.

In 1940 the musical theater in the capital, Stalinabad (now Dushanbe), became an opera and ballet theater named after S. Aini, who had campaigned for progress in Tajikistan. The first national ballet, *The Two Roses,* was produced in 1941, choreographed by Kasyan Goleizovsky to music by Aleksandr Lensky. Set in the early years of Soviet Tajikistan, the story tells of two young girls who are so good and so beautiful that people call them roses. One is betrothed to an honorable man, but the other's fiancé is unwittingly involved with the *basmachis,* a group of counterrevolutionaries. Upon seeing them rob a rich landowner and try to run off with the two girls, the youth realizes the identity of his associates. Both fiancés help the border guards to unarm the gang and save the two roses. The opposing sides are characterized by differing musical and choreographic themes: "Rakcikamchin," a dance with whips, communicates the anger of the *basmachis;* the dances "Panj-gul" (Five Roses) and "Merzon" (Trembling) are the basis of the women's movement, and "Striking Eagles" the men's. The genre scenes include a bazaar, a holiday concluding with a dance on stilts, a dance with clay pots, and a performance of traveling comedians and mummers.

Balamat-zade was chief choreographer of the company in the 1940s and staged a number of ballet classics. He also created new works, including *Leili and Medzhnun* (1947, reproduced by Goleizovsky in 1964 for the Bolshoi Ballet) to music by Balasanian, which was based on an oriental legend; *Dilbar* (1954) was set to music by Lensky, an early Tajik attempt to express a modern theme in classical dance. In 1965 Balamat-zade founded the Lola Tajik Dance Company to stage works based on oriental folk dance; the company has toured abroad.

In the 1950s and 1960s a number of young Tajik ballet dancers graduated from the Vaganova Ballet School in Leningrad and returned to Dushanbe to join their native ballet company. Among them was Malika Sabirova, who created a number of important roles. Her former partner, Muzafar Burkhanov, directed the company in the 1980s. Carefully maintaining continuity with the past, the company preserves Tajiki traditions and adapts them to meet modern sensibilities.

[*See also the entry on Goleizovsky.*]

BIBLIOGRAPHY

Azimova, A. *Tantsevalnoe iskusstvo Tadzhikistana.* Stalinabad, 1957.

Nurdzhanov, N. K. *Tadzhikskii narodnyi teatr.* Moscow, 1956.

YURI P. TYURIN
Translated from Russian

TAKARAZUKA (Takarazuka Girls' Opera) is a Japanese all-female company that presents musical shows. Founded in 1914 by Kobayashi Ichizo, the troupe was one of the attractions at his amusement park at Takarazuka, a suburb between Osaka and Kobe. Kobayashi owned not only the park but also the connecting Hankyu Railway; his intention in forming Takarazuka was to increase attendance at the park and use of the railway.

At first the company presented only Japanese dance, but in the early 1930s, the repertory was strongly influenced by Parisian revues. Through Takarazuka, many French *chansons* of that period became popular in Japan. Modified versions of European operettas and *kabuki* dance dramas were also staged.

The stars of the company, especially those playing male roles, attracted many female admirers, ranging from junior high school girls to rich housewives. Popular stars received showers of expensive gifts. During World War II, this "Takarazuka fever" caused concern to the government, which tried to restrain it, with only partial success.

After the war, Takarazuka flourished again, now under the influence of the Broadway musical. Its repertory, both Western and Japanese, became more varied and opulent, and Broadway directors and *kabuki* actors were often invited to supervise productions.

The stars of the company always retire at an early age, because the girls' youth is one of the troupe's main attractions and because company policy forbids Takarazuka actresses to marry. Some former Takarazuka stars, such as Koshiji Fubuki, have gone on to careers as popular singers; others, like Awashima Chikage and Otowa Nobuko, have become successful movie actresses.

Takarazuka has an affiliated school that gives the girls a two-year education in Western and Japanese music, ballet, modern and jazz dance, and traditional Japanese dance and acting. The girls range in age from fifteen to eighteen, and the school accepts forty to fifty girls annually, chosen from about ten times that many applicants.

The Takarazuka company toured Europe in 1938, 1965, and 1975, the United States in 1939, 1959, and 1992, and Southeast Asia in 1973, always with great success.

BIBLIOGRAPHY

Doraisamy, Cyril. "That's Entertainment, Japanese Style." *Dance Australia* (June–July 1995): 54–57.

Hirai, Takane. "External Influences in the Transformation of Japanese Dance." In *Culture Embodied,* edited by Michael Moerman et al. Senri Ethnological Studies, no. 27. Osaka, 1990.

Japan Centre, International Theatre Institute. *Theatre in Japan 1994.* Tokyo, 1995.

Newman, Barbara. "Takarazuka." *The Dancing Times* (September 1994): 1195–1197.

Ortolani, Benito. *The Japanese Theatre: From Shamanistic Ritual to Contemporary Pluralism.* Rev. ed. Princeton, 1995.

Shoemaker, Barbara. "The Takarazuka Dance Theatre." *Dance Magazine* (September 1959): 40–43.

Tobias, Tobi. "Wishful Thinking." *New York Magazine* (30 November 1992).

Wechsler, Bert. "Takarazuka." *Attitude* 9 (Winter 1993): 27–28.

USUI KENJI

TALE OF THE STONE FLOWER, THE. *See* Stone Flower, The.

TALLCHIEF, MARIA (Elizabeth Marie Tall Chief; born 24 January 1925 in Fairfax, Oklahoma), American ballet dancer, teacher, and company director. Although Maria Tallchief spent several seasons with the Ballet Russe de Monte Carlo, where she was a protégée of Bronislava Nijinska, and pursued an international career for twenty-five years, she will be best remembered for her association with George Balanchine during the New York City Ballet's early years of greatness, when she was the young company's first true star. She lacked the long-limbed proportions favored by Balanchine, but she personified another kind of Balanchine ideal: she moved with blazing speed, energy, unmannered brilliance—what the critics called "brio." At the height of her career, critic Walter Terry wrote that she could "spin across the stage faster and more accurately than any ballerina I [have] ever seen [and] flash through allegro passages with such authority that one [has] the feeling a partner [is] not necessary."

Daughter of an Osage Indian father and a Scotch-Irish mother, Tallchief trained in Hollywood with Ernest Belcher (father of Marge Champion) and Nijinska, joining the Ballet Russe de Monte Carlo as a teenager in 1942. (Nijinska was then in residence as guest choreographer.) At the age of eighteen, Tallchief appeared in Nijinska's *Chopin Concerto*, a performance that caused *New York Times* critic John Martin to refer to her as possible "ballerina material," with a "lovely simplicity of style and ease which certainly look hard to spoil." A year later she met Balanchine, who cast her as Alexandra Danilova's understudy in "Anitra's Dance" from *Song of Norway* and changed her life. With Ballet Russe, she performed solos in Balanchine's *Danses Concertantes*, *Ballet Imperial*, *Mozartiana*, and *Raymonda* and leading roles of the Coquette in *The Night Shadow* and the Fairy in *Le Baiser de la Feé* as well as roles in numerous other ballets in the repertory (including all the old chestnuts, such as *Schéhérazade* and *Gaîté Parisienne*).

At this time, in 1945, dance critic Edwin Denby noted her "thrilling power of momentum." In 1947, she became the first American since Augusta Maywood a century before to dance at the Paris Opera, where Balanchine staged *Serenade*, *Le Baiser de la Feé*, and *Apollo*. With Balanchine's tiny group called Ballet Society (1946–1948), Tallchief performed as ballerina in *Symphony in C*, *Symphonie Concertante*, and, perhaps most important, as Eurydice in *Orpheus*, the work that led to the formation of the New York City Ballet.

It was Balanchine's *Firebird* (1949) that established the reputation of the new company—and of its ballerina Maria Tallchief. Lillian Moore wrote that Tallchief danced the Firebird "like a flame." Walter Terry found her feats "breathtaking. In off-center spins, in sudden lifts, [her movements] seem to defy gravity, and in their alert, graceful, and sharp explorations of space, they define the characteristics of a magical, air-borne creature." It was at this time that she was referred to (not entirely accurately) as the first "homegrown" ballerina—an American of international stature who had neither trained in Europe nor made her reputation there.

For the next seven years or so, Tallchief was Balanchine's first dancer, creating roles in all of his virtuoso pieces, including *Sylvia: Pas de Deux* (1950), *Swan Lake* (1951), *The Nutcracker* (1954), *Pas de Dix* (1955), and *Allegro Brillante* (1956), among many others. Her frequent partner was André Eglevsky. Of *Pas de Dix*, Doris Hering wrote (in a comment typical of the time)—that "there was something almost crystalline in the way she moved through space—turning, tossing her head, arching her back . . . [with] a tantalizing combination of fire and detachment." Commenting on the art and philosophy of Balanchine, to whom she was married (1946–1950), and who was her greatest artistic influence, Tallchief said, "It's a way of timing, of attacking, of not holding back, of giving every ounce of your energy. You're never comfortable. To be comfortable and careful—that's not dancing."

Nevertheless, Tallchief's ethereal rendering of the Sylph in *Scotch Symphony* (1952) revealed that not everything about her art was hard brilliance. Dancing a version of *The Dying Swan* as Anna Pavlova in the Hollywood movie *The Million Dollar Mermaid* (1952), she displayed remarkable softness and a particularly graceful *port de bras*. These qualities were also notable in her portrayal of Ellida in Birgit Cullberg's *Lady from the Sea*, which she danced with American Ballet Theatre in the early 1960s.

TALLCHIEF. In 1950, Tallchief and André Eglevsky danced together for the first time, in Balanchine's *Sylvia: Pas de Deux*, a virtuoso showpiece. They subsequently performed it on stages all over the world. (Photograph from the archives at Jacob's Pillow, Becket, Massachusetts. Choreography by George Balanchine © The George Balanchine Trust.)

By the end of the 1950s, Tallchief's important years with Balanchine were over, although she remained with his company intermittently until 1965. Throughout her career, she made numerous television appearances and frequently danced as a guest artist with various companies, performing dramatic roles as well as virtuoso classics. With American Ballet Theatre (1960–1962), for example, her repertory included the title role in Cullberg's *Miss Julie* and Caroline in Antony Tudor's *Jardin aux Lilas* as well as Harald Lander's *Études* and the Black Swan pas de deux. At this time she renewed a partnership with Erik Bruhn. During a season with Ballet Russe de Monte Carlo (1954/55), she was reportedly the world's most highly paid ballerina. She appeared as well with Ruth Page's Chicago Opera Ballet, the Chicago Lyric Opera, the San Francisco Ballet, and the Royal Danish Ballet. One of her last roles was that of Cinderella in Peter van Dyk's production for the Hamburg State Opera in 1966. She retired from the stage soon thereafter.

In 1974, Tallchief established the Ballet School of the Lyric Opera in Chicago, and by 1980 she was able to form an independent school (affiliated with Balanchine's School of American Ballet in New York) and to found a company. The Chicago City Ballet, with Tallchief as artistic director, Paul Mejia as resident choreographer, and Suzanne Farrell and Balanchine as artistic advisers, produced its first season in June 1981. One of its principal successes was Mejia's version of *Cinderella* with Farrell, dancing as guest artist, in the title role. Although she was a fine teacher, Tallchief found herself unsuited to the role of artistic director. She severed her association with the company in 1987.

Over the years, many awards and honors have been bestowed upon Tallchief. Among the earliest was an achievement award presented by the Women's National Press Club in 1953, the same year in which she was elected an honorary princess of the Osage tribe. This was followed by a *Dance Magazine* Award in 1960 and the Capezio Award in 1965. In 1996 she was inducted into the National Women's Hall of Fame and was a recipient of a Kennedy Center Honor, awarded in recognition of a lifetime contribution to the nation's culture.

[*See also* New York City Ballet *and the entry on Balanchine.*]

BIBLIOGRAPHY

Anderson, Jack. *The One and Only: The Ballet Russe de Monte Carlo.* New York, 1981.

Cargill, Mary. "Talking with Maria Tallchief." *Dance View* 13 (Autumn 1995): 3–5.

Chujoy, Anatole. *The New York City Ballet.* New York, 1953.

Gruen, John. "Tallchief and the Chicago City Ballet." *Dance Magazine* (December 1984): HC24–HC27. Interview with Tallchief.

Hardy, Camille. "Chicago's Soaring City Ballet." *Dance Magazine* (April 1982): 70–76.

Hardy, Camille. "Tallchief on Balanchine: Passing on the Magic." *American Arts* (May 1984).

Livingston, Lili Cockerille. *American Indian Ballerinas.* Norman, Okla., 1997.

Maynard, Olga. *Bird of Fire: The Story of Maria Tallchief.* New York: 1961.

Reynolds, Nancy. *Repertory in Review: Forty Years of the New York City Ballet.* New York, 1977.

Tallchief, Maria, with Larry Kaplan. *Maria Tallchief: America's Prima Ballerina.* New York, 1997.

Taper, Bernard. *Balanchine: A Biography.* New rev. ed. Berkeley, 1996.

Tracy, Robert, and Sharon DeLano. *Balanchine's Ballerinas: Conversations with the Muses.* New York: 1983.

ARCHIVES. The Dance Collection of the New York Public Library for the Performing Arts has extensive holdings of still photographs of Tallchief and of materials pertinent to her performing career. The Barzel Collection, Newberry Library, Chicago, contains the archives of the Chicago City Ballet.

FILMS AND VIDEOTAPES. The Dance Collection of the New York Public Library for the Performing Arts has a large collection of videotapes showing, in whole or in part, Tallchief's performances in *The Firebird, Harlequinade Pas de Deux, Pas de Dix, Scotch Symphony, Symphony in C* (first movement), *Allegro Brillante, Don Quixote* (pas de deux), *Flower Festival in Genzano* (pas de deux), *The Nutcracker,* and *Sylvia: Pas de Deux,* among others. Anne Belle's *Dancing for Mr. B: Six Balanchine Ballerinas* (Seahorse Films, 1996), which contains a lengthy segment on Tallchief, is available commercially from Nonesuch/WarnerVision Entertainment. The George Balanchine Foundation Interpreters Archive, distributed to dance reference collections, includes several tapes of Tallchief coaching her important Balanchine roles.

NANCY REYNOLDS

TAMASHA. The popular musical theater of Maharashtra state, west-central India, tamasha is a kind of musical comedy with many racy songs and dances. The themes vary; they may deal with chiefs and kings, quarrels over land, domestic tales of henpecked husbands, historical romances, or stories from mythology.

Although today most of the performers in tamasha come from the lower-caste Mahar, Manj, and Kolhati communities, in the past a number of high-caste brahmans were celebrated as lyricists and composers of tamasha songs. Some of these brahman composers even formed their own tamasha troupes, although this usually resulted in their being ostracized by their families.

The history of tamasha (spelled *tamāśa* in Indian languages, *tamasha* in English) begins in the late seventeenth or early eighteenth century. It flourished for the next hundred years or so, but the takeover of the Maratha state by the British in the early nineteenth century put an end to court patronage of tamasha. Over the years, its popularity has waxed and waned. Today there are at least eight hundred established troupes, performing on tour in the countryside as well as in the cities. The troupes employ an estimated forty thousand actors, dancers, and musicians who make their living in this regional folk theater.

BIBLIOGRAPHY

Abrams, Tevia. "Tamasha: People's Theatre of Maharashtra State, India." Ph.D. diss., Michigan State University, 1974.

Gargi, Balwant. *Folk Theater of India.* Seattle, 1966.

Sawant, K. R. *Tamasha: A Unique Folk Theatre of Maharashtra.* Bombay, 1983.

Tendulkar, Vijay, and Kumud Mehta. "Dadu Indurikar." *Quarterly Journal of the National Centre for the Performing Arts* 2 (December 1973): 21–40.

CLIFFORD REIS JONES

TAMBOURIN. A lively duple-meter dance of Provençal origin, the *tambourin* was frequently used on the French stage during the eighteenth century. The *tambourin* was traditionally accompanied by a single musician playing pipe and tabor, or in French, the *galoubet* and *tambourin,* the large, double-headed drum that gave the dance its name. In orchestral settings of the dance, the drumbeats are imitated by the rhythmic repetition of a single bass note, thus providing a static but accented harmonic foundation over which the lively melody moves. The time signature of the *tambourin* is usually 2/4, and it was always described in the eighteenth century as quick and gay. Johann Joachim Quantz wrote in 1752 that the *tambourin* is to be played a little faster than the *bourrée* and *rigaudon,* thus making it one of the fastest of the French dances.

The *tambourin* made its first appearance on the French stage in Marin Marais's opera *Alcione* (1706). It reached the height of its success in the ballets and operas of Jean-Philippe Rameau, written for the Paris Opera between 1733 and 1760, in which the *tambourin* was one of the most frequently occurring dance types. Most of Rameau's *tambourins* come in pairs, one in a major key followed by one in a minor key, with a subsequent repetition of the first *tambourin.* Some of the *tambourins* were danced by Provençal characters, as in the first *entrée* ("Le Turc Généreux") in *Les Indes Galantes,* but most have no discernible connection with the regional origins of the dance. Rameau frequently used a pair of *tambourins* to end an act, which suggests that such *tambourins* were group dances. The scant stage indications in the scores and livrets, however, reveal little about the size or character of the performing forces for the dances and nothing at all about the choreography.

The only *tambourin* in Feuillet notation is a couple dance by Guillaume-Louis Pecour that appeared in the *Recüeil de danses pour l'année 1719,* one of a series of social-dance collections. It is a typical French couple dance with symmetrical figures based on the social dance step vocabulary and probably has a limited relationship with the stage *tambourins* of the following decades.

BIBLIOGRAPHY

Blades, James. "Tambourin. II (de Provence)." In *The New Grove Dictionary of Music and Musicians.* London, 1980.

Little, Meredith Ellis. "Tambourin. I." In *The New Grove Dictionary of Music and Musicians.* London, 1980.

Little, Meredith Ellis, and Carol G. Marsh. *La Danse Noble: An Inventory of Dances and Sources.* Williamstown, Mass., 1992.

Quantz, Johann Joachim. *On Playing the Flute* (1752). Translated by Edward R. Reilly. London, 1966.

Seefrid, Gisela. *Die Airs de danse in den Bühnenwerken von Jean-Philippe Rameau.* Wiesbaden, 1969.

REBECCA HARRIS-WARRICK

TAMIRIS, HELEN (Helen Becker; born 23 April 1903 in New York City, died 4 August 1966 in New York City), American dancer, choreographer, teacher, and theater director. During the late 1920s through the 1930s, Tamiris participated in the origin and development of the concert dance form of modern dance in the United States. Then, through the 1940s and 1950s, she solidified its place in the musical theater of New York's Broadway.

Trained in Italian ballet technique at the Metropolitan Opera, Russian ballet technique at Michel Fokine's studio, and natural dancing at an Isadora Duncan studio, Tamiris became a member of the corps of the Metropolitan Opera Ballet, a leading soloist in the Bracale Opera Company in a tour of South America, a specialty dancer in nightclubs and revues and in the stage shows of movie houses, and a featured dancer in the 1924–1925 Music Box Revue. Taking the name of "Ruthless Queen" Tamiris, and rejecting mimed stories, theatricality, and technical tricks, she turned to concert works by presenting a solo recital on 9 October 1927 at the Little Theater in New York (within a year of Martha Graham), with Louis Horst at the piano. "Dancing is simply movement with a personal conception of rhythm," she declared in a program note.

Tamiris created twenty-seven solo dances in two years and presented them in seven concerts—four in New York and three in Europe (Paris, Berlin, and the Salzburg Festival of 1938): a reflection of urban life in *Dance of the City* (1929) with siren accompaniment; the aura of Ernest Hemingway in *Impressions of the Bull Ring* (1927) with its flashing colors; a foreshadowing of concert jazz dance in *1927* (1927) to Gershwin rhythms; a summary of the 1920s "Champion of . . ." in *Prize Fight Studies* (1928) with its opening swagger performed to the beating of piano strings; a glimpse of Freud in *Subconscious* (1927), which included nudity; and a statement on sex in *Twentieth Century Bacchante* (1928), with its frank voluptuousness. Tamiris attacked affected Madonna interpretations in *Hypocrisy* (1928); she performed *The Queen Walks in the Garden* (1927) in silence; the spirit

TAMIRIS. A studio portrait of Tamiris in costume for one of her dances set to Negro spirituals. (Photograph from the Dance Collection, New York Public Library for the Performing Arts.)

of the Negro spiritual became her métier in *Nobody Knows de Trouble I See* (1928), *Swing Low, Sweet Chariot* (1929), and *Joshua Fit de Battle ob Jericho* (1928); and she sounded the call of the next decade in *Revolutionary March* (1929), using three kettle drums resounding alone and a flaglike costume: these were the awakenings of the social Tamiris. She was known as the "Harlem savage" who viewed life as conflict and said so verbally, physically, and artistically.

Tamiris was a leader in the development of the Dance Repertory Theatre of 1930 and 1931, during which the emerging modern dancers—Martha Graham, Doris Humphrey, and Charles Weidman (Agnes de Mille appeared in 1931)—banded together for financial reasons to give a series of their individual works at a common time in a common theater with a single staff. All did group works, Tamiris continuing to base hers on life as conflict. Accompaniment grew out of movement: in *Triangle Dance* (1930), instruments were carried; *Gris-Gris Ceremonial* (1932) used gourd rattles; and elbows beating on drums characterized *Mourning Ceremonial* (1931).

By 1934 Tamiris and Her Group was one of those forging the concert art called modern dance in *Walt Whitman Suite* (1934), a statement of yearning and being; *Toward the Light* (1934), a proccupation with freedom and existence; *Composition for Group* (1932), a sarcastic deriding of effeminacy and decadence; *Cycle of Unrest* (1935), a writhing manifesto of conflict and optimism; *Harvest 1935* (1935), a revolting denunciation of war; and *Momentum* (1936), a dramatic encounter between "haves" and "have-nots." The addition of *Crucifixion* (1931), *Git on Board, Lil Chillen* (1932), and *Go Down, Moses* (1932) completed what became her signature work, a suite of solos based on Negro spirituals, which, while expressing her sympathy for the oppressed human being, also reflected her own uninhibited nature and extemporaneous air and her love of the free flow of life, the impromptu, and the unpremeditated.

The concert dance *Mass Study* (1935) and the theater dances in the play *Gold Eagle Guy* (1934) were two results of Tamiris's affiliation with Group Theater, which developed into a reciprocal arrangement whereby she taught movement classes to its actors and the theater gave acting classes to her dancers. Lee Strasberg's adaptation of the Konstantin Stanislavsky method helped affirm and clarify Tamiris's approach to theatrical performance, direction, and choreography. It confirmed her search for specific human motivations for movement rather than reaching for abstract artistic applications.

Tamiris developed no characteristic technique that she could hand down to her followers. For her, no one way of moving could be true for everyone and for every moment. Instead she brought out the personal and existential style of each of her students, as she did for herself. Her own style became as immediate as her life itself—vital, warm, lusty, and powerful. She had sought and found movement, essentially primitive, that had the torso as its center, the face and limbs as the fringes of outflow. This movement grew out of her lusty affirmation of immediate life, a childlike wonder about its possibilities, and an innate respect for its endemic form. Thus Tamiris's style was found in her dance's dynamic actualities—the physicality of its movement, the forcefulness of its moment, and the clarity of its form.

John Martin described her impact in a review in the *New York Times:*

> What a really thrilling dancer she is when she breaks free from the moorings of sobriety and lets what a European critic once called 'the magnificent lust of motion' take possession of her! . . . there is a vitality, a warmth about her that relates her movements inevitably to human living. . . . What we need from her is more and more of that affirmation upon which she has laid so much stress; and we need it not only because it is part and parcel of her art but also, since she is interested in 'social content' in her dancing, because there is probably nothing anywhere to be found in the way of content that is more strongly social. (15 November 1936)

By contrast, critical reaction to Tamiris's choreography during the 1930s was limited and insular. Neither esoteric enough to be accepted by reviewers for the Louis Horst journal, *Dance Observer,* nor sufficiently submerged in social protest to be acceptable to the *Daily Worker,* her works adhered to no exterior law. Whether making solo dances for herself in the 1920s, ensemble work for Tamiris and Her Group or mass dances for the Federal Theater in the 1930s, or chorus dances for Broadway musical theater after World War II, she worked from the premise that the here and now determined her art. Because of her ephemeral approach, Tamiris left no technique *per se* and few dances. A molder of the art form of modern dance as much as Martha Graham, Charles Weidman, Doris Humphrey, or Hanya Holm, she was left out of the Bennington Group, a fact that has caused parochial historians to discount her contribution to the development of that art form.

Tamiris was the one who was driven to use the new form to shape the consciousness of people, not merely to make artistic statements for a narrow coterie. Thus for much of the 1930s she served as the catalyst for dancers in the Works Progress Administration (WPA) Federal Art Project. It was she who had the sense of mission required for advancing the welfare of dancers as individuals and the expansion of modern dance as art. Groups she supported included the Concert Dancers' League (fighting sabbath laws), the Dancers' Emergency Association (providing financial support), and the New Dance League (advocating social action), and she formulated and chaired the American Dance Association, which was successful in setting up the Federal Dance Project. In 1936 the project sponsored Tamiris's *Salut au Monde,* five episodes depicting race struggle, and in 1937 the double bill of Weidman's *Candide* and Tamiris's *How Long, Brethren?*. With the last, Tamiris achieved "status." Based on seven Negro protest songs and sung by a Negro chorus, its choreography was awarded *Dance Magazine's* first award for outstanding group choreography.

Financial cuts and infighting gradually hamstrung the project by 1939 but not before Tamiris had produced *Trojan Incident* (1938), a short play about the subjugation of Troy (set off by dancers and onstage singers), and *Adelante* (1939), a seventy-five minute, all-dance work on Loyalist Spain, subsequently recognized by Margaret Lloyd as the first of the big modern ballets.

From 1939 to 1944, Tamiris (who now added the name of Helen to her single name) found herself without a company (hers had disappeared into the Federal Dance Project; the other modern dancers had kept theirs distinct) and with a politically suspect reputation. Unions came in, ballet flourished, the war spurred the economy. After her work in the Federal Theatre Project, which drew masses of people to modern dance, Tamiris turned to Broadway as the best place to draw similar crowds to this new art. Between 1943 and 1957 she choreographed modern dances in eighteen musical comedies, six of which had long runs. Rather than using chorus lines or technical displays to advance the script or to enhance the music, Tamiris integrated dance into such theater pieces as *Up in Central Park* (1945) with its Currier and Ives "Skating Ballet"; *Annie Get Your Gun* (1946), with Daniel Nagrin in its

TAMIRIS. *How Long, Brethren?* (1937), with Helen Tamiris and Her Group. Produced by the Federal Dance Project as part of a double bill with Charles Weidman's *Candide,* Tamiris's suite of dances to Negro songs of protest had a long, successful run on Broadway. Although the work dealt with the plight of African Americans, it was originally performed by an all-white cast of women. In the early 1990s, the African-American choreographer Dianne McIntyre reconstructed this work for several U.S. student groups. (Photograph from the Dance Collection, New York Public Library for the Performing Arts.)

"Wild Horse Ceremonial Dance"; and *Inside U.S.A.* (1948), with Valerie Bettis in "Tiger Lily" and "Haunted House." *By the Beautiful Sea* (1954) had an underwater ballet, and *Plain and Fancy* starred Nagrin in the poignant "By Lantern Light." Instinctively, Tamiris integrated dance action with acting, speech, song, and stage pictorialism. All elements were equally fused for the whole that was musical theater in the 1940s and 1950s.

Tamiris's choreography for *Touch and Go* (1949) won the Antoinette Perry ("Tony") Award for the best choreography of the season. *Up in Central Park* had a national tour in 1946–1947 and then toured Europe after World War II; in 1948 it became a motion picture (Universal International) and included her dances. The string of Broadway performances of *Annie Get Your Gun*—1,147—was extended in 1947 to a London production as well as a U.S. tour in 1947–1948. The 1954 production *Fanny* also had a long run on Broadway and a U.S. tour in 1956–1957. Other musicals choreographed by Tamiris included *Stovepipe Hat* (1944); a new production of *Show Boat* (1946) with white and black member choruses; *Park Avenue* (1946); *The Great Campaign* (1947), which was staged by the Experimental Theater; *Great to Be Alive* (1950); *Bless You All* (1950); *Flahooley* (1951); *Carnival in Flanders* (1953); and, for Utah's centennial, *The Promised Valley* (1947).

Although she did not always have a studio, Tamiris continually taught not only dance but also body movement for actors and directors, including stage movement for directors at the American Dance Festival in Connecticut (1960), the Perry-Mansfield School of Theater and Dance in Colorado (1956–1958), the Tamiris-Nagrin Dance Workshop, which was based in New York and had summers in Maine (1957–1964), and C. W. Post College, on Long Island (summer 1962, 1963). Tamiris had returned to concert modern dance in 1957. The Tamiris-Nagrin Dance Company, formed with her husband, Daniel Nagrin (married 1946, separated 1964), who was co-director and leading dancer, performed intermittently between 1960 and 1964.

[*See also* Federal Dance Project *and the entries on the principal figures mentioned herein.*]

BIBLIOGRAPHY

Lloyd, Margaret. *The Borzoi Book of Modern Dance.* New York, 1949.

Markoff, Luba. "Dance in the Political Arena: The Federal Dance Project and Helen Tamiris." Master's thesis, San Jose State University, 1992.

McDonagh, Don, ed. *The Complete Guide to Modern Dance.* New York, 1976.

Nagrin, Daniel. "Helen Tamiris and the Dance Historians." In *Proceedings of the Twelfth Annual Conference, Society of Dance History Scholars, Arizona State University, 17–19 February 1989,* compiled by Christena L. Schlundt. Riverside, Calif., 1989.

Prickett, Stacey. "'The People': Issues of Identity within the Revolutionary Dance." *Studies in Dance History* 5 (Spring 1994): 14–22.

Schlundt, Christena L. "Tamiris: A Chronicle of Her Dance Career, 1927–1955." New York, 1972. Reprinted in *Studies in Dance History* 1 (Fall–Winter 1989): 65–154.

Sorell, Walter, ed. *The Dance Has Many Faces.* New York, 1951.

Tamiris, Helen. "Tamiris in Her Own Voice: Draft of an Autobiography." Edited by Daniel Nagrin. *Studies in Dance History* 1 (Fall–Winter 1989): 1–64.

Tish, Pauline. "Remembering Helen Tamiris." *Dance Chronicle* 17.3 (1994): 327–360.

FILM AND VIDEOTAPE. *Helen Tamiris in Her Negro Spirituals* (1959). "Trailblazers of Modern Dance" (1977).

CHRISTENA L. SCHLUNDT

TANAKA MIN (born 10 March 1945 in Hachioji-shi, Tokyo Prefecture, Japan), *butō* performer and choreographer. While at Tokyo Kyoiku University, which he had entered as a basketball player, Tanaka became a dancer. He studied ballet and modern dance, beginning his career as a professional modern dancer in 1966. Among his early works were *Dance-State Series* (1975), *Drive Series* (1977), and *Hyper-Dance* (1977).

In 1978, Tanaka created the Body Weather Laboratory, a sequenced series of exercises that he and others who have learned the technique teach in workshops. In 1981, he founded the Maijuku company in Tokyo, and in 1985 he established the Body Weather Farm in Yamanashi, a rural area several hours' drive from Tokyo. Tanaka has sought inspiration for his choreography in farming and communal life: he operates Body Weather as an organic farm; he established an annual festival, the Art Camp Hakushu, at the farm in 1988; and, every summer, he holds Body Weather Laboratory workshops there.

Tanaka first turned to *butō* in 1984, collaborating with Hijikata Tatsumi on the piece *Ren-ai Butō -ha* (Love *Butō*). Tanaka's later works have included two commissioned by the Paris Opéra-Comique: *Peut-on Danser une Paysage?* (Can We Dance a Landscape?, 1989), in collaboration with Dutch visual artist Karel Appel, and *Le Sacre du Printemps* (The Rite of Spring, 1990), in collaboration with sculptor Richard Serra; it has also commissioned *Tree* (1990). Tanaka has performed numerous times in the United States.

BIBLIOGRAPHY

Durland, Steven. "Weekend in the Country." *High Performance* (Summer 1990): 46–49.

"Min Tanaka at Bennington College." *Contact Quarterly* 19 (Summer-Fall 1994): 35–40.

Rouland, Katy. "Entretiens avec Min Tanaka." *Empreintes,* no. 6 (February 1984): 34–41.

Schmidt, Jochen. "The Individual as Microcosm." *Ballett International* 12 (November 1989): 18–21.

Stein, Bonnie Sue. "Min Tanaka: Farmer/Dancer or Dancer/Farmer." *Drama Review* 30 (Summer 1986): 142–151.

Tanaka Min. *Bodyprint.* Tokyo, 1981.

HASEGAWA ROKU
Translated from Japanese

TANGO. A complex popular genre in South America, tango involves dance, music, poetry, song, gesture, and narrative as well as philosophy and ethical values. During the late nineteenth century it was a vehicle that accelerated social integration in the Río de la Plata region of South America, weaving aesthetic and other cultural features from African, American, and European peoples. *Gauchos, criollos* (Creoles), European immigrants, and African Argentines participated in the formation of the genre.

Origins and Development of the Tango. The word *tango* is of Bantu origin (from central and southern Africa), meaning "drums" or "a social gathering with dances." Since the late 1700s, "tango" has referred to many different forms of dance and music (in chronological order): *tango de negros, tango americano* or *habanera, tango andaluz* or *tango español, tango criollo, tango rioplatense,* and *tango argentino.* The candombes, tambos, and tangos danced by Africans and African Argentines at the end of the eighteenth and the beginning of the nineteenth centuries were prohibited for "Christianizing" reasons by the viceroy and by the *cabildo* (town council). All these dances had no physical contact. The tango, as a dance of embrace, was born between 1860 and 1890 in the cities of Buenos Aires, Argentina, and Montevideo, Uruguay.

During this period when the tango crystallized as urban dance in the region of the Río de la Plata, Argentina was undergoing profound changes in the makeup of its population. In 1778 African Argentines constituted 29.7 percent of the population of Buenos Aires; by 1887 that percentage had declined to 1.8 percent, as African Argentines were displaced by European immigrants. Between 1821 and 1932 Argentina was second only to the United States among nations receiving immigrants (Canada was third). These immigrants came from all over Europe as well as from Lebanon and Syria, with the largest number coming from Italy and the second largest from Spain. In 1879, General Julio A. Roca's settlement program, the Conquest of the Desert, which attained land for cattle and agriculture, also contributed to the transformation of the Argentine population—it decimated a majority of the Araucanians, a native people. In 1880, the port city of Buenos Aires was named the federal capital of the Argentine Republic—*la Gran Aldea* would soon be a metropolis.

Until the middle of the nineteenth century, the European dances of the Río de la Plata region were the minuet, gavotte, contredance, and quadrille. From the 1840s until the end of the century, the waltz, polka, mazurka, and schottische were popular. In the 1830s African-Argentine dances and songs had begun to be imitated on stage. Between 1856 and 1865 the *compañías españolas de zarzuelas* performed *bailes de negros* and sang *tangos americanos* or Cuban *habaneras.* Minstrel shows, such as Christy's Minstrels (1869) from the United States, also imitated

TANGO. By 1920, from *barrio* to elegant cafe, the tango was danced at every level of Argentine society. On 6 September 1936 people danced it in the streets to celebrate the four hundreth anniversary of the founding of Buenos Aires. (Photograph from the Archivo General de la Nación, Buenos Aires.)

African dances and songs when they performed in Buenos Aires. At the same time, in their quest for social mobility, African Argentines began to imitate Europeans and incorporated the mazurka, the polka, and the waltz into their dances. The dance halls *(academias de baile)* provided the meeting place for the *candombe, habanera,* polka, mazurka, *milonga* (a form of improvised song to which choreography was added about 1860, it was first called the *habanera con cortes y quebradas* and later *baile con corte*), and the tango. The African-Argentine dances provided the movement and cadence of the tango and inspired the curves that form the tango poses. The figure called *ocho* ("eight") in the tango comes from the *candombe,* which is composed of a succession of eights drawn on the floor. The *ocho* is the base for all movements in the tango, as all other steps pass through it. The typical male dancers in the *academias de baile, compadres* (*gauchos* of the Argentine pampas who moved to the city but maintained their traditional attire and independent attitude), and *compadritos* (young men from the outskirts of Buenos Aires who imitated the attitudes of the *compadres*) mimicked and mocked the leg movements of the African Argentines.

Musical accompaniment to the *milonga tango* was played in 2/4 time on violin, guitar, and flute, with the harp sometimes replacing the guitar. Later the mandolin, the clarinet, the piano, and sometimes the accordion were added; at the turn of the century the *bandoneón* (large button accordion) was incorporated. In the 1910s the double bass, the violoncello, and the viola joined what had become a small orchestra. The tango, until then strongly influenced by the *habanera* and the *milonga,* began to assimilate Italian influences, as evidenced by the changing pathos of the music as well as the remarkable number of Italian surnames among the musicians.

TANGO. A popular aspect of feature films from the 1930s and 1940s, the tango was danced in RKO's *Flying Down to Rio* (1933) and Fox's *Down Argentine Way* (1940). In this photogaph, tango dancer and actor Elías Alippi holds an unidentified partner in the Argentine film *Así Es la Vida* (1939). (Photograph courtesy of María Susana Azzi.)

The tango was danced in urban neighborhoods and in the *arrabales* ("suburbs"). It was primarily a dance of the brothels but also was danced on *patios* of the *conventillos* ("tenements"), where Italian, Spanish, Polish, and other immigrants shared crowded living quarters. Until this point, the tango was considered to be a marginal, immoral, and indecent dance and as such was rejected by the *porteño*—the Buenos Aires high society. Nevertheless, the *niños bien* (sons of well-to-do families) frequented the brothels, where they danced and often fought with the *compadritos.*

In 1907 the tango made its way to Paris and from there spread to other European capitals as well as to New York City. In the aristocratic ballrooms, the tango became "decent" and stylized, leaving aside the *cortes y quebradas* (suggestive contorsions followed by a pause). Upon its return to Buenos Aires, the upper class took up this new, "clean" tango. The middle class of Buenos Aires also modified the tango in the dance halls of the Italian and Spanish associations, where they danced the *tango liscio* or *liso.* The dance no longer had complicated leg movements, but the dancers retained the stamp of elegance and the walk, and they executed the rhythm and tempo with exactitude. This smooth *tango de salón* replaced the tango *canyengue* and the *tango orillero* (both styles full of exaggerated steps and adornments), which could not be accommodated in crowded dance halls. In exhibitions, where there was more space, dancers continued to use more complicated movements, performing what was then called the *tango fantasía.* In the 1920s, the tango was as popular in the heart of the city as it was in the *barrios* ("neighborhoods"), although the styles remained distinct. In the city center, the dance was stylized; in the *barrios,* dancers continued to adorn it with curves. When the great internal migration of the 1940s brought thousands of people from the Argentine provinces to the capital city of Buenos Aires, the tango underwent another transformation. In the 1950s, 1960s, and 1970s, however, the popularity of the tango declined significantly.

The Dance. The tango is a dance of embrace, meaning that the woman dances in the man's arms (the embrace is borrowed from the waltz). Although the man is the engine that generates the movement—he leads—the work of the dance is shared equally by the man and the woman. Always moving counterclockwise, the man walks the tango, indicating the figures and the poses by gently pressing his right hand against the woman's back. With an attitude that is creative and active rather than passive or submissive, the woman intuits the movements her partner desires. She plays and adorns with her feet and must know how to turn and twirl. If the male dancer does not walk the tango, he does not dance it. If he only makes figures, he cannot pause, which is when the woman plays. If the man's role is more difficult because he leads, the woman must be a good solo dancer, to capture the moment in movement but bridle it when tempering is needed. The man proposes, and the woman offers counterproposals. The posture, the embrace, and the ability to place one's foot "just so" defines the good dancer. When danced slowly, simply, and elegantly, "the tango," as Jorge Luis Borges has written, "is a way of walking."

The tango is a dance with a non-rigid structure that developed through trial and error; it is continually transformed through improvisation and is passed on from generation to generation. Improvisation has come to lie in the order of the steps and figures and not in the conceptualization of the dance itself, as the movements have become substantially standardized. For example, the tango can open with a figure *ocho* forward or backward. Some tangos inspire the dancers to adorn it, others to just walk it; there are sad and joyful tangos. The dancer or choreographer creates the structures from which to improvise the steps and figures: *ocho, boleo, sentada, quebrada.* Dancing slowly is very difficult because the dancer has to feel the motion, cadence, and pauses; the movement is not continuous. The woman feels the man mark the movement according to what he feels; he transmits messages, she receives and interprets them. When danced smoothly, the tango is poetic. The good dancer has the capacity to arouse emotions in his or her partner and in an audience. Among the principal male dancers of the tango have been Casimiro Aín ("El Vasco"), José Ovidio Bianquet ("El Cachafaz"), Carlos Alberto Estévez ("Petróleo"), Ramón Ribera ("Fino"), Juan Carlos Copes, Jorge Orcaizaguirre ("Virulazo"), Pepito Avellaneda (José Domingo Monteleone), Antonio Todaro, and Miguel Angel Zotto. The principal female dancers have been Edith Peggy, Olga San Juan, Carmencita Calderón, María Nieves, Elvira Santamaría, and Milena Plebs.

The tango is different when it is danced in a dance hall than when it is performed onstage. In a dance hall (*milonga*) the man dances with a variety of partners and the woman dances with various men; there is no choreography, only improvisation. The dancers' intuitions must be keen. Each dancer marks and feels the tango distinctly. The woman adapts her body to what her partner tells her with his marks. The man guides, the woman accompanies. The woman can adorn this dance with wantonness, sentimentality, or other emotions—or, she can follow closely what the man feels. The *milonguero* is an artist produced by "authentic" conditions in the *milongas.* Onstage, professional tango partners do a gymnastic and acrobatic dance. The movements are choreographed, not improvised, richly adorned, and exaggerated—otherwise it becomes visually dull. Onstage stylization derives from the tango developed in Paris. Partners dance upright, and the poses are distinct. It is a technical and structured tango that does not transmit the popular sentiment, the cadence, the pause, or the adagio of the music; the manner of walking one sees in the *milongas* is not conveyed. Audiences like the display, the drama, the passion, the dips.

Music, Arts, and Literature. The rhythm of tango music reflects its Andalusian and its African roots, while the melody is Italian. Tango music has evolved dramatically since it was first played by small bands at the beginning of the twentieth century: from trios, quartets, sextets, and full orchestras to the avant-garde and the innovative musician Astor Piazzolla. When the *bandoneón* was incorporated, the joy of the tango music became solemn; the *bandoneón* produces a serious sound, and the tango has become a serious matter. "The tango is a sad thought that can be danced," Enrique Santos Discépolo, one of the most talented tango poets, has said. It has become impossible to separate the concept of the tango from the timbre of the *bandoneón*; the sound of this instrument has generated a cultural memory. The repertory of instrumental

TANGO. Premiered in Paris in 1983, *Tango Argentino* became a worldwide hit. "La Cumparsita," a turn-of-the-century tango danced by María and Carlos Rivarola, was an audience favorite. (Photograph © 1985 by Linda Vartoogian; used by permission.)

TANGO. One of the most dramatic and popular tango shows ever produced, *Tango Argentino* soon made its way to Broadway. In this 1985 photograph, Noanim Timoyko and Nélida Rodríguez perform a tango during one of the show's visits to New York City. (Photograph © 1985 by Jack Vartoogian; used by permission.)

and sung tango is vast, yet two of the great tango figures take center stage in Argentina's cultural memory. Carlos Gardel (1890–1935) developed a style of tango singing that brought him enduring renown as its greatest vocal interpreter—he embodied the tango-song; Astor Piazzolla (1921–1992), whose music synthesized tango, jazz, and classical music, revolutionized the way of playing the *bandoneón*.

Tango Argentino, the Broadway hit created by Claudio Segovia and Héctor Orezzoli, opened for six days at the Festival d'Automne, Paris, in 1983. In 1993 it completed a ten-year run of fifty-seven cities in the United States, Europe, Japan, and Latin America. Dancers in the original cast were Juan Carlos Copes and María Nieves, Virulazo and Elvira, Gloria and Eduardo, Nélida and Nelson, Mayoral and Elsa María, María del Carmen and Carlos Rivarola, and "Los Dinzel" (Gloria and Rodolfo). The show's great success resulted in a demand for additional professors of dance; the opening of Argentine tango schools in Argentina, Europe, Japan, and the United States; and the creation of other similar shows, such as *Tango × 2*. The rebirth of tango dance in Argentina has been directly related to the worldwide success of *Tango Argentino*.

The tango permeates the life and culture of the Argentine people (primarily the people in the Río de la Plata region), as one hears in frequent references to tango lyrics in daily life as well as in the works of many of the great twentieth-century Argentine writers, such as Roberto Arlt, Adolfo Bioy Casares, Jorge Luis Borges, Julio Cortázar, Ricardo Güiraldes, Leopoldo Lugones, Eduardo Mallea, Leopoldo Marechal, Ezequiel Martínez Estrada, and Ernesto Sábato. For Argentines, the tango continues to be both a central cultural reference and a strong source of cultural cohesion.

[*See also* Nieves and Copes *and* Plebs and Zotto. *For discussion in a broader context, see* Social Dance, *article on* Twentieth-Century Social Dance to 1960.]

BIBLIOGRAPHY

Andrews, George Reid. *The Afro-Argentines of Buenos Aires, 1800–1900.* Madison, Wis., 1980.

Azzi, María Susana. *Antropología del tango: Los protagonistas.* Buenos Aires, 1991.

Azzi, María Susana. "Multicultural Tango: The Impact and the Contribution of the Italian Immigration to the Tango in Argentina." *International Journal of Musicology* 5 (1996).

Azzi, María Susana. "The Golden Age and After: 1920s–1990s." In *¡Tango!,* by Simon Collier et al. London, 1995: 114–160.

Azzi, María Susana. "Tango Argentino." In *The Universe of Music: A World History,* vol. 11, *Latin America and the Caribbean,* edited by Malena Kuss. Washington, D.C. (forthcoming).

Borges, Jorge Luis. *Evaristo Carriego: A Book about Old-Time Buenos Aires.* Translated by Norman Thomas di Giovanni. New York, 1984.

Castro, Donald S. *The Argentine Tango as Social History, 1880–1955.* Lewiston, N.Y., 1991.

Collier, Simon. *The Life, Music, and Times of Carlos Gardel.* Pittsburgh, 1986.

Collier, Simon. "The Tango Is Born, 1880s–1920." In *¡Tango!,* by Simon Collier et al. London, 1995: 18–64.

Copes, Juan Carlos. *Let's Dance: Bailemos tango.* Buenos Aires, 1984.

Ferrer, Horacio. *El libro del tango.* Buenos Aires, 1980.

Gesualdo, Vicente. *Historia de la música en la Argentina.* Buenos Aires, 1961.

Hanna, Gabriela. *Así bailaban el tango.* Berlin, 1993.

La historia del tango. 19 vols. Buenos Aires, 1976–1987.

Jakubs, Deborah L. "From Baudy House to Cabaret: The Evolution of the Tango as an Expression of Argentine Popular Culture." *Journal of Popular Culture* 18 (Summer 1984): 133–145.

Novati, Jorge, et al. *Antología del tango rioplatense.* Vol. 1. Buenos Aires, 1980.

Savigliano, Marta. *Tango and the Political Economy of Passion.* Boulder, Colo., 1995.

Taylor, Julie M. "Tango: Theme of Class and Nation." *Ethnomusicology* 20.2 (1977): 273–291.

Tienken, Arthur A. "Carlos Gardel: Fifty Years Later." *Studies in Latin American Popular Culture* 7 (1988): 309–314.

Vass, Winifred Kellersberger. *The Bantu-Speaking Heritage of the United States.* Los Angeles, 1979.

Zlotchew, Clark M. "Tango, *Lunfardo,* and the Popular Culture of Buenos Aires." *Studies in Latin American Popular Culture* 8 (1989): 271–285.

María Susana Azzi
Translated from Spanish

TANKARD, MERYL (born 8 September 1955 in Darwin), Australian dancer and choreographer. Since 1989, when she was appointed artistic director of a permanent company, Tankard has emerged as one of Australia's most innovative choreographers of dance theater. She began her professional dance career with the Australian Ballet, which she joined in 1975 after graduating from the Australian Ballet School. She spent three years as a dancer with the company. During that time she choreographed her first piece, *Birds behind Bars,* for a special program presented by the Australian Ballet in 1977 as a tribute to retiring artistic director Dame Peggy van Praagh.

While on a study tour in Europe in 1978, Tankard's career moved in a major new direction when she encountered the work of the German choreographer Pina Bausch. Tankard joined Bausch's Tanztheater Wuppertal in 1978 and until 1984 performed as a soloist with the company, taking major roles in many of Bausch's works, including *Le Sacre du Printemps* and *Bluebeard.* While in Wuppertal she also co-wrote and performed in an experimental film, *Sydney on the Wupper,* which won a gold award at the Berlin Film Festival in 1983.

Tankard returned to Australia in 1984 to choreograph *Echo Point* and to freelance as a choreographer, performer, and director. Between 1984 and 1988 she also frequently returned to Bausch's company, touring with it as guest artist throughout Europe and in Canada and the United States. From 1989 to 1992 she was director of the Canberra-based Meryl Tankard Company. In 1993 she became director of the Australian Dance Theatre in Adelaide, which she renamed the Meryl Tankard Australian Dance Theatre.

Tankard's choreography builds on her experiences with Bausch. Some of her works stand in a direct line of descent from specific pieces in the Bausch repertory. Tankard's *Two Feet,* with its stress on the compulsive behavior often associated with performers and performances, recalls Bausch's *Bandoneon,* while the flooding of the stage with water in the final moments of *Two Feet* is reminiscent of Bausch's *Arien.* Like Bausch, Tankard also works from an emotional rather than a technical base. Bausch has remarked that she is not interested so much in how people move as what moves them, which could equally apply to Tankard.

Tankard builds her choreography from real experiences, often ones that develop during the rehearsal period. Her work is strongly image-based, with a new vocabulary emerging for each piece. In 1993 she made *Furioso* in which her dancers, attached to ropes and harnesses, were airborne for large sections of the piece. Since then, her choreography has continued to explore parts of the stage space not normally used in dance. She usually uses a collage of music taken from a variety of sources—although a number of her pieces, including *Songs with Mara* and *Banshee*—have involved collaboration with live musicians who have a distinct performing role in the works. An important influence on her work has been that of her associate artist, photographer, and scenic designer, Régis Lansac. Lansac's use of slide projections, exemplified by his work for *Nuti,* in which images are projected onto moving bodies, is often an intrinsic part of a Tankard production. Tankard's other credits include work for film and television and the choreography for two productions by the Australian Opera, *Death in Venice* (1989), *Orphée et Euridyce* (1993), and *The Deep End* (1996), a commissioned one-act work for the Australian Ballet.

BIBLIOGRAPHY

Halligan, Marion. "The Meryl Tankard Company." *Fremantle Arts Review* 5 (June 1990): 17–19.

Kiernander, Adrian. "Meryl Tankard's Australian Dance Theatre." *Theatre Forum,* no. 6 (Winter/Spring 1995): 5–11.

Nugent, Ann. "Meryl Tankard: An Impression." *Writings on Dance,* no. 5 (Autumn 1990): 52–62.

Potter, Michelle. *A Passion for Dance.* Canberra, 1997.

Potter, Michelle et al. "Meryl Tankard: The Canberra Record 1989–1992." *Brolga,* no. 3 (December 1995): 49–52.

INTERVIEW. Meryl Tankard, by Shirley McKechnie (July 1990), National Library of Australia, Canberra (TRC 2602). Meryl Tankard, by Michelle Potter (July 1996), National Library of Australia, Canberra (TRC 3477).

MICHELLE POTTER

TANZANIA. *See* Central and East Africa.

TAP DANCE. An American art form that fuses West African and British Isles dance traditions, tap dance slowly evolved between the mid-1600s and early 1800s from two sets of parent forms: British Isles soft-shoe and hard-shoe step dances, such as the jig, reel, and various clog dances, and a variety of secular and religious African step dances labeled *juba* and *ringshout* dances. In general, as tap's African elements became more formal and diluted, its European elements became more fluid and rhythmic. When African rhythms and performance styles fused with European techniques of footwork, the American tap hybrid was born.

What distinguishes tap from all other forms of dance based on percussive footwork is its unique jazz rhythms and syncopations. The rhythms, for example, of traditional clog dancing, classic flamenco *estampe,* or North Indian *kathak* sound very different from tap rhythms, yet all these dance styles share common techniques of footwork. Because their accent patterns, syncopations, and rhythm patterns differentiate one dance style from another, the polyrhythmic, multimetric African percussive sensibility is considered to have exerted the most profound influence on the development of tap.

Examples of tap's double heritage suggest ways in which African and European dance might have blended. Because it was done on the bare earth in bare feet, much African dance favored gliding, dragging, shuffling, and stamping footwork, with the body held in a gently crouched position. Tap's assimilation of these features is clear in its use of slides, drags, shuffles, and chugs and in its relaxed body attitude. Conversely, in step dances such as the jig and in clog dances the body was held erect; usually performed in hard-soled shoes or clogs on wooden floors, these dances favored the articulated and highly codified heel-and-toe actions that would provide the technical amplification for tap's percussive development. It is important to note that the old-style (*sean-nós* in Irish) step dances in England and Ireland were very different from later exhibition and competition forms. The old close-to-the-floor style of solo step dancing (and the step-dance vocabulary that occurs in the social form called set dances) was the main British Isles influence on the development of tap from 1600 to 1800. Theatricalized versions of step dances, such as the hornpipe and jig, only made their way to the United States (and began to influence the evolution of tap) with itinerant exhibition dancers after 1800. African dance, like African music, is polyrhythmic and multimetric, pushed forward by a propulsive tempo that accents the *offbeat* (the basis of jazz), a rhythmic signature whose imprint is seen in the performance of American social dance and heard in the percussions of tap. In African animal dances, details of the animal's behavior are realistically imitated in the whole body; these dances have enriched tap's vocabulary with such steps and gestures as pecking, shimmies, and snake hips. The term *buck-and-wing* described an early tap combination of shuffles and wings (in a "wing" the tapper jumps in the air while simultaneously executing a three-beat shuffle with the toes of one foot; excellent tappers can execute a five- or six-beat shuffle before landing), whereas *buck dancer* was an early term used to describe a solo male tap dancer, presumably because the rapid shuffling of the feet resembled pawing, prancing hooves.

TAP DANCE. A ninenteenth-century print by Matt Morgan of the flat-footed African-American step dancing that was a precursor to modern tap. Here, wooden planks supported by barrels serve as a resonant platform. Musicians are pictured playing banjo, fiddle, and tambourine, the typical accompaniment for this type of dance. (Collection of Sally R. Sommer and William G. Sommer.)

TAP DANCE. This postcard, captioned "Waiting for the Sunday Boat," shows a buck dancer "heel-and-toeing," c.1900. (Collection of Sally R. Sommer and William G. Sommer.)

Whites and blacks undoubtedly watched each other dance because between the seventeenth and nineteenth centuries blacks adapted the figures and partner relationships of European dances for their own use. Blacks adopted the form of men and women dancing together, following the figures of reels and quadrilles, but retained their African steps and rhythms. After 1825, with the rise of minstrelsy, the borrowing was reversed: white minstrelmen frankly copied African and African-American dance and musical styles and used them as their stage material, and after 1890 black social dances were rapidly assimilated into mainstream white culture—a trend that has dominated American social dancing in the twentieth century. [See United States of America, *articles on African-American dance traditions.*]

As the number of slaves in the colonies increased, so did the number of rules governing their behavior. One law in particular, first passed in 1739 in the Carolinas and soon legislated by the other colonies, directly affected the development of tap. As a result of a slave uprising known as the Cato Conspiracy or the Stono Insurrection, white slave masters, convinced (wrongly) that the sound of drums echoing throughout the countryside had called the slaves to revolt, made it illegal and punishable for slaves to play drums or congregate. In place of the forbidden drums, the slaves had to rely on tambourines, bones, banjos, fiddles, and "patting"—also known as "hamboning"—whereby the body is slapped as if it were a drum set. It was the feet, however, that became one of the most important of the slaves' percussive instruments, and this development was noted in contemporary accounts throughout the 1700s. Increasingly there were references to the popularity of "patting juba" and descriptions of feet slapping the floors at slave "frolics," beating against the ground like hail pounding on rooftops.

House slaves observed their masters dancing (or taking lessons from itinerant dancing masters) and may have seen some of the fine Irish step dancers who toured the South as entertainers. By the late 1700s and early 1800s, jig dancing contests were held between competing plantations, with owners placing bets on their favorite slave dancers. A couple of large planks were placed across supporting sawhorses or barrels to serve as a dancing platform and the winner was the dancer who executed the most complex footwork and daring turns without losing rhythm or balance. Similar contests took place on the docks and levees of the great rivers, and in urban centers jigging contests were held on market days, with the planks laid down on cobblestones in the city square.

By this time the term *jig* was beginning to be loosely applied to all African-American step dances, indicating, perhaps, that black and white styles looked similar and were blending together. It was with the rise of the minstrel show in the late 1820s, however, that tap quickly developed into a codified stage dance. White minstrelmen (usually Irish) blackened their faces with burnt cork and created stage performances based on their interpretations of plantation slaves and their music and dance forms—competing among themselves to see who had the most "authentic" material. Between 1840 and 1890 minstrel shows were the most popular form of American entertainment. Featuring a variety of songs, jokes, dancing, and music in a loose format, minstrel shows could have as few as four performers or as many as 150; at the peak of the shows' popularity, more than sixty companies crisscrossed the United States, and many regularly toured Europe. At best,

TAP DANCE. A portrait of Bill ("Bojangles") Robinson, who developed a light, crisp style by tapping up on his toes and departing from the flat-footed buck-and-wing tradition. (Photograph by James J. Kriegsmann; from the collection of Frankie Manning and Cynthia R. Millman.)

these minstrelmen could offer only pale copies of the African-American originals; at worst, they presented degrading racial stereotypes and caricatures. Nevertheless, the long-term popularity of the minstrel show testifies to the increasing influence of and interest in black culture in the United States, even in these whited-out formulas.

Before 1865 (and the end of the Civil War), black and white performers rarely were permitted to appear on stage together. One notable exception was Master Juba (William Henry Lane), an important figure in the history of tap dance. Born free in about 1825, Lane became a well-known dancer in the Five Points area of New York City when he was a teenager. A skilled Irish-jig and clog dancer, Lane was famous for his skillful and precise imitations of the best-known minstrel dancers of his day. Furthermore, he created his own rhythmically complex and virtuosic form of dance and was declared the champion dancer of his time, winning that title in the many minstrel dance competitions fiercely promoted by the various minstrel companies. Four of the best companies vied for his services, and they all gave him featured billing above his white colleagues. When Lane traveled to London with Pell's Ethiopian Serenaders in 1848, enthralled English critics—discerning judges of the traditional jigs and clogs—hailed Lane's dancing as unique both in its new rhythms and in his method of beating time with his feet. Clearly Lane had forged a style of dance that was neither African nor European but something in between. Grafting African-American rhythms onto the exacting techniques of the hard-shoe step dances and clogs, Lane set the standard for excellence. Although he died young (in about 1852), he was so respected that for years after his death minstrelmen would advertise their skills by announcing that they danced in the style of the late Master Juba. (*Juba* was an honorary name given to many fine minstrel dancers, but *late* referred specifically to Lane.) [*See the entry on Juba.*]

If Lane imitated white dance styles, white minstrelmen did the reverse. Skilled step and clog dancers hastened the development of tap every time they performed their imitations and interpretations of plantation dancing. Whether their intentions were parodic or purely derogatory, they internalized African-American rhythms and performance styles, thereby unintentionally contributing to the tap hybrid.

After the Civil War many black or mixed minstrel companies were founded—ironically, African Americans had to perform in blackface—and freshness and a new vitality were brought to the dance by performers in touch with their own culture. By the late 1890s the tap vocabulary included syncopated *stop times,* using silence to punctuate the rhythms; *sand dancing,* using the gritty abrasive sound of feet scraping on sand as the source of percussion; the *essence,* a rapid pigeon-toeing motion that made the dancer appear to slip across the stage as if on rollers; the *soft-shoe,* a graceful dance usually performed to a languid 4/4 tempo, originally done in soft-soled shoes and later with taps (later still, the soft-shoe became an elegant tap dance and style of performance); the *waltz clog,* a basic clog step done to an easy 3/4 tempo; and the *time step,* the most basic combination in tap, which uses syncopated accents in a 4/4 tempo.

Between 1890 and 1915 all sorts of steps and phrases from vernacular social dances—such as the cakewalk strut, rubber-legging, and the camel walk—were incorporated into tap. The body had softened and relaxed from the erect position of the clog dancer, the knees were slightly bent, and the shoulders and arms were used for witty and whimsical gestures. The term *tap* came into popular use very late; it may have been first used in public advertising by Ziegfeld Follies' dance director Ned Wayburn in 1902. Previously the dance had been called buck-and-wing, buck dancing, or flat-footed dancing (because of the shuffles, drags, and slides that differed from traditional clog steps); it also went by the older names step, clog, and jig dancing. Metal plates attached to the bot-toms of heel and toe did not come into common use until after 1910. Before then, a typical shoe had leather uppers and wooden soles split at the ball of the foot or soles with wooden pieces set into toe and heel. A variation was shoes with hobnails or pennies pounded into toe and heel (an old Irish practice that continued into the twentieth century); yet another shoe had soles made from several layers of leather covered at toe and heel with tiny nails sanded smooth.

With the rise of vaudeville and of traveling black road shows and Broadway revues and musicals, numerous performance opportunities opened up for tap as its haphazard but vigorous growth continued. [*See* Vaudeville.] Still, racism was insidious, and black and white performers essentially danced on different theatrical circuits for different audiences. In white vaudeville, several large syndicates (such as E. F. Albee and B. F. Keith's) linked hundreds of theaters together under a single artistic management. The Theater Owners' Booking Association (TOBA) was the single black syndicate; at its peak in the 1920s, TOBA controlled more than two hundred vaudeville theaters. The tap dance chorus line became entrenched on the larger stages of white, mainstream Broadway theaters where big-budget productions enjoyed long runs. Unrestrained by touring costs that limited the size of vaudeville shows, Broadway producers could hire professional dance directors and large chorus lines. Yet the quality of tap technique and choreography deteriorated. The reason is clear: the more dancers in a line, the simpler the rhythms tend to become, because complicated combinations are blurred by the multiplication of feet. The cycle of mediocrity continued as studios were established (often by the dance directors) to train the dancers with technique sufficient only to perform the simple routines and techniques necessary for chorus work.

Unlike other dance genres, tap has never been characterized by great teaching institutions where choreographers and dancers could go to learn the large and varied vocabulary that has evolved through the years. In the world of black tap dance in particular, traditions and techniques have almost always been learned through an informal process of observation and imitation followed by apprenticeship. In earlier decades, performance skills were sharpened in informal tap competitions or "tap-offs"; the winner was the dancer with the most daring improvisations and inventive step combinations. There was—and still is—an emphasis on developing individual styles. A tacit rule of this system is: you can copy my steps but not exactly, which bespeaks an attitude opposed to the practice of the well-drilled classroom.

Vaudeville, rather than Broadway, became the nursery for great tap-dancing talent. Indeed, the artistry of tap is perhaps best refined in the individual performer or in the small team of three to eight members, whose virtuosic rhythms can be clearly heard. The practice of playing before many different types of audiences enabled vaudeville performers to perfect their work, which kept the quality of their tap dancing extraordinarily high. The variety format was typical of all popular entertainment forms—on Broadway, in revues, and in vaudeville. In order to satisfy the public's taste and to define personal styles, performers drew on their imaginations to come up continually with something new. Gradually tap became roughly divisible into categories of performance styles. Good performers often merged different styles, and the lines that divide one classification from another are blurred at best.

Eccentric tap relied on idiosyncratic body movements: the body was almost as loose as a wet mop, unable to remain upright while the feet tapped out chattering rhythms below. This style was perfected by Ray Bolger and the lesser known but superb "Rubberneck" Holmes, a favorite performer on the TOBA circuit. *Comedy* tap always involved two or more dancers and often employed eccentric moves. The team of Bert Williams and George Walker personified this style: Williams's legs seemed to be

TAP DANCE. John W. Bubbles and Ford Lee ("Buck") Washington began collaborating in Louisville, Kentucky, in the 1910s, forming the famous singing-and-dancing act Buck and Bubbles. They are pictured here at the Zanzibar nightclub in 1943: Buck plays the piano as Bubbles dances. (Photograph from the collection of Sally R. Sommer and William G. Sommer.)

made of rubber, and as he did a slow and lazy hip grind he seemed on the verge of tripping over his rapidly shuffling feet. Walker, elegant in dress and manner, was a "class act" tapper and cakewalker who acted as a foil to Williams. *Flash* tap refers to spectacular tricks incorporated into tap phrases; done well, these touches add spice and visual interest.

Perhaps the best-known and most respected tap performers who used elements of flash techniques in their routines were the extremely elegant tap dance team known as the Nicholas Brothers (Harold and Fayard Nicholas). They would leap from platforms or stairs (one platform they used is said to have been more than ten feet high), land in full splits, bounce up, and continue with their tap phrases. [*See the entry on the Nicholas brothers.*] There were also acrobatic teams who extended flash tap by combining acrobatic maneuvers with their regular routines. The most elegant of these teams was the versatile Berry Brothers (Ananias, James, and Warren), who used many different stylistic elements in their dancing, including spectacular acrobatic work. [*See the entry on the Berry brothers.*] The art of acrobatic tap is to time each feat precisely and accurately so that the rhythms of the dance are not disturbed. *Class acts,* as the term suggests, were debonair in manner, sophisticated in dress, and charming, elegant, and casual in dancing style. Fred Astaire personified this tap style on film, and the equally remarkable Charles ("Honi") Coles epitomized it on the stage.

TAP DANCE. Ruby Keeler and Paul Draper in the Hollywood film *Colleen* (Warner Brothers, 1936). Keeler was an early tap star of the movies. Draper, who combined intricate footwork with smooth body movements, is noted for performing tap dance to classical music. (Photograph from the collection of Rusty E. Frank.)

The years 1920 to 1935 constituted the heyday of the Harlem Renaissance, the nightclub, black Broadway, and vaudeville, and throughout these years tap was the most popular of all the stage dances. The best known of all the tap dancers was Bill ("Bojangales") Robinson, who performed in each of these arenas as well as on film. Admired for his neat, clean footwork and for his style of dancing up on his toes with minimal heel taps, Robinson created dances that were brilliantly shaded with tonal nuance and dynamic shifts, using easily heard and economical rhythmic lines. Robinson's buoyant performances and style of phrasing set new standards in the evolution of tap; the typical patterning of the eight-bar phrase was three two-bar phrases followed by a two-bar contrasting phrase (known as the *break*). Considered to be the classic structure of tap, this pattern is still fundamental to the genre. Robinson always performed in split, wooden-soled shoes, preferring their mellow sound to the clatter of metallic plates. The stair dance may not have originated with Robinson, but he brought it to such a level of excellence that it has become synonymous with his name—perhaps the most famous example being the routine he performed with Shirley Temple in the 1935 movie *The Little Colonel.* [*See the entry on Robinson.*]

A younger man, John W. Bubbles (John ["Bubber"] Sublett), was known as the father of *rhythm* tap because he perfected this unique style and, like Robinson before him, influenced future generations of tappers. By bringing down his heels, Bubbles brought tap down from the toes; slapping his heels against the floor like a drummer hitting the bass drum, Bubbles added a new range of syncopated accents to his rhythmical lines. His rhythms were contemporary with—and in some cases preceded—the complex syncopations that developed in jazz music during the late 1920s and early 1930s and that would evolve further in bebop. Bubbles freed tap from the classic eight bar phrase ending in a two-bar break by "running" the bars, hooking together longer nonrepetitive phrases and lacing them across as many as sixteen bars. This style has continued to predominate in tap performances. [*See the entry on Bubbles.*]

A favorite offstage haunt for Bubbles and others of his generation was the Hoofers' Club, located on 131st Street in Harlem; it was really nothing more than a small back room that the sympathetic owner of a pool hall set aside for tap dancers. Open twenty-four hours a day, the club became the gathering place for tap dancers, the tap summit where famous improvisational contests were held. The best challenged the best, and because the aspiring dancers learned from the experts through observation and imitation, the Hoofers' Club earned its reputation as the best unofficial tap school in the country. The improvisational spirit comes from tap's African heritage and did much to foster its technical development, particularly among African-American tap dancers. When the Hoofers' Club closed in the late 1930s, something vital was lost, yet by then the tradition of the tap challenge had become part of tap's technique and performance, and it has remained one of the most important ingredients in the modern tap vocabulary.

With the rise of film and the demise of vaudeville during the 1930s, performers had to compete for audiences in a shrinking market. As a result, tap routines got trickier, filled with flash and increasingly dangerous acrobatics that kept audiences gasping. Writing in the *New Yorker,* prescient critic Robert Benchley discerned the trend:

> Up until three or four years ago I was the Peer of Tap-Dance-Enjoyers. . . . It didn't seem as if I could get enough tap-dancing. But I did. More than enough. With every revue and musical comedy offering a complicated tap routine every seven minutes throughout the program, and each dancer vying with the rest to upset the easy rhythm of the original dance form, tap-dancing lost its tang.

In the early 1930s, with the importation to Hollywood of Broadway dance directors, such as Sammy Lee, Seymour Felix, and especially Busby Berkeley, the tap dancing chorus line was taken to its surrealistic limit. Once again, as in the huge Broadway chorus lines, the artistry of tap was not enhanced by the chorus line numbers. The increasing mobility of the camera, as well as the ability of the editors to juxtapose and layer images in the cutting room, decreased, even further, the necessity for any tap technique. One of the notable exceptions to this declining excellence were the Russell Market Girls, a well-drilled and highly skilled tap-dancing chorus line. The quality of tap choreography inevitably suffered. However, Hollywood also preserved some of the finest tap dancing in the solo performances of Hal Leroy, Ann Miller, Buddy Ebsen, Ray Bolger, Eleanor Powell, Donald O'Connor, Vera-Ellen, Ginger Rogers and, above all, in the tap dance performances of Gene Kelly and the brilliant Fred Astaire. Astaire and Kelly epitomized the range of American tap styles. Kelly was athletic and smooth. The roles he usually played in film—reflected in his tap style as well—were unpretentious, everyday, working-class characters. In contrast, Astaire, whose tap style was elegant, classy and graceful, usually played debonair, charming characters who were themselves professional dancers. Astaire is certainly America's most famous tap dancer. Indeed, were it not for the continuing popularity of the Astaire films, the art of tap dancing probably would have been completely forgotten by the American public from the mid-1950s to the mid-1970s, when tap all but disappeared from public view.

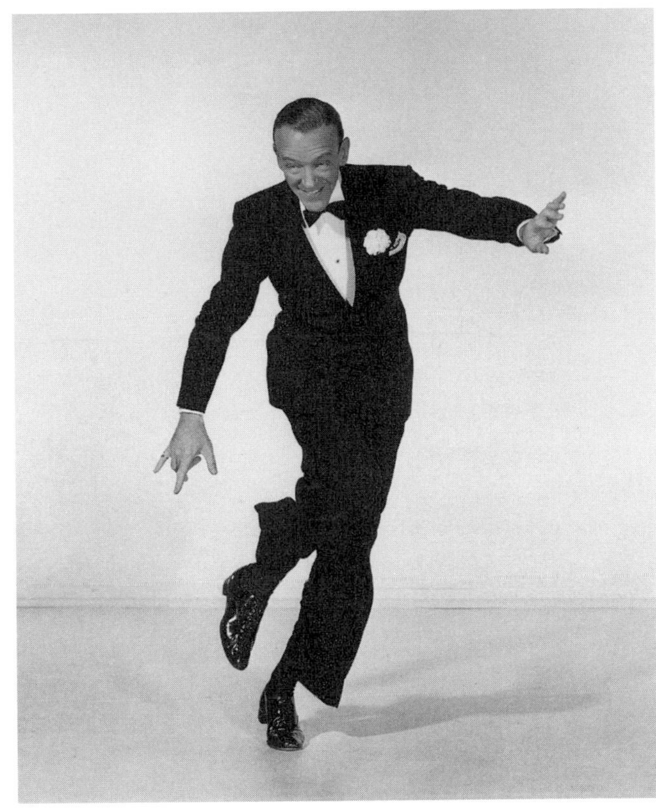

TAP DANCE. Fred Astaire in *Three Little Words* (MGM, 1950). (Photograph courtesy of the Kobal Collection, London.)

Broadway tastes shifted in the 1940s, when a new kind of dance, derived from ballet, modern-dance, and jazz-dance vocabularies, was introduced to audiences in *Pal Joey* and *Oklahoma!* Vaudeville was dead, and tap dancers had few places to perform. They traveled with the big bands as speciality acts and continued to appear in prologues, live entertainments that preceded the showing of films. Over the next twenty years tap gradually went into decline, kept alive only by a few remaining clubs and the reruns of Astaire's superb films.

The tap revival began slowly. The first flare was set off at the 1962 Newport Jazz Festival by jazz and tap historian Marshall Stearns when he brought eight of the older black tap percussionists back to the stage. Although the audience and the critics were dazzled, they believed that this was tap's swan song. In the 8 July edition of the *Boston Herald,* critic George Frazier praised the tappers, noting how "their Shim Sham sanctified the sunlight, so that if you had never seen this before, you could hardly believe that creativeness could seem so casual. Then for more than an hour these men—this dying breed—made a lithe litany." Fortunately, everyone was mistaken: these performances heralded a rebirth. In 1968 a series of concerts called *Tap Happenings* lit up the stage of the Dixie Hotel in Manhattan. Standing in the traditional semicircle, legendary figures of the African-American jazz-tap world each stepped out to take a solo riff. The success of this show reawakened the world of dance to the jazz-tap heritage it had almost let slip away. Suddenly the tap masters were teaching and performing once more.

The revival of *No, No, Nanette* with Ruby Keeler brought tap back to Broadway in 1971, followed by *The Wiz* (1975) and *Bubblin' Brown Sugar* (1976). Then, in quick succession, came *Sugar Babies* (1979), *42nd Street* (1980), *Sophisticated Ladies* (1981), *The Tap Dance Kid* (1982), and *My One and Only* (1983). Also during this period, tap dance was brought to dance concertgoers, thereby gaining new audiences and critical acclaim from a hitherto unexposed section of the dance world. Throughout its history, tap had been treated as entertainment, but now it was being considered as art, and a new generation of dancers began to study tap and to form small tap dance companies that performed in modern-dance concert halls.

TAP DANCE. Jimmy Slyde, a master of rhythm tap, in performance, c.1984. (Photograph from the collection of Sally R. Sommer and William G. Sommer.)

Jazz appealed to the minimalist aesthetic of the 1970s that revered improvisation and advocated an unstressed, pedestrian style of movement. The dexterous footwork of tap can be viewed as a flamboyant celebration of the walk. In tap, dancer and musician are the same, exemplified by the simple elegance of "tacet" tapping, with the sounds of taps as the only music.

Conspicuously, during the 1970s, the younger tap dancers actively sought out older African-American tap masters to teach them the jazz-tap or rhythm-tap style, strongly identified with John Bubbles, that flourished most markedly in the black tap and jazz communities. The traditional system of informal apprenticeship, with the tap competition or challenge as an essential evolutionary force, was maintained and refined. Instead of learning just an exacting tap vocabulary and unchangeable routine, the dancers were now taught to think of themselves as percussive instrumentalists with an improvisational sensibility. Although set routines are frequently used in jazz tap, the tapper does not necessarily need to adhere to the precise choreography. The routine may merely provide a structure within which the dancer creates improvisational rhythmic riffs—in the same way the jazz musician improvises with the well-known tune.

During the next fifteen years, extraordinary tap masters passed on the craft of jazz tap. Important mentors in New York were Charles ("Cookie") Cook, Charles ("Honi") Coles, Marion Coles, Chuck Green, Harriet Browne, Burt ("Gip") Gibson, Lon Chaney, Ralph Brown, Howard ("Sandman") Sims, Buster Brown; in Los Angeles, Eddie Brown, John Bubbles, and Jack Johnson; in Boston, Stanley Green, Leon Collins, Jimmy Slyde; in Florida, Steve Condos; in Chicago, Jimmy Payne.

From the mid-1970s through the mid-1980s, tap choreography was taken forward by a generation of dancers who were most often white, female, and trained in modern dance techniques. Although they learned jazz tap technique from the older Black tap masters, they choreographed by fusing traditional jazz-tap material with a modern-dance aesthetic, a fusion which shaped tap's concert presentation during the 1980s. Notable among these companies are Brenda Bufalino and the American Tap Dance Orchestra; Lynn Dally's Jazz Tap Ensemble; Heather Cornell's Manhattan Tap; and Linda Sohl-Donnell's Rhapsody in Taps.

In the 1980s and 1990s national tap festivals and conferences began to be held, initiated with By Word of Foot, organized by Jane Goldberg in 1981. These gatherings of venerated tap teachers, performers, and historians helped strengthen the community by offering opportunities for study, performances, and tap exchanges among tappers from all over the country. Concurrently, Europe slowly began rediscovering tap and appreciating its expatriot and younger tap dancers.

At the end of the 1980s, inspired by the Broadway success of *Black and Blue* (1989), and especially inspired by tap dancer Gregory Hines, who starred in *Sophisticated Ladies* (1983) and in *Jelly's Last Jam* (1991), along with Savion Glover, as well as in the Hollywood films *White Nights* (1985) and *Tap* (1989), many young African-American male dancers were attracted to tap.

The unquestioned leader of this youthful avant-garde was the brilliant Savion Glover. Profoundly influenced by the harsh vibrancy of 1990s hip-hop music with its heavy bass beats, political rap poetry, and fierce, inner-city sensibility, Glover's hip-hop–funk tap caused a major stylistic revolution within the field. Most importantly, it brought tap in line with the newest musical developments. Sometimes called "power tapping," the style is distinguished by dense, hard-hitting rhythms. The body hunkers over, the arms are used pragmatically to maintain balance, the knees are deeply bent, and the feet seem to attack and pound the floor. Little attempt is made to please the audience with smiles or eye contact and the dancer's focus remains inward as he searches to "find the groove." "Finding the groove" happens when the tapper plays with his rhythms until he creates a baseline beat, a rhythmic cadence around which he can weave his varied riffs. When the groove is good, it causes an almost trancelike state. The style—masculine, heavy, and fast—defines the George Wolfe–Savion Glover collaborative dance drama, *Bring in 'da Noise, Bring in 'da Funk: A Hip Hop Discourse on the Staying Power of the Beat,* which opened on Broadway in the fall of 1996.

TAP DANCE. The leader of a new generation of rhythm tappers, Savion Glover, in a 1991 performance. (Photograph © 1991 by Jack Vartoogian; used by permission.)

At the end of the twentieth century, tap continues to maintain a varied cultural tradition that is intergenerational, multiracial, and interdisciplinary, maintaining a high level of choreographic inventions. Tap has taken its place on concert as well as musical stages, in film, and in television. Its choreographic expressions range from traditional jazz tap to tap dance "orchestras" and experimental fusions of new music with tap performance. With the passing of the elder tap masters, the next generation of tap dancers has taken up the responsibility of keeping the legacy alive. In many respects tap seems new because it was virtually lost for two decades. Although tap is still a small part of the dance world, it continues to undergo vigorous change and growth; and because it has yet to discover its full potential, or reach its limitations, tap remains one of the more vital elements in the American dance world.

[*For related discussion, see also* United States of America, *article on* Musical Theater; *and the entries on Astaire, Baby Laurence, Bates, Berkeley, Bolger, Coles, Draper, Four Step Brothers, Green, Hines, Kelly, Miller, O'Connor, Powell, Sims, Temple, and the Whitman sisters.*]

BIBLIOGRAPHY

Balliett, Whitney. *Such Sweet Thunder.* Indianapolis, 1966.

Benchley, Robert. *The New Yorker* (16 May 1931).

Emery, Lynne Fauley. *Black Dance from 1619 to Today.* 2d rev. ed. Princeton, 1988.

Frank, Rusty E. *Tap! The Greatest Tap Dance Stars and Their Stories, 1900–1955.* Rev. ed. New York, 1994.

Frazier, George. *Boston Herald* (8 July 1962).

Gilbert, Douglas. *American Vaudeville: Its Life and Times.* New York, 1940.

Lahr, John. "King Tap." *New Yorker* (30 October 1995).

Murray, Albert. *The Omni-Americans: Some Alternatives to the Folklore of White Supremacy.* New York, 1983.

Nathan, Hans. *Dan Emmett and the Rise of Early Negro Minstrelsy.* Norman, Okla., 1962.

Sommer, Sally R. "Feet, Talk to Me!" *Dance Magazine* (September 1988): 56–60.

Southern, Eileen. *The Music of Black Americans.* New York, 1971.

Stearns, Marshall, and Jean Stearns. *Jazz Dance.* Rev. ed. New York, 1994.

Toll, Robert C. *Blacking Up: The Minstrel Show in Nineteenth-Century America.* New York, 1974.

Winter, Marian Hannah. "Juba and American Minstrelsy." In *Chronicles of the American Dance: From the Shakers to Martha Graham,* edited by Paul Magriel. New York, 1948.

FILM AND VIDEOTAPE. *History of American Tap,* series of documentaries on Louis DaPron, Nanette Fabray, Fred Kelly, Hal Leroy, Fayard Nicholas, and Jack Williams, held in the Dance Collection of the New York Public Library for the Performing Arts. Chris Bould and Bruce Goldstein. *The Nicholas Brothers* (EMI Records, 1992). George T. Nerenberg, *No Maps on My Taps* (1979). Christian Blackwood, *Tap Dancin'* (1980). Jolyon Wimhurst, *Masters of Tap* (1983). *About Tap* (Direct Cinema Ltd., 1985). *Tap* (Orion Pictures, 1989). "Tap," *Dance in America* (WNET-TV, New York, 1989). Robert Kuperberg, *Dance Crazy in Hollywood* (1990), a documentary on Hollywood choreographer Hermes Pan. Gerald Fox, *Opening Shot: Savion Glover* (1993).

ARCHIVES. Dance Collection, New York Public Library for the Performing Arts, Tap Dance clippings file. Schomburg Center for Research in Black Culture, New York Public Library. George T. Nerenberg Productions, New York.

SALLY R. SOMMER

TARANTELLA. Although the tarantella is firmly entrenched in the Western mind as an expression of the gaiety and vivacity of southern Italy, there is no set structure for the dance. The figures of the tarantella, which are made up of light hopping steps executed in 3/8 or 6/8 time, often in accelerating tempo, may be executed in any order the dancers please. In addition, there are regional differences in the number, sex, and demeanor of the dancers and in the musical instruments used to accompany the dance.

The tarantella has roots in ancient history; it is said to derive its name from the city of Tarentum (modern-day Taranto), formerly a Greek settlement on the southern coast of Italy. Historians have identified representations of the dance in ancient Greek vase paintings and on the wall paintings at Pompeii. Elba Farabegoli Gurzau (1981) notes, however, that the name *tarantella* came into use only within the last four or five centuries, and that the dance was formerly known as the *lucia, sfessania,* or *villanella,* among other names. She further observes that it became fused with the *fandango* and acquired the use of castanets when Spain dominated southern Italy in the late fifteenth century.

According to a widespread legend, the dance acquired its name because it was used as a cure for the poisonous bite of the tarantula spider. Gurzau reports that this etymological point was debated at the Venice Congress and Folk Festival in 1949, and the participants concluded that the legend was based on the similarity of the two words rather than actuality. In apparent contradiction to this conclusion is the fact that the tarantella is performed as a kind of exorcism by the practitioners of Tarantism, an Italian possession cult comparable to the *zār* cult of Ethiopia or Vodun in Haiti. Ernesto de Martino, whose *La terra del rimorso* (1961) is considered the principal monograph on Tarantism, has discovered, however, that the cult's association with the bite of the tarantula is more symbolic than real because its members, the majority of whom are women, tend to be concentrated in particular families, and their attacks usually occur annually around the time of the feast of Saint Paul.

W. G. Raffé's dictionary (1964), which contains three separate entries for the tarantella, identifies the dance with the *treguenda,* or *danza alla strega,* a witches' ritual in which an invisible web was woven to entrap unwary travelers, and the *danza dell'arco,* a mimed love story performed by pilgrims to Mount Virgine near Naples. The latter, he notes, is "not merely a technically executed folk-dance."

Gurzau (1981) records several regional variations of the tarantella as well as some modern-day arrangements created by folk dance groups. In Apulia (region on the southeastern coast of Italy, on the Adriatic Sea and Gulf of Taranto), the tarantella is usually danced by a man and a woman, with other dancers in a circle around them; when either partner tires, he or she is replaced from the circle. The women preserve a shy demeanor as they dance, keeping their heads bent and their eyes on the ground. Musical accompaniment is provided by the accordion, castanets, and tambourines. In Sicily, where the tarantella is often performed during wedding festivities, rhythmic clapping accompanies the dance instead of castanets or tambourines. The women of Campania (the region that includes Naples and Sorrento) dance with their heads up and a sense of self-pride. Two women may dance together as a third plays the tambourine; they may also make patterns with a long ribbon or sash. Bagpipes, tambourines, castanets, clapping, and finger-snapping accompany the dance.

Stylized tarantellas have been used to add a touch of local color to the ballet stage. An early example is the tarantella created for Fanny Elssler in Jean Coralli's ballet *La Tarentule* (1836), the plot of which centers around real and feigned bites of the tarantula. In making this dance, Coralli cannily exploited Elssler's previous success in character dances such as the *cachucha*. Inspired by his visit to Italy in 1841, August Bournonville's *Napoli* (1842) contained a tarantella that, as the master proudly notes, "was unanimously declared to be the finest composition of its kind" (1979). A comparison of his choreography

TARANTELLA. A nineteenth-century engraving showing a couple dancing the tarantella to the accompaniment of tambourines and a mandolin. Reflecting Spanish influence, the man dances with castanets. (Courtesy of Madison U. Sowell and Debra H. Sowell, Brigham Young University, Provo, Utah.)

with Gurzau's descriptions suggests that he may have conflated different regional variations of the dance.

Dolls dressed in Italian peasant costume performed a tarantella in Léonide Massine's *La Boutique Fantasque* (1919). George Balanchine's lively *Tarantella* (1964) was created as a display piece for two virtuosic dancers, Patricia McBride and Edward Villella. The choreographer modestly denied any claim of authenticity, stating, "[It] is 'Neapolitan' if you like and *'demi-caractère.'* The costumes are inspired by Italy, anyhow, and there are tambourines" (1977).

[*For related discussion, see* Character Dancing.]

BIBLIOGRAPHY

Balanchine, George, with Francis Mason. *Balanchine's Complete Stories of the Great Ballets.* Rev. and enl. ed. Garden City, N.Y., 1977.

Bournonville, August. *My Theatre Life* (1848–1878). Translated by Patricia McAndrew. Middletown, Conn., 1979.

de Martino, Ernesto. *La terra del rimorso.* Milan, 1961.

Gurzau, Elba Farabegoli. *Folk Dances, Costumes, and Customs of Italy.* 2d ed. Philadelphia, 1981.

Pillosu, Clotilde. "Deux danses de possession italiennes: La 'Tarentelle' des Pouilles et la danse de l''Argia' en Sardaigne." *Recherche en Danse,* no. 1 (June 1982): 133–138.

Raffé, W. G., ed. *Dictionary of the Dance.* New York, 1964.

Reynolds, Nancy. "Balanchine: An Introduction to the Ballets." *Dance Notation Journal* 6 (Winter–Spring 1988–1989): 15–74.

SUSAN AU

TARASOV, NIKOLAI (Nikolai Ivanovich Tarasov; born 6 [19] December 1902 in Moscow, died 8 February 1975 in Moscow), dancer and teacher. Tarasov developed an interest in ballet at an early age, influenced by his father, Ivan Tarasov, a dancer of note with the Bolshoi Ballet. In 1920 Nikolai graduated from the Moscow Ballet School, where he had studied under Nikolai Domashov and Nikolai Legat. Tarasov almost immediately became a principal dancer at the Bolshoi Theater, where he danced the male leads in ballets such as *Swan Lake, Giselle, La Bayadère, La Esmeralda, Coppélia, Raymonda, The Nutcracker, Don Quixote, The Red Poppy,* and *La Fille Mal Gardée.* He was partnered by some of the foremost ballerinas of the day, including Ekaterina Geltser, Viktorina Kriger, Marina Semenova, Liubov Bank, Margarita Kandaurova, and Nina Podgoretskaya. In her memoirs Viktorina Kriger recalled, "Tarasov was a superb dancer in the strict academic style. He never tried to dance for effect, for the sake of achieving quick success." Tarasov's precise, clean line and his unaffected manner sprang from a harmonious blend of technical brilliance and an intelligent, refined approach to the art.

Between 1923 and 1960 Tarasov taught at the Moscow Ballet School, from 1942 to 1946 holding the dual post of artistic director and managing director, and again in 1953 and 1954 serving as artistic director. A handsome man of noble stature, in class by his very presence Tarasov created a stimulating atmosphere conducive to the pursuit of artistic excellence. A paragon of punctuality and discipline, he felt he had a right to expect his students to measure up to his standards. Tarasov groomed his students to a high level of professionalism, putting them through a finely graded sequence of exercises and getting them to polish each element. He emphasized the barre exercises, seeing them as the foundation for mastery of the most complicated elements of classical technique, and loaded each combination with carefully selected movements that built in complexity. As a result Tarasov's students had an impressive range of sophisticated technique. Among the male dancers Tarasov trained were Yuri Zhdanov, Aleksandr Lapauri, Mikhail Lavrovsky, Maris Liepa, and Yaroslav Sekh. From 1923 to 1936 Tarasov had conducted the class for soloists of the Bolshoi Ballet; some of the best-known dancers, including Aleksei Yermolayev, Mikhail Gabovich, and Asaf Messerer, flourished under his competent guidance.

When the Lunacharsky Theater Technicum created a choreography department in 1947, Tarasov was appointed to teach the method and composition of classical dance. In 1958 he organized a choreographic training unit there, and in 1962 he received a professorship. Tarasov trained a great many ballet teachers, *répétiteurs,* and choreographers who went out to teach classical dance throughout the communist bloc. The wealth of experience he gained in teaching, coupled with that of his predecessors, enabled him to evolve his own philosophy and teaching method, both of which he described in detail in *Ballet Technique for the Male Dancer;* first published in 1971, the book won a national prize in 1975.

BIBLIOGRAPHY

Kholfina, Serafima. *Vospominania masterov moskovskogo baleta.* Moscow, 1990.

Puttke, Martin. "The Straight Line Is Godless." *Ballett International* 1 (January 1995): 26–31.

Struchkova, Raisa. "Nash liubimyi professor." *Sovetskii balet,* no. 1 (1983).

Tarasov, Nikolai. *Klassicheskii tanets, shkola muzhskogo ispolnitel'stva.* Moscow, 1971. Translated by Elizabeth Kraft as *Ballet Technique for the Male Dancer* (Garden City, N. Y., 1985).

RAISA S. STRUCHKOVA
Translated from Russian

TAVERNER, SONIA (born 18 May 1936 in Byfleet, Surrey), English-born Canadian ballet dancer. At age twelve Sonia Taverner began her dance studies in the weekly ballet classes of a local teacher, and at age sixteen she enrolled at the Elmhurst Ballet School, which offered a curriculum of academic courses combined with a program in the fine arts. Obviously talented, she was the 1954 winner of the Dame Adeline Genée silver medal for the most promising student. She also won a scholarship to the Senior School of the Sadler's Wells Ballet, where she continued her training and found her most inspiring instructor in Winifred Edwards, who had been a member of Anna Pavlova's company.

Taverner joined the corps of the Sadler's Wells Ballet early in 1955 and danced with the company, which was dubbed the Royal Ballet in 1956, for the next year and a half. Apprehensive about her chances for rising through the ranks of such a large organization, she was happy to join her family in relocating to a new home in Winnipeg, Canada. She was soon accepted into the Royal Winnipeg Ballet, where she was promoted to one of three leading female dancers for the season 1957/58. Among her first roles were leads in two early works by Brian Macdonald, *Aimez-vous Bach?* and *Pas d'Action,* which she created. Other works in which she danced leading roles were *Chinese Nightingale* by Heino Heiden, *Concerto* and *Romance* by Gweneth Lloyd, *Pas de Dix* by George Balanchine, and numerous pas de deux from the classical ballet repertory, in which her frequent partner was Fredric Strobel.

Aspiring to dance in full-length productions of the classics and attracted by the varied repertory of Les Grands Ballets Canadiens, Taverner moved in 1965 to Montreal and joined the company headed by Ludmilla Chiriaeff and Fernand Nault. In the classical repertory she shone in such works as *Giselle, The Nutcracker,* and *La Fille Mal Gardée.* She also found congenial roles in Nault's *Pas Rompu, Divertissement Glazounov,* and *Cérémonie;* in Balanchine's *Theme and Variations* and *Allegro Brillante;* and in Norman Walker's *Trionfo di Afrodite.* In classical and neoclassical works, she was often partnered by Richard Beaty, whose elegant style and looks provided a perfect foil for her own regal bearing and dark beauty.

After six years with Les Grands Ballets Canadiens, Taverner joined the Pennsylvania Ballet as principal dancer for the 1971/72 season and enjoyed the same success with American audiences as she had with those in Canada. She

TAVERNER. With Richard Beaty as her partner, Taverner danced a leading role in Fernand Nault's *Carmina Burana* during the Expo 67 season of Les Grands Ballets Canadiens. (Photograph © 1966 by Jack Mitchell; used by permission.)

gave notable performances in Balanchine's *Symphony in C* and *Raymonda Variations* and as the Innocent Girl in John Butler's *Villon.* Returning to Canada, she appeared with the newly formed Festival Ballet of Ottawa, dancing in Brydon Paige's *Songs for a Dark Voice,* and once again with Les Grands Ballets Canadiens. In February 1974 she gave a highly praised series of performances of *Giselle,* partnered by Vincent Warren.

Later that year Taverner relocated to western Canada and in 1975 was invited to head the ballet program at Grant MacEwan Community College in Edmonton, Alberta. For the next five years she taught classes, staged performances, and appeared as occasional guest artist with the Alberta Ballet and Les Grands Ballets Canadiens. Since 1980 she has taught at her own school near Edmonton.

BIBLIOGRAPHY

Goodman, Saul. "Sonia Taverner." *Dance Magazine* (October 1967): 58.

Maynard, Olga. "Idea, Image, and Purpose: Ballet in Canada Today." *Dance Magazine* (April 1971): 32–65.

CLAUDE CONYERS

TAYLOR, PAUL (Paul Bellville Taylor; born 29 July 1930 in Edgewood, Pennsylvania), American dancer and choreographer. During the first decade of Paul Taylor's dance career, he worked with several of America's most influential teachers and choreographers. Even his first steps in dance indicated his early eclecticism: Taylor's debut as a performer was in 1950 at Syracuse University—where he was studying painting, funded in part by a swimming scholarship—and his first choreography, *Hobo Ballet,* was created for students in the university's Dance department. Taylor has likened his training and competing with the Syracuse swim team to the commitment required in his early dance career. After moving to New York City in 1952, he trained for a year at the Juilliard School and also took classes with Margaret Craske and Antony Tudor at the Metropolitan Opera Ballet School; he performed in works by Doris Humphrey (1952), Merce Cunningham (1953–1954), Charles Weidman (1954), Martha Graham (1955–1962), and George Balanchine (1959); he worked in commercial theater and television; and from 1954 on, he created further performing opportunities for himself through his own choreography. Importantly, it was through these varied experiences that Taylor evolved his own pluralist aesthetic.

He was an extremely versatile performer. His tall, athletic physique created a striking presence on stage and he was particularly acclaimed in performances with the Martha Graham Dance Company; he created roles in *Clytemnestra* (1958), *Acrobats of God* and *Alcestis* (both 1960), *Visionary Recital* and *One More Gaudy Night* (both 1961), and *Phaedra* (1962). It was through this association that Taylor worked with George Balanchine on *Episodes,* the 1959 co-production which brought together Graham's company and the New York City Ballet.

During Taylor's formative years as a choreographer, he also collaborated with painter Robert Rauschenberg. In order to finance their early careers, both worked as window dressers (alongside another aspiring artist, Jasper Johns) at Tiffany's, the famous New York jewelers. After their first collaboration on *Jack and the Beanstalk* (1954) Rauschenberg designed all eleven works choreographed by Taylor during the 1950s, including *Three Epitaphs* (1956) and *Seven New Dances* (1957). Just as Rauschenberg's paintings challenged the lofty conventions of the abstract expressionists, Taylor's early choreography was seen as a rejection of mainstream American ballet and modern dance, and particularly of the highly codified styles developed by Balanchine and Graham.

Jack and the Beanstalk was the opening work in a Dance Associates program entitled A Theater for New Dance, Music, and Design. (Dance Associates was set up by choreographer James Waring to present shared programs of new, experimental work.) Previously, Taylor and Rauschenberg had worked separately at Black Mountain

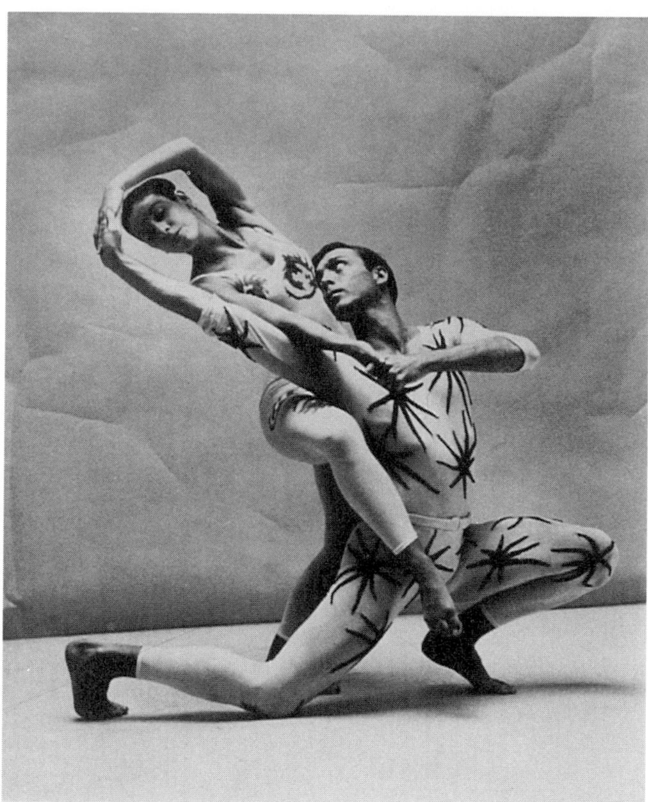

TAYLOR. Linda Hodes and Taylor in *Insects and Heroes* (1961). (Photograph by William Schipp; from the Dance Collection, New York Public Library for the Performing Arts.)

College in North Carolina where some of the earliest postmodern explorations occurred. It was there that John Cage developed and disseminated many of his ideas on chance, indeterminacy, and silence, the latter resulting in his 1952 work *4′33″*, created in response to a series of Rauschenberg's "white" paintings.

4′33″ was the inspiration for Taylor's *Duet,* part of his *Seven New Dances* concert. In the same way as Cage had experimented with music, ambient sound, and silence, Taylor was attempting to discover an individual vocabulary through a detailed study of stylized and pedestrian movement, and of stillness, in each of his seven dances. (He has described these studies as his "ABC" of dance postures, gestures, and steps.) While *Three Epitaphs,* his oldest surviving work, is now regarded as a Taylor classic, *Seven New Dances* is remembered for its single, controversial performance. The work that caused the greatest furor was *Duet,* Taylor's stage interpretation of Cage's score—four minutes and thirty-three seconds of silence and stillness. Relatively few people had attended the concert but Louis Horst's nonreview in *Dance Observer*—a blank column, identifying only the date and place of performance—was largely responsible for Taylor's first taste of fame (at a time when the choreographer had neither the administrative nor the financial resources to orchestrate his own publicity campaign) and, thus, he became the *enfant terrible* of the New York dance scene.

Critics and audiences were unable to reconcile Taylor's popularity as a performer in works by Graham and Balanchine with the seemingly nondance content of his choreography. His early works explored many of the ideas and practices of the American postmodernists but, even at his most experimental, Taylor never fully embraced their notion of performance—most particularly, their emphasis on process and their rejection of established theater venues. Nevertheless, he created ten further works following *Seven New Dances* and made two successful European tours with his own group of dancers (in 1960 and 1962) before establishing himself as a choreographer in New York. The turning point was *Aureole,* not least because audiences could applaud its seamless, skimming combinations of steps, set to music by Handel in five clearly structured sections. Moreover, the second movement featured Taylor in the work's main solo, an extended adagio in which his upper body virtually swims through space during an unbroken series of slow, controlled promenades and *penchées*, thereby highlighting his strong technique and lyricism. *Aureole* has become an enduring repertory favourite and, through its many restagings for other companies, it is one of Taylor's most performed works. Also, it was the success of this work that convinced him to leave Graham's company in order to work full time with his own group of dancers.

Today, the appeal of *Aureole* tends to overshadow other significant works created by Taylor during the same period, especially *Insects and Heroes* and *Junction* (both 1961), *Piece Period* (1962), and *Scudorama* (1963). It was undoubtedly this series of works that led critics to identify an alternating dark/light sequence in Taylor's choreography—he wanted *Scudorama* to be "as dark as *Aureole* is sunny"—and while the numerous works created since the 1960s cannot be confined to only two categories, the most telling and consistent aspect of Taylor's dancemaking is that he has resisted being pigeonholed by repeatedly doing the unexpected. (That the lyrical and plotless *Aureole,* danced to Baroque music, was created for the 1962 American Dance Festival was itself risqué because, at that time, the festival was predominantly a platform for America's more expressionist modern dance choreographers.)

Junction was Taylor's first choreography to Baroque music. Indeed, his aim in working with two of J. S. Bach's cello suites was to develop his musicality and, from 1961 on, a closer dance-music relationship can be detected in his work. (*Junction* was also the first work designed by Taylor's long-term associate, painter Alex Katz.) Musically, *Aureole* was an extension rather than a new direction for Taylor and he made further strides with *Piece Period.* The latter was a direct response to both the national and period styles of seven pieces of music by Beethoven, Haydn, Scarlatti, Vivaldi, and other pre-twentieth century composers, and it was this work that initiated Taylor's collaboration with designer John Rawlings. Subsequently, Rawlings designed such seminal Taylor works as *From Sea to Shining Sea* (1965), *Esplanade* (1975), and *Le Sacre du Printemps (The Rehearsal)* in 1980. (The latter was their last collaboration because Rawlings died later the same year.)

Scudorama, in its final form, was performed to a commissioned score by Clarence Jackson as part of Taylor's first Broadway season in December 1963. (The premiere, in August at the 1963 American Dance Festival, was performed without accompaniment because Jackson's score arrived too late. Also, although Katz's costumes were ready in time, his set for *Scudorama* was added later.) During rehearsals, Taylor worked with Igor Stravinsky's *Le Sacre du Printemps*. The aggression and dissonance of *Scudorama* stem largely from its original accompaniment and, typically, when Taylor returned to the two-piano version for his *Le Sacre du Printemps (The Rehearsal)* in 1980, he sought a completely different interpretation of Stravinsky's music. (Taylor's *Le Sacre*, set in a dance studio and Chinatown, is a double narrative in which the Chosen Maiden is, respectively, a dancer who submits herself to the daily ritual of rehearsals and a distraught mother whose baby has been kidnapped by gangsters.)

While *Piece Period* revealed Taylor's witty side, *Scudorama* was his first representation of evil and social disintegration. Whereas Graham chose allegory and ancient myths in order to critique human weakness, the most joyless and macabre of Taylor's dances are contemporary morality tales. Some could even be deemed futuristic, especially *Big Bertha* (1971) and *Last Look* (1986) where the abuse and destruction faced by present-day stereotypes are cautionary signs for tomorrow's world. Similarly, Taylor's treatment of history borders on the postmodern in its use of pastiche and irony: for example, in *From Sea to Shining Sea*, *Orbs* (1966) and the evening-length epic *American Genesis* (1974), his characterization of historical figures and natural phenomena—ranging from several biblical characters, the Statue of Liberty, and a Thanksgiving turkey to the planets, sun, and moons of the solar system—is irreverent and funny. The exception in Taylor's Americana series is *Speaking in Tongues* (1988), which some writers have compared to Graham's *Appalachian Spring* (1944). In both works, a religious protagonist controls the lives of a small-town community, but where Graham's work extols the simplicity and order of America's pioneer past, Taylor's is an indictment of such late twentieth-century ills as hypocrisy, evangelism, and violence. His Man of the Cloth is closer in kind to his Followers than to some divine power and is as prone as they are to temptation and prejudice.

Humor, doom, and ritual are recurrent themes in Taylor's choreography. However, particular ideas are most often suggested rather than described. Sometimes, Taylor identifies specific characters and provides clues such as

TAYLOR. The original cast of *Aureole* (1962), included (left to right) Sharon Kinney, Renee Kimball, Dan Wagoner, and Liz Walton. A series of clearly structured dances set to orchestral music by Handel, *Aureole* is one of Taylor's most popular works. It has been staged for many other companies, including the Royal Danish Ballet (1968) and the Paris Opera Ballet (1974). (Photograph © 1962 by Jack Mitchell; used by permission.)

subtitles in his program but he encourages an open interpretation of his dances. He believes that movement in itself is expressive and this is borne out by his ongoing interest in nonnarrative choreography. Possibly the most extreme example of this is the two-part *Polaris*, created in 1976 to a commissioned score by Donald York. Choreographically the second part is an identical repeat of the first but, by using two different casts and by responding to the contrasting dynamics of the music in the two sections, Taylor's aim was to highlight how individual dancers imbue movement with distinct nuances through their different physiques and personalities. In *Esplanade*, too, he shows how the same movement can appear very different by simply changing a dancer's stage position or facing, and how even the simplest, pedestrian actions are transformed into dance when set on a proscenium stage. Together with other devices, such as truncating or extending a gesture, altering its timing or directing it toward another dancer, Taylor captures the inherent dramatic potential of "pure" movement.

Throughout his career, Taylor has emphasized the theatrical possibilities of formalist choreography first explored in *Junction* and *Aureole*. Together, they can be seen as the prototype for *Airs* (1978), *Arden Court* (1981), *Mercuric Tidings* (1982), *Equinox* (1983), and *Brandenburgs* (1988), and it is no coincidence that these plotless works have all been choreographed to some of the finest pre–twentieth century music. By working closely with the orchestration and dynamics of his accompaniment, Taylor has developed a highly sophisticated sense of phrasing and sectioning. Other works, too, are essentially plotless. Only the dancers' costumes and certain associations—as suggested by Spinoza's "Man is a social animal" in the program for *Cloven Kingdom* (1976); by subtitles for *Musical Offering* (1986): "a requiem for gentle primitives," and *Syzygy* (1987): "the nearly straight line configuration of three or more celestial bodies in a gravitational system"; or by Taylor's structuring of six male-female duets in the romantic *Roses* (1985) and his dramatic use of a soloist/ensemble division in both *Spindrift* (1993) and *Moonbine* (1994)—make it possible for these works to be read as quasi narratives. There is no delineation of characters or situations; all of these works are a direct response to their musical accompaniment.

Several of Taylor's plotless works have been restaged by classical ballet companies around the world. After *Aureole* and *Company B* (1991), the most frequently performed works are *Airs, Arden Court, Cloven Kingdom, Esplanade,* and *Three Epitaphs*. While this has created international exposure for his choreography, it has popularized only part of Taylor's diverse style. (Conversely, only a few of his narrative works—specifically, *Big Bertha, Le Sacre du Printemps,* and *Speaking in Tongues*—have been restaged for other companies.) Such exposure has also highlighted certain aspects of Taylor's movement vocabulary more than others. Although some movements and step combinations do recur, both within and across works, his choreography incorporates an infinite number of pedestrian actions and postures, and a wide range of codified movements. Taylor has developed a technique—contrary to his

TAYLOR. *Esplanade* (1975), set to music by J. S. Bach, was Taylor's first major work created after his retirement from performing in 1974. It is generally considered his signature work. The pedestrian event of a girl running to catch a bus served as a starting image for the dance. Here, Lila York jumps over each of her fellow company members in series. (Photograph © 1977 by Jack Vartoogian; used by permission.)

earlier disclaimers. It is not a system of training, as are the techniques evolved by Graham, Cunningham, and other choreographers, but it comprises a clearly devised sequence of exercises and terminology. With elements such as "chugs," "paddle turns," and distinct C-arms, V-arms, and wrap-arms, Taylor's terminology is not so poetic as Graham's, nor as pragmatic as Cunningham's, yet it conveys both the type and quality of movement required. Also, it reveals Taylor's unpretentious attitude to his work.

The same is true of his views on dancers. Consistently, he has selected an unusual mix of personalities and physiques, with Taylor's female dancers often being both the shortest and tallest members of his company. He prefers to be inspired by their individual differences, rather than work with a homogenous group. A sense of unity stems from two common characteristics: Taylor's dancers manifest the same unmannered and athletic abilities as he did as a dancer; and they all share his fearless attitude to movement—not only when performing high-speed, high-risk traveling steps (in *Esplanade* and *Mercuric Tidings,* especially) but also in their commitment to other forms of abandoned movement, such as the disturbingly grotesque in *Dust* (1977), *Nightshade* (1979), and *Last Look,* and the extremely zany in *Aphrodisiamania* (1977), *Minikin Fair* (1989), and *Offenbach Overtures* (1995). Taylor describes this special quality as "zunch." In a letter to his dancers in 1975, he defined it as the "oomph that sets the exciting dancer apart from the adequate one"; "a kind of St. Elmo's fire that radiates all round the dancer, the defined space and the audience."

In 1974 Taylor collapsed during the New York premiere of *American Genesis,* his first full-evening work. (Taylor's 1974 New York season also marked the twentieth anniversary of his professional debut as a dancer-choreographer in *Jack and the Beanstalk.*) Initially, he anticipated only a short break from performing—with his roles "on loan" to other dancers—but within months, he decided to retire permanently. Thus, Taylor's letter was written at a crucial time in his career, in the year he retired from performing and immediately before the creation of *Esplanade.* Just as *Aureole* had launched his own full-time company and repertory, *Esplanade* confirmed that both of these could be successful without him at center stage. Also, after his retirement, Taylor began to tour less with his company and this enabled him to devote more time to the prerehearsal preparations for his next choreography. Listening to a wider selection of music was a significant part of this process, as can be seen in subsequent works by Taylor's more ambitious use of twentieth-century scores by Claude Debussy (*Images*), Francis Poulenc (*Dust*), Darius Milhaud (*House of Cards*), Edgard Varèse (. . . *Byzantium*), György Ligeti (*Counterswarm*), and Charles Ives (*Danbury Mix*); and his commissioning of contemporary composers Gerald Busby (for *Runes* later in 1975), Jan Radzynski

TAYLOR. Carolyn Adams and Christopher Gillis in a duet from *Airs* (1978), set to music by Handel. (Photograph © 1979 by Jack Vartoogian; used by permission.)

(*Profiles*), and Donald York (*Polaris; Diggity; Lost, Found and Lost; Snow White; Last Look;* and *Syzygy*).

Most importantly, Taylor's experience of choreographing *Esplanade* and then *Runes* "from outside" led to a new working relationship with his dancers and to a new phase of creativity. During the next decade, he developed a company of very talented dancers, several of whom he also encouraged as choreographers, while simultaneously choreographing some of his best works: *Esplanade* and *Runes* were followed by *Cloven Kingdom* and *Polaris* in 1976, *Images* and *Dust* in 1977, *Airs* and *Diggity* in 1978; and, during the early 1980s, by *Le Sacre du Printemps (The Rehearsal), Arden Court, Mercuric Tidings, Sunset* (1983), and *Last Look.*

The culmination of this stream of creativity was *Musical Offering,* choreographed in 1986 to one of J. S. Bach's last compositions. In its scale, complex musicality, and structure, *Musical Offering* was a high point in Taylor's career but it was also a watershed. Soon afterward, many of the dancers who had featured prominently as soloists in this work retired from performing or left to form their own companies. (Sadly, some have also died from AIDS-related illnesses.) Since 1986, Taylor's company has been transformed through a complete turnover of dancers; however, his curiosity about movement—the dance potential of particular ideas and personalities—remains undimmed. This is borne out by the creation of, on average, two works per year and, most notably, by *Speaking in Tongues, Company B,* and *Spindrift.* Like *Musical Offering,* all three recent works explore the physical possibilities and the inherent

TAYLOR. Three dancers in *Sunset* (1983): Kate Johnson, Jeff Wadlington, and Christopher Gillis. (Photograph © 1989 by Jack Vartoogian; used by permission.)

dramatic connotations of solo and group choreography: in *Musical Offering,* the female protagonist summons and controls the ritualized activities of the ensemble; in *Speaking in Tongues,* as well as Taylor's Man of the Cloth, other dancers emerge successively as archetypes, for example, A Mismatched Couple, A Party Girl, The Odd Man Out. In *Spindrift,* the leading male dancer often stands alone from the group, separated by distance (and possibly by a life/death divide), while *Company B,* taking its title from the Andrews Sisters' rendition of the song "Boogie Woogie Bugle-Boy" and the seventh section solo, illuminates various types of relationships (for example, the romantic contrasts between the male-female couple in "Pennsylvania Polka" and in "There Will Never Be Another You," and the soloist/group inversions of "Oh Johnny, Oh Johnny, Oh!" and "Rum and Coca-Cola."). As each song concludes, the slow-motion falling of the male dancers echoes Taylor's linking theme, namely the large-scale loss caused by war and its impact on loved ones.

Company B is one of Taylor's landmark dances. In this work, he began to feature several of his newest dancers as soloists—a policy that has proved highly successful in discovering and developing new talent. Today, these dancers have become Taylor's latest muses and, in working with him so closely, they have also assimilated the technical and performance styles of earlier choreography (as the revivals of *Junction* and *Private Domain* in 1992 and *Musical Offering* in 1995 confirmed). *Company B* was the first of a series of works set to popular songs, followed by *Field of Grass* (1993) and *Funny Papers* (1994). Furthermore *Company B,* which was made possible by a grant awarded to the Kennedy Center in Washington, D.C., brought Taylor considerable public acclaim. Six companies were selected to present new choreography there and, as part of the project, the Houston Ballet chose Taylor to create his first work for them. (Subsequently, the Houston Ballet has also performed *Sunset.*) *Company B* was the first premiere to result from the project, a high-profile event attended by then President George Bush and his wife, Barbara.

Most telling, however, was the genesis of *Company B.* Although commissioned and premiered by the Houston Ballet, Taylor created the choreography on his own company in New York. Taylor prefers to tease out movement ideas on dancers he knows well and, even though several of his works are performed by other companies, he has seldom assumed the role of guest choreographer. (None of the works created by Taylor for other companies have survived in repertory. Also, following his abortive attempt to choreograph *Airs* for American Ballet Theatre in 1978, he began anew with his own dancers. The Taylor company version was subsequently taken into American Ballet Theatre's repertory.)

Two other landmark dances of recent years are *Danbury Mix* and *Of Bright & Blue Birds & the Gala Sun.* The former was first performed during the 1988 American Music Festival, to a selection of music by Charles Ives. (The title makes reference to the composer's home in Danbury, Connecticut.) Choreographically, *Danbury Mix* resembles two of Taylor's former collages, *From Sea to Shining Sea* and *American Genesis.* Americana themes and characters have been borrowed from these earlier commentaries and, created in the same year as *Speaking in Tongues, Danbury Mix* presents a satirical, but equally probing, critique of American cultural mores.

Morality underpins much of Taylor's choreography. In *Of Bright & Blue Birds & the Gala Sun* (1990), his second full-evening work, journey, spiritual struggle, exorcism, and prodigal return are developed sequentially. As with *American Genesis,* narrative and scenic progression are of epic proportions and, like the hour-long *Orbs, Of Bright & Blue Birds* alludes to the scale and order of the solar system (with Heaven and Hell inspiring the strongest "planetary" activity). *American Genesis* had incorporated two recent dances *(So Long Eden* and *Noah's Minstrels);* similarly, *Of Bright & Blue Birds* evolved from *Syzygy.* It was first performed as part of the Taylor company's thirty-fifth anniversary season at City Center, New York and, as with *Syzygy,* it involved two of Taylor's longtime associates, music director and composer Donald York and lighting designer Jennifer Tipton. (Santo Loquasto, who has designed almost all of Taylor's work since 1988, created the costumes and sets.)

Now in his mid-sixties, Taylor is acutely aware of his place in America's ever-evolving dance tradition. Increasingly, he has involved himself in the retrieval of lost choreography: in 1986, he re-created his 1959 solo in *Episodes* for the New York City Ballet dancer Peter Frame; in 1992, he revived *Epic,* one of his early postmodernist experiments from the 1957 concert, *Seven New Dances.* Also in 1992, the National Endowment for the Arts awarded a challenge grant of $850,000 to help Taylor's company launch its Repertory Preservation Project. The aim of the five-year project is to document approximately thirty dances (on film, in written form, and in Labanotation) and this will involve the revival of lost works, such as other sections from the *Seven New Dances* program. A side outcome of the project has been the setting-up of a junior company, Taylor 2, which recruits its dancers from the Paul Taylor Dance School. Each year, this smaller group learns at least one of the works included in the project and, thus, these young dancers will not only preserve Taylor's choreography in performance but will also benefit from learning a series of major works at a crucial stage in their career.

The Paul Taylor Dance Company moved into improved premises in a building adjacent to their longtime home on Broadway in 1987 and here, as part of the Repertory Preservation Project, the company is establishing an archive. This is certainly timely because Taylor has been saving press cuttings, programs, and other important materials since the early 1950s. Moreover, though his work has been consistently well documented, by dance critics and by Taylor himself, access to information has been restricted. (Until the publication of Taylor's autobiography, *Private Domain,* in 1987, few comprehensive sources on his career were widely available, except as single-chapter accounts in dance texts, such as Mazo's *Prime Movers.*)

Taylor's sense of history is evident in several dances created during the last decade—. . . *Byzantium* (1984), *Kith and Kin* (1987), *Company B,* and *Field of Grass* are his most overt period pieces—and the historical importance of his work has been formally recognized through the Repertory Preservation Project. As he acknowledges on a videotape to promote the project, "My attitude is that I've been handed down so many wonderful things from the generations that came before me, it's a duty to keep doing that for others."

Undoubtedly, that duty, together with the many important works that constitute Taylor's legacy, will secure him a prominent place in America's dance history.

[*See also* Esplanade; Musical Offering; Spindrift; *and* Three Epitaphs.]

BIBLIOGRAPHY

Adams, Carolyn. "The Paul Taylor Mystique." *Dance Theatre Journal* 1 (Spring 1983): 7–9.

Anderson, Jack. "Taylor's Domain." *Dance Chronicle* 11.1 (1988): 130–132.

Coe, Robert. *Dance in America.* New York, 1985.

Croce, Arlene. *Sight Lines.* New York, 1987.

Dalva, Nancy. "Paul Taylor: A Very Appealing Genius." *Dance Magazine* (October 1991): 38–43.

Jacobson, Daniel. "Private Domains in Public Spaces." *Ballet Review* 17 (Spring 1989): 67–75.

Jowitt, Deborah. "A Fishy Conversation with an Obliging Giant." *Village Voice* (23 April 1979). Reprinted in *The Dance in Mind.* (Boston, 1985): 45–50.

Kane, Angela. "A Catalogue of Works Choreographed by Paul Taylor." *Dance Research* no. 2 (Winter 1996): 3–7.

Lobenthal, Joel. "Christopher Gillis: Dancing for Paul Taylor." *Ballet Review* 13 (Summer 1985): 10–22.

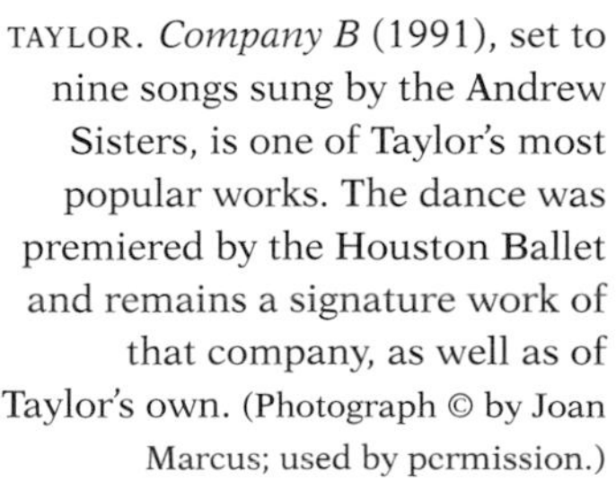

TAYLOR. *Company B* (1991), set to nine songs sung by the Andrew Sisters, is one of Taylor's most popular works. The dance was premiered by the Houston Ballet and remains a signature work of that company, as well as of Taylor's own. (Photograph © by Joan Marcus; used by permission.)

Lobenthal, Joel. "Victoria Uris: Dancing for Paul Taylor." *Ballet Review* 15 (Spring 1987): 26–37.
Mazo, Joseph. "Nikolais, Ailey, Taylor—Three Specialists." In *Prime Movers: The Makers of Modern Dance in America*. Princeton, 1977.
Reiter, Susan. "In Orbit." *Ballet News* 6 (April 1985): 16–19.
Reiter, Susan. "Baroque and Beyond with Paul Taylor." *Ballet Review* 14 (Fall 1986): 65–71.
Rosen, Lillie. "A Few Insights into Paul Taylor and One of His Finest, Longest Staying Dancers, Elie Chaib." *Attitude* 9 (Winter 1993): 6–15.
Sorens, Ina. "Taylor Reconstructs Balanchine." *Ballet Review* 14 (Summer 1986): 54–65.
Taylor, Paul. *Private Domain*. New York, 1987.
Tobias, Tobi. "A Conversation with Paul Taylor and George Tacit." *Dance Magazine* (April 1985): 54–60.

ANGELA KANE

TCHAIKOVSKY, PETR ILICH (Petr Il'ich Chaikovskii; born 7 May 1840 in Kamsko-Votkinok, Russia, died 6 November 1893 in Saint Petersburg), Russian composer whose three full-length ballets—*Swan Lake* (1877), *The Sleeping Beauty* (1890), and *The Nutcracker* (1892)—remain masterworks of the classical repertory. Tchaikovsky, the second son of a mining engineer, showed an interest in music at an early age. He started piano lessons when he was four and quickly showed exceptional skill. At the age of ten, he entered the School of Jurisprudence at Saint Petersburg and the same year was taken by his mother to see Mikhail Glinka's opera *A Life for the Tsar*, which made a deep and lasting impression on him. He spent nine years at the school, and his mother's death when he was fourteen was a shock that caused deep-rooted psychological disturbances. He sought emotional release by turning even more to music, adding singing lessons to piano studies and starting to compose.

He began work in 1859 as a clerk in the Ministry of Justice, giving up thoughts of a musical career for lack of financial support. Still, he involved himself socially in Saint Petersburg musical circles and took technique classes at the new conservatory there. During a tour to western Europe in 1861, he acted as interpreter for a friend of his father's and was greatly impressed by Germany, Belgium, Britain, and France. On his return, he joined the composition class taught by the conservatory's director, Anton Rubinstein, who in 1863 encouraged him to resign his job and concentrate on music study. Although this involved financial hardship, because his only income was from the private teaching of piano and theory, he managed to continue studies for two years, including flute and organ as well as composition. In 1864, he composed an overture on Aleksandr Ostrovsky's play *Groza* (The Storm), his first work of substance; a suite entitled *Characteristic Dances* then brought the first public performance of his music, in 1865, at an open-air concert conducted by the younger Johann Strauss, "The Waltz King."

Early Career. Tchaikovsky graduated in 1866, gaining a diploma and silver medal. He moved to Moscow as a teacher of harmony at the conservatory headed by Anton Rubinstein's brother Nikolai, with whom he lodged. He soon found the household distracting and the teaching duties irksome, but the experience brought him a new circle of influential acquaintances and the beginnings of a reputation.

The composition of Tchaikovsky's First Symphony ("Winter Daydreams"; 1866), at the insistence of Nikolai Rubenstein, was a long and difficult labor. Tchaikovsky's instinct was always much stronger for theater music than for symphonic discourse, and when his symphony was completed, in 1867, he turned to *Voyevoda* (Dream on the Volga), the first of his ten completed operas. Based on another Ostrovsky drama, it had no great success at its Moscow premiere in 1869; but a suite of "Hay Maidens Dances" from act 2 had made a favorable impression in concert performances beforehand, both in Moscow and Saint Petersburg. The dances, derived from his earlier *Characteristic Dances*, were published separately as a suite for piano duet. In David Brown's 1978 biography of Tchaikovsky, he writes of the "ravishingly chaste diatonicism" of the opening dance and declares that if the rest of the opera's invention had been as fine, it would have been a masterpiece. Tchaikovsky soon destroyed the *Voyevoda* score, although fragments were used in his 1877 ballet *Swan Lake*—the prelude to the opera's act 3 and a passage from that act are used in the entr'act before the ballet's act 4 and in the reunion of Prince Siegfried and Odette, respectively.

Tchaikovsky also destroyed his second opera, *Ondine* (1869), the romantic fairy tale of a water nymph, after it was turned down for production. Once again, fragments were salvaged for other purposes, the most notable being the final love duet from act 3. With its vocal themes transcribed for solo violin and cello, it achieved lasting fame as the White Swan pas de deux for Odette and Siegfried in *Swan Lake*, act 2 (no. 13e), which Lev Ivanov would one day choreograph.

From 1870 to 1872, Tchaikovsky wrote another opera, *The Oprichnik* (The Life Guardsman). Letters from this period mention a project for a four-act ballet, *Cinderella*, but nothing else survives to indicate its origins or whether any music was written. His letters and papers make no further reference to it.

The Oprichnik incorporates a round dance *(khorovod)* as the finale to act 1 and a suite of wedding dances in act 4, all based on themes from Russian folk songs. Five of these had been arranged by Tchaikovsky for piano duet in his *Fifty Russian Folksongs*, published in 1869. His next opera was *Vakula the Smith*, composed in 1874, and it incorporates earthy peasant humor and folk-tale fantasy. It features the Ukrainian *gopak*, danced in a variety of ways—as a Russian dance and as a Cossack dance in the ballroom scene of act 3, which itself begins with a *grande polonaise.*

Swan Lake. In the spring of 1875, Tchaikovsky was approached by the directorate of Russia's Imperial Theaters to compose the four-act ballet *Swan Lake* for production at Moscow's Bolshoi Theater. Tchaikovsky had attended ballets, but he was unimpressed by their prevailing musical standard. In a letter written later in 1875 to composer Nikolai Rimsky-Korsakov, Tchaikovsky wrote, "I accepted the work, partly because I want the money, but also because I have long had the wish to try my hand at this kind of music." The fee paid was eight hundred rubles, not a pittance but by no means generous.

A few years before this commission—probably in 1871—Tchaikovsky had himself staged another "Swan Lake," this one a domestic family entertainment. During one of several summer visits Tchaikovsky made to his married sister, Aleksandra (Sasha) Davydova, at her country home at Kamenka, near Kiev, Tchaikovsky contrived a dance pantomime based on the tale of the Swan Princess. He performed it for the entertainment of Sasha's children, and the event was long remembered in the family, with the story being passed on to Sasha's youngest son, Yuri (born in 1876). In a recollection published in 1962, he recounted what had happened:

> The staging of the ballet was done entirely by Pyotr Ilyich. He invented the steps and the pirouettes, and danced them himself to show the performers what he required of them. At such moments Uncle Pyotr, red in the face, wet with perspiration as he sang the tune, presented a pretty amusing sight. Yet in the children's eyes he was so perfect in the art of choreography that for many years the memories of this remained with them down to the finest details. (Davydov, 1962)

Davydov insisted that he recognized one tune in the mature ballet as having come from the earlier entertainment. This is thought to be the oboe tune in the finale to act 1 (no. 9), although no score for the entertainment has survived.

Tchaikovsky began work on *Swan Lake* in the summer of 1875. He sketched two acts by the end of September, scoring as he went along and, pressing himself, finished the ballet on 22 April 1876 at Glebovo, the country estate near Moscow belonging to his friend Konstantin Shilovsky. Earlier that month, a run-through of act 1 was held in the Bolshoi Theater school, the music played by a single *répétiteur* violinist, as was the custom for ballet rehearsals. He told his brother Modest that he thought it a rather ridiculous way to go about it, but that what was heard had been greatly admired.

How Tchaikovsky went about the composition of *Swan Lake* is uncertain. He must have had a scenario to determine the outline and some content for each act, as represented by the titles and descriptive cues in the score, but who was responsible for this remains unknown. Most sources suggest a collaboration among theater director Vladimir Begichev, dancer Vasily Geltser, ballet master and choreographer Julius (Wentzel) Reisinger, and the composer himself, who no doubt had his own ideas after devising the Davydov entertainment. What Tchaikovsky did not have was much experience of the way ballets were created and produced in the theater, how the music was expected to relate to the choreographer's intentions, or the leading dancers' prerogatives. As a result, *Swan Lake* is musically, in effect, a four-part tone poem, the narrative and mime scenes interspersed with set dances. It was composed with a degree of musical imagination that disconcerted both the orchestra and the dancers at first, introducing as it did a strong and organic element.

Swan Lake's score has a carefully organized and close-knit structure of key sequences and harmonic relationships around a central key (both major and minor) of B, the unison note on which the ballet ends. Within this scheme, Tchaikovsky reserved mainly flat keys for the forces of evil and bewitchment and sharp keys for the *divertissements*. Except for some recall of particular themes for reminiscence, the music is not concerned with symphonic devices and achieves continuity by repetition, as for example the "Dance of the Swans" in act 2 (no. 13) as a rondo, begun and linked by a waltz theme.

Roland Wiley's study of Tchaikovsky's ballets (1985) has much detail concerning the origins of *Swan Lake* and its composition. He explores the ballet's key relationships as a diagramed "circle of fifths," each with particular associations as to character and/or situation. In his study, David Brown drew particular attention to the range and variety of Tchaikovsky's abundant invention, especially in waltz rhythm, and "his ability to order different waltz themes to make a larger entity." Quoting opening bars from seven waltzes that occur in the ballet, Brown noted:

> The accompaniment is always of the simplest, always explicitly triple time, yet the themes themselves show endless rhythmic variety, partly through details of phrasing prescribed by Tchaikovsky, mainly by fertilizing the basic triple meter with duple-time inflexions. (Brown, 1978)

Other dance forms in *Swan Lake* include the czardas, bolero, tarantella, and mazurka among the national dances of act 3, to which Tchaikovsky added the "Russian Dance" for the benefit of Pelagia Karpakova, the first Odette-Odile. Her successor at the fifth performance, Anna Sobeshchanskaya, had gone to Saint Petersburg to obtain an extra pas de deux from the choreographer Marius Petipa, because Reisinger could not make it showy enough; it was choreographed to music by Léon Minkus, but Tchaikovsky found this unacceptable and wrote his own music to suit the choreography. The "Additional Pas de Deux," like the "Russian Dance," is published as an appendix to the full score in the complete Tchaikovsky edition. Only one version survived as Tchaikovsky's orchestration, however, the *Swan Lake* music having otherwise been replaced bit by bit until in the twentieth century a two-violin *répétiteur* score was found, bound into a score of the ballet *Le Corsaire*. The Tchaikovsky score was then re-orchestrated by Vissarion Shebalin for a Bolshoi Ballet production in 1953.

Tchaikovsky's refusal to accept another composer's music for his *Swan Lake* makes it unlikely that there was even one alien interpolation at the ballet's first performance. Nikolai Kashkin (1896), who did the first piano arrangement of the full score, wrote that with later performances "nearly one-third of the music of *Swan Lake* was replaced by extracts from other ballets which were, to say the least, mediocre." Most of these were probably occasioned by the change of choreographer, to Joseph Hansen, for the 1880 Moscow production. The ballet then continued in repertory until 1883, after which it was not seen again during Tchaikovsky's lifetime. Tchaikovsky seems not to have concerned himself with the Hansen production. By then Tchaikovsky had endured the trauma of his disastrous marriage and consequent mental breakdown, had resigned his conservatory post, and had found himself the beneficiary of unsolicited but welcome financial support from a wealthy widow, Nadezhda von Meck. Her assistance, however, was accompanied by the delicate stipulation—rigidly kept—that they never meet. [*See* Swan Lake.]

The Sleeping Beauty. Twelve years elapsed between *Swan Lake* and Tchaikovsky's next involvement with dance. Between European conducting tours in 1888 and 1889, he received a letter from the director of Russia's Imperial Theaters, Ivan Vsevolozhsky, proposing *The Sleeping Beauty* as a subject for ballet and inviting him to compose its music. Vsevolozhsky, appointed in 1881, was a man of taste and discernment, and a great admirer of Tchaikovsky's music. He helped to bring about the 1884 double production of the composer's opera *Mazeppa* at Moscow and Saint Petersburg only a few days apart, an unusual occurrence. In 1886, he abolished the post of staff ballet composer (then held by Minkus) in the interests of raising the standard of ballet music and sought to interest Tchaikovsky, who, however, had turned down the suggested subjects, *Ondine* and *Salammbô*.

The Sleeping Beauty (1889) was much more to Tchaikovsky's taste. Vsevolozhsky had sketched the scenario (he was also a playwright), and the composer was delighted. Evidence from Galina von Meck, granddaughter of Tchaikovsky's patroness, indicates that the subject had already been treated as another family entertainment at Kamenka years before; Tchaikovsky again retained some of its music for the mature ballet (Warrack, 1979).

To avoid any conflict of form and content between music and dance, as had been a factor in *Swan Lake*, Vsevolozhsky arranged for Petipa to be involved with the composer from the outset, and thus a collaborator in the fullest sense. Petipa wrote a detailed plan for each act, a working draft describing the narrative and the dances, with suggestions for the length and character of the music desired. Tchaikovsky noted progress in his diary, showing no evidence that he found Petipa's requirements irksome, as some historians have supposed; rather, the music would seem to indicate that the method was more a help than a hindrance.

Without slavishly following Petipa, Tchaikovsky worked close to the ideas, modifying them when he thought the musical interest was justified. In his four-part score (prologue and three acts), the discipline of the key relationships that was basic to *Swan Lake* was changed to a musical structure built from the contrast of narrative and dance character. Thematic references were confined to the Lilac Fairy and to Carabosse, as symbols of good and evil, presented clearly in the introduction and skillfully worked together at crucial dramatic moments. The role of Princess Aurora was associated not with a theme but with the waltz rhythm, which presented some of Tchaikovsky's most fertile invention, both for solo and ensemble purposes. His other formal dances are the act 2 minuet, gavotte, and so-called farandole (as named in the score, which is musically a mazurka); a polonaise, saraband, and mazurka are in act 3. The Sapphire Fairy variation (no. 23c) early in act 3 is in the unusual 5/4 meter that Tchaikovsky later employed in his Symphony no. 6 ("Pathétique") for the celebrated "limping waltz" movement (*allegro con grazia*) and in his "Valse à Cinqtemps" for piano (op. 72, no. 16). In *The Sleeping Beauty*, his only quotation from elsewhere is the old French song "Vive Henri Quatre," for the ballet's apotheosis (no. 31), which brings about the odd effect of a happy ending in a minor key. [*See* Sleeping Beauty, The]

The Nutcracker. Following the shock of von Meck's withdrawal of financial support, Tchaikovsky was asked for a one-act opera and a two-act ballet to be performed as a double bill at the Maryinsky Theater. The opera became *Iolanta* (1891), derived at three removes from a Hans Christian Andersen tale; the ballet was *The Nutcracker* (1892), adapted from one of the tales of E. T. A. Hoffmann.

Tchaikovsky began with the ballet and sketched act 1 before leaving for Paris on his way to the United States for his only visit in May of 1891. He conducting concerts in New York, Baltimore, and Philadelphia. He continued to compose while traveling and, having complained in a letter about "the absolute impossibility of depicting the Sugarplum Fairy in music," found the answer to his problem in Paris on discovering Auguste Mustel's newly invented keyboard instrument, the celeste, with distinctively bell-like tones. His anxiety to keep the celeste from rival composers so that he could be the first to use it perhaps led him to take the unusual step of performing a concert suite of music from *The Nutcracker,* including the Sugarplum Fairy's dance, some nine months before the ballet's production. The suite comprised "Overture," "March," "Waltz of the Flowers," and five character dances from act 2; almost every number was encored.

Tchaikovsky had considered using toy instruments as an element in the music, after the manner of Leopold Mozart's *Toy Symphony* (then attributed to Haydn), but decided to achieve his effects through his orchestration, such as leaving out all low-register instruments from the overture. The remaining fifteen numbers, in two acts as prescribed and again composed to a Petipa plan, include folk song themes from Germany ("Grossvatertanz," no. 5), France ("La Mère Gigogne," no. 12g), and Georgia ("Arabian Dance," no. 12b); otherwise the music is Tchaikovsky's invention. He looked on the suite with childlike imagination and with the intention of being charming rather than dramatic, avoiding the most sinister aspects of Hoffmann's tale. An optional wordless vocalise of children's voices is written into the "Waltz of the Snowflakes" (no. 9). An English dance in the form of a jig was originally composed among the act 2 character dances, but it seems to have been dropped before the first performance; it was not included in the published score, surviving only in a piano version, from which it was orchestrated for inclusion in later productions of the ballet. For various reasons, more visual than musical, the ballet, choreographed by Lev Ivanov, was only a partial success at its premiere performances. [*See* Nutcracker, The.]

The Final Years. Tchaikovsky made one more journey to England, conducting a Philharmonic Society concert (shared with Camille Saint-Saëns) in London and his tone poem *Francesca da Rimini* (1876) in Cambridge as part of a concert marking the university's conferral on him of an honorary doctorate in musical. Back in Russia, he conducted the premiere of his Symphony no. 6 in Saint Petersburg at the end of October 1893. Nine days later, he died; the cause of death given was cholera. It has been claimed that he actually died from arsenic poisoning, an act of suicide carried out in the threat of scandal about a homosexual relationship with a prominent nobleman (Orlova, 1979). Whether his alleged suicide was committed at the instigation of a "kangaroo court" or "court of honor" of his friends and associates has also been suggested but also remains unproven.

Contributions. What can be accepted is that the character of Tchaikovsky's music, theatrical and symphonic, was to a great extent formed by his acknowledged homosexuality, sternly repressed as it was by the laws and social conventions of his time. His music became a means of expressing thoughts and feelings that could not otherwise have found an outlet. A century later, his listeners are vastly the richer for the musicality, wealth, and candor of his emotions, put into forms that are universally accessible and as universally cherished.

The close relationship that exists between much of Tchaikovsky's ballet music and his concert music has led almost every choreographer of note in the twentieth century to make use of his concert music. Some of Tchaikovsky's concert pieces have suggested narrative themes, such as *Hamlet,* choreographed by both Serge Lifar and Robert Helpmann; *Romeo and Juliet,* by Lifar; *Manfred,* by Rudolf Nureyev; *Francesca da Rimini,* by both Michel Fokine and David Lichine; *Onegin,* by John Cranko (to the nonoperatic pieces); and *Anastasia,* by Kenneth MacMillan (to Symphonies 1 and 3). Music utilized for plotless ballets includes "Serenade for Strings," set by both Fokine and George Balanchine; Piano Concerto no. 1, by Bronislava Nijinska; Piano Concertos 2 and 3, by Balanchine; Symphony no. 1, by both Vladimir Burmeister and Peter Martins; Symphony no. 3, by Balanchine; Symphony no. 5, by Léonide Massine; and Symphony no. 6, by Serge Lifar, by Maurice Béjart, and by George Balanchine. In 1981, George Balanchine and the New York City Ballet staged a Tchaikovsky Festival for ten days at the New York State Theater. Twelve premieres were among the twenty-four ballets presented, and Balanchine then declared, "If it were not for Tchaikovsky, there wouldn't be any dancing."

BIBLIOGRAPHY

Acocella, Joan. "The Mystery, Magic, and the Majesty of Tchaikovsky and the Ballet." *Dance Magazine* (June 1981): 53–56.

Brown, David. *Tchaikovsky: The Early Years, 1840–1874.* London, 1978.

Brown, David. *Tchaikovsky: The Crisis Years, 1874–1878.* London, 1983.

Davydov, I. L. *Zapiski o P. I. Chaikovskom.* Moscow, 1962.

Kashkin, Nikolai. *Vospominaniia o P. I. Chaikovskom.* Moscow, 1896.

Kendall, Alan. *Tchaikovsky: A Biography.* London, 1988.

New York City Ballet program (June 1981).

Orlova, Alexandra. "Tchaikovsky: The Last Chapter." *Music and Letters* 1 (1979).

Tchaikovsky, Petr Ilich. *To My Best Friend: Correspondence between Tchaikovsky and Nadezhda von Meck, 1876–1878.* Translated by Galina von Meck. Oxford, 1993.

Warrack, John. *Tchaikovsky Ballet Music.* London, 1979.

Wiley, Roland John. *Tchaikovsky's Ballets.* Oxford, 1985.

Noël Goodwin

TCHAIKOVSKY PIANO CONCERTO NO. 2. *See* Ballet Imperial.

TCHELITCHEV, PAVEL (Pavel Fedorovich Chelishchev; born 21 September 1898 in Moscow, died 31 July 1957 in Frascati, Italy), Russian-American painter, illustrator, and stage designer. The painter Pavel Tchelitchev brought many innovative ideas to his stage designs, introducing new uses of stage lighting and the first use of film projections in a ballet. He preferred to approach the stage as a sculptor rather than as a painter. His sets were not merely painted backdrops; they incorporated elements that became integrated with the action: for example, gauzes to diffuse the shapes made by dancers or ropes manipulated by dancers to create geometric forms in space.

Born into an aristocratic and wealthy Russian family, Tchelitchev was exposed to the fine arts at an early age. At one time he wished to become a ballet dancer, an ambition his father firmly discouraged. In 1918, the aftermath of the Russian Revolution forced his family to flee to Kiev, Ukraine, where he began formal art lessons. Two of his teachers, Alexandra Exter and Isaac Rabinovitch, fostered his interest in stage design. He was commissioned in 1919 to design an operetta, *The Geisha,* which was never produced.

In 1920 Tchelitchev left Ukraine for Turkey, where he designed ballets for Victor Zimine's Istanbul-based company. After moving to Berlin in 1921, he worked for the cabaret theater group Der Blaue Vogel and for the Russian Romantic Theater, for which he designed ballets choreographed by Boris Romanov. In 1923 Serge Diaghilev saw Romanov's *Bojarenhochzeit (*The Wedding Feast of the Boyar*)* and invited Tchelitchev to work for the Ballets Russes. At this time Tchelitchev was strongly influenced by constructivism (a style that combined geometric abstraction and the use of modern industrial materials) and Russian folk art; the latter dominated his designs for Rimsky-Korsakov's opera *Le Coq d'Or,* commissioned by the Berlin State Opera in 1923.

Tchelitchev's move to Paris in July 1923 was marked by a stylistic shift toward naturalism. His painting *Basket of Strawberries,* exhibited at the Salon d'Automne of 1925, won him the notice of art collector Gertrude Stein. He was briefly associated with the neo-Romantic group of painters (among them Eugene Berman and Christian Bérard) and shared in their exhibition in 1926. His first experiments with multiple images (best known through his painting *Hide-and-Seek,* c.1940) began at this time.

His long-awaited collaboration with Diaghilev was realized in 1928 with Léonide Massine's ballet *Ode.* He was deeply involved in this project and even made extensive changes in Nicholas Nabokov's scenario. With his technical assistant, Pierre Charbonnier, an expert in neon lighting, he introduced many novel effects, including the placement of lights behind onstage screens, the use of mannequins suspended from ropes to create false perspectives, and the projection of time-lapse films. The ballet's success won him his first one-man show, at the Claridge Gallery in London in July 1928.

In 1933 he collaborated for the first time with George Balanchine, on the ballet *L'Errante,* where he experimented with transparent fabrics and mobile lights. He helped Lincoln Kirstein persuade Balanchine to emigrate

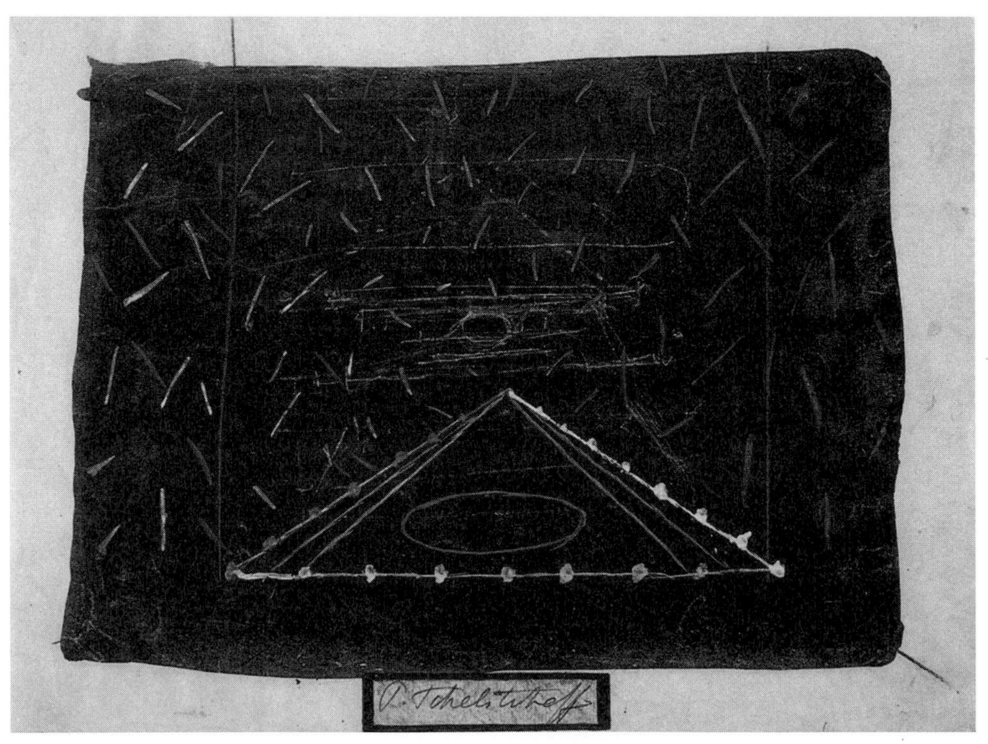

TCHELITCHEV. A design for Léonide Massine's *Ode* (1928), Tchelitchev's first project for Diaghilev's company. Interestingly, this gouache shows the triangular configuration of the stage space but omits the hanging mannequins considered a visual hallmark of the work. (Photograph from the Dance Collection, New York Public Library for the Performing Arts.)

to America; Tchelitchev himself first visited in 1934 and subsequently became a U.S. citizen. In 1936 he collaborated with Balanchine on the conception and design of Gluck's opera *Orfeo ed Euridice* for the Metropolitan Opera. Kirstein (1978) later described this controversial production as "a fusion of the Great Western traditions of myth which joined the mourning for Eurydice with Saint Veronica's Veil, and hell seen as a concentration camp." Tchelitchev also designed Balanchine's *Magic* (1936), *Balustrade* (1941), *Pas de Trois for Piano and Two Dancers, Apollon Musagète,* and *Concierto de Mozart* (all 1942; the latter two for the Teatro Colón, Buenos Aires). In *Apollon* he applied his experiments with multiple images to the ballet, using a single set that was transformed by lighting into a landscape of human faces. He had previously used similar transformations in Jean Giraudoux's play *Ondine,* produced in Paris in 1939.

Tchelitchev continued to advise Kirstein and Balanchine long after he gave up stage design in 1942. His scenario and sketches for the unrealized ballet *Cave of Sleep* (1941) were intended for them. He also designed Ruth Page's *Variations on Euclid* (1933) and Massine's *Saint Francis,* also known as *Nobilissima Visione* (1938).

[*See also* Scenic Design.]

BIBLIOGRAPHY. The most comprehensive analysis of Tchelitchev's stage designs is offered by Donald Windham, "The Stage and Ballet Designs of Pavel Tchelitchew," *Dance Index* 3 (January–February 1944): 4–32. Lincoln Kirstein, *Thirty Years: The New York City Ballet* (New York, 1978), gives many fascinating details about Tchelitchev's interaction with Balanchine and Kirstein. See as well Kirstein's most recent volume, *Tchelitchev* (Santa Fe, 1994). An extensive bibliography is provided in the exhibition catalog, *Pavel Tchelitchew: An Exhibition in the Gallery of Modern Art, 20 March through 19 April 1964* (New York, 1964), which also includes an excellent biographical essay by Kirstein and a chronology by Parker Tyler.

SUSAN AU

TCHERINA, LUDMILA (Monika [Monique] Avenirovna Tchmerzina; born 10 October 1924 in Paris), French ballet dancer, actress, painter, sculptor, and writer. Daughter of a Georgian father and a French mother, Monique Tchmerzina began her ballet training in the Paris studio of the great Russian dancer Olga Preobrajenska in 1931, when she was six. In 1933, at eight, she became a pupil of the Italian dancer Blanche d'Alessandri, who had been trained by Enrico Cecchetti. On holidays in Nice she took class with Ivan Clustine (who taught her Anna Pavlova's famous solo *The Dying Swan*), and she later studied with Julie Sedova and Gustave Ricaux, among others.

Perhaps because her family was poor, Tchmerzina became a performer for hire while still a child. Exhibiting unusual maturity, possessing formidable technical command, and already showing evidence of the stunning beauty she would eventually become, she led the life of a child prodigy, appearing at galas and salons in Paris and tea parties at the Nice Casino. At the age of twelve she met Michel Tverskoi, who had been a stage director in Moscow, and he began coaching her in the dramatic repertory. Her first important recitals as a dancer were in Paris, at the Maison de la Chimie in 1938 and at the École Normale de Musique in 1939.

The outbreak of World War II found Tchmerzina and her mother in Nice, where she met Marcel Sablon, then the manager of the Ballets de Monte-Carlo, who signed her as ballerina of the company. She was sixteen years old. In 1942 she met Serge Lifar, who gave her her big chance by choosing her to dance with him in his new ballet, *Romeo and Juliet.* She made her Paris debut in this ballet, set to Tchaikovsky's music, on 16 June 1942 at the Salle Pleyel. Lifar also chose the name by which she was to be known. At the Marseille Opera, where she danced in *Giselle, Swan Lake,* and several operas *(Manon Lescaut, Aida, Faust),* Tcherina met the dancer Édmond Audran, whom she married.

In 1945 Tcherina joined Roland Petit's Ballets des Champs-Élysées for its first season, dancing in *Les Forains* and pas de deux from *The Sleeping Beauty* and *Swan Lake.* She and her young husband put on dance concerts of their own from 1946 to 1951. In 1946 Audran choreographed *Madame La Lune* for her, to his own musical score, and *Le Loup et l'Agneau,* to music of Alessandro Scarlatti. That same year she created one of her favorite roles, the Young Bonaparte, in Lifar's *À la Memoire d'un Héros* for the Nouveaux Ballets de Monte-Carlo, where she and Audran were among the leading dancers.

At this time, Tcherina began a film career, appearing first in *Les Rendezvous,* directed by Christian Jacques, and then in two films directed by Michael Powell: *The Red Shoes* (1948) and *The Tales of Hoffmann* (1951), in which she co-starred with Moira Shearer, Robert Helpmann, and Léonide Massine. *The Tales of Hoffmann* would make her internationally famous and would bring her an Academy Award (an "Oscar") in 1952. Just when her career was in the ascendant, the tragic death of her young husband in an automobile accident in 1951 caused her to halt, as she was almost overwhelmed by grief.

She resumed performing as an international guest artist in 1954, when she appeared in *Giselle* at the Teatro alla Scala in Milan. In 1957 she appeared as a dancer and an actress in the title role of Lifar's production of *Le Martyre de Saint-Sébastien* at the Paris Opera, and in 1958 she founded her own company, which toured France, Britain, and Italy. The Ballets de Ludmila-Tcherina appeared in Paris in 1959 at the Théâtre Sarah-Bernhardt in a season of new productions that included Milko Šparemblek's *Les Amants de Teruel* and Paul Goubé's *Feu de Poudre.* The former work, which was called a *"ballet total"* at the time, was made into a full-length film and commercially distrib-

TCHERINA. In the film *The Lovers of Teruel* (1962), Tcherina appeared with the famous Spanish dancer Antonio, here pictured in a flying leap. Choreography was by Léonide Massine, set to music by Michel Theodorakis. Sets and costumes were designed by Evor Beddoes. (Photograph by Michael Powell Productions.)

uted in Anglophone countries as *The Lovers of Teruel.* In 1959 Tcherina went to Russia to dance in *Swan Lake* with both the Kirov Ballet in Saint Petersburg and the Bolshoi Ballet in Moscow.

During the 1960s, Tcherina was often to be seen in Italy. In 1960 she became a producer and principal dancer at the Teatro San Carlo in Naples; in 1961 she created the principal role in Maurice Béjart's *Gala,* presented by his Ballet du XXe Siècle at the Teatro La Fenice in Venice; and in 1967 she created a principal part in Ugo dell'Ara's historic revival of Luigi Manzotti's *Excelsior* at the Teatro Communale in Florence. That same year she appeared at the Metropolitan Opera in New York as principal dancer in Joseph Lazzini's production of *The Miraculous Mandarin* (1967), which was also filmed and televised. During the 1970s, she made numerous appearances on television and in films, and in 1972 she appeared in Palermo in the title role of Daniel Auber's opera *La Muette de Portici.*

As a dancer, Tcherina excelled in dramatic roles in ballets such as Lifar's *Le Martyre de Saint-Sébastien* and Goubé's *L'Atlantide* (both 1957); as an actress, she was admired as much for her exceptional beauty and strong presence as for her dramatic ability. She also established a reputation as a painter and sculptor, with several exhibitions of her work in Paris, Seville, and Strasbourg, and she is known as the author of two novels about the world of ballet, *L'amour au miroir* (1983) and *La femme à l'envers* (1986). She was named Officier des Arts et Lettres in 1979 and Officier de la Légion d'Honneur in 1980.

BIBLIOGRAPHY

Garaudy, Roger. *Ludmila Tcherina: Érotisme et mystique.* Paris, 1975.
Hirsch, Nicole. *Ludmila Tcherina.* Paris, 1958.
Lido, Irène, and Serge Lido. *Ludmila Tcherina: Tragédienne de la danse.* Paris, 1967.

MONIQUE BABSKY
Translated from French

TCHERNICHEVA, LUBOV (Liubov' Pavlovna Chernyshova; born 17 September 1890 in Saint Petersburg, died 1 March 1976 in Richmond, Surrey), Russian ballet dancer and teacher. A student of Michel Fokine at the Imperial Theater School in Saint Petersburg, Lubov Chernyshova entered the Maryinsky corps de ballet after her graduation in 1908. The following year she married Serge Grigoriev, who served as *régisseur* for the Ballets Russes de Serge Diaghilev during its spring and summer Saisons Russes in France. In 1911, she participated in Diaghilev's Paris season (with her surname spelled in the French fashion) and eventually became one the Ballets Russes' most popular dancers.

A woman of striking beauty with lovely hand and arm movements, Tchernicheva was a postwar favorite in the title roles of *Cléopâtre* and *Thamar* and as Chiarina in *Le Carnaval,* Zobeide in *Schéhérazade,* and Costanza in *Les Femmes de Bonne Humeur.* As Costanza, her solo of gently drifting *bourrées* on pointe was remembered by Lydia Sokolova as "truly exquisite" (Sokolova, 1960). Along with such *demi-caractère* parts as the Nursemaid in *Petrouchka,* the Tsarevna in *The Firebird,* the Principal Nymph in *L'Après-midi d'un Faune,* the Miller's Wife in *Le Tricorne,* and the Chanson Dansée in *Les Biches,* her repertory included classical solos in *Les Sylphides, The Sleeping Princess,* and *Apollon Musagète.*

In 1926, Tchernicheva succeeded Nikolai Legat and assumed the duties of ballet mistress for Diaghilev's Ballets Russes, a position she held until the company was disbanded upon Diaghilev's death in 1929. In 1932, Tchernicheva became ballet mistress for Colonel Wassily de Basil's Ballets Russes de Monte Carlo, where her coaching and teaching were highly esteemed. She remained in this position until 1952, throughout the life of the various companies managed by Colonel de Basil.

In 1935, Tchernicheva came out of premature retirement to dance her old roles in *Schéhérazade, Le Tricorne,* and *Thamar* (1936), earning critical praise for her powerful sense of theater and miming. In 1937, she created the title role in David Lichine's *Francesca da Rimini.* After the demise of the de Basil company, she settled in England, where she taught at the Sadler's Wells School and, with her husband, staged revivals of *The Firebird* (1954), *Les Sylphides* (1955), *Petrouchka* (1957), and the Polovtsian Dances from *Prince Igor* (1965) for Britain's Royal Ballet. In 1957, she made a last stage appearance as Juliet's mother in John Cranko's *Romeo and Juliet.*

BIBLIOGRAPHY

Anthony, Gordon. "Lubov Tchernicheva." *The Dancing Times* (February 1976): 248–249.

Beaumont, Cyril W. *Bookseller at the Ballet: Memoirs, 1891 to 1929.* London, 1975.

Garafola, Lynn. *Diaghilev's Ballets Russes.* New York and Oxford, 1989.

García-Márquez, Vicente. *The Ballets Russes: Colonel de Basil's Ballets Russes de Monte Carlo, 1932–1952.* New York, 1990.

Grigoriev, Serge. *The Diaghilev Ballet, 1909–1929.* Translated and edited by Vera Bowen. London, 1953.

Sokolova, Lydia. *Dancing for Diaghilev.* Edited by Richard Buckle. London, 1960.

Sorley Walker, Kathrine. *De Basil's Ballets Russes.* New York, 1983.

LYNN GARAFOLA

TEATRO ALLA SCALA. *See* Scala Ballet.

TEATRODANZA CONTEMPORANEA DI ROMA (Contemporary Dance Theater of Rome) is a modern dance company founded by Elsa Piperno in 1972 and directed by Piperno and the Italian-American dancer Joseph Fontano. The company and its school have been responsible in large measure for the diffusion of modern dance in Italy. This has been a difficult process in a country and a city where dance has traditionally been an elite enthusiasm, overwhelmed by the popular taste for opera and closed to the new forms of dance expression coming from the United States.

With determination and obstinacy, Piperno (a former pupil of the National Academy of Dance in Rome) went to London in 1967 to become a student of Robert Cohan, himself a disciple of Martha Graham, and later a dancer with his London Contemporary Dance Theatre. Upon her return to Italy in 1971, Piperno began a series of lecture performances designed to demonstrate and spread the teaching of the Cohan-Graham technique. She and Fontano, a student of Paul Sanasardo, constituted the nucleus of the Teatrodanza Contemporanea di Roma. The group and its school soon became the most important point of reference for modern dance in Italy. The doors of the Rome school opened to modern American artists of all stamps for seminars, lectures, and demonstrations.

The company's repertory was enriched by Piperno's choreographies, including *Stripsmania* (1980), set to selections from Luciano Berio's *Sequenza IV,* sung by Cathy Berberian; *Autofocus* (1981), to music by Brian Eno, J. S. Bach, and Nina Hagen; and *Aquile e Aquiloni* (1981), to music by J. M. Jarre, Genesis, A. Coppola, and P. Schiavoni. Also in the repertory are works by Fontano, including *Duetto in Nero* (1977), to the music of Jean Guillou; *On the Radio* (1980), set to pop and rock music by various composers; and *Sala B* (1982), to music by Eugenio Bennato and Toni Esposito. In the 1980s Teatrodanza Contemporanea has produced a number of modern dance teachers and dancers of great quality, who in Rome and other Italian cities continue to promote and popularize dance, as Elsa Piperno had done in the early 1970s.

BIBLIOGRAPHY

Bentivoglio, Leonetta. *La danza contemporanea.* Milan, 1985.

Doglio, Vittoria, and Elisa Vaccarino. *L'Italia in ballo.* Rome, 1993.

VITTORIA OTTOLENGHI
Translated from Italian

TECHNICAL MANUALS. [*To discuss the importance of published materials as aids in the understanding of technical requirements of early court and theatrical dance and ballet, this entry comprises three articles:*

Publications, 1445–1725
Publications, 1765–1859
Publications since 1887

For related discussion, see Medieval Dance; Renaissance Dance Technique; *and* Ballet Technique, History of.]

Publications, 1445–1725

A technical manual instructs the reader in the technique of dancing. In nearly all instances the technical portion of a manual contains sections on style, gesture, manners, the proper handling of accessories (swords, hats, fans, cloaks, gloves, kerchiefs, and so on) and on musical performance practice, meter, rhythm, and instrumentation. With few exceptions the technical manuals from the early Renaissance to the middle of the seventeenth century contain choreographic descriptions of dances, with or without musical accompaniment, in addition to their theoretical-technical introductions.

The first technical manual was the treatise of Domenico da Piacenza (c.1445), which was followed by Antonio Cornazano's manual (1455 and 1465) and Guglielmo Ebreo's treatises (1463 and undated exemplars). All three authors conceived of dance as an activity involving body, mind, and emotion. For this reason and because the treatises were addressed to persons who had already mastered the fundamentals of dancing, the technical information is embedded in a general discourse on dance, memory, space, and dance composition. A systematization of the steps is given by Domenico; all three fifteenth-century dancing masters dealt with the time values of the steps in relation to one another, with the combination of steps and ornamental motions into larger units (tempi), and with the interchangeability of the tempi in the various dance meters.

Compiled late in the fifteenth century but reflecting an earlier manner of dancing are the French Burgundian *bassedanse* sources, the Brussels manuscript, and Michel Toulouze's *L'art et instruction de bien dancer* (c.1488). The manual of Englishman Robert Coplande (1521) stands in the same tradition as does the so-called Moderne treatise (c.1540). In the theoretical introductions of all of these, the portions dealing with actual technique are often no more than a few sentences, but they are essential for understanding the dances themselves.

The dominant teaching method used in the technical manuals of the fifteenth century is direct didaxis: the teaching dialogue, a discussion between the master and his disciple. The device was first used by Guglielmo Ebreo in some of his treatises and was later used by Thoinot Arbeau and Fabritio Caroso.

Only two dance instruction books appeared during the century that separated the fifteenth-century treatises from the next group of major technical manuals, which begins with Caroso's *Il ballarino* of 1581. One was the *bassedanse*-related Moderne treatise; the other was Antonius de Arena's *Leges dansandi,* written in the macaronic Latin verse then fashionable in the literary circles of Avignon. Arena describes the steps one by one (the first viable reverence description for men and women comes from Arena) and gives extensive attention to manners. University students in the early sixteenth century obviously needed careful instruction in the social graces that a courtier acquired gradually as part of his education in his elevated social environment. Although the main focus of Arena's *Leges dansandi* is still the *bassedanse,* the dance types *branle, pavane,* and *tourdion* are mentioned for the first time.

Precise technical information is supplied by Fabritio Caroso and Cesare Negri, whose manuals appeared in the years 1581 to 1630. Large segments of their treatises describe steps in minute detail, each step in its own chapter *(regola).* Many chapters contain the authors' laments about dancers' bad habits and mistakes, making it possible to distinguish the proper version of a given step from an unsatisfactory one. Composite steps, like *galliard* and *canario* sequences, and step-units modeled after the meters of classical Greek verse (Caroso, *Della nobiltà di dame*) are all included in the *regole;* so too are chapters on men's and ladies' ballroom etiquette, as well as on sitting, walking, and greeting an equal or a superior. Negri's treatise *Le gratie d'amore* (1602) is especially rich in technical information, and it is Negri who gives the clearest images of the demanding theatrical dance technique of the Renaissance as it must have been employed in operas by Giulio Caccini and Claudio Monteverdi, in court ballets, *intermedi,* and other dance spectacles of the period.

Less technical manuals than technical reference books are Lutio Compasso's *Ballo della gagliarda* (1560), Prospero Luti di Sulmona's *Opera bellissima . . . di gagliarda* (1589), and Livio Lupi da Caravaggio's *Libro di gagliarda, tordiglione, passo è mezzo canario è passeggi* (1600, 1607). All three authors give almost no descriptions of steps or full choreographies, instead giving hundreds of step combinations to be used in the composition of new *galliards, tourdions, passo e mezzo*s, and *canaries* and in *passeggi,* the connecting passages between the figures of Renaissance dances that are performed hand-in-hand. Many of the step names mentioned are not described by Caroso and Negri.

The English *Treatise of Daunces* (1581) describes dances of the contemporary repertory and names the steps with which to do them, but it is not strictly speaking a technical manual.

The only technical manual from France in the late sixteenth century is Thoinot Arbeau's *Orchésographie* (1589, 1596). Arbeau, in a way, reaches back to the method used in the early Renaissance: his technical dance information is embedded in a teaching dialogue between himself and his student, Capriol, interwoven with remarks about style, manners, occasional excursions into history, and recurring statements about the benefits to be obtained from faultless mastery of the art of dancing. Arbeau's opening section—which deals with military movement and its music, with drum rhythms, signal tunes, and melodies for the fife *(arigot)*—is unique. In addition to the text Arbeau provides a series of pictures of dancers executing the most prevalent steps, a simple but effective teaching device that helps the reader now, as then, to understand the essential components of the French dance technique of the Renaissance.

In the first half of the seventeenth century, technical manuals were published in France and in Spain. François de Lauze's *Apologie de la danse* (1623) is, according to the full title, "the perfect method to teach [dancing] as much to the gentlemen as to the ladies." More than in any previous manual, emphasis is placed here on exercises, for the "assured grace and dignity" required for the flawless execution of the courante, branle, gavotte, and gaillard could only be acquired with diligent practice. The turnout from the hip is stressed again and again; attention is given to the glance and to facial expression; *révérence* steps for men and women in various social settings are dealt with extensively; the five positions, although not yet called by name, are clearly described, as are [bends] and rises that constitute the *mouvement* of the Baroque technique—all this makes de Lauze's *Apologie* the first technical manual of the Baroque era.

The same trend, although less pronounced, is evident in Esquivel de Navarro's *Discvrsos sobre el arte del dancado.* This manual also gives step descriptions and exercise sequences, but, as in de Lauze's manual, dance descriptions are kept to a minimum, and there is no music. Juan Antonio Jaque, in his *Libro de danzar* (c.1680), includes the descriptions of six fashionable social dances, together with instructions for steps and figures.

During the remainder of the seventeenth century, no further technical manuals were produced. The English country dance collections by John Playford (from 1651), Thomas Bray (1699 and later editions), and others exerted their influence on French ballroom practices, namely, André Lorin's *Livre de contredance présenté au Roy* (manuscript, c.1685) and his *Livre de la contredance du Roy* (1688). All contain some advice regarding the execution of steps; their main concern, however, is the transmission of choreographies, occasionally enhanced by elegant drawings of dancing couples (Lorin), not the teaching of dance.

The decade of the 1680s in France saw the eruption of an enormous concern with the creation of a viable dance notation. Lorin, Jean Favier, Pierre Beauchamps, and Sieur De La Haise each developed his own system (for details, see Harris-Warrick and Marsh, 1994, pp. 82ff.), but neither Lorin's nor Favier's notations (the latter summarized in the article "Chorégraphie" in volume 3 of Denis Diderot and Jean Le Rond d'Alembert's *Encyclopédie* of 1753) assumed the format of a technical manual. Beauchamps's efforts, in contrast, formed the background, albeit unacknowledged, to Raoul-Auger Feuillet's didactic masterpiece, the *Chorégraphie, ou L'art de décrire la dance* of 1700.

In Feuillet's *Chorégraphie,* which, as the title page states, is intended for the self-instruction of amateurs "in every kind of dance" as well as for the use of dancing masters, he takes his reader step by step through all the elements of his notational system. He deals with the dancing space, with the positioning of dancers in that space, and with floor patterns. He describes the five positions, the "good" ones as well as the *fausses,* with the toes turned in. He describes and notates a variety of ornamental leg gestures, explains the use of the arms, discusses *"la batterie des castagnettes,"* with practice sequences, and provides tables of hundreds of steps—*coupés, pas de bourrée,* pirouettes, cabrioles, and so on—in every direction. A relatively brief chapter is devoted to the correlation of the steps with the most common musical meters; practice phrases are included there also.

At the end of his treatise, Feuillet added a collection of fifteen notated *entrées de ballet* of his own composition, some of considerable difficulty, as a challenge to masters of the dance and to advanced students (see preface to *Chorégraphie*). This was followed by a separate collection of nine ballroom dances by Guillaume-Louis Pecour (see Witherell, 1983).

Not long after its first printing, *Chorégraphie* was translated into English in 1706 both by P. Siris and by John Weaver (whose later edition, with three additional dances, appeared in the early 1720s). Gottfried Taubert included a German translation in his *Rechtschaffener Tantz-Meister* of 1717.

The importance and viability of this dance notation was recognized immediately, as witnessed by the numerous dances that were published singly or in small groups each November, for the beginning of the "season" (see Annual Collections), and by the larger collections of choreographies for use in the ballroom and/or in the theater, such as the ones by Gaudrau (c.1712–1715) and Anthony L'Abbé, the last published by F. Le Roussau (c.1725; see Marsh, 1991; Little and Marsh, 1992). None of these is a teaching manual, strictly speaking; rather, each represents the repertory that dance enthusiasts in Europe could learn to master through diligent study of the instruction books and in their dancing schools.

The line of manuals devoted to the teaching of Beauchamps-Feuillet notation, not infrequently with modifications (as, for example, the detailed treatment of arms, hands, and fingers in Malpied, c.1780), continued through the entire eighteenth century. It included works by authors from Germany, England, Italy, Spain, and Portugal, all attesting to the far-reaching influence of the French style of dancing during the Baroque era (for individual listings and commentaries, see Schwartz-Schlundt, 1987).

In addition, a large group of instruction manuals describe in words the technique and style of the *danse noble* as well as, with increasing frequency, the *danse haute* of the theatre, nearly always in combination with directives for proper etiquette, descriptions of festivities of all kinds, excursions into history, and the like.

To this group belong Pierre Rameau's *Le Maître à danser* (1725; translated as *The Dancing Master* by John Essex, 1728), the textbook *par excellence* for early eighteenth-century social dancing; Louis Bonin's *Die Neueste Art zur Galanten und Theatralischen Tanzkunst* (1711); Gottfried Taubert's *Tantz-Meister* (1717); Kellom Tomlinson's *The Art of Dancing Explained* (1724/1735); Giambatista Dufort's *Trattato del Ballo Nobile* (1728); and, later in the century, Gennaro Magri's *Trattato* (1779) and Malpied's *Traîté* (c.1780).

Not quite satisfied with the purely verbal explanations of the dance technique of his time as he gave them in *Le maître à danser,* Rameau also published in 1725 his *Abbrégé de la nouvelle méthode dans l'art d'écrire ou de traçer toutes sortes de danses de ville,* a notation book intended as an aide-mémoire for persons who may have interrupted their dance studies but also useful for dancing masters. Tables of steps were given in a manner similar to that of Feuillet, but in each case Rameau juxtaposed the "ancienne Chorégraphie avec la nouvelle" (p. 85 ff), and he accompanied the notations with verbal descriptions of each step. Twelve dances by Pecour in "the new corrected and augmented" notation form part 2 of *Abbrégé.*

In many of these publications, the explanatory text was enhanced by engravings, showing persons in the execution of individual steps (Rameau) or step-sequences (Tomlinson), depicting arm and wrist motions (Rameau), arm and leg positions (Behr), dancing couples (Tomlinson, Rameau, Bickham, Dubois, Guillaume), an entire grand ball presided over by the king (Rameau), and so on. A particularly lovely set of illuminations can be found in Pablo Minguet e Yrol's *Arte de danzar à la francesa* (1758/1768). Practically all the manuals mentioned contain one or more sample dances in notation.

Volumes are also devoted to one dance type only, such as George Bickham (1738) and G. M. de Chavanne (1767) on the minuet; or Simon Guillaume (1769) and Dubois (late eighteenth century) on the allemande.

The minuet, which has enjoyed a lasting popularity since the 1660s, and demanded the utmost in control and elegance from those who dance it, normally one solo couple (see Hilton, 1981, p. 191ff. for details), occupies large sections of the more general instruction books as well (Tomlinson, Malpied, Magny, and others).

The technique of stage dancing, serious as well as grotesque, was given full attention in the writings of John Weaver (see Ralph, 1985) and Louis Bonin (1711), in book 2 of Taubert's *Tantz-Meister,* in Noverre's *Lettres* (1760), in Gaspero Angiolini's extensive forewords to his ballets *Don Juan* (1760) and *Semiramis* (1765; for both, see Brown, 1991 and Brainard, 1996) and in Gennaro Magri's *Trattato* (1779). The instruction manuals for actors cited in Dene Barnett's important study on gesture on the eighteenth-century tragic stage (1987) provide us with the material needed to fill in the gaps that the dance treatises left open.

Theater dances for all kinds of personages are depicted in Gregorio Lambranzi's *Neue und Curieuse Theatrialische Tantz-Schul* (Nürnberg, 1716). On the title page, next to a portrait of the author, is a scroll with one figure of a *loure* for a couple in Feuillet notation; no other example of that notation appears in the 101 engravings that make up the two parts of the book. Printed at the top of each page is the tune for each dance; below that is the image of a stage with a few flats and the dancing figures; at the bottom is a decorative medallion that frames the names of the steps the performers are to execute, with directives for the action, some very brief, some extensive enough to amount to small scenarios.

As Lambranzi explains in his foreword to part 1, his

> aim is not to describe in detail the choreography of these dances or any particular *pas,* still less to depict all their possible variations. . . . I shall portrait a principal character in appropriate costume, the style of his dance and the manner of its execution. . . . However, it is not my intention to restrict anyone to my method, but to leave each dancer free to adapt it as he pleases. (Beaumont edition, p. 15)

Lambranzi's opus is a treasure-trove of information on the dancing style and technique of Italian *commedia dell'arte* characters, on that of various professions and trades, on highly acrobatic buffoonery, and on the dancing of persons of elegance who move in the manner of Spain, of Rome, and, of course, of France.

National and regional dances are taught in a number of technical manuals from Spain by Juan Antonio Jaque (c.1680; see Subirá, 1950 and Gingell, 1991), Pablo Minguet and Minguet E Yrol (1750s), Felipe Rejo de Flores (1793); German, Polish, Hungarian and "a multitude of English dances" (eine Unzahl Englischer Tänze) appear in C. J. Feldtenstein's *Erweiterung der Kunst nach der Chorographie* [sic] *zu tanzen* (1772; 1775; 1776).

Parallel to the manuals that teach the technique and style of noble and theatrical dancing were publications devoted to the increasingly popular, more relaxed *contredanses,* country dances, quadrilles, and cotillons, some in verbal descriptions such as the Playford series and the Caledonian dances from Scotland, others in simplified Feuillet notation in which mainly the dancers' path is given and steps are written in only at crucial moments. Feuillet's own *Recüeil de contredances* (1706) is followed by similar collections by Jacques Dezais (1712), John Essex (1710), Ernest August Jayme (1717), Pablo Minguet e Yrol (1758), and De La Cuisse (1762), all the way to Gennaro Magri (1779) and beyond. Choreographies for *contredanses* are also included in many of the other instruction books, usually at the end, after the more formal dances have been presented (see Schwartz-Schlundt, 1987; also Guilcher, 1969).

Finally, a large number of publications have main objectives that are the aesthetics, and often the history, of the performing arts—of dance, music, and theater. These provide us with innumerable, valuable details concerning topics that are treated elsewhere in more or less cursory fashion, and they throw light on some of the heated discussions that occupied the minds of theorists and practitioners of the dance in the seventeenth and the eighteenth centuries. These include the manufacturing and wearing of masks, the execution of gestures in various dramatic situations, the relationship of music and dance, the composition of ballets, the education and training of dancers, the role of the grotesque versus that of the serious dancer on the Baroque stage, and so on.

There are far too many authors to mention them all by name (see Schwartz-Schlundt, 1987; Harris-Warrick and Marsh, 1994; among others). The list, of necessity, includes Marin Mersenne, Claude-François Ménestrier, Louis Bonin, Louis de Cahusac, Michel de Pure, John Weaver, Gaspero Angiolini, Jean-Georges Noverre, Giovanni Andrea Gallini, and Gennaro Magri; and, on the musical side, Michael Praetorius, Johann Mattheson, Thomas Mace, George Muffat, and Jean-Philippe Rameau. Important information is also transmitted in the Diderot-d'Alembert *Encyclopédie* and in the many dictionaries on music and dance subjects published during the Baroque period.

BIBLIOGRAPHY

Barnett, Dene, with Jeanette Massy-Westropp. *The Art of Gesture: The Practices and Principles of 18th Century Acting.* Heidelberg, 1987.

Beaumont, Cyril W., ed., and Derra de Moroda. *Gregorio Lambranzi: New and Curious School of Theatrical Dancing.* New York, 1966.

Brainard, Ingrid. "Die Choreographie der Hoftänze in Burgund, Frankreich und Italien im 15. Jahrhundert." Ph.D. diss., University of Göttingen, 1956.

Brainard, Ingrid. "Bassedanse, Bassadanza, and Ballo in the Fifteenth Century." In *Dance History Research: Perspectives from Related Arts and Disciplines,* edited by Joann W. Kealiinohomoku. New York, 1970.

Brainard, Ingrid. *The Art of Courtly Dancing in the Early Renaissance.* West Newton, Mass., 1981.

Brainard, Ingrid. "Der Höfische Tanz: Darstellende Kunst und Höfische Repräsentation." In *Europäische Hofkultur im 16. und 17. Jahrhundert,* edited by August Buck et al. Hamburg, 1981.

Brainard, Ingrid. "The Speaking Body: Gaspero Angiolini's *Rhétorique Muette* and the *Ballet d'Action* in the Eighteenth Century." In *Critica Musica: Essays in Honor of Paul Brainard.* Amsterdam, 1996.

Brown, Bruce Alan. *Gluck and the French Theatre in Vienna.* Oxford, 1991.

Chadima, Helen Gower. "The Use of Castanets in Baroque Dance." In *Proceedings of the Sixth Annual Conference, Society of Dance History Scholars, the Ohio State University, 11–13 February 1983,* edited by Christena L. Schlundt, pp. 84–94. Riverside, Calif., 1983.

Crane, Frederick. *Materials for the Study of the Fifteenth-Century Basse Danse.* Brooklyn, 1968.

Francalanci, Andrea. "The *Copia di M^o Giorgio del Guido di ballare basse danze e balletti* as Found in the New York Public Library." *Basler Jahrbuch für Historische Musikpraxis* 14 (1990): 87–179. Italian text only.

Gallo, F. Alberto. "Il 'ballare lombardo,' circa 1435–1475." *Studi musicali* 8 (1979): 61–84.

Gerbes, Angelika. "Gottfried Taubert on Social and Theatrical Dance of the Early Eighteenth Century." Ph.D. diss., Ohio State University, 1972.

Gingell, Jane. "Spanish Dance in the Golden Age: The Dance Text of Juan Antonio Jaque." In *Dance in Hispanic Cultures: Proceedings of the Fourteenth Annual Conference, Society of Dance History Scholars, New World School of the Arts, Miami, Florida, 8–10 February 1991,* compiled by Christena L. Schlundt. Riverside, Calif., 1991.

Goff, Moira. "Edmund Pemberton, Dancing-Master and Publisher." *Dance Research* 9.1 (1993): 52–81.

Goff, Moira, and Jennifer Thorp. "Dance Notations Published in England c.1700–1740 and Related Manuscript Material." *Dance Research* 9.2 (1993): 32–50.

Goff, Moira. "'The Art of Dancing Demonstrated by Characters and Figures': French and English Sources for Court and Theatre Dance, 1700–1750." In *The British Library Journal* 21.2 (1995): 202–231.

Goff, Moira. "George Bickham Junior and the Art of Dancing." In *Factotum* 34 (1993): 14–18.

Guilcher, Jean Michel. *La contredanse et les renouvellements de la danse française.* Paris, 1969.

Guthrie, John, and Marino Zorzi. "Rules of Dancing: Antonius Arena." *Dance Research* 4 (Autumn 1986): 3–53. Original text with English translation.

Harris-Warrick, Rebecca, and Carol G. Marsh. *Musical Theatre at the Court of Louis XIV: Le Mariage de la Grosse Cathos.* Cambridge, 1994.

Helwig, Christine, and Marshall Barron. *Thomas Bray's Country Dances, 1699.* New Haven, 1988.

Hilton, Wendy. *Dance of Court and Theatre: The French Noble Style, 1690–1725.* Princeton, 1981.

Hudson, Richard. *The Allemande, the Balletto, and the Tanz.* 2 vols. Cambridge, 1986.

Inglehearn, Madeleine, and Peggy Forsyth. *The Book on the Art of Dancing: Antonio Cornazano.* London, 1981. English translation only.

Jones, Pamela. "The Relation between Music and Dance in Cesare Negri's 'Le gratie d'amore' (1602)." 2 vols. Ph.D. diss., University of London, 1988.

Keller, Kate Van Winkle, and Genevieve Shimer. *The Playford Ball.* 2d ed. Northampton, Mass., 1994.

Kendall, Yvonne. "*Le gratie d'amore* (1602) by Cesare Negri: Translation and Commentary." Ph.D. diss., Stanford University, 1985. Original Italian text in facsimile with English translation.

Little, Meredith Ellis, and Carol G. Marsh. *La Danse Noble: An Inventory of Dances and Sources.* Williamstown, 1992.

Marrocco, W. Thomas. *Inventory of Fifteenth-Century Bassedanze, Balli, and Balletti in Italian Dance Manuals.* New York, 1981.

Marsh, Carol. "French Court Dance in England, 1706–1740: A Study of the Sources." Ph.D. diss., City University of New York, 1985.

Marsh, Carol G., and John M. Ward, eds. *Anthony L'Abbé, A New Collection of Dances.* Facsimile. Music for London Entertainment, 1660–1800, series D, vol. 2. Boston 1991.

Mather, Betty Bang, with Dean M. Karns. *Dance Rhythms of the French Baroque: A Handbook for Performance.* Bloomington, 1987.

Ralph, Richard. *The Life and Works of John Weaver.* New York, 1985.

Rebman, Elizabth Huttig. "Chorégraphie: An Annotated Bibliography of Eighteenth Century Printed Instruction Books." M.A. thesis, Stanford University, 1981.

Sasportes, José. *História de dança em Portugal.* Lisbon, 1970.

Schwartz, Judith L., and Christena L. Schlundt. *French Court Dance and Dance Music: A Guide to Primary Source Writings, 1643–1789.* Stuyvesant, N.Y., 1987.

Smith, A. William, trans. and ed. *Fifteenth-Century Dance and Music: The Complete Transcribed Italian Treatises and Collections in the Tradition of Domenico da Piacenza.* 2 vols. Stuyvesant, N.Y., 1995.

Sparti, Barbara. *Guglielmo Ebreo of Pesaro: On the Practice or Art of Dancing.* Oxford, 1993. Original Italian text with English translation.

Sparti, Barbara. *Ballo della Gagliarda: Lutio Compasso.* Freiburg, 1995. Italian text only.

Subirá, José. "Juan Antonio Jaque: Libro de Danzar de Baltazar de Rojas Pantoia." *Anuario musical* 5 (1950): 190–198.

Sutton, Julia. "Reconstruction of Sixteenth-Century Dance." In *Dance History Research: Perspectives from Related Arts and Disciplines,* edited by Joann W. Kealiinohomoku. New York, 1970.

Sutton, Julia. "Arbeau, Thoinot," "Caroso, Fabritio," and "Negri, Cesare." In *The New Grove Dictionary of Music and Musicians.* London, 1980.

Sutton, Julia. *Fabritio Caroso: Nobiltà di Dame (1600).* Music transcribed and edited by F. Marian Walker. Oxford, 1986. English translation only.

Taubert, Karl Heinz. *Höfische Tänze: Ihre Geschichte und Choreographie.* Mainz, 1968.

Tomlinson, Kellom. *A Work Book by Kellom Tomlinson: Commonplace Book of an Eighteenth-Century English Dancing Master (c.1708–1722).* Edited by Jennifer Shennan. Stuyvesant, N.Y., 1992.

Wilson, D. R. *Domenico of Piacenza (Paris, Bibliothèque Nationale, MS ital. 972).* Corr. ed. Cambridge, 1995. Italian text only.

Witherell, Anne L. *Louis Pécour's 1700 Recüeil de dances.* Ann Arbor, Mich., 1983.

INGRID BRAINARD

Publications, 1765–1859

The period from 1765 to 1859 marks a transition from the dance of the Baroque court and theater to the Romantic ballet; thus, the technical manuals of the time reflect both the old style and the new. Books devoted to theatrical dance technique, rare in previous periods, appear with more frequency, if mostly in numerous editions and translations of a few works, often still containing chapters on social, or "private," dancing. In the absence of any extant ballet repertory from the period preserving a semblance of its original choreography (with the possible exception of Vincenzo Galeotti's *The Whims of Cupid and the Ballet Master,* 1786), the value of the following technical manuals, with their insights into the changes that were occurring, is considerable.

The most important manual treating theatrical dance technique and execution in the latter part of the eighteenth century is Gennaro Magri's *Trattato teorico-prattico di ballo* (Naples, 1779). Magri discusses steps familiar from earlier in the century, usually giving French terms and their Italian equivalents, but his extensive list includes many later steps and exercises that reappear in the manuals of the next century. He often suggests which movements are appropriate for the various types of dancer—the serious, the *demi-caractère,* and the comic. Of particular interest is his information about the steps and style of the *grotteschi,* an impressive account of the skill and dexterity their art demanded. In contrast, the treatises by Claude Marc Magny (1765) and Malpied (c.1789) closely follow Raoul-Auger Feuillet's early text, *Chorégraphie* (1700). Although some additional steps are included, the predominant emphasis is on older forms, with special attention given to the minuet. The technical descriptions in Charles Compan's *Dictionnaire de danse* (1787) also reflect the style of the early eighteenth century. The *Encyclopédie méthodique* (1786), acknowledging its debt to the *traité* of Pierre Rameau as well as to the work of Louis de Cahusac and Jean-Georges Noverre, includes, among its technical material, an extensive discussion of arm movements.

The first important text devoted exclusively to theatrical dancing in the nineteenth century was written in 1820 by Carlo Blasis, *Traité élémentaire théorique et pratique de l'art de la danse.* The young author explains and illustrates many of the requisites still observed in ballet technique today, including complete turnout of the legs. His outline of "the lesson" provides some description of the "elementary exercises" to be "performed with the hand resting upon something firm," and a listing, but not an explanation, of the exercises to be practiced in center floor.

Although Blasis's is the first nineteenth-century account of the ballet lesson, his preface indicates that his instructions emanate "from the schools of leading masters who have contributed immensely to the progress and beauty of modern dancing." Indeed, an almost identical format of elementary exercises had been described earlier by J. H. Gourdoux-Daux (1817). His *Principes et notions élémentaires sur l'art de la danse,* published in 1811, had been preceded by a private printing in 1804. It clearly demonstrates the continuity between social and theatrical dancing.

In *Notes upon Dancing, Historical and Practical,* Blasis (1847) recalls the various translations of his *Traité* into Italian, Danish, Spanish, English, and French. His *The Code of Terpsichore,* written in England, was prepared for a printing in 1828, but because of the publisher's financial straits only a few copies were bound. The book finally appeared in 1830, with a French edition, *Manueal complete de la danse,* published that same year. The chapters on technique are virtually identical with those in the *Traité,* with the addition of a section on the "New Method of Instruction" and different engravings. [*See the entry on Blasis.*]

For this period, social dance publications continue to be helpful in explaining the step vocabulary found both on the stage and in the ballroom. Examples include *Elements of the Art of Dancing* by Alexander Strathy (1822) and *A Short Essay on the French Danse de Société* by Charles Mason (1827). The most extensive description of steps of the period appears in Giacoma Costa's *Saggio analitico-pratico intorno all'arte della danza per uso di civile conversazione* (1831). Although written as a text for social dancing, Costa's manual contains highly complex steps and some charming combinations *(ligazione).* Costa is easier to decipher than Magri, and his illustrations resemble those of Blasis.

E. A. Théleur's *Letters on Dancing* (1831) tried to accommodate the changing technical style with new nomenclature for the positions of the feet and arms. Although his efforts failed to be adopted, his technical descriptions, along with his two easily diciphered notation systems, his explanations of proper execution, and his illustrations (including the first depiction in a technical manual of a dancer on full pointe) give the clearest account of early nineteenth-century technique. His description of the dance lesson closely resembles Blasis's, but Théleur's account is more explicit. Included in the manual is the duet "Gavotte de Vestris," notated in both of Théleur's systems.

Although never published, the four handwritten notebooks by Léon Michel (who preferred to be known as Michel St. Léon) include numerous exercises, *enchaînements*, and *entrées* (and their music) for one to three dancers, composed or compiled during his tenure as dancing master at the court of Würtemberg. St. Léon also includes some solo and pas de deux selections from the Paris Opera ballet repertory by Pierre Gardel, Jean-Pierre Aumer, and Albert (François Decombe). These notebooks, together with works by August Bournonville, particularly his manuscript, *Méthode de Vestris* (c.1826) and his later published works on dance theory and notation, *Études chorégraphiques* (1855, 1861), provide important insights into the teaching methods developed by Jean-François Coulon and most especially by Auguste Vestris at the Paris Opera's School of Dance.

For a more complete understanding of the actual performance of ballet technique in the early nineteenth century, later texts must be consulted. Two especially pertinent ones are Arthur Saint-Léon's *La sténochorégraphie* (1852) and Giovanni Léopold Adice's *Théorie de la gymnastique de la danse théâtrale* (1859). Saint-Léon both describes and notates in his own system classroom combinations mentioned earlier by both Blasis and Théleur, as well as *enchaînements* from the collection of his father, Léon Michel. His notation is correlated with music for the *enchaînements* as well as for a pas de six from his ballet *La Vivandière*.

One section of Adice's book is devoted to the explication of Blasis's classes, which Adice extols over lessons of his own day. In the chapter on Blasis's *barre* work, Adice enumerates the repetitions of each exercise—altogether some 648 gymnastic movements. Substantial portions of this section are translated in *Dance as a Theatre Art*, edited in 1974 by Selma Jeanne Cohen. Some of the material from Adice, Blasis, Saint-Léon, and Théleur, is correlated and reconstructed in Sandra Noll Hammond's *Ballet: Beyond the Basics* (1982).

BIBLIOGRAPHY

Adice, G. Léopold. *Théorie de la gymnastique de la danse théâtrale.* Paris, 1859. Excerpts translated by Leonore Loft in *Dance as a Theatre Art*, edited by Selma Jeanne Cohen (New York, 1974).

Blasis, Carlo. *An Elementary Treatise upon the Theory and Practice of the Art of Dancing* (1820). Translated by Mary Stewart Evans. New York, 1944.

Blasis, Carlo. *The Code of Terpsichore: A Practical and Historical Treatise on the Ballet, Dancing, and Pantomime.* London, 1828.

Blasis, Carlo. *The Art of Dancing Comprising Its Theory and Practice, and a History of Its Rise and Progress, from the Earliest Times.* Translated by R. Barton. London, 1831. Second edition of *The Code of Terpsichore* (above).

Blasis, Carlo. *Notes upon Dancing, Historical and Practical.* Translated by R. Barton. London, 1847.

Bournonville, August. *Méthode de Vestris.* Undated manuscript located in Copenhagen, Royal Library, NKS 3285 4°.

Bournonville, August. *Etudes Chorégraphiques.* Copenhagen, 1855 and 1861.

Compan, Charles. *Dictionnaire de danse.* Paris, 1787.

Costa, Giacomo. *Saggio analitico-pratico intorno all'arte della danza per uso di civile conversazione.* Turin, 1831.

Encyclopédie méthodique: Arts académiques, équitation, escrime, danse, et art de nager. Paris, 1786.

Feuillet, Raoul-Auger. *Chorégraphie, ou L'art de décrire la dance, par caractères, figures et signes démonstratifs, avec lesquels on apprend facilement de soy-même toutes sortes de dances.* Paris, 1700. Translated by John Weaver as *Orchesography, or, The Art of Dancing* (London, 1706).

Flindt, Vivi, and Knud Arne Jürgensen. *Bournonville Ballet Technique.* London, 1992.

Gallini, Giovanni. *Critical Observations on the Art of Dancing, to Which Is Added a Collection of Cotillons or French Dances.* London, c.1770.

Gourdoux-Daux, J. H. *Principes et notions élémentaires sur l'art de la danse.* 2d ed. Paris, 1811. Translated by Victor Guillou as *Elements and Principles of the Art of Dancing* (Philadelphia, 1817).

Hammond, Sandra Noll. *Ballet: Beyond the Basics.* Palo Alto, Calif., 1982.

Jürgensen, Knud Arne and Ann Hutchinson Guest. *The Bournonville Heritage, A Choreographic Record 1829–1875.* London, 1990.

Magny, Claude Marc. *Principes de chorégraphie, suivis d'un traité de la cadence.* Paris, 1765.

Magri, Gennaro. *Trattato teorico-prattico di ballo.* Naples, 1779. Translated by Mary Skeaping as *Theoretical and Practical Treatise on Dancing* (London, 1988).

Malpied. *Traité sur l'art de la danse.* Paris, c.1785. 2d ed., rev. and enl. Paris, c.1789.

Mason, Charles. *A Short Essay on the French Danse de Société.* London, 1827.

Noverre, Jean-Georges. *Lettres sur la danse et sur les ballets.* Stuttgart and Lyon, 1760. Translated by Cyril W. Beaumont as *Letters on Dancing and Ballets* (London, 1930).

Saint-Léon, Arthur. *La sténochorégraphie.* Paris, 1852.

St. Léon, Michel. *Exercices de 1829, cahier d'exercices pour LL. AA. Royalles les Princesses de Würtemburg 1830, 2me cahier exercises de 1830.* Untitled volume containing Exercises de 1833, 1834, and 1836. Manuscripts located in Paris, Bibliothèque de l'Opéra, Res. 1137 and 1140.

Strathy, Alexander. *Elements of the Art of Dancing.* Edinburgh, 1822.

Théleur, E. A. *Letters on Dancing, Reducing This Elegant and Healthful Exercise to Easy Scientific Principles.* London, 1831.

Warner, MaryJane. "Gavottes and Bouquets: A Comparative Study of Changes in Dance Style between 1700 and 1850." Ph.D. diss., Ohio State University, 1974.

Winter, Marian Hannah. *The Pre-Romantic Ballet.* London, 1974.

Sandra Noll Hammond

Publications since 1887

From the late nineteenth century until World War I, ballet manuals were not widespread; however, books on natural movement and social and folk dancing became increasingly popular. Natural movement or physical culture manuals described various approaches to movement intended to create total body coordination. Social dance manuals described dances and discussed steps, styles, etiquette, and even the cost of holding social evenings. Recording folk dances was an aspect of the developing interest in heritage preservation.

In 1887 Friedrich Zorn published *Grammar of the Art of Dancing.* The industrious author is responsible for the last manual in the "old" style, in which a single author explained all aspects of dancing—history, technique, theatrical and social dance, and his own notation system. Subsequent technical manuals discussed fewer topics in more depth. In 1890 Berthe Bernay produced *La danse au théâtre,* a general educational reader. Probably around this time, Eugène Giraudet published his *Traité de la danse* (5th ed., 1891), collecting his many lectures on dance. Although mainly a description of social dances, it includes a section on theatrical dance, obviously inspired by Carlo Blasis.

Dictionnaire de la danse (1895) was written by G. Desrat to update the 1787 Compan book. It included a compendious bibliography of books written on dance.

Perhaps because of World War I, and because the presentation of Serge Diaghilev's Ballets Russes demanded a new evaluation of ballet technique, the decade 1910–1920 was sparse in manuals. In 1913, teacher Édouard Espinosa had his *Technical Dictionary of Dancing* published by the *Dancing Times* in London. His discussions of technique and ballet principles helped stimulate the English dance world to organize, leading to the formation of what is now the Royal Academy of Dancing (RAD). The popular *First Steps in Ballet* (1934), followed by *Intermediate Steps in Ballet* (1947) and *Advanced Steps in Ballet* (1950), by Ruth French and Felix Demery, updated Espinosa's discussion of technique and his terminology.

The teaching methods of Enrico Cecchetti, ballet master of the Ballets Russes, were published in 1922 as *A Manual of The Theory and Practice of Classical Theatrical Dancing (Méthode Cecchetti)* (1922), the most important technical manual of the time. The balletomane and publisher Cyril Beaumont, aided by the former Diaghilev dancer Stanislas Idzikowski, deciphered and analyzed Cecchetti's Italian-Russian mixture of ballet technique under the master's close guidance. This is a more detailed study than the 1894 *Manuel des exercices de danse théâtrale* (Saint Petersburg), handwritten by Cecchetti and including exercises notated in Arthur Saint-Léon's Sténochorégraphie. The 1922 book was complete in its discussion, from *barre* to *adage.* The *allegro* section was supplemented by *The Theory and Practice of Allegro in Classical Ballet (Cecchetti Method)* by Beaumont and Margaret Craske (1930), and *The Theory and Practice of Advanced Allegro in Classical Ballet (Cecchetti Method)* by Craske and Friderica de Moroda, (1956). The last book lists Cecchetti's *enchaînements* of center pirouettes as well as his daily combinations. Cecchetti's and Espinosa's books helped to establish a new foundation for ballet technique in England.

During the same period in New York, the Russian-trained teacher Louis H. Chalif wrote a series of three technical manuals: *The Chalif Text Book of Dancing, Book I* (1914), *Book II* (1915), and *Book III, Greek Dancing* (1920). Written from an experienced and successful teacher's point of view, the texts are spirited and straightforward. A practice exercise accompanies each step, which is then described both technically and aesthetically. Although the terminology may be outdated, his philosophies remain valid. In 1923 Luigi Albertieri published *The Art of Terpsichore,* a book inspired by Cecchetti's but with its many helpful line drawings and commentary not so dry.

Although a spate of technical manuals was published between 1930 and 1934, it was not until 1934 that the next definitive work appeared. In Basic Principles *of Classic Ballet* (1934), outstanding Russian teacher Agrippina Vaganova reevaluated ballet technique from an anatomical perspective. This manual has become the basis for Russian teaching methods and helped to create a new Russian style. The pre-Soviet style of Nikolai Legat was not published until *Ballet Education* (1947) was written by his wife, the former dancer Nadine Nikolaeva Legat; it was later discussed by André Eglevsky and John Gregory in *Heritage of a Ballet Master: Nicholas Legat* (1977) and updated with Gregory's *The Legat Saga: An Anecdotal Study of the Life and Times of Nicolai Legat* (1995).

Until the end of World War II the publication of ballet manuals was limited. In 1943 Kay Ambrose's *Ballet-Lover's Pocket-Book, Technique without Tears* included a section on ballet technique written in popular style. Its wide success was matched in 1951 by *Ballet For Beginners* by Nancy Draper and Margaret F. Atkinson.

In the 1950s detailed ballet studies were made from various perspectives. The anatomist Celia Sparger discussed technique in *Anatomy and Ballet* (1949). Joan Lawson continued this anatomical approach in *Teaching of Classical Ballet* (1973) and *Teaching Young Dancers* (1975). Former Ballets Russes members who turned to teaching published works explaining the principles of technique that guided them through their careers. In *Lifar on Classical Ballet* (1951), Serge Lifar explained, through text and line drawings, the subtleties of technique and style that separated great from good dancers. Tamara Karsavina, in *Ballet Technique* (1956) and *Classical Ballet: The Flow of Movement* (1962) offered practical solutions to specific movement problems. Historically valuable is Olga Spessivtseva's *Technique for the Ballet Artiste* (1967).

The most important technical manual published in the 1950s was *The Classical Ballet: Basic Technique and Termi-*

nology (1952), written by Muriel Stuart with Lincoln Kirstein and associated with George Balanchine's School of American Ballet. Although the emphasis is on Russian methods (the author was trained by Pavlova), Cecchetti material is also included. Highlighting clean, detailed line drawings are near-mathematical analyses of a vast catalog of ballet movements.

Asaf Messerer in *Classes in Classical Ballet,* originally published in Moscow in 1967, and Nikolai I. Tarasov in *Ballet Technique for the Male Dancer,* published in Moscow in 1971, chose to elucidate specific areas of Vaganova's training methods. It was becoming clear, however, that there was a need for new discussion of Russian technique. This came in the exhaustive *School of Classical Dance* (1978) by Vera Kostrovitskaya and Alexei Pisarev, which provides hundreds of step combinations as well as a detailed eight-year syllabus.

There are also technical manuals written from a historical perspective. Documenting the Bournonville method of training are two books, Erik Bruhn and Lillian Moore's *Bournonville and Ballet Technique* (1961) and Kirsten Ralov's *The Bournonville School* (1979). The Ralov manual is a set of four books, one for classwork music and three describing technique—one in words, one in Benesh notation, and one in Labanotation. As well, *Bournonville Ballet Technique: Fifty Enchaînements,* selected and reconstructed by Vivi Flindt and Knud Arne Jürgensen (1996) is presented in both book and video formats.

More and more, movement notation systems, especially Benesh and Labanotation, are being included in technical manuals, augmenting, or sometimes replacing verbal descriptions. Two good examples of other new directions in the explanation of technique are Merrill Ashley's *Dancing for Balanchine* (1984) with its hundreds of rapid-sequence photographs demonstrating subtleties of the Balanchine style, and *The Video Dictionary of Classical Ballet* (1983) a four-videotape set produced in association with the Metropolitan Opera Guild. In the latter, the former Royal Ballet principal dancer Georgina Parkinson elucidates the classical technique as superbly demonstrated by Merrill Ashley and Kevin McKenzie.

There is a plethora of new video studies, analyzing every aspect of ballet for all ages. David Howard's tapes *Ballet Class for Beginners* (1986); *Intermediate and Advanced* (1986); and *Take a Master Class with David Howard* (1991) are popular, as is *Pointe by Pointe* (1990) by Barbara Fewster OBE.

[*See also the entries on the principal figures mentioned herein.*]

BIBLIOGRAPHY

Albertieri, Luigi. *The Art of Terpsichore.* New York, 1923.

Ambrose, Kay. *The Ballet-Lover's Pocket-Book: Technique without Tears.* 2d ed. New York, 1945.

Ashley, Merrill. *Dancing for Balanchine.* New York, 1984.

Beaumont, Cyril W., and Stanislas Idzikowski. *A Manual of the Theory and Practice of Classical Theatrical Dancing.* London, 1922.

Bernay, Berthe. *La danse au théâtre.* Paris, 1890.

Bruhn, Erik, and Lillian Moore. *Bournonville and Ballet Technique.* London, 1961.

Cecchetti, Enrico. *Manuel des exercices de danse théâtrale.* St. Petersburg, 1894.

Chalif, Louis H. *The Chalif Text Book of Dancing.* 5 vols. New York, 1914–1924.

Craske, Margaret, and Cyril W. Beaumont. *The Theory and Practice of Allegro in Classical Ballet (Cecchetti Method).* London, 1930.

Craske, Margaret, and Friderica Derra de Moroda. *The Theory and Practice of Advanced Allegro in Classical Ballet (Cecchetti Method).* London, 1956.

Desrat, G. *Dictionnaire de la danse.* Paris, 1895.

Draper, Nancy, and Margaret F. Atkinson. *Ballet for Beginners.* New York, 1951.

Eglevsky, André, and John Gregory. *Heritage of a Ballet Master: Nicholas Legat.* New York, 1977.

Espinosa, Édouard. *Technical Dictionary of Dancing.* London, 1913.

French, Ruth, and Felix Demery. *First Steps in Ballet.* Rev. ed. London, 1938.

French, Ruth, and Felix Demery. *Intermediate Steps in Ballet.* London, 1947.

French, Ruth, and Felix Demery. *Advanced Steps in Ballet.* London, 1950.

Giraudet, Eugène. *Traité de la danse.* 2 vols. Paris, 1890–1900.

Gregory, John. *The Legat Saga: An Anecdotal Study of the Life and Times of Nicolai Legat.* New York, 1995.

Karsavina, Tamara. *Ballet Technique.* London, 1956.

Karsavina, Tamara. *Classical Ballet: The Flow of Movement.* London, 1962.

Kostrovitskaya, Vera, and Alexei Pisarev. *School of Classical Dance.* Translated by John Barker. Moscow, 1978.

Lawson, Joan. *The Teaching of Classical Ballet.* London, 1973.

Lawson, Joan. *Teaching Young Dancers.* New York, 1975.

Legat, Nadine Nikolaeva. *Ballet Education.* London, 1947.

Lifar, Serge. *Lifar on Classical Ballet.* Translated by D. M. Dinwiddie. London, 1951.

Messerer, Asaf. *Classes in Classical Ballet.* Translated by Oleg Briansky. Garden City, N. Y., 1975.

Parkinson, Georgina. *The Video Dictionary of Classical Ballet.* 1983.

Ralov, Kirsten, ed. *The Bournonville School.* 4 vols. New York, 1979.

Sparger, Celia. *Anatomy and Ballet.* London, 1949.

Spessivtseva, Olga. *Technique for the Ballet Artiste.* London, 1967.

Stuart, Muriel, et al. *The Classic Ballet.* New York, 1952.

Tarasov, Nikolai. *Ballet Technique for the Male Dancer.* Translated by Elizabeth Kraft. Garden City, N.Y., 1985.

Vaganova, Agrippina. *Basic Principles of Classical Ballet: Russian Ballet Technique* (1934). Translated by Anatole Chujoy. Edited by Peggy van Praagh. 2d ed. London, 1953.

Zorn, Friedrich Albert. *Grammar of the Art of Dancing* (1887). Translated by Benjamin P. Coates. Boston,1905.

VIDEOTAPES. Ashley, Merrill, and Suki Schorer. *The Balanchine Essays: Arabesque* (1995); *Bournonville Ballet Technique. Fifty Enchaînements* (Dance Horizons, 1992), performed by principals of the Royal Danish Ballet; *Bujones in Class* (Kulthur, 1986), featuring Fernando Bujones; Dickinson, Patricia. *Basic Principles of Pointe* (Dance Horizons, 1994) and *Pointe to Pointe* (Dance Horizons, 1994); Mahler, Roni. *How to: Improve your Ballet Technique* (1991), *How to: Improve your Pirouettes* (1993), and *How to: Improve your Pointe Technique* (1994).

KENNETHA R. MCARTHUR

TELEVISION. [*This entry comprises articles surveying the history of dance on television in three areas of the Western world where coverage has been especially rich: Canada, Europe, and the United States.*]

Dance on Television in Canada

Television came to Canada with the opening of CBFT in Montreal on Saturday, 6 September 1952. Ballet made its appearance the next evening with the beginning of a Sunday series from French television featuring Janine Charrat and her Ballets de France. On the following day, Monday, 8 September 1952, CBLT in Toronto began broadcasting. These two stations, CBFT and CBLT, thus became the flagships of the publicly owned television network called, in the country's two official languages, Société Radio-Canada (SRC) and the Canadian Broadcasting Corporation (CBC). Each organization maintains its own stations and affiliates, broadcasts in its own language, and is responsible for its own programming. Although SRC/CBC is funded by the federal government, the network also generates revenue from commercial advertising.

Variety programming, a staple of early television, was instrumental in developing a roster of versatile choreographers able to work in any style, be it classical, contemporary, or musical comedy. Alan and Blanche Lund, Don Gillies, Gladys Forrester, and Willy Blok Hanson created dance segments for the CBC. Hanson's *Maria Chapdelaine*—based on the novel by French-Canadian author Louis Hémon, set to a commissioned score by Calvin Jackson, and directed by Norman Campbell—was the first complete modern dance work shown on Canadian television when it aired on 12 December 1952 on the CBC. In Montreal, Ludmilla Chiriaeff and, later, Brian Macdonald, choreographed for SRC variety shows. Program directors at both the CBC and the SRC early on mastered the craft of capturing dance effectively on camera. In fact, the dance programs of Campbell (CBC) and Pierre Morin (SRC) would be acclaimed for their innovative camera work and imaginative special effects and would earn them many awards for excellence.

In those heady, early days of television, network executives such as Gabriel Charpentier, head of the SRC's Organisation et Direction Artistique (Télévision), and Franz Kraemer, CBC's executive producer of features, mandated that the performing arts be given prime-time exposure. What is interesting is the difference in emphasis. Charpentier, a well-known composer, focused on concert music, opera, and dance in the SRC's *L'Heure du Concert*, which premiered on 14 January 1954. In the CBC's *Scope*, which first aired on 19 December 1954, Kraemer showcased a potpourri of drama, music, dance, and documentary. In the former show, dance was featured once or twice a month; in the latter, dance averaged two programs a season.

The remarkable *L'Heure du Concert* was unique to North American television. Each week producers such as Pierre Mercure (another well-known composer), Noël Gauvin, Françoys Bernier, and Pierre Morin would set

TELEVISION: Dance on Television in Canada. In the 1950s, one of the most popular programs on Montreal's French-language public television service was *L'Heure du Concert*. Regular performers on this weekly program were a group of dancers formed by Ludmilla Chiriaeff. She is pictured here with Roger Rochon (left), Brydon Paige (right), and members of the ensemble in Eric Hyrst's *Variations sur un Thème de Haydn* (1955). (Photograph by Henri Paul; from the archives of Les Grands Ballets Canadiens, courtesy of Ludmilla Chiriaeff.)

opera, concert music, or dance within an artistic presentation. As well as showcasing original Canadian ballets by Chiriaeff, Macdonald, Fernand Nault, and Eric Hyrst and presenting original Canadian modern dance works by Françoise Sullivan, Jeanne Renaud, and Françoise Riopelle, *L'Heure du Concert* featured works by choreographers and their companies from the United States and Europe. Indeed, the list of choreographers whose works appeared on *L'Heure du Concert* reads like an international Who's Who, including George Balanchine, Jerome Robbins, Murray Louis, Alwin Nikolais, Janine Charrat, and Roland Petit. The SRC archives are a rich repository of notable performances captured on film and videotape, including, for example, the only extant footage of the New York City Ballet's Tanaquil Le Clercq and Jacques d'Amboise performing Robbins's *Afternoon of a Faun,* recorded on 6 October 1955.

Among the Canadians, Ludmilla Chiriaeff was remarkably creative, participating in some three hundred programs broadcast on the SRC. She gradually withdrew from choreographing for variety programs to concentrate on creating ballets for *L'Heure du Concert* and on building up a group of classically trained dancers. Her version of *Les Noces,* set to Igor Stravinsky's familiar score, was presented for the first time in Canada on the broadcast of 8 March 1956. The following autumn, Les Ballets Chiriaeff scored a triumph when it presented this work during the Montreal Festival season, a success that led the mayor of Montreal to suggest the formation of a permanent ballet company for the city. When Les Grands Ballets Canadiens gave its first performance in April 1958, dance historians noted the astonishing fact that a television network had given birth to a ballet company. [*See* Grands Ballets Canadiens, Les; *and the entry on Chiriaeff.*]

In September 1966, *L'Heure du Concert* was replaced with the weekly *Les Beaux Dimanches,* but the high quality and frequency of dance programming remained. Performances by Canadian and international ballet and contemporary companies were often featured. The first full-length ballet to be broadcast in color on either the English or the French network was Brian Macdonald's *Rose Latulippe.* Choreographed to an original score by Harry Freedman, it was performed on 7 May 1967 by the Royal Winnipeg Ballet under the direction of Pierre Morin. Other Morin highlights include the world television premiere of Maurice Béjart's Le Ballet du XXe Siècle performing *Messe pour le Tempes Présent* (1972). Morin ended his distinguished career in 1992 with the Emmy-nominated film of *Na Floresta,* choreographed by Nacho Duato and performed by Les Grands Ballets Canadiens.

The National Ballet of Canada made its first appearance on CBC's *Scope* in a performance of act 2 of *The Nutcracker* on Sunday, 26 December 1954. *Scope* (1954–1955) was followed by arts programs variously called *Folio* (1955–1959), *Festival* (1960–1969), *Musicamera* (1973–1978), and *Spectrum* (1979–1980). The first of Campbell's three productions of *Swan Lake* featuring the National Ballet made its live debut on *Folio* on 12 December 1956, starring Lois Smith and David Adams. This production

TELEVISION: Dance on Television in Canada. In a studio of Société Radio-Canada, Ludmilla Chiriaeff strikes a pose for the television camera during the same performance pictured opposite. During the 1950s, before widespread use of videotape, dancers performed on "live television," hampered by limited performance space and unyielding concrete floors. (Photograph by Henri Paul; from the archives of Les Grands Ballets Canadiens, courtesy of Ludmilla Chiriaeff.)

was the first full-length televised ballet by a Canadian company and the first North American television presentation of the beloved Russian classic. (Taped versions would follow in 1961 and 1967, the latter of which was the Erik Bruhn production.) Campbell's first non-studio production was the National Ballet's *Sleeping Beauty,* choreographed by Rudolf Nureyev; this Emmy-winning program was captured with six cameras at Toronto's O'Keefe Centre in 1972.

Producer Harvey Hart, who was primarily interested in modern dance, was responsible for the appearances on *Folio* of American companies such as those of José Limón, Pearl Lang, Donald McKayle, and Katherine Dunham as well as for commissioning original works from Canadian choreographers such as Gladys Forrester. Vancouver's Anna Wyman Dance Theatre was given national exposure via regional director Keith Christie's *Anna in Graz* (1974) and *Klee Wyck: A Ballet for Emily* (1975). Dance documentaries also played an important part in CBC programming, including the profile of Mikhail Baryshnikov by famed filmmaker Harry Rasky made shortly after the Russian dancer defected from the Soviet Union in Toronto in the summer of 1974.

By the 1980s, the CBC was losing viewers to the more popular, lowbrow programs available on American television and two competing private Canadian networks. The ratings game forced CBC to relegate arts programming to Sunday afternoon or the occasional prime-time special. This decade saw Norman Campbell capture on camera an average of one ballet production a year, mostly from the repertory of the National Ballet of Canada, although performances by the Royal Winnipeg Ballet and Les Grands Ballets Canadiens were also featured. Contemporary dance was given exposure in *Canadance* (1985), showcasing Montreal's La La La Human Steps, the Winnipeg Contemporary Dancers, Vancouver's Judith Marcuse Repertory Company, and Toronto's National Ballet in the work of Constantin Patsalas—with each segment produced by different regional teams.

As funding began to decline in the 1980s, CBC/SRC joined with other broadcasters or production companies as co-producers or pre-buy licensees. In 1985, the SRC co-produced a two-part series featuring the New York City Ballet to do homage to Balanchine directed by Morin with WNET/Thirteen (New York) and the BBC. From 1986 to 1991, the last six Campbell ballet productions that aired on CBC were the National Ballet in John Cranko's *Onegin,* Ronald Hynd's *The Merry Widow,* and Glen Tetley's *La Ronde* and *Alice;* the Royal Winnipeg Ballet in Jacques LeMay's *The Big Top;* and the documentary *Karen Kain: Prima Ballerina.* All were co-produced by Toronto's Primedia with the CBC and/or RM Arts of Britain. Ottawa's enterprising Sound Ventures co-produced with CBC/SRC an English and French version of Frank Augustyn's *The Tin Soldier / Le Soldat du Plomb,* featuring the Ottawa Ballet, which aired in 1992.

In the last decade of the century, there is only one prime-time show on CBC devoted to the arts. The magazine format *Adrienne Clarkson Presents* has featured profiles on such Canadian choreographers as Montreal's Gilles Maheu of Carbon Quatorze, Toronto's Baroque-period Opera Atelier, and Vancouver's John Alleyne of Ballet British Columbia. In-house programming has moved away from capturing extant works to focus on artists or special events. Vancouver-based Tony Papa has produced a documentary on ballet superstar Vladimir Malakhov, formerly of the National Ballet, while *A Salute to "Dancers for Life,"* produced by former National Ballet ballerina Veronica Tennant, recreated a studio version of an annual Toronto AIDS benefit presented by dance artists and companies from across Canada.

While facing stiff competition from the private French-language TVA network and dubbed American programs, SRC has not been dragged to quite the level of the common denominator as has the CBC. As the century turns, *Les Beaux Dimanches* is still a going concern despite cutbacks. SRC remains committed to dance, airing approximately seven or eight programs a season, but the majority of these are acquisitions. The focus is on dance that is out of the ordinary or that represents a new current, such as a program of highlights featuring international companies and artists appearing at Montreal's biennial Festival International de Nouvelle Danse. A limited number of in-house programs is being realized by a new generation of gifted directors such as Bernard Picard, who has filmed Jean-Pierre Perreault's *Joe,* and Jocelyn Barnabé, who has presented *Infante C'est Destroy* with Édouard Lock and his La La La Human Steps.

Cable television has widened the horizons of dance on television. Provincial educational broadcasters—Radio-Québec (1968), TVOntario (1970) and its French wing TFO (1987), ACCESS in Alberta (1973), and Knowledge Network (KNOW) in British Columbia (1980)—have shown dance, either produced, co-produced, or acquired, on a continuing basis. It is of interest to note that the French educational networks follow SRC in scheduling such programs dedicated to the performing arts as TFO's *Dimanches Classiques* and Radio-Québec's *Samedi C* and *Hors-Circuit.*

The educational networks have also functioned as producers and co-producers. Radio-Québec's archive includes profiles on dancers Marie Chouinard and Margie Gillis; a profile on Martine Époque, one of the founders of the seminal Montreal modern dance company Le Groupe Nouvelle Aire; and the documentary *Les Vingt-cinq Ans des Grands Ballets.* KNOW has produced *Point of Depar-*

ture, a six-part series that demonstrates imaginative use of the camera with dance.

TFO is working with producer Mark Hammond to bring together three directors and three choreographers to produce original dance film as a pilot for a new series. With various partners, TVO co-produced the six-part series *The Dancemakers* (1988), directed by Moze Mossanen, which profiles contemporary choreographers David Earle, Christopher House, Danny Grossman, Constantin Patsalas, James Kudelka, and Ginette Laurin. It was also responsible for independent filmmaker Anthony Azzopardi's *Making Ballet,* which documents the creation of James Kudelka's *The Actress* (1994), starring Karen Kain and the National Ballet of Canada. TVO is currently planning to commit funds that once purchased Euro-dance productions to filming small-scale Canadian dance works.

Two other cable networks feature dance programming. Vision, which first went on the air in 1988, is mandated to schedule television shows motivated by spiritual or humanitarian concerns. A wide range of acquisitions includes *Shumka: Return of the Whirlwind,* focusing on the Edmonton-based Shumka dancers and documenting their emotional 1990 tour of the Ukraine, the company's ancestral homeland. Vision has also co-produced such documentaries as *Making of a Dancer: Stephane Léonard,* profiling a Montrealer who attended the Vaganova Ballet School in Saint Petersburg, and *Moment of Light: The Dance of Evelyn Hart.* Francophones across Canada have access to TV5, which features programming from the best of French-language television around the world. This network is noted for its magazine shows, particularly *au current reportage* of rehearsals in progress and interviews with choreographers and dancers in the Francophone world.

The two most famous production companies in Canada are Toronto's Rhombus Media, headed by Niv Fichman, Barbara Willis Sweete, and Larry Weinstein, and Montreal's Ciné Qua Non, run by Bernar Hébert. Each company has won numerous awards and has attracted co-producers from around the world. Both companies produce work for television of innovative brilliance and have demonstrated that creating dance film is an art in its own right. Hébert productions include *Déluge* (1995), with choreography by Ginette Laurin, and *Le Petit Musée de Vélasquez,* based on Édouard Lock's *Infante C'est Destroy* (1994). Willis Sweete, who has become the dance specialist of Rhombus Media, has produced Purcell's *Dido and Aeneas* (1995), a "danced opera" with choreography by Mark Morris, and *The Sorceress* (1993), starring Kiri Te Kanawa, with arias interpolated from Handel's "magic operas" and choreography by Toronto's Opera Atelier, which specializes in works of the Baroque era.

With the publicly funded networks in a financial squeeze, the great hope of dance on television in Canada lies with Bravo!, the specialty arts cable network that began broadcasting on 1 January 1995. An earlier television service offering arts programming on a pay-per-view basis, C Channel, lasted only six months in 1983 because of a lack of subscribers. Bravo! is not pay-per-view television and is readily available on extended cable service. The name is licensed from its U.S. counterpart, but the Canadian Bravo! is an independent entity. In its brief lifetime, C Channel did present a wide range of dance programming, including Canadian premieres of works by Alvin Ailey, George Balanchine, and John Neumeier. Original C Channel productions included Brian Macdonald's *Newcomers,* created for the National Ballet, which uses the music of four Canadian composers to depict nineteenth-century immigration, and *I Am a Hotel,* a dance drama set to music by Leonard Cohen and featuring choreography by Ann Ditchburn.

Bravo! presents the arts in themes, and one day a week is devoted to dance, where the programming runs the gamut from conventionally staged ballet to experimental dance film. The backbone of programming is made up of international acquisitions and works from the Rhombus, Primedia, and National Film Board of Canada catalogs. (The catalog of the National Film Board lists over fifty dance films.) Bravo! creates new dance films by underwriting short video productions from its Bravo!Fact foundation or by supporting projects through development grants or pre-buy license fees. Original series, in conjunction with Sound Ventures of Ottawa, include the thirteen-part *Foot Notes: The Classics of Ballet with Frank Augustyn,* hosted by a former star of the National Ballet of Canada. Within its second year of operation, Bravo! was involved with the production of eighteen new Canadian dance films from experienced directors like Sweete, Fichman, and Hébert to a new generation of filmmakers from Winnipeg, Halifax, Regina, Vancouver, and Whitehorse in the Yukon.

One cannot leave a discussion of dance on television in Canada without mention of the rise of Canadian dance film. The annual Moving Pictures Festival of Dance on Film and Video, the first in North America to be dedicated to the art form, began in Toronto in 1992 and has become an important national and international showcase. The Media and Visual Arts Department of the Banff Centre for the Arts in Alberta is co-producer for approximately ten dance films a year, and the annual Banff Film and Video Festival is one of the most important in the world. Workshops on dance and the camera given by the Banff Centre (1992), Vancouver's Dance Centre (1994), and Toronto's Dance Umbrella (1996) invited choreographers to receive hands-on training from Sweete, Hébert, and Bob Lockyer, the BBC producer who is largely responsible for the growth of dance film in Britain. These workshops are already bearing fruit. In 1996 Lee Eisler, a workshop trainee and Vancouver choreographer, was given money to make a Bravo!Fact based on her previous output.

[See also Canada, *articles on theatrical dance.*]

BIBLIOGRAPHY

Canadian Broadcasting Corporation. *CBC Times* 4.1 (July 1951–July 1952); 22.27 (July 1969–December 1969). Toronto, 1948–1970.

Carpenter, Bernadette. *SPOTLIGHT newsletters 1951–1959.* Toronto, 1995.

McClelland & Stewart, Inc. *The Canadian Encyclopedia Plus* (CD-ROM). Toronto, 1996.

Officer, Jill, ed. *The Encyclopedia of Theatre Dance in Canada* (electronic). Toronto, 1989.

Tembeck, Iro. *Dancing in Montreal: Seeds of a Choreographic History.* Studies in Dance History, vol. 5.2. Madison, Wis., 1994.

PAULA CITRON

Dance on Television in Europe

The world's first high-definition television transmissions were started by the British Broadcasting Corporation (BBC) on 2 November 1936. They continued until the outbreak of World War II in 1939. Between November 1936 and September 1939 Ballet Rambert, Ballets Russes, and the Vic-Wells Ballet made regular telecasts. As early as 1926, dance first appeared on television. In 1928, the BBC authorized experimental regularly scheduled broadcasts, after tests that had begun in 1925. On 15 March 1933 Dame Adeline Genée gave her farewell performance for John Logie Baird, one of the inventors and pioneers of early television. The audiences for these early telecasts were very small—limited to those who had purchased television sets (receivers) or who built home receivers—those who could receive the signal transmitted from the Alexandra Palace on a hill in North London. After World War II, the BBC resumed television transmissions on 7 June 1946, and on 21 June, it broadcast Antony Tudor's ballet *Gala Performance.*

TELEVISION: Dance on Television in Europe. Margot Fonteyn and Michael Somes in the BBC Television broadcast of the Royal Ballet production of *The Sleeping Beauty,* in 1955. (Photograph from the Dance Collection, New York Public Library for the Performing Arts.)

Regularly scheduled telecasts began in the USSR (1931), France (1934), and Germany (1935). In 1936 the Olympic Games were telecast from Berlin. After World War II, general European programming began. Where dance was already established, as in Denmark, it found a place in the schedules of this new form of public entertainment. Until the 1950s all shows were broadcast live, however, the arrival of kinescope (the recording of the electronic pictures on 35-millimeter black-and-white film) made it possible to record performances and start an archive. The first complete dance performance in the BBC Film and Video Library is a performance of *Les Sylphides* with a cast that included Alicia Markova. The arrival of videotape recording in the 1960s and its subsequent development changed the nature of dance on television.

For dance on television the relationship between the program's director and the choreographer or company is most important. In the United Kingdom, Margaret Dale, a former dancer with Sadler's Wells Ballet, did pioneer work transferring works from the Royal Ballet repertory to television. These programs were made in television studios and included Frederick Ashton's *La Fille Mal Gardée* (1962) and Dame Ninette de Valois's *Checkmate* (1963). Later Colin Nears developed a close working relationship with Ballet Rambert and its choreographer Christopher Bruce, winning the Prix Italia in 1982 with *Cruel Garden,* a ballet based on the works of Spanish poet Federico García Lorca as choreographed by Bruce and directed by Lindsay Kemp. The Prix Italia has done much to promote television dance; it is an annual competition established in 1948 at the instigation of RAI (Radiotelevision Italia) to stimulate radio's music, drama, and documentary, and is open to broadcasters throughout the world. With the inclusion of television in 1957, dance played an important part in this competition. Bob Lockyer, working with Robert Cohan and the London Contemporary Dance Theatre, transferred to television many of Cohan's dances. In Denmark, Thomas Grimm has had a similar relationship with the Royal Danish Ballet, winning the RAI Prize with Glen Tetley's *The Firebird* at the Prix Italia in 1982.

In the United Kingdom, dance programs (not including dance acts or light entertainment routines) fall into three main types: documentaries, performances, and created works. Documentaries are either portraits of stars, such as *Markova,* a portrait of Alicia Markova produced by Keith Cheetham (BBC, 1980), and *All the Superlatives,* a portrait of Anthony Dowell by Colin Nears (BBC, 1976); films about companies, such as Margaret Dale's history of the Ballet Rambert, *Rambert at Fifty* (BBC, 1976); or programs like *MacMillan's "Mayerling,"* a documentary that included the historical background to the ballet. This program, made for London Weekend Television by Derek Bailey, won the Prix Italia in 1978.

Dance performances are either recorded as outside broadcasts, taking the television cameras and equipment into the theater and recording the program, often at a public performance, or taking the production into a television studio. For the great nineteenth-century ballets that demand theatrical effect, a television recording from the theater usually produces the best result. For the modern works and the shorter classical works the best results are obtained by taking the dance into the studio and remaking the ballet for television. However, this takes time. Rehearsal in the studio is important because dance is the hardest of the performance arts to televise, requiring an understanding between dancer, choreographer, cameraman, and director—unlike music recitals or opera where stand-ins for rehearsals are typical.

Dance made specially for television has been rare. An early example was Antony Tudor's *Fugue for Four Cameras,* which he created on 2 March 1937 as a solo for Maude Lloyd. In it she was first seen dancing in the center screen; then, as the second theme was introduced in the music, her movement took her to one side, and she was joined by a replica of herself, and so on, until she was dancing in quadruplicate.

When the Swedish choreographer Birgit Cullberg was asked to transfer her ballet *Miss Julie* to television, and wanting to retain control of the ballet in this new medium, she devised the idea of a single fixed camera; she changed the choreography to fit into the camera's unchanging field of view. With the advent of color television and the use of chroma key, Cullberg again broke new ground with *Red Wine in Green Glasses* (1971), a pas de deux where the performers danced inside the paintings of, among others, Jean-Antoine Watteau, Jean Honoré Fragonard, and Jan and Pieter Bruegel.

In Denmark, Flemming Flindt's ballet *The Lesson* (1963), an adaptation of the Ionesco play, was made for television before being remade for the stage. In the following years Flindt worked on many television ballets, including *The Young Man Must Marry* (1968) and *Felix Luna* (1973). In the United Kingdom, the BBC has not commissioned many dance works in recent years, but in 1970 Alwin Nikolais made *The Relay,* one of the most exciting and successful creative uses of dance and television.

TELEVISION: Dance on Television in Europe. Ross Parkes, Lynn Kothera, and members of the Glen Tetley Dance Company in a performance of Tetley's popular ballet *Mythical Hunters,* broadcast on West German television in 1969. (Photograph from the Dance Collection, New York Public Library for the Performing Arts.)

In the late 1970s increasing production costs caused broadcast and production companies to look for partners to share costs. In many cases this led to only the "safe" works being televised and recorded, often using the same international dance stars. Since the arrival of lightweight video equipment it has now been possible for smaller independent program makers and the dance companies themselves to make videos of exciting dance works or make dance for the camera. This work is then sold to major distributors and broadcasters.

Because of this, in 1988 IMZ (International Music Center, based in Vienna) in association with CID-UNESO, set up the Grand Prix International Vidéo Danse. It was held first at Nîmes and is now in Sète in the south of France.

In 1990, IMZ broke away and founded Dance Screen. The first was held at the Alte Oper Frankfurt and since then six other festivals have been held around Europe. The published catalogs show a move away from large-scale productions made by national broadcasters to smaller projects made by independent production compa-

TELEVISION: Dance on Television in Europe. Birgit Keil found one of her best roles as Mathilde Wesendonk in Heinz Spoerli's *Traume,* first performed on Swiss television in October 1979. Set to Richard Wagner's "Wesendonk Lieder," this ballet was later staged in both Basel and Stuttgart. (Photograph by Schweizer Fernsehen DRS, Zurich; courtesy of Heinz Spoerli.)

nies with the help of a mix of funders. In 1992 the Arts Council of England and BBC Television set a trend when it transmitted *Dance House*—a series of twelve short dance films made collaboratively by various choreographers and directors. This was followed by *Dance for the Camera,* and to date twenty-eight short dance film/videos have been commissioned. This example has been followed in many other countries including Spain, the Netherlands (Four TokenS), and Australia (Macrodance).

Choreographers' and directors' interest in film and video as a tool to make dance works has also led to a growing number of master classes and workshops to be held around the world. Many of these have been run by Elliot Caplan from the Cunningham Foundation or Bob Lockyer. Nearly all the major dance festivals worldwide include video dance showcases. Sadly, major changes in public broadcasting, film production, and television distribution are putting these exciting projects in jeopardy just as this new art form begins its emergence.

BIBLIOGRAPHY

Cullberg, Birgit. "Television Ballet." In *The Dance Has Many Faces,* edited by Walter Sorell. 2d ed. New York, 1966.

Dale, Margaret. "Ballet and BBC-TV." *The Dancing Times* (March 1963): 332–334.

Davis, Janet Rowson. "Ballet on British Television, 1933–1939." *Dance Chronicle* 5.3 (1983): 245–304.

Davis, Janet Rowson. "Ballet on British Television, 1932–1935: A Supplement." *Dance Chronicle* 7.3 (1984–1985): 294–325.

Davis, Janet Rowson. "Ballet on British Television: Christian Simpson, Producer, 1949–1959—Divine or Diabolic?" *Dance Chronicle* 19.1 (1996): 17–92.

IMZ *Dance Screen Catalogues* (1990–). Vienna.

Jordon, Stephany, and Dave Allen, eds. *Parrallell Lines.* London, 1993.

Penman, Robert, comp. *A Catalogue of Ballet and Contemporary Dance in the BBC Television, Film, and Videotape Library, 1937–1984.* London, 1987.

Bob Lockyer

Dance on Television in the United States

Dance, in one form or another, has been part of North American television since the 1930s. Dancers began appearing regularly on experimental television broadcasts in 1931. The medium's limitations at this stage were formidable, and it would take decades before many of its problems were satisfactorily overcome. Studio size was restricted; screen clarity was minimal; and directors and technicians often butchered the choreography by a combination of poor framing and graceless camera movement.

Nevertheless, the future for dance broadcasts was heralded with enthusiasm—the manager of the National Broadcasting Corporation (NBC) in 1939 proclaimed that television would do for dance what radio had done for speech. When commercial transmission began in 1941, dance programs were scheduled frequently. The Columbia Broadcasting System (CBS) offered several dance shows featuring the work of Erick Hawkins, Agnes de Mille, Katherine Dunham, Ruth Page, and Eugene Loring. In 1946 Pauline Koner and her partner Kitty Doner began a successful weekly program that was one of the first to experiment with television choreography. Dances were specially staged for the camera, and special effects, such as superimpositions, were selectively employed.

Television's enormous postwar expansion was accompanied by an increase in dance programming. The networks, not quite locked into their lowest common-denominator orientation, experimented with occasional offerings of ballet. Alicia Markova and Anton Dolin appeared on *NBC Concert Hall* in 1948. In 1949 the Ford Motor Company sponsored a weekly series of half-hour programs on CBS under the title *Through the Crystal Ball,* each of which consisted of an original ballet choreographed for television. Before being abruptly suspended, the series opened with *Robinson Crusoe,* choreographed by Michael Kidd and Talley Beatty, and went on to present a *Cinderella* by George Balanchine, to music of Tchaikovsky, *Ali Baba* by Helen Tamiris, *The Wild West* by Todd Bolender, *Alice in Wonderland* by Pauline Koner, *Fiesta* by Anna Sokolow, and *Casey at the Bat* by Paul Godkin. American Ballet Theatre was seen in a full-length presentation of *Giselle* (featuring Nora Kaye and Igor Youskevitch) in 1950.

The chief forum for television dance in the 1950s was the popular variety programs. Most shows had their own five- or six-member dance company and a resident choreographer responsible for staging several new dances each week. Cramped for space and forced to deal with a frenzied rehearsal schedule and the pressures of live performing, choreographers such as James Starbuck on *Your Show of Shows,* Tony Charmoli on *Your Hit Parade,* and Peter Gennaro on *The Perry Como Show* perfected a lighthearted, casual dance style that suited the medium's small-scale visual demands.

Beginning in the mid-1950s, the commercial networks started to restrict ballet to one of three different formats. The most popular was a five- or six-minute number in variety shows seeking an occasional dose of high culture. Programs such as *The Bell Telephone Hour, The Voice of Firestone,* and even *The Ed Sullivan Show* frequently featured *The Nutcracker* and *Swan Lake* pas de deux danced by such performers as Margot Fonteyn and Michael Somes, André Eglevsky and Melissa Hayden, and Edward Villella and Patricia McBride.

Once or twice a year the networks also offered special events designed to boost their cultural prestige. In 1955 NBC imported the Royal Ballet from London to present *The Sleeping Beauty* adapted by Frederick Ashton, which surprised everyone by attracting an audience of thirty million viewers. Two years later the Royal Ballet was brought back to perform Ashton's *Cinderella* in a version that used many electronic effects. Perhaps the most famous, or notorious, dance presentation of the period was CBS's 1962 broadcast of Igor Stravinsky and George Balanchine's *The Flood,* which was widely attacked for its twenty minutes of undistinguished abstract choreography and forty minutes of pretentious lecture material and rehearsal footage that surrounded it.

However, other than these scattered prime-time appearances, serious dance, like most cultural programming, was increasingly pushed to Sunday morning and afternoon time slots, where ratings were not as important. The most notable, semi-regular forum during the 1950s was *Omnibus,* an arts magazine supported by funds from the

TELEVISION: Dance on Television in the United States. Peter Gennaro was the choreographer and featured dancer on *The Perry Como Show* for several years. Seen here in his number set to "South Rampart Street Parade," he displays his characteristic charm. (Photograph © by Jack Mitchell; used by permission.)

TELEVISION: Dance on Television in the United States. In the 1950s the June Taylor Dancers were a regular feature of *The Jackie Gleason Show*, opening the program with precision tap routines, like the "bellhop" number seen here. (Photograph by Herb Flatow; from the archives of the Museum of Television and Radio, New York.)

Ford Foundation. Among its many dance programs were a 1953 version of *Billy the Kid* narrated by Eugene Loring, two lively shows on the history of ballet and choreography written and presented by Agnes de Mille, and a lecture-demonstration by Gene Kelly proving that male dancers are just as skilled (and manly) as male athletes. CBS's Sunday morning schedule was a rare haven for new dance. Its religious programs, such as *Lamp unto My Feet*, offered many commissions for original choreography based on biblical themes, and its innovative culture series, *Camera Three*, provided one of the few places on television hospitable to modern dance.

The formation of National Educational Television (NET) in the mid-1950s offered an alternative to choreographers unable or unwilling to work within restricted commercial demands. Martha Graham, who first appeared on television in an experimental NBC broadcast in 1939, was seen on several NET programs beginning in 1957. In the mid-1960s NET launched a pioneering series, *USA: Dance*, produced by Jac Venza, that demonstrated the expressive possibilities of videotaped dance performances. Among the program's highlights were a striking rendition of Anna Sokolow's *Rooms* and a collection of Balanchine pas de deux danced by the New York City Ballet, with occasional commentary by Balanchine, Arthur Mitchell, and Jacques d'Amboise.

Nevertheless, many choreographers were still reluctant to let their work be seen on television because of the medium's technological limitations and economic pressures. The small screen size made it difficult to see more than four or five dancers on stage at any one time. Further, the often gimmicky camera work directors employed to promote visual interest, the lack of adequate rehearsal time, and the inherent distortions of television's two-dimensional space posed serious obstacles. These problems were compounded by the fact that most television ballet and dance consisted of performances of existing repertory, rather than attempts to choreograph works specifically for the medium. Although calls have been raised since the 1940s for original dance created expressly for the camera, this has remained an infrequently fulfilled dream on broadcast television because of budgetary restrictions and a programming philosophy that favors the known and the safe over the new and the experimental.

A turning point, at least for the reproduction of repertory dance on television, occurred in 1976 when the Public Broadcasting Service (PBS, the successor to NET) initiated *Dance in America* as a showcase for the best dance companies in the country. Each program offered a bit of company choreographic philosophy, a little history, some documentary footage, and unusually intelligent television translations of repertory pieces. Producers Emile Ardolino and Merrill Brockway worked closely with each choreographer to reshape his or her work for the best possible television presentation. This often meant changing the lines and movements of individual dances to accommodate screen size and camera perspective, and the results, aided by sensitive direction, were frequently impressive.

Not the least of the achievements of *Dance in America* has been the diversity of its focus. The series not only lured mainstream choreographers who had remained skeptical of television's abilities, such as Jerome Robbins, Graham, and Balanchine, but it also examined companies that had rarely, if ever, received national exposure, including Paul Taylor, Pilobolus, the Pennsylvania Ballet, the Dance Theatre of Harlem, and Feld Ballet. Programs have also been devoted to the life and work of Katherine Dunham, a survey of avant-garde dancing in New York, a special rechoreographed-for-video sampler by Merce Cunningham, and works by Balanchine and Graham reconceived for television by their creators.

Dance in America was not the only innovative PBS program that looked at dance. Thanks to new low-light cameras, series such as *Live from Lincoln Center* and *In Performance at Wolf Trap* could telecast live events without disturbing the audience in the theater. The network also aired a few programs exploring video dance. WGBH in Boston produced several dance programs that used video technology as a direct choreographic tool, and Twyla Tharp's *Making Television Dance* was the result of her experiments with the equipment and facilities of WNET in New York. *Alive from Off Center,* from KTCA in Minneapolis, and *New Television,* from WGBH in Boston, have both served as showcases for experimental dance videos.

There is little doubt that the creation of PBS in 1967 freed the commercial networks from a sense of responsibility toward cultural programming. The number of shows featuring dance on CBS, NBC, and ABC (American Broadcasting Corporation) since the late 1960s has been minimal. Other than a few broadcasts of *The Nutcracker* at Christmas time, and a well-meaning but ill-fated experiment by NBC, *Live from Studio 8H,* dance has been left to fend for itself on PBS and a few upscale cable networks.

TELEVISION: Dance on Television in the United States. George Balanchine as Herr Drosselmeyer, with children and members of the New York City Ballet, in the CBS-TV production of *The Nutcracker,* broadcast Christmas Day, 1958. (Photograph from the Dance Collection, New York Public Library for the Performing Arts. Choreography by George Balanchine © The George Balanchine Trust.)

TELEVISION: Dance on Television in the United States. A cameraman filming members of the Paul Taylor Dance Company in *Company B,* one of three of Taylor's dances on a program entitled "Wrecker's Ball," presented as part of the *Dance in America* series. (Photograph © 1996 by Johan Elbers; used by permission.)

Over the last decade, even these environments have provided less and less of a welcome. Though they began in the 1980s with some original dance programming, cable networks like Bravo! and the Arts and Entertainment network now rely on a very limited menu of imported dance fare. More troubling is the diminished state of the once trailblazing PBS. Continuing budgetary cutbacks have led to a severe reduction of its dance commitment. At a time when American choreographers are being celebrated throughout the world, *Dance in America's* presentations are increasingly foreign co-productions, with only a few original domestic programs.

Dance has never been a staple on American television, but it has often been approached with freshness and sophistication. U.S. producers and directors discovered innovative methods to translate the sweep of choreography to the limitations of the small screen. Their contributions have played an important role in changing the face of dance on television.

[*For related discussion, see* American Bandstand.]

BIBLIOGRAPHY

Balanchine, George, and Bernard Taper. "Television and Ballet." In *The Eighth Art,* edited by Robert L. Shayon. New York, 1962.

Barzel, Ann. "Looking at TV." *Dance Magazine* (March 1953–December 1969). Monthly column on television dance, renamed "Reviewing the Tube" when Norma McLain Stoop became critic in December 1971 and changed to "Dancevision" under John Gruen in September 1980.

Bettis, Valerie, et al. "Dance on Television." In *Television: The Creative Experience,* edited by A. William Bluem and Roger Manvell. New York, 1967.

Bohen, Tullia. "Making Television Dance." *Ballet News* 1 (May 1980): 26–29.

Dance Theatre Journal (Summer 1988). Dance and television issue.

Feigay, Paul. "The Dance of 'Omnibus.'" *Dance Magazine* (March 1955): 23–27.
Grossman, Peter Z. "Video and Dance." *Videography* 2 (September 1977): 16–19.
Grossman, Peter Z. "Talking with Merce Cunningham about Video." *Dance Scope* 13 (Winter-Spring 1979): 56–68.
Koner, Pauline, and Kitty Doner. "Technological Progress and the Dance in Television." In *The Dance Has Many Faces,* edited by Walter Sorell. New York, 1951.
Lorber, Richard. "'Dance in America' on TV in America." *Dance Scope* 10 (Spring–Summer 1976): 19–28.
Lorber, Richard. "Experiments in Videodance." *Dance Scope* 12 (Fall–Winter 1977–1978): 7–16.
Mueller, John. "Twyla Tharp and the Wide-Angle Lens." *Dance Magazine* (September 1977): 99.
Mueller, John. "Martha Graham, Then and Now." *Dance Magazine* (December 1977): 107.
Mueller, John. "The Close-Up, the Dissolve, and Martha Graham." *Dance Magazine* (January 1978): 94–95.
Neal, Nelson D. "Early Television Dance." *Dance Scope* 13 (Winter–Spring 1979): 51–55.
Rose, Brian. *Television and the Performing Arts.* Westport, Conn., 1986.
Rose, Brian. *Televising the Performing Arts: Interviews with Merrill Brockway, Kirk Browning, and Roger Englander.* Westport, Conn., 1992.
Simpson, Herbert. "American Dance on Television: The Changing Picture." *Dance Magazine* (January 1977): 41–45.
Simpson, Herbert. "WNET TV's Dance in America." *Dance Magazine* (January 1977): 45–50.
Vaughan, David. "TV." *Ballet News* (May 1979–). Monthly column examining dance on television.
Venza, Jac. "Educational TV Loves Dance." *Dance Magazine* (September 1965): 43.

VIDEOTAPES. The following is a selected list of videotapes available for screening in the Dance Collection of the New York Public Library for the Performing Arts: Eugene Loring, "Billy the Kid," *Omnibus* (CBS, 8 November 1953). "Appalachian Spring" (National Educational Television, 1959). Alvin Ailey, "Revelations," *Lamp Unto My Feet* (CBS, 3 March 1962). George Balanchine, "Noah and the Flood" (CBS, 14 June 1962). "Four Pioneers," featuring a re-creation of Doris Humphrey's *Pasacaglia, USA: Dance* (National Educational Television, 1965). "New York City Ballet," featuring four Balanchine pas de deux (National Education Television, 1966). Twyla Tharp, "Bix Pieces," *Camera Three* (CBS, 7 October 1973). "Merce Cunningham: A Video Event," *Camera Three* (CBS, 27 October and 3 November 1974). *Dance in America* (WNET-TV, New York, 1976–). The following are available from the Museum of Television and Radio, New York and Los Angeles: Agnes de Mille, "The Art of Choreography," *Omnibus* (CBS, 30 December 1956). Frederick Ashton, "Cinderella," *Producer's Showcase* (NBC, 29 April 1957). Gene Kelly, "Dancing: A Man's Game," *Omnibus* (ABC, 21 December 1958).

BRIAN ROSE

TEMPLE, SHIRLEY (Shirley Jane Temple; born 23 April 1928 in Santa Monica, California), child tap dancer, singer, and actress. Shirley's trademarks were dimples, bright eyes, and curly golden hair, and she had a film musical named for each. Throughout her childhood, her fame was colossal.

When barely three years old, Shirley became a student at the Ethel Meglin Dance Studio and simultaneously a "Famous Meglin Kiddie." There she was discovered for Educational Films, for a new series of 1932 and 1933 one-reel comedies called *Baby Burlesks.* Temple soon astounded the film industry with her featured spot in *Stand Up and Cheer* (1934) for Fox with James Dunn. She performed with him again in *Baby Take a Bow* (1934).

From 1934 to 1940, Temple made twenty-four films; of those, fifteen included musical sequences in which she tap danced. When not performing alone, she was accompanied by first-rate veteran tap talent and vaudevillians. She has said:

> I didn't really have any dancing teachers, per se, at the time I was working on these films. My dancing "teachers" were just the ones I was working with . . . Bill [Robinson], or Buddy [Ebsen], or George [Murphy]. (Frank, 1994)

TEMPLE. With the eccentric tapper Buddy Ebsen, Temple is pictured here in the number "At the Codfish Ball," from the film *Captain January* (Fox, 1936). (Photograph from the collection of Rusty E. Frank.)

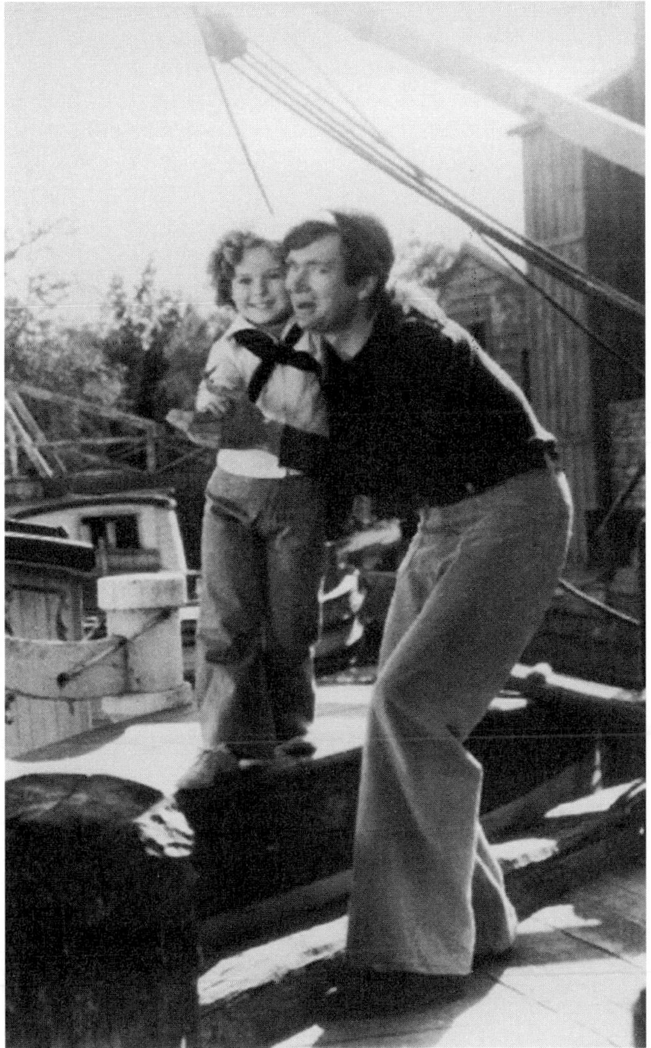

Temple was first paired with Bill ("Bojangles") Robinson in *The Little Colonel* (1935). The combination proved so winning, they were featured together in three more films: *The Littlest Rebel* (1935), *Rebecca of Sunnybrook Farm* (1938), and *Just around the Corner* (1938). Not only did she and Robinson become great friends, they were the first interracial couple in films. Explained Temple:

> Everyone I danced with was wonderful to work with . . . Buddy and George were certainly two of the finest ones. But Bill Robinson was my favorite. He was the easiest teacher I had, because we could do it by holding hands. I learned most of it by listening to the sounds of the taps. (Frank, 1994)

She danced with Ebsen in *Captain January* (1936) and with Alice Faye and Jack Haley in *Poor Little Rich Girl* (1936). She danced with Murphy in *Little Miss Broadway* (1938), with Arthur Treacher in *The Little Princess* (1939), and with Charlotte Greenwood and Jack Oakie in *Young People* (1940).

Temple's movies were magic at the box office—she was the top box-office attraction from 1935 to 1938. At the beginning of her success, the *Motion Picture Herald* listed her as number eight of the top ten money-making stars for 1934. One year later, she skyrocketed in popularity to become the number one box-office star and held that position through 1938, ranking above Clark Gable, Fred Astaire and Ginger Rogers, Joan Crawford, Gary Cooper, and Spencer Tracy. Temple's intelligent but unaffected personality and her uncanny abilities charmed audiences and critics alike. Temple continued making films until 1949 but her adolescent and adult films did not feature her dancing.

[*See also* Tap Dance.]

BIBLIOGRAPHY

Black, Shirley Temple. *Child Star.* New York, 1988.

Frank, Rusty E. *Tap! The Greatest Tap Dance Stars and Their Stories, 1900–1955.* Rev. ed. New York, 1994.

Stearns, Marshall, and Jean Stearns. *Jazz Dance: The Story of American Vernacular Dance.* Rev. ed. New York, 1994.

Thomas, Tony. *That's Dancing.* New York, 1984.

RUSTY E. FRANK

TENNANT, VERONICA (born 15 January 1947 in London), British-Canadian ballet dancer. As one of a new generation of Canadian dancers to emerge during the 1960s, Veronica Tennant demonstrated that it had become possible to have a distinguished and fulfilling international career without having to abandon her adopted homeland.

Tennant began her training at the Cone-Ripman School in London. When her family moved to Toronto in 1955, she continued her studies and joined the newly created National Ballet School of Canada, from which she was graduated in 1963. An injury delayed her entry into the National Ballet of Canada until 1965. Hired as a principal dancer, Tennant quickly established herself as a dancer-actress of extraordinary intensity and individuality in the role of Juliet in John Cranko's *Romeo and Juliet.* She soon built a repertory that included the leading roles in almost all the National Ballet's full-length classics, proving herself as adept in roles in the Petipa repertory—Aurora, Odette-Odile, and the Sugarplum Fairy—as in the Romantic roles of Giselle and La Sylphide.

As the leading ballerina of the company, Tennant starred in several award-winning CBC-TV ballet presentations, including *Romeo and Juliet* (Prix René-Barthélemy, Monte Carlo, 1965), Celia Franca's *Cinderella* (Emmy award, 1968) and Rudolf Nureyev's *The Sleeping Beauty* (Emmy award, 1972). She was the first to dance with Mikhail Baryshnikov after his defection from the Soviet Union, as his partner in a CBC-TV production of Erik Bruhn's *La Sylphide,* broadcast 26 July 1974, the day before Baryshnikov's American stage debut.

A knee operation in December 1976 kept Tennant from the stage for fourteen months, but she returned with deepened maturity and a newly refined musicality that was particularly apparent in such roles as Lise in Frederick Ashton's *La Fille Mal Gardée* and Titania in his *The*

TENNANT. An action photograph of Tennant in the title role of Celia Franca's *Cinderella,* in 1968. A broadcast of this production by CBC-TV helped make Tennant a household name throughout Canada. (Photograph by Ken Bell; used by permission of the National Ballet of Canada.)

Dream. Always a strong supporter of choreographers emerging from the ranks of the National Ballet, Tennant created numerous roles in works by James Kudelka, Constantin Patsalas, and David Allan. Among her most notable later roles were Tatiana in John Cranko's *Onegin*—acquired by artistic director Alexander Grant in 1985 as a particularly suitable vehicle for Tennant's dramatic talent—and Hanna in Ronald Hynd's *The Merry Widow,* which she danced in 1986.

Although she was most often partnered by Raymond Smith, Tennant danced with all the National Ballet's principal men and with numerous international guest stars, among them Anthony Dowell, Rudolf Nureyev, Fernando Bujones, Iván Nagy, Edward Villella, Peter Schaufuss, and Jean-Charles Gil. Her compatibility with dancers of such varied styles and dispositions is indicative of her own mastery of the stylistic spectrum of the National Ballet's repertory. She was as much at home playing the lighthearted heroines of *Coppélia, Napoli,* and *Don Quixote* as she was portraying an enchanted princess in *Swan Lake* or *The Sleeping Beauty.* Having announced her retirement in 1988, she recreated the role of Juliet for her final performance with the National Ballet of Canada on 12 February 1989.

Tennant is the author of two children's books, *On Stage, Please* (1977), a novel, and *The Nutcracker* (1985). She was the subject of a CBC-TV documentary, *Veronica Tennant: A Dancer of Distinction* (1983), and she became a frequent host and interviewer of radio and television arts programs. She is now an arts producer for CBC Television. The first dancer to be invested with the Order of Canada, in 1975, and the recipient of the Toronto Arts Award for the Performing Arts, she holds several honorary doctorates from Canadian universities.

BIBLIOGRAPHY

Howard, Sebastian. "Veronica Tennant: A Dancer of Distinction." *Dance in Canada* (Autumn 1989).

Kelly, Deirdre. "Dancing on the Town." *Performing Arts in Canada* (Summer 1992).

Maynard, Olga. "Veronica Tennant, a Canadian Ballerina." *Dance Magazine* (May 1972): 40–44.

Neufeld, James. *Power to Rise: The Story of the National Ballet of Canada.* Toronto, 1996.

Odom, Selma Landen. "Spotlight on Veronica Tennant." *Dance Magazine* (March 1977): 68-70.

MICHAEL CRABB

TERABUST, ELISABETTA (Elisabetta Magli; born 5 August 1946 in Varese, Lombardy), Italian ballet dancer and company director. Raised and educated in Rome, Elisabetta Terabust received her dance training at the ballet school of the Teatro dell'Opera under the direction of Attilia Radice, one of the last pupils of Enrico Cecchetti. Upon her graduation in 1962, Terabust was immediately engaged for the corps de ballet of the theater. She caught the public's attention when she first performed as a soloist, particularly in the role of Myrtha in *Giselle,* in which she was pallid, sublime, and merciless, with an excellent technique evidenced in her jumps and turns. She also triumphed in the spirited role of a Silver Sole in *Roi des Gourmets* by Jean Babilée, presented at the Teatro dell'Opera in 1964.

Terabust first danced the title role in *Giselle* at the Opera in 1965, partnered by Gianni Notari; she subsequently danced this role with several other illustrious partners, including Paolo Bortoluzzi, Peter Schaufuss, and Rudolf Nureyev. Small, slender, and graceful, with large black eyes, she was sought by Erik Bruhn in 1967 as a partner in *Flower Festival in Genzano,* for which she was taught the basics of the Danish technique and many aspects of the role of Giselle.

Dissatisfied with the scarce scheduling of dance in the lyrical seasons of the Rome Opera, Terabust followed the example of Carla Fracci and left her country. She first went to France, where she was the star (1974–1977) of the Ballet National de Marseille under the direction of Roland Petit. She appeared in revivals of his *Carmen* and *Nôtre-Dame de Paris,* as well as the new *Schiaccianoci.*

Terabust then became a star with London Festival Ballet in 1977. Here she refined the quality of her technique, which in her long association with Peter Schaufuss, her favorite partner, reached the highest level in both the classical tradition of Italy, France, and Russia and in the Bournonville tradition of Denmark. She appeared in revivals of Schaufuss's *La Sylphide,* with the London Festival Ballet (1978) and of *Napoli* with the National Ballet of Canada (1981). In 1982, Kenneth MacMillan created *Verdi Variations* for Terabust and Schaufuss; Glen Tetley created the role of Pimpenella in *Pulcinella* for her in 1984.

Within the framework of London Festival Ballet, where she danced the full classical and modern classical repertory, Terabust began to address herself to innovative contemporary productions—for example, the revival of Glen Tetley's *Sphinx* (1979), which was one of her best interpretations. This modern direction, although still within pure academic foundations, was confirmed and broadened in the early 1980s, when she was a guest start with Aterballetto in Reggio nell'Emilia. With this young and dynamic Italian company, Terabus danced many of the creations of Amedeo Amodio, notably *Psiche a Manhattan* (1984), and of William Forsythe, including *Artifact 2* (1984).

During the 1980s Terabust appeared as a guest artist with the National Ballet of Canada, with the Rome Opera Ballet, and with the ballet companies of the Teatro Comunale di Firenze, the Arena of Verona, the Teatro San Carlo in Naples, and the Teatro alla Scala in Milan. In 1990, she returned to Rome to direct the Rome Opera Ballet and its associated school. She effected great improvements in a short time, but she failed to win the support of the public or the officials of the Opera. She resigned her post in 1993 to go to Milan as artistic director of La Scala Ballet.

BIBLIOGRAPHY

Agostini, Alfio. "Elisabetta, Giuletta et Figlio prodigo." *Balletto oggi* (February 1987).

Doglio, Vittoria, and Elisa Vaccarino. *L'Italia in ballo.* Rome, 1993.

Fitzgerald, Brendan. "Rome's Prima Ballerina Finds Stardom in Paris." *New York Times* (27 February 1977).

Ottolenghi, Vittoria. "Elisabetta, la nostra stella." *Balletto oggi* 2 (March–May 1981).

Ottolenghi, Vittoria. "1983: L'anno di E.T." *Musica viva* 2 (February 1983).

Ottolenghi, Vittoria. "Elisabetta Terabust e Roland Petit." *Balletto oggi* (March 1992):12–13.

"London Festival Ballet: The Biographies." In *Ballet in London Year Book 1988/89.* London, 1988.

"Terabust, Elisabetta." In *Enciclopedia dello spettacolo.* Rome, 1954–.

Testa, Alberto, et al. *Il balletto nel novecento.* Turin, 1983.

Testa, Alberto. "Elisabetta Terabust." *Danza & danza* (November 1991).

VITTORIA OTTOLENGHI
Translated from Italian

TER-ARUTUNIAN, ROUBEN (born 24 July 1920 in Tiflis, died 17 October 1992 in New York City), Armenian-American stage designer. An extremely prolific and eclectic designer, Rouben Ter-Arutunian worked in every aspect of theater, from opera to television, from Shakespeare to Broadway musicals. He had his greatest effect, however, as premier designer for the New York City Ballet, in a long series of collaborations with George Balanchine.

Educated in Berlin, Vienna, and Paris, Ter-Arutunian worked in the theaters of these cities before emigrating to the United States in 1951. His German experience served him in his first work with Balanchine, the honky-tonk expressionism of the revival of *The Seven Deadly Sins* (1958). He went on to work in a spare, abstract idiom with choreographers such as Martha Graham, Paul Taylor, and Glen Tetley, but it is his grandly traditional redesign of Balanchine's *The Nutcracker* for the New York State Theater (1964) that has endured. The first act is a masterpiece of domestic poetry, a perfect unity of choreography and design; the setting is vividly detailed, faithful to what Balanchine called "a bourgeois Biedermeier home," yet more atmospheric than realistic, suffused with a nostalgic warmth which gives way before one's eye to the vast blue-white realm of the Snowflakes.

Never classifiable in style, Ter-Arutunian's designs for Balanchine range from the toy theater of *Harlequinade* (1965), adapted from opera scenery, to the comic grotesquerie of the stage-consuming cape in *Variations pour une Porte et un Soupir* (1974). His diversified scenery for *Vienna Waltzes* (1977), combined with Barbara Karinska's costumes, provided the most successful stage designs for the New York City Ballet since *The Nutcracker.* Once again there is theatrical magic in onstage transformation: as the dappled trees of the first scene rise into the flies, their dangling roots become decorative hangings of a *fin-de-siècle* salon. The last scene's glittering, mirrored ballroom doubles the full-company surge of dancers in Balanchine's great finale.

[*See also* Scenic Design.]

BIBLIOGRAPHY

Baker, Rob. "Designing Articulate Space." *Soho Weekly News* (18 May 1978).

Current Biography (June 1963). Includes an extensive list of works through the early 1960s.

Ter-Arutunian, Rouben. "In Search of Design." *Dance Perspectives,* no. 28 (Winter 1966).

Ter-Arutunian, Rouben. "Elegant Minimal Settings." *Theatre Crafts* (October 1971). Interview.

ARCHIVE. Dance Collection, New York Public Library for the Performing Arts.

CLAUDIA ROTH PIERPONT

TERPSICHORE, one of the Muses (or Moisai) of Greek mythology, has come to be known as the patroness of dance. In the earliest extant account of the Muses in Greek mythology, Hesiod describes them as the nine daughters of Zeus and Mnemosyne (Memory), who danced and sang atop Mount Helicon (*Theogony* 1–100). In poets' stories they were credited as the sources of inspiration: the epic, lyric, and dramatic authors called upon a Muse but did not invoke her by a specific name. Hesiod in his *Theogony* cited their names as Calliope, Clio, Erato, Euterpe, Melpomene, Polyhymnia (or Polymnia), Terpsichore, Thalia, and Urania. Later, less celebrated versions (for example, Diodorus Siculus) accounted for only three or four Muses, often with different names and different parentage.

Designating a fixed domain of patronage to each Muse was not a preoccupation until Roman times. Diodorus Siculus, writing in the first century BCE, attempted to assign different functions to each Muse by analyzing the supposed etymological components of her name (4.7). For example, he maintained that Terpsichore's name derived from the way she delighted *(terpein)* her followers with good things that came from education, and Polyhymnia's from the acclaim she brought to writers through her great *(pollē)* praises *(hymnēsis).*

In the same way, Plutarch in the first to second century CE treats the name Terpsichore as a compound of the words for enjoyment *(terpsis)* and seeing *(horan)*—thus, she is the Muse governing the visual delights ("Quaestiones convivales" 9.14). Ausonius's fourth-century poem on the Muses arbitrarily names Erato as patroness of the dance and Terpsichore as governess of emotions (*Appendix* 3). Only the latest classical references link Terpsichore with the dance and confirm Polyhymnia as mistress of the Roman pantomime (*Greek Anthology* 5.504–505). Western writers on dance have since appropriated Terpsichore for their discipline and use the word "terpsichorean" to indicate an association with dance.

In addition to the Muses, the ancient Greeks perceived the three Graces (Charitēs) as another divine dancing chorus, and they are represented frequently in epic and lyric poetry. While the Muses are led in dance by Apollo, the Graces have Pan as their leader in literature and art. As William Mullen has noted, Pindar seems to distinguish between the Muses and the Graces when invoking them in his lyric poetry (*Olympian Odes* 14).

[*See also* Greece, *article on* Dance in Ancient Greece.]

BIBLIOGRAPHY

Mullen, William. *Choreia: Pindar and Dance.* Princeton, 1982.

LIBBY SMIGEL

TESHIGAWARA SABURŌ (born 15 September 1953 in Sendagaya, Tokyo Prefecture, Japan), Japanese modern dancer and choreographer. After studying sculpture at an art institute, Teshigawara studied ballet with Saiga Toshiko. He began to give solo dance concerts in 1981, and in 1985 he founded the Teshigawara Saburō and Karas Dance Company. It performed its inaugural dance, *The Pale Boy,* as part of the Tokyo Scene Dance Series of 1986. Following this successful performance, his work *The Point of the Wind* was nominated for the international choreography competition in Bagnolet, France, in 1986 and won the silver prize. That same year, Teshigawara performed in France, at Éspace Quiron in Paris and at the Festival d'Aix in Aix-en-Provence.

Returning to Japan, Teshigawara presented new works including *The Arm of the Blue Sky* (1987), *The Moon Is Quicksilver* (1987), and *A Thought in the Night* (1988). More recent works include *Dah-Dah-Sko-Dah-Dah* (1991), *Bones in Pages* (1991), and *Noiject,* which premiered in 1992 and was also performed at the Brooklyn Academy of Music's Next Wave Festival in 1994 and at the Festival d'Avignon. *Noiject,* whose name is a coinage in English combining "noise" and "object," is considered one of Teshigawara's masterpieces; its score—noise blasted at excruciatingly high volume—contributes to a mood of crisis that is often present in Teshigawara's work.

Teshigawara has also directed a film, *Keshioko* (1993), and written a book, *Hone to Kuki* (Bone and Air), published in 1994.

BIBLIOGRAPHY

Boxberger, Edith. "A Change of Paradigms in Dance." *Ballett International/Tanz Aktuell* 2 (February 1994): 28–32.

Boxberger, Edith. "Expeditions into the Essence of Time." *Ballett International/Tanz Aktuell* 8 (August-September 1994): 64–69.

Durland, Steven. "Making the Air Dance." *High Performance* (Summer 1990): 38–43.

Hughes, David. "Ishi-No-Hana (Stone Garden)." *Dance Theatre Journal* 7 (February 1990): 16.

Hunt, Marilyn. "Saburo Teshigawara." *Dance Magazine* (April 1991): 50–53.

Hunt, Marilyn. "A Terrible Beauty Attenuated." *Dance Theatre Journal* 9 (Spring 1992): 28–29.

Kennedy, Gilles. "Escaping from the Swans." *Ballett International* 13 (January 1990): 111–115.

Nugent, Ann. "Through a Wide-Angled Lens." *Dance Now* 2 (Winter 1993–1994): 22–27.

Slater, Lizzie. "Rising Post-Butoh Dance Artist Saburo Teshigawara." *Dance Theatre Journal* 7 (Winter 1989): 7.

Svane, Christina. "The Pro Series." *Contact Quarterly* 18.2 (1993): 15–20.

Tsuki wa suigin: Teshigawara Saburō no buyō. Tokyo, 1988.

HASEGAWA ROKU
Translated from Japanese

TETLEY, GLEN (Glenford Andrew Tetley, Jr.; born 3 February 1926 in Cleveland, Ohio), American choreographer. In Europe, where his choreographic career has been centered, Tetley is rightly regarded as one of the pivotal figures in the emergence of a vigorous contemporary ballet idiom. His idiosyncratic, highly personalized vocabulary evolved from his eclectic background as an American performer with both ballet and modern companies, as well as on Broadway.

After pre-medical studies at Franklin and Marshall College, Tetley moved to New York and began studying modern dance with Hanya Holm and Martha Graham, later adding classes in classical technique from Margaret Craske and Antony Tudor at the Metropolitan Opera Ballet School. He received a bachelor of science degree from New York University in 1948 and became a teacher at Holm's School of Contemporary Dance. He appeared in Holm's Broadway productions of *Kiss Me Kate* (1948) and *Juno* (1959), among others, and danced in the premiere of Gian-Carlo Menotti's *Amahl and the Night Visitors* (NBC Television, 1951), choreographed by John Butler. Tetley's performance career also included seasons with the New York City Opera Ballet (1952–1954) and John Butler's American Dance Theatre (1951–1955). He was one of the original members of the Joffrey Ballet (1956–1957) and appeared with Martha Graham from 1957 to 1959, creating roles in *Clytemnestra* and *Embattled Garden.* He also danced with American Ballet Theatre (1959–1961) and with Jerome Robbins's Ballets: USA (1961–1962).

Tetley formed his own chamber company in 1962, for which he created *Pierrot Lunaire,* his first major work. Set to Arnold Schoenberg's 1912 song cycle, this often ribald, occasionally wistful series of vignettes used *commedia* archetypes. Tetley already showed a flair for the theatrical and a tendency to mix ballet and contemporary idioms without strict allegiance to the conventions of either. Originally danced by Tetley, Linda Hodes, and Robert Powell, this work has become a repertory staple for many European ballet companies. In 1969, following a government-sponsored tour of Europe, the company was officially disbanded.

Concurrent with the formation of his own troupe, Tetley accepted an appointment with the Netherlands Dance Theater. A guest choreographer, he also danced with the company (1962–1965), and in 1969 he became codirector with Hans van Manen. His major Netherlands contributions include *The Anatomy Lesson* (1964), inspired by the Rembrandt painting; *Mythical Hunters,* originally created in 1965 for Batsheva Dance Company; *Arena* (1968), a sextet for men; and *Embrace Tiger and Return to Mountain,* inspired by *taijiquan* and first staged for Ballet Rambert in 1968.

Begun in 1967 at the invitation of Norman Morrice, Tetley's ongoing association with Ballet Rambert has often been cited as one of the major contributing factors in Rambert's development of a new contemporary performance style. Tetley has staged ten ballets for Rambert, notably *Embrace Tiger, Ziggurat* (1967), *The Tempest* (1979)—his only full-length ballet to date—and *Murderer Hope of Women* (1983). The last was inspired by Oskar Kokoschka's brief expressionist pageant of 1909; it includes almost the entire Kokoschka text, interspersed throughout the dancing and chanted by the performers. The work was created with the support of the 1983 Tennent Caledonian Award for premiere at the Edinburgh Festival.

The Tempest (original score by Arne Nordheim) was also created through a commission, this one given to Tetley by the Schwetzingen Festival in Germany. Awarded during his tenure as artistic director of the Stuttgart Ballet (1974–1976), it was not realized until 1979 with Ballet Rambert. Tetley's replacement of John Cranko as head of the Stuttgart company led to the creation of *Voluntaries* (a memorial to Cranko), (1973), *Greening* (1975), and *Daphnis and Chloe* (1975).

After 1976 he worked extensively as a freelance choreographer. During the late 1970s several of his works, including *Rite of Spring* (originally staged for Munich State Opera, 1973) were taken into the repertory of American Ballet Theatre, for which he also created *Sphinx* (1977) for Martine van Hamel, and *Contredances* (1979) for Natalia Makarova and Anthony Dowell. Tetley's association with the Royal Ballet began with *Field Figures* (1970) and *Laborintus* (1972); the choreographer can be seen rehearsing the former in the Rudolf Nureyev film *I Am a Dancer.* Other stagings and creations for the Royal Ballet include *Dances of Albion–Dark Night: Glad Day,* for which he received the Queen Elizabeth II Coronation Award in 1981. Several of his Royal Danish Ballet productions, including *The Firebird* (1981), have been filmed for television. Tetley was artistic associate of the National Ballet of Canada from 1987 through 1989, choreographing several

TETLEY. In 1973, Tetley created his version of Stravinsky's ballet *The Rite of Spring* for the Bavarian State Opera Ballet in Munich. In 1976, he mounted it for the Stuttgart Ballet and cast Richard Cragun in the pivotal role of The Sacrifice, here seen tossed overhead by members of the male ensemble. Minimal scenery and costumes were designed by Nadine Baylis. (Photograph © 1976 by Leslie E. Spatt; used by permission.)

works for the company including *Alice* (1986), *La Ronde* (1987), and *Tagore* (1989). He has created or staged works for nearly every major ballet company in the Western world.

Tetley's work is characterized by fervid intensity, sinuous nonstop propulsion, and voluptuous physicality. A stance of epic grandeur (not unlike Graham's) can be found in his approach to ballet. He rarely creates abstract ballets, but rather utilizes movement as a means to convey his meditations on themes from myth, music, theater, and literature. Tetley's tendency toward abstruse intellectualism, coupled with the openly sexual impetus of his movement vocabulary, has sometimes been derided by American critics who find his stylistically distinct work overly mannered; in Europe, however where he is regarded as one of the major innovators of the century, his critical and popular reputation is of the highest order.

BIBLIOGRAPHY

Brinson, Peter, and Clement Crisp. *The Pan Book of Ballet and Dance.* Rev. ed. London, 1981.

Christofis, Lee. "Glen Tetley: Fusing Classical and Modern." *Dance Australia,* no. 57 (1991–1992): 33–36.

Crabb, Michael F. "Tetley Makes La Ronde Go 'Round." *Dance Magazine* (July 1988): 36–40.

Rogosin, Elinor. *The Dance Makers: Conversations with American Choreographers.* New York, 1980.

Williams, Peter. "Prospero's Island: Glen Tetley Talks to Peter Williams." *Dance and Dancers* (May 1979): 20–21.

ALLEN ROBERTSON

TEYYAM. The term *Teyyam* denotes both a Hindu festival and the deity propitiated in it. Teyyam festivals are held in both private and community Hindu shrines throughout the northern part of Kerala state and in contiguous parts of South Kanara and Coorg in southwestern India.

The festival is organized around the invocation of village ancestors, local heroes, and Puranic deities, who are worshipped with the whole spectrum of performing arts—drumming, singing, processions, feasting, and entertainment. The central performance progresses through a series of stages in which the low-caste dancer is transformed into a deity. Each stage has its own particular text, costume, ritual objects, and interactions among participants. In the first stage, the dancer calls down the spirit of the deity. In the second, the history and origin of the deity are recited. Wearing elaborate costume and makeup, the performer becomes possessed and dances in the third stage. Finally, he calls members of the community in order of their ritual and social importance and blesses them. Individual or communal problems can be brought up before the deity, who sometimes takes the role of mediator.

Until the 1960s and before the government redistributed land in the area, Teyyam performances could be seen as expressive of the local hierarchy. Elaborate rituals of deference, asymmetrical reciprocity, and ritual inversion sanctified the power and authority of the high-caste landowner, while allowing for the controlled aggression of the lower caste (in the person of the dancer) toward a rigid power structure. With the end of the old feudal order in 1972, however, and the concomitant freeing up of the social structure and reallocation of wealth from landowners to tenants, Teyyam performances have begun to assert different messages. They are now saying less about caste hierarchy and interdependence and more about caste mobility and independence.

BIBLIOGRAPHY

Kurup, K. K. N. *The Cult of Teyyam and Hero Worship in Kerala.* Calcutta, 1973.

WAYNE ASHLEY

THAILAND. A constitutional monarchy, the Kingdom of Thailand was formerly known as Siam. Thais are ethnically related to the Shan of Myanmar (Burma) and the Lao of Laos. Thai state religion is Theravāda Buddhism. The Thais moved south to this area from China in the thirteenth century, establishing kingdoms at Sukhothai in 1238 and Ayudhayā in about 1350. Portuguese traders in the 1500s marked the beginning of Siam's relations with the West. Although threatened by French and British colonization, Thailand retained its independence through the centuries.

Dance Genres. The major genres of Thai dance are *rambam phün muang* (folk dance), *nātasin* (classical dance), and *lakhǭn ram* (dance drama). Although at times these Thai arts have suffered from a lack of appreciation and understanding among some political authorities, they have been revived by traditionalists, and Thai classical and folk dance as well as dance drama remain living arts.

In both the folk and the classical style Thai dancers hold their bodies straight from the neck to the hips and move up and down, with knees bending and extending to the rhythm of the music. The arms and hands are kept in curves *(wong)* at various levels—high, medium, or low—and the legs are bent with knees opening outward to make an angle *(liem)*. The grace and beauty of the dancer depend on how well the *wong* and *liem* are kept in relationship and proportion to the whole body. The *wong* and *liem* of male dancers and characters are wide and open, while those of the female are narrow and closed.

For Thai dance, the symbolic hand gestures (*mudrā*s) of dance from India are simplified to a few basic gestures, such as the *čhip,* in which the thumb and index finger are pinched together; in other gestures all the fingers are held away from the thumb. The foot movements are slower in Thai dancing than in Indian dancing, with the toes mostly flexed upward or kept flat at an angle with the legs, never pointed as in Indian dance and Western ballet. Head and neck movements are slight, while the shoulders remain horizontal, resulting in their being at different angles to the moving body. The body moves in diagonal lines to the left and the right; it is rarely twisted in curves—one exception is the *nōrā chātri,* a southern dance drama. These rules apply to most Thai dance, with some variations.

Folk Dance. Each of the four regions of Thailand has its own folk dances, usually associated with agricultural and social activities such as rice planting, harvest festivals, and religious celebrations. The styles of these regional dances are unique to their localities and societies.

Northern folk dance, called *fōn,* is slow and graceful, with simple hand, arm, and leg movements to the musical accompaniment of the *khōng* (gong), *klōng* (drum), *pi* (oboe), and *chāp* (cymbals). Northeastern dance, called *soeng,* is faster in steps and tempo. Hand and leg movements remain simple, with the addition of sensual hip-shaking and swaying. The major instruments accompanying these dances are *khaen* (pipe flute), *klōng,* and *khōng.*

The folk dances of the central region, such as *ram srinuan* and *ram prop kai,* are more refined. Around the time of World War II, *ram wong* was created by Premier Phibulsongkhram's government to counteract the popularity of Western ballroom dancing. *Ram wong* is now a national folk dance.

Southern dances are closer in origin to Indian and Sri Lankan (Ceylonese) dance, as reflected in their fast rhythms and swift hand and leg movements. The southern style of dancing is called *ram sat.* The *ram sat chātri*'s movements are sensual, imitating the natural movements of mating birds and animals. The dance is accompanied by *pi, klōng tuk* (a pair of drums), *mong* (gong), *ching* (small cymbals), *thap* or *thōn* (a pair of one-faced drums), and *krae* (bamboo-stick castanets). Dancers of both the north and south usually wear long, curved bronze fingernails.

Classical Dance. *Nātasin* developed from the basic movements of Thai folk dances, later incorporating the elaborate hand gestures and arm and leg movements of the Indian *bharata nāṭyam* transmitted either directly or through the ancient Mons and Khmers. Although influenced by Indian dance, Thai *nātasin* maintains its own national characteristics.

The development of *nātasin* can be traced to the Sukhōthai period of the thirteenth and fourteenth centuries. The terms *rabam* (choreographed dances for specific functions or occasions), *ram* (dancing with emphasis on hand movements), and *ten* (dancing with emphasis on leg and foot movements) are first mentioned in a stone inscription from the reign of King Rāmkhamhaeng the Great (1279–1300). *Ten* probably refers to *khōn* (masked dance drama) and *nang* (shadow-puppet dance drama), because these two arts use foot movements in a martial style. However, it was probably not until the Ayudhayā period (1351–1767) that Thai classical dance and dance drama fully developed the forms and styles that continue to the present.

The long reign of King Boromakōt of Ayudhayā (1732–1758), a time of peace and prosperity, was also a golden age of Thai classical dancing and the dance drama of the royal court. The dance teachers and members of the royal family, who were responsible for the training of Ayudhayā court dancers, carried on the tradition through the Thonburi period (1767–1782) and the Ratanakōsin period (1782 to the present) after the fall of the ancient capital in 1767 in a war with the Burmese. Then, a large number of Thai court dancers were taken to the Burmese royal court; they settled in Yodia (Ayudhayā) village and taught Thai *nātasin* to the Burmese.

Dance Drama and Masked Dance Drama. Dance theater developed in the Ayudhayā period in the forms of *lakhọn* (dance drama) and *khōn* (masked dance drama). One of the oldest forms of *lakhọn* is the *nōrā chātri* of the south, which incorporates movements from Thai *nātasin,* Indian *bharata nāṭyam,* and the indigenous naturalistic style of southern dance. Other subgenres of dance theater are *lakhọn nōk* (folk dance drama, originally performed by male dancers, and later by a mixed ensemble) and *lakhọn nai* (female dance drama of the royal court). In

THAILAND. An early twentieth-century portrait of two *khōn* dancers of the royal court. (Photograph from a private collection.)

THAILAND. Performers of *Manōhrā,* a dance drama depicting the romance between a mythical bird-maiden and a human prince, are called *nōrā* dancers and are traditionally all male. Golden headdresses and long golden fingernails are characteristic items of their costumes. (Photograph from the archives of The Asia Society, New York.)

the nineteenth century many new styles were developed from these traditional dances—for example, *lakhǭn dư̆kdamban* (from *lakhǭn nai* and *lakhǭn nōk*), *lakhǭn phanthāng* (from *lakhǭn nōk*), *lakhǭn rōng* (Thai operetta), and *liké* (folk dance drama). *Liké,* because of its popular themes, wit, and humor, is the only form that survives as a people's art; the others are performed by the National Theater as classical dance drama.

The first Western-style theater building with a proscenium stage, called the Prince Theater, was constructed in the nineteenth century by Čhao Phrayā Mahin. Tickets were sold for the first time in the history of Thai theater. Other troupes followed suit and theater houses proliferated. Modern painted architectural sets with three-dimensional perspectives were introduced by Prince Narisaranuwadhiwong (1863–1947). Dance drama from this period onward was divided into acts and scenes, following Western tradition, a change from the traditional, free performance that was presented continuously for three to seven days and nights. The modernization and expansion of classical dance and dance drama in the reigns of King Chulalongkorn (1868–1910) and King Vajiravudh (1910–1925) enabled this centuries-old cultural heritage to survive through the era of westernization and into the present.

All the kings from King Tāksin, the sole monarch of the Thonburi period, to the present king, Bhūmiphol Adulayadēj, contributed in one way or another to classical dance and dance drama. In preserving the classical tradition, many talented artists and dramatists introduced new dimensions and directions to the content, style, form, expression, and stage presentation of Thai dance. The royal court maintained its role as the center of Thai classical dance and dance drama and set the royal style as the national model for public troupes and theaters.

King Rama II (1809–1824) was responsible for most of the royal choreographies and dramatic texts for *khōn* and *lakhǭn* that are preserved by the royal and national dance troupes today. Teachers of the National Academy of Dance and the National Theater come from a long line of artists of the royal courts of Ayudhayā, Thonburi, and Ratanakosin that has continued without interruption despite wars and political crises.

Dance Education. After the revolution of 1932, the government's Department of Fine Arts, under the Ministry of Education, took over the function of training dancers and producing dance and dance drama. Thai *nātasin, khōn, lakhǭn,* music, and art are now taught by modern methods along with academic subjects from the elementary to the college level. The natural, lifelong method of teaching used by traditional artists was changed to a system with a rigid curriculum for each academic year, dur-

THAILAND. *Khōn* perfomance at the National Theater, Bangkok. A masked dance drama, *khōn* enacts stories from the *Rāmakian,* the Thai version of the *Rāmāyaṇa.* Here, Phra Ram (Rāma), Phra Lak (Lakṣmaṇa), and the monkey army progress to the battlefield. (Photograph © Jukka Miettinen; used by permission.)

ing which students take academic courses in the morning and dance, music, and art in the afternoon. Both teachers and students participate in the National Theatre productions for the public. A graduate of the National Academy and College of Dance receives either a certificate of dance or a bachelor's degree in education with a specialization in *nātasin.* Thailand's Ministry of Education now prescribes Thai classical dance and music as compulsory courses in elementary and secondary schools. The National Academy of Dance has branches in the four major regions of Thailand to teach or to advise local schools, and the academy's traveling dance troupes perform in the country's provinces and abroad in Asia, Southeast Asia, Europe, and the United States.

Many universities and colleges offer elective courses in Thai classical dance and dance drama or extracurricular dramatic activities. During the 1990s, two leading universities, Chulalongkorn and Thammasat, began to offer bachelor degrees in Thai and Western dance. The Thammasat Faculty of Fine and Applied Arts emphasizes research, choreography, notation, theory, and methodology for the teaching of Thai classical, modern, and contemporary dance.

Students of Thai classical dance start their training at the age of eight to ten, learning the basic dance movements, called *phlēng chā* (series of slow movements) and *phlēng reo* (series of fast movements). They repeat the sounds of the *taphōn* (one-faced drum), which provides the rhythm for the dance while they do their daily exercise routine, chanting "čha-čhong-čha, thing-čhong-thing" for the *phlēng chā* and "tup-thing-thing" for the *phlēng reo.* Then they proceed to learn the basic patterns of dance for each character, called *mae bot* (mother chapter).

The next phase for students of classical dance drama is to learn the *ram nā phāt* (dances for specific actions and occasions in a play or ceremony). The most basic *nā phāt* (dance tunes and patterns for these actions) are *smoe,* used for walking and going from one place to another in a slow or moderate tempo, and *choet,* used for fast entrances or exits or other rapid actions, such as fighting. More elaborate *nā phāt* are for special kinds of actions, such as *tra nimit* for supernatural actions, *kuk phāt* for very violent and forceful actions, and *rua* to presage magical or supernatural actions. Each type of *nā phāt* is again divided into subtypes for specific purposes, occasions, and characters. All *nā phāt* are revered as sacred and must be performed with great respect, concentration, and care—as if the dancer were in a magical or religious trance.

THAILAND. Students who specialize in the portrayal of noble male characters practice at the College of Dramatic Arts, Bangkok. (Photograph © by Jukka Miettinen; used by permission.)

Certain *nā phāt* are considered very powerful, to the extent that they could cause accidents or even death to dancers who perform them improperly. An example is the "Dance of Phra Phirāp," performed in the dancers' invocation and initiation ceremony. Phra Phirāp is a god of dance, a destructive, monstrous form of the Hindu god Śiva (Shiva), the creator and destroyer, whose dance gives both life and death to the universe. Phirāp is also the name of a demon guardian of Śiva's garden in the *Ramakian,* the Thai version of India's *Rāmāyana* epic.

To perform well in dance drama, performers have to learn the language of gestures, *phāsā thā.* The narratives and dialogues in classical dance and dance drama of all forms are interpreted with gestures by the dancer, either word by word or phrase by phrase. The expression of emotions is also mimed with elaborate hand movements. These gestures are more fixed in the classical dance forms than in the folk and modern forms. The gestures have even influenced the daily language and expression of Thai people.

Each dancer has to practice *ti-bot,* the interpretation of scripts and characters. Dancers and actors who succeed in interpreting well are said to "smash the script and character to pieces." Although strict patterns of movement and gesture must be observed as an artistic skill, dancers can still explore their individual talents and ingenuity as creative artists.

Present trends include experimentation with adapting Thai classical dance to contemporary music, thus giving modern interpretations to classical dance drama. Examples are Professor Mattani Rutnin's *Busaba-Unakan* (1994) and *Rama-Sida* (1996), his modern version of the *Rāmakien;* Parichart Jungwiwattanaporn's *Phimphilalai* (1995), based on *Khun Chang Kun Phaen;* and *Savitri* (1996), performed under the title of *Love and Death* by a British-educated contemporary dancer, Nuchawadee Bamrungtrakul, and graduates of Chulalongkorn University.

[*See also* Khōn; Lakhǫn; *and* Manōhrā.]

BIBLIOGRAPHY

Maha Vajiravudh. "Notes on the Siamese Theatre." *Journal of the Siam Society* 55.1 (1967): 1–30.

Miettinen, Jukka O. *Classical Dance and Theatre in South-East Asia.* New York, 1992.

Rutnin, Mattani, Mojdara ed. *The Siamese Theatre.* Bangkok, 1975.

Rutnin, Mattani Mojdara. *Dance, Drama, and Theatre in Thailand.* Tokyo, 1993.

Rutnin, Mattani Mojara. "Phatthanākān Khǫng Lakhǫn Thai Smai Mai." In *Arayatham Thai.* Bangkok, 1997.

Morton, David. "Thailand." In *The New Grove Dictionary of Music and Musicians.* London, 1980.

Virulrak, Surapone. "Theatre in Thailand Today." *Asian Theatre Journal* 7 (Spring 1990): 95–104.

Yupho, Dhanit. *Classical Siamese Theatre.* Bangkok, 1952.

MATTANI MOJDARA RUTNIN

THARP, TWYLA (born 1 July 1941 in Portland, Indiana), American dancer and choreographer. Best known as a modern dance choreographer, Twyla Tharp has also worked in ballet, film, theater, television, and even sports. In all these venues her choreography is characterized by wit, inventiveness, complexity, and physical rigor. The glamor and daring of her movement style, as well as her frequent use of American popular music from rags to rock, have made her dances appealing to a wide audience; at the same time, they are works of scrupulous logic, demanding extraordinary technique.

Born to a Quaker family of farmers and entrepre-neurs, Tharp was the oldest of four children. When she was eight the family moved to southern California, eventually settling in San Bernardino. Her parents ran several businesses in the area, including—most important for Tharp—a drive-in movie theater. She began helping out at the drive-in as a child and continued through high school, absorbing the Hollywood movies of the 1950s.

Tharp's mother, who had studied to be a concert pianist, started her on a variety of music and dance lessons. Tharp had been introduced to ear training and piano by her mother while in Indiana, where she also studied "Hawaiian tap" in a neighbor's garage. In California she continued piano lessons with a professional teacher, studied ballet with one of Anna Pavlova's former company members, Beatrice Collenette, and later undertook violin, viola, drums, tap, and baton. Her daily practice schedule was formidable, but she developed habits of discipline and concentration that still influence her work in the studio.

After graduating from Pacific High School, Tharp entered Pomona College, planning to become a psychiatrist. The summer following her freshman year, however, she took classes at the Los Angeles studios of Lester Horton, Eugene Loring, and John Butler. She spent one more semester at Pomona before committing herself to dance and moving to New York, where she entered Barnard College. While majoring in art history at Barnard she studied at numerous schools of modern dance, including those of Martha Graham, Merce Cunningham, Alwin Nikolais, and Erick Hawkins; she also studied jazz with Luigi and ballet with Igor Schwezoff and Richard Thomas.

By the time Tharp graduated from Barnard in 1963 she was already a member of the Paul Taylor Dance Company. Although she spent less than two years with Taylor and had only small parts, her dancing won considerable praise; nonetheless, she was too independent and ambitious to be content working for someone else. On leaving the company she choreographed her first work, *Tank Dive,* which premiered on 29 April 1965 at Hunter College. It lasted only a few minutes and made up the entire program: highlights included Tharp in a diver's pose wearing outsized flippers, and Tharp holding a *relevé* in second position while Petula Clark's "Downtown" was played.

Tharp's work over the next five years came in the wake of the Judson Dance Theater but was only partially associated with the postmodern sensibility that reigned at the time. These early pieces were performed dispassionately to silence, metronomes, or spoken counts. They were structured so precisely and rigorously that Tharp could, and often did, diagram the dance on paper, using numbers, colors, and geometrical figures.

Like many others in this era, Tharp preferred nonproscenium spaces, staging events in gymnasiums, museums, and parks. *Medley* (1969), commissioned by the American Dance Festival, had six company members and about thirty students working in squadrons on a huge parade ground. *Dancing in the Streets of London and Paris, Continued in Stockholm and Sometimes Madrid* (1969), the biggest and most elaborate work of these years, took place simultaneously in different areas of the Hartford Atheneum in Hartford, Connecticut; closed-circuit television augmented the performance, and there were opportunities for audience participation.

THARP. Mikhail Baryshnikov and Marianna Tcherkassky in *Push Comes to Shove* (1976). (Photograph © by Herbert Migdoll; used by permission.)

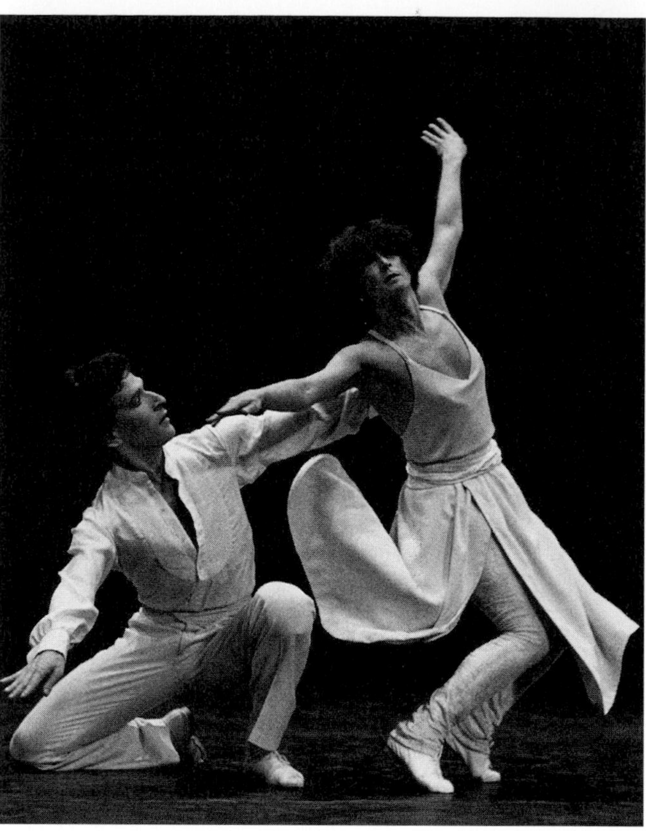

THARP. Richard Colton and Tharp in her *Baker's Dozen* (1979), an upbeat dance for twelve performers that is filled with flowing movement. (Photograph © 1979 by Jack Vartoogian; used by permission.)

Unlike many postmodernists, Tharp still believed in classical technique and in dance movement as distinct from pedestrian activity. From the beginning she worked with distinguished dancers, including Sara Rudner, Rose Marie Wright, and Kenneth Rinker; some of the most notable dancers she worked with later included Shelley Washington, Richard Colton, Tom Rawe, Jennifer Way, John Carrafa, Christine Uchida, and William Whitener.

By 1969 critics saw in Tharp's work a mixture of ballet, athletics, and knockabout play, with a style described by Deborah Jowitt in the *Village Voice* as "acquiring a strong classical technique and then learning to fling it around without ever really losing control." Arlene Croce—discussing *Group Activities* (1969), performed at the Brooklyn Academy of Music with the audience seated on two sides of the stage and the dancers working in the space between—noted "the near-collisions, the sudden crowding or circling in a gang (in a jumping phrase), the as-sudden dispersals," and said it looked "brilliantly irrational."

During this period Tharp was working to develop movement as intrinsically logical as music, with a structure based on retrograde, inversion, reversal, and other manipulations of the phrase. The culmination of this work, and of all Tharp's Judson-era dances, was *The Fugue* (1970), a trio performed in boots on a miked stage and displaying the unadorned architecture of a series of intricately related phrases.

With her next dance Tharp turned a corner. She kept the mathematical surety of musical structure but let the music itself be heard; she also freed her sense of humor and her affection for American popular culture, both historic and contemporary. *Eight Jelly Rolls* (1971), choreographed to the music of Jelly Roll Morton, was called by critic John Rockwell "an astounding masterpiece which pays tribute to jazz dance and a whole era and stratum of American life without ever slipping away from Tharp's own style." Later Tharp used the music of Bix Beiderbecke, Scott Joplin, Fats Waller, and Willie ("The Lion") Smith, as well as Chuck Berry and Paul Simon; in addition, she has choreographed to Bach, Mozart, Haydn, and Brahms.

As Tharp's style took shape in the 1970s, it came to be identified with risky, intricate partnering, sudden leaps and lifts, offhanded virtuoso displays, and a relentless urge to keep moving. Sometimes frantic, often funny, the movement seems spontaneous (audience members at lecture-demonstrations used to ask if the dances were improvised) because the counts and the phrasing are invisible. Yet the effect is harmonious, as if rules of classical propriety were operating covertly.

With *Deuce Coupe* (1973) Tharp became the first modern dance choreographer of her generation to cross over to ballet. Commissioned by the Joffrey Ballet and choreographed to songs of the Beach Boys, *Deuce Coupe* was performed by Joffrey and Tharp dancers together. Tharp also choreographed *As Time Goes By* (1973) for the Joffrey. Her works for American Ballet Theatre include *Push Comes to Shove* (1976), a witty and vigorous reassessment of balletic behavior set to rags and Haydn; *The Little Ballet* (1984) to music by Aleksandr Glazunov; *Sinatra Suite* (1984); and *Bach Partita* (1984). All but the last were made for Mikhail Baryshnikov, whose work with Tharp has been deeply illuminating for both artists. In collaboration with Jerome Robbins she created *Brahms/Handel* (1984) for New York City Ballet.

In 1986 Tharp altered the format of her company to include several classically trained ballet dancers so that she could choreograph ballet as well as modern styles for her own dancers. Her best-known work from this period was *In the Upper Room* (1986), to a score by Philip Glass. In 1988 she disbanded her company, despite its critical and popular success, because she felt that the burdens of administration and fundraising were making it impossible for her to work creatively. She joined American Ballet Theatre as an associate artistic director, and several of her dancers followed her. After Baryshnikov left the company in 1989, Tharp's formal association with it ended. She went on to create works for the Boston Ballet, the Paris Opera Ballet, and the Royal Ballet, as well as choreographing for American Ballet Theatre; and she has toured widely with pickup companies of ballet and modern dancers. In 1990 she granted permission to Chicago's Hubbard Street Dance Company to perform several of her early works.

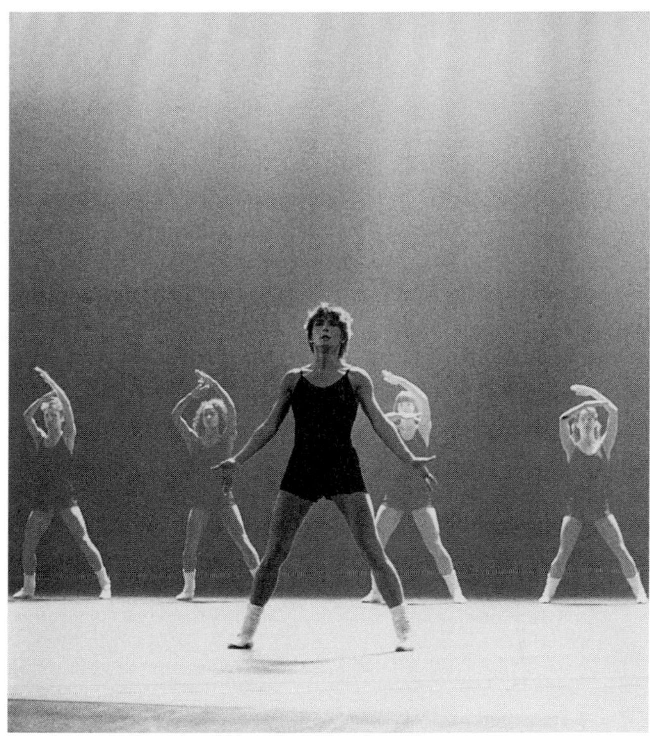

THARP. A personal characteristic of Tharp's choreography is her willingness to draw on movement from all sources. *Fait Accompli* (1983), pictured here with Tharp at center, features movement derived from boxing. Lighting designer Jennifer Tipton created brightly lit haze, evoking the feel of a sports arena. The designs for *Fait Accompli* evolved into the most famous Tharp-Tipton collaboration, *In the Upper Room* (1986). (Photograph © 1984 by Beatriz Schiller; used by permission.)

Long attracted to the idea of presenting a full-evening theater piece, Tharp created *When We Were Very Young* (1980) with playwright Thomas Babe, to a score by John Simon. The piece was based on the A. A. Milne poem "Disobedience," and the company portrayed a chaotic family, with Tharp as the crazed, courageous mother. A bigger, more complex theater piece followed a year later—*The Catherine Wheel,* with music by David Byrne. Densely symbolic but rich with dancing and theatricality, the piece has another tormented family, this time struggling with apoca-

THARP. *In the Upper Room* (1986) is perhaps Tharp's most popular work. In her autobiography, Tharp says that it is her only dance that consistently receives a standing ovation. A craftily constructed dance, set to a driving score by Philip Glass, *In the Upper Room* features a mixed cast of ballet and modern dancers. In this scene, Christine Uchida (left) and Shelley Washington (right), whose roles were inspired by black-and-white china bulldogs, guard the stage. (Photograph © 1987 by Jack Vartoogian; used by permission.)

lypse both inside and out. Turning to more traditional theater, Tharp directed and choreographed a Broadway production of *Singin' in the Rain* (1985), employing members of her company in the chorus. The show received poor reviews but ran successfully for nearly a year.

Early in her career Tharp became interested in the possibilities for video in creating, sustaining, and conveying dance. During her pregnancy (1970–1971), she videotaped herself doing the same movement every day; elements of these phrases appeared in her 1979 dance *Baker's Dozen.* Her first major television project was the award-winning "Making Television Dance" (1977), a co-production with WNET, in which she applied various video techniques to movement as well as providing an introduction to her company at work. Since then she has directed several video productions of her work, including a restaging of *The Catherine Wheel* (1983). For "Baryshnikov by Tharp" (1985), a public television production of three of her ballets for Baryshnikov, Tharp and co-director Don Mischer won two Emmy awards and a Directors' Guild of America award.

Tharp's fascination with film dates back to her childhood, and she has choreographed the dances for three films directed by Milos Forman—*Hair* (1979), *Ragtime* (1980), and *Amadeus* (1984); for the last she also staged the opera sequences. She also supplied some choreography for the film *White Nights* (1985), starring Baryshnikov and Gregory Hines.

Tharp has undertaken two special projects in the sports world. *After All* (1976) was choreographed for Olympic gold medal–winning figure skater John Curry, and "Dance Is a Man's Sport, Too" (1980), made for ABC's *Omnibus,* featured Peter Martins and football player Lynn Swann.

Tharp's numerous honors include the Brandeis University Creative Citation in Dance (1972), the Dance Magazine Award (1981), the Barnard College Medal of Distinction (1982), the New York City Mayor's Award of Honor for Arts and Culture (1984), the Columbia University Medal of Excellence (1986), and the Samuel H. Scripps American Dance Festival Award (1990).

BIBLIOGRAPHY

Acocella, Joan. "Balancing Act." *Dance Magazine* (October 1990): 54–59.

Albert, Steven. "Utopia Lost—and Found? A Look at Tharp's Way." *Ballet Review* 14 (Spring 1986): 17–35.

Croce, Arlene. "Twyla Tharp's Red Hot Peppers." *Ballet Review* 4.1 (1971): 33–40.

Foster, Susan Leigh. *Reading Dancing: Bodies and Subjects in Contemporary American Dance.* Berkeley, 1986.

Jowitt, Deborah. "Far-Out Ladies." *The Village Voice* (13 February 1969).

Jowitt, Deborah. "Twyla Tharp's New Kick." *New York Times Magazine* (4 January 1976).

Macaulay, Alastair. "Let's Twist Again." *New Yorker* (17 February 1992).

Nugent, Ann. "*Till* and Twyla: A Myth and a Legend." *Dance Now* 3 (Spring 1994): 10–17.

Reynolds, Nancy, and Susan Reimer-Torn. "Push Comes to Shove." In *Dance Classics.* Pennington, N.J., 1991.

Rockwell, John. "Tharp Troupe in L.A. Debut." *Los Angeles Times* (11 April 1972).

Rogosin, Elinor. *The Dance Makers: Conversations with American Choreographers.* New York, 1980.

Shapiro, Laura. "Something in the Way She Moves." *Rolling Stone* (2 June 1977).

Tharp, Twyla. *Push Comes to Shove: An Autobiography.* New York, 1992.

LAURA SHAPIRO

THEATERS FOR DANCE. In Western cultures, dance has been performed in every kind of space, indoors and out. With few exceptions, theatrical dance is performed in borrowed spaces because it does not have sufficient mass appeal to support a permanent home. Companies and choreographers who have home theaters, however, may shape their works for a particular stage, demonstrating that the dance space itself is an important determinant of style. For touring companies, the conditions of presentation are always changing; the same work can vary greatly in different spaces or even when viewed from different places in the same theater. The style of a work arises from what the dancer does with the body, how it relates to space, and how the audience sees the body in space. These factors are inextricably connected to the place of performance.

The general characteristics of the performing space for Western theatrical dance have evolved over the centuries. At the same time the relationship between audience and dancers also evolved.

Classical Antiquity. The space for choral performance in ancient Greek theaters is well known. One example, the theater at Epidauros (c.350 BCE), reflects the order and harmony of the classical style. It has a circular orchestra about sixty-seven feet (about 20 meters) in diameter set well into a *cavea* (amphitheater) accommodating fourteen thousand in fifty-five rows of stone seats. Privileged members of the audience sat in the lower seats with an excellent view of the dithyrambic and dramatic choruses, while the lowest class, the slaves, viewed the performance from a great distance.

In a theater where the orchestra was more than half surrounded by an audience seated in a graded construction, movement would have been seen from many points of view. We have limited knowledge of ancient choreographic method; sculptural (three-dimensional) movement by individuals or massed groups, gestural movement, rank-and-file figures, and circular figures were probably all used, but it is not known how these movements were connected in space or time.

Eventually the orchestra was reduced to a semicircle, and the *cavea* no longer "engulfed" the dance space. Audience and player were thus separated; seats of honor were moved to higher rows for a better perspective on the raised stage. The chorus exited when not performing, and its importance in the play was gradually reduced. The action was increasingly confined to the stage, where any danced movement would have taken a different form than it had in the orchestra. The long, narrow stage with a frontal aspect may have called for a more upright, two-dimensional use of the body, probably limited in range of motion and force.

The Romans made pervasive structural contributions to theater-building. They connected and enclosed the stage and auditorium, developed sophisticated audience circulation systems, and made the theater a free-standing edifice.

Inside the theater, the orchestra was walled off from the spectators. The movement emphasis shifted to the personal expressiveness of the solo performer instead of groups in formations. The rise of the pantomimist can thus be understood in a spatial context: this popular performer mimed on a shallow stage against a background of an elaborate *scaenae frons* (a wall with architectural embellishments) several stories high. Individual virtuosity could be accommodated in the limited space.

In the Middle Ages, before architecturally specific spaces began to be built, performances were held in basilicas, marketplaces, ceremonial halls, and other multipurpose sites. Performers and audience were often mobile, creating an individualized viewing perspective in which the movement was multivalent in style and meaning.

Renaissance Italy. The revival of classical theater-building in Renaissance Italy in the late fifteenth century was intended for the presentation of plays, but the scenic and architectural activity that ensued influenced all types of formal spectacle. There were two spaces available for theatrical dancing: the open space, or pit, in front of the stage; or the raised stage also occupied by painted, illusionistic perspective scenery, machines, and traps.

THEATERS FOR DANCE. The Theater of the Sanctuary of Apollo (fourth century BCE) at Delphi, Greece, a prototype for theaters in the Western world. (Photograph from a private collection.)

THEATERS FOR DANCE. This engraving in *Orbis sensualium pictus* (translated into English in 1658) shows a seventeenth-century raised stage surrounded by painted scenery. The audience gathered in front of the stage to view the performance. (Reprinted from Allardyce Nicolle, *Stuart Masques and the Renaissance Stage*, New York, 1938.)

Illustrations of court entertainments show steps or ramps connecting stage to pit, leading to an earlier assumption that steps were used. However, Nagler's descriptions of the Medici entertainments (1539–1637) indicate that steps were often painted on the front of the raised stage (the trap room), and stairs were actually built only if the choreography required it. The open space was not always available for dancing, because the patron and his entourage could be seated there on their own platform. In this case, the dancing was confined to about a twenty-foot (6-meter) depth of the raised stage. A famous Callot etching of the Uffizi in Florence in 1617 shows the use of the pit for a ballet, but this does not suggest an unvarying practice. In *Le Nozze degli Dei* (The Marriage of the Gods; 1637), the final scene used the entire stage to show a "celestial ballet" in layers of vertical space created by four levels of cloud machines. [*See* Nozze degli Dei, Le.]

Patrician families of Venice began producing opera not just for amusement of the private patron but also for a wider audience that paid to attend. To cover costs and return a profit, the maximum number of paying customers had to be accommodated; to this end, the pit filled with benches and multiple tiers of boxes replaced the galleries and graduated constructions derived from the classical *cavea*. The musicians were placed between audience and stage, further reducing access to the pit. The first theater so designed was the Teatro San Cassiano (1637); by 1699, Venice had sixteen such theaters.

France in the Baroque Era. Theater for profit had important implications for the expressive and technical use of the body. In France, it forced a transition between about 1615 and 1650 from the figured dance tradition of the *ballet à entrée* to the step tradition of the *danse d'école*.

The French were using ceremonial halls, tennis courts, or parks as theaters, temporarily arranged for each event. All of the interiors were in the *teatro da sala* tradition of rectangular rooms with one or two tiers of permanent galleries. The Palais du Louvre had five areas suitable for theatrical presentation, but none of them were used exclusively for that purpose. At Versailles most performances were held in a park theater, although in the late seventeenth century, plans were drafted for a *salle des ballets*. The spaces in regular use were the Grande Salle du Louvre, the Salle du Petit Bourbon, and the Palais Royal (home of the opera from 1673).

The Petit Bourbon was a huge room in the Hotel de Bourbon (now the site of the colonnade of the Louvre). Here *Le Balet Comique de la Royne* (1581) was produced, as were balls and other spectacles. Patin's well-known etching of the opening scene from the *Balet Comique* is drastically out of scale. Other illustrations of the Petit Bourbon suggest more plausible proportions and volume for this space. For example, a 1615 etching shows a room 221 by 48 feet (70 by 15 meters) with ground-level seating, an apse, and a vaulted ceiling that accommodated the machines omitted from the Patin etching. The king sat in the apsidal east end opposite Circe's garden, which rested on a sloped platform one foot (0.3 meter) high in front. A true raised stage with traps and machines underneath was not introduced in French court entertainments for another thirty-three years. Until then the settings were one with the dance space in the central area.

In 1596 Tomaso Francini, an Italian architect and engineer, came to France, where he created scenes and machines for several court ballets. Among the ballets was the *Triomphe de Minerve* (1615) produced in the Petit Bourbon, which used a six-foot-high (2-meter-high) raised stage or trap room with ramps to the floor on either side so that characters entering through the scene could descend to the floor for dancing. The raised stage effectively separated the decor from the audience, but the dancers still used the pit until the 1640s. When Giacomo Torelli was hired in 1645 to convert the Petit Bourbon fully to the Italianate style, his production of *La Finta Pazza* set a precedent for confining action to the stage. Performers were now on display in a new sense in the raised, picture-frame stage, which came to be regarded as a place distinct from the theatrical and social settings of the court. While amateurs retreated from such situations, professional dancers developed their art to be seen in Torelli's venue.

Illustrations of subsequent French court productions show a raised stage without ramps or steps into the pit. The orchestra pit begins to appear in its present position early in the eighteenth century. At the back of the pit was an amphitheater of ten or more rows of graded construction. The unfurnished front section was a pit for standing spectators in the public theaters, but at court it was reserved for the king. The Petit Bourbon was torn down in the 1660s to make way for an addition to the Louvre.

A magnificent but bizarre theater, Gaspare Vigarani's Salle des Machines (or Théâtre des Tuileries), was built for production of lavish machine plays (those using elaborate special effects). The stage of the new theater was the largest in Europe at 132-feet (40-meters) deep and had one machine that could hold as many as three hundred people. The theater had severe acoustic problems and fell into disuse, leaving only one theater in Paris—the Palais Royal—suitable for fully mounted productions of opera and opéra-ballet.

Paris Opera. Built during Cardinal Richelieu's residence (c.1640), the Palais Royal was the Paris Opera's first permanent home. It had a raised stage with flat wings, a proscenium arch, and steps into the pit. The painting *Le Soir* shows the theater with Richelieu and Louis XIII at a performance. Remodeled by Torelli in 1646 for Mazarin's Italian opera productions, it reverted to use for the more popular *ballet à entrée.* This space was home to many distinguished artists and their collaborators, notably Molière and Lully. A late plan of this theater (1745) shows a narrowing of the horseshoe toward the back of the house, possibly an attempt to improve sightlines.

From the late seventeenth century until the late eighteenth, choreography at the opera revolved around displays of steps in formal, stiff costumes including wigs, masks, armor, panniers, and heeled shoes. Changing subject matter included heroic pantomime and exotic and folk themes. These added variety to the *danse d'école,* but until dresses became soft at the end of the eighteenth century, the use of the body in the picture-frame stage could not have changed a great deal.

While the architect Pierre-Louis Moreau-Desproux built a new theater on the ruins of the old, the Opera was housed at the Théâtre des Tuileries (1764–1770). The new theater, still called the Palais Royal, measured 180 by 92 feet (about 57 by 30 meters). Formed on a truncated oval, it lost the look of a remodeled ceremonial hall. The house measured 48 by 46 feet (about 15 by 14 meters), with four tiers of boxes; the stage was 36 by 56 feet (about 11 by 17 meters). It lasted eleven years (1770–1781). Compared to other theater plans in the opera-house tradition, Moreau's was a compromise. His wider and shallower

THEATERS FOR DANCE. A vertical section of an eighteenth-century theater in Stuttgart shows two tiers of boxes, for viewing, and the orchestra, which is separated from the audience by a barrier. This is one of the theaters used by Jean-Georges Noverre during the time he served as *maître de ballet* to the court of the duke of Württemberg. (Reprinted from Jean-Georges Noverre, *Letters on Dancing and Ballet,* translated by Cyril W. Beaumont, London, 1951, p. 94.)

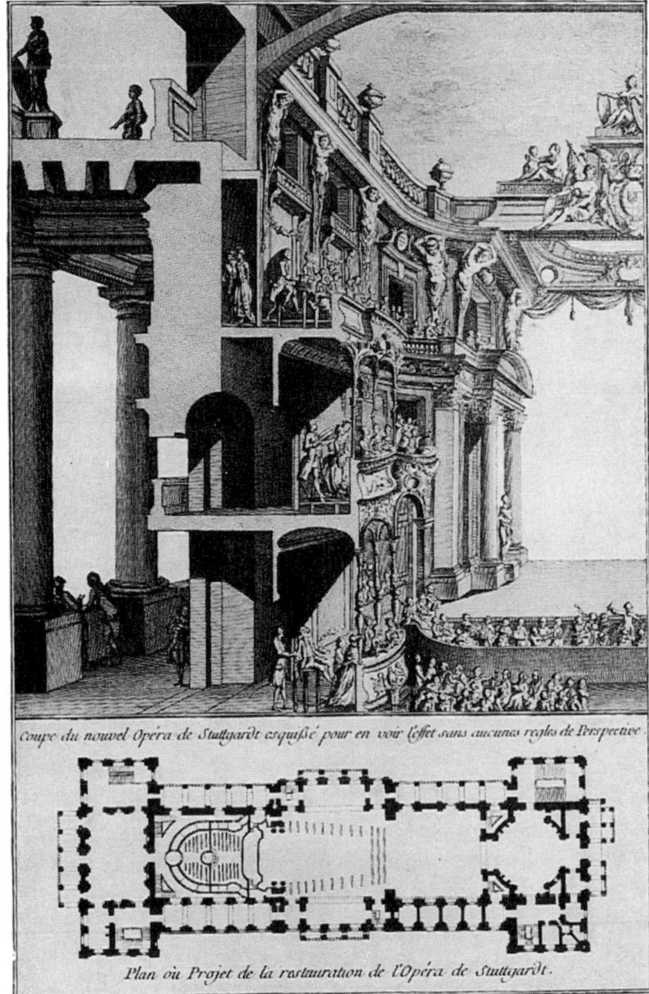

Coupe du nouvel Opéra de Stuttgardt esquissé pour en voir l'effet sans aucunes regles de Perspective.
Plan où Projet de la restauration de l'Opéra de Stuttgardt.

THEATERS FOR DANCE. Architect François Debret created a home for the Paris Opera by dismantling and reconstructing the Théâtre des Arts in the 1820s. This lithograph, made c.1850 by Jean-Baptiste Arnout, shows an 1831 performance of the "Ballet of the Nuns" in Meyerbeer's opera *Robert le Diable.* The theater burned in 1873. (Photograph from the Dance Collection, New York Public Library for the Performing Arts)

stage house and auditorium brought spectator and performer closer together. The stage itself had more functional space because new angled perspectives claimed less depth.

Jean-Georges Noverre's ill-fated years (1776–1779) as ballet master of the Paris Opera were spent in this theater. His *ballet d'action* repertory had been developed on well-equipped provincial and foreign stages. The ballets required a set with props to establish locale and situation, but open space was also needed for the danced parts. Such an arrangement was perfectly compatible with the opera, with which ballet always shared the evening. At Stuttgart (1760–1766) Noverre had had virtually everything he needed under the patronage of the duke of Wurtemberg, including a theater with a deep stage for the "new style of ballet." As in Moreau's theater, elaborate three-dimensional Italian vistas gave way to a more painted environment in which there was functional space available for the dance.

Again between homes after the new Palais Royal burned in 1781, the Opera was situated uncomfortably in the Porte Saint-Martin until 1793. A new theater had just opened, built by Marguerite Brunet Montansier for her own company, which included Charles Didelot. It had been designed to order by Victor Louis expressly for plays, operas, and dance on a grand scale. Louis's theater at Bordeaux (1772), where *La Fille Mal Gardée* premiered, was already famous for its grand staircase and circular plan. He had solved the problem of supporting a massive domed ceiling by a complex system of vaulting and semidomes that rested on giant columns encircling the audience. This technical masterpiece was widely imitated by subsequent architects and was used in the Montansier theater, which became the Opera's home in 1794 when the revolutionary government removed Montansier and her company. The building was renamed the Théâtre des Arts and alterations were made to the pit. In 1820, after the duc de Berry was assassinated there, the building was ordered demolished. Instead, the architect François Debret dismantled and reconstructed much of it in another part of Paris, creating a magnificent home for the Romantic ballet. Debret's theater also became a test house for gas lighting, already used in street lighting. All this brought the Opera back to artistic dominance during the years 1821–1850. This building was to have been a temporary house (though it lasted until it burned in 1873), and in 1860 plans were made for a new theater. Charles Garnier's theater building in the Place de l'Opéra, much in debt to Victor Louis, opened in 1875 after years of delays. Garnier's opera house remains one of the best-equipped and most admired in all of Europe.

England and the United States. The home of ballet and opera in England was London's Italian Opera House, built in 1705 in the Haymarket. The house was called the King's or Her Majesty's, according to the gender of the monarch, throughout its existence. It was a fashionable house requiring formal dress even for the pit. After it burned, a new theater opened in 1791 with a 37-foot (12-meter) proscenium opening and a deep, rather old-fashioned forestage which thrust the performers well past those seated in the stage boxes.

The English forestage was a desirable feature of the King's because of the building's poor acoustics and because it provided space for the danced sections of the *ballet d'action.* The stage boxes, which became popular in opera houses after Louis Véron introduced them in Paris in 1830, were a negative feature of the theater. Named after the new public transit vehicles, these "omnibus boxes" held large parties of subscribers who often became rowdy. The house could hold 2,500 people in five closely spaced tiers with a huge gallery. The pit was raked and filled with benches, leaving a wide center aisle known as "Fop's Alley."

In the United States, foreign dance artists first appeared in English-style theaters. Philadelphia's Chestnut Street Theatre, New York's Park Theatre, and Charleston's City Theatre were the major houses from the 1790s through

THEATERS FOR DANCE. Built in 1778 and renovated in 1838, the Teatro alla Scala in Milan is, like most Italian theaters, primarily an opera house, although dance performances are regularly presented. This photograph was shot at a performance of *Swan Lake* during the 1963/64 season. (Photograph from the Dance Collection, New York Public Library for the Performing Arts.)

the mid-1800s. Fanny Elssler appeared at all these theaters, beginning with her debut at the Park in 1840.

Russia. From the late eighteenth century, dance activity in Russia was housed in permanent public theaters in the opera-house tradition. Today the Bolshoi Theater in Moscow and the Maryinsky in Saint Petersburg are notable for their enormous stages and large companies of 180 to 250 dancers, which have developed an expansive style of dancing to fill and command the dance space.

In 1860 the Maryinsky Theater was built by Alberto Cavos with a capacity of more than 1,760 and a stage 97 feet wide and 72 feet deep (31 by 23 meters). The pit is nearly flat; the auditorium is bell-shaped, with five tiers of boxes and a gallery in the topmost tier offering the lowest-priced seats. In the center there is a royal box rising three tiers from the floor.

In the Bolshoi Theater of Saint Petersburg (1783–1889), the works of Charles Didelot were produced during the years 1801–1811 and 1816–1833. When Didelot first went to Russia, the Bolshoi was the only theater with the flight machinery and understage space needed for production of his Anacreontic ballets. In the new theater Marius Petipa created *The Sleeping Beauty* (1890) and, with Ivanov, *The Nutcracker* (1892) and *Swan Lake* (1895). The theater has had four name changes since the 1917 revolution; long known as the S. M. Kirov State Theater of Opera and Ballet, it reverted to the name Maryinsky Theater in 1992.

The name *Bolshoi* ("great") identifies both the theater and its company. The present building in Moscow (two have burned on its site) was built in 1865, seats two thousand, and has a stage 85 feet (28 meters) wide and 77 feet (25 meters) deep. Its predecessor, the smaller Petrovsky Theater (1780–1805), was intimate by comparison, seating eight hundred in three tiers of boxes and a gallery. The pit had benches and armchairs for special guests and could be raised to stage level for use as a ballroom, a common feature in opera-house design.

When Serge Diaghilev took his Ballets Russes to Paris in 1909, he transformed the Théâtre du Châtelet, which by Russian standards was primitively equipped. Elaborate hatches, traps, and fountains were installed for Mikhail Fokine's *Le Pavillon d'Armide.* The whole stage floor was then relaid and the interior of the auditorium redecorated for the premiere. Diaghilev took complete charge of productions, especially the lighting, seeking to provide the right environment for each ballet. The huge painted canvases used as backdrops provided the dance with space, color, and atmosphere in a manner previously unseen in the West.

Evolution of European Theater Design. By the mid-eighteenth century there were permanent theaters in the Italian opera-house style all over Europe; however, they were judged not by the appropriateness of their function but by the opulence of their interiors. Theatergoing was primarily a social activity, and elegant interiors and grand staircases were places for meeting and gathering, for reinforcing class distinctions, and for displaying fashion and wealth. The idea of the theater thus became definitively linked with the box-tier system.

In practice, however, the box-tier has never provided an adequate auditorium for viewing a performance. In any horseshoe-shaped house with a picture-frame stage, 25 to 40 percent of the audience have an impeded view of the stage. Architectural theorists and theater designers have since 1771 criticized this system as inappropriate for illusion theater, while others have justified its continued use on socioeconomic grounds. Recent study shows that the box-tier system was a structural development in which two performance types of the Renaissance were combined—the "motion theater" of outdoor tournaments and entries, and the picture-frame "illusion theater" for simu-

THEATERS FOR DANCE. This view from the stage of Saint Petersburg's Maryinsky Theater, built in 1869, shows the large royal box (located in the center), which rises through three tiers from the floor. (Photograph reprinted from Matilda Kshessinska, *Dancing in Petersburg,* translated by Arnold Haskell, London, 1960, p. 25.)

lation of reality. While the two types coexisted, their physical spaces were joined by ramps. By about 1650, the three-dimensional, corporeal motion theater had been entirely replaced by the simulated reality of illusion theater. The action moved to the stage and the ramps were removed, but box-tier seating did not change for more than two hundred years.

Theatrical dance developed in service of the illusion theater. The use of the body on the picture-frame stage may be seen as a series of transitions centering on costume. Body movement was inhibited by the stiff dresses in vogue from 1650 to 1750, but dance acquired a fuller use of expressive gesture by the late 1700s. The extension of the limbs, flights, and pointe and partner work developed with the softening of dress in the early nineteenth century. The Romantic tutu completed the costume repertory as ballet crystallized on the picture-frame stage. Ballet remained the pervasive style until the twentieth century, when modern dance and its experiments looked ahead to an exploration of the absolute values of the stage space.

The problem of sightline distortion was finally addressed by the composer Richard Wagner in the context of total musical-dramatic theater. Opening in 1876 in Bayreuth, Wagner's Festspielhaus was the most revolutionary theater in four centuries; it featured "continental seating," a fan-shaped pit with all seats facing the stage. The rows were spaced well apart to allow transverse access to side aisles. The orchestra, unseen by the audience, performed in a deep pit within an open acoustic shell. As a result of these innovations, the audience had an unimpeded view of the stage with no visual distractions caused by the shape of the auditorium.

Two other improvements influenced auditorium design. One, the dish-shaped pit with seating alternated so that patrons were never seated one exactly behind the other, was an innovation by the French architects Gabriel Davioud and J. D. Bourdais in 1875. The second involved a major change in engineering and materials. The use of iron in place of wood made possible deep balconies supported with bracketlike structures. G. H. Holloway designed such a cantilevered system in 1891 for what is now London's Palace Theatre. Balconies could be extended out over the pit, increasing auditorium capacity, yet all the seats faced the stage and provided a full view. With these changes the alternative shapes of the auditorium in the bipartite theater were established.

A coincident impetus in expressionist architecture was the People's Theater movement in Europe, especially Germany, from the 1890s to the 1920s. Repudiating the theater as elitist, directors such as Max Reinhardt provided large auditoriums, inexpensive seats, and thrust or arena stages to break down barriers between art and the people. The movement generated architectural experiments and alternative spaces intended to move and involve the viewer spiritually.

For the movement artist, there was an increasing acceptance of the whole body and a willingness to experiment both within and apart from tradition. There was a growing awareness of the stage as an environment, and concern that it be appropriate for the art form presented.

Twentieth-Century Innovations. The American dancer Isadora Duncan disliked opera houses, preferring to dance in the open-air space of the Greek theater. To achieve a neutral background for her performances, she toured with her own blue-grey draperies; to protect her bare feet, she laid groundcloths on the distressed opera-house stages.

Loie Fuller had her own theater built for the Paris Exposition of 1900. The theater was designed in Art Nouveau style by Henri Sauvage for her *Danses Lumineuses*. Fuller's unique lighting, costuming, and staging methods could be effective only under strictly controlled conditions, necessitating a custom-made theater. Perhaps no dance artist before her had achieved such precise fulfillment of production and artistic requirements.

Adolphe Appia, in collaboration with Émile Jaques-Dalcroze and other designers, created a theater for Dalcroze's lecture demonstrations at Hellerau in 1910, in a large hall with six hundred seats in continental arrangement. There was no proscenium arch and no sunken pit, and the walls were covered with transparent canvas which masked light sources, resulting in an ambient space with a one-room effect. The stage was arranged in levels of varying heights, its space further defined by light to create a three-dimensional environment for human movement.

The architect Norman Bel Geddes envisioned a theater that Rudolf Laban later recognized as an ideal space for his "plastic forms" (works that could be seen from all sides). Bel Geddes designed his "intimate" Theatre 14 in 1922 and submitted it for the Chicago World's Fair of 1933 and 1934. This was a theater-in-the-round with concentric circles of steep raked seating; all viewers were about the same distance from the stage. Laban wrote:

> Of all the arts dance suffers most from the inability of the audience to see properly. In most halls . . . the dancers' legs are hidden up to the knees by the heads of people sitting in front. The subtlety of gesture gets lost as the distance from the stage increases while those sitting in front, see details of mime too clearly and at the same time do not have full view of the whole dance area. (Laban, 1975, p. 162)

Based on his own architectural background and his theoretical study of space, Laban planned several performance environments, none of which was ever built. He recognized the need for a variety of dance spaces for different uses: theaters for stage dance; open-air pavilions ("dance temples") for choric dance by lay performers; and to fend

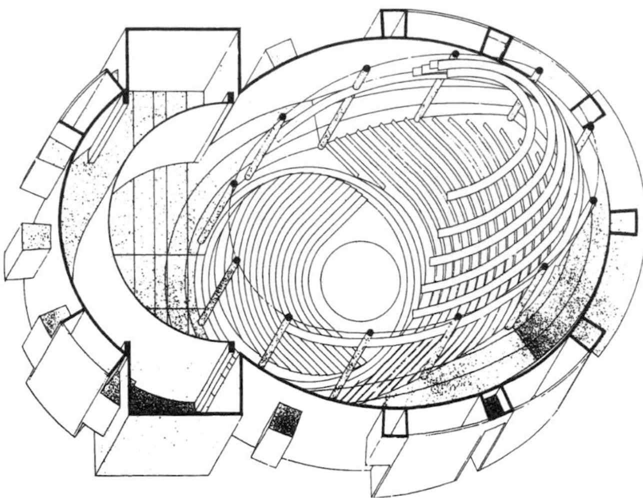

THEATERS FOR DANCE. A view into the auditorium, as seen from above, for the Total Theater (1926) of Bauhaus founder Walter Gropius. By rotating the big stage platform, the small proscenium stage is moved to the center of the theater. Scenery can be projected on screens that are placed between the twelve main columns. (Reprinted from Gropius, 1961, p. 13.)

off the weather for mass performances, a vault-like Kilometrehouse in the spirit of Buckminster Fuller's geodesic domes.

The Total Theater (1926) of Bauhaus founder Walter Gropius was a multiform design in response to the post-World War I demand for new performance spaces. The theater's mechanized stage and seating areas made it possible to alter the relationship of viewing and playing areas even during a production.

Oskar Schlemmer, a colleague of Gropius, sought a three-dimensional use of the body through a nonnarrative, nondecorative approach to movement. He experimented with studies in line, color, form, and space in an effort to eliminate all but absolute values. Schlemmer's work is better understood in the context of Rudolf Laban's polyhedral analysis of the kinesphere, known as *choreutics*. Out of the same "man in space" concept, Schlemmer sought ideas to generate movement and Laban created a tool for analysis, observation, and communication about movement.

The expressionist viewpoint which encouraged dance artists to work from the "inside out" also let them eschew the traditional theater both as content and as space. In the 1930s in New York City, modern dancers often performed on concert hall stages. Enclosed on three sides by a dark velour drape, the space presented a "strident bareness" in keeping with the artistic focus on the movement rather than on the decoration. This "symbolical stage," according to George Beiswanger (1939, p. 221) "lasted only until the dancer had become conscious of the fact that movement was doing something to the space . . . articulating it in terms of direction and level, radiation and bounds, channels and focal spots, points of energy flow and places of climax." Hanya Holm, by virtue of her German training, was perhaps the most articulate and intellectual in her recognition of the use of space. In 1938 the designer Arch Lauterer created a stage for Holm's work *Trend,* "geometrically parsed," functional, and clean as a movement environment. The amorphous folds of the draperies were replaced by flat panels angled like fins at the sides for entrances and exits. The use of low upstage platforms and a downstage open dance space was reminiscent of Adolphe Appia's spatial sensibilities.

About 1928 Doris Humphrey began using a collection of boxes and platforms designed by Erika Klein. These could be arranged in a multitude of ways to create representational, symbolic, or practical definitions of the stage space. For Martha Graham, Isamu Noguchi's sculp-

THEATERS FOR DANCE. Using the Piazzo San Marco in Venice as an alternative theater, the Merce Cunningham Dance Company performed *Event,* a program consisting of sections of pre-existing works spliced together, on 14 September 1972. (Photograph © by James Klosty; used by permission.)

THEATERS FOR DANCE. (*top*) Loft spaces have historically served as performance venues for modern and postmodern dance. In *Spiral* (1974), Trisha Brown utilized support pillars, an architectural feature of many lofts, by having her dancers, suspended in harnesses, wind their way around them. *(bottom)* Brown has designed works for other unconventional settings, including *Raft Piece* (1989) in the Hudson River at Battery Park City, New York. (Top photograph © 1974 by Babette Mangolte; used by permission. Bottom photograph © 1989 by Johan Elbers; used by permission.)

tural sets served "to wed the total void of theatre to form an action" and were symbolic participants in the work. Other artists, such as Jean Rosenthal, explored the effects of color and body definition through the use of light.

From 1930 to 1960, modern choreographers generally maintained the convention of frontal viewing and sought theaters that could provide at least an approximation of the proscenium space. Beginning with more experimental activity in the 1960s, there was a move away from design values and frontal viewing to street theater, loft concerts, and even rooftop performances. Merce Cunningham led a trend in the use of alternate spaces which was exploited by the choreographers of the Judson Dance Theater. The lighting designer Jennifer Tipton (1970) commented that such choreographers "are concerned with the spaces they're in, not stages but gyms, forests, lawns. They do not make it look always the same." Cunningham was among the most flexible in this respect, accepting that old dances in new places were in fact new dances.

Lacking mass appeal, modern dance in the twentieth century held little interest for theater owners primarily concerned with profit. The audience had to be built over three-quarters of a century, an effort bolstered by the fitness movement which became popular in the United States in the mid-1970s.

During that period dance artists and architects continued planning, adapting, and dreaming about ideal performance conditions. These were first provided by colleges and universities where dance was a part of the curriculum. In 1952 Marcel Breuer designed for Sarah Lawrence College a five-hundred-seat multipurpose theater with a steeply raked auditorium and a low stage to improve audience perspective.

Theaters in the opera-house style continue to be used and built in the service of tradition and public expectations. The New York State Theater at Lincoln Center (1964) is a throwback to the nineteenth-century neo-Baroque auditorium. At the same time, it is the only theater in a major North American city that provides a permanent home for its dance company, the New York City Ballet.

There is sparse but significant evidence of substantial architectural change for dance. Two renovated New York theaters provide intimate seating and excellent sightlines—the Joyce Theater (1981; a former movie house) and The Space at the City Center for Music and Dance (1982). Premiere Dance Theatre, opened in Toronto in 1983, was expressly designed for choreographic performance. These efforts indicate a new public and corporate willingness to support dance as an art form by providing permanent space for its performance.

[*See also the entries on the principal figures mentioned herein.*]

BIBLIOGRAPHY

Armstrong, Leslie, and Roger Morgan. *Space for Dance: An Architectural Design Guide.* New York, 1984.

Arnott, James F., et al., eds. *Theatre Space/Des Raum des Theaters.* Munich, 1977. See articles by Baldry, Zielske, Izenour.

Beiswanger, George. "The Stage for the Modern Dance." *Theatre Arts Monthly* 23 (March 1939).

Campbell, Larry G. "Finding a Home for Dance." *Dance Scope* 7.1 (1972–1973): 19–28.

Coeyman, Barbara. "Theatres for Opera and Ballet during the Reigns of Louis XIV and Louis XV." *Early Music* 18 (February 1990): 22–37.

Craig, Gordon. "Some Old Theatre Plans." *The Mask* 13.4 (1927).

Evans, Mary Stewart. "London Homes of the Romantic Ballet." *The Dancing Times* (March 1966): 294–297.

Foster, Susan Leigh. *Reading Dancing.* Berkeley, 1986.

Geddes, Norman Bel. *Horizons.* Boston, 1932.

Gropius, Walter, ed. *The Theater of the Bauhaus.* Translated by Arthur S. Wensinger. Middletown, Conn., 1961.

Hedstrom, Cynthia, and Judy Padow. "Space and Support." *Dance Scope* 14.4 (1980): 8–17.

Izenour, George. *Theatre Design.* New York, 1977.

Laban, Rudolf von. *A Life for Dance: Reminiscences.* Translated and edited by Lisa Ullmann. New York, 1975.

Lauterer, Arch. "Stage Design in Our Time." *Impulse* (1959): 56–58.

Lawler, Lillian B. *The Dance of the Ancient Greek Theatre.* Iowa City, 1964.

Lawrenson, T. E. *The French Stage in the XVIIth Century.* 2d ed. New York, 1986.

Leclerc, Hélène. *Les origines italiennes de l'architecture théâtrale moderne.* Paris, 1946.

Lloyd, Margaret. *The Borzoi Book of Modern Dance.* New York, 1949.

Lynham, Deryck. *The Chevalier Noverre: Father of Modern Ballet.* London, 1950.

MacClintock, Carol, and Lander MacClintock, trans. *Balet Comique de la Royne, 1581.* N.p., 1971. English translation and modern transcription of the music.

McGowan, Margaret M. *L'art du ballet de cour en France, 1581–1643.* Paris, 1963.

Nagler, A. M. *Theatre Festivals of the Medici, 1539–1637.* New Haven, 1964.

Nicoll, Allardyce. *The Development of the Theatre.* 5th ed., rev. New York, 1967.

Patté, Pierre. *Essai sur l'architecture théâtrale.* Paris, 1782.

Pehnt, Wolfgang. *Expressionist Architecture.* New York, 1973.

Prunières, Henry. *Le ballet de cour en France avant Benserade et Lully.* Paris, 1914.

Rice, Paul F. *The Performing Arts at Fontainebleau from Louis XIV to Louis XVI.* Ann Arbor, 1989.

Sachs, Edwin O. *Modern Opera Houses and Theatres.* New York, 1896.

Silin, Charles I. *Benserade and His Ballets de Cour.* Baltimore, 1940.

Silverman, Maxwell. *Contemporary Theatre Architecture.* New York, 1965.

Southern, Richard. *The Seven Ages of the Theatre.* New York, 1961.

Swift, Mary Grace. *A Loftier Flight: The Life and Accomplishments of Charles Louis Didelot.* Middletown, Conn., 1974.

Tipton, Jennifer. "Innovation in Lighting Design." *Theatre Design and Technology* 22 (October 1970).

Troili, Giulio, et al. *The Italian Baroque Stage.* Translated and edited by Dunbar H. Ogden. Berkeley, 1978.

Worsthorne, Simon T. *Venetian Opera in the Seventeenth Century.* Oxford, 1954.

DIANNE L. WOODRUFF

THERAPY. *See* Dance and Movement Therapy.

THREE-CORNERED HAT, THE. *See* Tricorne, Le.

THREE EPITAPHS. Choreography: Paul Taylor. Music: early New Orleans jazz music as recorded by the Laneville-Johnson Union Brass Band. Costumes: Robert Rauschenberg. First performance: 27 March 1956, Master Institute of United Artists, New York City, Dance Associates. Dancers: Paul Taylor, Carol Rubenstein, Therese Cura, Doris Thurston.

Paul Taylor's *Three Epitaphs* was first performed at a Dance Associates concert, as part of a shared program of new choreography. It is his oldest surviving work: a telling example both of his early choreography and of enduring Taylor-style traits. *Three Epitaphs* was created primarily as a performance vehicle for Taylor himself and three women, and like much of his early choreography, it was regarded initially as yet another of his avant-garde experiments. In this work, however, Taylor began to explore body stance, stillness, and postural changes, and to juxtapose large and small gestures—choreographic ideas that he would pursue more fully in *Seven New Dances* the following year. Moreover, it was in *Three Epitaphs* that he introduced signature traits such as the contracted, concave torso with its correspondingly weighted, parallel legs and relaxed wrists. Described by Taylor's dancers as "the Slump," it recurs in many subsequent works, most notably in *Cloven Kingdom* (1976). In *Three Epitaphs*, the Slump is often seen in profile. As the dancers recover from it by first lifting then twisting at the waist, the upper body turns *en face*, thereby presaging another aspect of Taylor's style: his use of two-dimensional movement, as seen in *Images* (1977), *Profiles* (1979), *Le Sacre du Printemps (The Rehearsal)*, (1980) and *Moonbine* (1994).

Similarly, although the music for *Three Epitaphs* seemed typical of Taylor's eclectic and unconventional choices during the 1950s, it also reveals a great deal about his ability to find meaning and an appropriate movement vocabulary from particular sound stimuli. And, as with later works such as *Scudorama* (1963) and *Field of Grass* (1993), *Three Epitaphs* evolved in rehearsals through a radical change of accompaniment. Taylor started choreographing the work to music by Debussy but then switched to early jazz music, a form played at weddings and funerals in the southern United States. This slurred, syncopated music, with its contrastingly funny and dirgelike tone, influenced a dynamic change in Taylor's choreography (and most probably contributed to the "Epitaphs" of his title).

The title also reflects the A-B-A structure of the final, five-minute version of *Three Epitaphs*. (A first reworking was *Four Epitaphs* in May 1956 and further revisions were made to the work, under its original title, during the late 1950s and early 1960s. Taylor's last reworking of *Three Epitaphs* included the addition of a second male dancer.) The first and third sections feature the full ensemble, all clad identically in dark, hooded leotards and tights designed by Robert Rauschenberg. The dancers are costumed from head to foot, their faces covered completely, with only small mirrors to suggest eyes and to distinguish the palms of their hands. Taylor and Rauschenberg collaborated many times during the 1950s, one of their shared aims being to challenge the modernist aesthetic of the New York mainstream. The choreography and costumes for *Three Epitaphs* certainly challenged established notions of body design, image, and projection. Even some of Taylor's dancers became disillusioned with such pre-Judson, postmodern ideas, thus prompting several cast changes during the work's early days.

Despite the anonymity of Rauschenberg's costumes, Taylor's powerful, triangular physique was unmistakable in *Three Epitaphs*. Through differentiating individual dancers by height, he not only distinguished himself as the leader of an otherwise indiscernible group; he also provided the work with many of its humorous moments. (Since Taylor retired from performing in 1974, his role has been danced by one of his tallest male dancers.) *Three Epitaphs* begins and ends with the most marked tall/small contrast: the "leader" is positioned downstage left, towering over the slouched contour of the group's smallest dancer, the runt of the litter who spends much of the work following two steps behind. Taylor's opening phrase—a series of arm gestures and shifts of weight *sur place*—is a synthesis of the work's main vocabulary and, as other dancers enter upstage left and start to echo many of his movements, the follow-the-leader theme of the work is further established. (Follow the leader is also a recurring structural device in Taylor's choreography.)

Taylor's role was most strongly differentiated in the short solo that forms the central section of *Three Epitaphs*. Performed without accompaniment, it is essentially a mime section in which, on reentering the stage, the dancer adopts a confident, upright stance—the most vertical of the entire work—before realizing that he has misjudged his stage position. Slightly unsettled, he steps into the center-stage spotlight and, after resuming his previous stance, rolling his shoulders alternately and raising one arm, he starts to groom himself as if reacting to the reflection in his mirrored palm. It seems to be a prelude to more complex dance movement until unexpectedly, he shrugs his shoulders and walks offstage. Only then do we realize that this brief, twenty-second sequence *was* the second epitaph.

Throughout his career, Taylor has continued to do the unexpected. In 1991, having established *Three Epitaphs* as a repertory classic, he attempted to rekindle some of its early, experimental appeal. One of his two premieres that year was *Fact and Fancy*. It begins with a complete performance of *Three Epitaphs*, followed by six new sections for Taylor's now much enlarged company of eighteen dancers. As the last drones of *Three Epitaphs* come to an end, the stage is transformed into a rehearsal studio. The backdrop and side flats disappear; towels, newspapers and furniture litter the floor; the dancers engage in various nondance activities—all accompanied by reggae music.

In its pluralist, pedestrian style, *Fact & Fancy* recalls Taylor's early postmodernist work. Aptly subtitled *3 Epitaphs & All*, it is a return to some of the ideas that he explored as a young choreographer during the 1950s, especially the distinctions between dance process and performance; between natural and stylized movement; the contrasting effects of metric, nonmetric, and unaccompanied choreography. Such fundamental ideas not only inspired *Three Epitaphs* but launched Taylor on his long, prolific career.

BIBLIOGRAPHY

Guthman, Louise. "Dance Associates." *Dance Observer* (May 1956): 73–74.

Jowitt, Deborah. "A Fishy Conversation with an Obliging Giant." *Village Voice* (23 April 1979). Reprinted in *The Dance in Mind.* (Boston, 1985): 45–50.

Manchester, P. W. "Dances by Paul Taylor and James Waring." *Dance News* (June 1956): 8.

Mazo, Joseph. "Nikolais, Ailey, Taylor—Three Specialists." In *Prime Movers: The Makers of Modern Dance in America.* Princeton, 1977. 231–270.

MacDonagh, Don. *The Complete Guide to Modern Dance.* New York, 1976: 313–325.

Taylor, Paul. *Private Domain.* New York, 1987: 75, 99.

ANGELA KANE

TIBET. A high plateau surrounded by mountain ranges including the Himalayas, Tibet is today an autonomous region of the People's Republic of China. It has some two million people in 475,000 square miles (1.2 million square kilometers) and is bordered by India, Bhutan, and Nepal to the south, Kashmir to the west, Myanmar (formerly Burma) to the southeast, and China to the north and northeast. The Tibetans are mainly pastoral people, raising yaks and other livestock and growing barley and vegetable crops. A Tibetan kingdom was flourishing by the seventh century CE. It came under the control of China in the seventeenth century and remained so until the overthrow of the emperor in 1911. Tibet was then independent until 1950, when the newly established People's Republic of China invaded and instituted repressive measures against Tibetan Buddhism, which is called Lamaism.

Ritual Dance. Ritual has played a major role in Tibetan life since ancient times. Scholars have limited knowledge about the indigenous pre-Buddhist religion known as the "religion of men," but its successor has been well documented—the shamanistic Bon religion, which is still practiced. Elaborate Bon rituals include dance. For example, when a Tibetan king was crowned, accompanied by a Bon priest of the royal household, he performed a dance to generate the supernatural power vested in the ruler and to maintain the cosmic and social order. Oral tradition relates that Bon priests, carrying drums, performed ritual dances on ceremonial occasions. Some say that these are the predecessors of the Buddhist Black Hat Dance. Other Bon ritual dances were performed by lay men and women (not of the priesthood), and some dances with animal costumes may have come from as far away as Persia.

Buddhism, which first came to Tibet from India in the seventh century, was not firmly established until the eighth century, when Padmasambhava, the great tantric master, was invited from India to subdue the forces that opposed the new religion. He introduced Vajrayāna Buddhism, which is based on a body of esoteric texts (*tantras*) that include ritual practices using *mudrās* (ritual gestures), *mantras* (symbolic incantations), visualizations of the deity, and *maṇḍalas* (sacred squared circles). Padmasambhava demonstrated the efficacy of these practices in eliminating the obstacles which threatened to halt the construction of the first Buddhist monastery in Tibet. Dance was not considered contrary to religion but rather an integral part of its worship: Padmasambhava rose into the sky, where he performed a threatening dance that dispelled the opposition, and the shadow he cast on the ground marked the boundaries of Bsam-yas monastery.

The oral tradition and the texts agree that the first known Buddhist dance in Tibet was performed during the time of Padmasambhava. However, other forms of masked dance and musical and theatrical events have appeared in documents covering the royal dynastic period from the seventh to the ninth centuries. Tibetans claim the lineage of the masked monastic dances can be traced back through a succession of deities to Padmasambhava, while scholars maintain that these dances are based on early Buddhist texts translated and taught in Tibet during the time of Padmasambhava.

Some ritual dances are also performed by the lay community; however, of those performed by the religious order, the monastic dances attributed to Padmasambhava have become known to the world through the photographs and writings of Western explorers.

Ritual dance in Tibet most probably developed from Indian ritual dance and theater and Bon dance. Indian dances are known to have been performed in front of statues of the Buddha portraying different gestures that may, themselves, have been inspiration for the dance. Masked dances rooted in Indian Tantrism, such as the Buddhist *cham,* spread from India to Tibet, China, Korea, and Japan, where they were adapted within the several cultural environments.

Dances in the Tibetan Buddhist style are performed by Tibetans and among the indigenous Buddhist peoples of the Himalayas in the areas of Ladakh, Sikkim, Bhutan, and in the Buddhist areas of Nepal; there are scattered Tibetan refugee settlements throughout these areas and in India.

In Tibet, mime dance, drama, and folk opera were developed and presented as a skillful means of transmitting Tibetan history and customs in what was predominantly an illiterate society. Ritual dances symbolically presenting esoteric teachings, through gesture and dance, varied in date of presentation, content, and style of presentation among the four Tibetan Buddhist sects, from area to area, and from monastery to monastery. These dances, representing the earliest type of Tibetan theatrical presentation, are similar to medieval European Christian mystery plays; however, they have no plot or story, but the dances and characters (well-known Tibetan deities) are symbolic. The performance is an extension of the Buddhist liturgy, which consists of creating the pure realm *(maṇḍala)* of the deity.

Tibetan dance rituals have all been composed by great teachers who recorded the dances of celestial figures they had seen in dreams or during meditations. Although the music and movements have been precisely recorded in texts, the secret information, such as the meaning of the ritual and the proper interpretation of the movement, is orally transmitted—this, to ensure that only those chosen to perform a dance will be able to execute it perfectly, for the entire ritual must be performed without error to be efficacious.

Tibetan dance rituals are presented with the objective of attaining special goals; for example, to eradicate negative forces and engender positive circumstances—long life, wealth, or inner transformation. All forms of Tibetan ritual dance are considered the vehicles of instantaneous enlightenment, since any spectator might spontaneously comprehend the otherwise secret meaning of the ritual. The dances are aural and visual offerings to a deity, enticing him or her to attend the dance and bless all present. As the dancers offer the beautiful movements of their bodies, their melodic speech (*mantra*s or song), and the devotional thought of their minds, these are ritually transformed into the *maṇḍala*s of the body, speech, and mind of the deity.

The *maṇḍala,* a sacred squared circle, is an important symbol in Vajrayāna Buddhism. It can represent the temporal world, with the sacred mountain at its center, or, in its purified form, the Buddha realm, with the palace in which the deity resides at the center. Practitioners engage in the *maṇḍala* through ritual practices that reveal to them that the deity is a reflection of one's own mind. Tibetan ritual dance is mandalic in form. The dancers whirl in a pattern that circles the deity, who is at the center of the dance ground, until they become united as the deity-and-his-retinue in their pure land.

The first part of any Tibetan Buddhist ritual is the creation of the *maṇḍala;* this sacred space is specially created by purifying and protecting it from hostile outside forces through exorcism, ritual offerings, incantations, and ritual gestures made to pacify the local spirits. Ritual dancers move in a clockwise manner, creating a boundary around the sacred space, protecting it from harmful influence, and thereby allowing the ritual of transformation to take place. The *maṇḍala* space is sanctified by the circling of the dancers, who empower both themselves and the space they enclose by revolving around the center—in the same direction as they perceive the planets revolving around the sun.

Monastic Dance. There are two main types of Tibetan monastic dance: *gar* and *cham.* The highest meditative ritual dance, *gar,* is the more complex and esoteric of the two and is performed privately for the initiates within the monastery. The movement is focused in the hands, which execute a series of stylized ritual gestures in an increasing tempo. This type of dance is generally performed by an individual or by a small group of dancers.

Cham is a large public ceremony of many dancers performing one or more dances, and most of the movement is executed with the feet. The performance lasts from sunset to sundown during a period of one to seven days. Originally the *chams* were performed secretly for the initiates within the monastery. Now, rehearsals may be private, but the lay community is welcomed into the monastery for the performance.

Different *cham*s are performed at different ceremonial occasions throughout the year. Their subjects range from the lives of the saints to the expulsion of negative influences. For example, a *cham* to ward off evil is the highlight of the lunar New Year celebration. Dancers in a variety of costumes and masks enact the different sections of the liturgy. In some dances, the performers wear heavy brocade gowns and oversized wooden or *papier-mâché* masks that personify sublimely peaceful or fiercely compassionate or wrathful deities. For example, the skeleton costume for the Lords of the Cemeteries—a dance common to all four sects of Tibetan Buddhism—consists of a skull-shaped mask and pajamas with bones painted on them. The Black Hat Dance, which is performed without masks but with elaborate headresses, is also common to many *chams.* [*See* Black Hat Dance.]

In the New Year *cham,* dancers make offerings to the deities and local spirits and eventually the ceremony culminates with the exorcistic stabbing of a dough effigy of a demon (representing the ego) into which all harmful forces have been conjured. When the figure is dismembered by a ritual dagger, misconception and negativity are annihilated and dispelled for the next year. Thus, the communal psyche is restored to balance; peace, health, happiness, and prosperity are ushered in.

Performance takes place in the courtyard of a monastery. The temple serves as a dressing room for the dancers. First the musicians and monks file into the courtyard to begin the ceremony with music and chanting. Led by the music master, an orchestra of horns, drums, cymbals, and conch shells accompanies the dancers as they circle the courtyard in a series of stamps, steps, and hops. These movements, which have names such as "half-thunderbolt," are to be performed smoothly and gracefully by a dancer who should have a gentle demeanor. The dancers have been chosen for their interest, dancing skill, and degree of meditative realization. They have prepared for their performance by meditating on the

TIBET. Itinerant performers of Tibetan folk opera. The masks worn by two of the group may be guises of divinities. (Photograph by S. Singh; from the Dance Collection, New York Public Library for the Performing Arts.)

deity they are to portray and by spiritually identifying with the deity. Through meditation they must come to understand and be able to demonstrate in dance the principles of detachment, clarity, and emptiness. As they dance, they must execute the correct movements, sing or recite *mantras*, and focus their thoughts on the deity. They study with a dance master, who is in charge of the technical details of the performance. He accompanies the dancers in rehearsal with cymbals to help them count the beat.

Some performances of *chams* contain dramatic comic interludes sandwiched between ritual dance sequences. The actors, who are often chosen from the lay community, portray through mime such stock characters as the stupid servant; some even mock the deities of the *cham* itself. The audiences of lay persons particularly enjoy performances that serve to attract attention and hold interest.

Ritual dances are not only performed by monks and nuns but also by devoted members of the lay community who are not confined by monastic restrictions; so, in costume, the lay population of men and women perform together. In one such dance, called "Ling-dro-dechen-rolmo," the dancers perform movements similar to folk dance and accompany themselves with a song of praise and devotion to the deity. Another *cham,* one of an exorcistic nature, is performed as an offering to increase the lifespan of a great teacher. The performers, young women or monks, portray celestial female messengers *(dakinis)* who have gathered to escort the teacher to the Buddha realms, symbolic of his death. They conclude the dance by accepting an effigy as a substitute for the teacher's person.

The number of Tibetan ritual dance performances has diminished since the Chinese occupation in 1959 (after an anti-Chinese uprising was put down). Some monasteries that have been modestly resettled in India have continued to carry on the dance tradition despite a lack of costumes and financial resources. Dance performances may often be shortened; sections may be omitted with the death of a dance master, or the loss of a text, or because many monks now must work as farmers. However, the long tradition of ritual dance—which includes various forms of *cham, gar*, and *dro* (the dance of lay people)—continues to develop through the new dreams and meditational visions of Tibetan teachers.

Folk Opera. There are two types of Tibetan dance drama: *chams* and *ache lhamo,* Tibetan folk opera (a choral dance drama). Named after sister goddesses, *ache lhamo* was created in the late fourteenth century by the great mystic, deified saint, and god of drama, Than-tog-gyal-po. To this day all performances of it are dedicated to him and offerings are made to him during each performance at an altar erected in the center of the performance area.

In the past, the performances were presented both as popular entertainment in central Tibet and as an offering to please the spirits of the soil, to secure the well-being of the community, and to ensure a plentiful harvest. In Tibet, troupes of *lhamo* performers wandered from village to village. The actors were usually peasant farmers or small shopkeepers who closed up shop once or twice a year to present their day-long performances. Gradually, some of these companies developed into professional troupes that performed for profit in monasteries and private homes.

The plots of the operas range from national history to Buddhist themes. Buddhism, which pervades Tibetan thought, has been integrated into the plays. Often their themes are about the life and former lives of the Buddha and other religious figures, and the moral message they convey is the triumph of good over evil. The deified characters wear masks, whereas the Tibetan and Chinese characters do not. The main plot is interspersed with satirical skits and parody. A dance precedes each opera and is performed between sets of operatic singing. The dramatic structure seems to have originated in India, while the style of song, makeup, and gesture are similar to those of regional Chinese opera.

The script is based on literary texts. From these are extracted the dialogues for the actors and the descriptive materials for the narrators. The more traditional troupes closely follow the original text, while others use it as a basis for improvisation. The dramatic portion of the opera is presented in a series of tableaux, in which one or two actors sing and the chorus echoes the last phrase of each line or stanza. A narrator presents the background of the story and describes each main character in an extremely rapid recitation.

For a change of scene or a new character, the actors dance into new positions on the stage. They move in a clockwise direction toward the back of the altar, for the action is performed in the round. Each character in the play has his or her own costume, mask, and characteristic musical theme to which he or she enters; the characters' movement styles reveal their personalities. The performers dance on stage in single file. A chorus of "hunters"—distinguished by large flat masks with stylized eyes and mouth, a triangular nose, moustache, and beard—enters, executing a leaping-and-turning dance accompanied by drums and cymbals. Often two groups of male dancers compete by leaping around the performance area. A group of young women, who compose the main part of the chorus, perform restrained flowing movements to music; they represent the sister goddesses for whom *ache lhamo* is named.

Folk Dance. In Tibet, the people danced whenever an occasion arose: to celebrate the harvest, the lunar New Year, gatherings of friends and relatives, and receptions for important personages. The dance genre they performed, *dro,* had no choreographers or oral or written directives and was thus flexible, vital, and strongly influenced by regional variation.

The folk dance styles and costumes varied from place to place. Western and central Tibetan dances emphasized

TIBET. A troupe from Lhasa dancing the ritual overture that traditionally begins a Tibetan opera performance. (Photograph from the archives of The Asia Society, New York.)

complex footwork in rhythmic patterns, while the phrases of eastern Tibetan folk dance were longer and slower, and the movements were more simple and flowing. Since folk songs have been said to travel from west to east in Tibet, it is assumed that the dances they accompany have followed the same route.

Tibetan folk dancers are most often accompanied by a capella singing or by the music of one or a few instruments. On occasion, however, the dancers remain silent as an ensemble or an orchestra of flutes and/or strings plays; the instruments are most often the long-necked, plucked lute that sounds like a banjo, and the transverse and vertical flutes. The songs that accompany folk dances are drawn from daily activities such as traveling, herding, churning butter, and winnowing or from such universal topics as love and thanksgiving.

As they perform the vigorous stamps and turns that distinguish *dro* movement style, the dancers make either circular or linear floor patterns that often cross, intermesh, or unravel.

[*See also* Costume in Asian Traditions.]

BIBLIOGRAPHY

Aris, Michael. "Sacred Dances of Bhutan." *Natural History* 89 (March 1980): 28–37.

Fantin, Mario. *Mani Rimdu, Nepal.* Singapore, 1976.

Hoetzlein, Nanci A. "Sacred Dances of Tibet's Gelugpa Sect." In *Hong Kong International Dance Conference.* Hong Kong, 1990.

Jerstad, Luther. *Mani Rimdu.* Calcutta, 1969.

Lerner, Lin. "Lingdro Dechen Rolmo: A Tibetan Ritual Dance in Mandalic Form." In *A Spectrum of World Dance,* edited by Lynn Ager Wallen and Joan Acocella. New York, 1987.

Nebesky-Wojkowitz, René de. *Oracles and Demons of Tibet.* The Hague, 1956.

Pearlman, Ellen. "Tibet: At the Crossroads of the Global Village." *Ear Magazine* 15 (October 1990): 16–23.

Samuel, Geoffrey. "Songs of Lhasa." *Ethnomusicology* 20 (September 1976): 407–449.

Snellgrove, David L., and Hugh E. Richardson. *A Cultural History of Tibet.* New York, 1968.

Snyder, Jeanette. "A Preliminary Study of the Lha Mo." *Asian Music* 10.2 (1979): 23–62.

Tethong, Rakra. "Conversations on Tibetan Musical Traditions." *Asian Music* 10.2 (1979): 5–22.

LIN LERNER

TIGUA DANCE. At Ysleta del Sur pueblo near El Paso, Texas, live about six hundred Tigua, descended from Isleta people, who were relocated there by the Spanish in the late seventeenth century. Tigua ceremonial culture features many dances, both masked and unmasked, largely associated with agriculture and the *kachina* (*katsina*) dance culture of the peoples of the southwestern pueblos. Masked dances are performed by young men known as "grandfathers" (*awelos,* from Spanish *abuelos*); in Ysleta del Sur these characters strongly resemble *kachinas* in that they descend from nearby mountains to lead dancers and impose social sanctions. Other than the grandfathers, the dancers are unmasked; unmasked clown society members participate as ceremonial police.

The dancers of Ysleta del Sur traditionally performed for major Roman Catholic festivals. Today, the ceremony of the feast day of Saint Anthony, 13 June, is the most regularly performed of their rituals. Surrounding the ceremonial drum, a chorus of male singers provides the music. Both the drum and the songs are said to have been brought by the original inhabitants of the pueblo. Other instruments include rattles worn by male dancers and a shotgun fired at the conclusion of each song.

Both men and women take part in the dances, sometimes jointly, as in their round dances and the Greeting, Hovina (Charging of the Drum), and Figura dances; or in paired duets, as in the Evergreen Dance. Dancing is always performed by the group, never by individuals. The dance movements for women are usually limited to the lower arms and legs, with straight, stiff torsos. Men's movements are also limited to the lower arms and legs, but the torsos are slightly hunched. The arms move from the elbows, causing the forearms to raise and lower. The legs alternately lift from one side to another. This stepping movement is subdued for women but almost a prance when performed by men.

The Tigua of Ysleta del Sur are no longer an agrarian people and, as a result, the meanings of their ceremonies have changed. The dances are now prayers and affirmations of Tigua identity. The participants have individual reasons for dancing: to acknowledge answered prayers, to pray for strength to overcome a problem, or to answer the call of the drum; but the format of the prayer—through dance—has not changed. Taking part in the ceremony reminds the individual of his or her Tigua past, ancestors, duties, and uniqueness in the world.

[*See also* Matachins, *article* on Matachines Dances in the Southwest United States; *and* Native American Dance.]

BIBLIOGRAPHY

Diamond, Tom. *The Tigua Indians of El Paso.* New York, 1966.

Griffith, James Seavey. "Kachinas and Masking." In *Handbook of North American Indians,* vol. 10, *Southwest,* pp. 764–777. Washington, D.C., 1983.

CARLOS LOZANO

TIKHOMIROV, VASILY (Vasilii Dmitrievich Tikhomirov; born 17 [29] March 1876 in Moscow, died 20 June 1956 in Moscow), Russian dancer and teacher. Tikhomirov studied from 1886 to 1891 at the Moscow Imperial Theater School under Ivan Yrmolov, and from 1892 to 1893 at the Saint Petersburg Imperial Theater School, where his teachers were Pavel Gerdt, Platon Karsavin, and Aleksandr Shiriaev. Beginning in 1893 he was the leading dancer of the Bolshoi Theater ballet company, performing mainly roles in the classical repertory. He was an ardent champion of preserving intact ballets of the classical heritage and objected to innovations introduced by the chief choreographer Aleksandr Gorsky. In Gorsky's original ballets he danced less often and not always in principal roles, for example, Narr-Avas in *Salammbô* in 1910. A classical dancer of the strictly academic school, Tikhomirov demonstrated a strong and refined technique, an elegant but virile manner of execution, and a somewhat static image. A skillful partner, he danced often with his wife, Ekaterina Geltser, beginning in 1898. At a mature age he created several noble characters: Conrad in *Le Corsaire* in 1912; Phoebus in *Esmeralda* in 1926.

Tikhomirov held a number of administrative posts at the Bolshoi: assistant *régisseur* of the ballet (1908), *régisseur* of the ballet (1909), assistant choreographer (1913), and chief ballet master of the company (1925–1930). He staunchly pursued his own line, struggling to preserve ballet in its traditional forms, and opposed in particular Kasyan Goleizovsky's experiments of the 1920s. He revived a number of productions: Kingdom of the Shades from *La Bayadère* in 1923, *The Sleeping Beauty* in 1924, and the second act of *La Sylphide* in 1925. In 1926 he revived *Esmeralda,* with music completed by Reinhold Glière, and reinforced the social message of the ballet.

In 1927 Tikhomirov collaborated in the staging of *The Red Poppy,* to music by Glière. He was responsible for the second act, "The Dream of Tao-Hoa," which he developed as a choreographic and mime *tour de force* for Geltser. He himself was one of the interpreters of the Captain. His dances drew a negative press; they were judged archaic and in bad taste. Nevertheless, Tikhomirov had a point when he sought to prove the right of classical dance to exist as extended ensembles and complex choreographic forms at a time when choreography of this kind was being renounced, but his example demonstrated that replication alone was lifeless.

Tikhomirov had started teaching in 1896 and brought to the Moscow ballet the style knowledge that he had gained during his training at Saint Petersburg. He taught until the 1930s and was director of the school from 1917 to 1931. All dancers of the Bolshoi, male and female, studied in his class or at the theater at various times. The strong and elegant style of dance demonstrated by Mikhail Mordkin, Laurent Novikoff, Viktor Smoltsov, and others was largely developed at lessons directed by Tikhomirov. He also regularly coached Geltser.

BIBLIOGRAPHY

Abolimov, P. F., ed. *Vasilii Dmitrievich Tikhomirov.* Moscow, 1971.
Guest, Ivor. *Ballet in Leicester Square.* London, 1992.
Krasovskaya, Vera. *Russkii baletnyi teatr nachala dvadtsatogo veka,* vol. 2, *Tantsovshchiki.* Leningrad, 1972.
Roslavleva, Natalia. "Moscow Assoluta." *Dance and Dancers* (April 1963): 23–25.
Smakov, Gennady. *The Great Russian Dancers.* New York, 1984.
Souritz, Elizabeth. *Soviet Choreographers in the 1920s.* Translated by Lynn Visson. Durham, N.C., 1990.
Swift, Mary Grace. *The Art of the Dance in the U.S.S.R.* Notre Dame, 1968.

ELIZABETH SOURITZ

TILLER, JOHN. *See* Precision Dancing.

TIMOFEYEVA, NINA (Nina Vladimirovna Timofeeva; born 11 June 1935 in Leningrad), dancer. Timofeyeva graduated in 1953 from the Leningrad Choreographic Institute, where she studied under Natalia Kamkova. In 1952, when she was still a student, she made her debut at the Kirov Theater as Masha in Vasily Vainonen's version of *The Nutcracker.* In 1953 she joined the Kirov company, and in 1954 danced Odette-Odile in *Swan Lake.* In 1966 Timofeyeva moved to the Bolshoi Ballet and became a leading soloist of the company. A virtuoso in command of all the subtleties of technique, she was considered too bold in the early years of her career. Eventually she learned to blend her academic precision with emotional truth and was well received in classical roles. But it was as an exponent of Soviet choreography that she made her name. She created the roles of the Girl in Leonid Lavrovsky's *Night City* (1961, set to Béla Bartók's *The Miraculous Mandarin*), the title role in Oleg Vinogradov's *Asel* (1967), Aegina in Yuri Grigorovich's *Spartacus* (1968), and Lady Macbeth in Vladimir Vasiliev's *Macbeth* (1980). Her talent as a tragedian was revealed with great force in one of her best roles, Mekhmene-Banu in Grigorovich's *Legend of Love.* Timofeyeva created a total of fifty roles in the classical and modern repertory. She also has fifteen films to her credit, among them *Fedra and the Twilight Nights* (1971), after Dostoyevsky, *Raymonda* (1974), and *The Three Cards* (1983), after Aleksandr Pushkin's *Queen of Spades.*

Timofeyeva was named People's Artist of the USSR in 1969 and was chosen a deputy of the Supreme Soviet of the USSR. In 1980 she graduated from the Choreography Department of the Lunacharsky Theater Technicum in Moscow, where she studied under Rostislav Zakharov. She retired in 1988 but has frequently returned to the Bolshoi as a coach.

BIBLIOGRAPHY

Demidov, Alexander P. *The Russian Ballet: Past and Present.* Translated by Guy Daniels. Garden City, N.Y., 1977.
Grigorovich, Yuri. "Edva li ne samaya sovremennaya." *Teatralnaia zhizn,* no. 13 (1969).
Lvov-Anokhin, Boris. "Nina Timofeyeva of the Bolshoi Ballet." *Ballet Today* (July 1960): 14–15.
Timofeyeva, Nina. *Mir baleta.* Moscow, 1993.

YURI P. TYURIN
Translated from Russian

TINIKLING. A performance by members of the Philippine Dance Company of New York. (Photograph courtesy of Reynaldo Gamboa Alejandro.)

TINIKLING. Among the many mimetic bird dances of the Philippines, the most famous is the *tinikling,* named after the *tikling* bird, which has long legs and a long neck. This dance, which originated on the island of Leyte, has two versions—the regular *tinikling,* danced between two bamboo poles, and one danced between two long pestles, called *tinikling ha bayo.* This dance is usually performed by a couple to the accompaniment of singers and guitar players.

The *tinikling* imitates the movements of the *tikling* birds as they walk and prance in the forest and ricefields. Some say the movements imitate the hopping and jumping of these birds as they try to escape bamboo traps hidden in the grass.

In the old days the *tinikling* was usually accompanied by a song with a slow 3/4 beat. Bamboo poles are struck together in time to the music while the dancers perform between the poles. In the 1950s the beat was accelerated, and the dance was stylized for the stage, an innovation by the dance scholar Leonor Orosa Goquingco.

The *tinikling* was once part of a curing ceremony, much like the rites observed by the Spanish, who colonized the Philippines in the 1500s. In Sitio Tubig-ginoo in Kawayan, Leyte, a curing ceremony was witnessed by Father Richard Arens of the Society of the Divine Word in 1950. In the second part of this ceremony, called *pana-ad,* women with red kerchiefs on their heads danced around the fire, and the men danced a kind of *tinikling.* The source of *tinikling* may therefore have been a pre-Hispanic ritual dance.

[*See also* Philippines.]

BIBLIOGRAPHY

Alejandro, Reynaldo Gamboa. *Philippine Dance: Mainstream and Crosscurrents.* Quezon City, 1978.

Arens, Richard. "Folk Practices and Beliefs of Leyte and Samar." *Leyte Samar Studies* 5 (1971): 107–121.

Baty, Gregoria. "Tinikling in Labanotation: A Search for Transcribing a Non-Western Dance." In *Hong Kong International Dance Conference.* Hong Kong, 1990.

Enriquez, Marge. "Orosa-Goquingco, Leonor Luna." In *Encyclopedia of Philippine Art.* Manila, 1994.

Joaquin, Nick. *La Orosa: The Dance-Drama That Is Leonor Goquingco.* Manila, 1994.

Reyes Tolentino, Francisca. *Philippine National Dances.* New York, 1946.

REYNALDO GAMBOA ALEJANDRO

TIV DANCE. The Tiv are an energetic and fiercely egalitarian people, about four million of whom live mostly in the valley of the Benue River in central eastern Nigeria. They work at fishing or as farmers on the open savanna land, living in small rural communities, each based on an extended polygamous family.

Their social organization features age sets, through which men close in age help one another in work and dance together in teams. The wives of men married within the same three-year period also dance together; unmarried girls from the husbands' compounds may join these teams.

Dance plays a central role at marriage and funeral ceremonies and is a popular form of entertainment at the lavish feasts held by elders to gain prestige and entertain visitors. The same styles of dance may be used for a variety of occasions. At village markets, held every five days, men and women perform in their separate teams for hours, encircled by dense crowds of enthusiastic spectators. Gifts of money are lavished on skilled performers, who hold a position of prestige because their dance has the power to dispel witchcraft and "mend the earth."

A dance song, "The Sun Is a Man, the Moon Is a Woman," voices the contrast between men's and women's dance. Men express their strength in a variety of dance styles. In the *ingough,* they circle around four drummers in a dance divided into a number of sections, each with its own rhythm, initiated by the master drummer and accompanied by a gong. The leader starts each rhythm with a walk, accelerating into a loping run that ends in a different movement pattern for each section. The first is a stamping pattern; the second is based on leaps ending with a turn; and in subsequent patterns the dancers take a stance that allows for repetitive contractions in the torso and shoulders. This is a familiar style in Tiv men's dance, but the *ingough* ends each section with the dancers abruptly adopting a grotesque posture with abdomens distended and faces distorted, creating a comic dramatic effect—to distance disease-causing painful deformities by satirizing them. The dancers wear amulets and charms, and each carries a small animal skin stuffed with protective medicine to negate the power of wizards who cause disease. Solo dances, such as the *ibiamegh,* are performed by a male elder who carries two long spears as he performs the strong, sustained body rhythms and arm gestures from a static position.

The *ajo* dance combines two styles. The master drummer plays a snare drum *(kunkun)* at the center of a circle of men squatting on low stools; their costume is characterized by two decorative crossed sticks tied to the upper back with leather thongs hanging down over the shoulders. They sing and drum as a chorus, beating tension drums *(ajo),* as two men move center to dance with powerful shoulder thrusts, causing the thongs to whirl. Two *ajo* players join them as partners in an intense rhythmic exchange between drummer and dancer, which mounts as the dancers compete in a spectacular performance revealing the Tiv talent for invention, often based on skillful adaptation of their neighbors' arts. On an important occasion, the *ajo* circle is surrounded by an outer circle of men dancing a simple foot pattern to the *kunkun.*

During the dry season when work lightens, the leaders of the women's *icough* teams compose new songs referring to recent events, each with a distinctive rhythm. The Tiv are perfectionists and spend months practicing the new dance for performance. The dance is not entirely innovative, but rather continues the *icough* style, with variations of gesture, movement patterns, and tempo that follow the rhythm of the drums *(agbande)* or flute *(agya).*

The outstanding feature of *icough* is the sustained, controlled flow of the movement through the body and limbs as the dancer passes through the basic positions of the dance. In the stance, the weight is placed on the whole foot, the knees are flexed, and the upper body moves from an upright position to a slight or deep forward inclination, according to the dance pattern. A gentle contraction-release of the shoulders extends into the body, creating a wavelike motion as the weight is used positively in pressing and wringing or released in light floating and gliding gestures.

Many teams include a section in which the women kneel on the ground throughout the dance. In a standing posture, the performers may remain stationary, either facing the drummers or along the line of the circle. In some sequences they progress slowly, using an elementary step pattern; in others, each dancer turns to face a partner with whom she exchanges position once or twice during the sequences.

The dancers on the circle perform the contrasting patterns of the dance sections in rhythmic unison. The leader, however, dances as a soloist within the circle, moving around to supervise their movement with an upright posture. Meanwhile, an elderly "mother of the dance" encourages the performers with ululation from outside the circle. (These *icough* styles were recorded between 1963 and 1965.)

In 1966 the Tiv tradition of expressing important events in dance was evident in the *gburka,* a soldiers' dance popular during the Nigerian civil war. The leader was dressed in a uniform and the women carried small wooden guns. A male "commander" joined the circle to shout drill commands to start the dance, to which the dancers responded with comic stiffened gestures. On the command "Fire!" the drums took over as the women held the guns forward with a series of abrupt gestures, after which the rhythm developed into a recognizable *icough* style.

In 1976, a spectacular *suwa* dance was created in the Gboko district for competition at FESTAC 77 in Lagos. Their song related to fishing activities; the team leader danced within the circle carrying a small replica of a fishing net. The best dancer on the circle led twenty women in unison, using rhythmic patterns from a stationary position. In place of a rattle, each woman carried a minute calabash in one hand. The "dance mother" moved around the outside gesturing with a hoe to encourage her dancers. The rhythms were far more complex than usual, and the tempo accelerated and declined twice within each rhythmic section. The sections were also longer, allowing the dance patterns to elaborate. The movements demanded great physical virtuosity, resulting in the development of a style that could be described as theatrical. The dance theme was based on a fishing experience: when the women found the river flowing too swiftly to catch fish, they built a dam with hand tools, emptied out the water with calabashes, and caught the stranded fish in their nets. The stylization of working movements is a conscious source of dance postures, movements, and gestures in Tiv women's dance.

By 1983, the *icough* dance in the Gboko district had lost much of its flow, subtlety, and invention. A more upright posture using walks and runs alternated with rhythmic patterns in a stationary position—reminiscent of the men's dances, as marked differences eroded between male and female dancing under urban influences.

Dance clubs have been popular in Tiv towns since the 1950s. There, young people perform simple adaptations of traditional dances, as recreation, to highlife beats played on a combination of Tiv, Hausa, and Western instruments. In the 1960s, cabaret dance by solo virtuoso dancers was performed with great skill in improvisation in a style called *swange*. Their influence may still be seen in the popular styles at present-day clubs.

[*See also* West Africa.]

BIBLIOGRAPHY

Harper, Peggy. "Dance in Nigeria." *Ethnomusicology* 13.2 (1969): 280–295.

Harper, Peggy. "Icough: A Tiv Dance." *African Notes* 6 (1970).

Harper, Peggy. *Dance: The Living Cultures of Nigeria*. N.p., 1975.

Keil, Charles. *Tiv Song*. Chicago, 1979.

Kerr, Julie A. "Tiv Dance Aesthetics." In *Congress on Research in Dance: Progress and Possibilities*. New York, 1987.

PEGGY HARPER

TODD, MABEL ELSWORTH. *See* Body Therapies, *overview article.*

TOMASSON, HELGI (born 8 October 1942 in Reykjavik, Iceland), dancer, choreographer, and company director. A dancer who would be noted for the clarity, refinement, and musicality of his dancing, Tomasson began training at age ten in Iceland. In 1958 he began performing with the Tivoli Pantomime Theater in Copenhagen. With the support of Jerome Robbins, he studied for several months at the School of American Ballet, and with the encouragement of Erik Bruhn he was invited to join the Robert Joffrey Theatre Ballet in 1962. He danced successfully there in a wide-ranging repertory until 1964, when he joined the newly formed Harkness Ballet. In 1969 he won the silver medal (to Mikhail Baryshnikov's gold) at the International Ballet Competition in Moscow.

TOMASSON. Jerome Robbins created *A Beethoven Pas de Deux* for Tomasson and Gelsey Kirkland in 1973. It was later retitled *Four Bagatelles*. (Photograph from the Dance Collection, New York Public Library for the Performing Arts.)

In 1970 Tomasson joined the New York City Ballet as a principal dancer; he flourished there until his retirement as a performer in 1985. Considered to be one of the finest male dancers of his generation, he acquired a large and varied repertory and was known as an exemplar of style in works by both George Balanchine and Robbins. Balanchine created numerous roles for him, including an unusual solo in *Divertimento from "Le Baiser de la Fée"* (1972) and the *demi-caractère* role of Franz in his new staging of *Coppélia* (1974). Robbins also created parts for him in numerous works, including the pure dance *The Goldberg Variations* and the dance drama *Dybbuk Variations*. Tomasson performed the role of Albrecht in *Giselle* with American Ballet Theatre in 1977 and a few years later with the Royal Danish Ballet.

Although relatively short for a dancer (five feet, seven inches), Tomasson was a handsome young man with good proportions. He became an excellent partner, working with Violette Verdy, Melissa Hayden, Gelsey Kirkland, and especially Patricia McBride.

Tomasson began his choreographic career with a work for the School of American Ballet Workshop performance in 1982. His second work, *Ballet d'Isoline* (1983), was later taken into the repertory of the New York City Ballet. His choreography, like his dancing, is noted for its formal refinement and musicality. He has been especially successful in creating roles for men.

In 1985 Tomasson was invited to become the artistic director of the San Francisco Ballet. He is credited with raising the technical standards of the company and providing it with a cohesive look. He developed a balanced repertory, including works by such masters as Marius Petipa, Balanchine, and Frederick Ashton, as well as such innovators as William Forsythe, James Kudelka, and Mark Morris. He has continued to choreograph many works of his own for the company. His *Handel—A Celebration* (1989) was particularly successful. He has also staged notable productions of *Swan Lake* (1988), *The Sleeping Beauty* (1990, later added to the repertory of the Royal Danish Ballet), and *Romeo and Juliet* (1994). In 1995 he sponsored UNited We Dance, a festival in honor of the fiftieth anniversary of the signing of the United Nations Charter that featured premiers by thirteen international companies.

His awards include Iceland's Knight of the Order of the Falcon (1974; he was its youngest recipient) and Commander of the Order of the Falcon (1990) as well as the 1992 *Dance Magazine* Award. He has been married since 1965 to former Harkness dancer Marlene Rizzo and has two sons.

BIBLIOGRAPHY

Current Biography. New York, 1982.

Gruen, John. "Interview with Helgi Tomasson." In Gruen's *The Private World of Ballet.* New York, 1975.

Hellman, Eric. "Tomasson's Coming of Age." *Ballet Review* 19 (Spring 1991): 85–87.

Kisselgoff, Anna. *Helgi Tomasson.* Brooklyn, 1975.

Mason, Francis, ed. *I Remember Balanchine.* New York, 1991.

Ross, Janice. "San Francisco Ballet: Helgi's Domain." *Dance Magazine* (September 1991): 38–45.

Tomasson, Helgi, et al. "The Male Image." *Dance Perspectives* (Winter 1969).

KATY MATHESON

TOMASZEWSKI, HENRYK (born 20 November 1925 in Poznań), Polish dancer, mime, choreographer, teacher, and company director. Tomaszewski studied dance with Feliks Parnell and acting with Iwo Gall. After performing as a soloist of the Wrocław Opera Ballet from 1949 to 1955, he established a mime studio, converted in 1958 into the Wrocław Mime Theater.

As a dancer, Tomaszewski always preferred dramatic, mimic, and character roles. He was expressive, full of invention, and talented in improvisation. He created many leading roles in his own dance dramas, shaping the style of interpretation in Polish mime theater. Early in his career as a choreographer for his mime company, he created short, strict mime in the style of Marcel Marceau. Later he developed an original type of narrative theater of movement based on his own scenarios, utilizing mime, modern dance, ballet, and acrobatics. The music in Tomaszewski's works fulfills an illustrative, ornamental function.

Among Tomaszewski's more important works are *A Harlequin's Masks* (1959), *The Sorcerer's Apprentice* (1960), *The Peculiar Closet* (1961), *Entrance to the Labyrinth* (1963), *The Minotaur* (1964), *The Rocking Horse* (1965), *The Garden of Love* and *The Dress* (both 1966), *Gilgamesh* and *Bagage* (both 1968), *Faust's Departure* (1970), *A November Night's Dream* (1971), *The Menagerie of Empress Philissa* (1972), *I Am Coming Tomorrow* (1974), *Fantastic Scenes from the Legend of Pan Twardowski* (1976), *The Dispute* (1978), *Hamlet—Irony and Mourning* (1979), *King Arthur's Knights* (1981), and *The Prodigal Son* (1983).

Tomaszewski also occasionally choreographed ballets for Polish opera companies or for foreign ballet companies. For the Dutch National Ballet, he created *The Bull* (1965), to music by Augustyn Bloch; *Labyrinth,* performed in silence, *Pit and Bolster,* to music by Charles Mingus, and *The Dream,* to music by Bloch (all 1969); and *Before Five Passed* (1972), set to music by Juliusz Luciuk. For the Royal Danish Ballet, he set *Bagage* (1969) to music by Giovanni Pergolesi.

Many films of Tomaszewski's dance dramas were broadcast in Poland and other European countries. His work also became known outside Poland through his company's regular tours and frequent appearances in various festivals. The Wrocław Mime Theater won the Critics Prize at the Parisian Festival of the Theater of Nations in 1962 and the Gold Star at the Festival International de Danse in Paris in 1970.

BIBLIOGRAPHY

Hausbrandt, Andrej. *Tomaszewski-pantomima.* Warsaw, 1974.

Neuer, Adam, ed. *Polish Opera and Ballet of the Twentieth Century: Operas, Ballets, Pantomimes, Miscellaneous Works.* Translated by Jerzy Zawadzki. Kraków, 1986.

PAWEŁ CHYNOWSKI

TOMLINSON, KELLOM (also known as Kenelm, Mr. Kellom; born c.1690, died after 1753), English dancing master and choreographer. Tomlinson is best known as the author of *The Art of Dancing* (1735). He was apprenticed to Thomas Caverley at his ladies' dancing and boarding school on Bedford Street in London in April 1707, where he remained until 1714. His instructor in theatrical dancing at that time was René Cherrier. Tomlinson also knew Anthony L'Abbé and was a contemporary at Caverley's with John Shaw, the theatrical dancer.

Tomlinson set himself up as a genteel dancing master at his lodgings on the corner of King's Gate Street, Holborn, and immediately began to notate and publish his own annual dance, following the examples of Mister Isaac, L'Abbé, P[eter?] Siris, and others. A series of six dances, for the years 1715 to 1720, was issued in a collected edition in 1721 as *Six Dances Composed by Mr. Kellom Tomlinson,* including "The Passepied Round O" (1715); "The Shepherdess" (1716); "The Submission" (1717), which was performed by Marie and Francis Sallé at Lincoln's Inn Fields theater as "Mr. Kellom's New Dance"; "The Prince Eugene" (1718); "The Address: A New Rigadoon" (1719); and "The Gavot" (1720). In 1721 he also published his "Passacaille Diana," dedicated to L'Abbé. These dances were for the "use and improvement" of his students and "for the further Encouragement of dancing." His most successful pupil was John Topham, who first appeared on the stage as "Mr. Kellom's scholar" and later danced in John Weaver's *Orpheus and Eurydice* (1718).

Tomlinson moved into his own house on Southampton Street, Holborn, in 1717 or 1718 after marrying Mary Alston (25 July 1717), and in 1719 they moved to Devonshire Street, near Queen's Square, Holborn. Although this suggests increasing prosperity, Tomlinson's failure to obtain enough subscribers led to a crucial delay in the publication of his major work *The Art of Dancing.* He finished the book in 1724 and advertised it as ready for press in October 1726, but it was not actually published until 1735.

The expense of Tomlinson's work (which accounted for

the long delay) was due to the cost of the fine plates by Gerard Vandergucht, George Bickhan, George Vertue, and others. The novel idea of the treatise, for which Tomlinson was eager to take credit, was to make the notation of dances more useful to the amateur and student: the manner of performance was described in words and dancers performing the steps were depicted graphically in addition to the steps being notated. The work is clearly set out and written in accordance with the principles and rules that Tomlinson had garnered from observing the outstanding masters of genteel dancing, including Caverley and others. Thirty named dances by English and French dancing masters published since 1700 are referred to in the text. The work was reissued as a second edition in 1744 and was one of the most finely produced of all dance books, subscribed to by the greatest in the British world of dance; it has continuing importance and interest for students of dance technique and bibliography.

Tomlinson disclaimed all knowledge of Pierre Rameau's *Le maître à danser* (1725) and maintained that John Essex's translation, *The Dancing-Master: or, The Art of Dancing Explained* (1728), which had a larger format than the original and sold at half the proposed cost of Tomlinson's book, was designed to destroy his market. A workbook apparently compiled by Tomlinson between 1708 and 1721 has come to light in New Zealand that contains six previously unknown dances by Tomlinson. Three of those dances were performed in London in a 1716 production of *The Island Princess* and used again, with two additional dances, in 1721. The collection also contains a solo *sarabande* for a man, performed in 1716, and a hitherto unknown version of Caverley's "Slow Minuet," which differs in several respects from Pemberton's engraved version.

BIBLIOGRAPHY

Brinson, Peter, ed. *The Ballet in Britain*. London, 1962.

Marsh, Carol. "French Court Dance in England, 1706–1740: A Study of the Sources." Ph.D. diss., City University of New York, 1985.

Petre, Robert. "Six New Dances by Kellom Tomlinson: A Recently Discovered Manuscript." *Early Music* 18 (August 1990): 381–390.

Scott, Edward. "Notes on the Minuet as Represented by Kellom Tomlinson." *Dancing Times* (December 1922): 243–245.

Shennan, Jennifer. "Discovery of New Kellom Tomlinson Manuscript." *Dance Research Journal* 22 (Spring 1990): 58–61.

Tomlinson, Kellom. *A Work Book by Kellom Tomlinson: Commonplace Book of an Eighteenth-Century English Dancing Master* (c.1708–1722). Edited by Jennifer Shennan. Stuyvesant, N.Y., 1992.

RICHARD RALPH and JENNIFER THORP

TONGA. The Kingdom of Tonga, in Polynesia, is in the southern Pacific Ocean, southwest of Samoa; it is an independent member nation of the British Commonwealth, composed of some 150 islands with about 100,000 people. Its parliamentary political system is headed by a king who traces his ancestry back to the Polynesian gods who are

TONGA. Men from Lapaha performing the *m'etu'upaki* at the centenary celebration of the Tongan constitution, at Nuku'alofa, 1975. (Photograph © 1976 by Adrienne L. Kaeppler; used by permission.)

said to have created and peopled the islands. Dance is a functional part of the present sociopolitical system, which combines traditional social stratification with a system of appointed nobles.

No notable occasion, from national celebration to informal get-together, is complete without the performance of some kind of dancing. The most important dances performed on formal occasions can be characterized as metaphorical danced speeches. These include *lakalaka,* usually a standing dance ideally performed by all the men and women of a village, and *mā'ulu'ulu,* a sitting dance performed by many individuals of one or both sexes from a school, church, village, or other corporate group. In these dances the basic text is structured along the lines of a formal speech in a series of concepts and references to past and present events, places, and people. Movements allude to selected words of the poetry or to underlying concepts to which the poetry alludes. Thus, Tongan dance creates a double abstraction; while movements are in themselves abstract, they also allude to multiple words, meanings, and concepts.

The aesthetic concept of *heliaki* (to say one thing but mean another) is found both in the melodically and rhythmically rendered poetry and in the movements that allude to it. Another aesthetic element, *fakateki* (side head tilt), expresses a state of inner exhilaration called *māfana.* In *lakalaka,* leg movements are primarily a series of sidesteps executed nearly in place, while in *mā'ulu'ulu* and other seated dances no leg movements are made except for a rhythmic pulse kept with one foot. Thus the most important movements are those of the hands and arms, which form a series of movement motifs—movements interpreting a selected word or concept, beautiful movements that ornament or complete certain phrases, and motifs that divide stanzas or sections of poetry.

Movement motifs are based on flexible wrists and the rotation of the lower arms, in conjunction with various finger movements and positions and palm facings, which occur in a limited number of arm positions. These motifs are known by the general term *haka,* and a number of the motifs also have specific names. For example, *milolua* is a movement that derives from the wringing of *kava (Piper methysticum),* plant material used to make a ceremonial drink. Arm movements for women are soft and graceful, and foot and leg movements are small, in keeping with the stricture of always keeping the thighs parallel and close together, even while seated. Men's movements are larger and more virile, delivered with stiffer wrists; the steps are wider and the legs more separated, and there is more body movement, including moving to one knee, striking the ground with feet or hands, and even rolling on the ground.

TONGA. Men and women from Kanokupolu performing a *lakalaka* at the centenary celebration of the Tongan constitution, at Nuku'alofa, 1975. (Photograph © 1976 by Adrienne L. Kaeppler; used by permission.)

Older dances that are still performed but no longer created include *me'etu'upaki,* a men's standing dance in which dance paddles are manipulated; and a women's dance, *fa'ahiula,* which includes a seated section called *'otuhaka* and a standing section called *ula.* The *ula* has been largely replaced by *tau'olunga,* an acculturated dance that combines Tongan and Samoan movements with Tongan poetry rendered in a form based on European melodic contours and played on stringed instruments.

[*For general discussion, see* Oceanic Dance Traditions *and* Polynesia. *See also* Music for Dance, *article on* Oceanic Music.]

BIBLIOGRAPHY

Kaeppler, Adrienne L. "Tongan Dance: A Study in Cultural Change." *Ethnomusicology* 14.2 (1970): 266–277.

Kaeppler, Adrienne L. "Aesthetics of Tongan Dance." *Ethnomusicology* 15.2 (1971): 175–185.

Kaeppler, Adrienne L. "Method and Theory in Analyzing Dance Structure, with an Analysis of Tongan Dance." *Ethnomusicology* 16.2 (1972): 173–217.

Kaeppler, Adrienne L. "Melody, Drone, and Decoration: Underlying Structures and Surface Manifestations in Tongan Art and Society." In *Art in Society: Studies in Styles, Cultures, and Aesthetics,* edited by Michael Greenhalgh and Vincent Megaw. London, 1978.

Kaeppler, Adrienne L. "Structured Movement Systems in Tonga." In *Society and the Dance: The Social Anthropology of Process and Performance,* edited by Paul Spencer. Cambridge, 1985.

Kaeppler, Adrienne L. *Poetry in Motion: Studies in Tongan Dance.* Nuku'alofa, Tonga, 1993.

ADRIENNE L. KAEPPLER

TOPÉNG. *See* Indonesia, *article on* Balinese Mask Theater.

TORDION (also Eng., *turgion;* Fr., *tourdion;* It., *tordiglione, dordigilone*), a lively triple-meter sixteenth-century dance type of unknown origins, similar to the galliard. French and Italian sources first mention the tordion in 1499, in *La grant danse macabre* (see Heartz, 1949–1979, p. 590) and in a letter to Isabella d'Este, which refers to a drummer playing a *dordoglione* in an *intermedio* (Pirrotta and Povoledo, 1982, p. 50). An early English reference appears in Thomas Elyot's guide to a prince's education, the *Boke Named the Gouvernour* (1531): "We have nowe, base daunsis, bargenettes, pavions, turgions, and roundes." There is no choreography, however, before 1581. The dance seems to have died out in Italy and France shortly after 1600, although references to it continue in Spain.

In musical collections of the early sixteenth century, the tordion was often an after-dance to the *bassedanse* (e.g., Pierre Attaingnant, *18 basses dances,* 1530), but the only contemporary choreographic reference, in Antonius de Arena's treatise *A suos compagnones studiantes* (1528), merely gives comical hints of sprightly "passages" in macaronic verse.

Choreographic details appear much later in Fabritio Caroso (1581, 1600), Thoinot Arbeau (1588), Cesare Negri (1602, 1604), and Livio Lupi (1600, 1607). Whatever the tordion was originally, it and the galliard are, by this time, recognized as related, if not actually identical. Arbeau equates the dances musically and choreographically but distinguishes between them also by saying that the tordion follows the *retour* of the *bassedanse.* He states further that it differs from the galliard because it is "danced close to the ground to a light, lively beat and the galliard is danced higher off the ground to a slower, stronger beat." He also supplies two simple variations.

The far more complex Italian choreographies blur even these small distinctions. Caroso's (two) and Negri's (one) *tordiglione* have passages and variations couched entirely in galliard terms; because all three dances have the same short music, whose six-beat units may be read as needed in triple (3/2) or duple (6/4), the Italian *tordiglione* may simply be a galliard to a specific tune or chord scheme. Caroso, however, has *tordiglione* variations (for the lady) in galliard movements of *balletto* suites to other music, such as "Nido d'Amore" (Caroso, 1600, p. 290). He says, in fact, that the *tordiglione* is a galliard (Caroso, 1600, p. 320). Nevertheless, Lupi's long lists of *tordiglione* variations (100 in 1600 and 140 for the gentleman and 30 for the lady in 1607) are kept separate from his even longer lists of galliard passages and variations. Thus, differences were apparently perceived by some that are not now evident but that more study and statistical analyses may yet reveal.

The mystery of the dance is further deepened by John Florio's definition of the *tordiglione* as "a kind of dance in Spaine" (Florio, 1598, 1600); yet Spanish references to this dance are from the seventeenth century only (Esses, 1992).

[*For related discussion, see* Galliard.]

BIBLIOGRAPHY: SOURCES

Arbeau, Thoinot. *Orchesographie et traicte en forme de dialogve, par leqvel tovtes personnes pevvent facilement apprendre & practiquer l'honneste exercice des dances.* Langres, 1588, 1589. Facsimile reprint, Langres, 1988. Reprinted with expanded title as *Orchesographie, metode, et teorie en forme de discovrs et tablatvre povr apprendre a dancer, battre le Tambour en toute sorte & diuersité de batteries, Iouët du fifre & arigot, tirer des armes & escrimer, auec autres honnestes exercices fort conuenables à la Ieunesse.* Langres, 1596. Facsimile reprint, Geneva, 1972.

Arbeau, Thoinot. *Orchesography.* 1589. Translated into English by Mary Stewart Evans. New York, 1948. Reprint with corrections, a new introduction, and notes by Julia Sutton, and representative steps and dances in Labanotation by Mireille Backer. New York, 1967.

Arena, Antonius. *Ad suos compagnones studiantes.* Lyon, 1528. Translated by John Guthrie and Marino Zorzi in "*Rules of Dancing* by Antonius Arena." *Dance Research* 4 (1986): 3–53.

Caroso, Fabritio. *Il ballarino* (1581). Facsimile reprint, New York, 1967.

Caroso, Fabritio. *Nobiltà di dame.* Venice, 1600, 1605. Facsimile reprint, Bolgona, 1970. Reissued with order of illustrations changed as *Raccolta di varij balli.* Rome, 1630. Translated into English with eight introductory chapters by Julia Sutton, the music transcribed by F. Marian Walker. Oxford, 1986. Reprint with step manual in Labanotation by Rachelle Palnick Tsachor and Julia Sutton, New York, 1995.

Florio, John. *A World of Wordes.* London, 1598. Facsimile reprint, Hildesheim, 1972. 2d ed., *Queen Anna's New World of Words.* London, 1611. Facsimile reprint of 1611 ed., Menston, England, 1973.

Lupi, Livio. *Libro di gagliarda, tordiglione, passo e mezzo, canari e passeggi.* Palermo, 1600. Rev. ed., Palermo, 1607.

Negri, Cesare. *Le gratie d'amore.* Milan, 1602. Reissued as *Nuove invenzione di balli.* Milan, 1604. Translated into Spanish by Don Balthasar Carlos for Señor Condé, Duke of Sanlucar, 1630. Manuscript located in Madrid, Biblioteca Nacional, MS 14085. Facsimile reprint of 1602, New York and Bologna, 1969. Literal translation into English and musical transcription by Yvonne Kendall. D.M.A. diss., Stanford University, 1985.

BIBLIOGRAPHY: OTHER STUDIES

Brooks, Lynn Matluck. *The Dances of the Processions of Seville in Spain's Golden Age.* Kassel, 1988.

Esses, Maurice. *Dance and Instrumental Diferencias in Spain during the Seventeenth and Early Eighteenth Centuries.* Stuyvesant, N.Y., 1992.

Heartz, Daniel. "Sources and Forms of the French Instrumental Dance in the Sixteenth Century." Ph.D. diss., Harvard University, 1957.

Heartz, Daniel. *Preludes, Chansons, and Dances for Lute Published by Pierre Attaingnant, Paris, 1529–1530.* Neuilly-sur-Seine, 1964.

Heartz, Daniel. *Keyboard Dances from the Earlier Sixteenth Century.* American Institute of Musicology, Corpus of Early Keyboard Music, 8. Dallas, 1965.

Heartz, Daniel. "Tourdion." In *Die Musik in Geschichte und Gegenwart.* 1st ed., vol. 13, 1966. Kassel, 1949–1979. Recast in *The New Grove Dictionary of Music and Musicians.* London, 1980.

Pirrotta, Nino, and Elena Povoledo. *Music and Theatre from Poliziano to Monteverdi.* Translated by Karen Eals. Cambridge, 1982.

Tani, Gino. "Tourdion." In *Enciclopedio dello spettacolo.* 9 vols. Rome, 1954–1968.

JULIA SUTTON
with David Hahn

TORNEO. *See* Barriera, Torneo, and Battaglia.

TORVILL AND DEAN. Jayne Torvill (born 7 October 1957 in Nottingham) and Christopher Dean (Christopher Colin Dean, born 27 July 1958 in Nottingham), English ice dancers and choreographers. Torvill and Dean revolutionized ice dancing, bringing it closer to art while indirectly casting doubt upon its viability as a sport. During their amateur career, which culminated with a gold medal at the 1984 Olympic Games, the couple amassed more perfect scores than any other competitors in skating history and transformed the sport through Dean's choreography, its imitation by others, and the rules changes aimed at reducing its influence. As professionals, Torvill and Dean's skating remained at the highest standard. In 1994 they returned to the Olympics under new eligibility rules, and their technically challenging and charismatic performance to "Let's Face the Music and Dance" was awarded a bronze medal for third place. The decision of the judges was highly controversial, and the suspicion that Torvill and Dean had been unfairly penalized renewed speculation that the highly subjective sport might be eliminated from Olympic competition.

Both Jayne Torvill and Christopher Dean started skating at about age ten, and both quickly achieved recognition in amateur competitions: Dean won a British junior dance championship (1974) with Sandra Elson, whereas Torvill won the British senior pairs championship (1971) with Michael Hutchinson. When both were left by their partners, they formed a dance team in 1975. In 1980, they were able to leave their jobs (Torvill was an insurance clerk, Dean, a policeman) to train full-time on a grant from the Nottingham City Council. They won four consecutive world championships, starting in 1981.

Their 1982 programs set new standards of artistry for the sport. "Summertime," a required Blues number, conveyed a feeling of passionate desolation, and its intriguing air of intimacy became a hallmark of the Torvill and Dean mystique (genuine, but also carefully cultivated). The desire of audiences to see them as a couple remained undisturbed by their subsequent marriages to others. The popularity of their free dance based on the failed Broadway musical *Mack and Mabel* stimulated revivals of the show. The 1983 free dance "Barnum" tightly integrated mime and dance, and was polished with the assistance of the show's London star, Michael Crawford. Their amateur competitive career climaxed at the Sarajevo Olympics in 1984. Their required Paso Doble strikingly depicted a bullfighter (Dean) and his cape (Torvill), but it was the free dance to Ravel's *Boléro* that captured a perfect score for artistic impression as well as the world's attention, becoming not just a sporting event but part of a collective cultural consciousness. As professionals, Torvill and Dean mounted their own ice shows and made several television specials. The most lavish of these was *Fire and Ice* (1986), which featured choreography by Graeme Murphy and, uniquely, Dean dancing without skates.

Christopher Dean's choreography contains several identifiable traits: carriage is straight-bodied and open; skaters frequently skate between or underneath each other's feet; and besides the traditional holds derived from ballroom or folk dancing, he employs three distinctive types—"behind-the-back," "leg," and "neck" holds. In the first, one partner holds the other with one or both arms behind the back; in the other two, one partner is held and guided by the leg (now illegal in amateur competition) or the neck (sometimes the cheek), often with the supported

TORVILL AND DEAN. Noted for elegance and precision, Torvill and Dean also excelled in dramatic numbers. "Missing" (1987), inspired by news stories of the fate of political dissidents in South America, was skated to "Dolencias," a song composed and performed by the popular South American music group Incantation. (Photograph courtesy of Torvill and Dean.)

partner stretched at an angle to the ice. The partners are equal in choreographic interest, and the woman frequently supports or guides the man. Overall, Dean's choreography gives a sense of continuously evolving movement that tends to relate literally to music. A striking exception is "Oscar Tango" (1990), with the sound largely provided by the skaters' blades.

Other significant choreography includes "Encounter" (1984), a highly detailed dance based on the simple motif of a bent knee; "Tribute to Fred and Ginger" (1987), a modernist's analytical interpretation of the Astaire-Rogers style; "Tribute to John Lennon" (1990), an exploration of action and reaction with overt physical aggression influenced by Édouard Lock; "Hat Trick" (1990), an intricate, amusing competition for a shiny red hat; "Iceworks" (1991), a choreography for video, incorporating skate sounds into the original music; and "Missing" (1987), a controversial piece that, despite Dean's refutation, draws on the theme, music, and choreographic motifs of Christopher Bruce's "Ghost Dances" (1981). Considered as "Dean after Bruce," however, "Missing" is a masterly synthesis of the multicharacter one-act ballet into a brief duet. A revised version was performed in 1990 by the French-Canadian team of Paul Duchesnay and his sister Isabelle, to whom Dean was briefly married. The Duchesnays won the world championships in 1991 with a hastily choreographed "sequel," after judges and audiences resoundingly rejected the abstract "Mirror Image," which highlighted the siblings' physical similarity. Other notable choreography created by Dean for the Duchesnays includes two 1988 programs, a comic tango and "Tribal [Savage] Rites," skating's equivalent to *Le Sacre du Printemps*. Dean has also choreographed for other dance and pairs teams and has received a commission to create works for the English National Ballet.

TORVILL AND DEAN. The famous couple in "Rumba," an original dance performed to "History of Love" by Carlos Almaran. This number was part of their 1994 program at the British championships, where they won the gold medal; at the European championships, where they won the gold medal; and at the Winter Olympic Games in Lillehammer, Norway, where, to the dismay of millions of television viewers, they were denied the gold medal and were awarded the bronze instead. (Photograph courtesy of Torvill and Dean.)

BIBLIOGRAPHY

Copley-Graves, Lynn. *Figure Skating History: The Evolution of Dance on Ice.* Columbus, Ohio, 1992.

Hennessey, John. *Torvill and Dean.* London, 1983.

Hilton, Christopher. *Torvill and Dean: The Full Story.* London, 1994.

Torvill, Jayne, and Christopher Dean. *Facing the Music.* London and New York, 1995.

VIDEOTAPES. *Path to Perfection* (1984). *Fire and Ice* (1986). *Torvill and Dean and the Russian All-Stars* (1990). *The Best of Torvill and Dean* (1994), which includes *Path to Perfection, Fire and Ice,* and the 1994 British National Championships.

ROBYNN J. STILWELL

TOTENTANZ. *See* Dance of Death.

TOULOUSE-LAUTREC, HENRI DE (Henri-Marie-Raymond de Toulouse-Lautrec-Monfa; born 24 November 1864 in Albi, France, died 9 September 1901 in Malrome, France), French painter. The name Toulouse-Lautrec evokes one of the most memorable and crucial eras in the history of both art and dance. The artist's celebrated images of Parisian life during the city's Belle Époque captured the excitement and, at times, despair of a modern France emerging. Toulouse-Lautrec's art had its own modernity. In 1891 he was asked to design a poster for the highly contemporary nightclub Moulin Rouge. The poster, with its bold color, sensuous line, and distorted space, revolutionized poster design and not only succeeded in advertising the dance hall but also brought immortality to the dancer it pictured, La Goulue (Louise Weber). Toulouse-Lautrec's reputation was secured; from then on, despite repeated critical attacks for his unconventional painting style and indecorous subject matter, he was in great demand. His posters, paintings, and prints of leading dance halls and their stars ensured the widespread popularity of both the artist and his work throughout Paris and abroad.

Born into one of the oldest noble families in France, Toulouse-Lautrec enjoyed a childhood typical of his class. However, as an adolescent he broke his legs in two successive accidents only months apart. His legs ceased to grow, leaving him permanently deformed. Deprived of the sport and hunt he loved so well, he turned instead to art, and what was once a leisure activity became a serious pursuit.

At the urging of fellow students at the school of Fernand Cormon, Toulouse-Lautrec settled in the bohemian Montmartre section of Paris in 1884. He had received some formal academic training but now looked more toward the innovative approaches of contemporary illustrators, Édouard Manet and the impressionists, Japanese art, and the painter he most admired, Edgar Degas. Subscribing to the modern theories of such writers as the French symbolist poet Charles Baudelaire, who insisted that truth and beauty could exist only in an art based on direct experience, Toulouse-Lautrec immersed himself in the night life of Paris and portrayed its most celebrated as well as its most downtrodden residents and places.

With a sardonic wit and the sharp eye of a journalist, he pinpointed the salient aspects of character, movement, and ambience in each subject. More than a mere observer, Toulouse-Lautrec identified personally with the entertainers, prostitutes, and clowns he portrayed. They, too, were considered misfits and "could stand as equivalent to the derided, unrecognized artist" (Thompson, 1977).

Among his most memorable subjects, however, are images of dancers and the dance. Like Degas, Toulouse-Lautrec studied ballerinas but preferred the wild contortions of *quadrille* dancers such as La Goulue and her partner Valentin le Désossé. Sketching horses as a child had developed his lightning skill at capturing movement, and he would spend hours sketching in his favorite dance halls or cabarets. Among the sights that caught his attention were the spectacular theatrics of Loie Fuller's skirt dance. Her innovative lighting effects and undulating drapery are rendered with an economy of means in his famous lithograph *Miss Loie Fuller* (1893). He also went numerous times to see operetta star Marcelle Lender dance the bolero in Chilpéric: "I came only to see [her] back! Look at it, you will hardly ever see anything so wonderful again" (Sorell, 1953). Yet Toulouse-Lautrec was concerned with more than mere movement, stage effects, or physiognomy. His artistic greatness rested on his ability to express the character and soul of his subject, be it person or place. Jane Avril's face reveals the hardships of her early life, whether she is depicted dancing, entering the Moulin Rouge, or sitting in attendance at the Divan Japonais.

The art and life of Toulouse-Lautrec are inextricably linked. Unfortunately, the same lifestyle that produced such an original, poignant body of work eventually destroyed the artist. He continued to work after suffering a nervous breakdown in 1899 but died two years later from the effects of alcohol abuse.

[*See also* Prints and Drawings. *For related discussion, see* Artists and Dance.]

BIBLIOGRAPHY. The basic text for the study of Toulouse-Lautrec is the comprehensive catalog in six volumes of all his work, M. G. Dortu, *Toulouse-Lautrec et son oeuvre* (New York, 1971). A useful, annotated list of characters and places that recur in Toulouse-Lautrec's work appears in *The Complete Paintings of Toulouse-Lautrec,* introduced by Denys Sutton (rev. ed., New York, 1987). Other sources include the following.

Adhémar, Jean. *Toulouse-Lautrec: His Complete Lithographs and Drypoints.* New York, 1965.

Amaya, Mario. "The Dance in Art, 1: 1850–1925" and "The Dance in Art, 3: The Little Genius of Montmartre." *Dance and Dancers* 11 (December 1960): 18–23+; 12 (April 1961): 18–21+.

Goldschmidt, Lucien, and Herbert Schimmel, eds. *Unpublished Correspondence of Henri de Toulouse-Lautrec.* London, 1969.
Murray, G. B. "The Theme of the Naturalist Quadrille in the Art of Toulouse-Lautrec: Its Origins, Meaning, Evolution, and Relationship to Later Realism." *Arts Magazine* 55 (December 1980).
Sorell, Walter. "The Dancers of Toulouse Lautrec." *Dance Magazine* (March 1953): 26–29.
Stuckey, Charles F. *Toulouse-Lautrec: Paintings.* Chicago, 1979. Exhibition catalogue.
Thompson, Richard. *Toulouse-Lautrec.* London, 1977.

ELLEN BREITMAN

TOUMANOVA, TAMARA (Tamara Vladimirovna Tumanova; born 2 March 1919 in Tyumen, Siberia, died 29 May 1996 in Santa Monica, California), Russian-American ballerina. Toumanova was born near Shanghai in a boxcar of a train in which her parents were leaving Russia after the Revolution. In China, where the family stayed for a few years, she received her first lessons in ballet when she was barely more than a toddler. After the family moved to Paris, she renewed her ballet training with Olga Preobrajenska in 1924, when she was five years old. The following year she was chosen by Anna Pavlova to dance in a benefit performance at the Trocadéro, and by the time she was ten, in 1929, she had developed such a formidable technique and charismatic presence that she was cast in a leading role in *L'Éventail de Jeanne,* a ballet with a cast of children, at the Paris Opera. André Levinson, a leading critic of the time, declared that the extraordinary virtuosity of this "prodigious child" was not only astounding but also somewhat frightening.

In 1931 Toumanova was invited to join the Ballets Russes de Monte Carlo by George Balanchine, ballet master of the company being formed under the direction of René Blum and Colonel Wassily de Basil. When the company made its debut in the spring of 1932, Toumanova, at age thirteen, was one of its three "baby ballerinas" (along with Irina Baronova, thirteen, and Tatiana Riabouchinska, fifteen). She created roles in four works by Balanchine—*Cotillon, La Concurrence, Le Bourgeois Gentilhomme,* and *Suite de Danse*—and in Léonide Massine's *Jeux d'Enfants.* When Balanchine left the company at the end of 1932 to form Les Ballets 1933, Toumanova went with him as leading dancer, appearing in Paris and London and creating principal roles in his *Mozartiana* and *Les Songes.* She returned to the Ballets Russes de Monte Carlo in October 1933, during its first London season at the Alhambra, and created roles in the first and fourth movements of Massine's *Choreartium.*

For the next several years Toumanova remained with the de Basil company, which from 1934 to 1937 was billed as the Ballets Russes de Colonel W. de Basil, dancing leading roles in the repertory and creating roles in several important new ballets, among them, Massine's *Le Bal* (1935) and *Symphonie Fantastique* (1936). In 1938 she joined the new Ballet Russe de Monte Carlo, headed by Massine as artistic director and Sergei Denham as managing director. During this company's famous London season in June 1938 she appeared for the first time in the title role of *Giselle,* for which she was to be acclaimed throughout her career. The following year, 1939, found her in New York in a supporting role in the Broadway musical *Stars in Your Eyes,* directed by Joshua Logan and starring Ethel Merman and Jimmy Durante.

TOUMANOVA. A studio portrait, posed *sur les pointes,* reveals Toumanova's fabled beauty. (Photograph by Maurice Seymour; used by permission.)

At the end of 1939, as war threatened to engulf Europe, Toumanova rejoined the de Basil company, by then called Original Ballet Russe, and appeared with it on tour in Australia, the United States, and Canada. Her affinity for Balanchine's choreography and his appreciation of her as a performer were notable in the dances he created for her in the third and fourth movements of his *Balustrade* (1941), set to Igor Stravinsky's Concerto in D for violin and orchestra. When her contract with de Basil expired in March 1941, she left his company to rejoin Denham's Ballet Russe de Monte Carlo, where she remained as ballerina until the end of the 1942 season.

Thereafter, Toumanova became internationally famous as a guest artist with numerous ballet companies in North and South America and in Europe. Among others, she danced with Ballet Theatre (1944–1945), in New York; with the San Francisco Ballet (1948); with the Paris Opera Ballet (1947, 1950, 1959); with Le Grand Ballet du Marquis de Cuevas (1949); with La Scala Ballet (1951, 1952, 1956), in Milan; and with London's Festival Ballet (1952, 1954–1955). In 1947, at the Paris Opera, she created the spectacular adagio role of the ballerina in the second movement of Balanchine's *Le Palais de Cristal* (later called *Symphony in C*). From 1959 onward she made frequent appearances in concert performances, often with her partner Vladimir Oukhtomsky. Acclaimed for her beauty and her acting skills as well as her dancing, Toumanova also appeared in numerous films: *Days of Glory* (1944, the producer of which, Casey Robinson, she married that year), *Tonight We Sing* (1953), *Deep in My Heart* (1954), *Invitation to the Dance* (directed by Gene Kelly; 1956), *Torn Curtain* (1966), and *The Private Life of Sherlock Holmes* (1970) as well as *Spanish Fiesta* (1941), the film of Massine's *Capriccio Espagnol.*

Toumanova's beauty and virtuosity as a ballerina were coupled with great versatility. Although her popular image was as a tragic or romantic dancer in the grand manner, she danced comedy roles with great success. Among her finest creations were the Girl in Balanchine's *Cotillon* (1932), the Beloved in Massine's *Symphonie Fantastique* (1936), and Potiphar's Wife in Margarete Wallmann's production of *Legend of Joseph* (1951), at La Scala in Milan. One of her greatest triumphs was the title role of *Phèdre,* staged at the Paris Opera in 1950 by Serge Lifar and Jean Cocteau to a score by Georges Auric. In addition to her Giselle, Toumanova was widely recognized as one of the foremost interpreters of Odette-Odile in *Swan Lake* and of the Miller's Wife in Massine's *Le Tricorne.*

BIBLIOGRAPHY

Anastos, Peter. "A Conversation with Tamara Toumanova." *Ballet Review* 11 (Winter 1984): 33–57.

Anderson, Jack. *The One and Only: The Ballet Russe de Monte Carlo.* New York, 1981.

Finch, Tamara. "The First Baby Ballerinas." *The Dancing Times* (August 1985): 952–954.

García-Márquez, Vicente. *The Ballets Russes: Colonel de Basil's Ballets Russes de Monte Carlo, 1932–1952.* New York, 1990.

García-Márquez, Vicente. *Massine: A Biography.* New York, 1995.

Healy, Katherine. "The Baby Ballerina on Trial." *Dance Now* 2 (Summer 1993): 19–27.

"An Informal Interview with Tamara Toumanova" (parts 1–2). *Dance Digest* (March–April 1957).

Lesser, Wendy. "Tamara Toumanova: Portrait of a Ballerina." *Dance Ink* (Fall 1994): 4–5.

Mason, Francis. "Tamara Toumanova (1916–1996)." *Ballet Review* 24.3 (Fall 1996): 35–62.

Sorley Walker, Kathrine. *De Basil's Ballets Russes.* New York, 1983.

Swisher, Viola Helgi. "Tamara Toumanova." *Dance Magazine* (September 1970): 46–63.

Tracy, Robert, and Sharon Delano. *Balanchine's Ballerinas: Conversations with the Muses.* New York, 1983.

KATHRINE SORLEY WALKER

TOURS EN L'AIR. *See* Ballet Technique, *article on* Turning Movements.

TOVIL. In Sri Lanka, one of the most dramatic forms of dance occurs in exorcist healing rituals variously called *tovil, thovil, toile, yakuma, yakun-natima,* and *yakun-natanava.* The *tovil* is part of the folk tradition of Sinhala-speaking Buddhists, and though not officially a part of Buddhism has been greatly influenced by it.

Techniques of *tovil* singing and dancing are handed down from teacher to pupil and from father to son (women do not perform); these traditions are said to be two thousand years old. Influences that are also identifiable come from South India, Malaysia, and Europe (the Portuguese established colonies on the island of Ceylon [now Sri Lanka] in 1505).

The *tovil* is performed by exorcists, combatting diseases believed to be caused by demons and ghosts. A temporary arena symbolizing the forest, a favorite haunting place for demons, is prepared on level ground near the patient's house, with a canopy, shrines, and trays for spirit offerings decorated with leaves, strips of banana stem, and coconut fronds. A pallet for the patient is set at one end of the arena. Relatives and friends gather around to offer their sympathies to the patient and to enjoy the performance, which runs from dusk to dawn.

The senior exorcist is usually accompanied by several younger men, who do most of the singing and dancing, and by one or two drummers. The dancers wear costumes and facial makeup; they frequently hold tufts of young coconut leaves or burning torches soaked in coconut oil. Smoke and the smell of incense fill the air.

The dancing begins slowly and grows progressively more energetic, sometimes led by the beat of the drums and sometimes in counterpoint to it. Singing, the chanting of spells and charms, and presentations to gods and demons are interlaced with vigorous dancing and loud drumming. The atmosphere is informal, with people coming and going, visiting and sleeping, eating and playing cards; yet excitement and tension build as the ceremony progresses to a dramatic conclusion. The patient may become possessed by a demon and dance to the rhythm of the drums. The patient must be settled, the gods appeased, and the demons conjured, all before sunrise, if a cure is to be achieved. The conclusion to the ceremony is a series of comic masked dances designed to depict and to placate a particularly nasty set of disease-causing demons.

TOVIL. The exorcist-dancer Samapala, performing the *pandam paliya* (torch ritual). (Photograph from the archives of The Asia Society, New York.)

The *tovil* drum, the principal musical instrument, is cylindrical, about one foot in diameter and three feet long; it is fitted with leather and strung together with hide, which can be tightened or loosened to vary the sound. A reed flute, bells, and jingles tied to the arms and ankles complete the dancer's equipment.

The *tovil* is a multipurpose performance: a socially integrative and entertaining public gathering of friends and relatives, a ritual dramatization of illness, a cathartic and therapeutic encounter for the patient, and a theological discourse. As monstrous as the demons may appear, they can be combated and subjugated if the proper procedures are followed, and so, by analogy, can other misfortunes of daily life.

Tovil is today thought to be a dying art, gradually being replaced by Buddhist pietism, Western medicine, and faith-healing cults. The drums can still be heard occasionally in rural areas, however, and—as one of the ironies of the modern world—*tovil* may be undergoing a modest revival as a form of tourist entertainment in urban areas.

[*For articles on other dance traditions in Sri Lanka, see also* Kandyan Dance; Kandy Perahera; Kohomba Kan Kariya; *and* Ves Dance. *For related discussion, see* Costume in Asian Traditions *and* Mask and Makeup, *article on* Asian Traditions.]

BIBLIOGRAPHY

Ames, M. M. "Tovil: Exorcism by White Magic." *Natural History* 87.1 (1978): 42–49.

Ames, M. M. "Tovil: The Ritual Chanting, Dance, and Drumming of Exorcism in Sri Lanka." *International Journal of Asian Studies* 2.2 (1982).

Gunawardana, A. J. *Theatre in Sri Lanka.* Colombo, 1976.

Loviconi, Alain. *Masques et exorcismes de Ceylan.* Paris, 1981.

Obeyesekere, Gananath. "The Ritual Drama of the Sanni Demons: Collective Representations of Disease in Ceylon." *Comparative Studies in Society and History* 11.2 (1969): 174–216.

Pertold, Otaker. *Ceremonial Dances of the Sinhalese* (1930). Colombo, 1973.

Seneviratna, Anuradha. *Traditional Dance of Sri Lanka.* Colombo, 1984.

FILM. Yvonne Hannemann, *The Work of Gomis* (Oakland, Calif.: Serious Business Co.).

ARCHIVES. The following museums contain major collections of Sri Lankan dance masks: American Museum of Natural History, New York; Canadian Museum of Civilization, Hull, Quebec; Chicago Field Museum; Ethnographic Museum, Stockholm; Hamburgisches Museum für Volkerkunde, Hamburg; Horniman Museum, London; Museum für Volkerkunde, Berlin; Museum für Volkerkunde, Leipzig; Museum of Anthropology, Vancouver, B.C.; Museum of Mankind, London; National Museum, Colombo; Science Museum, London; Smithsonian Institution, Washington, D.C.; Ubersee Museum, Bremen.

M. M. AMES

TRADITIONAL DANCE. *See* European Traditional Dance; Folk Dance History. *See also* Methodologies in the Study of Dance, *article on* Ethnography; *and the folk and traditional dance articles within individual country entries.*

TRANCE DANCE. An altered (or alternate) state of consciousness (ASC) is frequently associated with dance, particularly in the context of religious rituals. The result is often called *trance dance.* Gregory Bateson (1975) writes, "The use of dance as an entry into ecstasy and an egoalien world is ancient and perhaps worldwide." Adrienne Kaeppler (1978) describes the aesthetic experience connected with dance as "a heightened state of experience [that] may be related to trance." "Ecstasy" and "trance" as used here refer to forms of ASC.

An ASC is characterized as a deviation from the ordinary states in any or all aspects of mental functioning; it may involve changes in sensations and perceptions, including perceptions of time and space, or modifications of thought processes, memory, and awareness of self and others. Arnold Ludwig (1966) notes changes in meaning or significance, a sense of the ineffable, feelings of rejuvenation, and hypersuggestibility.

ASCs have been classified by different criteria, such as the manner of induction, the sociocultural context, or the categories used in native explanatory systems. Ludwig, who groups ASCs by the means used to produce them, distinguishes between states induced by altered levels of either internal or external stimuli and those induced by somatopsychological factors. The latter include drugs, physical disease (such as fever), and mental illness (such as hallucinatory or delusional states of psychosis).

The states treated here, even those that may be considered pathological in nature, are culturally interpreted, patterned, and controlled. They may be grouped by sociocultural context as either sacred or profane. In the sacred sense, trance dances are most frequently found in connection with either worship or curing; in secular contexts, they are usually forms of entertainment. Sacred ritual, however, often evolves into entertainment, and often the line between the two cannot be clearly drawn.

When ASC is linked to dance, it is usually also related to music. Gilbert Rouget (1985) established a music-based classification. More restricted than Ludwig's, it deals primarily with intentionally produced states. Rouget distinguishes between two states, ecstasy and trance. Ecstasy is characterized by immobility, silence, solitude, sensory deprivation, absence of seizures, heightened memory, and hallucination. Ecstatic states result from various types of meditation and are experienced by mystics in certain religions. Ecstasy thus defined is not included in this discussion.

In contrast to ecstasy, Rouget defines trance as typically involving movement, noise, sensory overstimulation, seizures, amnesia, and the absence of hallucination. Possession trance and shamanistic trance are the two principal subtypes, and each relates distinctively with the invisible world. In possession trance, spirits are believed to visit humans, acting through the bodies of possession trancers. In shamanistic trance, the shaman leaves the body to encounter various spiritual forces or beings. Because the shaman typically brings back messages from these spirit journeys, the absence of hallucination and memory is a questionable criterion for this classification. Rouget also finds a difference between the use of music in the two trance forms: the shaman is his own musician, usually singing and drumming, whereas the music for possession trance is provided by others.

Rouget's classification largely parallels one by Bourguignon (1973) based on native categories. She distinguishes between those states interpreted by participants as due to possession by spirits and those not so interpreted. Rouget's "ecstasy" and "shamanistic trance" belong to this second category, as do many nonintentional states, whether they are religious or secular. Bourguignon's classification depends not on features visible to or measurable by an observer, but on the explanation of the states by the cultural group in which they occur.

Possession trance in this classification is not simply an impersonation of other beings by a human actor but rather is a behavior that is culturally defined as being caused by the actual presence of these beings in the actor. Such a trance, which is frequently followed by amnesia, may include activities uncharacteristic of the individual: transsexual behaviors, eating foods considered repulsive, or performing spectacular feats. Such activities provide evidence to trancers of the presence of other beings in their own bodies. As such, possession trance is quite distinct experientially and cognitively from other forms of impersonation, such as conscious imitation or impersonation in a theatrical performance or a masking ritual. A mask may simply hide the identity of the actor or serve as an aid to imitation; if a spirit is believed to be present, it is generally thought to reside in the mask, not in the impersonator's body as in possession trance. Masked actors may experience an ASC, but this phenomenon has not been thoroughly investigated.

An ASC may be voluntary or involuntary. The demonic possessions recorded in the European and Euro-American Christian and Jewish traditions are typically, in their first manifestations, involuntary. Attempts at exorcism generally involve inducing an ASC (calling the spirits to be expelled). Such possessions—which are negative, undesired states, whether spontaneous or voluntary—do not involve music or dance. Apparent exceptions are the dancing manias of the late Middle Ages in Germany and the Low Countries and twentieth-century tarantism of southern Italy. In these cases, the sound of music was said to cause uncontrollable dancing, but music and dance were also used to cure the possessed.

Possession trance rituals occur in all parts of the world, all periods of history, and societies of various degrees of complexity and modernization. They are widespread in Africa—examples include Hausa *bori; zār* in Ethiopia, Somalia, Sudan, and Egypt; and *orisha* rituals among the Yoruba of Nigeria, among many others. African rituals were brought to the Americas with the slave trade and now appear in newer forms such as Santería in Cuba and Florida, Vodun *(vodoun)* in Haiti and New York, Shango in Trinidad and in a great variety of Afro-Brazilian religions, such as Candomblé, Macumba, Umbanda, Xângo, and others. Throughout Southeast Asia, possession trance is present in Bali, Malaysia, Thailand, Myanmar (formerly Burma), Vietnam, Cambodia and Laos, as well as in Sri Lanka. Such practices are known from European antiquity—for example, in the Dionysian cults of Greece. They also occur in movements of radical religious innovation, such as the eighteenth-century Shakers in England and America, and in nativistic movements, such as the Ghost Dance of the Plains Indians in the late nineteenth century. [*See* Ghost Dance.] Nonpossession trance is characteristic of Native American societies. It is often linked to hunting and gathering societies, while possession trance is typical of agricultural and pastoral groups.

Shamanism is or was widespread in northern Europe and Asia and among the native peoples of the Americas, Australia, and New Guinea. In Korea and Nepal, for example, some ritual practices combine features of both shamanistic and possession trance. Nepalese shamans experience possession trance early in their spiritual development; after additional levels of initiation, they engage in spirit voyages as part of their healing rituals.

Dance and ASCs typically occur in the larger context of rituals that may include sacrifice, feasting, curing, divining, praying, preaching, dramatic performances, spectacular acts (including proofs of invulnerability), acrobatics, and sleight-of-hand. They thus constitute a narrow range of activities within a larger field.

The relationship between dance and ASC is complex and variable. Adrienne Kaeppler (1978) notes that "trance and other altered states of consciousness are often associated with structured movement systems, yet they usually are not dance." She asks whether dance is created only when the participants themselves consider the movements to belong to a stylized category that corresponds to the Western concept of dance. Judith Lynne Hanna (1979) introduces a related problem by describing dance as involving the "manipulation of ordinary motor activities within an aesthetic domain." Although some structured movements occur frequently in conjunction with ASCs, they may not be defined by the participating group as dance or as occurring in an aesthetic domain.

Jeannette Henney (1973) has described possession trance in a fundamentalist Christian church on the Caribbean island of Saint Vincent, in which worshipers seek to experience the presence of the Holy Spirit during certain rituals. At the incipient stage of possession trance, individuals exhibit random behavior, such as bending at the waist or flexing the knees. At the second stage, each person repeats his or her own action pattern in unison with the movement and breathing of others. Although Henney writes that "people move as if in a dance line," depicts a "choral dance aspect of the possession trance phenomenon," and elsewhere refers to the patterns of movement as "aesthetically pleasing," neither she nor the participants appear to consider possession trance behavior as a form of dance. Nonetheless, it incorporates both ASC and a structured movement system.

Central to the experience reported by these Saint Vincent possession trancers is the sense of "being shaken," which starts as a "trembling within." The tremor is visible to the observer. Trembling as a feature of ASCs, at significant stages or throughout the experience, has been reported in many parts of the world.

Describing the ceremonial dances of the Kwakiutl of British Columbia, Franz Boas (1972) notes the "quivering of hands as well as the entire body." He remarks that "all these vibrations require a definite ecstatic quality in order to be executed." The participants recognize that the vibrations result involuntarily from a certain level of excitement that is recognized and named as an aspect of the dances.

Among the Kwakiutl, quivering is a patterned part of the dance. Elsewhere it is a sign that an ASC has been achieved, but it is not part of any choreography. Quivering can be seen vividly in a film by Jean Rouch, *Les maîtres fous,* which records possession trance rituals of the Haouka cult in Accra, Ghana. Here the only element resembling dance consists of a group of participants walking around in a circle to the sound of a violin. Those about to go into trance drop out of the circle. When the ASC begins, the camera clearly shows a series of small tremors, beginning in the feet and fingers of a seated individual, rising through the legs and arms to the trunk and the head. The tremor is typical and expected, but neither rhythmical nor a dance pattern. It does modify the behavior of the possession trancers while the ASC lasts: ordinary motor behavior, such as walking, becomes extraordinary, modified by the tremor and by a certain staccato quality that reveals a substantial effort to maintain control.

Tremor may also be used as an intentional means to induce trance. Bateson describes how little girls in Bali are put into trance in order to dance as if possessed by *dedari* ("angels"). Puppets, representing the angels, are made to dance by involuntary twitching (clonus) in the arms of the two men who support them suspended on a string between two bamboo poles. Grasping one of the poles, a girl is shaken violently by the twitching of the men's arms. With the pole, she beats out a few bars of the song being sung, falls back in a trance, is dressed for her role, and then dances in trance. She has been entered by the spirit of the angels, the state being induced through the pole by a form of contagion. An illustration (Bateson, 1975, plate 18) shows several Balinese girls being put into trance simultaneously. Here, shaking, brought about externally and mechanically, is preliminary to the trance. Child possession trancers are rare in any society. The Balinese girls dance with great balance and grace, often standing on the shoulders of men.

As they relate to ASCs, shaking and tremors may also occur outside the context of dance, as in the seated drumming of Nepali shamans. Larry Peters (1981) describes how his own conscious shaking developed into an automatic process, so that "after a few moments my whole body began to shake and I bounced all over the room."

Another frequent and characteristic motor pattern associated with ASCs is motion of the head. Eric Dodds (1951) notes that maenads, ancient Greek possession trancers, are often depicted in Greek art with tossed-back heads and hair swinging loose. Similar trance behavior is observed in ritual states in many parts of the world (for example, in Balinese *keris* dancers) as well as in nineteenth-century French clinical observations of hysterics.

Three types of relations between dance and ASC can be distinguished—dance as an expression of an ASC, as a means of producing an ASC, and as a means of controlling an ASC. Such distinctions are useful for ordering available information, although some categories inevitably overlap.

Dance as expression of an ASC occurs in two subforms, spontaneous trance dancing and intentionally induced ASC. In the first, the ASC is accompanied by extraordinary motion patterns such as whirling, hopping, jumping, trembling, twitching, staccato motions, convulsive movements, crawling, head-tossing, and grimacing. The interpretation of such behavior depends on the cultural context. Does it appear to be uncontrolled? Does it deviate significantly from behavior patterns deemed appropriate for the occasion? Are uncontrolled deviations interpreted as spirit interventions? Do they occur in the presence of music? If so, they may be considered dance of either human or supernatural origin. Spirit entities reveal themselves by the dancer's behavior, which mimes spirit characteristics.

The actions of Saint Vincent possession trancers include singing and clapping, and the extraordinary motion patterns are said to be caused by the presence of the Holy Spirit in the participants. In medieval dancing manias and southern Italian Tarantism, dance is the irresistible response to music. Included in Tarantism, as Michell and André Martin (1975) observe, was imitation of the behavior of the tarantula, whose bite was believed to cause the condition. [*See* Tarantella.]

In an example of an ASC resulting from intentional induction, Balinese girl-trancers express ASCs as complex acrobatic dancing after an initial seizure revealed by a fall. Bourguignon (1965) describes the hopping and whirling that result from the hypnotic induction of a Haitian possession trancer. Barbara Wright (1980) notes that in the *main petri* healing rituals of Kelantan, Malaysia, the onset of possession trance is signaled by dancing. At different points in the rituals the male healer or the female patient dance in trance.

In many possession trance rituals, the behavior of the dancers reveals the characteristics and identity of the individual spirit entities who are impersonated. In Greece, especially Macedonia, firewalking is practiced annually in honor of Saint Constantine and Saint Helen by dancers in trance who believe they are under the saints' control and protection. Firewalking occurs in many parts of the world and in different systems of belief. Like other spectacular trance activities, such as balancing on blades or stabbing oneself without experiencing harm, it involves both skill and fearlessness. [*See* Anastenáridēs.]

Michael Lambeck (1981) describes a possession trance ritual in the Comoro Islands. Those who are possessed dance in the fashion characteristic of a particular group of spirits, yet each adds personal touches as well:

> They moved in short steps or hops, a kind of light bounce, as if they were not touching the ground. Each dancer faced in one direction, moving two or three steps to the right, then rotating the upper part of the body, went two or three steps to the left, rotated again and turned to the right, so that the eventual path was a series of zigzags. (Lambeck, 1981)

This ritual focuses on healing, but at the end of a long night of dance, sacrifice, and personal consultation, it ends in lively entertainment.

Dance may be used formally to train dancers to enter an ASC, as is done by the Mevlevi dervishes of Konya, Turkey, who induce an ASC by means of a vigorous whirling dance. Esther Pressel (1974) observed special training sessions for novices in the Umbanda cult of São Paulo, Brazil. Among the dance-related techniques used are several leading to disturbances of balance and a loosening of contact with the environment, by spinning or rocking on the heels, followed by head- and chest-jerking movements that signal possession. Dancers also learn the special characteristics of each class of spirits, such as the stooped postures of old black spirits *(prêtos velhos),* or the upright, virile carriage of Indians *(caboclos).*

In ceremonial settings, induction of possession trance by a spinning dance is usually accompanied by polyrhythmic drumming, singing, and handclapping. Besides affecting balance and contact with the environment, vigorous dancing may also cause hyperventilation and euphoria.

Self-torture to induce visionary trance is rare in dance, with the important exception of the Sun Dance of the Great Plains, in which male supplicants for power sometimes danced while attached to a central pole by thongs passed through the skin of the breast or back until the skin broke. Attempts have recently been made to revive this practice, which was prohibited by the U.S. government at the beginning of the twentieth century.

The imposition of rhythm and structure on involuntary movement exercises an important control function, so that individual erratic behavior becomes structured and responsive to external cues. This control may be achieved through collective behavior, as in Saint Vincent, or through the use of music and ritualization, as in Tarantism.

Trance dance in some cultures is used as therapy. In the Brazilian Umbanda cult, possession trancers are mediums who deal with the afflictions of others. Many, however, join the cult to mitigate their own problems, and one of the symptoms of undeveloped mediumship is a spontaneous, uncontrolled ASC. Learning trance dancing in a controlled ritual environment offers a way to transform an involuntary state into a controlled, voluntary one. David Akstein (1974), a Brazilian psychiatrist influenced by Umbanda, reports on a method called terpsychore-trance therapy, which applies trance dance techniques to secular psychotherapy.

Trance dance also functions as entertainment in both traditional and modern contexts. Most possession trance rituals, in which diverse characters are acted out, are likely to include amusing or trickster personages. For observers, possession trance rituals often serve as entertainment. In Java and Bali, performances by folk trancers who act out various animal-spirit roles are popular. Balinese traditional kris trance rituals are now sometimes performed for tourists, as are staged ceremonies of Haitain Vodun. Firewalking is frequently performed for entertainment and, in the United States, as a sport as well as a spiritual exercise in the context of New Age religions, as described by Danforth.

An ASC may occur in the context of secular dancing, such as rock dancing, with loud and rhythmic music and large crowds in prolonged contact, to which young people come with high anticipation. In such cases, dance appears to be secondary to other factors in inducing the ASC.

[*For further discussion of related issues, see* Brazil, *article on* Ritual and Popular Dance; Shamanism; Vodun; *and* Zār.]

BIBLIOGRAPHY

Akstein, David. "Psychosocial Perspectives on the Application of Terpsychoretrancetherapy." *Psychopathologie Africaine* 10 (1974).

Bateson, Gregory. "Some Components of Socialization for Trance." *Ethos* 3 (Summer 1975).

Boas, Franz. "Dance and Music in the Life of the Northwest Coast Indians of North America (Kwakiutl)." In *The Function of Dance in Human Society,* edited by Franziska Boas. 2d ed. Brooklyn, 1972.

Bourguignon, Erika. "The Self, the Behavioral Environment, and the Theory of Spirit Possession." In *Context and Meaning in Cultural Anthropology,* edited by Melford E. Spiro. New York, 1965.

Bourguignon, Erika. Introduction to *Religion, Altered States of Consciousness, and Social Change,* edited by Erika Bourguignon. Columbus, Ohio, 1973.

de Martino, Ernesto. *La terra del rimorso.* Milan, 1961.

Dodds, E. R. *The Greeks and the Irrational.* Berkeley, 1951.

Hanna, Judith Lynne. *To Dance Is Human.* Austin, 1979.

Hecker, J. F. C. *The Dancing Mania of the Middle Ages* (1837). Translated by B. G. Babington. New York, 1970.

Henney, Jeannette H. "The Shakers of St. Vincent: A Stable Religion." In *Religion, Altered States of Consciousness, and Social Change,* edited by Erika Bourguignon. Columbus, Ohio, 1973.

Kaeppler, Adrienne L. "Dance in Anthropological Perspective." *Annual Review of Anthropology* 7 (1978).

Lambeck, Michael. *Human Spirits: A Cultural Account of Trance in Mayotte.* Cambridge, 1981.

Ludwig, Arnold M. "Altered States of Consciousness." *Archives of General Psychiatry* 15 (1966).

Martin, Michelle, and André Martin. *Les noires vallées du repentir.* Paris, 1975.

Peters, Larry. *Ecstasy and Healing in Nepal.* Malibu, 1981.

Pressel, Esther. "Umbanda Trance and Possession in São Paulo, Brazil." In *Trance, Healing, and Hallucination,* by Felicitas D. Goodman et al. New York, 1974.

Rouget, Gilbert. *Music and Trance.* Chicago, 1985.

Wright, Barbara S. "Dance Is the Cure: The Arts as Metaphor for Healing in Kelantanese Malay Spirit Exorcisms." *Dance Research Journal* 12 (Spring-Summer 1980): 3–10.

FILMS. Maya Deren, *Divine Horsemen: The Living Gods of Haiti* (1947–1952). Gregory Bateson and Margaret Mead, *Trance and Dance in Bali* (1951). Jean Rouch, *Les maîtres fous* (1954). John K. Marshall, *N/um T'chai* (1957). Peter Adair, *The Holy Ghost People* (1967). P. C. Haramis and K. Kakouri, *The Anastenaria* (1969). Karen Kramer, *The Jolo Serpent Handlers* (n.d.). Karen Kramer, *To Serve the Gods* (n.d.). *Sucking Doctor* (n.d.).

ERIKA BOURGUIGNON

TRAVESTY originally signified a male playing a female role *(en travesti).* This Western tradition of female impersonation originated in ancient Greece, where women were excluded from the stage and male actors and the chorus made use of masks and female costumes to portray women. The early Christian church perpetuated and dogmatized the prohibition of women onstage while, despite antitheatrical polemics, incorporating dramatic forms in its liturgy—mimetic processions, morality plays, and the like. Priests used music, dance, mime, costume, masks, and eventually elaborate scenic effects to vivify biblical history and to celebrate feast days within the cathedral.

Women played no part in the services or offices of the church, so the acting was done by clerics and choir boys; when such presentations were expanded to take place in the open air, away from church ritual, religious content and custom ensured the continuation of an all-male tradition. Yet records show that women occasionally took part. In doing so they were caught in a stigmatic double bind: considered unworthy of the somewhat priestly function of impersonating biblical characters, at the same time they were considered in jeopardy by association with the so-called unchaste and immodest practices of the theater. Because the idea was repugnant (running counter to anything that ordinary Christian folk felt about women) and because actors had no social standing outside the arena in which they played, women who joined them were regarded as disreputable. Until the late seventeenth century in Europe, it seemed quite natural and acceptable for men to play female parts.

In Shakespeare's time (1564–1616), boys were trained in the techniques of female impersonation. In Renaissance court spectacles, masks permitted young men to convincingly portray women in danced *entrées* and tableaux. In these private entertainments, women performed alongside men as well as with men *en travesti,* avoiding only the comic or grotesque roles that were generally taken by professional male performers. Men danced female roles without the embarrassment of any sexual ambiguity or social stigma as a matter of theatrical convention that was disassociated from private conduct.

The English Puritans of the seventeenth century became responsible for the demise of boy actors *en travesti* and the gradual substitution of women playing female roles throughout most of Europe. They based their attack on the theater, and on female impersonation in particular, on the Bible: "The woman shall not wear that which pertaineth unto a man, neither shall a man put on a woman's garment; for all that do so are abomination unto the Lord thy God" (*Deut.* 22.5). English theaters were closed and all public playgoing and acting banned between 1642 and 1660, the period of the Commonwealth. This brief period of prohibition seems to have been sufficient to interrupt the tradition of female impersonation. After it for the first time actresses came into vogue—even playing boys' parts on occasion and to some degree avoiding the brunt of antitheatrical stigma. By the end of the seventeenth century, men *en travesti* ceased to perform on the refined, serious level that derived from the Elizabethan period and began to burlesque female characters. Very soon the unprecedented popularity of female ballet dancers (Marie Sallé, Marie Camargo, Marie-Madeleine Guimard, among them) further diminished the demand for men *en travesti.* The prohibition against actresses persisted in Italy, however, and male travesty remained a matter of papal preference there until the close of the eighteenth century.

The biblical proscription against cross-dressing was applied with full force to women and interpreted to mean that pants were an absolute masculine prerogative not to be imitated by women, even concealed under skirts as underclothing. The separation of a woman's legs by any form of clothing was thought to be obscene and unholy, and underdrawers were not accepted as a respectable and conventional necessity until the middle of the nineteenth century. However, from the beginning of the eighteenth century, dancers and acrobats wore precautionary drawers *(caleçon de précaution)* while performing. These were a feature of European theatrical life that contributed to the association between sexual depravity and performers in the public's imagination.

The slightly perverse eroticism of this concealed transvestism—especially stimulating because it was revealed only now and then—was the basis on which actresses and female dancers began to impersonate men on the stage toward the end of the eighteenth century. Wearing "false disguise" with no pretense at concealing their real sexual identity, they exploited the salacious attitude that men held toward women in any form of male garb. Their costumes were androgynous adaptations of historical male fashions, designed to emphasize female proportions and, in particular, to show the forbidden upper leg to advantage in tights.

For about thirty years (1780–1810), male and female dancers impersonating one another performed together, sharing the stage with dancers not *en travesti.* Gradually, however, through this same period female dancers began to develop the use of pointe work, and by the 1830s the Romantic period found its fullest expression in the *ballet blanc*—legions of white-clad sylphs floated in nocturnal light. Except for a few male dancers of extraordinary talent, women dominated the Romantic ballet; male dancers were relegated to the role of *porteur,* whose function was to make the ballerina appear weightless and effortless in her performance. Since supported adagio and lifts were such an essential factor in the choreographic illusion of weightlessness, male dancers, though somewhat ignored by audiences, remained essential to the *ballet blanc* and women *en travesti* appeared in numbers only after *ballet blanc* began to go out of fashion.

TRAVESTY. Janet Hiligsberg *en travesti* in the ballet *Le Jaloux Puni,* which premiered 1 June 1793 at the King's Theatre, London. This engraving is by Jean Condé after H. de Janvry. (Courtesy of Madison U. Sowell and Debra H. Sowell, Brigham Young University, Provo, Utah.)

In the meantime, actresses *en travesti* were by no means a novelty. In the 1817 London production of *Giovanni in London,* the actress-singer Madame Vestris played in doublet and hose, sporting a plumed hat and brandishing a riding crop with such success that she continued in similar roles for twenty years.

About 1860, when the public began to tire of the ballet, choreographers experimented freely with novelty, such as *danseuses de travesti.* Because two women could not execute the lifts that were possible with a male partner, pas de deux *en travesti* required a more even distribution of choreographic display. Ballet masters concentrated on the acrobatic possibilities of sustained pointe work, such as multiple pirouettes, extended balances, and hops on toe, new steps of tour de force that could be done in unison to display the rather full-blown charms of both dancers. Female ballet costumes became somewhat abbreviated and frankly erotic, and the style favored for travesty was a loosely adapted version of the already anachronistic *style troubadour* worn by male actors. This was a fanciful combination of medieval and Renaissance fashions—a tunic or a doublet and hose, padded, puffed, or slashed, with a plume-decorated beret. In adapting this costume to women, personal attraction played a more important part in the choice of design than did historical accuracy. Instead of any effort to simulate masculine proportions, waists were corseted, hips were padded, and everything possible was done to enhance the curvilinear proportions of the female anatomy.

The ballet spectacles that followed the Romantic period—those produced by Luigi Manzotti in Italy, those of the Paris Opera and London's Alhambra and Empire theaters, and *The Black Crook,* which toured the United States—all featured legions of *danseuses de travesti* in every conceivable adaptation of male dress. Because male ballet dancers were at the time practically unemployable, their training was neglected, and the antitheatrical prejudice against them became more firmly fixed in Western culture than at any previous time.

TRAVESTY. In this scene from a Royal Ballet production of *La Fille Mal Gardée,* Merle Park appears as Lise with Stanley Holden, *en travesti,* as Lise's mother, the Widow Simone. David Blair observes from the loft. (Photograph by Houston Rogers; used by permission of the Board of Trustees of the Theatre Museum, London.)

Fortunately, the ballet in Russia had taken its own course; the tradition of strong male dancing survived there, to be reintroduced throughout Europe and America in the early twentieth century by Michel Fokine, Vaslav Nijinsky, and Serge Diaghilev. After seeing Diaghilev's Ballets Russes, audiences were never again willing to accept the substitution of women in men's roles.

Travesty survived into the twentieth century as a comedic tradition in vaudeville, in music halls, in the principal boys and dame comedians of English pantomime, and in the female impersonators of drag shows. (The term *drag* originated in the 1800s, derived from the dragging trains of women's dresses.)

In contemporary ballet, travesty roles for women are rare, with the exception of those roles that call for a temporary disguise that is not intended to deceive the audience as to the performer's true identity. Freudian self-consciousness about sexuality seems to have diminished the possibility of suspended disbelief when it comes to travesty, male or female. Cross-dressing (transvestism) is now considered a more serious psychological aberration than in the past, and any form of sexual ambiguity on the stage is apt to provoke distaste, uneasy laughter, or lecherous sneers. The exception is male travesty, providing that it offers a comic or grotesque impersonation far enough removed from reality and broad enough in its techniques or portrayal.

Male travesty roles still have an important place in ballet repertories. In *La Fille Mal Gardée,* the part of the heroine's mother, a comic peasant farmer, is often taken by a man. The great Italian ballet master Enrico Cecchetti danced this role and originated that of the wicked fairy Carabosse in *The Sleeping Beauty.* In the Kingdom of Sweets scene in *The Nutcracker,* Mother Ginger, a towering figure played by a man in a massive farthingale, enters and releases a horde of small children from beneath her skirts. The Headmistress in David Lichine's *Graduation Ball* is an absurdly flirtatious spinster, always danced by a man, whose pratfalls and broadly burlesqued choreographic gaffs leave no doubt as to his real identity. In 1948 Frederick Ashton choreographed *Cinderella* to the music of Prokofiev for the Sadler's Wells Ballet, casting himself and Robert Helpmann as the Stepsisters. The hilariously subtle characterizations of these two expert mimes contributed substantially to the success of the ballet.

In 1974 Les Ballets Trockadero, a company of male

TRAVESTY. Olga Tchikaboumskaya of Les Ballets Trockadero de Monte Carlo, a company of male dancers who perform classical ballets *en travesti*, in Peter Anastos's parodic work *Yes, Virginia, Another Piano Ballet.* (Photograph © 1977 by Jack Vartoogian; used by permission.)

dancers *en travesti* performing abbreviated, comedic versions of the classics, attracted attention in New York City; within a few seasons it was successful internationally with both critics and dance audiences. Most of the dancers in the company were poorly equipped for the arduous ballerina roles on pointe that they danced, and few of them had physical characteristics that would make it possible to pass for women onstage should they have wished to. Their subtle comic mime and attention to balletic nuance achieved something unique in the history of travesty—sometimes they conveyed the essential artistry and beauty of the balletic tradition while sending it up as broad comedy in performances that were both poignant and hilarious.

BIBLIOGRAPHY

Baker, Roger. *Drag: A History of Female Impersonation on the Stage.* London, 1968.

Baker, Roger. *Drag: A History of Female Impersonation in the Performing Arts.* London and New York, 1994.

MALCOLM MCCORMICK

TREFILOVA, VERA (Vera Aleksandrovna Trefilova; born 29 September [8 October] 1875, died 11 July 1943 in Paris), Russian ballet dancer and teacher. Destined to become one of the great Maryinsky ballerinas of the first decade of the twentieth century, Vera Trefilova graduated from the Imperial Theater School in Saint Petersburg in 1894 and joined the corps de ballet at the Maryinsky Theater. She enjoyed her first success in the title role of *Graziella* in 1900, and after her promotion to soloist in 1901 she received important parts in *Le Corsaire, The Naïad and the Fisherman, Bluebeard, The Tulip of Haarlem,* and *Coppélia.* Classes with Enrico Cecchetti, Rosita Mauri, and Caterina Beretta strengthened her technique. Following triumphs in the roles of Aurora in *The Sleeping Beauty* (1904), Kitri in *Don Quixote* (1906), and Odette-Odile in *Swan Lake* (1906), she was promoted to the rank of ballerina. In 1910, Trefilova retired prematurely, perhaps driven away by the jealousy of Matilda Kshessinska, who would brook no rival, or perhaps dissatisfied by the innovations then being introduced by Michel Fokine and others. She returned to the stage of the Mikhailovsky Theater in 1915 as a dramatic actress.

Having emigrated after the Russian Revolution, Trefilova danced Aurora in Serge Diaghilev's production of *The Sleeping Princess* at London's Alhambra Theatre (1921/22) and Odette-Odile in his shortened version of *Swan Lake,* presented in Monte Carlo in 1924. Of her performance in *Aurora's Wedding* at the Paris Opera (1922), André Levinson wrote, "Her technique is absolute . . . the total expression of a harmonious being. In the adagio, the play of curves and verticals is of unequaled purity; her *developpé* is like an opening flower. She is a . . . dancing Stradivarius." Settling in Paris, she served as ballet mistress of the Théâtre du Châtelet and opened a studio where she taught such well-known dancers as Nina Vyroubova and Marina Svetlova. She married the ballet critic Valerian Svetlov, her third husband, in emigration.

BIBLIOGRAPHY

Haskell, Arnold L. *Vera Trefilova: A Study in Classicism.* London, 1928.

Ivchenko [Svetlov], Valerian. "The Recent Creations of Vera Trefilova." *The Dancing Times* (December 1928): 343–345; (January 1929): 517–522.

Krasovskaya, Vera. *Russkii baletnyi teatr nachala dvadtatogo veka,* vol. 2, *Tantsovshchiki.* Leningrad, 1972.

Levinson, André. *La danse au théâtre.* Paris, 1924.

Smakov, Gennady. *The Great Russian Dancers.* New York, 1984.

LYNN GARAFOLA

TREND. Choreography: Hanya Holm. Music: Wallingford Riegger. Scenery: Arch Lauterer. First performance: 1937, Vermont State Armory, Bennington, Hanya Holm Company. Principals: Eve Gentry, Louise Kloepper, Bernice van Gelder, Lucretia Wilson, Elizabeth Waters.

Trend, the signature work of Hanya Holm, was choreographed and first performed during the Bennington Summer School in 1937. A fifty-five-minute epic of heroic proportions, *Trend* used a large all-female group (because male dancers were not available) juxtaposed against a series of solos depicting a society being destroyed by false values. The multilevel, double stage set of ramps, steps, and platforms by Arch Lauterer was hailed by John Martin of the *New York Times* as "the first truly modern stage setting that the dance has seen."

Trend is divided into six major sections: "Mask Motions," "Episodes," "Cataclysms," "The Gates Are Desolate," "Resurgence," and "Assurance." The "Episodes" section was further subdivided into solo themes: "The Effete" (Louise Kloepper), "Lucre Lunacy" (Bernice van Gelder), "From Heaven Ltd." (Lucretia Wilson), "Lest We Remember" (Elizabeth Waters), and "He the Great" (Eve Gentry). According to John Martin, "The sections are independent though related, treated more as if they were several acts in a drama, steadily carrying forward the central theme to its resolution. . . . There is a superb organization of material and a masterly instinct for balancing the values of group movement."

Company member Eve Gentry recalls one section:

> An endless line of tall women in long dresses, shoulder to shoulder, moved with their backs to the audience. They slowly inched sidewards, subtly, almost imperceptibly, shifting weight from one foot to another, a curtain of movement. The whole atmosphere was permeated with a tense excitement and vibration. It grew in volume; it became a wave of people breathing together.

The original score for *Trend* was by Wallingford Riegger; the "Resurgence" section added "Ionization" by Edgard Varèse, and the music for "Assurance" was Varèse's "Octandre." The score makes much use of percussion instruments, a Holm trademark.

When *Trend* was transported from Bennington to the Mecca Auditorium (now City Center) in New York in December 1937, Holm closed off the orchestra seats so people could only sit in the mezzanine and balconies and look down on the full architectural design. The work has never been remounted owing to its cost and to Holm's desire to rechoreograph sections for men as well as women. It was never recorded and is documented only in photographs.

BIBLIOGRAPHY

Martin, John. Review. *New York Times* (2 January 1938).

Sorell, Walter. *Hanya Holm: The Biography of an Artist.* Middletown, Conn., 1969.

Tobias, Tobi. "Hanya Holm: A Young Octogenarian." *Dance News* (March 1979): 1.

INTERVIEWS. Eve Gentry, Louise Kloepper, and Bernice van Gelder (Peterson), by Theresa Bowers, Oral History Research Office, Columbia University.

VIDEOTAPE. Marilyn Cristofori, "Hanya: Portrait of a Dance Pioneer" (1984), Dance Collection, New York Public Library for the Performing Arts.

NANCY MASON HAUSER

TRICORNE, LE. Ballet in one act. Choreography: Léonide Massine. Music: Manuel de Falla. Libretto: Martinez Sierra. Scenery and costumes: Pablo Picasso. First performance: 22 July 1919, Alhambra Theatre, London, Ballets Russes de Serge Diaghilev. Principals: Léonide Massine (The Miller), Tamara Karsavina (The Miller's Wife), Leon Woizikowski (The Corregidor), Stanislas Idzikowski (The Dandy).

Le Tricorne (The Three-Cornered Hat) is a signature piece of Léonide Massine's career. The ballet was born from the collaboration of Massine, Pablo Picasso, and Manuel de Falla under the direct supervision of Serge Diaghilev.

While the Ballets Russes was immobilized in Spain during World War I, Diaghilev began sowing the seeds for a Spanish ballet. Massine was enraptured by Spanish flamenco dance and began intensive training in that style, while Diaghilev engaged the talents of Falla to compose an authentic Spanish score. As Falla integrated basic forms of Spanish music, Massine translated ethnic dance onto the ballet stage. The artistic exchange began in 1917, but progress on the ballet was halted until 1919. When the work resumed, Diaghilev employed Picasso to design the sets and costumes.

The ballet, set in a small, eighteenth-century Spanish village, centers around the flirtations between the Miller, his Wife, and the Corregidor, who wears a three-cornered hat emblematic of his position and social class. Picasso effectively captured the essence of the Spanish temperament in the drop cloth; black borders denoting Spanish dignity enclosed bold colors reflecting the gaiety of the people. The costumes were based on authentic eighteenth-century styles.

The dancing was lively, to an underlying *jota* rhythm. Massine's understanding of the use of groups on the stage and the coordination of their movements as a congruent whole was very evident. The crowds were necessary within the story to create atmosphere, but there was always a logical reason for the group to exit when a solo was to be performed. The Miller's Wife had a brilliant *fandango* solo heavily laced with traditional Spanish steps yet in keeping with the theatrical setting. The pas de deux between the Miller and his Wife was also a kind of *fandango*, but it had more classical steps in its teasing, flirtatious content. Finally, the Miller's solo was an explosive, fiery *farruca.* With rapid staccato footwork, great jumps, and *tours en l'air,* this solo, like the *fandango,* integrated authentic Spanish, classical, and theatrical dance.

Massine was highly acclaimed for the rhythmic nature and musicality of the choreography in *Le Tricorne.* The *demi-caractère* quality of the work created a new subgenre in ballet.

[*See also the entry on Massine.*]

BIBLIOGRAPHY

Balanchine, George, with Francis Mason. *Balanchine's Complete Stories of the Great Ballets.* Rev. and enl. ed. Garden City, N.Y., 1977.

Fusillo, Lisa A. "Léonide Massine: Choreographic Genius with a Collaborative Spirit." Ph.D. diss., Texas Woman's University, 1982.

García-Márquez, Vicente. *Massine: A Biography.* New York, 1995.

Massine, Léonide. *My Life in Ballet.* New York, 1968.

LISA A. FUSILLO

TRIPUDIUM (plural, *tripudiī*) is a Latin term important to the history of Christian liturgical dance, related to the intransitive verb *tripudiō, tripudiāre,* with an occasional variant, *tripodium,* found in written sources from c.200 BCE to 1600 CE.

Etymology and Usage. No single term adequately translates *tripudium;* in various contexts *tripudium* may mean (1) "dance," generally (and at times metaphorically, as in "dancing for joy"); (2) "rejoicing" or "jubilation" (du Cange); or (3) an auspicious omen in Roman augury rites, which overlaps in usage with the first two meanings from at least 100 to 15 BCE but is obsolete after c.400 to 600 CE. This favorable omen is also seen as *tripudium solistimum,* for example in Livy's reference to a rite in which "the sacred chickens ate so greedily that the grain dropped [Foster et al. has "danced"] on the ground."

Despite the word's syllabic composition (see below), no primary texts positively support the widely held notion of *tripudium* as a "three-step dance," or *Dreischritt* (Pauly, Sachs); or as having "return" or "recovery" motifs in its step formulation (Sachs, Adams); nor is there adequate justification for generalizing the rebounding movement qualities suggested both by the augury ritual and some other instances of the term to all interpretations of it (Backman); these are all contextual rather than connotational associations. Especially to be resisted is the attempt to define a reconstructible "*tripudium* step" with "three steps forward, one step back . . . done over thousands of years" (Adams), a description championed in the mid- to late 1900s as part of a larger effort to insinuate modern liturgical dance into contemporary Christian worship as the recovery of a lost traditional practice rather than as the revelatory *novum,* with historical precedents and precursors, which it more likely is (La Rue, 1995, 1996).

Classical writers, including Livy, Cicero, and Seneca used *tripudium* infrequently; however, both Livy and Cicero used the word in all three of its meanings throughout their oeuvres. It appears twice in the instructions to the *Arval Brethren Hymn* (see below), once in the Latin Vulgate Bible (*Esther* 8.32), and in the retrospective etymologiara of the fifth to seventh centuries by Festus and Isidore of Seville (Migne). Later it occurs in the lyrics to Christian hymns such as "Tripudians Martyr," a tenth-century hymn to Saint Martial of Limoges (Dreves), "Stella Splendens," from the thirteenth-century Spanish *Llibre Vermell* (Brainard), and others; in the title of Guglielmo Ebreo's 1463 treatise, *De practica seu arte tripudii,* and, most problematically for recent writers, in a series of references to the "hopping saints" or *springenden Heiligen* of Echternach, which Backman connects with a processional folk dance observed in the town around 1940.

Tripudium's derivations as well as its meanings are uncertain. It may have come from the Greek τρίποδον *(tripodon),* "to trot" (Pauly), or from τρίποδίος *(tripodios),* "a poetic line of three metrical feet." Cicero's derivation from *terripavium,* "to strike the ground" (*De divinatione,* 2.34.72), is considered contrived. Some scholars associate specific dance movements such as "three-step," "hop-dance," "line-" or "circle-dance," and "religious dance" with *tripudium.* While no primary source positively defines the word thus, the segments *tri-, tres-* ("three") and *-pud, -pes, -pedis* ("foot" or "feet" or, possibly, "steps") and the possible derivation from *tripodios* appear to many writers to suggest a step with a pattern of three footfalls, or three beats, or both. Evidence from the *Carmen Fratrem Arvale* (Arval Brethren Hymn), a cryptic inscription from Rome dated to 218 CE that appears to provide instructions for a danced hymn whose refrains repeat three times (Ernout), taken together with the *tripodios* definition, might support this view, but the hymn's meter does not allow us to make assumptions about any movement that may have accompanied it, as Sachs implies. It should also be noted that this cluster of references alluding to the Salii of the late Roman republic (in Livy and Seneca) and to the Arval Brethren deserves attention. Both involved a sacred priesthood of twelve members dedicated to the cult of Mars, whose ceremonies are described as including a processional *tripudium;* it is slightly possible that the Fratres Arvales represent a revival of an earlier priesthood, perhaps undertaken as an act of piety in the turbulent days of the late empire.

Leaping or hopping steps associated with *tripudium* might explain the augur's use of the term to describe bouncing grain (in the third definition above); they would also be consistent with such Indo-European roots as *trep-,* "trepidation," and *trem-,* "to tremble"; this etymology for *tripudium* would moreover contradict the syllabic division of the word often used to suggest "triple steps." The *tripodon* derivation seems more likely in this case; even Cicero's intent in providing an etymology through *terripavium* becomes plausible. An eleventh-century reference to the procession of Saint Willibrod also uses the term, as

Backman demonstrates, although his irregular treatment of *tripudium* throughout his work is probably one cause of confusion among contemporary liturgical writers on the subject.

The range of formal shapes and movement patterns associated with *tripudium* varies widely as well. Some *tripudia* are clearly processionals, either linear or in phalangeal array (close ranks); however, "line dance" is conjectural. Translating *tripudium* as "circle dance" is probably also too specific. In the qualified phrase *tripudium rotundum,* which appears in the rubrics of the fourteenth-century hymn "Stella Splendens," if *tripudium* means "circle dance," then *rotundum* is superfluous (or perhaps pleonastic). But cases where *tripudium* is best rendered simply "dance" (Ebreo's title, *De practica seu arte tripudii,* for one) make a translation with fewer formal movement implications more useful.

Many but not all *tripudia* have religious associations. These include Roman "armed or victory dances" (Livy, 21.42.3; 23.26.9; Aeppli; Brainard), "funeral dances" (Livy, 25.17.5), the honorific dances of an elect priesthood like the Salii, and the cosmic dance of Roman mythological figures, glorified Christian saints, and angels delighting in the joys of Creation, as related in *De nuptiis* (Miller) and "Tripudians Martyr." *Tripudii* in these contexts are spiritually or emotionally expressive dances, often but not exclusively of a communal nature. There are also no grounds for accepting Chailley's effort to locate celebrative dances called *tripudii* in any specific part of the pagan calendrical or Christian liturgical year, especially as opposed to those called *caroles,* which are known to have occurred throughout the year.

It is important to remember that *tripudium* may not always mean "dance," but may mean "rejoice," especially in religious sources, where figurative or symbolic language often occurs: a "dance of joy," for example, may be a metaphoric image for joy and not an actual dance at all. In the hymn cited above, for example, *tripudians* may as easily mean "rejoicing" as "dancing" martyr; and its presence in the lyrics in no way proves the hymn was ever danced, as Backman claims.

No one meaning can be imposed on every source in which *tripudium* occurs. Throughout its currency, the uses of *tripudium* range with the uses of dance itself; this alone favors a general over a specific meaning for the term. It seems wisest to leave the question open to further research and to urge a contextually sensitive, conservative approach to the sources themselves.

Historiography. As a historiographic case, the study of *tripudium* is also instructive. As Lawler notes, confusion about early terms takes a particular turn where an ephemeral, nonartifactual medium such as dance leaves only a few enigmatic clues behind. Paucity of information pressures the analyst to wrest as much meaning as possible from a given source; a scarcity of correctives leaves the field open to a variety of interpretations.

The clearest example of this attends the contemporary introduction of liturgical dance noted above. Danced exposition of the tenets of Christianity, regularly approved and encouraged by an ecclesial hierarchy responsible for planning services of worship, has appeared sporadically in the past (though the written record is probably biased in favor of upper-class ecclesiastical references during much of the period of *tripudium*'s usage, since most lettered historians were in the employ of the church, the courts, or both). Nor can liturgical dance be said to occupy a central place in the life of most congregations today.

Proponents of an epiphanic event like danced worship, which interrupts but does not rupture the fabric of traditional Christianity, have introduced it as a restoration, rather than a revelation, of a vital practice of faith to a church historically suspicious of enthusiastic liturgical innovation. This must be considered in terms of the philosophical and theological beliefs that prevailed during the period in question. Creedally, the church holds that the human spirit is incarnate—not incarcerate—in the human body. Yet the church has only rarely and ineffectually attempted to dispel the strong current of Gnostic antimaterialistic dualism riding along on the underbelly of popular theology. [*See* Christianity and Dance.]

In addition, the references to such a supposed tradition are both geographically and chronologically disparate, and the original compendium of these references (Fiske-Taylor, as cited or reprinted in Adams, and in Apostopoulos-Cappadona) requires intensive review. These sources—anecdotal references, hymn lyrics, misunderstood visual sources (the dancing angels in Fra Angelico's *Last Judgment,* for example, are probably heavenly courtiers, not exponents of liturgical practice), misinterpreted florilegaic articles on dance from late nineteenth-century liturgical dictionaries, and disconnected local dance and processional practices scattered about western Europe from the tenth to the eighteenth century—each require better analysis on their own terms before they can be described as fitting into the historical sequence of repeated events that the term *tradition* usually implies (the liturgical term *traditio* actually represents a much broader concept). As a dynamic ethical icon, modeling an active response to faith and a valuation of the physical body as a fit vessel for praise, danced prayer functions well within the range of self-understood Christian creedal affirmations emphasizing a holistic cosmology and anthropology.

Moreover, there is no need to overdetermine words such as *tripudium* or to overinterpret sources referring to religious dance simply to assuage the fears of those who are wary of the new. Developing a functional theology of applications for liturgical dance (Rock, 1978, 1988; La Rue 1995, 1996), educating congregations and dancers alike to the many ways beyond a fundamental gestural literalism in which dance can communicate meaning, and attending to areas of resonance within the broader understanding of *traditio* offers a more balanced approach. Careful attention to the quality of danced worship as well as to its proper function—of forwarding the intentions of the gathered assembly through prayerful submission to both the craft and the expressive potential of the work—is less disruptive to the fabric of dance history in general and the understanding of terms like *tripudium* in particular, is more respectful of the richer historical situation, and may best establish the place of liturgical dance.

BIBLIOGRAPHY

Adams, Doug. *Congregational Dancing in Christian Worship.* North Aurora, Ill., 1980.

Aeppli, Fritz. *Die wichtigsten Ausdrücke für das Tanzen in den romanischsen Sprachen.* Halle, 1925.

Apostopoulos-Capadona, Diane, and Doug Adams, eds. *Dance as Religious Studies.* San Francisco, 1992.

Backman, Eugène Louis. *Religious Dances in the Christian Church and in Popular Medicine.* Translated by E. Classen. London, 1952.

Brainard, Ingrid. "Dance: Middle Ages and Early Renaissance." In *The New Grove Dictionary of Music and Musicians.* London, 1980.

Chailley, Jacques. "La danse réligieuse au Moyen Âge." In *Arts libéraux et philosophie au Moyen Âge: Actes du quatrième congrès international de philosophie médiévale.* Montreal, 1969.

Cicero. *De divinatione.* Translated by William Armistead Falconer. Cambridge, Mass., 1979.

Dreves, Guido Maria, and Clemens Blume, eds. *Analecta Hymnica Medii Aevi.* Vol. 49, no. 372. Leipzig, 1922.

Du Cange, Charles Du Fresne. *Glossarium mediae et infimae latinitatis.* Paris, 1937.

Ernout, Alfred. *Recueil de textes latins archaïques.* Paris, 1973. See entry 146.

Fiske-Taylor, Margaret. *A Time to Dance.* North Aurora, Ill., 1976.

La Rue, Donna. "Tripudium: Its Uses and Meanings from 200 BCE to 1600 CE, or, More Than Just Another Pretty Word Study." *ARTS Journal* (September 1995).

La Rue, Donna. "Both a Performance and a Prayer: Towards an Aesthetic and Theology of Liturgical Dance." Unpublished seminar paper, January, 1996.

Lawler, Lillian. *The Dance in Ancient Greece.* Seattle, 1967.

Livy. *Ab urbe condita.* Translated by B. O. Foster et al. Cambridge, Mass., 1970.

Miller, James. *Measures of Wisdom: The Cosmic Dance in Classical and Christian Antiquity.* Buffalo, 1986.

Migne, J.-P. *Patrologiae cursus, series Latina.* "De Ecclesiasticus Officis Lib. I." Vol. 83, col. 775.

Pauly, August Friedrich von. *Real-Encyclopädie der klassischen Altertumswissenschaft.* Stuttgart, 1894.

Rock, Judith. *Theology in the Shape of Dance.* Austin, Tex., 1978.

Rock, Judith, and Norman Mealey. *Performer as Priest and Prophet.* San Francisco, 1988.

Sachs, Curt. *World History of the Dance.* Translated by Bessie Schönberg. New York, 1957.

Seneca. *Epistolae morales.* Translated by Richard M. Gummere. Cambridge, Mass., 1979.

DONNA LA RUE

TUDOR, ANTONY (William John Cook; born 4 April 1909 in London, died 19 April 1987 in New York City), British choreographer. Tudor created a new dance genre, the psychological ballet, in which the characters' inner states were externalized through movement. Though Tudor himself asserted that "principles from other choreographers did not actively or consciously affect my works," he carried to its ultimate conclusion Michel Fokine's "second principle," that dance movement and gesture should be expressive of the characters' thoughts and feelings. It is probable that he was also influenced by Sigmund Freud and Konstantin Stanislavsky.

As a child Tudor was captivated by dancers he saw in music halls and Christmas pantomimes, but he did not study dance seriously until he was about twenty. At that time he was working as a clerk in London's Smithfield meat market. After a few classes at adult education institutions, he presented himself to Marie Rambert, who took him on as a pupil.

In spite of his late start, Tudor quickly became proficient enough to pass the Cecchetti examination in 1929 and that of the Imperial Society of Teachers of Dancing a year later. He danced in the performances by Rambert's dancers at the Lyric Theater, Hammersmith, and at the Ballet Club, and at the beginning of the Ballet Club's second season he choreographed his first ballet, *Cross-Garter'd,* to music by Girolamo Frescobaldi (1583–1643), based on an episode from Shakespeare's *Twelfth Night.* Tudor himself danced the role of Malvolio.

Like Frederick Ashton, Tudor learned two important lessons in ballet making from working on the tiny stage of what came to be called the Mercury Theater: how to achieve his effects with the utmost economy of means and how to build the structure of a ballet on the basis of the chosen musical score. Tudor's approach was quite different from Ashton's; he was intellectual, whereas Ashton was intuitive. Ashton used a basically classic vocabulary with some jazz and Latin American elements, while Tudor incorporated natural movement and colloquial gesture, eventually finding his way to what is now recognized as a modern dance idiom. He briefly studied central European dance and saw performances by Mary Wigman, Harald Kreutzberg, and Les Ballets Jooss; at Rambert's studio he met Agnes de Mille and worked with her.

Tudor's second ballet, *Lysistrata, or The Strike of Wives* (March 1932), was also based on a literary source, Aristophanes' comedy. For this Tudor selected piano pieces by Sergei Prokofiev, which Rambert considered unsuitable, as did the composer when he saw the ballet. But again Tudor successfully conveyed the comedy of character through movement, and the ballet remained in the repertory of the Ballet Rambert until 1940.

Male dancers were in demand in the early days of British ballet. In January 1932 Tudor began dancing with

TUDOR. *The Descent of Hebe,* set to Ernest Bloch's Concerto Grosso no. 1 in B Minor, was created for the Ballet Club in 1935. In a 1940 performance by Ballet Rambert, Leo Kersley and Lisa Serova appeared in the roles of Mercury and Night, originally danced by Hugh Laing and Maude Lloyd. (Photograph by Cyril Arapoff; from the Dance Collection, New York Public Library for the Performing Arts.)

the Vic-Wells Ballet and also appeared in the Camargo Society's performances. He choreographed a ballet for the society, *Adam and Eve* (December 1932), to the music by Constant Lambert that Serge Diaghilev had used for Bronislava Nijinska's *Romeo and Juliet.* At Sadler's Wells Tudor was allowed to choreograph the ballet in *Faust* (1933), but its artistic director Ninette de Valois refused to let him choreograph for the ballet company proper, advising him to join the Ballets Russes du Colonel W. de Basil for a year or two to learn his craft by working with such esteemed choreographers as Michel Fokine and Léonide Massine. Tudor declined to take this advice, and it was not until Ashton succeeded de Valois as director more than thirty years later that Tudor was invited to choreograph for the company, which by then had become the Royal Ballet.

Tudor's next two ballets at the Ballet Club, although unsuccessful, were important because they marked the beginning of two important artistic and personal associations. In *Pavane pour une Infante Défunte* (1933), he worked for the first time with designer Hugh Stevenson, and in *Atalanta of the East* (May 1933), Hugh Laing danced for the first time.

It was in his next ballet that Tudor's genius began to manifest itself. This was *The Planets* (October 1934), to three movements from the orchestral suite of that name by Gustav Holst. Both the designs and the concept were by Stevenson, and each scene showed the influence of the planet on mortals born under it: Venus on a pair of lovers; Mars on a young man (Laing) whose conflict was as much within himself as with an external enemy; Neptune on a mystic who "longs to unit herself with the infinite." This last role was created by Kyra Nijinsky, Vaslav Nijinsky's daughter. The movement ranged from the lyricism of "Venus" through the pounding, percussive modern idiom of "Mars" to the austere, reductive tranquility of "Neptune."

Although Tudor was often emotionally remote and at times cruel in his comments, he began to collect around himself a group of dancers who were in all of his ballets and were deeply devoted to him: Laing, Maude Lloyd, and Peggy van Praagh. When Tudor found a flat with a studio large enough to rehearse in, the group worked long hours away from Rambert's watchful and jealous eye.

Tudor started dancing too late to become a virtuoso and probably had no ambitions in that direction, but he was an authoritative performer of character roles in his own and other choreographers' ballets and was also an excellent teacher. A trained musician, he chose unusual, often difficult scores for his ballets. His approach to the music was not analytical: he knew it thoroughly and choreographed in long phrases that went "through" the music. An exception to this practice was the final section of his next ballet, *The Descent of Hebe* (April 1935), to Ernest Bloch's Concerto Grosso no. 1, a choreographic fugue that exactly mirrored the musical one.

Rambert paid her choreographers one British pound per minute for a staged ballet, with no royalties, so Tudor augmented his income by choreographing elsewhere. In the summer of 1935 he arranged the ballets for Thomas Beecham's opera season at Covent Garden, and he also began to work in the commercial theater and in the earliest British Broadcasting Corporation (BBC) television transmissions. He did pioneering work in the new medium, such as the *Fugue for Four Cameras* with Maude Lloyd in 1937.

In January 1936 Tudor produced his first unquestionable masterpiece, *Jardin aux Lilas,* to music by Ernest Chausson (*Poème* for violin and orchestra). Again Stevenson not only designed the ballet but had much to do with its final form. The action devised by Stevenson and Tudor can be summarized in the descriptions of the four main characters: Caroline, the bride-to-be (Lloyd); Her Lover (Laing); The Man She Must Marry (Tudor); and An Episode in His Past (van Praagh). The various emotions flowing among these four people were expressed in dance movement and in small, subtle gestures. Supported adagio was used not for acrobatic effects but to heighten the drama of a moment—Caroline's lover steps in from the wings to stop her at the end of a solitary pirouette; the Other Woman throws herself headlong into the bridegroom's arms. The most audacious stroke occurs at the point of crisis, coinciding with the highest climax in the music. All the characters who have been seeking and avoiding each other in the moonlit garden, snatching moments together or being torn apart, suddenly coalesce in a frozen group, from which Caroline alone detaches herself, moving slowly in a circle as though in a trance, overcome by a despair she cannot outwardly express. As Lloyd has said, "she walks out of time." It was Tudor's boldest use so far of stasis as a positive choreographic element.

Tudor's last ballet for Rambert was *Dark Elegies* (February 1937), to Gustav Mahler's *Kindertotenlieder.* The choice of music was a daring one for the time. Tudor did not make the mistake of pantomiming the words: the ballet is an abstraction of grief, of mourning, and of eventual resignation. Nor did he attempt a slavish visualization of the music; more than ever the movement parted company with the music and went its own way, coming together with it at certain key points. The ballet's lineage may be traced back both to Nijinsky's *Le Sacre du Printemps* and to Nijinska's *Les Noces*. Like those works, it depicts a community confronted with a momentous event, in this case, the death of its children. The community enacts a ritual in which individuals emerge from the group only to be absorbed back again. Although the women were on pointe, the vocabulary is not that of the classic dance. The feet are usually in parallel, and the thrust of the movement is downward into the floor. Much of the movement was developed from folk dance or everyday gesture; for all intents and purposes, *Dark Elegies* is a modern dance work.

By this time Tudor was ready to strike out on his own, in part because Rambert was a difficult person to work with. In the summer of 1937, he and Agnes de Mille joined forces in a company called Dance Theatre, which gave a short season at the Playhouse in Oxford and then promptly folded. He took with him some of his favorite dancers (not including Lloyd), and some of his most important ballets, and he made one new one—*Gallant Assembly,* which the painter Lawrence Gowing described as "an inconsequent and pleasantly disreputable Rococo frolic."

During the following season Tudor worked in television to accumulate funds for a more permanent company of his own. As a curtain raiser to a production of Nikolai Gogol's play *Marriage,* Tudor choreographed the bitterly sardonic *The Judgment of Paris,* set in a sleazy French bordello, to a suite from Kurt Weill's *Dreigroschenoper;* de Mille was the voluptuous, vacuous Venus.

In December 1938 Tudor's new company, the London Ballet, opened after months of rehearsal in the new four-hundred-seat theater at Toynbee Hall, an adult education institution where Tudor had been lecturing on dance history. This time Lloyd was with him, as were Laing, van Praagh, and some new dancers. In addition to *Hebe, Jardin aux Lilas, Elegies,* and *The Planets* (with a new fourth scene, "Mercury"), the repertory included *Gallant Assembly* and *The Judgment of Paris* as well as two new ballets—*Soirée Musicale,* to music by Gioacchino Rossini as augmented by Benjamin Britten, a charming *divertisse-*

TUDOR. The four principal dancers in the original cast of *Jardin aux Lilas* (1936): Maude Lloyd (second from left) as Caroline, Hugh Laing as Her Lover, Antony Tudor as The Man She Must Marry, and Peggy van Praagh as An Episode in His Past. Scenery and costumes were designed by Hugh Stevenson. (Photograph from the Dance Collection, New York Public Library for the Performing Arts.)

TUDOR. *Dark Elegies,* set to Gustav Mahler's *Kindertotenlieder,* was first performed by Ballet Rambert at the Duchess Theatre in London in 1937. After immigrating to the United States, Tudor staged it for Ballet Theatre in 1940 and appeared with Nora Kaye in "Second Song." (Photograph by Carl Van Vechten; used by permission.)

ment, and *Gala Performance,* to music of Sergei Prokofiev. *Gala,* about the rivalry of three ballerinas from Moscow, Milan, and Paris, provided a witty commentary on the different styles of classic ballet that they exemplified.

The company's first season ran through April 1939, with weekly performances, and in the spring Tudor again choreographed the opera ballets at Covent Garden for his company (Margot Fonteyn was guest artist in *Aída*). He was already preparing new works for the following season, among them a ballet to Arnold Schoenberg's *Verklärte Nacht* (Transfigured Night), but the London Ballet did not present another season under his direction. Soon after the outbreak of war in Europe in the fall of 1939, Tudor, Laing, and Andrée Howard, another of Rambert's choreographers, sailed for New York to join the newly formed Ballet Theatre. Lloyd and van Praagh kept the London company going for a season or two; it was then reabsorbed into the Ballet Rambert.

Tudor immediately set to work rehearsing three of the most successful ballets he had made in London, *Jardin aux Lilas* (its title usually given in English as *Lilac Garden*), *The Judgment of Paris,* and *Dark Elegies,* all of which were given during the first two weeks of Ballet Theatre's inaugural season in January 1940 at the Center Theater. On opening night, 11 January 1940, Tudor danced a leading role in Eugene Loring's *The Great American Goof.*

The first new ballet that Tudor choreographed in the United States was a minor work, *Goya Pastoral,* given at the College of the City of New York's Lewisohn Stadium that summer. The work's primary *raison d'être* was to make use of some beautiful scenery and costumes that Nicholas de Molas had designed for an unsuccessful ballet, *Goyescas,* by José Fernandez, which had been on the same program with *Jardin Aux Lilas.* Tudor's ballet survived into the following season, when it too was called *Goyescas.*

No new ballet by Tudor was presented during Ballet Theatre's second season. *Gala Performance* was revived in February 1941. His first truly "American" ballet was made at the invitation of Lincoln Kirstein, for the American Ballet Caravan's goodwill tour of South America in the summer of 1941. *Time Table,* another minor work, set in a railroad station during World War I and danced to Aaron Copland's *Music for the Theatre.* It was shown at an open dress rehearsal in New York before the company left and was briefly revived in 1949 during the first season of New York City Ballet.

In the meantime Tudor had resumed work on his ballet to *Verklärte Nacht,* which finally reached the stage as *Pillar of Fire,* first performed at the Metropolitan Opera House on 8 April 1942 after being in rehearsal for more than a year. It immediately established Tudor as a choreographer of the first rank and Nora Kaye as the greatest dramatic ballerina of her time. Kaye had danced a small role and later that of Caroline in *Jardin aux Lilas* and the role of the Russian Ballerina in *Gala Performance.* Critic Walter Terry had described *Jardin* as "almost a psychological ballet"; *Pillar* went further, a danced case history of Hagar, whose repressed emotions and desires are made clear to the audience in her smallest gestures. Critical reception to Tudor's earlier ballets had been only moderately enthusiastic, but in the light of this new, great work, they were reassessed. Critic John Martin proclaimed Tudor to be "the most important figure in the contemporary ballet."

Certainly it was Tudor's ballets that gave artistic stature to Ballet Theatre, even after Sol Hurok took over management of the company in the 1941/42 season and, advertising it as "the greatest in Russian Ballet," started to bring in new and old ballets by Fokine, Massine, George Balanchine, Nijinska, and David Lichine and the ballerinas Alicia Markova and Irina Baronova. Tudor often performed in his own ballets, but both he and Laing had leading roles in Massine's *Aleko* (1942), and Tudor sometimes played the king in Fokine's burlesque, *Bluebeard.*

Tudor was never a prolific choreographer, and his next ballet, *Romeo and Juliet,* was still incomplete at its scheduled premiere, 6 April 1943; the finished ballet was not given until four nights later. It was danced not to Prokofiev's famous score, then unknown in the West, but to a selection of orchestral pieces by Frederick Delius, which proved to be surprisingly apt for Tudor's approach, described by dance critic Edwin Denby as "a meditation on the play." Originally, the ballet was to be designed by Salvador Dali, but Tudor rejected his sketches and insisted that the commission be given to Eugene Berman. The result was one of the most beautiful scenic investitures in modern ballet. Laing was a natural choice for the impetuous, passionate Romeo, but Tudor's casting of Juliet was much less obvious: Markova danced the role in a red wig; it was one of her greatest roles outside the classic repertory. Kaye later took it over, with Tudor himself as Tybalt.

Tudor's *Dim Lustre* (October 1943) was a ballet on the Proustian theme of "mixing memory and desire." The action takes place at a ball where the scent of a woman's perfume and the sight of a man's white tie trigger memories of previous loves in the minds of a couple (Laing and Kaye). Some of the episodes were amusing, and Tudor devised some brilliant dance passages to the *Burlesca* of Richard Strauss, but the stagecraft of the transitions from present to remembered action was surprisingly clumsy. Tudor revived *Dim Lustre* for New York City Ballet in 1964, but its 1985 revival by American Ballet Theatre was unsuccessful.

The intervals between Tudor's new ballets became longer. After *Dim Lustre* a year and a half passed before the appearance of *Undertow* (April 1945), Tudor's only work to a commissioned score, by William Schuman. The theme, a kind of Freudian analysis in dance terms, was suggested by playwright John van Druten. The protagonist, a young man (Laing), is driven to commit what Martin called "a sordid sex murder" as a consequence of a traumatic experience in childhood. The ballet is full of sensational incidents, beginning with as realistic a depiction of birth as is possible on the ballet stage and going on to scenes involving prostitutes, drunken bawds, the gang rape of a vicious little girl (danced by Alicia Alonso), and the seduction of the transgressor by the temptress who became his victim. To convey universal significance, the characters had names from Greek mythology. Again Kaye was not in the original cast but later took over the role of the seductress Medusa, first danced by Nana Gollner, who was previously known for such roles as Odette-Odile in *Swan Lake.*

Three years elapsed between *Undertow* and Tudor's next ballet, although in 1945 he choreographed several musical comedies (so-called serious choreographers were in demand on Broadway after de Mille's success with *Okla-*

TUDOR. The principal dancers in the original cast of *Pillar of Fire,* created for Ballet Theatre in 1942: Annabelle Lyon as The Youngest Sister, Antony Tudor as The Friend, Lucia Chase as The Eldest Sister, Nora Kaye as Hagar, and Hugh Laing as The Young Man from the House Opposite. Scenery and costumes were designed by Jo Mielziner. (Photograph from the Dance Collection, New York Public Library for the Performing Arts.)

homa!). In the summer of 1946 Ballet Theatre visited London for the first time, and Tudor's major American works *Pillar of Fire, Romeo and Juliet,* and *Undertow* were seen at Covent Garden. In the following season Lucia Chase and Oliver Smith, who had taken over the direction of Ballet Theatre in 1945, named Tudor its artistic administrator.

As early as the late 1930s, Tudor had considered making a ballet to Gustav Mahler's symphony *Das Lied von der Erde,* and he finally succeeded in 1948 with *Shadow of the Wind.* Although the piece had its adherents, the combination of Chinese poetry in Mahler's setting with a largely ballet dance idiom was criticized by others. It did not survive beyond the season of its creation.

After restaging *Time Table* for New York City Ballet, Tudor spent most of the 1948/49 season in Stockholm, where he revived *Jardin aux Lilas* and *Gala Performance* for the Royal Swedish Ballet. He returned briefly to Ballet Theatre the following year and, in May 1950, produced a slight piece, *Nimbus,* to music by Louis Gruenberg, in which Kaye portrayed a Working Girl and Laing her "Dream Beau."

In the 1950/51 season Laing and Diana Adams, who had married, left Ballet Theatre to join New York City Ballet; they were followed a few months later by Kaye and Tudor. Tudor's first work for New York City Ballet was *The Lady of the Camellias,* presented in February 1951 to a selection of music by Giuseppe Verdi (but none from *La Traviata*). Its main *raison d'être,* other than as a vehicle for Adams and Laing, was to make use of scenery and costumes designed by Cecil Beaton for an earlier *Camille* ballet by John Taras for Original Ballet Russe. Tudor, who appeared under a pseudonym in the role of Armand's father, later described his task as that of "a short order cook." Given the circumstances, except for the lovers' pastoral duet, the result was mediocre.

Tudor's attempt to provide a vehicle for Kaye was not much better. In *La Gloire* (February 1952), Kaye portrayed a Sarah Bernhardt-like actress both onstage (as Lucretia, Phaedra, and Hamlet) and off (with her lovers). The work was in three scenes, and the music consisted of three

TUDOR. *Gala Performance,* made for the London Ballet in 1938, was restaged and revised for Ballet Theatre in 1941. A spoof of mannerisms of rival *prima ballerinas* from Russia, Italy, and France, it remained a repertory staple for many years. In a 1946 performance, the three ballerinas were portrayed by Nora Kaye (kneeling, at left of center), as La Reine de la Danse (from Moscow); Alicia Alonso (center), as La Déesse de la Danse (from Milan); and Norma Vance (bowing, at right of center) as La Fille de Terpsichore (from Paris). They are flanked by Tudor (at left) and Hugh Laing (at right) as their cavaliers. (Photograph from the Dance Collection, New York Public Library for the Performing Arts.)

Beethoven overtures, which tended to overwhelm the dance action.

Tudor's most successful work for New York City Ballet was a 1951 revival of *Jardin aux Lilas* (restaged as *Lilac Garden*), with Kaye, Laing, and Tudor in their familiar roles and with Tanaquil Le Clercq as the Other Woman. The elaborate decor by Horace Armistead was later used for several other ballets in the repertory. Kaye and Laing did not stay long with New York City Ballet, but Adams remained and became one of Balanchine's favorite ballerinas. Tudor also severed his connection with the company.

For the next few years Tudor devoted himself chiefly to teaching. He was an extraordinary teacher who challenged his students intellectually as well as physically. He had been spending summers at Jacob's Pillow in Massachusetts since the late 1940s; in 1950 he had become director of the Metropolitan Opera Ballet School; and he joined the faculty of the Juilliard dance department when it opened in 1951. Starting in 1973 he was a frequent guest instructor at the University of California, Irvine. He also served as administrative director of the Metropolitan Opera Ballet but refrained from choreographing any of the operas himself (although he had choreographed three during the 1949/50 season). Most of his choreographic work in this period consisted of small pieces for his students.

Tudor was also teaching in Philadelphia and in 1954 put on a program of ballets there, including revivals of *Les Sylphides* and Nijinsky's *L'Après-midi d'un Faune* and a new ballet, *Offenbach in the Underworld,* to the arrangement of Offenbach tunes originally used by Massine for his *Gaîté Parisienne.* This ballet subsequently went into the repertories of the Komaki Ballet, Tokyo (where Kaye was a guest artist later in 1954), of the National Ballet of Canada (1955), of Ballet Theatre when Kaye and Laing returned (1956), and of the Joffrey Ballet (1975). The piece is a hybrid: a Tudor treatment of a Massine subject, with a rowdy can-can and a characteristic passage where the various denizens of the "Bar du Can-can" wonder if they have paired off with the right partners.

Others of Tudor's ballets were revived over the years in many places, but new ballets were few: in Buenos Aires, a version of Strauss's *Die Josephslegende* (Teatro Colón, 1958); for ballet evenings at the Metropolitan Opera, *Hail and Farewell* (1959), also to music of Strauss, including his *Four Last Songs,* with Kaye as guest artist, and *Concerning Oracles,* to music of Jacques Ibert (1966); for the Royal Swedish Ballet, where Tudor returned as guest choreographer and artistic adviser from 1961 to 1963, *Ekon av Trumpeter* (1963), to music of Bohuslav Martinů. Of these, only the last was of consequence, and under the name *Echoing of Trumpets* it was taken into the repertories of American Ballet Theatre in 1967 and London Festival Ballet in 1973. Some considered this ballet, based on the massacre of the Czech village of Lidice by the Nazis in World War II, a great dramatic work; others thought it synthetic and exploitative.

TUDOR. *Dim Lustre* (1943), set to Richard Strauss's Burlesque in D Minor for Piano and Orchestra, was a ballet about love and illusion, about old, fragile passions vaguely recalled and glimpsed through the scrim of memory. Tudor staged it for the New York City Ballet in 1964, with Patricia McBride as The Lady with Him and Edward Villella as The Gentleman with Her. Costumes were designed by Beni Montresor. (Photograph by Fred Fehl; used by permission.)

When Frederick Ashton became director of the Royal Ballet in 1963, he wanted to correct the injustice of the company's neglect of Tudor, the other great contemporary British choreographer. Tudor finally went to London in 1966 to create a new ballet, *Shadowplay,* which had its premiere in January 1967. The libretto was suggested by Rudyard Kipling's *The Jungle Book,* as was the music by Charles Koechlin. Tudor cast Anthony Dowell as the Boy who undergoes an initiation at the hands of a Terrestrial (Derek Rencher) and a Celestial (Merle Park). The ballet itself is unsatisfactory, but under Tudor's coaching Dowell gained considerable artistic maturity, making the role his own in a way that Mikhail Baryshnikov failed to do in a subsequent revival by American Ballet Theatre.

Tudor's association with the Royal Ballet continued the following year; in November 1968 the main company revived *Jardin aux Lilas* at Covent Garden (even with Svetlana Beriosova as Caroline it was unsuccessful), and the touring section presented a new ballet, *Knight Errant,* to music of Richard Strauss, with a libretto drawn from Pierre Choderlos de Laclos's *Les liaisons dangéreuses.*

Again Tudor made a central role that brought out the talent of a young male star, in this case David Wall, who played the Philandering Hero (though not at the first performance, when he was out with an injury. Neither of these ballets remained for long in the respective repertories; in 1980 the Royal Ballet revived *Dark Elegies*, with no greater success.

In the summer of 1969 Tudor was invited by the Australian Ballet to revive *Pillar of Fire* and to make a new piece, *The Divine Horsemen*, with music by Werner Egk, based on the book by Maya Deren. Both were designed by Hugh Laing, who had designed the original costumes for *The Judgment of Paris* and in 1970 designed *Gala Performance* for the Royal Danish Ballet.

Tudor often made small pieces for his students. Among these, *Little Improvisations*, to music by Robert Schumann, given at Jacob's Pillow in 1953 and at Juilliard in 1960, and *Fandango*, to music by Antonio Soler, given at the Metropolitan Opera Ballet Studio in 1963, have gone into the repertories of several companies. In 1971 Tudor received a choreographic grant from the National Endowment for the Arts, in fulfillment of which he made three short, originally untitled, ballets for his Juilliard students.

TUDOR. Created in 1967 for the Royal Ballet, *Shadowplay* was revived in 1975 for American Ballet Theatre. Mikhail Baryshnikov is pictured here in the principal role of The Boy with Matted Hair; behind him stands Danilo Radojevich as the dominating figure of The Terrestrial. Set to music by Charles Koechlin, the scenario is an allegory of life based loosely on Rudyard Kipling's *The Jungle Book*. (Photograph © 1976 by Linda Vartoogian; used by permission.)

Later called *Sunflowers*, to music of Leoš Janáček; *Cereus*, to music by Geoffrey Guy; and *Continuo*, to music by Johann Pachelbel, these were made available to virtually any company that wanted to do them.

In 1974 Tudor was appointed associate director of American Ballet Theatre, and in the company's 1975 summer season at the New York State Theater two of his ballets were added to the repertory, *Shadowplay* and the new *The Leaves Are Fading*, a lyrical, even rhapsodic work about young love. The story depicted in the ballet seems to take place in the memory of a woman who passes across the stage at the work's beginning and end. Like many people, Tudor was apparently captivated by the fullness and fearlessness of Gelsey Kirkland's dancing at that stage of her career, for he cast her both as The Celestial in *Shadowplay* and as the woman in the leading couple in *Leaves*. The new ballet suffered from an excessive evenness of texture, induced perhaps by the music, a selection of Antonín Dvořák's lesser string pieces.

The Tiller in the Fields (December 1978), also to Dvořák (movements from two symphonies and an overture), was a kind of sequel. Again the leading role was danced by Kirkland and seemed to be built around her offbeat personality as much as her gifts as a dancer. She played the Gypsy Girl who is seduced by (or who seduces) the Peasant Lad, and she appears at the end with padding to simulate pregnancy. The theme recalls Janáček's song cycle *Diary of One Who Vanished*. Unlike its predecessor, which has returned to the American Ballet Theatre repertory from time to time (and was revived by the Royal Danish Ballet in 1984), *The Tiller in the Fields* was soon dropped. It was Tudor's last ballet, though he continued to be listed as choreographer emeritus by American Ballet Theatre.

In February 1985 the Paris Opera Ballet presented an evening in homage to Tudor, whose works were hardly known in France. The program consisted of *Shadowplay*, *Jardin aux Lilas*, *Continuo*, and *Dark Elegies*. Tudor was not in attendance.

Any study of Tudor's career must ask why his creativity faded after producing a handful of masterpieces in his first fifteen years as a choreographer? Was this a deliberate abdication on his part—a withdrawal from the spotlight? Always reclusive, Tudor was for years a resident of the First Zen Institute in New York, and he seems to have been convinced that he had nothing more to express. Lack of movement invention was not his problem, but too often in his later ballets the subject matter was not made manifest through the dancing itself. As Denby wrote of *Undertow*, "one keeps watching the movement all through for the intellectual meaning its pantomime conveys more than for its physical impetus as dancing." Even in his most productive period Tudor was never prolific in the way that his contemporaries, Ashton and Balanchine,

TUDOR. Gelsey Kirkland, Tudor's last muse, with Iván Nagy in a 1980 performance of *The Leaves Are Fading,* created for her in 1975 to music by Antonín Dvořák. Costumes were designed by Patricia Zipprodt. (Photograph © 1980 by Max Waldman; used by permission.)

were, and it may be that a failure to exercise the craft of choreography in the end caused a stoppage of his creativity.

Nevertheless, any choreographer will be ultimately judged on only a few works. It is tragic that Tudor's *The Planets, The Descent of Hebe,* and above all *Romeo and Juliet*—the finest of all ballets on that overworked subject—have been lost. Tudor's reputation must rest on the few ballets that survive: judged by such works as *Jardin aux Lilas, Dark Elegies,* and *Pillar of Fire,* Tudor's status as one of the greatest choreographers of the twentieth century beyond dispute.

In 1986 Tudor received the Capezio Dance Award and New York City's Handel Medallion, and he was a recipient of the Kennedy Center Honors. At the Capezio award ceremony, Mikhail Baryshnikov, then artistic director of American Ballet Theatre, said, "We do Tudor's ballets because we must. Tudor is our conscience." Until a day or two before his death Tudor was rehearsing a new cast for *Pillar of Fire* with American Ballet Theatre.

[*See also* Dark Elegies; Jardin aux Lilas; *and* Pillar of Fire.]

BIBLIOGRAPHY

Chazin-Bennahum, Judith. *The Ballets of Antony Tudor: Studies in Psyche and Satire.* New York, 1995.

Cohen, Selma Jeanne. "Antony Tudor: The Years in America and After." *Dance Perspectives,* no. 18 (1963).

Coton, A. V. *Writings on Dance, 1938–1968.* Edited by Kathrine Sorley Walker and Lilian Haddakin. London, 1975.

Heppenstall, Rayner. *Apology for Dancing.* London, 1936.

Jordan, Stephanie. "Antony Tudor: His Use of Music and Movement." *Eddy,* no. 8 (Spring–Summer 1976): 18–23.

Lloyd, Maude. "Some Recollections of the English Ballet." *Dance Research* 3 (Autumn 1984): 39–52.

Percival, John. "Antony Tudor: The Years in England." *Dance Perspectives,* no. 17 (1963).

Perlmutter, Donna. *Shadowplay/The Life of Antony Tudor.* New York, 1991.

Van Praagh, Peggy. "Working with Antony Tudor." *Dance Research* 2 (Summer 1984): 56–67.

Vaughan, David. "Antony Tudor's Early Ballets." In *The Myriad Faces of Dance: Proceedings of the Eighth Annual Conference, Society of Dance History Scholars, University of New Mexico, 15–17 February 1985,* compiled by Christena L. Schlundt. Riverside, Calif., 1985.

DAVID VAUGHAN

TULSA BALLET THEATRE. Since its inception in 1956, the thirty-member Tulsa Ballet Theatre, based in one of the major cities of Oklahoma, has been characterized by fine, classical training and a conservative approach to repertory selection. Its founding directors, Roman Jasinski and Moscelyne Larkin, married in 1943 when they were dancers with Colonel de Basil's Original Ballet Russe. They later joined Sergei Denham's Ballet Russe de Monte Carlo. Outstanding works from the repertories of these companies have gained a home with the Tulsa Ballet Theatre.

The company has also revived ballets that otherwise might never have been seen again. In 1978 David Lichine's version of *The Prodigal Son,* originally danced by Jasinski, was revived for his son, Roman L. Jasinski. Serge Lifar's *Icare* was also revived. In 1982 the "Hand of Fate" pas de deux from George Balanchine's *Cotillon* received avid critical attention when the company took it to New York. The same was true in 1987, when Balanchine's *Mozart Violin Concerto* was revived. In 1990 Michel Fokine's *Paganini* was also returned to the stage.

Until his death in 1991, Jasinski was the company's principal choreographer. Although he preferred to create abstract works, such as *Tribute, Convolutions,* and *Zingara,* one of his most successful productions was *The Bamboo Princess,* a dramatic ballet created in 1983 in collaboration with Sahomi Tachibana. Jasinski's early training was at the Warsaw Opera Ballet School, whereas Larkin's training began in Tulsa at the school of her mother, Eva Matlagova, and later continued in New York. From the outset the couple's Tulsa school was characterized by their mutually high standards.

Unlike most other regional companies in the United States, Tulsa Ballet Theatre does not have a substantial nucleus of Balanchine ballets, nor does it foster new or experimental choreographers from outside the company or from within its ranks. Its specially commissioned works have included *Cinderella* and *Romeo and Juliet,* staged by Alun Jones, director of the Louisville Ballet. It also has acquired such repertory staples as Eugene Loring's *Billy the Kid,* Lew Christensen's *Con Amore,* the Ruth Page–Bentley Stone *Frankie and Johnny,* Agnes de Mille's *Rodeo,* and Léonide Massine's *Gaîté Parisienne.* Of more recent vintage are Peter Anastos's *Yes, Virginia, Another Piano Ballet* and Lisa de Ribere's *Casey at the Bat.*

Because of its somewhat popular approach to repertory, Tulsa Ballet Theatre's finances have remained unusually stable. In 1992, it was able to dedicate a handsome new home structured from a former public school building.

In 1991, after his father's death and a relatively brief career with the Cincinnati Ballet and American Ballet Theatre, Roman L. Jasinski became artistic director, and his mother functioned actively as artistic director emerita. Jasinski's tenure was turbulent. He resigned in 1994, as did the company's longtime general manager Connie Cronley. In 1995, Marcello Angelini, a dancer with the Cincinnati Ballet, became Tulsa Ballet Theatre's new artistic director.

BIBLIOGRAPHY

Anderson, Jack. *The One and Only: The Ballet Russe de Monte Carlo.* New York, 1981.

Anderson, Jack. Obituary: Roman Jasinski. *New York Times* (17 April 1991).

Garafola, Lynn. "Fokine's *Paganini* Resurrected." *Ballet Review* 14 (Spring 1986): 69–71.

Livingston, Lili Cockerille. "Tulsa Ballet Theatre's Ballet Russe Renaissance." *Dance Magazine* (February 1988): 54–63.

Livingston, Lili Cockerille. "Jasinski Leaves Tulsa Ballet Theatre." *Dance Magazine* (February 1995): 28–34.

Souvenir Program. Tulsa Ballet Theatre, 1992.

INTERVIEW. Roman Jasinski, by Doris Hering (July 1976), Dance Collection, Oral History Tapes, New York Public Library for the Performing Arts.

DORIS HERING

TUNE, TOMMY (Thomas James Tune; born 28 February 1939 in Witchita Falls, Texas), American director, choreographer, and dancer. As a youngster, Tune studied ballet and produced theatrical entertainments in his family's garage in Witchita Falls. By the time he reached his full height—six feet, six inches—in high school, he had grown too tall for a classical dance career and instead set his sights on the theater. He took courses at Lon Morris Junior College, earned a Bachelor of Fine Arts degree in dramatic arts from the University of Texas at Austin in 1962, and pursued graduate studies the following year at the University of Houston.

New York City seemed a better venue than Houston for pursuing stardom, and Tune got a job on his first day in town with a U.S. touring production of the Broadway musical *Irma La Douce.* His New York debut was on 16 February 1965, when he appeared as a chorus dancer in *Baker Street* at the Broadway Theater. During the following year he appeared in *A Joyful Noise,* with dances by Michael Bennett, and was given a solo in the 1967 *How Now Dow Jones?*

Tune choreographed a tour of *The Canterbury Tales,* then moved to Hollywood in 1969 to play Ambrose Kemper in the film *Hello, Dolly!,* remaining in California as a television series regular on *Dean Martin Presents the Golddiggers.* He was cast in the 1971 film version of *The Boyfriend,* starring the willowy former model Twiggy. While shooting the movie in London, lean and lanky Tune recognized Twiggy as his perfect dancing partner, although the two did not appear together onstage until the 1983 production of *My One and Only.*

Back in New York, he was cast as David in Bennett's production of *Seesaw,* which opened on 18 March 1973 at the Uris Theater and subsequently moved to the Mark Hellinger. Troubled with money problems, *Seesaw* was still a significant critical success, completing a respectable Broadway run and national tour. For it, Tune won his first Tony Award as Best Supporting or Featured Actor in a Musical.

Tune's first New York directing assignment came in 1976, for Eve Merriman's satirical *The Club* at Circle in the Square. His colorful sex-role charades gave a light touch to sometimes dark material, which became a hallmark of his work. The following year he directed *Sunset* at the Studio Arena in Buffalo and began a collaboration on what would become his first blockbuster, *The Best Little Whorehouse in Texas.*

With co-director Peter Masterson and co-choreographer Thomie Walsh, Tune was able to capitalize on his Texas heritage. Among many colorful numbers, the dance he devised for football players, cheerleaders, and stuffed dummies is probably the most memorable. The popular success of *The Best Little Whorehouse in Texas* at the Entermedia caused the production to be moved to Broadway's Forty-sixth Street Theater. For it, he won a 1978 Tony as Best Director of a Musical.

Again collaborating with Walsh, Tune was recognized during the following season for direction and choreography for *A Day in Hollywood/A Night in the Ukraine,* notable for its inventive "ankle stage." For this production he won two 1980 Tonys, as Best Director of a Musical and as Best Choreographer, and he received the 1979/80 Drama Desk awards for Best Choreography and Best Staging of a Musical.

Caryl Churchill's nonmusical *Cloud 9* (1981) was Tune's next success. Produced off-Broadway at the Theatre de Lys, the play was given a strongly visual interpretation by Tune, who again used gender-changing role modeling as a technique for revealing both text and subtext. In the spring, he directed and choreographed *Nine,* adapted from Fellini's film *8½. Nine* won five Tonys, including for Tune Best Musical and Best Director of a Musical; he also accepted Drama Desk awards as Best Director of a Musical *(Nine)* and Best Director of a Play *(Cloud 9).* With a 1982 Obie as Best Director for *Cloud 9* as well, Tune's was a distinctive triple-crown Broadway achievement.

The sweetness of Tune's onstage persona was best expressed in the role of Captain Billy Buck Chandler in *My One and Only* (1983), in which he starred, directed and co-choreographed with Walsh. At last paired with Twiggy, Tune evoked the romance of an earlier era in top hat and tails, dancing to the silky tunes of George Gershwin from *Funny Face,* with a new book by Timothy Mayer. An effervescent sense of theatrical wonder and joy permeated *My One and Only,* presenting theatergoers with a perfect prescription for elegant escape. Tune and Walsh shared Tony and Drama Desk Awards for Choreography, and Tune received a 1983 Tony for Best Actor in a Musical. In that same year he directed the initial, problematic version of *Steppin' Out.* He was presented the *Dance Magazine* Award for 1984, and Twiggy attended the ceremony to take photographs from the first row of the audience.

With co-choreographer Marge Champion, Tune directed another edition of *Steppin' Out* in 1987 that received neither critical nor popular endorsement. He soon turned his creative sights from frothier confections to darker flirtations with the lavish and compelling *Grand Hotel* (1989). Set in the gilded decadence of 1920s Berlin, *Grand Hotel* presented some of Tune's most vivid couple dances (partly inspired by the triumphant 1985 New York appearance of *Tango Argentino*). The titilating presentation of feminine charms was a highlight of *The Will Rogers Follies,* which opened at the Palace Theater on 1 May 1991; the production won six Tony awards and Tune was honored as Best Choreographer.

The film *That's Dancing* (1984) and the television special "Irving Berlin's 100th Birthday Salute" (CBS, 1988) gave Tune opportunities that have continued with other television experiments. Besides the creativity of his tap and softshoe compositions, Tune is credited with breaking up and opening out the narrow range of body types that had become associated with chorus lines. His own height made him especially sensitive to size, and his productions have focused on dancers of many shapes and lengths, rather than on a single profile. He is noted principally for his innovative choreography and musical staging, for stylish comedy, and for adapting material from other media for the theater.

TUNE. *My One and Only* (1983) featured Tune and Twiggy singing and dancing to a selection of show tunes by George Gershwin. With Tune not only co-starring but co-choreographing, the dancing vied with Gershwin's beloved melodies as the highlight of the show. (Photograph by Kenn Duncan; used by permission of Virginia Duncan Shearer.)

BIBLIOGRAPHY

Bordman, Gerald. *American Musical Theatre: A Chronicle.* 2d ed. New York and Oxford, 1992.

ARCHIVES. Dance Collection and Theater Collection, New York Public Library for the Performing Arts.

CAMILLE HARDY

TUNISIA. Once part of Phoenician Carthage, Tunisia was conquered by Rome in the second century BCE and by the Muslims spreading Islam in the seventh century CE. The Ottoman Empire ruled from the sixteenth century until the *beys* (governors) gained their independence and founded a center for corsairing in the eighteenth and nineteenth centuries. France established a protectorate in 1881; it was the site of fierce battles during World War II, and Tunisia became independent in 1956.

A small North African country with a fairly homogeneous population, Tunisia has extensive contact and interchange among its various regions, which accounts, at least in part, for the similarity of its traditional dance styles. In general, many dances typical of North Africa are also found in Tunisia. Rifle and sword dances, once common throughout the country, can still be seen in isolated areas, such as the southern oasis town of Nefta. The exorcistic rites of the sub-Saharan brotherhoods, called *stambeli* in Tunisia, consist primarily of singing. Their dance is a simple procession in which they accompany themselves with the typical *chakchakas* (forged iron percussion instruments).

On the islands of Djerba and Kerkenna, male musicians dressed in nineteenth-century costumes dance while playing the *tbal* (large two-headed drum) and the *mizwid* (bagpipe) or the *darabukka* (clay goblet drum) and the *zikra* (folk oboe). Their dancing includes complex pelvic rotations, graceful walking, and smoothly executed squat turns. In the southern coastal area, around Medenine, male dancers dressed in flowing robes dance with canes and handkerchiefs to a drum made from a shallow bowl covered with a skin. The dance consists primarily of simple walking and running steps.

In Tunisia, as in North Africa generally, numerous ecstatic brotherhoods are attached to the shrines of local saints. They hold special commemorative gatherings during which they sing, speak in tongues, mortify the flesh, or dance. One of the brotherhoods of Sidi Alī in Nefta is an example of the latter. Their meeting takes place in a courtyard. The members dance in a loose line, facing a row of musicians playing *bendirs* (circular frame drums). The dancers throw their torsos violently, but rhythmically, up and down. Their heads move reciprocally, producing a slight undulating quality. This motion is similar to a movement common in Moroccan Berber dances but is more extreme. As the dance progresses, the drummers shift into different rhythmic patterns, producing a gradual acceleration and growing excitement. The dancers repeat the same movement over and over until some fall to the ground unconscious. The dancing may go on all night.

In the small towns of Tunisia, song and dance play an especially important role. They occur at every wedding and at most large celebrations, as well as at home. Often, after the family dinner is over, someone may sing a popular song or two. If the mood is festive enough, dancing will begin. All present—men, women, and children—are urged to participate.

Traditional social dancing is an improvisational form performed as a solo or duo. Tunisian dancing does not differ appreciably whether performed by a male or a female (as is true generally in North African dance). The movements of the torso are so integral a part of the folk culture that country people use them unself-consciously. Although performing this style of dance in public is frowned upon, almost anyone can enjoy dancing among friends and family.

Tunisians dance to the music of the *darabukka* and the *mizwid* and, especially at large outdoor celebrations, the *tbal* and the *zikra*. The most usual dance rhythms are 6/8 and 12/16. The dance style is characterized by light, glid-

TUNISIA. The Ali Suissi ensemble from the island of Kerkenna, in a 1977 performance at the Dar Shaab in Sfax. In North Africa, it is not uncommon for dancers to play musical instruments while dancing. (Photograph by Aisha Ali; from the collection of Mardi Rollow.)

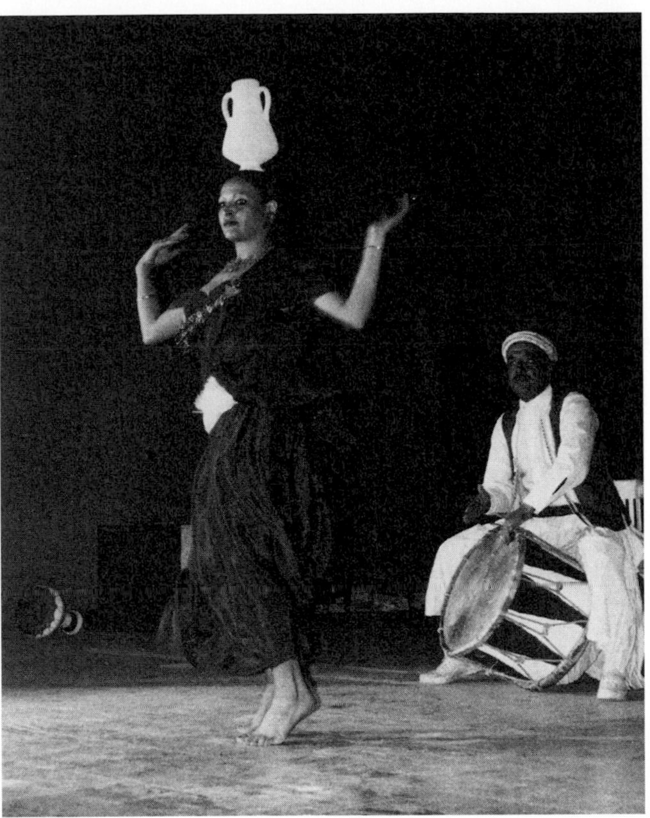

TUNISIA. Nabila, a professional dancer, demonstrates the Tunisian women's style at a performance at the Dar Shaab in Sfax, 1977. (Photograph by Aisha Ali; from the collection of Mardi Rollow.)

ing steps and vigorous horizontal hip movements, which are accentuated by the fullness of the traditional dress, called *melia* or *palla,* and the flying ends of the yarn belts commonly worn. The rural women have excellent carriage; the vigor of their hip movements does not interfere with the gliding character of their steps.

A Tunisian woman dances with her arms held slightly forward and to the sides, with fingertips up and palms away from the body. Her arms are relaxed, although she sometimes accentuates the sharp movements of her hips with strong reciprocal arm motions.

Occasionally, a woman will dance with scarves, moving them from side to side and up and down, in a manner complementary to the hip accents. Professional dancers sometimes add sharp shimmies to the usual repertory of movements. They may sit and perform a number of simple mimetic movements, such as preparing a meal of couscous, combing the hair, and applying makeup. Balancing a water jar on the head is a popular embellishment.

Tunisia has a national folk-dance company, the National Ensemble of Popular Arts, based in Tunis, that presents highly choreographed versions of folk styles. Although company members have been recruited from all over Tunisia, they do not necessarily perform dances from their own regions. Fortunately, there are still places, such as Djerba, Medenine, and Nefta, where the local inhabitants perform their dances much as they may have done for centuries.

[*See also* North Africa.]

BIBLIOGRAPHY

Rollow, Mardi. "Traditional Dance in Tunisia." *Arabesque* 5 (May–June 1979): 10–15.

RECORDING. *Music of the Shikhat and Dance Music of Tunisia* (Disques Maghrébins 5001).

VIDEOTAPE. *Dances of North Africa: Vol. 1, Morocco and Tunisia* (Araf, 1995).

AISHA ALI, MARDI ROLLOW, and LEONA WOOD

TURCZYNOWICZ, ROMAN (born 14 March 1813 in Radom, Poland, died 21 May 1882 in Warsaw), Polish dancer, choreographer, and ballet director. Turczynowicz trained at the ballet school attached to Warsaw's Wielki Theater, where he performed as a principal dancer from 1825 to 1843. Although he preferred character roles, he also played classical roles, such as James in *La Sylphide,* Alidor in *Fee und Ritter,* and Alvar in *Hertha's Sacrifice.*

In 1843 Turczynowicz began choreographing with the support of Filippo Taglioni, the newly engaged director of the Warsaw Ballet. Three years later he made his choreographic debut with *Peasant Feast near Kielce.* His interest in Romantic and national themes continued throughout his career. As second company choreographer he staged his own versions of *Le Diable à Quatre* (1847), *Giselle* (1848), *Catarina, ou La Fille de Bandit* (1850), and *Esmeralda* (1851). His stagings maintained a balance between mime and pure dance and between male and female dancing.

From 1853 to 1866 Turczynowicz served as director of the school and company. Although the Russian authorities forbade ballets on national themes, he set stage versions of national dances in almost every ballet in the repertory, crowning the whole series with *mazur, polonez,* and Highlanders' dances for Stanisław Miniuszko's opera *Halka* in 1858, which remained in the repertory until 1917. He also emphasized character dancing in the curriculum of the school.

Turczynowicz's wife, Konstancja (1818–1880), was a principal dancer from 1832 to 1853 at the Wielki Theater, excelling in both character and classical roles. She taught Marie Taglioni the *mazur.* In 1842 she appeared with her husband in a program of Polish national dances at the Paris Opera. From 1832 to 1853 she taught at the ballet school affiliated with the Wielki Theater.

BIBLIOGRAPHY

Chynowski, Paweł, and Janina Pudełek. *Almanach baletu warszawskiego, 1785–1985/Le ballet de Varsovie, 1785–1985.* Warsaw, 1987.

Pudełek, Janina. *Warszawski balet romantyczny, 1802–1866.* Warsaw, 1968.

Pudełek, Janina. *Two Hundred Years of Polish Ballet, 1785–1985.* Warsaw, 1985.

JANINA PUDEŁEK

TURKEY. The Turks, descendants of nomadic peoples of Central Asia, had been living on the Anatolian Plateau for centuries before they began an agressive advance into neighboring eastern Europe, the Levant, northern Africa, and western Asia to create an empire—the Ottoman Empire—which lasted from the fourteenth to the twentieth century. The Turks had practiced shamanism, then Buddhism and Manichaeism, but with their conquest of Constantinople in 1453, then capital of the Byzantine Empire, they accepted Islam. The city was renamed Istanbul and it became the capital of both their empire and the Islamic caliphate. With the demise of the empire after World War I, the Republic of Turkey, with its new capital at Ankara, was founded as a secular, Western-style country.

Traditional Dance. Because many cultures have lived in and crossed Anatolia, the dances of Anatolian Turkey possess a rich heritage of movement and gesture. Even with this heterogeneous heritage, Turkish folklore never lost the flexibility to add new components. Turkish folk dances are therefore a blend of the cultural traditions of several folk cultures.

After the Anatolian tradition, the two most important influences on Turkish dance come from Asia, including one directly from the shamanistic rituals of the Ural-Altaic region [*see* Shamanism], from which the Turkish peoples originated, and one indirectly from other Asian cultures, such as the Chinese. The dances of Turkestan (a region between the Caspian Sea and the Gobi Desert), which were brought west to Turkey, were probably introduced to China as well, where dances from Central Asia had been enjoyed in antiquity. Contemporary Anatolian folk dances bear myriad signs of shamanistic influences. The most important of these is dancing to the accompaniment of the drum in which the Anatolian drum *(davul)* is the primary instrument. Also widespread in both urban and rural Turkey is animal mimicry—simulated by gesture or by masks and other disguises, just as shamans donned animal skins. Some of these dances are relics of ancient Anatolia, but others reflect a synthesis of Anatolian and Central Asian cultures.

The third major influence on Turkish dance is that of Islam. Because Islam is fundamentally antagonistic to dance, its influence has been largely negative. (There is a ban against women dancing with men, for example.) Positive aspects, however, have been acquired from increased contact with other Islamic traditions—mainly the Arab and Persian. Islamic puritanism did not greatly affect Turkish peasants, who retained both their ethnic unity and their dancing. Despite Islamic bans, in many of the peasant dances, men and women do dance together, especially among the heterodox (non-Sunni Islamic) tribes. The fourth influence was caused by the expansion of the Turkish empire, with ensuing cultural exchanges among its varied peoples.

TURKEY. A member of the Mevlevi order of Sufis, performing the whirling dance characteristic of the order, founded in the thirteenth century by the poet-philosopher Jalāl al-Dīn Rūmī. Through their revolving dance, the dervishes (the word refers to a person on the threshold of enlightenment) strive to detach themselves from earth and become spiritually united with a nonpersonified God. (Collection of Metin And.)

The fifth has been the influences of Western civilization. From the Republic of Turkey's modern and secular beginnings under Kemal Atatürk in the 1920s, westernization has set Turkey apart from the other Muslim nations. Modern improvements in communications and other factors have been lessening the practice and purity of folk dancing, yet more than a thousand traditional Turkish dances remain. The heterodox Turkish tribes living across Anatolia, some still seminomadic, have preserved a form of traditional Turkish culture.

The Turkish word *oyun,* for "dance," covers a wide field of concepts that have little to do with dance; Turkish *raks* (from Arabic *raqş*) means both "dancing" and "a form of dance." In 1975 the State Folk Dance Company was formed to present Turkey's rich heritage of dance at home and abroad.

Ecstatic and Sacred Dance. Despite Islamic bans, the Sufi concept of music and dancing as part of religious experience gained acceptance in Turkey; various Muslim religious orders of dervishes practice Sufi mysticism. The central Asian shamanistic influence may still be felt most strongly in the quasi-religious dances of these orders, especially the Bektaşi and Kalendar dervishes, who had a powerful influence among nomadic heterodox tribes and people of the Alevi sect, an Anatolian offshoot of Shiism. In Sufism, *sema* (Ar., *samāʿ*) is the practice of listening to music, singing, and chanting to attain a state of religious ecstasy; *zikr* (Ar., *dhikr*), the repeated recital of short invocations to Allah with movements to vocal or instrumental accompaniment, helps to free physical effort from conscious thought. The complex ceremonial dances of the dervish orders usually begin with a slow movement that increases in speed. The Mevlevi (Mawlawīyah) order (the "whirling dervishes") was founded by the poet and mystic Jalāl al-Dīn Rūmī (known in Turkish as Mevlana Celaleddin Rumi) in the thirteenth-century city of Konya, then the capital of the Seljuk Turks. The dancers are first blessed by their leader. Then, with arms crossed on their breasts, heads bent, and feet close together, they turn very slowly, resting on each heel in turn. As the speed of their spinning increases, their long white skirts flare outward. Sometimes the right hand is raised, palm upward, and the left lowered, palm downward, symbolizing the belief that the influence of heaven is handed down to the world. The whirling symbolizes the celestial motions—the earth turning on its axis as it revolves around the sun. As the dervishes spin, they circle the hall (termed "the hall of celestial sound").

The quasi-religious dances of the Alevi (see above) parallel these. Some of these people are still seminomadic and hold indoor parties at which there is male-female dancing. These carefully guarded dances are performed in secrecy from fear of the Sunni bans. As the Alevi do not intermarry with other sects, their cultural unity has preserved their dances. Despite the sacred air of these mixed-sex dances, they usually have a social nature. Two to sixteen dancers take part. Sometimes a master of ceremonies invites both men and women, who sit on opposite sides of the room, to dance. They face each other, extend their arms forward, cross them on their chests, and dance without ever touching each other. When a dancer is tired, a man goes to a man, and a woman to a woman, inviting the person to replace him or her with a kiss on the knees, called *niyaz.*

TURKEY. Unlike most devout Muslims, members of the Alevi sect, an offshoot of Shiism, enjoy male-female dancing on social occasions. These dancers are from one of the seminomadic groups of Alevi who live in rural Turkey. Characteristically, they do not touch each other while dancing. (Photograph from the collection of Metin And.)

Professional Dancing. Some Turkish dancing is primarily designed to entertain spectators; it is performed by professional boy and girl dancers, buffoons, grotesque dancers, and dancers in theatrical performances. Like most Asian theater, traditional Turkish theater fuses dance, music, acrobatics, song, and story. Turkish shadow puppet theater seems to have borrowed movements and costumes from the Ottoman jesters and grotesque dancers who entertained long before the shadow theater. Also, throughout rural Anatolia countless unsophisticated dramas are enacted, accompanied by singing, dancing, and mime; some use masks and animal mimicry—probably a legacy of ancient shamanistic and religious rites.

TURKEY. Often performing acrobatic and virtuosic dances, buffoon characters were popular acts in Ottoman processions. This eighteenth-century buffoon carrys an implement used to strike the small drum worn at his waist. (Collection of Metin And.)

Dancing by buffoons, wandering dervishes, and boys dressed as females was an important part of Ottoman spectacular processions, both in cities and villages. Comic dancers, *curcunabaz,* were members of the same companies as boy dancers, acrobats, and tumblers; their grotesque costumes and postures contrasted with the boys' artistic eroticism. The buffoons sometimes wore masks and sometimes imitated animals. The dancers displayed their virtuosity: the *kasebaz* danced and twirled *majolica* plates on their fingers, while other dancers performed acrobatics and contortions, and still others danced on stilts.

Boy and girl dancers, hired for exhibition dancing, are still an established institution throughout the Middle East. In Ottoman Turkey the word *çengi,* which referred both to the boys and the girls, was basically synonymous with the French terms *comédiant(e)* and *joueur de farce.* A "company" of these boys or girls was a *kol,* their "leader" was the *kolbşı.*

The dancing boys called *köçek* cultivated a feminine appearance; they often grew their hair long and dressed like girls, dancing with languid movements and suggestive gestures, and marking time with clappers or by finger snapping. They danced rapidly, with somersaults, wrestling, and mimicry; in the dance *tavşan raksı,* they sprang lightly and moved the muscles of their faces like rabbits *(tavşan).* Their popularity among the urban population caused trouble, so *köçek* performances were banned by the sultan in 1857. Nevertheless, in Anatolian villages both amateur and professional *köçek* still perform at weddings and other parties, some wearing wide, multicolored skirts. When these boys are older, they often become drummers for younger *köçek.*

The *çengi* dancing girls were very popular. Holding a silk scarf, they performed sensuous contortions and pantomimes of physical love—alternatively acting coy or alluring. The *kolbaşı* was an older woman, and a *kol* usually included twelve dancing girls and four musicians playing a fiddle, a double drum called a *nekkare,* and two tambourines. In addition to dancing for male audiences, they danced in women's public bathhouses and in the women's quarters in the houses of the wealthy. The *çengi* girls often dressed as boys or men and were believed to arouse lesbian desires among women in their audience. First

TURKEY. A nineteenth-century print of a dancing girl with finger cymbals. (Collection of Metin And.)

they sang, saluted the audience, and marched around in rhythm. Then, with finger cymbals clicking, they quivered and gyrated their bodies in sensuous undulations. In the third part of their performance, in the *tavşan rakşı,* they wore trousers and whirled and jumped. The final part of the performance was more a pantomime with singing. A favorite role was the *kalyoncu* (galley sailor), in which the principal dancer mimed a braggart captain challenging his rivals.

Although the dancing girls were not banned in 1857, as the boys were, their popularity has waned. Today, their dancing is merely the corrupt belly dancing [*see* Danse du Ventre] of nightclubs; in Anatolian villages, however, female *çengi* still perform occasionally.

Nonprofessional Dancing. As a reflection of the pure joy of dancing, and not for the admiration of spectators, dancing by nonprofessionals serves to reinforce social solidarity. Such dances include all folk dancing and those dances with magico-religious purposes whose origins are lost in antiquity. The dances easily disappear in urban surroundings but have survived in great variety in the Turkish countryside. Turkish folk dances are regional, but among some common elements of basic movement the most widespread is crouching or kneeling, possibly a central Asian influence. Other characteristic movements are lifting one knee to a half-bent position; the sole of the foot remains parallel to the ground while the other leg supports the weight of the body. One arm is extended above the shoulder while the other points downward. Heavy foot stamping is also typical. In many dances, for both men and women, either every dancer holds a handkerchief in the right hand or the leader of the line holds it. There are line, ring, couple, and solo dances, some danced only by men, some only by women, and some by both—although the sexes rarely touch. The accompaniment may be instrumental or vocal.

In eastern Anatolia, the word for "group dances" is *bar.* In central Anatolia the most popular dances are *kaşık oyunu,* in which each dancer uses a pair of wooden spoons like castanets, and *halay,* in which the dancers hold one another's hands or shoulders in a line, from which the leader may break away to perform a solo. In the north of Turkey and on the Black Sea coast the typical dance is the *horon;* in southwest Anatolia, it is the *teke;* and in western Turkey and on the Aegean coast, it is the *zeybek.* One of the best-known Turkish dances can be performed by one dancer or by several, in a special solemn, heroic style; in Turkish Thrace, the word for this dance is *karşılama* (a solo) or *sirto* (usually a chain dance). Considerable regional overlapping exists, however, so one word may be used to describe different dances in the different regions.

Turkish dances may be themeless or mimetic. The latter can be categorized in five groups, by the subject imitated:

TURKEY. Women from the Black Sea area performing a line dance. (Photograph from the collection of Metin And.)

the actions of animals; the daily routine of village life or seasonal work; the personification of nature; combat, with or without weapons; and courtship. In the first group of dances the performer is disguised as an animal or uses stylized movements to suggest the animal. Both may be vestiges of ancient rites. The trembling movements in the *horon* are thought to symbolize the local *hamsi* ("anchovies")—the dance being a vestige of a fertility or an abundance rite. There are many variants of an eagle dance, *kartal halayı,* that depict the hopping, sidling advance of the bird toward its prey, while the arms of the dancers mimic wings. In a *kartal halayı* from Tokat, a hat placed in the circle symbolizes the prey; near the end of the dance one dancer attacks this and grasps it with his teeth.

A typical mimetic dance of everyday life is the *köy halayı* from the Sivas area, in which the dancers mime various village tasks and conclude with a lively dance called *hoplatma,* a kind of thanksgiving. In *esnaf* ("craftsman"), a mimicking song and dance from Kastamonu performed by women and children, the gestures reflect movements used in various trades—there are countless dances of this type.

Of dances personifying nature, a graceful chain dance for women is "Ben Bir Kavak" (I Am a Poplar Tree). In it, the dancers glide sideways, gently swaying their bodies and arms. A typical combat dance is the *hançer barı* from Erzerum, in which two dancers, each holding a dagger in both hands, depict movements of attack and defense. In Giresun on the Black Sea, a rifle dance, *çandırlı tüfek oyunu,* is danced before the bride's house when the crowd comes to take her to her groom's village. There are many sword and shield dances, for couples and for lines facing each other. In a popular Anatolian dance, *sinsin,* dancers form a ring around a bonfire and each in turn stands in the center. In turn, the dancer in the center hits another

TURKEY. Combat dancers that utilize rifles or swords are popular, as seen in this photograph of men from eastern Anatolia. (Photograph from the collection of Metin And.)

on the back, to signal his turn in the center. The encircling dancers increase their speed, with each in turn leaping over the fire.

In courtship dances, the man seldom touches his partner—and sometimes a man dressed as a woman dances the female part. In many dances from eastern Turkey the man follows the woman closely, with open arms (like barriers encircling her), while the woman makes expressive movements with her hands and wrists.

Theatrical Dance. Before 1947 in Turkey, classical ballet was known from a few performances by visiting companies. In that year, Dame Ninette de Valois was invited by the Turkish government to visit the country and study the feasibility of setting up a ballet school within the existing State Conservatory of Music and Drama. The school officially opened in Istanbul in 1948, but in 1950 it moved to the Ankara State Conservatory. Its first professional performance as a full company took place in 1960, when Robert Harrold mounted Manuel de Falla's *El Amor Brujo* with all Turkish dancers. The company is now known as the Ankara State Ballet; in 1970, a second company was founded, the Istanbul State Ballet.

In the 1965/66 season, the first large-scale ballet was set to music by a Turkish composer, Ferit Tüzün. The production, *Çeşmebaşı* (At the Fountain) was choreographed for the company by de Valois using elements of Turkish folk dance. The 1967/68 season presented *Sinfonietta,* choreographed by de Valois to music by Nevit Kodalı. The work combines classical ballet with Turkish folk dance steps in a lighthearted romantic intrigue. *Hançerli Hanım* (The Lady with the Dagger), choreographed by Richard Glasstone to music by Bülent Tarcan, was also performed. In it, a legend of love, jealousy, and murder in seventeenth-century Istanbul is reenacted in a dream sequence. These ballets paved the way for an indigenous Turkish ballet style. The company now has its own choreographers, who work with both Turkish and non-Turkish material. At the same time, the company is constantly enlarging its repertory of the great classical ballets.

In 1968, for the first time, the company performed a ballet by a native choreographer, Sait Sökmen. His ballet *Çark* (The Wheel), an abstract work, visually follows the musical line and structure of Maurice Ravel's String Quartet in F. In 1973, Oytun Turfanda choreographed *Pembe Kadın* (A Woman Called Rosy), set to music by Necil Kazim Akses and based on Hidayet Sayın's drama depicting the ignorance and hopelessness of Turkish peasant women. Turfanda has also choreographed *Yoz Döngü* (Vicious Circle), an exciting abstract ballet set to Turkish folk melodies; *Güzelleme;* and the three-act *Hürrem Sultan,* the story of the second wife of the emperor Süleyman the Magnificent. The individual style of Duygu Aykal, another choreographer, combines classical technique with free modern dance forms. *Çoğul* (Plurality), set to music by Cengiz Tanc, concerns the metamorphosis of a miniature world. Her second ballet, *Oluşum* (Evolution) to music by Ilhan Uzmanbaş, resembles *Çoğul* in style, since both deal with people as symbols of time and events and their struggles with the elements of life. Later ballets by Aykal are *Bulutlar Nereye Gidiyor* (Where Do the Clouds Go?) and *Insan-Insan* (Human, Human).

Geyvan Yılmas McMillan, a Turkish modern dance

choreographer, has created four one-act ballets: *Baharda Duet* (Spring Duet), *Anadolu Gecesi* (Anatolian Night), *Mavı Düşler* (Blue Dreams), and *Delta.* Other additions to the Ankara company's repertory are *Köçekce,* choreographed by Oya Aruoba to a dance rhapsody composed by Ulvi Cemal Erkin in 1943; *Ebru,* the stormy love affair and dethroning of Sultan Selim III, by Altan Tekin to music by Kodalı; and *Saray Eğlenceleri* (Istanbul Palace Amusements) by Aruoba to music by Evinç Sunal.

BIBLIOGRAPHY

And, Metin. "Dances of Anatolian Turkey." *Dance Perspectives,* no. 3 (Summer 1959).

And, Metin. *A Pictorial History of Turkish Dancing.* Ankara, 1976.

And, Metin. "Opera and Ballet in Modern Turkey." In *The Transformation of Turkish Culture: The Atatürk Legacy,* edited by Günsel Renda and C. Max Kortepeter. Princeton, 1986.

And, Metin. "Les rituals et les danses extatiques mystiques de la Confrérie des Bektachis et des Alevis d'Anatolie." In *Transe, Chamanisme, Possession: De la fête à l'extase; Actes des deuxièmes rencontres internationales sur la fête et la communication, Nice Acropolis, 24–28 avril 1985.* Nice, 1986.

Arabesque. New York, 1975–.

Berger, Morroe. "A Curious and Wonderful Gymnastic: The Arab Danse du Ventre." *Dance Perspectives,* 10 (Spring 1961): 4–41.

Faruqi, Lois Lamya' al-. "Dances of the Muslim Peoples." *Dance Scope* 11.1 (1976–1977): 43–51.

Faruqi, Lois Lamya' al-. "Dance as an Expression of Islamic Culture." *Dance Research Journal* 10.2 (1978): 6–13.

Halman, Talat Sait, and Metin And. *Mevlana Celaleddin Rumi and the Whirling Dervishes.* Istanbul, 1983.

Haq, Sirajul. "Samāᶜ and Raqṣ of the Darwishes." *Islamic Culture* 18.2 (1944): 111–130.

James, D. W. "Some Turkish Folk Dances." *The Dancing Times* (October 1946): 14–15.

Masᶜūdī, Abū al-Ḥasan ᶜAlī al-. *Les prairies d'or (Murūj al-dhahab wa maᶜādin al-jawhar).* Vol. 8. Translated by C. A. C. Barbier de Meynard. Paris, 1874.

Molé, Marijan. "La danse extatique en Islam." In *Les danses sacrées,* edited by Jean Cazeneuve. Paris, 1963.

Rezvani, Madjid K. *Le théâtre et la danse en Iran.* Paris, 1962.

Saygun, Ahmed Adnun. "Des danses d'Anatolie et de leur caractère rituel." *Journal of the International Folk Music Council* 2 (1950): 10–14.

Shiloah, Amnon. "Réflexions sur la danse artistique musulmane au moyen âge." *Cahiers de Civilisation Médiévale* 6 (October–November 1962): 463–474.

Tabbārah, Shafīq. *Al-raqṣ fī lubnān.* Beirut, 1957.

Yönetken, Halil. "Turkish Folk Dances." *Rosin the Bow* 4.7 (1952).

METIN AND

TURKMENISTAN. Sharing a long northern and eastern border with Uzbekistan and a corner of Kazakhstan, with Afghanistan and Iran on the south and the Caspian Sea on the west, Turkmenistan, in Central Asia, is largely covered by a desert, the Kara Kum. Long occupied by fiercely independent horse-riding tribes, it became a province of ancient Persia, then passed successively to Arab, Mongol, and Uzbek Khiva khanate rule to become a Turkic-speaking Muslim nation. It became part of Russian Turkistan in the late 1800s, and a constituent republic of the USSR in 1925. With the dissolution of the USSR in 1991, Turkmenistan became an independent state.

Turkmenistan has no documented history of dance prior to the early twentieth century. The feudal system, tribal strife, oppression by the khanate, predatory raids by foreigners, and restrictive national and religious customs precluded a focus on dance.

In 1936 a group of Turkmen children was sent to the Leningrad Choreographic Institute, and two years later the first Turkmenian ballet school and workshop was established in the capital, Ashkhabad, with the assistance of Russian teachers. In 1939 the workshop's choreographer, Leonid Yakobson, created the first Turkmenian piece, *Ak-Eshekli.* Further work was carried out by Nikolai Kholfin at the Ashkhabad Opera and Ballet Theater, which opened in 1941; the first full evening of ballet took place that year. Also in 1941 the Turkmenian folk dance company was established under the leadership of Ivan Boiko. The first dances he staged were based on traditional folk art motifs: carpet weaving, carving, games, and rituals. The company gave its first concert in 1942.

The first ballet on a national theme was Kholfin's *Aldar Kose* (1942) to music by Klimenty Korchmarev. It tells the story of the folk hero of Turkmenistan, who is the protector of the poor; thanks to his courage he conquers the khan. For the idolized hero Kholfin created stylized Turkmenian folk dances and incorporated innovative narrative passages, familiar folk games, and imitations of work movements. A later version by Kosha Japarov enriched the movement vocabulary of the ballet, which deepened and consolidated its message. Still a favorite, the production is considered a landmark in the history of Turkmenian ballet.

In the 1980s the dancers Gulbakhar Musaeva and Akhmed Pursianov enjoyed special popularity, creating roles in both the national and classical repertories. During the early 1990s, there was practically no ballet activity.

BIBLIOGRAPHY

Ataev, S. A. *Tantsuet Turkmenistan.* Ashkhabad, 1965.

Uralskaya, Valeria. "Sozdanie traditsii." *Sovetskii balet,* no. 5 (1982).

N. P. RADKINA
Translated from Russian

TURNER, HAROLD (born 2 December 1909 in Manchester, died 2 July 1962 in London), British dancer, teacher, and ballet master. Turner began his training at sixteen with Alfred Haines and made his debut with the Haines English Ballet; encouraged by Léonide Massine, he studied next with Marie Rambert in London. In 1930 Tamara Karsavina joined Rambert's company as a guest artist and chose Turner to partner her in *Le Spectre de la Rose* and *Les Sylphides.* During the next several years, after dancing his first dazzling Bluebird and a Harlequin of overflowing gaiety to Karsavina's Columbine in *Le Carnaval,* Turner emerged as the first male virtuoso produced by British training.

Previously a guest artist, he joined the Vic-Wells Ballet as a principal in 1935, creating both the elegant Dancing Master and the crazed Gentleman with a Rope in *The Rake's Progress.* He followed these in 1937 with his two most important creations: the impudent Blue Skater in Frederick Ashton's *Les Patineurs* and the grim, zealous Red Knight in Ninette de Valois's *Checkmate.* He stamped all his roles with classical virtuosity and personal magnetism.

Turner left the company during the 1940s to perform and choreograph for the Arts Theatre Ballet and International Ballet and complete his military service; he returned in 1945, danced his first Rake, and then became the first British dancer to portray the Miller in *Le Tricorne,* succeeding Massine in 1947. He chose this vigorous *demi-caractère* role for his farewell performance in 1950.

Upon retiring, Turner became the ballet master of the Covent Garden Opera Ballet, an honored teacher at the Sadler's Wells School, and an occasional guest artist with the Sadler's Wells Ballet. Enlisted to appear as the old Marquis di Luca in the 1962 revival of Massine's *The Good-Humored Ladies,* he died on the way to his dressing room after a rehearsal.

BIBLIOGRAPHY

Anthony, Gordon. "Harold Turner." In Anthony's *A Camera at the Ballet: Pioneer Dancers of the Royal Ballet.* Newton Abbot, 1975.

Turner, Harold. "Ballet in Opera." *The Dancing Times* (April 1958): 315–316.

Vaughan, David. *Frederick Ashton and His Ballets.* London, 1977.

BARBARA NEWMAN

TURNOUT. [*This entry comprises two articles. The first examines physical turnout of the dancer's legs and the second surveys the history and aesthetics of the practice.*]

Physical Mechanics

In dancers' parlance, "turnout" refers to a position of the legs that is effected by lateral rotation of the hip joints.

Anatomically, the form of the hip joint is analogous to a ball and socket. This form provides the greatest mobility of all the body's joints, in all three dimensions: forward and backward, side to side, and rotationally outward and inward. Many athletic activities, and dance in particular, exploit the mobility of the ball and socket joints; even walking requires the rhythmic motions of these joints for smooth striding over changing terrains.

Lateral rotation is measured in degrees of the arc through which the toes pass as the ball of the hip swivels in the socket of the pelvis. Zero degrees is indicated where the toes are oriented straight forward. This basic anatomical position is referred to as "parallel." From parallel, each leg is normally capable of lateral rotation of between 15 and 50 degrees.

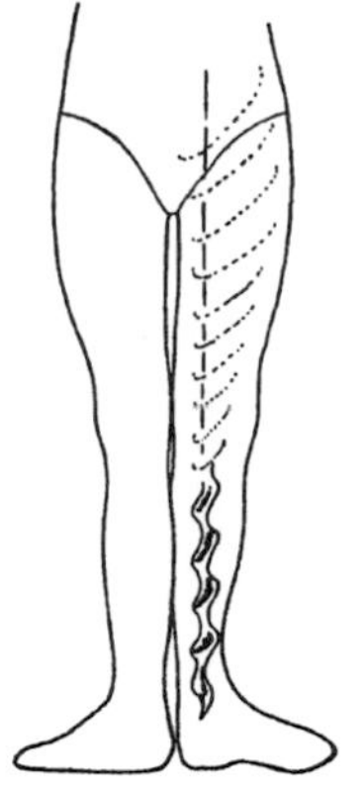
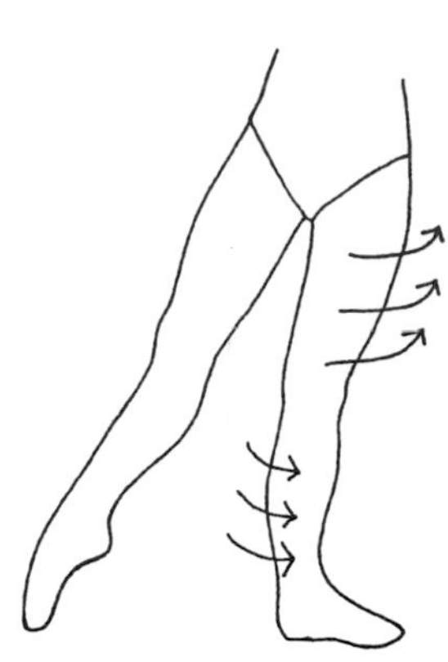

TURNOUT: Physical Mechanics. Turnout comes from the rotation of the femur (thigh bone) in the hip socket and is an active movement rather than a static placement of the leg. (Drawing by Naomi Rosenblatt; reprinted by permission from Valerie Grieg, *Inside Ballet Technique,* Pennington, N.J., 1994, p. 53.)

The parallel position provides a convenient but inexact standard. The numerous bones and many joints of the leg all affect the alignment and movement of the limb. Genetic variations from one individual to another are manifold, so the range of "normal" bone alignment and joint configuration is necessarily broad.

It is normal for the foot to be oriented 15 to 30 degrees laterally from the anterior orientation of the knee. The knee may also be oriented between five degrees medial or inward rotation to 15 degrees lateral rotation within the normal genetic range. Therefore, an absolute parallel alignment of the foot and knee with the anterior or forward aspect of the hip is a rare anatomical configuration. Furthermore, the science of arthrometry (joint measurement) has identified nine independent genetic factors at the hip alone that delimit the motions of the entire leg.

Positions in dance techniques, although absolute in the manuals, are actually different for each body, in much the same way that anatomical parallel is different from person to person. Turnout in ballet and most modern dance techniques is, optimally, 50 degrees for beginning students and 90 degrees for advanced students. Considering that 50 degrees of rotation is the maximum normal range, anything approaching optimal turnout must be achieved by compensating elsewhere, often by hyperextending the lower back or rolling inward on the arches of the feet.

Turnout training emphasizes use of the twelve small muscles deep within the pelvis that are the prime movers for lateral rotation of the hips. Because these muscles are neither visible beneath the skin nor clearly and independently sensed by feedback mechanisms, the dancer has no direct image of their sizes, insertions, or feeling of their force of contraction. Therefore the dancer must learn to judge proper placement from external appearances and from hands-on instruction.

Increases of from 5 to 10 degrees in turnout are not unusual as a result of careful training of adults. Greater increases almost invariably impose stresses on the weakest joints of the leg, on the ligaments, tendons, and cartilages. Turnout in children can be increased by as much as 30 degrees, but this should be done slowly and with great care. The individual's structure might not be genetically designed to operate efficiently in that altered configuration, and the consequences of forcing the turnout can be severe and irreversible.

BIBLIOGRAPHY

"A Guide to the Impairment of the Extremities and Back." *Journal of the American Medical Association* (15 February 1958): 82–83.

Moore, Margaret L. "Clinical Assessment of Joint Motion." In *Therapeutic Exercise,* vol. 6.1, edited by John V. Basmajian. 5th ed. Baltimore, 1990.

Napier, John. "The Antiquity of Human Walking." *Scientific American* 216 (April 1967): 56–66.

Steindler, Arthur. *Kinesiology.* Springfield, Ill., 1955.

Stuart, Muriel, et al. *The Classic Ballet.* New York, 1952. See pages 26–27.

Wilson, John M. "Kinesiology for Dance." *Arts* 2.2 (1981): 8–14.

JOHN M. WILSON

History and Aesthetics

Turnout is the rotation outward, or *en dehors,* of the legs from the hip joints. For contemporary classical ballet, ideal turnout allows the feet to form a straight line, or a 180-degree angle, when the heels are placed together in first position. To be fully turned outward was deemed the "first essential for the legs" by Carlo Blasis in 1820. However, the desirability of performing social and theatrical dances with turned-out legs can be documented for the two hundred years preceding Blasis, for aesthetic as well as utilitarian reasons.

François de Lauze, writing in 1623, advised that steps be made with "the toes well outward" so that movements "free from all timidity, proceed from the hip." Even though a lady's feet might not show beneath her long gown, they should be turned outward, for it was much more graceful to dance in that manner, according to de Lauze.

Earlier indications of turnout appeared in the 1589 publication of *Orchesography* by Thoinot Arbeau, who suggested that the degree of the angle of the feet be left to the discretion of the dancer. However, he believed that the "natural rotation of the leg will not permit it to exceed a right angle." Furthermore, a gentleman's toes should not be "too positively turned out," for that gave a "feminine appearance." However, as Ingrid Brainard (1983) notes, fifteenth-century Burgundian gentlemen posed, stepped, and danced with feet turned outward as a matter of expediency when wearing shoes with fashionably long points. Italians of the same period, in more modest footwear, are pictured with their legs and feet in parallel positions. Indeed, any degree of turnout was discouraged by Italian dancing masters of the sixteenth and early seventeenth centuries. Fabritio Caroso, for instance, cautioned that, whether dancing or not, it was a most ugly sight to "point one foot south and the other north," as if the feet were misshapen by nature (Caroso, 1600).

Despite such objections, turnout of the legs was incorporated in the codification of the five positions of the feet by the end of the seventeenth century. As depicted in Feuillet's *Chorégraphie* (1700), the angle of turnout in first position was about ninety degrees and remained no more than an obtuse angle throughout most of the century.

In the mid-eighteenth century, Jean-Georges Noverre, an advocate of a return to more "natural" movement and gesture, nevertheless believed that "in order to dance well . . . nothing is so important as the turning outward of the thigh" (Noverre, 1760). Elegance and grace made it imperative "to reverse the order of things and force the limbs, by means of exercise" into a "totally different position from that which is natural to them." Condemning the use of the *tourne-hanche,* or hip-turner machine, Noverre advocated regular practice of *ronds de jambe* and *grands battements tendus,* "working from the hip" in order to become well turned outward.

By the nineteenth century, it was so essential to be turned out that Blasis advised aspiring dancers be given careful physical examinations before being allowed to "embark upon a career which demands certain natural endowments," such as the capacity for extreme turnout (Blasis, 1820).

In the twentieth century, complete 180-degree turnout continues to be espoused for both aesthetic and practical purposes. According to Edward Villella (1992), "Turnout initiates movement; turnout extends movement." Thus, he believes that turnout "isn't a position. It's the constant rotation of the body outward from the center." For André Levinson (1925) a completely turned out fifth position is the very "spirit of classic dancing."

Rebellion against the strictures of classic dancing led early twentieth-century choreographers to abandon turnout as they sought new, freer approaches to dance movement. By the 1950s, however, turnout of the legs had been incorporated into most modern-dance techniques, again justified by both aesthetic and practical considerations.

[*See also* Ballet Technique, *article on* Feet Positions.]

BIBLIOGRAPHY

Arbeau, Thoinot. *Orchesography* (1589). Translated by Mary Stewart Evans. New York, 1948. Reprinted with introduction, corrections, and notes by Julia Sutton, New York, 1967.

Beaumont, Cyril W., and Stanislas Idzikowski. *A Manual of the Theory and Practice of Classical Theatrical Dancing (Méthode Cecchetti).* London, 1922. New York, 1975.

Blasis, Carlo. *An Elementary Treatise upon the Theory and Practice of the Art of Dancing* (1820). Translated by Mary Stewart Evans. New York, 1944.

Brainard, Ingrid. "Modes, Manners, Movement: The Interaction of Dance and Dress from the Late Middle Ages to the Renaissance." In *Proceedings of the Sixth Annual Conference, Society of Dance History Scholars, Ohio State University, 11–13 February 1983,* compiled by Christena L. Schlundt. Milwaukee, 1983.

Caroso, Fabritio. *Nobiltà di dame* (1600). Translated and edited by Julia Sutton. Oxford, 1986.

Feuillet, Raoul-Auger. *Chorégraphie, ou L'art de décrire la dance, par caractères, figures et signes démonstratifs, avec lesquels on apprend facilement de soy-même toutes sortes de dances.* Paris, 1700. Translated by John Weaver as *Orchesography, or, The Art of Dancing* (London, 1706).

Lauze, François de. *Apologie de la danse, 1623: A Treatise of Instruction in Dancing and Deportment.* Translated by Joan Wildeblood. London, 1952.

Levinson, André. "The Spirit of the Classic Dance" (1925). In *Dance as a Theatre Art,* edited by Selma Jeanne Cohen. New York, 1974.

Noverre, Jean-Georges. *Lettres sur la danse et sur les ballets.* Stuttgart and Lyon, 1760. Translated by Cyril W. Beaumont as *Letters on Dancing and Ballets* (London, 1930).

Rameau, Pierre. *Le maître à danser.* Paris, 1725. Translated by Cyril W. Beamont as *The Dancing Master* (London, 1931).

Villella, Edward. *Prodigal Son.* New York, 1992.

SANDRA NOLL HAMMOND

TUTU. Claude Bessy, a *première danseuse étoile* at the Paris Opera (1956–1971), in a typically French tutu, somewhat shorter and puffier than the platelike tutus usually worn in such Russian classics as *Swan Lake* and *The Sleeping Beauty.* Note that the bodice, made in several sections and heavily boned, is perfectly fitted to the dancer's torso. (Photograph by Studio Liseg, Paris; from the Dance Collection, New York Public Library for the Performing Arts.)

TURNS. *For discussion of turning movements in ballet, see* Ballet Technique, *article on* Turning Movements.

TUTU. A woman's ballet costume, a tutu consists of a closefitting bodice and a bouffant skirt made of many layers of tarlatan, muslin, tulle, gauze, silk, nylon, or other thin, lightweight fabrics. The word, which is said to derive from French children's slang for the human buttocks, is sometimes used to indicate the skirt only. The length of the skirt varies; it is often called a "classical" tutu if it is knee-length or shorter and a "Romantic" tutu if it reaches to the midcalf or ankle. Although the tutu, along with toe shoes, has come to symbolize ballet to the popular mind, it did not make its appearance until the nineteenth century and is no longer considered compulsory by today's choreographers and costume designers, having been superseded to some extent by softer, more free-flowing skirts of chiffon, nylon, or other fabrics.

The Romantic tutu, so called because of its association with the Romantic period in ballet, developed first. It originated in the late 1820s, probably evolving gradually out of the costumes of the time. The basic silhouette of the Romantic tutu appears in a costume designed by Hippolyte Lecomte for Pauline Montessu to wear in *La Somnambule* (1827). Marie Taglioni wore a similar costume as the Naiad in Jean Aumer's *La Belle au Bois Dormant* (1829) and as Flora in a revival of Charles-Louis Didelot's *Flore et Zéphire* (1831). The origin of the tutu is sometimes traced to the costume worn by Taglioni in the title role of *La Sylphide* (1832), and its invention is sometimes credited to Eugène Lami, the costume designer of the ballet. However, no actual design for the Sylphide was found among Lami's sketches for the ballet. Ivor Guest (1981) believes that the Sylphide costume "differed little from the basic costume that a ballerina would have worn in class," and that it was distinguished from its predecessors mainly by its simplicity and white color.

The tutu proved to be the perfect costume for the supernatural creatures that dominated the Romantic ballet, for its floating skirts lent them a weightless quality and its white color symbolized their pure, ethereal nature. It could also be adapted for the use of more earthly beings by altering the cut and color of the bodice and skirt and by adding details and accessories that suggested national or period costumes. The shape of the skirt was influenced by contemporary women's fashions such as the crinoline; it became shorter and more bouffant, and when the bustle came into vogue in the 1870s, the tutu showed a corresponding fullness in back. The Italian ballerinas of the mid-1870s shortened their skirts to several inches above the knee in order to display their virtuosic technique. Necklines were lowered as the dancers strove to emphasize their sexual attractiveness.

By the late nineteenth century the tutu had become the ballerina's uniform. Although the corps de ballet and supernumeraries might be dressed in costumes closely approximating the authentic, the ranking ballerina wore a tutu regardless of the ballet's period or setting. The Egyptian princess in Marius Petipa's *La Fille de Pharaon* (1862) wore a tutu with an overskirt bearing "Egyptian" decorations. When Michel Fokine began to call for reforms in ballet, he protested against this practice.

In the twentieth century the so-called classical tutu achieved its platelike form, standing out stiffly from the hips. The French critic André Levinson remarked upon the contrast between the immobile skirt and the active movement performed in it.

The use of the tutu in contemporary ballet is often dictated by the mood or style the choreographer wishes to convey. Lyrical works often use the drifting, flowing Romantic tutu; an example is George Balanchine's *Serenade* (1935), which was originally costumed in brief tunics. A ballet that emphasizes academic formalism may use the more revealing classical tutu, as does Harald Lander's *Études* (1948). The tutu may also evoke a specific historical period. Fokine used the Romantic tutu in *Les Sylphides* (1909), his tribute to Taglioni's era. Balanchine's *Ballet Imperial* (1941), intended as a tribute to the late nineteenth-century classicism of Petipa and the Imperial Russian Ballet, was costumed in classical tutus. When he stripped the ballet of its imperial associations in 1973, retitling it *Tchaikovsky Piano Concerto No. 2,* the tutus were replaced by soft chiffon skirts.

[*For related discussions, see* Costume in Western Traditions *and* Designing for Dance.]

BIBLIOGRAPHY

Chaffee, George. "Three or Four Graces: A Centenary Salvo." *Dance Index* 3 (September–November 1944): 136–211.

Guest, Ivor. "Costume and the Nineteenth-Century Dancer." In *Designing for the Dancer,* by Roy Strong et al. London, 1981.

Kahane, Martine, and Delphine Pinasa. *Le tutu guide.* Paris, 1997.

Lawson, Joan, and Peter Revitt. *Dressing for the Ballet.* London, 1958.

SUSAN AU

TWO PIGEONS, THE. Original title: *Les Deux Pigeons.* Ballet in two acts. Choreography: Frederick Ashton. Music: André Messager, arranged by John Lanchbery. Libretto: Frederick Ashton, after La Fontaine. Scenery and costumes: Jacques Dupont. First performance: 14 February 1962, Royal Opera House, Covent Garden, London, Royal Ballet Touring Company. Principals: Christopher Gable (The Young Man), Lynn Seymour (The Young Girl), Elizabeth Anderton (A Gypsy Girl), Richard Farley (Her Lover).

Ashton's ballet was not the first to be mounted to Messager's score, which had been commissioned for an 1886 production at the Paris Opera. Choreographed by Louis Mérante, starring Mérante and Rosita Mauri, and with a libretto by Mérante and Henry Régnier, *Les Deux Pigeons* was an elaborate three-act ballet based on a fable by La Fontaine. Pepino, longing for a life of adventure, leaves his fiancée, Gourouli, to join a band of Gypsies. But Gourouli disguises herself as a Gypsy and wins him back. A one-act version was staged by Albert Aveline for Carlotta Zambelli at the Paris Opera in 1919.

For his version, Frederick Ashton also drew upon La Fontaine's fable, but his treatment was allegorical, set in

THE TWO PIGEONS. Lynn Seymour and Christopher Gable in the final pas de deux, in which the young lovers are reconciled. (Photograph © by Zoë Dominic; used by permission.)

late nineteenth-century bohemian Paris. In his studio, a young painter tires of the young woman who is both his model and his mistress. When a group of Gypsies enters, he is at once attracted to an alluring Gypsy girl and eventually leaves the studio in pursuit of her. In act 2, scene 1 (the Gypsy camp), the Gypsy girl encourages the rivalry of the artist and her own lover. Eventually the Gypsies manhandle the artist and throw him from the encampment. He returns to his studio to find his old lover alone. Their pas de deux of reconciliation, reaching heights of passion and intimacy, ends the ballet.

Ashton uses the classical ballet vocabulary, with entirely different inflections for the tender, intimate "pigeons," his protagonists—who use pigeonlike movements at many points—and the bold, sensual Gypsies. Comedy and pathos are combined and contrasted. The narrative theme of a man learning the nature of love from his experiences with more than one woman, treated several times by this choreographer, is developed with particular poetic precision in this work.

Jacques Dupont, in his only collaboration with Ashton, produced very successful designs, including a studio with a broad view of Parisian rooftops and Degas-style dresses for the heroine and her friends. The two leading roles were choreographed for Lynn Seymour and Donald Britton; at the first performances, however, the injured Britton was replaced by Christopher Gable. As a result, the original concept of an older man irritated with his youthful girlfriend was replaced by the story of an immature man's experience.

Retitled *The Two Pigeons* when Ashton staged it for the main company of the Royal Ballet in October 1962, the ballet quickly became popular and was frequently performed in London and in other cities of Great Britain. It has been mounted for CAPAB Ballet (1968), the Australian Ballet (1975), the National Ballet of Canada (1978), the Houston Ballet (1983), Les Ballets de Monte Carlo (1987), and the ballet company of the Teatro Regio in Turin (1992).

BIBLIOGRAPHY

Macaulay, Alastair. "Performing Pigeons." *Ballet Review* 8.1 (1980): 85–95.

Macaulay, Alastair. "Taking Flight." *Ballet News* 4 (May 1983): 33–35.

Vaughan, David. *Frederick Ashton and His Ballets*. London, 1977.

VIDEOTAPE. "A Real Choreographer," BBC-TV (1979).

ALASTAIR MACAULAY

U

UBAKALA DANCE. One of about two hundred formerly politically autonomous Igbo groups in Nigeria, the Ubakala are a patrilineal, egalitarian, achievement-oriented agricultural people. Reincarnation and ancestor honor are key tenets in their traditional polytheistic religion, which persists to some degree even among Christian converts. The most important Ubakala dance form is the dance play *nkwa,* which encompasses all phases of Ubakala life.

Although Ubakala groups transmit dance plays from one generation to the next, innovation through individual or group creation and borrowing from others are common. Social, psychological, or ecological factors catalyze the performance of a dance play. A village market, family birth or death, or festival celebration makes participation in a dance play as a performer or spectator virtually obligatory. The dry season or a moonlit night provides an opportunity for the pleasure of a *nkwa.* Motivations and desired rewards for participating in a dance play include fear of being shamed for not meeting expectations; enjoyment, social approval, prestige, or money received for a praiseworthy performance; promotion of positive social relations; the desire to introduce novelty; and the opportunity to present publicly a grievance, mediate conflict, or keep informed of current events. Furthermore, once a performance is successfully underway, it commands attention.

The Ubakala dance plays both reflect what is and suggest what might be. They send messages through rich symbolism—about values (fertility, egalitarianism, innovation, respect, and reciprocity), beliefs, and norms—which is clarified and dramatized. Movement, song texts, costume, music, and action (who does what, when, where, why, and how) clarify social relationships and their transitions. The *nkwa* delineates the roles of child, wife, mother, husband, father, grandparent, and ancestor, and promotes interdependency within and between families.

Young people of both sexes have relatively similar dance movements. Elderly men and women have their own patterns. However, when the age of both sexes is close and the biological and social sex role differentiation is greatest, there is strong contrast in the dance-movement patterns between women as life-creating and nurturing and men as life-taking warriors, actually or symbolically. Men's directional changes are more angular, their body shapes more varied and complex. Men dance in a circle extrusively, stepping in and out, leaping up and down, and moving on the ball of the foot; in contrast, women use the circle intrusively, have a more homogeneous spatial level, and move predominantly on the whole foot. Rapid speed and varied spatial use connote destruction, while more deliberate movements and limited spatial use connote construction. The warrior's killing thrust is swift; he ventures abroad. A woman's gestation-and-suckling period (about two and three-quarters years) somewhat restricts her mobility.

Because women and youths are excluded from formal ritual and political decision-making organizations, the dance play offers these groups an accepted means of demanding redress of grievances. The so-called Women's War of 1929, which was sparked by what Ubakala women believed to be unfair taxation, illustrates the *nkwa*'s potential for social drama and change. When the women's complaints expressed through the *nkwa* went unresolved, they went on a rampage, inciting riots, releasing prisoners, and attacking European trading stores. These actions moved the British to alter their colonial administration of eastern Nigeria.

[*See also* Sub-Saharan Africa *and* West Africa.]

BIBLIOGRAPHY

Hanna, Judith Lynne. *To Dance Is Human: A Theory of Nonverbal Communication* (1979). Chicago, 1987.

Hanna, Judith Lynne. "African Dance Frame by Frame: Revelation of Sex Roles through Distinctive Feature Analysis and Comments on Field Research, Film, and Notation." *Journal of Black Studies* 19 (June 1989): 422–441.

JUDITH LYNNE HANNA

UGANDA. *See* Central and East Africa. *See also* Pokot Dance.

UKRAINE. [*To survey dance in Ukraine, this entry comprises two articles: the first article discusses traditional dance; the second traces the history of ballet.*]

Traditional Dance

One of the largest countries of Europe, Ukraine occupies 233,000 square miles (600,000 square kilometers) and has a population of some fifty-two million. It borders on Poland, Belarus, Russia, the Slovak Republic, Hungary, Romania, and Moldova; the Black Sea and the Sea of Azov are to the south. The complex history of Ukraine involves numerous changes in political sovereignty and territorial definition since Neolithic pastoralists first settled in the Dnipro and Dnister valleys. Most of Ukraine was ruled by Scythia from the eighth to the first century BCE. Scythians, Sarmatians, Goths, Huns, Avars, Khazars, and other groups lived in these territories over the centuries. The leaders of Kyivan Rus' (Kievan Rus or Kievan Russia; c.900–1240) adopted Eastern Christianity and ruled a large and powerful state. The Mongols of the Golden Horde conquered Ukrainian territory in the thirteenth century, and Poland-Lithuania ruled from the fourteenth to the seventeenth century. A Cossack state was established in the mid-seventeenth century, but most of Ukraine came under the control of the Russian and Austro-Hungarian empires by the late eighteenth century. During World War I, Ukraine was the battleground of the Eastern Front. The collapse of tsarist Russia resulted in an independent Ukrainian National Republic until 1922, when Ukraine became part of the new Soviet Union. After World War II, Ukraine remained within the Soviet bloc after treaties enlarged it and gave it a seat in the United Nations. Since 1991, Ukraine has been independent.

The majority of Ukrainian territory consists of fertile steppes drained by major rivers that empty into the Black Sea and the Sea of Azov. The Carpathian mountain range crosses a small area in the southwest and the Polissian lowlands (Prypiat Marshes) lie in the northwest. Agriculture has provided good subsistence for several mellennia.

Ukraine was industrialized in the second half of the nineteenth century. This and other factors contributed to the retention of a relatively integrated and archaic peasant culture longer than in some other areas of Europe. The rich folk tradition has led to a strong emphasis on folklore and ethnography in the development of Ukrainian national consciousness.

Some 27 percent of the population of Ukraine constitute minority ethnic groups, including Russians, Jews, Belorusians, Romanians, and others. Some 14.5 million people of Ukrainian origin live outside the borders of Ukraine, either because the political boundaries do not now correspond with historical ethnolinguistic patterns or as a result of immigration since the 1880s to European Russia, Siberia, the United States, Canada, South America, western Europe, and other destinations.

Ritual and Participatory Dance. In Ukrainian territory the beginnings of human habitation are known through archaeological evidence. Speculation on dance types, functions, and contexts in the prehistoric and pre-Christian times is based on extrapolations from comparative studies and the remnants of old rituals. Since the acceptance of Christianity in 988, churchmen fighting paganism have noted that ritual ceremonies involved dance. Frescoes help shed some light on dance as part of the performances of *skomorokhy,* palace entertainers in the time of Kyivan Rus'.

UKRAINE: Traditional Dance. A nineteenth-century woodcut showing two villagers from west-central Ukraine dancing outdoors after an engagement ceremony. The dancer on the left is performing a *prisiadka,* a step typical of Ukrainian and Russian folk dances done by men. (Photograph reprinted from I. Belichko and A. V'iunyk, *Ukrains'ke narodne vesillia,* Kiev, 1969, fig. 12.)

UKRAINE: Traditional Dance. A bride, Svitlana Rusnak, dancing *rus'ka* with her brother Iurii (center) and their friends at the commencement of her wedding ceremonies in the village of Toporivtsi, Bukovina, in August 1995. (Photograph by Andriy Nahachewsky; from the Ukrainian Folklore Archives, University of Alberta.)

The oldest Ukrainian dances are characterized by circle, chain, and line formations, now preserved primarily in lyrical ritual dance-songs *(vesnianky, haivky, khorovody)* and in children's games. Dances during midwinter ritual visitations (*plias, malanka* mumming) and for wedding processionals are also seen as remnants of the ancient culture. In western Ukraine, old circular dance forms *(kolomyika, hutsulka)* continue to be common. Dances with a virtuosic improvisatory focus *(hopak, kozachok)*, most characteristic of central and eastern Ukraine, seem to constitute a slightly newer style of dance connected with the Cossack baroque. The whirling couple dances (many polka derivatives, the waltz), quadrille-forms *(kateryna, lintsei)* and new improvisatory dance styles (rock-and-roll) are common in all parts of Ukraine. This basic historical pattern correlates with the rest of Europe.

Geographic boundaries did not limit the spread of dance in Ukraine; shifting political boundaries often allowed direct contact with western Europe, Russia, the Caucasus, and Asia Minor. Common dance elements can therefore be observed with neighbors in all directions. Cosmopolitan aspects of elite dance culture were sometimes adopted by the lower classes—for example by servants in the palaces of their landlords. Contact of all kinds has increased since the 1700s through experiences at marketplaces, factories, and military service in distant lands. The spread of dance styles from the peasantry to members of the elite occurred mostly in the second half of the 1800s, inspired by the growing romantic nationalism of the time; this occurred again but somewhat differently in the time of Soviet socialist realism. Peasant dances were sometimes adapted for the ballroom but more often, they were portrayed onstage. The Soviet policy of raising the culture of the masses to so-called higher forms supported the development of stage dance.

Ritual dances continue to have their place during rites of passage. The elaborate wedding ritual involves dance, as do christenings, farewell parties for emigration and military conscription, and even funerals in some areas. Nowadays, dance events for adolescents and dance traditions associated with holidays of the calendar cycle remain numerous. *Haivky* were performed across western Ukraine on the traditional three days of Easter; in central and eastern Ukraine, similar dance-songs were performed, generally, throughout the spring season. Minor dance traditions are related to Pentecost, Kupalo (the Feast of Saint John the Baptist near midsummer), harvest, Christmas, New Year's, and before Lent in the spring and Advent in the fall. At some ritual occasions, the actual dances performed are the same as those danced during social events.

A great diversity of dance forms have been documented in Ukraine. Couple dances predominate in a variety of forms (polka, *hutsulka,* waltz). Some dances are structurally simple to allow a fair amount of improvisation. In western Ukraine, many couple dances are performed in a large circle. Some circular dances survive from older tra-

UKRAINE: Traditional Dance. Four members of the Ukrainian Dance Company perform acrobatic leaps in a Cossack dance, a *zaporozhtsi*. (Photograph from the Dance Collection, New York Public Library for the Performing Arts.)

ditions (*holubka, metelytsia,* some *hutsulka* variants), but others are newly popular forms (*sim-sorok,* often rock-and-roll). Dances for men only *(arkan, kozak,)* are less common, as are trio dances *(ocheret, verkhovyna),* and thematic forms (*shevchyky* [shoemakers], *holiar* [barber]).

Traditionally, social dancers were held on village commons or in homes on Sunday afternoons and on other holy days, except during lenten periods. In the Soviet era, the organization of social events was taken over by local branches of the Communist youth organization or other official institutions. Dances took place in "palaces of culture," in schools, and in other facilities with large rooms. Although the Soviet authorities tried to limit access to rock-and-roll, Western genres of music and dance, including rock, jazz, disco, break dancing, rap, and heavy metal, have became extremely popular—attendance at this type of dance event was usually limited to adolescents and young adults.

Wedding dances involve a much greater age range. Rural weddings typically take place in a large tent constructed near the host's house; urban weddings often take place in rented restaurants. Most ritual and participatory dance forms in Ukraine are learned informally, by observation and participation. Adolescents and unmarried adults dance most often, but married people and even seniors participate at weddings and other family-based events. In Ukrainian diaspora communities, remnants of participatory dance forms that were popular prior to emigration may be seen in Canada, Brazil, the United States, and other countries. Of particular note is a virtuosic *kolomyika* form that evolved in North America in the 1960s.

Musical traditions are very rich and vary according to region, time, and rural/urban customs. Traditional musical groups typically involved three or four performers. Violins and, more recently, accordions, carry the melody line, while flutes, hammer dulcimers, double basses, drums, tambourines, small cymbals, and other instruments are also played. Clarinets, saxophones, banjos, guitars, electronic keyboards, and many other instruments have become popular since the 1960s. Musical groups remain most desirable for weddings and other traditional dance occasions, though recorded music is less expensive and has been used on occasion. Discotheques play recorded popular music for evenings of dancing.

Folk Dance Onstage. The first Ukrainian dance performed onstage was most probably during the 1819 premiere of Ivan Kotliarevsky's play *Natalka Poltavka*. Theater was important to the growth of the Ukrainian national (independence) movement in the late 1800s and early 1900s. Comedies and melodramas with village settings were popular, and they established the tradition of presenting peasant customs, dress, song, and dance onstage. Staged folk dances evolved into a variety of formats, including folkloric-ethnographic tableaux, dramas, variety concerts, and cabarets.

After the establishment of the Soviet Union, policy required that nationalistic elements in all forms of Ukrainian dance be severely downplayed, although the great local popularity of dance and its potential for international public relations continued to be exploited. For example, the State Folk Dance Ensemble of the Ukrainian S.S.R. was formed in Kyiv (Kiev) in 1937 under the direction of Mykola Bolotov and Pavlo (Pavel) Virsky. The movement to establish this professional ensemble was based on 1930s developments in local ballet and the success of the Ukrainian performers at the 1936 International Festival of Folk Dance in London. It was also related to general developments in Soviet art dance at that time. After World War II, professional folk-stage ensembles were founded in almost all of the twenty-five provinces in Ukraine; thousands of amateur ensembles were organized through the Ministry of Culture, the Ministry of Education, and the Workers' Unions. The Ukrainian State Dance Ensemble (later named for long-time director Pavlo Virsky) has become well known. Since the 1950s, many of Virsky's choreographies have become classics, inspiring imitative compositions both in Ukraine and abroad. [*See the entry on Virsky.*] Other key choreographers include Klara Balog, Lidia Cherneshova, Iaroslav Chuperchuk, Leonid Kalinin, Anatolii (Anatole) Kryvokhyzha, Darii (Dare) Lastivka, Volodymyr Nerodenko, Mykola Vantukh, and Kim Vasylenko. By 1983, the organized amateur dance movement in Ukraine involved an estimated 425,000 participants; folk-stage dance (as it is called) was more popular than the classical ballet, ballroom, and historical dance whose ranks were also included within this number. Thousands of trained professional choreographers, rehersal directors, administrators, educators, accompanists, and wardrobe managers were employed in the industry. Dance attracted many as a form of healthy exercise, a chance for socializing, and particularly as an opportunity to travel, sometimes even abroad. With the dissolution of the Soviet Union, the cultural industries have experienced a sharp decline in funding, resulting in instability and disenchantment. If opportunities for travel have increased for some, many dance collectives have become smaller or disbanded completely.

With a few notable exceptions, the early leaders of the Ukrainian folk-stage dance movement approached this activity from the perspective of ballet professionals. The Soviet tradition of folk-stage dance *(narodno-stsenichnyi tanets')* evolved as a semi-autonomous genre related to character dance *(kharakternyi tanets')*, which itself had always been a part of ballet. The choreographers and dancers were not so much concerned with reproducing village forms but instead placed their emphasis on creating theatrical art. The extended visual line of ballet, its postures, movements, and terminology all strongly influenced the style of folk-stage movement, as did ballet's strong frontal orientation to the proscenium, its concern with monumentality, massiveness, compositional density, and technical virtuosity. High energy and color were prized, with great variety developing from the diversity of the cultures represented and the range of repertory within each. By the late 1980s and early 1990s, a rethinking of aesthetics occurred in some quarters, resulting in a slightly greater appreciation of intimacy over bravado, plus a striving for greater connection with earlier village forms and with the rising national consciousness of an independent Ukraine.

In diaspora communities, Ukrainian stage dance is extremely popular, a visible symbol of Ukrainian ethnicity owing to the efforts of Vasile (Vasily) Avramenko as early as the 1920s and the several generations of enthusiasts that followed. In the diaspora, choreographers and audiences generally declare a concern for heritage retention and fidelity to village prototypes. This stated concern for authenticity is often not reflected in the dances, however, which since the 1960s have been increasingly influenced by the appeal of technically virtuosic Soviet-style folk-stage dance.

In Soviet Ukraine, ballroom dance and the related *estrada* were popular for theatrical, participation, and competition purposes.

Institutional Structures and Research. As in other European countries, the major impetus for studying traditional dance in Ukraine was nineteenth-century Romanticism—the links to ones rural past—and the associated growth of a national consciousness, and independence movement. Song texts and music connected with peasant dance were collected, arranged, and published increasingly by the end of the 1800s. Oskar Kolberg and Volodymyr Shukhevych contributed early descriptions of such dances. This movement also gave rise to both the study of participatory dance traditions and the stage dance movement. The first book on traditional dance was published in 1919 by V. Verkovynets'. Hundreds of Soviet publications later dealt with the theatrical presentation of Ukrainian dance, and they include descriptions of repertory as well as methodological advice for leaders of dance collectives. Roman Harasymchuk (Harasymczuk) and Andrii (Andre) Humeniuk, both with ethnomusicological training, are the most important researchers of participatory dance. Harasymchuk's work remains largely unpublished, however. Some field notes and films of ritual and participatory dancing are found in archives, but these remain scattered and unsystematized, while a great deal remains in private collections. English publications on Ukrainian dance are few at this time.

Except for Harasymchuk and Humeniuk's work at Ukraine's Institute of Art Studies, Folklore, and Ethnography, and for incidental archival support, almost all institutional involvement in dance in Ukraine is connected with stage presentation and the training of performing artists. The department of dance at the Institute of Culture grants postsecondary diplomas, and dozens of pedagogical institutes and specialized high schools prepare professional dancers for work in schools as well as for amateur and professional ensembles. Research on staged dance activity has been conducted in the offices of the Ministry of Culture, the Ministry of Education, and the Workers' Unions for the republic and for provincial and local levels, since folk-stage dance had been financed by these organizations during the Soviet period. The most important authors on methodology are Iroida Antypova, Luidmila Bondarenko, and Kim Vasylenko.

BIBLIOGRAPHY

Avramenko, Vasile. *Ukrains'ki natsional'ni tanky, muzyka i strii.* Winnipeg, 1947.

Borymska, Henrietta. *Samotsvity ukrains'koho tantsiu.* Kiev, 1974.

Harasymczuk, Roman. *Tance Huculskie.* Prace Etnograficzne, vol. 5. Lvov, 1939.

Hnatiuk, Volodymyr. *Haivky.* In *Materiialy do ukrains'koi etnolohii.* Vol. 12. Lvov (Lemberg), 1909.
Humeniuk, Andrii. *Narodne khoreohrafichne mystetstvo Ukrainy.* Kiev, 1963.
Humeniuk, Andrii. *Ukrains'ki narodni tantsi.* 2d exp. ed. Kiev, 1968.
Klymasz, Robert B., ed. *The Ukrainian Folk Dance: A Symposium.* Toronto, 1961.
Nahachewsky, Andriy. "The Kolomyika: Change and Diversity in Canadian Ukrainian Folk Dance." Ph.D.diss., University of Alberta, 1991.
Nahachewsky, Andriy. *Bibliography of Ukrainian Dance: Materials Available in Canada.* Edmonton, 1993.
Shatulsky, Myron. *The Ukrainian Folk Dance.* Toronto, 1986.
Verkhovynets' [Kostiv], Vasyl'. *Teoria ukrains'koho narodnoho tanka.* 5th rev. ed. Kiev, 1990.
Zaitsev, Ievhen. *Osnovy narodno-stsenichnoho tantsiu.* 2 vols. Kiev, 1975–1976.
Zerebecky, Bohdan. *Ukrainian Dance Curriculum and Teacher's Guide.* Ukrainian Dance Resource Booklets, Series 3. Saskatoon, 1988.

ANDRIY NAHACHEWSKY

Theatrical Dance

Ukrainian dances were first seen on the professional stage in 1780 in Kharkov, at the Gorodsky (City) Theater, where a ballet company led by P. I. Ivanitsky, a dancer from Saint Petersburg, performed *divertissements* based on folk song motifs. In 1819 I. P. Kotliarevsky's drama *Natalka Poltavka,* including many round dances, the Kasachok tap dance, and comic dances, was staged at the City Theater of Poltava. A few years later, in 1823, a number of national dances by an unknown choreographer were included in a production of the opera *A Ukrainian Maiden, or The Magic Castle,* staged at the opening of the City Theater in Kiev.

Thereafter, throughout the 1820s and 1830s, Ukrainian dances and ballets were often performed in the cities of Kharkov, Kiev, and Odessa by touring theatrical companies led by I. F. Stein and L. I. Mlotkovsky. After 1840, Russian and Polish ballet companies began to make fairly frequent tours in Ukraine, and during the 1860s ballets from the standard repertory (e.g., *Esmeralda, Giselle,* and *Catarina, ou La Fille du Bandit*) were seen on the stage of the Italian Opera House in Kiev. A permanent Russian Opera House was opened in Kiev in 1867, but the resident ballet company was too small to mount major dance works. In 1893, however, the ballet company was expanded and, under the direction of various Polish choreographers, gave regular performances for the next twenty-five years. Works bearing such titles as *The Ukrainian Ballet, A Holiday at the Seaside, Harvesting in the Ukraine,* and *Festival of Hungarian Gypsies* typically included Ukrainian folk dances. More modern works were introduced in 1915, when Bronislava Nijinska and her husband, Aleksandr Kochetovsky, spent two years in Kiev staging ballets from the repertory of Diaghilev's Ballets Russes.

The development of Ukrainian theatrical dance was associated with the activities of the Ukrainian classical theater in the late nineteenth century, especially with the musical dramas and operas produced by M. L. Kropivnitsky and M. P. Staritsky. In 1899 Kropivnitsky successfully collaborated with the Polish dancer and choreographer Foma Nijinsky, who produced dances for Nikolai Arkas's opera *Katerina.* This work, which is among the earliest Ukrainian operas, was based on a poem by Taras Shevchenko, generally considered the father of Ukrainian

UKRAINE: Theatrical Dance. Members of the Virsky Academic Dance Company of Ukraine in a scene from the last act of *The Sleeping Beauty,* performed in Kiev in December 1938. (Photograph by B. Kosiuk; from the Dance Collection, New York Public Library for the Performing Arts.)

UKRAINE: Theatrical Dance. Members of the Donetsk Ballet in *Paquita*. (Photograph © 1989 by Jack Vartoogian; used by permission.)

national literature. Productions of Shevchenko's plays also often included folk dances.

In the early twentieth century, the Ukrainian permanent theater in Kiev staged not only dramas and comedies but also many national operas and operettas with dances created by the choreographer and folklorist V. N. Verkhovinets. In 1919 the first Ukrainian opera and ballet theater, called the Ukrainian Musical Drama, was opened in Kiev, where ballets were staged by Mikhail Mordkin and others. In 1924, in Kharkov, the first production of the Ukrainian heroic opera *Taras Bulba,* composed in 1890 by Mykola Lysenko, was a significant event. It included dance scenes staged by the choreographers R. I. Balanotti, M. A. Sobol, and V. N. Verkhovinets. The following year, 1925, the first national opera and ballet theater was opened in Kharkov, and the dance company, led by Balanotti, Sobol, and Verkhovinets, soon built up a repertory of both classical and national choreography.

In 1926 the theaters of Kharkov, Kiev, and Odessa formed an association under the guidance of artistic director I. M. Lapitsky. The Kharkov company, led by Mikhail P. Moiseyev, was the first in Ukraine to stage the Soviet ballet *The Red Poppy* (1927). Other companies soon followed with versions of their own. In 1931 Vasily Litvinenko, collaborating with Verkhovinets, staged in Kharkov the heroic ballet *Pan Kanevsky* to music by M. I. Velikovsky. This was the first Ukrainian ballet to integrate the language and forms of classical dance and Ukrainian folk dance, the traditions of ballet and the national musical drama theater. Theatrical folk dance was further developed in operas such as Boris Liatoshinsky's *The Golden Hoop* (1929), in which the dances were staged by Pavel Virsky, Verkhovinets, and Sobol. The latter two were invited to Kiev in 1934, and Virsky was appointed head of the ballet company of the opera house there in 1936. The following year, with N. A. Bolotov, Virsky founded the Ukrainian State Folk Dance Company, for which he tapped the roots of Ukrainian folkore in choreographed works such as *Zaporazhe Cossacks, Polzunets,* and *Why Is the Willow Tree Weeping?* After his death in 1979 Miroslav Vantukh was appointed artistic director of the company; he maintains the Virsky repertory and adds new works of his own in the same style.

In 1940 the ballet *Lilea* was presented in Kiev with choreography by G. A. Berezova and Sobol. The score by Konstantin Dankevich was based on motifs in Shevchenko's poems, and the story of the ballet is dramatic. A landlord separates a loving peasant couple, Lilea and Stephan. She becomes a dancer in the serf theater; he goes to the Cossack War and, after losing his sight in a battle, becomes a musician. Some time later, rebels burst into the home of the landowner, where guests are being entertained by his dancers. Stephan is with the rebels, but Lilea perishes in the skirmish. The rebels raise her corpse overhead and carry her as a symbol of undying love and freedom.

Lilea is important because of the way in which folk elements form the dramatic base of the choreography, defining the distinctiveness of the work as a whole. The search for a modern, national choreographic language was continued in the heroic ballet *Svetlana*, staged in Kharkov by Pavel Yorkin in 1941.

Meanwhile, works from the classical repertory were also staged in various Ukrainian cities. In 1940 the Franko Opera and Ballet Theater was opened in Lvov. In 1943 in Kharkov the composer and conductor Grigory Veriovka formed a choral and dance group to celebrate pan-Ukrainian indigenous culture. Called Veriovka Ukrainian National Dance Company, now under the direction of Anatoly Avdevsky, the dance portion of the company comprises young, ballet-trained dancers. Touring the United States in 1996, the company presented theatricalized folk dances, such as the "Gopak," "Taras Bulba," and dances of the Carpathian region, as well as folk-based scenes staged by the chief choreographer, Aleksei Gomon (who had worked with Virsky's company), and works by other choreographers—Anatoly Shekera's "The Fern Is Blooming" and Yaroslav Chuperchuk's "Turtle-Dove."

During the years of World War II, the ballet companies of Kiev and Kharkov worked in Irkutsk, while the groups of Odessa and Dnepropetrovsk went to Krasnoiarsk. After the war, a number of large-scale ballets based on Ukrainian literary sources were staged—for example, *The Forest Song* (1946), *Marusya Boguslavka* (1951), *Rostislava* (1955), *The Shadows of Forgotten Ancestors* (1960), and *Oksana* (1964)—and more works from the classical repertory—*Romeo and Juliet, Cinderella, The Stone Flower, Spartacus,* and, of course, *Swan Lake, The Sleeping Beauty,* and *Raymonda*—were produced by Russian ballet masters. In the 1960s and 1970s principles of symphonism enriched the choreography of the national ballets, with new works being created by Vakhtang Vronsky, Virsky, and Anatoly Shekera. Shekera's *The Stone Ruler* (1972), based on the drama by Lesya Ukrainka, was important in this development. At the same time, the process of gathering and analyzing national folklore continued, as it does today.

Since the 1960s Ukrainian companies have made frequent tours abroad. They have won numerous awards, and in 1964 the company of the Shevchenko Opera and Ballet Theater in Kiev won first prize at the International Dance Festival in Paris. There are now six opera and ballet theaters in Ukraine, and the Kharkov, Odessa, and Lvov theaters have associated ballet schools. The State Ballet School, established in Kiev in 1934, trains dancers for both ballet and folk dance companies, and the Department of Theatrical Arts at the M. F. Rylsky Institute of Art Research, Folklore, and Ethnography, with branches in Kiev and Lvov, has long been the center for the study of the history of theatrical dance in Ukraine.

[*See also the entry on Virsky.*]

BIBLIOGRAPHY

Schreyer-Tkachenko, A., ed. *Istoriya ukrainskoy muzyki.* Moscow, 1981.

Stanishevsky, Yuri. *Ukrainsky radyansky balet.* Kiev, 1963.

Stanishevsky, Yuri. *Ukrainsky radyansky muzychny teatr, 1917–1967.* Kiev, 1970.

Stanishevsky, Yuri. *Baletnyi teatr Sovetskoi Ukrainy, 1925–1985.* Kiev, 1986.

Warrack, John, and Ewan West. *The Oxford Dictionary of Opera.* Oxford and New York, 1992.

ARCHIVES. The Ukrainian State Museum of Theatrical, Musical, and Cinematographic Art and the Karpenko-Kary State Theatrical Institute, both in Kiev, contain extensive holdings of books and archival materials.

YURI A. STANISHEVSKY
Translated from Russian

ULANOVA, GALINA (Galina Sergeevna Ulanova; born 8 January 1910 in Saint Petersburg), Russian ballet dancer. Ulanova was born into a family of dancers. Her father, Sergei Nikolaevich Ulanov, was a dancer and ballet master; her mother, Maria Fedorovna Romanova, was a dancer and her daughter's first teacher at the Petrograd (Leningrad) Choreographic Institute. In the advanced class Ulanova's teacher was Agrippina Vaganova. From the beginning Ulanova was a hard worker at the ballet barre, and her talents were soon recognized. For her graduation performance in 1928 she danced the waltz and mazurka from Michel Fokine's *Chopiniana.* In her first season as a member of the Kirov Ballet, she danced Princess Florine in *The Sleeping Beauty;* in her second season, she danced Odette-Odile in *Swan Lake* and Aurora in *The Sleeping Beauty.* At the beginning of World War II she was evacuated with the company to Tashkent and then to Perm. In 1944 she was transferred to the Bolshoi Ballet, where she was *prima ballerina* until she retired in 1962; thereafter she served as the company's ballet mistress and coach.

Ulanova danced leading roles in many ballets of the standard repertory. After *Swan Lake* and *The Sleeping Beauty,* she danced *Giselle* in 1932 and *The Nutcracker* in 1934. She became best known, however, for her creation of roles in new ballets, especially Maria in Rostislav Zakharov's *The Fountain of Bakhchisarai* (1934) and Juliet in Leonid Lavrovsky's *Romeo and Juliet* (1940). She was also instrumental in the shaping of new versions of Soviet ballets, including Zakharov's *Cinderella* (1945), and Lavrovsky's *The Red Poppy* (1949) and his *The Tale of the Stone Flower* (1954). Notable among her concert numbers was her rendition of Fokine's *The Dying Swan.*

Ulanova was widely praised for her musicality. She described dance as the movement of music, that which makes music visible (Kahn, 1962, p. 31). She seemed to respond to the subtlest nuances of music not only in the precise rhythm of her dancing but also in the play of her arms and hands, and even her glances, pauses, and the inclination of her head. Her dramatic ability was equally notable. Each movement, each fleeting glance, was an im-

ULANOVA. Thanks to the 1954 Soviet film of Leonid Lavrovsky's production of *Romeo and Juliet,* Ulanova can still be seen in one of her greatest roles. This still photograph, taken from the film, shows her as Juliet with Yuri Zhdanov as Romeo. (Photograph from the Dance Collection, New York Public Library for the Performing Arts.)

portant link, defining the meaning of the sequence to follow. In the words of Konstantin Stanislavsky, she strove to express the life of the human soul. Seeking inspiration in the works of Aleksandr Pushkin and Shakespeare, she created profound tragic images, conveying through dance the most complex dramatic conflicts.

With Ulanova, the almost imperceptible moment of suspended animation was neither an interruption of the dance nor an ending; rather, it seemed as if the moment were gradually fading, melting, and dissolving into the air. This unique art in her plastique of *ritardando* or fading away created a *pianissimo* effect of great expressiveness. Ulanova avoided abrupt stops; her dance flowed freely, reflecting the movements of the spirit. Her virtuosity, not flamboyant, gave priority to the living, vibrating flexibility of line. Without sharp accents or staccato rhythms she embodied the most delicate, tremulous images of femininity, weightlessness, and softness. Truly Russian, her art combined the poetic lucidity of Pushkin with the modesty and laconic manner of Chekhov—a perfect match for the music of Tchaikovsky.

Ulanova wrote that she loved the role of Maria in *The Fountain of Bakhchisarai* because it expressed Pushkin's poetry so well. She felt at once that the character of the captured princess had to be individualized, but her concept of the character developed over the years. At first, she felt, her portrayal of Maria was one of all-pervading grief. The portrait later changed, becoming more intricate and brighter, with hints of joy and youth in the first act. The character of Juliet developed from the music, although Ulanova found Prokofiev's music difficult, often abrupt, and bewildering with its frequent changes of rhythm. Nevertheless, she soon found in the score a harmony of thought and action. For her, Juliet appeared as a character of strong will, ready to fight and die for happiness, like the contemporary "heroine of the people" ready to die for a patriotic cause. This made the centuries-old tragedy seem new. This kind of concern also attracted her to the character of Tao-Hoa in *The Red Poppy,* a role requiring both lyricism and valor.

A traditionalist, Ulanova excelled in dance drama, appearing uninterested in abstract works or in the modern experiments that were prevalent in the Soviet Union in her time. An isolated venture into the latter was the role of Komsomolka in Vasily Vainonen, Leonid Yakobson, and Vladimir Chesnakov's *The Golden Age* (1930). She told Albert Kahn (1962): "For me, the value of my work lies in the conviction that the language of the ballet can convey to people great and vital truths about life, about the beauty in life and in the human heart."

ULANOVA. The British film *The Bolshoi Ballet,* released by the Rank Organisation in 1957, contains a complete performance of *Giselle,* with Ulanova in the title role. (Photograph from the Dance Collection, New York Public Library for the Performing Arts.)

In the 1950s Ulanova's art won her worldwide recognition in places as farflung as Egypt and China. She first danced in western Europe at the Maggio Musicale Fiorentino in 1951. This was followed by performances with the Bolshoi Ballet in Berlin (1954), London (1956), Japan (1957), Paris (1958), and the United States and Canada (1959, 1962). In a London review Richard Buckle wrote of her Giselle that she "painted all the shyness, doubts and delicate hesitations of first love and at times she conveyed rapture. . . . There was a delicious exhilaration in her *petits battements,* and her *pas ballonnés* were like a draft of mountain air." In New York the *New York Times* critic John Martin described her Juliet as one of the greatest, spoken or unspoken. Seeing her when she was nearly fifty years old, he claimed that her youthfulness in the role transcended in artistic values the youthfulness of nature.

After retiring from the stage Ulanova dedicated herself to directing and teaching. Among her students who became major figures in Soviet ballet are Nina Timofeyeva, Ekaterina Maximova, Vladimir Vasiliev, Ludmila Semenyaka, Malika Sabirova, and Nina Semizorova. In her role as mentor Ulanova has said that she wanted to develop the imagination of the young dancers, to help them to think creatively. "The artist creates the role; the teacher molds the personality of the artist into one capable of creating an artistic image," she wrote (1959). Maximova has testified to Ulanova's emphasis in coaching on the development of the character of the role, a task requiring not only physical effort, for perfect technical control, but emotional and intellectual work.

As chairman of the Bolshoi Ballet Council, Ulanova participated in the programming of performances and casting and was involved in the general supervision of the company's affairs. She was also chairman of the examining board of the Bolshoi school, and she frequently served as both the chairperson and a member of the jury of the international ballet competitions held in Moscow and Varna. She received numerous honors in the USSR and internationally: Honored Artist of the USSR (1939), National Artist of the USSR (1940), states prizes (1941, 1946, 1947, 1950), People's Artist of the USSR (1951), the Biotti Prize in Italy (1959), honorary memberships in the Academy of Arts of the German Democratic Republic (1959) and the American Academy of Science and Art (1960), and Hero of Socialist Labor (1974, 1980).

In 1981 in Paris, UNESCO sponsored a gala in honor of Ulanova for which Vasiliev created *Tribute to Ulanova.* In 1984 in Stockholm and in Leningrad sculptures of her were installed.

BIBLIOGRAPHY

Bogdanov-Berezovskii, V. M. *Ulanova and the Development of the Soviet Ballet.* Translated by Stephen Garry and Joan Lawson. London, 1952.

Brinson, Peter, ed. *Ulanova, Moiseyev, and Zakharov on Soviet Ballet.* Translated by E. Fox and D. Fry. London, 1954.

Clarke, Mary. *Six Great Dancers.* London, 1957.

Golubov, Vladimir. *Tanets Galiny Ulanovoi.* Leningrad, 1948.

Gould, Susan. "Talking with Galina Ulanova." *Dance Scope* 14 (September 1980): 8–15.

Ilupina, Anna. *Ballerina: The Life and Work of Galina Ulanova.* Philadelphia, 1965.

Kahn, Albert E. *Days with Ulanova.* New York, 1962.

Potapov, Vladimir. "Galina Ulanova." In *The Soviet Ballet,* by Yuri Slonimsky et al. New York, 1947.

Lvov-Anokhin, Boris. *Galina Ulanova* (in English). 2d ed. Moscow, 1984.

Smakov, Gennady. *The Great Russian Dancers.* New York, 1984.

Swift, Mary Grace. *The Art of the Dance in the U.S.S.R.* Notre Dame, 1968.

Ulanova, Galina. *The Making of a Ballerina.* Translated by S. Rosenberg. Moscow, 1959.

BORIS A. LVOV-ANOKHIN
Translated from Russian

ULRICH, JOCHEN (born 3 August 1944 in Osterode), German dancer, choreographer, and company director. Having studied at the Cologne Institute of Theater Dance from 1964 to 1967, Jochen Ulrich became a member of the Cologne State Opera Ballet in 1967. A talented dancer, he was soon cast in soloist roles. He was also quickly given the opportunity to try his hand at choreography, which allowed him to experiment with modern forms of dance movement. With the support of some of his colleagues in the company, Ulrich managed over the next few years to transform the opera ballet company into a contemporary dance company. Although still attached to the Cologne opera house, the company was modeled on such experimental troupes as the Netherlands Dance Theater and Ballet Rambert. The daily classes for the dancers came to be less strictly based on the classical ballet vocabulary and increasingly influenced by the modern technique of Martha Graham.

In 1971 the company was officially renamed the Tanz-Forum der Oper der Stat Köln (Dance Forum of the Cologne State Opera). Ulrich functioned as first among equals in a tripartite directorship shared with Helmut Baumann—later replaced by Jürg Burth—and Gray Veredon. Since the 1978/79 season, Ulrich has been the sole director and chief choreographer of the Cologne Dance Forum, which he has developed into one of the foremost modern-oriented German dance companies, frequently collaborating with such international choreographers as Glen Tetley, Hans van Manen, and Christopher Bruce. Under his aegis, the company has performed in many countries. In 1995, the Cologne Dance Forum became an independent company, with a guaranteed number of performances at the Cologne opera house but otherwise detached from it.

Ulrich has created a large repertory of works for the

Cologne Dance Forum and has served as guest choreographer for the Wiesbaden, Munich, and Vienna State Opera ballet companies. His ballets—many of them full-length productions—shun all classical academic material. They are rather lean and somewhat strenuous, coolly sensual, lissome, and elastic. When Ulrich has occasionally dealt with topical subjects, he has always sided strongly with the socially underprivileged and economically deprived. His musical taste is catholic, and he has worked with very different kinds of music by various composers.

Notable among Ulrich's earlier works are *Lewis C.* (1970; music by Ivo Malec), *Waltz Dreams* (1977; music by Kurt Schwertsik), *The Miraculous Mandarin* (1980; music by Béla Bartók), *American Landscapes* (1983; music by George Gershwin and Charles Ives), *Lyric Suite* (1984; music by Alban Berg), and *Der Wanderer* (1984; music by Wilhelm Killmayer and Franz Schubert). His works from more recent years include *Neue und Curieuse Theatralische Tanz-Schul* (1988; music by Mauricio Kagel), *Lulu* (1990; music by Nino Rota), *Graf Dracula* (1991; music by Samuelina Tahija), *Yerma* (1992; music by Salvador Pueyo), *Carmen* (1993; music by Egberto Gismondi), *Peer Gynt* (1994; music by Jean Sibelius and Henryk Gorecki), *Goya* (1995; music by Bo Spaenc), and *Get Up Early* (1996; music by Joachim Kühn).

BIBLIOGRAPHY

Nevill, Timothy, trans. *Ballet and Dance in the Federal Republic of Germany.* Bonn, 1988.

Weigelt, Gert. *Tanz-Forum Köln.* Cologne, 1986.

HORST KOEGLER

UMEWAKA MAKIO (born 11 February 1941 in Tokyo), *nō* actor of the Kanze school, fourteenth headmaster of the Kichinojō branch of the Umewaka family, leader of the Umewaka Kennōkai troupe. Makio is the great-grandson of Umewaka Minoru I (1828–1909), who with Hōshō Kurō (1837–1917) and Sakurama Bamba (1835–1917) preserved *nō* at the beginning of the Meiji era and who taught *nō* to Ernest Fenollosa (1853–1908), the first foreigner to study it as a performing art. Makio is also the elder son of Umewaka Manzaburō II (1908–1991), who in 1956 was designated Bearer of an Important Intangible Cultural Asset by the Japanese government and whose dream was to spread *nō* around the world. (It was Manzaburō who in 1979 accepted the first non-Japanese, Stephen Comee, to train as a professional *nō* actor.)

The earliest known reference to the Umewaka family appears in a diary kept by Emperor Go-Komatsu (ruled 1392–1412) in the entry for 9 March 1416. Descended from the medieval Tamba *sarugaku* troupe, the Umewaka family also claims descent from Prince Regent Shōtoku (572–621) through Tachibana no Moroe (684–757), famous as one of the compilers of the *Man'yōshū* (Anthology of Ten Thousand Leaves for Ten Thousand Ages). The family, which had been established as the *tsure* (accompanying actor) branch of the Kanze school in 1868 by warlord Toyotomi Hideyoshi (1536–1598), broke away from the Kanze school when its headmaster fled with the defeated shogun; it remained in Tokyo, where it struggled to preserve *nō* and its traditions. In 1921 the Umewaka family, supported by the Kanze school's Tetsunojō branch, declared itself an independent school, but it again rejoined the Kanze school in 1954.

Makio debuted on the *nō* stage at the age of three, performed his first *shite* (main actor) role at seven, and at fourteen gave his first performance with a mask (indicating that a youth is now a full-fledged *nō* actor) in the play *Okina*. He participated in the official *nō* tours to Europe six times (1967–1975); led a cultural tour that performed in the United States, Canada, and Mexico (1978); performed at the University of British Columbia (1984); gave

UMEWAKA MAKIO. As the beautiful Spirit of the Wisteria *(fuji)*, Umewaka is shown dancing with joy after having attained buddhahood, in the *nō* drama *Fuji*. (Photograph by Morita Toshiro; used by permission.)

lecture-demonstrations at the Vancouver Museum (1985); and led the official Japanese delegation to perform *nō* at Canada's World's Fair in Vancouver in 1986. Makio also participated in Belgium's Europalia '89–Japan, led his troupe on a tour through France (1990), and performed and gave lecture-demonstrations throughout the United Kingdom as part of Japan Festival '91. He was dispatched by the Japan Foundation to perform *nō* for the first time in Moscow (1991). Since 1992, he has toured Hong Kong, Italy, Germany, and other countries, while remaining active in Japan, not only performing in theaters all over the country but also participating in an overwhelming number of popular torch-lit *nō* performances each year.

Makio's art is especially characterized by the flowing, balletic grace of his "dance of the angel" *(tennyo-no-mai)* and the shimmering yet dark elegance of his women, as well as by the intense power of his evil spirits (as in *Aoi no Ue* and *Dōjōji*). The fluidity of his movement adds depth and dimension to his dancing. His chanting is sung in a lyrical yet powerful manner, and the intensity of his acting draws the audience deep within its vortex. He both studied the works of Zeami and often performed with the great Kanze Hisao. At present, he is recognized as one of Japan's leading *nō* actors and often performs with Hisao's younger brother, Kanze Tetsunojō VIII.

Among the numerous awards he has received is the Prix d'Honneur of the Osaka Cultural Prize (1988); he was designated Bearer of an Important Intangible Cultural Asset by the Japanese government in 1991.

[*See also* Kanze School *and* Nō.]

BIBLIOGRAPHY

Keene, Donald. *Nō: The Classical Theatre of Japan*. New York, 1966.

Kodansha Encyclopedia of Japan. Tokyo, 1983. See the entries "Kanze School," "Nō," and "Zeami."

Komparu Kunio. *The Noh Theater: Principles and Perspectives*. Translated by Jane Corddry and Stephen Comee. New York, 1983.

Nishino Haruo and Hata Hisashi, eds. *Nō, kyōgen jiten* (Dictionary of Noh and Kyogen). 2d ed. Tokyo, 1988.

Shirasu Masako. *Umewaka Minoru kikigaki*. Tokyo, 1951.

Umewaka Kennōkai, ed. *Nō: Umewaka Kennōkai*. Tokyo, 1990.

Umewaka Manzaburō. *Manzaburō geidan*. Osaka, 1946.

STEPHEN COMEE

UNDINE. *See* Ondine.

UNITED STATES OF AMERICA. [*To survey the dance traditions of the United States of America, this entry comprises nine articles:*

An Overview
African-American Dance Traditions
African-American Social Dance
Regional Dance Companies
Musical Theater
Ballet Education
Social, Folk, and Modern Dance Education
Dance Research and Publication
Contemporary Criticism

The introductory article views dance in the context of recurring cultural contacts and assimilation; the second and third explore the syncretism of African and European forms in theatrical and social dance traditions; the fourth focuses on the development of regional dance companies; the fifth discusses the development of American musical theater and attendant forms of theatrical dancing; the sixth and seventh articles consider the diversity of dance education; the concluding articles examine dance scholarship and writing. For a discussion of dance traditions of indigenous peoples, see Native American Dance.]

An Overview

Dance in the United States is a culturally diverse and complex phenomenon. Woven into its development are all the strands of American cultural history: patterns of immigration, settlement, and cultural contact; shifts of geographical boundaries; developments in transportation and communication; growth of industry, economy, and business life; diverse religious and philosophical attitudes; and varied expressions in social life and amusements. What we call dance in the United States is bound by two central problems that must be examined in order to understand historically patterned expressive movement experience: human physiognomy, both in terms of developing medical knowledge and the general assimilation of that knowledge by populations, and cultural perceptions and attitudes toward the human body.

More particularly, the history of dance in the United States is a story of recurring cultural contacts and assimilation through the most direct channel available to people, their bodies. It is also the story of the creation and rationalization of forms of amusement and theatrical performances by people who saw these innovations as broadly and democratically contributing to the concept of a national character and the growth of the nation.

The study of dance in the United States begins with the dances of Native Americans. The written record on dance commences with the first sustained European contact with the native peoples of the North American continent. Not until the United States developed a national identity, however, were dominant political and social groups able to reach a tacit consensus and communicate an "American" style of dance. Prior to the early decades of the nineteenth century, descriptions of dance were shared by and associated among people sharing similar ethnic background and social class. Nevertheless, while there was not yet a wholly American dance in 1800, unique experiences in the nation's development were molding the culture of the new nation and creating the basis for its dance.

The Colonial Period. From 1492 to 1660 early European colonial ventures in Virginia, Georgia, South Carolina, Massachusetts, and Connecticut, as well as those in what is now Mexico and California, served commercial purposes for their mother countries and provided political and religious asylum for many settlers. Diverse immigrants, brought together in the common necessity to survive, included military men, aristocrats, traders, adventurers, prisoners, slaves, and indentured servants, predominantly from England, France, and Spain but also from Holland, Sweden, and Africa. Residents of these first settlements maintained their indigenous dance traditions and behavioral expressions, but they sometimes responded to their frontier isolation and spare, marginal living conditions with keen observation and adaptations. Native American dancing and ceremonies, as well as the dancing and ceremonies of foreign neighbors, inspired some early cross-cultural exchanges. Noteworthy examples come from accounts of fur trappers and traders who associated with both Native American tribes and the predominantly white, Anglo-Saxon world.

Immigrants, however, often reacted to the wilderness and the freedom of the American frontier—as they would a century later in the wilderness of crowded urban environments—by projecting notions of proper and improper behavior on the bodily expression and dancing of others in order to fortify and separate their own community values. Historian Michael Zuckerman has drawn the portrait of Thomas Morton, a trader who, after erecting a Maypole at Merry Mount, Massachusetts, in 1626, fell to "frisking," reviving the early, roisterous English holidays. Zuckerman showed that the merriment, which included dancing, was emblematic of the clash of consciousness between Elizabethan traditions and Puritanism.

Relatively few sources of later seventeenth- and early eighteenth-century settlements mention dance. Those rare observations are by predominantly Anglo-Saxon and upper-class writers. Prominent among these are the sermons of New England Puritans (for example, Reverend Increase Mather [1639–1723] and later his son Cotton Mather [1663–1728]); diaries and letters of middle-colony and southern plantation owners; observations by European and colonial travelers; and court records dealing with infractions of community laws regarding public gatherings. Historical methods, such as demographics, that attempt to define the activities of "invisible" (middle-, lower-class, and illiterate populations) have not yet been applied to dance in the United States. Consequently what emerges as dance in these early years of the colonial period is a view biased by the thin historical record created by literate, Anglo-Saxon, upper-class witnesses.

European theatrical performers who came to the colonies in the late seventeenth and early eighteenth centuries encountered widely separated, culturally diverse, and generally sparse populations with few of the refinements common in Europe. Yet, like European cities, the Atlantic seaboard communities were multicultural, had many of the same religious and political strictures, and provided a range of audiences comparable to those in Europe. Early theatrical dancers were itinerants who performed on the tight and slack ropes, enacted comic sketches, and exhibited their virtuoso physical skills and feats in solo dances—such as hornpipes, *galliards*, jigs—and acrobatics. They often joined acting companies as actors. Historical records in southern colonies show instances in which these itinerant performers entertained at plantation parties. For the most part, early itinerant theatrical performers have not been systematically investigated and remain anonymous.

Fashion and taste in Europe influenced both theatrical trends and social amusements in the United States. Formal occasions for performances of such court dances as the *pavane, allemande, corrante, sarabande, galliard, passepied,* and *menuet* were, at first, infrequent, and musicians and dancers competent to perform them were scarce. After the mid-eighteenth century, gains in population, growing local economies encouraging varied occupations especially within towns, and rising standards of living gradually supported hierarchical social strata and styles of living closer to those of Europe. A white, Anglo-Saxon society whose wealth, power, and status arose from trade and political influence with European powers dominated the colonies. At the higher end of the social scale more leisure time was available for dances of society. People of the middle class who wished to make an impression on more powerful individuals and obtain the attention of their peers emulated the manners, dance fashions, and tastes of the colonial aristocracy.

Among religious liberals (particularly in the middle and southern colonies), a kind of consumer class for "the art of dancing" began to form. The growth of dancing as an amusement, social accomplishment, symbol of gentility, and occasion for meeting favorable marriage partners is evidenced by the growing number of references about teachers of dancing in newspapers, diaries, and letters. Among the names are George Brownell, Peter Pelham, and Charles and Mrs. Stagg. Occasions vary from military tributes and encampment celebrations to birthnight balls and festivities for visiting dignitaries. The increasing number of music and dancing masters attests to the growth of general interest in court dances of the eighteenth century, such as the *menuet, rigaudon,* and *gavotte,* which required professional instruction. Dance publications from Europe, such as John Playford's *The English Dancing Master* (1651–1726), and, after 1720, sheet music and other notes for informal French dances were available to purchasers. The availability of published guides and music led to country dance versions performed with little or no knowledge of formal steps by an untutored general public. Books found in estate inventories of the period reveal the close connection between European and American dance tastes and fashions. For example, the inventory of Virginian Charles Stagg's estate made after his death in 1735 contained two dance instruction books: one by John Weaver, *Orchesography* (1706), and the other by John Essex, *For the Further Improvement of Dancing* (1710). Both these volumes are translations of Raoul-Auger Feuillet, and both are entitled in the inventory as *The Art of Dancing*.

Throughout the early eighteenth century slow transatlantic travel (and consequently, slow communication) resulted in a time warp for fashions and styles from one side of the Atlantic to the other. Coupled with the colonists' adherence to traditions (first- and second-generation American customs), this situation sometimes caused theatrical and social dance fashions and tastes to become curiously combined and layered. For example, as late as 1770 a "banqueting house" reminiscent of sixteenth-century entertainments was erected in Virginia for "good Neighborhood" and fit to entertain annually the subscribers and their wives, sweethearts, and friends. At the same time, a colonial governor might have been receiving his order for a suit tailored in the latest English fashion or a list of the dances performed at the yearly Birthnight Ball of the English court just a few weeks or months before. Meanwhile, outbreaks of Maypole dancing in various colonies shocked those members of the population who viewed such dancing as primitive and ritualistic.

Other socioeconomic and ethnic communities had their own dance expressions. For example, sailors danced their competitive jigs and hornpipes (official exercises aboard ship), and African slaves performed tribal animal-imitation dances and ritual dances for special occasions such as marriages and harvest. Although the dances of such subcultural groups have not been thoroughly investigated, scholars assume that they were important to their performers in maintaining social solidarity in an alien environment and that they may have influenced individuals outside the group. These early, overlapping patterns of diversity of physical movement created the foundation for an emerging American consciousness—attitudes and responsiveness—to all types of dance and tolerance or aversion to the physical expressions and behaviors entailed therein.

Theatrical dance shared an early and parallel development with the beginnings of theater in the United States. European theatrical dance traditions presented in the United States range from the early touring of itinerant performers whose various dancing skills did not necessarily include classical training to highly trained, professional classical dancers such as Londoner Henry Holt (1738), "Monsieur Denoier" (Philip Desnoyer, 1751), Pietro Sode (1774), and Louis Roussel (1783). It was not uncommon to have a rope dancer on the same program with a ballet performance. The colonial period in the United States witnessed the introduction of dancers in groups (later called "ballet companies") associated both with early acting companies and with the construction of permanent theaters.

Tradition has it that theater in the United States dates from 1716, when William Livingston established the first playhouse in Williamsburg, Virginia. However, evidence exists of earlier banqueting halls with social entertainments that featured the talents of paid performers and gentlemen amateurs. Later, urban musical societies and clubs, like the Philadelphia Dancing Assemblies (founded in 1748) and the Saint Cecilia Society of Charleston, South Carolina (1762), sanctioned private and exclusive social and theatrical performances of music and dance. The musical concert coupled with a dancing party continued well into the nineteenth century as a refined and respectable evening entertainment in which professional musicians and amateur dancers (both men and women) might have appeared. During these entertainments, dancing masters would often exhibit the most skilled of their young pupils.

The American Revolutionary era, from 1760 through 1789, had its effect on dancing in society and in the theater. In October 1774 the First Continental Congress passed a resolution that strongly recommended the closing of all public places of amusement. In this time of political unrest, public theatrical performances and dancing were considered not only unrefined but likely to be emotionally and politically inflammatory. As a result, Loyalists in the dancing profession returned to England. Some antitheatrical laws remained in effect until 1789. Similarly, court dances, such as *menuets* and *gavottes,* carried a controversial message. They were reminders of hierarchical power relationships at a time when American's democratic republic was being tested. French quadrilles and cotillions and English country dances and reels were less exclusive and more neutral forms to which "as many as will" could be added. These dances symbolized the democratic ideals of the new nation. After the Revolutionary War, British dancers returned and French expatriates began to seek refuge in America.

Prior to 1815, four major theater companies with affiliated dancers presented dance events periodically. The American Company (1783) formed the basis of a permanent theater in New York City. Beginning in 1796 a Frenchman named Jean-Baptiste Francisqui, previously a member of Alexandre Placide's Charleston, South Carolina, company, became its ballet master. The Chestnut Street Theatre (1794–1815) in Philadelphia, managed by Thomas Wignell and Alexander Reinagle, retained William Francis as ballet master. The Federal Street Theatre (1793) in Boston also presented ballet. French expatriate Alexandre Placide (c.1750–1812), manager of the City Theatre (1795) in Charleston from 1798 to 1812, danced in all these theaters and was perhaps the single most influential theatrical dance figure of the post-Revolutionary period in America.

From these four theatrical centers emanated four major touring circuits before 1815: Charleston north to Richmond; Philadelphia south to Baltimore, Annapolis, and Washington, D.C.; New York City and environs; and Boston, including New England. Performances were given usually three times a week, and typical programs are described in a monograph (originally published 1960; reprinted 1976) that dance historian Lillian Moore titled *New York City's First Ballet Season*. The John Street Theatre opened on a night in January 1792 with projected programs that included a play, a ballet or pantomime, interludes of dancing or acrobatics, and sometimes a farce. Ballets and pantomimes like *The Bird Catcher; The Two Philosophers, or The Merry Girl;* and *Harlequin Protected by Cupid, or The Enchanted Nosegay* mixed with interlude dances, such as "Menuet de la Cour," "a Gavotte," "an Allemande," "a Sabottiere Dance," and "a Hornpipe."

It is useful to note that both dancers and teachers from the mid-eighteenth century are conventionally distinguished in newspapers as professional dancers touring from Europe, or immigrants, or native-born. This information is a clue to the historian regarding the establishment of beginnings of "an American dance," that is, one rising from a native-born population and not imported from Europe.

Early touring dancers, such as the popular Madame Anna Gardie and the immigrant dancer and choreographer William Francis, are familiar because of extant comments made by their contemporaries. Many other dancers, like Mr. and Mrs. Aivre, Monsieur Lege, and Mr. and Mrs. Oscar Byrne, remain more obscure. The first American-born theatrical dancer is generally considered to be John Durang (1768–1822). [*See the entry on Durang.*] His son Charles Durang (1794–1870) performed with Placide's company and at New York City's Bowery Theatre. Actor, ballet and social dancing master, stage manager, author and early critic, Charles Durang wrote several guides to the dances of society that reveal his familiarity with the principles of continental ballet technique of Jean-Georges Noverre and Carlo Blasis. The many names of and references to dances and dancers in newspapers and letters after 1800 attest that theatrical dance had appreciative and large audiences and that the business of teaching society to dance was a widely acceptable occupation in early America.

Prominent choreography by native-born Americans, unlike dramatic works, appears to have been sparse. At least four choreographers of this period were well known,

UNITED STATES OF AMERICA: An Overview. A watercolor self-portrait of John Durang (1768–1822), considered the first American-born theatrical dancer, performing a hornpipe. (Courtesy of the Historical Society of York County, Pennsylvania.)

Placide, Francisqui, Byrne, and Francis. European ballets were restaged in the United States. Moore credited *La Fôret Noire* as "the first serious ballet to be given in this country" (Magriel, 1948). Patriotic pantomimes with ballets—"a medley of plot, singing, and dancing, adorned with elaborate scenery and costumes, and using complicated mechanical devices to produce spectacular effect"—like *American Independence, or The 4th of July 1776* (1794) by French choreographer Jean-Baptiste Val—were a genre with symbols of liberty and national meaning that appealed to American audiences (Cohen, 1976). Pantomimes like *Harlequin Panattaha, or Genii of the Algonquins,* presented in 1810 at the Park Theatre in New York City, and dances like the Indian Dance in the opera *Tammany* (1794)—the first opera ballet in America—helped audiences assimilate their own unique American experiences.

A major issue in the study of dance of the early nineteenth century in the United States is the change of performance technique and style from the classical presentation of the body and steps formulated in French court dancing beginning in the mid-seventeenth century to the Romantic ideal of the early nineteenth century developed in the theater schools of Europe. Another issue is the fact that the *danse d'école,* or ballet, and the dancing of the society were inextricably meshed throughout the late eighteenth and the early nineteenth century. The last dancing master in the United States to teach French court dancing to both performers and society died in the 1840s. Curiously, in the mid-nineteenth century, both in Europe and the United States, a revival of French court dancing mixed with the Romantic ballet as the latter began to wane.

Theatrical ballet stars and society personalities were models for performance, and they popularized the dances with which they were identified. Examples taken from sheet music popular in the early part of the nineteenth century include "Commodore Perry's March," by P. L. Duport (Baltimore, 1813); "Miss M. A. Cowper's Favorite Waltz," by Frederich L. Abel (Philadelphia, 1819); the "Elssler Quadrilles, Selected from her Favorite Dance," composed by C. T. Geslain (New York, 1840); the "Ravel Polka Quadrilles," composed by M. Keller (c.1847); and "The Cally Waltz," by Allen Dodworth, named in honor of his wife in the 1840s.

Dancing masters often taught both members of society and aspirants to the stage. Often teaching both theatrical and social dancing contributed to the mixing of conventions, techniques, and forms. Elite clientele demanded the newest and most respected social dances, and they had the leisure time to learn some technique. Complications and competition in the teaching profession resulted when dance exponents had sparse training and experience. Exotic, foreign-sounding names often disguised their lack of experience. Dance instruction was competitive both in quality and in the variety of prices established for the diverse customers who might decide that knowledge in dance, as well as access to proper social customs and individuals associated with dancing circles, was worth the price.

The Nineteenth Century. Tremendous national growth marked the years from 1789 to 1865. In 1803 the Louisiana Purchase doubled the size of the United States. With the later annexation of territories as states, such as California in 1850, the young country extended west to the Pacific and south to Mexico. Significant to the development of dancing in the United States were the cultures that these new annexations officially brought into the country: Native American; Spanish and, later, Mexican-owned parts of the Southwest and California; and French interests in New Orleans, Florida, and the Northwest. Russian contact occurred in northern California and the Pacific Northwest. Although not annexed territory, the French and English colonies of Canada also influenced the northeastern region of the United States. Settlements in these borderlands were characterized by specific cultural tastes and dancing customs, and therefore became distinctive regions of cultural contact that have continued to be influential. In contrast to these borderlands and to isolated cultural pockets like the Appalachian Mountains, seaport cities and junctions along major transportation and trade routes were more cosmopolitan. Also in this period, certain preferences—stemming from the dominant political, religious, and social values of the old colonial gentry and the *nouveaux riches* of the rapidly growing northeastern postindustrial society—controlled and shaped the development of dance in the United States.

One such trend during this early period was widespread religious evangelism, which had been unevenly fanned by the flames of revivalism since the mid-eighteenth century. Perhaps as a result of social conservatism and its recoil from sensuality rekindled by the Second Great Awakening, which began in New England in the 1790s and spread with the westward expansion of settlements in the early decades of the nineteenth century, from about 1820 to 1835 some dancing masters found themselves no longer as essential to the old colonial gentry and to the relatively small urban elite. Performance of quadrilles, cotillions, and country dances—the hallmarks of the new republic—had become repetitious, even stagnant; the waltz had not become the mania in America that it was in Europe. The polka had yet to burst upon the popular stage. Conservative Americans disapproved of the potential immorality presented by closed couple dances and of what a closed couple symbolized as a loss of control over previously dominant community values.

UNITED STATES OF AMERICA: An Overview. A watercolor painted c.1830 depicting members of the Moravian community of York, Pennsylvania, dancing to a small instrumental ensemble and mixed chorus. (Courtesy of the Historical Society of York County, Pennsylvania.)

By 1835 both of America's leading evangelists, Lyman Beecher and Charles G. Finney, had abandoned their urban outposts to take up academic chairs in colleges in the West. Thereafter second-rate men and reform crusades diluted revivalism, yet they brought the Christian gospel to broader and more dispersed audiences. In this less intense and more receptive social environment teachers of dance found another opportunity to expand their profession. Just as Beecher and Finney changed their focus to become lecturers—moving from conducting revivals (inspiration) to delivering advice on how to conduct revivals (methodology)—dancing masters moved to conduct "proper" dancing parties and to teach "correct techniques" for achieving what they collectively agreed was "morality in motion." To complement this more conservative social milieu, dancing masters advocated physical education and such related social reforms as functional dress and outward displays of social grace and gentility as a national standard of etiquette. By the 1850s, when new social dances such as the mazurka, *redowa,* and five-, three-, and two-step waltzes were becoming familiar to more people, a wider populace accepted the dancing master as a social arbiter between the potentially volatile expressions of the human body and its practiced control.

Early social reform and educational crusades encouraged American intellectual and cultural institutions to support dance in education by using the argument of the benefits of physical education. They also made later serious study of dance possible. Self-education systems—the Lyceum movement (1826–1861), the Transcendentalist philosophy of "self-culture," and the beginnings of free public education—focused the nation on the significance of physical training and supported the consideration of exercise programs, gymnastics, and dancing as means to physical improvement. The rhetoric of physical education for a healthier body and a healthier nation persuaded the general population to accept dancing as a legitimate cultural amusement and theatrical art form. The moral and healthful virtues of gymnastic movements thus carried over into social dancing.

The vocabulary of simple rhythmic steps used in physical exercise and gymnastic programs such as Catharine Beecher's 1837 calisthenic exercises, Dio Lewis's New Gymnastics, and Adolph Spiess's revival of the folk roundel paralleled the move of social dance from classical ballet terminology and theatrical standards of execution. Dancing masters were believed to be necessary to teach deportment and refinement of steps and for chaperoning couple dancing, but mass audiences on their own increasingly could find refuge and a easy level of competency in the simple stepping patterns of standardized social dances.

Social movements against slavery, nativism, anti-Catholicism, and the struggle for women's rights also had their effects on the formation of an American dance. These and other issues and reforms tacitly called attention to deviancy in appearance and behavior from an implied national norm. The appearance and expressive display of the human body had long been a means to assess the inner morality of people. Such focus on the human body and its movements supported interest in social and cultural stereotypes, for example, the simple morality involved in the contrasts between thrift and idleness, temperance and intemperance. These moral directives appeared in novels and popular prints and were put into movement on the stage in character delineations and satires. Blatant ill manners, some uncontrolled body gestures, certain crooked postures, excessive display of emotions and "humors," and overly sloppy, gaudy, or inappropriate dress and conduct expressed bad character. Exaggerated self-control of emotions, severely plain and simple dress, which the wearer's "good nature" was supposed to ornament, and proper conduct (often perceived as tight and formal) expressed good character.

Physical expressions of moral lessons were also acted out in real life by assigning body movements certain cultural meaning. Restrictions of movement (such as that between the rib cage and pelvis, thus presenting the torso as a single unit) and the rigid prescription of gender roles (for example, stereotypical ways that men physically displayed strength and independence and that women exhibited dependency) affected how dancing was perceived and to be performed. Clothing proper to the occasion of dancing supported preferred body movement patterns.

Led by the steamboat, canal systems, toll roads, and railroads, new means of transportation and communication instigated a great social and economic expansion in antebellum America. In the first decade of the nineteenth century this expansion opened the West for settlement and encouraged new theatrical touring circuits as well as created new employment possibilities for dance instructors. Itinerant dancing masters, traditionally respected for their offerings of "gentility" and "polite education," brought cosmopolitan culture to remote geographic areas. They plied their trade in the expanding frontier areas of the Ohio Valley, the Mississippi River, the Old Northwest, and California to bring the socially useful, external displays of virtue and grace, or "manners," to the new social leaders of these rough-hewn communities. Middle- and upper-class social circles in well-established smaller towns retained respectable and long-tenured dancing teachers who taught what their clientele needed, and wanted, to participate in "polite society." At the same time, powerful oral and participatory instruction introduced traditional dances to the young of immigrant and ethnic communities and, as a consequence, initiated them to their native customs of social interaction and preferred patterns of deportment. Traditional culture and new-forming society had to mediate between behavioral options; for many the dance floor was a sanctioned space for trying on new and different movement fashions.

Growth of industry and commerce, of occupations, and of the labor force assisted by influxes of new immigrants (notably from Ireland and Germany) supported larger towns and dense population areas that, in turn, created new customers for a growing form of respectable amusement, the social dance party. Those of the middle classes who wished to capture respectability felt that socially controlled dancing parties (or balls) ensured properly conducted courtships and marriages and, in turn, the continuance of the positive socializing influence of the family. All this was to lead spirally to the proper conduct and refinement of the community, city, and nation. The more people understood the beneficial aspects of social dance—its gentle form of physical exercise and its containment of undesirable behaviors in aesthetic form—the more they would understand the rationale and beauty of theatrical dance. There were also larger audiences for theatrical dance, particularly the morally didactic and "family entertainment" of companies such as the Ravels. [*See the entry on the Ravel family.*]

Some Europeans and dissenters against centralized power continued to regard the United States as an asylum and a place for utopian experimentation. Thus religious communal societies and various religious and social utopian models—as widely diverse as the religious sect called Shakers (founded c.1777) and Pullman, Illinois, a community planned for laborers (founded in 1880 on the outskirts of Chicago by railroad magnate George Pullman)—condoned expressive physical activities, some of which included dance. These communities were artificial environments whose social and religious rationales supported dancing and other physical activities. [*See Shaker Dance.*]

At mid-nineteenth century, the fear of urban violence erupting uncontrolled from groups of dislocated and dissatisfied peoples began to threaten traditional authority and power. Nativism and fear of social contamination encouraged society's upper strata to use organized, private dancing classes and complicated dance forms, such as the

UNITED STATES OF AMERICA: An Overview. Couples dancing at "The Great Russian Ball," held at the Academy of Music, New York, on 5 November 1863. (Reprinted from *Harper's Weekly*, November 1963; courtesy of Elizabeth Aldrich.)

German cotillion, as a social defense. Knowledge of an elaborate dance was a password as well as certification of social acceptance. The upper classes believed that pure dance forms and polite manners would cement class loyalty and keep the impure elements of society from contaminating "the right people." Dances from the eighteenth century, such as *menuets* and *gavottes,* which were reminiscent of a seemingly more virtuous and simple time, were thought to promote the gentility and refinements necessary to a moral and polite society.

Also at mid-century, burgeoning population—particularly in the cities—created favorable conditions for more and larger theaters and for more theatrical touring. Itinerant musical and dancing masters continued to follow the same routes as did itinerant theatrical and ballet companies. New roads, more efficient modes of water transportation, and the new railroad lines supported two major theatrical touring routes: the Ohio River Valley circuit established by Samuel Drake (1769–1854) and the Mississippi Valley circuit controlled by James H. Caldwell (1793–1863) from 1825 to 1835 and after 1835 by Noah Ludlow (1795–1886) and his partner, Solomon Smith (1801–1869).

The social and cultural climate of the United States—embroiled in such issues as public education, temperance, peace, rights for women, abolition, criminal reform, workers' rights, and domesticity, and preoccupied with social purity and law and order—did not view the theatrical arts, especially dancing, as a cultural or social imperative in national progress. As a consequence, Americans did not support the training of American theatrical dancers. Because the U.S. government did not support national academies devoted to the theater arts as in Europe, and because there were widely divergent ideas on the legitimacy and morality of dancing, foreign dancers continued to dominate the American stage well into the twentieth century. A sampling of these foreign classical dancers—initially and largely English and French, later Italian, and finally Russian—includes some of the century's most brilliant stars: Edmund H. Conway (1824–?), Claude and Madame Labasse (1822–1831), Fanny Achille (1827–?), Charles and Maria Ronzi Vestris (1828–1829), the Ravel family (1823–1868), Paul and Amalia Galster Taglioni (1839), Madame Augusta (1836–1839), Fanny Elssler (1840–1842), the Montplaisir Ballet (1847–1856), Domenico Ronzani and the Ronzani Ballet (1857–1868), Madame Celeste (1827–1866), whom Charles Durang, in his *The Philadelphia Stage* (1854), described as "probably the most successful female star ever to appear on the American boards," Giuseppina Morlacchi (1866–?), Anna Pavlova (1910–1916), and Serge Diaghilev's Ballets Russes (1916).

The nineteenth century was distinguished by a few prominent native-born dancers: Mary Ann Lee, whom Moore credited with being "the first American dancer to attain nation-wide fame as an exponent of the classical ballet" (Moore, 1948), Julia Turnbull (1822–1887), and Augusta Maywood (1835–1876?), America's first internationally famous *prima ballerina*. The life of George Washington Smith (1825–1899) exemplifies the versatility expected of an American dancer. He danced in *grand ballet*, opera, and the circus, working for both P. T. Barnum and Edwin Booth. Smith did entr'actes, clowned, and partnered almost every great ballerina who visited the United States from 1840 to the end of the century. He also choreographed, taught social dancing, and trained dancers for the theater. [*See the entries on Lee, Maywood, and George Washington Smith.*]

UNITED STATES OF AMERICA: An Overview. The Italian dancer Giuseppina Morlacchi, one of a number of European ballet stars to tour the United States, made her New York debut on 23 October 1867. This portrait shows her in costume for the can-can she created several months later during a stay in Boston. (Photograph by L. R. Burnham; from the Hotlibzelle Theatre Arts Library, University of Texas at Austin.)

In popular theatrical dance, William Henry Lane (c.1825–1852), an African American known as Master

Juba, took the uniquely American theatrical dance art of African Americans to Europe. The emergence of black musicians, dancers, and actors on the American stage in the late 1830s marked the historical beginnings of one of the most original contributions of the United States to dance, an aspect of the jazz idiom that historians Marshall and Jean Stearns have termed "American vernacular dance." [*See the entry on Juba.*]

UNITED STATES OF AMERICA: An Overview. William Henry Lane, known as Master Juba, is an important figure in the development of American dance. As a skilled Irish jig and clog dancer, as well as a virtuosic minstrel dance competitor, Lane fused African-American rhythms with the techniques of hard-shoe step dancing. He traveled to London with Pell's Ethiopian Serenaders in 1848, where he was hailed by critics. This print shows him performing a jig at Vauxhall Gardens, London. (Reprinted from *Illustrated London News,* 5 August 1848.)

Those Americans in the middle and upper social strata continued to be more attracted to European tastes and fashions than to their own creative potential until after the Civil War. Spectacle productions with dance and acrobatics, like those of the Ravels, and the Romantic ballets, such as *Giselle* (1841), *La Esmeralda* (1844), and *Le Corsaire* (1856), were more prominent in the theater.

The Civil War had a positive effect on one particular aspect of dancing: revivals of dances from the eighteenth century—symbolic of the nation's genesis and union—achieved their greatest impetus during the campaign, beginning in the 1850s, to purchase and preserve George Washington's home, Mount Vernon, as a symbol of national unity. In the wake of this movement, eighteenth-century dances, again fashionable, spread to a popular audience. The American Centennial Celebration in 1876 further continued support of this early preservation movement of "old-fashioned" (eighteenth-century) dances. This new interest in history, as expressed by attention to a national folklore, to the English Arts and Crafts Movement in the United States, and to the need for models of a national standard of etiquette and manners, sustained this dance revival to the turn of the century.

The Civil War also marked the culminating point of the American brass band movement. Brass bands and the concomitant establishment of town bands and professional organizations of musicians contributed to the general spread of popular musical arts in America. These orchestras and bands provided music for both social and theatrical dance. New York musician and society dancing master Allen Dodworth and his family represented the popularity of all types of music and dance during this period. The beginnings of a professionalized American musical community drew dance and music more closely together and created conditions necessary for dance innovations.

The period from 1865 to 1900 marks the rise of "modern America." Characterized by the establishment and consolidation of business and social hierarchies and the stabilization of social, economic, and political relationships, thc nation knit farming, ranching, and industry and brought the New South, the mining frontiers, the expansion of the railroad West, and agriculture to new power an influence. The period marks the advent of great cities and associated problems aggravated by increasing numbers of immigrants, including massive influxes of peoples from middle and eastern Europe. The U.S. political policy of economic isolationism ended, and this brought the country in closer diplomatic and commercial contact with foreign cultures, particularly those in East Asia.

Like benign rulers, the new wealthy industrialists of the 1870s and 1880s focused a portion of their influence on what they considered to be their moral responsibility and duty to the nation. Their idea of *noblesse oblige* motivated cultural philanthropy. Beautiful public structures, such as libraries, and cultural arts programs and events including dance and dance-related arts were to transform cities and regenerate the spiritual lives of their inhabitants.

The "modern America" period also introduced a new focus on child nurturing. This new attention developed largely through the work of theologian Horace Bushnell and in education through the model of the German kindergarten. Childhood education brought new regard to the importance of children's play, games, and dances. Accompanying this interest in children was a generalized fear that industrialization and modernity were ending a cultural age of innocence: old traditions were dying and needed to be saved. One response to this fear was an emphasis on physical regeneration as implied by the support of adult physical education and sports, which included new programs of exercise and spectator events.

The configuration of cultural interests in this period encouraged new attitudes toward the function of dance in American life. Four key trends in this transformation were the movement to professionalize teachers of dancing; the development of physical education in public schools and in community recreation programs that included forms of dance; the widespread popularity of systems of physical expression; and a new appreciation of history and culture consciousness in broad segments of the population, which led to the revival and popularity of dances from the past and from other cultures. These trends resulted in new attitudes toward all kinds of dancing and catalyzed the attention and concern of a mass, popular audience toward dance. The perception that dance was not only morally but socially useful began the process through which dance education and dance arts gained credibility and became more popular after the middle of the twentieth century.

Dancing masters, like architects, doctors, and lawyers, did not have any nationwide guild structures in the early decades of the nineteenth century. Two emerging phenomena, the dance teaching family and the professional and national organization of dancing masters, pointed to the professionalization of dancing masters at midcentury. Just as small "dynasties" of theatrical and stage dancing families like the Booths and the Ravels began to appear on the American theatrical scene, urban social dancing families (like the Durangs, the Dodworths, the Bourniques, the Ferreros, and the Carusis) became involved in teaching social dance. These family "businesses" had respectability and, unlike theatrical families, geographical stability.

Three professional organizations formed in the last quarter of the nineteenth century represent the first formal and broadly inclusive attempts to organize, standardize, and professionalize dance teaching and teachers in the United States. In Europe such organization had begun much earlier with government-established and tightly controlled theaters and academies. The American Society of Professors of Dancing was founded on 19 January 1879 and incorporated 20 October 1883. The American National Association of Masters of Dancing, United States and Canada, was founded in Boston on 15 June 1883. The Western Association Normal School, Masters of Dancing was started in Saint Louis in June 1894. Membership in all three groups reflected a broad geographical membership—for example, from Toronto; Louisville, Kentucky; and Oakland, California. Some members made regular trips to New York City and regularly corresponded in order to learn new dances, exchange ideas about dance, and keep up on musical and dance trends. By 1896 all three societies were flourishing. *The Director* (December 1987–November 1898), believed to be the first magazine devoted to dances published in America, gave a subtle sense of the relationship between these groups that begs further inquiry when it reported a bit too positively that "although the societies are distinct and working upon somewhat different principles, they should be in harmony and in friendly relation with each other. We have no reason to doubt that such a relation does exist, and we trust that it may continue."

Dancing masters such as E. B. Reilley and Judson Sause pointedly related their art to healthful exercise, physical culture, and gymnastics in order to stress its moral necessity to society. Like other dogma, gospel, rituals, and literature from the fields of business, medicine, and the publications industry that claimed to make Americans more successful, wealthy, and better persons, dancing manuals and the American Society of Professors of Dancing professed to accomplish similar transformations.

Dancing masters also capitalized on dance literature to influence their audiences. Dance, like other literature, was made possible at a reasonable cost because of mid-nineteenth-century inventions and improvements in printing presses that boosted production capabilities. Among the diverse books and pamphlets whose numbers steadily increased after the Civil War was a genre of technical manuals on a wide range of how-to subjects, from horseshoeing to beekeeping. How-to dance literature superficially mirrored the scientific, technical approach of these publications and made dance available to a large reading audience. Whether or not Charles Durang's *Terpsichore* (1847), Thomas Hillgrove's *Scholar's Companion and Ball-Room Guide* (1858), Elias Howe's *American Dancing Master* (1862), and Edward Ferrero's *Art of Dancing* (1859), as well as hundreds of anonymously written dance manuals, were read and used, they had the effect of standardizing and systematizing specific dances, like waltzes and quadrilles, and stimulating interest in popular American social and theatrical dance forms. The American body as well as character was being shaped through a common set of instructions.

Publications on dance burgeoned particularly after 1870, when new federal copyright laws permitted dance teachers to better protect their writings and notations (both written and shorthand methods) of their dances. Grassroots-oriented programs such as the ongoing Chautauqua movement, which began in 1874 as a Sunday school assembly in upstate New York and later became a forum for education, religion, arts, and public issues, were among the many educational projects that depended upon a variety of publications for lectures and correspondence courses. The Chautauqua School of Physical Education was founded in 1886 and directed until 1904 by William G. Anderson. Among his course offerings to the twelve to fifteen hundred physical education teachers who came to Chautauqua from all regions of the United States was an "Americanized Delsarte" system of expression. Continuing earlier self-culture attitudes and Lyceum programs from the first half of the century, Chautauqua also brought the subject of the moral and healthful benefits of dance to widely dispersed audiences across the country. It supported ideas about and provided a forum for the integration of dance into education as a vital aspect of American life.

Systems of physical expression contributed to the changing attitudes of Americans toward the morality of the human body and, by extension, of dance. The term *expression* in the nineteenth century included "physical culture, pantomime, dramatics . . . interpersonal communication, [and] . . . professional training for public speaking" (Ruyter, 1979). Expression was taught by instructors of elocution who emphasized the role of posture and gesture in effectively communicating with others in a variety of settings, from legal courts to public balls. As the Lyceum movement and later the Chautauqua movement provided more opportunities for both men and women to persuade and to teach their peers, the subject of expression became appropriate for all ranks of people.

The most popular of these expression systems used in the United States was the Delsarte system, developed by François Delsarte (1822–1871). As a professor of music, Delsarte developed a system of rhythmic exercises that combined singing, declamation, gymnastics, and dancing. Key to its broad acceptance in the United States was the Reverend William R. Alger, a Boston Unitarian clergyman, who, in his lectures, advocated the system's appeal to morality. He saw Delsartism as a religious culture that would redeem the earth. Delsartism brought broad segments of the population into contact with physical culture and dance, and it sanctioned dancelike activities in respectable homes, places of business, and educational institutions. [*See* Delsarte System of Expression.]

Marches and formations of the "musical drill" were another contribution to the creation of an American dance style. From approximately 1865 to 1885 drills evolved in civilian life in conjunction with English and American fraternal militias. Musical drills, more or less artistically arranged exercises set to music, not infrequently included dance steps and relied for effect on spatial patterns and, like chorales, upon large numbers of persons. German cotillions that were "staged" for several hundred participants often used drill formations and spatial emblems. The musical drill appeared simultaneously in several aspects of American culture: military training for the Spanish-American War; physical education in public schools and on public playgrounds; historical pageantry; stage dancing; social dancing; and rituals involving sororal and fraternal organizations. Wherever large crowds had to be managed with some degree of order, the musical marching drill was effective because it could be either called by simple "left" and "right" directions or comprehended easily by simple diagrams.

As dances incorporated physical exercise and gymnastic elements, physical educators began to use dance in their programs. In 1887 the director of the Boston Turnverein, a Mr. Eberhard, taught a new genre called "Fancy Steps" at the Harvard Summer School of Physical Education. Also in 1887, Dr. W. G. Anderson began a new genre called "gymnastic dancing." As head of the Brooklyn Normal School of Gymnastics, he believed that dancing could be used to arouse greater interest in gymnastics, and so he introduced jigs, reels, and clogs (an umbrella term he used for any ethnic dance) into the school's exercise program in order to develop the ear as well as the grace of his students (many of whom were the sons and daughters of immigrants). Anderson's and Eberhard's approaches were ways in which the new muscular morality was made to fit into the performance of American social dances.

After 1890 Elizabeth Burchenal and Dr. C. Ward Crampton, both of New York City and leaders in the new folk dance movement, began to collect and preserve European folk dances. Once considered a resource for the steps of gymnastic dancing, folk dances and their steps now became a separate and legitimate area of study. In 1918 Burchenal published the first modern book of traditional American dances, *Twenty Eight Contra Dances, Largely from the New England States*. Dr. Luther Gulick, a medical doctor as well as a leader in the profession of physical training, published *The Healthful Art of Dancing* (1910), through which he united, with new authority, the ideas of healthful exercise, folk dance, and public morality. Other university-educated instructors, such as M. B. Gilbert (Harvard Summer School of Physical Education) and O. L. Herbert (physical director of the Providence YMCA), further united social dancing with physical exercise and the concepts of folk dancing.

The Twentieth Century. By 1901, continuing demands for political, economic, and social change had ushered in the Progressive Era, a period of massive collective efforts to correct inequities caused by corruption in big business and by increasing waves of immigration. President Theodore Roosevelt led the attack against immorality in American society by calling for physical fitness and exercise. Progressive educational theory—espoused by philosopher Herbert Spencer, psychologist and educator G. Stanley Hall, philosopher William James, philosopher and educator John Dewey, and psychoanalyst Sigmund Freud—developed previous arguments for the rationalization of dance through art and physical education programs as a necessary means to healthy personal development.

UNITED STATES OF AMERICA: An Overview. Classical Greek sculpture and philosophy inspired many American dancers, choreographers, and dance educators in the late nineteenth and early twentieth centuries. Greek ideals of sport and education were part of the Progressive Era philosophy that brought dance into college and university settings. Pictured here are students at Barnard College's annual Greek dance competition in 1927. (Photograph by White Studios, New York; from the collection of Sally R. Sommer and William G. Sommer.)

Reactions against old definitions of the arts and social life, which characterized the period up to World War I, heightened contrasts and created concepts of "high" and "low" culture as well as of tradition and modernism. In the arts, the era has been defined as the "American Renaissance." Guided by the Pre-Raphaelites, who extolled the sixteenth century as a golden age of integrity in workmanship, American architects, city planners, mural painters, and dramatists tapped the ideals of Renaissance Europe to enrich what they felt were thin artistic currents in the United States.

In the area of dance, inspiration came from bygone eras in which the spirit as well as the body was honored. Elizabethan England bestowed the idea of wholesome pastimes and reinforced Anglo-American identity and traditions—especially in folk dance, and English folk dance in particular. Ancient Greece projected compelling images of serenity, the preciousness of youth before its decay, and the promise of light—inspiration—in contrast to the public image of American corruption. The Orient bequeathed mystery, eccentricity, and a kind of antimasque—

"unimaginable antiquity, inhuman beauty, boundless distance" (Said, 1978)—to the Anglo-European experience.

The ideals of the Progressive Era forged the concept of a "modern dance" in two areas: aesthetics and the theater, and education. Through programs in colleges and universities, a uniquely American vision of dance emerged. Gertrude Colby of Teacher's College, Columbia University, and Margaret H'Doubler of the University of Wisconsin took the theories of the new philosophers, educators, and artists and brought those ideas to fruition in dance curricula. [*See the entry on H'Doubler.*] The discipline heralded dance as a nurturing and spontaneous activity and as preparation for democracy by "strengthening body, cultivating love of beauty, stimulating imagination, challenging the intellect and social capabilities, and prompting individualization and self-expression" (Ruyter, 1979). The growth of dance in education continued to nourish a new professional modern dance by providing teaching and performing opportunities as well as informed audiences for new directions in dance as art.

Beginning in 1915 and extending through 1930, the rise in theater ticket prices, competition from spectator sports, and the appearance of films caused the popularity of big Broadway theaters to decline. As a consequence, there was little support for theatrical dancing scenes associated with expressive and elaborate productions and realistic spectacles, which had been used to provide touches of mood and verisimilitude to such shows as Augustin Daly's *Frou-Frou* (1870) and *The Taming of the Shrew* (1892) and David Belasco's *The Heart of Maryland* (1895) and *A Girl of the Golden West* (1905). Prior to this period, theatrical dancing had moved from the Romantic ballets of the 1840s and 1850s to the spectacle feats and chorus-line patterns of *The Black Crook* (1866) to the technically faultless, but emotionally arid, skill of the Italian ballerinas of 1860–1880, Marie Bonfanti, Giuseppina Morlacchi, and Rita Sangalli. Various kinds of popular dancing—like the chorus line and revue—gradually began to dominate the turn of the century. [*See* Black Crook, The; *and the entries on Bonfanti, Morlacchi, and Sangalli.*]

New popular entertainment genres—vaudeville, burlesque, and carnival and tent shows—that used precision, tap, and ethnic dances, ballet, and specialty acts and dances (acrobatics, adagio, exhibition ballroom, and striptease) absorbed hopeful theatrical dancers. The chorus line and precision dancing, a major choreographic attraction, dominated musical comedies and revues (particularly those mounted by Florenz Ziegfeld [1869–1932] as the *Ziegfeld Follies*). Theater audiences who had been exposed to dance through physical education and military training had an immediate appreciation for staged choreographic figures of columns and lines. Later, New York City's new Radio City Music Hall (1932), with its chorus line of thirty-six precision dancers, would carry this dance genre into present times. [*See* Radio City Music Hall *and the entry on Ziegfeld.*]

At the same time, a variety of public programs continued to expose mass audiences to new visions of dance in relation to American social reform, national unity, morality, and health. These public programs included the Playground Association of America (later the Playground and Recreation Association of America) founded in 1906; the American Pageant Association, officially founded in 1913; and more strongly developed German *Turnverein* and gymnastic exercise programs, begun in earnest after 1850. Further refinements in the training and certification of dancing teachers legitimized theatrical as well as social and folk forms of dancing and earned the broad support of participants as well as political and social audiences. Proponents of these public performances were firmly united in their social interests in public art, physical education, recreation, medicine, and ceremonies supporting nationalism. Traditional dances were supported by wealthy industrialists and cultural philanthropists such as Henry Ford and John D. Rockefeller. Ford became keenly interested in early American and international dances and music as a means to "Americanize" factory workers. His sense of duty to a seemingly nonexistent American dance catalyzed the attention of the nation through publicity in magazine and newspaper articles and, later, radio and Edison cylinders. Dances made up of simple lines and emblems and featuring large groups of performers created a positive and orderly image that could assuage the fears that American manufacturers had of managing dissimilar populations, riots, and disruptive union activities.

In the first decade of the twentieth century, just as Henry Ford had streamlined production techniques with the assembly line, standardized and published versions of teaching "methods" and dances—whether the mechanized chorus line or square dancing—spread to broader audiences across the country. Dance teachers as different as theatrical chorine trainer and choreographer Ned Wayburn and society dancing masters T. George Dodworth of New York and Alvar Bournique of Chicago turned away from the earlier dance "academies" toward modern dance "schools"—literally factories—run on business principles. At a different level of society, taxi dance halls wherein one could buy a dance and syndicated dance studios made their appearance.

In the first quarter of the century social dancing expressed two directions of American society: Traditional dancing masters, their businesses built on the needs of the social elites—clients preoccupied with the display of wealth, style, and fashion—moved to find novel attractions to counteract the staleness of old society dances and to keep their consumers conspicuous and stylish. Audiences at the new places of entertainment—first hotel ballrooms, then, in the 1920s, nightclubs—began to move to new, expressive dance rhythms originating in the various ethnic communities of the city and from countries such as Cuba and Central and South America, with whom the United States was, for the first time, exploring diplomatic relations, policies, and markets. Black American and American Creole communities were the source of the cakewalk. The syncopated rhythms of the one-step (its variants including the Turkey Trot and Bunny Hug), the Argentine tango, and the fox trot contrasted sharply with the smoothness of society dance. Dancing teams, especially that of Irene and Vernon Castle, promoted these new dances internationally in hotel ballrooms, nightclubs, and vaudeville houses. [*See the entry on Irene and Vernon Castle.*]

One of America's first independent artists in dance—Isadora Duncan—exemplified the spirit of a new form of American dance. Duncan's revolution can be best understood against the American compulsion to systematize and standardize expressive bodily movement. An aversion to "schools," systems, and artifices and an underlying anxiety about the loss of cultural innocence, symbolized by the expressive freedom of a child, motivated a few socially conscious and liberal thinkers of Duncan's era. In an age when most people turned to revivals of the past for guidance, Duncan, and later Ruth St. Denis, found more than old form: they found their own unique inspirations to create new dances. Duncan equated natural and freely expressive body movements in dance with hope for modern humanity. Her art was a reaction to the hegemony of the French academy, with its rules of proportion, composition, suitable subjects, and other matters that together legitimized "the academy" approach to general education and traditional art. Reactions against the status quo were not yet widespread. It was too early for Duncan to find support for her modern art in the United States, so she turned to Europe. [*See the entries on Duncan and St. Denis.*]

On 13 February 1913 a select group of progressive painters organized the Armory Show in New York City as a means of combating the doldrums of the artistic spirit in the United States. Called "pathological" by the *New York Times,* the show included for the first time in the United States the work of European postimpressionists and futurists. In an era when "the academy" had a corner on respectability in all arts, including dance, this exhibition focused the attention of the art world on the tension between traditionalism and modernism. The influence of both reached the art of dance through aesthetic principles of abstraction and expressionism. Both guided the tastes of new audiences in appreciating form and content in abstract representations of the body and its emotions. What was novel was that modern intellectual currents supported self-expression that promised both creative and psychological well-being.

The earlier appearance of Russian dancers Anna Pavlova and Mikhail Mordkin at the Metropolitan Opera House in New York in 1910 had exposed American audiences to the expressive, new vitality in classical ballet; but when Serge Diaghilev's Ballets Russes came to the United States in 1916, the company's modernism "rocked a widespread minority of interested people all over America to their imaginative foundation" (Kirstein, 1967). Russian dancers who stayed in America, like Michel Fokine and Léonide Massine, revitalized ballet teaching with Russian technique but were not able to capture the electric modernism of Diaghilev's repertory. It would be seventeen more years before Russian George Balanchine, influenced by American culture, would infuse vital new choreography into classical ballet in the United States. In 1916 insufficient organization and management of opera houses, inadequately trained dancers, and the need for permanent dance companies—all necessary to support ballet's theatrical illusion—were still underdeveloped. [*See the entries on Balanchine, Fokine, Massine, Mordkin, and Pavlova.*]

An accretion of dance types, both traditional and modern, meshed into a new wave of theatrical dance. Around 1912, and in emulation of the independent theaters of Europe, several so-called little theaters and art schools became established in the United States. Significant to the dance world was the momentum of the movement, as it supported the creative inclinations of individual dance artists upon whom modernism was having an effect. Exemplary was the Neighborhood Playhouse, established by Irene and Alice Lewisohn in 1915 in New York City as an adjunct to the Henry Street Settlement. Originally designed not as a social experiment but to serve the needs and creative interests of residents of the area, the Neighborhood Playhouse evolved out of festivals for children of the settlement. Individual dance artists also started their own little theaters and schools. In 1914 Nellie Cornish established the Cornish School in Seattle, and in 1915 the Ruth St. Denis School of Dancing and Its Related Arts opened in Los Angeles as Denishawn. [*See* Denishawn.]

In 1912 Jesse L. Lasky, Samuel Goldwyn, and Cecil B. De Mille headed west to make the film *The Squaw Man.* Early American cinema included the first recording of dance in the United States. Theatrical dancing depicted in Hollywood films provided mass audiences with images—albeit stereotypic—of dance in the lives of Americans. These first films included Broadway musical comedies and revues adapted for the silver screen as well as scenes set in nightclubs and frontier towns. A major resource for dance historians, early films have provided the history of other forms of dance, often inadvertently caught in newsreels, home movies, and early documentaries. [*See* Film musicals, *article on* Hollywood Film Musicals.]

After World War I—a point that conventionally marks the end of American cultural näiveté and of the massive

UNITED STATES OF AMERICA: An Overview. Students at the Denishawn school in Los Angeles, c.1920. This canopied, open-air studio provided the perfect environment for the Denishawn curriculum, which included at various times courses in dramatic gesture, assorted "Oriental" dance techniques (Indian, Arabian, Siamese, et al.), ballet, "Greek" dancing, music visualization, piano, the French language, and craft-work. (Photograph from the archives at Jacob's Pillow, Becket, Massachusetts.)

immigration from eastern Europe that began in the 1880s—new emphasis was put on an "American-styled" dance. By performing American and European folk dances in their mass-participant, outdoor spectacles and civic pageants, both the American Pageant Association and the community theater movement had served to define these dances to a general public. Both agencies renewed audience and producers' interests in programs that acknowledged cultural roots of the United States and those of recent arrivals. These civic programs aroused interest in and directed research of historical American dress, dances, and folklore.

A kind of forced self-consciousness caused by being relegated to overcrowded urban and northern ghettos, such as New York City's Harlem, contributed to the emergence of a new black American assertiveness and intellectualism. Black Americans uncovered their own historical and cultural motifs and incorporated them into new forms of artistic expression. For white intellectuals, Harlem was an opportunity to discover and experience the exotic in an otherwise staid, conformist, and mechanistic world. The Harlem Renaissance of the late 1910s and the 1920s brought to popularity social dances of ragtime and early jazz, like the Black Bottom, the Shimmy, and the Charleston. The Cotton Club, a Harlem night spot, is notable for having introduced black performers such as Ethel Waters, Cab Calloway, Maude Russell, and Bill Robinson. Gramophone recordings and national radio broadcasts brought the new dance sounds to popular attention.

By 1928 the juncture of the development of modern aesthetic theories and the support of the intellectual community; the emergence of "new schools" (some of which supported dance performances); the extraordinary appearance of expressionism in dance in Diaghilev's Ballets Russes; and the awareness brought to "an American dance" by civic festivals and film created a receptive environment for independent and nonconformist young dancers to experiment with modernism in dance. Four such individuals are exemplary: Doris Humphrey and Charles Weidman, Martha Graham (with composer and music director Louis Horst), and Helen Tamiris. All choreographed, performed, and taught in a network of "new schools" and, on occasion, in the Neighborhood School of the Theater. All anchored, in their individual ways, their choreographic ideas in the expression of American culture. For example, the titles of Graham's early works—*Immigrant, Revolt, Four Insecurities,* and *Heretic*—evoke both the social consciousness and the psychological issues that were current in the late 1920s and early 1930s. Similarly, Graham's pieces of the 1930s—*Primitive Mysteries* and *Ceremonials,* followed by *Frontier* and *American Document,* demonstrate the influence of American themes. [*See the entries on Graham, Horst, Humphrey, and Weidman.*]

The invention of synchronous sound for motion pictures in 1927 and the Great Depression that followed the stock market crash of October 1929 were serious blows to Broadway theaters. In the 1930s, as part of President Franklin Roosevelt's New Deal to American artists, the Federal Dance Project (1935–1939), subsidized by the Works Progress Administration (WPA), attempted to cut unemployment drastically in the theatrical dance field. Although administered in various cities, the Federal Dance Project was most active in Chicago and New York. Also in the early 1930s, numerous groups in New York City, including the Red Dancers and the New Dance Group, joined to form the Workers' Dance League. Dedicated to making dance a weapon in the class struggle and a means of social protest, the league produced dances of revolution. As the decade went on, however, its themes shifted to issues of war, fascism, and censorship. [*See* New Dance Group.]

The accomplishments of the Federal Dance Project reflected the variety of directions that theatrical dancing took after the turn of the century. There was a children's festival, entitled Folk Dances of All Nations, choreographed by Lillian Mehlman, and there were perfor-

UNITED STATES OF AMERICA: An Overview. Maude Russell and Her Ebony Steppers, who were a featured act at several Harlem clubs in the 1920s. (Photograph from the Dance Collection, New York Public Library for the Performing Arts.)

UNITED STATES OF AMERICA: An Overview. A former Denishawn dancer, Martha Graham was one of the most influential, and long-lived, modern dance pioneers. She swirls here in *Letter to the World* (1940), a work inspired by the life and poetry of Emily Dickinson, which premiered at the Bennington Festival in Vermont. (Photograph © by Barbara Morgan; used by permission of the Barbara Morgan Archives, Hastings-on-Hudson, New York.)

mances by the new modern dancers Humphrey, Weidman, Tamiris, and Katherine Dunham. The project brought together the diverse forms of theatrical dance that had developed over the previous fifty years and presented many of them side by side on the same stage. For instance, tap and chorus line routines were mixed with classical ballet in a Chicago revue called *O Say, Can You See?* Current social and political issues were expressed in movement, for example, Tamiris's *How Long Brethren?* (1937). Most importantly, in many cities the records of the region's performing arts were brought together in research studies for the first time, and the WPA led to the development of some of the first modern chronologies of early American dance, music, and theater history. [*See* Federal Dance Project; *and the entry on* Tamiris.]

The swing-band era of Benny Goodman, Glenn Miller, and others introduced social dances such as the boogie-woogie and jitterbug. These dances, free and improvised, further marked the move away form the close embrace of couple dancing. New sounds of maracas, claves, and Cuban drums popularized Latin American dances like the rumba, samba, and *maxixe*.

Dance increasingly became a more serious subject in colleges and universities as well as in the scheme of national cultural life. The first modern studies of the history of dancing began to appear in the 1930s: Lincoln Kirstein's *Dance: A Short History of Classical Theatrical Dancing* (1935) was closely followed by the English translation of the musicologist Curt Sachs's pioneering study *World History of the Dance* (1937). Sachs's book had been published in Germany just before he took up residence in New York City as professor of music at the Graduate School of Liberal Arts, New York University, and as music consultant to the New York Public Library.

The WPA had identified and made legitimate, if only briefly, federal responsibility for the nation's arts. The 1930s also witnessed renewed attempts to establish American professional dance companies and schools for classical ballet training. The founding of the School of American Ballet in 1933 and of the American Ballet in 1934 by Lincoln Kirstein and Edward M. Warburg with George Balanchine (whom they had invited to the United States to direct and organize the company) reflected a growing

UNITED STATES OF AMERICA: An Overview. Katherine Dunham was director of the Negro Unit of the Federal Dance Project in Chicago for a period in the late 1930s. During her tenure there, she presented her ballet *L'Ag'ya* under the FDP's auspices. She appears here, at center, with three male dancers of her company, in this work inspired by her research in Martinique. (Photograph from the Dance Collection, New York Public Library for the Performing Arts.)

interest in American ballet. In 1946 Balanchine and Kirstein also organized Ballet Society, a membership organization for the encouragement of lyric theater; in 1948 it was renamed New York City Ballet. Three brothers, who epitomized the development of dance in America—Willam, Lew, and Harold Christensen—established ballet schools in the far western United States. [*See* American Ballet; New York City Ballet; *and the entries on the Christensen brothers and Kirstein.*]

To some, ballet remained controversial until the 1950s. Essentially an assertion of high culture in a country whose population and potential audiences responded to popular entertainments and pastimes, ballet was not a standard aspect of university and college dance programs until the 1960s. Connoisseurship of classical dance, the result of exposure and education, grew steadily as a consequence of early dance tours like those of Ballet Caravan and that company's exploration of American subjects in choreography. Ballet Caravan's innovative repertory included *Pocahontas* (1936) by Lew Christensen, with music by Elliott Carter; *Yankee Clipper* (1937) by Eugene Loring, with music by Paul Bowles; *Filling Station* (1937) by Lew Christensen, with music by Virgil Thomson; and *Billy the Kid* (1938) by Eugene Loring, with music by Aaron Copland. [*See* Ballet Caravan.]

Also in the 1930s, American square dancing began as a nationwide recreational dance movement, having received impetus from the back-to-the-land movement prior to the stock market crash of 1929 and from the emergence of middle-class vacationers and auto tourists. Vacationing created a demand for "country customs" and brought local performers to the attention of travelers on holiday. Out of this trend arose a number of dance enthusiasts from all ranks who began "collecting" early dances on the model provided by English musicologist Cecil Sharp, who had founded the English Folk Dance Society of America in 1915, simultaneously in New York, Boston, Chicago, and Pittsburgh. In 1932 the English group became the English Dance and Song Society; later the United States branch became the Country Song and Dance Society of America.

Several books published after 1930 attest to the vitality of the country dance movement: Beth Tolman and Ralph Page's *The Country Dance Book* (1937), Lloyd Shaw's *Cowboy Dances* (1939), Grace L. Ryan's *Dance of Our Pioneers,* and Lucile K. Czarnowski's *Dances of Early California Days* (1950). These enthusiasts responded to the belief that they were preserving the dances of older members of their communities. They sponsored traditional dances at new-fashioned dude ranches and ski resorts, and they joined together to make a tacit folk community whose

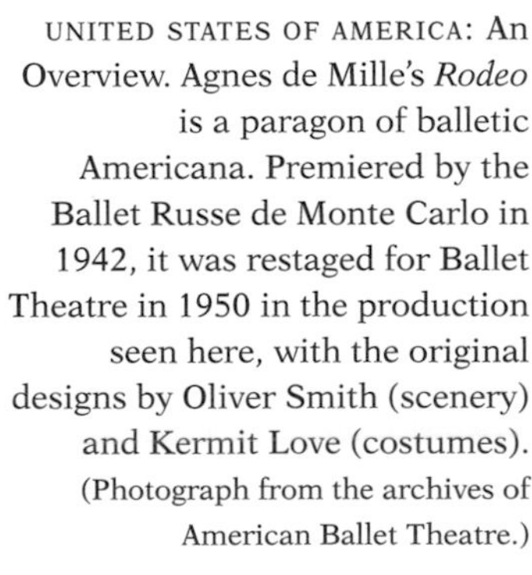

UNITED STATES OF AMERICA: An Overview. Agnes de Mille's *Rodeo* is a paragon of balletic Americana. Premiered by the Ballet Russe de Monte Carlo in 1942, it was restaged for Ballet Theatre in 1950 in the production seen here, with the original designs by Oliver Smith (scenery) and Kermit Love (costumes). (Photograph from the archives of American Ballet Theatre.)

networks have since grown steadily, some of whose members have emerged as professional performers.

Summer festivals and dance camps for all varieties of dance put young dancers together with mature performing artists and subject specialists. Beginning with summer pageants, Charlotte Perry and Portia Mansfield's summer dance camp in Steamboat Springs, Colorado (1914), Cecil Sharp's camps in Eliot, Maine, and Amherst Agricultural College, Massachusetts (1915), and later, the modern dance sessions at Bennington College in Vermont (1934–1946) and Mills College in California (1934), these intensive periods of study drew dancers and increased slowly in number and geographical location until their peak in the mid-1970s.

Against the background of these developments up to World War II, the Broadway musical *Oklahoma!* (1943), choreographed by Agnes de Mille, appeared as a milestone in American theatrical dance. In de Mille's choreography, elements of the growing traditional dance movement were united with classical ballet steps in a popular musical theater production on an American theme. The production brought many diverse aspects of American dance together, and the result was a dance form that attracted a large and popular audience. [*See the entry on de Mille.*]

American theatrical dance continued to attract large audiences after World War II, when ethnic, folk, and social genres began to support intellectual, social, and aesthetic diversity. Developments in national cultural life again guided the dance's multifarious directions. Foreign policy debates, the escalating Cold War between the USSR and the United States, loyalty checks and other ramifications of McCarthyism, economic and political reconstructions abroad, and the post–New Deal economy combined to create an aura of insecurity at home and abroad.

The population of the United States in 1952 was double that of 1900. Only 10 percent depended upon farming for their livelihood. Beginning in the 1950s, white collar workers outnumbered manual laborers, and manufacturers and suppliers in all professions increased markedly. Social progress began to be made in the fields of civil rights, health, and welfare. After 1950 dancing as an art form—enhanced by government support to arts and phys-

UNITED STATES OF AMERICA: An Overview. A scene from Yvonne Rainer's *Carriage Discreteness*, from *Nine Evenings: Theater and Engineering* (1966), a series of performances in which avant-garde artists collaborated with engineers from Bell Telephone Laboratories at the Sixty-ninth Regiment Armory, New York. (Photograph © 1966 by Peter Moore; used by permission.)

UNITED STATES OF AMERICA: An Overview. Trisha Brown devised the movement for *Locus* (1975) by assigning letters to points on an imaginary cube surrounding her body and then "spelling" out an autobiographical text through actions directed at these points. From left to right, Brown, Elizabeth Garren, Mona Sulzman, and Judith Ragir appear in different phases of this articulation. *Locus* was pivotal in the development of Brown's efficient, yet fluid, style of movement, which has been influential among dancers and choreographers throughout the world. (Photograph © by Babette Mangolte; used by permission.)

ical education programs in colleges and universities; growing national economic security; an increase in the number of educated viewers; television exposure; and finally the establishment of the national endowments—entered a period of growth that exploded by the mid-1970s.

Classical ballet companies began to develop all over the world and by the 1960s had become international symbols of national or civic prestige. The successful visit of Great Britain's Sadler's Wells Ballet (renamed the Royal Ballet in 1956) from Covent Garden to New York City in 1949 marked the beginning of regular international cultural exchanges of dance companies. Impresario Sol Hurok (1888–1974) was a major figure in these exchanges. In the 1950s he arranged for visits by the Bolshoi Ballet, the Kirov Ballet, the Moiseyev Dance Company, and the Azumi Kabuki troupe as well as tours by American artists such as Martha Graham to Europe and East Asia.

Beginning in 1956, with the first regional ballet festival in Atlanta, Georgia, the regional ballet movement began to provide one solution to the problem of training young dancers for ballet companies, nationally and abroad. Consisting of nonprofessional companies attached to schools, the activity complemented the earlier civic theater movement. It brought support to its members, served the communities with which it was affiliated, and was one answer to the need for developing young talent for professional careers. After the formation of the Regional Ballet Festival Association (later the National Association for Regional Ballet), the design spread to the Northeast (1959), Southwest (1963), Pacific Western (1966) and Middle States (1972) regions.

Against the canvas of expanding professional dance organization and touring companies, the off-Broadway movement, whose performances took place in out-of-the-way theaters and improvised auditoriums in order to cut production costs, supported new waves of young modern dancers who pursued the path of individual expression established by Graham, Humphrey, Tamiris, and Hanya Holm. Dancers such as Merce Cunningham, Alwin Nikolais, and Paul Taylor began to steer choreography and performance technique away from its expressionist focus. Cunningham created a style of dancing that embodied flexibility, multiplicity change, and idiosyncrasy. Other modern dancers, like Anna Halprin, explored the cacophony of modern life and found new ways to create sense from its diverse elements with happenings, wherein any raw material—simultaneous phenomena, sounds, or objects—could become part of the dance event. [*See the entries on Cunningham, Halprin, Holm, Nikolais, and Taylor.*]

A simplified version of the jitterbug, the jive, and "smooch" dancing to quiet music characterized post–World War II social dancing. Soon, however, rock-and-roll (popularized by Bill Haley and the Comets in 1955) became the rage, and dances like the Twist (popularized by Chubby Checker in the early 1960s) and the Shake became the popular "fast" dances. All could be danced in groups without partners. Electric guitars and organs, along with rhythm and sometimes brass instruments, created a new dance sound that entertained widespread audiences through records played at home, at school proms, on jukeboxes, and on the radio. [*See* Social Dance, *article on* Social Dance since 1960.]

From 1961 through 1968, the presidencies of John F. Kennedy and Lyndon Johnson, the population of the United States increased by twenty-four million—with 60 percent living in metropolitan areas, 5 percent on farms. In a phantasmagorical scene induced by national and international events, the country witnessed domestic wars on poverty and racism convergent with U.S. involvement in Vietnam. A confrontation on a national scale over the potential end of the world's natural resources coincided with and exacerbated the media images and felt consequences of environmental destruction and the sacrifice of lives in war as a means to peace. By 1970 American society appeared to have stalled: within ten years it had confronted the paradox of being both the best and the worst of nations. Dancing reflected the times in terms of choreographic themes and artistic approaches as well as through its growth boosted by federal programs for the arts and humanities. In 1966 the U.S. Congress initiated governmental support of the nation's arts with passage of the National Foundation on the Arts and Humanities Act. Touring and funding for dance projects began in 1966, and in the early 1970s the National Endowment for the Arts (NEA) Dance Program became a special umbrella for dance as a performing art.

The increasing diversity of dance styles and genres after 1960 was met by a conscious joining of styles and the disassembling of dance movements—directions in dance that have served to create expressive new dimensions in the arts. Examples can be drawn from divergent levels of society and training. Inspired by choreographer Cunningham, artists Allan Kaprow, Robert Rauschenberg, and Jasper Johns, and composer John Cage, postmodern dancers such as Steve Paxton, Yvonne Rainer, Trisha Brown, and David Gordon explored invention and change as a means of disengaging from ideas of tradition, personal expression, craftsmanship, and composition. Their dances not only evaluate space, time, and weight; but they also play with perception, arbitrary assemblages, fragmentation, and juxtaposition; movement is demystified and allowed to be ordinary, mundane. [*See the entries on Trisha Brown, Cage, Gordon, Johns, Paxton, Rainer, and Rauschenberg.*]

UNITED STATES OF AMERICA: An Overview. Zydeco is a Cajun couple dance performed to lively two-step music. Pictured here are dancers doing the Nouveau Zydeco at the Twelfth Annual Original Southwest Louisiana Zydeco Music Festival in Plaisance, Louisiana, in 1994. (Photograph © 1994 by Jack Vartoogian; used by permission.)

UNITED STATES OF AMERICA: An Overview. Catherine Turocy's New York Baroque Dance Company and James Richman's Concert Royal revived Rameau's 1745 *opéra-ballet Le Temple de la Gloire* in 1991. Here, Venus (dancer Patricia Beaman) and Mars (dancer Todd Putman) crown the Roman emperor Trajan (tenor Frederick Urrey) with a laurel wreath in an allegory of ideal kingship; Glory (soprano Christine Brandes) observes from the clouds above. (Photograph © 1991 by Jack Vartoogian; used by permission.)

American dance after the 1960s reflected the work of choreographers like Glen Tetley, who, trained in both classical and modern styles, brought the rational and cool steps, position, and attitudes of ballet together with the free and independently expressive use of space, time, and rhythm in modern dance. [*See the entry on Tetley.*] In a similar vein, but from another dance community, break dancing—a movement art that used wrists, shoulders, and heads more than feet in a stunning array of twists, kicks, and spins—superseded "dancing" on roller skates as the urban dance art of the 1980s. Most break dancers were black or Hispanic male teenagers who gathered on the streets or in discos to display their talents. Frequently accompanied by a "rapper," a nondancer who gave a "soliloquy in rhyme about the hard knocks, crime, and life in the ghetto" (Sandler, 1984), the dancing incorporated movements similar to gymnastics, wrestling, and martial arts. [*See* Break Dancing.]

In the 1960s and early 1970s, social dances like the Frug, the Hustle, and salsa moved into discotheques. A revival of rock-and-roll and renewed interest in country-western music rejuvenated dances from the 1950s as well as country swing, the Texas Two-Step, Cotton-Eyed Joe, and clogging. Late 1950s and early 1960s Latin dances such as the cha-cha and the bossa nova infused more formal ballroom practices, and a revival of "tea dancing" in urban hotels renewed interest in the fox trot, waltz, and other ballroom dances.

Professional associations founded since the 1960s express contemporary and burgeoning diversity of dance interests, from dance history to movement therapy to aerobics. These groups reflect developments in physical education, ethnic and traditional dancing, dance criticism, dance therapy, cheerleading, dance music, dance revivalism, games, and play. Dance revivalism, the impulse to preserve dances from the past—a phenomenon in American dance history as far back as the eighteenth century—has become almost a science, involving a combination of sensitivity to theatrical and social history with procedures of analysis, scholarship, and expressive movement reconstruction. As a result, an ironic situation has developed: American scholars in historical dance have played an important role in bringing forth reconstructed early court dance choreographies to European audiences. The Baroque Dance Ensemble under the direction of Shirley Wynne was the first such American company in Europe at Spoleto, Italy, in the summer of 1979. Two of her company members, Catherine Turocy and Ann Jacoby, co-founders of the New York Baroque Dance Company, presented the premiere performance in Europe of Jean-Philippe Rameau's opera *Les Bordéades* in Aix-en-Provence, France, in the summer of 1982.

As the turn of the twenty-first century approaches, dance art in the United States is like any other medium and cultural commodity that must keep pace in both the intellectual marketplace and the supermarket of consumerism. Performers, musicians, choreographers, choreographies, and audiences are globally accessible and performers interchangeable within a vast array of professional movement styles. A good theatrical dance experience, like most American cars, may have performers, director, and expressive and technical components from multiple international communities. Like postmodern choreographer and dancer Mark Morris, American dance artists have played an increasingly significant role in the development of dance arts in Europe. In 1984, the American Dance Festival in Durham, North Carolina, produced its first International Modern Dance Festival and its first International Choreographers Workshop, which led to the formation of the International Choreographers Commissioning Program in 1987. The year 1993 saw the first International Dance Critics Conference. Activities were not limited to the United States; by 1994, twenty-four foreign countries had offered classes and workshops led by American Dance Festival faculty. [*See* American Dance Festival; *and the entry on Morris.*]

In 1985, New York's Dance Theater Workshop founded The Suitcase Fund: A Project of Ideas and Means in Cross-Cultural Artist Relations. The Fund was organized to assist independent professional artists and their progressive producers in overcoming the economic and political barriers that deny artists access to other cultures. In addition, the fund now also helps producers and writers travel to major meetings and festivals in order to build ongoing relationships with their peers. By 1995 both the American Dance Festival and Dance Theater Workshop were sponsoring cooperative activities with Africa, Asia, Europe, and Latin America.

U.S. dance magazines and scholarly publications regularly cover international dance in Denmark, France, the Netherlands, and some Asian countries. There are now international ballet seminars. A child studying dance in

UNITED STATES OF AMERICA: An Overview. Mark Morris set his *Pièces en Concert* to selections from François Couperin's work of the same title. Pictured here, in the 1986 premiere performance at the Brooklyn Academy of Music, are Susan Hadley, Morris, and Rob Besserer. (Photographs © 1986 by Jack Vartoogian; used by permission.)

UNITED STATES OF AMERICA: An Overview. The Pacific Northwest Ballet, directed by Kent Stowell and Francia Russell, is one of the most successful dance companies in the United States. In Stowell's production of *Cinderella* (1994), Ross Yearsley as the Prince partnered Louise Nadeau in the title role. (Photograph courtesy of Pacific Northwest Ballet.)

Omaha, Nebraska, can aspire to join a dance company in almost any part of the globe. Likewise, complementing fine televised programming of all types of dance—accessible to countless audiences worldwide—the World Wide Web and internet permit audience, performer, and choreographer to exchange information instantly and to see bodies move across their computer screens. In such a frantic and fragmented world, meaning in expressive body gestures and dance language is one of "references," a postmodern trend that lets us view body movement from our theater seats much as we view scenery from a fast-moving car. The embodied performance—not self-conscious—is the *rara avis,* and yet it is sought out by ethnologists and sociologists and can, when captured, become, in an Erving Goffman manner, a kind of theater experience in itself. As Adam Gopnik remarked in the *New Yorker,* "Post-modernist art is, above all, post-audience art."

The broad acceptance of American dance, its diverse manifestations and definitions, expresses a uniquely American cultural consciousness. Dance historians examine past webs of ideas, and the pathways that dancers have been asked by their society and culture to travel. Dance anthropologists and musicologists challenge the public to see the movement performance of others within the performers' own cultural systems. Sociologists urge spectators to find structured relationships in vernacular dancing events. Folklorists and psychologists show how dance events and interpersonal behaviors create vital circuits of communication between participants and how the values and attitudes related to dance postures and gestures are encoded in culture and society so that they are saved, used, and perpetuated. Dance therapists call attention to how body-movement patterns and preferences impede or assist growth, development, and perception. The history of dance in the United States is thus best understood from a broad, interdisciplinary base of inquiry that seeks to define and explain dance expressions in the tangled variety of cultural situations that are the American experience.

BIBLIOGRAPHY. Primary sources available for the study of dance in the United States are virtually without limit. The ephemeral and all-encompassing activity of dance makes it necessary to consider a broad variety of sources in order to understand what diverse groups of Americans have thought about their bodies and those of others, and what principles have helped to shape people's expressive postures and gestures as well as forms in dance. Standard documents for the investigation of dancing include diaries and journals, letters, newspapers, magazines, and books. Graphics such as paintings, magazine and newspaper illustrations, and photographs—though laden with artistic conventions and limited by the medium as well as by the artist—reveal cultural ideas about dancing and the body. Film is one of the most immediate, but least available, records of dance. Oral histories can provide information to the folklorist as well as to the historian in dance. Less obvious sources are municipal, state, and federal records, ship passenger lists, and legal records.

Abrahams, Roger D. "Moving in America." *Prospects* 3 (1977): 63–82.

"American Dancing." *Dance Magazine* (July 1976): 44–78.

Andrews, Edward D. *The Gift to Be Simple: Songs, Dances, and Rituals of the American Shakers.* New York, 1940.

Aschenbrenner, Joyce. *Katherine Dunham: Reflections on the Social and Political Contexts of Afro-American Dance.* CORD Dance Research Annual, 12. New York, 1981.

Banes, Sally. *Terpsichore in Sneakers: Post-Modern Dance.* Boston, 1980.

Barker[-Warner], Barbara. *Ballet or Ballyhoo: The American Careers of Maria Bonfanti, Rita Sangalli, and Giuseppina Morlacchi.* New York, 1984.

Barzel, Ann. "European Dance Teachers in the United States." *Dance Index* 3 (April–June 1944): 56–100.

Benson, Norman A. "The Itinerant Dancing and Music Masters of Eighteenth-Century America." Ph.D. diss., University of Minnesota, 1963.

Blaustein, Richard J. "Traditional Music and Social Change: The Old Time Fiddler's Association Movement in the United States." Master's thesis, Indiana University, 1975.

Brockett, Oscar G. *History of the Theatre.* 7th ed. Boston, 1995.

Brooks, Lynn Matluck. "The Philadelphia Dancing Assembly in the Eighteenth Century." *Dance Research Journal* 21 (Spring 1989): 1–6.

Brown, Richard D. *Modernization: The Transformation of American Life, 1600–1865.* New York, 1976.

Cohen, Selma Jeanne. "The Fourth of July, or, The Independence of American Dance." *Dance Magazine* (July 1976): 49–53.

Dance Research Journal (Spring 1983). Special issue entitled "Popular Dance in Black America."

Delamater, Jerome. *Dance in the Hollywood Musical.* Ann Arbor, Mich., 1981.

de Mille, Agnes. *Dance to the Piper.* Boston, 1952.

Emery, Lynne Fauley. *Black Dance from 1619 to Today.* Rev. ed. Princeton, 1988.

Garafola, Lynn, ed. *Of, By, and For the People: Dancing on the Left in the 1930s.* Madison, Wis., 1994.
Glassberg, David. "Restoring a 'Forgotten Childhood': American Play and the Progressive Era's Elizabethan Past." *American Quarterly* 32 (Fall 1980): 351–368.
Handlin, Oscar. *The Uprooted: The Epic Story of the Great Migrations That Made the American People.* 2d enl. ed. Boston, 1973.
Harris, Neil. *The Artist in American Society: The Formative Years, 1790–1860.* Chicago, 1966.
Haskins, James. *The Cotton Club: A Pictorial and Social History of the Most Famous Symbol of the Jazz Era.* New York, 1977.
Haskins, James. *Black Dance in America: A History through Its People.* New York, 1990.
Hazzard-Gordon, Katrina. *Jookin': The Rise of Social Dance Formations in African-American Culture.* Philadelphia, 1990.
Howe, Daniel Walker, ed. *Victorian America.* Philadelphia, 1976.
Humphrey, Doris. *Doris Humphrey, an Artist First: An Autobiography.* Edited by Selma Jeanne Cohen. Middletown, Conn., 1977.
Kirstein, Lincoln. *Ballet, Bias, and Belief: Three Pamphlets Collected and Other Dance Writings.* New York, 1983.
Lally, Kathleen A. "A History of the Federal Dance Theatre of the Works Progress Administration, 1935–1939." Master's thesis, Texas Women's University, 1978.
Lehman, Rhea H. "Virtue and Virtuosity: America's Vision of the Romantic Ballet, 1827–1840." Ph.D. diss., University of Wisconsin, Madison, 1986.
Lynes, Russell. *The Tastemakers.* New York, 1954.
Magriel, Paul, ed. *Chronicles of the American Dance: From the Shakers to Martha Graham.* New York, 1948.
Marks, Joseph E. III. *America Learns to Dance: A Historical Study of Dance Education in America before 1900.* New York, 1957.
Marks, Joseph E. III. *The Mathers on Dancing.* Brooklyn, 1975.
Martin, Carol. *Dance Marathons: Performing American Culture of the 1920s and 1930s.* Jackson, Miss., 1994.
Martin, John. *The Modern Dance.* New York, 1933.
Matlaw, Myron, ed. *American Popular Entertainment: Program and Papers of the Conference on the History of American Popular Entertainment.* Westport, Conn., 1979.
McDermott, Douglas. "The Development of Theatre on the American Frontier, 1750–1890." *Theatre Survey* 19 (May 1978): 63–78.
Moore, Lillian. "Moreau de Saint-Méry and 'Danse.'" *Dance Index* 5 (October 1946): 232–260.
Moore, Lillian. "Some Early American Dancers." *Dancing Times* (August 1950): 668–671.
Moore, Lillian. "The Duport Mystery." *Dance Perspectives,* no. 7 (1960).
Moore, Lillian. "New York's First Ballet Season, 1792." *Bulletin of the New York Public Library* (September 1960).
Moore, Lillian. *Echoes of American Ballet: A Collection of Seventeen Articles Written and Selected by Lillian Moore.* Edited by Ivor Guest. Brooklyn, 1976.
Moulton, Robert D. "Choreography in Musical Comedy and Revue on the New York Stage from 1925 through 1950." Master's thesis, University of Minnesota, 1957.
Nye, Russell Blaine. *The Cultural Life of the New Nation, 1776–1830.* New York, 1963.
Nye, Russell Blaine. *The Unembarrassed Muse: The Popular Arts in America.* New York, 1970.
Nye, Russell Blaine. *Society and Culture in America, 1830–1860.* New York, 1974.
Oliver, George B. "Changing Pattern of Spectacle on the New York Stage, 1850–1890." Ph.D. diss., Pennsylvania State University, 1956.
Prevots, Naima. "American Pageantry and American Modern Dance." In *Proceedings of the Sixth Annual Conference, Society of Dance History Scholars, the Ohio State University, 11–13 February 1983,* compiled by Christena L. Schlundt. Milwaukee, 1983.
Richman, Marjorie L., and Gertrude R. Schmiedler. "Changes in a Folk Dance Accompanying Cultural Change." *Journal of Social Psychology* 42 (1955): 333–336.
Ruyter, Nancy Lee Chalfa. *Reformers and Visionaries: The Americanization of the Art of Dance.* New York, 1979.
Said, Edward W. *Orientalism.* New York, 1978.
Sandler, Ken. "Breakdancing! Spinning into the Big Time." *Washington Post* (January 1984).
Schneider, Gretchen. "Dance as an Expressive Response to Frontier Life in the Mining Camps of California, 1848–1855." Master's thesis, University of California, Los Angeles, 1968.
Schneider, Gretchen. "Pigeon Wings and Polkas: The Dance of the California Miners." *Dance Perspectives,* no. 39 (1969): 1–57.
Schneider, Gretchen. "Using Nineteenth-Century American Social Dance Manuals." *Dance Research Journal* 14.1–2 (1981–1982): 39–42.
Seeger, Mike. *Talking Feet: Buck, Flatfoot, and Tap: Solo Southern Dance of the Appalachian, Piedmont, and Blue Ridge Mountain Regions.* Berkeley, 1992.
Shelton, Suzanne. *Divine Dancer: A Biography of Ruth St. Denis.* Garden City, N.Y., 1981.
Stearns, Marshall, and Jean Stearns. *Jazz Dance.* New York, 1968.
Theeman, Margaret. "Rhythms of Community: The Sociology of Expressive Body Movement." Ph.D. diss., Harvard University, 1973.
Thompson, Robert Farris. *African Art in Motion: Icon and Act.* 2d ed. Los Angeles, 1979.
Van Cleef, Joy. "Rural Felicity: Social Dance in Eighteenth-Century Connecticut." *Dance Perspectives,* no. 65 (Spring 1976): 3–45.
Van Cleef, Joy, and Kate Van Winkle Keller. "Selected American Country Dances and Their English Sources." In *Music in Colonial Massachusetts, 1630–1820,* vol. 1, *Music in Public Places.* Boston, 1980.
Van Dyke, Jan. *Modern Dance in a Postmodern World: An Analysis of Federal Arts Funding and Its Impact on the Field of Modern Dance.* Reston, Va., 1992.
Winter, Marian Hannah. "American Theatrical Dancing from 1750 to 1800." *Musical Quarterly* 24 (January 1938): 58–73.
Wynne, Shirley S. "From Ballet to Ballroom: Dance in the Revolutionary Era." *Dance Scope* 10 (Fall–Winter 1975–1976): 65–73.
Zuckerman, Michael. "Pilgrims in the Wilderness: Community, Modernity, and the Maypole at Merry Mount." *New England Quarterly* 50 (June 1977): 255–277.

RECORDINGS. *Nineteenth-Century American Ballroom Music* (Nonesuch, 1975). *Come and Trip It: Instrumental Dance Music, 1780s–1920s* (New York, 1978).

VIDEOTAPES. Catherine Turocy, *The Art of Dancing: An Introduction to Baroque Dance* (New York, 1979). Mike Seeger, *Talking Feet: Buck, Flatfoot, and Tap* (El Cerrito, Calif., 1987).

GRETCHEN SCHNEIDER

African-American Dance Traditions

African-American dance, a syncretism of African and European dance, evolved in the United States out of plantation and frontier life and came to the popular stage through minstrelsy. Its path and pattern of development delineate the tenor of American racial segregation and discrimination. The progression from minstrelsy to the concert stage—from mid-nineteenth century to the present—parallels the availability to African Americans of additional performance environments in successive eras of American history.

The earliest outlets were tent shows, road shows, and the minstrel stage, followed by white burlesque houses—the lowest rung on the white show business ladder. (Nineteenth-century burlesque was a variety entertainment genre. Striptease developed in the twentieth century.) Next came segregated theaters on African-American vaudeville circuits (1900–1940s). A few black Americans performed in white vaudeville and on Broadway during the first few decades of the twentieth century, but only occasionally were they so engaged. Community-based college and repertory theater productions of African-American concert dance (beginning in the 1920s) preceded the earliest professional concert recitals (1930s).

Additional performance outlets stimulated experimentation, innovation, and the creation of new dance genres, but the root connection with African and plantation forms remained. Refined and developed, the earliest African-American form, plantation dance, was the basis for minstrel dance. With the advent of drinking houses and dance halls in southern and frontier labor communities during Reconstruction, new dances—social dances—evolved. African Americans on Broadway and in vaudeville created a generous variety of theatrical and social dances in the 1920s and 1930s. Drawing upon its rich legacy of a past rooted in vernacular and popular stage traditions, African-American concert dance comprises a wide variety of styles and approaches and represents a healthy interchange between theatrical and vernacular, African and European, forms.

Minstrelsy. The most popular genre of American entertainment during the mid-nineteenth century, minstrelsy was the first professional performance outlet for African Americans, and the training ground for early vaudevillians. It carried African-American vernacular forms into American popular culture, preserved plantation dances, and laid the groundwork for the creation of new dances. It also sanctioned the use of white forms (jig, clogging, ballads, arias) by black Americans and offered them employment and the opportunity to develop theatrical talent. On the other hand, minstrelsy established and perpetuated the negative character stereotypes that have haunted African Americans and continued to circumscribe their social and theatrical achievements into the present. This overriding characteristic of the genre looms large enough to neutralize its positive contributions.

William Henry Lane, known as Master Juba (c.1825–c.1852), was one of the few African Americans in antebellum minstrelsy. Blending jigs and clogging with African-based rhythm and syncopation, he created a new dance style and came to be considered the father of tap dance. [*See the entry on Juba.*]

African Americans did not gain general access to the minstrel stage until after the Civil War. Setting a precedent that continued into vaudeville, minstrel performers were multitalented. They danced, sang, and played one or more musical instruments and were comedians as well as masters of ceremonies, managers, and directors.

Plantation dances that were preserved and developed in minstrelsy include the Virginia Essence, the cakewalk, the buck-and-wing, Pattin' Juba, and the walk-around. The Virginia Essence was a refined shuffle in which the performer's feet moved so smoothly as to appear not to move at all. Billy Kersands was famous for his development and performance of this dance, which is the precursor of the vaudeville soft-shoe as well as the first African-American dance to gain popularity on the American stage. The plantation buck dance, another variation on shuffle steps (which form a fundamental component in African-American vernacular dance), was combined with hopping—or wing—steps and became the minstrel buck-and-wing, a major early form of tap dance. Pattin' Juba developed out of a West African ceremonial dance called Giouba. Plantation owners outlawed the use of drums, so ingenious slaves substituted interrelated systems of syncopated foot patting, vocal punctuation, and the patting or clapping of various parts of the body. This dance, known as Pattin' Juba, was transposed to the minstrel stage as a specialty number involving the rhythmical patting of chest, hips, and thighs. Remnants exist in children's handclapping games and in the hambone routine that is performed to the folk rhyme of the same name.

The cakewalk, a plantation challenge dance, with a cake as the prize, was a paradigm of African-American continuity with African forms and syncretism with European forms. It contained elements of competition and improvisation basic to African dance. The characteristic strutting steps originally parodied the plantation owners, whom slaves observed dancing European forms at social functions. Forerunner of the strut and the jazz walk familiar to musical comedy and jazz dance, it was used for the finale in African-American minstrelsy. By the 1890s it became the first social fad dance to gain popularity in both black and white circles, with cakewalk contests a common occurrence.

The cakewalk finale was performed as a walk-around, the secular equivalent of the plantation ring shout, which replicated the structure of traditional West African dance: onlookers stood or moved in a circle around a soloist or couple who improvised in the center, then joined the circle to be replaced by someone else. It continued into early vaudeville and was replaced by the Shim-Sham finale of the swing era of the 1930s and 1940s. [*See* Cakewalk.]

Of the many outstanding African-American minstrels, mention must be made of Sam Lucas, Tom Fletcher, and Billy Kersands. Others who began their careers as min-

UNITED STATES OF AMERICA: African-American Dance Traditions. A parade of cakewalk dancers depicted in a photo-montage by H. M. Pettit, after a film made by Thomas Edison, c.1896. The cakewalk, which began as a competitive plantation dance, became a popular feature of many theatrical entertainments. (Collection of Sally R. Sommer and William G. Sommer.)

strels include James Bland, W. C. Handy, Gussie L. Davis, Ernest Hogan, George Walker, Bert Williams, and Dewey ("Pigmeat") Markham. After leaving minstrelsy, Williams and Markham continued to perform in burnt-cork makeup as vaudevillians.

Greatly reduced in scope and concept and overshadowed by new theatrical genres, minstrelsy declined in national popularity but survived through the 1960s as road-show fare in the rural South.

Vaudeville and Social Dance. Dance formed the matrix of African-American performance in minstrelsy, musical comedy, and vaudeville. Stars such as Ethel Waters, Ralph Cooper, Lena Horne, and Dorothy Dandridge all began as dancers. In turn, concert dancers such as Katherine Dunham and Lavinia Williams-Yarborough spent part of their career on the popular stage. [*See the entries on Dunham and Williams-Yarborough.*]

Minstrelsy declined as the all-male format was challenged externally by the rising interest in female performers, the film industry, and the cabaret and internally by repetitiveness and lack of innovation. By 1890 African-American minstrel shows had added women, forerunners of the chorus line, and ushered in the "coon show" era, exemplified by productions such as *The Creole Show* (1890); *The Octoroons* (1895); *Oriental America* (1896), the first African-American show to run on Broadway; and *Black Patti's Troubadours* (1897), which subsequently toured for eighteen seasons as a road show. *A Trip to Coontown* and *Clorindy, or The Origin of the Cakewalk* (both 1898) were the first African-American shows to make a complete break with the minstrel format. These productions laid the groundwork for the contributions of George Walker and Bert Williams, multitalented African-American performers, producers, and directors who created a series of operettas (1897–1907) and popularized the cakewalk.

During this period African-American song and dance became trendsetters for white American popular culture. Through popular entertainment outlets of the 1900s and 1920s white audiences learned such plantation-derived dances as the cakewalk, the Turkey Trot, the Grizzly Bear, the Black Bottom, Ballin' the Jack, the Charleston, the Shimmy, and the Mooche. African-American songwriters such as Perry Bradford ("The Bullfrog Hop," 1912; "The Original Black Bottom Dance," 1919), Chris Smith ("Ballin' the Jack," 1913), and Sheldon Brooks ("Walkin' the Dog," 1917) wrote dance instruction songs that were sold in sheet form.

African Americans performed in road shows, medicine

shows, carnivals, and circuses throughout the South and the Midwest, either in the segregated units of white companies or as part of independent African-American outfits, such as the *Whitman Sisters' Roadshow* (1910s–1930s), Salem Tutt Whitney's *Silas Green from New Orleans* show (1904–1940s), and Irvin C. Miller's *Brownskin Models* (1920s–1950s).

By 1920 African-American theaters that had been built in the South and the Midwest early in the twentieth century were organized into the Theater Owners' Booking Association (TOBA), which booked complete shows and independent acts through the 1930s. Ethel Waters, Bessie Smith, Willie Bryant, Bill Robinson, Eddie Rector, and the Berry Brothers were but a few of the many performers who began their career on "TOBY-Time." Its demise was owed, in part, to the expanding influence of white managers and to the growth of the film industry (double features meant the end of the movie-with-variety-show format). [*See the entries on the Berry Brothers and Robinson.*]

After George Walker retired from the stage in 1907, Bert Williams joined the *Ziegfeld Follies*. African-American shows disappeared from Broadway (until 1921, with the opening of *Shuffle Along*) and survived in African-American repertory theaters across the nation. In Harlem, the Lincoln, Crescent, Alhambra, and Lafayette theaters, which originally produced farces, serious dramas, and variety shows, by the 1920s had become vaudeville houses. The Lafayette Theater's 1913 production of *Darktown Follies* featured Eddie Rector, whose tapping was characterized by light-footed grace and elegance—instead of a shuffling stereotype—and who was the predecessor of the swing-era "class act." This *Follies* also featured Toots Davis, whose acrobatic tapping foreshadowed the swing-era "flash act," and it introduced an African-American dance hall favorite, the Texas Tommy, forerunner of the Lindy Hop. It was one of the last shows to feature a cakewalk finale. The show's final act was bought by Florenz Ziegfeld and used for his *Follies* in 1913, with no credit given to J. Leubrie Hill, who was director, writer, and producer of the original, or to cast members (such as dancer Cora La Redd) who taught the new routines to Ziegfeld's white, downtown dancers.

The co-opting of African-American choreography and music by the white world began in white minstrelsy and continued in vaudeville and on Broadway. Choreographer Buddy Bradley created routines for stars such as Adele Astaire and Clifton Webb but was given no credit. [*See the entry on Bradley.*] James Reese Europe's Memphis Students Band was the first "big band" and in 1912 was the first to play jazz music in a concert setting, although the Paul Whiteman 1921 concert generally is cited as the first such instance. African Americans also initiated the "dancing conductor," later epitomized by musicians such as Cab Calloway. It was Europe and Ford Dabney's band that played for Irene and Vernon Castle, created the fox trot for them, and initiated the custom of African-American musicians playing at white social dance events. This trend was reversed by the mid-1930s. The white world turned away from African-American bands after white bands, led by Benny Goodman and others, had mastered the sound that had once been the exclusive domain of bands led by the likes of Fletcher Henderson, Duke Ellington, and Jimmie Lunceford. African-American nightclubs fell into decline as whites took their business to white clubs.

The 1920s and 1930s was a period of dense cultural interchange between blacks and whites. African-American choreographers opened dance studios and created routines for white performers. White composers, including Harold Arlen, Jimmy McHugh, and Dorothy Fields, contributed music to the New York Cotton Club revues; Cotton Clubs and Plantation Clubs in cities across the United States offered exclusively African-American entertainment for exclusively white audiences. White choreographers such as Jean De Meaux and composers such as Armand Lamet devised routines and musical arrangements for the white ballroom repertory (waltzes, tangos, and so forth) of African-American dance teams, such as Norton and Margot. Whites wrote black Broadway shows; and black arrangers, such as James Mundy, Billy Strayhorn, Benny Carter, Will Vodery, and Don Redman—to name only a few—were behind the swing music of many white big bands.

Big band music and ballrooms evolved out of a need for sound to accompany and space to accommodate the various social dance crazes that began at the turn of the century and peaked in the 1920s and 1930s. Americans of both races danced in Harlem ballrooms such as the Savoy, Alhambra, and Renaissance.

A healthy interchange took place between the ballroom and nightclub dance floor and the vaudeville and Broadway stage. Updated, theatricalized versions of age-old African and plantation steps were introduced to whites by African-American performers who used them as the basis for their routines. White audiences took these steps back to their ballrooms. Broadway shows such as *Runnin' Wild* (1923), which introduced an old African-American dance, the Charleston, and *Dixie to Broadway* (1924), which introduced another vintage African-derived dance, the Black Bottom, served the same function. The African American performing to white audiences was the means of dissemination from black world to white. As choreographer Buddy Bradley later recalled:

> We thought nothing of the fact that everybody in and out of colored show business seemed to know a million old jive steps. . . . We all knew those movements as kids . . . they were a part of our life that we took for granted—and it was some time be-

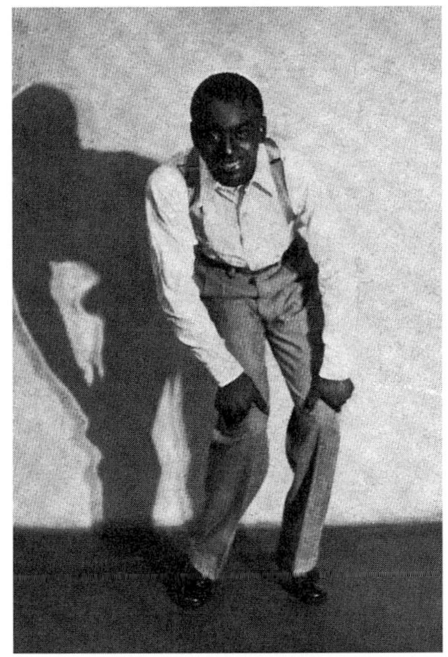

UNITED STATES OF AMERICA: African-American Dance Traditions. Choreographer Buddy Bradley taught African-American dance steps to many of the white stars of musical theater. He is seen here, c.1927, demonstrating Ballin' the Jack (left), the Baltimore Jazz (center), and the Breakdown (right). (Photographs by Nasib; collection of Sally R. Sommer and William G. Sommer.)

> fore I realized that they were pretty new to Broadway and that most white people couldn't begin to do any of them.
>
> (Quoted in Stearns, 1994, p. 165)

Fad dances such as Truckin', the Susie Q, the Shorty-George, Peckin', and the Scronch originated as Cotton Club production numbers and subsequently caught on as ballroom dances. By the time they reached white circles, they had been simplified and toned down—and replaced by new fad dances created in African-American circles. [*For discussion of social dances see* Big Apple, Lindy Hop, *and the entry on Frankie Manning.*]

The influence of African-American "dance directors" on Broadway changed the nature of American musical comedy dance and introduced the precision chorus line to Broadway. These "directors" included Bradley, Clarence Robinson, Leonard Harper, Elida Webb, Charlie Davis, Herbie Harper, Charlie White, Addison Carey, Leonard Reed, Sammy Dyer, and Frank Montgomery. By the 1930s, however, black Broadway's heyday was over, killed by the Great Depression and by white lyricists and composers who produced their own versions of materials originally generated by the likes of Sissle and Blake, Miller and Lyles. As in minstrelsy, the churning out of formula shows led to self-induced obsolescence. [*See the article on* Musical Theater, *below.*]

Vaudeville dance acts manifested a staggering variety of genres, including tap, eccentric, comedy, acrobatic, exotic, social (fad dances), and ballroom. As with pure acrobatics, ballroom was a small category, epitomized by the team of Norton and Margot, who dared to break the stereotype of speed, rhythm, or exoticism and who danced in the style and repertory of white teams such as Veloz and Yolanda.

As big bands declined, so did the dances they accompanied. In the late 1940s, after a major depression and two world wars—crises spanning three decades through which Americans sang, danced, and reveled in spite of themselves—the American temperament experienced a major shift from an outgoing to an introspective national personality. This shift was marked by such diverse cultural trends as widespread ownership of the automobile; television viewing; small-group, bebop music; mass migration to the suburbs (a reversal of urban migration patterns of the preceding half-century); xenophobia elicited and revealed by McCarthyism; and increased use of psychoanalysis.

African-American dance lost its national footing in the 1950s. It receded from white scrutiny and survived on the so-called Chitlin' Circuit comprising neighborhood bars in the various Harlems throughout the nation. Resurgent national attention to African-American vernacular forms was occasioned by the animal dance craze of the 1960s (the Monkey, the Pony, the Philly Dog, and other spinoffs of the Twist), the Hustle of the 1970s, and disco dancing in the 1970s and 1980s. [*See* Social Dance, *article on* Social Dance since 1963.]

Vaudeville dance and the vaudeville stage no longer exist. The concert dance arena, including modern dance, ballet, and staged versions of African-based ceremonial dance, is the contemporary frontier for African-American dance.

Theatrical Dance. In 1932, reviewing an African-American recital, critic John Martin termed concert dance "the white man's art" (quoted in Emery, 1972, p. 314). This subjective value judgment aptly reflects the prevailing biases to which African Americans were subjected when they entered the concert dance arena. It was an updated version of the point of view that had obtained in minstrelsy, on Broadway, and in vaudeville: African Americans fit certain stereotypes and nothing more. As late as the 1960s Martin and Ernestine Stodelle asserted that the African American was culturally and anatomically unfit for ballet (Emery, 1972, pp. 282, 287). This myth, which has persisted in the world of classical ballet, conceals the fundamental problem, the root racism that pervades American culture and society. Despite the fact that African-American dance types have influenced every type of white dance, the black dancer has not been considered fit to dance "the white man's art."

> The success of a dancer depends on whether he has lived up to the audience's expectations. If the dancer is black, the audience frequently has a preconceived notion of the type of dance he should be performing. (Emery, 1972)

In 1931 Hemsley Winfield and his New Negro Art Dancers gave a concert dance recital in New York City. The program reflected Denishawn, African, and African-American themes. Company member Edna Guy was one of the first to dance to Negro spirituals in the genre that became known as the dance spiritual.

Winfield was preceded (in the 1920s) by Charles H. Williams's Hampton Institute Creative Dance Group. Through contact with African exchange students, they staged reconstructions of traditional African dances, thereby setting a precedent that was followed by Asadata Dafora in the 1930s. Williams's group reconstructed traditional African-American dances, such as the Juba and the cakewalk; they also established the prototype for African-American, college-based concert dance groups, such as those established at Spelman, Howard, Fisk, and Tuskegee. In 1934 Dafora produced *Kykunkor,* the first professional concert version of traditional African dance and the forerunner of the stage genre embraced by African national dance companies and African-American groups, such as those of Michael Olatunji, Nana Dinizulu, Chuck Davis, and Charles Moore, to name but a few.

Eugene Von Grona's American Negro Ballet premiered in 1937, performing modern ballets (barefoot, on *demi-pointe*) to the music of Bach, Ellington, and Gershwin. The same year, Katherine Dunham presented her first New York concert, a shared bill at the Ninety-second Street Young Men's and Young Women's Hebrew Association (YM-YWHA). A trained anthropologist, Dunham based her productions on original field material, and her unique combination of ballet, modern, and traditional Caribbean dance became famous as the Dunham technique. The Dunham School of Dance in New York City

UNITED STATES OF AMERICA: African-American Dance Traditions. Hemsley Winfield (on the floor) with members of his New Negro Art Theater Dance Group in *Life and Death.* From 1931, when he founded his company, to 1934, the year of his premature death, Winfield presented concert works that probed issues of black aesthetics. (Photograph from the Dance Collection, New York Public Library for the Performing Arts.)

(1940–1955) and the company's Broadway and film appearances had a pervasive influence on American dance, black and white. Often the style was appropriated, with no credit given to Dunham. Just as J. Leubrie Hill and Buddy Bradley had taught white Broadway dancers, Dunham dancers taught in Hollywood and New York City and saw their technique reappear in all-white films and routines. [*See the entry on Dunham.*] Talley Beatty, Lavinia Williams-Yarborough, Vanoye Aikens, Carmencita Romero, Tommy Gomez, Lucille Ellis, Syvilla Fort, Lenwood Morris, Claude Marchant, Hope Clarke, and Jean-Léon Destiné are among Dunham's legatees.

In 1943, Pearl Primus, also a trained anthropologist, debuted at the Ninety-second Street YM-YWCA with a program including staged West African dances as well as protest dances highlighting the plight of black Americans. Although African-American dancers have since explored many styles and themes, unsolved problems of racism have compelled many to reaffirm connections with Africa and New World African cultures while protesting the oppression of blacks.

White critics have often concluded that black artists only deal adeptly with recognizably "black" material, which is interpreted as making a social statement in itself. Donald McKayle's *Rainbow 'Round My Shoulder* (1959), a testament to the suffering of Southern chain gangs, fits this critical framework; yet his *Games* (1951) and *District Storyville* (1962), based on African-American folklore, are political works only in that showing a previously underrepresented social reality on stage is a necessarily political act.

Many black choreographers since Primus have made dances without particular social content or African-derived movement, such as Eleo Pomare's dance drama *Las Desenamorados* (1967), based on Federico García Lorca's play *The House of Bernarda Alba*. Gus Solomons, Jr., is known for abstract essays in a style related to that of Merce Cunningham, with whom he performed. By contrast, Garth Fagan, celebrated for his lyrical athleticism, mines diverse sources of motion and music from the African diaspora in such pieces as *From Before* (1978), which abstracts and isolates African movements and regroups them in a minimalist framework. Postmodern dancers such as Blondell Cummings and Bebe Miller approach movement conceptually, with a basis in improvisation. Even in *The Hendrix Project* (1992), celebrating Jimi Hendrix, an iconic black musician, Miller's vocabulary owes little to black dance forms. Ralph Lemon, known for his expansive, release-oriented idiom, has examined such varied themes as the *commedia dell'arte* and the myth of Persephone; he exemplifies the freedom many black choreographers of his generation feel from an obligation to focus on political content.

Other choreographers stress political commitments perhaps even fiercer than Primus's. Rod Rodgers's *Box* (1971) is a non-narrative social commentary inspired by the jailing of black militant George Jackson. Bill T. Jones's *Still/Here* (1994) concerns heroism, mortality, and survival among sufferers of AIDS and cancer; while his sprawling *Last Supper at Uncle Tom's Cabin/The Promised Land* (1990) mines diverse sources of myth, as well as his family history (his mother appears in the work) to confront racial stereotypes. Like Jones, Ron Brown examines homophobia and sexism as often as racism and invokes both his family and racial heritage in such dances as *Combat Review/Witches' Response* (1992–1993). Yet both choreographers are also preoccupied with movement invention and problems of formal structure. The range of approaches represented by Louis Johnson, Dianne McIntyre, Fred Benjamin, Arthur Hall, and Donald Byrd is similarly diverse.

Given that white companies tend to exclude black dancers, African-American companies would be justified in employing only blacks. Ironically, the only major integrated American dance company is the (African-American) Alvin Ailey American Dance Theater, truly American and truly representative of the multicultural ideal.

UNITED STATES OF AMERICA: African-American Dance Traditions. Eugene Von Grona, founder of the American Negro Ballet, 1938. (Photograph by Carl Van Vechten; used by permission.)

UNITED STATES OF AMERICA: African-American Dance Traditions. (*left*) Maxine Sherman and Donna Wood (right) of the Alvin Ailey American Dance Theater in a 1980 performance of George Faison's *Suite Otis*. (*below*) Ralph Lemon in his solo *Joy* (1990). (*above*) A scene from Bill T. Jones's *Havoc* (1992) with Seán Curran (left) and Odile Reine-Adelaide. (Photographs left and above © 1980 and 1992 by Jack Vartoogian; photograph below © 1993 by Beatriz Schiller; all used by permission.)

At the end of the century ballet was still a no-man's land for the African-American dancer. Neither Arthur Mitchell's entry into New York City Ballet in 1956 nor the creation of his company, the Dance Theatre of Harlem in 1969, paved the way for meaningful black entry into white ballet despite the professional talent of, among others, Ronald Perry, Kevin Pugh, Virginia Johnson, Mel Tomlinson, and Christopher Boatwright as well as their illustrious predecessors Billy Wilson, Sylvester Campbell, Delores Brown, Raven Wilkerson, Paul Russell, Keith Lee, Christian Holder, and John Jones.

Dance is a measure of society. The history of African-American dance is a measure of the history of American racial oppression. The survival and proliferation of African-American dance is thus a testament to its substantive strength and indestructibility.

[*See also* Alvin Ailey American Dance Theater; Dance Theatre of Harlem; Tap Dance; Vaudeville; *and the entries on Beatty, Dafora, Fagan, Bill T. Jones, McKayle, Mitchell, Primus, and Zollar.*]

BIBLIOGRAPHY

Aschenbrenner, Joyce. *Katherine Dunham: Reflections on the Social and Political Contexts of Afro-American Dance.* CORD Dance Research Annual, 12. New York, 1981.

Dixon-Stowell, Brenda. "Dancing in the Dark: The Life and Times of Margot Webb in Aframerican Vaudeville of the Swing Era." 2 vols. Ph.D. diss., New York University, 1981.

Dixon Gottschild, Brenda. *Digging the Africanist Presence in American Performance: Dance and Other Contexts.* Westport, Conn. 1996.

Emery, Lynne Fauley. *Black Dance in the United States from 1619 to 1970.* Palo Alto, Calif., 1972. Rev. ed. Princeton, 1988.

Malone, Jacqui. *Steppin' on the Blues: The Visible Rhythms of African American Dance.* Urbana and Chicago, 1996.

Sampson, Henry T. *Blacks in Blackface: A Source Book on Early Black Musical Shows.* Metuchen, N.J., 1980.

Stearns, Marshall, and Jean Stearns. *Jazz Dance* (1968). New York, 1994.

Toll, Robert C. *Blacking Up: The Minstrel Show in Nineteenth-Century America.* New York, 1974.

ARCHIVES. Dance Collection, New York Public Library for the Performing Arts. Katherine Dunham Collection, Morris Library, Southern Illinois University, Carbondale. Hatch-Billops Collection, New York. Joseph Nash Collection, New York. Schomburg Center for Research in Black Culture, New York Public Library.

BRENDA DIXON GOTTSCHILD

African-American Social Dance

In the sub-Saharan African population groups from which slaves were taken, dance was integrated with daily life. Ceremonial dance expressed philosophical ideas, community attitudes, and individual identities. The brutality of the slave experience, regardless of where it was, transformed Africans' cultural lives and dance. This experience of slavery varied somewhat from place to place, country to country, or colony to colony. For the most part, slaves from several African societies lived and worked together, often in all-male units. On plantations, males and females worked both in the master's house and on the land. This article describes the situation in the colonies that became the United States, and emphasizes the evolution from plantation dances to contemporary social dances. Slavery existed in the British colonies of the 1600s and lasted legally in the United States until 1 January 1863.

New African-American dances emerged and varied according to context and with the work rhythms of the tasks performed. On the plantation, the slaves' social activities were restricted, but they took every opportunity to create new alternatives. Slaves used dancing to perform a variety of functions: education, resistance, community sanction, and the establishment of social norms. Dances were held in the woods or in other isolated locations when the slave owners were least vigilant. Although most masters permitted dancing on Saturdays, Sundays, and holidays such as Christmas, Thanksgiving, and the Fourth of July, they also encouraged dancing to increase their own profits, for example, dances were held to stimulate the shucking of corn. Of all the types of plantation dances, corn-shucking dances were the slaves' favorite. Held after work, shuckings involved teams of slaves from two or more plantations. The corn was divided, and each team competed to finish first. During and after the work, dancing contributed to an atmosphere of frolic and release.

Urban slave dances were more heterogeneous than plantation dances. Held on the edge of a town, these dances could attract two hundred to seven hundred slaves, both agricultural and urban. Like the smaller secret dances, the larger urban gatherings provided rare opportunities to plan and stage acts of resistance. Dance was the natural camouflage most frequently chosen to stage acts of self-determination, such as setting a fire, running away, or organizing a rebellion. These dances often took place near major cities, such as Charleston, South Carolina, and Mobile, Alabama, but the most famous occurred at Congo Square in New Orleans. Even after the Emancipation of 1863 and until about 1890, blacks gathered until sunset on Sundays, drumming and dancing the calenda, the bamboula, and the chica-congo.

Emancipation, including the breakup of both rural and

UNITED STATES OF AMERICA: African-American Social Dance. A characteristic depiction of early African-American step dancing. The dancer plays castanet-like bones, to the accompaniment of banjo and fiddle. The "get-down" position of his body and the angular arrangment of his limbs show a strong African influence, whereas the position of his arms overhead, framing the body, reveal the influence of European folk dancing. (Engraving c.1888 by G. W. Breeneman; collection of Sally R. Sommer and William G. Sommer.)

urban slave quarters and the reorganization of black labor under the sharecropping system, contributed to the transformation of the nature of African-American dance. During the period following Emancipation, African-American dance experienced accelerated cross-fertilization, reworking, and fine-tuning. The primary institutional context for most social dance was called the jook, a poorly constructed shelter used for dancing, drinking, and social activity. At the jooks, older plantation dances such as the Buzzard Lope, Snake Hips, the Breakdown, the Juba, and the Buck Dance could combine with new, urbanized forms. From the jooks came great American dance crazes: the Black Bottom, the Charleston, and the Twist, as well as the Turkey Trot and the Big Apple.

Between the end of Reconstruction—the reorganizing of the states that had seceded and reestablishing them in the Union (1867–1877)—and the beginning of World War I in 1914, African-American social dance became better known among the general public. Dance experienced a new level of development as Southern black migration to urban areas and then a rapidly changing war economy influenced black Americans—who created new music and new fashions while experiencing new economic and cultural demands. The dances from the plantations and the jooks were rapidly redefined in the cities. New social institutions provided African-American dance with additional variations on an already richly varied tradition. Urban dance halls, membership clubs, and honky-tonks provided places in which dances could relinquish some of their rural characteristics, such as flatfootedness, and acquire a more urbane polish. The institutional complex formed by the jooks, honky-tonks, dance halls, and membership clubs enabled African Americans to experience an ever-widening variety of sociocultural options; these were directly reflected in the proliferation of and variations on African-American dance.

After World War I, when some social and cultural choices for blacks increased, social dance became more sophisticated. Cabarets and "rent parties" (gatherings to contribute to a friend's monthly rent, when needed) provided new situations for social interaction. Although dancing had been unrefined and intimate, public expectation influenced cabaret dancing, frequently rendering it self-conscious, theatrical, and performance-oriented. During the Great Depression of the 1930s and as World War II approached, black migration to the industrial North intensified. The jook-house tradition also went north and cross-fertilized the dances developing among northern urban blacks.

Among the characteristics of African-American social dance are competition, dancing apart (couples do not touch), improvisation, call and response, mimicry, and derision. These elements can be observed in the competitive high kicking of the cakewalk, the apart dancing of the Black Bottom and the Charleston, and the improvisational Lindy Hop breakaway. The Susie Q, Truckin', the Shorty-George, and the Slop are all dances that have been used in a competitive, improvisational manner. Along

UNITED STATES OF AMERICA: African-American Social Dance. Whitey's Lindy Hoppers, a group of Savoy Ballroom dancers organized by Herby ("Whitey") White, performed their synchronized Lindy routines in nightclubs, theaters, revues, and films. The three couples pictured here are (left to right) Norma Walker and Frankie Manning, Lucille Middleton and Jerome Williams, and Billy Williams and Mildred Cruse. (Photograph from the collection of Frankie Manning.)

UNITED STATES OF AMERICA: African-American Social Dance. Robert Taylor demonstrates three characteristic break dancing moves: the Turtle (left), Back Spin (center), and Downrocking (right). (Photographs by Michael Ginsburg; courtesy of Sally R. Sommer and William G. Sommer.)

with dances from the plantations, these formed the core vocabulary of African-American social dance. Nevertheless, negative influences limited the structural development and content of African-American social dance.

Although a good amount of American social dance has resulted from African-American culture, for nearly a century after Emancipation, blacks were barred (in the segregated South) from public social activity with whites. In the first half of the twentieth century, however, in New York, Chicago, Saint Louis, New Orleans, and other cities with large African-American populations, jazz flourished and nightclubs and theaters were patronized by whites as well as blacks; here, on phonograph records, and in Hollywood films, African-American music and dance entered the American mainstream. Not until the 1960s, however, were the final vestiges of legal segregation at all public facilities in the United States removed by act of Congress. And in that decade African-American dance rediscovered and reestablished some of its original characteristics. Dancing apart characterized many of the popular dances of the decade: the Twist, Boogaloo, African Twist, Sophisticated Sissy, Philly Dog, Horse, Chicken, Watusi, Shing-a-ling, Monkey, Swim, Waddle, Mashed Potato, and Four Corners. This period of intense social change renewed and strengthened black identification with African-American social dance traditions.

In the 1970s, a trend toward intense competition culminated in the development of break dancing. "Breaking," a predominantly male activity, demonstrates through the characteristic use of competition, mimicry, and derision an acrobatic, theatricalized, and highly self-conscious cultural response. Breaking has also altered the traditional male-female partnering relationship; dancers compete to outdance one another in a fashion reminiscent of the corn-shucking dances and the dance contests engaged in at rent parties.

Many contemporary African-American dances may be recycled versions of older ones. A good example is Pop Locking, a variation on the old plantation dance Snake Hips. Done in the Georgia Sea Islands prior to emancipation, Snake Hips was popularized in the 1920s by performer Earl ("Snake Hips") Tucker. In the 1950s, it reappeared in the urban Midwest as Poppin' the Hips. The Jerk of the 1960s appropriated part of its technique and vocabulary. Its snapping and joint-locking technique was utilized in the Robot of the 1970s, and its fluidity was redefined in the break dancing of the 1980s.

[*See also* Cakewalk *and* Lindy Hop. *For general discussion, see* Social Dance, *article on* Twentieth-Century Social Dance to 1960.]

BIBLIOGRAPHY

Begho, Felix D. "Black Dance Continuum: Reflections on the Heritage Connection between African Dance and Afro-American Jazz Dance." Ph.D. diss., New York University, 1985.

Emery, Lynne Fauley. *Black Dance from 1619 to Today.* 2d rev. ed. Princeton, 1988.

Hanna, Judith Lynne. "Moving Message: Identity and Desire in Popular Music and Social Dance." In *Popular Music and Communication,* edited by James Lull. 2d ed. Newbury Park, Calif., 1992.

Hanna, Judith Lynne. "What Is Black Dance? Report on 'Choreographing the Future: Dance, Politics, and the African Diaspora.'" *Dance Teacher Now* 16 (October 1994): 69–72.

Hazzard-Gordon, Katrina. *Jookin': The Rise of Social Dance Formations in African-American Culture.* Philadelphia, 1990.

Perpener, John O. "African-American Dance and Sociological Positivism during the 1930s." *Studies in Dance History* 5 (Spring 1994): 23–30.

Stearns, Marshall, and Jean Stearns. *Jazz Dance.* Rev. ed. New York, 1994.

Szwed, John F., and Morton Marks. "The Afro-American Transformation of European Set Dances and Dance Suites." *Dance Research Journal* 20 (Summer 1988): 29–36.

KATRINA HAZZARD-DONALD

Regional Dance Companies

Decentralized or regional dance takes place outside New York City. The companies discussed herein have additional identifying characteristics. They are resident in their communities, which means that the core of their performing takes place in the home city, usually with a subscription series as the basis of their earned income. Outside their home communities they tend to perform under regional consortia, such as the Southern Arts Federation, either as part of tour plans initiated by their state arts agencies or as the guests of local sponsors. Regional ballet companies usually identify with the home city or state by using geographically related titles, whereas modern dance companies tend to use the names of their directors, although some, such as the Dayton Contemporary Dance Company and Philadanco (Philadelphia Dance Company), prefer geographical nomenclature.

Despite a heartening increase in the quantity and quality of televised dance, millions of Americans would see little live dance were it not for regional companies. The high costs of widespread touring have curtailed the itineraries of major New York companies. More and more, regional companies are filling this gap. The touring of regional companies, though, even in the case of a well-traveled ensemble like the Bella Lewitzky Company, is rarely national. The closest to national in exposure are the Boston Ballet, the Houston Ballet, the Pacific Northwest Ballet, and the San Francisco Ballet.

Despite the economic hazards, more young people than ever before are looking to dance as a career. New York City cannot accommodate them all. Regional companies not only provide needed employment, they also help to identify dance artists not as nomads but as respected members of their communities. The companies help provide sociological identity for the American dancer.

Twentieth-century America has fostered a unique group of dance pioneers. They were and are the founders of regional dance companies. As individuals they have shared certain traits: they were receptive to all forms of dance; they had taste; and they were dedicated teachers who not only imparted technique but knew how to shape artists. All had boundless energy and strength of character. Most important, they related effectively to their communities and their trustees. The leaders were Dorothy Alexander (Atlanta), Josephine and Hermene Schwarz (Dayton), and Willam Christensen (Salt Lake City). All were determined to make dance happen in their communities at a time when there were no precedents.

The Atlanta Ballet, founded in 1929, is the oldest ballet company in the United States. The Dayton Ballet came along in 1937. Christensen organized the San Francisco Ballet in 1934. In 1951 his brothers Lew and Harold took over the company and school while Willam moved to their native Salt Lake City and formed what is now Ballet West. Other distinctive companies, such as the Littlefield Ballet and the Pavley-Oukrainsky Ballet, also emerged during the 1930s but did not survive.

World War II meant an inevitable hiatus in the formation of dance companies. It was not until the 1950s that a crop of new pioneering directors emerged. Among them were Thomas Armour (Miami Ballet, 1951), Barbara and Deane Crockett (Sacramento Ballet, 1954), Jan Collum (Balletacoma, 1955), Lisa Gardiner and Mary Day (Washington Ballet, 1956), Moscelyne Larkin and Roman Jasinski (Tulsa Ballet Theatre, 1956), and E. Virginia Williams (Boston Ballet, 1958). From the 1960s one might add Jeraldyne Blunden (Dayton Contemporary Dance Company), Madeline Culpo (Berkshire Ballet), Lila Zali (Ballet Pacifica), Loyce Houlton (Minnesota Dance Theatre), Audrée Estey (American Repertory Ballet), Leona Norman (Marin Ballet), and Barbara Weisberger (Pennsylvania Ballet). Younger artistic directors, while sharing many traits with their predecessors, have had the benefit of role models and service organizations.

In the Southwest, a once-strong Ballet Russe influence was stimulated by the extensive touring in that area of the Ballet Russe de Monte Carlo. The Houston Ballet, for example, did not begin under a pioneering director. Instead, the company was initiated by a board of trustees that first selected Tatiana Semenova and then Nina Popova as artistic director. Both had Ballet Russe credentials. The company's artistic identity did not take shape, however, until the advent of artistic director Ben Stevenson, whose background is British. The Dallas Ballet began with a sequence of guest artistic directors, all of Ballet Russe origin. These included Marina Svetlova, Nathalie Krassovska, Mia Slavenska, Alexandra Danilova, and eventually George Skibine. Not long after Skibine's death in 1981, the company was dissolved. In 1993 the Fort Worth Ballet was renamed Fort Worth–Dallas Ballet. Under Moscelyne Larkin and Roman Jasinski, Tulsa Ballet Theatre conscientiously revived pillars of the Ballet Russe repertory, such as Léonide Massine's *Gaîté Parisienne* and *Le Beau Danube*, David Lichine's *Prodigal Son*, and Michel Fokine's *Schéhérazade*. With Jasinski's death in 1991, the company's focus began to shift.

Since the mid-1980s, the strongest influence on American regional companies has been that of George Balanchine. His death expanded that influence because the Balanchine Trust under Barbara Horgan has made his ballets readily available. Furthermore, former Balanchine dancers are directing companies all across the United States. The earliest seeds of the Balanchine influence were sown with the celebrated Ford Foundation Program. This included the establishment in 1960 of regional scholarships for promising young dancers to study in New York at the School of American Ballet. The following year introduced the first of a series of free teachers' seminars conducted by Balanchine. In 1963 the foundation distributed $7,756,000 to seven ballet companies: New York City Ballet, San Francisco Ballet, Boston Ballet, Pennsylvania Ballet, Houston Ballet, National Ballet, and Ballet West.

In addition to underscoring Balanchine's contribution to American dance, the plan also encouraged the entire dance world to pay more attention to the need for fiscal stability. Until that time, most companies had been rather haphazardly funded or had depended upon a single benefactor. Now these same organizations began to augment their boards of trustees and to engage experienced executive directors. For better or for worse, dance began to assume the characteristics of the corporate world.

UNITED STATES OF AMERICA: Regional Dance Companies. Members of the Atlanta Civic Ballet Junior Group in *The Princess's Magic Mirror* (1954), choreographed by Merrilee Smith and Marie Ellen Roberts to music from Josef Bayer's *Rouge et Noir.* By 1954, its twenty-fifth year, the Atlanta Civic Ballet had developed three distinct sections of its repertory: adult programs, children's programs, and lecture-demonstrations. This three-act ballet was based on the children's story "The Plain Little Princess" by Phyllis McGinley. (Photograph by Ben Damon; reprinted from a souvenir program, courtesy of Claude Conyers.)

The earliest Balanchine dancers to head regional companies were Fred Danieli (Garden State Ballet), Robert Barnett (who, in 1963, succeeded Dorothy Alexander in Atlanta), and Robert Lindgren (North Carolina Dance Theatre). In the mid-1990s the ranks were led by Todd Bolender (State Ballet of Missouri), Daniel Duell (Chicago City Ballet), Paul Mejia (Fort Worth–Dallas Ballet), Bryan Pitts and Laura Flagg (Ballet Oklahoma), Francia Russell and Kent Stowell (Pacific Northwest Ballet), Helgi Tomasson (San Francisco Ballet), Edward Villella (Miami Ballet), and Patricia Wilde (Pittsburgh Ballet Theatre).

While the Balanchine repertory exercised its influence, it was *The Nutcracker* that continued to be performed by more ballet companies than any other work, and audiences for *The Nutcracker* proved to be double that for any other program. Also in demand were *Romeo and Juliet* and *Cinderella*.

In modern dance, Martha Graham stands equal to Balanchine as a twentieth-century influence. But because she did not allow her works to be set on any American company other than her own, her influence has not become choreographic. There is, however, a strong stylistic impact because so many directors and choreographers of modern companies have studied with Graham or her disciples.

It is easy to trace choreographic trends filtering down from the top, and to credit regional companies with producing at least three generations of impressive American dancers, but what has been the imprint of these regional companies on American choreography? One of the most distinctive voices was that of Loyce Houlton. Her works abounded in surreal, free-associative imagery enhanced by sophisticated theatrical effects. Among the most prolific of the company directors are Heinz Poll, Dennis Nahat, and Helgi Tomasson. All three work in the classical mold, Poll with great vigor and energy; Nahat in a flowing, musically aware style; and Tomasson with elegance and structural finesse. Other company directors who create a substantial portion of each season's repertory are Martin Fredmann (Colorado Ballet), Ronn Guidi (Oakland Ballet), Alun Jones (Louisville Ballet), Lambros Lambrou (Ballet Austin), Paul Mejia (Fort Worth–Dallas Ballet), David Nixon (BalletMet), Kirk Peterson (Hartford Ballet), Kent Stowell (Pacific Northwest Ballet), and Septime Webre (American Repertory Ballet).

Most modern companies, such as Garth Fagan Dance and the Margaret Jenkins Dance Company, are centered around the creative output of a single choreographer. Others, like Dance Kaleidoscope, Oberlin Dance Collective, and the Hubbard Street Dance Company, rely upon several. Some of the freelance and resident choreographers, now deceased, who initially developed their skills on regional companies were Choo San Goh, Patricia Olalde, Tom Pazik, Stuart Sebastian, and Norbert Vesak. Heading the later generation are Peter Anastos, Jill Eathorne Bahr, Val Caniparolli, Lisa de Ribere, Bill Evans, Jon Rodriguez, Bess Saylor, Lynne Taylor-Corbett, and Bruce Wells.

Making quality choreography available to regional companies was one of the principal concerns of the National Association for Regional Ballet. The evolution of this service organization for decentralized companies began in 1955. Anatole Chujoy, then publisher of *Dance News,* had previously attended regional ballet festivals in Canada. He suggested to Dorothy Alexander that she initiate a similar project in Atlanta. In April 1956, with the Atlanta Ballet as host, Alexander invited the companies she knew in the Southeast for a weekend of performing, classes, and social activities. The impact of the event was so strong that it provided the impetus for Alexi Ramov (Scranton Ballet), with Barbara Weisberger (Wilkes-Barre Ballet Guild), to host the first Northeast Festival in 1959. The Southwest followed in 1963, with Barbara and David Carson (Austin Civic Ballet) as hosts. In 1966 the Sacramento Civic Ballet, under Deane and Barbara Crockett, brought the Pacific region into the fold. In 1972 the Mid-States began in Kansas City under Tom Steinhoff (Kansas City Civic Ballet).

With continuity apparent, it was deemed wise to consolidate the regions under a national office with a professional staff. Funding from the National Endowment for the Arts stimulated this move in 1972. Doris Hering, who had just completed three terms as the association's president, became its first executive director, with Dorothy Alexander as founder-consultant and Barbara Crockett as president. While some of the members' choreographic needs were already being addressed, the national office widened their scope. For example, the Craft of Choreography Conferences had begun in 1960. Under the guidance of Josephine Schwarz, the directors in the Northeast region had come together in the summer to work intensively at their craft. Gradually the project was expanded to the other regions, and it began to attract not only the directors but the young choreographers rising through their companies, plus a nucleus of freelance choreographers.

The National Endowment for the Arts, several state arts agencies, and the Monticello College Foundation were instrumental in the development of the conferences and in the allocation of scholarships to dancers and emerging choreographers. Among the artists who have served as creative directors of the conferences are Salvatore Aiello, Martha Hill, Saeko Ichinohe, Elizabeth Keen, Phyllis Lamhut, Bella Lewitzky, Dennis Nahat, Lynne Taylor-Corbett, Glen Tetley, and Norman Walker.

To help meet the constantly growing repertory needs of its member companies, the national association evolved additional programs. The National Choreography Plan, formed with the aid of the Andrew W. Mellon Foundation, offered an index of the strongest works performed at festivals since the beginning. Forty-three companies received ballets of their choice, with the national office subsidizing the choreographers' fees and expenses.

While these and several other related projects were designed to strengthen the companies artistically, another evolving need began to be addressed. Initially the role of the artistic director had been that of pioneer and leader. During the early 1970s the identity began to change from leader to employee of the board of trustees, with the executive director often exceeding the artistic director in institutional prestige. To help correct this imbalance and to redefine and strengthen the role of the artistic director, the National Association for Regional Ballet, with the aid of the Andrew W. Mellon Foundation and the L. J. and Mary C. Skaggs Foundation, initiated the Artistic Directors Seminar in 1985.

In 1987 the office and services of the National Association for Regional Ballet were for the most part discontinued. The organization, retitled Regional Dance America, returned to functioning as it had initially, with the festivals as the primary focus. But it had already made its impact. Whereas there had been virtually no professional dance companies outside New York City in the early 1960s, by the 1990s there were approximately fifty fully professional companies, plus another two hundred that were engaged in serving their communities on substantial technical and creative levels. Decentralization had indeed proven to be a major force in twentieth-century American dance.

[*See also* Atlanta Ballet; Boston Ballet; Cleveland–San Jose Ballet; Dayton Ballet; Dayton Contemporary Dance Company; Houston Ballet; Ohio Ballet; Pacific Northwest Ballet; Pennsylvania Ballet; Pittsburgh Ballet Theatre; San Francisco Ballet; Tulsa Ballet Theatre; *and* Washington Ballet.]

ARCHIVES. Records of the National Association for Regional Ballet (NARB) reside in the Dance Collection of the New York Public Library for the Performing Arts, Lincoln Center. They include festival souvenir programs for the five regions—Mid-States (1972–1987), Northeast (1959–1987), Pacific (1966–1987), Southeast (1956–1987), and Southwest (1963–1987)—as well as company souvenir programs (1956–1987), NARB brochures, NARB Choreography Conference brochures (1972–1987), National Choreography Plan (1976–1987), rosters of member companies (1972–1987), Twenty-fifth Anniversary Press Kit (1981), national board of directors fiscal information and minutes of semi-annual meetings, pictures of festivals and choreography conferences, records of Artistic Directors Seminar (1986).

Records of Regional Dance America, also held in the Dance Collection, New York Public Library for the Performing Arts, Lincoln Center, consist of festival souvenir programs for the five regions (1988–1996). Other archival materials are held in the homes of various officers; locales change as the officers change.

DORIS HERING

Musical Theater

Two productions in the middle of the nineteenth century laid the foundation from which the American musical comedy, and its attendant forms of theatrical dancing, evolved. When *The Black Crook* opened at Niblo's Garden on 12 September 1866, spectators witnessed a lush extravaganza designed by W. T. Voegtlin, the acrobatic contortions of the Majilitons, and classically trained Italian *danseuses* Marie Bonfanti and Rita Sangalli along with a corps of Amazons, girls with shields and helmets whose drills used simple steps to execute complicated patterns. All of this splendor was unified by a complex, slightly moralizing plot. *The Black Crook* was so popular that it could be seen in revivals until 1929, when the young Agnes de Mille appeared in the Bonfanti role. [*See* Black Crook, The.]

With the opening of *Ixion* at Wood's Museum on 28 September 1868, Lydia Thompson and Her British Blondes showed New Yorkers that ladies in fleshings, as the pink tights were called, could provide innocently titillating entertainment. The battalion of chorines, or "ballet girls," who subsequently trooped across American stages needed good legs rather than technique to retain a spot in the limelight. The taste for foreign extravaganza and Victorian burlesque established the practice of alternating precision drills by large female choruses with variations by legitimate ballerinas.

The season of 1879 brought two additional shows to New York that greatly influenced the next phase of development. *The Brook* (12 May 1879) incorporated a flimsy plot device to string together vaudeville turns, thus providing the seeds for both the revue format and the much later book musical. Gilbert and Sullivan's *H.M.S. Pinafore* introduced operetta to an audience with whom it remained fashionable, particularly in Viennese editions, until 1930, when realistic techniques of the legitimate theater and the new "talking" motion pictures made the romantic fantasies of operetta seem naïve.

The operetta was a nineteenth-century phenomenon that had multinational roots in the Italian *opera buffa,* the German *Singspiel,* and the British ballad opera. Among its illustrious antecedents was Adam de la Halle's play *Le Jeu de Robin et de Marion,* into which the author inserted songs during the 1283 presentation for the French court at Naples. Dancing was an integral part of a later French variant—*comédie-ballet*—of which the best example is Molière's *Le Bourgeois Gentilhomme,* first performed for Louis XIV on 14 October 1670, with a score by Jean-Baptiste Lully and steps by the royal ballet master Pierre Beauchamp. John Gay's *The Beggar's Opera,* produced in London at Lincoln's Inn Fields in 1728, added provocative, low-life characters such as Peachum and Macheath to the milieu, and Mozart's *Le Nozze de Figaro* (1786) centered all actions on the peasant hero of Pierre-Augustin Caron de Beaumarchais's comedy.

Hundreds of operettas were composed between 1855 and 1930. The earliest center was Paris, where some elements from the boulevard theaters, vaudeville, and the magical transformations of Romantic ballet fused into a new form. Composer Adolphe Adam and playwright Eugene Scribe (both well known to French balletomanes) contributed to several of the earliest productions. The real

UNITED STATES OF AMERICA: Musical Theater. Members of the female ensemble of *The Black Crook* chorus as they appeared at Niblo's Garden, New York, in 1866. (Photograph from the Dance Collection, New York Public Library for the Performing Arts.)

master was Jacques Offenbach (1819–1880), whose *La Vie Parisienne* (1866) owed as much to the waltzes, polkas, and formal quadrilles of the public balls as it did to the risqué can-can of café society. Offenbach's *Tales of Hoffmann* has been the basis for theater, film, and ballet productions.

The waltz transformed the operetta in Vienna into a distinctive world standard. *Die Fledermaus,* by Johann Strauss the younger, had its premiere in April 1874 and remains a classic of the genre. *Fledermaus* has the requisite satire, romance, and mistaken identities that later joined with exotic locales to become hallmarks of operetta. This popular entertainment brought complex variants of social dances out of the grand salons and into the theaters. While the swirling patterns of ländlers, polkas, and waltzes were common on Continental stages, the real impact of couple dances—particularly the waltz—did not peak in the United States for another thirty years, until Franz Lehár's *The Merry Widow.*

British productions by William Gilbert and Arthur Sullivan offered other links to operetta practices in Paris and to the emerging concert stage. In 1871 John D'Auban staged the first Gilbert and Sullivan collaboration. D'Auban was a British dancer who had been employed at Paris's Théâtre de la Porte-Saint-Martin; in the cities of Saint Petersburg, Saint-Quentin, and Brussels; and in sixteen English theaters, including the Alhambra, the Gaiety, and Drury Lane. It was D'Auban who experimented with his sister on a dance that featured the manipulation of her long skirt in a sketch titled "'Ain't She Very Shy." He later coached Kate Vaughan, who became the leading British skirt dancer. Following its London premiere on 25 May 1878, *H.M.S. Pinafore* opened on 25 November at the Boston Museum. Its popularity with American audiences was so great that by March 1879 eight separate companies were performing *Pinafore* in New York alone.

During the last decade of the nineteenth century, several events occurred in the United States that caused the walking and marching of chorines to be superseded by buck-and-wing, jig, cakewalk, high kicks, skirt dancing, and other artful innovations. Spanish dancer Carmencita made her American debut in August 1889 and a year later gained a rival in the fiery Carolina Otéro. Carmencita and Otéro introduced the sensuous and expressive potential of the solo female form to a wide spectrum of dazzled viewers. The Chicagoan Loie Fuller was the first of the extraordinary trio of artists (including Ruth St. Denis and Isadora Duncan) to perform an experimental dance in the commercial theater. Fuller (1861–1928) was an actress-singer-dancer who created a sensation with her *Serpentine Dance,* seen originally in the play *The Quack M.D.* (1 October 1891). The magical impression of her solo was effected by colored light projections onto yards of silk that she manipulated around her body while she dipped and turned. On 24 February 1892, as featured dancer, she joined the cast of Charles Hoyt's smash hit *A Trip to Chinatown,* the show that set the record for the longest Broadway run of the nineteenth century. By the time Fuller left the production the following spring to go to Europe, her dance discovery had gained acceptance and inspired a host of imitators. [*See the entry on Fuller.*]

Julian Mitchell (c.1854–1926), who staged most of Hoyt's innovative musical farce-comedies, was the earliest example of the successful Broadway director-choreographer and was one of the period's most sought after dance arrangers. He helped to create vehicles for Loie Fuller, Maud Allan, Mademoiselle Dazie, and scores of other luminaries, and he staged the American debuts of Anna Held and Adeline Genée. As burlesque, spectacles, and operettas grew to number as many as one hundred and fifty in their choruses, Mitchell had to deal simultaneously with an entirely different theatrical dimension. Between 1895 and 1904, the golden years of Weber and Fields's memorable partnership at the Music Hall, Mitchell staged several successful productions there despite the tiny stage, which could accommodate fewer than a dozen members of the music hall's adulated Beauty Chorus. Mitchell and another colleague, Gus Sohlke, compensated for the small scale by incorporating more complicated steps and combinations into the dances. Mitchell's Broadway blockbusters—among them Victor Herbert's *The Idol's Eye* (25 October 1897) and *The Fortune Teller* (26 September 1898) along with the director's hits of the 1903/04 season *The Wizard of Oz* and *Babes in Toyland*—made him the highest-paid person in the business. Because of this reputation, the young Florenz Ziegfeld hired him as general director for all of his productions. Among other Ziegfeld assignments, Mitchell conceived and staged the first seven editions of the annual *Follies,* which began in 1907.

The extravaganza began to lose favor at the end of the century, although one of the last and most acclaimed of these productions, George Lederer's *The Man in the Moon* (24 April 1899), introduced a new trend setter. Not the little-known Ruth St. Denis, who appeared in the chorus, but the Pony Ballet—eight petite dynamos from the John Tiller School in England—caused the excitement. The crisp precision routines of the Tiller Girls became a mainstay of theatrical dancing. Welcomed in New York intermittently until after World War II, they were the model for the American Rockettes.

The influence of realism and the fascination with settings that sported verisimilitude led to the use of narrative as a device for unifying music, drama, and dance in musicals. Economic as well as aesthetic factors reduced the size of the female chorus, which in turn raised the level of skill that was demanded. The appeal of variety was maintained in the more sophisticated revue, in which recherché themes, often centering on the battle of the sexes, served as a framework for specialty numbers. The prototype for the American revue, a genre that amused audiences for the next fifty years, was *The Passing Show* (12 May 1894). Produced by George Lederer and Sydney Rosenfeld, the production mingled French nuances with elements from English music halls and Yankee vaudeville houses.

The late nineteenth-century obsession with hygiene, coupled with the connection that had been made between dance and healthful exercise, helped to alter earlier biases against dancing and expand the number of teaching studios. A wave of gifted immigrants, products of the great European academies, arrived to teach classes and to arrange dances for the stage. They included Marie Bonfanti, Mamert Bibberyan, Léon Espinosa, Luigi Albertieri, and Louis Chalif along with the revered native George Washington Smith, who in 1881 had partnered Fanny Elssler on her legendary American tour as well as opened his studio in Philadelphia.

New Dimensions and Inspirations. The technical level of theatrical dancing was not high at the turn of the century, but by then the commercial stage offered a variety of styles that were vigorous, highly expressive, and appealing to an audience just beginning to develop its tastes.

Besides the smaller (though by no means small) groupings, a new dimension was added to the female chorus in 1900. Again inspiration came from a British import: *Floradora* (12 November) boasted a sextet of tall, willowy redheads who established the statuesque charms of the "show girl," known above all else for her visual allure. The distinction of the "broiler," a girl of action, a vivacious category of chorine noted for actual dancing skills plus a winsome figure, developed that same season.

The musical adventure stories of Reginald De Koven, operettas by Victor Herbert and Franz Lehár, as well as George M. Cohan's distinctive shows enlivened Broadway during the first decade of the twentieth century. A production with far-reaching influences, Ziegfeld's *A Parisian Model* (27 November 1906) touted glamour on a lavish scale. A superficial plot provided the structure for what was, in fact, a revue. The ultimate showman was a trend setter. In addition to dozens of the most beautiful girls—who danced on roller skates with delectable Anna Held—Ziegfeld inserted a ballroom number. Held performed the *maxixe* with Gertrude Hoffman in travesty. Hoffman, a talented dancer and choreographer, was the first in a distinguished group of art dancers whom Ziegfeld presented in his revues and musicals. Some of these include Mademoiselle Dazie, Bessie Clayton, Adeline Genée (the only genuine ballerina most Americans had seen), and, in 1927, Ruth St. Denis and Ted Shawn. Julian Mitchell's staging of *A Parisian Model* inspired the choreographer's greatest brainchild: in the following year Ziegfeld premiered his unmatched series with the *Follies of 1907*.

The other smash of that season—affecting everything from fashions to bonbons—was Lehár's *The Merry Widow* (21 October 1907). Overnight the popularity of Viennese operetta soared. Everyone waltzed. The number of male

UNITED STATES OF AMERICA: Musical Theater. George M. Cohan as the title character in *Little Johnny Jones* (1904). The first of Cohan's shows with a theme of American patriotism, *Little Johnny Jones* featured two unforgettable numbers: Cohan's flag-waving song and dance to "The Yankee Doodle Boy" (or "I'm a Yankee Doodle Dandy") and a spectacular "transformation scene" set to "Give My Regards to Broadway." (Photograph from the Museum of the City of New York; used by permission.)

dancers slowly increased along with the demand for couples in ballroom displays. The *apache*, the tango, the fox trot, the *maxixe*, the polka, and other dance inventions blossomed. Nearly all were demonstrated by Irene and Vernon Castle, who personified the crest of ballroom fervor from their marriage in 1911 until Vernon's death in 1918.

The Metropolitan Opera Ballet School opened in 1909 under the direction of Malvina Cavallazzi to offer first-rate, professional training. Instruction was free, though graduates were expected to remain for three years, with pay, in the opera's corps de ballet. Some did; many others defected to higher-paying Broadway ventures. One of the decade's most sensational dances was produced at the Met. Biancha Froelich's "Dance of the Seven Veils," an erotic solo that was widely parodied in the commercial theater, caused such a furor that Richard Strauss's *Salomé* was taken out of the Metropolitan repertory until 1934. Audiences also got their first glimpse of Russian classicism at the Met. Anna Pavlova, partnered by Mikhail Mordkin, made her American debut there on 28 February 1910. During the next season, Gertrude Hoffman presented a Russian ballet ensemble headed by Theodore Koslov and Maria Baldina. Spectators' standards for technical execution rose considerably.

The second decade of the twentieth century was the last period in which the American musical theater depended to any appreciable extent on foreign imports. Significant elements emerged that became characteristics of the lyric stage after World War I. As operettas flourished and the book musical made some appreciable progress, revues gained ascendancy. Actors' Equity was founded in 1912, and some of the vagaries of the profession began to be addressed. Low pay was not as burning an issue as the policy of no rehearsal pay. Under the common practice, it was possible to rehearse for months without a salary. If the show closed after a single night, no recompense other than for one performance was required. In its earliest days Equity began efforts to improve standards of safety for dancers as well as negotiations with producers to provide rehearsal shoes, among other compensations. Attaining these ends took decades.

One of the true masterworks of the musical stage opened in 1910. Victor Herbert's *Naughty Marietta* (7 November) was commissioned by Oscar Hammerstein I for his Manhattan Opera Company. Herbert (1859–1924), the leading composer of the New York theater, was the only U.S.-based musician to gain an international reputation for his operettas. Among his many achievements, Herbert wrote cohesive scores to support plots that centered, eventually, on romance rather than on the antics of comics. *Naughty Marietta* was a transitional production that pointed the way toward a more integral relationship between libretto and accompanying music. Pauline Verhoeven, a Belgian classicist, staged the dances. She had made her New York debut in 1904 at the Metropolitan Opera House. Verhoeven subsequently became ballet mistress to Hammerstein's ensemble and eventually directed the Metropolitan Opera Ballet School. With *Naughty Marietta* she set an important precedent: it was the first time that a choreographer and dancers associated, primarily, with a ballet troupe were used in a commercial production. Theatergoers saw the Danish ballerina Adeline Genée, once again, in *The Bachelor Belles*, which had its premiere on the same evening as Herbert's triumph.

In the next year *The Pink Lady* (13 March) was praised for the fact that its songs developed logically out of dramatic situations. As staged by Julian Mitchell, this Ziegfeld show capitalized on the passionate craze for ballroom dances. Eccentric routines were featured in his contribution to *Follies of 1911*, which introduced New Yorkers to the dancing Dolly Sisters. An updated revival of Charles Hoyt's *A Trip to Chinatown*, retitled *A Winsome Widow* (11 April 1912), gave Mitchell and Ziegfeld another success. Mitchell, who had collaborated with Hoyt on the original, staged a dance on ice for the new production, and the graceful skaters astonished the crowds. Equipment was installed in the theater to freeze the one-inch-thick sheet of ice for this number.

The Shubert organization (run by brothers Sam, Lee, and J. J.) offered the greatest Broadway competition to Ziegfeld's enterprises. To ensure summer business at their major house, the Winter Garden, and to take advantage of the innovations of the *Follies*, the Shuberts inaugurated *The Passing Show of 1912*. It, too, was a revue but remained closer than the *Follies* to the format established by Weber and Fields at the Music Hall. The first edition offered "The Ballet of 1830," originally mounted in London, as its first act. In the *Follies of 1913*, Ziegfeld introduced the dancing soubrette Ann Pennington. The Shuberts countered in *The Passing Show of 1914* by presenting the Broadway debut of Marilyn Miller, who became one of the most beloved dancing stars.

"The Dance Craze," as the demand for ballroom shenanigans was termed, was abetted on 3 February 1913 by the premiere of *The Sunshine Girl*. An English import with American performers, the production starred Julia Sanderson and featured Irene and Vernon Castle as well as the venerable Joseph Cawthorn. The plot revolved around a soap factory and the stipulation that its heir not become engaged or marry for a period of time. Castle, as the young lord "Bingo," impersonated the new owner of the establishment. He performed a tango with Sanderson and a Turkey Trot with his wife, establishing, in the words of critic Charles Darnton, "a new reputation for himself as a dancer." Presidents Roosevelt, Taft, and Wilson were portrayed in ballet skirts in a comic number called "Who's the Boss?"

A hit show by twenty-six-year-old Irving Berlin, *Watch Your Step* (8 December 1914), ensured the ambitious musician's tenure on Broadway. The syncopation of ragtime and a complete score based on native rhythms and melodies were Berlin's chief aims. The presence of the Castles at the head of the cast and the centerpiece number "The Syncopated Walk" were evidence of the production's dance emphasis. In "I'm a Dancing Teacher Now," Vernon Castle parodied the burgeoning number of dance studios that had been established to meet the national demand for private lessons, and Irene Castle led the troops in "Show Us How to Do the Fox Trot."

The *Follies of 1914* was a turning point for Ziegfeld. A quarrel with Mitchell caused a rift in their relationship that lasted until 1924, and comic Leon Errol staged most of the numbers for this edition. With an arrangement of "The Star Spangled Banner" in its first-act finale, the *Follies of 1914* presaged the patriotism and preoccupation with the military that characterized the World War I era. Typical of many hits of the period, the highlight of *Hip-Hip Hooray* (30 September 1915) was music by "the March King," John Philip Sousa. Entrepreneur and choreographer Ned Wayburn left the Shuberts to join the Ziegfeld team in 1915. Along with Viennese set designer Joseph Urban, Wayburn helped to take Ziegfeld's revues into the realm of legend. [*See the entry on Wayburn.*]

Scores by Rudolf Friml and Sigmund Romberg strengthened Broadway's operetta holdings. Some of the most influential music in the teens was written by Jerome Kern (1885–1946) for *Nobody Home* (20 April 1915), the first of the Princess Theater shows that launched the intimate musical. These productions were stripped of the huge number of chorus members, the preoccupation with lavish spectacle, and many of the other aspects that had linked the American musical stage with native and European extravaganzas. Located on West Thirty-ninth Street in Manhattan, the Princess had only 292 seats and a diminutive stage to match. There Kern, teamed with wordsmith Guy Bolton, helped to create in *Nobody Home* the theatrical prototype that integrated both songs and jokes into the dramatic action. The practice was unheard of at the time either in British music halls or on American stages, and Kern worked on both sides of the Atlantic.

What was trimmed in quantity was made up for in quality. The sets and costumes for *Nobody Home* were beautifully executed on a small scale that prized elegance and charm. Like many of Mitchell's choreographic innovations that were the result of the tiny dimensions of Weber and Fields's Music Hall, the staging for *Nobody Home* emphasized inventiveness rather than large audiences. The popularity of *Nobody Home* was exceeded by its successor, *Very Good Eddie*. P. G. Wodehouse, the British critic for *Vanity Fair*, joined Bolton and Kern to compose additional shows for the Princess, among which were *Oh, Boy!* and *Oh, Lady! Lady!!* The rehearsal pianist for the latter was the youthful George Gershwin. Produced by Bessie Marbury and Ray Comstock, the Princess musicals foreshadowed the first great masterpiece of the American lyric theater: Ziegfeld's *Show Boat* (27 December 1927), composed by Kern, was both landmark and harbinger of the book musical that evolved into the exquisitely integrated productions of the 1940s.

UNITED STATES OF AMERICA: Musical Theater. Irene and Vernon Castle in the Broadway musical *Watch Your Step* (1914), with book by Charles Dillingham and music by Irving Berlin. (Photograph from the Dance Collection, New York Public Library for the Performing Arts.)

Some of the greatest composers for the musical stage were already working on Broadway in the teens. Besides Kern and Berlin, two younger musicians began making their mark, Gershwin and Cole Porter. Oscar Hammerstein II was at the beginning of his extraordinary career as a lyricist. Visually, audiences at the Metropolitan Opera House were taken by storm by the 1916 appearance of the Ballets Russes de Serge Diaghilev. Vaslav Nijinsky gave a considerable boost to the image of the *danseur* and excited the growing interest in ballet.

The number of revues—wonderful vehicles for soloists, stars, and chorus dancers—began to escalate. Kern composed the majority of songs for the *Follies of 1916.* George M. Cohan got in on the act with *The Cohan Revue of 1916* (9 February). Florence O'Denishawn, a product of the Denishawn school founded by Ruth St. Denis and Ted Shawn in California, appeared in *Kitchy-Koo of 1918* and in its sequel the following year. O'Denishawn reaffirmed the link for dancers between the concert stage and the commercial theater. Former hoofer George White (born Weitz) instituted a revue notable, above all, for its dancing sequences. The *Scandals of 1919* was the maiden production of the annual series to which White later gave his name. Tapping, shimmying, and acrobatic feats delighted viewers and provided more competition for Ziegfeld. *Greenwich Village Nights,* renamed *Greenwich Village Follies* (15 July 1919), added to the revue's development.

Two book musicals in 1919 advanced that evolving genre. Victor Herbert's *The Velvet Lady* (3 February) was not one of his finest scores, but Julian Mitchell's direction turned it into a dancing phenomenon, especially for Georgia O'Ramsey. *Irene* (18 November) was a significant benchmark because its plot dealt with realistic characters who took believable actions that provided logical situations and motivations for songs as well as dances. Meanwhile, the Actors' Equity strike of 1919 resulted in bitter recriminations as performers attempted to improve their salaries and working conditions.

The Innovative Twenties. The 1920s ushered in the jazz age, which was more idiosyncratically American than any previous era. World War I had solidified a national identity that firmly recognized the United States as a leading world power. Syncopated rhythms, art deco visuals, and an explosion of dance styles set a racy pulse. The revue reached its zenith, a level that has never been equaled. In spite of scores of imitators, Ziegfeld's *Follies* reigned supreme. Nearly fifty new musicals were produced in the 1920/21 season alone, most of them revues. Some emphasized music; a few showcased dance, comedy, or even nudity. The Shuberts' *Passing Show,* White's *Scandals,* and Ziegfeld's *Follies* plus his *Midnight Frolics* continued to dominate the scene, but there were some notable additions—and incidents.

The 22 September 1921 premiere of *The Music Box Revue* was a spectacular christening for the Music Box Theater. For the *Greenwich Village Follies of 1923* (20 September), Martha Graham danced in a Spanish fiesta number and in "The Garden of Kama," an exotic replication from her Denishawn days. Earl Carroll's *Vanities* (5 July 1923) appeared with the 1923 production. *The Grand Street Follies* were so successful as a private event that the series went public with *The Grand Street Follies of 1924* on 20 May. The Shuberts flirted with nudity in *Artists and Models of 1924* (15 October). *The Garrick Gaieties* (17 May 1925) affirmed the songwriting abilities of young Richard Rodgers. One of the best and most remarkable revues, *Blackbirds of 1928,* featured the footwork of Bill ("Bojangles") Robinson. Jazz and the black performer were acclaimed, respected, and legitimized on the Great White Way. By 1929 Broadway was so saturated that *Ned Wayburn's Gambols* ran for only thirty-one nights.

The *Charlot Revue of 1926* received some unusually negative press coverage. The roster for this British import was headed by Gertrude Lawrence, Beatrice Lillie, and Jack Buchanan, who also staged some of the dances and several of the Noël Coward songs. A letter from "a Wrathful Playgoer" to the management of the Selwyn Theater complained about the lackluster entertainment and uninspired cast. Journalist Alexander Woollcott gave Miss Lawrence space in his column so that she could reply

UNITED STATES OF AMERICA: Musical Theater. Chorus girls in *Shuffle Along* (1921). Josephine Baker stands sixth from the right. This show was the first all-black "smash hit" on Broadway, thanks mainly to the danceable tunes of Eubie Blake. (Photograph from the archives of Noble Sissle and Eubie Blake; reprinted from Robert Kimball and William Bolcom, *Reminiscing with Sissle and Blake,* New York, 1973, p. 128.)

UNITED STATES OF AMERICA: Musical Theater. An English precision dance group founded by John Tiller in 1901, the Tiller Girls were a popular attraction at the *Zigfield Follies* in 1922, 1924, and 1925. (Photograph by White Studio, New York; from the Dance Collection, New York Public Library for the Performing Arts.)

publicly to her detractors. The lady confessed to exhaustion, due to her intensive effort to make a good impression on New Yorkers.

Magnificent music seemed to be everywhere. Three operettas, *The Student Prince, The Vagabond King,* and *The Desert Song,* exemplified the genre's last glorious blaze before losing favor to more realistic lyric theater pieces and to films. Both Rudolf Friml (1879–1972) and Sigmund Romberg (1887–1951) were Europeans who had trained as classical musicians in Prague and Vienna, respectively, before immigating to the United States. The two also contributed significantly in the transition from operetta to musical comedy that took place in the 1920s. Romberg's *Student Prince* (2 December 1924) retained the aura of unrequited love in a Ruritanian setting, but his *Desert Song* (30 November 1926), with its contemporary French North Africa locale, moved closer to the realm of musical drama. In *The Vagabond King* (20 September 1925), Friml dealt with issues surrounding political upheaval, an indication that serious ideas were being tested on the lyric stage. With *Rose-Marie* (2 September 1924), he struck a balance between Old World romance and contemporary accents, captivating spectators and setting a box office record that remained unbroken for nearly twenty years. Melody and beat propelled the dancers in David Bennett's *Rose-Marie,* its choreography including the Charleston, the Black Bottom, and the Lindy Hop plus adagio, toe-tapping, and Tiller Girl precision routines. The "Totem Tom-Tom" production number in act 1 presented one hundred dancers in formations that are associated with a later era of Hollywood musicals.

The book musical coalesced in the 1920s and proved to be the American musical theater's vehicle of the future. *Irene* and George M. Cohan's *Mary* (18 October 1920) piqued the taste for heroine-centered sagas. Ziegfeld's *Sally* (21 October 1920) was a runaway favorite, with Marilyn Miller as star, Jerome Kern as composer with additional ballet music by Victor Herbert, and Joseph Urban as designer. Miller's performance in the "Butterfly Ballet" was so enchanting that the entire number was interpolated into a subsequent edition of the *Follies.* Miller triumphed again in *Sunny* (22 September 1925), produced by Charles Dillingham and directed by Julian Mitchell not long before his death. *Sunny* was the first Kern-Hammerstein collaboration and was staged by Mitchell in conjunction with David Bennett, Alexis Kosloff, and John Tiller. The altering relationship between book and music did not affect Ziegfeld's production methods. For one of Miller's numbers in Romberg and Gershwin's *Rosalie* (10 January 1928), he surrounded his star with fifty beauties adorned in "simple peasant costumes of satin and chiffon."

The 2 February 1927 premiere of *Rio Rita* opened the exquisite, egg-shaped Ziegfeld Theater. For all the future-shock elegance of the auditorium and settings, *Rio Rita* was something of a dated, swashbuckling operetta, with one exception: Albertina Rasch fashioned a stunning ballet for the Albertina Rasch Girls, who wore black-and-white costumes by Joseph Urban. Many of the other sequences were staged by Sammy Lee, who had succeeded Ned Wayburn as Ziegfeld's dance director in 1923. [*See the entry on Rasch.*]

In a decade brimming with hits, some unusual talents and new themes emerged. Fred Astaire, who gave up

UNITED STATES OF AMERICA: Musical Theater. Marilyn Miller in the title role of *Rosalie* (1928), with music by Sigmund Romberg and George Gershwin. As a princess from the Ruritanian country of Romanza who falls in love with a West Point cadet, Miller danced in several elaborate numbers staged by Seymour Felix. (Photograph from the Billy Rose Theater Collection, New York Public Library for the Performing Arts.)

vaudeville and between 1917 and 1932 appeared in ten Broadway shows with his sister Adele, began choreographing and performing his own solos in George and Ira Gershwin's *Lady, Be Good!* (1 December 1924). The Astaires displayed their enormous charms in *Funny Face* (22 November 1927) and took three of their New York successes to London during the 1920s. Tap dancing was eulogized by adorable flappers in the frothy, amusing *No, No, Nanette* (16 September 1925). At the opposite end of the spectrum *Show Boat,* with dances by Sammy Lee, examined tough social issues such as racism and divorce. Based on Edna Ferber's novel, the book by Oscar Hammerstein II and Jerome Kern's score set a precedent for revealing the interplay of serious emotions on the musical stage. The same season introduced Vincent Youman's talent in *Hit the Deck!* (25 April 1927). Staged by Seymour Felix, the show featured an eccentric, "knee-twisting" ballet performed by Madeline Cameron. *The Three Musketeers* (13 March 1928) allowed Ziegfeld and Urban to dabble with historical settings, and it provided the occasion for Rasch to insert a *ballet de cour* in act 2 of Friml's score. In *Whoopee* (4 December 1928), Ziegfeld explored the Wild West, Urban reinvented the Grand Canyon, and Eddie Cantor pranced his way to stardom.

Two shows were outstanding for the work of their choreographers rather than for breathtaking box office records. *The Street Singer* (17 September 1929), a Shubert venture that borrowed heavily from the Folies-Bergère, was co-produced by Busby Berkeley, who created a touching "Green Room Ballet" for Queenie Smith. Best remembered as a singer, Smith actually began her career as a soloist with the Metropolitan Opera Ballet. Ziegfeld's *The Show Girl* (2 July 1929) allowed Rasch to cap the decade in which she had begun choreographing so successfully. With a Gershwin score and Ruby Keeler in the lead, Rasch had glorious material to work with. Her coup was a ballet to Gershwin's *An American in Paris* that featured Harriet Hoctor.

Rasch, known as the "Czarina of Broadway," was a classically trained Viennese dancer who had appeared in major opera houses, in vaudeville, and as the entr'acte entertainment on a South American tour with Sarah Bernhardt. A brilliant teacher and choreographer, she created dances for the Hippodrome for fifty of her dancers and sent out groups of "Albertina Rasch Girls" numbered to suit the scale of specific stages. She helped, also, to convince Sol Hurok to bring the German expressionist Mary Wigman to the United States for a tour in 1930. Both she and Berkeley became major influences in film choreography during the 1930s.

The invention of the talkies collided with the stock market crash of October 1929, and the bright lights dimmed on Broadway.

Experimentation and a Seriousness of Purpose. The Great Depression had a profound effect on the American theater, contributing to one of the most creative periods in its history. Whereas the 1920s had witnessed the culmination of innovations begun at the turn of the century, the 1930s marked radical changes in the nation's social, economic, and political fabric that were reflected in the highly experimental nature of the era's theatrical achievements. Productions that confronted pressing social and labor issues were mounted simultaneously with those that offered purely escapist fare. The seriousness of purpose and rich quantity of talent caused this decade to uncover ideas that were refined for many years afterward.

A Gershwin score was teamed with a book by George S. Kaufman for *Strike Up the Band* (14 January 1930), a musical that dealt with war, international politics, and big business. Jazz syncopations were exchanged for "swing" melodies. A few of the pit musicians for the production

UNITED STATES OF AMERICA: Musical Theater. *(above)* The Albertina Rasch Dancers and soloist Harriet Hoctor (right) in Rasch's ballet set to Gershwin's *An American in Paris,* in Ziegfeld's production of *Show Girl* (1929). *(below)* In *The Band Wagon* (1931), Rasch choreographed an inventive number to "Dancing in the Dark" for Tilly Losch, in the role of a glamorous ballerina, and Fred Astaire, as a stagedoor beggar who dances with her in a dream. They performed the number on a raked stage with a mirrored floor. (Photographs from the Billy Rose Theater Collection, New York Public Library for the Performing Arts.)

were Benny Goodman, Gene Krupa, Glenn Miller, and Jimmy Dorsey. George Hale arranged the dances for this show, which set a new tone for Broadway.

The golden days of the revue were over, although the genre was still in evidence. In *The Band Wagon* (3 June 1931), Tilly Losch danced on a raked, mirrored floor in a set that incorporated revolving stages. Albertina Rasch choreographed, and the Astaires appeared together for the last time, as Adele Astaire was about to exchange her stage career for marriage. The last *Follies* that Ziegfeld supervised personally was in 1931. After his death in 1932, editions were produced sporadically—usually staged by Robert Alton—but these never equaled the standard set by Ziegfeld himself. Another revue, *Hellzapoppin* (22 September 1938), established a box office record and featured a precedent-setting use of film footage in its opening production number. [*See the entry on Ziegfeld.*]

Of Thee I Sing (26 December 1931) was the first musical to win a Pulitzer Prize. Collaborators George and Ira Gershwin, George S. Kaufman, and Morrie Ryskind were floored, as was George Hale, their choreographer.

Broadway began losing many of its finest talents to more lucrative film ventures in Hollywood, a situation

that enhanced the abundance of movie musicals that were produced over the next two decades. Typical of this exodus are the examples of Fred Astaire and Albertina Rasch. Astaire's last stage musical was *Gay Divorce* (29 November 1932) with Claire Luce. Appearing for the first time in a book show with a woman who was not his sister, Astaire began, in *Gay Divorce,* to explore the deft, romantic comedy that became the framework for all his films: sophistication rather than sentiment is the touchstone, and the most important love scenes are the danced duets. *The Great Waltz* (22 September 1934) was an operetta produced, like earlier behemoths, on an extravagant scale. The lives of the Johann Strausses—father and son—served as plot and motive for using the Waltz King's superb music. On stage, the show incorporated two hundred performers, several sweeping numbers by Rasch, and $250,000 worth of sets and costumes. In the 1938 Metro-Goldwyn-Mayer (MGM) movie, Rasch was able to mount her dance sequences on an even more lavish scale.

The days of great producers in the Ziegfeld mold were over. Yet an interesting roster of producing organizations emerged. The Works Progress Administration (WPA) Federal Theatre and Dance Projects supported new composers, such as Eubie Blake in *Swing It* (22 July 1937) and Lehman Engel in *A Hero Is Born* (1 October 1937). Under Federal auspice, *The Swing Mikado* (1 March 1939) was produced in Chicago, inspiring Michael Todd's *The Hot Mikado* (23 March 1939) in New York City with Bill Robinson. The Group Theater produced Paul Green's *Johnny Johnson* (19 November 1936). The Mercury Theater and the Theater Guild joined the action. Plays with music and dance were mounted, such as the 1933 productions *Run, Little Chillun* and *School for Husbands* for which Doris Humphrey created the dances. The Ladies Garment Workers Union renamed the Princess Theater the Labor Stage and on 27 November 1937 opened the politically activist *Pins and Needles,* which included some dances by Katherine Dunham.

Many figures from the concert field came to work on Broadway. José Limón staged the Dance of the Seven Mannequins in *Roberta* (18 November 1933), which featured Bob Hope and Fay Templeton and used only twenty-eight chorus girls. George Balanchine made history with "Slaughter on Tenth Avenue" for *On Your Toes* (11 April 1936), introducing Ray Bolger and proving that dance could be integrated with the dramatic plot. Balanchine asked to be billed as "choreographer" for the show, the first listing of the term in a Broadway program.

The Russian genius began his forrays into the commercial theater in London, where he created dances for

UNITED STATES OF AMERICA: Musical Theater. Two jazz versions of Gilbert and Sullivan's comic opera *The Mikado,* with all-black casts, opened on Broadway in March 1939. *The Hot Mikado,* produced by impresario Mike Todd, starred Bill Robinson, who strutted through his role wearing a gold suit, gold shoes, and a gold hat and carrying a gold cane. He is pictured here with an unidentified player and the "three little maids from school": Gwendolyn Reyde, Frances Broch, and Rosetta Le Noire. After its Broadway run, the show moved to the grounds of the World's Fair in Flushing, Queens. (Photograph from the Museum of the City of New York.)

UNITED STATES OF AMERICA: Musical Theater. The "Pernambuco" number from *Where's Charley?* (1948), choreographed by George Balanchine. Ray Bolger as a *caballero* is seen at center wooing Allyn Ann McLerie. (Photograph by Eileen Darby, Graphic House, Inc.; used by permission.)

Charles B. Cochran's *Revue* (1930 and 1931) and for Sir Oswald Stoll's *Variety Show* (1931). In the United States Balanchine staged or made dances for five movies and nearly twenty musicals, casting leading ballet performers and bringing up the standards of choreography to a par with those for musical composition. For *Babes in Arms* (14 April 1937) he made Broadway's first dream ballet: "Peter's Journey" in act 2 took the hero to Hollywood, Europe, and Africa and ultimately returned him to reality. Balanchine's association with black dancers began with the tap dancing Nicholas Brothers in *Babes in Arms.* He later worked with Katherine Dunham in the stage and movie versions of *Cabin in the Sky* (1940) and the film *Star Spangled Rhythm* (1942). During his association with *House of Flowers* (30 December 1954)—the cast of which starred Pearl Bailey and Diahann Carroll and included Arthur Mitchell and Alvin Ailey—Balanchine designed the staging and was instrumental in Geoffrey Holder's arrangement of the Banda Dance. Besides using ballerinas Tamara Geva and Vera Zorina on Broadway, Balanchine cast Alexandra Danilova and Frederic Franklin, along with an entire ensemble from Ballet Russe de Monte Carlo, in *Song of Norway* (21 August 1944). He choreographed for Ray Bolger in *On Your Toes, Where's Charley?,* and *Keep Off the Grass,* in which José Limón and Jerome Robbins also appeared. Young chorus dancers in *Great Lady* included Robbins and, in *The Lady Comes Across,* the youthful Gower Champion. Among Balanchine's greatest musical theater successes were *I Married an Angel* (11 May 1938), *The Boys from Syracuse* (23 November 1938), and *The Merry Widow* (4 August 1943). [*See the entry on Balanchine.*]

Development of Theatrical Choreography. Serious theatrical choreography began to develop almost simultaneously with the demise of a leading American composer, the death of George Gershwin in Hollywood in 1937. Initially inspired by Jerome Kern's songs, Gershwin had entered the musical theater at a time when most of its scores were trite, old fashioned, or cliché-ridden. He fused jazz syncopations, big symphonic arrangements, and an often-haunting lyricism into distinctive scores, many of which are equally at home in a concert hall or in a Broadway orchestra pit. The last Gershwin shows coincided with the first of Cole Porter's long string of hits, beginning with *Anything Goes* (21 November 1934), for which Robert Alton arranged numbers for the chorus and leading lady Ethel Merman. Another Porter show, *DuBarry Was a Lady* (6 December 1939), introduced the novice dancer Betty Grable.

The book musical clearly defined itself as a distinguished art form during the 1940s, when all production elements were organically integrated and the form reached the sort of apex attained by the revue in the 1920s. There were several strong forerunners to the new importance of librettos created by serious writers.

UNITED STATES OF AMERICA: Musical Theater. Agnes de Mille's landmark choreography for *Oklahoma!* (1943) fused ballet and modern dance idioms to create a new-style Americana musical. The original cast members seen here include, at left, Katherine Sergava as Laurey and Bambi Linn as Child. Marc Platt as Curley heads the cowboys on the right. (Photograph by Vandamm Studio, New York.)

Maxwell Anderson had joined Kurt Weill to create *Knickerbocker Holiday* (19 October 1938), and Gertrude Stein had collaborated with Virgil Thomson on *Four Saints in Three Acts* (20 February 1934), "an opera to be sung," as Stein described it. The positive national image following World War II contributed to the blossoming of theatrical expressiveness. The first major-league American ballet troupes—now known as New York City Ballet and American Ballet Theatre—came into being in the forties and evinced strong classical training and technique. Modern dancers added their singular gifts as both choreographers and performers.

Three productions opened new 1940s directions. *Cabin in the Sky* (25 October 1940), with Ethel Waters and Katherine Dunham as stars and Balanchine as choreographer, took a close look at black lifestyles. Robert Alton's dances for Gene Kelly in *Pal Joey* (25 December 1940), along with the show's script and score, brought three-dimensional characters to life in a situation that engendered cynicism rather than idealized love. Like numerous other musicals in this period, both became popular movies. For *Lady in the Dark* (23 January 1941), Albertina Rasch used dance to explore the psychological ramifications of dreams. The most famous dream ballet ever created was staged two years later by Agnes de Mille.

De Mille's choreography for *Oklahoma!* (31 March 1943) elaborated character as well as plot, used idiomatic American gestures and folk forms, and firmly allied Broadway with professionals from ballet and concert stages. In the celebrated sequence "Laurey Makes Up Her Mind," de Mille cast dancers in roles that paralleled the principal characters and had them demonstrate the interior struggle Laurey experienced in choosing her beau. Directed by Rouben Mamoulian, *Oklahoma!* transformed Alfred Drake, Celeste Holm, and Joan Roberts into leading stage personalities. The original cast for the dream ballet comprised Katherine Sergava as Laurey, Bambi Linn as Child, George Church as Jud, and Marc Platt as Curley. The two men were subsequently replaced by Vladimir Kostenko and Erick Hawkins. Other *Oklahoma!* dancers who were part of the relatively recent practice of incorporating serious dance artists in commercial ventures included Diana Adams, John Butler, Marian Horosko, Joan McCracken, and later, Gemze de Lappe and Mavis Ray. [*See the entry on de Mille.*]

This pattern continued and expanded in *One Touch of Venus* (7 October 1943), Cheryl Crawford's production that combined the experimental approach of the Group Theater with the proven attraction of de Mille's choreography. Elia Kazan directed the show—his first musical—that had a book by S. J. Perelman with Ogden Nash and a score by Kurt Weill. Mary Martin starred as Venus, and Sono Osato was featured as *première danseuse.* Kermit Love designed the dance costumes. De Mille staged, among other numbers, the ballets "Forty-five Minutes for Lunch," "Foolish Heart," and "Venus in Ozone Heights." Some of the dancers were Diana Adams, Ann Hutchinson, Pearl Lang, Duncan Noble, Welland Lathrop, and, briefly, Merce Cunningham, who appeared in the cast for a week in Boston.

At thirty-four, de Mille had impressive credentials. She had already completed a Charles Cochran revue in London for Gertrude Lawrence; dances for the 1936 film version of *Romeo and Juliet* with Norma Shearer and Leslie Howard; *Drums Beat in Hackensack* for Les Ballets Jooss; *Three Virgins and a Devil* for Ballet Theatre; and *Rodeo* for Ballet Russe de Monte Carlo. Her "Civil War Ballet" in *Bloomer Girl* (5 October 1944) had less to do with the plot than with touching national consciousness with regard to grief for husbands and sons who were fighting overseas and in its plea for racial tolerance. With the ballet-pantomime to the overture of *Carousel* (19 April 1945), de Mille set a poetic dimension for the entire production. Teamed with Frederick Lowe and Alan Jay Lerner for *Brigadoon* (13 March 1947), she again extended the range of feeling and mood that could be sustained by dance in the musical theater, especially with the chasing of Harry Beaton and the mourning ritual for his death.

With Sono Osato and Nancy Walker as winsome principals, *On the Town* (28 December 1944) was the first Broadway show to evolve from a ballet, Jerome Robbins's *Fancy Free*. It also was the debut of what became a spectacular theatrical partnership between Robbins and Leonard Bernstein. Next, Robbins choreographed the ballet *Interplay*—for himself, Janet Reed, John Kriza, and Michael Kidd, among others—for Billy Rose's *Concert Varieties* (1 June 1945), which had an exceedingly short run. He scored another hit with his hilarious "Mack Sennett Ballet" in *High Button Shoes* (9 October 1947), which had music by Jule Styne. In *Look, Ma, I'm Dancin'* (29 January 1948) Robbins spoofed the ballet world with a cast featuring Nancy Walker and Harold Lang. [*See the entry on Robbins.*]

Another influx of dancemakers came to Broadway from the concert circuit. Helen Tamiris evoked pure magic in her Currier and Ives "Skating Ballet" for *Up in Central Park* (27 January 1945); she enlivened the Wild West with *Annie Get Your Gun* (16 May 1946), Irving Berlin's tailor-made score for Ethel Merman; and she staged dances for a revival of *Show Boat* in the same season. Michael Kidd also demonstrated a flair for blending ballet with theatrical dance forms. One of his earliest achievements was *Finian's Rainbow* (10 January 1947), an unusual mixture of serious issues and escapism; Kidd created an entire

UNITED STATES OF AMERICA: Musical Theater. The final tableau of the "Mack Sennett Ballet" from *High Button Shoes* (1947), choreographed by Jerome Robbins. (Photograph reprinted from a souvenir program.)

role for the speechless character Sharon out of dance and mime passages. Some of his best work was done in the film *Seven Brides for Seven Brothers* (1954), which utilized company members from both Ballet Theatre and the New York City Ballet. *Kiss Me, Kate* (30 December 1948), widely considered to be one of the most perfect musicals, matched the gifts of Shakespeare with those of Cole Porter and Hanya Holm, who used preclassic dance forms (pavane and tarantella) to lend a Renaissance dimension to her choreography.

Concert soloists also made an impact on the commercial theater. Katherine Dunham appeared in several revues and in *Carib Song* (27 September 1945). Pearl Primus led the cast for *Caribbean Carnival* (5 December 1947), an artistic and aesthetic breakthrough even though it was not well received at the box office, an indication that audiences were not yet comfortable with the exuberance of African and Latino exoticism. Modern dancer Valerie Bettis stunned spectators in the revue *Inside U.S.A.* (30 April 1948).

The American Society of Composers, Authors and Publishers (ASCAP), the composers' union, called a strike during the 1948 season. Despite complaints against it, ASCAP had been instrumental in bringing about an important artistic change, beginning in the 1930s. Until then, it was common to have several composers contribute to a production, a situation that stemmed both from the revue format and from the custom in nineteenth-century opera houses of having several staff musicians write part of the music for a ballet. Even a major accomplishment such as Ziegfeld's *Rosalie* incorporated melodies by Sigmund

UNITED STATES OF AMERICA: Musical Theater. The pavane from Cole Porter's *Kiss Me, Kate* (1948), choreographed by Hanya Holm. Decor and costumes were designed by Lemuel Ayres. (Photograph by Eileen Darby, Graphic House, Inc.; used by permission.)

Romberg and George Gershwin, and Jerome Kern's *Show Boat* included Charles K. Harris's period song "After the Ball." The move to have an entire score written by one composer was a crucial step in unifying musical productions. ASCAP's efforts at one-show-one-composer were abetted by the strong personalities and musical gifts of Kern and Gershwin. Kern's work at the Princess Theater and Gershwin's score for *Strike Up the Band* provided favorable evidence in support of change. Kern's *The Cat and the Fiddle* (15 October 1931) and Gershwin's *Of Thee I Sing* (26 December 1931) helped to establish this practice, which was standard procedure by the late 1940s.

Rodgers and Hammerstein finished the decade with their Pulitzer Prize–winner *South Pacific* (7 April 1949). Anderson and Weill collaborated for the last time before Weill's death with their poignant *Lost in the Stars* (30 October 1949). Carol Channing began her long love affair with theatergoers in *Gentlemen Prefer Blondes* (8 December 1949), with steps made to measure by de Mille.

Emergence of the Director-Choreographer. The concept of the single director-choreographer—another attempt at production unity—began in the 1950s and became increasingly prominent in subsequent decades. Writing in *And Promenade Home,* de Mille attributed this, primarily, to a choreographer's need to have control over his or her work without interference from a director or producer. Both Julian Mitchell and Gus Sohlke had functioned in this solo capacity at the turn of the century. The advantage of a single creative vision is, normally, a tightly integrated production. During the 1950s, Jerome Robbins and Michael Kidd took over directorial and choreographic responsibilities, often producing their own shows as well.

A harsher realism entered the theater in the 1950s and slowly supplanted the apple-pie values and traditional American idioms that had been so well served in the 1940s. The "beat generation" grooved to rock-and-roll. The scope of the lyric stage widened to encompass ethnic variety as well as streetwise figures and tactics. When exotic locales were featured, they usually provided background for the encounters of three-dimensional characters. Choreographers were able to add a kinetic veracity in the process of role development. The time span between *Oklahoma!* (1943) and *Fiddler on the Roof* (1964) is the richest period in American musical theater. A growing emphasis on human values and an onstage synthesis of the performing and visual arts produced a body of work that has yet to be matched in substance or number.

The modest appeal of the immodest *Michael Todd's Peep Show* (28 June 1950) revealed the by-then limited draw of revues. That same year witnessed the premiere of one of the masterpiece musicals, *Guys and Dolls* (24 November 1950), with a book by Abe Burrows, score by Frank Loesser, and dances by Michael Kidd, whose crap game for Sky Masterson and his friends to "Luck Be a Lady Tonight" is a pinnacle of choreography for males on the musical stage, rarely equaled except for Kidd's ensembles in the film *Seven Brides for Seven Brothers,* Fred Astaire's movie dances, and some of Robbins's work. For *The King and I* (29 March 1951), Robbins used poses from Siamese classical dance to fashion "The Small House of Uncle Thomas," a complete miniature ballet that could stand alone as a concert piece. Although de Mille's dance hall girls in *Paint Your Wagon* (12 November 1951) were fully realized characters, the Old West had lost the power to rivet popular imaginations. Two foreign-flavored offerings sparked the 1953 season. Kidd racked up another winner in *Can-Can* (7 May), starring Lilo and Gwen Verdon and brandishing a fine Cole Porter score. *Kismet* (3 December), with its seductive themes borrowed subtly from Aleksandr Borodin, was enhanced by Jack Cole's choreography. A former Denishawn member, Cole was a pioneer of jazz dancing. He trained Verdon and Carol Haney as well as many other dancers, coached Marilyn Monroe, and collaborated on several movies. [*See the entry on Cole.*]

The Pajama Game (13 May 1954), Richard Adler's first hit with Jerry Ross, employed two directors, George Abbott and Jerome Robbins. Bob Fosse staged the dances, and his "Steam Heat" brought instant recognition for himself and Carol Haney, his leading dancer. Fosse brought his tight-bodied jazz to Broadway again almost immediately with *Damn Yankees* (5 May 1955), a baseball spoof with Gwen Verdon as the sexy vamp Lola. David Merrick began to develop a reputation as a producer that was reminiscent of the 1920s' theater tycoons and of Ziegfeld. His *Peter Pan* (20 October 1954), conceived and staged by Robbins with Mary Martin as the eternal youth, became an all-time classic.

Robbins's greatest musical theater achievement to date was accomplished with Leonard Bernstein on *West Side Story* (26 September 1957). Created with Peter Gennaro, the dances and fights proved that gesture could convey the full range of emotion from tenderness to violence, providing spectators with an Aristotelian catharsis along the way. Its foundation based in Shakespeare's *Romeo and Juliet, West Side Story* transposed the noble houses of Capulet and Montague—as well as their transgressions—to the warring street gangs of Sharks and Jets. As drama critic Walter Terry observed in the *New York Herald,* "The great wonder of *West Side Story* is that realistic action flows into dancing and out of it again without a hitch or break, just as speech swells or snarls its way into poetry and song." Throughout the production, music and dance heightened adolescent interactions, vividly articulating feelings that the young are unable to express. Male dancers gained a new macho dimension in the public eye. These were not street toughs but kids from the corps de ballet, notably, in the film, Russ Tamblyn and Eliot Feld. Both the stage and film versions of *West Side Story* continue to fill theaters around the world because of its timeless power as a metaphor of youth and death. The show also brought a new lyricist to Broadway, Stephen Sondheim.

Other interesting and off-beat attractions included *House of Flowers*, with a book by Truman Capote; the dancerly spy thriller, *Silk Stockings* (24 February 1955), with choreography by Eugene Loring, which was appropriate as the Cold War commenced; and *Flower Drum Song* (1 December 1958), one of several attempts to reinvoke the lucrative Oriental splendors of *The King and I.*

My Fair Lady (15 March 1956), one of the great box office colossuses, was a musical theater jewel in its original production. Again, the principal librettist was a man of letters: George Bernard Shaw's *Pygmalion* was adapted by Lerner and Lowe into a witty, sophisticated tryst for Rex Harrison and Julie Andrews. Hanya Holm, a wizard with period movement, exceeded her own standards with the bustling Covent Garden sequences, the understated "Ascot Gavotte," and the ripsnorting "Get Me to the Church on Time."

With *Gypsy* (21 May 1959), Robbins staged the last of the big, traditional musical comedies. The wonderful burlesque-hall tale of Mama Rose and her fetching daughter Gypsy Rose Lee had a score by Jule Styne and lyrics by Stephen Sondheim. The great-hearted *Fiorello!* (23 November 1959), with dances by Peter Gennaro, marked the end of an era. The decade's finale, *The Sound of Music* (16 November 1959), immortalized the Trapp family in a production that placed top value on music rather than dance.

Radical Concepts and New Energy. The 1960s brought on a severe crisis in American confidence and a splintering of national identity that was disorienting on nearly all levels. The early optimism that began with the Kennedy administration was gradually eaten away by the emotional and financial costs of the war in Vietnam. Civil rights, political assassinations, street violence, campus rebellions, women's liberation, and flower children further fragmented traditional alliances. Acid rock and psychedelic imaginings expressed a free-falling loss of innocence that characterized the decade. The stage, as a result, produced an eclectic assortment of odd bed fellows: the avant-garde flourished next to the traditional. A great deal of experimentation took place with radical concepts and energy coming from communal performance groups, postmodern artists, and pop culture.

Escalating costs that continued to push ticket prices up caused cast numbers to shrink in most productions. Appropriately, the music that holds the record for the longest off-Broadway run helped to christen the decade. *The Fantasticks* (3 May 1960), Tom Jones and Harvey Schmidt's romance for seven players, echoed the simplicity of a parable and became a touchstone for the sixties' generation. Stock production numbers were hardly the point with such a tiny cast, yet this entire show was conceived in dance terms, and one of the seven characters is a white-faced mime. Like the functional, unpretentious props that were taken out of an onstage trunk as needed, the choreography wove simple steps and movement into lyrical sequences that bound together the dramatic action. The Boy (Matt) and The Girl (Luisa) had a fanciful turn of swirling embraces in "Soon It's Gonna Rain," the two fathers executed a soft-shoe routine in "They Did It 'Cause We Said No," and the first act ended with "The Rape Ballet." The initial production investment was $16,500. *The Fantasticks* was still running in 1997, demonstrating the antitraditional stance and creative vitality that still permeates off- and off-off-Broadway venues.

One of the liveliest of these was the Judson Poets' Theatre, housed in the Judson Church at 55 Washington Square South. Under the stewardship of its associate minister, Al Carmines, an insouciant musician and composer, the arts program at the church added the Judson Dance Theater to its aegis in 1962. New programs of dance, theater, and musical theater were given every month or so. *What Happened* (October 1963), which typified the Judson participatory democracy, won the annual Obie award for best production of a musical. The Gertrude Stein script was directed by Lawrence Kornfeld and had a score that was composed and performed by Carmines. Three male singers and five female dancers—Joan Baker, Lucinda Childs, Aileen Pasloff, Yvonne Rainer, and Arlene Rothlein—performed postmodern games and tasks. Five separate sections were sorted out by Jerry Tallmer in the *New York Post:* skipping rope and chases; counting sweet cadence; wedding and slicing; hop-scotch and crossings; and falling down and photographs. The James Waring Dance Company appeared in *Poet's Vaudeville* on the same bill. By scrutinizing the essence of movement and dissecting all styles of dance, these artists pushed out the boundaries of the art form.

The success of Judson's *In Circles* (13 October 1967) caused the production to be moved from the church to the Cherry Lane Theater and, ultimately, to Grammercy Arts. Stein's syllabic collisions that made up the script of *In Circles* were again staged by Kornfeld and accompanied by a Carmines score. The singing-dancing company included Rothlein, Theo Barnes, Elaine Summers, and David Vaughan, who performed an overture out of the phrase "Poppa knowses that Momma blows her noses." Carmines's whimsical *Promenade* (4 June 1969) opened the Promendade Theater and helped to propel some of the experimentation uptown. The pattern of moving popular experimental productions into commercial houses, inaugurated in the 1960s, was refined over the next decade into a standard operating procedure by Joseph Papp's Shakespeare Festival.

On the mainstream musical front, Gower Champion

joined the front ranks of Broadway creators with *Bye Bye Birdie* (14 April 1960), which he choreographed and directed. *Birdie* dealt with the generation gap, motorcycles, television, and Shriners. Dick Van Dyke and Chita Rivera starred.

At the opposite extreme were the presentations of idealized worlds. *Camelot* (3 December 1960) brought Holm back into the theater to create May dances and medieval games for a cast headed by Richard Burton, Julie Andrews, and Robert Goulet. Based on *The Rainmaker, 110 in the Shade* (24 October 1963) was de Mille's last Broadway original. Jones and Schmidt retained their delicacy in libretto and score. With "Everything Wonderful Happens at Night," de Mille conjured up a spell of ice cream socials and fragile first love—quaint, but too tame and too distant to fire audience imaginations. Jack Cole left Hollywood temporarily to stage *Man of La Mancha* (22 November 1965). This musical tale of Don Quixote is one of the most chivalrous of love stories. Canadian Onna White fashioned period steps to contemporary melodies both for *Half a Sixpence* (25 April 1965), which introduced British teen idol Tommy Steele to Americans, and for *1776* (16 March 1969), which presented the nation's founding fathers in a historic gambol. *George M!* (10 April 1968) brought director-choreographer Joe Layton out of his television studio and back into the limelight. Layton combined patriotism, zippy theatrics, and tap dancing in his brash and sassy view of vaudeville.

Reversing the former stage-to-screen route, a number of sixties' musicals were adaptations from films. *Sweet Charity* (29 January 1966), based on Federico Fellini's *Le Notti di Cabiria* (Nights of Cabiria), was one of the most successful of these and brought a great deal of acclaim to choreographer-director Bob Fosse. Neil Simon Americanized the script into a saga of Charity (Gwen Verdon) and her more worldly cohorts (Helen Gallagher and Thelma Oliver) at the Fan-Dango Ballroom. For "Hey, Big Spender" Fosse lined up his tough corps of hostesses along a railing just over the orchestra pit and gave them the twitchy, grinding posturings that became his choreographic signature. The Cy Coleman score with Dorothy Fields lyrics provided springing-off points for everything from a hippie spiritual, "The Rhythm of Life," to a showstopping soft-shoe for Charity, "If They Could See Me Now." Among other achievements, *Sweet Charity* refurbished the Palace Theater, reclaiming the famed pinnacle of vaudeville as a legitimate Broadway house.

The blockbusters of the 1960s were nearly all built around a single star. In these productions, Broadway capitalized on the early phase of the dance boom that trained high-caliber performers and inspired a massive following of fans who adored watching them. The 1964 season alone produced three of the biggest shows. Champion directed and choreographed the first. *Hello, Dolly!* (16 January 1964) brought Carol Channing back to her adoring fans and, in a later all-black cast, did the same for Pearl Bailey. The script, adapted from Thornton Wilder's *The Matchmaker*, was accompanied by a Jerry Herman score. In the irrepressible "Waiters' Gallop," Champion had his male dancers leaping back and forth across the orchestra pit from the stage to a ramp in the front rows of the auditorium. *Funny Girl* (26 March 1964), choreographed by Carol Haney, was a star vehicle for Barbra Streisand based on a period telling of the life of comedienne Fanny

UNITED STATES OF AMERICA: Musical Theater. The "Big Spender" number from a 1986 revival of *Sweet Charity* (1966), directed and choreographed by Bob Fosse. (Photograph by Alan Pappé, Lee Gross Inc.; from the Billy Rose Theater Collection, New York Public Library for the Performing Arts.)

Brice. The third and most sensationally popular of the three was *Fiddler on the Roof* (22 September 1964). Directed and staged by Robbins as a lyrical paean to the Jewish family, the cast was headed by Zero Mostel. Another later production in this category was *Mame* (24 May 1966), in which Angela Lansbury played everybody's favorite auntie. Onna White's dances included a death-defying fox hunt and smoothie, 1920s ballroom routines.

Musicals that heralded the future were those that dealt acerbically with the perils of urban life. These were the "now" shows that focused on fast-paced banter, rhythms, and steps. *How to Succeed in Business without Really Trying* (14 October 1961) was staged by Bob Fosse with Hugh Lambert. *Subways Are for Sleeping* (27 December 1961) was choreographed by Michael Kidd. *Promises, Promises* (1 December 1968) introduced another candidate for the top echelon of director-choreographers in Michael Bennett and a composer new to Broadway in Burt Bacharach. Satire and nostalgia were served by *You're a Good Man, Charlie Brown* (7 March 1967) and *Dames at Sea* (20 December 1968). No two choreographers could have been less alike. Patricia Birch, a former Graham dancer, set the rompish movement for the "Peanuts" gang of Charles M. Schulz's comic strip. Neal Kenyan directed and staged the delicious period tap routines for Bernadette Peters and her cronies in *Dames at Sea.*

German decadence with Bertolt Brecht–Kurt Weill overtones set the atmosphere for *Cabaret* (20 November 1966). Ron Field choreographed absinthe-etched numbers, and Joel Grey hosted the proceedings with chilly precision. Grey, an example of the triple-threat singing-dancing actor, gained prominence during the 1960s with spectators who developed a taste for virtuosity. The "Age of Aquarius" arrived with Tom O'Horgan's *Hair* (29 April 1968), the archetypal communal love orgy. To diminish barriers between art and life and to decry the need for technique, the cast invited the audience onstage to participate in the finale.

Rock and Revivals. Economic constrictions became an even greater factor during the 1970s. Inflation spiraled, and the energy crisis affected nearly every aspect of social and professional life. For most of the decade, four patterns could be identified. Rock music and country-western music became increasingly popular in various manifestations. Several outstanding black musicals were mounted. The single director-choreographer retained favor as a cost-effective method of evolving an integrated show. Original scripts and scores were fewer, with producers relying on the revival of proven bonanzas as the way to make profits on their investments.

Gaudy, irreverent *Jesus Christ Superstar* (12 October 1971) not only epitomized the fervency of rock fans, it also heralded the growing preoccupation with technology over human talent in musical theater. The *Superstar* concept started as a two-volume record album of this cultish dramatization of the last seven days of Christ. Andrew Lloyd Webber's music and Tim Rice's lyrics depicted long-haired Jesus, played by Jeff Fenolt, as a poet-prophet whose awesome howls riveted his followers. Staged by Tom O'Horgan, the over-amplified production made it necessary for practically the entire cast to carry hand-held microphones with long, sinewy gray chords. Machines and hallucinatory imagery were the keys to O'Horgan's movement. Ben Vereen as Judas made an entrance on the wings of a gigantic butterfly. At one point the stage floor itself rose in three sections to become a vertical field for crawling and wiggling. Smaller, more trenchant rock productions were *Grease* (14 February 1972) and *Godspell,* the latter an experimental show developed in 1971 at Café La Mama out of a retelling of the gospel according to Matthew. Its success transported it first to the Cherry Lane Theater and then uptown, where it ran until 1977.

The influx of musicals starring black performers began with the near failure of *Ain't Supposed to Die a Natural Death* (20 October 1963). An advertising campaign conducted in black neighborhoods to boost attendance succeeded in attracting a significant new audience to the theater district. Black patrons grew in number with *Purlie* (15 March 1970), a less controversial production with choreography by Cleavon Little. Veteran dance man Donald McKayle did the musical numbers for *Raisin* (18 October 1973), the lyrical version of Lorraine Hansberry's *A Raisin in the Sun,* which had originated at the Arena Stage in Washington, D.C., to open as a successful Broadway show in 1959. A wonderful extravaganza, *The Wiz* (5 January 1975), directed by Geoffrey Holder with dances by George Faison, was a funky retelling of Frank Baum's *The Wonderful Wizard of Oz.* Stephanie Mills, as Dorothy, led the cast in everything from boogie-woogie and tap routines to the latest disco dance fads. Among the shows that capitalized on earlier black dance and music traditions were *Bubblin' Brown Sugar* (2 March 1976), choreographed by Vernon Washington with tap sequences by Bill Robinson; the Fats Waller tribute *Ain't Misbehavin'* (9 May 1978), staged by Arthur Faria; and *Eubie!* (20 September 1978), with dances by Billy Wilson.

Risks were taken with a number of shows. Bob Fosse chose an unlikely hero for *Pippin* (23 October 1972) in the historically curious figure of Charlemagne's young son. The *Pippin* innovation that was to have the greatest consequence was the use of television advertising to sell a musical to the public, a factor that increased ticket sales but also drove up production costs considerably. Another Fosse brainchild was *Dancin'* (27 March 1978), a plotless production led by Ann Reinking in which sixteen performers capitalized on America's absorption with dance. [*See the entry on Fosse.*]

Dancin' had been inspired by the record-breaking bo-

UNITED STATES OF AMERICA: Musical Theater. The original cast of *A Chorus Line* (1975). Donna McKechnie is the eighth from right. (Photograph © by Herbert Migdoll; used by permission.)

nanza of the 1970s, Michael Bennett's *A Chorus Line,* originally produced under the auspices of Joseph Papp's Shakespeare Festival. The script was based on improvised material from biographical sketches of dancers—gypsies whose dreams of stardom began, and sometimes ended, by making it into a Broadway chorus lineup. On 29 September 1983 *A Chorus Line* completed its 3,389th performance, establishing it as the longest-running legitimate musical on the American stage. (It would later be overtaken by *Cats* in the summer of 1997.) At the June 1984 ceremonies in the Gershwin Theater, Bennett received a special Tony award and was treated to an unusual accolade. The finale from *A Chorus Line* was presented as the evening's climax, with 332 performers who had appeared in various editions of the show. [*See the entry on Bennett.*]

Bennett had additional successes, some, financial, others, artistic. *Company* (26 April 1970) used a Sondheim score to reveal the perils and lonely victories of the urban swinging singles' scene. The "Tick-Tock Dance" commented wryly on the so-called sexual revolution. *Follies* (4 April 1971), another collaboration with Sondheim, was a ghostly and beautiful invocation of the Ziegfeld productions as "remembered" by former stars, dancing acts, and the exquisite show girls who drifted through the Winter Garden Theater like mythic godesses. The realization of his short-lived *Ballroom* in 1979 cost Bennett $2 million of his own money. Although it was a box office disaster, *Ballroom* was critically acclaimed for its sensitive treatment of middle-aged romance and for its dancers. Most of this lively corps—all of whom were well past forty—had been young gypsies in the halcyon days of *Oklahoma!* and *South Pacific.* Youth, they proved, was but one aspect of theatrical magic.

At least one other venturesome production was a big-scale experiment. *Pacific Overtures* (11 January 1976), a lavish, sophisticated amalgam of Japanese and American elements, featured choreography by Patricia Birch, who had also contributed to the surprising popularity of the 1974 Leonard Bernstein hit, *Candide.* Eighteen years earlier the show had flopped badly, but the peripatetic staging, which took the cast around and through the audience, and Birch's loosely structured dances, added to the compelling music, gave the newer production its bittersweet appeal.

Less daring revivals of, among others, *Oklahoma!, Peter Pan,* and *Kismet* (the last disguised as *Timbuktu*), were gauged to make profits out of nostalgia. Notable among these was the 1971 revival of *No, No, Nanette,* for which Busby Berkeley, the legendary mogul of 1930s' movie musicals, came out of retirement to supervise production numbers. Choreographer Larry Fuller received praise for both *Sweeney Todd* (1 March 1977) and Andrew Lloyd Webber's *Evita* (25 September 1979), though neither was a dance-oriented show. Staging for the musical numbers in *Annie* (21 April 1977) was created by Peter Gennaro, whose major work at the time was done with the Rockettes at Radio City Music Hall.

Two of the freshest talents on Broadway were Tommy Tune and his sometimes choreographic collaborator Thommie Walsh. *The Best Little Whorehouse in Texas* (19 June 1978), the first popular country and western musical, started its run at the Entermedia Theater and then moved to Broadway. The musical showcased two of Tune's funniest dances. One took place in a men's locker room. The other, a parody of football cheerleaders, mixed pneumatic, life-sized puppets with dancers who personified vacuously charming bubbleheads. Tune's lanky ease as a performer was matched by his facility for producing colorful and inventive staging. Two small, madcap productions—*A Day in Hollywood, A Night in the Ukraine* (1 May 1980), created with Walsh, and *Cloud 9* (18 May 1981)—won Tune a considerable following. The production of *Nine* (9 May 1982), directed by Tune and choreographed by Walsh, won five Tony awards. As the star with Twiggy, the British model with whom he had appeared in Ken Russell's film version of *The Boy Friend,* Tune had a resounding success in the updated period musical *My One and Only* (1 May 1983). This production, adapted with Walsh, included songs from Gershwin's 1927 *Funny Face.*

Commerce over Creativity. Recalling Broadway of the Roaring Twenties reveals a sharp contrast with that of the 1980s. Whereas in 1920 there had been premieres of fifty new musicals, the 1982/83 theatrical lineup reflected the worst financial slump in a decade. The fewest premieres in Broadway history were staged the following season. There were only fifteen musicals; four were revivals, and only five of the remainder ran for more than one hundred performances. In a hotly debated 1985 decision, no Tony was awarded for musical theater choreography because no entry in the 1984/85 season was deemed worthy of recognition.

Musical production costs had escalated astronomically because of the rising price of materials, the high wages demanded by union designers and stagehands, and the expense of advertising. Producers appealed to the spectator's visual sense, made keener by film and video spectacles, with hundreds of thousands of dollars worth of scenery, costumes, and special effects. Choreographers had learned how film techniques of montage and cross cuts could be used effectively on stage. The integrated book musical coexisted with less linear narratives that used flashbacks, simultaneous sequences, and fast-forwards at a relentless pace that simulated urban lifestyles.

The average ticket price for a musical had reached $28, and choice seats were $47.50. The financial situation placed strict limits on experimentation and put live Broadway performances out of the reach of thousands of theatergoers. Ironically, this occurred at a time when New York was heralded as the world capital of dance in terms of both creative and performance capabilities. If life in the 1980s was more expensive, it also was more stressful because of new anxieties over the federal budget deficit and random acts of violence by international terrorists. The American Dream seemed to be giving way at the seams. This tension, along with an obsessive drive to succeed, was evident in the theater. Interest in creating productions of high quality was less evident than the commercial urge to latch onto a Broadway jackpot.

Michael Bennett's *Amadeus* (17 December 1980), a stunning stage production on the life of Mozart, subsequently enjoyed a truly cinematic transposition to the screen. Dances for the movie were created by Twyla Tharp and performed by her company with a sly, tongue-in-cheek nod to eighteenth-century technique and practices. With *Dreamgirls* (20 December 1981), Bennett captured the scheming competition in the Motown capital of the rock empire. His synthesis of black styles with rock and musical theater dance was accomplished in a glittering array of scenic spectacle and special effects.

Another shrewd and glamorous idea was the jazz musical *Sophisticated Ladies* (1 March 1981). Conceived by Donald McKayle, the show had difficulty reaching its premiere and was unable to sustain a satisfying run. Many talented artists were involved. Michael Smuin, then artistic director of the San Francisco Ballet, collaborated with McKayle on direction and choreography; Henry Le Tang staged the tap numbers. Cast members included Hinton Battle, Mercedes Ellington, Gregory Hines, and Judith Jamison, a principal member of the Alvin Ailey American Dance Theater.

The standout seller of the early 1980s was *Cats* (7 October 1982), a bold adaptation of T. S. Eliot's *Old Possum's Book of Practical Cats,* with a score by Andrew Lloyd Webber. Gillian Lynne's choreography had the feline dancers slinking into every cranny of the Winter Garden Theater—even the balcony rail. Her emphasis was on acrobatics and sex appeal, a high-voltage combination that thrilled viewers but resulted in a high incidence of turnovers in the dance corps because of injuries.

An accent on acrobatics and slapstick was Joe Layton's concept for *Barnum* (30 April 1980), built around the British comedian and dancer Jim Dale. Travesty was the gimmick in *La Cage aux Folles* (21 August 1983), with its chorus line of male dancers in show-girl attire. Hinton Battle personally triumphed in *The Tap Dance Kid* (21 December 1983), which featured choreography by Danny Daniels. Graciela Daniele staged dances in the short-lived *The Rink* (9 February 1984), for which Chita Rivera won a Tony.

There were gratifying attempts to reignite a partnership between the commercial and concert stages. The revival of *On Your Toes* (1 May 1983), with musical numbers by Donald Saddler, called on the talents of both the New York City Ballet and American Ballet Theatre. Balanchine's choreography was reconstructed with additional ballet sequences by Peter Martins, by then a ballet master in chief of City Ballet. Ballet Theatre principal George De La Pena appeared in the Ray Bolger part, and Russian *prima ballerina* Natalia Makarova starred. The legendary

"Slaughter on Tenth Avenue" was introduced to a new generation and reentered the New York City Ballet repertory. Two years later Martins choreographed the second, all-dancing act of *Song and Dance* (18 September 1985), with Bernadette Peters and Christopher d'Amboise in the leading roles.

A pair of stage musicals that originated as films reflected a growing demand for novel material that nonetheless had a record of strong audience appeal to protect backers' interests. *Forty-second Street,* adapted from the Berkeley film starring Ruby Keeler, opened in Washington at the Kennedy Center to an unfavorable response. Producer David Merrick and director-choreographer Gower Champion doctored the whole considerably, adding dances and cutting some of the expository material. In one of the more macabre incidents in musical comedy history, Merrick announced Champion's death from the stage following the New York premiere on 25 August 1980. The show was a hit.

Singin' in the Rain (2 July 1985), directed and choreographed by Twyla Tharp, was the most costly production in Broadway history. Its $5-million tab seemed particularly exorbitant when compared to the Ziegfeld spectacles, none of which exceeded $300,000. Based on the all-time favorite movie musical from 1952 starring Gene Kelly, Donald O'Connor, and Debbie Reynolds, the stage version—with Don Correia, Peter Slutsker, and Mary D'Arcy—reconstructed most of the original choreography by Kelly and Stanley Donen. Tharp's skill at making dances for the concert stage, screen, and television was evident only in the second act, which opened with a zany parade of live Hollywood toys that skittered around the stage to several tunes, including "Wedding of the Painted Doll." Later, a wacky interpolation in the movie-within-the-show, *The Dancing Cavalier,* mixed roller skates with the "movie's" period French costumes; and in the finale the full cast cavorted to the title song in bright yellow slickers.

This was Tharp's first directorial assignment. Some of the high points and some of the inherent difficulties stemmed from the problematic relationship between screen and stage. The rushes of *The Dancing Cavalier,* designed and shot by Gordon Willis, were delightfully satiric. The overall production was staged in a style consistent with the pageant approach of musical theater in the mid-1950s, which obliterated the cinematic qualities of the script and many of the musical numbers. *Singin' in the Rain* drew crowds to the 1,992-seat Gershwin Theater largely on the basis of its technology: the famous soft-shoe number in the rain was danced in the most spectacular man-made shower ever produced on stage.

Noncommercial dancing that also mesmerized theatergoers included 1985 appearances by Grand Kabuki of Japan at the Metropolitan Opera House and *Tango Argentino* at City Center. Under the direction of Claudio Segovia and Hector Orezzoli, the Argentinian dancers and musicians were such a success in initial New York performances that the ensemble opened at the Mark Hellinger Theater on 9 October 1985 for a six-month run and subsequent national tour.

Bob Fosse's short-lived *Big Deal* (10 April 8–June 1986) won him the 1986 Tony award for Best Choreography, which he shared with his associate Christopher Chadman, and a revival of Fosse's *Sweet Charity* on 27 April at the Minskoff brought additional accolades. The 1986/87 season was notable for the success of *Me and My Girl* (10 August 1986) at the Marquis Theater, with dances by Gillian Gregory, and the failure of *Steppin' Out* (1 January-15 March 1987), a choreographic collaboration by Tommy Tune and Marge Champion. *Starlight Express* (15 March 1987) brought the avant garde focus at the time on stamina and risk to the Great White Way. Arlene Phillips staged the entire production on roller skates, with far more brutal routines than those done three years earlier by Graciela Daniele for *The Rink.*

Modern dance choreographer Lar Lubovitch added hops, skips and gentle jumps to the grownup fairy tales by Stephen Sondheim (music and lyrics) and James Lapine (book and direction) for *Into the Woods* (5 November 1987) at the Martin Beck Theater, with a stunning cast headed by Bernadette Peters as the wicked and very funny witch. The traditional stories of archetypal heroines like Cinderella and Rapunzel were assigned contemporary outcomes, with adultery and random death given equal time to the quiet heroism of peons and mankind's courage to carry on against the emptiness of the unknown. Partly influenced by the October 1987 plunge of the New York Stock Exchange, some of the most admired musicals for the next two years were preoccupied with less-than-gleeful subject matter. Especially distinguished for choreography were Tommy Tune's *Grand Hotel* (12 November 1989) and *City of Angels* (12 December 1989), with musical staging by Walter Painter.

Almost as a talisman, *Singin' in the Rain* seemed to signal the opening of an obsessive Broadway emphasis on revivals, encompassing everything from *Oklahoma!* to Michael Bennett's quite recent *Dreamgirls.* With some significant exceptions between 1984 and 1994, productions from bygone eras seemed to alternate most frequently with new works by Andrew Lloyd Webber, whose scores leave little space outside the emotional pyrotechnics for dancing. Gillian Lynne's staging for *Phantom of the Opera* (26 January 1988) flirted with figures from nineteenth-century Parisian stages and ballrooms, and *Sunset Boulevard,* which reached New York in 1994 by way of London and Los Angeles, was a harmonized version of the movie. The February 1997 announcement by director Harold Prince that Lloyd Webber's *Whistle in the Wind* was "not ready" to open on Broadway as scheduled seemed to herald the end of the British tunester's influence on American audiences.

During the last two decades of the twentieth century, some of the most innovative dance influences in musical theater came from multicultural productions that focused on ethnic styles. *Flamenco Puro* (19 October 1986) was the second offering by Argentinian producers Segovia and Orezzoli, switching in this instance from tango to dazzling flamenco forms. *Oba Oba* (29 March 1987), a Brazilian extravaganza with choreography by Roberto Abrahao, brought Carnival themes and rhythmns to Broadway. *Sarafina!* (28 January 1988) was a presentation from South Africa with dances by Ndaba Mhlongo. *Black and Blue* (26 January 1989), an African-American revue, embellished the stardom of Savion Glover and sported staging and routines by Cholly Atkins, Henry Le Tang, Frankie Manning and Fayard Nicholas of the legendary Nicholas Brothers. Choreographed and directed by Graciela Daniele, *Once on This Island* (18 October 1990) was a Caribbean tale told exclusively through music and dance. Glover was again the headliner for *Jelly's Last Jam* (26 April 1992), with choreography by Hope Clarke and Gregory Hines, and for *Bring in 'da Noise, Bring in 'da Funk*, which moved from the Public Theater—where the production originated—to Broadway in April 1996. *Tommy* and *Grease* in revivals and *Stomp* were principal theatrical interests for rock music lovers.

UNITED STATES OF AMERICA: Musical Theater. Pierre Dulaine as the Gigolo and Yvonne Marceau as the Countess in *Grand Hotel* (1989), directed and choreographed by Tommy Tune. (Photograph by Martha Swope © Time Inc.; used by permission.)

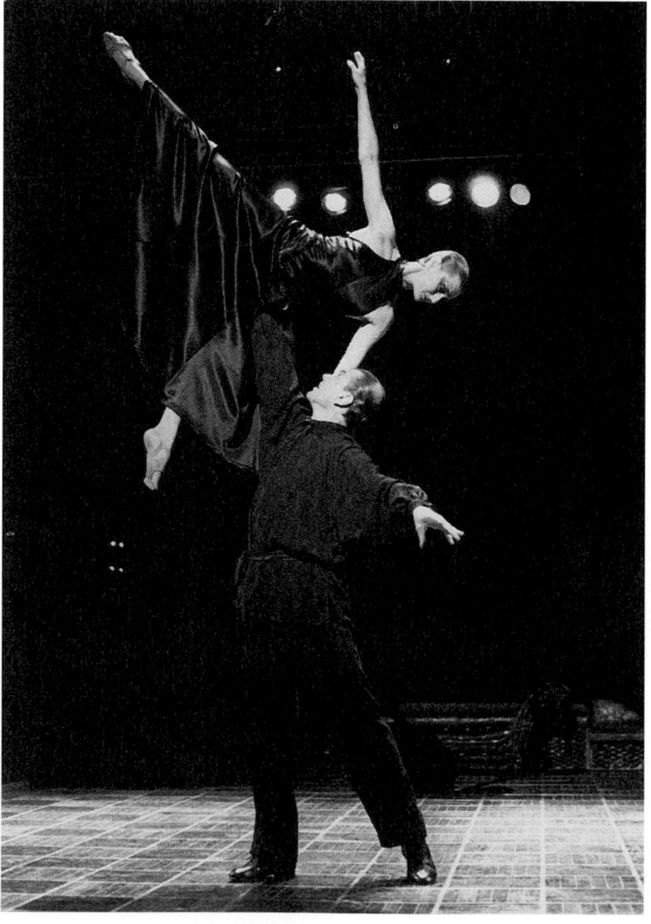

Other sources beyond Broadway also contributed to dance vitality in the 1990s. American Ballet Theatre acquired Lar Lubovich's *Ballet of the Red Shoes* from the ill-fated musical that closed after a handful of performances in December 1993 and added the piece to the company's spring 1994 season at the Metropolitan Opera House. In that year City Center began Encores!, concert productions of musicals from previous eras that might have limited audience appeal, yet represent significant milestones in the evolution of the American form. *Fiorello!*, featuring a high-stepping number by Christopher Chadman for Donna McKechnie, launched the series. The 1996 Encores! presentation of *Chicago* with Bob Fosse's original choreography, restaged by Ann Reinking, gained such a following that moves to the Richard Rodgers Theater and on to the Shubert Theater were necessary to accommodate crowds that had been missing in the original run in 1975. San Diego's Old Globe Theater brought a delightful revival of *Damn Yankees* to the Marquis Theater in 1994, with dances by Rob Marshall (who staged some of the numbers for *Kiss of the Spider Woman*, the 1993 Tony award for Best Musical), but without the distinguished Fosse choreography. A beautiful 1994 version of Rodgers and Hammerstein's *Carousel* at Lincoln Center's Vivian Beaumont Theater also appeared with some dances by Sir Kenneth MacMillan, yet minus the glorious work of Agnes de Mille. In a day of widespread notation, recording devices and living resources, it seems appropriate to treat a production's choreography with the same respect given to the score and book. While updating may be critical in some instances, in others—especially with regard to work by giants like de Mille and Fosse—re-exposure of the original choreography could prove enlightening to contemporary spectators.

For more than fifty years, Jerome Robbins has been an exalted creative presence in American musicals on stage and screen. His *Jerome Robbins' Broadway*, which opened at the Imperial Theater on 26 February 1989, featured a collection of his finest Broadway choreography mounted under his own supervision. From that production, *West Side Story Suite* entered the repertory of the New York City Ballet. Subsequent editions of his choreography were also seen in revivals that included *Fiddler on the Roof* (1990), *Gypsy* (1991), *Peter Pan* (1991), and *The King and I* (1995).

UNITED STATES OF AMERICA: Musical Theater. Savion Glover as Young Jelly and Gregory Hines as Jelly Roll Morton in the number "The Whole World's Waitin' to Sing Your Song" from the musical *Jelly's Last Jam* (1993). (Photograph by Martha Swope © Time, Inc.; used by permission.)

With a facility that may some day match Robbins's, Susan Stroman gained experience making dances in regional theater, on television, and for such New York City Opera enterprises as the 1991 production of *A Little Night Music*. She choreographed *Crazy for You* (a retake on George Gershwin's *Girl Crazy* that was the recipient of the 1992 Tony award for Best Musical), was also represented on Broadway by Jerome Kern's *Show Boat,* and has won Tony, Drama Desk, and Outer Circle recognition. Stroman made the dances for *Steel Pier* (24 April 1997), which centered on a 1933 dance marathon in Atlantic City. With a background similar to Stroman's, Lynne Taylor-Corbett choreographed *Titanic* (23 April 1997).

The New Forty-Second Street, a ten-year urban renewal project undertaken by the City of New York, implies a lively and changing profile for musical theater in Times Square. Following an $11.5 million renovation, the New Victory Theater opened on 11 December 1995 with a mandate to commission and to produce entertainment for children and families. On 29 April 1996, *Rent*—acclaimed as the most creative musical of the 1990s—opened one block away on Forty-first Street at the Nederlander Theater. In April 1997, Disney reopened Florenz Ziegfeld's fabled New Amsterdam Theater with *The Lion King* in a production for the stage by Julie Taymor, whose *Juan Darién* won critical praise during a short holiday run in 1996 at the Vivian Beaumont Theater. Another milestone in this undertaking, the Ford Center for the Performing Arts opened with a production of *Ragtime* on 26 December 1997. While a low point for dance on Broadway may have occurred when Stephen Sondheim's *Passion,* winner of the 1994 Tony for Best Musical, had no dancing at all, the direction for the twenty-first century points to increased collaboration among dance artists in commercial, film, and concert performance venues.

[*See also* Film Musicals, *article on* Hollywood Film Musicals; Tap Dance; Vaudeville; *and the entries on Astaire, Berkeley, Bernstein, Dunham, Hines, Holm, Kidd, McKayle, Martins, Primus, Tharp, and Tune.*]

BIBLIOGRAPHY

Block, Geoffrey. *Enchanted Evenings: The Broadway Musical from "Show Boat" to Sondheim.* New York, 1997.

Bordman, Gerald. *American Musical Theatre: A Chronicle.* New York, 1978.

Gänzl, Kurt. *The Encyclopedia of Musical Theatre.* 2 vols. New York, 1994.

Hardy, Camille. "Bessie Clayton: An American Genée." *Dance Chronicle* 2.4 (1978–1979): 251–278.

Hardy, Camille. "The American Debut of Adeline Genée." In *New Directions in Dance,* edited by Diana Theodores Taplin. Toronto, 1979.

Hardy, Camille. "Ballet Girls and Broilers." *Ballet Review* 1.1 (1980): 96–127.

Hardy, Camille. "Art Dancing on Broadway: Loie Fuller in *A Trip to Chinatown.*" In *Musical Theatre in America,* edited by Glenn Loney. Westport, Conn., 1984.

Kirstein, Lincoln, et al. *Choreography by George Balanchine: A Catalogue of Works.* New York, 1983.

Smith, Cecil, and Glenn Litton. *Musical Comedy in America.* 2d ed. New York, 1981.

Traubner, Richard. *Operetta: A Theatrical History.* Garden City, N.Y., 1983.

ARCHIVES. Dance Collection and Theater Collection, New York Public Library for the Performing Arts.

CAMILLE HARDY

Ballet Education

The teaching of classical ballet in the United States began around 1830. Before then, retired dancers occasionally took pupils, most often the children of theatrical families, to train in their own sitting rooms, and professional performers and ballet masters trained apprentices on dimly lit, off-duty theater stages. In 1837, Paul H. Hazard, a retired dancer trained at the Paris Opera, established a ballet school in Philadelphia. Augusta Maywood and Mary Ann Lee were among his first pupils. French-trained ballet dancers Jules Martin and Eugénie Lecomte (his sister) also opened a school in Philadelphia. Charles Durang, son of America's first native dancer, John Durang, added ballet to the ballroom dancing he and his wife taught in Philadelphia. Pauline Desjardins, a member of Fanny Elssler's company, remained after the 1841 tour to teach in New York. All through the 1840s, European ballet dancers toured America. Most of them took themselves and their dollars back across the Atlantic, but a few remained to teach French, fencing, and dance.

In 1852, Léon Espinosa, then twenty-seven years old and finished with his studies at the Paris Opera, was the ballet master for a troupe that danced a varied repertory for an entire season in the Varieties Theatre in Saint Louis, Missouri. Espinosa enlarged his company, teaching the Americans he recruited with a notice that read, "Young ladies wanted to dance in *La Bayadère.*" Giuseppina Morlacchi, trained at the Teatro alla Scala in Milan, came to New York in 1867 to dance in *The Devil's Auction,* and subsequently headed her own company. In the 1880s she taught in Lowell, Massachusetts. These teachers were all trained in the methods and traditions of the Paris Opera and Milan's La Scala with its roots in the codified technique of Carlo Blasis. Their students, however, were not motivated by anything beyond the elementary dance training needed for a career in the music halls. J. F. Cardella, who reported in an interview that he had studied with Blasis, was ballet master of the Theatre Comique in Saint Louis in 1879, where he directed and taught the locally recruited corps de ballet. He gave three-hour classes but deplored the lack of technique and noted that there was no "sideboard practice." Indeed, *barre* work was a rarity in American dance schools until the twentieth century.

A demand for female dancers developed when versions of *The Black Crook,* a musical extravaganza, proliferated and toured. Because badly trained female dancers were employed, the public gained an inaccurate idea of ballet. The original *Black Crook* ballerina, La Scala–trained Marie Bonfanti, opened a school in New York in 1897, where she taught until 1916. In the wake of *The Black Crook,* extravaganzas were popular and toured the country in the last decades of the nineteenth century. In 1876, Elizabeth Menzeli was the dance star of *Ali Baba.* She retired to teach in New York and New Jersey (and, much later, in Cleveland). The Bonfanti and Menzeli schools had stability, and ballet was taught in a manner consistent with academy traditions. To judge from pictures of the classes and the caliber of the students, their activities could honestly be regarded as classical ballet.

The political upheavals in Europe in the 1870s sent many immigrants to the United States. Among these were dance masters who brought with them the new educational idea of "aesthetic gymnastics." The new Americans established dancing academies in many cities, especially in the Midwest. They featured ballroom dancing and included drills and "fancy dancing," the latter being neither ballroom nor folk but a free form that had elements of ballet and *demi-caractère.* The clientele of these academies was middle class, and the dance masters were respected members of the community, socially notches above the theatrical "maestros" who were never part of the mainstream.

In 1879, the American Society of Professors of Dancing was formed, followed in 1883 by the American National Association of Dancing Masters (later Dancing Masters of America). At their annual conventions, ballroom dance trends were a major concern, but, aware of changing demands, the organizations also engaged experts to teach dances suitable for fancy dancing. Eventually, the need for instruction of technique was recognized, and the only technique known was that of classical ballet. Therefore, the organizations hired noted ballet masters such as Stefano Mascagno to teach the dance masters during the convention. For many years, Mascagno was "convention principal" of the Dancing Masters of America.

At these conventions some of the dancing masters acquired the fundamentals of ballet technique to bring back to their pupils in such cities as Omaha, Kansas City, Cincinnati, and Portland. Friedrich Albert Zorn's *The Grammar of the Art of Dancing* (1887) was the authoritative reference for terminology and technique. By 1930, members in the dance masters' organizations numbered in the hundreds and, although the classical ballet taught in their schools was limited and quite elementary, the associations invited fine teachers to serve on the convention faculties. Such artists as Michel Fokine, Adolph Bolm,

UNITED STATES OF AMERICA: Ballet Education. Young pupils of "Miss Dorothy" Lister in a demonstration class at the Joffrey Ballet School, New York, c.1980. (Photograph by Iris Fodor; courtesy of Jody Sperling.)

Muriel Stuart, and Catherine Littlefield planted seeds that later bore fruit.

New theories of child psychology and new ideas about physical education for girls developed at the turn of the century. Dance was recommended for both the naturally active child and for girls, who now attended high schools and colleges in greater numbers. "Normal" courses for teachers offered a dilute form of ballet with simple steps and positions; *jeté, arabesque,* and *pirouette* were taught with no *barre* work and nary a thought of placement. The subject matter was "material," that is, these were simple dances with no concern for technique. However, with the normal courses, dance attained a measure of respect in the educational world.

Inevitably, individual interest and ambition were aroused. Some pupils sought more exact training. They went to the professional dancing academies, where astute ballroom teachers included classical ballet in their offerings. The teachers of ballet classes were too often poorly prepared. Conditions were aggravated by cement-hard toe shoes. Toe dancing of an excruciatingly bad type discredited classical ballet.

However, a distinctly new type of American dance instructor developed: young women trained as physical education teachers who became deeply interested in dance, studied more, and gained honest perceptions of the art. They became excellent teachers, left the gymnasiums, and opened their own dance studios. Edna McRae of Chicago is a notable example.

To train dancers for opera ballets, the Metropolitan Opera Ballet in New York started a school in 1909, directed first by Malvina Cavallazzi, who taught ballet of a decent level. The Chicago and San Francisco operas had no official schools until the 1920s. However, when Andreas Pavley and Serge Oukrainsky became the ballet masters of the Chicago Grand Opera Company in 1916, they conducted their own school, which trained dancers for the opera ballet. As they expanded, many American teachers studied with them, especially in their summer quarters in South Haven, Michigan. The South Haven location was one of the first vacation-site dance schools, initiating a fashion for dance camps.

Classical training in the United States received its greatest impetus from Russian ballet. First came Anna Pavlova, whose dancing struck sparks wherever she appeared. The 1917 Russian Revolution led several noted ballet dancers to settle eventually in the United States, conduct classes in established schools, and found their own schools. These included Fokine, Bolm, Theodore Koslov, Mikhail Mordkin, and Bronislava Nijinska. They focused attention on classical ballet as an art.

From 1910 to 1930, opportunities for careers in dance attracted many students to dance schools. Vaudeville, which presented theatrical acts of many kinds, was America's most popular entertainment. The existence of several hundred vaudeville theaters in the land created a demand for performers, and ballet dancers, both excellent and mediocre, worked regularly. Another prime source of employment was the "stage show" or "prologue" presented between film screenings in dozens of magnificent new "cinema palaces." Many theaters hired ballet groups for year-round work, while others brought in touring units or shows that included ballet groups.

In the fall of 1933, Colonel W. de Basil's Ballets Russes de Monte Carlo appeared in New York and then toured the country. It toured annually, soon followed by the Littlefield Ballet, Lincoln Kirstein's Ballet Caravan, Ballet Theatre, and Serge Denham's Ballet Russe de Monte Carlo. These touring companies had a profound effect on the teaching of classical ballet. Inspired students came to ballet schools with ambitions to dance in companies. Though male students did not exactly flock to classes, the number studying classical ballet increased. More attention was paid to strengthening and purifying technique, particularly in the matter of turnout, line, and footwork. Virtuosity was encouraged. The practice costume changed. Gone were the tunics, tutus, bloomers, and rompers. Tights and leotards became the rule.

Of special significance was the founding of the School of American Ballet in 1934 under the direction of Lincoln Kirstein and George Balanchine with a faculty that included George Balanchine, Pierre Vladimiroff, and then Muriel Stuart, Anatole Oboukhoff, and Dorothie Littlefield, among others. The prime function of the school is the training of dancers for the New York City Ballet in the style developed by Balanchine. In the decades since its founding the faculty has been increased, especially with retired New York City Ballet dancers. The prestige of the school, the quality of the teachers, and the standards of technique affected the teaching of ballet, especially with new summer courses for dance teachers. At the School of American Ballet, more attention was paid to placement and turnout. Footwork was fastidious. Speed and suppleness were cultivated. Line became more elegant. Variations from classical repertory and supported adagio were taught, influencing scores of schools to do the same. There was a new selectivity of students: the petite feminine female was superseded by the sleek, long-limbed young woman with high extensions.

The School of American Ballet trains dancers in the Balanchine-approved style of dancing that company's repertory. Other companies have developed similar schools. Many ballets including the Joffrey, San Francisco, Boston, Houston, Pittsburgh, Tulsa, Colorado, and Milwaukee train students to perform in their companies.

Because of the expanding interest and respect for classical dance, ballet has been invited into U.S. colleges. An academic interest has legitimated the history of ballet and the philosophy of its styles. More surprising is the acceptance of ballet as a physical movement science to be taught by a knowledgeable faculty.

Ballet teachers in colleges often are retired dancers whose prestigious performing, directing, or choreographing careers are accepted as experience in lieu of the academic degrees required of most university faculty members. Notable among them have been Willam Christensen (University of Utah), George Verdak and William Glen (Butler University), Lawrence Rhodes (New York University), Elisabeth Carroll (Skidmore College), Jean-Pierre Bonnefous (Indiana University), Igor Youskevitch and Leon Danielian (University of Texas at Austin), George Zoritch (University of Arizona), Nicholas Petroff and Kenneth Johnson (Point Park College), and Carol Walker (succeeding Royes Fernandez at the State University of New York at Purchase).

Many performing artists have recently settled down as teachers. Their broad experiences, including dancing in ballets by several imaginative choreographers, are reflected in an eclectic style of ballet that recognizes many new elements. Increasingly lithe and freer torsos are emphasized, and some teachers cultivate greater virtuosity—multiple pirouettes, high extensions, and great jumps.

The faculty of the School of the Arts at the University of North Carolina, Chapel Hill, originally directed by Robert Lindgren, exemplifies many of these trends. Although they did not emphasize virtuosity, an appreciation of a wide range of ballet influences was taught by Bentley Stone and Walter Camryn, who conducted a school in Chicago for forty years and whose many students, now teachers, are carrying on these precepts. One of Camryn's innovative courses was American Character Dance, in which the gait and style of folk dances of several regions was taught. Among the teachers with original and eclectic styles have been Benjamin Harkarvy, Maggie Black, Carmelita Maracci, and Loyce Houlton. Eclecticism is common, but some do teach distinctive methods and styles. From England's Royal Ballet have come Margaret Craske in New York, Stanley Holden in California, Christine DuBoulay and Richard Ellis in Chicago, and several, such as Ben Stevenson in Houston, who conduct schools in connection with companies. The Bournonville style is not the sole one in any school as yet, but guests such as Kirsten Ralov and Kirsten Simone have introduced the style in several schools. The former Soviet style of Russian ballet, as distinct from the Imperial Ballet style of the first wave of Russians, was taught by Valentina Pereyaslavec and Alexander Mintz; with freedom to travel after the breakup of the Soviet Union in 1991, many Soviet-trained teachers came to the United States.

Modern dance has been finding ballet amenable and has in turn influenced classical ballet. Some of its elements were in the plastique exercises once presented by Muriel Stuart at the School of American Ballet. Many ballet schools now have special classes of modern dance. But more noteworthy is the fact that modern dance has influenced the range of classical ballet. Some teachers introduce subtle modifications into the execution of standard steps, and they also invent movements based on ballet technique that employ a more lithe torso and expressive arms.

The study of classical ballet has emerged from the sitting rooms and twilight theater stages of colonial times to large, airy studios with special floors and competent faculties. Hundreds of dedicated students perform their *pliés, battements tendus,* and so on—and not exactly in the same old ways.

BIBLIOGRAPHY. Ann Barzel, "European Dance Teachers in the United States," *Dance Index* 3 (April–June 1944): 56–100, is the only systematic history of classical training in America. But various articles and particularly the advertisements in dance teacher periodicals reveal a great deal about the teaching of ballet in America from the turn of the century. Some of these are *The Two Step* (Buffalo, N.Y., 1890s); *The Ballroom* (Kansas City,

Mo., 1896–1897); *The Dancing Master* (St. Joseph, Mo., 1900–1901); *Terpsichorean* (Chicago, c.1918–1920s); *The Dancing Master* (Chicago, 1920s); *Dance Lovers* (New York, 1920s); *The Dance* (New York, 1929–1931); *The American Dancer* (Calif. and New York, 1930s); and *Dance Magazine* (New York, 1940s–). The Newberry Library, Chicago, contains an extensive archive of such periodicals, as well as other dance memorabilia.

ANN BARZEL

Social, Folk, and Modern Dance Education

In the United States, dance training exists in general education, recreational, and professional contexts. Dance in general education has been important since colonial times with each era focusing on what would best reflect the predominant ideals of the day. Recreational dance has been enjoyed by people of all classes also from colonial times and may or may not involve formal training. The preparation of professional dancers for the stage, while introduced on a limited basis early in the nation's history, has proliferated in the twentieth century.

Ballroom dance, for example, was important to the colonial aristocracy and to succeeding social elites as well as those who aspired to them. Folk and popular dances were adapted to educational purposes in the wake of nineteenth-century democratization. Modern and creative dance came to the fore with middle-class progressive education of the twentieth century. Related, but not always parallel to general education curriculums, private teachers and specialized institutions have offered a range of techniques, including social dances; theatrical dance forms; and, to a lesser extent, dances from the international arena. Recreation departments and some religious organizations similarly have covered the gamut of dance genres but with emphasis on social and folk dance.

The development of dance education has been cumulative. By the 1980s all kinds of dance were being offered in the various settings. Popularity makes some genres more available at certain times than others, but in major urban areas classes in all types of dance are offered.

Social Dance. The colonists brought their social dances with them from the Old World, and by the late seventeenth century American society was sufficiently developed to support formal training in the art. Despite sporadic attacks by moralists, the urban and rural gentry followed European tradition and included dance in their children's education. Dance was justified in terms of educational functions: it fostered good carriage and gentle manners, instilled a sense of form in life, and prepared one to be an acceptable member of society.

Proper dance skill and behavior were taught by English, French, and American dance masters in pupils' homes, in taverns or other rented rooms, and in schools, colleges, and military academies. Basing his instruction on European theory and practice, the master taught his students the minuet, cotillon, rigaudon, hornpipe, and country dances, and he also served as master of ceremonies at balls. Colonial diaries, letters, wills, financial records, and newspapers contain numerous references to dance masters and dance occasions as well as some mentions of dance treatises.

Throughout the nineteenth century, social dancing continued to be a popular activity for all classes of Americans in every region. As the new nation grew, so did the number of dance teachers and schools to serve those who could afford such training: the wealthy, of course, and the growing middle class. Despite some opposition, social dancing was still promoted for training in grace and manners—and for its value as exercise. It continued to be offered in private schools and academies, but for many leaders in the burgeoning field of public education, it was frivolous, had an elitist orientation, and was suspected of posing a risk to public health and morals. When dance finally entered nineteenth-century public education, it was in the context of physical education; social aspects of the dance experience were minimized.

By the end of the nineteenth century, dance teaching was an established profession with organizations and a growing body of literature. With the founding in 1879 of the American Society of Professors of Dancing and of other national organizations, dance teachers gained a means of accreditation, a forum for the exchange of ideas and dances, and the strength of numbers to promote policies and standards. The publication of numerous articles and books by dance teachers also contributed to the respectability of the profession and to the level of knowledge and theory within it.

Important leaders in nineteenth-century dance education included Melvin Ballou Gilbert, Allen Dodworth, A. E. Bournique, and Carl Marweg. Gilbert (1847–1910) taught for forty years in New England, wrote books, and founded and edited *The Director* (1897–1898), one of the earliest known dance magazines in the United States. Gilbert was typical of his profession in that he taught not only ballroom dance but also related subjects, such as etiquette, stage and exhibition dancing, teaching methods, and what he called "aesthetic calisthenics."

Interest in social dance continued in the twentieth century, and the rapid succession of new dance fashions usually ensured the stability of social dance teaching as a profession. Also since many of the popular dances of the twentieth century were first danced on stage or screen in forms too difficult for the public, the professional teacher has profited from adapting such dances for general use. A temporary decline was suffered from the 1950s to the 1970s, however, when dance styles became improvisatory.

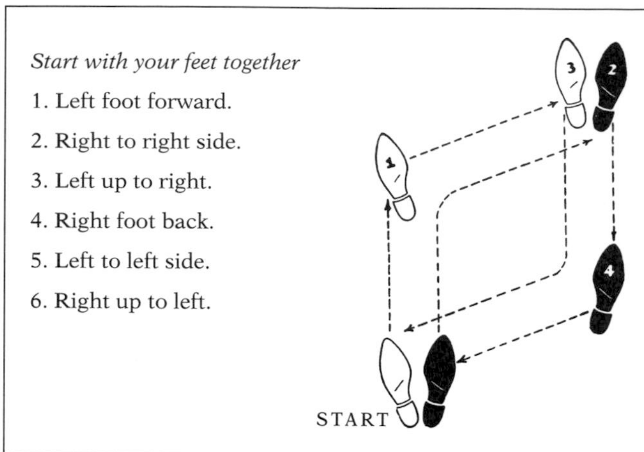

Start with your feet together
1. Left foot forward.
2. Right to right side.
3. Left up to right.
4. Right foot back.
5. Left to left side.
6. Right up to left.
START

UNITED STATES OF AMERICA: Social, Folk, and Modern Dance Education. Drawings of footprints were a signature part of Arthur Murray's instructional method, allowing students to learn dances on their own. The diagram here shows the box step of the rumba. (Reprinted from Arthur Murray, *How to Become a Good Dancer*, New York, 1947, p. 140.)

The twentieth-century social dance teacher taught in many contexts: secondary schools, in higher education, and for recreation departments, churches, and community centers. By far the most important setting has been the private studio or dance studio chain (such as those associated with Fred Astaire and Arthur Murray). In contrast to earlier times—when social graces were perceived as the concomitants of social dance skill—twentieth-century ballroom dance schools emphasized attractiveness to the opposite sex in their advertising.

In the late twentieth century, mature adults sought instruction in what were by then thought of as "classical" ballroom dances, such as the waltz, fox trot, and tango. Young people, in contrast, usually only wanted to learn what was new and popular. After nearly two decades of individual improvisation in the rock-and-roll era, young people in the late 1970s were drawn to dances that once again involved skill and coordination with a partner. Both disco dancing and country and western dances required instruction and practice. At the same time, young people developed a new interest in traditional ballroom dances and in certain "fad" dances of the past, such as swing, Lindy Hop, mambo, and cha-cha. As a consequence of both developments, the ballroom dance teacher regained importance in the social dance scene. [*For related discussion, see* Social Dance, *articles on nineteenth- and twentieth-century social dance.*]

From Gymnastics to Folk Dance. Physical education began to develop in the 1820s in tandem with public education, and it featured heavy gymnastics training for robust men and lighter programs for women, children, and sedentary men. The latter systems, as exemplified by Catharine Beecher's calisthenics and Dio Lewis's "New Gymnastics," were accompanied by music, but their creators disclaimed any relation to dancing. After 1865 heavy gymnastics for men began to include exercises that were based on folk dance steps. This "gymnastic dance" was eventually introduced into physical education training schools, and from there it made its way into the public school curriculum. Modern counterparts to such conditioning exercise set to music are jazzercise and aerobic dance.

From the 1880s onward, educators sought to adapt known dance material to educational goals. In these early years there was apparently no interest in presenting authentic folk or popular dances as cultural artifacts or artistic entities. Rather, selected patterns were extrapolated for their presumed effectiveness in physical training and conditioning. In 1887, for example, William G. Anderson introduced at his Brooklyn Normal School of Gymnastics a dance course incorporating step patterns he had learned from his study of Irish, Dutch, and southern black folk dances. In the same year, Dudley A. Sargent engaged Christian Eberhard of the Boston Turnverein to teach gymnastics dance at the Harvard School of Physical Education. Then, in 1894, Sargent introduced Gilbert's "aesthetic calisthenics" (later called "aesthetic dancing"), which was an adaptation of ballet, social, and folk dance steps and was widely used in women's physical education courses until approximately 1915.

After 1900 folk dance continued to be important in the curriculum. Specialists began to collect and notate actual dances from various nationalities. The material came to be valued educationally not only for its contribution to physical conditioning but also for the understanding it provided of different cultures and past eras. Early leaders of the folk dance movement, such as Elizabeth Burchenal, Mary Wood Hinman, and Louis Chalif, conducted research, published collections of dances, trained teachers, and were active in professional organizations.

Folk dance instruction takes place in various settings. In elementary education it is often tied in with multicultural studies and the production of festivals. The majority of U.S. colleges and universities have folk dance courses or clubs where dances are regularly taught. Churches or fraternal organizations with a national orientation—such as Greek, Armenian, or Russian—and synagogues often provide training to strengthen cultural identity, and the traditional dances usually are enjoyed by those of all ages at both religious and secular festivities. In addition a nationwide network of recreational folk dance clubs and organizations sponsors dance events and courses, publishes magazines, directories, and dance descriptions, and sets standards of teaching and authenticity. Teachers of folk dance include nonspecialists, such as elementary school teachers; international or area folk dance specialists who constantly increase their own repertory by attending special courses both in the United States and abroad; and native dancers who have inherited a folk dance tradition and teach solely from their own heritage.

Folk dance as it has been described herein is a social activity for the participants, not a display for observers. Character dance (balletic versions of folk dance patterns) was a part of ballet from its beginning, and dances with various national motifs were featured in popular stage entertainments. Only in the twentieth century were folk or ethnic dance ensembles established. Training for participation in an ensemble is specialized, rigorous, and performance-oriented and usually is conducted or at least supervised by the ensemble director. Although some of these ensembles are professional, most are amateur and connected with a university, church, recreation center, or national community group. A prominent example is the Duquesne University Tamburitzans, which is made up of young dancers and musicians who receive university scholarships in exchange for their participation.

Modern and Creative Dance. By the early twentieth century, dance was generating much interest among educators. In 1905 it was chosen as a theme for the American Physical Education Association's New York convention, which featured folk and popular dances and Gilbert's aesthetic dance. The cause of dance was taken up also by such figures as G. Stanley Hall, leading Darwinian educator and psychologist, who widened the perspective on dance by emphasizing that its benefits were not necessarily limited to the physical but could be psychological, intellectual, moral, and emotional as well.

With the progressive education movement that reached full development in the twentieth century came an emphasis on self-direction, self-expression, and creativity in the educational process. Seeking a more creative approach to dance, physical educators sought ideas from American Delsartism, Dalcroze eurhythmics, the dancing of Isadora Duncan, and the productions of Denishawn. They developed a kind of dance that was educational but included theatrical performance, emphasized expression but also included technique, and offered creative opportunities but also developed discipline.

The first influential figure in the new educational dance was Gertrude Colby of Teachers College, Columbia University. Active from 1913 to 1931, Colby trained hundreds of teachers in a nontechnical approach to movement expression that she called "natural dance." The most important center for the continuing development of what was new and progressive in educational dance was the University of Wisconsin at Madison. In 1917 Margaret H'Doubler began to work on an approach to educational dance based on scientific physical principles, a problem-solving instructional method, and a belief in the value of individual creativity. It was soon offered in a physical education course and then in a teacher-training program. Finally, in 1927, Wisconsin established the first dance major to be offered in an institution of higher education.

An important aspect of the Wisconsin program was Orchesis, a club first organized in 1918 to present performances in the new idiom. The result of learning and creativity was the finished dance piece—an art product. The Orchesis idea stimulated much interest among students in the new dance and spread to other institutions. Dance courses and Orchesis groups began to appear in colleges and universities throughout the country from the early 1920s on.

Since that time dance departments and major programs have proliferated in colleges and universities. The main offering has continued to be some form of modern dance, although the curriculum often includes other dance techniques, theory and history courses, notation, and related subjects. Some of the historically influential dance departments have been at Bennington College (Bennington, Vermont), Ohio State University (Columbus), Mills College (Oakland, California), Sarah Lawrence (Bronxville, New York), the University of California at Los Angeles, and, in the conservatory setting, at the Juilliard School in New York City.

Summer schools of dance have been particularly important in promoting modern dance along with other theatrical dance forms. The Bennington School of Dance (1934–1939), for example, offered instruction and new works by the great modern dance innovators such as Martha Graham and Doris Humphrey. Also important have been the American Dance Festival (first at Connecticut College), the Perry-Mansfield School, Jacob's Pillow, and the summer program at Colorado College under the direction of Hanya Holm. Countless teachers as well as performers have been trained in these programs. The consequent effect on dance education has been enormous, as the aesthetic principles, artistic standards, technical systems, and choreographic approaches of the professional dance world have been disseminated to educational institutions throughout the United States. [*See* American Dance Festival; Bennington School of the Dance; *and* Jacob's Pillow.]

From the beginning there has been a close collaboration between modern dance departments in higher education and professional modern dance artists. The professionals have depended on the universities for teaching stints and performance engagements, and the educators have valued the stimulus from the professional world—even though at times they have questioned how closely educational dance should emulate the professional. That question has receded, however, as professional training in the arts has gradually made a place for itself in the academic setting. As a result, dance departments have moved from physical education into the fine arts and have begun to train to professional standards and for professional careers.

Modern dance in higher education has been a nationwide phenomenon. The important and influential departments are scattered throughout the country, and there is a network of communication through organizations, publications, conferences, touring groups, visiting teachers, and changing personnel. The educational dance world has variety, optimism, dynamic growth, and artistic validity that makes it a significant element in the United States cultural scene.

Modern dance has been offered in other educational settings but to a lesser degree. Private studios offering modern dance can hardly exist outside of urban areas, such as New York or Boston. Modern dance, however, is often a part of high school physical education programs, some of which include the Orchesis type of public presentation. There are also a few professional performing arts high schools, the High School of Performing Arts in New York City, for example, where modern dance is featured. Creative children's dance, an offshoot of modern dance, is sometimes offered in primary schools, in recreation programs, or by private dance teachers.

At the end of the twentieth century, except among those communities whose religion forbids dancing, almost every American was in contact with some facet of dance education. In its many manifestations, training in dance has become a ubiquitous part of American culture.

[*See also* Delsarte System of Expression.]

BIBLIOGRAPHY

Casey, Betty. *International Folk Dancing U.S.A.* Garden City, N.Y., 1981.

Dancemagazine College Guide 1996–1997: A Directory to Dance in North American Colleges and Universities. New York, 1996.

Kraus, Richard, Sarah Chapman Hilsendagger, and Brenda Dixon. *History of the Dance in Art and Education.* 3d ed. Englewood Cliffs, N.J., 1991.

Marks, Joseph E., III. *America Learns to Dance: A Historical Study of Dance Education in America before 1900.* New York, 1957.

O'Brien, Dorothy Adella. "Theoretical Foundations of Dance in American Higher Education, 1885–1932." Ph.D. diss., University of Southern California, 1966.

Rogers, Frederick R., ed. *Dance: A Basic Educational Technique.* New York, 1941.

Ruyter, Nancy Lee Chalfa. *Reformers and Visionaries: The Americanization of the Art of Dance.* New York, 1979.

NANCY LEE CHALFA RUYTER

Dance Research and Publication

As in most other countries, dance scholars in the United States began with enthusiasm and learned their skills along the way. As late as the 1930s, American universities offered no courses in dance history, and those libraries that possessed a few serious books on dance shelved them next to treatises on other "physical" activities, such as basketball and swimming, where casual researchers would hardly be likely to discover them.

But in 1928, Lillian Moore, then a young dancer with the Metropolitan Opera Ballet, found her way to the New York Public Library and between rehearsals began investigating her professional heritage. After old newspapers and magazines yielded their treasurers to her, she traveled to find descendants of legendary performers and sought out long-forgotten names and dates on long-neglected gravestones. Although she did not live to complete her comprehensive history of American dance, her individual studies in Americana remain invaluable, as do her essays on styles of ballet technique. [*See the entry on* Moore.]

Also in the 1920s, a young graduate of Harvard had discovered the ballet. Lincoln Kirstein involved himself in many forms of art as producer, director, and writer but still found time to publish America's first major book of dance history in 1935. From the beginning he favored classical ballet—its discipline, clarity, and purity. In later books he continued his proselytizing as he developed his early themes with fervor and erudite brilliance. [*See the entry on* Kirstein.]

Countering Kirstein's preference for ballet, John Martin promoted the new modern dance, not only in the pages of the *New York Times* but also in books, such as *The Modern Dance* (1933), that allowed him to probe more deeply into the nature of this expressive style and into the kinesthetic experience of its audience. Martin was the first American to formulate a theory of dance based on its communicative powers and, as such, deserves more attention than he has received from aestheticians. From 1934 to 1937 Martin taught a course in dance history at the Bennington School of the Dance in Vermont. [*See the entry on* Martin.]

Paul Magriel's pioneering effort in documenting American dance, *A Bibliography of Dancing,* was published in 1936, but few serious dance books appeared in the 1930s and 1940s. The field was not ready for them.

The dance audience was growing, however, and in time the fan books began to appear—ballet stories, elementary technique manuals, picture books, and biographies full of adulation but often lacking accurate, factual information. *Dance Magazine* (then titled *The American Dancer*), the oldest and long the most popular dance publication, began in 1927 under the aegis of Ruth Eleanor Howard. At first focused on the needs of the teacher and later of the performer, the periodical soon sought to serve the dance audience as well by offering reviews. *Dance News,* started in 1942 by Anatole Chujoy, who was later joined by P. W. Manchester, favored an elitist, ballet-oriented readership; although concerts in other dance forms were reviewed, they were not featured. For future historians these early publications would provide significant insights into America's attitude toward theatrical dance in the early decades of the twentieth century. A beginning had been made.

As the dance audience grew in size, it became more heterogeneous. New members of that audience—teachers and scholars working in such fields as art, music, and theater history—were disappointed to find so little academic discipline applied to their new area of interest. Unable to find the books they wanted, they set out to write their own. Musicologists explored the dances of the Middle Ages and the Renaissance. Some mavericks appeared: a professor of ancient Greek, Lillian Lawler, produced the authoritative study of Grecian dance, *The Dance in Ancient Greece* (1954); a nun, Sister Mary Grace Swift, wrote the authoritative biography of Charles-Louis Didelot, *A Loftier Flight* (1973).

The group of dancers interested in dance history grew as well and, in time, they had more opportunities to pursue their interests. By the mid-1990s more than one hundred American colleges and universities offered at least a one-year survey course in dance history, and many had graduate courses. The University of Chicago pioneered graduate study with three summer seminars from 1974 to 1976. York University in Toronto, Canada, was the first to offer a continuing graduate program, initiated in 1971 by Grant Strate. Christena Schlundt established a master's degree curriculum at the University of California, Riverside, in 1981; a Ph.D. program was launched there in 1993. New York University also began to offer degrees in dance through its departments of education and performance studies.

Although extensive interest in dance scholarship is of recent origin, enterprising individuals have been sponsoring serious periodicals for some time. In 1934 Louis Horst founded the *Dance Observer,* a monthly magazine devoted primarily to modern dance. The magazine survived until Horst's death in 1964. Although it consisted largely of reviews, some theoretical and analytical articles appeared as well; a notable contribution was "Symbolism and the Dance" by mythologist Joseph Campbell. From 1942 to 1948 Lincoln Kirstein, assisted for some years by Marian Eames, edited *Dance Index,* which presented the results of important historical research and original theorizing, most of it devoted to classical ballet. In its seven years of publication, only a single issue—the last in the entire series of monthly monographs—was devoted to non-Western dance: Colin McPhee's "Dance in Bali."

Dance Perspectives (1959–1976) also published monographs. Founded by A. J. Pischl and edited by Selma Jeanne Cohen, the quarterly journal covered a wider range than had *Dance Index* and devoted one issue each year to a form of ethnic dance. It also produced several symposium-like issues, such as those on music for dance, dance films, and dance aesthetics. *Ballet Review* (1965–), edited first by Arlene Croce and later by Francis Mason, has specialized in well-written, often provocative, articles dealing with contemporary issues and performances.

Dance Research Journal has been published by the Congress on Research in Dance since 1974. Its early issues, co-edited by Lois Andreasen and Elizabeth Burtner, concentrated on educational and ethnological subjects. In the 1980s the scope widened to cover theatrical dance. Since its founding in 1977, *Dance Chronicle,* which is focused on Western theatrical dance, with forays into music and scene design, has been co-edited by Jack Anderson and George Dorris. Although *Ballet News* (1979–1986) was devoted largely to reviews, editor Karl Reuling managed to produce some special issues dealing with historical context, as in the issue devoted to the August Bournonville centennial.

As interest in dance developed, more periodicals were produced. Among them was *Studies in Dance History,* a biannual series of monographs, initiated in 1990 by the Society of Dance History Scholars and first edited by Barbara Palfy. Most of the issues have been devoted to in-depth research of areas of Western theatrical dance. Two provocative journals dealing with the contemporary dance scene are *Dance Ink,* edited by Lise Friedman from 1990 to 1996, and *Dance View,* edited by Alexandra Tomalonis since 1992.

American dance historians have made their primary contributions in the area of fact-finding. The methodologies that were initially applied to dance research evolved from other disciplines. The first model came from anthropologists who incorporated analyses of dances into their investigations of ethnic groups. A prominent example was Ruth Benedict's *Patterns of Culture* (1934). What followed were studies that concentrated on the role of dance in particular societies. The acknowledged American pioneer in this field was Gertrude Prokosch Kurath, who, beginning in the 1940s, published numerous works on Native Americans.

Most of those who followed concentrated on particular ethnic areas, seeking through direct observation, as well as through the study of documents and artifacts, to determine the original purposes and structures of the dances of a society and then to pursue their history and development. This field grew with increasing vigor in the 1980s; both dancers and anthropologists were attracted to the tasks of refining research techniques and extending the areas of exploration.

Less formal in their methodology, many folk dance researchers have based their studies on seeing and performing the recreational dances of many lands. Fascinated by discoveries of cross-cultural themes, they have also sought the specific movement flavor of individual cultures and countries. Mary Ann Herman wrote extensively on pervasive patterns and their national variations.

Growing numbers of scholars are concerned with dances of the past. Using notated records (when they exist), technical manuals, costume designs, and written commentaries, these researchers have sought out contemporary clues not only to steps but also to performance styles. In addition to writing about their discoveries, they perform them: for example, Ingrid Brainard's group does European court and urban dances of the fifteenth to eighteenth centuries, and Catherine Turocy leads the New York Baroque Dance Company.

In 1973 Dance Perspectives Foundation established the de la Torre Bueno Prize, honoring the late J. R. de la Torre Bueno, who founded the dance book program at Wesleyan University Press. The prize is awarded annually for what is judged the best work of dance scholarship published in the preceding year. Other university presses have also become increasingly interested in the subject. Important books from the past have been reprinted by Dance Horizons, whereas the Princeton Book Company has published both historical treatises and technical guides for young readers.

In the 1990s an important move was made toward interdisciplinary approaches to dance scholarship. Viewed within the contexts of culture or gender studies, dance takes on new kinds of significance. [*See, for example,* Methodologies in the Study of Dance, *article on* New Areas of Inquiry.] It has also gained respect in academia, where scholars in other disciplines have discovered that dance can provide them with sources of fresh insights relevant to their own fields. Journals published by the American Society for Aesthetics, the Society for Ethnomusicology, and the American Society for Theatre Research frequently publish articles on dance. In 1996 the Society of Dance History Scholars became the first dance organization to be admitted to membership in the American Council of Learned Societies.

The comprehensive history of American dance that Lillian Moore had been planning has yet to be written. Now, however, that history may take a number of forms, each viewing its subject from a different perspective, within a different context, and reaching an audience larger than earlier writers would ever have imagined.

[*For repositories and locations of major collections, see* Libraries and Museums.]

SELMA JEANNE COHEN

Contemporary Criticism

American dance criticism developed in tandem with the emergence of dance as a performing art, to be considered as refined and richly varied as were music and drama. Few indications remain of how professional writers viewed staged dance in the 1790s, fifty years after the first recorded performance of ballet in America. Ballet was a very popular entertainment, however, with French ballet dancers performing on theatrical circuits from Boston to New Orleans. Their activities can be charted in brief newspaper items on performers, upcoming performances, duels, and deaths; in the letters to the editor from critical readers; and in the detailed advertisements that appeared in the newspapers of the nine major touring cities. Actual reviews tended to be "vague and pretty and not at all definite," as dance historian Lillian Moore observed of American dance reviewing in the mid-nineteenth century. "Madam Gardie . . . gave us a delight altogether new," *New York Magazine* reported in a review of a 1794 performance by Anna Gardie, the first ballet star to appear in the United States. "Her face, figure, and action were . . . prepossessing beyond any example on our stage." Boston critics observed that Gardie had "a certain something in her action and expression, which ravishes the senses," and they delighted in the ballerina's power "to melt, to fascinate, and astonish." Perhaps these were, after all, critical enough responses to dance performed generally for simple amusement and entertainment.

Gardie's murder in 1794 was reported in every newspaper in cities along the circuit, and ballet would not receive quite such widespread publicity until the mid-nineteenth century, when the European soloist Fanny Elssler swept through the United States on a wave of adulation. Although the level of ballet dancing had declined at the beginning of the nineteenth century, new European touring companies soon arrived, most notably those of Eugénie Lecomte and Paul and Amalia Taglioni, whose popularity among Americans was enhanced by the news that they were related to the great soloist Marie Taglioni. If the Taglionis noted with disgust the low quality of corps dancers they were forced to enlist on their American tour, so did the writers of the time. Nevertheless, the 1830s were a time of renewed popularity for ballet in America. "Why cannot the ballet be attached permanently to our theaters?" an anonymous critic wrote plaintively in 1839, in the *Spirit of the Times;* it was one of several popular theater journals then published in New York City, each with regular commentary on dance in America and abroad. Reviews from the 1830s show an increased awareness of "the scientific quality and brilliant execution" of ballet, as a reviewer of the ballet *La Fille Mal Gardeé* put it in 1838, in Philadelphia's *Public Ledger,* casually using such technical terms as pas de deux and pirouette.

Americans were thus ready to see—and write about—Elssler when she arrived in 1840. No dancer of her caliber had yet performed in the United States, and she was greeted with incessant, gossipy publicity of a kind not repeated in the nation until the arrival of Anna Pavlova in 1910. Some American writers pressed the "peerless Fanny" to their readers' hearts through breathless exclamations, but others described her dancing with the sense of occasion and poetics that existed in English and French dance writing of the time. The critic of New York's *Evening Post,* for example, compared Elssler to Taglioni in vivid but telling prose. Critics became sufficiently confident and well versed in the art of ballet to suggest, in reviews in New York publications, that a visiting foreign star limit himself to comic rather than Romantic-hero roles and to write about improvements in the technique of various young American dancers or to compare them favorably with foreign visitors

The long success of *The Black Crook* (1866)—an American extravaganza that was performed continuously into the early twentieth century—and its vaudevillian successors helped revive the American puritanical spirit that had objected to stage dancing a century before. At the same time, the style of much mid-nineteenth-century dance writing cheapened, wavering among the empty praise of earlier years, pompous declamations, and what read like perfumed parodies of Théophile Gautier. With a few exceptions, writing on dance would not take itself seriously in America until the late 1920s, when it began to become the specialized (if poorly remunerated) profession it would be by the end of the century.

Early in the twentieth century, foreign ballet flourished in the United States, when highly popular tours by Anna Pavlova and the Ballets Russes de Serge Diaghilev drew sensational, innocently idolatrous, and even serious coverage from U.S. newspapers and journals. The Metropolitan Opera Company, founded in 1883, offered a continuous dance presence throughout the early years of the twentieth century. Isadora Duncan and Ruth St. Denis also performed in America during the century's first decade, and their innovative work initiated the stirrings of a new American dance that would require new scrutiny and new sympathy from the music, drama, feature, and sports writers who commonly served as dance reviewers. An iconoclastic modern dance pioneer named Martha Graham gave her first solo recital in New York City in 1926, and ballet created and performed by Americans began to come into its own in the 1930s.

There were music and drama critics who wrote perceptively and intelligently about dance, among them H. T. Parker of the *Boston Evening Transcript* (1904–1934), Carl Van Vechten of the *New York Times* (1906–1907 and 1910–1913), Alfred Frankenthaler of the *San Francisco Chronicle*, and Cecil Smith of both the *Chicago Daily Tribune* and *Theatre Arts Monthly*. Claudia Cassidy, who succeeded Smith at the *Tribune* in 1942, brought notoriety to dance in Chicago through her acid but very popular reviews.

Van Vechten, the nation's first acknowledged critic of dance, wrote about dance events of the early twentieth century with sophisticated enthusiasm, knowledge, and a poetically evocative style, and he thereby played an important part in the creation of public taste. Mary F. Watkins of the *New York Herald Tribune* (1927–1934) became the nation's first full-time dance critic employed on a daily newspaper, switching from music to dance a few weeks before the hiring of John Martin at the *New York Times* in 1927. Martin, whose tenure at the *Times* did not end until 1962, established dance criticism as a profession. That seal was set in 1976, when dance critic Alan Kriegsman, who had been at the *Washington Post* since 1966, was awarded the Pulitzer Prize for criticism.

Watkins brought a distanced eye and a tart, polished writing style to dance criticism. Martin saw himself as an educator, helping in particular to explain the unfamiliar art of modern dance to early audiences and encouraging young dance revolutionaries to form their own choreographic styles. His successor, Allen Hughes, who was at the *Times* only until 1965, brought a similarly open mind to the early experimentation of postmodernism. For many years dance critics perceived their primary responsibility as one of education and advocacy, a position exemplified in the work of Margaret Lloyd of the *Christian Science Monitor* (1936–1960).

Walter Terry—critic for the *Boston Herald* (1936–1939), the *New York Herald Tribune* (1939–1942 and 1945–1967), the *World Journal Tribune* (1967–1968), and the *Saturday Review/World* (1968–1982)—was dance's popularizer. Like Martin and most of the critics who followed him, Terry had had some training in dance. Also like Martin, he wrote prolifically on dance in reviews, features, and books and lectured extensively throughout the United States. Terry's genial style, which made him an exceptionally popular public figure both in the United States and abroad, was characterized by a high level of enthusiasm that occasionally masked the abundance of firsthand knowledge he brought to his work. Clive Barnes, also a popularizer, wrote for the *New York Times* from 1965 to 1977, then joined the *New York Post*. Reversing the traditional process, Barnes became the *Times*'s drama critic in 1967, bringing a consequent celebrity as well as a witty style to his reviewing. He was succeeded as dance critic by Anna Kisselgoff, who had been at the *Times* since 1968. Her reviews were distinguished by their sense of the historical context of a given dance event.

Although generally plainspoken and optimistic, American dance criticism has had its idiosyncratic stylists, most notably B. H. Haggin of the *Hudson Review* (1958–1972) and Jill Johnston, who covered postmodernist dance for the *Village Voice* in the 1960s. It has had its essayists, too. Arlene Croce, who joined the *New Yorker* in 1974, stood out for her rigorous, meditative writing that addressed both the event and the field itself from the viewpoint of an informed observer. George Beiswanger of *Theatre Arts Monthly* (1939–1944) and the *Atlanta Journal* (1967–1972) offered journalistic analyses that were particularly thoughtful. Equally thoughtful was the work of Nancy Goldner, whose analytical reviews and features for a number of nondance publications in the 1970s and 1980s revealed both an extrinsic and an intrinsic knowledge of dance.

Edwin Denby of *Modern Music* (1936–1942) and the *New York Herald Tribune* (1942–1945) was, along with Martin and Terry, a dean of American dance criticism. Dancer, choreographer, and poet, Denby was the influential founder of the intrinsic school of criticism. He brought to reviewing a vivid sense of how it feels to move through space, the ability to describe that, and the objective analysis of ballet in technical, stylistic, and psychological terms. More explicitly a critic with a highly developed sense of kinetic empathy was Deborah Jowitt of the *Village Voice,* who, beginning in 1967, brought to reviewing the perceptions of a former dancer and choreographer.

Jowitt and Marcia B. Siegel have been influential in training dance reviewers—first in private, informal classes that the two taught in the late 1960s and later through seminars conducted at the various critics' conferences that flourished briefly across the nation during the "dance boom" years of the 1970s. The most established of these seminars, the Critics Conference of the American Dance Festival, grew out of a dance festival course taught by Selma Jeanne Cohen in 1967. Still held each summer, the conference first convened in 1970 under the aegis of the Dance Program of the National Endowment for the Arts.

Dance of new and greater variety was touring nationally in the 1970s, under the auspices of the endowment's Dance Touring Program; regional dance companies, particularly ballet, then flourished and became important alternatives to performing in the nation's urban dance capitals. The conference worked to train regional critics to respond with sophistication to this proliferation of dance, some of it new and unfamiliar. By the 1980s, dance criticism had become a highly specialized profession. Critics shared a body of knowledge that was once unimaginable and they had begun to meet yearly at conferences conducted in New York City by the Dance Critics Association, a national group formed in 1974. Increasingly, dance criticism became part of university dance curricula.

Landmarks in U.S. dance publishing had been John Martin's *The Modern Dance* (1933) and *The Dance Encyclopedia* (1949). Dance books proliferated in the 1980s and were regularly reviewed in the national and dance media; opportunities for the study of dance history became available at the Dance Collection of the New York Public Library and other archives. Numerous specialty publications—the oldest and most popular is *Dance Magazine,* which dates from 1926—offer reviews, news, and historical features. Critics of major newspapers across the country were regularly expected to contribute interviews and essays to them on the dance. More and more, dance was preserved on film, most popularly in the Public Broadcasting Service (PBS) series *Dance in America,* which brought dance to vast national audiences beginning in 1975.

During this heyday of dance writing, the movement was away from the traditional, judgmental role of the critic and toward the attempt to report objectively on movement in dance, emphasizing choreography over performance and description over overt analysis. By the end of the 1980s, dance criticism had become more institutionalized and dance critics generally brought more specialized cultural perspectives to the field than did the music and drama writers of previous decades. Jobs for dance critics continued to be scarce in America, and writers outside the nation's biggest cities often found themselves having to adopt, once again, the roles of advocates and educators, which had been so much a part of the earlier dance criticism.

Once again, dance writing had thrived with the prospering fortunes of American dance; yet by the early 1990s, the scene had begun to change drastically, both for dance and dance writing. Increased cutbacks in government funding for dance were followed by the cutbacks and revamping of private aid, especially for programs that advocated crossover dance—dance that blurred the distinctions between classical ballet and modern dance. Most major American dance institutions struggled to survive. Newspapers did, too, as electronic media (television and interactive computers) became the media of choice. With general staff cutbacks and retirements, the number of jobs for dancers and dance writers decreased. By the late 1990s, the *New York Times* was the only national newspaper still to have full-time staff critics whose sole job was to write about dance.

Dance publishing in the 1990s, both of books and general dance periodicals, also decreased. University critical writing courses, like the dance departments, were being phased out. The scarcity of places to publish thinned the ranks of the new generation of dance writers. At the same time, however, new (but unpaid) possibilities emerged on the Internet for dance writing, from the simple publicizing of dance events to reviews and features. By the late 1990s, even small dance institutions had their own websites, and information about dance could be shared within minutes with readers throughout the world.

Writing for Dance Online was still unpaid by 1997, two years after the start of this pioneering major dance website. Nevertheless, the new electronic media promise new ways of looking at and studying dance; the potential also exists for the development of a new generation of dance writers whose shorter reviews, relatively informal personal styles, and international readership should bring profound changes to the field of dance criticism.

JENNIFER DUNNING

UNIVERSITY OF CAPE TOWN BALLET. *See* CAPAB Ballet.

URUGUAY. The Republic of Uruguay was a Spanish colony in South America until independence in the early 1800s; it has about 72,000 square miles (187,000 square kilometers) located on the Rio de la Plata between Brazil to the northeast and Argentina to the southwest. Its population, some 3.1 million, mainly Roman Catholics, is about 90 percent of European descent. There has been no indigenous population since the late nineteenth century, when mass European immigration began (to serve the grazing and meat-packing industries). The Europeans are mainly Spanish and Italian but also German, eastern European, and British. The other 10 percent of the population are of African descent, mulattos (mixed European and African), and *mestizos* (mixed European and Native American). The capital city of Montevideo is the major cultural center, where more than half the people live.

Folk Dance. In 1943 the eminent musicologist Lauro Ayestaran began collecting Uruguayan folk dances and classifying them in four major categories. The four thousand field recordings he made, now in the Museo Histórico Nacional in Montevideo, reveal that the music of the old European dances has been preserved in Uruguayan folk tradition. Ayestaran's wife, Flor de María Rodriguez de Ayestaran, was able to reconstruct twenty dances by using various archival sources. In 1973 she founded the Ballet Folklórico del Uruguay, which has made Uruguayan folk dances better known both within the country and abroad and has won her many prizes. In 1977 she established the Ballet Flor de Ceibo, which is sponsored by both Uruguay's Ministry of Culture and the Argentine embassy in Uruguay; it also performs in Argentina. In all nineteen of the departments (provinces) of Uruguay there are "nativist societies" working to preserve the "native" colonial culture. All have folk dance groups specializing in dances of the Rio de la Plata region.

In 1975 the Ministry of Education and Culture established the National Dance School in Montevideo, with two sections: ballet, under the direction of Margaret Graham, and folklore, under the direction of Flor de María Rodríguez de Ayestaran. The school trains dancers and dance teachers from the nation's secondary schools. Unfortunately, no dance is taught at the university level, even as an extracurricular subject.

Uruguay has an African minority that dances the *candombe,* the country's only "living" folk dance. This African-Uruguayan dance originated in Montevideo and is the only one of its kind in the Rio de la Plata region. *Candombe* characters still dance in the streets and in nightclubs in the city. During Carnival there is a parade called Llamadas ("calls") in which descendants of African slaves dance while drums beat continuously. The *candombe*'s standard characters are La Mama Vieja (The Old Mother), El Escobero (The Broom Man), El Gramillero (A kind of witch doctor), La Dama Joven (The Young Woman), and the Vedette, a glamorous female character who entered the repertory in the 1940s because of the popularity of Josephine Baker, the beautiful African-American entertainer who performed in Paris nightclubs.

Other ethnic communities also have dance groups in Uruguay. Dances from the different regions of Spain are represented by the groups of Rosario Penalver, Lydia Revilla, Spikerman Reyno, Pepe Montoya, and other ensembles. There are Italian, Tyrolese, Scottish, Yugoslavian (the Balkan states), and Jewish folk dance groups; particularly noteworthy is the Lithuanian ensemble Azuolinas, under the direction of J. A. Stanevicius, which has performed successfully in the United States and Canada. The Indio-American Folklore Association collects Native American folk dances from all of Latin America.

SODRE Ballet. Uruguay has a state ballet that operates under the auspices of the state radio system, SODRE (Servicio Oficial de Difusión Radio Eléctrica). The radio system was established in 1929, its ballet in 1935. The SODRE Ballet was first led by the Uruguyan Alberto Pouyanne, then by numerous directors of international repute, including Gala Shabelska, Tamara Grigorieva, Vaslav Veltchek, Roger Fenonjois, Alexander Sakharoff, and Clotilde Sakharoff. The Pole Yurek Shabelevsky directed the SODRE Ballet from 1954 to 1957, and from 1965 to 1980 it was under the direction of the Argentine Eduardo Ramírez. In 1980 the *prima ballerina* Margaret Graham assumed directorship; then, following a short interval in which the Argentine Amalia Lozano was in charge, the Uruguayan José Brum was appointed director in 1982.

The SODRE Ballet has had no home since a fire destroyed its theater in 1973. As a result, it is unable to have long seasons and is generally scheduled to take advantage of available dates at other state theaters, which are, however, unsuitable for dance performances. The SODRE Ballet also performs outdoors during summer seasons and tours the country. Its international repertory includes *Giselle, Les Sylphides,* act 2 of *Swan Lake,* the pas de deux from *Le Corsaire* and *Don Quixote, Aurora's Wedding, Boléro, Capriccio Espagnol, La Fille Mal Gardée, The Firebird, The Duel,* and *Graduation Ball.* These works alternate with choreographies by Amalia Lozano, Tito Barbon, Margaret Graham, Adriana Coll, and Eduardo Ramírez, and the Uruguayans Elsa Vallarino, Domingo Vera, and Alejandro Godoy. Worthy of mention is the Uruguayan choreographer Violeta López Lomba, whose *Contemporary Suite* was first performed in 1959, to music by Héctor Tosar. Although not performed again and ceasing to be part of the usual repertory, this piece is significant as a relevant work by the pioneer of Uruguayan contemporary dance, who died in 1968.

Vilen Galstian came to the SODRE Ballet from the Soviet Union in 1986 and 1987 to stage productions of *Don Quixote, Giselle,* and *Gayané.* In 1986 Alberto Alonso came from Cuba to choreograph the new ballet *Delmira Agustini,* based on Uruguayan themes; and Uruguayan choreographer Domingo Vera went to Cuba to stage his *Retrato* (Portrait), based on songs of Edith Piaf.

In 1988 the Cuban teacher Lydia Díaz became director of the SODRE Ballet. During her tenure the company staged several works by the Cuban Gustavo Herrera, one of which, *Candomballet,* used both academic dance and African folk dance. During this time also, Romanian choreographer Gheorghe Caciuleanu produced three important ballets, *The Four Seasons* (1988) to music by Vivaldi, *Symphonie Fantastique* (1989) to music by Berlioz, and *Mozartissimo* (1991) to music by Mozart.

Since 1994, the SODRE Ballet has been directed by the Cuban teacher Olga Madan Vera. She has presented a new version of *Les Sylphides,* based on choreography by Alicia Alonso, and a series of renowned pas de deux. Uruguayan choreographer Domingo Vera presented *Canto Hondo a España* in 1992 and *Gloria* in 1995 (to music by Vivaldi), both with the SODRE Ballet. SODRE House is being rebuilt; this began in 1995, to be completed about 1999. Until completion, the ballet continues to work out of its provisional home.

Independent Groups. Violeta López Lomba, student of Alexander and Clothilde Sakharoff, was one of the first people in Uruguayan dance to come into contact with North American contemporary dance. During that period, the 1950s, independent groups devoted to new dance genres began to appear.

The first of these, DALICA (Danza Libre de Cámara, or Free Chamber Dance), directed by the dancer, choreographer, and painter Elsa Vallarino, was founded in 1957. Since then it has performed in uninterrupted seasons throughout the country. It has its own dance school. Vallarino has made many trips to the United States, Brazil, Costa Rica, and other countries. Some of her students are now part of the SODRE Ballet or have formed their own small dance groups abroad. Her dance often uses themes from popular music, and on several occasions she has presented choreographies with Uruguayan musicians playing on stage.

The Ballet de Cámara de Montevideo (Montevideo Chamber Ballet) has been directed since its founding in 1958 by Hebe Rosa. At first the group danced in a neoclassical style, but Rosa, influenced by German dance technique and by José Limón, turned to expressionist choreography, although her dance school still includes ballet in its curriculum.

The Taller Mouret (Mouret Workshop) gave its first performance in 1966 under the direction of Iris Mouret, formerly with the Ballet de Cámara. It maintains the expressionist tendency of the latter both in its performances and in its dance school.

The Teatro Danza Company (Dance Theater Company) was founded in 1968. Its first performance was *Danza, Luz, Sonidos* (Dance, Light, Sound), under the direction of Julia Gade and her husband, José Claudio. An experimental group, it incorporates all branches of theater and is producing video performances. The style of Teatro Danza is personal, achieving an integration of balance, sound, and silences in purely regional abstract works. It has performed throughout Uruguay and in Argentina. Since 1974 the artist Fernando Álvarez Cozzi has been a third creative member of the group and has contributed films, slides, and video recordings. In 1978 the group opened a contemporary dance school to promote its experimental work.

Grupo Moebius was formed in 1974 under the direction of Cristina Martínez. It performs contemporary and experimental dance and also operates a school. Grupo Gestus is an expressionistic group created by the former SODRE ballerina María Minetti. Its first performance took place in 1980.

Group Concertante de Balle (Ballet Concert Group) is the only academic dance group independent of the state. Under the direction of former SODRE Ballet director Eduardo Ramírez, it has its own repertory, which is performed by pupils of its own school together with SODRE's star dancers.

On 1 March 1985 Julio María Sanguinetti was elected president of Uruguay, ending almost twelve years of military dictatorship. The new political situation stimulated developments in the arts, and independent dance prospered with the return of artists who had left Uruguay during the period of the dictatorship. Choreographers Ema Häberli and Numen Vilariño have created the Center of Contemporary Art in Montevideo. Teresa Trujillo, the modern dance teacher, has returned from Europe. Florence Varela, influenced by both American and German modern dance, founded the Contradanza Group. Dancers from several schools joined together to form the Babinka Group. Babinka and Contradanza merged in 1991, and work under the name Contradanza. Uruguayan dancer and choreographer Graciela Figueroa (who danced for Twyla Tharp in 1969) has returned to Uruguay; she directs her own Dance Group in Montevideo after spending many years traveling, dancing, and teaching in Chile, Brazil, and Europe (mainly Spain). Teresa Trujillo is teaching Eutony, a body technique based on the studies of Gerda Alexander (1908–1994).

Since December 1985, Ana Rosa Rodríguez Cravanzola has conducted a weekly program on SODRE television;

called "El Mundo de la Danza" (Dance World); it includes dance news, interviews with artists, and filmed dance.

BIBLIOGRAPHY

Assunção, Fernando O. *Evolución de los bailes populares tradicionales en el Río de la Plata.* Buenos Aires, 1978.

Carvalho Neto, Paulo de. "The Candombe: A Dramatic Dance from Afro-Uruguayan Folklore." *Ethnomusicology* 6 (September 1962): 164–174.

"Entretien avec Lolita Parent." *La Danse* (March 1957): 29–30.

Figari, Pedro, and Fernando Guibert. *Tango y candome en el Río de la Plata, 1861–1979.* Río de la Plata, 1979.

Gilbert, Isabel. "Teresa Trujillo, bailarina y coreógrafa." *Cuba en el Ballet* 3 (May 1972): 36–39.

Gimelfarb, Norberto. "Le tour du monde en quatre-vingts tours de piste." In *La danse: Art du XXe siècle.* Lausanne, 1990.

Lauro Ayestaran, Flor de Maria R. de Ayestaran. *Las musicas infantiles en el Uruguay* (includes coreografia). Montevideo, 1995.

Legido, Juan Carlos. *La orilla oriental del tango: Historia del tango uruguayo.* Montevideo, 1994.

Omara, Grania. "Panorama del ballet en el Uruguay." *Ballet* (Lima) 2.3 (1953): 10–11.

Rodríguez de Ayestarán, Flor de María. "Methodology in the Reconstruction of Extinct Folk Dances." *Dance Studies* 8 (1984): 67–74.

Rodríguez de Ayestarán, Flor de María. *La danza popular en el Uruguay.* Montevideo, 1994.

Sclavo, Jorge. *Los tangos del Cuque.* Montevideo, 1990.

El tango uruguayo. Montevideo, 1994.

CLAUDIO SANGUINETTI GAMBARO
Translated from Spanish

USTINOVA, TATIANA (Tat'iana Alekseevna Ustinova; born 19 December 1908 in Tver [formerly Kalinin], Russia), choreographer and teacher. Ustinova graduated from the Moscow ballet school in 1931. From 1931 to 1938 she was a choreographer and dancer at the Moscow Theater of Young Audiences. From 1938 onward she was chief choreographer for the Piatnitsky State Academic Russian Folk Choir.

Ustinova created more than one hundred original dance scenes and various dances during her long career, using elements of Russian folk dances as a primary means of expression. She studied original folk dances for many years, beginning with her first ethnographic expeditions to the villages of her native Kalinin region. She gradually expanded her expeditions to include other areas of the Soviet Union. Ustinova's intimate knowledge of the folk material, coupled with her mastery of all its nuances, have lent a sense of authenticity to her stage compositions. Ustinova's dances are all original works, which she choreographs explicitly for the stage and according to her personal vision of the world. Ustinova founded the school of academic-style Russian folk dance.

"Northern Round Dances," staged by Ustinova in 1954, portrayed the Russian North, with its serenely flowing rivers and vast expanses. The majestic and tranquil movements of the region's women, wrapped in large embroidered shawls, the fluid transitions between dance numbers, and the rhythms of the North were all depicted on the stage. An entirely different rhythm carried the spectator away in the rollicking *chastushka* dance "Timonya" (1947). The gaiety that erupts from the circle of dancers creates a festive atmosphere characteristic of the southern regions of Russia. In Kursk and Belgorod it is precisely in this way that people celebrated—openly and sincerely, alternating the vivacious *chastushka* with the diversified rhythmic and improvised round dance. Ustinova's dances, united in a single program, conveyed the diversity of Russia.

"Siberian Polka" (1957) and "The Golden Chain" (1959) were built on elements characteristic of Siberian dances. "The Ural Shestera" is a quadrille characteristic of that region. The Kalinin (1938) and Yaroslavl (1950) quadrilles are lyrical and ornate, and capture the essence of the central regions of European Russia. "Voronezh Round Dance" (1944), "The Smolensk Goose Dance" (1945), "Moscow Round Dances" (1952), "Vologda Naparochka" (1963), "The Bryansk Igrishcha" (1978), "Kaluga Perebory" (1980), and many other dances incorporate characteristics of the folk cultures of the cities and villages of Russia.

Ustinova also had a keen sense of the present. Consequently, among her creations there are a number of compositions that in form are close to ballet, although these numbers are usually performed in variety shows by ensemble groups. Such dances include "The Star Round Dance" (1961), "Bloom" and "Springtime Land" (1963), "The Red Carnation" (1976), "Greetings, Volga!" (1978), "A Tale of the Russian Land" (1978), and "Zimushka" (1980). In her productions Ustinova also made use of the imagery of Russian folk poetry: "Willow Tree," a personification of woman, mother, the motherland; "White Swans," beautiful maidens; "Evil Kites," an enemy force; "Fearless Falcons," brave youths. *A Tale of the Russian Land* had three scenes: peace, war, and again peace. This structure was at once characteristic of the folk dance tradition and profoundly contemporary, expressing ordinary people's eternal yearning for peace and evoking memories of the dead. The poetic image of the Russian woman, the chastity of her dance, represented a special theme in Ustinova's work, which found expression in the woman's role in the dance "And I Walk in the Meadow" (once performed by Ustinova herself), "Ivushka," *A Tale of the Russian Land,* "Carnations," and others.

Ustinova wrote many books on dance. The major ones include *Russkie tantsy* (Russian Dances), 1950; *Berech krasotu russkogo tantsa* (To Preserve the Beauty of Russian Dance), 1959; *Zvezdnie khorovody* (The Star Round Dance), 1964; and *Russkii narodnyi tanets* (Russian Folk Dance), 1976. Ustinova has also written numerous articles in journals, anthologies, and newspapers. She has been a prominent public figure and the founder of folk dance studios, and created a curriculum for Russian dance that is taught at dance schools and institutes of higher education. Ensembles that perform her dances have enjoyed success. Ustinova is People's Artist of the USSR (1961), Laureate of the State Prize (1949, 1952), and winner of the Glinka Prize (1971).

BIBLIOGRAPHY

Klimov, A. A. Article in *Sovetskii Balet,* no. 6 (1983).

Uralskaya, Valeria. *Poiski i resheniia: Tanets v russkom khore.* Moscow, 1973.

Ustinova, Tatiana. *Russkie tantsy.* Moscow, 1955.

Ustinova, Tatiana. *Berech krasoty russkogo tantsa.* Moscow, 1959.

VALERIA I. URALSKAYA
Translated from Russian

UTHOFF, ERNST (born 28 December 1904 in Duisburg, Germany, died 19 February 1993), dancer, teacher, director, and choreographer. As a youth, Uthoff was initially interested in acting. His parents did not object as long as he also acquired a "serious profession." Hence, Uthoff served a two-year apprenticeship with an import-export firm and then joined the Bank of Dresden. At the same time he studied with Rudolf Laban. After obtaining a scholarship to study with Kurt Jooss, Uthoff devoted himself to dancing full-time.

UTHOFF. Oscar Escauríaza and Hans Züllig of the Ballet Nacional Chileno in Uthoff's late-1950s ballet *Wunder auf der Alameda,* based on *Die Puppenfee.* (Photograph by Bob Borwicz.)

In 1932, when Les Ballets Jooss won the Archives Internationales de la Danse choreographic competition with *The Green Table,* Uthoff danced the role of the Standard Bearer; he also created other roles, such as the Libertine in *Big City.* The company, supportive of its Jewish members, emigrated from Nazi Germany to England in the mid-1930s. On one of its tours (1940), it performed in Chile; a year later, when the company returned to England, Uthoff—with Lola Botka, whom he had married in 1938, and another dancer, Rudolf Pescht—settled in Santiago to found the University of Chile's dance school.

The success of Uthoff's version of *Coppélia* (1945) established the budding dance school on the local scene. It became the Ballet Nacional Chileno and, until his retirement in 1965, Uthoff's career was linked with it. As director and chief choreographer, he formed a compact company of approximately thirty dancers, trained in the Kurt Jooss–Sigurd Leeder technique. At first, several of Uthoff's ballets *(Drosselbart, Petrouchka, The Prodigal Son)* were on themes already choreographed by Jooss; later, however, he struck out on his own with works such as *Alotria,* a humorous circus ballet, and his greatest success, a ballet to Carl Orff's oratorio *Carmina Burana* (1937, 1960).

Uthoff's work, which in its later phase incorporated elements of classical technique, is best described as dance theater, defined by a clear and logical development of character and story line. A meticulous worker, he spent months on the preparation and rehearsal of each of his ballets, constantly demanding that the dancers not only perform the steps but interpret their roles, giving each instant its precise meaning. During the late 1950s and early 1960s, Uthoff and the Ballet Nacional Chileno undertook several very successful Latin American tours. In 1964, the company also performed at Lincoln Center in New York City. Uthoff retired in 1967 and, in 1984, belatedly received Chile's National Art Award.

BIBLIOGRAPHY

Cánepa Guzmán, Mario. *El Teatro Municipal en sus 125 años de sufrimientos y esplendor.* Santiago, 1985.

Ehrmann, Hans. "A Descendant of the Jooss Ballet Thrives in Chile." *Dance Magazine* (April 1957): 30–33.

Ewart, Germán. "Ernesto Uthoff." *El Mercurio* (24 September 1961).

HANS EHRMANN

UZBEKISTAN. The dance traditions of present-day Uzbekistan have been enriched by numerous cultures over the centuries because of the country's central location on the Silk Road, the ancient trade routes that linked China with the Mediterranean. Formerly known as Bactria, Transoxiana, Maveranaher, and Turkestan, the area was inhabited at least fifty-five thousand years ago. The ancient tribes that lived in Central Asia left petroglyphs, bas-reliefs, clay sculptures, and other artifacts depicting dancers and musicians. Later peoples continued to portray dancing figures in wood and clay sculptures, wall paintings, ornaments, and drawings on serving vessels of precious metal. Pictures dating from the first centuries CE show religious, mythological, and secular subjects in which dancing figures play an important part. From the fourth to eighth centuries CE the professional dancers of Samarkand, Bukhara, and Tashkent were so well known that they were in demand at the court of the Chinese emperor. The Arab invasion of Central Asia in the seventh century and the adoption of Islam promoted sexual segregation and the practice of veiling. Women danced for each other in the *ich kari,* or women's quarters. Public performances of dance were the domain of the *batcha,* or dancing boy, who dressed in women's clothing, wore makeup, and mimicked female behavior. A notable exception to this practice were the female court dancers depicted in miniature paintings produced from the Middle Ages until the nineteenth century.

The surviving dance heritage of the Uzbek people includes both folk and professional traditions. Folk dances fall into two general categories: dances performed at a specific time and linked to specific occasions, and dances performed at any time for entertainment. The first group consists of ritual dances performed at festivals associated with the seasons and reflecting humans' relationship with nature. Especially popular are the songs and dances devoted to the pre-Islamic festival Navruz (Nawrūz), which takes place on the spring equinox. In addition to an all-night ritual of stirring a large caldron to make *sumelek,* a special dish made from seven grains, festivities also include the *suskhotin,* a dance asking for rain, and the *mazhnun tal,* a dance by girls with fluffy willow buds woven into their braided hair. Other folk dances depict daily chores, seasonal work, or important events. Some dances relate to ceremonies such as weddings and funerals. Vestiges of Central Asian shamanism can be linked to the incantational dances of healers and fortunetellers, which were still common at the beginning of the twentieth century. Also still performed is the *zikr, (dhikr),* a Sufi ritual in which dancers travel in a circle with repetitive movements, accompanied by chanting and percussion, and sometimes reaching a trance state.

Entertainment dances include the *koshuk* and *kairakufari,* each distinctive to a particular area, which feature the playing of *kairok,* castanets made from smooth, flat river stones or metal. The *lapar* is a duet to sung couplets; the *yalla* is a solo dance accompanied by song. *Gul ufari* (jocular rhythms) or *khaivonlar ufari* (animal rhythms) are sometimes obvious imitations of animals, birds, or fish; at other times they are sophisticated dances representing stylized images of wild or domesticated animals.

"Tanovar", a classical dance from the Ferghana Valley, exists in at least twelve different variations. It expresses the hopes and longings of women and is somewhat melancholy in nature. Another classical dance, "Munadzhat", reflects the sentiment of an eponymous poem by Alisher Navoi, a prayerful lament entreating God for succor.

Uzbek dance is characterized by intricate arm and hand movements, a variety of spins and turns, backbends, shoulder isolations, and animated facial expressions. Portions of the dance are often performed kneeling on the floor. Footwork is relatively simple; high leaps and pelvic isolations are absent. Dancing is done mostly by women and girls. Musical accompaniment takes many forms, ranging from purely rhythmic patterns and melodies of narrow tonal range perfomed by a single percussion instrument or two-stringed instruments, to classical *maqom* (complex compositions of many parts), or even music performed by a large orchestra of folk instruments with singers.

The professional dance tradition falls into three categories. The first includes *raqș, oyin,* and *ufari,* technically sophisticated dances performed by virtuosos who may improvise on the basic patterns. The second group is *gul ufari,* a humorous, imitative form developed by dancers of the Uzbek theater of Maskharaboz. The third category consists of dances performed by traditional circus artists that include various acrobatic stunts.

Three regional styles of Uzbek dance, each with clearly defined styles and systems of training, developed in the separate political entities that existed in Turkestan prior to its incorporation into the Soviet Union. The Khanate of Kokand in the Ferghana Valley, the Khanate of Khiva in the Khorezm region, and the Emirate of Bukhara produced the Ferghana, Khorezm, and Bukharan styles, respectively. The most lyrical of the three schools, Ferghana dance, is characterized by intricate wrist circles and undulations of the hands and arms, with pliant bending of the spine and a shy yet playful demeanor. Khorezm dances often feature trembling of the hands and torso, side-to-side movements of the head, and comic elements. The most popular Khorezm dance, the *lazgi,* was originally a healing dance, traditionally performed with the dancer standing on a large platter. Dances from Bukhara feature a proud carriage and the juxtaposition of soft, undulating movements with crisp, staccato ones. The Bukharan style is the most acrobatic of the three, requiring fast spins, sudden drops to the floor, and deep backbends. In all three schools, dancers sometimes wear wrist bells to add a percussive element to their movements. Traditionally, both folk and professional Uzbek dance were solos, group dances being virtually nonexistent.

Although Russia conquered Turkestan in the mid-nineteenth century, local traditions went largely undisturbed until 1924, when the region was incorporated into

UZBEKISTAN. Dressed in traditional Uzbek costume, Mukarram Turgunbaeva (left) and Tamara Khanum (right) in a photograph from the 1920s perform a dance from the Ferghana Valley. (Photograph by K. Romeev; courtesy of Laurel Victoria Gray.)

the Soviet Union. The Bolshevik campaign to eliminate the custom of veiling soon led to public performances of dance by women. Born in Margillan in 1906, Tamara Khanum (*khanum,* an honorific meaning "madame" or "lady," was her sobriquet) was one of the first women to defy tradition and perform unveiled, often courting death at the hands of fundamentalists. In 1924 she performed Uzbek dance at the World Exposition in Paris, the first time in modern history that Central Asian dance had been seen in the West. One of Tamara Khanum's colleagues, a young dancer named Nurkhon, was murdered by her own brother for dishonoring the family by dancing in public. Nurkhon later became the subject of a musical drama by Kamil Yashin. [*See the entry on Khanum.*]

The Uzbek Ethnographic Company was established in 1926 to create concerts staged by masters of traditional dance. Ten years later the first Uzbek folk song and dance ensemble was formed; in 1956 another collective, Shodlik (Joy), was established. In 1958 an ethnographic song and dance company was created in Khorezm. The most celebrated of all Uzbek dance ensembles, Bakhor (Spring), was founded in 1957. Under the artistic direction of Mukarram Turgunbaeva, Bakhor developed a repertory of group and solo dances based on Uzbek traditions but employing Western techniques of staging and choreography. Bakhor has toured throughout the world and at its zenith consisted of forty-five young dancers who performed with an orchestra of native musicians. Nearly one hundred amateur companies exist, some of which perform dances reflecting local themes and genres.

The first contemporary dance studios were founded between 1927 and 1932. Isadora Duncan performed in Tashkent and Samarkand in 1924; one of her adopted daughters later taught special classes at the Tashkent Choreographic Institute. In 1947 the Tashkent ballet school was founded, with departments for both classical and folk dance. Since 1970 folk dance choreographers have been trained at the Tashkent Institute of Culture under teachers from Leningrad and Moscow as well as Tashkent. The first Uzbek musical theater was established in 1929. The pantomime *Pakhta* (Cotton) was staged there in 1933, with choreography by Konstantin Bek, Usta Kamilov, and Turgunbaeva. Five years later the theater staged *Shakhuda,* a ballet on the theme of the struggle against the Basmachi bandits, with choreography by Kamilov, Turgunbaeva, and Aleksandr Tomsky. In both cases, the dances were based on folk idioms with classical elements introduced. In 1939 the State Academic Bolshoi Theater of Opera and Ballet (Uzbek Opera and Ballet Theater), named for Alisher Navoi, opened in Tashkent. Two of Uzbekistan's first native ballerinas were Galiya Izmailova and Bernara Karyeva, who performed traditional Uzbek dance as well as classical ballet.

In addition to ballets from the classical repertory, Uzbek choreographers have created their own works, developing new forms through a synthesis of classical and traditional dance. *Amulet of Love, Poem of Two Hearts,* and *Tomiris* are examples. One of the most popular is *Guliandom* (1940) by Vera Gubstkaya, Ilya Arbatov, and Tamara Khanum. On the basis of folk melodies collected by

UZBEKISTAN. Galiya Izmailova in a dance from the Khorezm region. (Photograph by K. Romeev; courtesy of Laurel Victoria Gray.)

Gavkhar Rakhimova, the composer Evgeny Brusilovsky created the score, introducing quotations from folk themes. The choreographers created the character of the hero by combining classical ballet with traditional Uzbek dance elements. Leading contemporary choreographers of classical and traditional dance are Galiya Izmailova, Ibraghim Yusupov, Kadir Muminov, Viktoria Akilova, Yulduz Ismatova, Damira Sagirova, Akbar Muminov, Sonmas Burkhanov, Takhir Dusmetov, and Inna Gorlina.

Uzbekistan declared its independence on 31 August 1991 and annually celebrates this event with festivities in which dance plays a central role. Each year members of Tashkent's professional dance ensembles participate in a mass dance, with specially created music and choreography. The ancient celebration of the spring holiday, Navruz, has also enjoyed a renaissance in the post-Soviet era, with numerous concerts featuring dance and a competition between professional dance companies for the best new festival program. Economic reforms have forced many companies to reduce their size and some professional dancers and musicians to seek employment outside the arts. Small, privately sponsored dance groups have sprung up to entertain tourists, foreign business people, and nightclub audiences. Traditional Uzbek dance has become more commercial in nature, abandoning many of the older dances in favor of lively numbers performed to ethno-pop-style music. Access to foreign materials has resulted in traditional-style costuming being replaced by sequined gowns and rhinestone tiaras. Arabic and Turkish-style dances and more revealing costumes have also become popular at concerts. Some professional companies and numerous amateur ensembles, however, endeavor to preserve Uzbek dance traditions. Dance remains central to Uzbek life; no wedding is complete without it, and televised dance performances enjoy great popularity, giving leading dancers celebrity status.

Expanded contact with the outside world, especially in the 1980s, encouraged Western dance forms to flourish in Uzbekistan, including ballroom dance and American break dancing, aerobics, and hip-hop. Cultural exchange, notably through the sister-city relationship between Tashkent and Seattle, resulted in an increased interest in Uzbek dance abroad, with non-Uzbeks in the United States and Europe studying and performing traditional dances. In 1985 the Uzbek Dance and Culture Society was founded in the United States to preserve and promote Central Asian culture; today it has members in the United States, Europe, Canada, and Australia.

BIBLIOGRAPHY

Allworth, Edward. *The Modern Uzbeks*. Stanford, Calif., 1990.

Avaz, Sotim, and O. Madrakhimov. *Madrakhim sherozii*. Tashkent, 1991.

Avdeeva, Lubov. *Tamara Khanum*. Tashkent, 1959.

Avdeeva, Lubov. *Tantseval'noe iskusstvo Uzbekistana*. Tashkent, 1960.

Avdeeva, Lubov. *Balet Uzbekistana*. Tashkent, 1973.

Avdeeva, Lubov. *Tanets Bernary Karyevoi*. Tashkent, 1973.

Avdeeva, Lubov. *Galiia Izmailova*. Tashkent, 1975.

Avdeeva, Lubov. *Tanets Mukarram Turgunbayevoi*. Tashkent, 1989.

Cohen, Selma Jeanne. "Report from Tashkent: East Meets West in Central Asia." *Dance Magazine* (July 1990): 45–48.

Gray, Laurel Victoria. "A Living Legacy: Women's Dances in Uzbekistan." *Arabesque* (January–February 1983): 6–7.

Gray, Laurel Victoria. "Tamara Khanum: Uzbekistan's Heroine of Dance." *Arabesque* (January–February 1985): 14–15.

Gray, Laurel Victoria. "Uzbek Women Dance through Time." *Middle Eastern Dancer* (April 1985): 17–20.

Gray, Laurel Victoria. "Uzbek Women's Dances, Past and Present." *Viltis* 43 (March–April 1985): 7–9.

Gray, Laurel Victoria. "Dancing Boys." *Arabesque* (May–June 1986): 8–11.

Gray, Laurel Victoria. "Americans Dance in Uzbekistan." *Dance Magazine* (September 1988): 10.

Gray, Laurel Victoria. "Poesie und Anmut des Herzens." Part 1: "Ferghana." Part 2: "Bukhara." Part 3: "Khorezm." *TanzOriental* (1994).

Gray, Laurel Victoria. "Uzbeks Adapt to Independence." *Dance Magazine* (August 1994): 22–23.

Gray, Laurel Victoria. "The Splendor of Uzbek Dance, Part 1: Khorezm." *Habibi* (Spring 1995): 12, 27.

Gray, Laurel Victoria. "The Splendor of Uzbek Dance, Part 2: Ferghana." *Habibi* (Summer 1995): 14, 31.

Karimova, Roziia. *Ferganskii tanets*. Tashkent, 1973.

Karimova, Roziia. *Khorezmskii tanet*. Tashkent, 1975.

Karimova, Roziia. *Bukharskii tanets*. Tashkent, 1977.

Karimova, Roziia. *Tantsy ansamblia Bakhor*. Tashkent, 1979.

Karimova, Roziia. *Tanovar*. Tashkent, 1993.

Lakov, Nikolai A., and Vera P. Sokolovskaia. *Kostiumy k tantsam narodov SSSR*. Moscow, 1964.

Khamrayeva, Gul'sum R. "Obshche Zakony Stsenicheskoi Khoreografii i Natsional'nyi Obraz Tantsa." Ph.D. diss., Khamza Institute of Art Studies, Tashkent, 1986.

Pulatova, Ogulkhon M. *Istoki Formirovaniya i Dal'neishego Razvitiya Terminologii Tantseval'nogo Iskusstva Uzbekskogo Yazyka*. Tashkent, 1992.

Shirokaia, O. I. *Al'bom Tamara Khanum*. Tashkent, 1972.

Swift, Mary Grace. *The Art of the Dance in the U.S.S.R.* Notre Dame, 1968.

Tkachenko, Tamara. *Narodnyi tanets*. 2d ed. Moscow, 1967.

VIDEOTAPES. "An Introduction to Uzbek Dance" (Uzbek Dance Society, 1986). "In Concert: The Bakhor Ensemble" (Uzbek Dance Society, 1989). "The Mukhimi Theatre Presents: Nurkhon" (Uzbek Dance Society, 1989).

ARCHIVE. Museum of Tamara Khanum, Tashkent.

LAUREL VICTORIA GRAY
With material provided by Lubov Avdeeva

V

VAGANOVA, AGRIPPINA (Agrippina Iakovlevna Vaganova; born 14 [26] June 1879 in Saint Petersburg, died 5 February 1951 in Leningrad), dancer, choreographer, and teacher. Vaganova studied at Saint Petersburg's theater school under Aleksandr Obladov, Lev Ivanov, Ekaterina Vazem, Christian Johansson, and Pavel Gerdt, and later under Olga Preobrajenska and Nikolai Legat. Upon graduation in 1897 she joined the corps de ballet of the Maryinsky Theater, where, despite her superlative technique, she made slow progress in her stage career (*coryphée* from 1903, soloist from 1906, *prima ballerina* from 1915). Vaganova danced leading roles in Marius Petipa's versions of Arthur Saint-Léon's *The Little Humpbacked Horse* and Jean Coralli and Jules Perrot's *Giselle;* Petipa's own *Les Caprices du Papillon* and *Le Talisman;* Petipa and Lev Ivanov's *Swan Lake* and *Le Réveil de Flore* as well as their version of Jean Dauberval's *La Fille Mal Gardée;* Aleksandr Gorsky's *Don Quixote;* Saint-Léon's *La Source,* restaged by Achille Coppini; Nikolai Legat's revival of Petipa's *Les Saisons;* and Michel Fokine's *Le Carnaval* and *Chopiniana.* Legat also staged for her in 1910 "The Whisper of Flowers," to Franz von Blon's eponymous waltz.

Critics invariably emphasized Vaganova's energetic style. Describing her as the "queen of variations," Valerian Svetlov pointed out in her dancing its chiseled precision, attention to detail, and ease of execution. Vaganova's achievements, such as the role of Odette-Odile in *Swan Lake* in 1913, came at the end of her stage career. She retired from the stage in 1916 and devoted herself to teaching.

One of Vaganova's first works in choreography was the miniature *The Visions of a Poet* (1927), to music by Arseny Gladkovsky, at the theater of the Leningrad ballet school. Vaganova revived Fokine's *Chopiniana* at the same theater in 1931; it was later staged at the Leningrad Opera and Ballet Theater. As the art director of the ballet company of the Opera and Ballet Theater from 1931 to 1937, Vaganova gave every encouragement to the company's interest in the modern repertory and revived two classic ballets: *Swan Lake* in 1933 and *La Esmeralda* in 1935. In these productions Vaganova sought to achieve the integrity of choreographic drama, to sharpen the dramatic conflict (social conflict in *La Esmeralda*) by enhancing the role played by mass scenes and consistent psychological motivation of the action. The scene of the first meeting between Siegfried and Odette, which she staged anew, was included in subsequent versions of the ballet; in act 2, the "swan act," Vaganova carefully preserved Ivanov's choreographic text.

Vaganova began teaching at the School of Russian Ballet run by Akim Volynsky in Petrograd. From 1921 to 1951 she taught at the Petrograd ballet school; she was named professor in 1946. In 1957 the school was renamed after Vaganova. From 1934 to 1941 she also taught in the ballet teachers' department of that school, and from 1943 to 1944 she taught at the Bolshoi Theater in Moscow. From 1946 to 1951 she was the chair of choreography at the Leningrad Conservatory.

As a teacher, Vaganova contributed to the survival of classical ballet in the complex conditions of the emergence of a new culture in the country. The efficient and well-planned system of instruction in classical dance that she had established became the foundation of Soviet ballet art and training. This system was based on both the traditions of pure academic dance that Vaganova had adopted from her teachers and the selection of the finest achievements of the past, with a critical revision of what had been introduced into Russian ballet by representatives of various European schools in the late nineteenth century. Vaganova rejected the outward decorative effects and mannerisms that were characteristic of the French school of the late nineteenth century as well as the self-centered technique of the Italian school, with its exaggerated, angular dance style. She summed up and imaginatively used in her teaching the experience of the distinctive Russian school of dance and choreography that had taken shape at the turn of the century. At the same time she took into account the innovations of the Russian choreographers who had succeeded Petipa. Following Johansson, Vaganova interpreted virtuosity not as an aim in itself but as a means of artistic expression, subordinated to the general conception of a role and the choreography of the ballet as a whole.

Vaganova attached great significance to the strict carriage of the body and to its core of stability, the spine. This theoretical prerequisite played an important part in her pedagogical practice. For Vaganova, movement necessarily began from the body, for this gave support and artistic freedom to dance. At the beginning stage of training she also gave considerable attention to *épaulement*—the skill to hold the head and shoulders freely, not straining the muscles of the neck—as the first sign of future artistry. The correctly placed body, leading to perfect aplomb, was the foundation for steps of elevation, including turns and complicated jumps in allegro. In Vaganova's pedagogical system, steely aplomb was connected to correctly placed hands and the natural beauty of their movements, and to unconstrained *port de bras* and its organic connection with the control of the head. The hands, in Vaganova's opinion, should not only complete the contour of the visual image but also actively help the movement in jumps and turns. Vaganova's method enables ballet dancers to use the time-tested technique of academic style to adapt freely to the sophisticated tasks set in modern choreography. It has indirectly influenced the development of male dance by the universality of its main principles.

Vaganova described her system in her book *Fundamentals of the Classic Dance,* published in Russian in Leningrad, 1934, which has been translated into many languages. She greatly influenced the pedagogical principles of the Soviet and world school of classical ballet. Most of Vaganova's pupils were not only outstanding dancers but also teachers who imaginatively used her experience in their own work. Vaganova was awarded the title of People's Artist of the Russian Federation in 1934 and the State Prize of the USSR in 1946.

BIBLIOGRAPHY

Bogdanov-Berezovskii, V. M. *A. Ia. Vaganova.* Moscow, 1950.

Gregory, John. *The Legat Saga.* 2d ed. London, 1993.

Greskovic, Robert. "Ballet, Barre, and Center, on the Bookshelf." *Ballet Review* 6.2 (1977–1978): 1–56.

Iuzhina, Kamila. "Agrippina Vaganova and the Art of Teaching." *Dance Magazine* (November 1979): 36.

Kendall, Elizabeth B. "In Search of the Classichiski." *Dance Connection* 11.4 (1993–1994): 13–16, 53–54.

Krasovskaya, Vera. *Agrippina Iakovlevna Vaganova.* Leningrad, 1989.

Kremshevskaia, G. D. *Agrippina Iakovlevna Vaganova.* Leningrad, 1981.

Vaganova, Agrippina. *Stati, vospominaniia, dokumenty.* Leningrad, 1958.

Vaganova, Agrippina. *Basic Principles of Classical Ballet: Russian Ballet Technique* (1934). Translated by Anatole Chujoy. Edited by Peggy van Praagh. 2d ed. London, 1953; reprint New York, 1969.

Volkov, Nikolai D. "Agrippina Vaganova." In *The Soviet Ballet,* by Yuri Slonimsky et al. New York, 1947.

VALERY A. KULAKOV
Translated from Russian

VAINONEN, VASILY (Vasilii Ivanovich Vainonen; born 8 [21] February 1901 in Saint Petersburg, died 23 March 1964 in Moscow), dancer, choreographer, and librettist. Vainonen graduated from the Petrograd ballet school, where he studied under Vladimir Ponomarev, in 1919. From then until 1933 he danced with the Petrograd/Leningrad Opera and Ballet Theater, mainly in character roles. He started to work as a choreographer in the early 1920s and during the ensuing decade staged a few dances, including *Nocturnes* (1923), to Chopin; the Russian sailors' dance "Yablochko" (Little Apple; 1927); *Moszkowski Waltz* (1930); and *The Musical Snuffbox* (1932), to music by Anatol Liadov. These works evidenced his fascination with Isadora Duncan's art and also that of Michel Fokine. In addition to his work in ballet, Vainonen staged dances in operas. He was choreographer at the Leningrad Opera and Ballet Theater from 1930 to 1938 and at Moscow's Bolshoi Theater from 1946 to 1950 and 1954 to 1958.

Vainonen's first significant choreographic work was *The Golden Age,* to Dmitri Shostakovich's score, which he created with Vladimir Chesnakov and Leonid Yakobson at the Leningrad Opera and Ballet Theater in 1930. The production was largely experimental, with parody and the grotesque prevailing. Vainonen relied on his experience in variety dance and made an attempt to enrich the dance vocabulary with that of related arts: cinematography and propaganda posters. Vainonen's 1932 premiere of *The Flames of Paris,* to Boris Asafiev's score, at the Leningrad Opera and Ballet Theater was a milestone event in the history of Soviet ballet. (A new version was presented in 1936 and 1950; restaged at Moscow's Bolshoi Theater 1933, 1947, 1960, and at the National Opera House in Budapest in 1950.) Turning to the historical theme of the French Revolution, Vainonen made the people the protagonist; in his development of mass dance scenes the influence of gala performances of the early post-Revolutionary years could be noted. In his choreography, with its action dance and quest for a new plastique language containing elements of folk dance as well as virtuosic leaps and spins, he pursued the aim of presenting the image of a new hero: vigorous, rebellious, and determined to act. That was of major significance for the advancement of Soviet ballet, and largely anticipated the heroic style of Vakhtang Chabukiani's productions. [*See* Flames of Paris, The, *and* Golden Age, The.]

In later years Vainonen turned to modern themes in *Partisan Days* (1936, revised 1937) and *Militsa* (1947), both to scores by Asafiev and presented at Leningrad's Opera and Ballet Theater; *The Coast of Happiness* (1952), to music by Antonio Spadavecchia, in Novosibirsk; and Aram Khachaturian's *Gayané* in 1957 at Moscow's Bolshoi Theater. Using classical dance enriched with elements of comedy and drama, Vainonen choreographed *Mirandolina* (1949), to music by Sergei Vasilenko and a libretto based on Carlo Goldoni's play *La Locandiera,* for the Bolshoi Theater in Moscow.

Vainonen also produced original versions of the classics, such as *The Nutcracker* in 1934 for the Leningrad Opera and Ballet Theater, and Riccardo Drigo's *Har-*

lequinade in 1945 for the Belarussian Opera and Ballet Theater. For *The Nutcracker* Vainonen revised Marius Petipa's libretto, eliminated the naive doll-like character of the ballet, enriched the psychological motivations of the protagonists, and presented a new choreographic interpretation of Tchaikovsky's score. Other Petipa ballets that Vainonen restaged were *Raymonda* in 1938, with a new libretto by himself and Yuri Slonimsky, for the Kirov Opera and Ballet Theater, and *The Sleeping Beauty* in 1952 for the Novosibirsk Opera and Ballet Theater. He collaborated on the libretto for Aleksandr Radunsky's new version of *The Little Humpbacked Horse* in 1960. An article, "Notes on the Language of Choreography," was published in the September 1940 issue of the journal *Teatr.* Vainonen was awarded Merited Artist of the Russian Federation in 1939 and the State Prize of the USSR in 1947 and 1949.

BIBLIOGRAPHY

Armashevskaia, Klaudiia, and Nikita Vainonen. *Baletmeister Vainonen.* Moscow, 1971.

Roslavleva, Natalia. *Era of the Russian Ballet* (1966). New York, 1979.

Swift, Mary Grace. *The Art of the Dance in the U.S.S.R.* Notre Dame, 1968.

VALERY A. KULAKOV
Translated from Russian

VAIN PRECAUTIONS. *See* Fille Mal Gardée, La.

VALBERKH, IVAN (Ivan Lessogorov; Ivan Ivanovich Val'berkh; born 3 [14] July 1766 in Moscow; died 14 [26] July 1819 in Saint Petersburg), dancer, choreographer, teacher, and man of letters. Valberkh graduated from the Saint Petersburg Theater School in 1786 and was immediately appointed a soloist with its ballet troupe. Studying under Gaspero Angiolini and Giuseppe Canziani, he developed a taste for pantomime and mastered its technique. Charles Le Picq, the famous French dancing master, exercised a great influence on the young Valberkh. An inquisitive and thoughtful dancer, Valberkh took a creative approach to whatever he was learning by executing the dance in his own new way.

With his polished technique and attractive stage presence, Valberkh quickly made his mark as *premier danseur,* with a special gift for dramatic roles. He is best remembered for his brilliant Jason in *Médée et Jason,* choreographed by Le Picq after Jean-Georges Noverre; Alexis in *Le Déserteur,* choreographed by himself after Jean Dauberval; Romeo in his own *Romeo and Juliet;* and Ivan in *Russians in Germany, or The Effects of Love for the Motherland,* mounted by himself and Auguste Poireau. Press reviews praised him as a first-class dancer whose pantomime and dance technique were faultless.

An adherent of eighteenth-century theatrical aesthetics, Valberkh shared Noverre's views on the *ballet d'action.* In his compositions Valberkh freely alternated dances with dramatized mime scenes. He was fully aware of literary and artistic trends of the day and was open to them, but he rejected both the rationalism of Noverre's ballets and the limitations of mythological themes. He was the first in Russia to present on the ballet stage the heroes of Shakespeare and Jean-Pierre Bernardin de Saint-Pierre. The content of his ballet *The New Sterne* (1801) was drawn from Laurence Sterne's novel *A Sentimental Journey.* Valberkh kept a close watch on the repertory and stage practices of the dramatic theater of the period; as a result, melodrama had profound influence on the style of his productions.

Valberkh produced thirty-six original ballets, revived ten ballets staged by other choreographers, and composed and arranged dances and mime scenes for forty-two grand operas. His ballets varied widely in genre and theme, including mythological subjects (*Orpheus and Eurydice,* 1808) and fairy tales (*Raoul Barbe-Bleue,* 1807). But Valberkh was proudest of his "moral" ballets, products of the sentimental trend in choreography. In these he departed from mythological themes and titanic images, instead drawing empathetic inspiration from the experiences of ordinary people. He praised virtue, repentance, and the triumph of justice, and often resorted to melodramatic effects. Moralizing and edifying principles dominated his productions, as even the titles indicate, from his debut as a choreographer on 8 February 1795 with *A Happy Repentance,* a pantomime-ballet, through *Blanca, or A Marriage of Revenge* (1803), *The Count Castelli, or The Criminal Brother* (1804), *Clara, or Return to Virtue* (1806), *Romeo and Juliet* (1809), *An American Heroine, or Treachery Punished* (1814), and *Henry IV, or Virtue Rewarded* (1816). All were marked by sentimentality and the praise of virtue.

Valberkh's *The New Werther* (1799) had a libretto based on a true story of two lovers who committed suicide in a cemetery in Moscow. The wealthy parents of the young woman opposed the marriage because the young man was only a poor infantry officer. The idiom of the dances was subordinated to the theme, especially in the duets, and the dancers performed in contemporary dress. Valberkh's quest to link ballet with the arts of his epoch was crowned by the great success of *A New Heroine, or The Cossack Woman* (1811). The libretto was based on another true story, that of Nadezhda Durova, a girl who disguised herself as an army officer and took part in the difficult battles waged by the Russians against Napoleon's encroaching army. The ballet had a long run at theaters in Moscow and Saint Petersburg. During the 1812 war, Valberkh initiated a new genre—a folk *divertissement* as an organic blend of dances, songs, and music. The war inspired him to produce *Russians in Germany, or The Effects of Love for the Motherland* (1813) and several other patriotic ballets.

From 1794 to the day he died, Valberkh taught at the Imperial Theater School. Evgenia Kolosova, Arina Tukmanova, Agrafina Makhayeva, Constance Pletin, Isaac Ablets, and Adam Glushkovsky were among his pupils. An active dancer, choreographer, and teacher, Valberkh also found time to pursue the career of a man of letters. He knew several languages, translated twenty-seven plays staged by Russian theaters, and left informative memoirs of early nineteenth-century French ballet, in which he presented his philosophy of art. In dancing he valued, above all, harmony and the ability to express ideas; he opposed those who saw these qualities only as a way to display a dancer's technical brilliance.

BIBLIOGRAPHY

Bakhrushin, Yuri. *Istoriia russkogo baleta.* 3d ed. Moscow, 1977.

Roslavleva, Natalia. *Era of the Russian Ballet* (1966). New York, 1979.

Sorley Walker, Kathrine. "Ballet in Imperial Russia." *Dance Gazette* (October 1982): 38–40.

Swift, Mary Grace. *A Loftier Flight: The Life and Accomplishments of Charles Louis Didelot.* Middletown, Conn., 1974.

Valberkh, Ivan. *Iz arkhiva baletmeistera.* Moscow, 1948.

Winter, Marian Hannah. *The Pre-Romantic Ballet.* London, 1974.

NIKOLAI I. ELYASH
Translated from Russian

VALLI (Alarmel Valli; born 14 September 1956 in Madras), Indian dancer. Trained in the Pandanallur technique of classical *bharata nāṭyam* by the guru Chokkalingam Pillai, Valli began her studies at the age of seven. Later she expanded her repertory with her master's son, Subbaraya Pillai. She studied *abhinaya* (expressive dance) with Kalanidhi Narayanan. Like many of her contemporaries, she also studied Oḍissi dance, but she decided to concentrate solely on *bharata nāṭyam.*

Valli's dancing is marked by a sparkling quality. To the typically forceful movement style of Pandanallur dance, she brings a refreshing approach which adds grace without stripping the style of its grandeur. Her style is not a forceful one, either in the movements of the arms or in the execution of *adavus*, the dance units that build up the architectonic structure of *bharata nāṭyam.* Rather, her signature lies in softening the movements gracefully while preserving the essential vigor. Her steps uncoil and flow, revealing beauty in the dance's unfolding. Her *utplavans* (jumps) are light and her landings perfect, drawing exquisite, lingering curves. Her dancing is playful; her eyes do not move as prescribed in the classical treatises but rather enhance the movements and give a joyous touch to the presentation. Nonetheless, both her repertory and performance adhere to tradition. Studying music has developed in her the keen musicality essential to a *bharata nāṭyam* dancer.

Valli has also choreographed several *bharata nāṭyam* works that recast traditional sequences to create beautiful movement patterns. She has participated in many national and international festivals and conferences, winning critical acclaim. She has explored the combination of *bharata nāṭyam* and Oḍissi dance with Oḍissi exponent Madhavi Mughal, but she is best known as a soloist.

Valli lives in Madras, where she trains young dancers at her academy. Her performances were filmed by Prakash Jha in a series produced for the Festival of India. Her honors include the Nritya Choodamani award from Shri Krishna Gana Sabha, Madras, and the Kalaimamani award from the Tamil Nadu State Sangeet Natak Akademi, as well as many other honors from various arts organizations.

BIBLIOGRAPHY

Kliger, George, ed. *Bharata Nāṭyam in Cultural Perspective.* Manohar, 1993.

Kothari, Sunil, ed. *Bharata Natyam: Indian Classical Dance Art.* Bombay, 1979.

Meisner, Nadine. "Festival of India." *Dance and Dancers* (June 1982): 31–32.

SUNIL KOTHARI

VAN PRAAGH, PEGGY (born 1 September 1910 in London, died 15 January 1990 in Melbourne, Australia), British dancer, teacher, and ballet director. Van Praagh studied with Aimée Phipps, Margaret Craske, Lydia Sokolova, Vera Volkova, Tamara Karsavina, Gertrud Bodenwieser, and Agnes de Mille. She made her debut at the Coliseum Theatre in London on 16 September 1929 in a company formed by Anton Dolin, and in 1932 she passed her advanced Cecchetti examination. Subsequently she danced in Camargo Society performances and then as a soloist with the Ballet Club/Ballet Rambert (1933–1938), working particularly with Frederick Ashton and Antony Tudor. She also danced in many musicals, in opera ballets at Covent Garden, and in some of the earliest television transmissions. In 1938 she joined Tudor's London Ballet, where she created roles in his *Jardin aux Lilas* (1936), *Dark Elegies* (1937), *Soirée Musicale* and *Gala Performance* (both 1938), and *The Planets* (extended version, 1939).

At the beginning of World War II, van Praagh took over the Craske studio in London and became joint director with Maude Lloyd of the London Ballet, revived initially for lunchtime performances during the blitz. When the company was absorbed into Ballet Rambert in 1941, she joined Sadler's Wells as teacher and principal dancer, later making a particular impression in *demi-caractère* and virtuoso roles such as one of the Blue Girls in Ashton's *Les Patineurs* and Swanilda in *Coppélia.*

Van Praagh was appointed ballet mistress of the newly established Sadler's Wells Theatre Ballet in 1946 and was assistant director to Ninette de Valois from 1951 to 1955. In that position she nurtured the early choreographic works of John Cranko and Kenneth MacMillan and the early careers of many dancers who became leaders of the Royal Ballet. She also pioneered many outreach programs to popularize and explain classical ballet through lectures and lecture-demonstrations.

After she left Sadler's Wells in 1955 to freelance, van Praagh staged ballets by Ashton, de Valois, and Tudor in Canada, West Germany, Sweden, Norway, the United States, and France. She also produced many ballets for BBC Television between 1949 and 1958 and directed the Edinburgh International Ballet in 1958.

In 1960 she went to Australia as guest teacher for the Borovansky Ballet, for which she staged *Coppélia* and *Les Rendezvous*. She was appointed artistic director of the Australian Ballet for 1963–1974 and 1978–1979. As such she is considered the principal influence in the development of classical ballet in Australia, where she fostered dancers, teachers, and choreographers and continued her outreach work on television as well as in personal lectures and demonstrations.

An examiner and London committee member of the Cecchetti Society since 1937, she was considered one of its leading teachers and achieved an international reputation as an exponent of the Cecchetti method of training. She received many honors, including the Queen Elizabeth II Coronation Award, Royal Academy of Dancing (of which she was vice president), 1965; Commander of the Order of the British Empire (CBE), 1966; Dame Commander of the Order of the British Empire (DBE), 1970; honorary doctor of letters, University of New South Wales, Armidale, 1974; Distinguished Artist Award of Australian Art Circle, 1975; honorary doctor of laws, Melbourne University, 1981.

[*See also* Australia, *article on* Ballet.]

BIBLIOGRAPHY

Brinson, Peter. "Married to the Ballet." *Brolga*, no. 3 (December 1995): 24–48.

Pelly, Noël. "A Tribute to Dame Peggy." *Dance Australia* (April–May 1990): 31–34.

Sexton, Christopher. *Peggy van Praagh: A Life of Dance*. South Melbourne, 1985.

Sorley Walker, Kathrine. "A Sort of Dedication." *The Dancing Times* (December 1974): 128–130.

van Praagh, Peggy. *How I Became a Ballet Dancer*. New York, 1954.

van Praagh, Peggy, and Peter Brinson. *The Choreographic Art*. London, 1963.

van Praagh, Peggy. *Ballet in Australia*. Melbourne, 1965.

van Praagh, Peggy. "Working with Antony Tudor." *Dance Research* 2 (Summer 1984): 56–67.

Woodcock, Sarah C. *The Sadler's Wells Royal Ballet*. London, 1991.

PETER BRINSON

VANUATU. *See* Melanesia.

VASILIEV, VLADIMIR (Vladimir Viktorovich Vasil'ev; born 18 April 1940 in Moscow), Russian dancer, choreographer, and teacher. Vasiliev graduated from the Moscow Ballet School, Mikhail Gabovich's class, in 1958 and became a leading soloist of the Bolshoi Ballet. His ballet teachers and coaches were Aleksei Yermolayev, Asaf Messerer, and Galina Ulanova. He graduated from Rostislav Zakharov's course in choreography at the Lunacharsky Theater Technicum in 1981.

Vasiliev's talent combined consummate technique with highly artistic and original acting. He made a brilliant debut in the 1959 Bolshoi staging of Yuri Grigorovich's *The Stone Flower*, portraying the leading role of Danila, a Russian folk artist. Vasiliev's Ivanushka in Aleksandr Radunsky's *The Little Humpbacked Horse* and Petrouchka in Michel Fokine's eponymous ballet, revived by Konstantin Boyarsky for the Bolshoi, were distinctive for their rich national coloring. Another of his remarkable roles was Medzhnun, which was created for him by Kasyan Goleizovsky in *Leili and Medzhnun* (1964). In this ballet Vasiliev mastered a style of choreography unusual for its variety in nuances, just as he later did in Maurice Béjart's productions of *Romeo and Juliet* and *Petrouchka*. Able to immerse himself in his roles and evince each character

VASILIEV. Cast in the title role of Leonid Lavrovsky's *Paganini* in 1962, the youthful Vasiliev relished the opportunity to display his exceptional elevation and virtuosity. (Photograph reprinted from a Bolshoi Ballet souvenir program, 1962.)

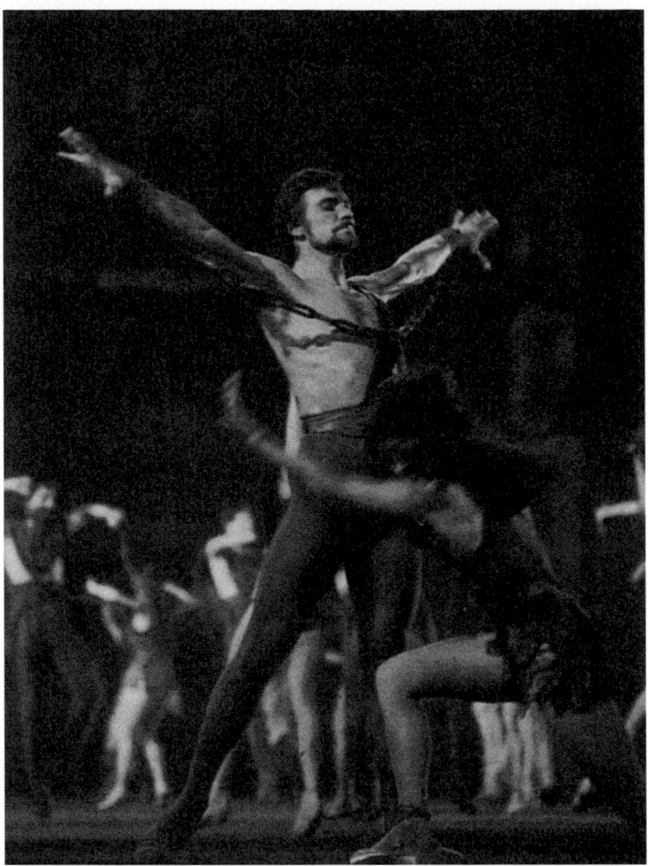

VASILIEV. In 1968, Vasililev created the title role of Yuri Grigorovich's *Spartacus.* This photograph, taken during a performance, captured a dramatic moment when Spartacus's wife Phrygia (Ekaterina Maximova) throws herself at the knees of her husband to make an impassioned plea. (Photograph from the Dance Collection, New York Public Library for the Performing Arts.)

through movement, Vasiliev gave an innovative interpretation to the roles of Romeo in Leonid Lavrovsky's *Romeo and Juliet* and the Prince in Zakharov's *Cinderella.* His virtuosity was seen in the traditional role of Basil in Marius Petipa's *Don Quixote.* He brought to Albrecht in *Giselle* and Désiré in *The Sleeping Beauty* the spirit of classicism and poetry in motion. Vasiliev became the exemplary interpreter of Grigorovich's ballets, creating the principal roles in *Spartacus, The Nutcracker, Ivan the Terrible,* and *The Angára.*

Vasiliev's dancing influenced the contemporary artistic criteria of ballet. Fedor Lopukhov passed on to Vasiliev from Vakhtang Chabukiani the title "god of the dance." Yermolayev said that with each role Vasiliev adopted a new persona and especially commended his "soft" and "hard" *pliés,* which allowed him a limitless range of movement and of roles. Lopukhov (1974) commented with professional delight on Vasiliev's technique: "His *double tours* to left and right, *entrechats,* simple and *double cabrioles,* and *double ronds de jambe* are of an amazingly noble pattern. He performs, for example, the following unique combination in the pas de deux coda from *Don Quixote:* after making two *jetés en tournant* from the right leg, he makes a *tour en l'air en attitude* and during the turn performs an ordinary *rond de jambe.* This combination is repeated several times *en manège,* and the audience feels enraptured by the soaring dancer whose feet touch the floor almost imperceptibly."

Vasiliev displayed his mature skill as a choreographer in productions staged at the Bolshoi. Remaining loyal to classical dance and realistic art, he regarded form as the flesh and blood of an idea and sought to polish realistic images into symbols of significance. In his full-length story ballets *Icarus* (1971) and *Macbeth* (1980) he relied on sophisticated technique, which he performed. The flight of Icarus, for example, is an unusual combination: from a swift, springy *chassé* he soared in a high *saut de basque en dedans* on the right leg and, at the moment of turning at the acme of the jump, changed the position of his legs in midair to execute a *grand rond de jambe* with his left leg, then landed in a broad fourth position; this was performed twice. In his plotless ballet *These Charming Sounds* (1978) Vasiliev revealed his search for a wider range of classical dance technique. His work as choreographer and dancer in his ballet film *Aniuta* (1982, expanded for the stage in 1986), based on Anton Chekhov's *Anna Round the Neck,* and his one-act productions *I Want to Dance* (later called *Suite Nostalgique*), created in honor of Ulanova, and *Fragments of a Biography,* set to music by Russian and Argentine composers, were acclaimed; *Correo Musical Argentino* magazine wrote that he "created a truly Argentinian elegy by the wonderful singing of his dance. There is no archaeological reconstruction, no ethnic documentality. Vasiliev has offered us a bunch of Argentinian flowers chosen by an artist in spirit and a universal man in art. His perfect dance, the dignity and integrity of his art, is evidence that he is the greatest dancer of our day."

During the 1980s, while retaining his position at the Bolshoi, Vasiliev was often invited as a guest choreographer to companies outside and inside the Soviet Union—Berlin, Budapest, Naples, Riga, Cheliabinsk, Kasian—as well as performing as a guest artist, usually with his wife, the ballerina Ekaterina Maximova. By the end of the 1980s his disaffection with the Bolshoi had become patent, so that he and Maximova were no longer welcomed. In 1990 Vasiliev joined the board of the Kremlin Ballet, reviving for the new company his *Macbeth* and creating his version of *Cinderella* (1991), in which he and Maximova danced. Always a champion of the Russian, as opposed to Soviet, style of dancing, Vasiliev formed a small company of dancers, drawn from the Bolshoi and Kirov companies and representing diverse republics, and toured the United States in 1991 in a program of excerpts from his ballets complemented by classical pas de deux. Vasiliev's nomadic existence came to an end when in 1995 Grigorovich was made to step down as director of the Bolshoi Ballet. Vasiliev was named joint director with Vladimir Kokonin of the Bolshoi Theater, overseeing the opera, ballet, and theater companies. His immediate aims are to stabilize the theater's finances, to open the Bolshoi Ballet repertory to foreign choreographers' and new young choreographers' works, to associate the school more directly with the company, and to foster international exchange.

BIBLIOGRAPHY

Avaliani, Noi, and Leonid Zhdanov, comps. *Bolshoi's Young Dancers.* Translated by Natalie Ward. Moscow, 1975.

Belinskii, A. A. "Odin takoi tsantsovschik." *Sovetskii balet,* no. 6 (1983).

Ben-Itzak, Paul. "Vladimir Vasiliev: Hauling the Bolshoi into the Twentieth Century." *Dance Magazine* 70.2 (February 1996): 74–77.

Demidov, Alexander P. *The Russian Ballet: Past and Present.* Translated by Guy Daniels. Garden City, N.Y., 1977.

Garafola, Lynn. "Vladimir Vasiliev." *Dance Magazine* (November 1990): 50–53.

Ignatov, Victor. "Entretien: Vladimir Vassiliev au Bolchoi." *Danser* (June 1995): 34–35.

Kisselgoff, Anna. *Vladimir Vasiliev.* Brooklyn, 1975.

Lazzarini, Roberta. *Maximova & Vasiliev at the Bolshoi.* London, 1995.

Lidova, Irène. "Volodia, il gigante buono." *Ballettoggi* (July–August 1988): 15–18.

Lopukhov, Fedor. "Vladimir Vasiliev." In *Muzyka i khoreografiia sovremennogo baleta.* Leningrad, 1974.

Lvov-Anokhin, Boris. "Vladimir Vasiliev." In Lvov-Anokhin's *Mastera Bolshogo Baleta.* Moscow, 1976.

Ottolenghi, Vittoria. "Vladimir Vassiliev: Autoritratto in due parole." *Ballettoggi* (July–August 1988): 12–14.

Smakov, Gennady. *The Great Russian Dancers.* New York, 1984.

Willis, Margaret E. "Vasiliev through the Viewfinder." *Dance Magazine* (January 1988): 48–51.

GALINA V. BELYAYEVA-CHELOMBITKO
Translated from Russian

VAUDEVILLE. [*This entry is limited to discussion of vaudeville in the United States. For related discussion of European traditions, see* Music Hall.]

Variegated performances of song, dance, comedy, and tumbling had held the American stage since colonial times, but not until the period following the Civil War were they commonly called variety shows. Usually presented within the precincts of a barroom, honky tonk, or concert saloon, these entertainments had to amuse a rowdy and impatient crowd of male boozers. There was no place for the finer points of dance. Ballerinas, imported from Britain or Europe for extravaganzas such as *The Black Crook* and burlesques such as *Ixion,* danced in variety theaters in the off-season or when the taste for such shows faded, but these former *coryphées* merely had to display their stockinetted legs in a few energetic steps. Tony Pastor's more ambitious Opera House boasted its regular corps de ballet of ten "soloists" under the direction of a Monsieur Szollosy.

VAUDEVILLE. The Four Cohans were one of the best-known family acts to tour the vaudeville circuits. George M. Cohan is pictured here with his sister Josephine, his father Jerry J., and his mother Helen. (Photograph from the Museum of the City of New York; used by permission.)

VAUDEVILLE. The specialty act of Earl ("Snake Hips") Tucker exploited his unique, seemingly boneless way of moving. As his nickname suggests, he popularized the Snake Hips—in origin a plantation dance—and was also noted for his undulating Belly Roll. One of the foremost African-American entertainers of his day, Tucker was a regular at Harlem clubs, including the Cotton Club and Connie's Inn. (Photograph from a private collection.)

Most variety dancing was more athletic than aesthetic. Clogging contests, popularized by the phenomenal John Queen, were judged on time, style, and execution. Introduced in 1876 by Jimmy Bradley, sand jig dancing, a style tripped on the balls of the feet in 4/4 time like a schottische, was appraised from beneath the stage in order to gauge the accuracy of cadence. Kitty O'Neill was the first female sand jigger; the Barlow Brothers and the Girard Brothers, the first double acts to perform it. The Majiltons launched "legmania," a frenetic display of high kicks, splits, and three-hand reels played in grotesque wigs and tights; they were widely imitated by, among others, the Daly Brothers, the first act to kick at inanimate objects, such as hats and cigar boxes. In 1877 the Poole Brothers combined legmania and clogging, thereby creating the first acrobatic clog dance.

Throughout the 1870s, variety dancing stressed gimmickry and vigor over technique. Prime novelties were the Egg Dance, a series of pirouettes, dips, and hops carried out among two dozen raw eggs; the Spade Dance, in which the blade served as a kind of pogo stick on which the dancer hopped through an obstacle course; and the Transformation Dance (especially popular with male impersonators), in which costumes were yanked off the performer from the wings by means of strings, enabling her to perform, in succession, a military drill, an Irish jig, and a skipping rope dance, each time clad in appropriate garb. Charlie Dimond started the vogue for soft-shoe, accompanying himself on a harp slung over his shoulder. According to Joe Laurie, Jr. (1953), the Turkey Trot was introduced by Johnny Lorenze in 1886, the same year the first "break" was danced on a piano, by Guy Hawley. In 1888 buck-and-wing dancing was initiated, by Lew Randall; roughhouse dancing, by Charles Guyer and Nellie O'Neill; and double one-legged song and dance, by Harper and Stencil. Dancers working the big time during this period made at most $70 a week in tandem and performed under less than ideal conditions. The brother-sister team of Johnny and Bertha Gleason, wooden-shoe dancers, traveled with their own pianist to ensure accurate music cues and were the first dance team to use a mat of hardwood slats to correct the lack of resilience in the double stage flooring of most theaters. Amateurs had to rehearse for auditions and contests in empty grain cars that had hard, smooth floors.

The opening of Tony Pastor's Fourteenth Street Theatre in 1881 signaled the use of "vaudeville" to imply a higher grade of entertainment, one that was clean and refined. As managers wooed family audiences by promising high-toned amusements, they screened variety dancing for any salacious or sensual overtones. Bubble dances with or without fans and doves, striptease, and *danses du ventre* were strictly relegated to burlesque. Censors were quick to jib at any suggestion of licentiousness in dance. The Cubanola Glide, a cakewalk, was, complained the *American Magazine* in 1909, "a dance so suggestive and so reeking of implied indecency that it is an insult to any respectable woman who happens to hear it." Later, hints of passion in *apache* dances would be attacked by local moralists as overtly sensual, even bestial.

Conversely, children's troupes were thought to guarantee wholesomeness. The Hengler Sisters; Harry Delf "The Kid Romeo"; Elseeta, "The American Dancing Girl"; Eva and Harry Puck; and Rae Dooley had successful careers as juvenile dancers until the "Geary society" (American Society for the Prevention of Cruelty to Children) cracked down on full-time employment of minors.

African-American dance was never presented in the early days of white vaudeville because at first such dances were interpreted by white performers in blackface. Cakewalks came to vaudeville by way of the minstrel show. Johnson and Dean were the earliest black dance team to feature the cakewalk in variety, but it was Irish Dan Burke who spiced the cake with high kicks. The shuffle and sway was first danced by the white George Primrose. The finest black performers were eventually able to break in but initially only in the unpopular number two spot on the bill: Phina and Her Picks (short for *pickaninnies*), George Cooper, and Bill ("Bojangles") Robinson, who developed the stair dance (initiated by Al Leach in 1899) into a full-fledged art form. Exclusively black vaudeville helped to cultivate the talents of Ulysses ("Slow Kid") Thompson, with his legmanic tap dance, the high kicks and leaps of Peg Leg Bates, and the Duo Éclatant of Ollie Burgoyne and Usher Watts. Buck and Bubbles began as ushers at B. F. Keith's in Louisville, Kentucky, before becoming the first black team to perform there (although under burnt cork masks). Long after white vaudeville had entered its decline, the Apollo Theater in Harlem provided a showcase for Snake Hips Tucker and the Berry Brothers, with their combination of acrobatics, soft-shoe, and strut. [*See the entries on the Berry Brothers, Peg Leg Bates, and Robinson.*]

Vaudeville audiences, even in the gilded palaces managed by Keith, E. F. Albee, and F. F. Proctor, remained indifferent to dance as an art but responded enthusiastically to successive waves of novelties. Spanish dance became a rage in 1890, when Carmencita did a *cachucha,* a Santiago waltz, and a *fandango* with castanets at Koster & Bial's in New York City. She was widely imitated, burlesqued, and, six years after her death, impersonated by an imposter in a "farewell" performance at Hammerstein's theater. Her chief rival was Carolina Otéro, known in Paris as La Belle Otéro. The skirt dances and graceful glides of England's Kate Seymour and Kate Vaughan were Americanized at about this time by Amelia Glover and Bessie McCoy. The replacement of gas by electric lighting enabled the experiments of Loie Fuller in manipulating translucent gauze in colored light, and in her wake followed a spate of serpentines, fire dances, and butterfly dances. A certain Papinta embellished her serpentines with mirrors and a glass trapdoor through which she fell in 1895. [*See* Skirt Dance *and the entry on Fuller.*]

In 1894 a performer called Ayesha conveyed to vaudeville a laundered hootchy-kootchy from its birthplace, the World's Columbian Exposition in Chicago. The number was then headlined at Hammerstein's by one "Rajah," formerly of Huber's Museum on the Bowery, where she had danced with a chair in her teeth. Hammerstein's later featured Djemille Fatimah in Algerian dances. Hawaiian dancing arrived in 1908 with Toots Paka's company, and by 1916 Doraldina was packaging an act comprising the hula, a harem dance, and similar exotica.

Bare feet were given a veneer of scriptural authority in 1908 with the Salome that Gertrude Hoffman (Kitty Hayes) copied from Maud Allan (who was prevented by a booking war from dancing it in the United States). Once again the pattern of imitation, exaggeration (Eva Tanguay omitted the veils), and derision (Fanny Brice as a Yiddish Salome) continued for years, eventuating in the Salome of La Belle Marie (Marie Gillian), a "Terpsichorean Dream" that verged on striptease. The Salome craze ushered in a series of symbolic storytelling dances, obvious allegories readily comprehended, such as Joseph Herbert and Lillian Goldsmith's *Dance of the Siren* and Alice Eis and Bert French in *Rouge et Noir* (1912), a gambling scenario. More cryptic and hence less popular were Valeska Suratt's *Black Crepe and Diamonds* and the Orientalia of Ruth St. Denis, who loathed performing for vaudeville audiences.

By 1915 ragtime dominated, with shoulder shaking, finger snapping, wriggling, the fox trot, the Turkey Trot, and the one-step. A leading exponent was Joe Smith of the Avon Comedy Four, a specialist in step dances and the buck-and-wing. Later Bee Palmer and Gilda Gray would perform a toned-down Shimmy. During World War I dance halls lost appeal, as young men vanished from the

VAUDEVILLE. A nightclub performer whose heyday was in the 1910s, Gilda Gray became famous as the inventor of the Shimmy. She is seen here in a 1940 portrait. (Photograph by Carl Van Vechten; used by permission.)

floors and paid partners were scorned as shirkers. Social dancing found a haven in vaudeville, where in the 1920s the Charleston, the Black Bottom, or the Toodle-oo would be exhibited, albeit in expurgated versions.

Before World War I, Maurice Mauvet and Florence Walton were among the earliest teams to demonstrate genteel with ballroom techniques to middle-class audiences. Their well-tailored demeanor contrasted sharply with that of Irene and Vernon Castle, with their "languid energy, drooping strenuousness [and] whimsical seriousness" (Caffin, 1914, p. 103). In her autobiography, however, Irene Castle claimed that she and Vernon "only went into vaudeville when we were hard up." On the Orpheum circuit, Ivy and Douglas Crane were billed as "The Vernon and Irene Castle of the West." Jack Clifford and Evelyn Nesbit exploited her involvement in the sensational Harry Thaw murder trial by creating a "modest and proper" act that played the Keith circuit from 1913 to 1917. Between film engagements, Mae Murray and Clifton Webb toured in *Society Dances,* disseminating throughout the provinces such urban fads as a "Valse d'Arlequin," a "Brazilian Maxixe," a "Cinquante-Cinquante Tango," and a "Barcarole Waltz." Other popular teams included Mr. and Mrs. Carter De Haven, the "Beau Ideals"; the French Mitty and Tillo; the English Ted Trevor and Diane Harris; the suave and syncopated Tony and Renée De Marco; and Fred and Adele Astaire. The Astaire siblings played vaudeville as early as 1908 (Hudson Theater, New York City) in an act written by Ned Wayburn; their steps ranged from toe to the more popular hard-shoe, but they displeased the variety public: Fred seemed too effeminate. This was a frequent charge leveled at male exhibition dancers, who often were stigmatized as "lounge lizards" and "gigolos."

VAUDEVILLE. Edna Covey developed a comedic act that showed her special skills as a ballet-dancing contortionist. She was a featured performer in several editions of the *Ziegfeld Follies* in the 1920s. (Photograph from the Dance Collection, New York Public Library for the Performing Arts.)

VAUDEVILLE. Acts featuring Oriental or exotic themes were a staple of variety shows. This alluring, barefoot dancer was billed as Mademoiselle Armen Ohanian, "The Dancer of Shamahka." An advertisement in *The Morning Telegraph* announced her appearance at the Aeolian Hall, New York, in April 1924. (Photograph from the Dance Collection, New York Public Library for the Performing Arts.)

The ballet school tradition was perpetuated by La Petite Adelaide (Mary Dickey) in her dollie act and by Mademoiselle Dazie (Daisy Peterkin), originally known as Le Domino Rouge, expert at the *eschoppe,* or rock step. To keep from seeming stilted or mechanical, vaudeville toe dancing had to be a sprightly form of acrobatics. Mazie King was the first to jump off a table several feet in the air and come down on pointe, whereas Titenia would trip up and down stairs on her toes. Bessie Clayton, described by Caroline Caffin (1914) as a "sportive, laughing elfin creature" in a Pierrot costume, performed eccentric toe steps in unblocked shoes. Even Sally Rand, later notorious for her fans, toe danced at the Palace in New York City, waving ostrich plumes to Debussy's *Clair de Lune.*

The influence of Diaghilev's Ballets Russes was to be diffused throughout vaudeville. Gertrude Hoffman presented picturesque Russian dance dramas, and a number of authentic émigrés, such as Anna Pavlova and defectors from the Ballets Russes as well as Americans with Slavic sobriquets offered cut-rate renditions of Russian ballets to one-horse towns across the nation. Shura Rulowa's Ballet Russe, for example, toured the Pantages, Orpheum, Loew, and Keith theater circuits from 1922 to 1926, showering the fruits of enlightenment upon flocks of corn-fed ballerinas. Mockery ensued, often on the same bill. Sammy Krevoff did an infant travesty of Michel Fokine's *Le Spectre de la Rose,* and Fanny Brice dealt the *coup de grâce* to *The Dying Swan.*

The old standbys of acrobatic and comic dancing maintained a tenuous hold. Even the Albertina Rasch Dancers with its pastel, pompadour ambience had to feature a contortionist, for refinement was commercial only if it was enlivened by physical exertion. Legmania was revitalized by Evelyn Law and Charlotte Greenwood; wooden-shoe acts, by Pat Rooney and Marion Bent; and the Texas Tommies flung one another around with frank good humor. There were dancers who imitated animals (Arthur Borani and Annie Nevaro, Rita Le Roy), scarecrow dancers (Montgomery and Stone; Macmahon, Diamond, and Clemence), and performers who specialized in drunken falls down staircases (Leon Errol, Willie Solar). When adagio dancing came into favor it was teeming with acrobats: Percy Oakes spun his partner Pamela Latour over his head, threw her on his back, and then whirled over the stage. The craze for the *apache* dance, launched by Giovanni Molasso, was capitalized on by French and Eis in their *Vampire Dance* (1909). [*See* Apache Dance.] Even in the late 1920s Janette Hackett stunned audiences with her "bad girl" act melding stunt work with tendentious allegory: upon finding her partner (Cesar Romero) to be Death, the fast-living siren rushes up a flight of stairs, clutches a heavy drape, and, swathed in it, rolls back down to the bottom.

The hoofer (a term coined about 1890 by the minstrel Billy Emerson but not heard commonly until the 1920s) did not necessarily specialize. Almost every comic could "shuffle off to Buffalo" to get offstage, and virtually every singer could fill in between verses with a sketchy soft-shoe. Some celebrities, such as the Dolly Sisters, could

VAUDEVILLE. The sight of two identically clad dancers moving in perfect synchrony has always held an appeal for the American public. *(left)* Inez Courtney and Gertrude McDonald holding a pose from their "Broadway Whirl" number, c.1921. *(right)* The young Verlon and Berlon Griffin are seen here in a mirror-image "Egyptian" pose, c.1923. The Griffin Twins were headliners on B. F. Keith's vaudeville circuit. (Photograph at right by Progress Studio, New York; both from the Dance Collection, New York Public Library for the Performing Arts.)

barely move in time to the music, but their looks and charm were adequate recompense. It was a comedian, Joe Frisco, who originated the bent-knee jazz dance accompanied by cigar and derby. By 1923, the peak revenue year of vaudeville, usually three or four dance acts, the best earning upward of $250 a week, were on a "class" bill and scheduled in a strong spot directly after intermission. The dancers' technical expertise improved over the decades as audiences became more adept at distinguishing finesse from flat feet.

But vaudeville's yearning for sophistication and refinement proved to be its undoing. Large ensembles, tasteful costumes, and elaborate sets began to cut into profits: expenses of the Albertina Rasch Dancers totaled $2,500 a week. In 1921 the critic Marsden Hartley wrote how he regretted that

> now we get little more in the field of acrobatics beyond a varied buck and wing; everything seems tuxedoed for drawingroom purposes. (*Adventures in the Arts,* p. 156)

Audiences began to drift away, first to the automobile, now a viable commodity, which emptied theaters on weekends; then to the radio, which had the audacity to broadcast unseen tap dancers; and, most definitively, to the movies, where the lavish theatrics of a Busby Berkeley spectacular could be amplified by the live musical numbers, or "prologs," that preceded the films. The Palace Theater in New York stopped playing two-a-day vaudeville in 1932, and after an interim of mixed live and filmed entertainment, converted exclusively to movies in 1934.

As a result of this waning, many who had started as dancers metamorphosed into actors, the most conspicuous examples being George Raft, the hottest of Charlestoneers; James Cagney; and Buddy Ebsen, a popular adagio dancer. Adagio teams moved to the nightclubs, which had proliferated with Prohibition (1920–1933), and beat out the clean-cut varsity acts that had predominated there; ballet dancers found a berth in revue, a form intended for smaller, more elite audiences; and eccentric dancers received featured spots in musical comedy. A recrudescence of sorts occurred in the early 1940s, when the Palace revived vaudeville for a wartime public; and again during the 1950s on television, when it relied heavily on variety programming. Then, such troupers as the June Taylor Dancers and Mata & Hari garnered a vast new public for time-honored precision dancing and for spoofs of outdated styles. As Bernard Sobel (1961) has written, "Vaudeville is dead, but vaudevillians live on."

[*See also* Fan Dance; Tap Dance; United States of America, *articles on African-American dance traditions.*]

BIBLIOGRAPHY

Caffin, Caroline. *Vaudeville.* New York, 1914.
Castle, Irene. *Castles in the Air.* Garden City, N.Y., 1958.
Cooper, H. E. "Variety, Vaudeville, and Virtue: From the Naughty Nineties to Respectability." *Dance Magazine* (December 1926): 31–32.
Donahue, Jack. *Letters of a Hoofer to His Ma.* New York, 1931.
Fletcher, Tom. *One Hundred Years of the Negro in Show Business.* New York, 1954.
Laurie, Joe, Jr. *Vaudeville.* New York, 1953.
Martin, John. "Variety Revival Finds New Blood in an Old Medium." *New York Times* (10 May 1942).
Sampson, Henry T. *Blacks in Blackface: A Source Book on Early Black Musical Shows.* Metuchen, N.J., 1980.
Slide, Anthony. *The Vaudevillians: A Dictionary of Vaudeville Performers.* Westport, Conn., 1981.
Smith, Bill. *The Vaudevillians.* New York, 1976.
Sobel, Bernard. *A Pictorial History of Vaudeville.* New York, 1961.
Stearns, Marshall, and Jean Stearns. *Jazz Dance* (1968). New York, 1994.
Stein, Charles W., ed. *American Vaudeville as Seen by Its Contemporaries.* New York, 1984.
Terry, Walter. "Variety Dancers." *Dance Magazine* (July 1942): 12–13.
Terry, Walter. "Vaudeville Dance." *New York Tribune* (16 May 1942).
White, Stanley. "The Art and Agony of Toe-Dancing." *Royal Magazine* (June 1902).

FILMS. The following films may be found at the New York Public Library for the Performing Arts, unless otherwise noted. *Amy Muller* (Edison, 1896), featuring legmania, George Eastman House, Rochester, N.Y. *Annabella* (Edison, 1897). *Fougère* (American Mutoscope and Bioscope Co., 1902), with the ragtime cakewalk. *A "Tough" Dance* (American Mutoscope and Bioscope Co., 1902), with Kid Foly and Sailor Lil performing an *apache* dance. *Ameta* (American Mutoscope and Bioscope Co., 1903). *Franchonetti Sisters* (American Mutoscope and Bioscope Co., 1903). Edwin S. Porter, *Uncle Tom's Cabin* (Edison, 1903), with the time step, breaks, and street cakewalk. *She Would Be an Actress* (Lubin, 1907). *Tillie's Punctured Romance* (Sennett, 1914), featuring exhibition ballroom dancing and a parody by Marie Dressler and Charlie Chaplin, Museum of Modern Art, New York. Michael Curtiz, *Yankee Doodle Dandy* (Warner Brothers, 1942), featuring reconstructed and modernized vaudeville dance routines performed by veteran vaudevillians James Cagney and Walter Huston. *Dance Program* (George Amberg, c.1945), with clips of the Sisters Daineff, Loie Fuller, Alla Nazimova, and the Charlestons.

VIDEOTAPE. *The History of Jazz Dancing* (KQED-TV, San Francisco, 1970), Dance Collection, New York Public Library for the Performing Arts.

LAURENCE SENELICK

VEDANTAM SATYAM (Vedantam Satyanarayan Sarma; born 15 August 1934, Kuchipudi, Andhra Pradesh), Indian dancer. Vedantam Satyam is renowned for his enactment of female roles in traditional Kuchipudi dance drama. Trained from early childhood by his elder brother Prahlad Sarma and other teachers, he soon attracted the attention of connoisseurs with his exceptional expressive talent. His portrayals of Satyabhama in *Bhama Kalapam* and of Usha in *Usha Parinayam* have been universally hailed as the finest. He imparts an uncanny authority and assurance to his female roles and commands style, empathy, and erudition. His total identification with his roles draws crowds again and again. Many wonder how his masculine mind can comprehend and elicit the intensity of expression and ethos so intimately associated with women; however, the questions become irrelevant when one witnesses his compelling and communicative female portrayals that bring forth the essence of a *nāyikā* (heroine in a Sanskrit drama) with remarkable ease and abandon. Indeed, he belongs to the class of legendary dancers such as the Oḍissi guru Kelucharan Mahapatra and the late Balasaraswati and Mylapore Gauri Amma. Even when the physical form is no more than that of a young maiden, Vedantam Satyam's metamorphosis and evocation of female roles continue to surprise audiences.

Regarded as the foremost Kuchipudi dancer of recent times, Vedantam Satyam also served as principal of the Kuchipudi Art Academy and as a lead actor in the Venkataram Natya Mandali company of traditional male performers. In recognition of his rare gifts, he was made a fellow of the Central Sangeet Natak Akademi at the young age of twenty-six and received the academy's major aware. The government of India bestowed the Padamshri award on him; he also received the prestigious Kalidasa Sanman award for his services to Kuchipudi. Married and the father of two daughters and a son, Vedantam Satyam lives in Kuchipudi village, from which he travels to perform throughout India and abroad.

BIBLIOGRAPHY

Jonnalagadda, Anuradha. *Kuchipudi Who is Who.* Hyderabad, India, 1993.

Ragini Devi. *Dance Dialects of India.* 2d rev. ed. Delhi, 1990.

SUNIL KOTHARI

VEIGL, EVA MARIA. *See* Violette, Eva Maria.

VEMPATI CHINNA SATYAM (born 28 October 1929 in Kuchipudi, Andhra Pradesh), Indian dancer, choreographer, and teacher. Born into a traditional family of Kuchipudi performers, Vempati Chinna Satyam was trained by the legendary Vedantam Lakshminarayan Sastri, Tadepalli Pariya Satyam, and others from early childhood. Like other traditional male dancers, he began by performing female roles and later took male roles.

In the late 1950s Vempati moved to Madras to choreograph for films. In 1965 he established the Kuchipudi Art Academy, where he trained many young female dancers, an innovation in a dance drama genre which until then had been the preserve of men. His disciple Shobha Naidu interpreted his solo dances remarkably, establishing him as a brilliant choreographer.

Soon Vempati began choreographing dance dramas on mythological themes, working with a team of musicians to build up a large repertory of both solo and group works. His solo numbers featured lilting music, an arresting dance style, rapid footwork, and undulating vertical movements. What had begun as a folk genre three decades before, with loose, ill-defined movements, acquired sophistication in his hands. He applied the principles of classical Indian dance manuals to Kuchipudi technique, raising it to the level of such classical genres as *bharata nāṭyam, kathakaḷi,* and *kathak.* His dance dramas, especially *Krishna Parijata, Padmavati Srinivasa Kalyanam, Hara Vilasa, Ramayana,* and *Chandalika,* are a precious legacy.

The many dancers who studied with Vempati have transformed Kuchipudi dance; notable are Shashikala, Bala, Padma Menon, Kamala Reddy, and the late Kamadeva. His son Vempati Ravi Shankar is also a noted dancer and teaches with his father at their academy in Madras. Among Vempati's honors are the Central Sangeet Natak Akademi award, the Kalidasa Sanman, and many awards from art institutions in Andhra Pradesh.

BIBLIOGRAPHY

Misra, Susheela. *Some Dancers of India.* New Delhi, 1992.

Ramachandran, Anandhi. "Interview: Vempati Chinna Satyam." *Sruti* (Madras), no. 13 (November 1984): 32–34.

Satyanajayana, Andavilli, and Premaraju Surya Rao. *Dr. Vempati—Maestro with a Mission.* Vijaywordan, 1993.

SUNIL KOTHARI

VENDA DANCE. Most of the traditional dances of the Venda, a Bantu people, were developed in an enclave within the Transvaal, South Africa, that was declared an independent republic in 1979. This is a lush, mountainous region directly south of Zimbabwe, between the South African town of Louis Trichardt and Kruger National Park. Its 1987 population of approximately six hundred thousand included minorities speaking Tsonga and Northern Sotho (Pedi). Several hundred thousand Venda live in the Republic of South Africa, especially in Soweto, where some fine performances of men's dances can be seen because of the many dance teams that rehearse and perform regularly.

The teams are organized in much the same way as those in the rural areas but with the difference that the dancing is the focus of social activity, rather than a part of rituals and social events organized by rulers and healers. Team members contribute regularly to the general expenses and particularly to the cost of beer. Each team has a manager and an assistant manager, a musical director and his assistant, and a dance director and his assistant, who are responsible for demonstrating the steps. This system of organization existed in Venda before the arrival of Europeans, as did indigenous terms for the officers, their functions, the accompanying musical instruments, and the music played on them.

Two types of dance are performed, and teams generally specialize in one or the other; both are circle dances. The dancers move counterclockwise around the drums, and each dancer blows a single pitch on a stopped pipe so that the whole ensemble produces sequences of melody that are filled out with chords. The *givha, visa,* and related dances are played on pipes tuned to a pentatonic scale, while the pipes of the *tshikona* are heptatonic. Traditionally, the two sets of pipes are made from different types of reed and tuned to different pitches, so that pentatonic melodies cannot be played on heptatonic pipes; this distinction is observed even when the pipes are made from pieces of tubing or hose.

The *tshikona* is the most sacred and important of the Venda dances and was originally performed by adult men and women on state and ritual occasions. The *givha* and *visa* are comparatively new versions of ancient play dances for young people. Various tunes are used for the *visa, mutshaini, givha,* and *tshikanganga,* but many dance steps are common to all of them. There is only one *tshikona* melody but many different steps, some representational and others abstract and named after their inventor, or after a ruler whom the choreographer wanted to honor. The representational steps portray baboons, the gathering of peanuts, sowing seeds, and other horticultural activities related to the first-fruits rites at which *tshikona* is performed.

Dzhombo (children's dances) and *tshigombela* (a recreational dance for adolescent and preadolescent girls) are classified as games *(mitambo)* and are similar in form to the *givha* and *visa*. In contrast, the *domba* premarital initiation dance, the female puberty rites *vhusha* and *ndayo* (which resembled physical-training exercises), the *ngoma dza midzimu* dances of spirit possession, the dances of the *sungwi* girls' initiation, and the *tshikona* are all classified as sacred, serious acts *(dzingoma)*.

There are contrasts within many events between communal dancing in a circle or spiral (expressed by the lexical root *-mona*)—which is also referred to by the general word meaning "to dance" *(-tshina)*—and improvised solo exhibition dancing *(-gaya)*. In *tshigombela,* girls dance *gaya* in groups of two, three, or four and always rehearse their coordinated step routines. In dances of spirit possession, which are performed by cult members and are centered on medicine, healing, and ancestral spirits, *tshina* and *gaya* are condensed into sequences of steps danced by individuals who come out in turn into the arena. Each one alternately spins around for sixteen beats and dances toward three drummers for another sixteen beats. In the important dancing to *malende* beer-drinking songs, however, the style is that of solo *gaya,* but it is always called *tshina*.

The basic posture in Venda dances for both men and women is relaxed, with feet parallel and a slight tilt forward from the hips. Dancers never try to fight against gravity, except when men and youths leap high in *malende* or *gaya*. The legs and arms are not fully extended, although girls and women often flex the foot when lifting it so that the sole is nearly parallel to the ground. The men's style contrasts with that of women; it is light and opposed to the ground, while the women's is sharp and earthbound, with the feet kicking the ground. Men move outward, perform bigger movements, and use all available space; women use the more limited space underneath themselves, using the front-back plane without extending their limbs.

In traditional Venda society, everyone dances during childhood and youth, and most men and women dance *tshikona* or *malende,* or both, whenever they can. Dancing is an integral part of both informal and formal education. It can also help people achieve the transcendent states necessary for direct experience of the "real world" of the spirit.

[*See also* South Africa, *article on* Indigenous Dance; *and* Southern Africa.]

BIBLIOGRAPHY

Blacking, John. "An Introduction to Venda Traditional Dances." *Dance Studies* 2 (1977): 34–56. Contains photographs and Benesh notation of dances by Dora Frankel.

Blacking, John. "Songs and Dances of the Venda People." In *Music and Dance,* edited by David Tunley. Nedlands, W.A., 1982.

Blacking, John. "The Context of Venda Possession Music: Reflections on the Effectiveness of Symbols." *Yearbook of the International Council for Traditional Music* 17 (1985).

Grau, Andrée. "Some Problems in the Analysis of Dance Style, with Special Reference to the Venda of South Africa." Master's thesis, Queen's University of Belfast, 1979.

Stayt, Hugh A. *The Bavenda.* Oxford, 1931.

JOHN BLACKING

VENEZUELA. During the precolonial era, dance in Venezuela was associated with religious ceremonies. In the early years of independence and throughout the nineteenth century, dances were performed for entertainment, among them zarzuelas, *sainetes,* and musical comedies. Ballet was not then a part of the national culture.

The visit of Anna Pavlova and her ballet company in 1917 marked the first time Venezuelans saw ballet in their own country. In 1930 Gally de Mamay, a former member of Diaghilev's Ballets Russes, arrived in Caracas. She taught private classes for the city's privileged youth, usually using large rooms in their own homes.

From 1864 to 1935 Venezuela had been ruled by a military dictatorship. During a brief democratic spell, Nena Coronil, who had studied with de Mamay, founded the National School of Ballet in 1948. There were scholarships for selected students, with each of the nation's twenty states contributing financial support. By 1953 the school had one hundred pupils. The faculty consisted of

William Lundy, an American, the Russians Irina Yovanovitch and Lila Nikolska, and Miro Anton, a Czech.

In 1953, Henry Danton from England's Sadler's Wells Ballet headed the school, and Coronil established the Ballet Nena Coronil. This was the nation's first professional company, but its repertory was limited by the elementary level of the dancers. Progress was also impeded by the lack of a sense of organization and risk, typical of the country at that time. In addition, Coronil and Danton relied on the standard European ballet heritage rather than attempting to create an image more appropriate to the regional culture. In 1954, Coronil staged fragments of the classics—*Swan Lake, Giselle,* and *The Sleeping Beauty.* Nevertheless, Coronil's efforts were important: they familiarized the Venezuelan audience with the art of ballet; they also formed a generation of Venezuelan dancers, among them Graciela Henríquez, Julián Pérez, Belén Lobo, Vicente Nebrada, Maruja Leiva, Margot Contreras, and Irma Contreras.

Meanwhile, Grishka Holguín, a student of Waldeen and Guillermina Bravo, arrived in Caracas from Mexico. He and Conchita Crededio founded the Venezuelan School of Contemporary Dance, which functioned from 1948 to 1959. Among Holguín's best choreographic works were *Mampulorio* (1956), *Hiroshima* (1957), and *Medea* (1957) His student Sonia Sanoja established her own group in 1963, but her idiosyncratic style hindered the formation of a lasting company.

Another attempt at founding a company supported by a school was made in 1957 by Irma Contreras. The National Ballet of Venezuela began with members of the newly disbanded Coronil company and was associated with the Interamerican Academy of Ballet. In addition to staging classics and fragments, Contreras sought to create new works; however, the dancers, not yet fully attuned to the classical tradition, were not ready for this move, nor was the public. The company disbanded in 1968. The Interamerican Academy of Ballet and the National Ballet had, however, achieved one exceptional result: they produced Zhandra Rodríguez. After six years at the school, Rodríguez began dancing major roles with the company at the age of fourteen. She then studied at the School of American Ballet in New York and danced with American Ballet Theatre before returning to Venezuela in 1975.

Irma Contreras resigned from the National Ballet in 1968. Her place was taken by Elías Pérez Borjas, who had been the company's *régisseur* since its founding. Seeking to establish a national identity, Pérez Borjas introduced the company to modern dance. As the Ballet del INCIBA (Instituto National de Cultura y Bellas Artes), the group was a success despite the desertion of many of the original dancers. Pérez Borjas became an important presence on the cultural scene. He brought to Venezuela a new way of viewing dance and of organizing a company.

VENEZUELA. Zhandra Rodríguez was Venezuela's leading ballerina from the 1960s to the 1980s. Partnered by Zane Wilson, she appeared in Vicente Nebrada's neoclassical *Nuestros Valses* in a 1977 performance with the Ballet Internacional de Caracas. (Photograph by Miguel Gracia, courtesy of Belén Lobo.)

In 1968 the Ballet del INCIBA staged the debut of the choreographer Graciela Henríque. With her first work, *Tres,* she established her position in the vanguard of Venezuelan dance and achieved her desire, to reveal through movement the personality of a human being—dancer, woman, or worker. Another of her works, *Mujeres,* was more polemical.

A new policy of subsidizing arts groups was announced by the National Institute of Culture and Fine Arts in 1974 but was not immediately put into practice. As a consequence, unemployed dancers looked for new ways to continue their professions, and a new kind of organization, the independent group, emerged. Among them were the Taller de Danza Contemporánea, founded by José Ledezma; Macrodanza, directed by Norah Parissi; and Contradanza, directed by Hercilia López. These remain active and are now supported by the state.

The 1970s were marked by the reshaping of concepts of modern dance, influenced by the work of Martha Graham, Merce Cunningham, and Alwin Nikolais. Drama, gesture, and daily actions were incorporated. The sisters Adriana and Luz Urdaneta, who had graduated from The

Place in London, formed the group Danzahoy in 1980. The Urdanetas' search for a Latin American style was embodied in such successful Venezuelan works as Henríquez's *Oraciones* (1982), Carlos Orta's *Un Modo de Andar por la Vida* (1980), and the collective creations *Selva* (1981), *Momentos Hostiles* (1987), *40 Grades de la Sombra* (1988), and *Ventana* (1990).

Two companies had important impacts on dance in Venezuela. Both the Ballet Internacional de Caracas, founded in 1975, and the Ballet Fundación Teresa Carreño, founded in 1980, enjoy substantial financial support. The Ballet Internacional had Zhandra Rodríguez as principal ballerina and Vicente Nebrada, who had been with New York's Harkness Ballet, as artistic director and resident choreographer. Essential to Nebrada's work was a corps of strong, athletic dancers, most of whom he recruited from the defunct Harkness group. Only a few Venezuelan dancers were able to work in the new company. The Americans Alvin Ailey and Margo Sappington were invited to stage their works for the BIC, as was the Canadian Brian Macdonald. The company toured Europe, performed at the Spoleto Festival in Italy, and danced in New York. Disunity undermined the company, however, as Rodríguez came into conflict with Nebrada.

In 1983, the Ballet Nuevo Mundo (Ballet of the New World) emerged from the BIC with Rodríguez and Dale Talley as artistic directors and principal dancers. The company gathered many of the BIC dancers and reserved the rights to certain of its choreographic works. While the Ballet Internacional de Caracas oriented itself in the direction of the Harkness Ballet and American Ballet Theatre, the Ballet of the New World commissioned occasional works from new choreographers and from Carlos Orta. In 1987 the Ballet of the New World toured Europe and Asia.

The Teatro Teresa Carreño opened in 1983, providing a cultural and theatrical complex comparable to New York's Lincoln Center, with technologically sophisticated scenographic devices. It became the home of La Fundación Ballet Teresa Carreño, founded by the Argentinian teacher Rodolfo Rodríguez. With the intention of staging the classical repertory, Rodríguez invited such foreign stars as Rudolf Nureyev, Ekaterina Maximova, and Fernando Bujones to interpret principal roles, letting the Venezuelans dance in the corps. This procedure was in contrast to that of the Ballet of the New World, where only Venezuelan dancers performed.

With Pérez Borjas in charge at the Teresa Carreño, Nebrada returned to choreography with great success in his 1984 version of *The Firebird,* which featured elaborate scenery and a brilliant company. Nebrada clearly revealed the neoclassical direction of the company by staging his choreographies such as *Géminis, Percussion for Six Men, Nuestros Valses, Doble Corchea, George Sand,* and, later, versions of *Romeo and Juliet, Coppélia, Don Quixote, Swan Lake,* and *Cinderella.* The Teresa Carreño Foundation successfully blended dancers from different companies and schools, including the Metropolitan Ballet, directed by Keyla Ermecheo; the Ballet Nina Novak, directed by Nina

VENEZUELA. Dancers of the Ballet Nacional de Caracas Teresa Carreño (originally the Ballet Fundación Teresa Carreño) in a 1986 performance of Vicente Nebrada's *Doble Corchea,* set to music by Benjamin Britten. (Photograph by Miguel Gracia, courtesy of Belén Lobo.)

VENEZUELA. Members of the Danzahoy group perform Adriana Urdaneta's *Huespedes* (1994), to music by Aquíles Báez. (Photograph by Ana María Yánez, courtesy of Adriana Urdaneta.)

Novak; Ballet Arte, directed by Lidija Franklin; Conjunto Coreográfico (Choreographic Alliance) of the state of Carabobo, directed by Nina Nikaronova; and the Ballet School of Taormina Guevara, directed by Taormina Guevara until her death. In 1986 Danzahoy became the resident company of the Teatro Teresa Carreño.

Additional small groups were formed. Danza Teatro, directed by Abelardo Gameche, formerly with the Taller de Danza Contemporánea, was oriented toward experiments with postmodern tendencies. While also dancing with the José Limón company in the United States, Orta established a group of his own, Choreoarte, planning to develop choreography based on folklore.

La Fundación Ballet Teresa Carreño, called Ballet Nacional de Caracas Teresa Carreño since 1984, participated in the United We Dance festival held in 1995 in San Francisco, California. In the area of modern dance, Venezuela's encouragement for young choreographers has seen notable development as a result of the Festival de Jóvenes Coreógraphos. At this time in Venezuela there are six active classical dance companies and thirteen active modern dance companies, all subsidized by the Consejo Nacional de la Cultura.

BIBLIOGRAPHY

Alvarenga, Teresa. *Zhandra Rodríguez y el Ballet de Caracas*. Caracas, 1980.

Barrios, Maria Eugenia. *Por amor a la danza*. Caracas, 1985.

Danzaluz. *Directorio latinoamericano*. Maracaibo, 1991.

Danzaluz. *Cuadernos de danza (Terminología de danza académica y contemporánea)*. Maracaibo, 1991.

Fernandez Palazzi, Federico. *Las dos caras de la danza*. Caracas, 1990.

Ferrari, Marisol. *Danzaluz: Veinticinco aniversario*. Maracaibo, 1994.

Guerra, Ramiro. *Apreciación de la danza*. Maracaibo, 1990.

Leon, Carlos Augusto. *Vivencia de la danza*. Caracas, 1974.

Lobo, Belén. "La danza en Venezuela: De Gally de Mamay a Vicente Nebreda." *Enciclopedia conocer a Venezuela*, 1986.

Lobo, Belén. *Pasión de la danza*. (Revista M. 93) Caracas, 1990.

Lobo, Belén. "La danza clásica y contemporánea en Venezuela." *Enciclopedia temática de Venezuela*. Caracas, 1993.

Lobo, Belén. *Nebreda/Nebrada*. Caracas, 1996.

Monasterios, Ruben. *B.I.C. Imágen de un ballet perdido*. Caracas, 1981.

Monasterios, Ruben. *Cuerpos en el espacio*. Caracas, 1986.

Perez Borjas, Elias. *La danza en Venezuela*. Caracas, 1966.

Sanoja, Sonia, *Duraciones visuales*. Caracas, 1963.

Sanoja, Sonia. *A través de la danza*. Caracas, 1971.

Sanoja, Sonia. *Bajo el signo de la danza, 1992*. Caracas, 1992.

Sassone, Helena, and Roland Streuli. *La danza en Venezuela*. Caracas, 1989.

Stahl, Steffy. *El amanecer de la danza en Venezuela*. Caracas, 1992.

Viana, Luis. *La metáfora de la violencia*. Caracas, 1994.

Womutt, Andreina. *Movimiento perpetuo*. Caracas, 1991.

BELÉN LOBO

VERCHININA, NINA (Nina Verchinina de Beausacq; born 1912 in Moscow, died 16 December 1995 in Rio de Janiero, Brazil), dancer. By the first half of the twentieth century many ballet companies were touring Brazil, and some of the dancers stayed to open schools and found companies. Until the arrival of the Russian dancer Nina Verchinina in 1954, Brazil's exposure to theatrical dance was almost exclusively to classical ballet. After arriving in the country as an independent choreographer, Verchinina became a pioneer, introducing the basic principles of modern dance.

Nina Verchinina had a noble background. Born in Moscow and raised in Shanghai, she held the title of countess of Beausacq. As a child she began taking dance lessons with two of the most prominent Russian instructors of the time, Olga Preobajenska, master of the classical technique, and Bronislava Nijinska, one of the first to introduce modern dance worldwide. After absorbing Nijinska's teachings, Verchinina went to Germany to study with Rudolf Laban.

Verchinina began her professional career in 1929 as a member of Ida Rubinstein's dance company. At that time, the company had Nijinska as a choreographer and Igor Stravinsky and Maurice Ravel as contributing composers. Verchinina soon became a soloist for the Ballets Russes de Monte Carlo, and when the company split, Verchinina stayed with Colonel Wassily de Basil's group, then called the Original Ballets Russes. She danced intermittently for the company from 1933 to 1937, 1939 to 1941, and 1946 to 1947.

During her years with the Ballets Russes, Verchinina was known for her idiosyncratic style, juxtaposing classical pointe technique with dramatic gesture and modern angular steps. Because of these characteristics, she was often referred to as "Mary Wigman on pointe."

VERCHININA. As one of the picnickers in the third movement, "In the Country," of Léonide Massine's *Symphonie Fantasque* (1936). (Photograph from the Dance Collection, New York Public Library for the Performing Arts.)

Beginning in 1937, while dancing with the Original Ballet Russe, Verchinina began experimenting with choreography. She worked initially as invited choreographer for the San Francisco Ballet in the 1937/38 season, and later at the Ballet Opera of Havana, from 1942 to 1945.

In 1949, while established in Madrid, Spain, Verchinina founded her own dance group. Works such as *The Quest* and *Valsa Triste*, created then, are now part of the repertory of many companies worldwide.

During the 1950s Verchinina built an independent career in South America. In 1950 she went to Argentina and worked in Buenos Aires, La Plata, and Mendoza. Four years later, she settled in Brazil. In 1954 and 1955, Verchinina was based at the Rio de Janeiro City Theater as invited choreographer. There she was responsible for the *mise-en-scène* of *Narciso* and *Rhapsody in Blue*. From 1957 to 1960, Verchinina began creating dances for the same company, based on the work of Brazilian composers. The results included *Tahina Can*, to music by Heitor Villa-Lobos, and *Zuimaaluti*, to music by Claudio Santoro.

In the 1960s, Nina Verchinina stopped choreographing and dedicated her time exclusively to teaching dance. Her style, combining a strong classical background with modernist movement and an expressionist repertory of gestures, was carried into her teaching. It has been of incomparable value to the development of theatrical dance in Brazil.

BIBLIOGRAPHY

Faro, Antonio José. *Pequena história da dança*. Rio de Janeiro, 1986.
Faro, Antonio José. *A dança no Brasil e seus constructores*. Rio de Janeiro, 1988.
Portinari, Maribel. *História da dança*. Rio de Janeiro, 1989.
Sucena, Eduardo. *A dança teatral no Brasil*. Rio de Janeiro, 1988.

KATIA CANTON

VERDON, GWEN (Gwyneth Evelyn Verdon; born 13 January 1925 in Culver City, California), American dancer, singer, actress, choreographer, and dance educator. Because she was "knock-kneed," Verdon began to study dance with her mother, Gertrude, a Denishawn dancer, while very young. She continued with the Cecchetti, method taught by Ernest Belcher and Aida Broadbent and explored Spanish dance with Eduardo Cansino (Rita Hayworth's father). Chosen "Miss California" at the age of fourteen, she danced with Broadbent's ballet corps in Los Angeles Civic Light Opera productions of *Rosalinda* and *The Three Musketeers* (1947) and even formed a comedy ballroom team, Verdon and Del Velle.

After a brief marriage at the age of sixteen, motherhood, and a three-year interlude from dance, she returned to study ballet with Carmelita Maracci and East Indian dance with La Meri. She joined Jack Cole's landmark dance company in nightclubs and on stage in *Bonanza Bound* (out of town, 1947) and *Alive and Kicking* (Broadway, 1950). With her strong technique and immaculate isolation, she became one of the leading exponents of Cole's inventive jazz style, first assisting him on *Magdalena* (Broadway, 1948).

Under contract to Twentieth Century–Fox, Verdon and Cole, who was the dance director, explored erotic honesty in onscreen dance, often causing havoc with the censors. In 1951 she blistered the screen as a slave girl in *David and Bathsheba,* was featured with Betty Grable in *Meet Me after the Show,* and led the ensemble of *On the Riviera.* After choreographing and dancing in *Dreamboat,* she was back illuminating Cole's work in *The "I Don't Care" Girl* and *The Merry Widow* (1952). In 1953, she had an acting role and again danced with Grable in *The Farmer Takes a Wife* and performed a steamy Voodoo-ceremony dance (which she choreographed) in *Mississippi Gambler.*

At the invitation of choreographer Michael Kidd, she auditioned for the role of Claudine in *Can-Can* (1953). On opening night on Broadway, she created a sensation, and she subsequently won her first Tony award for her performance. Hollywood lost its best dancer, although she did briefly rejoin Cole for *Gentlemen Marry Brunettes* (1955). Cast next as the temptress Lola in *Damn Yankees* (1955), Verdon collaborated with another film expatriate, choreographer Bob Fosse. With her impudent explosion of flame-red hair, uniquely lovable squeaky voice, and innocent farm-girl face, Verdon, planted firmly on her well-controlled and well-proportioned body, became the definitive dancing-singing star of American musicals.

With Verdon as his inspiration and muse, Fosse continued to experiment and define his style. Together they created a succession of hit shows, with Verdon as their star, as the Broadway musical moved into its choreographer-as-director era: *New Girl in Town* (1957), *Redhead* (1959), *Sweet Charity* (1966), and, finally, *Chicago* (1975). Verdon and Fosse had married in 1960 and had a daughter together in 1963. Although they subsequently divorced, Verdon continued to assist Fosse on the film version of *Sweet Charity* (1969, for which she coached Shirley MacLaine), staged the second company of *Chicago,* and served as dance mistress on *Dancin'* (Broadway, 1978).

In addition to multiple Tony, Donaldson, Grammy, and *Dance Magazine* awards for her stage performances, Verdon also has the distinction of being the quintessential interpreter of the work of two of the twentieth century's most innovative stage and film choreographers. One of her stage roles, in *Damn Yankees* (1958), was captured on film: the crispness and clarity of her technique and her unique vulnerability and sense of humor and style are riveting.

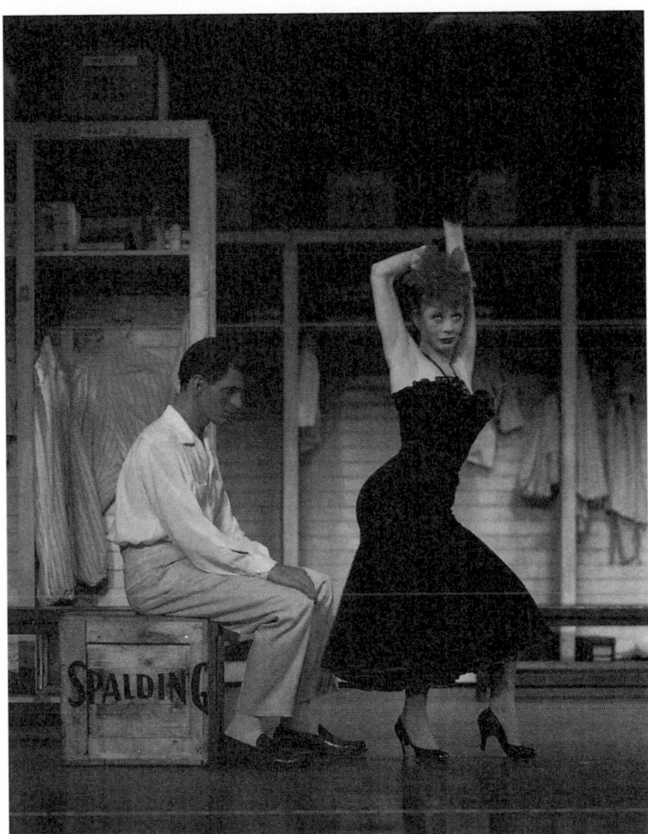

VERDON. The sultry "Whatever Lola Wants," choreographed by Bob Fosse, was one of the hit numbers of *Damn Yankees* (1955). Verdon is pictured here as Lola, a 172-year-old witch sent by Satan to seduce an uncooperative baseball player (Stephen Douglass). Her provocative striptease was an extraordinary mix of East Indian hand gestures, flamenco-like footwork, French burlesque, and purely American jazz dance. (Photograph by Photofest, New York; used by permission.)

BIBLIOGRAPHY

"1961 Award Winner Profile." *Dance Magazine* (March 1962).

Grubb, Kevin Boyd. *Razzle Dazzle: The Life and Work of Bob Fosse.* New York, 1989.

Mordden, Ethan. *Broadway Babies.* New York, 1983.

Who's Who in Entertainment, 1992–1993. Wilmette, Ill., 1993.

LARRY BILLMAN

VERDY, VIOLETTE (Nelly Armande Guillerm; born 1 December 1933 in Pont l'Abbé), French dancer and teacher. Verdy began ballet lessons at the age of eight. Following studies with Carlotta Zambelli and Rousanne Sarkissian, she made her professional debut in 1945 in Roland Petit's *Le Poète,* soon afterward becoming a member of his Ballets des Champs-Élysées. For three years she

VERDY. Her vivacity and extraordinary musicality made Verdy an audience favorite wherever she appeared. She is pictured here in an exuberant *saut de chat* in George Balanchine's *Donizetti Variations,* in 1960. (Photograph by Fred Fehl; used by permission. Choreography by George Balanchine © The George Balanchine Trust.)

danced cameo roles until chosen by film director Ludwig Berger to star in his 1950 release *Ballerina.* It was at this time that she adopted the stage name of Verdy.

Although *Ballerina* was generally considered an insignificant film, Verdy's sincere acting and pure technique led to numerous guest appearances at festivals and galas and to contracts with the reorganized Ballets des Champs-Élysées, the Ballet de Marigny, and the Ballets de Paris de Roland Petit. While with the latter group she created the embattled heroine in Petit's *Le Loup* (1953), a portrayal that marked her artistic coming-of-age. After the Ballets de Paris disbanded, Verdy toured the United States with the London Festival Ballet. Injury temporarily interrupted her career, but by 1957 she was appearing with the Ballet Rambert in her first full-length *Coppélia* and *Giselle.*

An amateur film made during Verdy's Festival Ballet tour and shown to Nora Kaye led, in 1957, to an invitation for Verdy to join American Ballet Theatre. Thereafter, with brief exceptions, the focus of her career shifted to the United States. Her ability to adapt herself to the tastes of the American public in such works as *Gala Performance, Offenbach in the Underworld,* and *Theme and Variations* was summed up by a reviewer for *Dance News* (November 1957): "Violette Verdy has acclimatized herself to the company and is part of the repertory with no ado. Her unmannered style is the secret of the ease with which she fits into British, French, and American Ballet." Beside dancing the standard repertory, Verdy also created the title role in the American Ballet Theatre production of Birgit Cullberg's *Miss Julie* (1958).

With the temporary disbanding of American Ballet Theatre in autumn 1958, Verdy became the only company member invited to join the New York City Ballet. Although her physique and training set her apart from the majority of the New York City Ballet dancers, her musicality and intelligence enabled her to blend harmoniously into George Balanchine's choreographic conceptions. For close to two decades she brought vitality and incisive musical understanding to her interpretations of *Symphony in C, Divertimento No. 15,* Polyhymnia in *Apollo, Stars and Stripes, Scotch Symphony,* and *Allegro Brillante.* Her longtime partner Edward Villella commented on her "extraordinary, complete musical understanding, almost like Balanchine's. The remarkable thing . . . is that a French dancer coming here to another style and another repertoire has pointed up Balanchine's intentions . . . more than any of his other dancers."

In addition to her roles in the standard repertory, Verdy had Balanchine parts crafted for her in *A Midsummer Night's Dream, Episodes, Liebeslieder Walzer, Jewels, La Source,* and *Sonatine.* Throughout the same period she also created roles by other choreographers, including that of Creusa in the American premiere of Cullberg's *Medea* and a solo (op. 25, no. 4) in Jerome Robbins's *Dances at a Gathering,* beside making guest appearances dancing the classics with such companies as England's Royal Ballet, the Paris Opera Ballet, and the Boston Ballet. Her portrayal of Giselle was hailed as one of the finest of her generation, while her partnership with Villella approached the legendary. She also served as a roving talent scout for the School of American Ballet's scholarship program.

Verdy's last years with Balanchine were punctuated by recurrent injuries and by a growing distance between herself and the choreographer, largely because of her independent thinking. In 1977 she left the New York City Ballet to become the first female director of dance at the Paris Opera. For three years she attempted, against some opposition, to bring flexibility into the Opera's rigid hierarchical system, as well as to promote youthful dancers and choreographers. She was also instrumental in obtaining the ballet company's first musical director. When a change of administration necessitated her departure in 1980, Verdy returned to the United States, where she became artistic co-director, later full director, of the Boston Ballet, a position in which she served until 1984. She then rejoined the New York City Ballet, where she is a teaching associate. Known for her broad-ranging skills in the field, Verdy also receives frequent invitations to teach, choreograph, and lecture at other institutions, including England's Royal Ballet, the Paris Opera Ballet school, and Ballet West. She is also active in regional ballet. She has written a book for children, *Of Swans, Sugar Plums, and Satin Slippers,* which was published in 1991.

BIBLIOGRAPHY

Dekle, Nicole. "Summer Secret." *Dance Magazine* (February 1994): 88–93.

Garis, Robert. "The Balanchine Enterprise." *Ballet Review* 21 (Spring 1993): 24–44.

Haggin, B. H. *Ballet Chronicle.* New York, 1970.

Huckenpahler, Victoria. *Ballerina: A Biography of Violette Verdy.* New York, 1978.

Marks, Marcia. "Violette—'Because She Is So Modest.'" *Dance Magazine* (February 1972): 47–62.

Mason, Francis. "The Paris Opéra: A Conversation with Violette Verdy." *Ballet Review* 14 (Fall 1986): 23–30.

Verdy, Violette. *Giselle: A Role for a Lifetime.* New York, 1977.

Verdy, Violette. "Violette Verdy on the Bolshoi." *Ballet Review* 15 (Summer 1987): 15–38.

Whitney, Mary. "Homecoming." *Ballet News* 2 (September 1980): 18–21.

VICTORIA HUCKENPAHLER

VES DANCE. The Sri Lankan ritual dance drama called Kohomba Kankariya, dating to the fifth century BCE, is the spiritual home of the *ves* dancer. The *ves* regalia *(suseta abarana)* is that of a priest-king. No fewer than sixty-four items make up this costume, which is believed to belong to the deity Kohomba and is regarded as a replica of costume of the royal magician Male Rajjuruwo, who was supernaturally lured to the island of Sri Lanka to heal King Panduvasdeva of an incurable malady.

The impressive headgear is a crown of several parts: a silver tiara *(sikha-bandanaya);* a forehead plate fringed with silver *bo*-leaves *(netti malaya);* and seven silver spokes rising like rays above the dancer's head. Intricate silver ear plates *(thodupath)* adorn his ears; ornamental plates *(urabahu)* of silver or brass cover his shoulders. He wears three sets of broad silver armlets *(bandi wallalu),* six on each arm, and necklaces of colored beads *(karapatiya).* His bare chest is covered with strings of beads, held together with clasps of carved ivory ornamented with silver. He wears elongated silver wrist plates about two inches (five centimeters) wide.

The clothing of the dancer is called *hangalaya.* From waist to ankle he wears a white cloth *(ududaya)* intricately pleated, about three and a half yards (three meters) in length. Over this he puts another cloth, the *devalla,* which is twenty yards (twenty meters) long, heavily pleated, and extends to the knees. Around the waist he wears yet another cloth *(yoth pota)* of fine material folded to a width of two inches (five centimeters) and flounced at the end to form layers of frills *(neriya).* A strong string forty-two feet (fourteen meters) long, the *hangal lanuwa,* is wrapped around the dancer's waist to secure the layers of pleated fabric, and a silver belt with a decorated clasp is worn over the cloth. From the center of this belt down to the knees is a drape of bright red velvet decorated with heavy silver bosses *(inahedaya),* fashioned into nineteen tasseled corners to simulate an elephant's trunk. Around the calves are several sets of brass jingles *(rasu pati),* and on the feet are anklets *(silambu)* rounded and filled with bells, anchored to the second toe of each foot.

After several years of apprenticeship under a revered *mulyakdessa,* the *ves* dancer *(yakdessa)* is crowned with his silver headgear at an auspicious time with much ceremony; traditionally, this initiation occurs at a Kohomba Kankariya ceremony. The *ves* dancers and drummers display their talents in competitive performances at the Kohomba Kankariya. [*See* Kohomba Kankariya.]

Ves dance has a highly developed classical technique with many variations and synchronizations of mood and rhythm. Its elements include invocatory chants, perfect synchronization of hand and foot movements, and vigorous embellishments. The dancer has to be equally proficient in dancing, drumming, and singing before his initiation.

VES DANCE. Wearing an elaborate traditional costume, the *ves* dancer Surasena demonstrates a characteristic jumping movement. (Photograph from the archives of The Asia Society, New York.)

Ves dancers from traditional families, such as the Nittawela, Thiththapajjala, Rangama, and Amunugama families of the Kandy district, were given lands and settled in certain villages by the Kandyan kings. These masters have passed down their art form in its purity from father to son for perhaps two millennia. The Beravaya community of shamans today preserves the highly evolved art of Kandyan dance. [*See* Kandyan Dance.] In recent times they have provided a grand finale to any public performance of Kandyan dancing, welcomed state guests, and participated in the famous annual street pageant, the Kandy Perahera, held in August.

[*For articles on other dance traditions in Sri Lanka see* Kandy Perahera *and* Touil. *See also* Costume in Asian Traditions *and* Mask and Makeup, *article on* Asian Traditions.]

BIBLIOGRAPHY

Amunugana, Sarath. *Notes on Sinhala Culture.* Colombo, 1980.

Bowers, Faubion. *Theatre in the East: A Survey of Asian Dance and Drama.* New York, 1956.

de Zoete, Beryl. *Dance and Magic Drama in Ceylon.* London, 1957.

Disanayaka, Mudiyanse. *Udarata santikarma saha gami natya sampradaya.* Colombo, 1990.

Gunasinghe, Siri. *Masks of Ceylon.* Colombo, 1962.

Kotelawala, Sicille P. C. *The Classical Dance of Sri Lanka.* New York, 1974.

Makulloluwa, W. B. *Dances of Sri Lanka.* Colombo, 1976.

Nevill, Hugh. "Sinhalese Folklore." *Journal of the Royal Asiatic Society, Ceylon Branch* 14 (1971): 58–90.

Pertold, Otaker. *Ceremonial Dances of the Sinhalese* (1930). Colombo, 1973.

Raghavan, M. D. *Dances of the Sinhalese.* Colombo, 1968.

Sarachchandra, Ediriweera R. *The Folk Drama of Ceylon.* 2d ed. Colombo, 1966.

Sedaraman, J. I. *Nrtya ratnakaraya.* Colombo, 1992.

Sedaraman, J. I., et al. *Udarata natum kalava.* Colombo, 1992.

Seneviratna, Anuradha. *Traditional Dance of Sri Lanka.* Colombo, 1984.

SICILLE P. C. KOTELAWALA

VESTRIS FAMILY, Italian-French family of dancers, of Florentine origin, originally surnamed Vestri. Because of difficulties arising from business irregularities, the Vestri family was forced to leave northern Italy in the late 1730s. The head of the family, Tommaso Maria Ippolito Vestri, and his wife, Beatrice Bruscagli, took refuge in Naples, along with their seven children, Giovanni Battista, Teresa, Gaetano, Angiolo, Maddalena, Francesco, and Violante. Schooled in music and dancing, the older children soon began to appear on stage in Naples and Palermo. After a time, the family left Naples and pursued theatrical work in Bologna, Venice, Genoa, and Vienna. Then the family split, to look for work elsewhere. The mother, Teresa, and Gaetano went to Dresden, and the father and the other children went to Milan. In Dresden, Teresa and Gaetano were hired for the opera, but by the late 1740s both had settled in Paris, where they were joined by Angiolo and Giovanni Battista. Under the French spelling of *Vestris,* the family name was to become famous throughout Europe, thanks chiefly to the genius of Gaetano and his son Auguste.

Jean-Baptiste Vestris (Giovanni Battista Vestri; born 1725 in Florence, died 1801 in Paris). The eldest of the children, Jean-Baptiste retired from the stage in 1753 to maintain the home of his famous brother Gaetano, known as Gaëtan, and later to devote time to the education of his nephew and godchild Auguste. Possessing a good nature and an even temperament, Jean-Baptiste managed the affairs of the family with exceptional skill, always maintaining harmonious relations with the often impetuous and scheming personalities typical of the theatrical world in eighteenth-century Paris.

Thérèse Vestris (Maria Teresa Francesca Vestri; born 1726 in Florence, died 18 January 1808 in Paris). After the family left Italy, Teresa performed for a time in Vienna, but, when her love affair with Prince Esterházy aroused the displeasure of the empress Maria Theresa, she found it prudent to leave the city. She went first to Dresden, then spent eighteen months in Florence, and finally settled in Paris in 1746. She used her social connections to obtain positions for her brothers Gaetano and Angiolo with the Paris Opera, where she herself made her debut on 17 March 1751 in *Le Carnaval du Parnasse.* She also performed in court spectacles. Like her brothers, she reinforced her position at the Opera with backstage intrigues, aimed particularly at her rival Mademoiselle Puvigné, whom she desired to supplant, frequently complaining to the director of the Opera that Puvigné was unfairly favored by the ballet master. After creating a number of incidents, Thérèse and her brothers left the Opera in December 1754 and went to Berlin.

One year later they were back in Paris, appearing in *Roland,* an opera by Robert Quinault and Jean-Baptiste Lully. "The Italian Beauty," as Thérèse was called, often danced as the partner of her famous brother Gaëtan. She performed in Bernard's *opéra-ballet Les Emprises de l'Amour* (In the Grip of Love) and in Lully's *Armide,* and she scored triumphs in Lully's *Alceste* and *Amadis.* Jean-Marie Clément referred to "signorina Teresina" as

> the most pleasant ballerina. What legs! — a joy to look at! She has an admirably slender waist, her head is held high and is well positioned. Her eyes, teeth, and lips are charmingly expressive. Her smile is so gracious, there is something so tender, something so voluptuous in all her movements, a graciousness so smooth that it permeates your fantasy: I think of it constantly. (Clément,1754)

Other reviewers similarly praised her grace and loveliness. Until 1766 she ruled the Opera stage with a seductiveness that won her many admirers.

Gaëtan Vestris (Gaetano Apolline Baldassare Vestri; born 18 April 1729 in Florence, died 23 September 1808 in Paris). After his engagement at the Dresden Opera, Gaëtan went to Paris, where he studied dance with Louis Dupré and was admitted to the ranks of dancers at the Opera. He made his debut in 1749 as a sailor in the comic ballet *Le Carnaval et la Folie.* As few dancers of the day could equal him, he was immediately welcomed and enjoyed great success. In 1750 he appeared in no fewer than six major productions of opera and ballet—Royer's *Almasis,* Campra's *Les Fêtes Vénitiennes* and *Tancrède,* Rebel and Francoeur's *Ismène,* Brassac's *Léandre et Héro,* and Collasse's *Thétis et Pélée*—and was highly acclaimed in them all. Appointed *premier danseur* in 1751, he performed chiefly in works by Lully (e.g., *Alceste, Prosperine,* and *Armide*) and Rameau (e.g., *Les Indes Galantes, Castor et Pollux, Platée,* and *Dardanus*). He also danced in court spectacles with his sister Thérèse and his brother Angiolo. Clément wrote that "the *premier danseur* after Dupré, and of his type, now dancing at the Opera is a young Florentine named Vestris. He is quite tall and long-legged, and nobly built, and he cuts a dashing figure in the theater" (Clément, 1754).

Gaëtan was dismissed from the Opera in 1754 after an awkward incident involving his fellow dancer Jean-Barthélémy Lany. During a rehearsal, a quarrel broke out between Mademoiselle Puvigné and Thérèse Vestris. Lany sided with Puvigné and Gaëtan with his sister. In the heat of the moment, Gaëtan challenged Lany to a duel. Things were smoothed out and the duel did not take place, but some days later, on a report from guards posted at the Opera, Gaëtan was confined to the prison of Fort l'Évêque, where he lived in high style. On his release he accepted an engagement in Berlin. His exile from the Opera was, however, brief. In December 1755 he rejoined the company and appeared with his sister Thérèse in Lully's *tragédie-lyrique Roland.*

By the mid-1750s Gaëtan's public life was becoming increasingly important, and his name was often mentioned in the newspapers. *Le Mercure* of 31 May 1757 praised his performances in Bernard's *opéra-ballet Les Emprises de l'Amour* and in Lully's *Alceste* and *Amadis.* In *Les Indes Galantes* he was greatly admired in the role of Borée for "the brilliance of his steps, the precision of his positions, and the picturesque genius of his dancing." He was called *l'homme à la belle jambe* ("the man with the beautiful legs") and, after Dupré, *le dieu de la danse* ("the god of dance"). In her memoirs (1835–1837) the painter Élisabeth Vigée-Lebrun noted that "he was a very handsome man and perfect in *la danse noble.* I can hardly describe the grace with which he took his hat off and put it back on, and the bow that preceded the minuet."

With each success, Gaëtan's sense of self-importance and his demands for preference increased in proportion to his triumphs, and his romantic affairs supplied much material for the scandal sheets. His numerous liaisons included affairs with Marie Allard, the mother of his son Auguste (born 1760), and Anna Heinel, who also bore him a son, Adolphe (born 1791), and whom he married in 1792, when he was sixty-three.

Between 1760 and 1766 Gaëtan Vestris often danced at the Hoftheater in Stuttgart under the direction of Jean-Georges Noverre. There he created roles in a number of Noverre's ballets, including Admète in *Admète et Alceste* (1761), Hercules in *La Mort d'Hercule* (1762), Jason in *Médée et Jason* (1763), and Orpheus in *Orpheus und Eurydice* (1763), among others. In France he continued to make frequent appearances at the Opera and at the court theater at Fontainebleau. In 1767, he mounted a version of *Médée et Jason,* with choreography "after Noverre," in Vienna, and in Paris, dancing with Marie-Madeleine Guimard, he had a great success in what Gaston Capon (1908) called the "pantomime très voluptueuse" in the ballet *Dardanus.*

Having been assistant ballet master at the Paris Opera since 1761, Gaëtan succeeded Jean-Barthélémy Lany as ballet master in 1770. He lost little time in mounting yet another version of *Médée et Jason,* which by then had become a favorite work. He choreographed a mediocre ballet, *Endymion,* in 1772 and danced in it in March 1773, along with Mademoiselle Guimard and his son Auguste, who by then was a boy of thirteen. In 1775, dancing the role of Jason with Guimard or his sister Thérèse as Medée, he gave still another version of Noverre's *Médée et Jason.* In 1776 he turned over the post of ballet master to Noverre. After a triumphal tour of England with Auguste in 1781, he retired in 1782 but reappeared in 1800 to dance a minuet in Maximilien Gardel's *Ninette à la Cour.*

Gaëtan Vestris began his career as a burlesque dancer, but he adopted to perfection the serious style that had been the glory of his teacher, the great Louis Dupré. A noble reserve lent harmony to his steps, and Noverre said that "while he does the pirouette much better than his son, he is sparing of it; he leaves the audience wanting more." But he was also able to humanize his art by adopting the reforms recommended by such innovators as Gardel and Noverre. Like Gardel, he abandoned the use of masks, and, following Noverre's principles, he "combined with extremely noble and easy execution the rare merit of moving and involving the spectators and speaking to their passions."

Well aware of his talent and popularity, Vestris once declared, "There are only three great men in Europe: the king of Prussia, Monsieur de Voltaire, and me." Despite his vanity and egoism, he nevertheless served the cause of dance with passion, contributed to its growth, and paved the way for his son Auguste, who can justly be considered the first modern dancer.

VESTRIS FAMILY. Auguste Vestris depicted at a gleeful moment during his first visit to London, in 1780–1781. This etching was made from a sketch by Nathaniel Dance that is now in the Fitzwilliam Museum, Cambridge. (Reprinted from Cecil J. Sharp and A. P. Opie, *The Dance: An Historical Survey of Dancing in Europe*, London, 1924.)

Angiolo Vestris (Angiolo Maria Gasparo Vestri; born 1730 in Florence, died 10 June 1809 in Paris). A handsome, blue-eyed blond, Angiolo played the flute in the Concerts de la Reine in Paris, studied dance with Louis Dupré, and joined the Opera as a soloist in 1753. He remained with the Opera until 1757, with an interruption in 1754. Fearing that his brother Gaëtan's fame would overshadow his own, he continued his career in various European theaters before being hired in 1761 for the Stuttgart Opera as *premier danseur*, under the direction of Noverre. There he spent six years and married the comic actress Françoise Rose Gourgaud, a sister of the celebrated mezzo-soprano Louise Dugazon. In 1767 he returned to Paris, where he became an actor, first with the Comédie Italienne and then with the Comédie Française.

Auguste Vestris Marie-Jean-Augustin Vestris; born 27 March 1760 in Paris, died 5 December 1842 in Paris). The son of Gaëtan Vestris and Marie Allard (whence his nickname, Vestr'Allard), Auguste studied dance with his father and showed exceptional gifts at a very early age. As a prodigy of twelve, he appeared on stage at the Paris Opera on 18 September 1772 during the performance of a pastorale called *La Cinquantaine.* Presented by his father in court dress, a sword at his side, the young boy immediately won the hearts of the audience. *Le Mercure* declared that he combined "brilliance of execution, personal grace, the finesse of art, beauty of bearing, intelligence, and all the advantages of a felicitous nature and a consummate talent." Baron Grimm, a prominent reviewer, noted that Auguste "danced with the same precision, the same aplomb, and almost the same strength as the great [Gaëtan] Vestris" (Grimm, 1812).

Having been applauded at court on 14 November 1772 and admitted to the Opera as a pupil, Auguste danced the role of Eros beside his father and Marie-Madeleine Guimard in *Endymion* in March 1773. Hired for the Opera in 1775, he became a solo dancer in 1776 and performed in *Les Petits Rien, Alceste,* and *Les Caprices de Galathée* of Noverre. He was named *premier danseur* in 1778 and *premier sujet de la danse* in 1780. He then took a six-month leave of absence and toured England with his father. At the King's Theatre in London he triumphed in

VESTRIS FAMILY. Auguste Vestris as the lead dancer in *Les Amans Surpris* (1780), which was first performed at the King's Theatre, London, during Vestris's tour of England. This contemporary lithograph, by J. Thorthwaite after James Roberts, was published in Bell's *British Theatre* (London, 1781). (Courtesy of Madison U. Sowell and Debra H. Sowell, Brigham Young University, Provo, Utah.)

Noverre's *Les Caprices de Galathée* and *Médée et Jason* and in Maximilien Gardel's *Ninette à la Cour* and *Mirza et Lindor,* all of which he had performed at the Paris Opera with Guimard, with whom he had a brief love affair. In addition, Auguste shown in such Gardel ballets as *La Chercheuse d'Esprit* (1778), *La Rosière* (1784), *Le Premier Navigateur, ou Le Pouvoir de l'Amour* (1785), and *Le Coq au Village* (1787). After the French Revolution in 1789, he returned to England and performed at the King's Theatre, where Noverre was directing the ballet.

A man of many love affairs, Auguste married a young Opera dancer, Anne-Catherine Augier (1777–1809), who had made her debut in 1795 under the name of Mademoiselle Aimée, but marriage did not prevent him from continuing his many amorous liaisons. Among others, he had a notable affair with Marie-Adrienne Chameroy (1779–1802), a pupil of Gardel, a charming dancer, and a rival of Auguste's famous partner Guimard. Chameroy accompanied him on one of his tours of the provinces—he repeatedly scored triumphs in Lyon, Montepellier, and Bordeaux—and they enjoyed particular success in Pierre Gardel's ballet *Psyché* (1790). After Pierre Gardel succeeded his brother Maximilien as ballet master of the Opera in 1786, he made a number of ballets that included roles worthy of Auguste's special abilities, among them *Télémaque dans l'Île de Calypso* (1790), *La Dansomanie* (1800), *Achille à Scyros* (1804), and *Paul et Virginie* (1806).

By 1803 Auguste had a rival: the twenty-two-year-old Louis-Antoine Duport, who gradually won the public adulation that Vestris had earlier enjoyed. Their rivalry was a juicy subject for the gossip sheets. Although Vestris was no longer able to astonish spectators as he had in his youth, he was still capable of moving them in such ballets as Pierre Gardel's *L'Enfant Prodigue,* which he created in 1812 and which he danced for his farewell performance on 27 September 1816. Almost twenty years later, at the age of sixty-five, he made his last appearance on the Opera stage, dancing a courtly minuet with Marie Taglioni during a gala performance on 8 August 1835.

The heir to his father's majesty and his mother's sprightliness, noble and charming, full of imagination, Auguste Vestris did not fit into any of the customary classifications. Noverre valued his gifts as a dancer and his knowledge as a performer, stating that "his debut in the serious dance was a triumph; this young dancer was distinguished by the rare qualities of aplomb, daring, sureness, brilliance, beautiful formation of steps, and a sensitive and delicate ear." Speaking of a *pas de pâtres* (shepherds' dance) created by Lany for Vestris and Mademoiselle Théodore, Noverre noted that

> our young Proteus [Auguste] grasped this new genre, so completely opposed to the one taught him by his father, with as much taste as intelligence, and was extremely successful in it. I used him in *Le Bergère Héroïque,* a fine, delicate, and characteristic work, in which he demonstrated the naive graces and all the expressiveness that could be desired. (Noverre, 1760)

Regarded as a prodigy and proclaimed the greatest dancer in Europe, Vestris aroused enthusiasm whenever he appeared.

A dancer of great virtuosity as well as artistry, Vestris inspired numerous imitators. Although he was, ultimately, inimitable, his example set a high standard for male dancers of his day. Particularly noteworthy were his cabrioles, his *entrechats* (Serge Lifar [1950] said he could perform the *entrechat douze*), and his pirouettes, although with these he was, according to Noverre, "too generous,"

VESTRIS FAMILY. A much publicized rivalry existed between Auguste Vestris and the younger star of the Paris Opera, Louis-Antoine Duport. In this engraving, Duport is pictured triumphant, as he extends his leg—in perfect *écarté* position—over the fallen body of Vestris. (Engraved frontispiece from Joseph Berchoux's *La danse, ou Les dieux de l'Opéra,* Paris, 1806; courtesy of Madison U. Sowell and Debra H. Sowell, Brigham Young University, Provo, Utah.)

performing them with extraordinary speed if not perfect balance when he stopped. His exceptional elevation was also particularly admired. In her memoirs Madame Vigée-Lebrun (1835–1837) noted that "he was the most amazing dancer to be seen, such was his grace and lightness at one and the same moment. . . . He rose toward the sky in such a prodigious manner that he was believed to have wings."

Vestris was also a choreographer and a teacher. His few choreographies, several *divertissements* and a ballet called *The Nymphs of Diana* (1781), were all presented at the King's Theatre in London and, in sum, added nothing to his glory. As one of the most famous teachers of his day, however, Vestris was able to transmit his art to a significant number of dancers worthy of his lessons, including Charles-Louis Didelot, August Bournonville, and Jules Perrot. But it was as a dancer that Auguste Vestris was indeed supreme. He revealed to audiences that the miraculous emanates from the dance itself, from man transfigured by the conquest of his art. Therein resided his characteristic genius, originality, and modernity.

Armand Vestris (Armand-Auguste Vestris; born 1795 in Paris, died 17 May 1825 in Vienna). Son of Auguste Vestris and Anne-Catherine Augier, Armand Vestris studied dance with his grandfather, Gaëtan. In 1800, at the age of four, he was presented to the Paris Opera audience by his grandfather, still elegant despite his seventy-one years, and his father, then at the height of his glory. Armand followed the family tradition by training as a professional dancer, but in later life he spent little time in Paris. After touring in Italy and Portugal, he went to England in 1809 and stayed for some years in London. There, on 28 June 1813 he married the comic actress Lucia Elizabetta Bartolozzi (1797–1856), who as Madame Vestris became a well-known figure on the London stage. Vestris himself served as choreographer at the King's Theatre from 1813 to 1816, where he successfully mounted several ballets. These included *Le Calife Voleur, Mars et l'Amour,* which was performed by Auguste Vestris, and *Gonzalve de Cordoue,* his most important work. A handsome dancer, Armand Vestris was pleasant to watch, but he did not have the genius of his famous predecessors. He deserted his wife in 1820, left England, and spent the last years of his life in Italy and Vienna.

BIBLIOGRAPHY

Beaumont, Cyril W. "Gaetano and Auguste Vestris in English Caricature." *Ballet* 5 (March 1948): 19–29.

Berchoux, Joseph de. *La danse: Les dieux de l'Opéra.* Paris, 1806.

Campardon, Émile. *L'Académie Royale de Musique du XVIIIe siècle.* 2 vols. Paris, 1884.

Capon, Gaston. *Les Vestris: Le dieu de la danse et sa famille.* Paris, 1908.

Chapman, John V. "Auguste Vestris and the Expansion of Technique." *Dance Research Journal* 19 (Summer 1987): 11–18.

Clément, Pierre. *Les cinq années littéraires.* 2 vols. The Hague, 1754.

Fenner, Theodore. "Ballet in Early Nineteenth-Century London as Seen by Leigh Hunt and Henry Robertson." *Dance Chronicle* 1.2 (1978): 75–95.

Grimm, Friedrich Melchior von. *Correspondance littéraire philosophique et critique.* 17 vols. Paris, 1812–1814.

Guest, Ivor. *The Romantic Ballet in England.* London, 1972.

Guest, Ivor. *The Romantic Ballet in Paris.* 2d rev. ed. London, 1980.

Guest, Ivor. *Jules Perrot: Master of the Romantic Ballet.* London, 1984.

Hammond, Sandra Noll. "The 'Gavotte de Vestris': A Dance of Three Centuries." In *Proceedings of the Seventh Annual Conference, Society of Dance History Scholars, Goucher College, Towson, Maryland, 17–19 February 1984,* compiled by Christena L. Schlundt. Riverside, Calif., 1984.

Lifar, Serge. *Auguste Vestris, le dieu de la danse.* Paris, 1950.

Migel, Parmenia. *The Ballerinas: From the Court of Louis XIV to Pavlova.* New York, 1972.

Moore, Lillian, "Gaetan Vestris and the Vestris Family." In Moore's *Artists of the Dance.* New York, 1938.

Noverre, Jean-Georges. *Lettres sur la danse et sur les ballets.* Stuttgart and Lyon, 1760. Translated by Cyril W. Beaumont as *Letters on Dancing and Ballets* (London, 1930).

Price, Curtis A., et al. *Italian Opera in Late Eighteenth-Century London,* vol. 1, *The King's Theatre, Haymarket, 1778–1791.* London, 1995.

Swift, Mary Grace. *A Loftier Flight: The Life and Accomplishments of Charles Louis Didelot.* Middletown, Conn., 1974.

Vigée-Lebrun, Élisabeth. *Memoirs of Madame Vigée Lebrun* (1835–1837). Translated by Lytton Strachey. London, 1903.

Winter, Marian Hannah. *The Pre-Romantic Ballet.* London, 1974.

JEANNINE DORVANE
Translated from French

VIENNESE KINDERBALLET. Children's theater, in which children play the roles of adults, has a long history. Organized by impresarios with a good business sense, or by choreographers, children's ballet (German, *Kinderballett*) touched feelings in adults that perhaps combined sentimentality and perversity. Vienna appears to have been particularly fruitful soil for this genre: the two most famous children's ballet groups were the Friedrich Horschelt Kinderballett, which performed in the Theater an der Wien, and Josefine Weiss's Danseuses Viennoises.

In the late eighteenth century Vienna had a children's ballet that was artistically quite sophisticated, using choreographers of the stature of Franz Hilverding and Jean-Georges Noverre. To ensure a regular supply of dancers, in 1771 Noverre founded a dance school from which he recruited dancers for his company. The children, who included Antoine and Théodore Bournonville, danced in regular court productions as well as in children's ballets.

When Friedrich Horschelt, who as a child had danced in the Theater an der Wien, returned to work for the theater in 1813, he found that a number of children were dancing there as well as in the court opera house, the Kärntnertor Theater. In 1814 Horschelt became deputy ballet master and in 1816 full ballet master for the Theater an der Wien, which was then under the same management as the Kärntnertor Theater.

On 14 November 1816 Horschelt presented the first production of the children's ballet in a pantomime, *Die Kleine Diebin,* to music by Joseph Kinsky. After the great success of this ballet, a team was formed to adapt existing ballets for children's performances. The two best-known such adaptations were Louis-Antoine Duport's *Aschenbrödel* (Cinderella), performed by as many as 174 children, and *Der Blöde Ritter* (The Bashful Knight), with new music.

In 1815 there were twenty dancers in the children's ensemble. The stars of the troupe were Therese Heberle, Angioletta Mayer, the Schröder sisters Wilhelmine, Betty, and Auguste, Michael Johann Laroche, and Anton Stuhlmüller. Heberle later made a career in Italy; Stuhlmüller became a well-known dancer in central Europe and a partner of Fanny Elssler.

In 1818 this extremely popular and profitable undertaking received its first setback. The Inspectorate of the Vienna Police conducted an investigation and found that the children were in danger of "corruption of morals." Although the investigation was quickly forgotten, Empress Caroline Augusta herself issued a prohibition against the children's ballet, claiming that the children's morals were seriously threatened by "epicures." Count Ferdinand Pálffy, then director of the theater, tried to postpone the decision, arguing that the productions of the children's ballet occupied such an important place in the repertory that it was out of the question to drop them.

Furthermore, he argued, if they were all dismissed immediately, thirty or forty families would be left destitute. An investigation of the domestic conditions of the children in 1820 revealed that the children's ballet had fifty-two members, thirty-seven girls and fifteen boys; the youngest child was eight, the oldest nineteen, and most were between twelve and fifteen. Only thirteen children could return to proper households if dismissed. Most of the others supported their families with their earnings. It was also rumored that a few were supported by "highly placed people," including Count Pálffy.

These findings did nothing to prevent the dissolution of the children's ballet. Horschelt accepted a post as ballet master in Munich in 1822. Apparently the management of the Kärntnertor Theater did not feel that the imperial prohibition applied to it, for by 1824 there were fifty-one child dancers in the theater's employ; however, only dancers who had reached the age of fifteen were allowed to remain in the company.

Children's ballet in Vienna was not revived until 1841, when the dancer Josefine Maudry Weiss accepted the post of a ballet mistress of the Theater in der Josephstadt. She had herself danced at the Kärntnertor Theater and held the post of ballet mistress in the 1830s. As she had already worked with children in Hamburg, she immediately began creating children's dances for the Theater in der Josefstadt. Unlike Horschelt, who created full-length ballets for his children, Weiss limited herself to the composition of short character and national dances, for which she was well known. She inserted them into fairy-tale extravaganzas, musical plays, and other ballets. The music for these dances was written by composers such as Johann Strauss the elder or Joseph Lanner, but chiefly by Anton Emil Titl, conductor at the theater.

VIENNESE KINDERBALLET. This lithographed music cover, published in the 1840s, shows children of the Danseuses Viennoises in *The Harvest Fête,* performed to music by Max Maretzek at Her Majesty's Theatre, London. (Courtesy of Madison U. Sowell and Debra H. Sowell, Brigham Young University, Provo, Utah.)

In June 1842 Weiss signed contracts with the parents of twenty-eight children, committing the children to a five-year ballet training program. She saw to the physical well-being of the children and guaranteed the parents a payment for each performance. Late in 1844, she took thirty-six female dancers on tour along with her twelve-year-old son Franz, who had been a dancer at the Theater in der Josefstadt since 1843. During the next eight years, the children astonished audiences with the incredible precision of their performances. They toured Austria, Germany, and northern Italy. As the Danseuses Viennoises, the troupe visited Paris (1845, 1846, and 1850), London (1845, 1846, and 1849), and the United States, Canada, and Cuba (1846 and 1847). On tour Weiss had to contend with changes of corrupting the children's morals and problems with immigration authorities.

In December 1852, Weiss unexpectedly died. The director of the Theater in der Josefstadt temporarily became the children's guardian, but the troupe was dissolved later that month. A few Viennese children obtained posts with the Kärntnertor Theater, but most of them—including French, English, and even American children—returned to their parents.

[*See also the entry on the Horschelt family.*]

BIBLIOGRAPHY

Dieke, Gertraude. *Die Blütezeit des Kindertheaters: Ein Beitrag zur Theatergeschichte des 18. und beginnenden 19. Jahrhunderts.* Emsdetten, 1934.

Feigl, Susanne, and Christian Lunzer. "Der Fall Alois Fürst Kaunitz-Rietberg." In *Das Mädchenballett des Fürsten Kaunitz.* Vienna, 1988.

Seyfried, Ferdinand von. *Rückschau in das Theaterleben Wiens seit den letzten fünfzig Jahren.* Vienna, 1864.

GUNHILD OBERZAUCHER-SCHÜLLER
Translated from German

VIENNESE WALTZ. *See* Ballroom Dance Competition *and* Waltz.

VIETNAM. Situated on the east coast of the Indochinese Peninsula, the Socialist Republic of Vietnam was formed in 1976, uniting the northern and southern regions after some twenty years. This Southeast Asian region had been colonized by France in the nineteenth century and was divided into three administrative regions (empires) at that time: Tonkin in the north, Annam in the center, and Cochin China in the south. The three were formed into French Indochina between 1859 and 1887. During World War II, Japan invaded and occupied the country. In 1945, Vietnam was made an independent nation, but French attempts at regaining authority led to the French Indochina War (1946–1954). A Geneva Conference in 1954 divided the country along the seventeenth parallel, with communist rule in North Vietnam and a noncommunist regime in South Vietnam. Efforts by North Vietnam to reunify led to the Vietnam War (1957–1975). Today, some seventy million people live in about 130,000 square miles (330,000 square kilometers), bordered by China in the north, Laos in the west, and Cambodia in the southwest. The South China Sea lies to the east. About nine million tribal peoples live in the northern and central highlands, and about two million Chinese descendants of precolonial families continue to live in the country. Mahāyāna Buddhism, Confucianism, and Daoism are the prevailing religions.

The region had a neolithic rice-growing society in the Red (Hong) River Delta before it became a province of China from 221 BCE to 939 CE, and again in the fifteenth century. The Vietnamese expanded their own territory gradually, taking the southern portion in the late fifteenth century and incorporating the Mekong Delta from Cambodia in the seventeenth and eighteenth centuries. Beginning in the sixteenth century, however, European traders and clerics had begun their commerce with Southeast Asia.

Traditional dance in Vietnam reflects the various elements that have contributed to the nation's culture—indigenous, Chinese, and Buddhist. Four categories of traditional dance may be distinguished: folk dance, religious dance, court dance, and dance in the traditional music theaters.

Folk Dance. Throughout Vietnam, folk dances are performed by nonprofessional dancers in everyday dress, using simple gestures and few stage properties. The musical accompaniment is from songs sung by the dancers in unison, or from a few drums or clappers. Some of the dances concern the peasants' work in the fields, such as the *mua chay cay* ("dance of the plough") done at Phu Tho in northern Vietnam, or work on the rivers, such as the *mua ba trao* ("rowing dance") done at Knanh Hoà, Huê, and Binh Dinh in central Vietnam. Others are related to folk games, such as the *mua du tiên* ("dance of the fairy swing") or the *mua co nguoi* ("dance of the human chess pieces") in northern Vietnam; to seasonal feasts, such as the *mua lân* ("dance of the unicorn") on New Year's Day in southern Vietnam; to folk customs or beliefs with a ritual character, such as the *mua cau ngu* ("dance in honor of the whale"), performed by fishermen, *mua dua linh* ("funeral dance), *mua dèn* ("dance of the oil lamp"), *mua dâng ruou* ("dance to offer rice wine"), and *mua dao vo* or *mua câu mua* ("dance to implore the rain") in Thanh Hoa in northern Vietnam.

Religious Dance. These dances are performed by dancers who are possessed by spirits or gods and by monks or members of a religious community. In the *mua phu thuy* ("sorcerer's dance"), a sorcerer dances with incense (joss) sticks, a small bell, or a small drum to cure a disease or to chase away evil spirits. *Mua bong* and *mua châu van* are shamanistic dances of southern and northern Vietnam, respectively, performed by a female medium (shaman). In northern Vietnam the shaman performs different dances depending on which deity possesses her: the *mua kiêm* ("sword dance") for the First, Second, Third, and Fourth High Dignitaries; the *mua môi* ("torch dance") for the First Mother in the Sky; the *mua cheo do* ("boat girl dance") for the Mother of Water; the *mua quat* ("fan dance") for the Fourth Ambassador to the Sky; the *mua cung* ("arch dance") and the *mua hèo* ("stick dance") for the Third, Seventh, and Tenth Princes; the *mua thanh long* *dao* ("blue dragon's saber dance") for the Fifth Dragon King; and the *mua lân* ("unicorn dance").

Another religious dance, the mua luc cung ("six offerings dance") is performed by priests in Buddhist temples or by young girls twelve or thirteen years of age. The six offerings are incense, flowers, candles, tea, fruit, and rice cakes.

Court Dance. Certain dances were performed at various ceremonies at the courts of the ancient Vietnamese emperors. The "Bat Dât" dance originated in China and was performed by 128 court dancers—sixty-four for the civilian segment *(van vu)* and sixty-four for the military *(vo vu)*. Other court dances are "Tam Tinh Chuc Tho" (Three Stars Present Wishes for Longevity), "Mua Tu Linh" (Four Fabulous Animals—the dragon, unicorn, phoenix, and tortoise), and "Mua Hoa Dang" (Flowery Lantern Dance). "Nu Tuong Xuat Quan" (Female Warriors' Dance) is performed by female dancers.

Dance in Music Theater. There are two kinds of music theaters in which dances are performed in Vietnam: *hat cheo,* the folk-music theater of the north, and *hat tuông* or *hat bôi,* the classical-music theater of central and southern Vietnam.

Folk and religious dances are disappearing from Vietnam today. Court dances are being restored for study purposes, however, and theatrical dances are still being performed.

BIBLIOGRAPHY

Cuisinier, Jeanne. *Danse sacrée en Indochine et en Indonésie.* Paris, 1957.

Do Bang Doàn and Do Trong Huê. *Nhung dai le ya yu khuc cua yua chua Viet Nam.* Saigon, 1967.

Ky yeu hoi nghi mua dan toc Viet Nam. Hanoi, 1979.

Lâm To Loc. *Nghe thuat mua dan toc Viet.* Hanoi, 1979.

TRÂN VAN KHÊ

VIGANÒ, SALVATORE (born 25 March 1769 in Naples, died 10 August 1821 in Milan), Italian ballet dancer, choreographer, and composer. Salvatore Viganò was a son of Onorato Viganò, a skillful choreographer, and Maria Ester Viganò (née Boccherini), a talented dancer and mime who was a sister of the composer Luigi Boccherini. Initiated into the art of dance by his parents, Viganò also became an avid student of history, the pictorial arts, and literature, gaining knowledge and insights that would win him the esteem of the major cultural figures of the times. The study of music also occupied an important place in his artistic training, and he became a good violinist and an accomplished composer. (It is likely that his uncle, the celebrated Boccherini, contributed to his development.) When he was just seventeen years old, Viganò presented an *opera buffa* in Rome. Thereafter, he frequently composed or adapted the music for his father's ballets as well as his own.

Viganò's dancing debut took place in 1783, when he was fourteen years old. He appeared with his father's company at the Teatro Argentina in Rome in a female role, because women were still forbidden to appear in the theaters of the Papal States. Salvatore performed in his father's company until 1788, then went to Madrid, where he took part in the festivities surrounding the coronation of Charles IV and where he performed until 1789. This was his chance to study Spanish dance and also to meet Jean Dauberval, a follower of Jean-Georges Noverre. Under Dauberval's guidance, Viganò danced in Bordeaux and London, improving his technique and delving deeper into Noverre's concepts of the *ballet d'action.* In Madrid, Viganò had met and then married Maria Medina, a Spanish dancer, whom he subsequently partnered in many successful productions until they separated at the end of the century.

The influence of Dauberval's teachings marked Viganò's first works. In Italy once again, Viganò's presented *Raul, Signore de Crechi,* a ballet based on the plot of an *opéra comique* by Jacques-Marie Monvel and Nicolas Dalayrac but set to his own music. This, the first of Viganò's works shown alongside his father's works, was mounted in 1791 at the Teatro San Samuele in Venice and was followed in 1792 by his revival of Dauberval's *La Fille Mal Gardée,* staged at the Teatro La Fenice.

Shortly afterward, in 1793, the Viganòs moved to Vienna, where his fame became such that it even influenced the style of the times: "There was no hairdo, footwear, or new *contredanse* that was not 'in the manner of Viganò,'" reports Henry Prunières (1921); even the young Ludwig van Beethoven composed a "minuet in the manner of Viganò." Still under the influence of Dauberval, and having assimilated from his father the tradition of grotesque dancing and pantomime, Viganò presented in 1794 his comic ballet *La Fiera di Barcellona* in Vienna, incurring for it the censure of Cornelius von Ayrenhoff, an advocate of Antonio Muzzarelli. During his career, Viganò composed in the comic genre with no less care than in the serious, demonstrating his knowledge and appreciation of comedy in the traditions of dance theater. The characters in his *Mazilli und Orisko,* staged at the Hoftheater in Vienna in 1800, are, for example, directly linked to the figures of sixteenth-century *commedia dell'arte.*

Among other works produced while Viganò was in Vienna, *Richard Löwenherz, König von England* (Richard Lionheart, King of England), to music by Joseph Weigl, stands out. Inspired by Michel-Jean Sedaine and André-Ernest-Modeste Grétry's *opéra comique,* it was first performed at the Kärntnertor Theater in 1795. It evidenced moments of remarkable intensity, a skillful interplay of groups, and use of the leitmotif as a function of dramatic structure. Viganò further developed these devices in subsequent works.

Between 1795 and 1798, Viganò and his wife frequently

toured central Europe, going to Prague, Dresden, Berlin, and Hamburg. In 1798 and 1799 Viganò staged some of his ballets at the Teatro La Fenice in Venice, and in 1799, separated from Medina, he returned to Vienna, where he remained until 1803. His first major work after his return to the Austrian capital was *Die Geschöpfe des Prometheus* (The Creatures of Prometheus; 1801), set to the score by Ludwig van Beethoven. This work, an exaltation of music and dance, was inspired by the heroic myth of Prometheus and was turned into a grand allegory that dramatized universal themes. [*See the entry on Beethoven.*] Some years later, it became the point of departure for Viganò's *Prometeo,* a major work staged at the Teatro alla Scala in Milan in 1813.

Viganò's work in Vienna makes it clear that he was already developing his own poetics, which were destined to surpass those of the *ballet d'action* and even the *divertissement.* His ballet *Die Spanier auf der Insel Christina* (The Spaniards of Christina Island) was performed in 1802 and *I Giuochi Istmici* in 1803. Both were set to music by Weigl. Also in 1802 appeared *Die Zauberschwestern im Beneventer Walde,* set to music by Franz Xaver Süssmayr. (Viganò staged a revised version of this ballet, *Il Noce di Benevento* [The Walnut Tree of Benevento], at La Scala in 1812. Carlo Ritorni, Viganò's biographer, gives a detailed account of this production, asserting that it was received in Milan by some as "an outstanding, pleasantly eccentric, work" and by others as a "hodgepodge of diabolical and grotesque inventions" [Ritorni, 1838]. Stendhal, however, compared Viganò's ballet to Shakespeare's *The Tempest* and to the last act of *The Merry Wives of Windsor.*)

Viganò's debut in Milan took place at the Teatro Carcao with *Marzio Coriolano,* to music composed by Weigl, in 1804. In this work Viganò sacrificed pure dance in favor of dramatic coherence. During the years that followed, some of Viganò's productions were performed in Venice, Milan, Rome, Padua, Bologna, and Turin. He composed *Gli Strelizzi* for the Teatro La Fenice in Venice in 1809. The subject was the Strelitz conspiracy, which occurred in Russia during the reign of Peter the Great, and was portrayed by Viganò with strong emotional energy. Mass movements alternated with pas de deux, among which was that of the Tsar (Viganò) and Elisabetta (Amalia Muzzarelli). The historian Prunières (1921) saw in this ballet "gestures, subordinated to the imperious need of the rhythm," the path that later led to Vaslav Nijinsky's research and to the theories of Émile Jaques-Dalcroze.

After 1811, Viganò worked almost exclusively for the Teatro alla Scala. In Milan, with its lively cultural milieu, he found fertile soil for the creation, with the assistance of a select group of dancer-actors, of a new form of danced drama, which Ritorni (1838) defined as *coreodramma.* This was because of Viganò's way of composing ballets, utilizing solutions adopted by the contemporaneous musical theater. Thus his drama was neither "quiet, mimed tragedy . . . nor dumb acting, but mute singing."

The most illustrious writers of his time lauded what was one of Viganò's masterpieces, *Prometeo,* performed in 1813—not a revival but a completely new version of *Die Geschöpfe des Prometheus.* The remake used some numbers from Beethoven's score as well as pieces of music by Joseph Weigl, Franz Joseph Haydn, and Viganò himself. Among the scenes at which audiences most marveled was the opening one, which set a powerful image for the ensuing action.

> The first scene of act 1 takes place on a desolate heath. Men drag themselves around in a brutish state while Prometheus, surrounded by Virtue, the Arts, and the Muses, contemplates the moment with commiseration, wondering how to awaken their reason. Act 2 shows, with a marvelous use of machinery, the fall of the Titan from Minerva's chariot after the theft of the celestial fire. In act 3, the sparks from the fallen torch give birth to innumerable Cupids, symbolizing the spread of reason among human beings. The men then rescue Prometheus and will be led by him to the Temple of Virtues. Act 4, set in Vulcan's furnace, shows the gods' reaction to Prometheus's theft of fire. In act 5, again in the Temple of Virtues, the Muses, Sciences, Arts, and Graces are about to educate the humans when Cupid, with an arrow, excites love between a man and a woman. The idyll is broken by the appearance of the Cyclopes, who carry Prometheus underground with them. The final act, closer to the traditional myth, shows the men sympathizing with Prometheus, now the bound and tortured Titan. They ask Hercules to free him. In an apotheosis, Prometheus is crowned with immortality by an appeased Jupiter.

The ballet was a resounding success and was repeated in the autumn season. Ritorni (1838) wrote, "I consider myself lucky to have seen, with my own eyes, the *Prometeo,* of which people have a false idea: that it is a spectacle of machines. . . . To the contrary . . . it was a moral spectacle, that is to say a sublime and surprising expression of poetic ideas and dramatic situations."

Several years later, in 1817, Viganò produced another masterpiece, *Mirra, o sia La Vendetta di Venere.* According to the critics, *Mirra* was greater than the tragedy by Count Vittorio Alfieri that had inspired it. Viganò was able to render in the mute language of gestures the torment of the heroine, Mirra, who is secretly in love with her father. The obvious difficulties inherent in the scabrous subject held the risk of being accentuated by the pantomime; Viganò, however was able to sublimate the action to the dancing and obtain a cathartic effect. The internal drama of Mirra was interpreted by Antonia Pallerini, Viganò's favorite artist.

Among Viganò's other outstanding works was the triad *Otello* (Othello), *Dedalo* (Daedalus), and *La Vestale* (The Vestal Virgin) of 1818, all with scenery by Alessandro Sanquirico. In *Otello,* Viganò concentrated the action on the core of the drama. In *La Vestale,* Pallerini created one of her most celebrated characterizations, as Viganò had provided her with yet another role that transcended the division between pantomime and dance. These three works were followed by *I Titani* (The Titans), staged in 1819. Set at the dawn of humanity, this work, the fruition of Viganò's long career, was richly invested with imagination and fantasy, merging classical myths and biblical themes. Although somewhat uneven, it contained moments of rare beauty. After *I Titani,* Viganò composed *Alessandro nelle Indie,* a ballet showing a mature and articulated use of music for dramatic purpose, as well as *Le Sabine in Roma* and *Giovanna d'Arco,* all mounted in 1820.

A painstaking, tireless artist, Viganò died the following year, while he was trying to finish his *Didone.* "A new art died with this great man," said Stendhal (1826). Nonetheless, Viganò left a rich heritage of research and innovations. He was to become the emblem of the choreodramatic genre, his work a lasting touchstone. An imaginative librettist and a poetic visionary, he based his dance dramas on a skillful play of contrast, on the combination of differing elements into a coherent whole. His choreodramatic pieces were animated in successive scenes, always changing for the eyes of the audience. In a process that blended the actions of separated scenic planes, he combined the Baroque legacy of the "marvelous" with the requirements of dramatic verisimilitude that was being pursued by the new theater of his time.

BIBLIOGRAPHY

Ayrenhoff, Cornelius von. *Über die teatralischen Tänze und die Balletmeister Noverre, Muzzarelli und Viganò.* Vienna, 1794. Reprinted in Ayrenhoff's *Sämmtliche Werke,* vol. 5 (Vienna, 1814).

Brinson, Peter. *Background to European Ballet: A Notebook from Its Archives.* Leiden, 1966.

Celi, Claudia. "Il balletto in Italia: Il Ottocento." In *Musica in scena: Storia dello spettacolo musicale,* edited by Alberto Basso, vol. 5, pp. 89–138. Turin, 1995.

Celi, Claudia. "Verso il 'canto muto': Dal danzatore pittore al danzator musico." In *Proceedings of the Conference "Naturale e artificiale nel teatro veneziano del secondo Settecento," Venezia, 10–11 November 1995.* Venice, 1997.

Cohen, Selma Jeanne, ed. *Dance as a Theater Art.* New York, 1974. Reprint, Princeton, 1992.

Guest, Ivor. "L'Italia e il balletto romantico." *La danza italiana* 8–9 (Winter 1990): 7–25.

Ferrari, Donatella. "I libretti comici di Salvatore Viganò." *La danza italiana* 7 (Spring 1989): 79–97.

Girardi, Maria. "I balli di Onorato Viganò a Venezia." *La danza italiana* 5–6 (Autumn 1987): 89–119.

Hadamowsky, Franz. *Die Wiener Hoftheater (Staatstheater),* vol. 1, *1776–1810.* Vienna, 1966.

Kirstein, Lincoln. *Dance: A Short History of Classical Theatrical Dancing.* New York, 1935.

Krasovskaya, Vera. "Ballet Changes, Shakespeare Endures." *Ballet Review* 19 (Summer 1991): 71–80.

Levinson, André. *Meister des balletts.* Potsdam, 1923.

Milloss, Aurelio. "La lezione di Salvatore Viganò." *La danza italiana* 1 (Autumn 1984): 7–19.

Monaldi, Gino. *Le regine della danza nel secolo XIX.* Turin, 1910.

Moore, Lillian. "Salvatore Viganò." In Moore's *Artists of the Dance.* New York, 1938.

Mori, Elisabetta. *Libretti di melodrammi e balli del secolo XVIII.* Florence, 1984.

Mori, Elisabetta. "Dove gli eroi vanno a morir ballando, ovvero la danza a Roma nel Settecento." *La danza italiana* 4 (Spring 1986): 27–47.

Prunières, Henry. "Salvatore Viganò." *La revue musicale* (December 1921): 71–94.

Raimondi, Ezio, ed. *Il sogno del coreodramma: Salvatore Viganò, poeta muto.* Reggio Emilia, 1984.

Ritorni, Carlo. *Commentarii della vita e delle opere coreodrammatiche di Salvatore Viganò e della coreografia e de' corepei.* Milan, 1838.

Rossi, Luigi. *Il ballo alla Scala, 1778–1970.* Milan, 1972.

Saint-Léon, Arthur. *Portraits et biographies des plus célèbres maîtres de ballets et chorégraphes anciens et nouveaux de l'école française et italienne.* Paris, 1852.

Stendhal (Marie-Henri Beyle). *Rome, Naples et Florence.* Paris, 1826.

Terzian, Elizabeth. "Salvatore Viganò: His Ballets at the Teatro La Scala (1811–1821), the Attitudes of His Contemporaries." In *Proceedings of the Tenth Annual Conference, Society of Dance History Scholars, University of California, Irvine, 13–15 February 1987,* compiled by Christena L. Schlundt. Riverside, Calif., 1987.

Winter, Marian Hannah. *The Pre-Romantic Ballet.* London, 1974.

Zambon, Rita. "Sulle traccie dell'immortale Astigiano." *Chorégraphie* 2 (Autumn 1993): 73–84.

CLAUDIA CELI
Translated from Italian

VILLELLA, EDWARD (born 1 October 1936 in Bayside, New York), American ballet dancer, teacher, and company director. Referring to the "dazzling antics" of Edward Villella, Lincoln Kirstein once described him as "born to be both Arlecchino and Pulcinella" (Kirstein, 1973, p. 244). A strong, athletic little boy with a scrappy nature and a cocky attitude, Villella began his dance studies with a local teacher in Bayside, Queens, a suburban neighborhood of New York City. When he was ten, he was awarded a scholarship to the School of American Ballet, where he continued his studies until 1952, when he was sixteen. Then, in what Kirstein further describes as "more than five long and unprofitable years in the Merchant Marine Academy," the young dancer's progress was halted. With his return to the School of American Ballet in 1956, he began to make up for lost time.

Villella joined the New York City Ballet in 1957, on his twenty-first birthday, and soon made his solo debut in Jerome Robbins's *Afternoon of a Faun,* partnering Allegra Kent. In 1958, his natural and remarkable elevation won him the jumping roles of Robert Barnett, such as Candy Cane in *The Nutcracker,* the third movement in *Symphony in C,* and the Thunderer in *Stars and Stripes.* In 1959 George Balanchine cast Villella in the title role of *The Prodigal Son,* which he performed with enormous success, putting his personal stamp on the role to such an extent that his interpretation established a new, definitive

VILLELLA. In *Harlequinade* (1965), George Balanchine made the roles of Harlequin and Columbine especially for Villella and Patricia McBride. Of all the roles they danced together, none suited them better than the sweethearts of the *commedia dell'arte.* (Photograph by Fred Fehl; used by permission. Choreography by George Balanchine © The George Balanchine Trust.)

model. The following year, 1960, he danced the first role that Balanchine created expressly for him, the Prince of Lorraine in *The Figure in the Carpet.*

New, major roles followed, nearly one a year for the next decade, in works created by Balanchine or Jerome Robbins: *Electronics* (1961), *A Midsummer Night's Dream* (1962), *Bugaku* (1963), *Tarantella* (1964), *Harlequinade* (1965), *Brahms-Schoenberg Quartet* (1966), *Jewels* (1967), *Dances at a Gathering* (1969), *Suite No. 3* (1970), and *Watermill, Symphony in Three Movements,* and *Pulcinella* (all 1972). In these and other works in the repertory Villella often danced opposite Patricia McBride, Allegra Kent, or Violette Verdy. With McBride he formed a special partnership and gave unforgettable performances in *Tarantella,* the *Rubies* section of *Jewels,* and *Tchaikovsky Pas de Deux,* to name only three of the many works they danced together. In *Harlequinade,* McBride was the quintessential Columbine (Colombina) to his definitive Harlequin (Arlecchino), perpetrator of the dazzling antics that so charmed Kirstein, along with everyone else who saw them. During these peak years, Villella also made numerous television appearances, including *A Man Who Dances,* a 1968 NBC film with himself as the subject.

In 1962, Villella appeared in the musical *Brigadoon,* in the dancing role of Harry Beaton, at the City Center of Music and Drama in New York. His success was such that he was invited to perform the role in several subsequent revivals of the show. In 1966, he created his first ballet, *Narkissos,* but soon realized that choreography was not his forte. He was, essentially, a performer. Throughout the late 1960s, he not only performed regularly in numerous roles with the New York City Ballet, but he often made guest appearances with other companies, frequently dancing in such nineteenth-century classics as *Giselle* and *La Sylphide.*

By the early 1970s, Villella was beginning to feel the full effects of his late return to dance, of an early injury, and of dancing on concrete surfaces in television studios. In 1973, at the age of only thirty-six, he began the struggle of dancing a physically demanding repertory despite persistent pain in his back and hip. For the Ravel Festival in 1975, Balanchine used him only sparingly in a work set to Ravel's *Shéhérazade,* and in subsequent years he was forced to relinquish a number of his more exuberant roles. He made his last appearances as a member of the New York City Ballet in Robbins's monumentally static *Watermill* in 1979, performing an essentially mime role. Eleven years later, in June 1990, he reprised his role as the principal figure in this mesmerizing work in an official farewell performance. He was fifty-three years old, but the power and nobility of his portrayal were undiminished.

Seeing Villella as the perfect embodiment of both Arlecchino and Pulcinella, as Lincoln Kirstein did, is certainly justifiable, but such a view falls far short of giving a full picture of his artistry. To understand the breadth of his range one must also consider him as the protagonist of *Watermill,* as the Prodigal Son, and as Apollo, which he first performed in 1964 and in which he won great acclaim. In comic roles, he was the epitome of merriment; in dramatic roles, he could be profoundly moving. Perhaps, of all his roles, his part in the third movement of *Brahms-Schoenberg Quartet* best examplifies his style: elegant yet impetuous, powerful yet delicate, straightforward yet sly, romantic yet classical.

After leaving the New York City Ballet, Villella did not immediately stop dancing. Although physically unable to perform a full-scale repertory with a ballet company, he continued to give lecture-demonstrations with ballet students and to teach master classes. In 1980 he became artistic director of the Eglevsky Ballet, on Long Island, New York, a post he held for the next four years, and in 1981 he served for a year as visiting artist at the U.S. Military Academy at West Point, New York. He also served during this period as artistic adviser to Ballet Oklahoma and the New Jersey Ballet, and he worked both as a consultant and as a producer-director for the *Dance in America* series on public television. In 1986, Villella founded the Miami City Ballet, which today he continues to develop and direct. In addition to commissioning new ballets for his dancers, he has restaged a good number of Balanchine works, including *The Prodigal Son, Apollo, Bugaku, The Nutcracker,* and *Jewels.*

Villella's accomplishments have been officially recognized by a *Dance Magazine* Award (1965); an Emmy award (1976), from the Academy of Television Arts and Sciences; the Capezio Award (1989); the National Medal of Arts (1997); and a Kennedy Center Honor for lifetime achievement (1997).

BIBLIOGRAPHY

Barnes, Clive. "Edward Villella." *Dance Magazine* (November 1989).

Bland, Alexander, and John Percival. *Men Dancing: Performers and Performances.* New York, 1984.

Croce, Arlene. "Edward Villella: A Man and His Roles." In *Edward Villella: American Dancer.* West Point, N.Y., 1982. The catalog of an exhibition of photographs, sponsored by the Cadet Fine Arts Forum, 2–28 May 1982, Class of 1929 Gallery, Eisenhower Hall, U.S. Military Academy.

Croce, Arlene. "Slower Is Faster." *The New Yorker* (21 November 1988, 28 November 1988).

Kirsten, Lincoln. *The New York City Ballet.* New York, 1973. With photographs by Martha Swope and George Platt Lynes.

Terry, Walter. *Great Male Dancers of the Ballet.* New York, 1978.

Villella, Edward. "The Male Image." *Dance Perspectives,* no. 40 (Winter 1969).

Villella, Edward, with Larry Kaplan. *Prodigal Son: Dancing for Balanchine in a World of Pain and Magic.* New York, 1992.

ROBERT GRESKOVIC

VILZAK, ANATOLE (Anatolii Iosifovich Vil'tzak; born 29 August 1896 in Vilnius, Lithuania), Russian-American ballet dancer and teacher. Vitzak studied under Michel Fokine at the Imperial Theater School in Saint Petersburg, entering the corps de ballet of the Maryinsky Theater upon his graduation in 1915. He soon came to the attention of Matilda Kshessinska, and with her backing he stepped into leading classical roles, becoming a soloist in 1917.

In 1921, Vilzak left Russia and, with his wife Ludmilla Schollar, joined the Ballets Russes de Serge Diaghilev, dancing the role of Prince Charming in Diaghilev's production of *The Sleeping Princess* at London's Alhambra Theatre (1921/22). Between 1922 and 1925, he became the company's leading male classicist, performing principal roles in *Aurora's Wedding, Les Sylphides, Schéhérazade, Le Carnaval,* and *Les Biches.* Dismissed from the company for supporting a threatened strike in 1925, he appeared in Fokine's *Frolicking Gods* at the London Hippodrome and danced in a number of the choreographer's ballets at the Teatro Colón in Buenos Aires. In 1928, he became Ida Rubinstein's premier danseur, creating the leading male roles in Bronislava Nijinska's *Le Baiser de la Fée, Boléro, La Bien-Aimée,* and *La Valse.*

A matinee idol among the *danseurs nobles* of his generation, Vilzak appeared with Ida Rubinstein's troupe (1931, 1934), the State Opera House in Riga, Latvia (1932), Nijinska's Théâtre de Danse (1932–1934), and the Levitov-Dandré Russian Ballet (1934–1935). For René Blum's Ballet Russe de Monte Carlo, he danced the title role in Fokine's *Don Juan* (1936) as well as the leading role in Fokine's version of the *Polovtsian Dances* from *Prince Igor.* From 1935 to 1937, Vilzak appeared with Balanchine's American Ballet at New York's Metropolitan Opera, creating roles in many *divertissements.*

Retiring from the stage, Vilzak became one of the most prominent Russian teachers in the United States, serving on the faculties of the School of American Ballet, the Ballet Russe de Monte Carlo School, the Ballet Theatre School, and the Washington School of Ballet, in addition to conducting his own school in New York with his wife. From 1966 until 1996, when he was one hundred years old, he taught at the San Francisco Ballet School. His *Vilzak Variations after Petipa* for the San Francisco Ballet was premiered in 1982.

BIBLIOGRAPHY

Denny, Carol H. "Viva Vilzak: On His Toes at Eighty-Six." *San Francisco Sunday Examiner and Chronicle* (31 January 1982).

Heymont, George. "A Real Charmer." *Ballet News* 4 (February 1983): 14–18.

Karsavina, Tamara. "Vilzak, Dolin, Malcolm Sargent and Others." *Dancing Times* (May 1968).

Moore, Lillian. "Diaghileff Teachers in America: A Study in Constructive Guidance." *Ballet Annual* 10 (1956): 75–77.

Newman, Barbara. *Striking a Balance: Dancers Talk about Dancing.* Boston, 1982.

Ross, Janice. "Vilzak Variations." *Dance Magazine* (July 1988).

LYNN GARAFOLA

VINOGRADOV, OLEG (Oleg Mikhailovich Vinogradov; born 1 August 1937 in Leningrad), Russian choreographer. Upon graduation in 1958 from the Leningrad Choreographic Institute, where he studied with Aleksandr Pushkin, Vinogradov joined the Novosibirsk Opera and Ballet Theater as a dancer and later assistant choreographer until 1965. From 1968 to 1972 he was choreographer at the Kirov Opera and Ballet Theater in Leningrad, from 1973 to 1977 he held the same post at Leningrad's Maly Opera and Ballet Theater, and since 1977 he has been artistic director and chief choreographer of the Kirov Ballet.

Vinogradov produced Prokofiev's *Cinderella* (Novosibirsk, 1964; Odessa, 1970; Dresden, 1973; Leningrad's Maly Theater, 1977; Budapest, 1983) and *Romeo and Juliet* (Novosibirsk, 1965; Sofia, 1971; Erevan, 1972; new version at the Maly Theater, 1976), and Vladimir Vlasov's *Asel* (for the Bolshoi Ballet, Moscow, 1967). For the Kirov Theater he produced Murad Kazhlayev's *The Mountain Girl* (1968; new versions 1973 and 1984), Prokofiev's *Aleksandr Nevsky* (1969), Arif Melikov's *Two* (1969), Benjamin Britten's *The Prince of the Pagodas* (1972), Tikhon Khrennikov's *The Hussar's Ballad* (1979; with Dmitri Briantzev, new version for the Bolshoi Ballet, 1980), *The Fairy of the Rond Mountains* to Grieg (1980), *The Inspector-General* to

Tchaikovsky (1980), and *Testaments of the Past* (1971), to a pastiche score, for the bicentennial of the Kirov Theater. For the Maly Theater he produced *La Fille Mal Gardée* (1971; Odessa and Saratov, 1973; Berlin's Komische Opera, 1974; Frunze and Riga, 1976; Minsk, 1979; Tallinn, 1980), *Coppélia* (1973), Boris Tishchenko's *Yaroslavna* (1974), and *A Pedagogical Poem* (with Leonid Lebedev to Lebedev's music, 1977). On his return to the Kirov he produced Aleksei Machavariani's *The Knight in Tigerskin* (1985), *Battleship Potemkin* to Tchaikovsky (1986), his own version of *Petrouchka* (1990), which the company presented in Paris, and Samuel Barber's *Adagio* (1991), among others. Vinogradov has been the librettist and designer of many of his own productions.

Vinogradov has clearly tended toward large-scale compositions, in which the corps de ballet is assigned a considerable role and characterization is imaginative and inventive. At the same time his ballets have been quite varied. Besides classical ballets (*The Prince of the Pagodas* and *The Fairy of the Rond Mountains* as well as the standard repertory) he has done experimental productions *(Yaroslavna, A Pedagogical Poem, The Inspector-General)* that have stretched the boundaries of modern choreography, as well as ballets that are tragic *(Romeo and Juliet)*, comic *(La Fille Mal Gardée)*, and even satirical *(The Inspector-General)*. He has believed that the struggles of everyday life can be resolved in ballet, as reflected in *Asel, A Pedagogical Poem,* and *The Mountain Girl.* The latter is especially interesting for its skillful use of the rich folk dance idiom of Daghestan, as is *The Knight in Tigerskin* for its incorporation of Georgian and Indian dances.

The plots of most of Vinogradov's ballets were not previously choreographed, but even with traditional subjects the choreographer's point of view has been manifested. For example, his *Cinderella* is not simply a story of virtue rewarded but of the confrontation between two outlooks on life, the philistine and the artistic. In *Romeo and Juliet,* which is addressed to young audiences, the accent is on the protagonists' travails and the constancy with which they are surmounted, set in a timeless context. Vinogradov's translation into dance of the classic comedy *The Inspector-General,* a text which had seemed inseparable from the caustic and pictorial language of Nikolai Gogol, was daring yet preserved something greater than words: the spirit of Gogol's satire, his famous "laughter through tears."

Vinogradov's choreography and Tishchenko's music for *Yaroslavna* were new in Soviet ballet, in their spirit of bold experimentation, use of modern theater techniques, and rich content. The creators viewed *The Lay of Igor's Campaign* (against the Polovtsians), the remarkable twelfth-century epic on which the ballet is based, through the eyes of modern artists and called on the spectator to reflect on the lessons of history. The dance movement, costumes, and design were pervaded with themes and symbols characteristic of ancient Russian art. Vinogradov has formulated his credo as follows: "In my opinion, a spectator coming to the ballet to admire only the beauty of the dancing deprives himself of what matters most. Modern ballet can and must stir not only emotions, but also thoughts."

As artistic director and chief choreographer of the Kirov Ballet, Vinogradov has also devoted attention and effort to preserving and restoring the classical repertory, especially the Petipa corpus, with emphasis on the intrinsic style of each ballet. Thus he has restored *The Sleeping Beauty* and *Le Corsaire* and set a *divertissement* from *Paquita* for the Paris Opera Ballet. At the same time he was the first Soviet director to bring ballets by Western choreographers into a Russian company's repertory. He is credited by many historians with having raised the Kirov Ballet from a state of decline in the early 1970s to its original eminence. In 1995 Vinogradov was replaced at the Kirov by Valery Gergiev. In 1990 Vinogradov opened a school in Washington, D.C., the Universal Ballet Academy, of which he remains director. Since 1991 he has also been head of the Saint Petersburg Chamber Ballet. Among his awards are the title People's Artist of the USSR (1983), the Petipa Prize in Paris (1979), the Order of Friendship of Nations (1984), and the Nijinsky Prize (1991).

BIBLIOGRAPHY

Alovert, Nina. "An Interview with Oleg Vinogradov." *Dance Magazine* (July 1989): 42–44.

Gregory, John. "Vinogradov's Testament." *The Dancing Times* (August 1982): 822–823.

Ilicheva, Marina A. *Oleg Vinogradov.* Hamburg, 1994.

Krasovskaya, Vera. "V seredine veka, 1950–1960." In *Sovetskii baletnyi teatr, 1917–1967,* edited by Vera Krasovskaya. Moscow, 1976.

Roslavleva, Natalia. "The Cause of Controversy: Oleg Vinogradov." *Dance and Dancers* (November 1967): 24–26.

Universal Ballet Academy. *Oleg Vinogradov: Portrait of a Contemporary Classicist.* Washington, D.C., 1990.

ARSEN B. DEGEN
Translated from Russian

VIOLETTE, EVA MARIA (Eva Maria Veigl [Weig(e)l or Faig(e)l]; born 29 February 1724 in Vienna, died 16 October 1822 in London), Austrian dancer. The daughter of Johann Veigl, valet of the Viennese Count von Paar, Eva Maria obtained ballet lessons at an early age from the prominent Austrian dancing master and choreographer Franz Hilverding. From about 1734 to 1745 she was attached to the ballet companies of the two leading Viennese theaters, the Kärntnertor Theater and the Burgtheater, both of which were under the management of the ballet master Joseph Sellier, perhaps another of her teachers. During this time she changed her name to Violette (*Veigl* is the Viennese dialect word for the German *Veilchen,* "violet").

Early in 1746, Eva Maria Violette and her younger

brother Ferdinand, a dancer who also took the name Violette, accepted an invitation to the London Theatre in the Haymarket. Charles Burney, in his *General History of Music,* erroneously states that Violette's London debut was on 7 January 1746 in the dances between the acts of Christoph Willibald Gluck's opera *La Caduta de' Giganti.* According to some contemporary reports and documents, Violette's arrival in London cannot be dated before the end of February 1746. Burney's comment on "the new dances by Auretti and the charming Violetta, afterward Mrs. Garrick" may well correspond to Violette's real London debut in Gluck's second London opera, *Artamene,* on 4 March 1746.

From that time onward she was extremely successful, both on the London stage and in London society. Her very close connection with the powerful Burlington family, which had taken the young dancer under their wing soon after her arrival in London, gave way to rumors that she might have been Lord Burlington's illegitimate daughter. Violette's contemporaries had little that was specific to say of her style of dancing. In *The Letters of Horace Walpole* she is said to be "the first and most admired dancer in the world" (1903, vol. 2, p. 230). Steedman (1979) quotes others as calling her "exquisite" and one who "inimitably" expresses the role of her character. Her marriage to the great English actor and playwright David Garrick on 22 June 1749, which created a sensation, ended Violette's stage career. The happy marriage ended only when Garrick died in 1779. Eva Maria, who never returned to her home country, outlived her husband by forty-three years and was buried next to him in London in Westminster Abbey.

BIBLIOGRAPHY

Burney, Charles. *A General History of Music.* 4 vols. 2d ed. London, 1789.

Derra de Moroda, Friderica. "The Dancer in Westminster Abbey: Eva Maria Garrick." *The Dancing Times* (June 1967): 476–477.

Garrick, David. *The Letters.* Edited by David M. Little and George M. Karl. London, 1963.

Parsons, Clement. *Garrick and His Circle.* London, 1906.

Steedman, W. "The Early Years of Mrs. Garrick." *Theatre Research International* 4 (February 1979).

Walpole, Horace. *The Letters of Horace Walpole.* London, 1903.

SIBYLLE DAHMS

VIRSALADZE, SIMON (Soliko Bagratovich Virsaladze; born 13 [26] January 1909 in Tbilisi, died 9 February 1989 in Tbilisi), Russian scenery and costume designer. Virsaladze trained at the Tbilisi (1926) and Leningrad (1928–1931) academies of art, and from 1932 to 1936 he was chief designer of the Paliashvili Theater in Tbilisi, where he designed operas as well as ballets. The most distinctive were *Heart of the Hills* (1936) and over twenty years later *Othello* (1957), both choreographed by Vakhtang Chabukiani. At the Kirov Theater in Leningrad he created the decor for the restaging of Chabukiani's *Heart of the Hills* (1938) and his new *Laurencia* (1939). After becoming chief designer there in 1945 he designed Fedor Lopukhov's *Spring Tale* (1947); Konstantin Sergeyev's *Raymonda* (1950), *Swan Lake* (1950), and *The Sleeping Beauty* (1951); and Vasily Vainonen's *The Nutcracker* (1954). In the same period Virsaladze also provided scenery for ballets at Leningrad's Maly Theater, and he later designed decor for theaters in Baku, Novosibirsk, and abroad. Between 1930 and 1950 the art of Virsaladze, along with that of other outstanding artists (Fedor Fedorovsky, Vladimir Dmitriev, Petr Williams, and Vadim Ryndin), largely defined the main principle of ballet design: realism coupled with a creative interpretation of the dramaturgy and characters.

From 1957 until his death Virsaladze worked in ballet exclusively with the choreographer Yuri Grigorovich, at the Kirov until 1962, and at the Bolshoi Theater in Moscow thereafter. His art was inseparably linked with the new principles Grigorovich introduced into ballet. The Grigorovich ballets designed by Virsaladze—*The Stone Flower* (1957), *Legend of Love* (1961), *The Sleeping Beauty* (1963 and 1973), *The Nutcracker* (1966), *Spartacus* (1968), *Swan Lake* (1969), *Ivan the Terrible* (1975), *The Angara* (1976), *Romeo and Juliet* (1979), *The Golden Age* (1982), and *Raymonda* (1984)—largely determined the development of Soviet choreography.

Virsaladze was thoroughly familiar with the requirements of dance design. Leaving the center of the stage free for the choreography, he usually found an expression for the ballet as a whole, which might also appear in specific scenes as the action unfolded. In *The Stone Flower,* for example, the repository of fairy tales in *The Malachite Casket* on which the ballet is based incorporates pictures of every act. Virsaladze's costumes were invariably integral to the character as well as convenient for dancing. He never oversimplified a costume or converted it into a uniform or an abstract sketch. His costumes reflected the traits of the character or had historical and social appropriateness; at the same time the color and cut revealed and emphasized the plastique. They were also related to the scenery in color, thus creating "symphonic paintings" that were integral with the music and dance. Virsaladze was a People's Artist of the USSR and a Fellow of the Soviet Academy of Art. He won the Lenin Prize in 1970 and the State Prize of the USSR in 1949, 1951, and 1977.

BIBLIOGRAPHY

Berezkin, Viktor. "Khudozhnik v sovetskom balete." In *Sovetskii baletnyi teatr, 1917–1967,* edited by Vera Krasovskaya. Moscow, 1976.

Karp, Poel M. "Simon Virsaladze." In *Leningradskie khudozhniki teatra,* edited by E. A. Davydova. Leningrad, 1971.

Obituary. *Dance Magazine* (June 1989): 28–29.

Vanslov, Victor V. *Simon Virsaladze* (in Russian). Moscow, 1969.

VICTOR V. VANSLOV
Translated from Russian

VIRSKY, PAVEL (Pavlo Vir'skyi, known in Russian as Pavel Pavlovich Virskii; born 12 [25] February 1905 in Odessa, Ukraine, died 5 June 1975 in Kiev), dancer and choreographer. Virsky graduated in 1926 from the dance department of the Odessa School of Music and Drama, where he studied under Vladimir Presnyakov, and in 1928 from a theater school in Moscow, where his teachers were Asaf Messerer and Kasyan Goleizovsky. Between 1923 and 1926 Virsky was a ballet dancer, but his interest soon turned to choreography. From 1928 to 1933 he served as chief choreographer of the Odessa Opera and Ballet Theater and 1933 of the Kharkov Opera Theater. In 1935 he worked in the same capacity in Dniepropetrovsk and in 1936 in Kiev.

In 1932, with Nikolai Bolotov, Virsky produced the heroic ballet *La Carmagnole* for the Moscow Art Theater Ballet, then under the directorship of Viktorina Kriger. While relying on the classical tradition, Virsky boldly introduced into his ballet productions the advancements of the contemporary dramatic stage, the latest achievements of folk dance choreography, and modern plastique in an effort to achieve clear-cut dramatic development and to create vivid characters and ensemble dances with full-blooded emotional and substantive content. Some of his best ballet productions created in collaboration with Bolotov are noted for vivid and original dance imagery. They include *The Red Poppy* (1928), *The Little Humpbacked Horse* and *La Esmeralda* (1929), *Swan Lake* (1932), and *Le Corsaire* (1933) in Odessa; *La Esmeralda* (1933) and *Raymonda* (1934) in Kharkov; and the comic ballet *The Burgess from Tuscany* (1935) in Dniepropetrovsk and 1936 in Kiev).

In 1937 Virsky founded a Ukrainian dance ensemble for which he labored to collect, systematize, and realize on the stage the rich heritage of Ukrainian folk dance. He also staged a series of narrative dance numbers and the ballet *Bondarivna* (Kiev, 1938) based on the folk dance idiom with elements of classical dance. In the 1920s and 1930s Virsky also produced dances for Soviet, Ukrainian, and contemporary operas, of which the most significant were the large-scale scenes in Mykola Lysenko's *Taras Bulba*, Semen Gulak-Artemovsky's *The Zaporozhe Cossack beyond the Danube*, and Boris Liatoshinksy's *The Golden Ring* and *Shchors*. Between 1939 and 1943 Virsky was chief choreographer of the song-and-dance ensemble of the Kiev military district, and from 1943 to 1955 he served in the same capacity with the Anatoly Aleksandrov ensemble of the Soviet Army, staging numerous military dances and choreographed scenes.

From 1955 to 1975 Virsky was the artistic director of the State Academic Dance Ensemble of the Ukraine. The ensemble has borne his name since 1975. During this period Virsky displayed every facet of his talent as choreographer. A connoisseur of Ukrainian folk dance, he skillfully theatricalized it by using a combination of dramatic techniques, modern ballet, and pantomime. The large-scale works he staged—*The Zaporozhe Cossacks, We Remember, Why Is the Willow Weeping?*, and *The Guelder Rose*—are noted for a wide range of themes, genres, and styles. He also devised delightfully vivid dance miniatures, such as "Chumak Joys," "Podolyanka," "Polzunets," "Kozachek," and "The Dolls," which revealed new expressive dimensions in Ukrainian dance, reflecting various facets of the distinctive national character, artistic traditions, and folk dance heritage. In 1960 Virsky produced a modern Ukrainian heroic ballet, *Black Gold*, at the Kiev Opera and Ballet Theater, and in 1967 he created the ballet *October Legend*. In 1962, on Virsky's initiative, the ensemble opened a folk dance studio, which has since produced many first-class performances.

For his distinguished services Virsky was honored in 1960 with the title People's Artist of the USSR. He was also awarded state prizes of the USSR in 1950 and 1970 and the Shevchenko State Prize of the Ukrainian SSR.

BIBLIOGRAPHY

Lawson, Joan. "The Ukrainians Return to London." *The Dancing Times* (November 1961): 83.

Stanishevsky, Yuri. *Pavlo Pavlovych Virskyi*. Kiev, 1962.

Stanishevsky, Yuri. *The Ukrainian Ballet, 1786–1986*. Kiev, 1986.

Zürner, Inge. Obituary. *Dance News* (September 1975): 6–7.

YURI A. STANISHEVSKY
Translated from Russian

VLADIMIROFF, PIERRE (Petr Nikolaevich Nikolaev [Vladimirov]; born 1 [13] February? 1893 in Saint Petersburg, died 26 November 1970 in New York), Russian dancer and teacher. Vladimiroff was the prototype of the imperial Russian dancers who found a second career in the West after the Bolshevik Revolution. As the successor to Vaslav Nijinsky at the Maryinsky Theater, he was the favorite partner of the leading Saint Petersburg ballerinas and the object of legendary outbursts of balletomania. He danced in Serge Diaghilev's and Anna Pavlova's companies before settling in the United States, where he taught at the School of American Ballet in New York from its founding until his retirement in 1967.

Vladimiroff trained with Sergei Legat, Samuil Andreonov, and Mikhail Obukhov in the Imperial Theater School. In 1911 he graduated into the Maryinsky company and became *premier danseur* in 1915. In the Fokine repertory he danced *Le Carnaval, Chopiniana, Le Pavillon d'Armide*, and *Le Spectre de la Rose*, and he created the title role of *Eros*. Urged by Michel Fokine, he also performed the classics: *Giselle* with Olga Spessivtseva, *Swan Lake* with Lubov Egorova, and *Paquita, Raymonda, Le Corsaire*, and *The Talisman*.

During leaves of absence in 1912 and 1914, Vladimiroff

danced for Diaghilev, who attempted to recruit him as Nijinsky's permanent replacement, but he refused at the request of his partner, Matilda Kshessinska. Last appearing at the Maryinsky in 1918, he fled the Soviets with his wife, the dancer Felia Doubrovska, in 1920. He danced for Diaghilev as Prince Désiré in *The Sleeping Princess* and with Tamara Karsavina in European and American concerts. In the United States he toured with Adolph Bolm's Ballet Intime and Mikhail Mordkin's Russian Ballet. He was Pavlova's last partner and was said to have been her favorite. Touring with her company from 1928 to 1931 he danced *Dionysus, Chopiniana, Grand Pas Hongrois, The Fairy Doll,* and *Autumn Leaves.*

Vladimiroff returned to the United States in 1933 with a troupe organized by Serge Lifar. In 1934 George Balanchine engaged him for the School of American Ballet, where he taught for thirty-three years. Vladimiroff had been a favorite dancer of Balanchine's at the Maryinsky and transmitted to American dancers the pure classicism of the Russian tradition.

VLADIMIROFF. With Anna Pavlova in *Chopiniana*, photographed during a South American tour in 1928. (Photograph by Nicholas Yarovoff; from the Dance Collection, New York Public Library for the Performing Arts.)

BIBLIOGRAPHY

Barzel, Ann. "European Dance Teachers in the United States." *Dance Index* 3 (April–June 1944): 56–100.

Borisoglebsky, Mikhail. *Proshloe baletnogo otdeleniia Peterburgskogo teatral'nogo uchilishcha, nyne Leningradskogo gosudarstvennogo khoreograficheskogo uchilishcha: Materialy po istorii russkogo baleta.* Vol. 2. Leningrad, 1939.

Como, William, and Richard Philp. "Pavlova." *Dance Magazine* (January 1976): 43–74.

Doubrovska, Felia. "Pierre Vladimiroff: A Memoir, as Told to Marian Horosko." *Dance Magazine* (February 1971): 43–45.

Krasovskaya, Vera. *Russkii baletnyi teatr nachala dvadtsatogo veka,* vol. 2, *Tantsovshchiki.* Leningrad, 1972.

Relkin, Abbie. "In Pavlova's Shadow." *Ballet News* 2 (January 1981): 26–29.

Smakov, Gennady. *The Great Russian Dancers.* New York, 1984.

SUZANNE CARBONNEAU

VODUN. The dance culture of Haiti is inseparable from the pervasive Africa-based folk religion of the nation, Vodun. Misunderstood and labeled "Voodoo" by outsiders, this tradition is not mere witchcraft based on superstition but a highly structured system fulfilling social and psychological needs. Slaves brought to the Spanish and French colonies on the island of Hispaniola from various regions of sub-Saharan Africa experienced terrible dislocation and nostalgia as well as physical suffering. They were deprived of the family and community in which elders provided security, linking them together. Their land and family spirits were far away. To reconstruct an emotional African background was essential for psychological survival in their new milieu, but that could not be done without the unity possible only through traditional religion.

This religion has survived despite the efforts of slaveowners to suppress it and the desire of some Haitian governments to eradicate it. Today, Vodun constitutes vivid testimony to the African presence in Haiti.

Vodun is an amalgam of the religious practices of several African cultures, including Yoruba, Fon, Congo, Igbo, Bamana, Adja, Akan, Asante, Wolof, Mandinka, Hausa, Mahi, and Ewe. Its greatest influence came from the Fon people of Benin (formerly Dahomey), from whom most Haitians are descended. Vodun is one of the best-preserved Africa-based religions systems in the Americas. Although it has much in common with other New World Africa-based religions—Santería or Lucumi of Cuba; Candomblé, Macumba, and Batuque of Brazil; Kumina of Jamaica; Shango and Nago of Trinidad and Tobago—it differs in some respects. The others are derived to a large extent from the Yoruba (with the exception of Kumina of Jamaica, which is influenced mostly by the religious systems of the Akan and Asante [Ashanti] peoples of Ghana).

VODUN. A man, his face puckered in the throes of possession, dances during a Vodun ceremony in 1960. (Photograph by Pierre Verger; used by permission.)

The word *vodun* means "spirit" in the Fongbe language of Benin. Vodun involves rites of birth, initiation, marriage, death, and burial in conjunction with the worship of its pantheon. (Contrary to popular belief, Vodun is not malevolent but harmless and benevolent in character.) As a religious system, Vodun uses ritual songs and dances that are accompanied by a sacred drum and other musical instruments. A clear picture of this religion is given by Harold Courlander:

> Vodun is clearly more than ritual of the cult temple. It is an integrated system of concepts concerning human behavior, the relation of mankind to those who have lived before, and to the natural and supernatural forces of the universe. It relates the living to the dead and those not yet born. It explains unpredictable principles. In short, it is a true religion which attempts to tie the unknown to the known and thus create order where chaos existed before. (Courlander, 1960, p. 9)

Many students of Vodun conceive of it as geocentric and anthropocentric, unlike Christianity, which is theocentric. The Vodun practitioner is not interested in heaven but believes that humans must do good deeds on earth to join the world of the spirits, where they may be able to help the living. This basic concept is shared by most African religious systems.

The Vodun temple, called a *hounfor,* consists of three sections. In the peristyle (courtyard), where public ceremonies are held, there is a center post, called *poteau mitan,* down which spirits descend during ceremonies. The *jevo* is a special sanctuary for confining devotees during initiation and for curing serious illness. The *bagui,* commonly called *kay-miste* or *kay loa* ("house of the spirits"), is a sanctuary room that contains one or more altars *(pe)* on which are arranged a large number of ritual objects. The *hounfor* serves not only as a place of worship but also as a shelter for the homeless; nonmembers are welcome as long as there is enough space.

The *houngan* (Vodun priest) and the *mambo* (Vodun priestess) are the spiritual leaders who officiate at all ceremonies. They are helped by members of the congregation, called *hounsis;* there are two categories, *hounsis bossales* and *hounsis kanzo,* the former noninitiated and the latter initiated. Some of the initiated *hounsis* hold special positions in the congregation's hierarchy. The *laplace,* chief assistant to the *houngan,* ordinarily acts as a master of ceremonies, often carrying a sword or a machete while leading processions within the *hounfor.* The *houngenikon,* a special assistant, leads the choir and assists the *houngan* during sacrifices, taking the *houngan's* place when necessary, especially when the *houngan* is possessed. (Both assistants are final steps before becoming a *houngan.*)

Not every Vodun practitioner belongs to a particular congregation. Some go to a *hounfor* often, but others seek help from a *houngan* or a *mambo* only when faced with a crisis. The *houngan* functions in the community not only as a spiritual leader but also as a medicine person, counselor or social worker, judge, political leader, and policymaker. Not everyone can become a Vodun priest or priestess; one must either inherit knowledge from parents or relatives or be chosen by a spirit—mainly from among the family spirits.

Ritual Objects. A good Vodun priest knows about all the aspects of the Vodun rituals, including the meaning and significance of the ritual and its sacred objects. The drums are the most sacred and the most common musical instrument in African religions. In Vodun their use is specific to certain ceremonies. For example, a Rada drum is not to be used in a Petro ceremony.

The *assoto* drum, the most sacred drum in Vodun, is seven feet (two meters) high. There is a special ceremony held in its honor every year, or every two or three years, depending on the locality. Rada drums are a set of three. The largest, three to four feet (one meter) high, is called *maman;* the middle sized is *segond,* and the smallest is *bula* or *bébé.* They are made of wood, with stretched cowhide skins affixed to the body with wooden pegs. The Rada drums are used during ceremonies honoring the Rada spirits. Petro drums are a set of two. The larger is called *maman* or *gro baka,* and the smaller *pitit* or *ti baka.* They have stretched goatskin attached to the wooden body with sisal strings. The Petro drums are used during ceremonies in honor of the Petro gods.

There are also drums for lesser groups of deities, such as Congo drums or *juba* drums, but these drums are seldom used because some of these spirits belong to the Rada group. The drums also have their own spirit, called Hunto.

The *asson,* another important ritual object, is a pear-shaped gourd rattle covered with multicolored beads that represent the colors of the Vodun deities. It is used by the priest and priestess to help summon the spirits.

The *gavi* is a ritual clay pot into which spirits are drawn down by the priest or priestess. It is also used to house the spirit *mait-tête* ("master of the head") of a deceased devotee. The priest takes the spirit off the corpse's head in a ceremony called *dessounin* and puts it in the *govi.* It also functions as *pot de tête* ("head pot"), holding hair strands and nail parings of the initiated (personal matter that can be used for either good or bad magic).

The *zin,* used during initiation and funeral rites in a ceremony called *boule zin* (pot burning), is usually made of clay but sometimes of iron. The *plate marassa* (twin's dishes and pitchers) are also of clay, but sometimes of wood. They are used to hold offerings of food and drink for the spirits of twins. The *cruche* or *criche* is a clay pitcher that holds water for libations during ceremonies and sometimes fulfills the function of *pot de tête.*

Vodun Pantheon. The Vodun religion has a large pantheon of deities called *loa* (a Congo word meaning "spirit"). Most of them are syncretized with Roman Catholic saints, owing to the pressure on the slaves by their masters who wanted them converted. Early Vodun practitioners first used Catholic elements as camouflage; later they became integral to the religion. Syncretism in Vodun is not limited to saints/*loas*; it plays an important role in the liturgy, with most Vodun ceremonies begun with Catholic prayers.

The Vodun pantheon has two main categories. Rada deities consist mostly of African entities, whereas Petro deities comprise mostly local or Creole deities. The deities are intermediaries between humans and God, whom Vodun practitioners call Grand Mait' (Great Master).

Rituals and ceremonies in honor of the spirits are an integral part of Vodun. These are called *service loa:* the two most common are the Mange Marassa (food for the twin spirits) and the Mange Yams (eating yams)—a thanksgiving ceremony. There are also ceremonies honoring a *loa*'s day, which often coincides with the celebration of the corresponding Catholic saint; for example, Saint Patrick's day is also Damballah's, and Saint James's day is also Oggun's. Depending on the preference of the spirit, goats, roosters, pigs, pigeons, or occasionally a cow may be offered as sacrifice during a ceremony.

Ceremonies. At the beginning of every ceremony the priest draws symbols on the ground of the *hounfor* with corn flour, especially around the *poteau mitan.* These symbols, called *veves,* are emblems of the deities; they help attract the spirits. Legba, the oldest deity of the pantheon, is the first to be honored in any ceremony.

Songs, rhythmic drumbeats, and especially dance are also attractive forces to the spirits during the ceremony. Each deity has a specific rhythm and dance to attract him or her. The *yanvalou* rhythm and dance, for example, attract Agwe, the spirit of the sea, and Damballah, the snake spirit of fertility; *nago* rhythm and dance attract Oggun, the spirit of war and iron. In the former dance, the devotee mimes the undulating movements of a snake and the waves of the sea by moving gracefully forward and backward. In the second dance, however, the participant's movements recall those of a slave trying to break the chains or a warrior attempting to crush an enemy. In both cases there is a correlation between the character of the deity and his favorite dance.

Vodun is a family religion, and the hereditary element is used to acquire help from a spirit. Each person may inherit a spirit from his mother's or father's side—sometimes from both. In order to benefit fully from the protection of a particular spirit, the protégé must establish a forceful rela-

VODUN. A man dancing in a *hounfor* (temple) during a Vodun ritual. (Photograph by Pierre Verger; used by permission.)

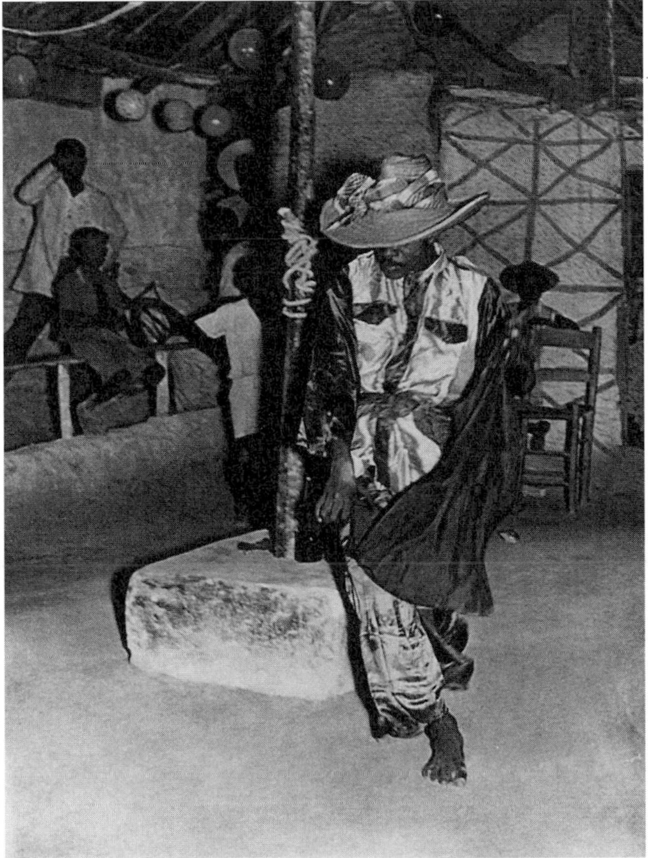

tionship between himself and this spirit protector through initiation. The complex initiation rite, called *kanzo,* lasts twenty-one days and is the first step toward becoming a priest.

Possession by a spirit is one of the main features of Vodun. The gods communicate with devotees either by entering their bodies or in dreams. Possession occurs when the *loa* moves into the individual's head. The person becomes the "horse" of the god, his mouthpiece. The actions and words of the possessed are those of the spirit by whom the devotee is mounted. Possession is not regarded as evil; for the worshipper it is a blessing, because it enables him to carry out difficult tasks such as curing disease or protecting the life of one in great danger. During initiation, a neophyte may be possessed by his spirit two or more times, a good sign, showing communication between the protégé and the protector.

[*See also* Haiti.]

BIBLIOGRAPHY

Bastide, Roger. *African Civilisations in the New World.* Translated from the French by Peter Green, with a foreward by Geoffrey Parrinder. New York, 1971.

Bascom, William R. "The Focus of Cuban Santería." *South Western Journal of Anthropology* 6.1 (1950).

Bastien, Remy, and Harold Courlander. *Religion and Politics in Haiti; Two Essays.* Washington, D.C., 1966.

Cabrea, Lydia. *El Monte.* Miami, 1971.

Courlander, Harold. *The Drum and the Hoe: Life and Lore of the Haitian People.* Berkeley, 1960.

Deren, Maya. *Divine Horsemen: The Living Gods of Haiti.* New York, 1953.

Franck, Harry A. *Roaming through the West Indies.* New York, 1920.

Frank, Henry. "African Religion in the Caribbean: Santería and Voodoo." *Carib* 2.1 (1982).

Gonzalez-Wippler, Migene. *Santería: African Magic in Latin America.* New York, 1973.

Gonzalez-Wippler, Migene. *The Santería Experience.* New Jersey, 1982.

Gonzalez-Wippler, Migene. *Rituals and Spells of Santería.* New York, 1984.

Herskovits, Melville J. *Life in a Haitian Valley.* New York, 1937, reprinted 1964.

Hurbon, Laennec. *Dieu dans le Vaudou Haitien.* Paris, 1972.

Jahn, Janheiz. *Muntu, the New African Culture.* New York, 1961.

Maximilien, Louis. *Le Voudou Haïtien: Rite Radas-Canzo.* Port-au-Prince, 1945.

Métraux, Alfred. *Vaudou in Haitien.* Translated from the French by Hugo Charteris. New York, 1958.

Murphy, Joseph M. *Santeria, an African Religion in America.* New York, 1988.

Moreau de Saint-Mery, M. L. E. *A Topographical and Political Description of the Spanish Part of Saint-Domingo, Containing General Observations on the Climate, Population, and Productions; on the Character and Manners of the Inhabitants.* Translated from the French by William Cobbett, Philadelphia, 1796.

Planson, Claude. *Voodoo, Un Initié Parle.* Paris, 1974.

Rigaud, Milo. *La Tradition Voudoo et le Voudoo Häitien: Son Temple, Ses Mysteres, Sa Magie.* Paris, 1953.

HENRY FRANK

VOLININE, ALEXANDRE (Aleksandr Emel'ianovich Volinin; born 4 [16] September 1882 in Moscow, died 3 July 1955 in Paris), Russian-French ballet dancer and teacher. Born to a family of engineers, Volinine received his dance training from Vasily Tikhomirov and Aleksandr Gorsky at the Imperial Theater School in Moscow. Entering the Bolshoi Ballet as a soloist in 1901, he quickly established himself as one of the company's leading classical dancers, admired for his beautiful, flowing line and adagio. In 1904, he replaced Tikhomirov in *The Goldfish,* which led to his promotion to principal dancer. In subsequent years, he added the major classical ballets to his repertory: *Raymonda, La Fille du Pharaon, La Fille Mal Gardée, Coppélia, The Sleeping Beauty,* and *Swan Lake.*

In 1910, Volinine left Russia to dance in Serge Diaghilev's Saison Russe in Paris partnering Ekaterina Geltser in *Les Orientales* and also appearing in *Les Sylphides, Le Carnaval,* and *Schéhérazade.* With Lydia Lopokova, her sister Evgenia, and her brother Fedor Lopukhov, he left Europe on a tour of the United States, subsequently performing in Gertrude Hoffmann's Saisons Russes (1911) and Mikhail Mordkin's All-Star Imperial Russian Ballet (1911–1912). He partnered Adeline Genée on her American and Australian tours (1912–1913) as well as during her farewell season at the London Coliseum (1914).

Later in 1914 Anna Pavlova invited Volinine to join her company, initiating a partnership that lasted with few interruptions until 1926. During these years, Volinine appeared as Pavlova's *danseur noble* in *Giselle, The Sleeping Beauty, The Awakening of Flora, Raymonda, The Fairy Doll,* and *The Magic Flute,* also performing various solo *divertissements.* For P. J. S. Richardson, editor of *The Dancing Times,* he was "the finest male dancer of [his] generation. He has a magnificent presence, and is always manly. His 'Bow and Arrow' dance shows a poise and elevation coupled with a purity of line and perfection of pose that make most *premiers danseurs* seem very small beer indeed." In 1926, Volinine opened a school in Paris where he taught such well-known dancers as Jean Babilée, Zizi Jeanmaire, George Skibine, Janine Charrat, and André Eglevsky. In 1946, he staged *Giselle* for the Royal Danish Ballet.

BIBLIOGRAPHY

Cross, Julia Vincent. "A Volinine Vignette." *Dance Magazine* (February 1957): 42–43.

Krasovskaya, Vera. *Russkii baletnyi teatr nachala dvadtatogo veka,* vol. 2, *Tantsovshchiki.* Leningrad, 1972.

Lazzarini, John, and Roberta Lazzarini. *Pavlova: Repertoire of a Legend.* New York, 1980.

Michaut, Pierre. "Parisian studios de danse." *Ballet Annual* 4 (1950): 124–129.

Money, Keith. *Anna Pavlova: Her Life and Art.* New York, 1982.

Volinine, Alexandre. "My Dance of Life" (parts 1–4). *Dance Magazine* (January–April 1930).

"Volinine at Work." *The Dancing Times* (January 1929): 548–551.

LYNN GARAFOLA

VOLKOVA, VERA (born 7 June 1904 in Saint Petersburg, died 5 May 1975 in Copenhagen), Russian ballet teacher. Volkova was born into the Russian aristrocracy and had her formal education in the Smolny Institute for Young Girls in Saint Petersburg. She started dancing at the age of fourteen. Stimulated by the influential critic Akim Volynsky, she became a pupil at his private school, the Russian School of Choreography. Agrippina Vaganova was a teacher there, and Volkova was a member of the group of pupils on which Vaganova tested her theories. Also among Volkova's teachers was Maria Romanova, the mother of Galina Ulanova.

Volkova danced with the Kirov Ballet, but her performing career was brief. She had intended to go to the West and join Serge Diaghilev's Ballets Russes, but when Diaghilev died in 1929, she defected while on tour with a group of colleagues in Vladivostok. She then settled in Shanghai, where she met the English architect and painter Hugh Finch Williams. They moved to Hong Kong, where they married in 1932, and she established her own school. Among her earliest pupils there was the young Margot Fonteyn, who also studied with Volkova later in England.

In 1937, Volkova moved to London and established an academy on West Street, which for years was attended by the most important English dancers of the period. From 1943 to 1950 she also taught for the Sadler's Wells Ballet. Volkova had great influence on the generation that shaped English ballet after World War II. She was the first and most important exponent of Vaganova's method of training in the West.

In the late 1940s, Volkova went to the Teatro alla Scala in Milan; not satisfied with conditions there, she allowed the head of the Royal Danish Ballet, Harald Lander, to persuade her to join his company in Copenhagen. Volkova organized the training at the Royal Ballet School, combining the Vaganova system with the traditional Danish Bournonville method. She was of decisive importance in setting the technical and spiritual standard that led the company to international fame during the following decade. Among her pupils in Copenhagen was Stanley Williams; in his later position as a teacher she was of great inspiration. Volkova also profoundly influenced such Danish soloists as Kirsten Simone, Erik Bruhn, Henning Kronstam, Peter Martins, Peter Schaufuss, Adam Lüders, and Lis Jeppesen. The American-born choreographer John Neumeier, head of the Hamburg Ballet, also said that his conversations with Volkova in Copenhagen were decisive in his decision to start choreographing. From 1950 to 1957 Volkova watched the Royal Danish Ballet from her seat in the stalls at almost every performance, in order to prepare for her teaching the next day.

From 1958 until 1970 Volkova also taught at Kurt Jooss's Folkwang Schule in Essen, Germany. She was a guest teacher in the United States on several occasions, most often with the Harkness Ballet. In 1956 she was named a Knight of the Order of Dannebrog.

BIBLIOGRAPHY

Aschengreen, Erik. "Hommage à Vera Volkova." *Saisons de la danse*, no. 75 (June 1975): 28.

Hering, Doris. "America Meets Vera Volkova." *Dance Magazine* (September 1959): 36–38.

Kragh-Jacobsen, Svend. "Interview with Vera Volkova." *Ballet Review* 5.4 (1975–1976).

Volkova, Vera. "Agrippina Vaganova." *Ballet Annual* 7 (1953): 44.

EBBE MØRK

VOLTA (Fr., *volte*) is a word used in Italian and French technical terminology for dancing, fencing, and horsemanship (three closely associated "manly arts," many of whose traditions and terms have descended from the Renaissance). *Volta* ("turn") appears in dance terminology as early as the first Italian manuals of the fifteenth century. It is still a standard term in the Italian dance vocabulary, frequently used with modifiers to indicate the degree of turn—for example, *mezza volta* ("half turn") or *volta tonda* ("full turn").

Volta also means "time," in the sense of frequency; its usage in dance is customary, as in *una volta* ("once") and *due volte* ("twice"). In this sense it also appears regularly in Italian Renaissance dance terminology, as in the instruction, in Cesare Negri's dance manual of 1602, *si levarà il salto intorno due volte alla sinistra* ("jump and turn around twice to the left").

The term *volta*, when it means "the turn" (Eng., *the lavolta;* Fr., *la volte;* Prov., *la volto*), seems to have been used generically by a few Renaissance writers for any turning couple dance in any meter; Rinaldo Corso (1555), for example, used the term in this broad sense, saying, "Begin the ball with a *passo e mezzo* [a duple-meter dance related both to the pavan and the galliard], which is a pleasing *volta* halfway between moderate and lively. At the end join together and do the *volta* that is now in fashion." Clearly, in this case the term refers simply to the large group of rapid turning dances that are documented from the Middle Ages to the present in iconography and literature throughout Europe and Scandinavia. The dances are distinguished by the partners, who face and hold one another firmly in embrace position—coordinating their steps to produce the centrifugal force for a full turn or pivot, with or without a lift (e.g., Swedish *polsks,* German *Zwiefacher,* Viennese and French waltzes).

References to the *volta* as a specific dance appear in print and in musical and iconographic sources on courtly life between about 1550 and 1650. Despite the dance's apparent popularity throughout western Europe, Thoinot Arbeau's *Orchésographie* (1588) is the only major dance manual to describe it in detail and correlate it with music. Arbeau says it is a triple-meter couple dance, a variant of the immensely popular galliard. Its distinguishing feature is a leap-turn by the lady, during which the man pivots on one foot while assisting his partner to leap. With one hand he grasps the bottom of her busk (a long rigid piece of thin metal or bone inserted or sewn into the corselet and extending from the breastbone to the crotch) and with the other he presses her back at the waist. At the same time, he turns her around with his other (lifted) knee just under her buttocks. The lady contributes to the lift by jumping strongly off one foot while she simultaneously presses one arm or hand forcefully down on her partner's shoulder using her other arm to keep her skirts from flying too high. She remains absolutely erect during the lift, with her legs straight down but not together. She is set down at the end of each turn. With a preparation, the whole pattern takes six beats and is to be repeated or else done to the other side *ad libitum.*

Arbeau gives two different rhythms for the changes of weight (one verbal and another in tabulation) and two different paths to alternate (one moving forward with a simple galliard variant, the other with the lift-turn). In the turning version, the preparation consists of two kicks, and the assisted lift and turn take the place of the *saut majeur* and *posture* of the last three or four beats of Arbeau's basic galliard pattern. These instructions are briefly confirmed by John Ramsey in about 1606 (Manuscripts of the Inns of Court, Douce 280).

There are numerous musical examples of the sixteenth- and seventeenth-century *volta* from France, England, Italy, and Germany. Like the galliard, it is in 6/2 or 3/2 time, and frequently the second half of its six-beat pattern contains the dotted rhythm of that dance: | 𝅗𝅥 𝅗𝅥 𝅗𝅥 𝅗𝅥. ♩ 𝅗𝅥 |. Unlike the galliard, however, the music for the *volta* never became increasingly complex polyphonically and rhythmically (and, hence, slower) as it aged, but remained a plain tune or a tune with simple harmonies. Its slow harmonic rhythm of only one or two chords to a bar continued to indicate a brisk tempo. As the dance itself retained its focus on the preparation and lift, which was its constant and tempo-controlling feature, so did a number of *volta* melodies also emphasize the leap to the fourth beat of every six. (See Example 1.)

No *volta* instructions appear in Italian large or small dance manuals, although Negri gives a related dance, "La Nizzarda" (The Girl from Nice), a fast and energetic turning dance in embrace position with small jumps and other hopping steps. Some scholars claim that it is the same as the *volta* (Donington, 1980). Negri's rather ambiguous description of "La Nizzarda," however, with its low hopping turns and embrace position, shows only a familial relationship to Arbeau's *volte.* However, a later description by Federico Zuccari in his travel memoirs (1608) describes a *nizzarda* with high lifts and turns that seems closer to Arbeau's choreography. The precise relationship between *volta* and *nizzarda,* both of which may be of Provençal origin, seems still to be in question.

The *volta's* lusty and erotic nature caused it to figure frequently in moral, salacious, or humorous texts that appeared during its greatest popularity at European courts (c.1550–1650). The suggestive embrace position and the spin and lift of the dance provided ample fodder for commentary: for example, Abbé Pierre de Bourdeilles de Brantôme (*Les vies des dames galantes,* c.1570), says of it, "The *volta,* as it swirls the dress up, always shows something delightful to the eye, and as I have seen, has caused many to lose their heads and to be utterly transported"; Guillaume Bouchet (*Les Serées,* 1597) says, "The *volta* [and] the *courante,* . . . which magicians have brought from Italy to France, besides their rude and bold movements, have the misfortune of causing an infinite number of murders and miscarriages, killing and destroying all who are yet unborn"; and the diary of "R. Z." (c.1600) in the Biblioteca di Modena says that the lift involves a tight pivot and is dangerous because if the dancers "are not fast [enough], they may both fall; nor must they allow them-

VOLTA. Example 1. A *volta* from William Byrd's *Fitzwilliam Virginal Book* (c.1612–1619). Note the melodic leap to the fourth beat in three of the four bars.

selves to get dizzy." Even Arbeau, despite his carefully detailed and practical instructions, seems to feel it his churchman's duty to warn his student, Capriol:

> After having spun round for as many cadences as you wish, return the damsel to her place, when, however brave a face she shows, she will feel her brain reeling and her head full of dizzy whirlings; and you yourself will perhaps be no better off. I leave it to you to judge whether it is a becoming thing for a young girl to take long strides and separations of the legs, and whether in this *lavolta* both honour and health are not involved and at stake. (Arbeau, 1588, pp. 119–121)

Shakespeare, in *Henry V* (act 3, scene 5), is much more approving:

> They [the English] bid us, "to the English dancing-schools,
> And teach lavoltas high and swift corantos—
> Saying, our grace is only in our heels,
> And that we are most lofty runaways.

Early records reveal two assumptions about the *volta*'s origins, one Italian, the other Provençal. Certainly the earliest known references to it are in Italian, or speak of it as Italian: in 1556 Carlois, the secretary of Vielleville, says it has been brought to France from Italy and popularized by Catherine de Médicis and Henri III (Tani, 1954); Bouchet says it is Italian; Arbeau, however, says it is Provençal. In fact, it has been reported in Provence from the sixteenth century to the present day. Whatever its origins, for nearly a century the *volta* at court represented those vigorous and earthy pleasures not yet defeated by Puritanism's proprieties.

The name *volta* (Ger., *wältzen,* "to roll" or "to revolve") was given by the French in the nineteenth century to perhaps the most popular couple dance in the world, the nineteenth-century waltz. At the height of its popularity, the French were delighted to discover that they had an ancient dance of the same name and claimed the *volta* as the French ancestor of the waltz (Desrat, 1895). The claim seems highly unlikely, for the sixteenth-century *volta,* along with the elongated busk it required, had died out by the middle of the seventeenth century; furthermore, the waltz was never characterized by a high lift. Many turning couple dances, with and without lifts, however, had remained important in Scandinavian and German-speaking countries, even in "polite" society (among them the *Weller,* the *Deutscher,* the *Drehtanz,* and the *Ländler*). The *volta* and the waltz may have shared a common ancestor and been equally dizzying, intimate, and sensuous, but they were as different from one another in affect as exuberant lustiness is from ecstatic lyricism.

BIBLIOGRAPHY: SOURCES

Arbeau, Thoinot. *Orchesographie et traicte en forme de dialogve, par leqvel tovtes personnes pevvent facilement apprendre & practiquer l'honneste exercice des dances.* Langres, 1588, 1589. Facsimile reprint, Langres, 1988. Reprinted with expanded title as *Orchesographie, metode, et teorie en forme de discovrs et tablatvre povr apprendre a dancer, battre le Tambour en toute sorte & diuersité de batteries, Iouët du fifre & arigot, tirer des armes & escrimer, auec autres honnestes exercices for conuenables à la Ieunesse.* Langres, 1596. Facsimile reprint, Geneva, 1972.

Arbeau, Thoinot. *Orchesography.* 1589. Translated into English by Mary Stewart Evans. New York, 1948. Reprint with corrections, a new introduction, and notes by Julia Sutton, and representative steps and dances in Labanotation by Mireille Backer. New York, 1967.

Corso, Rinaldo. *Dialogo del ballo.* Venice, 1559. Facsimile reprint, Bologna, 1969.

Manuscript of the Inns of Court. Located in Bodleian Library, Bodleian, Douce 280, ff.66av-66bv (202v-203v).

Negri, Cesare. *Le gratie d'amore.* Milan, 1602. Reissued as *Nuove invenzione di balli.* Milan, 1604. Translated into Spanish by Don Balthasar Carlos for Señor Condé, Duke of Sanlucar, 1630. Manuscript located in Madrid, Biblioteca Nacional, MS 14085. Facsimile reprint of 1602, New York and Bologna, 1969. Literal translation into English and musical transcription by Yvonne Kendall. D.M.A. diss., Stanford University, 1985.

BIBLIOGRAPHY: OTHER STUDIES

Bragaglia, Anton Giulio. *Danze popolari italiane.* Rome, 1950.

Desrat, G. *Dictionnaire de la danse.* Paris, 1895.

Donington, Robert. "Volta." In *The New Grove Dictionary of Music and Musicians.* London, 1980.

Heartz, Daniel. "Volte." In *Die Musik in Geschichte und Gegenwart.* 1st ed., vol. 14, 1968. Kassel, 1949–1979.

Palisca, Claude V. "The Beginnings of Baroque Music: Its Roots in Sixteenth-Century Theory and Polemics." Ph.D. diss., Harvard University, 1953.

Palisca, Claude V. *Humanism in Italian Renaissance Musical Thought.* New Haven, 1985.

Sachs, Curt. *World History of the Dance.* Translated by Bessie Schönberg. New York, 1937.

Tani, Gino. "Nizzarda" and "Volta." In *Enciclopedio dello spettacolo.* 9 vols. Rome, 1954–1968.

Tennevin, Nicolette, and Marie Texier. *Dances of France II: Provence and Alsace.* Vol. 2. Translated by Violet Alford. London, 1951.

Wilson, D. R. "Dancing in the Inns of Court." *Historical Dance* 2.5 (1986–1987): 3–16.

JULIA SUTTON
with Patricia Weeks Rader

VOLYNSKY, AKIM (Akim L'vovich Flekser; born 11 April 1865 in Zhitomir, Russia, died 6 July 1926 in Leningrad), Russian literary and ballet critic and art historian. Volynsky venerated the classical tradition and sought to elevate ballet to a status equal to that of the other arts. He wrote extensively on literature, aesthetics, and art, including a monumental study of Leonardo da Vinci for which he was proclaimed an honorary citizen of Milan.

Volynsky's sharply worded polemics in support of the classical tradition appeared in a number of leading periodicals, including *Birzhevye vedomosti, Zhizn' iskusstva,* and *Severnyi vestnik.* Among his many targets over the years was Boris Romanov, whom he forcefully upbraided, describing his works as "expressive bordering on grotesque" and "barbarically breaking the rules" of classical dance. He later criticized Michel Fokine as well as George Balanchine and his Molodoy Balet (Young Ballet) on similar grounds.

In 1921 Volynsky founded the School of Russian Ballet in Petrograd. Many teachers from the Maryinsky Theater Ballet School, including Nikolai Legat and Agrippina Vaganova, taught there. On the basis of his lectures at the school, Volynsky wrote *Kniga likovanii: Azbuka klassicheskogo tantsa* (The Book of Exultation: A Primer in the Classical Dance), published in 1926. This work attempts a formulation of his philosophy of ballet and aesthetics. It includes an examination of ballet in contrast to the other arts and in terms of metaphysics. Additionally the work outlines a basic, suggested ballet school program, including aspects of theory and aesthetics. Volynsky's other major book on dance was *Problemy russkogo baleta* (Problems of the Russian Ballet), published in 1923.

From 1920 to 1922 Volynsky engaged in a fierce debate on the pages of *Zhizn' iskusstva* concerning performances by the Maryinsky Theater and ballet training at its ballet school. He particularly assailed Leonid Leontev, whom he blamed for much of the decline of the Petrograd ballet. Volynsky advocated radical reforms in the school's teaching methodology and changes in the troupe's leadership in order to breathe new life into the company. His attack included an open letter to Anatoly Lunacharsky, the commissar for enlightenment.

Volynsky was likewise embroiled in administrative disputes following Fokine's departure from the Maryinsky Theater. Volynsky wrote a series of articles in 1922–1923 asserting that Nikolai Legat was the only ballet master capable of leading the troupe. He and Legat were united in their belief that Fokine and his experimental diversions had been leading ballet away from its true path of development.

Volynsky's importance rests on his articulate, unflagging defense of classical dance theory and forms. In the words of Fedor Lopukhov, Volynsky was the "first who attempted an explanation of the meaning of each movement in dance . . . and who revealed the wonderful essence of the choreographic art."

[*For similar discussion, see the entries on Koni, Levinson, Svetlov, and Zotov.*]

BIBLIOGRAPHY

Souritz, Elizabeth. *Soviet Choreographers in the 1920s.* Translated by Lynn Visson. Durham, N.C., 1990.

Leontev, L. V. "V zashchitu padaiushchego Gosudarstvennogo baleta." *Zhizn' iskusstva* (26–27 June 1920).

Volynsky, Akim. "Baletmeisterskii vopros (B. G. Romanov)." *Birzhevye vedomosti* (20 February 1915).

Volynsky, Akim. "Reforma Gosudarstvennogo baleta: Otkrytoe pis'mo narkomu prosveshcheniia A. V. Lunacharskomu." *Zhizn' iskusstva* (29–31 May 1920).

Volynsky, Akim. *Leonardo da Vinchi.* St. Petersburg, 1922.

Volynsky, Akim. "Gde byt' russkomu baletu?" *Zhizn' iskusstva* (11 December 1923).

Volynsky, Akim. "Khoreograficheskie arabeski." *Zhizn' iskusstva* (17 April 1923).

Volynsky, Akim. *Problemy russkogo baleta.* Petrograd, 1923.

Volynsky, Akim. *Kniga likovanii: Azbuka klassicheskogo tantsa.* Leningrad, 1926. Translated by Seymour Barofsky as "The Book of Exultation," *Dance Scope* (Spring 1971).

Susan Cook Summer

VOODOO. *See* Vodun.

VYROUBOVA, NINA (Nina Goursoff; born 4 June 1921 in Crimea), Russian-French dancer and teacher. Vyroubova was a naturally gifted dancer and an heir to the imperial Russian style. In 1924, with her grandmother and widowed mother, she immigrated to Paris, where they lived the difficult life of penniless émigrés. Vyroubova dreamed of dancing from the time she saw Anna Pavlova in *The Fairy Doll* and *The Dying Swan* in 1931 at the Théâtre des Champs-Elysées.

Her career took shape quickly. She began by studying with Olga Preobrajenska; later teachers included the Russian dancers Vera Trefilova and Lubov Egorova. Discovered by Elvira Roné, a pupil and longtime assistant of Preobrajenska, Vyroubova was performing at sixteen as Swanilda in *Coppélia* at the ballet festival in Caen; her partner was Aubrey Hitchins, formerly of Pavlova's company. In 1940 she danced with the Ballets Polonais and the Ballets Russes de Paris; in 1945 she was one of the young dancers who participated in the Dance Fridays at the Théâtre Sarah-Bernhardt (another was Roland Petit, Vyroubova's partner in *Giselle*). In the first production of Petit's *Les Forains* (1945), she created the role of the Sleeping Beauty, also dancing it at the Ballets des Champs-Élysées, which she joined in 1946. In December 1946 she danced the title role in *La Sylphide,* perhaps the peak of her career.

In fall 1949, Vyroubova made her debut as a *première danseuse étoile* at the Paris Opera in the *Divertissement d'Aurore.* Director Serge Lifar called on her to replace Yvette Chauviré; in 1950, Vyroubova triumphed in *Giselle* in Monte Carlo and performed in works of the repertory ranging from *Swan Lake* to George Balanchine's *Le Palais de Cristal.* Edwin Denby (1950) spoke of her as "the brightest hope in Europe for another great ballerina five years from now," adding:

> [She has a] delicious figure, limpid style, sweet absorption. . . . She has the sweetest Russian-style virtues. A long foot, quick thigh, delicate bust, small head far from the shoulder. The step has edge, the arms are a classicist's dream, the carriage of the head has distinction, the face makes sense. She is unusually accurate and musical.

VYROUBOVA. As La Dame in Serge Lifar's *Dramma per Musica*, at the Paris Opera in 1950. (Photograph by Roger-Violett © Lipnitzki-Viollet; used by permission.)

Vyroubova became particularly associated with Lifar's work, dancing in *Suite en Blanc, Romeo and Juliet, Dramma per Musica,* and *La Mort du Cygne*, as well as in *Phèdre,* in which she succeeded Tamara Toumanova. Lifar also made roles for Vyroubova in *Blanche-Neige* (Snow White; 1951), *Fourberies* (1952), *The Firebird* (1954), and *Les Noces Fantastiques* (1955).

In 1956 Vyroubova left the Opera, appearing as a leading dancer with Le Grand Ballet du Marquis de Cuevas from 1957 to 1962. There she performed the great Romantic roles and established a partnership with Serge Golovine. She had roles created for her by Ana Ricarda (in the 1957 *La Chanson de l'Éternelle Tristesse*) and by Lifar (the 1957 *L'Amour et Son Destin*). She created an unforgettable portrayal of the Sleepwalker in Balanchine's *La Sonnambula* and performed the title role of *The Sleeping Beauty* with Rudolf Nureyev as her partner. From 1962 to 1966 she performed as a guest artist throughout the world in such widely dissimilar roles as the ethereal Taglioni in Anton Dolin's *Pas de Quatre* and the fatally seductive Bellastriga in Peter van Dyk's *Abraxas*.

Since 1986 Vyroubova has taught privately in Paris and at the Conservatory of Troyes. Reflecting her personality, her technique combines vivacity and legato, lightness and passion, ease of movement and the slow flowering of the adagio.

In 1957 Vyroubova was awarded the Prix Pavlova for her interpretation of Giselle and the Petipa Prize for her teaching. In 1980 she received the Italian prize Una Vita per la Danza. She is a Chevalier de l'Ordre National du Mérite.

BIBLIOGRAPHY

Denby, Edwin. *Dance Writings*. Edited by Robert Cornfield and William MacKay. New York, 1986.

Dorvane, Jeannine. "Hommage à Nina Vyroubova." *Saisons de la danse*, no. 128 (November 1980): 24–29.

Laurent, Jean. *Nina Vyroubova et ses visages*. Paris, 1958.

Perrin, Olivier. "The Art of Ballet: Interviews." *Opera, Ballet, Music-Hall*, no. 1 (1952): 33–52.

Swinson, Cyril, ed. *Dancers and Critics*. London, 1950.

Zürner, Inge. "Nina Vyroubova." *Ballet Today* (January–February 1964): 14–16.

FILMS. Dominique Delouche, *Le spectre de la danse* (1960) and *L'adage* (1965).

JEANNINE DORVANE
Translated from French

W

WALDEEN (Waldeen Falkenstein; born 1 February 1913 in Dallas, Texas), Mexican dancer, choreographer, ballet director, and teacher. Waldeen received classical ballet lessons from Theodore Koslov and Vera Fredowa. At thirteen she made her debut as a soloist with the Koslov Ballet Company and at the Los Angeles Opera. At fifteen she studied modern dance with Benjamin Zemach—an exponent of the school of Rudolf Laban and Mary Wigman—the director of the Russian Habimah Theater. She also took intensive courses from Harald Kreuzberg at his school in Bern, Switzerland. She joined Michio Ito's dance company on a three-year tour of the United States, Canada, Japan, and Mexico, visiting the last in 1934. In 1939 Waldeen returned to Mexico, where the government commissioned her to form a modern dance company, the Ballet de Bellas Artes.

WALDEEN. Guillermina Bravo and Ricardo Silva in Waldeen's *En la Boda* (1954), set to music by Blas Galindo, with costume designs by Carlos Mérida. (Photograph reprinted from *Artes de Mexico,* August 1955.)

Waldeen was a pioneer of the Mexican modern dance movement of the 1940s and 1950s. During this period she directed a group of young dancers who produced works stressing nationalistic and Mexican approaches to history and art. In 1940, she presented the ballet *La Coronela* (The Lady Colonel) to Silvestre Revueltas's music; in 1942 she presented the mass ballet *Siembra* (Sowing Time), danced by five thousand people. Her choreography (including *Suite de Danzas, Cinco Danzas en Ritmo Búlgaro, Alegretto,* and *Elena la Traicionera*) provides aesthetic models for many modern Mexican choreographers, incorporating and reflecting the Mexican spirit on the stage. Waldeen was the teacher of Mexico's first generation of modern dancers.

Strongly influenced by Mexican nationalistic painting and music, Waldeen successfully used the themes and images of Mexico's peoples and cultures. From 1940 to 1942, she took her Ballet de Bellas Artes, as well as her later group, the Waldeen Ensemble, on tours through the United States. In 1946 she went back to New York, where she joined the Choreographers Workshop and the New School for Social Research. In 1948 she returned to Mexico, where she successively directed the Modern Ballet Company, the Bellas Artes Ballet Company, and the Waldeen Ballet Company. In 1962 she traveled to Cuba, where she directed a modern dance school and produced several ballets.

Waldeen returned to Mexico in 1966 to resume her work in choreography and teaching. She also served in an advisory capacity to various government organizations, as well as at her own academy. She now lives in Cuernavaca, Mexico, where she directs a choreography workshop.

[*See also* Mexico, *article on* Theatrical Dance.]

BIBLIOGRAPHY

Dallal, Alberto. *La danza contra la muerte.* 3d ed. Mexico City, 1993.
Dallal, Alberto. *La danza en México.* 3 vols. 2d ed. Mexico City, 1995.

Razetti, Ricardo. *"La coronela": Ballet del Teatro de las Artes.* Mexico City, 1940.

Waldeen. *La danza: Imagen de creación continua.* Mexico City, 1982.

ALBERTO DALLAL

WALKAROUND TIME. Choreography: Merce Cunningham. Music: David Behrman; ". . . for nearly an hour. . . ." Scenery supervised by Jasper Johns; based on Marcel Duchamp's unfinished work *The Large Glass* (1913–1923). Costumes (uncredited): Jasper Johns. First performance: 10 March 1968, Upton Auditorium, State University College at Buffalo, New York, Merce Cunningham Dance Company. Dancers: Merce Cunningham, Carolyn Brown, Barbara Lloyd, Sandra Neels, Valda Setterfield, Meg Harper, Albert Reid, Gus Solomons, Jr., Jeff Slayton.

Walkaround Time is essentially an *hommage à Marcel Duchamp.* In having such a central focus, it differs from most Cunningham collaborations in which artist, composer, and choreographer create relatively independently, their efforts coming together only in performance. Duchamp's interest in pure chance ("a way of going against logical reality") made him a role model or hero figure for John Cage and Cunningham. Like Duchamp's work, Cunningham's choreography is enigmatic. It is laced with references to Duchamp the man, to his work, and specifically to his work *The Large Glass,* or *The Bride Stripped Bare by Her Bachelors, Even.* The dance is divided into two sections by an unchoreographed entr'acte which, according to Cunningham, is "straight out of *Relâche,*" a Dadaist ballet in which Duchamp performed. In the entr'acte the dancers may walk around on and off stage, practice steps, rest, talk with musicians and stage hands, or do anything they choose. This improvisatory section is in sharp contrast to parts 1 and 2, which are characterized by clearly articulated, precisely timed, exacting movement, ranging from basic unadorned classroom material (Duchamp's "readymades") to technical, highly demanding material (Duchamp's "mechanical apparatus"). The title of Behrman's music refers to an earlier Duchamp painting, *To Be Looked at with One Eye, Close to, for Almost an Hour.* The set, which *New York Times* critic Clive Barnes called "the finest decor American dance has ever known," consists of seven vinyl boxes of varying shapes and sizes onto which Jasper Johns transcribed images from *The Large Glass.* The audience looks through the dance to see the painting and through the painting to see the dance, each absorbing the other into its world.

> "*Walkaround Time* is, purely and simply, a masterwork. . . . The entire choreographic aesthetic . . . at once austere, whimsical, transparent and meticulous, is like that of *The Large Glass.*" (John Mueller, *Dance Magazine,* June 1977)

Walkaround Time also exists as a forty-eight minute, 16mm color film performed by the Merce Cunningham Dance Company, with cinematography by Charles Atlas, filmed at the Brooklyn Academy of Music in 1969 and the Théâtre de la Ville, Paris, in 1972.

BIBLIOGRAPHY

Cunningham, Merce. *Changes: Notes on Choreography.* Edited by Frances Starr. New York, 1968.

Cunningham, Merce, in conversation with Jacqueline Lesschaeve. *The Dancer and the Dance.* New York, 1985.

Mazo, Joseph H. *Prime Movers: The Makers of Modern Dance in America.* New York, 1977.

Tomkins, Calvin. *Duchamp.* New York, 1996.

CAROLYN BROWN

WALKOWITZ, ABRAHAM (born 1878 in Tyumen, Siberia, died 27 January 1965 in New York), creator of drawings and watercolors of Isadora Duncan. Walkowitz gained recognition in the dance world for his numerous drawings and watercolors of Isadora Duncan. In his lifetime he made thousands of sketches of the dancer ("more than I have hairs on my head"), which allegedly inspired her to remark, "Walkowitz, you have written my biography in lines without words."

Walkowitz was born in Tyumen, a small city in Siberia. After his father's death, the family immigrated to New York in the late 1880s and settled on the Lower East Side. The young artist enrolled in the National Academy of Design at the age of sixteen and subsequently saved enough money for European travel and two years of study at the Académie Julien in Paris.

Isadora Duncan and Walkowitz were introduced at the studio of the sculptor Auguste Rodin in 1906; the following day Walkowitz saw her perform in a private salon. He saw her dance again in Paris and during Duncan's American tours in 1908 and 1909. "She was an inspiration . . . a Muse," said Walkowitz in an interview in 1958. "She didn't dance according to rules. She created. Her body was music."

Walkowitz's studies of Duncan explore seemingly endless variations of her dance figure. The drawings were done from remembered impressions and sought to convey the visual equivalent of his personal experience. With expressive draftsmanship and fluid lines he summarized the essence of Duncan's form and movement.

Themes other than dance also figured in Walkowitz's art, particularly Manhattan street life and architecture. His early works dating from 1913 and 1914 reveal an interest in and understanding of the rhythm, tensions, and dynamics that were just then beginning to absorb progressive American artists. This same understanding underlies his interpretation of Duncan's art.

The artist's first one-man exhibition in New York in 1908 was followed by several shows between 1912 and

1917 at Alfred Stieglitz's famed "291" gallery. In 1913 he participated in the celebrated Armory Show, and in his lifetime he was accorded retrospectives by the Brooklyn Museum (1939) and the Jewish Museum (1949). Failing eyesight, which began in his fifties, prevented Walkowitz from pursuing his profession in later life. A prodigious body of early work, however, indissolubly links him to the dance and choreography of Isadora Duncan.

BIBLIOGRAPHY

Walkowitz, Abraham. *Isadora Duncan in Her Dances*. Girard, Kansas, 1945.

Werner, Alfred. "Abraham Walker Rediscovered." *American Artist* 43 (August 1979): 54–59.

NANCY VAN NORMAN BAER

WALL, DAVID (born 15 March 1946 in London), British dancer and teacher. A *premier danseur* with a noble manner and a flowing classical technique, Wall was completely trained at the Royal Ballet School, which he entered at the age of ten. Graduating into the Royal Ballet Touring Company in 1963, he informed his dancing with such authority and intelligence that he was promoted to soloist in 1965 and to principal—then the youngest in the history of the Royal Ballet—in 1966.

Wall's meteoric progress seemed inevitable. He won his first solo, in *Napoli,* within months of joining the company, and he followed it swiftly with sharply contrasted debuts as the Young Man in *The Two Pigeons* and as Her Cousin in *The Invitation.* Guided by the company teacher Erling Sunde and company director John Field, he danced the leading male roles in *Giselle, Swan Lake, La Fille Mal Gardée,* and *The Rake's Progress* in 1965, often partnering Doreen Wells. He moved on confidently to *The Dream* and *Coppélia* in 1966 and *The Sleeping Beauty* in 1967. By then he was the mainstay of the company and an experienced and gracious partner.

When the Touring Company disbanded in 1970, Wall transferred to the Royal Ballet at Covent Garden and continued to stretch himself technically and emotionally with debuts as Romeo in *Romeo and Juliet* and Solor in *La Bayadère.* A pure and natural classicist in *Symphonic Variations, Song of the Earth,* and *Agon,* he played the role of Petruchio in *The Taming of the Shrew* with robust delight. His compelling gifts as a dramatic actor, which he first tested as the Rake and developed further as Mercutio and the Prodigal Son, blazed into full maturity with his creation of Lescaut in *Manon* (1974) and the tortured Crown Prince Rudolf in *Mayerling* (1978).

Wall was the company's principal *danseur* through the 1970s. In 1978 he won the *Evening Standard* Award for "the most outstanding achievement in dance in 1977" and was awarded a CBE (Commander of the Order of the British Empire) in 1985. He retired from dancing in 1984 and joined the Royal Academy of Dancing as associate director the same year; he became director in 1986 and retained that position until 1991.

BIBLIOGRAPHY

Maynard, Olga. "David Wall: England Made Him." *Dance Magazine* (August 1974): 53–59.

Newman, Barbara. *Striking a Balance: Dancers Talk about Dancing.* New York, 1982.

Percival, John. "A Whole Dancer." *Dance and Dancers* (August 1984): 24–29.

Woodcock, Sarah C. *The Sadler's Wells Royal Ballet.* London, 1991.

BARBARA NEWMAN

WALLMANN, MARGARETE (also known as Margarita Wallmann; born 22 July 1904 in Vienna, died 2 May 1992 in Monte Carlo), Austrian dancer and choreographer. Wallmann attended the ballet school of the Berlin State Opera and studied with Evgenia Eduardova, Olga Preobrajenska, and Matilda Kshessinska and, starting in 1920, with Heinrich Kröller at the Munich State Opera Ballet school. In 1923 she began studying with Mary Wigman in Dresden; she took over the Wigman school in Berlin in 1929.

In 1930 in Munich, Wallmann and her Tänzer-Kollectiv ensemble performed with Ted Shawn the movement drama *Orpheus Dionysos* to music by Gluck. In the summer of 1931 Wallmann and her troupe were guest performers at the Salzburg Festival, where, as an exponent of contemporary expressionist dance, she staged the premiere of *The Last Judgment* to music by Handel. Thanks to this success, Wallmann was a regular guest at the Salzburg Festival until 1937, where she made her debut as an opera producer in 1933 with Gluck's *Orpheus and Eurydice.* From 1934 to 1938 she was also the leading house choreographer at the Vienna State Opera. Since she was Jewish, she left Vienna after the annexation of Austria by Nazi Germany in 1938.

Wallmann turned away from modern dance and arranged sumptuously staged spectacles to pleasant music with Austrian themes in *divertissement* form, such as *Austrian Farmer's Wedding,* to music by Franz Salmhofer; this had its premiere 6 October 1934 at the Vienna State Opera. In addition, she created dance scenes for Hollywood films, notably *Anna Karenina* (1935). From 1938 to 1948, at the Teatro Colón in Buenos Aires, she presented *Josephslegende* and *Don Juan* as well as ballets with South American themes. After 1949 she choreographed for Teatro alla Scala in Milan and again for the Salzburg Festival before returning to opera production. She was associated with the Metropolitan Opera in New York from 1964 to 1977 and presented numerous productions, with varying degrees of success, in Milan, Rome, Vienna, Paris, Chicago, Naples, Palermo, and elsewhere. Wherever she worked, Wallmann was recognized for her theatricality, her knowledge of stage effects, and her characteristic block use of groups of performers.

BIBLIOGRAPHY

Amort, Andrea. "Die Geschichte des Balletts der Wiener Staatsoper, 1918–1942." Ph.D. diss., University of Vienna, 1981.

Amort, Andrea. "Die Tänze oder Verfewden." *Ballett International/Tanz Aktuell* 8–9 (1995): 64.

Amort, Andrea. "Margarete Wallmann." *Pipers Enzyklopiëdie des Musiktheaters, Oper, Operette, Musical, Ballett.* Vol. 6. Zurich, 1996.

Basaldua, Emilio. "Hector Basaldua and the Colón Theater." *Journal of Decorative and Propaganda Arts* 18 (1992): 32–53.

Shawn, Ted. "Germany's Newest Genius," *Dance Magazine* (August 1930).

"Margarete Wallmann: Zum Tode der Choreographin und Regisseurin." *Tanzdrama,* no. 19 (1992): 8–11.

Wallmann, Margarethe. *Les balcons du ciel.* Paris, 1976.

ANDREA AMORT
Translated from German

WALTER, ERICH (born 30 December 1927 in Fürth, near Nuremberg, died 23 November 1983 in Herdacke), German ballet dancer, choreographer, and company director. Having been trained in ballet by Olympia Alperova in Nuremberg, Erich Walter joined the opera ballet there in 1946. He was with the Göttingen Opera Ballet from 1950 to 1951 and the Wiesbaden Opera Ballet from 1951 to 1953. He was ballet master and choreographer in Wuppertal from 1953 to 1964 and then ballet director and chief choreographer of the Deutsche Oper am Rhine (German Opera on the Rhine), Düsseldorf-Duisburg, from 1964 onward, with numerous guest engagements in Germany (West Berlin, Munich) and abroad (Vienna State Opera, Teatro alla Scala, Zurich Opera). The first classically trained German choreographer to emerge after World War II, Walter became known for his musically am-

WALTER. A scene from Georg Reinhart's production of Hans Werner Henze's *Boulevard Solitude,* first mounted at the Hanover Opera in 1952. Uniting ballet and lyric drama, realism and surrealism, nineteenth-century conventions and modern cinematic illusion, the seven scenes of this evening-length work derived meaning as much from Walter's choreography as from Henze's music, Grete Weil's libretto, or Reinhart's production values. (Photograph by Saurin-Sorani; reprinted from Horst Koegler, *Ballett International,* Berlin, 1960, fig. 142.)

bitious, perfectly integrated ballet productions, which were a product of his close collaboration with the designer Henrich Wendel.

In the course of Walter's long, consistent, and distinguished career there were certain mainstays: the classics (*Giselle, Swan Lake,* and *The Sleeping Beauty,* on all of which he collaborated with Ruzena Mazalová from Prague, an authority on traditional choreography); the Prokofiev full-length ballets *(Romeo and Juliet, Cinderella,* and *The Stone Flower);* and full-length productions based upon musical selections from an individual composer (Monteverdi's *Orfeo,* in a fully choreographed version; *Fantasies,* dealing with episodes from the life of Tchaikovsky; and *Kalevala,* with music by Sibelius). These were, however, far outnumbered by his one-act ballets, choreographed to concert music ranging from Albinoni and Vivaldi to contemporary composers such as Wolfgang Fortner, Hans Werner Henze, and Aribert Reimann. Walter's special sympathies were reserved for Berlioz, Debussy, Janáček, Stravinsky, and Bartók. Among his best ballets must be counted "Dance around the Golden Calf" (1968) in the Düsseldorf production of Schoenberg's opera *Moses und Aron* and his version of Stravinsky's *Le Sacre du Printemps* (1970).

Walter was born in the same year as Maurice Béjart, John Cranko, and Yuri Grigorovich. His ballets may lack the strongly individual flavor of those of his eminent contemporaries, but his choreographies are imprinted with his impeccable musical taste and demands, in which he was obviously schooled by George Balanchine. He was a lyricist rather than a dramatist and always favored a beautiful line and decorous group arrangement rather than striving for originality through distorted movements. At the peak of his career Walter was Germany's most classically minded choreographer.

BIBLIOGRAPHY

Barfuss, Grischa, et al. *Ein Ballett in Deutschland.* Düsseldorf, 1971.

Koegler, Horst. "Ballettgeschichte an der Rheinoper." In *Die Deutsche Oper am Rhein 1964–1980,* pp. 10–11. Düsseldorf, 1986.

Kügler, Ilka, et al. *Poet des Tanzes: Der Choreograph Erich Walter.* Düsseldorf, 1993.

HORST KOEGLER

WALTZ. The word *waltz* is derived from German *wälzen,* meaning "to turn," "to revolve," or "to wander." This European couple dance in triple measure reached its zenith in the nineteenth century, in the capitals of Europe and the Americas. It captivated all strata of society with its heady, romantic rotations, a contrast to the precise protocol of the earlier minuet and the confining geometry of the cotillon and the contradance. Initially, however, genteel society was rather shocked by the intimacy implied by the waltz's embracing position.

Much has been preserved of the nineteenth-century waltz, but its origins are unclear. The waltz cannot be attributed to the inspiration of a specific dancing master or associated with any notable event. Dance historians have traced general similarities to the *volta,* a sixteenth-century court dance done by couples turning and striding to triple measure. The *Weller,* a German peasant turning dance, was mentioned in 1525 by the Nüremberg Meistersinger Has. A dance in which a couple turned together, face to face with hands placed on each other's shoulder or waist is depicted in engravings of the late Renaissance; it is identified as Alpine peasant dancing.

In regard to the music, a seventeenth-century lute manuscript preserved in an Austrian monastery at Kremsmuenster contains melodies that closely resemble the musical form later identified as *Walzer;* they are entitled "Laenderli" and "Steyerische," words associated with Austrian peasant dances in which couples pursue and capture each other, entwine arms in a series of courtship postures, and finally revolve together in unison.

Joseph Schmelzer (1623–1680), *Kapellmeister* to the court of Vienna from 1665, composed music for a "Ballet d'Amoretti e Trattore" performed in the opera *Le Disgrazie d'Amore,* in the form of a *Ländler.* In 1679 Schmelzer's music for the opera *Baldrucca,* performed at the Viennese court of Leopold I, included music to which Schwabian peasants danced in triple time to an aria with clear waltz characteristics.

An obstacle confronting dance historians researching the early waltz is the various applications of words meaning "German" (such as *Allemande* and *Deutscher*) in seventeenth- and eighteenth-century dance description. *Allemande,* for example, originally denoted a processional court dance of the late Renaissance, bearing little resemblance to the waltz. In mid-eighteenth-century France the same word was applied to a different court dance in which partners turned one another with interlaced arms, with steps possibly derived from the *Ländler.* In Austria, *Ländler* were Alpine peasant dances from the Landl district, while *Deutscher* encompassed all Germanic dances. Finally, *walzen, drehen,* and *spinneren* were verbs of general usage describing various motions of turning not necessarily related to dancing.

Around 1750 numerous comedies staged in Vienna were interspersed with musical pieces called *walzer.* In 1760, "waltzende Taenze" were publicly cited there as licentious.

Although dance historians are reluctant to draw connections between minuet and waltz, it is true that Viennese composers of the eighteenth century included rustic *Ländler*-like trios as a contrast to the grand style of the minuet, both in their symphonic minuet arrangements and in music intended solely for dancing. A sonatina by Franz Joseph Haydn, written in 1776, included a "mouvement de valse"—perhaps the first waltz specifically scored for piano. In 1784 an "air pour valser" appeared in André-Ernest-Modeste Grétry's ballet *Colinette à la Coeur,* presented by the Opéra Comique of Paris. In 1786 the comic opera *Una Cosa Rara* by the Spanish composer Vicente Martín y Soler (1754–1806) had its first performance in Vienna; the sensation it created was due less to the music than to the simple peasant turning dance incorporated in it.

The music associated with turning dance of this period, variously labeled *Walzer, Ländler, Allemande,* or *Deutsche,* was usually in the form of two eight-measure phrases in triple measure, repeated as AA/BB. Each beat of the bar was accented more or less evenly, although there are early examples of typical waltz characteristics—anticipation of the first beat, elongation of the second beat, and rubato. Occasionally several *Walzer* were strung together, forming a rudimentary suite.

In 1787, Mozart's opera *Don Giovanni* presented a minuet, *contredanse,* and waltz ingeniously combined. Mozart also wrote numerous "Deutsche Tanze" and *Ländler* intended for social dancing. Beethoven composed twelve *Deutscher* for the Redoutensaal balls in 1795.

Johann Nepomuk Hummel (1778–1837), Mozart's best-known pupil, is credited with introducing dance music to the concert salon in 1808. Joining six somewhat programmatic waltzes with trios to a coda, he expanded the waltz to a form that a decade later was taken up by Carl-Maria von Weber in his *Invitation to the Dance.*

In 1800, a waltz was danced at the Paris Opera, in Étienne-Nicolas Méhul's ballet *La Dansomanie.* By 1804 "une valse, encore une valse" was the cry of young dancers in Paris. The court of Russia succumbed to its charms after the death of Catherine the Great in 1798, but the court of Berlin, though exposed to waltzing by 1794, never entirely accepted this innovation. Although the waltz was danced at Almack's Assembly Rooms by foreigners prior to 1812, London society resisted it until its appearance on the program of a ball given in July 1816 by the Prince Regent.

In the same year, Thomas Wilson, dancing master at the King's Theatre, London, published *A Description of the Correct Method of Waltzing,* giving instructions for three French waltzes and one German waltz, complete with illustrations and music, and a refutation of the evil influence ascribed to waltzing.

- In Wilson's Slow French Waltz, the man steps with the left foot from fourth position behind to the second position with a turn of the body clockwise; then he executes a slow pirouette on the right foot to fifth position behind the left; he continues turning on both feet (always on the toes) until the right foot comes around in front of the left. He then executes the three steps of the *pas de bourrée* (already known to dancers in the *menuet*), beginning with the right foot (R,L,R) on the counts 4, 5, 6. The woman performs first the *pas de bourrée* (R,L,R) on counts 1, 2, 3, and then the steps first executed by her partner. In the first measure they dance half a circle, and in the second measure the other half, moving around the ballroom in a counterclockwise direction.
- In Wilson's second waltz, called the Sauteuse Waltz, the man springs into second position with the left foot, turning clockwise; then springs again into second position with the right foot, continuing the turn, and places his left foot in fifth position behind, still turning, (counts 1, 2, 3). He then executes the same *bourrée* as above, commencing with a spring. The woman dances the counterpart, beginning with the *bourrée.*
- In the Jetté or Quick Sauteuse Waltz, the music accelerates as the man leaps to second position with the left foot, turning clockwise. He rests the right foot behind the left ankle and hops on the left foot, still turning. He then leaps to second position with the right foot. The woman executes the reverse at the same time.
- In the German Waltz, the man steps with the left foot into second position and performs a coupé with each foot in sequence. He then steps forward through fourth position with the right foot forward, then fifth, then fourth again. The woman mirrors these steps. The woman begins by stepping forward with the right foot forward. Wilson provides engravings showing a variety of positions for holding partners in each of the waltzes.

Despite the apparent dissimilarity between waltz and minuet, it is interesting to note that Thomas Wilson used the word *bourée* (or *bourrée*) to describe the *enchaînement* of three steps used in the second measure of the waltz. This same basic *bourrée* sequence is used in the second measure of the minuet step as described by eighteenth-century dancing masters. Wilson points out that the waltz *bourrée* should be danced on the toes and does not include the "sinks" *(pliés)* required in the *bourrée* of the minuet.

The Slow French Waltz became known to dancing masters as the *"trois-temps* waltz." Wilson states that the three waltzes should be danced as a suite, with couples moving in regulated semicircles around the ballroom. To dancers restricted to the confining dimensions and exacting technique of earlier dances, the waltz represented a newfound spatial freedom. The new spirit of liberty also inspired radical shifts of fashion.

Joseph Lanner (1801–1843) and Johann Strauss the elder (1804–1849) were both members of a Viennese dance band. In 1821, Lanner established a small band of his own, to be joined later by Strauss. As their popularity grew, the band was enlarged and finally divided into two separate orchestras, with Strauss leading one and Lanner the other. Eventually rivalry separated the two partners, and their individual fame paralleled the exploding popularity of the waltz. Beginning with Weber and his *Invitation to the Dance* (1819), a series of major composers—

including Frédéric Chopin, Franz Schubert, and even Richard Wagner—wrote waltzes.

During the early nineteenth century, the original 3/8 signature time was changed to 3/4, and the typical Alberti bass gave way to a strong emphasis on the first beat, shortening the second and third beats. The melody was now expressed in the Romantic style, varied in rhythm and temperament to counteract the steady repetition of the triple beat.

The Viennese waltz was exported to all the capitals of Europe and the Americas. Johann Strauss the younger (1825–1899) conducted his first public concert at the age of nineteen, despite his father's disapproval, and took over the orchestra following his father's death five years later. His two brothers Eduard and Josef became composers of waltz music as well received as that of their father and elder brother. [*See* Strauss Family.]

The principle of couples turning together *à la valse* was soon applied to other dance steps in 2/4, 4/4, and 6/8, rhythms. The ancient *chassé* step, for instance, when danced by couples turning became the *galop,* popular in ballrooms of the 1820s. The *chassé-sauté en tournant* became the basis of the polka. The *pas de basque* step danced by couples turning became the *redowa.* The mid-century schottische probably owes its inspiration to the Scottish strathspey step so similar to the *enchaînement* of *temps-levé, chassé, jeté,* and *assemblé,* which formed the basic step of the French quadrille.

The exciting, erratic rhythms and exotic harmonies of the dashing mazurka (brought to France by Polish emigrés serving in Napoleon's campaigns against Russia) rivaled the waltz briefly but proved too difficult for ballroom dancers to master. The "Cellarius Waltz," introduced in the 1850s, was an attempt to combine waltz and mazurka in a dance simple enough for all. The five-step waltz applied the turning principle to music in 5/4 time, an interesting if short-lived innovation. The polka-redowa and polka-mazurka were more successful, satisfying the mid-century craze for turning by combining simplified polka and mazurka steps to waltz tempo.

By the early 1840s, the old *trois-temps* waltz was giving way to the *deux-temps* waltz. This simplification of steps allowed dancers to turn to and fro, in and out, in all direc-

WALTZ. In the early nineteenth century, the waltz was frequently performed with a variety of steps and arm positions. Pictured here are nine of these, recommended by English dancing master Thomas Wilson in his 1816 manual *A Description of the Correct Method of Waltzing.* (Private collection.)

tions, relieving the endless, dizzying, somewhat monotonous rotations by half-circles which were often awkward in crowded ballrooms. The *deux-temps* waltz should not be confused with the two-step, a later dance. Waltzers often elongate the second beat of the measure to extend the length of the turn and shorten the third beat by quickening the close, a characteristic of the mazurka as well. The *deux-temps* waltz discarded the *bourrée* of Thomas Wilson's era in favor of a step and pivoting *chassé*. Both partners executed this maneuver in unison and in one measure.

By the 1870s, dancing masters were introducing variations of the waltz step, among which the Boston merits attention because of its direct relevance to the hesitation waltz, popular at the turn of the century. The Boston was a kind of limping *chassé;* the hesitation waltz called for a distinct pause on counts two and three, lending a certain languor to the endless turning motion.

Although superseded during the twentieth century by many newer dances, the waltz has continued to be taught in ballroom dancing schools and is still performed, especially by older couples, at formal occasions. It also survives in certain rural regions and among ethnic minorities who adopted it during its heyday. Several stylistic variants form part of the repertory of competitive ballroom dancers, including Viennese Waltz and American Waltz.

[*See also* Social Dance, *article on* Nineteenth-Century Social Dance.]

BIBLIOGRAPHY

Carner, Mosco. *The Waltz.* New York, 1948.

Cellarius, Henri. *The Drawing-Room Dances.* London, 1847.

Dodworth, Allen. *Dancing and Its Relations to Education and Social Life.* New York, 1885.

Nettl, Paul. *The Story of Dance Music.* New York, 1947.

Richardson, Philip J. S. *The Social Dances of the Nineteenth Century in England.* London, 1960.

Wechsberg, Joseph. *The Waltz Emperors: The Life and Times and Music of the Strauss Family.* London, 1973.

Wilson, Thomas. *A Description of the Correct Method of Waltzing.* London, 1816.

DESMOND F. STROBEL

WARING, JAMES (born 1 November 1922 in Alameda, California, died 2 December 1975 in New York), American dancer, choreographer, teacher, and designer. Waring's early dance training was in San Francisco, first with Raoul Pausé, who taught both ballet and plastique dance, and later with Welland Lathrop, the Christensen brothers, and Gertrude Shurr (for Graham technique). His first choreography was the 1946 *Luther Burbank in Santa Rosa,* to music by Gioacchino Rossini, at the Halprin-Lathrop Studio Theater in San Francisco.

In the late 1940s Waring moved to New York, where he studied at the School of American Ballet and, later, with Anatole Vilzak and Antony Tudor. His first full-scale ballet, *The Wanderers,* with music by Marga Richter, was presented in New York by the Choreographers' Workshop at the Ninety-second Street YM–YWHA, on 23 March 1952; the cast included Aileen Passloff and Marian Sarach. Like many of Waring's later ballets, this one was about performers: Passloff danced the role of a young woman who runs away from a traveling circus.

The following winter Waring and several other young choreographers, including Alec Rubin and David Vaughan, formed Dance Associates, a cooperative that presented works by themselves and others (among them Shirley Broughton and, later, Paul Taylor). For the first concert, at the Ninety-second Street Y in January 1953, Waring made *The Prisoners,* a ballet concerning "three young people introduced abruptly into an asylum," with music by Rudy Crosswell. Waring continued to present work in Dance Associates concerts, and when it ceased to operate in 1957, he gave concerts with his own company until 1969.

Many of his early dances had similarly fantastic or macabre subject matter, such as *Pastorale* (1953) to music by Hy Gubernick, and *Freaks* (1954) to music by MacRae Cook, but some were more purely romantic, such as the duet *Lamento,* (1953) suggested by a poem of Théophile Gautier to music of Croswell, or abstract, such as *Intrada* (1957) to music by Gubernick, and *Phrases* (1957) to music by Erik Satie. *Burlesca* (1953) to music by Claude Debussy was again about a company of players, but without narrative content.

Dances before the Wall (1958), Waring's first evening-long contemporary dance work, decisively established him as a leading figure in the New York avant-garde. He had always sought out young composers and painters. In 1956 he worked for the first time with the composer John Herbert McDowell, on *Adagietto: Flakes of Chance,* a solo for Toby Armour; in 1959 he first worked with the composer Richard Maxfield, on *Lunamble,* a solo for himself. Waring was to collaborate frequently with both composers. He also continued to work with existing music, especially that of Wolfgang Amadeus Mozart. In 1955, the painter Jasper Johns designed costumes for Waring's *Little Kootch Piece,* to music by Olivier Messiaen, several years before Johns first designed for Merce Cunningham. *Peripateia* (1960) with music by Maxfield had decor by George Brecht. *At the Hallelujah Gardens* (1963), to music by Maxfield, was a seventy-five-minute piece with "scenery, objects, and events" by Al Hansen and costumes and other props by Brecht, Red Grooms, Robert Indiana, Larry Poons, Robert Watts, and Robert Whitman. In the early 1960s, works such as these influenced the painters involved, and others, to create their own happenings and performance pieces.

Poet's Vaudeville (1963) to music by McDowell was another large-scale piece, with text by the poet Diane

DiPrima. Waring's company for these and other pieces at this period included David Gordon, Valda Setterfield, Yvonne Rainer, Deborah Hay, Arlene Rothlein, and Lucinda Childs. His classes in technique (an idiosyncratic yet rigorous approach to classic ballet) and in composition had a tremendous influence on those who were to be the founders of the Judson Dance Theater and subsequently the leaders of the postmodern movement in dance. (Waring gave concerts of his own at the Judson Church in New York City but was never formally part of the Judson group; in both 1978 and 1990 retrospectives of his work were presented at the Judson Church.)

In the last years of his life Waring worked with various companies, among them the Manhattan Festival Ballet, for which he made *Phantom of the Opera* (1966) to music by McDowell, *Northern Lights* (1967) to music by Arnold Schoenberg, and *Arena* (1967) to music of Igor Stravinsky. In 1969, *Purple Moment* was made to a combination of popular songs and selections from J. S. Bach and *Spookride* to music by Chopin and Ezra Sims, both for the New England Dance Theater; in 1970 they were revived, respectively, by the Netherlands Dance Theater and by the Pennsylvania Ballet. In 1971, for the Netherlands Dance Theater, Waring also made *Variations on a Landscape,* to music by Schoenberg. For New England Dinosaur, he choreographed *Novelty Sweets* (1971) to music by Scott Joplin, *A New Kind of Love* (1974) to popular music, and in 1975 a new version of *Arena.* Also in 1975 he made *Sinfonia Semplice,* to Mozart, for the Eglevsky Ballet Company.

Waring had the gift of being able to show dancers of relatively little technical accomplishment to the best advantage; for several years he taught at the arts summer school at Indian Hill (Stockbridge, Massachusetts), where he produced exquisite, witty dances for the teenage students. He was also able to perceive and utilize a professional dancer's unique qualities of physique and personality, especially in solos. As early as 1954, his *Three Pieces for Solo Clarinet* (to music of Stravinsky), for Paul Taylor, defined that dancer's individual style. Later Waring made equally personal solos for many other dancers, among them Vincent Warren, Aileen Passloff, Toby Armour, Richard Colton, Gretchen MacLane, Deborah Lee, Ze'eva Cohen, Rachel Browne, Raymond Johnson, and Elizabeth Walton.

In addition to being a dancer, choreographer, and teacher, Waring was also an accomplished collagist, and much of his choreography had the character of that medium, bringing together disparate elements. This and his use of popular music and movement led to the characterization of his work as "neo-Dada" and even as "camp," but whether in the Duncanism of *Mazurkas for Pavlova* (1967) to music by Chopin or in the pastiche of popular styles in such works as *Musical Moments* (1965) to music

WARING. In a straw hat and bow tie, Waring appeared with Deborah Lee in his *Musical Moments* (1965), a play on popular dance styles of the past. (Photograph from the Dance Collection, New York Public Library for the Performing Arts.)

by various composers or *At the Café Fleurette* (1968) to music by Victor Herbert, Waring's re-creations of past styles were free of condescension. He never had the lack of faith in the material that would justify the use of such epithets. Although it was only in his later works that he sometimes choreographed in a balletic idiom, classic ballet was always the technical base for his style; to this he added other elements, drawn from modern dance, musical comedy, vaudeville, social dance, natural movement—whatever suited his immediate purpose.

A designer and maker of costumes for his own and others' pieces, Waring was also a director and the author of plays, poems, criticism, and essays; on occasion, he was even a composer of music. Although he was a consummate craftsman and a thorough professional, his work never received the wider recognition it deserved. Yet it can safely be said that the life of anyone who knew him—as a choreographer, teacher, or friend—was deeply affected, and even changed, by the experience.

BIBLIOGRAPHY

McDonagh, Don. *The Rise and Fall and Rise of Modern Dance.* New York, 1971.

McDonagh, Don, ed. *The Complete Guide to Modern Dance.* New York, 1976.
Vaughan, David. "Remembering James Waring." *Ballet Review* 5.4 (1975–1976): 102–107.
Waring, James. "Five Essays on Dancing." *Ballet Review* 2.1 (1967): 65–77.
Waring, James. "My Work." *Ballet Review* 5.4 (1975–1976): 108–113.

DAVID VAUGHAN

WARREN, VINCENT (Vincent de Paul Warren; born 31 August 1938 in Jacksonville, Florida), Canadian-American dancer and teacher. Having begun dance training at age twelve with a local teacher in his hometown, Warren subsequently studied with a variety of internationally known teachers, including Peter Appel, Tatiana Grantzeva, Ludmilla Chiriaeff, Merce Cunningham, and Anatole Oboukhoff. Early in his career, he danced with the Metropolitan Opera Ballet (1957–1959), the Santa Fe Opera, and the performing groups of contemporary choreographers James Waring and Aileen Passloff. In 1961, Warren joined Les Grands Ballets Canadiens in Montreal, where, except for a leave of absence in 1969–1971, he remained until his retirement from the stage in 1979.

WARREN. John Butler's *Carmina Catulli,* staged for Les Grands Ballets Canadiens in 1968, provided Warren with one of his most effective roles. His heroic physique and expressive performing style made him well suited for Butler's dramatic choreography. (Photograph © 1968 by Jack Mitchell; used by permission.)

Warren, who was noted for his fine looks, noble bearing, and dramatic gifts, performed roles in most of the wide-ranging repertory of Les Grands Ballets Canadiens, including male leads in such classical works as *Giselle, Swan Lake,* and *The Nutcracker* as well as roles in works by George Balanchine, John Butler, and other contemporary choreographers. Notably, Warren created many roles for the artistic directors and resident choreographers of the company: Ludmilla Chiriaeff, Fernand Nault, and Brian Macdonald, whose *Adieu Robert Schumann* (1978) was made for Warren's farewell performances. Warren appeared in televised performances of this and numerous other works and in the award-winning film *Pas de Deux* by Canadian animator Norman MacLaren.

During his leave of absence from Les Grands Ballets Canadiens, Warren danced with the Théâtre Français de la Danse in Paris (1969–1970) and with the Cologne Opera Ballet (1970–1971). As a guest artist, he also appeared with the Pennsylvania Ballet, the National Ballet of Guatemala, and the avant-garde Canadian company Groupe de la Place Royale.

A much-loved and respected figure in Canadian dance, Warren was awarded the Queen's Jubilee Medal in 1977. After he ceased performing, he served as chairman of the Dance in Canada Association in 1981–1982. He has since taught ballet and dance history at various institutions in Montreal, principally for the École Supérieure de Danse du Québec, where today he serves as curator of the dance library.

BIBLIOGRAPHY

Stoop, Norma McLain. "Spotlight on Vincent Warren." *Dance Magazine* (August 1973): 64–69.
Tembeck, Iro Valaskakis. *Dancing in Montreal: Seeds of a Choreographic History.* Studies in Dance History, vol. 5.2. Madison, Wis., 1994.
Warren, Vincent. "Archives of the Dance: La Bibliothèque de la Danse et l'École Supérieure de Danse du Québec, Montréal." *Dance Research* 13 (Winter 1995): 89–94.
Windreich, Leland. "Collector and Archivist Vincent Warren." *Dance International* 22.4 (1994–1995): 26.
Wyman, Max. *Dance Canada: An Illustrated History.* Vancouver, 1989.

MICHAEL CRABB

WARSAW BALLET. In 1818 Ludwik Osiński, director of the National Theater in Warsaw, founded a ballet company under the directorship of the French choreographer Louis Thierry. The company moved into Warsaw's new

Teatr Wielki (Great Theater) in 1833. Since then it has been the cradle and center of ballet in Poland. Officially named the Balet Teatru Wielkiego w Warzawie, it is known in English as the Warsaw Ballet or as the Wielki Theater Ballet.

During the Romantic period the company enjoyed special glory under the directorships of Maurice Pion (1826–1843), Filippo Taglioni (1843–1853), and Roman Turczynowicz (1853–1866). Although these choreographers closely followed the French style, they never neglected male dancing in favor of the cult of the ballerina. They also promoted character dancing and emphasized expression and action in their ballets. Most of their works were produced on a lavish scale, with a large, well-trained corps de ballet, sumptuous costumes and scenery, and ingenious stage machinery. The repertory included restagings of such famous Romantic ballets as *La Sylphide, Giselle, Esmeralda, Faust,* and *Le Corsaire,* as well as original works. [*See the entries on Pion and Turczynowicz.*]

A series of Italian ballet masters led the company beginning in 1869: Virgilio Calori (1869–1874), Pasquale Borri (1875–1878), José Mendes (1878–1888), Raffaele Grassi (1892–1902), and Enrico Cecchetti (1902–1905). The general decadence of western European ballet, compounded by the company's own long-standing conflict between the French and Italian traditions and its deepening financial difficulties, caused a gradual decline in its artistic standards despite the success of such works as *Jotta, Coppélia, Brahma,* and *Swan Lake.*

In the early twentieth century, the rising popularity of operetta, the mass exodus of dancers to the touring companies of Serge Diaghilev and Anna Pavlova, and the onset of World War I in 1914 dealt heavy blows to the company. Although it survived this severe crisis (from 1905 to 1918), the only high points of the period were its performances of Michel Fokine's *Eunice, Chopiniana,* and *Schéhérazade.*

From the early days of the company, the Russian rulers of Poland had stringently repressed ballets that expressed a sense of national identity. The few existing works of this nature—among them *Kraków Wedding, Pan Twardowski,* and *The Fire Feast*—were extremely popular, as were stage versions of Polish national dances executed within foreign ballets and in operas such as Stanisław Moniuszko's *Halka.* This situation changed after Poland regained its independence in 1918, and the company began to recover its brilliance under the leadership of Piotr Zajlich (1917–1934). Nationally inspired ballets, including a completely new version of *Pan Twardowski* and *The Highlanders,* now had priority in the repertory, which also included the classics and restaging of Diaghilev's ballets.

During World War II, the Wielki Theater was destroyed, and most of the company was dispersed. After 1945 Zajlich reassembled a small company, which worked in temporary quarters, gradually rebuilding its staff and repertory. Among the ballets produced at this time were *Romeo and Juliet* and *Le Sacre du Printemps.*

In 1965 the company returned to a restored Wielki Theater, having once more achieved a high artistic level. Its present repertory includes the classics (among them Frederick Ashton's production of *La Fille Mal Gardée*), ballets based on Polish themes (*Pan Twardowski, Kraków Wedding, Stanisław and Anna Oświęcim,* and *The Highlanders*), and contemporary works, including ballets by Serge Lifar, Maurice Béjart, Brigit Cullberg, John Neumeier, and Hans van Manen.

In 1985 the company was honored by the organization of the two-hundredth jubilee of the Polish ballet. Since then political and economic difficulties have limited its activities, and the Warsaw Ballet is fighting to survive.

[*See also* Poland, *article on* Theatrical Dance.]

BIBLIOGRAPHY

Chynowski, Paweł. "The Anniversary of Polish Ballet." *Ballet International* 8 (May 1985): 18–21.

Chynowski, Paweł, and Janina Pudełek. *Almanach baletu warszawskiego, 1785–1985 / Le ballet de Varsovie, 1785–1985.* Warsaw, 1987.

Drabecka, Maria. *Choreografia baletów warszawskich za Sasów.* Kraków, 1988.

Jasinski, Roman. "Some Recollections of *Swan Lake* in Warsaw." *Dance Chronicle* 14.1 (1991): 102–107.

Karsavina, Tamara. *Theatre Street.* Rev. and enl. ed. London, 1948.

Kinel, Lola. "Ludomir Rozycki and His *Pan Twardowski:* The First Polish Ballet Produced at the Warsaw Opera." *Musical Standard* 17 (1921): 209–210.

Mamontowicz-Łójek, Bożena. *Terpsychora i lekkie muzy.* Kraków, 1972.

Neuer, Adam, ed. *Polish Opera and Ballet of the Twentieth Century: Operas, Ballets, Pantomimes, Miscellaneous Works.* Translated by Jerzy Zawadzki. Kraków, 1986.

Pudełek, Janina. *Warszawski balet romantyczny, 1802–1866.* Warsaw, 1968.

Pudełek, Janina. *Warszawski balet w latach 1867–1915.* Warsaw, 1981.

Pudełek, Janina. *Z historii baletu.* Warsaw, 1981.

Pudełek, Janina. *Two Hundred Years of Polish Ballet, 1785–1985.* Warsaw, 1985.

Pudełek, Janina, and Jacek Lumiński. "Poland: Anniversary Celebrations of Polish Ballet." *Ballett International* 9 (May 1986): 38–41.

Pudełek, Janina. "The Warsaw Ballet under the Directorships of Maurice Pion and Filippo Taglioni, 1832–1853." *Dance Chronicle* 11.2 (1988): 219–273.

Pudełek, Janina. "*Swan Lake* in Warsaw, 1900." *Dance Chronicle* 13 (Winter 1990–1991): 359–367.

Pudełek, Janina. "Crisis of Polish Dance." *Ballett International* 14 (July–August 1991): 56.

Pudełek, Janina. "Fokine in Warsaw, 1908–1914." *Dance Chronicle* 15.1 (1992): 59–71.

Pudełek, Janina, with Joanna Sibilska. "The Polish Dancers Visit St. Petersbourg, 1851: A Detective Story." *Dance Chronicle* 19.2 (1996): 171–189.

Rambert, Marie. *Quicksilver: The Autobiography of Marie Rambert.* London, 1972.

JANINA PUDEŁEK

WASHINGTON BALLET. An outstanding school has always been at the heart of the Washington Ballet. The current school was founded in 1944 by Mary Day and Lisa (Elizabeth) Gardiner, both District of Columbia natives. Day still directs both school and company.

Gardiner, a former member of the Anna Pavlova Company and a concert artist in her own right, opened her first school in 1922 and incorporated a small company called the Washington Ballet in 1938. Day had studied with Gardiner and was a member of the company. World War II put a halt to its performing until 1946. The title of Washington Ballet was resumed in 1956. A year later Gardiner became artistic adviser; she died in 1958.

In the meantime, Frederic Franklin had joined Day as co–artistic director, and for a brief time the company bore the aesthetic imprint of the Ballet Russe de Monte Carlo, with which Franklin had long been associated. By 1961, Franklin had left to form his own company, the National Ballet, also in Washington, D.C. Day meanwhile put the Washington Ballet on hold and turned her attention to developing a resident school of ballet and academic studies. It quickly earned an outstanding reputation, but a lack of funds forced its closure in 1977. The demise in 1974 of the National Ballet led Day to reestablish her Washington Ballet. Currently a twenty-four-member ensemble, the Washington Ballet is known for its fine classical style. In addition to grooming dancers, it is consistent in its encouragement of emerging choreographers.

In 1976, while the company was deeply occupied in rebuilding its identity, Day engaged a young Sinhalese choreographer named Choo San Goh. The eleven years until his untimely death in 1987 were vital to the growth of the Washington Ballet. His presence was also beginning to be felt throughout the entire ballet world. Goh's choreographic style was both passionate and challenging. Although his ballets were in essence abstract, a strongly subjective current coursed through them. In addition, he enjoyed working with large groups of dancers and magnetizing them into vibrant responsiveness. Among his most substantial works are *Birds of Paradise, In the Glow of the Night,* and *Double Contrasts.*

Works from Goh's entire repertory are constantly being revived by the Washington Ballet. It also maintains a more modest selection of Balanchine ballets, such as *Allegro Brillante, Concerto Barocco, The Four Temperaments, Serenade,* and *Square Dance.* It is to guest choreographers, however, that the company more consistently turns. Its choices tend to be relatively conservative and have included Christian Holder, Judith Jamison, Alonso King, Monica Levy, Graham Lustig, Rick McCullough, and Martine van Hamel. The choreographic aspirations of company dancers like Lynn Cote and John Goding are also fostered.

In 1991, Mary Day began to groom her former student Kevin McKenzie to be the next artistic director of the

WASHINGTON BALLET. Choo San Goh's *Momentum,* set to Sergei Prokofiev's Piano Concerto no. 1 in D-flat, entered the company's repertory in 1983. Costumes were designed by Carol Vollet Garner. (Photograph 1990 by Richard N. Greenhouse; used by permission of the Washington Ballet.)

Washington Ballet, but American Ballet Theatre selected him for this position in 1992. Since then Day and general director Elvi Moore have worked in tandem to assure a serene future for the company.

[*See also the entry on Day.*]

BIBLIOGRAPHY

Elliot, Laura. "Dancing with Miss Day." *Washingtonian* (March 1988).

Fiorillo, Kathy. "The Woman Who Brought Ballet to Washington." *Washington Times* (3 October 1984).

Hering, Doris. "Washington Ballet's Mary Day." *Dance Magazine* (March 1992): 58–59.

Marshall, Leslie. "Mother Courage." *Washington Post* (20 November 1983).

Obituary: Choo San Goh. *New York Times* (30 November 1987).

Obituary: Lisa Gardiner. *Washington Star* (5 November 1958).

DORIS HERING

WATER STUDY. Choreography: Doris Humphrey. First performance: 28 October 1928, Civic Repertory Theater, New York City. Dancers: sixteen members of Doris Humphrey's Concert Group.

A product of Doris Humphrey's early explorations into the nonballetic possibilities of movement, *Water Study* appeared on the first program that the Humphrey-Weidman company performed independently. Although Humphrey shared Ruth St. Denis's and Isadora Duncan's interest in the flow of natural phenomena as a source for movement, her earliest experiments on nature themes were strikingly different from either the Art Nouveau–like aestheticism of St. Denis or the wholesome, bucolic youths suggested by Duncan.

In *Water Study* the movement of the individual dancer, the collective phrasing of the group, and the progression of the dance over space and time are all crafted to create water imagery on simultaneous levels of perception. The dancer's body unfolds and folds, in primal pulsations that grow from risings and sinkings to stretches, jumps, and collapsing falls. Each new movement travels through the members of the group on rhythmic upsurges that are produced and sustained by the dancers' breath—there is no musical or other accompaniment. The overall dance is a progression from slow, heavy stirrings on the floor to running leaps and falls, circling eddies, and subsidence to the floor again.

Although all the movement is "natural," *Water Study* takes great skill to perform. The dancers must have an acute sensitivity to one another and an ability to produce the dynamic cycle within themselves while also remaining responsive to the larger demands of the group.

BIBLIOGRAPHY

Davis, Martha, and Claire Schmais. "An Analysis of the Style and Composition of 'Water Study.'" *CORD Dance Research Journal* 1 (1968): 105–113.

Humphrey, Doris. *Doris Humphrey, an Artist First: An Autobiography.* Edited by Selma Jeanne Cohen. Middletown, Conn., 1977.

Kagan, Elizabeth. "Towards the Analysis of a Score: A Comparative Study of 'Three Epitaphs' by Paul Taylor and 'Water Study' by Doris Humphrey." *CORD Dance Research Annual* 9 (1978): 75–92.

Marion, Sheila. "Studying *Water Study.*" *Dance Research Journal* 24 (Spring 1992): 1–11.

Siegel, Marcia B. *The Shapes of Change: Images of American Dance.* New York, 1979.

Siegel, Marcia B. *Days on Earth: The Dance of Doris Humphrey.* New Haven, 1987.

MARCIA B. SIEGEL

WAYANG. [*This entry is limited to discussion of Balinese shadow-puppet theater and related forms of Balinese dance drama. For similar traditions in other parts of Indonesia, see* Indonesia, *article on* Javanese Dance Traditions. *For related discussion, see* Asian Dance Traditions, *article on* The Influence of Puppetry.]

In any discussion of Balinese dance and dance theater, attention must be given to the shadow-puppet theater, *wayang,* which is a major influence on most Balinese performance genres. *Wayang* is looked upon by performers as a source and guide with respect to thematic content, dramatic plot construction, vocal and movement characterization, poetic and classical language, and visual aspects such as costume and facial expression.

Balinese *wayang* is performed by a solo puppeteer, or *dalang,* who animates in movement and voice a large cast of characters, accompanied by a quartet of ten-keyed bronze metallophones *(gendér).* The puppets *(ringgit)* are elaborately cut flat figures of buffalo- or cow-skin parchment, painted in bright colors and perforated in delicate patterns through which the light from a coconut-oil lamp

WAYANG. Children watch a daytime *wayang kulit* performance sometime in the 1920s or 1930s. The daytime *wayang,* given without lamp or screen, is said to be held for an invisible audience of the gods. (Photograph by Walter Spies / Beryl de Zoete; reprinted from Hitchcock and Norris, 1995, fig. 75.)

passes. They are silhouetted against an illuminated screen and articulated at the shoulders and elbows, punctuating their dialogue with stylized gesticulation. Some puppets have movable jaws, lips, or legs, often used for comic effect. They are manipulated by three rods fashioned from water-buffalo horn, wood, or bamboo.

Wayang performances generally last about three hours, beginning around eleven o'clock at night, though in the past performances could last until dawn. The stage is a raised bamboo platform erected for the event in the outer courtyard of a temple or palace, or on the roadside by the home of a family sponsoring the event. When the *dalang* arrives, he sits down crosslegged behind the coconut-oil lamp, which is hung just beside the white screen, and begins his preparations by reciting *mantra* prayers. Meanwhile, the musicians play introductory pieces called *gending pategak.*

WAYANG. Master puppeteer I Wayan Wija in a *wayang kulit* performance in New York City in 1992. This behind-the-scenes photograph shows how the puppeteer positions himself behind the traditional flaming lamp to keep his own shadow from falling on the screen. (Photograph © by Jack Vartoogian; used by permission.)

When the *dalang* is ready to begin the *wayang,* he signals the musicians by hitting the wooden *kropak* box in which the puppets are stored. The *kropak,* or *gedog,* lies within reach of his right foot and is hit with a wooden mallet held between the *dalang*'s two larger toes to signal sudden dramatic impulses and conduct the *gamelan* music. The opening music *(pemungkah)* is played as the Kayon puppet is waved, fluttered, twirled, and inched along the screen. The word *kayon* is derived from *kayu,* ("wood") and refers to the Tree of Life. Gunungan, another name for the same puppet, derives from *gunung* ("mountain") and refers to the mountain of the gods, Meru or Mahameru. As well as preceding the *wayang* story in a stylized dance, the Kayon serves throughout to suggest various forces of nature, unrest, or transition from a cosmic perspective.

After the Kayon is removed, the *dalang* takes his puppets one by one from the *kropak* box and assembles them side by side at either end of the screen, according to each character's allegiance in the ensuing story. Once all the Pandawa clan or Prince Rāma's followers (depending on whether the episode being enacted is from the *Mahābhārata* or *Rāmāyaṇa*) are assembled on the right, and the Kurawa clan or the demon-king Rawana and his followers) are on the left, they are all removed and the story begins.

The plays *(lampahan)* are most often taken from the Indian *Mahābhārata* epic, known in Bali as *Astadasa parwa* (The Eighteen Books). In fact, Old Javanese poems, based on episodes in the *Mahābhārata,* are the direct literary source. The most popular is *Bharata yuddha* (The Great War), dealing with the rival houses of Pandawa and Kurawa. Other *Mahābhārata*-derived stores are *Bimaswanga* and *Arjuna wiwaha.*

The other major source of *wayang* literature is the Indian *Rāmāyaṇa* epic, which requires a different set of puppets and an expanded gamelan ensemble, *wayang batel,* to portray the battles between Rawana and Rāma's allies, particularly Anoman and his army of monkeys. There are also indigenous *wayang* stories, such as *Cupak* and *Calonarang,* dealing with witchcraft. These stories utilize the *parwa* puppets, merely adding a few main characters.

A purely ritual context may require *wayang lemah,* generally performed in the afternoon using the same puppets but no screen. This brief and less dramatic genre is performed in connection with such ceremonies as tooth-filing, cremation, consecration of a building, temple anniversaries, or the blessing of a child on one of its first three birthdays.

The skills of a *dalang* are extensive, and long training and experience are necessary before one is considered adept. A mystical understanding of *wayang* is crucial, and the teachings of the *Dharma pawayangan* text are generally studied in depth for this purpose. Before embarking on a performance career, a *dalang* (like other performers) goes through a *mawinten* ceremony, during which a Pedanda priest inscribes magic syllables on his tongue with the stem of a *cempaka* flower dipped in honey. The *taksu,* or psychic energy, of a *dalang* is looked for and valued by the Balinese audience.

Facility with Kawi (the old Javanese literary language) must include the ability to construct plots and subplots, *(carangan)* utilizing excerpts of poetry *(cecantungan)* to illuminate a mood or action. A *dalang* must be able to translate spontaneously back and forth between classical Kawi, High Balinese, and vernacular Balinese, since characters address each other in these varieties according to rank. The *dalang* should also be able to quote freely from Middle Javanese (Malat) poetry.

Fluency in the musical repertory enables the *dalang* to fit his singing *(tandak)* to the pentatonic tuning and melodic flow of the four *gendér;* his *tandak* phrasing has its own melodic contours which overlap the instrumental melody without joining it, pitch by pitch. A crucial aspect of the *dalang*'s art is that of movement and vocal characterization *(masolah).* In the physical and spiritual relationship initiated when the *dalang* picks up a puppet, he must "enter the soul" of the puppet and bring it to life, while the puppet in turn speaks through the *dalang* as if he were its spiritual medium. A *dalang* must have a grasp of the techniques of vocal production that will enable him to embody the particular characters at hand. Each puppet's distinct movement and gestures are coordinated with stylized voice, rhythm, and dramatic qualities.

The most important criterion of a *dalang*'s skill at characterization is his relationship with the characters Tualen, Wredah, Sangut, and Delem. These four Panakawan, comic servants to the principal rival clans, are the most popular characters in the *wayang.* With their flexible jaws, these puppets have the role of translating other's Kawi language into vernacular Balinese for the audience and interpreting the story's philosophical and practical content. Although they can provide the crudest humor and silliest slapstick, the Panakawan are considered to be of divine origin, most often associated with Balinese ancestors; the other characters are all of Indian origin.

There are divergent opinions concerning the origins of *wayang.* A Central Javanese stone inscription issued by King Balitung and dated 907 CE mentions *mawayang,* the performing of *wayang,* although this does not necessarily refer to shadow-puppet theater. A Javanese charter issued by Mahārājā Sri Lokapala in 840 CE refers to *aringgit* performers. In the eleventh-century Old Javanese poem *Arjuna wiwaha, ringgit* is the term for leather shadow-puppets, as it is today. The origin of Indonesian *wayang* is often traced to India, where shadow theater is believed by

WAYANG. Rāma and Sītā are portrayed as extremely refined characters in *wayang wong* dramas. Both wear elaborate gilt headdresses, with winglike side pieces and bird decorations at back. (Photograph by Walter Spies / Beryl de Zoete; reprinted from Hitchcock and Norris, 1995, fig. 190.)

some to have existed at least as early as the first century BCE; others argue for independent invention, theorizing that ancient indigenous initiation or ancestral rites gave rise to Indonesian *wayang.* In any case, with the advent of Indian influence in the area, Hindu gods and legends were gradually superimposed on older Malay-Polynesian myths. Even if, as some scholars suggest, *wayang* arrived in Bali via East Java as late as the fifteenth century, it is now a distinctly Balinese genre, both ritually and dramatically.

Wayang shadow-puppet theater has influenced dance-drama characterization in general, and most profoundly in *wayang wong,* which owes its themes entirely to the *Rāmāyaṇa. Wayang,* literally meaning "shadow," here refers to the dramatic presentation of stories, while *wong* means "human," referring to the actors.

Wayang wong is performed in a small number of villages, the best-known groups being in Mas, Batuan, Tejakula, and Tunjuk. It is most commonly presented in connection with specific *odalan* temple festivals and during the Galungan and Kuningan holiday season, when the ancestors descend for a time to inhabit shrines. Particularly sacred are the numerous *wanara,* including the monkey army led by Anoman. *Wanara* are considered to be animals of divine origin; some are combinations of different creatures and are often linked with the sacred *barong.*

The monkey king Subali and his brother Sugriwa are strong character types, whereas Anoman (Hanumān) is of a more refined type. Other animals are lion, birds, deer, elephant, dog, pig, and snake. Jatayu, the bird hero, and the deer, which is actually the man Marica in disguise, are also important in the drama.

The principal male characters with noble, refined qualities include Rāma and his brother Laksmana, as well as Wibisana, brother of the demon-king Rawana. Refined female characters are Rāma's wife Sītā, her attendant Condong, Dewi Tara, wife of Sugriwa, and Çurpanakha, sister of Rawana. The strong *(keras)* male types are the *raksasa* king Rawana, his accomplice Marica, and Kumbakarna. Although masks for all *wayang wong* characters exist, in performance, masks are generally restricted to the animals, and the four Panakawan and are considered religious heirlooms. The music for *wayang wong* is performed by the *wayang batel* ensemble, the same collection of *gendér* and assorted percussion used for *wayang Rāmāyaṇa.*

Parwa is a dance theater genre very similar to *wayang wong* but based on the *Mahābhārata* epic. In both genres, the actor-dancers use sung Kawi poetry for entrances, exits, and occasional proverbial quotations and stylized speech in dialogue. The poetry and text are of particular prominence, distinguishing these from other dance theater forms. In most versions of *wayang wong* and *parwa,* the dancers' movements are not as closely synchronized with the gamelan music as in other forms.

[*See also* Indonesia, *articles on Balinese dance traditions.*]

BIBLIOGRAPHY

Becker, A. L. "Text-Building, Epistemology, and Aesthetics in Javanese Shadow Theater." In *The Imagination of Reality: Essays in Southeast Asian Coherence Systems,* edited by Aram A. Yengoyan and A. L. Becker. Norwood, N.J., 1979.

Hitchcock, Michael, and Lucy Norris. *Bali, the Imaginary Museum: The Photographs of Walter Spies and Beryl de Zoete.* New York, 1995.

Hobart, Angela. *Dancing Shadows of Bali.* London, 1987.

Hooykaas, Christiaan. *Kama and Kala: Materials for the Study of Shadow Theatre in Bali.* Amsterdam, 1973.

Keeler, Ward. *Javanese Shadow Plays, Javanese Selves.* Princeton, 1987.

Keeler, Ward. "Release from Kala's grip: ritual uses of shadow plays in Java and Bali." *Indonesia* 54 (October 1992): 1–25.

McPhee, Colin. *Music in Bali.* New Haven, 1966.

Lysloff, René T. A. "A Wrinkle in Time: The Shadow Puppet Theater of Banyumas (West Central Java)." *Asian Theater Journal* 1 (Spring 1993): 49–80.

McPhee, Colin. "The Balinese Wayang Kulit and Its Music." In *Traditional Balinese Culture,* edited by Jane Belo. New York, 1970.

Pucci, Idanna. *Bhima Swarga: The Balinese Journey of the Soul.* Boston, 1992.

Robson, S. O., ed. and trans. *Wañbañ Wideya: A Javanese Pañji Romance.* The Hague, 1971.

Robson, S. O. "The Kawi Classics in Bali." *Bijdragen tot de Taal-, Land- en Volkenkunde* 128 (1972).

Sugriwa, I Gusti Bagus. *Ilmu Pedalangan/Pewayangan.* Denpasar, 1963.

Sumandhi, I Nyoman. "Gending Iringan Wayang Kulit Bali." In *Pakem wayang parwa Bali.* Denpasar, 1978.

Yayasan Pewayangan Daerah Bali. *Pakem wayang parwa Bali.* Denpasar, 1978.

Zoetmulder, P. J. *Kalangwan: A Survey of Old Javanese Literature.* The Hague, 1974.

Zurbuchen, Mary S. *The Language of Balinese Shadow Theater.* Princeton, 1987.

Zurbuchen, Mary S. "Internal Conversion in Balinese Poetry." In *Writing on the Tongue,* edited by A. L. Becker. Ann Arbor, Mich., 1989.

EDWARD HERBST

WAYBURN, NED (Edward Claudius Weyburn; born 30 March 1874 in Pittsburgh, Pennsylvania, died 2 September 1942 in New York City), American dance director of

WAYBURN. Processionals were a Wayburn trademark. In various editions of the *Ziegfeld Follies* and *Midnight Frolics,* he displayed remarkable ingenuity in creating scenes that culminated in a parade of beautiful girls in beautiful costumes. These young lovelies appeared in "Bring on the Girls" in the *Ziegfeld Follies of 1922.* (Photograph reprinted from Wayburn, 1925, p. 186.)

musical shows and vaudeville acts. One of the most prolific dance directors of the twentieth century, Wayburn staged more than three hundred musical shows and two hundred vaudeville acts. His New York studios trained numerous performers by implementing a system he devised for teaching his specialties: musical comedy dance, tap and step dancing, acrobatic work, "modern Americanized ballet," eccentric toe routines, and exhibition ballroom displays.

As a young man in Chicago, Wayburn worked as a draftsman for the 1893 World's Columbian Exhibition and as an accompanist and assistant instructor at the Hart Conway School of Acting. It was at this time that he came into contact with the theories of François Delsarte and the Per Henrik Ling gymnastic exercises, both of which he incorporated into his dance training methods.

In 1896 Wayburn became a vaudeville pianist and soon was known for his syncopation of classical music. Three years later he choreographed his first chorus numbers for *By the Sad Sea Waves* (opened 28 February 1899 at the Herald Square). The cast included Kitty Hays, who, as Gertrude Hoffman, worked with him on several productions. Between 1901 and 1913 Wayburn created vaudeville acts for Oscar and William Hammerstein as well as for the theatrical syndicate of Klaw and Erlanger. He staged spectacles in New York, Chicago, and London and directed shows for Lew Fields and the Shubert Brothers. Wayburn also founded the Headline Vaudeville Production Company.

Wayburn's celebrated association with Florenz Ziegfeld and Joseph Urban began when Wayburn staged the *Ziegfeld Follies of 1916*. He contributed to six editions of the *Follies* (1916–1919, 1922, 1923), five seasons of the *Midnight Frolics* (1915–1919), and three of Ziegfeld's book musicals. The alluring step sequence known as the "Ziegfeld walk" was a Wayburn invention.

Adept at codifying many types of information, Wayburn established a hierarchical system for training chorus members that made his prodigious output possible. He divided the chorus girls into five categories based on height and at his studios had each group trained in a specific and different technique. These classes, along with his book—with tips on everything from diet and makeup to sample contracts—supported his claim that he regarded "the training of chorus girls strictly as a science." Performers who completed some portion of their training with Wayburn included Adele and Fred Astaire, Earl Carroll, Marion Davies, the Dolly Sisters, Mary Eaton, Gilda Gray, Gertrude Lawrence, Evelyn Law, Marilyn Miller, and Ann Pennington.

After 1918 Wayburn experimented with the prolog, a live performance designed to introduce a film. His efforts in this field and the fact that most of his own choreography involved geometrical patterns best seen from overhead contributed to his influence on early movie musicals.

WAYBURN. Fanny Brice was one of the stars of the *Ziegfeld Follies of 1916*, singing and clowning in two of her vaudeville numbers, "The Hat" and "The Dying Swan," in which she satirized Anna Pavlova's famous solo. Brice also appeared in "The Blushing Ballet," a scene staged by Wayburn that was a send-up of Vaslav Nijinsky's most famous roles. Brice sang Gene Buck's comic song "Nijinsky" and wore this sylphide-like costume. Nijinsky had made his American debut with Diaghilev's Ballets Russes at the Metropolitan Opera House only a few months before the 1916 *Follies* opened. (Photograph by White Studios, New York; from the Billy Rose Theater Collection, New York Public Library for the Performing Arts.)

[*For related discussion, see* United States of America, *article on* Musical Theater; *and* Vaudeville.]

BIBLIOGRAPHY

Cohen[-Stratyner], Barbara Naomi. "The Dance Direction of Ned Wayburn: Selected Topics in Musical Staging, 1901–1923." Ph.D. diss., New York University, 1980.

Wayburn, Ned. *The Art of Stage Dancing*. New York, 1925.

CAMILLE HARDY

WEAVER, JOHN (born July 1673 in Shrewsbury, England, died 24 September 1760 in Shrewsbury), English dancing master, dancer, and theoretician. Weaver was responsible for rethinking the theoretical and theatrical nature of dance in the early eighteenth century. His writings influenced the social acceptance of dance, the professional training of dancing masters, and the way in which dance would be written about in England for nearly two hundred years. His many publications are a valuable repository of information about dance in his era.

As a teacher of dance to young gentlemen and ladies throughout his life, Weaver was conversant with all aspects of his subject. During his many years as a theatrical dancer and dancing master, he introduced serious dramatic dance entertainments into the English theater, basing his experimental productions on the practice of ancient pantomimes and contemporary Italian harlequin dancers from French fairs. Those entertainments are thought to have influenced the development of the *ballet d'action* and to have introduced comic pantomime to England. Weaver wanted theatrical dance to share the lofty and edifying aims of tragic drama.

As a dancing teacher, Weaver was concerned with professional standards and the social status of dance and spent much of his career seeking to regulate, improve, and explain the practices of his colleagues. He always sought to justify the social and historical importance of dance.

Weaver was educated at Shrewsbury School, where he gained a command of ancient and modern languages and became interested in the liberal arts, science, and philosophy. Part of his childhood was also spent in Oxford, where his father was a university dancing master. In about 1696, after an apprenticeship, Weaver began his career as a dancing master in Shrewsbury. He retained his practice in the town for most of his life and in a variety of schools; even at the height of his theatrical career in London he returned to Shrewsbury for half of each year. His provincial location explains much about his need to publish and about his practical involvement with notation.

Weaver went to London in about 1700 as a theatrical dancing master; shortly thereafter he met Mister Isaac, the queen's dancing master, who became his patron. In 1706, Weaver notated and published a collection of six ball dances by Mister Isaac and in that same year, Mister Isaac also encouraged Weaver to translate Raoul-Auger Feuillet's notation manual *Chorégraphie* (Paris, 1700) under the title *Orchesography*.

An Essay towards an History of Dancing (1712) and *Anatomical and Mechanical Lectures upon Dancing* (1721), Weaver's two important theoretical publications, were both dedicated to Thomas Caverley, who led the metropolitan profession with Isaac. The former work was promoted by Richard Steele in *The Spectator*, an influential journal that also published other contributions by Weaver.

In 1717, Steele gave Weaver the opportunity to produce a serious entertainment in dancing at Drury Lane. *The Loves of Mars and Venus* was succeeded by *Orpheus and Eurydice* (1718) and *The Judgement of Paris* (1733). Weaver also produced numerous humorous entertainments, notably *The Shipwreck, or Perseus and Andromeda* (1717), *Harlequin Turned Judge* (1717), and *Perseus and Andromeda* (1728), for which Monsieur Roger provided the serious scenes.

Weaver's Work in the Theater. Beginning with the 1699/1700 season, Weaver appeared as a dancer in several London theaters, mostly in short comic interludes, character pieces, and special features such as the original Yorkshire version of the "Roger a Coverly." *The Tavern Bilkers* (1702–1703) was Weaver's first attempt at comic scene dancing and probably used characters from the *commedia dell'arte.*

More important and well documented were Weaver's experiments in serious narrative dance, all of which were performed at Drury Lane. *The Loves of Mars and Venus* (1717) was loosely based on Peter Motteux's play set to music of the same name. The part of Venus was danced by Hester Santlow, a dramatic dancer of true quality who had a principal role in Weaver's three major productions. Weaver himself danced the semicomic role of Vulcan, the cuckold. A Monsieur Dupré, a French dancer, was Mars, but it is not possible to confirm whether this was Louis Dupré.

The Loves of Mars and Venus served Steele's purpose by attracting audiences from Lincoln's Inn Fields, with which Drury Lane was in direct competition. However, Weaver was disappointed by his dancers' inability to respond fully to the unfamiliar dramatic demands of his work. The novelty of the piece lay in its lack of spoken or sung explanation: the story was conveyed by explicit manual gestures and physical expression. In addition, the plot and narrative were dramatically advanced by means of group dances, duets, and solos that established the atmosphere of each scene, as did the introductory symphonies composed for each scene by Henry Symonds.

In the scenes involving the two best dance actors, Weaver and Santlow, a complex interaction of personalities was attempted: motive was explained, the action was advanced, and the course of the plot affected. Venus performed a stylized dance, to which Vulcan reacted. His gestures became less formal and more spontaneous and instinctive as his exasperation at her insouciant disdain increased. The music for the action of each scene was supplied by Charles Fairbank, who was a dancing master as well as a composer.

Orpheus and Eurydice (1718) enjoyed comparatively little success, although Weaver prepared it meticulously.

Classical sources were established for every part of the action; the intention was to re-create an ancient fable so fully that no subtlety was lost. Weaver danced the role of Orpheus himself, incorporating some of the gestures from *The Loves of Mars and Venus.* Santlow's part, Eurydice, was relatively small, and the greater part of the entertainment depended on Weaver himself.

Weaver appeared as a comic and character dancer in the 1720s, but rather than attempt his own major works, he supported John Thurmond's rise to fame as an exponent of pantomime and collaborated as a dancer and coauthor with Monsieur Roger, also at Drury Lane. Under the influence of Thurmond, John Rich, and Lewis Theobald, the serious aims of dramatic dance were supplanted by grotesque comedy and spectacular scenic display. This genre of entertainment became known as pantomime and established itself as a permanent feature of English theatrical performance.

The Judgement of Paris (1733), adapted from William Congreve's masque of 1701, with a new score by Seedo, consisted of a succession of tableaulike scenes supported by gesture, dance, and song. Weaver demonstrated that he could adapt his theatrical principles and aims to changed circumstances. The cast was led by Philip Desnoyer as Paris and Santlow as Helen of Troy. In a variety of dramatic settings, the entertainment enjoyed sustained success.

It was Weaver's misfortune to work in a period of bitter theatrical rivalry. In addition, his theatrical career was intermittent, and his reformative ideas were hampered by the conservatism of his dancers and the vulgar expectations of London audiences. The main influence of his theatrical work was indirect: the vitality and verve of English comic pantomime as it developed under Rich, Thurmond, Theobald, and others created a dynamic dramatic impetus for theatrical dance to which even Jean-Georges Noverre and his European contemporaries, for all their high-minded disclaimers, may have been indebted.

Weaver's Publications. Weaver's theatrical works were designed to follow classical themes and methods and to promote the narrative element in dance, enabling it to convey emotions, character, and plot without spoken or sung explanation. The books published as accompaniments to Weaver's three major serious entertainments are valuable historical sources, as are those written by the exponents of comic pantomime who followed him.

The book of *The Loves of Mars and Venus* (1717) includes historical material from *An Essay towards an History of Dancing* (1712), illustrating and justifying the action and graphically describing the demonstrative gestures Weaver advocated to convey twenty-four of the "passions" and "affections" specified in the piece. The book of *Orpheus and Eurydice* (1718) includes an exhaustive historical discussion of the myth, with extensive quotations from classical sources. The printed version of *The Judgement of Paris* (1733) is little more than an abridgment of Congreve's masque, from which Weaver's entertainment is adapted.

Weaver's nontheatrical publications are concerned with dance notation and the historical, musical, and anatomical understanding of his art. In all that he wrote, his concern was with regulating practice and with the social and artistic justification of dance.

Feuillet's *Chorégraphie* (see above) represented the most widely used system of dance notation in the eighteenth century: all dance steps in common use could be indicated by carefully contrived marks on a line, or tract, that suggested the floor pattern of the dance. The ground plan was explicitly related to the musical accompaniment, the tune of which was shown above the diagram. For its time it was an effective system, and Weaver's excellent translation (*Orchesography,* 1706) was in use for the greater part of the century. *A Small Treatise of Time and Cadence in Dancing* (1706) supersedes the brief musical section translated in *Orchesography:* Feuillet had improved his own system and published it in the preface to his *Recüeil de dances* (Paris, 1704), from which Weaver translated it. [*See* Feuillet Notation.]

A Collection of Ball-dances Perform'd at Court also appeared in 1706; Weaver's finely produced work of notation is an invaluable record of Isaac's compositions for the later Stuart court. (His notated version of Isaac's royal dance for 1707, "The Union," was published separately.)

Weaver was the champion of the provincial master; indeed, he was one himself. Notation enabled exemplary compositions to be widely studied and performed, and the possibility of teaching the most fashionable social dances gave the provincial dancing master an added claim on his pupils' patronage. The tendency to uniformity encouraged high standards of composition and performance; the very disciplines of notating and of deciphering notation made dancers and dancing masters more aware of style and precision of execution. The establishment of a body of specialized knowledge in which dancing masters required a practical working competence was part of Weaver's plan to retrain the profession. The same is true of Weaver's work in anatomy.

Weaver's lectures on anatomical and mechanical aspects of dance were read to leading members of the profession in an academy in Chancery Lane in about 1721. Weaver expected his colleagues to understand the human body in a fairly comprehensive way if they wished to train it properly and set unforced and unaffected movement on it. He therefore gave a purely anatomical description of the body and outlined the mechanical principles governing movement. From this he derived a set of reflections on the art of dance, "Rules and Institutions for Dancing," which appear at the end of the printed version of his lectures.

As early as 1706 Weaver was planning a history of dancing that would correct English social assumptions about the art that led most cultured people to dismiss it as nugatory and unworthy of serious thought. Extracts from the unfinished text of Weaver's work were freely incorporated in several issues of *The Spectator,* and Steele assiduously promoted Weaver's essay before and after its publication.

When it was finally published in 1712, *An Essay towards an History of Dancing* consisted of a conflation of sources of varying accuracy and authority that nevertheless gave the most complete account of dancing that had yet appeared in English. The essay contained a full account of Greek and Roman dance and pantomimes and sought to demonstrate, through a survey of its religious use and symbolism, that dance was one of the oldest and most fundamental human activities. Weaver also gave a full defense of dance as a social accomplishment for both gentlemen and ladies. Some of his arguments were current in courtesy literature, but they had not been fully marshaled before. Weaver found an unexpected ally in the philosopher John Locke, whose ideas on the educational benefits of dance he quoted at length, and in Francis Fuller, a physician whose fashionable promotion of exercise for purposes of health buttressed Weaver's thesis. Many other English and classical writers were cited to establish a wide and serious context for the acceptance of dance. Weaver also addressed himself to the religious and moralistic opponents of dance whose proscriptive activities were coextensive with the history of his art.

Weaver was able to draw on an impressive, if rather carefully qualified, philosophical countertradition, notably represented by Sir Thomas Elyot, that supported dance. The misgivings of ancient writers were presented as pertaining to the conditions of a different epoch. The concluding account of modern dancing is suffused with the wish to relate ancient patterns of narrative dance to contemporary practice: dance should convey meaning and address itself to matters of human moment and dignity; it should be able to encompass important themes from classical mythology and to rise to the level of the most serious art. (He regarded French figure dancing, as practiced in London by Claude Ballon and others, as contrary to his reformative purposes, calling it "meaningless motion.")

An Essay towards an History of Dancing is a remarkable document that uses material from a wide range of sources, many of them recondite and in Latin. It established a new framework within which dance could be assessed and was regarded as the standard English text on the history and defense of dancing until the late nineteenth century. (Most English works published up to that time contain either references to or extracts or borrowings from *An Essay.*)

Weaver's *History of the Mimes and Pantomimes* (1728) consists of an edited reprint of the last two chapters of *An Essay,* which deal with ancient mime and pantomime and modern dancing. It was designed to take advantage of the popularity of pantomimes, then at its height, and to make money for the author. At the same time, it recalls in a salutary way the dignified origins of mimic performance (with which many of the farcical contemporary pantomimes had little in common). The concluding "List of the modern entertainments that have been exhibited on the English stage; either in imitation of the Ancient pantomimes or after the manner of the modern Italians" is marred by several deliberate falsifications of date, designed to emphasize Weaver's priority and to represent the exponents of pantomime at Lincoln's Inn Fields as slavish imitators of the work of their rivals at Drury Lane. *The History of the Mimes and Pantomimes* has the hallmarks of a work published simply for gain; Weaver, twice married, had a large family and extravagant tastes.

Weaver was both a representative and a visionary figure; many of his ideas were not realized in his lifetime but were echoed by later writers with widely different technical and theatrical backgrounds. At the least, Weaver's publications contain a unique record of the practice of his contemporaries; at their best, his writings give a rare sense of the full potential of dance and of its capacity to serve people's physical, artistic, and spiritual natures in a socially valuable way. His apologetic methods were widely imitated for almost two hundred years. His theatrical reforms had less impact, although his part in introducing pantomime to the English stage was a permanent legacy to the theater. His anatomical lectures pointed the way to more systematic and professional teaching methods and to the further development of virtuosic performing skills.

BIBLIOGRAPHY

Chatwin, Amina, and Philip Richardson. "The Father of English Ballet: John Weaver." *Ballet Annual* 15 (1961): 60–65.

Cohen, Selma Jeanne. "Theory and Practice of Theatrical Dancing: II. John Weaver." In *Famed for Dance,* by Ifan Kyrle Fletcher et al. New York, 1960.

Dorris, George. "Music for the Ballets of John Weaver." *Dance Chronicle* 3.1 (1979): 46–60.

Foster, Susan Leigh. *Reading Dancing: Bodies and Subjects in Contemporary American Dance.* Berkeley, 1986.

Goff, Moira, and Jennifer Thorp. "Dance Notations Published in England, c.1700–1740." *Dance Research* 9 (Autumn 1991): 32–50.

Marsh, Carol. "French Court Dance in England, 1706–1740: A Study of the Sources." Ph.D. diss., City University of New York, 1985.

Ralph, Richard. *The Life and Works of John Weaver.* London, 1985.

Weaver, John. *An Essay towards an History of Dancing.* London, 1712.

Weaver, John. "The Loves of Mars and Venus" (1717). In *Dance as a Theatre Art,* edited by Selma Jeanne Cohen. New York, 1974.

Weaver, John. *The History of the Mimes and Pantomimes.* London, 1728.

RICHARD RALPH

WEDDING BOUQUET, A. Choreography: Frederick Ashton. Music: Lord Berners [Gerald Tyrwhitt]. Libretto: Lord Berners, with text by Gertrude Stein. Scenery and costumes: Lord Berners. First performance: 27 April 1937, Sadler's Wells Theatre, London, Vic-Wells Ballet. Principals: Ninette de Valois (Webster), June Brae (Josephine), Margot Fonteyn (Julia), Robert Helpmann (The Bridegroom), Mary Honer (The Bride).

The score of *A Wedding Bouquet* is a choral setting of Stein's text "They Must.Be Wedded.To Their Wife" as considerably edited and abridged by Berners, who changed words and sequences, adding or deleting repetitions to suit his musical purposes. He concocted a scenario with Ashton and Constant Lambert, not in the form of a logical narrative but rather as a series of incidents that take place at a provincial wedding in France around the turn of the twentieth century. *A Wedding Bouquet* is not a character ballet in the manner of Léonide Massine or Ninette de Valois but rather a classic ballet. The Bride and Bridegroom have a pas de deux that does not celebrate the wedding as much as prefigure the marriage—everything goes wrong; the Bride is turned upside down or faces the wrong way. There is also a pas de trois for two of the male guests and Julia's dog Pépé (named for a Mexican terrier owned by Miss Stein and her companion, Alice B. Toklas), who dons a tutu.

Among those present are the slightly demented Julia, who seems to have been seduced by the Bridegroom at some earlier date, and Josephine, who drinks too much champagne and has to be removed. The maid, Webster, whose character was evidently based on that of her original interpreter, runs the household with iron discipline.

That Ashton sometimes let the words point up a character or a situation became clear during World War II, when it was impossible to perform the ballet with a singing chorus (the ballet was no longer sharing the theater with the opera and general musical forces were reduced). Instead, Lambert recited the words while sitting at a table on one side of the stage and sipping champagne: the words were even more audible in his clear and caustic delivery. When the ballet was revived at the Royal Opera House in 1949, the chorus was briefly restored; then again, at Ashton's request, in 1983, for the centennial of Berners's birth. The ballet was in the repertory of the Royal Ballet touring section in the 1974/75 season and was revived by the Joffrey Ballet in 1978. Both productions used spoken, not sung narration. (The score has been recorded, with chorus, by the RTE Chamber Choir and Sonfonietta, conducted by Kenneth Alwyn, on a Marco Polo CD.)

BIBLIOGRAPHY

Barnes, Clive. "Ballet Perspectives No. 10: *A Wedding Bouquet.*" *Dance and Dancers* (April 1959): 20–21.

Stein, Gertrude. "They Must.Be Wedded.To Their Wife" (1931). In Stein's *Operas and Plays*. Barrytown, N.Y., 1987.

DAVID VAUGHAN

WEEME, MASCHA TER (born 17 October 1902 in Amsterdam, died 31 July 1995 in Amsterdam), Dutch dancer and ballet director. Ter Weeme received her first dance training in the schools of Mary Wigman and Émile Jaques-Dalcroze. She went regularly to Paris to study classical dance. After performing mostly in solo programs, she joined, as a soloist, the newly formed company of Yvonne Georgi, whose assistant she became. She stood out as a strong performer in character parts, which she gave a stylish, elegant flavor.

After a conflict with Georgi, ter Weeme left in 1944, started her own school, and appeared with another Georgi soloist, Tony Raedt, in dance recitals. In 1947 she and others founded the Ballet der Lage Landen; ter Weeme directed that company until it was amalgamated in 1959 with the Ballet of the Netherlands Opera to form the Amsterdam Ballet. Thus it formed a direct link between the artistic ideas of Yvonne Georgi and the new developments in Dutch dance after World War II.

Ter Weeme had no ambition to be a choreographer, a unique exception among ballet directors in the Netherlands. Her importance lies in the fact that she ascribed great value to, and had a remarkable feeling for, the emotional and theatrical side of dance. Her refined taste and eye for detail found expression in the conscientious care she gave to interpretation, decor, and costumes. This made her company quite different from others.

In 1961 ter Weeme was appointed co-director, with Sonia Gaskell, of the newly formed National Ballet, and the differences in their artistic ideas became so evident that the collaboration lasted only one season. Ter Weeme withdrew and devoted her time to teaching.

BIBLIOGRAPHY

Schaik, Eva van. *Op gespannen voet: Geschiedenis van de Nederlandse theaterdans vanaf 1900*. Haarlem, 1981.

Sinclair, Janet. *Ballet der Lage Landen*. Haarlem, 1956.

Sinclair, Janet. "A Dutch Pioneer." *The Dancing Times* (December 1982): 200–201.

INE RIETSTAP

WEIDMAN, CHARLES (Charles Edward Weidman; born 22 July 1901 in Lincoln, Nebraska, died 16 July 1975 in New York City), American dancer and choreographer. Weidman was reared and educated in Lincoln, Nebraska. He was considered a bright student and received several awards for his academic achievements. His interest in the history of architecture benefited him in the preparation, in 1919, of his first solo concert—nine ethnic dances choreographed in the style of Ruth St. Denis—whom Weidman had seen in concert in Lincoln in 1916; Weidman had been able to explain to his schoolmates the historical and architectural influences on St. Denis, those from which he drew for his own choreography.

On the basis of Weidman's solo performance, a local dance instructor invited him to study classical dance at her studio in exchange for his services as a teacher of ballroom dance. In 1920, Weidman had saved enough money for transportation to Los Angeles and tuition for summer study at Denishawn; he embarked upon a course that would change his life. Ted Shawn auditioned the tall, gawky boy with craggy eyebrows and a bony facial structure, and Weidman became a scholarship student. Before the summer session was over, Shawn sent Weidman to Tacoma, Washington, to replace a dancer who had broken his foot in the dance drama *Xochitl.*

From 1921 until 1928, Weidman's Denishawn years, his career took him to England, France, Asia, and many cities in the United States. He also served as a teacher at the Denishawn school in New York City. In 1928, Weidman and Doris Humphrey formed the Humphrey-Weidman Studio and Company. They had hoped to incorporate their ideas into Denishawn, but founders Ruth St. Denis and Ted Shawn were not receptive to their proposal.

Among Weidman's extensive contributions to American dance, his masculine approach to movement and his unique and individualistic abilities in pantomimic dance, enabled many men to enjoy dancing without following a lyrical and romantic path that some found distasteful. Some male audience members are also better able to identify with Weidman's style of dance than with much of ballet.

As a dancer, Weidman was hailed by the critic John Martin as "the most promising masculine dancer in America." He was in demand as a dance partner and it was on one such occasion that his concept of "kinetic pantomime" was brought to fruition. In a dance with Agnes de Mille, Weidman, disturbed by the use of tangible objects, replaced them by translating ideas into movement, which gave animation to the feeling behind an idea.

WEIDMAN. In this scene from *On My Mother's Side* (1940), a satirical suite about family members, Weidman portrayed his grandfather as a man who never relaxed—not even in death. (Photograph © 1980 by Barbara Morgan; used by permission of the Barbara Morgan Archives, Hastings-on-Hudson, New York.)

Weidman choreographed and performed all types of dances—dramatic, humorous, lyrical—and was comfortable with each. *On My Mother's Side* (1940), a solo he based on members of his mother's family, embraced movement that left no doubt in the viewer's mind that Grandmother Hoffman had nimble fingers and was an artist at stitchery. In this witty commentary, Weidman introduces Great-Grandfather Walcott, the young pioneer who is quite proud; Great-Grandfather and Grandfather Hoffman; and Grandmother Hoffman, each of whom he portrays in turn. His Aunt Jessie appears next, dancing daintily to the strains of "Dear Little Buttercup," indicative of the fact that she appeared as Buttercup in one of her theatrical adventures. The final character of the dance is Weidman himself, who showed, through dance and pantomime, the young "Sonny" of Lincoln, Nebraska, who studied at Denishawn and learned Oriental dance and ballet but was not quite satisfied that this was his style of dance. He contemplates the predicament and decides that he wishes to move more freely; then, in a reminiscent fashion, he performs a few excerpts from the Humphrey-Weidman repertory while the members of the speaking chorus sum up the dance: "Then the modern creed it got him / And some think they / Might have shot him / As a leader / Of the bare / Foot and Soul."

Flickers (1942), an affectionate burlesque of silent motion pictures, was choreographed in a jerky style to approximate the movements of early moving pictures. The four scenes included in this dance were "Hearts Aflame," a takeoff on the mortgage plot of Mary Pickford movies; "Hearts Courageous," a cowboys-and-Indians western; "Flowers of the Desert," a spoof of Rudolph Valentino's sheik sagas; and "Wages of Sin," a satire on the Theda Bara–type of seductress.

Fables for Our Time (1947), a suite of four dances based on James Thurber's stories about impressionable birds, animals, and people, was the result of Weidman's being awarded a Guggenheim fellowship. The four fables Weidman included in the suite were "The Owl Who Was God," "The Shrike and Chipmunks," "The Unicorn in the Garden," and "The Courtship of Arthur and Al." *Fables* was considered one of Weidman's best efforts and received rave reviews from the critics.

Two of Weidman's later works, *Saints, Sinners, and Scriabin* and *Liebeslieder Waltzes,* both created in 1961, indicated that the master choreographer was still at work. The former work was a solo piece in which Weidman presented portrait studies of memorable characters from the past whom historians had classified as either saints or sinners. *Liebeslieder Waltzes,* dedicated to Humphrey's memory, did not contain a single traditional waltz step;

WEIDMAN. Weidman choreographed his first version of *Candide* in 1933 for a week-long Broadway run, produced by Michael Myerberg. He later restaged it for the Federal Dance Project's first season in 1936 and again in 1937 as a part of a double bill with Helen Tamiris's *How Long, Brethren?*. Pictured here is the South America scene from the 1937 production. (Photograph from the Dance Collection, New York Public Library for the Performing Arts.)

while reviewing Humphrey's beautiful fall-and-recovery technique, Weidman recalled how he had rebelled because he thought the falls were too feminine, so he decided to choreograph a suite of dances characterized by them.

When Humphrey retired as a dancer in 1945, Weidman formed the Charles Weidman Theatre Dance Company. He continued to teach and tour. For several years both his school and large company were successful, but by 1951 Weidman's alcoholism and poor management caused the company to disband. Weidman then undertook the teaching tours he continued until his death. In 1955 he joined Alcoholics Anonymous and successfully achieved sobriety, which he maintained for the remainder of his life.

In 1960 Weidman and a young avant-garde artist, Mikhail Santaro, joined forces and opened the Expression of Two Arts Theatre in New York City; Weidman's living quarters were in the rear of the second-floor loft. It was a small studio, but adequate for classes and small concerts. *Liebeslieder Waltzes* was the first major choreographic effort he made in his new quarters. Other works—*The Christmas Oratorio, The Marriage of Jacob, The Easter Oratorio, King David,* and *Visualizations from a Farm in New Jersey*—were also included in the repertory.

In 1969 a group of friends established the Charles Weidman Foundation and the Charles Weidman School of Modern Dance. In 1970 the Dance Division of the American Association of Health, Physical Education and Recreation presented Weidman with the Dance Heritage Award for his years of service to education.

[*See also entries on the principal figures mentioned herein.*]

BIBLIOGRAPHY

Becker, Svea, and Joenine Roberts. "A Reaffirmation of the Humphrey-Weidman Quality." *Dance Notation Journal* 1 (January 1983): 3–17.

"Chipmunk at Jacob's Pillow." *Time* (28 July 1947).

Code, Grant. "Humphrey-Weidman and Group." *Dance Observer* (January 1941): 8.

Hering, Doris. Review. *Dance Magazine* (April 1960): 26.

King, Eleanor. *Transformations: The Humphrey-Weidman Era.* Brooklyn, 1978.

Kriegsman, Sali Ann. *Modern Dance in America: The Bennington Years.* Boston, 1981.

Richards, Sylvia. "A Biography of Charles Weidman." Ph.D. diss., Texas Women's University, 1971.

Sherman, Jane. "Charles Weidman at Denishawn." *Ballet Review* 13 (Fall 1985): 73–82.

Smith, A. William. "*Flicker:* A Fifty-Year Old 'Flicker' of the Weidman Tradition." In *Dance Reconstructed,* edited by Barbara Palfy. New Brunswick, N.J., 1993.

Stodelle, Ernestine. "The First Duo-Drama." *Dance Observer* (December 1959): 154–155.

ARCHIVE. Humphrey-Weidman Collection, Dance Collection, New York Public Library for the Performing Arts.

SYLVIA PELT RICHARDS

WEIDT, JEAN (Hans Weidt; born 7 October 1904 in Hamburg, died 29 August 1988 in Berlin), German dancer and choreographer. Born into the working class, choreographer Jean Weidt dedicated his career to furthering the proletarian cause through dance.

Weidt first performed in a folk dance group sponsored by a youth club. (He later wrote in *Der Rote Tänzer* [1968] that he learned "the laws of choreography" from Anna Helms and Julius Blasche, leading members of the folk dance revival movement in Germany.) As a youth he also studied with the modern dancer Sigurd Leeder (before Leeder joined Rudolf Laban and Kurt Jooss) and with the ballet mistress at the Hamburg Opera, Olga Brandt-Knaack. Throughout his choreographic career, Weidt drew upon and fused classical, folk, and modern dance, for he believed that the content of a dance determined its form, not the reverse.

In 1925, Weidt gave his first solo concert in Hamburg, including the first of "ten to twelve" versions of *The Worker.* The same year he formed a group, which included many unemployed workers, that performed in conventional theater spaces as well as at Communist Party rallies. Weidt's later groups in Berlin and Paris also performed in both types of venues. (Although he converted to the Communist cause during a workers' uprising in 1923, Weidt did not become an official party member until 1931.)

In 1929, Weidt moved to Berlin, where his group became known as The Red Dancers. The political content of his work intensified as the politics of the time became increasingly factionalized. In one solo, *Member of Parliament,* Weidt wore a mask resembling Paul Löbe, the Social Democrat leader of the Reichstag. A group work, *Potsdam,* employed masks to represent politicians on the right: Hitler, Franz von Papen, and Alfred Hugenberg. Weidt became involved with circles of other leftist artists, and in 1931 he was invited to choreograph Friedrich Wolf's play *Tai Yang Awakes,* under the direction of Erwin Piscator.

After Hitler came to power in January 1933, Weidt was arrested and jailed for several weeks. Upon his release, he received permission to travel to Sweden, but instead he journeyed to the Workers' Theater Olympiade in Moscow. From there, he made his way to Paris and formed a group to work with the French Communist Party. (At this time Weidt changed his given name from Hans to Jean.) Because of his political activities his visa was not exended, so he returned to Moscow, and then moved to Prague, where he formed another dance group. In 1937, he returned to Paris and revived his earlier French group as Les Ballets 38; among the works premiered by his company were Satie's *Parade* and Prokofiev's *Prodigal Son.*

World War II interrupted his choreographic career, for Weidt was first interned by the French and later fought in the British forces. After the war, his Paris company appeared at the 1947 International Choreographic Competition in Copenhagen and won first prize for *The Cell,* described by an American observer as "a work portraying the aspirations, nightmares and death of a common man" (Hastings, 1947).

In 1948, Weidt returned from exile to East Berlin. From 1948 to 1950 he directed the Dramatic Ballet at the Volksbühne in East Berlin. He then took positions at the opera houses in Schwerin and in Karl-Marx-Stadt. In 1958, he choreographed a work for three hundred amateur dancers in Rostock, which set the course for the remainder of his choreographic career dedicated to lay dance. From 1958 to 1966 he directed a lay dance ensemble associated with Berlin's Komische Oper, and from 1978 to 1980 he directed a workshop for young choreographers there. Along with Gret Palucca, another survivor from the 1920s Weimer era, Weidt served as an inspiration to choreographers who came of age in the Democratic Republic before the reunification of Germany in 1990.

BIBLIOGRAPHY

Hastings, Baird. "Concours à Copenhagen." *Dance Magazine* (September, 1947).

"Jean Weidt." *Tanzdrama* 5 (1988): 14–15.

Reinisch, Marion. *Auf der grossen Strasse: Jean Weidts Erinnerungen.* Berlin, 1984.

Weidt, Jean. *Der Rote Tänzer, ein Lebensbericht.* Berlin, 1968.

SUSAN A. MANNING

WELCH, GARTH (born 14 April 1936 in Brisbane), Australian dancer, choreographer, director, and teacher. Although Garth Welch made his professional debut as a performer in musical comedy and has returned to that genre on occasions in recent years, he was also Australia's first true *danseur noble.* His classical line and strong technique were enhanced by a well-proportioned body and an elegant manner of moving that marked him as a potential principal artist from the earliest days of his career as a dancer with the Borovansky Ballet.

Trained by Phyllis Danaher in Brisbane, Welch joined the Borovansky Ballet in 1952 and, apart from a period in 1958/59 when he danced in Britain with Western Theatre Ballet, he performed with Borovansky until the company folded in 1961. He was promoted to principal in 1959. While negotiations were proceeding for the establishment of the Australian Ballet, Welch danced in Europe with Le Grand Ballet du Marquis de Cuevas, returning to Australia in 1962 to join the newly formed national company as its principal male dancer.

Early in his career Welch established a luminous partnership with Marilyn Jones, to whom he was also married for a number of years. Their dancing partnership, in which they exhibited a strong emotional rapport, continued during the 1960s and 1970s until Welch retired from full-time dancing in 1973. They gave especially memorable performances in John Cranko's *The Lady and the Fool,* in which Jones played La Capricciosa and Welch played Moondog. Welch also excelled in dramatic roles such as Albrecht in *Giselle* and The Outsider in Robert Helpmann's Australian ballet *The Display.* His dramatic abilities were never more apparent, however, than in Graeme Murphy's *After Venice,* created on Sydney Dance Company in 1984. Welch, at forty-eight, played the role of the aging Aschenbach with an overwhelming strength and presence that received critical acclaim both around Australia and in the United States and Europe.

Welch has also had an important career as a choreographer, director, and teacher. He began to choreograph in earnest after spending time in 1966 and 1967 studying in the United States on a Harkness Fellowship. In New York he was influenced by Martha Graham; his first work made after his return to Australia, *Othello* (1968), was, as he said in an interview in 1990, "almost a homage to the technique I learnt from her." Othello was mounted by the Australian Ballet in 1970. Since then Welch has made many works for the Australian Ballet, Sydney Dance Company, West Australian Ballet, Ballet Victoria, Queensland Ballet, and Ballet Philippines.

His first taste of artistic directorship came in 1974 when he was associate artistic director of Ballet Victoria, a company founded as Ballet Guild by Laurel Martyn in 1946. He was also artistic director of the West Australian Ballet from 1980 through 1982. As a teacher he has worked at the Victorian College of the Arts and in a school that he and Marilyn Jones founded in Sydney in 1883. In the 1990s he has freelanced as a teacher and has taken particular interest in the careers of young dancers on the verge of a professional career.

BIBLIOGRAPHY

Laughlin, Patricia. "Dance Greats: Garth Welch." *Dance Australia* no. 84 (June–July 1996): p 28.

Pask, Edward H. *Ballet in Australia: The Second Act, 1940–1980.* Melbourne, 1982.

INTERVIEW. Garth Welch by Michelle Potter (January 1990), National Library of Australia, Canberra (TRC 2545).

MICHELLE POTTER

WELLER. As Lise in a 1982 performance of Frederick Ashton's *La Fille Mal Gardée.* Weller performed the role of Lise for many years, during which she had ample opportunity to display her marked flair for comic acting as well as her talent for expressive dancing. (Photograph © 1982 by Nan Melville; used by permission.)

WELLER, DAWN (born 16 December 1947 in Durban, Natal), South African ballet dancer and company director. First enrolled in dance classes at age two and a half, Weller received her early ballet training from Iris Manning and Arlene Spear in Durban. In 1964 she was one of the first dancers to join a company formed under the aegis of the Natal Performing Arts Council (NAPAC), one of the four provincial arts councils in South Africa. With NAPAC Ballet, Weller toured for a few months and then, in 1965, joined the larger, more competitive ballet company of the Performing Arts Council of the Transvaal (PACT). With PACT Ballet, Weller made rapid progress; she was soon dancing soloist roles and in 1968 was named a principal dancer.

During her long career with PACT Ballet, Weller's growth as an artist was steady and determined. Although her body was not ideally formed for ballet dancing, her drive to succeed, her innate musicality, and rigorous coaching by such outstanding teachers as Faith de Villiers, Denise Schultze, and Lorna Haupt helped Weller to develop into a strong and much admired performer. It was not her technical mastery, however, that made her dancing truly memorable, but her individual style and her ability to project a character. Accordingly, she shone in such roles as Titania in Frederick Ashton's *The Dream* and as the heroines of such classic ballets as *Giselle, Romeo and Juliet, Coppélia,* and *Cinderella.* In 1980 André Prokovsky gave her one of the most acclaimed roles of her career as a dancer-actress in his ballet *Anna Karenina,* for which she received both the Lilian Solomon Award and the Friends of the Ballet Award. In other works in the repertory, Weller's distinctive sense of humor was displayed in such lighthearted roles as Lise in *La Fille Mal Gardée,* Rosalinda in Ronald Hynd's ballet of the same name, and Milady in Prokovsky's production of *The Three Musketeers.*

Early in her career, Weller found it difficult to approach ballets without characters or narrative, although she later became comfortable with portraying mood and emotion in abstract ballets. Apart from Frank Staff, who worked with Weller in her first three years with PACT Ballet, the only choreographer to work creatively with her was Ashley Killar, who was ballet master with the company from 1979 to 1985. After a difficult beginning, due partly to Weller's reluctance to dance in abstract works, the success of their first ballet, *Migrations* (1980), paved the way for others, many of them non-narrative works. *The Duenna, Overture, Forgotten Summer, Sarabande, Schubert Adage,* and *Camille* were all created between 1980 and 1983.

In 1983, Weller was appointed artistic director of PACT Ballet, and in 1986 the board of directors conferred on her the title of *prima ballerina.* Not long thereafter, she was involved in a serious automobile accident, which led to her decision to retire from the stage in 1987 and to focus her energies on direction of the company. To mark her retirement, the South African government honored her with the Order for Meritorious Service, a national award for distinguished service in the public interest.

Under Weller's direction, PACT Ballet grew from strength to strength. She not only continued the policy of inviting guest artists from abroad to dance with the company, but she augmented the practice of inviting guest choreographers to mount their works for the company. As well as many revivals produced under her direction, she was responsible for enriching the repertory with the works of numerous choreographers of international renown, ranging from August Bournonville to George Balanchine, John Cranko, Choo San Goh, and David Bintley.

In 1994, Weller became director of the new PACT Ballet School, while retaining the position of artistic director of the company. Also in that year she was appointed a trustee of the national Arts and Culture Trust, and the following year, 1995, she was the center of attention at a gala performance at the State Theater in Pretoria in honor of her thirtieth year of service with PACT Ballet.

Weller's skill in coaching and producing dancers and the dramatic flair she brought to her own performances were demonstrated in 1996 in her most important production, a full-length version of *La Bayadère,* originally choreographed by Marius Petipa in Saint Petersburg in 1877. At the time of its premiere in Pretoria, Weller's production was only the third staging of the complete ballet by a company outside the republics of the former Soviet Union.

[*See also* PACT Ballet.]

BIBLIOGRAPHY

Allyn, Jane, and Nan Melville. *Dawn Weller: Portrait of a Ballerina.* Johannesburg, 1984. Includes a chronological listing of roles performed.

Borland, Eve. "CAPAB and PACT Ballet, South Africa." *Dance Gazette* (March 1985).

Cooper, Montgomery, and Jane Allyn. *Dance for Life: Ballet in South Africa.* Cape Town, 1980. Photographs by Montgomery Cooper; text by Jane Allyn.

Hurwitz, Jonathan. "Thirty Years with PACT Ballet." Program notes, PACT Ballet, 1995 season. Pretoria, 1995.

NAN MELVILLE

WELLS, DOREEN (Doreen Patricia Wells; born 25 June 1937 in Walthamstow, London), English ballerina. Trained at the Bush Davies Schools, Doreen Wells won the Adeline Genée gold medal of the Royal Academy of Dancing in 1954, and the following year she joined the Sadler's Wells Theatre Ballet. In 1956 she moved to the Royal Ballet at Covent Garden and quickly became a soloist. Exceptionally musical, petite, and beautifully proportioned, she had a sure and elegant technique and a range that extended from soubrette roles (in which she showed a delicious sense of comedy) to the most demanding of the nineteenth-century classical roles.

After her promotion to principal dancer in 1960, she led the Royal Ballet Touring Company for ten years, with David Wall as her regular partner. They were ideally matched. From 1970 to 1974 she danced with both sections of the Royal Ballet. She took the title roles in Rudolf Nureyev's 1963 staging of *Raymonda* (replacing Margot Fonteyn) and in Peter Wright's 1968 production of *Giselle.* She was a radiant Aurora, a sparkling Swanilda, a gentle Giselle, and a distinguished Odette-Odile. She also danced a wide selection of the Frederick Ashton repertory, appearing in the first casts of new productions of *Sylvia* (1963), *The Dream* (1963, Titania), and *Monotones* (1968, *Trois Gnossiennes*). She was particularly associated with the heroine of *The Two Pigeons,* a role that suited the sunny sweetness of her stage personality.

Ashton created two ballets with Wells in leading roles: *Sinfonietta* (1967), in which she danced the mysterious central Elegy, lifted and partnered through multiple configurations by four men, and *The Creatures of Prometheus* (1970). She also created roles in ballets by Kenneth MacMillan (*La Création du Monde,* 1964), Wright (*Summer Night,* 1964), Joe Layton (Mary Pickford in *The Grand Tour,* 1971), and Geoffrey Cauley. She was in the Royal Ballet Touring Company's first productions of MacMillan's *Concerto* (1967, second movement) and *La Boutique Fantasque* (1968, Can-Can Dancer), and she frequently danced the role of the Girl in MacMillan's *The Invitation.*

In 1972 she married the marquess of Londonderry, and in 1974 she retired from the Royal Ballet to become the mother of two sons. Since then she has danced at galas, as a guest with several companies (including Sadler's Wells Royal Ballet from 1980 to 1982, when she made her first appearance as the Betrayed Girl in *The Rake's Progress*), in pantomime, and in the 1984 London production of *On Your Toes,* in which she successfully followed Natalia Makarova as the Russian Ballerina.

BIBLIOGRAPHY

Buckley, Peter. "A Royal Pair: Doreen Wells and David Wall." *Dance Magazine* (March 1971): 58–61.

Clarke, Mary. "Doreen Wells." *The Dancing Times* (March 1961): 347.

Herf, Estelle. "Doreen Wells of the Royal Ballet." *Ballet Today* (May–June 1969): 18–21.

Woodcock, Sarah C. *The Sadler's Wells Royal Ballet.* London, 1991.

MARY CLARKE

WEST AFRICA. The region known as West Africa includes along the Atlantic coast the countries of Mauritania, Senegal, Gambia, Guinea-Bissau, Guinea, Sierra Leone, Liberia, Côte d'Ivoire (Ivory Coast), Ghana, Togo, Benin, Nigeria, and Cameroon; the island republic of Cape Verde off the western coast of Senegal; in the northwestern interior of the continent, Mali, Burkina Faso (formerly Upper Volta), Niger, and Chad. With more claims to diversity than threads of unity, the region encompasses environments ranging from desert and savanna to dense tropical rain forest. Sustenance is mostly derived from fishing, herding, and crop cultivation. There are effervescent urban centers and scattered quiet villages, thriving markets and desolate outposts. Christianity and Islam vie to dominate religious life. Political structures historically varied from small-scale, simply organized communities to widespread kingdoms and empires, and today include both autocracies and democracies. The peoples speak languages belonging to the Niger-Congo, Afro-Asiatic, and Nilo-Saharan families.

In West Africa, the French and British dominated in the colonial period (nineteenth to mid-twentieth century); Portugal controlled Guinea-Bissau and Cape Verde; and Germany held Togo and Cameroon. Liberia, created for and settled by freed American slaves, has been independent since 1847.

Despite this variety, West Africa has some common characteristics. The region's history is a chronicle of great indigenous kingdoms between the Sahara and the Gulf of Guinea, the longest sub-Saharan African history of contact with Europeans, the densest population (with more than 30 percent of the continent's population), and the greatest number of urban centers. Europeans arrived on the Guinea coast in the mid-fifteenth century. Trade soon flourished in gold, grain, pepper, ivory, and palm oil, and in slaves. After World War II, colonial control ended and new nations emerged, most of them retaining the European-imposed boundaries of the colonies, ignoring the territories of indigenous ethnic groups, which today overlap national borders.

Stereotypes of African dance were created in Europe and the Americas that even some westernized Africans came to accept. The dances that evoked the strongest European reaction, those therefore brought to Western theaters, were hip-swinging, pelvic-thrusting, breast-bouncing, or spear-throwing types. Through such dances, unmarried youths showed their energy, coordination, and creativity, which are believed to predict their ability to cope with life's exigencies. Nonetheless, lyrical, reserved, and stylized dances also exist here.

Although dance is common throughout West Africa, not everyone in any one society dances or moves in the same way. There are gender and class differences. Among the Wolof, highborn girls do not usually dance publicly, and when they do, their dancing is restrained. By contrast, the

WEST AFRICA. These Maxi women of Benin are Nensuxhe priestesses, devoted to the cult of the water spirits. They have left the town of Savalou and are on their way to a neighboring village, where they will join initiates into the cult in a dance to invoke the power of the spirits. (Photograph © 1992 by Judith Gleason; used by permission.)

dances of lower-class women feature sexually suggestive movements and postures. In the town of Bida in Nigeria, class prejudice precludes a man of high status from joining a dance with people of lower station.

Because African tradition is not static, but rather a changing phenomenon related to time, place, and situation, dances reported by early observers may have undergone many traditional, neotraditional, and theatrical transformations. A dance that first existed in the village may have a second form onstage in the city, a third on television, and yet a fourth on tour abroad. In contrast with dance in industrial societies, African dance tends to be enmeshed in nondance aspects of life; the sacred often blends into the secular and the aesthetic into the utilitarian. Dances with the same purpose may take different forms, and those with the same form may have different purposes.

WEST AFRICA. A masked dancer of the Guro people of central Côte d'Ivoire. His raffia skirt, wristbands, and anklebands are a brilliant red; the covering of his legs, arms, and head is banded in bright red and blue; his shawl bears black and red stripes on a white ground. He wears a spray of black feathers at the back of his head and a sculpted crown of a leopard attacking an antelope. (Photograph © 1993 by Jenny Lynn McNutt; used by permission.)

In Western ethnographic literature, African dancing is often mentioned in conjunction with religious ritual, healing, music, storytelling, masking, dress, festivals, play, recreation, and war; the accounts of dance in these contexts vary in detail and sophistication. With growing understanding of both Africa and dance, however, reports have become less likely to stigmatize West African dance as pornography, conflict, or savagery; writers now tend to recognize the perspective of the indigenous dancer and audience. Some scholars seek to formulate a distinctly pan-African expression common to approximately a thousand societies, but such generalizations lack empirical support from ethnographic and film records.

Colonial administrators in West Africa were concerned about the propensity of music and dance to disturb the colonists' sleep, to distract Africans from going to work on time or even working for Europeans, or to ignite anti-imperialist sentiments (as in warrior dances)—so they imposed bans on dancing. The study of dance by Europeans, which might legitimize it as an art form, was not encouraged. In addition, Christian missionaries—who were aware of the deeply rooted integration of dancing with indigenous religion—tried to eliminate dancing, thereby to more easily spread Christianity.

Purposes of Dancing. Dance in West Africa conveys feelings, attitudes, concepts, and stories that emanate from everyday life, morality, myth, and legend. Dance also encapsulates essential aesthetic and social values and communicates systems of belief. Marcel Griaule (1965) recorded a Dogon elder's notions of dance as part of a coherent system of thought, a cosmological representation and vehicle for moving the world to order after the disorder of death. Team dance and masked choreography depict the Dogon conception of the world's progress. By extending movement beyond the human body, masks create the illusion or believed reality of the supernatural, inspiring reverence in performers and spectators alike. The Dogon "Storied House," one of some eight masks, rises more than ten feet (3 meters) above the dancer's head.

The dance of the Ubakala of Nigeria reflects the key tenets of their value system, mediates conflict, promotes social relations, and introduces change. The Mende, Bambara, Manika, and Nupe are among the groups that merge dance and economic activity. Dance may be intimately connected with work, interrupting or becoming part of daily tasks as an incentive to complete routine activities or initiate endeavors. Talented Nupe dancers may become professionals through the sponsorship of patrons.

Dance in West Africa plays an important educational role, too, providing a means whereby beliefs, mores, and cultural heritage are passed from adults to children. Initiation dances, performed when a boy or girl reaches puberty, usually celebrate the value of fertility, pass on lore about the initiate's new sexual powers, and describe the social responsibilities arising from the new status. For example, among the Wan, a hot and sweaty man dances with a cool and aloof female initiate on his shoulders. Opportunities for nearly mature Kuka adolescents to become acquainted and possibly marry occur in the *tadjo* dance.

In West Africa, the kind of dance that one performs expresses social rank. Prestige is usually associated with a restrained dance style. For example, the Bamana (Bambara) *segu-ka-bara* dance reflects the traditional aristocratic social structure based on gender, descent from nobility, and domestic slave status. Each Bamana social group has its own dance patterns. Low-status groups perform grotesque and obscene dances to entertain their masters; the upper-class Dahomean, however, does not dance to fast, compelling rhythms. Dances to send the deceased Igbo (Ibo) to the world of the ancestors are performed only for those believed to have earned such recognition. Dignity and age—beginning with the king, chiefs, priests and priestesses, and descending the social scale from the elderly to the young—determine the *igbin* dance sequence of the Yoruba.

In many cultures, dance promotes healing and preventive medicine. Expressing their grievances through dance is a way the Ubakala deal with stress that may lead to illness. Exercise, integral to dance, has been shown to help prevent such illnesses as heart disease, obesity, non-insulin-dependent diabetes, hypertension, and osteoporosis. In West Africa, the Tiv of Nigeria see dancing as a life force that counters disease and death, which are caused by sorcerers. The Dogon describe the rapid dance movement *gona* as "a relief, like vomiting." Possession dance is often related to physical or mental health as well as to supernatural sanction for resolving social conflict. Conversely, dance can spark conflict, as in the Ubakala second burial dances, which enact the deeds of the deceased and remind onlookers of unsettled scores.

Dance in West Africa is also linked to politics. Sponsorship of a costly dance production displays wealth and prestige and creates and validates leaders. Applying rules with sacred sanction while remaining above community factions, masquerade dancers are a medium of social control. Authorities sometimes use dance to redress grievances and control subordinates, who in turn use dance to constrain their leaders' exercise of power. For such groups as the Ubakala, Bamara, and Dahomeans, dance is a safe and sanctioned means of ridiculing the errant, conveying grievances, and proposing solutions.

As a coping mechanism for such life crises as marriage, birth, and death, dance helps individuals to contend with the foibles of humanity. For example, the *ikaki* ("tortoise") masquerade of the Kalabari presents human psychology in animal guise; the playing of *ikaki* is a taming of human behavior.

WEST AFRICA. Men of the Temne people in Sierra Leone instructing a group of boys in the coming-out dance that will be performed during the boys' initiation into adulthood. The boys wear woven caps and robes to protect them during the perilous, liminal state of transformation from child to adult; when the caps and robes are removed, the boys will emerge as men. (Photograph © 1975 by Frederick Lamp; used by permission.)

Changes in Dance Forms. European contact has led to syncretistic dance forms—those that blend traditional and outside concepts. In Ubakala villages, where public physical contact between the sexes was considered improper, a group of young girls performed their parody of the Western man and woman embracing style of dance. In "Come Waltz with Me," instead of the Western male-female couple or Ubakala traditional circular dance pattern, the girls formed couples and parodied the Western-style waltz, clasping one another's heads, necks, shoulders, waists, hips, backs, and buttocks. Urban Nigerians and Ghanaians have merged European ballroom dance position (the embracing couple) with traditional African dance movements from many villages to create the "high-life" dance. Accompanied by indigenous and English-

WEST AFRICA. *(top)* Rose Marie Guirand, leading choreographer of the Côte d'Ivoire, posing in an outdoor setting. Guirand is the founder of the dance company called Les Guirivoires and its associated school, the École de Danse et d'Echange Culturelle, in Abidjan. *(bottom)* N'Deye-Gueye, a well-known dancer and teacher in Senegal, performing a spirited "highlife" dance. Highlife dancing is popular on social occasions throughout sub-Saharan Africa. (Top photograph © 1993 by Jenny Lynn McNutt; bottom photograph © 1996 by Jack Vartoogian; both used by permission.)

language songs, highlife dances are seen at parties and in nightclubs.

After Europeans introduced West Africans to university-level education, Western dance styles and theatrical dance forms soon appeared alongside traditional festival, ritual, and social events. Professional touring companies were developed, such as the Ghanaian concert parties (similar to *commedia dell'arte* or vaudeville) and Nigerian folk opera troupes, which present dramas featuring music, dance, and mime. Renowned practitioners of folk opera include the dramatist Duro Lapido, the actor-playwright Kola Ogunmola, and Hubert Ogunde, who is often regarded as the founder of Nigerian theater.

Theatrical Dance. Theatrical dance in West Africa may be either an aside, as in the Ghana Drama Studio's presentation of *Mother's Tears,* or an integral part of the production, as in Wole Soyinka's plays, which are more westernized than Nigerian folk opera. Soyinka's *The Lion and the Jewel* uses several arts, including dance; his *A Dance of the Forests* presents its climax through dance; and his *Death and the King's Horseman* also draws on Yoruba dance. A common pattern in West African theatrical dance companies, such as the Guinea National Ballet, is the punctuation of a simple story line with a series of traditional dances that are shortened or otherwise modified.

Dances performed in a Western-type school, government-sponsored competition, festival, or national-independence celebration are other transformations of traditional dance presented in new contexts. Apart from its manifest function as entertainment, westernized theater has also developed the covert function of encouraging nationalism.

[*See also* Aesthetics, *article on* African Aesthetics; Costume in African Traditions; Mask and Makeup, *article on* African Traditions; Music for Dance, *article on* African Music; *and* Sub-Saharan Africa. *For related discussion, see* Bamana Dance; Cameroon; Dogan Dance; Ghana; Hausa Dance; Tiv Dance; Ubakala Dance; *and* Yoruba Dance.]

BIBLIOGRAPHY

Binet, J. *Sociétés de danse chez les Fang du Gabon.* Travaux et Documents de l'O.R.S.T.O.M., no. 17. Paris, 1972.

Drewal, Henry John. "Efe/Gelede: The Educative Role of the Arts in Traditional Yoruba Culture." Ph.D. diss., Columbia University, 1973.
Fortes, Meyer. "Social and Psychological Aspects of Education in Taleland." *Africa* 11 (1938).
Gamble, David P. *The Wolof of Senegambia.* London, 1967.
Gebauer, Paul. "Dances of Cameroon." *African Arts* 4 (1971).
Griaule, Marcel. *Conversations with Ogotemmeli: An Introduction to Dogon Religious Ideas.* London, 1965.
Hanna, Judith Lynne. "African Dance as Education." *Impulse* (1965): 48–56.
Hanna, Judith Lynne. "Africa's New Traditional Dance." *Ethnomusicology* 9 (January 1965): 13–21.
Hanna, Judith Lynne. "The Highlife: A West African Urban Dance." In *Dance Research Monograph One.* New York, 1973.
Hanna, Judith Lynne. "The Anthropology of Dance Ritual: Nigeria's Ubakala Nkwa di Iche Iche." Ph.D. diss., Columbia University, 1976.
Hanna, Judith Lynne. "African Dance: Some Implications for Dance Therapy." *American Journal of Dance Therapy* 2 (1978): 3–15.
Hanna, Judith Lynne. *To Dance Is Human: A Theory of Nonverbal Communication* (1979). Chicago, 1987.
Hanna, Judith Lynne. "From Folk/Sacred to Popular Culture: Syncretism in Nigeria's Ubakala Dance-Plays." *Critical Arts* 3 (1983).
Hanna, Judith Lynne. "Movement in African Performance." In *Theatrical Movement: A Bibliographical Anthology,* edited by Bob Fleshman. Metuchen, N.J., 1986.
Hanna, Judith Lynne. *Dance and Stress: Resistance, Reduction, and Euphoria.* New York, 1988.
Harper, Peggy. *The Irigwe Dancers of Miango Village on the Jos Plateau.* Ibadan, 1968.
Harper, Peggy. *Tiv Women: The Icough Dance.* Ibadan, 1968.
Hinckley, Priscilla Baird. "The Dodo Masquerade of Burkina Faso." *African Arts* 19 (February 1986): 74–77, 91.
Horton, Robin. *The Gods as Guests.* Marina Lagos, 1960.
Horton, Robin. "The Kalabari Ekine Society." *Africa* 33 (1963).
Horton, Robin. "Igbo: An Ordeal for Aristocrats." *Nigeria Magazine* 94 (1967).
Imperato, Pascal James. "The Dance of the Tyi Wara." *African Arts* 4 (Autumn 1970).
Keil, Charles. *Tiv Song.* Chicago, 1979.
Little, Kenneth. *The Mende of Sierra Leone.* Rev. ed. London, 1967.
Meillassoux, Claude. *Urbanization of an African Community: Voluntary Associations in Bamako.* Seattle, 1968.
Nadel, S. F. *A Black Byzantium: The Kingdom of Nupe in Nigeria.* London, 1942.
Nicholls, Robert W. "Igede Funeral Masquerades." *African Arts* 17 (May 1984): 70–76, 92.
Nketia, J. H. Kwabena. "Possession Dances in African Societies." *Journal of the International Folk Music Council* 9 (1957).
Ottenberg, Simon. "Afikpo Masquerades." *African Arts* 6 (1973).
Ottenberg, Simon. "Illusion, Communication, and Psychology in West African Masquerades." *Ethos* 10 (Summer 1982).
Ravenhill, Phillip L. "The Interpretation of Symbolism in Wan Female Initiation." *Africa* 48 (1978).
Tiérou, Alphonse. *Dooplé: The Eternal Law of African Dance.* London, 1992.
Warner, Mary Jane. *Laban Notation Scores: An International Bibliography.* New York, 1984.
Wescott, Joan. "The Sculpture and Myths of Eshu-Elegba, the Yoruba Trickster: Definition and Interpretation in Yoruba Iconography." *Africa* 32 (1962).

JUDITH LYNNE HANNA

WESTERN THEATRE BALLET. *See* Scottish Ballet.

WHITE-HAIRED GIRL, THE. Choreography and libretto: Hu Rongrong, Fu Aidi, Cheng Daihui, and Lin Yangyang. Music: Yan Dinxian. Scenery: Du Shixiang and Zhu Shichang. First performance: May 1965, Shanghai School of Dancing. Principals: Cai Kuoying (Xier), Ling Guiming (Dachun), Ga Xiamei (White-Haired Girl).

Taken from a 1945 Chinese folk opera, this ballet in eight acts tells the tragic tale of Yang Bailao, an elderly and poor peasant, and his daughter Xier, in the village of Yanggezhuang in northern China during the war against Japan (1937–1945). Cruelly exploited by his despotic landlord Huang Shiren, Yang lives in abject servitude and shame. With anger smoldering in his heart, he rises against the landlord's ruthless oppression and exploitation, only to be beaten to death. Xier is seized by Huang as payment for Yang's debt and is put to work as a slave in his household. Suffering terribly, she escapes to a barren mountain, where, in the wintery conditions, her hair turns white. Only after the Eighth Red Army liberates the village does she return home to begin a new and happier life.

The White-Haired Girl was an important new attempt by Chinese choreographers in the field of national ballet and followed a fruitful experiment with the ballet *Red Detachment of Women* (1964). That work featured the integration of many colorful and locally flavorful folk dances with European classical dance techniques and used a socially forceful theme—the old society turned men into ghosts, but the new society turned ghosts into men.

The White-Haired Girl was first presented in 1964 in Shanghai by the Shanghai School of Dancing. It was filmed there in color in 1969 by the Shanghai Film Studio and released for general distribution on the Thirteenth Anniversary of Mao's Talks on Literature and Art at Yenan, 15 February 1972. With this ballet, the Shanghai Ballet Troupe toured the Democratic Republic of Korea (North Korea) in 1972 and Canada in 1977.

[*See also* China, *article on* Contemporary Theatrical Dance.]

BIBLIOGRAPHY

Brown, Estelle T. "Toward a Structuralist Approach to Ballet: *Swan Lake* and *The White-Haired Girl.*" *Western Humanities Review* 32 (Summer 1978): 227–240.
Chang Keng. "My Recollection of the Production and First Performances of *The White-Haired Girl.*" *Chinese Literature,* no. 9 (1977): 99–105.
Chiang Ling-chih et al. "Comments on the Ballet *The White-Haired Girl.*" *Chinese Literature,* no. 8 (1966): 133–140.
Ho Ching-chih. "How *The White-Haired Girl* Was Written and Produced." *Chinese Literature,* no. 2 (1953): 110–114.
Li Hsi-fan. "An Artistic Gem Born in the Class Struggle." *China Reconstructs* 16 (September 1967): 39–43.

Snow, Lois Wheeler. *China on Stage*. New York, 1972.
Strauss, Gloria B. "Dance and Ideology in China, Past and Present: A Study of Ballet in the People's Republic." *CORD Research Annual* 8 (1977): 19–53.
Wan Kung. "How Our Revolutionary Operas and Ballets Were Produced." *Chinese Literature*, no. 5–6 (1977): 66–72.
Wan Kung. "What Chiang Ching Did to Culture." *China Reconstructs* 26 (May 1977): 2–6.
Yu Lu-yuan. "The Revolutionary Ballet *The White-Haired Girl*." *Chinese Literature*, no. 8 (1965): 117–132.

ZHU LIREN

WHITMAN SISTERS. A family of multitalented entertainers who owned and produced their own traveling show that played major U.S. cities from 1900 to 1943, the Whitman Sisters were one of the most popular acts in black vaudeville and one of the longest-running and highest-paid acts on the Theater Owners Booking Association (TOBA) circuit. **Mabel Whitman** (died 1942), the eldest, was a singer who also handled bookings and managed the company. **Essie Whitman** (born 1881, died 7 May 1963) was a singer and comedian who designed and made costumes. **Alberta Whitman** (died 1963) was a singer, dancer, and comedian who composed music and acted as financial secretary. "Baby" **Alice Whitman** (died 1969), a singer and versatile dancer, was the show's dancing star.

From a very young age the sisters performed at church socials at the African Methodist Episcopal Church in Lawrence, Kansas, where their father was bishop of the AME Church. Essie sang jubilee songs; Mabel and Alberta played the piano. After moving to Atlanta, Georgia, where the Reverend Whitman served as dean at Morris Brown College, baby sister Alice won amateur cakewalking contests. Inspired by the enthusiastic local reception to their musical talent, Mabel and Essie formed an act and toured abroad with their mother as chaperon. Alberta joined them on their return, and in 1904 they organized themselves as the Whitman Sisters' New Orleans Troubadours. Mabel, as organizer of the group, became the first black woman to manage and continuously book her own company in leading southern houses. In 1910, Mabel organized her own show, Mabel Whitman and the Dixie Boys, which toured Germany and Australia. On her return, Alice joined the company and the Whitman Sisters were reorganized as a road show featuring all four sisters. Mabel would soon retire from the stage to manage the company.

The sisters' fast-paced show, based on a variety format of songs, dances, and comedy skits, included a cast of twenty to thirty performers, a chorus of twelve to fourteen girls, and a five- or six-piece jazz band. Alberta, or "Bert," could stop the show by patting and stamping out a Charleston rhythm for the chorus or by dancing a flashy, high-kicking strut. She cut her hair short and dressed as a man to become one of the best male impersonators in vaudeville. Essie, who excelled as a comedian in a drunk act, became famous for belting out "Some of These Days" in a resonant contralto voice that could be heard at the last row of the theater. Alice, billed as the "Queen of Taps," sang and danced tap versions of such popular black social dances as Ballin' the Jack, Walkin' the Dog, Sand, and the Shim-Sham-Shimmy. Admired for her clean, clear taps, she was considered the best female tap dancer of the 1920s. Alice married tap dancer Aaron Palmer, and their son became the last member of the family to join the show. Billed as Albert ("Pops") Whitman (1919–1950), he became a notable acrobatic tap dancer who performed cartwheels, spins, flips, and splits to swinging rhythms.

The Whitmans are considered the greatest incubators of dancing talent in black vaudeville because they gave dozens of tap dancers their first professional break into show business. Bill Robinson, Maxie McCree, Jack Wiggins, Eddie Rector, Leonard Reed, the Berry Brothers, and the legendary dancer Groundhog all served an apprenticeship with the Whitman Sisters, whose show was built on the strength of its dancing talent.

[*See also* Tap Dance.]

BIBLIOGRAPHY

Millstein, Gilbert. "Harlem Stompers." *New York World Telegram Week-End Magazine* (23 January 1937): 3.
Stearns, Marshall, and Jean Stearns. *Jazz Dance: The Story of American Vernacular Dance*. Rev. ed. New York, 1994.

CONSTANCE VALIS HILL

WIESENTHAL, GRETE (born 9 December 1885 in Vienna, died 22 June 1970 in Vienna), Austrian dancer and choreographer. Grete Wiesenthal, the daughter of the painter Franz Wiesenthal, entered the ballet school of the Vienna Hofoperntheater in 1895. After studying with Karoline Ellend, Eduard Voitus van Hamme, and Camilla Pagliero, she was accepted into the corps de ballet of the Vienna Court Opera in 1901. Matilda Kshessinska's guest performance at the Opera in 1903 spurred Wiesenthal to undertake additional studies in classical ballet with Carl Raimund. With improved technique, she was promoted to *coryphée* in 1905.

Her slender body set Wiesenthal apart from the other dancers of the Court Opera Ballet; in addition, her alert mind, interest in art history, and above all her extraordinary musicality soon led her to recognize the limits of that context. She was particularly disturbed by the lack of connection between music and choreography. "It was only a hop, skip, and jump in time to the beat, without feeling and without any idea of the music," she later wrote in her book *Der Aufstieg* (The Ascent; 1919). During this period the prime movers of American modern dance were making guest appearances in Vienna (Loie Fuller in 1898; Isadora Duncan in 1902, 1903, and 1904; Maud Allan in

1903 and 1906; and Ruth St. Denis in 1907 and 1908), but they did not provide Wiesenthal the impetus to carve out her own career.

The dancer and her sister Elsa (1887–1967), also a *coryphée* at the Court Opera Ballet, were members of the artist's alliance known as the Viennese Secession, the imagery of which may have anticipated Grete Wiesenthal's dance style. Both sisters were eager to make their own way, and an occasion soon presented itself. Gustav Mahler, in 1907, his last year as director of the Court Opera, chose Grete Wiesenthal to dance the coveted role of Fenella in Daniel Auber's opera *Die Stumme von Portici.* Subsequently the director, ballet master Josef Hassreiter, and Wiesenthal clashed, and she departed. In the spring of the same year she gave her first private program. Already in 1904 she had choreographed a dance to Chopin's Waltzes in D-flat Major; it may be more than a coincidence that Isadora Duncan had performed her Chopin program in Vienna the same year. To this program Wiesenthal added two Beethoven pieces and the Johann Strauss waltzes "By the Beautiful Blue Danube" and "Roses from the South" (the latter choreographed as a solo for Elsa Wiesenthal). This program became the core of one given at the Wiener Werkstätte cabaret, Die Fledermaus, on 14 January 1908 by Grete and her sisters Elsa and Berta, with piano accompaniment by Gertrud, another sister. The Viennese, usually not open to new developments, immediately applauded the new style of dance, which departed radically from that of the Court Opera; it was perhaps not viewed as revolutionary solely because it was in three-quarter time.

With her interpretations Wiesenthal effected a congenial transformation of the Viennese waltz into theatrical dance. The waltz was now more than the monotonous "one–two–three" done on pointe by fixedly smiling dancers laced into corsets. For Wiesenthal, waltzes were a kind of ecstasy; with unbound hair and swinging dress, she danced with a flow of movement that seemed eternal. A multiplicity of the waltz's aspects were made visible in the choreography. Waltzing was bliss, but it was also dark suspicion and even menace—an aspect of the waltz that George Balanchine was later to embody in his choreography. The waltz had now ceased to be a couple dance in which the female partner was lifted into the air on a specific beat. It became an individual giving of the self, in which stresses could be indicated even with the fists. Small or large groups moved across a gigantic stage. Waltzing became expression and development of the individual personality.

The Wiesenthal sisters soon ended their successful program at Die Fledermaus and, on the recommendation of Hugo von Hofmannsthal, turned to Max Reinhardt in Berlin. He immediately incorporated the sisters into a production and gave them an opportunity to present their program to Berliners. In addition to their dance evenings, Grete Wiesenthal, who separated from her sisters in 1910, participated in pantomimes, a genre that Reinhardt subsequently cultivated, with great popular success.

Immediately after her Berlin debut, Wiesenthal began doing guest performances. In 1908 she danced in Russia and then in the Austrian provinces. In September 1909 she made her debut in the London Hippodrome and then in the Théâtre de la Vaudeville in Paris. In 1910 she designed the movements for Reinhardt's *Sumurûn* in Berlin, in which she danced the title role. In 1912 she danced for the first time in New York. In the same year she created the role of the Kitchen Boy in Reinhardt's Stuttgart production of *Der Bürger Edelmann.* She also signed a contract with Serge Diaghilev for 1913, which she was unable to fulfill for reasons of health. She played in the 1913 film *Das fremde Mädchen,* based on a pantomime by Hugo von Hofmannsthal, which had premiered in Berlin in 1911.

WIESENTHAL. Grete Wiesenthal in her joyful "Frühlingsstimmenwalzer" (Voices of Spring Waltz). This soft-focus photograph was meticulously retouched to bring out the details of Wiesenthal's features and her unusual feathered costume. (Photograph by Rudolf Jobst; reprinted from Fritz Klingenbeck, *Unsterblicher Walzer: Die Geschichte des deutschen Nationaltanzes,* Vienna, 1940, plate 51.)

Even during World War I Wiesenthal maintained her guest appearances. She danced for the most part alone, in small genre scenes with one partner, or in small pantomime ensembles. By 1919, when she founded her first school in her native city, she had become a Viennese institution. In the dancers Willy Godlewski and Anton Birkmeyer she found partners who adapted to her style of dance; she toured all of Europe with Birkmeyer. During the 1920s she did her first work for the Salzburg Festival and also worked with Reinhardt in Berlin. Her integrated ballet interludes in Reinhardt's 1929 production of *Die Fledermaus* became famous. Wiesenthal's choreography was danced in every subsequent staging of this opera; it was revised in 1942 by George Balanchine as *Rosalinda* for performances by the New Opera Company in New York.

In 1930 Wiesenthal returned to the Vienna State Opera with her choreography for the premiere of the ballet *Der Taugenichts in Wien,* based on Joseph von Eichendorff's novel and with music by Franz Salmhofer. After a guest appearance with Willy Fränzl in the United States in 1933, in 1934 Wiesenthal agreed to lead a master class at the Academy of Music and Performing Art in Vienna. In 1938 a dance department was established at the academy. In 1945 Wiesenthal became the director of the department, a post she held until 1951. Her assistant, Maria Josefa Schaffgotsch, taught the Wiesenthal technique in the department until 1972. Even during World War II the academy had a chamber dance group that danced Wiesenthal's works almost exclusively. Its most important members included Hertha Gindl, Lia Werner, and Grete Sellier. Lisl Temple was another important interpreter of the Wiesenthal style during this period. The Grete Wiesenthal Dance Group, established in 1945, existed until 1956 and appeared as guest artists in Europe and overseas; its most important members were Vilma Kostka and Erika Kniza. Since 1977 these two have repeatedly staged Wiesenthal dances for the Vienna State Opera Ballet. Elements of Grete Wiesenthal's dance style also survive in the waltz choreographies of Dia Luca and Gerhard Senft for the Vienna Folk Opera.

BIBLIOGRAPHY

Fiedler, Leonhard M., and Martin Lang, eds. *Grete Wiesenthal: Die Schönheit der Sprache des Körpers im Tanz.* Salzburg, 1985.

Huber-Wiesenthal, Rudolf. *Die Schwestern Wiesenthal.* Vienna, 1934.

Prenner, Ingeborg. "Grete Wiesenthal: Begründerin eines neuen Tanzstils." Ph.D. diss., 1950.

Wiesenthal, Grete. *Der Aufstieg.* Berlin, 1919.

Wiesenthal, Grete. *Der ersten Schritte.* Vienna, 1947.

Witzmann, Reingard. *Die neue Körpersprache: Grete Wiesenthal und ihr Tanz.* Vienna, 1985. Exhibition catalog, Historisches Museum der Stadt Wien.

GUNHILD OBERZAUCHER-SCHÜLLER
Translated from German

WIESENTHAL TECHNIQUE. In developing her revolutionary dance technique, Grete Wiesenthal (1885–1970) was not influenced, as so many of her contemporaries were, by gymnastics, Greek culture, or folk dance, but rather by her feeling for the ecstatic, her musicality, and her childhood ballet training. Designed for female dancers (men function only as partners), the Wiesenthal technique can only be mastered from a foundation of classical training.

Wiesenthal's primary goal was to overcome the static quality of classical ballet and to dissolve all traces of posing in an endless flow of movement. She specialized in translating into dance the flowing, wavelike quality of 3/4 time as embodied in Strauss waltzes.

Wiesenthal technique comprises four areas of instruction: ballet exercises, waltz movements, turns, and leaps. In class the dancers wear sandals or soft ballet shoes.

Exercises in both balance and waltzing begin with warmup at the *barre.* Balance exercises involve slow lifts from *demi-plié* to *demi-pointe,* with torso, head, and arms inclined forward; the face followed the movement. In Wiesenthal waltz movements, the torso extends horizontally, parallel to the floor. A typical Wiesenthal turn begins from a deep bend, with head and arms hanging down; in a dynamic rising movement, the head and arms unfold upward and the dancer swings out, reaching an explosive high point. The gaze must not be fixed. Wiesenthal used this turn to unforgettable effect in "Acceleration Waltz." Another kind of turn is performed with slightly bent knees, feet parallel and on *demi-pointe,* pelvis pushed forward, and upper torso bent backward; the turn is performed slowly and with a slide. In a turn to the right, the right foot must bear most of the weight while the left slides along lightly, in an action similar to skiing.

Wiesenthal also worked out a foot technique for small, quick, sliding leaps. It requires training in classical leaps, with modifications in style and stance. Photographs show Wiesenthal in her characteristic high leaps with knees drawn in, a position she also adopted for turns. She taught these refinements only to her leading dancers.

Effortlessness, flying and swinging movement, rapture, and the capacity to be deeply moved by music were the characteristics of Grete Wiesenthal. With her technique she succeeded in integrating these into a system that could be transmitted to later generations.

BIBLIOGRAPHY

Fiedler, Leonhard M., and Martin Lang, eds. *Grete Wiesenthal: Die Schönheit der Sprache des Körpers im Tanz.* Salzburg, 1985.

Wiesenthal, Grete. *Der ersten Schritte.* Vienna, 1947.

MARIA JOSEFA SCHAFFGOTSCH
Translated from German

WIGMAN, MARY (Marie Wiegmann; born 13 November 1886 in Hanover, died 18 September 1973 in West Berlin), German modern dance pioneer. Wigman was the eldest daughter of Amalie and Heinrich Wiegmann, a prosperous merchant in Hanover. The Wiegmanns had one son, also named Heinrich, and a second daughter, Elisabeth. When Mary was nine, her father died; her mother subsequently married her husband's twin brother and business partner.

Mary attended a private girls' school and studied piano at the Hanover Conservatory. When the school director suggested that Mary enroll in the first girls' gymnasium opening in Hanover, her mother and stepfather, appalled at the thought of their daughter becoming a bluestocking, decided to send her to an English boarding school instead.

After her sojourn abroad, Mary returned to Hanover, but the glimpse of a larger world now made her feel estranged from her peers. She took up singing, but when her teacher encouraged her to seriously pursue a musical career, her parents opposed the idea. Restless, she traveled to Switzerland and Holland, became engaged, and broke the engagement, resisting her family's wishes that she marry and settle into a bourgeois life. She was "seeking," as she later wrote; seeing performances by Dalcroze students in Amsterdam and by the Wiesenthal sisters in Hanover inspired her to become a dancer.

Wigman went to the Dalcroze School in Hellerau in 1910, the year the school opened. She was almost twenty-four years old and had had little previous dance training. This was not as unusual as it may appear, for during Wigman's childhood dance was not considered an art; it was not until the early 1900s that dance experienced a revival in Germany. Enthusiastic audiences applauded guest artists Isadora Duncan, Ruth St. Denis, and Anna Pavlova as well as the Wiesenthal sisters, Clothilde von Derp, and Gertrud Louis Leistikov. Critics debated whether dance reform should proceed along the lines of "natural" or "artificial" dancing. They argued their contrary visions of dance in a spate of books on dance history and aesthetics. This theoretical orientation remained characteristic of German dance during the years of the Weimar Republic (1919–1933).

Wigman remained at the Dalcroze School for two years and earned her teacher's certificate there. She later credited Émile Jaques-Dalcroze with little influence on her work, reserving praise for her subsequent teacher Rudolf Laban. Yet Dalcroze's teaching was Wigman's first exposure to the idea that dance does not necessarily involve predetermined steps and traditional forms; it can arise from the correspondence of gesture and an internalized sense of motion based on the rhythms of music.

Wigman learned of Laban through Suzanne Perrottet, an assistant teacher at the Dalcroze School, and through Emil Nolde, an expressionist painter. Visiting Hellerau, Nolde saw Wigman improvising and remarked that he knew a man who "dances as you do—without music." In the summer of 1913, Wigman went to Ascona, a retreat in the Swiss Alps, where Laban and his students lived communally and experimented with new ways of dancing. During this summer, the Dalcroze School asked Wigman to open a branch of the school in Berlin, but with Laban's encouragement Wigman turned down the offer, deciding to try the more uncertain career of stage dancer.

In the fall, Wigman followed Laban back to Munich to work with him there; when he fell ill, she took over his teaching for him. In the spring of 1914, for the first time, Wigman publicly presented her own compositions on a program at the Laban School. That summer of 1914, Laban and Wigman returned to Ascona for another workshop; when World War I broke out in August, the Hungarian-born Laban was stranded, and Wigman stayed with him. With few students to teach, Laban turned to work on his notation system, using Wigman as the instrument on which to test his ideas. Wigman had become not only Laban's colleague but also a collaborator.

Laban was Wigman's pedagogical model throughout her long teaching career. She adopted Laban's way of freeing students to discover their own movement through improvisation. Like Laban, Wigman based her training on gymnastics, believing that the student needed strength and flexibility to discover an individual style of movement. Like Laban, Wigman stressed the conceptual awareness demanded by dancing, an understanding of the dynamics of tension and relaxation and of the rhythms of movement through space.

Wigman was also influenced philosophically by Laban. The concept of dance as a language, as an organic unity of physical and spiritual forces, as an autonomous system with laws of its own—ideas first articulated by Laban—formed the basis of Wigman's aesthetics. Laban taught Wigman to appreciate the spatial dimension of movement as a realm independent of musical motion with a harmonic of its own. In emphasizing the spatial dimension of movement, Laban necessarily deemphasized the temporal dimension most closely akin to music, the area of Dalcroze's researches. This corresponded to Wigman's own proclivities; she later remarked that her intuitive creative work often led to discoveries paralleling Laban's theory.

Although Laban gave Wigman ways of thinking about and working with movement, he did not pass on specific structures for performance. Perhaps Wigman's first models for performance structure were the dances she and Laban saw at the Dada Gallery in Zurich in spring 1917. There, some of the dancers associated with Laban—Sophie Taeuber, Claire Walther, and Suzanne Perrottet—collaborated with Hugo Ball, Tristan Tzara, and other Dadaists in evenings of songs, dramatic sketches, and dances. The dancers were often masked and moved to the sound of a gong or a drum or in silence; the idea of the dance was primary, and all other elements—costume, scenery, music—were subordinated to it. This form seems to be the germ for the dances Wigman later evolved.

Wigman spent 1918 in solitary retreat in the Swiss mountains. She had stayed with Laban until she felt she had enough technical training to transform her body into an instrument of her creative process; like Isadora Duncan, Wigman felt compelled to create a new dance language on her own body. Having no dancers' bodies to mirror her creative process, Wigman took sole responsibility for the fusion of subjective and objective responses in the making of a dance. A special intensity marked her solos, which sprang from an inner tension. When dancing, Wigman appeared transfixed by an inner dialogue of unconscious inventing and conscious ordering.

At the end of her year of retreat, Wigman was ready to perform her dances for the public. It was at this point that she adopted the Anglicized version of her surname. Assisted by the Swiss dancer Berthe Trümpy, Wigman prepared a solo program to perform in Switzerland during the winter and spring of 1919 and then toured Germany with the program the following winter. Her first program included the solo cycles: *Dances of Night; Four Hungarian Dances* (based on Brahms); *Dance Songs,* comprising the solos "Marche Orientale," "Yaravi," and "Scherzo"; and *Ecstatic Dances,* comprising "Prayer," "Sacrifice," "Idolatry," and "Temple Dance."

The subjects of these early solos show Wigman striving toward an approach of her own. Cycles like *Four Hungarian Dances,* based on Romantic-era music, as were many Duncanesque dances, and *Dance Songs,* suggesting the pastiche of Oriental dance seen in exotic dances of the time, soon dropped out of her repertory. Increasingly, Wigman turned in the direction of *Ecstatic Dances,* where, rather than imitating religious dances of other cultures, as Ruth St. Denis often did, Wigman objectified spiritual experience without explicit reference to exotic traditions. Infused with Laban's ideas on the mystical connection between the dancer and the cosmos, Wigman continued to create dances in which "the personal life experience of the choreographer yields to the dance visualization of the incomprehensible and eternal" (Wigman, 1975, p. 93).

Within a short time Wigman found an approach of her own. She danced to silence or to a percussive accompaniment scored by Will Goetze, who joined her in 1921 as piano accompanist and composer. Wigman and Goetze collaborated in creating scores; during rehearsal Goetze would improvise accompaniment on various drums and a Javanese gong as Wigman danced, then later would set and notate the piece for performance.

Building on *Ecstatic Dances,* Wigman soon created mature works exemplifying her spiritual vision, such as the solos *Witch Dance* (1926) and *Monotony Whirl* (1926). In *Witch Dance,* the masked Wigman began by sitting on the floor. Convulsive jerks synchronized with percussive sounds from offstage animated her torso; it was impossible to tell whether the masked figure's movement created the sound or the sound impelled the movement. At one point the figure relaxed forward as the accompaniment of drum, gongs, and cymbals died away, and the energy of the dance seemed exhausted; but the figure came to life, swung itself to standing, then moved in circles, looming large in the space. Finally the figure sank back to the floor, but this time with its masked face staring out at the audience. In this dance Wigman did not impersonate a witch; she exemplified a spiritual state of demonism.

WIGMAN. An undated studio portrait of Wigman in "Song of Destiny" from her cycle *Dance Songs* (1919). (Photograph by Charlotte Rudolph; from the Dance Collection, New York Public Library for the Performing Arts.)

Similarly in *Monotony Whirl,* Wigman did more than

impersonate a whirling dervish, although this was certainly one level of association, since the dance comprised nothing but seven minutes of spinning onstage. Watching the repeated motion, the spectator could sense stillness at its center and could interpret the dance as the exemplification of the state of acting yet not acting, of being acted upon by a greater force. Like *Witch Dance, Monotony Whirl* built to several peaks of energetic motion, spinning faster and faster before subsiding; the dance ended as Wigman reached high into space and then collapsed.

Witch Dance and *Monotony Whirl* display a mode of dance that realized the theoretical ideal of the German dance movement in the early 1920s. In 1923, Laban had defined this ideal before an audience of philosophers as *Eigenkunst,* dance as "its own art"; the exemplary genre for *Eigenkunst* became dance in silence. Laban described the two-stage historical process leading to the new art: first, the rejection of ballet and dance as narrative; then, the rejection of Duncanesque dancing and music as compositional structure. Laban interpreted Wigman's dance as the exemplar of a third stage, dance discovering its own terms of expression.

Wigman ensured the independence of dance by emphasizing the spatial dimension of movement. Space became an active element in Wigman's solos; her body moved between the extremes of struggling against and giving into space. Wigman gave dramatic expression to her solo encounters with space by projecting the inner dialogue of composition in spatial terms.

Wigman achieved this mode of expressive yet absolute dance by focusing each solo around one basic movement motif and associated image, its theme. Wigman wrote that during the process of choreographing, the theme often took on a life of its own and imposed its own laws. In other words, Wigman built each dance from a motif specific to that dance rather than selecting motifs from a set vocabulary. She never codified a vocabulary, although she had a distinctive approach.

Characteristic of Wigman's approach was the cycle format, the arrangement of solos, each concentrated around a single theme, into a greater thematic whole. This format, apparent from the time of Wigman's first German tour, allowed for flexibility in building her repertory, for solos from a cycle could be presented alone or in the context of part or the whole of a cycle. To create *Witch Dance,* Wigman reworked a dance presented in 1914 at the Laban School as one solo in the *Visions* cycle (1925–1928); she then could perform *Witch Dance* either alone or in tandem with other dances from the cycle. Two years after creating *Monotony Whirl* as part of a two-dance cycle, Wigman incorporated it in the group work *Celebration* (1927–1928); once *Celebration* passed out of her repertory, Wigman still performed *Monotony Whirl* as a solo.

The cycle format reinforced other formal characteristics of Wigman's solo work. Solos arranged in a cycle displayed a series of beginnings and endings; these repeated starts and stops supported the extremes of energy marking Wigman's style. Drives toward a climax followed by a collapse often occurred; also common was the alternation of active states with periods of stillness that imperceptibly renewed the dancer's action. The arrangement of several themes into a greater whole emphasized two further structural principles in Wigman's dances: the juxtaposition of contrasting moods and movement qualities, and the recurrence of the opening image as the ending.

Wigman did not realize the possibilities of the cycle format all at once. Not until the late 1920s did she create cycles so tightly unified by interconnections from solo to solo that she could not perform the solos separately without significant loss of meaning. *Shifting Landscape* (1929) moved from an opening "Invocation" to a worshipful "Seraphic Song," then shifted to the darker mood of "Face of Night" before returning to the lighter tone of the opening, though now made more lively, in "Pastoral," "Festive Rhythm," and "Dance of Summer." "Storm Song," in which Wigman both experienced and embodied the storm, ends the idyll with a recall of the darker mood of "Face of Night."

Sacrifice (1931) reversed the pattern of light and dark presented in *Shifting Landscape.* The opening "Song of the Sword" set the note of struggle that dominated the work, then gave way to its antithesis in "Dance for the Sun"; one critic described the movement as going from the masculine to the feminine. The controlling motif of the cycle came to the fore in "Death Call," in which Wigman embodied both the force of death calling the living and the force of life resisting the call. In the following "Dance for the Earth," Wigman became a creature of nature, no longer a participant in ultimate human struggles; the critic likened this section to a Greek satyr play. "Lament" anticipated the end with a diagonal motion that became the dominant image of the final "Dance into Death." In her final solo, Wigman rushed down the diagonal against a presence that forced her to the floor, then rose and fell again, resigned to the presence.

Beyond noting the greater unity of the cycle format in *Shifting Landscape* and *Sacrifice,* critics detected a shift in the style of Wigman's solos from the early to the late 1920s. According to critic Rudolf Maack, Wigman's early dances explored pure form as a way of controlling an overflow of expressiveness, and her later dances explored the tension and reconciliation of pure form and expressiveness. Maack interpreted Wigman's early dances as the last wave of expressionism in German art and her later dances as moving toward classicism, paralleling the movement toward classicism in the other German arts.

It is clear that Maack considered Wigman's solos serious works of art. Her group works, however, received more ambivalent critical response. While some critics praised her group dances as the culmination of her art, other critics were disappointed that Wigman's group works did not achieve the heights of her solo works.

Once Wigman opened her school in Dresden in 1920 with Berthe Trümpy as codirector, a group of highly talented students gathered there, many of whom became leading dancers of their generation: Yvonne Georgi, Harald Kreutzberg, Gret Palucca, Vera Skoronel, Max Terpis. Within a few years these dancers had all left to take up positions elsewhere, mostly in opera houses. Other students left in order to open their own schools. Dance enjoyed a widespread popularity during the 1920s, which would have been unimaginable before World War I. In 1926, Trümpy decided to open her own school in Berlin, so Wigman's sister Elisabeth became codirector of the Dresden school. By 1925, Wigman's second performing group grew to about twenty dancers, including Hanya Holm, who became Wigman's assistant. This group disbanded three years later, and thereafter Wigman created new groups from among her students as needed.

Without a stable ensemble of dancers Wigman could not build a repertory to encompass works from a period of years, so her performance repertory comprised mostly current works. Usually, Wigman toured in the fall with new solos she had created the previous summer and then rehearsed a new group work to perform on tour in the spring. The group traveled as lightly as possible: black curtains to surround whichever stage they used; costumes with simple geometric lines, often made of rich satins and brocades; and an assortment of percussion instruments. Wigman's aesthetic of dance as an independent art had a practical as well as a philosophic basis. Like the Dadaists in 1917, Wigman turned necessity into art.

WIGMAN. Wearing a mask, Wigman appeared in a solo in her group work *Dance of Death* (1926). (Photograph from the Archiv der Akademie der Künste, Berlin; courtesy of Susan A. Manning.)

Wigman's first full-scale group work, *The Seven Dances of Life* (1921), was set to a score by Heinz Pringsheim that had been commissioned by Hans Niedecken-Gebhard, a director interested in revitalizing opera by emphasizing its dance elements. Here, Wigman set a cycle of solos for herself within the framework of an overall narrative of a dancer performing for a king (represented by an effigy on stage) who promised to free her if she can dance the meaning of life. The dancer appears to have failed: a demon speaks out of the darkness and four girls bring a black veil of death; but in the final "Dance of Life" Wigman returned in a golden garment and beckoned the girls to dance with her.

Wigman's next full-scale group work, *Scenes from a Dance Drama* (1923–1924), abandoned the explicit narrative frame in favor of a series of variations entitled with abstractions such as "Circle," "Chaos," and Vision." The changing relationship of the leader to the group became the central theme in this and in many later group dances. *A Dance Fairy Tale* (1925) burlesqued this theme, when Wigman, costumed as a black magician, transformed three girls into flowers and worked other wonders in a world of fantasy. The comic-grotesque costumes that distorted the dancers' shapes recalled Oskar Schlemmer's *Triadic Ballet,* which had premiered three years earlier.

Dance of Death (1926) returned to Wigman's preoccupation with the forces of life and death. Here, life did not emerge as the clearcut victor in the struggle. Wigman, the only dancer not masked, stood between a beastlike figure of death and the group of creatures the figure commanded.

Celebration (1927–1928), Wigman's last work for her dance group of the 1920s, moved away from dramatic images and toward a structure comparable to symphonic music, a movement anticipated by *Hymns in Space* (1926). In *Celebration,* the dance images themselves made the analogy between the structures of pure dance and music, as dancers entered in procession playing musical instruments. The work was created for the Second Dancers' Congress in Essen, for an audience of peers rather than for a wider public. At the congress Wigman announced

WIGMAN. Pictured here with members of her group, Wigman appears at center in "The Prophetess," the fifth section of her *Women's Dances* (1934). (Photograph from the Dance Collection, New York Public Library for the Performing Arts.)

that her dance group was disbanding because of financial difficulties.

Wigman next turned to another form of dance created among peers, the movement choir, a dance activity for a large group of nonprofessionals, first developed by Laban. In 1929, Wigman created three studies in choric movement for her students at the Dresden School. For the 1930 Third Dancers' Congress in Munich, she integrated choric movement into a theatrical spectacle to create *Totenmal,* based on a poem and musical composition by Albert Talhoff. The theme of the dance of death recurred, but it was given more explicit reference than it had in *Dance of Death;* here, the dead were the fallen soldiers of World War I, and the chorus that called them was the women they had left behind.

Totenmal disappointed the audience of dancers at the congress, an ironic response since many of the dancers at the 1928 congress had called for dance to realign itself with the theater. At that previous congress, Wigman had described her vision of a new form of theater based on dance, and *Totenmal* was her attempt to realize that vision.

Wigman's redefinition of her aesthetic ideal around 1930 recalled her earlier collaborations with theater artists. In the early 1920s, Wigman had choreographed *A Midsummer Night's Dream* for expressionist director Berthold Viertel's production at the Berlin Schauspielhaus. During the same period, she choreographed the dance interludes for the premier of Hans Pfitzner's opera *The Rose from the Garden of Love* in Hanover. After World War II, Wigman continued her work in choric and theatrical choreography.

Wigman's aesthetic shifted significantly under the impact of National Socialism (Nazism), which became Germany's ruling political party in 1933 under the leadership of Adolf Hitler. Like many other dancers, Wigman initially embraced the new aesthetic of art arising from the so-called spirit of the Aryan race, as evidenced in her essays collected in *German Dance Art* (1935). Her one involvement with Nazi spectacle came with *Olympic Youth,* a pageant staged in connection with the opening of the Berlin Olympic Games in 1936. Ten thousand young people executed choreography contributed by Wigman, Palucca, Kreutzberg, and other dancers. Like the Nazi-sponsored dance festivals of 1934, 1935, and 1936, *Olympic Youth* was a showpiece contrived for impressionable spectators. Rather than promoting experimental work, the National Socialist spectacles glorified the Germanic past.

Wigman's group dances created in the early 1930s and her solos prior to her farewell performance in 1942 reflect the new Germanic mood of retrospection. They seem to be pastiches of earlier works rather than new works. The group cycle *Women's Dances* (1934) picks up the earlier *Witch Dance* as well as the motif of mourning women from *Totenmal. Autumnal Dances* (1937), a solo cycle, picks up the images of nature from *Shifting Landscape.* Hanns Hasting, who had replaced Will Goetze as Wigman's accompanist and composer in 1929, wrote the music for these works.

Wigman did little touring outside of central Europe, with the exception of three extended and well-received tours of the United States in the 1930/31, 1931/32, and 1932/33 seasons. Wigman's repertory for the first of these, which was limited to the East Coast, included solos from the *Shifting Landscape* cycle, *Witch Dance, Monotony Whirl,* and several newly composed solos. The second U.S. tour, which took in all parts of the country, included the cycle *Sacrifice,* which Wigman created in response to seeing Niagara Falls, just as *Shifting Landscape* had been created in response to an earlier trip to France. On the third U.S. tour, Wigman brought along a group of twelve dancers in a cycle created for the occasion, *The Way.*

Sponsored by Sol Hurok, Wigman's tours created a sensation among U.S. dancers and critics; for the most part, American spectators interpreted Wigman in terms of the evolution of American modern dance; they saw her as the transitional artist between the solo genius of Isadora Duncan and the early Martha Graham and Doris Humphrey. They regarded Wigman as representing the theoretical ideal of dance as an absolute art; they had had no way of seeing the changes in Wigman's work over the years or of understanding how much she had in common with her German contemporaries. With Hurok's support, Wigman's assistant Hanya Holm stayed in New York City to open a branch of the Wigman School and reinterpret Wigman's approach for American dancers.

After 1936, Wigman received no further commissions for group works from the National Socialist party, although she continued to tour her solo programs with official support. In 1942, she gave her farewell concert and sold her school. She then moved to Leipzig, where she continued to teach through the last years and aftermath of World War II. In 1949, she moved to West Berlin and reopened her school there.

In the 1950s, Wigman staged operas at the National Theater in Mannheim as well as dance performances of *The Rite of Spring* and *Orpheus and Eurydice* in Berlin. No longer creating solos for herself, Wigman continued her work in choric theater. That Wigman now worked in the opera house says much about the changed conditions of dance in postwar Germany, since the modern dance movement was over, at least for a time. In the immediate

WIGMAN. "Men's Dance" *(below)* and "Mysterious Circle" *(opposite)*, two dances from Wigman's *Rite of Spring* (1957), set to the Stravinsky score. (Photographs by Siegfried Enkelmann; from the Dance Collection, New York Public Library for the Performing Arts.)

postwar years, German dance moved in the direction of modern ballet. Only in the 1970s did a new form of modern dance emerge that went under the rubric of *Tanztheater.* The movement was inspired in part by the teaching of "survivors" from the pioneering interwar period, including Wigman herself.

Wigman shared many concerns with her generation of dancers, who built the German modern dance movement of the 1920s. They were concerned with ideas as the controlling impulse of dance; with an expressive yet absolute mode midway between narrative and abstraction; with space as an active presence in dance; with the mask and costume as transformers for the human self; and with the theme of the dance of death.

Wigman had worked more intently and had pushed her work further than did other dancers of her generation. While during the Weimar years other dancers tended either to remain touring soloists or to become ballet directors, Wigman attempted the range of choreographic forms—from solo to group to choric to stage choreography. While other dancers turned to ballet as a necessary support for theatrical dance, Wigman resisted, sustaining a vision of modern dance as a fusion of the dancer's subjective and objective responses to the times. She did not resist the allure of National Socialist aesthetics. She presented, in dance terms, the spirit of her time and place, wavering as that spirit became transformed. Although difficult for us to accept, this fact testifies to her ability to sense and utilize the currents of her time.

[*See also* Artists and Dance, *article on* Artists and Dance, 1760–1929; Ausdruckstanz; Germany, *article on* Theatrical Dance, 1600–1945; Movement Choir; *and the entry on Laban.*]

BIBLIOGRAPHY

Bach, Rudolf, ed. *Das Mary Wigman-Werk.* Dresden, 1933.

Delius, Rudolf von. *Mary Wigman.* Dresden, 1925.

Howe, Dianne S. "The Notion of Mysticism in the Philosophy and Choreography of Mary Wigman, 1914–1931." *Dance Research Journal* 19 (Summer 1987): 19–24.

Howe, Dianne S. "Parallel Visions: Mary Wigman and the German Expressionists." In *Dance: Current Selected Research,* vol. 1, edited by Lynnette Y. Overby and James H. Humphrey. New York, 1989.

Kaut, Marion. "Lebensmoster Mary Wigman: Die Suche nach der verloren n welt." *Tanzdrama* 25 (1994): 14–19, 25 (1995): 16–19.

Linder, Kurt. *Die Verwandlungen der Mary Wigman.* Freiburg im Breisgau, 1929.
Maletić, Vera. "Wigman and Laban: The Interplay of Theory and Practice." *Ballet Review* 14 (Fall 1986): 86–95.
Manning, Susan A. *Ecstasy and the Demon: Feminism and Nationalism in the Dances of Mary Wigman.* Berkeley, 1993.
Müller, Hedwig. "At the Start of a New Era: Tenth Anniversary of the Death of Mary Wigman." *Ballett International* 6 (December 1983): 6–13.
Müller, Hedwig. *Mary Wigman: Leben und Werk der grossen Tänzerin.* Weinheim, 1986.
Müller, Hedwig. "Wigman and National Socialism." *Ballet Review* 15 (Spring 1987): 65–73.
Odom, Selma Landen. "Wigman at Hellerau." *Ballet Review* 14 (Summer 1986): 41–53.
Toepfer, Karl. "Speech and Sexual Difference in Mary Wigman's Dance Aesthetic." In *Gender in Performance,* edited by Laurence Senelick. Hanover, N.H., 1992.
Wigman, Mary. *Deutsche Tanzkunst.* Dresden, 1935.
Wigman, Mary. *The Language of Dance.* Translated by Walter Sorell. Middletown, Conn., 1966.
Wigman, Mary. *The Mary Wigman Book.* Translated and edited by Walter Sorell. Middletown, Conn., 1975.

FILM: Allegra Fuller Snyder, *When the Fire Dances between the Two Poles: Mary Wigman, 1886–1973,* includes most of the extant clips of Wigman dancing.

SUSAN A. MANNING

WILDE. A performance photograph of Wilde and members of the female ensemble of the New York City Ballet in George Balanchine's *Serenade,* c.1959. Strong and swift, with remarkable elevation, Wilde could blaze across the stage and soar through the air with thrilling effect, seeming to ride the crest of the surging strains of Tchaikovsky's "Serenade for Strings." (Photograph from the Dance Collection, New York Public Library for the Performing Arts. Choreography by George Balanchine © The George Balanchine Trust.)

WILDE, PATRICIA (Patricia Lorrain-Ann White; born 16 July 1928 in Ottawa), American ballet dancer, teacher, and company director. Patricia White began studying ballet at the age of three with Gwendolyn Osborne in Ottawa. When she was about eleven, she and her older sister Nora went to New York to continue their studies with Dorothie Littlefield. At age twelve Patricia enrolled at the School of American Ballet, where her teachers included George Balanchine and Muriel Stuart. She made her professional debut at age fifteen with the American Concert Ballet and the next year, 1944, danced in the corps de ballet of the Marquis de Cuevas's Ballet International.

In the summer of 1945 White was one a group of dancers, headed by Marie-Jeanne and William Dollar, that Balanchine took to Mexico City for a series of performances at the Palacio de Bellas Artes with the Ópera Nacional. There he mounted productions of Michel Fokine's *Les Sylphides,* his own *Concerto Barocco* and *Apollo,* and *Constantia,* a work he made jointly with Dollar, as well as staging dances in several operas. White danced a solo in the Walpurgisnacht scene in *Faust.* Upon returning from Mexico, White joined her sister Nora in the corps of Sergei Denham's Ballet Russe de Monte Carlo (changing her surname from White to Wilde to avoid confusion with her sister) and remained with this company until 1949. She then went to Europe, where she studied briefly with Olga Preobrajenska in Paris, performed as a guest artist with the Ballets de Paris de Roland Petit, and toured the Netherlands and England with the Metropolitan Ballet, a short-lived English company.

In 1950 Wilde joined the New York City Ballet. She spent the bulk of her career as a dancer with this company and with it danced many leading roles. Among those she created in Balanchine ballets were the third waltz in *La Valse* (1951), the soloist in *Scotch Symphony* (1952), the Scherzo in *Western Symphony* (1954), one of the five ballerinas in *Divertimento No. 15* (1956), and the principal female roles in *Square Dance* (1957), *Native Dancers* (1959), and *Raymonda Variations* (1961). She also originated and had great success in the pas de trois in Balanchine's staging of *Swan Lake,* which in 1959 was replaced by a solo for Prince Siegfried to the same music. She also choreographed a number of ballets, including some for the New York Philharmonic Promenade Concerts. Wilde was a mainstay of the New York City Ballet during its City Center period. She was an impeccable technician, unsurpassed in allegro, with a power and facility in aerial steps that are rare in a ballerina.

Wilde resigned from the New York City Ballet in 1965; retiring from dancing, she began a second career as an outstanding teacher by becoming director of the dance department of Harkness House for Ballet Arts, a position she held until 1967. In 1969, at Balanchine's invitation, she set up the school for the Ballet du Grand Théâtre de Genève. She was associated with the American Ballet Theatre School from 1967 until it closed in 1982—serving as director from 1979 to 1982—and between 1970 and 1976 she was a ballet mistress at American Ballet Theatre.

In September 1982 Wilde became artistic director of Pittsburgh Ballet Theatre. Her first priority as artistic director was to improve the company's technical ability so that the dancers could handle the Balanchine ballets she introduced into the repertory. She later focused on acquiring new works for inclusion in the company's mixed-bill programming.

In 1953 Wilde married George Bardyguine, at the time the New York City Ballet's production stage manager; they have two children. She became a U.S. citizen in 1957. She has served as an adviser to the New York State Council on the Arts and has been the recipient of a number of honors and cultural awards.

BIBLIOGRAPHY

Anderson, Jack. *The One and Only: The Ballet Russe de Monte Carlo.* New York, 1981.

Dacko, Karen. "Dancing on the Wilde Side: Full Steam Ahead for Pittsburgh Ballet Theatre." *Dance Magazine* (August 1986): 52–54.

Denby, Edwin. *Dance Writings.* Edited by Robert Cornfield and William Mackey. New York, 1986.

Gruen, John. *The Private World of Ballet.* New York, 1975.

Kirstein, Lincoln. *The New York City Ballet.* With photographs by Martha Swope and George Platt Lynes. New York, 1973.

Tobias, Tobi. "Patricia Wilde: A Full Life." *Dance Magazine* (September 1971): 68–74.

William James Lawson

WILHELM, C. (William John Charles Pitcher; born 21 March 1858 in Northfleet, Kent, died 25 March 1925 in London), British costume and stage designer. C. Wilhelm was the principal designer of English ballet during the late nineteenth century, when Victorian propriety had pushed it from the opera houses into the music halls. Beginning with costume design and advancing to whole productions, his spectacular showpieces for London's Empire Theatre helped preserve a local tradition of classical dance, embedded in popular entertainment, between the eras of the Romantic ballet and the Ballets Russes.

A self-trained draftsman, Wilhelm began his career designing costumes for pantomimes at the Theatre Royal, Drury Lane. His thirty-year association with the Empire began with its opening in 1884 and advanced in 1887 with *Dilara,* in which each *coryphée* wore a white cockatoo on her wrist. His collaborations with choreographer Katti Lanner and composer Leopold Wenzel were the basis of the Empire's success, although it was in stage design that the self-declared "home of ballet" was widely agreed to surpass the larger Alhambra.

"Color is the life-blood of my art," Wilhelm said. In *Rose d'Amour* (1888) the corps de ballet were costumed as variously colored flowers, coming together into one enormous bouquct. As important as color was the spinning of whole systems of finely elaborated fantasy. He devised *Les Papillons* (1901) for the Empire's ballerina Adeline Genée with fastidious attention to actual butterfly markings, with each costume representing a different variety: Genée was the Queen Butterfly *(Vanessa imperialis),* attended by a retinue of elves and glow-worms. The dancers were always resplendent, whether costumed as fish, birds, or even fruit. Wilhelm's watercolor sketches for these costumes are as exquisite in color and detail as they are exuberant in imagination.

Wilhelm designed many of the popular contemporary ballets, such as *The Paris Exhibition* (1889), which featured the brand-new Eiffel Tower, and *The Press* (1898), in which dancers wore the symbols of contemporary London newspapers. He preferred historical romance, however, and as he became the dominant figure at the Empire, inventing scenarios as well as designs, more traditional subjects were favored. His production of *Cinderella* (1906), set in the midst of a Watteau *fête galante,* had exceptional success. The appearance of the Ballets Russes de Serge Diaghilev in London damaged the glamorous appeal of the Empire, and during World War I the ballet company was disbanded. Wilhelm retired to his watercolors in 1919; he died two years before the Empire was converted into a movie theater.

BIBLIOGRAPHY

Beaumont, Cyril W. *Five Centuries of Ballet Design.* London, 1939.

Forsyth, Gerald. "Wilhelm: A Noted Victorian Theatrical Designer." *Theatre Notebook* 11 (January-March 1957): 55–58.

Guest, Ivor. *Adeline Genée.* London, 1958.

Guest, Ivor. *The Empire Ballet.* London, 1962.

Guest, Ivor. *Ballet in Leicester Square.* London, 1992.

Claudia Roth Pierpont

WILLIAMS, E. VIRGINIA (Virginia Ellen Williams; born 12 March 1914 in Stoneham, Massachusetts, died 8 May 1984 in Malden, Massachusetts), American ballet teacher, choreographer, and company director. Virginia Williams, who preferred to be known as E. Virginia, was the quintessential New England Yankee. Like her maternal grandfather, who owned five whaling vessels out of Salem, she was courageous and obdurate. She was also passionate about dance. This passion manifested itself early on, and although her parents frowned on a performing career, she was given the best training then available in Boston. Among her early teachers were Miriam Winslow, Dana Sieveling, and Jerrie Cragin. She also studied in New York City with Tatiana Chamié, Anatole Oboukhoff, and George Balanchine.

In 1937 Williams married Carl Nelson, with whom she had a daughter, Carla. For the next two decades she immersed herself in teaching. (Two of her early schools were in Malden and Stoneham, Massachusetts.) After divorcing Nelson, Williams married pianist Herbert Hobbs in 1955. Hobbs became musical adviser to the New England Civic Ballet, which Williams formed in 1958. When seen at the first Northeast Regional Ballet Festival in 1959, the company attracted immediate attention.

George Balanchine began to visit Williams's studio to recruit dancers for the New York City Ballet, and in 1962 he invited her to work with him privately once a month. A deep bond of mutual respect developed between them, and in 1963, with Balanchine's help, her company received a grant from the Ford Foundation that helped finance the shift from the nonprofessional New England Civic Ballet to the professional Boston Ballet. To her new status as director of the Boston Ballet Williams brought her special gifts as teacher, choreographer, and imaginative builder of repertory. She also had an infallible memory for the choreography of others.

Williams had daring dreams for the company. She invited contemporary choreographers such as Pearl Lang, John Butler, Talley Beatty, and Merce Cunningham to enrich the repertory. She also initiated the Vestris Prize Competition, which brought attention to little-known choreographers. And she encouraged well-known choreographers, such as Agnes de Mille and Choo San Goh, to take unaccustomed stylistic paths.

In 1980 Williams invited Violette Verdy to become associate artistic director of the Boston Ballet. In 1983 Williams retired, but her close connection with company and school ended only with her death the following year. Among her honors were a *Dance Magazine* Award (1976), the Distinguished Bostonian Award (1980), and several honorary doctorates.

[*See also* Boston Ballet.]

BIBLIOGRAPHY

Basco, Sharon. "E. Virginia Williams Dons New Hat." *Dance Magazine* (July 1983): 6–7.

Cash, Debra. "The Boston Ballet." *Ballet News* 5 (May 1984): 34.

Fanger, Iris M. "E. Virginia Williams." *Dance Magazine* (July 1984): 87–88.

Hering, Doris. "New England Civic Ballet: Sweet Compulsion." *Dance Magazine* (April 1960): 52–55.

Tobias, Tobi. "E. Virginia Williams and the Boston Ballet." *Dance Magazine* (June 1976): 47–58.

Williams, E. Virginia. "What Makes a Great Teacher of Classical Ballet?" *Dance Magazine* (August 1963): 20–21.

Doris Hering

WILLIAMS, PETR (Petr Vladimirovich Williams; born 17 [30] June 1902 in Moscow, died 1 December 1947 in Moscow), Russian scenery and costume designer. Williams

PETR WILLIAMS. One of the settings that Williams designed for Leonid Lavrovsky's production of *Romeo and Juliet* at the Kirov Theater, Leningrad, in 1940. The dancers pictured are Konstantin Sergeyev and Galina Ulanova in the title roles. (Photograph from the archives of the Maryinsky Theater, Saint Petersburg.)

studied painting with Wassily Kandinsky and Konstantin Korovin, among many others. From 1941 to 1947 he was chief decor designer at the Bolshoi Theater in Moscow. Williams's signature was decor as a huge easel painting framed by a giant three-dimensional portal. His finest achievements were his decors for *Romeo and Juliet* (Kirov Ballet, 1940) and *Cinderella* (Bolshoi Ballet, 1945).

The painted backdrops for *Romeo and Juliet* were framed with a richly ornamented portal that re-created the images of the Italian high Renaissance. Sometimes Williams incorporated compositions of the great painters into his designs, for example, a copy of Sandro Botticelli's *Primavera* appeared in the backdrop for Juliet's bedroom. The costumes were so authentic that they seemed to clothe personages from Italian paintings come to life.

For the ballroom scene in *Cinderella,* drawing on Baroque magnificence and the porcelainlike delicacy of the Rococo, Williams decorated his ornamental portal frame with mirrors, candles, and sculptured figures—a triumph of sumptuous stage design. The first act, however, had been completely realistic, in accordance with the conventions for drama ballet *(drambalet),* a genre of which Williams may be considered a typical representative in decor design. Williams was named Merited Art Worker of the Russian Federation and won the State Prize of the USSR in 1942, 1945, and 1946.

BIBLIOGRAPHY

Sidorov, Aleksandr. *Petr Viliams* (in Russian). Moscow, 1980.

Syrkina, F. Y. *Petr Vladimirovich Viliams* (in Russian). Moscow, 1953.

VIKTOR I. BEREZKIN
Translated from Russian

WILLIAMS, STANLEY (born 5 March 1925 in Chappel, England, died 21 October 1997 in New York), Anglo-Danish dancer and teacher. Son of an English father and a Danish mother, Williams immigrated with his parents to Copenhagen in 1932, when he was seven. Two years later he entered the school of the Royal Danish Ballet. There, in classes taught by Karl Merrild, Harald Lander, and others, he was thoroughly trained in the Danish school of dancing established in the nineteenth century by August Bournonville. Williams was accepted into the company in 1943, at age eighteen, and was appointed a *solodanser* (soloist, or principal dancer) in 1949, a rank he held until 1963. Among his leading roles in the Bournonville repertory were Vilhelm in *Far from Denmark,* James in *La Sylphide,* and the Ballet Master in *Konservatoriet.* He was also noted for his Mercutio in Frederick Ashton's *Romeo and Juliet,* for his Jailer in Léonide Massine's *Symphonie Fantastique* (fourth movement), and for the character role of Doctor Coppélius.

Early in his career, Williams began to go abroad for appearances as a guest artist. In 1947 and 1948, he made guest appearances in Iceland, Belgium, and Sweden, and in 1953–1954 he was the leading dancer and ballet master with George Kirsta's Ballet Comique in England. In 1955 he danced at Jacob's Pillow, in Becket, Massachusetts, with the first group of soloists of the Royal Danish Ballet to appear in the United States.

Although Williams was a skillful dancer, his greatest gift was for pedagogy. He began teaching under Lander's direction in 1950, at the age of twenty-four, but it was Vera Volkova, who came to the Royal Danish Ballet as artistic adviser in 1951, who was principally responsible for shaping him as an instructor. Volkova, a Russian dancer and teacher who had settled in England in the 1930s, was the leading authority in the West on the Vaganova system of instruction. Under her tutelage, and after an injury limited his roles onstage, Williams began to devote his energies to teaching, which he found that he greatly enjoyed. Subsequently, his teaching was influenced considerably by the work of George Balanchine, whom he met in 1956 during the New York City Ballet's visit to Denmark. Having observed Williams's classes, Balanchine invited him to come to America to teach. Williams served as guest teacher for the New York City Ballet for the 1960/61 and 1961/62 seasons, and in 1964 he became permanently affiliated with that company.

For many years Williams worked almost exclusively with the company's academy, the School of American Ballet. Long recognized as an outstanding teacher, he held for many years the prestigious appointment to the Senior Faculty Chair, an honor bestowed upon him in the 1980s. In addition to teaching daily classes, Williams frequently staged excerpts from Bournonville ballets for the school's annual Workshop Performances, and in 1977 he mounted a group of these pieces for the New York City Ballet under the title *Bournonville Divertissements.*

Williams also regularly taught company class for the New York City Ballet and served as a guest instructor with the Royal Danish Ballet and American Ballet Theatre. In class, his teaching manner was quiet and absolutely concentrated, his demeanor modest yet masterful. Over the years his reputation as a teacher achieved almost legendary status, as his skill and talent were praised by numerous famous dancers who were his students. Edward Villella, for one, credits Williams with extending his performing career by more than a decade (Villella, 1992); Peter Martins, for another, considers Williams preeminent among the world's great ballet teachers (Martins, 1982). All his students extol the fundamental simplicity of his teaching, his ability to transmit his knowledge of what has been called "the essence of technique." Yet, through his emphasis on technical purity, advanced students recognize that Williams took them beyond technique and confronted them squarely with the art of ballet dancing. Commenting on his company class for the New York City

Ballet, one dancer said that "it's like listening to Bach. It's pure, it's classical, it gets straight to the heart of things" (quoted in Schof, 1996).

BIBLIOGRAPHY

Martins, Peter, with Robert Cornfield. *Far from Denmark*. Boston, 1982.

Schof, Thomas W. "Master of the Barre." New York City Ballet *Stagebill* (January 1996): 12–13, 46.

Tobias, Tobi. "Stanley Williams: The Quality of the Moment." *Dance Magazine* (March 1981): 74–83.

Villella, Edward, with Larry Kaplan. *Prodigal Son: Dancing for Balanchine in a World of Pain and Magic*. New York, 1992.

CLAUDE CONYERS

WILLIAMS-YARBOROUGH, LAVINIA (born 1919 in Philadelphia, Pennsylvania, died 19 July 1989 in Haiti), American dancer, teacher, and choreographer. Trained in classical ballet, Williams-Yarborough performed in musical comedy and modern dance before turning to African-derived, New World dance forms as a means of reaffirming her cultural heritage. Following Katherine Dunham and Jean-Léon Destiné, she combined the religious and folkloric dances of the Caribbean—particularly those of Haiti—with European forms of theatrical dance and created a syncretic, contemporary, theatrical black dance style. She also helped to establish national dance academies in Haiti, Jamaica, Guyana, and the Bahamas.

Raised in Portsmouth, Virginia, and Brooklyn, New York, Williams-Yarborough began studying ballet when she was three years old. Tap, modern, acrobatics, singing, and acting classes soon followed. She graduated from Washington Irving High School in New York City and won a scholarship to the Art Students' League. Her dance teachers included Kay Perper (Denishawn School), Anna Sokolow, Martha Graham, Agnes de Mille, Katherine Dunham, Valerie Bettis, Lisan Kay, Helen Tamiris, African dancers Prince Almamy and Asadata Dafora, and Kyra Nijinsky (Antwerp). Her performing credits include Eugene Von Grona's American Negro Ballet (1937–1939), Ballet Theater's premiere season (in *Obeah*, choreographed by de Mille, 1940), and the Katherine Dunham Company (1940–1946, in New York City, on national tour, and in Hollywood). She appeared in the films *Stormy Weather* and *Carnival of Rhythm* (both 1943) and in several Broadway productions: *Blackbirds of 1939*, *Cabin in the Sky* (1940), *A Tropical Revue* (1943), *Blue Holiday* (1945), a 1945 United Service Organizations (USO) revival of *Shuffle Along*, *Showboat* (1946), *Finian's Rainbow* (1947), and *My Darlin' Aida* (1952).

With Haiti as her base, from 1953 to 1980 Williams-Yarborough also taught and choreographed in Jamaica (1958–1982), Guyana (1972–1976), the Bahamas (1976–1980), Antigua, Trinidad, Barbados, Montserrat, and Saint Kitts as well as in Sweden (1967) and Germany (1980–1981). She returned to the United States in 1980 and taught at the Alvin Ailey American Dance Center, Steps Studio 56, and at her own Brooklyn-based school, which opened in July 1983. In the mid-1980s she resettled in Haiti and taught at her school there until her death from food poisoning.

BIBLIOGRAPHY

Aschenbrenner, Joyce. "Katherine Dunham: Reflections on the Social and Political Contexts of Afro-American Dance." *CORD Dance Research Annual* 12 (1980).

Emery, Lynne Fauley. *Black Dance from 1619 to Today*. 2d rev. ed. Princeton, 1988.

MacDonald, Annette. "Madame Lavinia Williams: Conversations in Nassau." *Journal of Ethnic Studies* 13 (Summer 1985): 106–117.

Williams-Yarborough, Lavinia. "Haiti, Where I Teach Dance." *Dance Magazine* (October 1958): 42–44, 76–79.

ARCHIVES. Dance Collection, New York Public Library for the Performing Arts. Schomburg Center for Research in Black Culture, New York Public Library.

BRENDA DIXON GOTTSCHILD

WILSON, ROBERT (born 4 October 1941 in Waco, Texas), American theatrical designer and producer. Wilson attended the University of Texas for three years and received a bachelor of fine arts degree in 1965 from Pratt Institute in Brooklyn, New York. In 1962 he studied with George McNeil in Paris, and in 1966 with Paolo Soleri at the Arcosanti Community in Arizona. Wilson formed the Byrd Hoffman School of Byrds in 1969, a close-knit group of people from diverse backgrounds who experimented together in dance, theater, and movement.

Robert Wilson has been recognized internationally as a theatrical innovator, performer, director, writer, visual artist, and video artist. His works, which reflect his training as a painter and architect, are generally referred to as operas, although they lack the dramatic narrative and the correlation between the music and drama characteristic of traditional opera. Some of his works on an operatic scale produce the sense of total theater first described in Richard Wagner's formulation of the *Gesamkunstwerk*. Wilson's operas are structured as visual collages in which text, movement, and music are treated independently. The spectacular visual tableaux are developed through often imperceptibly slow movement by the performers, resulting in an unusual theatrical experience.

Because each tableau was complete in itself, Wilson's early productions could be rearranged, augmented, or condensed. *The King of Spain* (1969), for example, became the second act of *The Life and Times of Sigmund Freud* (1970), which was in turn incorporated into the first three acts of *Deafman Glance* (1970). *The Life and Times of Joseph Stalin*, first produced at the Brooklyn Academy of Music in 1973, was twelve hours long and included material from all five of Wilson's previous productions. His

ROBERT WILSON. A scene from Wilson's *Dr. Faustus Lights the Lights* (1992). Although few of his works include dances, Wilson exhibits a choreographic sensibility in the extreme precision with which he designs his performers' stage movement, tableaux, and abstract gestures. (Photograph © 1992 by Jack Vartoogian; used by permission.)

longest production, *Overture to KA MOUNTAIN AND GUARDenia Terrace* (1972), presented at the Shiraz Festival, Iran, lasted seven days and nights.

Einstein on the Beach (1976), one of Wilson's most celebrated works, was a collaboration with the composer Philip Glass, with choreography by Andy de Groat. The opera toured extensively in Europe before its American premiere on 21 November 1976 at the Metropolitan Opera House, New York. Revivals of *Einstein on the Beach,* with choreography by Lucinda Childs, were produced by the Brooklyn Academy of Music in 1984 and 1992.

Wilson's international opera, *the CIVIL warS: a tree is best measured when it is down,* which was to have its premiere at the 1984 Los Angeles Olympics, was canceled because of inadequate funding. Though yet to be seen in its entirety, segments of *the CIVIL warS* have been performed worldwide in Cologne, Rome, Amsterdam, Minneapolis, and New York. In 1986 Wilson was the sole nominee for the Pulitzer Prize for drama for *the CIVIL warS,* although the Pulitzer Board declined to give the award that year.

Wilson's most popular work to date was his 1990 production *The Black Rider,* with music by Tom Waits and texts by William Burroughs, for the Thalia Theater in Hamburg. Since its premiere the show has toured extensively worldwide. Wilson and Waits collaborated a second time on the Thalia's production of *Alice,* first performed in December 1992.

Among the awards and honors received by Wilson are the Bessie award (in 1984 for *the Knee Plays*); the Obie award for direction (in 1986 for *Hamletmachine*); and the Skowhegan Medal for Drawing (in 1987). He has also received fellowships from the Rockefeller Foundation (1975, 1981) and the Guggenheim Foundation (1971, 1980). In 1993 he won a Golden Lion award for sculpture at the Venice Biennale.

Major exhibitions of Wilson's work have been presented by the Museum of Fine Arts in Boston (*Robert Wilson's Vision,* 1991); the Centre Georges Pompidou in Paris (*Mr. Bojangles' Memory,* 1991); the Instituto de Valencia de Arte Moderno (1992); and the Boymans Museum, Rotterdam (1993). In 1993 Wilson was commissioned to design an installation for the Venice Biennale.

BIBLIOGRAPHY

Flakes, Susan. "Robert Wilson's *Einstein on the Beach.*" *Drama Review* 20 (December 1976): 69–82.

Kaplan, Peggy Jarrell. *Portraits of Choreographers.* New York, 1988.

Robert Wilson: From a Theater of Images. Exhibition catalog with essays by John Rockwell and Calvin Tomkins. Cincinnati, 1980.

Shyer, Laurence. *Robert Wilson and His Collaborators.* New York, 1989.

SILAS JACKSON and SETH GOLDSTEIN

WILSON, SALLIE (born 18 April 1932 in Fort Worth, Texas), American dancer and ballet director. The preeminent female interpreter of Antony Tudor's ballets during the 1960s and 1970s, Sallie Wilson became a leading dramatic ballerina during her thirty-year performing career. She began studying ballet at the age of twelve and later moved to New York, where she studied with Margaret Craske, Tudor, and Edward Caton. Accepted into Ballet Theatre in 1949, she joined the Metropolitan Opera Ballet, then under Tudor's direction, a year later. Her five years there inaugurated her intense and pivotal professional association with Tudor. Rejoining Ballet Theatre in 1955, she became a soloist the next year; her repertory included Myrtha in *Giselle* and Kristine in Birgit Cullberg's *Miss Julie.*

When the company suspended operations in 1958, Wilson joined the New York City Ballet, performing the Queen in Jerome Robbins's *The Cage,* Profane Love in Frederick Ashton's *Illuminations,* the Coquette in George Balanchine's *La Sonnambula,* and the Scherzo of his *Western Symphony.* Most notably, Martha Graham created the role of Queen Elizabeth in *Episodes* (1959) for her.

Returning to American Ballet Theatre in 1960, Wilson was promoted to principal in 1961. She had earlier danced Rosalind in *Romeo and Juliet* and "She Wore Perfume" in *Dim Lustre;* her Tudor repertory soon grew to include the lead roles in *Pillar of Fire, Jardin aux Lilas, Dark Elegies,* and *Undertow.* Hagar in *Pillar of Fire,* which she first danced in 1966, soon became Wilson's signature role; she was also acclaimed for her Lizzie Borden in de Mille's *Fall River Legend.* She danced lead roles in Fokine's *Les Sylphides,* de Mille's *Three Virgins and a Devil,* Tudor's *The Judgment of Paris,* José Limón's *The Moor's Pavane,* and Glen Tetley's *Sargasso.* She created roles in Robbins's *Les Noces* (1965), Alvin Ailey's *The River* (1970), and de Mille's *A Rose for Miss Emily.* She last performed with American Ballet Theatre in 1980.

Wilson often stages Tudor's ballets; she has assisted with American Ballet Theatre's revivals and has mounted productions for the Paris Opera Ballet and other companies worldwide. Her choreography includes *Liederspiel* (1978) and *Fête* (1979) for Arlington Dance Theatre, a three-act *Il Principe delle Pogode* (1979) featuring Carla Fracci, and *Idyll* (1986) for the Riverside Festival in New York. During the early 1980s she occasionally made guest appearances with smaller companies in New York and elsewhere.

BIBLIOGRAPHY

Gruen, John. *The Private World of Ballet.* New York, 1975.

Gruen, John. "Sallie Wilson Makes a Drama of Dance." *New York Times* (2 September 1979).

Wechsler, Bert. "Survivor: Sallie Wilson." *Ballet News* 3 (April 1982): 20–22.

SUSAN REITER

WINTERBRANCH. Choreography: Merce Cunningham. Music: La Monte Young; "Two Sounds" (April 1960). Costumes, object, and lighting: Robert Rauschenberg. First performance: 21 March 1964, Wadsworth Atheneum, Hartford, Connecticut, Merce Cunningham Dance Company. Dancers: Merce Cunningham, Carolyn Brown, Viola Farber, Barbara Lloyd, William Davis, Steve Paxton.

Winterbranch is the last of four Cunningham works named after the seasons and the most controversial. The dance occurs in darkness; the dancers' movements are often barely visible, caught as if by accident by abruptly changing lights similar to automobile headlights suddenly illuminating objects or animals on a road at night. Robert Rauschenberg's lighting, which often used hand-held lighting instruments, was different in every performance and made an important contribution to the ambience of the work. The costumes were ordinary navy blue sweat pants and shirts, white socks, and deck shoes. Rauschenberg had the dancers put black horizontal smudges under their eyes, like those worn by football players. The effect was likened to commandos or prisoners of war.

The dance begins in silence. The stillness is broken by one and then another tape-recorded sound played at an extremely high volume over loudspeakers. One of the sounds was produced by scraping ashtrays against a mirror; the other was made by rubbing pieces of wood against a Chinese gong. The resulting sounds were so egregious that they occasionally drove people out of the theater. The movement vocabulary consists primarily of different kinds of falling, with bodies often dragged offstage. Even the leaps end in falls. A Rauschenberg "monster" (the dancers' affectionate name for a sculpture made from objects found backstage), lit from within and created anew for each performance, was pulled across the back of the stage in darkness, adding yet another menacing and mysterious element to the dance. The twenty-minute length of the dance is permanent, but its internal divisions of time and space are flexible.

Much performed on the 1964 world tour, *Winterbranch* was found haunting, strange, dramatic, disturbing, sinister, frightening; it was even likened to the Holocaust. In Essen, Germany, it received eighteen curtain calls, boos and catcalls mingling with bravos. *The Indian Express,* New Delhi (30 October 1964), called it "The most powerful and interesting work of the evening. . . . there is no way to judge it except to be exposed to it and feel its primeval impact." *Winterbranch* has no specific story, presents no particular mood. Its impact, perhaps more than with many other Cunningham works, depends upon what the individual viewer brings to the experience.

BIBLIOGRAPHY

Cunningham, Merce, in conversation with Jacqueline Lesschaeve. *The Dancer and the Dance.* New York, 1985.

Cunningham, Merce. *Changes: Notes on Choreography.* Edited by Francis Starr. New York, 1968.

CAROLYN BROWN

WIRTSCHAFT. A German court masquerade and entertainment of the seventeenth to mid-eighteenth century, the *Wirtschaft* (also *Wirthschaft, Wirthschafft;* pl., *Wirtschaften*) is lighthearted in nature and therefore was widely favored as an antithesis to the more formal court ballet. The main difference between the two forms is that in a *Wirtschaft* all present participated actively, supported by the artistic staff of the court dancing masters and their families, poets, and musicians, whereas in a ballet only a select few were performers while the rest of the court provided the audience.

The name *Wirtschaft* means "inn" or "hostelry" and set the theme for the activities. The sequence of events—some metaphorically related to the occasion (such as a princely visit or a birthday), others outright humorous, even raucous—unfolded in the setting of an inn, a *Wirtschaft,* a stopping place for a diversity of lower-class personages such as milkmaids, chimney sweeps, fools, drunkards, traveling entertainers with their monkeys, and schoolchildren, all performed by the members of the court and their guests. Characters called the *Wirt* and the *Wirtin* (innkeeper and his wife) were the official hosts of the event, played by emperor and empress (as in Austrian *Wirthschafften*), duke and duchess, landgrave and landgravine (as in Darmstadt). Both assumed additional roles during the course of the evening, as did the more prominent of the participating nobles.

The locale for a *Wirtschaft* was usually the main hall of the palace, transformed by strategically placed backdrops and props into a semblance of a rugged dining room: that the crystal chandeliers and brocade wall-coverings contradicted the feeling did not bother anyone. For such an occasion the palace itself was called *Gasthaus zum Weißen Adler* (Dresden, 9 February 1728), *Gasthaus zum Schwarzen Adler* (Vienna, before and during the reign of Maria Theresa), and the like.

On arrival the guests, lavishly attired in previously determined national, regional, and "lower-class" costumes, were greeted at the door by the *Wirt* and *Wirtin* and led to their places on chairs placed along the walls or at tables in cases where the *Wirtschaft* provided the framework for a banquet. One of the charms of this entertainment was the temporary suspension of the rigidly maintained hierarchical seating order that governed other spectacles of the period. A space was left open for the actual performance, which consisted of spoken and sung verses, reminiscent of the French *récits,* alternating with danced *entrées,* some fully laid out and carefully prepared by the court dancing master, others allowing for audience participation (*contredanses, quadrilles, cotillons*). In spite of the tendency toward increased realism in costumes, decorations, and dramatic action, *Wirtschaften* made concessions to the taste prevalent in high society: after the relaxed hilarity of the grotesque *entrées,* the final number tended to be a formal ballet, sung by a chorus accompanied by the full orchestra and danced by shepherds and shepherdesses.

The music, in every case specially composed, was written by the court composer, who also conducted the *Hofkapelle* from the harpsichord or the first violin's stand; were the size of the resident orchestra insufficient for a particularly splendid occasion (such as the *Wirthschaft* given in Darmstadt, November 1658, in honor of the visiting Cardinal Friedrich von Hessen, brother of the ruling landgrave), additional musicians were hired as reinforcements from a neighboring court or metropolis.

With the invention of the *Wirtschaft* and the stylistically related *Bauern-Hochzeit* ("peasant wedding"; see Böhme, 1886, p. 144; Gregor, 1944, p. 226), the aristocracy initiated a movement toward democratization, a conscious, albeit still playful, acknowledgment of the fact that the world of account extended beyond the palace gates. Subsequent manifestations of the same spirit were the *réceptions dans la campagne* initiated in the salon of the marquise de Mauconseil (Bie, 1919, p. 108), the *fêtes champêtres* throughout the eighteenth century, Baroque literature, and Jean-Jacques Rousseau's maxim, "Retour à la nature."

BIBLIOGRAPHY

Bie, Oskar. *Der Tanz.* 2d ed. Berlin, 1919.

Böhme, Franz M. *Geschichte des Tanzes in Deutschland.* 2 vols. Leipzig, 1886.

Gregor, Joseph. *Kulturgeschichte des Balletts.* Vienna, 1944.

Kaiser, Hermann. *Barocktheater in Darmstadt.* Darmstadt, 1951.

Kindermann, Heinz. *Theatergeschichte Europas,* vol. 3, *Das Theater der Barockzeit.* Salzburg, 1959.

Pasqué, Ernst. "Geschichte der Musik und des Theaters am Hofe zu Darmstadt." *Die Muse* (1853–1854).

Tintelnot, Hans. *Barocktheater und barocke Kunst.* Berlin, 1939.

INGRID BRAINARD

WITH MY RED FIRES. *See* New Dance Trilogy.

WOIZIKOWSKI, LEON (Leon Wójcikowski; born 20 February 1899 in Warsaw, died 23 February 1974 in Warsaw), Polish dancer, ballet master, and teacher. Trained as a dancer at the Wielki Theater School in Warsaw, Woizikowski joined the ballet company of the Wielki Theater in 1914, leaving it the following year to go to France and join the Ballets Russes de Serge Diaghilev. With the Diaghilev company, Woizikowski's remarkable gifts as a character dancer soon revealed themselves, and in the next five years he created a number of important roles in ballets of Léonide Massine. In addition to principal parts in *Las Meninas* (1916) and *Contes Russes* (1917), he created the roles of Niccolò in *Les Femmes de Bonne Humeur* (1917), the Manager in Evening Dress in *Parade* (1917), the Tarantella Dancer in *La Boutique Fantasque* (1919), the Corregidor in *Le Tricorne* (1919), and Fourbo in *Pulcinella* (1920). He frequently danced as partner to Lydia Sokolova, his offstage companion during the 1920s. A performer of enormous fire and virility who rivaled Massine in such parts as the Miller in *Le Tricorne,* he was equally memorable as the Polovtsian Chief in *Prince Igor* and in the title role of *Petrouchka,* bringing to Michel Fokine's choreography an admirable feeling for style, period, and dramatic effect.

In 1922, Woizikowski left the Ballets Russes, appearing at the London Coliseum (1922) and with Massine and Lydia Lopokova in *You'd Be Surprised* at Covent Garden (1923). Rejoining Diaghilev in 1923, he established himself as the company's leading character dancer, creating major roles in Bronislava Nijinska's *Les Noces* (1923), *Les Biches* (1924), and *Le Train Bleu* (1924) and in several George Balanchine works, including *The Prodigal Son* (1929). After Diaghilev's death, he appeared with Anna Pavlova's troupe (1929–1931), with Ballet Rambert (for which he staged Vaslav Nijinsky's *L'Après-midi d'un Faune* in 1931), with the Opéra Russe (1931), and with Colonel Wassily de Basil's Ballets Russes de Monte Carlo (1932–1934), creating roles in Massine's *Les Présages* (1933), and Balanchine's *Cotillon* (1932) and *La Concurrence* (1932). In late 1934, he left de Basil, and after a brief association with the Ballets Russes de Paris, he formed the Ballets de Léon Woizikovsky, which toured Europe and Australia under de Basil's auspices from 1936 to 1938.

Woizikowski returned to his native country in the late 1930s, heading a company of Polish dancers that performed at the 1939 World's Fair in New York. After World War II, he served as ballet master at the Warsaw State Opera, where he staged revivals of *Schéhérazade, Petrouchka,* and *L'Après-midi d'un Faune.* Between 1958 and his death, he worked mainly in the West, reviving, thanks to an extraordinary memory, various Diaghilev-era works for London's Festival Ballet, the Cologne Opera Ballet, and the Rome Opera Ballet, and serving on the faculty of Bonn's Rheinische Friedrich-Wilhelms-Universität.

BIBLIOGRAPHY

Garafola, Lynn. *Diaghilev's Ballets Russes.* New York and Oxford, 1989.

García-Márquez, Vicente. *The Ballets Russes: Colonel de Basil's Ballets Russes de Monte Carlo, 1932–1952.* New York, 1990.

Gockel, Eberhard. "Leon Woizikovski." *Ballet Today* (July–August 1969): 17.

Grigoriev, Serge. *The Diaghilev Ballet, 1909–1929.* Translated and edited by Vera Bowen. London, 1953.

Hall, Fernau. "Men in Ballet: Leon Woizikowski." *Ballet Today* (October 1958): 4.

Sokolova, Lydia. *Dancing for Diaghilev.* Edited by Richard Buckle. London, 1960.

Sorley Walker, Kathrine. *De Basil's Ballets Russes.* New York, 1983.

LYNN GARAFOLA

WORSAAE, JENS-JACOB (born 19 April 1946 in Jutland, died 8 August 1994 in Copenhagen), Danish stage and costume designer. Worsaae's designs for dance, which spanned the Russian classics, the works of August Bournonville, and new ballets, were characterized by elegance, lightness and sumptuous imagination. Working in Scandinavia, the United States, and elsewhere, Worsaae delighted in the process of collaboration and in using the full range of theater's resources, often combining fantasy renderings of period styles with contemporary stagecraft, such as lightweight costume materials and projections. He made imaginative use of stage space, breaking it up with subsidiary flats yet keeping a clear space for dancing. His costumes moved beautifully with the dancers and flattered individual physiques. His eye for color and detail led to dyeing techniques that produced gradations of tones, as in his costumes for Toni Lander and Bruce Marks's reconstruction of August Bournonville's *Abdallah.* He handled large-scale productions with zest and could adapt them to touring conditions.

As a youth Worsaae wanted to become a film director and haunted Copenhagen's film museum. While at the University of Copenhagen, however, he became involved with an experimental theater. He later studied at the Academy of Stage Design in Prague and gained further practical experience there. He would continue to design for drama, but he liked the freedom of dance as a less realistic art form.

His first dance design, in 1974, was for Flemming Flindt's *Felix Luna* in Göteborg, Sweden, followed by the first two of several ballets with Bruce Marks. His work in dance gained impetus in 1979 with commissions for Bournonville productions by the Soloists of the Royal Danish Ballet. Among his other designs for Bournonville works were several stagings by Kirsten Ralov, including the scenery for *A Folk Tale* by the Bolshoi Ballet.

Another of Worsaae's repeated collaborators was Anna Lærkesen, a former ballerina of the Royal Danish Ballet, who worked with him in original ballets for both that company and the San Francisco Ballet. Other major Royal Danish Ballet productions included Yuri Grigorovich's *Don Quixote* and Flindt's *Caroline Mathilde.* Worsaae also worked in various theaters with Ib Andersen, Peter Schaufuss, Elsa-Marianne von Rosen, Egon Madsen, and others. An important series of collaborations was with Helgi Tomasson at the San Francisco Ballet on *Intimate Voices, Quartette, Con Brio, Swan Lake, The Sleeping Beauty,* and *Romeo and Juliet.* Their *Swan Lake* had a Watteau-like pastoral quality and conveyed an atmosphere of heartless flirtation in the palace scenes, underscored by the refined tactile sensuousness of the costume materials.

One of Worsaae's last productions before his untimely death was a somewhat revised version of Tomasson's *The*

Sleeping Beauty for the Royal Danish Ballet. Set in Russia, it moves from the Oriental seventeenth century to Peter the Great's French-influenced eighteenth century, tempering sumptuousness with fairy-tale lightness and grandeur with Danish intimacy, and reflecting the round of the seasons, all with Worsaae's typically gracious imagination.

BIBLIOGRAPHY

Hunt, Marilyn. "Jens-Jacob Worsaae Sets a Sparkling Stage: Designing the Light Fantastic." *Dance Magazine* (April 1987): 48–52.

Matthew, Alanna. "The Magical Spaces of Jens-Jacob Worsaae." *Vandance International* 20 (Summer 1992): 12–13.

MARILYN HUNT

WRIGHT, PETER (born 25 November 1926 in London), British dancer, choreographer, director, producer, and teacher. A choreographer and producer with a gift for revitalizing the classics, Wright received his early training from Kurt Jooss and Sigurd Leeder while performing with the Ballets Jooss in England (1945–1946 and 1951–1952). He also studied with Vera Volkova and danced with several small ballet companies, including the Sadler's Wells Theatre Ballet (1949–1951 and 1952–1955), and in musicals and revues, before turning to choreography.

He made his first ballet, *A Blue Rose* (1957), for the Sadler's Wells Theatre Ballet. He made four more—of which *Mirror Walkers* and *Quintet* are the best known—for the Stuttgart Ballet, where he served under John Cranko as associate choreographer, ballet master, and teacher from 1961 to 1966. His first classical recension, the Stuttgart production of *Giselle* (1966), opened an important new chapter in his career. Highly praised for its period atmosphere and dramatic logic, it was acquired by both sections of England's Royal Ballet and by companies throughout the world.

Wright quickly followed that success with a new *Sleeping Beauty,* mounted in Cologne in 1967 and revised for the Royal Ballet, with additions by Frederick Ashton, in 1968. In 1984 Wright's first production of *The Nutcracker* was staged for the Royal Ballet.

During the late 1960s he traveled in Europe and America, teaching, choreographing, and producing the classics and his own works. He also worked extensively as a guest producer for BBC (British Broadcasting Corporation) television, where he had previously trained under Margaret Dale.

Wright returned to the Royal Ballet in 1970, as associate director in charge of the Touring Company and then as administrator of both the resident and the touring companies. In 1976 he became director of the Sadler's Wells Royal Ballet (as the Touring Company was named in that year), and he remained at the helm of that company, renamed the Birmingham Royal Ballet, from its arrival in Birmingham in 1990 until his retirement in 1995. As a ballet director he devised educational programs for young audiences and mounted new productions of *Coppélia, Swan Lake, The Sleeping Beauty, Giselle,* and *The Nutcracker.* He was awarded a CBE (Commander of the Order of the British Empire) in 1985 and was knighted in 1993.

BIBLIOGRAPHY

Crisp, Clement. "Peter Wright." *About the House* 3.7 (1970): 16–17.

Meisner, Nadine. "No Strings." *Dance and Dancers* (November 1990): 10–13.

Newman, Barbara. *Swan Lake: Sadler's Wells Royal Ballet.* London, 1983.

Newman, Barbara. "Speaking of Dance: Peter Wright CBE." *The Dancing Times* (March 1986): 506–507.

Thorpe, Edward. "Peter Wright, Pre-eminent Producer of the Classics." *Dance Gazette* (March 1985): 16–19.

Woodcock, Sarah C. *The Sadler's Wells Royal Ballet.* London, 1991.

Wright, Peter. "*Quintet* and *Summer's Night.*" *About the House* 1 (December 1964): 15–16.

BARBARA NEWMAN

WU XIAOBANG (born 18 December 1906 in Taicang County, Jiangsu Province, China, died 8 July 1995 in Beijing), dancer, choreographer, teacher, theoretician, and promoter of dance. Originally given the name Zupei and later Qiming, Wu took Xiaobang as his final and stage name because it sounds like "Chopin," the Polish pianist and composer, whom Wu admired both for his works and for his patriotism. Influenced by the "May Fourth" New Culture Movement in his teens and by Marxism and the goals of Sun Yat-sen (founder of the first republic of China) in his college years, Wu became an enthusiastic patriot.

Between 1929 and 1936, he went to Japan three times and studied ballet and Mary Wigman's expressionistic modern dance at the Takada Masao Dance Institute and at the Eguchi Takaya and Misako Miya Modern Dance Institute. He performed a dozen self-choreographed dances back in Shanghai, including *In a Funeral Procession, Puppet, Peace Fantasy, Clown,* and *Misery of Love,* laying the cornerstone for his "new dance" movement, although interest was at the time limited to elite circles.

In 1937 when the war against Japan (1937–1945) began, Wu became an activist dancer, taking part in the Shanghai National Salvation Performing Team. His solos included *March of the Volunteers* (the music of which became the national anthem of the People's Republic of China), *March of the Broadsword, Killing the Traitor, Exile Trilogy,* and *Song of the Guerrillas.* The first was danced five times at the front lines at the soldiers' request. During China's War of Liberation (civil war, 1945–1949), Wu pursued the creative and scientific methodology of German modern dance and choreographed realistic dances, using inspiration from the Tang dynasty and exposing the dark side of prerevolutionary China in such dances as *Ugly Boast of a Traitor, Messenger, Earthly Inclination, Hungry Fire, Mongolian Dance, Mongolian People's Trilogy, March Dance,* and the full-length dance dramas *Poppy Flower, Lord Tiger,* and *Pagoda and Memorial Gateway.*

After the People's Republic of China was founded in 1949, Wu devoted more time to experimental choreography, especially from 1957 to 1960, with his small experimental company, the Heavenly Horse Studio. The dances were set mainly to Chinese classical music, as music was integral with dance in Chinese tradition. He also conducted scholarly research, founding the Chinese Dance Art Research Society in 1954, and encouraged a group of young scholars to become the foundation of the Dance Research Institute. Established in 1974, it began systematic, in-depth study into ancient Chinese dance history. Sheng Jie, Wu's wife, took another group of young teachers to collect Chinese folk dances in the countryside, which laid a solid basis for the folk dance curriculum of the Beijing Dance Academy, of which Wu was appointed director of the Preparatory Committee. Wu also filmed Taoist and Confucian dances in their temples, preserving the only live images of these valuable dance rituals. He continued to teach his German-based but more realistic and political "new dance" to the first group of dance leaders in the People's Republic. Representative dances of this period included *Wintersweet Trilogy, Wild Goose in Migration, Wintersweet Drills, Happy Fisherman,* and *Ambush in All Directions.* Before and during the Cultural Revolution (1966–1976), he was persecuted for his individualism, independent tendency, emphasis on ancient themes, and works that seemed to have little to do with the excessive revolutionary fervor of the Chinese people during that period.

In 1978, two years after the Cultural Revolution ended, the Chinese Communist Party and central government began to adopt a more open policy; Wu was then appointed chairman of the China National Dance Artists Association and founding director of the Dance Research Institute, which rejuvenated him and allowed him to resume promulgating the "new dance." Unfortunately, he was over seventy by then and unable to perform. In 1982, he became the first adviser to master of arts in dance programs in China.

Wu published six books on dance theory as well as his autobiography, *My Career of Dance Art.* He also worked as editor in chief of three monumental projects in contemporary Chinese dance history: *Collection of Chinese National Folk Dances* (in more than thirty volumes), *The Chinese Encyclopaedia: Music and Dance Volume,* and *Contemporary China: Dance Volume.* In 1985 and 1990, the China National Dance Artists Association held two symposia on his lifelong contributions to all aspects of contemporary Chinese dance. He is the founder of modern Chinese theatrical dance, in both practice and theory.

[*See also* China, *article on* Contemporary Theatrical Dance.]

BIBLIOGRAPHY

Ou Jian-ping. "Dance Scholarship in China: Yesterday, Today, and Tomorrow." In *Documentation of Beyond Performance: Dance Scholarship Today,* edited by Susan Au and Frank-Manuel Peter. Berlin, 1989.

Ou Jian-ping. *The Modern Dance: Theory and Practice,* vol. 1.5, *Oh, My Great Motherland* (in Chinese). Beijing, 1994.

Ou Jian-ping. "From 'Beasts' to 'Flowers': Modern Dance in China." In *East Meets West in Dance: Voices in the Cross-Cultural Dialogue,* edited by John Solomon and Ruth Solomon. Chur, Switzerland, 1995.

Wang Ke-fen et al., eds. *A Dictionary of Chinese Dance* (in Chinese). Beijing, 1994.

Wu Xiaobang. *Introduction to the New Dance Art* (in Chinese). Shanghai, 1950. Rev. ed. Beijing, 1982.

Wu Xiaobang. *My Career of Dance Art* (in Chinese). Hong Kong, 1980. Rev. ed. Beijing, 1981.

Wu Xiaobang. *New Theory on Dance* (in Chinese). Shanghai, 1985.

Wu Xiaobang. *Anthology of Dance Theory* (in Chinese). Chengdu, 1986.

Wu Xiaobang. *Wu Xiaobang on Dance Theory* (in Chinese). Beijing, 1988.

Wu Xiaobang. *New Anthology of Dance Theory* (in Chinese). Beijing, 1989.

OU JIAN-PING

X–Y

XIMÉNEZ-VARGAS BALLET ESPAÑOL. In 1955 a remarkable dance partnership was formed by Roberto Ximénez, a dancer of introspective dignity, and Manolo Vargas, who danced with a wild, highly personal style. Their Ximénez-Vargas Ballet Español, which lasted for a decade, was noted for its disciplined sense of theater and its attention to individual dancers. Over the years, they developed a repertory of great quality and dramatic power and some fine dramatic dancers, notably Maria Alba.

Both dancers are Mexican. Ximénez, the son of a businessman who loved the theater, attended the Escuela Nacional de Danza, studying Mexican, Spanish, Russian, and Asian dance, as well as Latin American folklore. He nearly completed a degree in chemical engineering before he returned to his interest in Spanish dance and formed his own company.

Unlike Ximénez, Vargas was discouraged by his rancher father from pursuing a dance career, but his mother, a former dancer, tutored him in secret. Later he took night classes at the Escuela Nacional. He took a job in a New York night club, where La Argentinita saw him and took him into her company in 1942.

After Argentinita's death, Vargas danced with Pilar López's Ballet Español, which Ximénez joined in 1948, replacing José Greco. The two Mexicans created a concert group in 1950 and left Lopez to form their own company in 1955, touring Europe, Asia, and the Americas. Their first United States appearance was in March 1958, and they gained immediate acclaim. Ted Shawn was particularly impressed, and they performed at Jacob's Pillow in the summers of 1958–1960, 1963, and 1964.

Both men acknowledge the profound influence Pilar López had on them, especially her uncompromising authenticity and her disciplined approach to every detail of a theatrical performance. Like Argentinita and Pilar López, their expressiveness was typical rather than individual; however, the style of their dances was very much their own and represented a new direction in the Spanish idiom. Whether tragic or humorous, their dances tended to be starkly, tersely dramatic. The two men spent hours with company members, learning their individual characteristics and exploring the motivation for each movement. The result, as critics observed, was that their dancers always seemed to know why they were onstage, and even very spare movements and gestures were highly expressive.

The most powerful of the Ximénez-Vargas dances were evocations of pure feeling. Of *Sin Quererlo Ni Buscarlo, Petenera, Petenera*—in which a courtesan meets her death in a jealous triangle—Doris Hering (*Dance Magazine*, April 1958) said, "The emotional line wove, like a surge of sea, through the innocent dance divertissements." The understated flaring and ebbing of emotional currents also characterized the humorous *De Querer Amores*, in which a rivalry between two women briefly sparks the interest of

XIMÉNEZ-VARGAS BALLET ESPAÑOL. Manolo Vargas and Roberto Ximénez in an athletic flamenco number. (Photograph from the archives at Jacob's Pillow, Becket, Massachusetts.)

men in a cafe. *La Monja Gitana*—in which two men come to life in a nun's memory, wrapping and unwrapping her in a long fabric like a cloud—is repeatedly cited for its taut symbolism.

Ximénez and Vargas were also known for their presentation of Latin American folk dances. The Spanish government granted them special permission to collect and record the regional dances of Spain.

The combination of Ximénez, Vargas, and Maria Alba, their leading female dancer from 1959 to 1963, was particularly felicitous; however, when Ximénez and Vargas began talking about retiring in late 1963, Alba and Ramon De Reyes left to form their own company. Ximénez and Vargas continued to perform in a quartet with Sara de Luis and Maria Dolores through 1964. Vargas now teaches yoga in Mexico City and continues to choreograph, including a solo version of *La Monja Gitana* for Pilar Rioja. Ximénez lives in Madrid, where he teaches dance in a private school.

BIBLIOGRAPHY

Marks, Marcia. "Ximénez-Vargas and the Dance of Spain." *Dance Magazine* (June 1962): 38–42.

Martin, John. "Dance: Spanish." *New York Times* (15 April 1962).

Pedroso y Sturdza, Dolores de. "Manolo Vargas." *Ballet* 11 (April 1951): 40–43.

Pohren, D. E. *Lives and Legends of Flamenco*. Madrid, 1964.

Reviews. *Dance Magazine* (August 1957, April 1958, January 1959, May 1962, January 1963, October 1964).

ARCHIVE. Dance Collection, New York Public Library for the Performing Arts.

JUDY FARRAR BURNS

XIMÉNEZ-VARGAS BALLET ESPAÑOL. *(above)* Manolo Vargas in a dance evoking the ancient indigenous cultures of Mexico. His elaborate ceremonial costume recalls figures from Aztec art. *(below)* Members of the Ximénez-Vargas company in a flamenco work. The couples awaiting their turn to dance provide the *palmas,* the syncopated handclapping accompaniment vital to many flamenco dances. (Photograph above by Anne-marie Heinrich; used by permission. Photograph below by John Lindquist; used by permission of the Harvard Theatre Collection, The Houghton Library.)

YAKKO AND KAWAKAMI, husband-and-wife *shinpa* company, the first Japanese theater group to tour abroad. Kawakami Otojiro (born 1 January 1864, died 11 November 1911) and his wife, Yakko (Kawakami Sadayakko; born 18 July 1871, died 7 December 1946), were colorful intercultural pioneers who opened bridges between Japanese and Western theatrical traditions at the turn of the twentieth century. While a knack for self-promotion and compromise may have resulted in an obscured place in modern theater history, their energies and achievements were significant.

Born into a poor samurai family, Kawakami came to Tokyo just as the shogunate was dissolving. Arrested numerous times for his political soapboxing, he began performing satiric songs, including his famous "Oppekeppe," as a way to continue his political attacks from a safe platform. Dabbling in *rakugo* storytelling and politics, he finally found his forte in *shinpa,* the nascent "new sect" theater movement that opposed *kabuki's* feudal themes and conservative stylization. Kawakami's barnstorming *shinpa* troupes achieved fame and intermittent fortune with productions based on contemporary political events. *Kawakami Otojiro's Battlefield Diary,* a production about Japan's success in the First Sino-Japanese War (1894–1895), featured realistic costumes and battle scenes, catapulting the young man to the largest theaters in Tokyo. *Shinpa* was highly naturalistic compared to *kabuki:* little makeup was used, the actors spoke fluidly, and stage assistants *(kurogo)* were not needed. So realistic were the costumes and acting style that there were reports that actors playing policemen and other villains were attacked by confused audience members.

Kawakami married Yakko, a spirited, high-class Tokyo geisha. In 1896, they raised funds to build the Kawakami-za, a European-style theater without the *hanamichi* (flower path) characteristic of *kabuki* theaters. Hoping to improve their flagging fortunes, husband and wife—along with a troupe of sixteen actors—embarked on a "study mission" to America and Europe in 1899. In San Francisco, Yakko joined the female impersonators onstage, to become the first Japanese woman to act since the shogunate had banned women from *kabuki* three hundred years earlier.

Attempting to distance themselves from the numerous Japanese vaudeville companies and to show their reformist interests, the troupe performed a mixture of ruthlessly edited *kabuki* standards such as *Dōjōji* and *Zingoro* (which they dubbed "A Japanese Pygmalion") and adaptations of Western drama *(Shylock, Sappho, Lady of the Camellias).* During their eight-month tour of the United States, Kawakami refined their repertoire to give the public what it wanted—the blood-and-guts of the sword fighting, the static power of the pantomime scenes, the elegance of Yakko's dancing, and numerous changes of gorgeous costumes.

Despite such exertions, the U.S. tour was poorly attended, although critics raved about Yakko's evocative dancing and heart-rending death scenes. Yakko appeared to use her geisha dance training to good effect, although the *kabuki*-like histrionics of Kawakami were often deemed unintentionally comic. Their most successful adaptation was *The Geisha and the Knight,* a combination of two *kabuki* plays, which displayed Yakko's dancing and acting talents as well as the troupe's acrobatic swordplay. The costumes, stage settings, and delicacy of emotional expression were well received, as critics marveled at these "woodblock prints come to life." Ironically, Yakko and Kawakami's "radical" *shinpa* troupe had become the promoter of *kabuki* tales of Japanese feudalism.

At the Paris Exposition of 1900, the American dancer, inventor, and producer Loie Fuller featured them at her theater, which was designed by Henride Toulouse-Lautrec. The hara-kiri death throes were so popular that Kawakami was asked to add them to every play. Fuller brought the company back a year later for a European tour, but, finding them expensive, she hired a Japanese dance-hall girl of fewer artistic pretensions, Hanako, and turned her into a star.

Meanwhile, Kawakami returned from his Western tours with pronouncements on the strengths of the European drama and a set of reforms: electric lighting, evening performances, tickets sold directly to customers (instead of through teahouse middlemen), and the separation of dance from drama. Trading on its firsthand experience with Western theater, the troupe produced Japanese versions of *The Merchant of Venice (Shylock), Hamlet*—with Hamlet riding a bicycle down the *hanamichi* dressed in a contemporary school uniform—and *Othello,* with the Moor transformed into a Formosan general (the island of Formosa, now Taiwan, was then occupied by Japan, after its success in the First Sino-Japanese War).

Abroad, Yakko had been warmly received by Fanny Kemble, Eleanora Duse, Henry Irving, and Ellen Terry. Encouraged by the high esteem with which women in the acting profession were held in the West, Yakko and Kawakami in 1906 established the first Japanese school for actresses (it was taken over by the Imperial Theater in 1911).

Kawakami died of complications from appendicitis suffered in the United States. Yakko remained active in various theater reforms, giving her farewell tour as an actress in *Aïda* in 1917. She answered critics who complained of her "advanced" age (then only forty-six) by citing Sarah Bernhardt as an example.

Meanwhile, *shinpa's* revolutionary naturalism quickly became stale. *Shinpa* had caused *kabuki* to define itself as the classical theater, but the "new sect" was in turn displaced by *shingeki* as the contemporary, modern theater. *Shinpa* does continue today—but only as frozen melodramas set in the Meiji period (1868–1911).

BIBLIOGRAPHY

Berg, Shelley C. "Sada Yacco: The American Tour, 1899–1900." *Dance Chronicle* 16.2 (1993): 147–196.

Fuller, Loïe. *Fifteen Years of a Dancer's Life* (1913). New York, 1978.

Kei Shionoya. *Cyrano et les samurai: Le Théâtre Japonais en France et l'effet de retour.* Paris, 1986.

Kikou Yamata. "Sada Yacco et le Théâtre Japonais." *La revue de France* 19 (January–February 1939): 65–109.

Otojiro Kawakami and Sada Yacco. *Jiden: Otojiro Sada Yakko.* Edited by Sotetsu Fujii. Tokyo, 1984.

Pronko, Leonard C. *Theater East and West: Towards a Total Theater.* Berkeley, 1967.

Salz, Jonah. "Intercultural Pioneers: Otojiro Kawakami and Sada Yakko." *Journal of Intercultural Studies,* no. 20 (Winter 1993): 25–74.

Sevarese, Nicolas. "La peritpazazi emblematica di Sada Yacco." *Cippario Anno* 35 (1980): 5–31.

Yoko Chiba. "Sada Yakko and Kawakami: Performers of *Japonisme.*" *Modern Drama* 35 (March 1992): 35–53.

JONAH SALZ

YAKOBSON, LEONID (Leonid Veniaminovich Iakobson; born 2 [15] January 1904 in Saint Petersburg, died 17 October 1975 in Moscow), Russian dancer and choreographer. Upon graduation from the Leningrad Ballet School, where he studied under Vladimir Ponomarev, Yakobson danced at the Leningrad State Academic Theater for Opera and Ballet from 1926 to 1933, later becoming its choreographer (from 1942 to 1950 and 1956 to 1975); from 1933 to 1942 he was the choreographer for the Bolshoi Theater in Moscow. Yakobson performed several classical and character dances and roles: Puss in Boots in *The Sleeping Beauty;* the Acrobat in *The Red Poppy;* the Guest Dressed as a Bat in Fedor Lopukhov's new version of *The Nutcracker.* While still a student he began to mount concert pieces for his fellow pupils at the ballet school. When he graduated he was already a member of the Leningrad troupe and continued (without pay) as choreographer for the school. Roles Yakobson created for the junior pupils exhibited a gift for comedy and satire, while those choreographed for the senior grades attested to his enthusiasm for athletic and acrobatic movement. The second act and the dances in the first act of the ballet *The Golden Age,* staged at the Leningrad Opera and Ballet Theater in 1930 with Vasily Vainonen as artistic director, was the first important choreographic production by Yakobson. [*See* Golden Age, The.] His athletic dances for the Workers' Sport Club stadium conveyed the energy and dynamism of sporting events, expressing their competitive spirit and tension. In his one-act *Till Eulenspiegel* (1933), set to Richard Strauss's score, which he choreographed for the graduation recital at the ballet school, Yakobson

YAKOBSON. A scene from the Moscow production of *Shurale,* mounted at the Bolshoi Theater in 1955, with members of the original Bolshoi cast: Vladimir Levashev as Shurale, the wood goblin; Yuri Kondratov as Ali-Batyr, the hunter; and Maya Plisetskaya as Syuimbike, the enchanted bird-maiden. (Photograph from the A. A. Bakrushin Central State Theatrical Museum, Moscow.)

blended all of his comic dance novelties into an integral choreographic program.

The creative ideals of Yakobson's art were rooted in the trends in Soviet art in the 1920s that repudiated everything that had been created before, including classical dancing; things of the past were seen as products of courtly culture that had to be replaced by a new dance idiom capable of expressing the reality of the new era. Yakobson's preference for situations of sharp conflict along strong social, class, and political lines; his repudiation of classical dance and of the right of modern choreographers to use it; and his search for a dance idiom of his own in which dance movements were to be blended with pantomime were all reflections of those trends. Yakobson was a champion of the idea, popular in Soviet ballet in the 1930s, of injecting drama into ballet theater. He sought to invest each action with dramatic meaning and to make the portrayal of each character psychologically convincing. However, the predominant form of ballet in those years was alien to him; its forms followed the canons of classical ballet, alternating dances and pantomime scenes, and it also transplanted onto the ballet stage some of the conventional mechanics of dramatic theater. Pantomime acquired a larger role in ballet productions.

So unconventional were Yakobson's experiments that they effectively frightened off the audience. He composed little at that time, and his dance engagements were infrequent, but by the end of the 1930s he decided to compromise and make peace with classical dance, which had in the meantime regained its lead as an expressive mode in the art of dancing. He arranged and composed several recital divertissements, and in 1941 he choreographed *Shurale,* a three-act ballet with music by Farid Yarullin to be staged in Kazan. But World War II broke out, and *Shurale* was performed only at rehearsals. In 1950 it was finally presented by the Kirov Theater in Leningrad with the title *Ali-Batyr* and in 1955 by the Bolshoi Theater in Moscow. [*See* Shurale.]

Yakobson's *Solveig (The Ice Maiden),* to Grieg's music, was produced in 1952 at the Maly Theater of Opera and Ballet in Leningrad. In it, Yakobson adhered to the themes and structure of Romantic ballet; *Shurale* had been conceived as a classical ballet. Yakobson gave a new meaning to each of these forms. The Ice Maiden, a fantastic being ruling over her kingdom, and Shurale, a wood goblin of Tatar lore, are both creatures inimical to humans. The kingdoms of ice and of the virgin forest, with evil reigning supreme in both, contrasted with the bright and merry worlds of the Norwegian and Tatar countryside. The classical dances in *Solveig* were reserved for scenes of fantastic imagery that gave beauty and an alluring appeal to the production. In *Shurale* the characters in the scene in which the forest comes to life were grotesque, while the classical dance was used to represent birds-turned-maidens and their floating dances; classical movements were also used in the love scenes of the ballet. Although traditional in structure, both ballets asserted a new aesthetic in that their content and characters were interpreted purely by dancing.

In Aram Khachaturian's *Spartacus,* staged at the Kirov Theater in 1956 and at the Bolshoi Theater in 1962, Yakobson introduced no classical dances. Instead he developed the principles of free plastique dance and ancient dance stylization originally introduced by Isadora Duncan and Michel Fokine but disregarded in Soviet ballet for more than thirty years. Yakobson mounted a spectacular gala parade in which he juxtaposed the victorious, bellicose, and harsh Rome of patricians, the military, the troop leader Crassus, his retinue, and his sweetheart Aegina with the slaves, who were sold in the marketplace or forced to kill each other in the circus. The theme of challenging a tyrant's power was consonant with the quest for new means of expression that characterized Soviet art of the period. [*See* Spartacus.]

The new ideas and approaches introduced by Yakobson in *Spartacus* were taken a step farther in *The Bedbug* (1962), set to a score by Otkazov and Firtich, based on Vladimir Mayakovsky's eponymous comedy and some of his other poems, and in *The Twelve* (1964), to music by Boris Tishchenko, based on Aleksandr Blok's eponymous poem and staged in Leningrad by the Kirov Theater. The two ballets represented contrasting trends in Soviet postrevolutionary life: the corrupting influence of philistinism and of vulgar conventionality were the subject of

YAKOBSON. The Battle of the Gladiators from the Leningrad production of *Spartacus,* created for the Kirov Ballet in 1956. The two gladiators pictured are Yuri Maltsev (left) and Yuri Grigorovich (right), in the role of Rietiari. Yakobson's *Spartacus* was mounted in Moscow at the Bolshoi Theater in 1962 but was replaced in 1968 by a new production staged by Grigorovich. (Photograph from the Dance Collection, New York Public Library for the Performing Arts.)

The Bedbug; The Twelve celebrated the emergence of a new outlook on life and of a sense of responsibility for progress. Mayakovsky in the 1920s considered philistinism and vulgar conventionality to be vestiges of the past. Yakobson in his ballet showed how tenacious such remnants of the past were and how easily they degenerated into readiness to prey on and prosper at the expense of others.

In *The Bedbug* Mayakovsky, the central figure of the ballet, is seen by the audience inventing his characters on the stage, only to lose control over them almost immediately. The story of Prisypkin's marriage is the focal point of the ballet, which unfolds amid parasites and moneygrubbers of all sizes and shapes. Marriage is the logical culmination of Prisypkin's entire life, throughout which he excelled only as a conformist. Yet another landmark on Prisypkin's inglorious path is the suicide of Zoya Berezkina, the girl he had seduced. The climax of Prisypkin's aspirations, the episode on the vast nuptial bed that takes up the greater part of the stage evokes in the audience a feeling of disgust from watching a heap of swarming, blood-soaked bedbugs. The primacy of personal over public interests is the theme of the Red Wedding Party scene, in which the philistines march in triumph across the stage holding aloft great chunks of ham and wine bottles. The march proceeds against the background of the Russian Revolution and the civil war that followed: struck down by an enemy bullet a Red Army man drops dead; a Communist is knifed to death; a husband and wife find themselves on opposite sides of the political fence. In the revised version of *The Bedbug* (1974), set to Dmitri Shostakovich's music, Yakobson deleted the revolutionary scenes and stressed situations in which the negative and the alien were exposed and denounced.

In *The Twelve* the dynamic force of the Revolution was embodied in the figures of twelve Red Guard fighters, headed by Petrukha. In the opening scenes they are treated as a formidable and unbridled force, symbolizing the dispossessed, that is ready to destroy the old world, which is stumbling helplessly in a raging snowstorm in need of someone to guide it. In a honky-tonk scene the bar patrons register universal bewilderment in the face of the oncoming revolution and drown their fears in alcohol. Petrukha's murder of Katka, his bride-turned-prostitute, exemplifies the destruction wreaked by the Red Guards. The pangs of remorse expressed in Petrukha's solo that follows the murder scene lead to his regeneration and make him see his responsibility for all that has happened. By the finale the twelve Red Guards have turned into a well-organized force of like-minded men, and the experiences they lived through and paid for in blood make them a conscious revolutionary force with a moral right to change the world.

A follower of Fokine, Yakobson always found himself swimming against the current. He was against clichés and stereotypes in art. A choreographer whose aesthetic was expressed through choreography itself, he sought new idioms and forms and introduced into ballet the imagery and methods of related arts. Denunciation of evil and social vice became the central theme of all his creations, in which the new moral ideal of the hero was taking shape. *Love Stories* (1963), to Maurice Ravel's music, and *The Land of Miracles* (1967), to Isaac Shvarts, were among the last ballets that he choreographed for the Kirov Theater.

In mounting his productions Yakobson always included choreographic miniatures, either to introduce a theme or expand an episode, or to present an image not directly related to the theme. At the Kirov Theater in 1958 Yakobson presented his *Choreographic Miniatures,* which included his best numbers from the past and new arrangements, each of which was a short but complete ballet. The tragedy, comedy, satire, dialogue, and fairy-tale pieces were set to the music of both classical and contemporary composers and bore titles such as *Meditation, Rodin Triptych, Alborada, Skaters, Gossip,* and *Stronger Than Death.*

In 1969 Yakobson formed the troupe Choreographic Miniatures, which made its first public appearance in 1971. Although Yakobson revived some of his old pieces, the repertory was dominated by his new one-act ballets: *Exercise XX,* to Bach; *Contrasts, Traveling Circus,* and *Ebony Concerto,* to Stravinsky; *Jewish Wedding,* to Shostakovich; *Symphony of Eternity,* to Tishchenko; *The City,* to Webern; *A Brilliant Divertissement,* to Glinka; *Surprise,* to Haydn; and *Six Pas de Deux,* to Rossini, Chopin, Britten, Honegger, Lehar, and Donizetti. The best Yakobson miniatures: *Pas de Deux* to music by Mozart, *Pas de Quatre* to Bellini; *Paolo and Francesca* and *Minotaur and Nymph* to Alban Berg; *Troika,* to Stravinsky; *Baba-Yaga* to Mussorgsky; and *Snow Maiden* to Prokofiev.

Relinquishing some of the ideas of his younger days Yakobson, in the last stage of his career, made use of classical dance along with other forms of expression. He developed, transformed, and burlesqued classical dances and mounted compositions the subject matter of which could only be guessed. In the 1970s Yakobson again found himself in the forefront of Soviet ballet, anticipating its subsequent interest in the abstract presentation of humankind's spiritual and moral aspects.

BIBLIOGRAPHY

Demidov, Alexander P. *The Russian Ballet: Past and Present.* Translated by Guy Daniels. Garden City, N.Y., 1977.

Dobrovolskaya, Galina N. *Baletmeister Leonid Iakobson.* Leningrad, 1968.

Koegler, Horst. "Guests from Leningrad: Leonid Jakobson and His 'Choreographic Miniatures.'" *Ballett International* 12 (December 1989): 56–58.

Roslavleva, Natalia. *Era of the Russian Ballet* (1966). New York, 1979.

Ross, Janice. "A Survivor's Story." *Dance Magazine* (April 1988): 76–79.
Swift, Mary Grace. *The Art of the Dance in the U.S.S.R.* Notre Dame, 1968.

GALINA N. DOBROVOLSKAYA
Translated from Russian

YAKṢAGĀNA. The term *yakṣagāna* refers to several styles of dance drama in South India; this article focuses on those prevalent in the North and South districts of Kanara, Karnataka. Male performers enact stories from sacred Hindu texts, mainly the *Mahābhārata* and the *Rāmāyaṇa;* modern performances may also include local legends and new themes, as well as variations on traditional ones.

The styles of the different regions all employ vocal and instrumental music, dance, costume, makeup, and extemporaneous dialogue to tell the story; however, regional styles differ markedly in some respects. The northern style of South Kanara is known for an intricately wrapped headdress, fast steps requiring quick shifts in balance, and distinctive choreography to introduce characters; there are competitive performances in which two or more troupes portray the same stories simultaneously before the same audience. The southern style of South Kanara is famous for detailed philosophical argument, the bravado of demonic characters in varied makeup, whirling dances, and performances depicting the origin of the temple of each troupe.

The North Kanara troupes, although loyal to particular temples, are mostly family-directed. They employ flamboyant body stances, exaggerated facial expressions, and dramatic delivery of dialogue. Each troupe expresses its individuality in choreography, characters, costumes, and makeup.

Basic to traditional *yakṣagāna* is the coordination of body movement with the rhythms of the vocal and instrumental music, the latter provided by two drums—*maddale* and *caṇḍe*—and a pair of small cymbals. The story is explained through extemporaneous dialogue after each segment of music and dance, and the characters are identified through conventional costumes and makeup.

There is no recorded or oral tradition of the origin and development of *yakṣagāna*. It is generally believed that the performance was intended as an offering to a god by a patron in return for a fulfilled request. Performances took place after the rice harvest in a field where the setting was simply an area of ground demarcated by bamboo poles covered with palm frond mats, with lighting provided by torches. The play was free to the public. Although a few troupes employ similar staging to this day, most perform on raised stages in tents with spotlights and audio systems; admission is charged. About twenty-five troupes regularly perform in both Kanara districts from the end of November through May.

In the past, students attended small schools, now nonexistent, to learn the sacred texts they used in improvising dialogue. They learned music and dance from mas-

YAKṢAGĀNA. A procession of dancers from South Kanara, India, wearing characteristically elaborate headdresses. (Photograph from the archives of The Asia Society, New York.)

YAKṢAGĀNA. A *yakṣagāna* troupe includes at least two actor-dancers specializing in demon roles: a *rākṣasa vēśa* (seen here in a daylight portrait) and his demoness counterpart, the *rākṣasi vēśa*. Both men must be tall and sturdy, with broad faces, to bear the characters' heavy crowns and intricate rice-paste-and-pigment makeup. Their entrances are heightened with flaming torches, showers of crackling sparks, even small fireworks. (Photograph from the archives of The Asia Society, New York.)

ter performers in their homes and on the road from one performance to another, and by observing and participating in performances. Today there are temple, government, and privately supported schools and tutors.

Yakṣagāna has undergone many changes. Contact with the West, the impact of modern technology, and a desire to discard the old and bring in the new have influenced and altered it considerably. The adopted foreign elements and techniques obscure the remaining traditions and authentic styles of the troupes. Nevertheless, it remains a popular form of dance drama in South India.

BIBLIOGRAPHY

Ashton[-Sikora], Martha Bush, and Bruce Christie. *Yakshagana: A Dance Drama of India.* New Delhi, 1977.

Karanth, Kota Shivarama. *Yakshagana Bayalata.* Mysore, 1976.

Massey, Reginald, and Jamila Massey. *The Dances of India: A General Survey and Dancer's Guide.* London, 1989.

Massey, Reginald. "Yakshagana Indian Dance Drama." *The Dancing Times* (August 1990): 1084.

MARTHA BUSH ASHTON-SIKORA

YAMADA SETSUKO (born 25 December 1950 in Nagano City, Japan), *butō* performer and choreographer. While a student in the drama department of Meiji University in 1971, Yamada entered the Tenshi-kan *butō* training center, where she studied with Kasai Akira until 1979. She presented her first performance, *Lilac Garden,* a solo, in 1977. This was followed by dances such as *Balance of Ship* (1980), *Lion Heart* (1982), and *Crystal Vagina* (1983).

Yamada danced in Europe for the first time in 1983, when she was invited to perform at La Chartreuse in Villeneuve-lès-Avignon, France and at two festivals in Barcelona. At La Chartreuse, she received acclaim from dancer Carolyn Carlson. She toured in Europe again in 1984, earning raves as "a dancer who possesses extraordinary delicacy."

Yamada performed solo works in Seoul, Korea, in 1986 and 1987. She also choreographed for the Chang mu Dance Company, a troupe of traditional Korean dancers, and performed with them in 1988 and 1989. She collaborated with Jean-Michel Jarre in London in 1988 and with composer Carl Stone in Tokyo in 1989. From 1989 to 1991, she presented seven works in the series *Tentai no*

YAMADA SETSUKO. Wearing men's shoes, the Japanese choreographer appears here in her solo *Father* (1991). (Photograph © 1994 by Jack Vartoogian, used by permission.)

Aki. She choreographed *Father* in 1991, presenting it in Saint Petersburg, Russia, in Bucharest, Romania, as a delegate from the Japan Foundation in 1992, and in New York City in 1994.

Although her dance originated in *butō,* Yamada has created her own style with her own spatial awareness. Yamada's dances, most of which are solos, transform her inner consciousness and memory into movement. For example, her highly acclaimed *Father* was based on her recollection of her father, who had been a dancer in the Ishii Baku Modern Dance Company. The piece calmly evoked her strong tie with her father, her love for him, and complications of their relationship that could not be expressed verbally. The performance ended with lamentation.

Audiences have consistently been amazed at the beauty of Yamada's subtle movement and tensed forms and by the magnitude of the momentary metamorphoses that appear in her dances. Yamada's art is a pure dance of detailed movement and form.

BIBLIOGRAPHY

Hering, Doris. Review. *Dance Magazine* (January 1995): 112–113.

Jennings, Bernadine. "The Spirit Moves, through Sand." *Attitude* 10.4 (1994–1995): 63.

HASEGAWA ROKU
Translated from Japanese

YANG MEIQI (born 20 September 1945 in Shanghai), Chinese teacher, educator, and promoter of dance. In 1956 Yang was admitted to the National Dance Drama Section of the Beijing Dance Academy. After her graduation in 1963 she was assigned to teach Chinese folk dance at the Guangdong Dance School, where she excelled in training folk dancers. She also collected and compiled the local folk dances from fifteen areas in Guangdong Province and systematized them for teaching. In 1979, she was invited back to the Beijing Dance Academy as co-author of college-level teaching materials on Chinese folk dance. In 1983, she was invited by the Hong Kong Dance Federation to teach Chinese folk dance. A year later she was promoted to principal of the Guangdong Dance School, a position that she held until the end of 1995.

As a member of delegations of Chinese dance teachers and choreographers, Yang visited North Korea and the former Soviet Union. Early in the 1980s, when China's central government began to adopt a more open policy, she was greatly stimulated by the information that began to be available on Western modern dance; its educational and creative potential was made known by Chinese who had lived in or visited the West.

In 1986, recommended by Chiang Ching, Yang's former classmate at the Beijing Dance Academy and a New York–based Chinese-American modern dancer and choreographer, Yang had the opportunity to observe American modern dance in New York City and at the American Dance Festival, through a grant from the Asian Cultural Council. On this tour she realized that Western modern dance was indeed what she, her students, and her colleagues at home badly needed, and she determined to do everything possible to bring this creative dance form into China in a systematic way. Strongly supported by Charles Reinhart, director of the American Dance Festival, and Ralph Samuelson, director of the Asian Cultural Council, and encouraged by the Guangdong People's Provincial Government, Yang planned a four-year cooperative project—the "Guangdong Dance School: Modern Dance Experimental Class"—between the American Dance Festival and her school, begun in September 1987.

In July 1990, the Guangdong Dance School Modern Dance Practice Company was formed for the purpose of getting more stage and touring experience. The company impressed audiences at the Fifth Hong Kong International Festival of Dance Academies in July 1990, the Indian International Dance Festival at the end of the same year, and the American Dance Festival in July 1991, performing the students' own compositions. In November 1990, Qin Liming and Qiao Yang, two student members, won a gold medal for pas de deux at the Quatrième Concours International de Danse de Paris with two dances—*Taiji Impression,* choreographed by themselves, and *Ancestral,* choreographed by Willy Tsao, founder, director, and choreographer of the Hong Kong City Contemporary Dance Company.

In May 1992, the first professional modern dance company in mainland China, the Guangdong Modern Dance Company, was officially founded in Guangzhou (Canton), the capital city of Guangdong Province, with Yang as its managing director and Tsao as artistic director. A celebration gala was staged on 6 June at the local Friendship Theater. Under the leadership of Yang and Tsao, the company has successfully toured Singapore, France, Germany, Austria, Korea, and other locales, receiving acclaim from both audiences and critics. As a result of Tsao's involvement, Yang frequently took the company to Hong Kong, where they danced both independently and with the City Contemporary Dance Company.

Yang has published many articles on folk and modern dance. Her recent "Chinese Characteristics Are the Creative Root of the Guangdong Modern Dance Company" is regarded as her public manifesto on Chinese modern dance. She has also served as vice-chairman of the Guangdong Provincial Dance Artists Association, a member of the Guangzhou Municipal Arts Educational Committee, deputy director of the China National Dance Teaching Society, and a member of the China National Dance Artists Association, the Hong Kong Academic Examination and Inspection Bureau, and the Guangdong Provincial People's Political Consultative Conference.

[*See also* China, *article on* Contemporary Theatrical Dance.]

BIBLIOGRAPHY

Ou Jian-ping. *The Modern Dance: Theory and Practice,* vol. 1.5, *Oh, My Great Motherland* (in Chinese). Beijing, 1994.

Ou Jian-ping. "From 'Beasts' to 'Flowers': Modern Dance in China." In *East Meets West in Dance: Voices in the Cross-Cultural Dialogue,* edited by John Solomon and Ruth Solomon. Chur, Switzerland, 1995.

Wang Ke-fen et al., eds. *A Dictionary of Chinese Dance* (in Chinese). Beijing, 1994.

World Ballet and Dance 1–4 (1989–1993). Each volume contains an annual overview of the national dance situation in mainland China by Ou Jian-ping.

Yang Meiqi. "Chinese Characteristics Are the Creative Root of the Guangdong Modern Dance Company" (in Chinese). *Guangdong Magazine,* no. 2 (1994).

Yang Meiqi. "Bringing Modern Dance to China." In *East Meets West in Dance: Voices in the Cross-Cultural Dialogue,* edited by John Solomon and Ruth Solomon. Chur, Switzerland, 1995.

Ou Jian-ping

YAP. *See* Micronesia.

YAQUI DANCE. The Yaqui homeland is in the state of Sonora, Mexico. They had their first significant contact with Jesuit missionaries in 1617. By the mid-1600s, the Yaqui had incorporated Roman Catholicism into their religious system and had developed a Passion play (a play enacting the Passion of Jesus) that is among the oldest still being performed.

There are several Yaqui villages in Arizona established in the nineteenth century, when hundreds of Yaquis crossed the border as political refugees. In order to maintain their tribal identity and their syncretic form of Catholicism, they fled from the repressive Mexican government of Porfirio Diaz.

Men take part in Yaqui Catholic ceremonies to fulfill a vow given by or for an individual. This involves participation in one of several ceremonial groups that require public performances. Women do not fulfill their vows by dancing; instead, they participate in work or singing groups. Among the Arizona Yaqui there are four ceremonial dance groups for men: the Matachini, Fariseo, Caballero, and Fiesta dancers.

The Matachini society, dedicated to the Virgin Mary, dances several times a year. Musicians accompany the dancing with song, guitars, violins, and the Yaqui harp, while the dancers shake rattles. Matachini dance choreography is reminiscent of European folk dances, exemplified by the maypole dance performed on Holy Saturday. The Matachini are considered to be forces for good in the conflict between good and evil of the Passion play.

The Fariseo (Pharisees) personify the forces of evil in the Passion play. Actually dedicated to Jesus, the members pretend that Judas is their patron saint. Some of the members, called *chapayeka,* represent the common soldiers of ancient Rome, then the occupying force in the Near East. These masked figures are both comic and sinister. Not allowed to speak, they communicate by pantomime, hitting wooden swords and daggers together and shaking belt rattles of animal hooves. This "language" is highly stylized and is limited to the *chapayeka.*

In the numerous processions of the Passion play, both the Fariseo and Caballero society members march in file to the sounds of drum, flute, and striking wooden swords and to the noises made by the *chapayeka.* At the conclusion of the Passion play on Holy Saturday, the marching is characterized by a variety of step and tempo changes. The Caballeros change allegiance from evil to good during the final stages of the Passion play and do not participate in the dramatic procession on Holy Saturday, so their dance performances are limited.

The Fiesta dancers include the Pascola group and the Deer dancer *(maso).* The Pascola have small masks that they wear on the sides of their heads while acting as ritual clowns and ceremonial hosts, and on their faces when they pretend to hunt the Deer dancer. During the unmasked dancing, the musicians play violins and harps. The dance includes rapid shuffling of the feet while the hands dangle near the knees. Ankle rattles and bells that hang from the waists of the Pascola dancers provide self-accompaniment. When they perform with the Deer dancer they play sistrums, and a single musician plays a flute and tambour simultaneously.

Shaking hand rattles made of gourds, leg rattles of cocoons, and hip rattles of deer hooves, the Deer dancer reacts to the music of the singers and musicians, who play rasps and a gourd water-drum. On a restricted ground space, with a deer head attached to the crown of his head, the Deer dancer combines dance movements with pantomime to suggest the motions of a deer. Like all Yaqui dancers, he dances in a ceremonial context. He and the Pascola dancers are considered to be magical forces for good.

[*See also* Matachins, *article on* Matachines Dances in the Southwestern United States; *and* Native American Dance.]

BIBLIOGRAPHY

Painter, Muriel T., and E. B. Sayles. *Faith, Flowers, and Fiestas: The Yaqui Indian Year.* Tucson, Ariz., 1962.

Painter, Muriel T. *A Yaqui Easter.* Tucson, Ariz., 1971.

Painter, Muriel T. *With Good Heart: Yaqui Beliefs and Ceremonies in Pascua Village.* Tucson, Ariz., 1986.

Carlos Lozano

YEMEN. Located at the southwestern corner of the Arabian Peninsula, Yemen borders on Saudi Arabia to the north and northeast, the Red Sea to the west, the Indian Ocean to the south, and Oman to the east. An estimated 13 million people live in about 205,000 square miles (528,000 square kilometers), stretching from an arid coastal zone to high mountains and a central plain. Before Islam there were a succession of wealthy South Arabian kingdoms, including the fabled home of the biblical queen of Sheba and the site of the Marib dam mentioned in the Qur'ān. In the medieval period Yemen was renowned for its agriculture and pivotal role in Red Sea–Indian Ocean trade, especially from the port of Aden. Yemen was isolated from the turmoil of the Crusades that influenced the history of much of the Middle East and the Mongol invasion that resulted in the destruction of the ʿAbbasid caliphate. The more populous North Yemen was dominated by a Zaydī religious imamate until the revolution in 1962 created the Yemen Arab Republic. The Zaydī imams, who claimed descent from the Prophet Muḥammad, were originally invited to Yemen by the tribes, who remain the dominant power brokers through the present. The South was colonized by the British in the early nineteenth century, owing to its strategic location on the sea route to India, until a Marxist revolution in 1967 created the Peoples' Democratic Republic of Yemen. Until recently, Yemen was a subsistence-based economy with few indigenous industries. During the 1970s and 1980s up to a third of the male labor force worked outside the country and sent back remittances. Oil was discovered in Yemen in 1984, although production is not as great as in the other states on the Arabian Peninsula. In 1990 North and South united into one country, the Republic of Yemen.

Traditional Dance. A strong, diverse dance tradition reflects the country's ecological and social diversity. Dancing and music are popular throughout Yemen, and the ability to dance is often equated with being Yemeni. Each community has its own dances, which may differ from each other in tempo, movements, and gestures; number and gender of performers; musical accompaniment; and in the appropriate occasions for their performance. Some dances are lively, with a fast tempo and many skips and jumps, whereas others are dignified and subdued, like the Bird Dance of Suḥār in the northern region. In this dance men, wearing robes with wide sleeves that fall like birds' wings, glide slowly and rhythmically, arms outstretched, in imitation of birds in flight. The dances may be performed by men or women. In some communities men and women dance together on a regular basis; in others they do so only in intimate contexts. Yemeni dancing is performed largely by nonprofessionals, although professional dancers are found in the southern highlands and on the Red Sea coastal plain, which is called the Tihama. As a rule, professional musicians accompany dancing on festive occasions.

Yemeni dances utilize weight shifts that are common to other Middle Eastern dance traditions, although the ways in which these are combined result in a typical Yemeni "look." The dances are characterized by intricate steps, outlined shapes on the ground, frequent turns, and moving forward and backward in a deep knee bend. Other steps include walking, the grapevine and its variations, hops, skips, and jumps. The torso is usually held erect, although some dances involve shimmying the hips or the shoulders, or swinging the head and hair with a movement initiated in the upper torso. The men usually carry daggers, sticks, or rifles when dancing. A number of dances accompany sung poetry, and most songs are set to dance music.

Traditional categories include men's dances performed to the accompaniment of drums or chanted poetry; couple dances; and dances in threes performed by men, women, or both. Solos may include the juggling of knives or other demonstrations of acrobatic skill. The religious dancing of the Sufi orders can be seen on the coastal plains and in parts of the southern highlands. *Zār* (the healing ceremony) is performed on the coastal plains. [*See* Zār.]

Dances in the eastern portions of the country include variations of the *bālah,* in which two lines of dancers are separated by a poet. The dancers repeat the verses recited by the poet and then move to the beat of drums (sometimes to other musical instruments as well), while the poet composes another verse. Several poets may compete in a contest of poetic repartee. This genre of dancing may be performed by men, women, or mixed groups, depending on the community and the context of the performance; it is known as *ẓaff* in Yafiʿ. In the northern Tihama region similar line dances, known as *farsānī,* are performed by men only.

The *zubayrī* is a couple dance performed in the evenings in the southern highlands. Another dance from this area is the *ḥawṭī,* performed by male professional dancers to the beat of drums. It involves high jumps and the twirling and juggling of daggers. In the northern highlands, only men perform line dances. Couple dances and dancing in threes are performed by men or women. In Razih, in the northernmost part of the country, the *ghārah* is performed by men to sung poetry, while the *darimah* involves shooting rifles in the air. Women perform a dance in threes called *mathlūth,* in which they weave slow figure eights.

In the Ḥaḍramawt region in southern Yemen, where social stratification was traditionally more rigid than in the north, dances were classified according to the performers' social strata. Traditionally, the *zarbādī* was performed during the ibex hunting season, and the *sharḥ al-rayyid,* in which dancers run across a circle, was performed by members of the elite. This dance included high jumps and deep knee bends. The women's version of this dance is similar to the men's, with smaller changes in level. Merchants and craftsmen performed the *shabwānī,* a line dance accompanied by responsorial poetry. Laborers performed a dance called *luʿbah,* characterized by swinging the body above the waist. Another version of this dance was performed by a man and woman in the midst of a circle of men. The *sharḥ dhāhirī* resembles the *bālah* described above.

Dances performed by men in the Tihama coastal region typically include juggling acts and high jumps. A line dance that has been compared to the Levantine *dabkah* is performed in the northern Tihama.

There are dances associated with various occupations—the tobacco dance, performed by tobacco farmers, and the dances performed by fishermen. Other activities, technically not dancing, are classified as dancing in Yemen. One of these is *raqṣat al-ḥammām,* the bath dance, performed to song and a rhythmic sh-sh-sh sound voiced by the performers. This dance is not aesthetic but a way for performers to work up a sweat before taking a traditional steam bath. Another example is the footwork involved in sowing seeds; the farmer's rhythmic step is considered dancelike.

Imam Yaḥyā, the Islamic ruler of North Yemen from 1914 to 1948, banned the playing of the oud (lute) and *mizmār* (double-reed pipe) and the dancing that accompanied them. The ban was made ostensibly on religious grounds, but apparently also in reaction to the criticism

YEMEN. *(top and bottom)* Men performing a traditional *baraʿ* in a cleared area used as a parking lot in the village of Al-Ahjur. They are wearing everyday dress—a robe or shirt and skirt under a Western-style jacket—and carrying knives in their right hands. (Photographs 1978 and 1979 by Daniel Martin Varisco; courtesy of Najwa Adra.)

and revolutionary ideas aired in songs and at musical sessions. This ban had the effect of forcing urban music and dancing underground. Ironically, Yemeni dancing continued to flourish even while the ban was in effect. Windowless basement rooms were furnished to permit music and dancing that would not be heard by the imam's guards; people also stuffed their windows with cushions so that the music could not be heard outside. A smaller oud, which could be hidden under clothing, was developed. Some musicians immigrated to Ḥaḍramawt, where they established schools of Yemeni classical music, each of which is associated with a particular dance. Rural dancing continued virtually undisturbed.

The ban on dancing did not include *baraᶜ*, a men's dance performed in the highlands to the beat of drums alone. Commonly, the dancers place themselves one behind the next in an open circle, wielding daggers in their right hands. They move forward, backward, and sideways. In parts of the dance they turn so that they are standing side by side and then all move together in one direction. The steps are variations of the grapevine, combined with step-together-step hops, punctuated by turns and deep knee bends. The dancers' eyes are focused on the leader, who dances near the middle of the line, directing movements and initiating changes in tempo. The performance is judged successful to the extent that the dancers achieve an extremely difficult coordination among themselves and with the drummers.

In some areas, the entire male population of a village or group of villages performs together; in others, *baraᶜ* involves only two or three men at a time. Each tribe's *baraᶜ* traditionally differed from that of others and served as one of the tribe's identifying markers. This dance is performed during religious and national holidays, at specific points during wedding festivities, on the road by traveling companions, at home to welcome important visitors, and during cooperative work projects (e.g., building a school or mosque, cleaning out cisterns used in agriculture). Traditionally, during work projects one half of the group would perform *baraᶜ*, while the other half worked (those who worked chanted short work songs); performers and workers alternated for the duration of the project. In Yemen, *baraᶜ* traditionally represented the concept of tribalism, with its emphasis on coordination and group cohesion (Adra, 1982, 1984). It does not share the connotation of frivolity that marks other genres of dancing; in fact, its performance in public is highly respectable. Even heads of state and other notables can be seen performing *baraᶜ* at official functions.

In opposition to *baraᶜ* are varieties of *luᶜbah* couple dances accompanied by song and oud in towns or the *mizmār* in rural areas. Appropriate songs include love songs as well as praises to the Prophet Muḥammad. In many cases, song lyrics speak directly to events in the lives of the dancers. These dances are performed indoors in the evenings at weddings and other celebrations but may be performed at any small gathering of friends or relatives. Traditionally, they were also performed after the harvest. Typically, *luᶜbah* is performed by two men at men's parties, two women at women's parties, or by a man and woman together in the intimacy of the home. Whereas performing *baraᶜ* is considered honorable and dignified, performing *luᶜbah* is considered frivolous—although not necessarily dishonorable when it is performed in appropriate contexts. Symbolically, these dances represent cultural emphases on personal autonomy and on sentiments of love and affection that stand in opposition to the ethic of responsibility and group cohesion signified by *baraᶜ*.

Rapid social and economic changes in Yemen have affected dancing behavior. The traditional couple dance of the northern highlands until the 1970s was the *lāᶜibīyah*. This dance is composed of a series of slow knee bends combined with small weight shifts from one foot to the other. In 1980, only older people were performing this dance. More popular dances, known simply as *luᶜbah* or *raqṣ* ("dance"), focus on complicated footwork performed to intricate cross rhythms. By the late 1980s, a couple dance originally from Lahj in southern Yemen had become popular in the northern cities, where it was known as *Laḥjī*. This dance is a fast-paced, light, gliding dance. It is easier to learn than the traditional northern *luᶜbah*.

Changes have not been limited to *luᶜbah* performance. There has also been a shift in performance contexts and in the significance of *baraᶜ* in many parts of Yemen. Where tribal government has declined in importance relative to that of the national government, the primary locus of identification has shifted from the tribe to the nation: Yemenis now see themselves as Yemeni nationals first and then as members of a particular tribe. Consequently, *baraᶜ* performance has shifted to towns and cities and is perceived as a national dance, representing the cohesiveness of the state.

Yemeni dancing has undergone further changes since the 1970s, with exposure to and influences from abroad. There is a decline in the amount of dancing performed at informal get-togethers at home, as television viewing fills leisure hours. The amount of dancing at formal celebrations has also declined. This is the result of both the significant rise in fees charged by professional musicians and of increased religious conservatism. Increased mobility and access to television have, however, expanded nearly everyone's knowledge of and repertory of dances, as Yemeni men and women learn to perform dances of other regions and other countries.

[*See also* Middle East.]

BIBLIOGRAPHY

Adra, Najwa. "Qabyala: The Tribal Concept in the Central Highlands of the Yemen Arab Republic." Ph.D. diss., Temple University, 1982.

Adra, Najwa. "Achievement and Play: Opposition in Yemeni Tribal Dancing." In *Proceedings of the Consulting Seminar on the Collecting and Documenting of the Traditional Music and Dance for the Arabian Gulf and Peninsula, 15–19 December 1984*. Doha, Qatar, 1984.

Adra, Najwa. "Tribal Dancing and Yemeni Nationalism: Steps to Unity." *Revue du Monde Musulman et de la Méditerranée* 67 (1993).

Botta, Paul-Émile. *Relation d'un voyage dans l'Yémen*. Paris, 1880.

Harris, Walter B. *A Journey through the Yemen and Some General Remarks upon That Country*. London, 1893.

Hunter, Frederick M. *An Account of the British Settlement of Aden in Arabia*. London, 1877.

Ingrams, Harold. "A Dance of the Ibex Hunters in the Hadramaut: Is It a Pagan Survival?" *Man* 37 (1937).

Lāmī, Majīd al-. "Al-Yaman wa-al-turāth al-shaʿbī." *Al-turāth al-shaʿbī* 5 (1974).

Myers, Oliver C. "Little Aden Folklore." *Bulletin de l'Institut Français d'Archéologie Orientale* 44 (1947).

Qāsimī, Khālid al-, and Nizār Ghānim. "Al-mūsīqā al-humāsīyah fī al-khalīj wa-al-Yaman." *Al-ma'thūrāt al-shaʿbīyah* 2 (1987).

Qāsimī, Khālid al-. *Awāṣir al-ghināʾīyah bayna al-Yaman wa-al-Khalīj*. Beirut, 1988.

Rihani, Amin. *Around the Coasts of Arabia*. London, 1930.

Scott, Hugh. *In the High Yemen*. London, 1942.

Serjeant, R. B., ed. *Prose and Poetry from Ḥaḍramawt*. London, 1951.

Serjeant, R. B. "The Ma'n 'Gypsies' of the West Aden Protectorate." *Anthropos* 56 (1961).

Serjeant, R. B. *South Arabian Hunt*. London, 1976.

Skene, R. "Arab and Swahili Dances and Ceremonies." *Journal of the Royal Anthropological Institute* 47 (1917).

Stark, Freya. *A Winter in Arabia*. London, 1941.

Stone, Francine, ed. *Studies on the Tihāmah: The Report of the Tihāmah Expedition 1982 and Related Papers*. Harlow, 1985.

NAJWA ADRA

YERMOLAYEV, ALEKSEI (Aleksei Nikolaevich Ermolaev; born 10 [23] February 1910 in Saint Petersburg, died 12 December 1975 in Moscow), dancer, choreographer, and teacher. Yermolayev studied from 1921 to 1926 at the Leningrad Choreographic Institute under the tutelage of Vladimir Ponomarev. Yermolayev's talent was manifested early. His intelligence, single-mindedness, and determination allowed him to complete in only five years the eight-year program at the school. His graduation performance was in the role of Vayu, god of the wind, in Marius Petipa's *The Talisman*, upon which he was taken into the parent company and immediately became a solo dancer.

While still a student, absorbing and perfecting the heritage of generations of dancers, he began to seek out the new. What fired his imagination was the challenge of expanding the language of male dancing by devising new movements and searching for heroic characters consonant with the new times. In 1930, when he joined the Bolshoi Theater troupe in Moscow, he was already a star. He danced the leading roles in the classical repertory but especially stood out for the range of major roles he created in his contemporaries' ballets, such as Vasily Vainonen's *The Flames of Paris* and *Mirandolina*, Rostislav Zakharov's *The Bronze Horseman* and *The Fountain of Bakhchisarai*, and Leonid Lavrovsky's *The Red Flower* and *The Tale of the Stone Flower*. The ballerina Marina Semenova, Yermolayev's contemporary, said of him that his uninhibited temperament, stamina, and technical brilliance roused audiences. His art heralded the advent of a new style that asserted the strong and heroic in classical dance. His dancing gave the impression of risk, of bold and innovative interpretations, which was true even of the traditional roles. Yermolayev's supremacy at characterization was unchallenged. The veteran Moscow Maly Drama Theater actress Elena Gogoleva said that he lived his roles; with his perfect command of technique he also offered a meticulously acted rendering of a role.

Although filled with advanced ideas, Yermolayev's choreographic output was small. At the Belarussian Opera and Ballet Theater he choreographed two ballets: *The Nightingale* (1939), to Mikhail Kroshner's score, and *Fiery Hearts* (1954), to Vasily Zolotarev's music. According to contemporary accounts, in staging these ballets he displayed daring and imaginative innovation. *Peace Will Prevail Over War* (1952) was a concert piece to the music of various composers. Directed, choreographed, and danced in by Yermolayev, it proved that modern themes could be adapted to the ballet stage. He also choreographed several *divertissements*.

Upon his retirement from dancing after a career at the Bolshoi that spanned the years 1930–1958, he channeled his energies into coaching the company from 1960 until his death, and teaching from 1968 to 1972 at the Moscow School of Choreography. There, he devised an unusual system of training dancers; his lessons and dance sessions resembled a creative laboratory in which new movements and means of expression were tested on a daily basis. Legends about Yermolayev's classes gained wide currency and are still in circulation. He schooled a galaxy of gifted dancers, among them Vladimir Vasiliev, Mikhail Lavrovsky, Vladimir Tikhonov, and Yuri Vladimirov. These dancers promoted the strong male dancing conceived by their teacher. They inherited from him a gallant attitude toward their art, a lack of complacency about their accomplishments, and the methods of rehearsing roles that he had perfected. Yermolayev is credited with instilling in them a savor for self-discovery and a stimulating creative drive, the qualities that were his hallmarks.

In 1970 Yermolayev was honored with the title People's Artist of the USSR after having won several state prizes.

BIBLIOGRAPHY

Bazhenova, T. P., ed. *Aleksei Ermolaev* (in Russian). Moscow, 1982.

Beaumont, Cyril W. "The Nightingale." In Beaumont's *Supplement to Complete Book of Ballets*. London, 1942.

Churova, Marina, ed. *Aleksei Ermolaev* (in Russian). Moscow, 1974.

Lawson, Joan. "A Short History of the Soviet Ballet, 1917–1943." *Dance Index* 2 (June–July 1943): 77–96.
Mamontov, George. "Two Dancers: Alexei Yermolayev and Vakhtang Chabukiani." In *The Soviet Ballet*, by Yuri Slonimsky et al. New York, 1947.
Smakov, Gennady. *The Great Russian Dancers*. New York, 1984.
Volkov, Nikolai D. "Distinguished Artists of the Moscow Ballet." *The Dancing Times* (October 1944): 13–14.

BORIS B. AKIMOV
Translated from Russian

YE SHAOLAN (born 1943 in Beijing), Chinese opera actor specializing in *xiaoshen* roles. Among the acknowledged stars of Chinese classical musical drama—in particular those who specialize in the *xiaoshen* role (young heroes, scholars, government officials, or generals)—Ye Shaolan is a premier artist, named by the People's Republic of China as a national treasure. Born in 1943 in Beijing, he is in the fourth generation of an established line of Beijing Opera performers, the tradition passing from father to son. His father, Ye Shenglan, was the leading man in a famous troupe that was invited to Paris, receiving adulatory critical response and the praise of Charlie Chaplin. He began to train his son in the art of young male roles when the boy was seven years old. Ye Shaolan remembers standing on one leg, the other on a high fence (undoubtedly as his father had before him), shivering in his underwear in the snow, sweating in padded winter garments in the heat of summer, training to concentrate on reciting lines and singing arias while disregarding physical discomfort. Until his father's death during China's Cultural Revolution of 1966 to 1976 (when classical opera was forbidden), the father continued to train his son secretly; with a return to normalcy, the son emerged in his father's place.

Ye Shaolan was formally educated at the Chinese Academy of Operas in Beijing, graduating in 1962; he completed further studies in the Directing Department of the Central Institute of Drama (1972). Throughout those years he was also tutored by Ru Fulan, Jiang Miaoxiang, Xiao Lianfang, Yu Zhengfei, and Yan Qinlin, all renowned artists in Beijing Opera. He had not only the best academic training available but also personal guidance from great performers. As a result, he excels in all aspects of his art, acting, singing (imitating and developing the voice skills of the great Beijing Opera actor Qiu Shengrong, especially in integrating voice and emotion), martial arts, and dance technique and interpretation. His comprehensive grasp of the form has made him a remarkable director as well; he has reworked old classics with fine dramatic effect.

Ye Shaolan's repertory includes his signature role as Lu Bu in *Lu Bu and Diao Chan*, an operatic adaptation of one of the early stories in *San Guo* (Three Kingdoms), which combine ambition and political strategy with a weakness for women, leading to subsequent downfall—a piece that provides a fine range for the *xiaoshen* performer. He has also starred with outstanding success in *An Assembly of Heroes*, another historical drama from the San Guo period; in *Liang Shanbo and Zhu Yingtai*, a Romeo and Juliet–style story; and in *The Legend of the White Snake*, an old folk tale. For these and other roles, he won the first Plum Blossom Award from the Chinese government.

In 1985, Ye was Fulbright Scholar and Artist in Residence at Bennington College in Vermont, teaching classes in movement and dance. He also gave public lectures and demonstrations: an excellent series on the art of Beijing Opera at Bennington, with shorter versions presented at nearby colleges. He adapted famous scenes from operas for his best students; toward the end of his stay, he incorporated their performances into his lectures, which he took farther afield to major universities, and to the Asia Society in New York City. He was received with popular and critical acclaim. Audiences that often had no previous experience of Beijing Opera were won over by Ye's mastery of his field, the brilliance and sincerity of his performance, and the accomplishments of the students, a real tribute to Ye as a teacher. He has made professional visits to Taiwan, Hong Kong, Singapore, Japan, Australia, and England, deepening the knowledge of cognoscenti, enlightening newcomers, and winning new fans for the art.

Ye is affiliated with the Zhan You Beijing Opera Company of Beijing. He is a member of the board of directors of the All-China Association of Dramatists and a member of the executive committee of the Conference on Political Consultation of China.

[*See also* China, *article on* Dance in Opera.]

BIBLIOGRAPHY

Arlington, L. C. *The Chinese Drama: From the Earliest Times Until Today.* Shanghai, 1930, New York, 1966.
Mackerras, Colin. *The Rise of the Peking Opera (1770–1870): Social Aspects of the Theatre in Manchuria.* Oxford, 1972.
Mackerras, Colin. *The Chinese Theatre in Modern Times: From 1849 to the Present Day.* Amherst, Mass., 1975.
Mackerras, Colin. ed. *Chinese Theater from its Origins to the Present Day.* Honolulu, 1983.
Scott, A(dolphe) C(larence). *The Classical Theatre of China.* Westport, Conn., 1957.
Yung, Bell. *Cantonese Opera: Performance as Creative Process.* Cambridge, 1989.
Zung, Cecilia S. L. *Secrets of the Chinese Drama: A Complete Explanatory Guide to Actions and Symbols, as Seen in the Performance of Chinese Dramas.* New York, 1937, 1964).

PHEBE SHIH CHAO

YOGA. The Sanskrit word *yoga* means "union with the higher reality." It is one of the six schools of Indian philosophy, and, unlike the other schools, it stresses practical methods of self-development. It advocates several paths toward the ultimate goal of communion with the Cosmic Being, the most common of which are *karmayoga,* the path of action, *bhaktiyoga,* the path of devotion, *jñānayoga,* the path of knowledge, and *haṭhayoga.* Hatha yoga is considered the lowest rung on this ladder of self-realization, but it is of particular interest to dancers and to those interested in the health and physiological condition of the human body and in the control of breath. It is not accepted as a formal school of philosophy, however, because its concentration is on *āsana*s (postures of the body), and *prāṇāyāma* (breath control).

Hatha yoga was codified systematically in the extensive work *Haṭhayogapradīpikā* by Svātmārāma between 1350 and 1550. The author of this text states that *ha* represents the sun, and *ṭha* the moon. They are also symbolic expressions of *iḍā* and *piṅgala,* the two main channels of subtle energy in the body, and of left and right, female and male, passive and active—the yin and yang of Chinese philosophy. Hatha yoga is the practice of uniting *prāṇa* and *apāṇa,* sun and moon.

This yoga, along with the others, finally leads to the highest yoga of all, the *rājayoga,* or "royal" yoga, which is also called *aṣṭāṅgayoga* (the Eight-Fold Path) and includes the teachings of all the paths of yoga. Hatha yoga should not be treated only as a method of bodily development, even though it expounds physical postures, but rather as the first key for the opening of the door of self-realization.

Hatha yoga prescribes from 84 to 108 *āsana*s. According to *Haṭhayogapradīpikā,* "*āsana*s make one firm, free from maladies and light of limb." This means that the body is made calm for the purpose of meditation, which is deepened if the body is in good health and free from aches and pains. In addition, the body and mind are both lightened by the removal of excess weight, and by the elimination of lethargy and depression.

YOGA. A yogin, or follower of yoga disciplines, adopts an immobile posture to isolate his mind from bodily functions. (Photograph by Associated Press of India.)

BIBLIOGRAPHY

Bharata-Muni. *The Nāṭyaśāstra Ascribed to Bharata-Muni.* Translated by M. M. Ghosh. 2 vols. Calcutta, 1951–1961.

Eliade, Mirca. *Yoga: Immortality and Freedom.* 2d ed. Princeton, N.J., 1969.

Himalayan International Institute of Yoga Science and Philosophy. *Hatha Yoga.* Honesdale, Pa., 1977.

Vatsyayan, Kapila. *Indian Classical Dance.* 2d ed. New Delhi, 1992.

RITHA DEVI

YORUBA DANCE. One of the largest ethnic groups of southwestern Nigeria, the Yoruba make up approximately 20 percent of that nation's estimated ninety million inhabitants. According to archaeological evidence, they have been traditionally traders and farmers and to some extent an urbanized people since at least the first millennium—their lifestyle was first described to Europeans by Portuguese traders in the fifteenth century.

According to a Yoruba adage, "not standing still is dancing." In its broadest sense, Yoruba dance expresses the vitality of existence and the individual's well-being (*iwapele,* literally, "gentle or prudent character"). Thus, one of the most valued traits of a Yoruba dancer is composure, which is registered in a rhythmically controlled body, a calm, expressionless face, and a motionless head. Robert Farris Thompson (1966) called this characteristic "the aesthetic of the cool." For the Yoruba, a collected, controlled appearance reflects a composed, prudent state of mind. In dance, technical proficiency combined with improvisational flair communicates this ideal inner state.

Because of its emphasis on technical mastery and improvisation, the formal and stylistic properties of Yoruba dances override concern with narrative content; indeed, rhythm and style provide the primary content. Therefore, two dancers performing simultaneously adhere to the rhythmic structure of the music in the style appropriate to a specific context, but what they actually do within that framework is always spontaneous. Performers dance at the same time—but not necessarily together—with little concern for strict spatial, dynamic, or even rhythmic uniformity. What is most crucial is the communication between each dancer and the musicians.

Yoruba dancing is inseparable from drumming. In fact, the most frequently mentioned criterion is that dancers understand the musical structure and phrasing of the drums and match their stepping to the drum rhythms. Although the music is percussive, the dancing that accompanies it varies from highly percussive to extremely fluid, depending on the gender and status of the dancer. Men's dancing is usually "hard," forceful, and energetic, while women's is "cool," fluid, and delicate. (These values remain in the Yoruba-derived Candomblé dances in the state of Bahia, northeastern Brazil.)

Yoruba dance is composed of discrete rhythmic units, which can be elaborated, repeated, deleted, or condensed. The outer features of Yoruba dance include spatial and temporal segmentation, discontinuity, repetition, spontaneity, and simultaneity. The more specialized dances are also rhythmically irregular. Dancers may perform relatively simple rhythms as long as they work up to their capacity; drummers respond to the level of the dancers' proficiency, either by progressively increasing the complexity and sophistication of the music or by simplifying it.

The basis of the rhythmic units is verbal, usually in the form of drummed aphorisms or proverbs. A strong correlation is often observed between the sound qualities of the drummed verbal texts and the effort (or dynamic) qualities of the dancer, particularly in the context of a possession-trance performance, in which the dancer "becomes" the deity, to express the essence of that deity's power. Thus, the verbal basis of the music is not merely mnemonic or semantic; rather, the verbal content, the music, and the dance together represent attitudes toward time, space, weight, and flow—that is, the effort qualities appropriate to a particular context. The Yoruba use effort qualities as an expression of the metaphysical concept of the vital life force *(ase)*.

Yoruba children frequently inherit the authority to perform specialized dances, but divination also plays a crucial role in identifying and authorizing performers. Generally, the learning process involves emulating the masters. During initiations into priesthoods, however, dance training is more formal. In other contexts, students learn stepping styles and rhythms by observing and imitating their elders. With regular, sustained exposure to performances, children assimilate particular dance techniques, structures, and drum phrases; by learning to mark simple stepping patterns, they begin to perform by the age of three. Encouraged to dance, they are then rewarded with small coins and cheers from the spectators. Older, more accomplished children are usually followed closely by an adult from their lineage who makes sure that they follow the rhythms of the drums and accent the proper beats. With preadolescents, the coach watches from the side but does not hesitate to rush forward to make a correction. The performance itself therefore functions as a training session for novices.

In the interplay among Yoruba dance participants, spectators become performers and performers become spectators. Dancers or family members can tell drummers what to play, or drummers can initiate music. Spectators are free to join in the dancing. Thus individuals shape performances spontaneously, making each one fluid and unique.

YORUBA DANCE. During a ceremony in Sakete, Benin, this young man was possessed by Ṣango, a powerful deity of the Yoruba people. With upraised arms, he dances in the guise of the god. (Photograph © 1981 by Pierre Verger; used by permission)

Through Yoruba dance, spiritual forces materialize for the community's benefit. Such materializations take the form of possession trances and masquerading; possession trance is primarily within women's domain, while masking is the prerogative of men. In possession trance, the god is said to mount *(gun)* the devotee (*elegun*, literally, "one who is mounted"), and, for a time, that devotee becomes the god. Whatever a priest does from the moment of entering the trance state is thought to represent a god's own actions. Such spirit mediumship is the most significant role of a priest.

Some traits and ideals of Yoruba dance have had a significant impact on certain dance forms in the Americas. This is especially evident in Brazil, Cuba, and the United States—where aspects of Yoruba belief and the tradition of danced worship survive and flourish.

[*See also* West Africa.]

BIBLIOGRAPHY

Abiodun, Rowland. "Identity and the Artistic Process in Yoruba Aesthetic Concepts of Iwa." *Journal of Culture and Ideas* 1 (December 1983).

Abiodun, Rowland, et al., eds. *The Yoruba Artist: New Theoretical Perspectives on African Arts.* Washington, D.C., 1994.

Ajayi, Omofolabo Soyinka. "Aesthetics of Yoruba Recreational Dances as Exemplified in the Oge Dance." *Dance Research Journal* 21 (Fall 1989): 1–8.

Drewal, Henry John, and Margaret Thompson-Drewal. *Gelede: Art and Female Power among the Yoruba.* Bloomington, 1983.

Harper, Peggy. "Dance in Nigeria." *Ethnomusicology* 13.2 (1969): 280–295.

Laoye I, Adetoyese. "Yoruba Drums." *Odu* 7 (1959).

Thompson, Robert Farris. "An Aesthetic of the Cool: West African Dance." *African Forum* 2.2 (1966).

Thompson, Robert Farris. *Black Gods and Kings: Yoruba Art at UCLA.* Los Angeles, 1971.

Thompson, Robert Farris. *African Art in Motion: Icon and Act.* 2d ed. Los Angeles, 1979.

Thompson-Drewal, Margaret, and Glorianne Jackson, comps. *Sources on African and African-Related Dance.* New York, 1974.

Thompson-Drewal, Margaret. "Symbols of Possession: A Study of Movement and Regalia in an Anago-Yoruba Ceremony." *Dance Research Journal* 7 (Spring-Summer 1975): 15–24.

Thompson-Drewal, Margaret, and Henry John Drewal. "More Powerful Than Each Other: An Egbado Classification of Egungun." *African Arts* 11 (Spring 1978).

Thompson-Drewal, Margaret, and Henry John Drewal. "Composing Time and Space in Yoruba Art." In *The Relationship of the Verbal and Visual Arts among the Yoruba,* edited by Rowland Abiodun. 1987.

Thompson-Drewal, Margaret. "Dancing for Ogun in Yorubaland and in Brazil." In *Africa's Ogun: Old World and New,* edited by Sandra T. Barnes. Bloomington, 1989.

Thompson-Drewal, Margaret. *Yoruba Ritual: Performers, Play, Agency.* Bloomington, 1991.

Verger, Pierre. "Role joue par l'État d'Hebetude au cours de l'initiation des novices aux cultes des Orisha et Vodun." *Bulletin de l'Institut Français d'Afrique Noire, Series B* 16 (1954).

Verger, Pierre. *Orixás: Deuses iorubás na Africa e no Novo Mundo.* Salvador, Brazil, 1981.

MARGARET THOMPSON-DREWAL

YOUSKEVITCH. In costume for one of the princely roles in which he excelled, Youskevitch posed for this studio portrait c.1940. (Photograph from the archives at Jacob's Pillow, Becket, Massachusetts.)

YOUSKEVITCH, IGOR (Igor' Ivanovich Iuskevich; born 13 March 1912 in Pieyatin, Ukraine, died 13 June 1994 in New York), Russian-American ballet dancer, choreographer, and teacher. Youskevitch was probably the single dancer most responsible for establishing ballet as an acceptable profession for a man in the Americas. He inspired many young people to enter the profession through his masculine, unmannered, naturally elegant, and ardently romantic approach, in contrast to the highly stylized and theatrical manner of many earlier European dancers. He was instrumental in setting the style of American male classical dancers and in gaining recognition for the classics, which in the Ballets Russes tradition tended to be overshadowed by modern *demi-caractère* ballets. Edwin Denby once summed him up as follows:

> His style is calm, rich and elastic. It is completely correct. . . . The trunk takes the main direction of the dance and the limbs vary the force and the drive by calculated countermovements. The changing shape of the dancing body is vigorously defined. The weight of the body and the abundant strength of it are equally clear; and the two aspects blend gracefully in the architectural play of classic sequences. The distribution of energy is intelligent and complex. In his leaps, for instance, the noble arm positions, the tilt to the head sideways or forward, make you watch with interest a whole man who leaps. . . .
>
> The completeness of his dance education is unique among our classic male dancers. His rhythm is free, his characterization economical, his lift gracious. His stage presence has none of that hard insistence on attention that breaks the illusion and the flow of a classic ballet. (Denby, 1949)

Backstage, Youskevitch's even temper, good manners, and detachment from petty rivalries were cited as an inspiration by his colleagues. The press made much of his athletic background (even claiming he had been in the circus) and his status as a family man. He was married to Anna Scarpova; she and their daughter Maria were both dancers.

He left his native Russia at the age of eight as a refugee from the revolution and settled in Belgrade, pursuing academic studies as far as the Royal University and becoming a champion amateur gymnast. Chosen by an adagio-style dancer, Xenia Grunt, as a concert partner, he began ballet training at age twenty, principally with Olga Preobrajenska. He overcame his late start in ballet through his gymnastics background, natural aptitude, analytical mind, and the experience gained under the guidance of Leon Woizikowski with the Ballets Russes de Paris (1934–1935), the Ballets de Léon Woizikovsky (1935–1936)—where Youskevitch became first classical dancer—and in a second company of Colonel Wassily de Basil (1936–1937) on a ten-month tour of Australia. He made an early reputation in Michel Fokine's *Le Spectre de la Rose* and danced it under the choreographer's direction as a guest with René Blum's Ballets de Monte-Carlo.

As a principal dancer of Serge Denham's Ballet Russe de Monte Carlo (1938–1944), Youskevitch created roles in such works as Léonide Massine's *Gaîté Parisienne, Seventh Symphony,* and *Rouge et Noir;* Bronislava Nijinska's *The Snow Maiden;* Aleksandra Fedorova's *Magic Swan* (*Swan Lake,* act 3); and Igor Schwezoff's *Red Poppy* (Ribbon Dance). He left the company to serve in the U.S. Navy, and upon his discharge after World War II he joined Massine's Ballet Russe Highlights (1946) and then (American) Ballet Theatre (1946–1955). He made later guest appearances with the latter, including a tour of Russia in 1960.

George Balanchine choreographed *Theme and Variations* for Youskevitch, capturing his nobility, *élan,* and technical control; the role, still a challenge to the best dancers, is considered one of his greatest, along with Albrecht in *Giselle.* He added to his repertory such varied ballets as *La Fille Mal Gardée,* the *Don Quixote* pas de deux, Nijinska's *Schumann Concerto,* Balanchine's *Apollo,* and Valerie Bettis's *A Streetcar Named Desire,* and formed an illustrious fourteen-year partnership with Alicia Alonso, both in the United States and Cuba. He appeared with Alonso's company from its inception in 1948, dancing the standard repertory, full-length classics, and Cuban works, and touring Latin America. He rejoined Ballet Russe de Monte Carlo from 1955 through 1957, becoming the company's artistic adviser. Gene Kelly's feature film *Invitation to the Dance* was released at this time, showcasing Youskevitch's dancing, of which the film remains the best record.

Youskevitch made a concert tour of South America with Nathalie Krassovska as his partner in 1961. He choreographed, restaged the classics, and established his own New York school (1960–1980), and was head of the dance program of the University of Texas at Austin (1971–1982), which honored him with a four-day tribute on his retirement. In 1983 he became the artistic director of the New York International Ballet Competition, a position in which he was active until his death. Youskevitch received a *Dance Magazine* Award in 1958 and the Capezio Award in 1992.

BIBLIOGRAPHY

Barker, Barbara. "Celebrating Youskevitch." *Ballet Review* 11 (Fall 1983): 27–29.

Cohen, Selma Jeanne. "Prince Igor: The Story of Youskevitch." *Dance Magazine* (May 1953): 14–17.

Denby, Edwin. *Looking at the Dance* (1949). New York, 1968.

Hunt, Marilyn. "Danseur Noble." *Ballet News* 3 (March 1982): 16–18.

Hunt, Marilyn. "Igor Youskevitch Dancing." *Ballet Review* 11 (Fall 1983): 32–63.

Newman, Barbara. *Striking a Balance: Dancers Talk about Dancing.* Rev. ed. New York, 1992.

Youskevitch, Igor. "Igor Youskevitch" in "The Male Image." *Dance Perspectives,* no. 40 (Winter 1969).

Youskevitch, Igor. "Former Soviet Stars as Seen by a Colleague." *New York Times* (21 February 1982).

Youskevitch, Igor. "Busing Les Ballets." *Ballet Review* 11 (Fall 1983): 30–31.

FILMS. *Seventh Symphony* (1938). *Ballets Russes de Monte Carlo* (c.1941). *Giselle,* NBC (1950). *Invitation to the Dance* (1956). Ann Barzel, *Youskevitch Gala* (n.d.), Dance Collection, New York Public Library for the Performing Arts.

MARILYN HUNT

YUAN XUEFEN (born 26 March 1922 in Zhejiang, China), Shaoxing Opera actress. One of the best known and founding actresses of *Yueju,* or Shaoxing Opera, an all-female theatrical genre and one of the most popular in China, Yuan was born into a rural teacher's family. She began her training at eleven, following a failed attempt at eight, with a male master in a local opera genre different from the then-embryonic Shaoxing Opera. Yuan played her first leading role in Hangzhou in 1936, shortly before her debut in Shanghai the same year. While her early performances were often with male partners in slightly different styles, she participated in China's first recording of the all-female Shaoxing Opera. She settled in Shanghai in 1938, concentrating on developing and refining the new female genre for urban audiences. In 1945, she founded her own Xuesheng company. In 1950, she became head of China's first state-sponsored Shaoxing Opera company—the East China Experimental Shaoxing Opera Company—and later headed the Shanghai Shaoxing Opera Theater (where she is now honorary head). She led her company on tour to East Germany and the Soviet Union (1955), Hong Kong (1960), North Korea (1961), France (1986), and to the United States (1989).

Compared to most older traditional Chinese theatrical genres, Shaoxing Opera is less conventionalized and more influenced by modern drama, especially in its use of scenery. But Yuan preferred suggestive sets, somewhere between modern drama's realism and Beijing Opera's bare stage. She also learned from *kunqu*'s (Kun opera) salient characteristic of simultaneous singing and dancing. Because in ancient China decent (noble) women were required to wear floor-length dress and walk in small steps (on bound lily feet), Yuan's characters seldom had large movements like jumping or running; instead they concentrated on the nuanced gestures of upper body, hands, and facial parts, and they played with small props such as a fan or letter. Because many of her performances were in love scenes with a male character played by a female actress, the exchange of expression between the performers was particularly delicate.

In 1953, Yuan helped conceive, choreographed, and starred in, *Liang Shanbo and Zhu Yingtai;* the subsequent film version won the Prague Film Festival prize for best musical film. In this tragedy of love, Yuan played Zhu Yingtai, who had to disguise herself as a man to leave home for school, where she fell in love with a schoolmate unaware of her feelings. Its best-known scene "Farewell," which has often been performed in excerpt, featured Yuan playing a woman faking a man trying every possible way to convey her love to a man played by a woman before leaving him. Slowly, they walked a meandering path, passing eighteen locales, such as a pond where couples of mandarin ducks swan, a well in which Zhu saw a wedding picture, and a temple with a fertility goddess. All these were indicated by Yuan's exquisite fingers, a fan, and her facial expressions mixing eagerness and bashfulness.

In Yuan's co-adaptation of the classic play *Xi Xiang Ji* (The West Chamber), she created the character of a vivacious matchmaking maid. Yuan also successfully created modern characters, the best known being Mrs. Xianglin in both stage and film versions, based on China's best writer Lu Xun's short story about a poor widow who lost everything to the oppressive society. In addition to the many young actresses trained in Yuan's theater, she also trained the first few male Shaoxing Opera actors.

BIBLIOGRAPHY

Yuan Xuefen. "Biography." Unpublished manuscript entry to *Shanghai Yueju Zhi* (records of Shanhai Shaoxing opera).

Zeng Bairong et al., eds. *Jingju Jumu Cidian.* Beijing, 1989.

Zhongguo Da Baikequanshu: Xiju, Quyi. Beijing, 1983.

WILLIAM H. SUN

YUGOSLAVIA. [*To survey the dance traditions of the former Socialist Federal Republic of Yugoslavia, this entry comprises five articles:*

The first article explores traditional dance in Macedonia and six zones that made up Yugoslavia; the second and third articles focus on the development of ballet and modern dance to 1991; the fourth article examines theatrical dance since 1991; the concluding article provides a brief history of scholarship and writing.]

Traditional Dance

The Socialist Federal Republic of Yugoslavia was created in 1918. Throughout its relatively brief national history, it was an uneasy union of diverse cultural groups critically in need of common denominators. The country comprised six republics (Croatia, Bosnia-Herzegovina, Slovenia, Serbia, Montenegro, and Macedonia) and two autonomous regions (Kosovo and Vojvodina), with three official languages (Serbo-Croatian, Macedonian, and Slovenian), two official alphabets (Latin and Cyrillic), three principal religious groups (Eastern Orthodox Christians, Roman Catholics, and Muslims), and a large number of ethnic minorities.

The scarcity of historical records prior to the ninth century makes it virtually impossible to determine what dance was like in the Balkans before the arrival of the Slavs in the sixth and seventh centuries; neither do we know what kind of dances the Slavs brought with them, or what the dance situation was in the fourteenth and fifteenth centuries, when most of the area fell to the Turks. Comparative (especially linguistic) studies, combined with empirical data collected over the past hundred years, indicate that communal group dancing was common to the Slavs in their original homeland north of the Carpathian Mountains. The chain dance (a closed or broken circle of dancers usually linked by joined hands) was the predominant form in Europe through the Middle Ages; among the Slavs it bore the name *kolo* ("wheel"). There may also have been an ancient type of couple dance without physical contact. It is highly likely, however, that the old Slavic repertory contained religious as well as purely social dancing, and that accompaniment was both vocal and instrumental. That the Slavs may not have distinguished clearly between the activities of dance and play is evidenced in the word *igra,* which has survived to the present with both meanings. In certain areas of Yugoslavia its meaning is limited to play or game, while in other areas, notably Serbia, it denotes both game and dance.

Traditional dance is defined here as folk dances, that is, social and ritual dances passed down from generation to generation primarily through imitation of culturally approved models. The period of collection of dances existing in actual practice or in the memories of the oldest informants began in the early 1930s. In remote areas, less touched by industrialization, the media, and urbanization, many of these dances survive in their latest evolved forms; in other areas they are rare in spontaneous contexts, but they are taught in schools and cultivated as living museum pieces on stage at folklore festivals. These gatherings were sponsored by the communist government for the purpose of preserving the dances under strictly-enforced rules of authenticity. The dances today thus represent an arbitrarily selected stage in the process of slow evolution.

In understanding traditional dance in Yugoslavia, it is important to bear in mind that one is seldom dealing with discrete data; rarely can one define a given dance with a single name and a single melody. Underlying structural patterns of movement have diffused over the area and beyond the national boundaries, assuming various names, tunes, styles, and modes of execution. Dances with different names found in different regions may be identical in structure and meter. The assignment of names is often an arbitrary recourse of the outsider or scholar.

The Yugoslavian dance ethnographer and choreographer Ivan Ivancan has defined six dance zones, the Dinaric, Morava, Vardar, Adriatic, Alpine, and Pannonian. (Macedonia also merits consideration as a separate zone.) The line that marks the division between the first three zones and the others coincides generally with the boundary that separated the Ottoman Empire from Europe from the fourteenth century to the late nineteenth century. In the Turkish-dominated region, the traditional patriarchal society of the Slavs remained stronger and the occurrence of ritual dances more frequent; under the Ottomans the medieval circle and chain dances continued to evolve. The other regions reflect the influence of Mediterranean and central European cultures, favoring the social and couple dances of the nineteenth and twentieth centuries. The Pannonian zone shows the influence of central Europe, often fascinatingly combined with the older *kolo* elements.

A phenomenon of the Dinaric, Morava, and Vardar regions is a rather small group of basic structural patterns upon which a larger number of discrete dances are built. For example, the *devojack* pattern has generated dozens of dances throughout the area, including some of the oldest. The *kokonjeste* pattern underlies the most famous family of dances in Serbia, variously known as *usest, sestica,* and *kukunjes.*

An important social element in these areas is the role of the male. A kind of Balkan cool and what social psychologists now call male bonding are operative, dating back to ancient times in a traditional patriarchal society. The male who pays the musicians has paid for the lead position in the dance. His performance in that role counts in acquiring and maintaining his position in the community and among his peers. The concept of the open circle, with a position for a male leader and an end man in a women's dance, is a development of this social attitude.

Dinaric Zone. The western mountain Dinaric area includes the Croatian hinterlands of Dalmatia, most of Bosnia-Herzegovina, and Montenegro. The area is rugged, life is hard, and stock breeding is the principal occupation. The dances of this area seem to be the most archaic in Yugoslavia. Chain dances made up of simple walking patterns, especially the ubiquitous Faeroe step, are performed along a curved path. They are found in other parts of the Balkans as well, and this and the features they share with the dances of other Slavs point to their great age.

In parts of Bosnia-Herzegovina, stringed instruments accompany the dances. Some of the dances are accompanied by singing for a portion and then continued in silence. Representative of this kind of dancing is *ličko kolo,* from the Dinaric highlands. As people gather after church, someone begins singing an old local song. A group of friends casually gathers in a long chain, all singing as they do the Faeroe step, moving clockwise in an ambling, casual manner. When the last verse is finished they continue dancing in silence, at first slowly, but gradually faster and with more energy. At the command of the leader they perform variations on the Faeroe step pattern in unison. The only sound is that of footfalls and perhaps the clinking of metal ornaments.

Various mimetic song-and-dance games are found everywhere in Yugoslavia, but nowhere as frequently as in the Dinaric zone. In some dance games a sole performer in the middle of a circle mimics the movements of birds or animals to the accompaniment of the circle's singing. Among the most popular of the dance games is "Paun Pase" (How the Peacock Grazes). Elaborate variants of these are practiced by the Muslim population of Bosnia-Herzegovina, among whom traditional segregation of the sexes is particularly strong.

Morava Zone. The fertile Morava zone consists of most of present-day Serbia and parts of eastern Bosnia-Herzegovina and was the route of many population shifts in the past. The open *kolo* predominates, with a leader and end man. The dances in the center of this region tend to be symmetrical; those of the eastern borderlands tend to be asymmetrical. Bagpipes, flutes, violin, and accordion provide the accompaniment. The repertory has diminished dramatically over the last two or three generations to a small number of basic patterns. *Čačak,* a

YUGOSLAVIA: Traditional Dance. Members of Tanec, the Macedonian professional folk dance ensemble, in a Croatian folk dance. (Photograph from the Dance Collection, New York Public Library for the Performing Arts.)

YUGOSLAVIA: Traditional Dance. In this exuberant folk dance, performed by the Tanec ensemble, the four couples in each group link arms in a circle and whirl around so fast that the women are able to lift both feet off the ground and fly through the air. (Photograph from the Dance Collection, New York Public Library for the Performing Arts.)

ten-measure dance, is widespread in the southeast. Turkish-dominated cities developed a culture with a strong Eastern influence. The Sumadijan style is widespread.

Vardar Zone. The Vardar zone contains all of present-day Macedonia and much of southern Serbia. Dances of this region are the open *kolo, tesko* dances in the southwest, and lighter dances in the east. There is a strict division between men's and women's dances. The most prevalent steps are *lesnoto* and Faeroe; basic patterns are Faeroe step, *berance,* and *malesevka. Zurla* (a shawm) and *tapan* (a large double-headed drum), *kavali* (a wooden, rim-blown flute), and bagpipes are used. A typical dance of the *tesko* type is performed exclusively by men. It begins slowly but then speeds up; the musicians follow the cues of the lead dancer, who sets the tempo and dynamics while the drummer matches his beats to the steps and pauses he sees performed. The music defies conventional notation.

Alpine Zone. The Alpine zone includes the republic of Slovenia and some contiguous areas of Croatia; historically it was part of the Hapsburg Empire. The dance repertory consists primarily of couple dances derived from eighteenth- and nineteenth-century central Europe, such as the polka, waltz, and mazurka, and local dances such as the *sotis, stajeris, sustarska,* and *potrkana polka.* There are also some traditional chain and circle dances, such as the *metliško kolo, žakle,* and *šivajo.* Accompaniment is provided by violin, accordion, clarinet, cymbalom, *sopile* (a double-reed wind instrument), and *mih* (bagpipe). The predominating rhythms are 2/4 and 3/4.

Pannonian Zone. The fertile plainland of northern Croatia, including Zagreb, and the autonomous region of Vojvodina make up the Pannonian zone. The most important dance type here is the *drmeš* (sometimes spelled *drmež*); the name is derived from the Serbo-Croatian verb *drmati,* meaning "to shake," "to tremble," "to vibrate," or "to bounce rapidly up and down." Its most common form is in two parts: in the first section the dancers execute some type of vertical bouncing step in place, and in the second section they spin counterclockwise. The *drmeš* is performed in couples, trios, and small circles. The closed, leaderless *kolo* is also found here.

Adriatic Zone. The Adriatic zone consists of the islands and coastal towns and villages of Croatia. The "older" dances generically known as *tanac* and *linđo* are within the repertory of the population born before the mid-twentieth century in rural, agriculturally based communities. North of Split, *tanac* dances are accompanied by *mih* or *sopile,* while in the south, *linđo* dances are accompanied by a *lijerica* (a bowed three-string instrument), although the oldest members of the population recall that the dancing was formerly accompanied also by the bagpipe. Dancing events are commonly organized during the winter season from Christmas to the beginning of Lent, also on village saints' days and at weddings. Dancing is considered a social event, which allows for acceptable contact between men and women.

Adult dancers (unmarried or married) dance in a file of side-by-side couples that traces a circular or serpentine path. During the dances there are usually reversals of direction, such as from clockwise to counterclockwise. *Tanac* and *linđo* dances have a flexible sequence of patterns in an improvised order, lead by a male (while dancing with his partner). He directs the ensemble with verbal cues or by initiating changes in pattern. Many *tanac* dances also include formations in which the men and women face each other in two lines; they all dance in place, then the members of each couple exchange places. Throughout this area, men also have an opportunity within the dance structure to demonstrate their expertise with solo dancing, performing quick footwork, lifting their arms above their heads, and spinning. The men also direct their partners into spinning turns, as well as performing pivot turns with their partners as a couple.

Under Austrian rule during the nineteenth century, the fashionable waltz *(valcer)* and polka became standard repertory at Adriatic dance events. These dances continue to be performed and in some villages have replaced the older *tanac* and *lindo*. In the second half of the twentieth century, particularly with the expansion of tourism and the construction of complexes of hotels, cafés, and nightclubs, amplified music has replaced the local instruments to cater to an international tourist clientele with contemporary pan-European music dancing. Only scattered pockets of rural communities continue to dance the older dances accompanied by traditional music. Tourism, however, is also responsible for the preservation of some dance types through seasonally organized performance groups that present programs of "traditional" dance and music for foreign visitors. Among these social dances adapted for stage performance are sword dances extant on the island of Korčula, called the *moreska* and *kumpanija*, whose roots go back at least to the fifteenth and sixteenth centuries. [*See* Moresca.]

Macedonia. Lying between Albania to the west, Bulgaria to the east, Greece to the south, and the rump Yugoslavia (Serbia and Montenegro) to the north, Macedonia has experienced successive waves of occupiers attracted by the area's ancient trade routes leading west toward the Adriatic seaports and north toward the interior of Europe as well as its rich agricultural lands and mineral deposits. The current population is composed two-thirds of Slavic, Macedonian-speaking people and one-quarter of ethnic Albanians, with Turkish, Romany (Gypsy), and Serbian minorities. The two major religions, Eastern Orthodox Christianity and Islam, are as influential in determining the types of dances performed and their social occasions as the population's various ethno-linguistic identities.

During the 1930s, more than two hundred dances were identified and described by the Janković sisters in the western, southwestern, and northern areas of Macedonia (then called South Serbia). Many of the dances tended to be segregated by sex, with the dancers linked by handholds or shoulderholds in open circles, whose path progressed counterclockwise. Tempos varied from extremely slow rubato dances to quick-paced irregular rhythmic patterns. Instrumentation for outdoor dances was usually *gajda* (bagpipe), or *zurla* (shawm) with *tapan* (drum). Urban centers with a middle-class supported mellower-sounding *calgija* orchestras (comprising violin, lutes, *kanon*, clarinet, and tambourine), which played indoors, accompanying singers for slow, walking-style dances *(lesnoto)*.

Until the 1950s the eastern, central, and western regions of Macedonia each had distinctly different dances. However, with the postwar migrations of population from mountain villages to plains areas and to urban centers, these distinctions became muted. By the 1980s a pan-Macedonian repertory had emerged at wedding celebrations, with dances (known as *oro*) often danced to newly composed songs. Weddings are lavish affairs that always feature hired musicians, and there is an expectation that everyone in attendance will dance, whether the wedding is held at the home, or in a public restaurant. Dancing is also popularly done during any public occasion when musicians are hired, such as warm evenings in the park, at a restaurant, or in an outdoor cafe, often accompanied by the singing of old and newly composed Macedonian songs.

At these occasions, a basic repertory of dance music and dances is performed by both the urban and rural populations throughout Macedonia. Men and women dance together in open circles, the dancers joined with hands held at shoulder level or with the arms down at their sides; short-phrased, repetitive step patterns progress the path of the circle in a counterclockwise direction. The pan-Macedonian dance repertory includes a variety of rhythmic patterns, for dances generically known as *lesnoto* (such as the *lesno*, *za ramo*, *teškoto*, and *pravoto*, all in 7/8 and/or 2/4 meters), *devetorka* (9/8), *beranče* (or *krsteno*, in 13/8), *eleno mome* (7/8), *pajduško* (5/8), *sitno*

YUGOSLAVIA: Traditional Dance. Dancers from the Tanec group performing a *rusalija*, a type of sword dance. (Photograph from the Dance Collection, New York Public Library for the Performing Arts.)

YUGOSLAVIA: Traditional Dance. A dancer perches atop a large drum *(tapan)* at a climactic moment in this Macedonian men's dance, the *teškoto,* performed by members of Tanec. The other musician plays a *zurla,* a loud shawm. The *tapan-zurla* repertory accompanies outdoor dancing at feasts, weddings, and circumcisions. (Photograph from the Dance Collection, New York Public Library for the Performing Arts.)

(2/4) and *čačak* (2/4). Music accompaniment tends to be by a folk orchestra composed of accordion, electric guitars, clarinet, saxophone, and trap set or *darabuka* (hourglass shaped drum) that plays newly composed music in the rhythms appropriate to each dance meter. The rhythm of the music, not the melody, determines which steps are executed.

Since 1945 Macedonian folk dances have also been performed on stage by the republic's sole professional ensemble, Tanec, as well as by a multitude of urban and village dance groups sponsored by the Cultural Artistic Societies (referred to by their collective Macedonian acronym, KUD). By 1995, approximately one hundred dance groups in Macedonian towns and villages were performing a similar choreographed repertory of Macedonian dances that represented the central, western, and eastern regions of the country. Although the population of Macedonia is multicultural, most of this stage repertory represents only the Slavic-speaking population. The principal influence on the standardization of these dances is the diffusion of the repertory of Tanec, which consists of a standardized set of regional dances established during the early 1950s from traditional sources, subjected to extensive choreographic elaboration during the 1970s and 1980s, and transmitted throughout the country. Tanec and many of the town-based KUD groups tour internationally with their programs, while other KUD and village-based groups perform in annually sponsored national and regional festival programs that offer nominally authentic dances, music, and costume to public view.

Urban Dances. In the late nineteenth century, as nationalist yearnings burgeoned among ethnic groups in the Balkans, it became clear that the only forms on which to found future national culture were the folk arts: colorful costumes, crafts, oral prose, epic poetry in the Homeric tradition, a rich stock of lyrical songs, and an immense stock of folk music and dance. One of the first things the new royal court in Belgrade undertook was the creation, based on native motifs, of dances "in the national spirit."

In their music and structure these dances reflect two main characteristics of the period: a romantic enthusiasm for the culture of the peasantry, and a desire to match the dances of the salons of Paris and Vienna. The Croatian ballroom *kolo,* for example, combined the multifigured structure of the French quadrille with movements emulating features of village dancing. From the court in Belgrade came a series of dances composed in honor of various members of the royal house. The opening dance at royal balls was "Kraljevo Oro" (The King's Solo), customarily led by the monarch himself. It consisted of the familiar Faeroe step, performed in a slow, elegant style. "Natalijino Kolo" (Queen Natalia's *Kolo*) gained immense popularity outside the court, its melody surviving as a dance tune as late as World War II, when, ironically, it was performed to the singing of patriotic revolutionary lyrics by Tito's partisans.

The Yugoslav people dance as much today as they did in the past—at family gatherings, social get-togethers, and holidays. But the types of dancing done today reflect the intense urbanization and internationalization of the country. The majority of the dancing population, the youth, now find it natural to dance their own versions of rock and roll, disco, and *sving.* In remote areas, however, many traditional dances still live.

BIBLIOGRAPHY

Dopuda, Jelena. *Narodni plesovi-igre u Bosni i Hercegovini.* Zagreb, 1990.

Dunin, Elsie Ivancich. *Dance Occasions and Festive Dress in Yugoslavia.* Los Angeles, 1984.

Dunin, Elsie. "Lindo in the Context of Village Life in the Dubrovnik Area of Yugoslavia." *Dance Research Annual* 16 (1987): 1–4.

Dunin, Elsie Ivancich and Stanimir Visinski. *Dances in Macedonia: Performance Genre—Tanec Ensemble.* Skopje, 1995.

Dunin, Elsie Ivancich, and Nancy Lee Chalfa Ruyter. *Yugoslav Dance: An Introduction and List of Sources Available in United States Libraries.* Palo Alto, Calif., 1981.

Dunin, Elsie Ivancich. "Yugoslav Dance Research Project." *Dance Research Journal* 22 (Spring 1990): 52–54.

Ivančan, Ivan. "Folk Dance among the Croats." *Narodna umjetnost,* special issue no. 2 (1988): 69–107.

Ivančan, Ivan. "Geografska podjela narodnih plesova u Jugoslaviji." *Narodna umjetnost,* no. 3 (1964–1965).

Ivančan, Ivan. "Folk Dances in Various Regions of Yugoslavia." In *The Folk Arts of Yugoslavia,* edited by Walter W. Kolar. Pittsburgh, 1976.

Janković, Ljubica S., and Danica S. Janković. *Narodne igre.* 8 vols. Belgrade, 1934–1964.

Janković, Ljubica S., and Danica S. Janković. *Dances of Yugoslavia.* New York and London, 1952.

Lawrence, Lee A. "News: Zagreb." *Dance Magazine* (November 1985).

Leibman, Robert. *Traditional Songs and Dances from the Soko Banja Area.* San Francisco, 1973.

Mladenović, Olivera. *Kolo u južnih slavena.* Belgrade, 1973.

Pajtondžiev, Gančo. *Makedonski narodni ora.* Skopje, 1973.

Ramovš, Mirko. *Plesat me pelji: Plesno izročilo na Slovenskem.* Ljubljana, 1980.

Ruyter, Nancy Lee Chalfa. "Some Musings on Folk Dance." *Dance Chronicle* 18.2 (1995): 269–279.

Elsie Ivancich Dunin
(Adriatic Zone)

Elsie Ivancich Dunin and Stanimir Visinski
(Macedonia)

Richard Crum
(all others)

Ballet

Although a permanent ballet company was not established in Zagreb until 1894, the city witnessed many performances by gymnasts, illusionists, and pantomime troupes before that time. Occasionally, foreign dancers made isolated appearances, and in 1876 the first full dance company, that of Pietro Coronelli, toured Yugoslavia. The group's ballerina, Ivana Freisinger, was engaged by the Zagreb Opera for the 1876/77 season. Remaining there into the 1880s, she provided several ballets for the standard opera repertory but attracted little interest.

In 1892 a Viennese ballet master, L. Gundlich, arrived in Zagreb and staged Josef Bayer's *The Fairy Doll* for the Croatian National Theater. Gundlich's staging repeated the success of Josef Hassreiter's original production at the Vienna Court Opera Ballet four years earlier—even though, because of the lack of a permanent ballet ensemble, he cast actors and actresses in all the roles. That situation changed two years later, when Stjepan Miletić took over the management of the National Theater and established not only a permanent dance ensemble, but also a ballet school.

Miletić engaged foreign dancers to fill the front ranks of the company, whose star became Erna Grondona, born in Budapest and trained at the Teatro alla Scala. During the next four years the company premiered *Coppélia* and *Giselle,* as well as ballets by Grondona, including *To the Plitvice Lakes* (1898), set to music by Sreácko Albini and based on a libretto by Miletić.

After Miletić left the National Theater at the turn of the century, the ballet company and school languished. Not until the 1920s, and Yugoslavia's emergence as an independent nation following the collapse of the Austro-Hungarian empire in World War I, did ballet become firmly established as a theatrical form in Zagreb, Ljubljana, and Belgrade. Immigrant dancers, mostly Russian, spearheaded the revival. While introducing works from the Russian repertory to the Yugoslav audience, they laid the groundwork for the development of a national repertory, a process that reached fulfillment after World War II.

In 1921 the Russian Margarita Froman arrived in Zagreb with her brothers Maksimilijan, Pavel, and Valentin. Maksimilijan took leading roles in her works, Pavel designed many of her productions, and Valentin followed her as a choreographer. For the National Theater Margarita staged many works from the Russian repertory, including *Schéhérazade* (1922), which Pavel designed and in which she and Maksimilijan appeared together, and *Petrouchka* (1923), also designed by Pavel after Alexandre Benois and including Valentin in the family-dominated cast.

Margarita Froman also staged works on Yugoslav themes to music by Yugoslav composers, notably *The Gin-*

gerbread Heart (1924); Krešimir Baranović wrote the libretto and composed the music, and Maksimilijan Vanka designed the scenery and costumes. Set at a Croatian village fair, the ballet shows a young man presenting a girl with a gingerbread heart and thereby winning her love. Whirling folk dances *(kolos)* echo their exuberance. *The Gingerbread Heart* became a staple in the Yugoslav repertory. [*See the entry on Froman.*]

At the opera house in Ljubljana a Czech, Václav Pohan, initiated a ballet revival and staged works from the international repertory, including *Coppélia* (1919) and *Swan Lake* (1921). Pohan was succeeded by choreographers who, following the lead of the Fromans in Zagreb, turned their attention toward contemporary themes. Aleksandar Trobisch staged *The Flowers of Little Ida* shortly after its Zagreb premiere in 1925, while Maria Tuljakova staged *The Matchmaker* (1925), *The Gingerbread Heart* (1925), and *Capriccio Espagnol* (1926) after Froman productions. Václav Vlček, also a Czech, took Bronislava Nijinska as precedent in his 1928 staging of Gabriel Piernés *Impressions de Music-Hall,* a "ballet à l'Américaine," just one year after its original production in Paris.

Jelena Poljakova, trained in Saint Petersburg, initiated the ballet revival in Belgrade with her stagings of *The Nutcracker, Schéhérazade,* and *Les Sylphides* in 1923. Although she turned her attention from choreography to pedagogy after this first season, she continued to influence the ballet revival for another two decades. Aleksandar Fortunato succeeded Poljakova as choreographer at the Belgrade Theater and staged additional works from the Russian repertory, including *Coppélia* (1924), the *Polovtsian Dances* from *Prince Igor* (1925), *Giselle* (1926), and *Swan Lake* (1926). In the late 1920s, Margarita Froman was invited to Belgrade and introduced ballets choreographed to music by contemporary composers, such as Manuel de Falla's *El Sombrero de Tres Picos* (1928), designed by Vladimir Zhedrinski.

Pia and Pino Mlakar were students of Rudolf Laban in Berlin. In 1933 they toured a program called New Ways and were invited the following year to stage Richard Strauss's *Die Josephslegende* and *Till Eulenspiegel* at the Belgrade Theater. At this time the Mlakars were ballet directors in Zurich, but they continued to stage works in Yugoslavia, notably *The Devil in the Village,* which was first performed in Zagreb in 1937 and in Belgrade in 1938. Set to music by Fran Lhotka, the full-length ballet integrated folk motifs, including a *kolo* in the concluding wedding festival. [*See the entry on Mlakar.*]

Meanwhile, Froman continued her choreographic efforts in all three centers of Yugoslavian ballet, and Nina Kirsanova in Belgrade joined the distinguished line of ballerina-choreographers who were also teachers. At the same time, the first generation of native dancers made its mark: Nataša Bošković, a student of Poljakova and of Olga Preobrajenska in Paris, who performed leading roles at the Belgrade Theater from 1918 to 1944; Mia Čorak-Slavenska, a student of Margarita Froman, who took leading roles in Zagreb from 1930 to 1937 (she later emigrated and became known as Mia Slavenska); and Ana Roje, a student of Froman and Poljakova who later assisted Nikolai Legat and, with her husband Oskar Harmoš, directed the Zagreb Ballet from 1945 to 1953. Roje was the last of the line of great female ballerina-choreographers who taught. Male dancers who attained distinction included Michel Panaiev and Igor Youskevitch.

After World War II, theatrical dance received generous government subsides following the Soviet model and expanded enormously. Ballet became established at theaters in Maribor, Novi Sad, Osijek, Rijeka, Sarajevo, Skopje, and Split. Audience surveys showed that in some areas interest in ballet equaled or surpassed interest in opera. The three traditional centers of Belgrade, Zagreb, and Ljubljana opened ballet schools offering extensive and rigorous training, and talented students received scholarships to finish their training in Russia. In 1959 Ljubljana became host to a biannual ballet competition.

Postwar choreography turned toward full-length contemporary ballets. Again Margarita Froman took a leading role with *The Legend of Ochrid* (1949). The action was set in the period of national struggle against Turkish oppression but alluded to the contemporary situation in Belgrade, which had nearly been destroyed in World War II. The work integrated folk motifs and classical ballet. The Janković sisters, early collectors of Slavic folk dances, had questioned the theatricalization of folk dances for the professional stage, but this theatricalization became an accepted practice in postwar choreography.

The Mlakars, whose *The Devil in the Village* had anticipated the new genre, made further contributions with *The Bow* (1946), *The Little Ballerina* (1947, and *Danina, or Jocko the Brazilian Ape* (1950). Other leading postwar choreographers were Franjo Horvat, who studied with Maletić and M. Zibine in Zagreb and later became director of the ballet in Sarajevo, and Dimitrije Parlić, who studied theater and dance at the Academy of Music in Belgrade and later choreographed for many theaters in Yugoslavia and abroad. [*See the entry on Parlić.*] Both Horvat and Parlić restaged what became the classics of the Yugoslav repertory, *The Gingerbread Heart* and *The Legend of Ochrid,* and choreographed original narrative works. Other choreographers explored the music of contemporary Yugoslav composers. Vera Kostić created *Vibrations* (1959) to music by Krešimir Fribec, while Nevenka Bidjin and Sonja Kastl created *Symphony of a Dead Soldier* (1959) to music by Branimir Sakač, *The Man and His Mirror* (1963) to music by Milko Kelemen, and *Symphony in D* (1965) to music by Luka Sorkočević.

Theatrical dance suffered a slump in the early 1980s. In the preceding decade Yugoslavia had become an exporter of dancers, but suddenly the country had to import dancers. Although technical standards remained high, artistic standards seemed to decline, except for the works of Milko Šparemblek. Especially notable were *Pjesme Ljubavi i Smrti* (Songs of Love and Death; 1981), set to music by Gustav Mahler; *The Soldier's Tale* (1983), to the score by Igor Stravinsky; and *Catulli Carmina* (1984), to the score by Carl Orff. [*See the entry on Šparemblek.*]

BIBLIOGRAPHY

Batušić, Nikola. *Hrvatsko kazaliste u Zagrebu, 1840–1992.* 2d ed. Zagreb, 1992.

Curcija-Prodanović, Nada. *Ballerina.* London, 1961.

Dragutinović, Branko. *Jedan vek Narodnog pozoriste u Beogradu, 1868–1968.* Belgrade, 1968.

Grbić-Softić, Slobodanka. *Osvajanje igre: Balet u Bosni i Hercegovini.* Sarajevo, 1986.

Gresserov-Golovin, Peter. *Moja ljuba Slovenija.* Ljubljana, 1985.

Hofmann, Wilfried. "Ballett in Belgrad." *Das Tanzarchiv* 25 (May 1977): 201–206.

Jovanović, Milica. *Balet Narodnog pozorišta u Beogradu izmedju dva rata.* Belgrade, 1976.

Lešić, Josip. *Narodno pozoriste Sarejevo, 1921–1971.* Sarajevo, 1972.

Luijdjens, Adriaan H. "Il balletto del Teatro Nazionale di Belgrado." *Balletto* 1 (November 1955): 55–63.

Magazinović, Maga. *Istorija igre.* Belgrade, 1951.

Maynard, Olga. "The Dance in Yugoslavia." *Dance Magazine* (May 1977): 67–82.

Mosusova, Nadezhda. "The Heritage of the Ballet Russe in Yugoslavia between the Two World Wars." In *Proceedings of the Eleventh Annual Conference, Society of Dance History Scholars, North Carolina School of the Arts, 12–14 February 1988,* compiled by Christena L. Schlundt. Riverside, Calif., 1988.

Rakić, Branka, and Radivoje Nikolajević. *Yugoslav Ballet.* Translated by Petar Mijušković. Belgrade, 1958.

Rakić, Branka. *Jugoslovenska baletna scena, 1950–1980.* Sarajevo, 1982.

Rakić, Branka. "Ballet." In *Zagreb Croatian National Theatre, 1860–1985.* Zagreb, 1985.

Ruyter, Nancy Lee Chalfa. "Pietro Coronelli, Dance Master of Zagreb." *Dance Research* 7 (Spring 1989): 78–81.

Sarabon, Mitja, ed. *Petdeset let slovenskega baleta.* Ljubljana, 1970. Contains Henrik Neubauer's "A Short History of the Slovene Ballet on Its Fiftieth Anniversary" (in English).

Turkalj, Nenad. "Opera and Ballet in Yugoslavia." *World Theatre* 15.5 (1966): 389–396.

Volk, Petar. *Beogradske scene.* Belgrade, 1978.

MILICA JOVANOVIĆ, PIA MLAKAR, and PINO MLAKAR

Modern Dance

In the 1930s, modern dance became an important influence on the Yugoslav dance scene. Although as early as 1921 Claudia Isačenko had introduced a Russianized form of Isadora Duncan's dancing to Belgrade, and by the mid-1920s Maga Maazinović had taught rhythmic dancing and plastique there, it was not until the 1930s that students of Rudolf Laban emerged as dancers of stature.

Ana Maletić was a student of Maazinović when she met Laban in 1924. After graduating from his school in Berlin, she returned to Zagreb, where she established a private school to teach his principles. Maletić also choreographed for her own company, staging works often based on national motifs and folklore, in close collaboration with Yugoslav composers. After World War II Maletić became attached to the Zagreb Music School. As a result of her efforts, a state school, the Zagreb School for Rhythmics and Dance, was established in 1955, the only one of its kind in the country. Some of the graduates of the school became eminent experts in their field. Among the most distinguished are Tihana Škrinjaric, Milana Broš, Lela Gluhak-Buneta, and Vera Maletić. Škrinjarić was one of the country's best-known modern dance choreographers. She also directed the school's dancers in the 1979 Mediterranean Games in Split and the 1984 Olympics in Sarajevo.

Ana Maletić's work was often inspired by national themes, as in her *Three Steles,* to music by Ivo Malec, a choreographic vision of the reliefs on medieval tombstones in Bosnia, or her choreographic satire, *Connections,* to a commissioned score by Boris Papandopulo, created in 1963 and performed in Zagreb and throughout Yugoslavia and then at Bayreuth. Her dramatic treatment of folkloric motifs is indeed her most notable achievement.

In 1962 Vera Maletić, Ana Maletić's daughter, opened the Studio of Contemporary Dance in Zagreb. The company's dancers experimented with sounds, the spoken word, and props as aural and visual components of dance. They created *Studies in Sound and Movement, After Love* (based on a poem by Vesna Parun), and *Skopje 63* (based on recollections of the disastrous earthquake in that city).

The 1960s were a decade of great experimentation and exciting innovations in the field of modern dance in Yugoslavia. Collaboration with television became an important part of the Studio's activities, and it found the demands of the medium to be very different from those of the theater. According to Vera Maletić, the International Music Council seminars and conferences in Zagreb, Vienna, and Salzburg, where numerous television ballets were screened and discussed, were tremendously stimulating and encouraging. Among the works that received critical and popular acclaim were *Connections* (Ana Maletić and Papandopulo) and *Formations* (Vera Maletić and Ruben Radica), the first co-production between TV-Zagreb and TV-Vienna, directed by Herman Lanske and presented at the Congress in Vienna in 1964; *Three Steles* (Ana Maletić and Ivo Malec) for TV-Zagreb, directed by Vladimir Seljan; and *Dessins Commentés* (Vera Maletić and Milko Kelemen), directed by Mladen Raukar; and *Équilibres* (Vera Maletić and Kelemen) for Stockholm television, directed by Arne Arnebom and screened at the Salzburg Congress in 1965.

From the beginning, the members of the Studio were aware of the need for a wider public appreciation of contemporary dance. To achieve this they started a successful collaboration with organizations concerned with arts appreciation for young people and with the wider public, such as the Musical Youth Organization, the Zagreb Theater of the Young, the Croatian State Ensemble of Folk Dance and Song, and People's University. Through these organizations they gave performances and lecture-demonstrations in schools, factories, and other places. They produced numerous programs sent on tour in Yugoslavia and abroad, consisting of works by the Studio members.

By the 1980s the Zagreb School was providing performers for Vera Maletić's company and two other professional modern dance troupes. The Studio for Contemporary Dance was then headed by Zaga Zivković and was no longer experimental, but more concerned with entertainment. Trained in both ballet and the Martha Graham technique, the dancers performed a wide-ranging repertory in concerts as well as in stage musicals and on television. The Ensemble for Free Dance (KASP), which also originated in 1962, was directed by Milana Bros. There, the emphasis was on minimalist concepts and improvisation. The Zagreb Dance Ensemble was founded in 1970 and headed by Mirna Zagar. The group performed modern works based on folk material. Zagar explained the use of folkloric themes: "These ideas are a part of our lives; they are the soul of our society and our land."

BIBLIOGRAPHY

Hofmann, Wilfried. "Ein Pionier des freien Tanzes: Smiljana Mandukic." *Das Tanzarchiv* 25 (April 1977).

Lawrence, Lee A. "News: Zagreb." *Dance Magazine* (November 1985).

Maletić, Vera. "Modern Dance Strives in Yugoslavia." *Dance News* (June 1966).

Mosusova, Nadezhda. "American Dance Abroad: A View from Yugoslavia." In *Proceedings of the Fifteenth Annual Conference, Society of Dance History Scholars, University of California, Riverside, 14–15 February 1992,* compiled by Christena L. Schlundt. Riverside, Calif., 1992.

JASNA PERUČIĆ NADAREVIĆ

Theatrical Dance Since 1991

The breakup of the former Yugoslavia began in June 1991 when Slovenia, soon followed by Croatia and later by Bosnia and Macedonia, became independent countries. Only Serbia and Montenegro continued to exist under the name Yugoslavia. Dance in Yugoslavia thus meant dance in Serbia, since Montenegro never developed professional theatrical dance.

Serbia. In Belgrade, the capital, and in Novi Sad, the second-largest city, the dance community struggled through difficult times but succeeded in maintaining a continuity in its work while the audience showed a renewed interest in theater, as is often the case in troubled times.

The cultural isolation that followed the imposition of United Nations economic sanctions created harsh conditions for dance in Serbia. While before the war a large and tightly knit dance community enjoyed frequent exchanges with a national and international dance scene, following the outbreak of hostilities Yugoslav dance activity was confined to the country's two largest cities. In Belgrade, the National Theater managed to maintain the classical repertory, though few new ballet productions were mounted. The survival of modern dance, known as "alternative dance," was assisted by the enthusiasm of individuals and the form's association with long-established traditions of avant-garde theater.

Ballet. The National Theater in Belgrade presented stagings of *Coppélia, Giselle, Don Quixote, La Bayadere,* and *Swan Lake.* Contemporary repertory consisted of pieces by Aleksandar Izrailovski, Krunislav Simić, and Lidija Pilipenko. Leading dancers were Ashen Ataljanc,

YUGOSLAVIA: Theatrical Dance since 1991. Andjela Todorović as Odette and Denis Kasatkin as Siegfried in a performance of *Swan Lake* at the National Theater in Belgrade in 1995. (Photograph courtesy of Xenia Rakic.)

Duška Dragicěvić, and Konstantin Koskjukov. The company's artistic directorship changed hands several times.

Elsewhere in Belgrade, Sava Centar presented an "Homage to Dimitrije Parlić," conceived and created by Višnja Djordjević, in 1993. This event was produced in an effort to conserve the work of Yugoslavia's most prolific and successful ballet choreographer. Several Broadway musicals were also staged.

In Novi Sad, the ballet company at the Serbian National Theater presented *Giselle, The Little Humpbacked Horse, La Fille Mal Gardée, Les Sylphides, The Nutcracker, Swan Lake,* and several contemporary pieces. Leading dancers included Rastislav Varga, Mihai Babuşka, Ana Kusnirova, and Oksana Storozuk.

Modern dance. Modern dance, commonly referred to as "alternative dance," developed mainly during the 1980s in Yugoslavia. By 1991 a number of modern companies and independent choreographers were established in Belgrade. Television, cultural centers, and presenters increasingly commissioned work by young modern choreographers. New dance venues included the Bitef Teatar and the Small Stage at the National Theater. There were performance spaces in concert halls (Sava Centar, Kolarac), cultural centers (the Students Cultural Center, Kud Abrašević), and traditional theaters (Atelje 212, Beogradsko Dramsko Pozorište, Yuglovensko Dramsko).

Smiljana Mandukić (1980–1992), teacher, choreographer, and founder of the Contemporary Belgrade Ballet, left a modern legacy that was developed by her students. Prominent among them is Nela Antonović, who established her own dance company, Mimart, in 1984. Other choreographers associated with Mandukić are Katarina Stojkov-Slijepčević, teacher at the Lupo Davičo National Ballet School; Vesna Milanović, who is with the Belgrade Dance Theater; and Vera Obradović, associated with the Ballet XXI Movement.

Under the auspices of the Belgrade International Theater Festival (BITEF) and its home theater, the Bitef Teatar, a number of evening-length works were created. These include *The Portrait of Dorian Grey* (1991) and *Macbeth against Macbeth* (1992), both choreographed by Dejan Pajović to music by Nenad Jeličić; *Medea* (1991), by Sonja Vukičević, former dancer at the National Theater, to music by Zoran Erić; and *Isadora* (1991), by Jelena Santić, another former National Theater dancer, to a score by Ivana Stefanović. Nada Kokotović, who left the country to work in Germany, is well known for her choreodramas, which were performed throughout the former Yugoslavia.

The Belgrade National Theater joined presenters of modern dance by offering its Small Stage to choreographers with the company's ranks of dancers. Aleksandar Israilovski began presenting work there annually after

YUGOSLAVIA: Theatrical Dance since 1991. Jelena Santić in the "Death of Isadora" scene from her evening-length dance-theater work *Isadora* (1991), set to a score by Ivana Stefanović. (Photograph courtesy of Xenia Rakic.)

1990; Violeta Andonović was another dancer who choreographed for the space. In 1994, Sava Centar presented Andjela Todorović's work *Island, Dance of Atoms,* performed by the Ister Theater.

Novi Sad has no modern dance tradition to speak of. However, after 1980 there was a surge of interest in contemporary dance forms. Jazz became popular, and several private studios that opened enrolled a large public. Choreographers organized showcases for their work and the community responded by including contemporary dance in many cultural programs and public celebrations. The gap between contemporary dance, regarded as popular entertainment, and ballet, perceived as high art, began to narrow. Most of the new studios and performing groups were directed by graduates of the national school and former members of the Serbian National Theater. At the national school itself, the curriculum was expanded to include jazz and modern dance. Excerpts from Mats Ek's *Giselle,* staged by Nada Dražeta, were performed to critical acclaim at the school's recital in 1994.

A local choreographer of outstanding achievement, Tatjana Grujić, won first and second prizes for choreographer at the Yugoslav Ballet Competition held in Novi Sad in 1990. Grujić cofounded Studio Rebis with Gordana Dean Gačić in 1989. A former gymnast, she included elements of formal ballet, jazz, and modern dance in her work. Other successful studios and schools include Partizan 2, founded in 1987 by Jelena Andrejev; Lala-Znanje, founded in 1990 by Dragan Rančev; City Dance Studio, founded in 1991 by Vesna Šećerov and Vera Markuš; and the Educational Group for Modern Dance, founded in

1991 at the College of Physical Education by Professor Ljiljana Mišić.

The first International Festival of Alternative and New Theater (INFANT) was held in July 1995 as part of the Novi Sad Summer Festival. Among the companies taking part were Mimart and Ister Theater from Belgrade.

Bosnia. From the time it was founded in 1946, the Sarajevo Opera possessed a ballet group, initially directed by Eduard Venier, a dancer from Zagreb. Ubavka Milanković, a dancer from Sarajevo, directed the ballet school. At first the ballet served exclusively the needs of opera productions, but this changed in 1949 when Jitka Ivelja was named principal dancer and Franjo Horvat, a Croat, became resident choreographer. Ivelja and Horvat presented the first ballet productions. *Žetva* (Harvest), premiered in May 1950, marked the professional coming of age of the Sarajevo Ballet. A full-length work, it was choreographed by Nina Kirsanova, a guest artist from Belgrade, to the music of Boris Papandopulo, a Bosnian composer.

Over the next four decades, the Sarajevo Ballet developed into a strong regional company. The school provided the company with young dancers, but principal roles were often given to guest artists from abroad and from republics of what was then Yugoslavia. In April 1992 war erupted in Sarajevo. The ballet was then directed by Nedžad Potogija, who oversaw a new production of *Swan Lake,* staged by visiting Russian Vladimir Riabov, in December 1991. The leading roles were danced by Tatiana Kladnikina and Vladimir Grigorjiev, both guests from Russia. War interrupted all the regular functions of the national theater in Sarajevo. Nevertheless, in May 1993 Potogija presented those dancers who remained in the city in excerpts from *Carmina Burana.* Since the building housing the National Opera was damaged, this performance took place in a small theater. Dancers continued to leave the city; by 1994, only six remained. Potogija presented these six in *Boléro,* choreographed by Dragutin Boldin, at the repaired Opera in May 1994. Following the peace accord of November 1995, the National Theater resumed work. Artistic director of the ballet was Bahria Bihorac. Independently, in November 1992 choreographer and director Slavko Pervan, the ballet's former artistic director (1975–1978 and 1980–1983), caused a sensation with a production of the musical *Hair* in Sarajevo.

Macedonia. National opera and ballet companies were founded in Skopje, the republic's capital, in 1948. A year later Georgije Makedonski, who had been trained in Zagreb and Belgrade, was appointed artistic director of the ballet. He soon established a national ballet academy affiliated with the company. In 1953, the company presented its first national full-length work, *The Macedonian Tale,* choreographed by Dimitrije Parlić to music by Gligor Smokvarski. The company became one of the major troupes in Yugoslavia. Its repertory consisted of traditional nineteenth-century classics and contemporary works. Macedonian choreographers were fostered, but guests from other Yugoslav republics and abroad were also invited. Parlić maintained a connection to the company throughout his career.

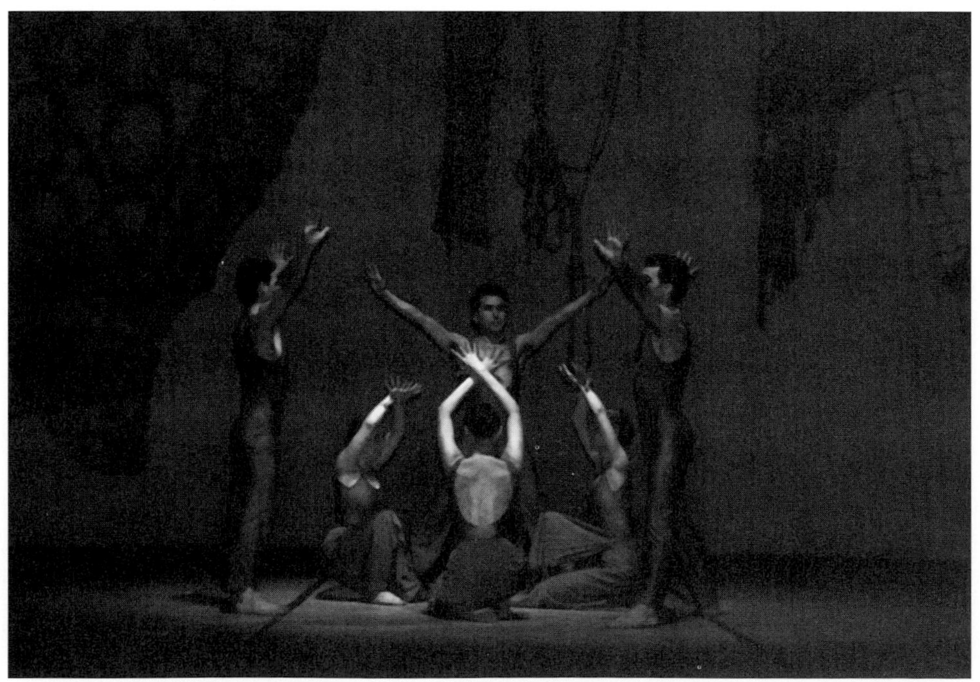

YUGOSLAVIA: Theatrical Dance since 1991. Dragutin Boldin choreographed his *Boléro,* to the music of Maurice Ravel, for the last six dancers remaining in Sarajevo in May 1994, after two years of brutal Serb bombardment. The dancers were (left to right) Haris Šabanović, Adnan Džindo, and Mensud Vatić, with (kneeling) Irma Ugrinčić, Brižita Karabašić, and Tefeda Abazović. (Photograph courtesy of Xenia Rakic.)

YUGOSLAVIA: Theatrical Dance since 1991. Vojko Vidmar, Marko Omerzel, Mojmir Lasan, and Tomaž Rode of the Ballet of Ljubljana in Milko Šparemblek's *Enigma Gallus,* in a 1989 performance. The set was designed by Nenad Fabijanić, with costumes by Mojca Makuc. (Photograph courtesy of Vojko Vidmar.)

Following Macedonia's independence in September 1992, the company continued to present ballets. Many guests from Russia were invited to stage works, and several ballets by Dragutin Boldin, Iskra Sukarova, and Ekrem Husein were produced. Leading dancers of the era included Goran Božinov, Zoica Purovska, Zoran Velevski, Tanja Vujisik.

Slovenia. Following Slovenia's withdrawal from Yugoslavia in 1991, the country continued to support two ballet companies. The Ballet of Ljubljana, in the capital, had about fifty dancers, or twice the number of the troupe in Maribor. Although government funding was reduced, the company in Ljubljana continued to produce two new works a year and that in Maribor one. The Ljubljana company, which has staged more than two hundred works in a history extending back to the early years of the twentieth century, is primarily a classical troupe. Native choreographers who have worked with the company include Pino Mlakar, Milko Šparemblek, Vlasto Dedović, and Ivo Kosi. Some of their works are set to music by Slovenian composers. Works by international choreographers include Birgit Cullberg's *Romeo and Juliet;* Irina Lukashova's stagings of *Giselle* and *The Nutcracker;* Croat Dinko Bogdanović's *Don Quixote;* Toer van Schayk's *Pyrrhic Dances II, Chimera,* and *Orpheus;* and Argentine Julio López's *A Midsummer Night's Dream.*

Ballet is often aired on television; consequently, most productions exist on videotape. Many ballets are co-produced with foreign television stations; Cullberg's *Romeo and Juliet,* for example, was taped in a co-production with Swedish television, and Valery Panov's *Dreyfus: J'accuse* was a coproduction with the Bonn Ballet and English, Swedish, and German partners. There are also some videodance festivals such as Dance Screen, Video Dance, and Prix Italia.

The country's leading ballet dancer is Vojko Vidmar, whose thirtieth year of dancing was celebrated in a telecast in which the dancer received the country's highest artist award, the Great Prešeren prize, named after France Prešeren, Slovenia's most famous poet. (Other twentieth-century ballet dancers who were similarly honored include Pia Mlakar, Pino Mlakar, Tatjana Remškar, and Mojmir Lasan.)

Maribor's renovated theater includes a modern stage and large auditorium. Major productions include *The Nutcracker,* staged by Vaslav Orlikovsky; *Don Quixote,* staged by Valery Panov; *Giselle* and *Romeo and Juliet;* and contemporary works by Vasily Solomon and Maja Milenović-Workman.

BIBLIOGRAPHY

Cerić, Zoran. "Šest 'Alternativaca'." *Borba, Kultura* (26 June 1995).

Jovanović, Milica. *Balet Narodnog Pozorišta u Beogradu.* Belgrade, 1994. See Chapter 1, "Prvih Sedamdeset Godina."

Katić-Serban, Minja. "Kako Postaješ Ratnik, ili o Sonji." *Orchestra,* no. 2 (Summer 1995): 34–35.

Maksimović, Bogdan. "Intervju Nada Kokotović." *Orchestra,* no. 3 (Winter 1996): 26–27.

Mandukić, Smiljana. *Govor Tela, Iskustvo Modernog Baleta.* Belgrade, 1990.

Marinković-Rakić, Branka, and Nikolajević Radivoje. *Yugoslav Ballet.* Belgrade, 1958.

Narodno Pozorište Sarajevo. *Sarajevski Balet 1950–1990.* Sarajevo, 1990.

Radmanović, Duška. "Pod Našim Krovom." *Pozorište,* no. 6 (February 1992): 17.

Savić, Svenka. "Studiske i Igračke Grupe u Novom Sadu." *Pozorište,* nos. 8–10 (April–June 1993): 30–31.

Savić, Svenka. "Balet Bez Pozorišta." *Pozorište,* nos. 1–2 (October–November 1994): 33.

Savić, Svenka. "Lepo I Umetnicki Ozbiljno." *Pozorište,* nos. 1–5 (September–December 1995, January 1996): 41.

"Slavko Pervan," *Svijet* (11 April 1996).

Srpsko Narodno Pozorište. "45 Godina Baleta Srpskog Narodnog Pozorišta (repertoar 1950–95)." *Pozorište,* addition to nos. 6–7 (March–April 1995): 47–78.

Zajcev, Milica. "U Devetoj Decenij Stvaralaštva." *Pozorište,* nos. 1–2, (September–October 1991): 35.

Zajcev, Milica. "Prednost Izražajnom Pokretu Tela." *Pozorište,* nos. 1–2, (September–October 1991): 36–38.

Zajcev, Milica. "Povratak Tradiciji." *Pozorište,* nos. 7–8 (March–April 1992): 61.

Zajcev, Milica. "Biliar Iza Zatvorenih Vrata." *Pozorište,* nos. 8–10 (April–June 1993): 33.

Zajcev, Milica. "Igra Uprkos Ratu." *Hello Belgrade,* no. 9 (December 1993–January 1994): 19.

Zajcev, Milica. "U Iščekivanju Novog Jutra. . . ." *Hello Belgrade,* no. 12 (April–May 1994): 21.

Zajcev, Milica. *Igra Što Život Znači: Zapisi O Beogradskim Baletskim Umetnicima.* Belgrade, 1994.

Zajcev, Milica. "Mladi Dolaze." *Pozorište,* nos. 1–5 (September–December 1995, January 1996): 41.

Xenia Rakic, Ani Udovicki, and Vojko Vidmar

Dance Research and Publication

Research in the field of dance in the Balkans has not been very extensive. Since universities have not offered dance curricula, teachers and choreographers, not to mention dance scholars, have not been able to study dance in an academic context. Young musicologists, later responsible for dance in theater museums, learned nothing of dance in their university years. The research that has been done is mostly by dancers, choreographers, and museum workers. Most has been in the history of development of regional dance, the work of certain dance companies, and personalities on the Yugoslav dance scene.

Research in Yugoslavia before 1991. Nearly all dance publications of the communist era were published on anniversaries or other festive occasions. No dance periodicals existed, probably because Yugoslavia was a multiethnic state with three mutually unintelligible languages. Furthermore, Yugoslavia did not have a ministry of culture on the federal level. The only scientific dance institutions in the country were the institutes for folk art and folk dance in Ljubljana, Skopje, Zagreb, Sarajevo, and other cities, which pursued research and were closely connected with folk dance groups in their respective regions. These institutes issued numerous publications describing in words and Labanotation the rich variety of national dances in Yugoslavia.

There were some attempts to assemble dancers, choreographers, dance teachers, and dance critics to discuss problems facing Yugoslavian ballet. Festival Ljubljana used the occasion of the Yugoslav Ballet Biennial to organize symposiums. Every two years, dance scholarship works were presented and discussed. Festival Ljubljana also started a short-lived quarterly newsletter on dance.

In 1958 the commission for cultural relations with foreign countries published the English-language book *Yugoslav Ballet.* The authors, Branka Marinković-Rakić and Radivoje Nikolajević, wrote about the origins of ballet in Yugoslavia and described the development of ballet companies. Some books and articles written later presented more facts on regional dance. Also worth mentioning is Slobodanka Grbić-Softić's *Osvajanje igre* (Conquering the Dance), published in 1958. This history of dance in Bosnia and Herzegovina spans the period from the appearance of the first dancers in that republic until the founding of the first professional company in 1950. To commemorate the twentieth anniversary of that company, Slobodan Spirić wrote an article in 1970, "Twenty Years of the Sarajevo Ballet." Two books published in 1968 describe theater life in Belgrade. The first is *One Hundred Years of the National Theater,* for which Veroslava Petrović and Ksenija Oreŋković contributed articles on the Belgrade Ballet from 1918 to 1941 and from 1944 to 1968. The other book, written by Belgrade Theater dramatist Branko Dragutinović, is *Jedan vek Narodnog pozorista u Beogradu, 1868–1968* (A Century of National Theater of Belgrade), with a section devoted to opera and ballet. In 1976 Milica Jovanović wrote an article in *Teatron 5* entitled "Ballet of the National Theater [Belgrade] between Two Wars," using documents of that time to chronicle the Belgrade Ballet between 1922 and 1941, when German bombs destroyed the theater. The Zagreb Theater's hundredth anniversary was commemorated in *Croatian National Theater 1860–1950,* with a short article by Josip Kavur, "Ballet of the Croatian National Theater from Its Foundation till Today." Nikola Batušić wrote *Hrvatsko kazaliste u Zagrebu, 1840–1992* (History of the Croatian Theater), which briefly mentions opera and ballet.

In Slovenia, most research work in dance history was done by Henrik Neubauer. His notable articles include "Ballet Problems in Yugoslavia," and "Slavko Osterc [a composer] and the Slovene Ballet," "A Chronicle on the Development of Ballet Art in Ljubljana," and "A List of Ballet and Dance Performances in Ljubljana from the Middle of the Eighteenth Century Onward" (all 1963); "Chronological Survey of the Development of Slovene Ballet" (1970), which included lists of performances by the ballet companies in Ljubljana and Maribor; "A Short History of the Slovene Ballet on Its 50th Anniversary" (in English, 1970); and "A Chronicle of the Ballet School in Ljubljana" (1970).

Also worth mentioning are memoirs of the Russian-born Peter Gresserov-Golovin, the late ballet master and choreographer in Ljubljana and Maribor. His book *Moja ljuba Slovenija* (My Beloved Slovenia), issued in 1985 in a translation from Russian by Henrik Neubauer, evokes his life and work. It includes descriptions of dancers, choreographers, singers, directors, conductors, composers, and designers during the period from 1924 to 1951. Pino Mlakar, another former ballet master of the Ljubljana Ballet, wrote "Ballet on the Slovene Stage" (1967) for the Slovene Theater Museum.

Various articles have also been published about personalities from different Yugoslav ballet companies—Margarita Froman, Pia and Pino Mlakar, Slavko Pervan, Katarina Kocka, Stane Polik, Lidija Sotlar, Tatjana Remškar, Lidija Wisiak, Jelena Poljakova, Nada Murašova, Erika Marjaš, Radomir Vučić, Ivanka Lukatelli, and others. There are also reference works dealing with dance personalities, such as *Slovene Biographical Lexicon, Slovene Theatrical Lexicon, Music Encyclopedia, Lexicon of Yugoslav Music, Encyclopedia of Croatian National Theater, National Theater of Sarajevo 1921–1971,* and *Slovene Encyclopaedia.*

Research dedicated to folk dance is also conducted in different regions of Yugoslavia, and many books and articles describing various folk dances have been issued. Notable among the folk dance books are the eight volumes produced by Ljubica S. Janković and Danica S. Janković from 1934 to 1964, *Narodne igre*.

Research in Slovenia since 1991. Since declaring its independence in 1991 Slovenia has reorganized the system of cultural institutions it had inherited from Yugoslavia. Under the direction of the new ministry of culture, progress is being made slowly to bring Slovenia in line with other European countries in the area of dance research. The Institute for Folk Art and Folk Dance is now attached to the Slovenian Academy of Art and Science, and the Slovenian Theater Museum is gradually collecting all the materials and documents concerning theater and dance.

Most dance research is still done by Henrik Neubauer. In 1992 he published "Balet ob 100-letnici" (Ballet at the Hundredth Anniversary), included in *One Hundred Years of the Opera House in Ljubljana,* published by the Slovenian National Theater in Ljubljana. In the same year the Slovenian Theater Museum published his *Glasbeno gledališka dela slovenskih skladateljev* (Music Theater Works of Slovenian Composers), a comprehensive survey of all ballets, operas, and operettas by Slovenian composers. The book includes a chronological list of 129 works performed between 1798 and 1992 with dates and venues of their premieres, and of ninety-three never-performed works. The book's second chapter includes an alphabetical listing by composer with the names of their works, dates of composition, names of librettists, and a brief synopsis for each work. Of the 222 compositions described, sixty are ballet scores. Neubauer's book *The Development of Ballet Art in Slovenia* was published in 1997 by the Association of Ballet Artists of Slovenia. He also contributed a short article entitled "Dance Theater in Slovenia" to the *World Encyclopedia of Contemporary Theater.*

In 1993 the Ballet School in Ljubljana issued a brochure for its forty-fifth anniversary, which included "Ljubljanasha baletna šola od 1970 do 1993" (Ballet School in Ljubljana from 1970 to 1993) by Alenka Tomc, a ballet teacher. In 1993 Breda Pretnar, a ballet and dance critic, wrote "Experimental Works and Renewals (Slovenian Dance Scene)," published in English by the Slovenian Center of the International Theater Institute (ITI) in a survey on the 1992/93 theater season under the title "Slovenian Theater 1993"; Neubauer's "A Good Sign for the Future" (also in English), was included in the ITI's survey for the following season.

Henrik Neubauer

Z

ZAÏRE. *For discussion of dance in Zaïre, renamed Congo in 1997, see* Central and East Africa. *See also* Mbuti Dance *and* Sub-Saharan Africa, *article on* Popular Dance in Sub-Saharan Africa. *For dance traditions in the African diaspora, see* Brazil, *article on* Popular and Ritual Dance.

ZAJLICH, PIOTR (born 26 June 1884 in Warsaw, died 18 April 1948 in Warsaw), Polish dancer, choreographer, and ballet director. A graduate of the ballet school affiliated with Warsaw's Wielki Theater, Piotr Zajlich performed with the Warsaw Ballet from 1900 to 1910. The following year he joined Serge Diaghilev's Ballets Russes for a season, and from 1912 to 1914 he worked with Anna Pavlova's company as both principal dancer and choreographer, often under the Russian pseudonym Shouvalov. Among the works he created for Pavlova were *Invitation to the Dance, Oriental Fantasy,* and a version of Petipa's *Halte de Cavalerie.*

Zajlich spent the years from 1914 to 1917 in a German prisoner-of-war camp. Upon his release he returned to Warsaw, where he took over the direction of the Wielki Theater school and company until 1934. He reformed the curriculum by adding rhythmic gymnastics and academic classes. His pupils included Ballets Russes stars Roman Jasinski, Yurek Lazowski, and Yurek Shabelevsky. He reestablished the artistic level of the Warsaw company, producing a large repertory. Among his works were revivals of classics such as *Swan Lake, Giselle,* and *Coppélia,* as well as a selection of Diaghilev ballets, including *Les Sylphides, Schéhérazade, Petrouchka,* and *The Firebird.* In addition, he created original ballets based on Polish national tradition, and these he cultivated with special care. As a choreographer he remained traditional, even in his revisions of the Diaghilev repertory. His 1921 version of *Pan Twardowski* was especially popular, although he also set works to music of contemporary Polish composers, such as Karol Szymanowski's *Songs of Hafiz* and Ludomir Rogowski's *The Fable.* For the Polish Ballet, Zajlich restaged *Kraków Wedding* in 1938/39. After World War II, he led a small company that performed with the opera in a Warsaw theater that had escaped major damage.

[*See also* Warsaw Ballet.]

BIBLIOGRAPHY

Dąbrowski, Stanisław, and Zbigniew Raszewski, eds. *Słownik biograficzny teatru polskiego.* 2 vols. Warsaw, 1973–1994.

Kinel, Lola. "Ludomir Rozycki and His *Pan Twardowski.*" *Musical Standard* 17 (1921): 209–210.

Kinel, Lola. "The Great Polish Ballet-Pantomime, *Pan Twardowski.*" *Poland America* 4 (November 1923): 287–291, 309–310.

Mamontowicz-Łojek, Bożena. *Terpsychora i lekkie muzy.* Kraków, 1972.

Pudełek, Janina. *Z historii baletu.* Warsaw, 1981.

Pudełek, Janina. *Two Hundred Years of Polish Ballet, 1785–1985.* Warsaw, 1985.

Rebling, Eberhard. "Pan Twardowski." In *Ballet von A bis Z.* Berlin, 1966.

JANINA PUDEŁEK

ZAKHAROV, ROSTISLAV (Rostislav Vladimirovich Zakharov; born 7 September 1907 in Astrakhan, Russia, died 14 January 1984 in Moscow), dancer, choreographer, teacher, art director, and artistic director. Zakharov graduated in 1926 from the Leningrad Choreographic Institute, where he trained under Vladimir Ponomarev. His first professional positions were as a dancer with the ballet companies of Kharkov and then Kiev, where he became a soloist and essayed his first choreography for amateur groups and students, and married ballerina Maria Smirnova. Aware of the prevailing trend toward dramatizing ballet, he returned to Leningrad in 1928 to study stage directing with Vladimir Soloviev at the Leningrad Institute of Theatrical Art, and graduated in 1932. He had continued to choreograph and also began to collaborate on stage productions with the director Sergei Radlov. At the time Radlov was artistic director of the State Academic Theater for Opera and Ballet; he brought Zakharov into the company as a dancer and choreographer.

Zakharov created his first and most outstanding ballet, *The Fountain of Bakhchisarai,* for the company in 1934. Set to a score by Boris Asafiev and a libretto by Nikolai Volkov based on Aleksandr Pushkin's eponymous poem, it tells an exotic and lustful tale of love and revenge. Zakharov wrote in 1977:

> After I had the good luck to mingle with the people and witness their everyday life, traveling from town to town and visiting workers' settlements, seeing how they lived and learning of their aspirations, I realized that our art failed to portray that

> seething life, those profound human emotions, but was confined to its narrow shell. I realized that ballet just as any dramatic or operatic production should have depth and should be comprehensible without recourse to program notes. The action had to be so organized that the plot could develop logically and consistently, that the protagonists could be lifelike characters in the process of interaction and conflict. I reasoned that since the ballet is theater, and theater is a public stage from which the people are told about themselves, about the beauty and cruelty of life, and about the variety of man's inner world that induces him to action, ballet has no right to stand aloof from real life.

Zakharov embodied these principles in *The Fountain of Bakhchisarai.* Before he began to choreograph he conducted research into pertinent historical material and literary sources. To prepare the work for the stage he introduced to the ballet world the principles of character development formulated by Konstantin Stanislavsky. Concepts such as "superobjective," "through-composed action," "the kernel of a role," and the actor's "period of study" were brought into play and the moral and philosophical foundations of the work explained, so that the dancers would not only dance but also act. So successful was the ballet at its premiere that it remained a company staple and was also restaged at the Bolshoi Theater in Moscow. [*See* Fountain of Bakhchisarai, The.]

In 1938 Zakharov joined the Bolshoi Theater, where he remained for twenty years, as choreographer for the ballet and the opera companies as well as a stage director for operas. There he produced other ballets based on Pushkin's works: *The Prisoner of the Caucasus* (1938) and *Mistress into Maid* (1946), both to music by Asafiev, and *The Bronze Horseman* (1949) to music of Reinhold Glière. All of them developed, each in its distinctive way, the genre of Soviet *dram-balet,* or dramatic ballet. The principles of dramatic ballet included a close link with literature, a clear-cut concept of dramaturgy and stage direction, and a reliance on the acting dancer. This implied a renunciation of the structural forms of traditional ballets: divertissements and a broad use of pantomime. In Soviet dramatic ballets the language of classical dance mingled with character dance, which was dictated by commitment to the people, realism, and social significance. Ballet sought to be lifelike and appeal to mass audiences.

In the chamber comedy ballet *Mistress into Maid* Zakharov was attracted by the lyrical theme of love, the atmosphere and style of Pushkin's epoch. The large-scale historico-philosophic ballet *The Bronze Horseman* conveyed the idea of Pushkin's poem: the indomitable Russian national spirit, symbolized by the image of Peter the Great and his capital Saint Petersburg. The ballet also incorporated elements of a fairy play. The production was replete with grandiose stage effects: scenes of a flood in Saint Petersburg, the launching of a ship, and the assembly of the statue of Peter the Great. There was also a clear dramatic line in the lyrical relations between the protagonists Yegeny and Parasha.

Realism was the hallmark of Zakharov's *Taras Bulba* (1941), to music by Vladimir Soloviev-Sedoi, and *Lost Illusions* (1936), to music by Asafiev, based on works of Nikolai Gogol and Honoré de Balzac, respectively; in *Taras Bulba* Zakharov worked on a synthesis of classical dance with Ukrainian folklore. He was further the first interpreter of Sergei Prokofiev's score *Cinderella* (1945); his production was in the repertory for almost thirty years and was filmed as *The Crystal Slipper.* He produced a new version of Glière's *The Red Poppy* in 1949 as well as a revival in 1939 of the classical favorite *Don Quixote,* which is still in the Bolshoi Ballet repertory. In it, while preserving what had been created by Marius Petipa and later Aleksandr Gorsky, Zakharov reinforced the plot and added a number of new dances: a jig, a dance with guitars, and a fandango.

As a choreographer Zakharov's principles set the guidelines for the development of multinational Soviet ballet. He choreographed for the new postrevolutionary audiences but at the same time recognized the historical traditions of ballet, which proved an effective choice. Early on he collaborated with fellow choreographers such as Vasily Vainonen, Leonid Lavrovsky, Vakhtang Chabukiani, and Konstantin Sergeyev, but in practice and in theory he was the most active and consistent champion of dramatic ballet. Thus, from the 1930s to the 1950s Zakharov's art played an important role in converting ballet from what was perceived as a narrow elitist art to a popular art, close to the people ideologically and aesthetically, and his ballets were the core of his companies' repertory. He also influenced a generation of outstanding dancers. Galina Ulanova, Olga Lepeshinskaya, Marina Semenova, Olga Jordan, Natalia Dudinskaya, Tatiana Vecheslova, Raisa Struchkova, Maya Plisetskaya, Konstantin Sergeyev, Aleksei Yermolayev, Mikhail Gabovich, and many others revealed their talents in Zakharov's productions. But by the onset of the 1960s his adherence to dramatic ballet as the only correct manifestation of socialist realism came to be increasingly criticized. Only his importance as head of prominent training schools protected his position: from 1945 to 1947 he was director of the Moscow School of Choreography, and from 1946 until his death head of the choreography department, which he had founded, at the Lunacharsky Institute for Theatrical Art.

Zakharov's staging of dances in operas such as *Ruslan and Ludmila, Ivan Susanin, Aïda,* and *Carmen* was distinguished. He was also acknowledged as a fine director of operas. His 1937 production of Mikhail Glinka's *Ruslan and Ludmila* at the Bolshoi Theater was famous. The stagings of Gioacchino Rossini's *William Tell* in Kuibyshev in 1942 and at the Bolshoi in 1944 won Zakharov the State

Prize of the USSR. His production of Georges Bizet's *Carmen* at the Bolshoi in 1943 was in the repertory for many years. Zakharov also demonstrated his talent as a director in productions of large open-air performances. At world festivals of youth and students in Prague (1947), Budapest (1949), Berlin (1951), Bucharest (1953), and Moscow (1957), he was the chief director of the Soviet delegation, organizing performances that combined elements of athletic parades, massive spectacles, dance festivals, and artistic political manifestations. As a principal director of the Sixth Moscow Festival he staged the ballet *Our Flourishing Youth* at the new Lenin Stadium, in which 2,500 performers from all Soviet republics participated.

Zakharov was a prolific and often contentious writer, using the medium as a means to answer his critics. Among his books are *Iskusstvo baletmeistera* (The Art of Choreography; 1954), *Besedy o tantse* (Conversations on Dance; 1963); *Rabota baletmeistera s ispolniteliami* (The Choreographer's Work with Dancers; 1967), *Zapiski baletmeistera* (A Choreographer's Notes; 1976), *Slovo o tantse* (A Word on Dance; 1977), and *Sochinenie tantsa* (Composition of Dance; 1983.) He won the State Prize of the USSR in 1943, 1944, 1945, and 1946, and was named People's Artist of the USSR in 1969.

BIBLIOGRAPHY

Anisimov, Aleksandr I., ed. *Balet Gosudarstvennogo Ordena Lenina Akademicheskogo Bol'shogo Teatr SSSR.* Moscow, 1955.

Barnes, Clive. "Kirov Ballet Backdrop." *Dance Magazine* (September 1961): 40–47.

Brinson, Peter, ed. *Ulanova, Moiseyev, and Zakharov on Soviet Ballet.* Translated by E. Fox and D. Fry. London, 1954.

Dementieva, N. "Tvorcheskaya neutomimost." *Sovetskii balet,* no. 6 (1983).

Ivashnev, Vitalii, and Kira Ilyina. *Rostislav Zakharov: Zhizn v tantse.* Moscow, 1982.

Krasovskaya, Vera. "New Thoughts in the USSR." *Dance Magazine* (February 1966): 33–35.

Roslavleva, Natalia. "Stanislavski and the Ballet." *Dance Perspectives,* no. 23 (1965).

Roslavleva, Natalia. *Era of the Russian Ballet* (1966). New York, 1979.

Slonimsky, Yuri. *Sovetskii balet.* Moscow, 1950.

Zakharov, Rostislav. "Dramaturgy of the Ballet." *Dance Magazine* (June 1953): 24, 46–47.

Zakharov, Rostislav. *Slovo o tantse.* Moscow, 1977.

Zakharov, Rostislav. *Sochinenie tantsa.* 2d ed. Moscow, 1989.

GALINA V. BELYAYEVA-CHELOMBITKO
Translated from Russian

ZAMBELLI, CARLOTTA (Carolina Celia Luigia Zambelli; born 4 November 1875 in Milan, died 28 January 1968 in Milan), Italian dancer. While a student at the ballet school of Teatro alla Scala in Milan, Zambelli studied under Cesare Coppini. In 1894 Pedro Gailhard hired her for the Paris Opera. Already possessed of an excellent technique, she was an immediate success in a variation with a mirror in *Faust.* After her interpretation of the Fairy of the Snows in *La Maladetta* (choreography by Joseph Hansen), in which she replaced Rosita Mauri, she was named *étoile* ("star"). She danced in numerous opera *divertissements,* including that of *La Favorite,* in which she executed fifteen *fouettés,* something never before achieved in France; in *Le Cid,* her spirit and provocative suppleness aroused wonder. She performed *L'Étoile* (choreography by Hansen) and *La Korrigane* (choreography by Louis Mérante). Invited to the Maryinsky Theater in Saint Petersburg in 1901, she danced *Coppélia, Paquita,* and *Giselle,* which she rehearsed with Enrico Cecchetti.

Zambelli stamped her personality on many ballets, including *La Ronde des Saisons* (choreography by Hansen), *La Fête chez Thérèse* (choreography by Madame Stichel), *Namouna* (choreography revised by Léo Staats), and *Suite de Danses* (choreography by Ivan Clustine). She was a graceful embodiment of the charming Gourouli of Mérante's *Les Deux Pigeons;* in his *Sylvia,* she ensured the

ZAMBELLI. From 1898 until 1930, Zambelli reigned supreme as *première danseuse étoile* at the Paris Opera. She posed for this charming publicity photograph around the turn of the century. (Photograph from the Dance Collection, New York Public Library for the Performing Arts.)

triumph of the haughty nymph. She was the Shade previously incarnated by Marie-Madeleine Guimard in *Castor et Pollux,* and Terpsichore (like her predecessor Marie Sallé) in *Les Fêtes d'Hébé,* performed in Monte Carlo, where she revived the French style of the eighteenth century.

Her performance in *Cydalise et la Chèvre-pied* (choreography by Staats) in 1923 remains memorable. *Impressions de Music-Hall* (choreography by Bronislava Nijinska) in 1927 was her last stage appearance. From 1920 to 1955 she taught the class of *grands sujets* and directed the training of the future dancers of the Paris Opera.

The last Italian star at the Paris Opera, Zambelli expressed herself in an incisive, pure language of movement. She was praised for her elegant precision, the vivacity of her *entrechats,* the infallibility of her acute pointe work, the audacity of her leaps, and the musical precision of her variations, which featured brilliant pirouettes and *déboulés.* As a student at the Maryinsky in 1901, Nijinska was fascinated by Zambelli's theatrical skills. Zambelli's Italian fervor was tempered by French moderation; in the words of André Levinson,

> Demonstration followed demonstration: the sparkling play of Coppélia, the radiant *entrée* of Sylvia and the liveliness of the famous pizzicato, the spiritual coquetry of Cydalise. The mischievousness of Mimi Pinson is replaced by tenderness in *La Fête chez Thérèse,* gaiety and audacity make way for a time for the romantic melancholy of Roussalka. (Levinson, 1924)

Levinson defined her art as "that clear awareness that causes the body to move like a precision instrument with a perspicacity and a spirit of finesse that never fail." Zambelli once wrote that "dancers know, or should know, that they cannot be mediocre," a belief that governed her entire career. She was the first female dancer to be recognized by France's Légion d'Honneur, an award the press warmly welcomed. Named Chevalier of the Légion in 1926, she was made an Officier in 1956.

BIBLIOGRAPHY

Garafola, Lynn. "Dancing for the Silent Screen." *The Dancing Times* (October 1981): 26–27.

Guest, Ivor. "Carlotta Zambelli" (parts 1–2). *Dance Magazine* (February–March 1974).

Levinson, André. *La danse au théâtre.* Paris, 1924.

Vaillat, Léandre. *Ballets de l'Opéra de Paris (ballets dans les opéras—nouveaux ballets).* Paris, 1947.

ARCHIVE. Walter Toscanini Collection of Research Materials in Dance, New York Public Library for the Performing Arts.

JEANNINE DORVANE
Translated from French

ZAMBIA. *For discussion of dance traditions in Zambia, see* Central and East Africa.

ZĀR is a healing ceremony for men and women believed to be possessed by malevolent spirits. Similar to other trance-dance traditions worldwide, *zār* is performed in many parts of the Middle East, in North Africa, and in East Africa. Dancing, often developing into trance, is an essential part of the ritual. Most of the dancing in *zār* ritual is adapted from local dance traditions and often includes parodies of stereotypical individuals.

The term *zār* refers to both the spirits and the cults dedicated to exorcising them. Individuals are said to be possessed if they are lethargic and depressed, if they lose their appetite, if they have fits of convulsion or rage, if their stomach or legs swell mysteriously, or if they display symptoms not known to be responsive to medical treatment. Women who are barren may be said to be possessed. In some regions both men and women participate in *zār,* whereas in others only women do so; however, in all regions where *zār* is practiced, most of those afflicted are women with marital problems.

Treatment for possession *(ḍarb al-zār)* includes, at a minimum, a *zār* healer-exorcist; an animal sacrifice (the patient is required to smear its blood on parts of her or his body or to drink some of the blood); dancing that leads to trance by those possessed; drums and other musical instruments; incense and other aromatics to attract spirits (jinn) and to draw the patient out of the trance; and gifts given to the possessing spirit in order to placate it. These gifts remain with the patient. The bowl lyre *(ṭanbūra)* is an integral part of *zār* ceremonies on the Arabian Peninsula and in parts of East Africa. Commonly, the healer and/or dancers wear a large belt made of goats' hooves or shells attached to leather. The hooves or shells rattle rhythmically when the pelvis is rotated in the dancing. In the Gulf region, a special house provides a focal point for the activities of the *zār* cult. In Egypt and elsewhere, special amulets made of silver and other silver jewelry are associated with the cult.

Details of *zār* ritual vary from place to place; yet the following generalizations apply to most *zār* cults. A person suspected of being possessed by spirits is taken to a healer. The healer will then ask the patient's family to arrange for a healing ceremony. This involves a large gathering with dancing and music. It may also involve sacrificing a chicken or lamb plus the giving of gifts to the healer and the patient. Guests include others who have been possessed by spirits, as well as the family and friends of the patient. The possessed are thought not to be responsible for their actions, thus unconventional behavior, such as smoking cigarettes, drinking alcoholic beverages, and/or cross-sex dressing is typical of *zār* ceremonies. Moreover, dancing during *zār* ceremonies may be less restrained than it is on other occasions.

The healer or drummers will play several rhythms. Guests who have been possessed will get up to dance to the particular beat that identifies their spirit. Eventually, the patient will begin to dance and continue dancing until she (or he) falls into a trance. The possessing spirit is identified both by the patient's symptoms and by the drum beat to which it responds. When the patient enters a trance, the spirit is questioned by the healer; it responds by presenting demands through the patient. Its demands are usually for gifts of jewelry or clothing or for family members to change their behavior toward the patient. These demands must be met by the patient's family. Failure to placate the spirit will ensure its return to plague the patient and, by extension, the family.

A special relationship is formed between the healer and a patient who has recovered. Initiates are expected to attend all *zār* ceremonies given by their healer, at which they often enjoy special status. *Zār* ritual often includes Muslim and Christian prayers, religious figures, and religious traditions; *zār* spirits are thought to respect the fasting months of Ramadan and Lent. Nevertheless, the *zār* cult is officially condemned by Muslim and Christian religious leaders.

The origin of *zār* is the subject of much scholarly debate; many believe it to have originated in Somalia or Ethiopia, where it was observed by Western travelers in the latter part of the eighteenth century. They argue that it then spread to the Niger basin, to Sudan, Egypt (where it was first reported in the late nineteenth century), the Arabian Peninsula, the Gulf region, southern Iran, Iraq, Turkey, Libya, Tunisia, Algeria, and Morocco. The presence of the bowl lyre in Mesopotamia, in ancient Sumerian inscriptions (c.3000 BCE), may indicate a possible earlier date for its spread in the region. Whatever the history of *zār*, elements of the cult appear to have been incorporated into the indigenous tradition of healing by sorcery.

[*See also* Egypt, *article on* Traditional Dance; *and* Middle East, *overview article.*]

BIBLIOGRAPHY

Ansaldi, Cesare. *Il Yemen nella storia e nella leggenda.* Rome, 1933.

Boddy, Janice. *Wombs and Alien Spirits: Women, Men, and the Zār Cult in Northern Sudan.* Madison, Wis., 1989.

Cloudsley, Anne. *Women of Omdurman: Life, Love, and the Cult of Virginity.* Rev. ed. London, 1983.

Fakhouri, Hani. "The Zar Cult in an Egyptian Village." *Anthropological Quarterly* 41 (1968).

Hadidi, Haguer el-. "The Zar Cult: An Aesthetic Expression." Master's thesis, American University of Cairo, 1996.

Hall, Marjorie, and Bakhita Amin Ismail. *Sisters under the Sun.* London, 1981.

Kahle, Paul E. "Zâr: Beschwörungen in Egypten." *Der Islam* 3 (1912).

Khoury, René. "Contribution à une bibliographie du 'zār.'" *Annales Islamogiques* 16 (1980).

Leiris, Michel. "Le culte des zárs à Gondar." *Aethiopica* 2 (1934).

Messing, Simon D. "Group Therapy and Social Status in the Zar Cult of Ethiopia." *American Anthropologist* 60 (1958).

Miṣrī, Fāṭimah al-. *Al-zār: Dirāsah nafsīyah tahlīlīyah anthrūpūlūjīyah.* Cairo, 1975.

Nelson, Cynthia. "Self, Spirit Possession, and World-View: An Illustration from Egypt." *International Journal of Social Psychology* 17 (1971).

Qāsimī, Khālid al-, and Nizār Ghānim. "Al-mūsīqā al-humāsīyah fī al-khalīj wa-al-Yaman." *Al-ma'thūrāt al-sha'bīyah* 2 (1987).

Racy, Ali Jihad. *Tanbura Music of the Gulf.* Doha, Qatar, 1988. Companion book to audiotape.

Saleh, Magda. "A Documentation of the Ethnic Dance Traditions of the Arab Republic of Egypt." Ph.D. diss., New York University, 1979.

Saunders, Lucy Wood. "Variants in Zar Experience in an Egyptian Village." In *Case Studies in Spirit Possession,* edited by Vincent Crapanzano and Vivian Garrison. New York, 1977.

Ṭayyāsh, Fahd 'Abdallah al-. "Ḥawl irtibāṭ aghānī al-zār bi-raqṣat al-sāmirī." *Al-ma'thūrāt al-sha'bīyah* 2 (1987).

Zenkovsky, S. "*Zār* and *Tambura* as Practiced by the Women of Omdurman." *Sudan Notes and Records* 31 (1950).

VIDEOTAPE. Magda Saleh, "Egypt Dances" (1979).

NAJWA ADRA

ZEAMI (born 1363 or 1364, died 1443 probably in Kyoto), Japanese performer, choreographer, playwright, and preeminent theoretician of *nō* theater. Together with his father Kan'ami, Zeami is credited with transforming the medieval performing art called *sarugaku* into *nō.*

Zeami, whose name has often been erroneously transliterated as "Seami" in Western publications, used several names in his lifetime. In his youth he was called Fujiwakamaru, and later Motokiyo; in his old age he signed his name as Zea, and also as Shio. Born in a family of *sarugaku* actors—who at the time were outcasts in Japanese society—he learned dancing and singing from the earliest years of his childhood. When he was eleven, he gave a performance at the Imanokumano Shrine in Kyoto that proved decisive for his career: the seventeen-year-old shogun, Yoshimitsu, was highly attracted by the beautiful and talented boy and invited him to live in the palace, starting a patronage of *nō* that became traditional at the shogun's court and among the samurai elite.

Zeami's contribution in the field of choreography was crucial in directing *nō* dance toward an ideal of highly polished, graceful elegance and simplicity with deep interior energy. As a dancer he achieved the highest recognition by the most powerful and sophisticated rulers of the time as well as by a wider public at more accessible shrine festivals. As a playwright, Zeami is credited with the authorship or adaptation of a large number of the finest *nō* dramas, including *Izutsu, Takasago, Kiyotsune,* and *Yuya.*

Beyond these achievements, Zeami is the most important author of performance theory in Japanese history. His treatises on the "Secret Tradition" of *nō,* such as *Kadensho* and *Kakyō,* reveal the pedagogical process used to train the highly talented performer who is destined to reach—and perpetuate—the sublime peak of the *nō* art. Zeami's elaboration of the central concepts of *nō* dra-

ZEAMI. A drawing, attributed to either Zeami or his brother-in-law Konparu Zenchiku, of a devil character from one of Zeami's treatises on the technique of *nō*. (Photograph from the archives of Nicola Savarese.)

maturgy *(monomane, hana, yūgen* and *kokoro),* his ranking of the styles of performance, and his insight into the essence of artistic performance are fundamental to an understanding of *nō*.

Zeami's life, after many fruitful years of favor at court, was marred by bitter disillusionment, caused by shifts of political power after Yoshimitsu's death (1408) and later by the early death of his beloved son, the heir to his art, Motomasa (died 1434). Banishment to the island of Sado (1434–1441) added new sadness to his old age. He eventually found new meaning and consolation in the art of his son-in-law Konparu Zenchiku, who became the heir to the Secret Tradition, and a great playwright and important theoretician of performance aesthetics in his own right.

[*See also* Konparu Zenchiku *and* Nō.]

BIBLIOGRAPHY

Hare, Thomas B. *Zeami's Style: The Noh Plays of Zeami Motokiyo.* Stanford, Calif., 1986.

Keene, Donald. *Nō: The Classical Theatre of Japan.* New York, 1966.

Komparu, Kunio. *The Noh Theatre: Principles and Perspectives.* New York and Tokyo, 1983.

Ortolani, Benito. *The Japanese Theatre: From Shamanistic Ritual to Contemporary Pluralism.* Rev. ed. Princeton, 1995.

Rimer, Thomas, and Yamazaki, Masakazu, trs. *On the Art of the Nō Drama: The Major Treatises of Zeami.* Princeton, 1984.

Sieffert, René, tr. *Zeami: La Tradition secrète du Nō, suivie de une journée de Nō.* Paris, 1960.

Smethurst, Mae J. *The Artistry of Aeschylus and Zeami: A Comparative Study of Greek Tragedy and Nō.* Princeton, 1989.

Thornhill, Arthur H. *Six Circles, One Dewdrop: The Religio-Aesthetic World of Komparu Zenchiku.* Princeton, 1993.

Tyler, Royall, tr.. *Japanese Nō Dramas.* London, 1992.

Yasuda, Kenneth. *Masterworks of the Nō Theater.* Bloomington and Indianapolis, 1989.

BENITO ORTOLANI

ZHOU XINFANG (born 14 January 1895 in Jiangsu, China, died 1975 in Shanghai), Chinese opera actor. A Beijing opera actor specializing in *laosheng,* old male characters, Zhou began training at six in Hangzhou and performing onstage at seven; this resulted in his stage name Qiling Tong (seven-year-old child) and later Qilin Tong (Qilin is an auspicious animal in Chinese mythology, akin to the dragon). He created the Qi school, one of the two most distinctive styles of Beijing Opera; the other is the Mei school of his frequent stage partner, Mei Lanfang.

Given the stylized nature of Beijing Opera, Zhou is best known in China for his realistic approach to characterization. He joined a modern drama group in his thirties, befriending many modern playwrights and actors. During the war against the Japanese invasion and the civil wars, he conceived and co-authored, as well as choreographed, many Beijing Opera pieces based on the ancient stories but alluding to contemporary issues, such as national defense and the peasant rebellion.

In Zhou's plays he mainly developed his robust and vigorous acting style of the righteous male hero. Zhou's voice was a bit harsh for an opera singer, but he turned this idiosyncratic feature to his advantage by integrating singing and movement as inseparable organic parts. For example, in one of his most memorable pieces, *Xu Ce Pao Cheng* (Xu Ce Runs on the City Wall), about a senior court official rushing to see the emperor for an emergency, he circles the stage alone, in various dance steps (in shoes with two-inch-thick hard soles) for about thirty minutes, while singing throughout to express his indignation, hesitation, and final determination. In indoor scenes requiring no large-scale movements, he concentrates on the dance of hands, face, and even beard and headset. In *Qingfeng Ting* (The Breeze Pavilion), when the old man he plays discovers that his wife has been murdered, his hands start trembling, pointing to her body, to the murderer, to the sky, and to his chest. Then all of a sudden he grabs some of his long beard and bites it in his mouth before crashing his head onto a pillar of the house. His other famous roles include Song Jiang, a peasant rebel leader from the classic novel *The Water Margin,* and Song Shijie, an exceptionally caring and wise official in *Si Jinshi* (Four New Officials).

Zhou was studious and learned extensively from numerous Chinese opera forms other than Beijing Opera in order to enrich his Qi school style and repertory, resulting in many of his best pieces being adaptations of other genres. In turn, his Qi school influenced generations of traditional Chinese performers of all types. He headed theater companies to tour in North Korea and the Soviet Union in 1953 and 1956, respectively. He was associate director of the Chinese Academy of Traditional Theater, head of the East China Academy of Traditional Theater, and later head of the Shanghai Beijing Opera Theater and vice-chairman of the Chinese Theater Artists Association until Mao Zedong's Cultural Revolution of 1966 to 1976, which destroyed all these and many other traditional institutions. During the Cultural Revolution, Zhou's early creation of historical character Hai Rui, a righteous official who risked his life to criticize the emperor on behalf of the people, became his "crime" against Mao. Ironically, Zhou, widely acclaimed as the reincarnation of heroes who brought justice to wronged people, was then unjustly persecuted, to die in grief.

BIBLIOGRAPHY

Liu Housheng. "Mei Zhou Xihuan Difanxi." *Xinmin Wanbao* (20 December 1994).

Zeng Bairong et al., eds. *Jingju Jumu Cidian.* Beijing, 1989.

Zhongguo Da Baikequanshu: Xiju, Quyi. Beijing, 1983.

WILLIAM H. SUN

ZIEGFELD, FLORENZ (Florenz Ziegfeld, Jr.; born 21 March 1867 in Chicago, died 22 July 1932 in Santa Monica, California), American theatrical producer. The number of his theatrical enterprises and the span of "Flo" Ziegfeld's professional career has yet to be equaled by an American. Son of the founder of the Chicago Musical College, he took the revue format from a series of topical novelty acts and developed it into a star-studded event. His productions set an unmatched standard for visual extravagance from pre–World War I seasons through the 1920s, the decade considered to have been the genre's zenith.

Ziegfeld's earliest success was as manager of the 1893 appearances of the Great Sandow, a charismatic muscle man. His first theatrical production was the 1896 revival of Charles Hoyt's *A Parlor Match* as a showcase for Anna Held (Ziegfeld's first wife), with Julian Mitchell as stage director. Teamed again with Ziegfeld and Held in 1906 for *A Parisian Model,* Mitchell evolved a formula for embellishing political and theatrical satire with musical numbers and beautiful girls. That idea later emerged as Ziegfeld's *Follies of 1907.* Influenced by Harry B. Smith

ZIEGFELD. The big hit of the *Ziegfeld Follies of 1927* was Irving Berlin's "Shaking the Blues Away." The stage setting, designed by Joseph Urban, featured a backdrop depicting a Southern plantation and a cut drop hung with skeins of Spanish moss. Singer Ruth Etting was backed up by the Jazzbow Girls (dressed entirely in red), the Albertina Rasch Dancers, the Banjo Ingenues, and Dan Healy. By the end of the number, staged by Sammy Lee, there were nearly eighty people on the stage. They were met by thunderous applause from the audience. (Photograph from the Billy Rose Theater Collection, New York Public Library for the Performing Arts.)

and later by Gene Buck, Ziegfeld adopted Mitchell's basic structure, elaborating and escalating its dimensions for his revues, which opened annually (except in 1925, 1929, and 1930) until 1931, the last edition under his personal supervision.

Known as the "Great Glorifier," Ziegfeld adorned his *Follies* with exquisite women whom he dressed in elegant gowns by Pascaud, Lady Duff-Gordon, or Erté and placed in sumptuous settings by Joseph Urban. Besides Mitchell, others who staged parts or all of the *Follies* included Leon Errol, Ned Wayburn, Ben Ali Haggin, and Michel Fokine. Singers, comics, and dancers—from art soloists to chorus girls—also were featured in Ziegfeld's book musicals. Among his headliners were Mademoiselle Daisy, Gertrude Hoffman, Bessie Clayton, Adeline Genée, Ann Pennington, Marilyn Miller, Adele and Fred Astaire, Irene Castle, Ruby Keeler, the Tiller Girls, and the Albertina Rasch Dancers.

With rare exceptions, the *Follies* were presented at the Jardin de Paris on top of the New York Theatre or at the New Amsterdam, where in 1915 Ziegfeld introduced his *Midnight Frolics* (forerunner of the modern floor show), an effort to capitalize on the era's taste for stylish naughtiness. As revues dwindled and a weakening national economy made it infeasible to stage flamboyant Broadway entertainments, many of his stars and his second wife, Billie Burke (whom he married 11 April 1914), entered films. Ziegfeld's only film was the disappointing *Glorifying the American Girl* (1929). It was live theater that kindled Ziegfeld's imagination and allowed his extraordinary abilities to mix politics, nudity, and art into a glamorous theatrical experience that subsequent revivals (1934, 1936, 1943, and 1957) have been unable to recapture.

[*For related discussion, see* United States of America, *article on* Musical Theater; *and* Vaudeville.]

BIBLIOGRAPHY

Baral, Robert. *Revue.* New York, 1962.

Carter, Randolph. *The World of Flo Ziegfeld.* New York, 1974.

Higham, Charles. *Ziegfeld.* Chicago, 1972.

Ziegfeld, Richard, and Paulette Ziegfeld. *The Ziegfeld Touch: The Life and Times of Florenz Ziegfeld, Jr.* New York, 1993.

CAMILLE HARDY

ZOLLAR, JAWOLE WILLA JO (born 1951 in Kansas City, Missouri), American dancer and choreographer. Emerging in the 1980s as one of the most innovative choreographers of modern dance, Zollar belongs to the cadre of black dancemakers whose work has avant-garde sensibilities and integrates cross-disciplinary theatrical forms. Her dances celebrate and examine the spiritual and folk traditions of the African diaspora. Her choreography is informed by grass-roots lifestyles and the musical and dance traditions of black America as well as by modern and African dance. She has cited modern dancers Dianne McIntyre, Blondell Cummings, and Kei Takei and African dancer-scholar Nontsizi Cayou as key influences.

Zollar's initial dance preparation began as a child under the direction of Joseph Stevenson, a former student of Katherine Dunham. Zollar's early training in Afro-Cuban and vernacular dance forms, supported by ample performing experiences in dance revues for social clubs and community events, began to shape her aesthetic. After graduating from high school in Kansas City, she decided to pursue a career in dance. She received a B.A. in dance from the University of Missouri at Kansas City and an M.F.A. from Florida State University.

In 1980 Zollar moved to New York City. There, she studied with Dianne McIntyre's Sounds in Motion Dance Company. She was introduced to the jazz improvisational aesthetic in modern dance and met dancers, vocalists, composers, and percussionists who were interested in performance collaboration. In 1984, a turning point in her career, she established the Urban Bush Women, a five-member ensemble whose New York premiere in July of that year received immediate critical acclaim. Revealing herself to be a cultural warrior with a strong sociopolitical consciousness, Zollar began to formulate evening-length works in which dance, a cappella vocalizations, live music, the spoken word, and visual art are assembled into multilayered dance-theater productions that explore struggle, growth, transformation, and survival of the human spirit. The work of Urban Bush Women has been described as hard-edged and straightforward. Some performances have been viewed as controversial because the company takes on such issues as abortion, racism, sexism, and homelessness. Zollar's work is characterized by a deep sense of commitment and responsibility to examine the lives of the disenfranchised, and through her choreography she seeks to "create poetry without words" based on the lives of people of color.

Zollar's creative process involves collaboration with composers, percussionists, vocalists, writers, scenic designers, and actors. She also relies on her dancers, whom she encourages to express their life experiences and choreographic voices, to help galvanize her vision. The dynamic of the dancing ranges from delicate and lyrical to bold and tough, and the content and form of the productions are based on an African-American female perspective. Recurrent themes in Zollar's work are discovery, redemption, loss, self-love, family, and survival.

Noteworthy evening-length works include *Anarchy, Wild Women, and Dina* (1986), based on the South Carolina Sea Islands folk culture; *Heat* (1988), a journey of women's lives through hope and despair, which included the acclaimed section Shelter, commissioned by the Alvin

ZOLLAR. The Urban Bush Women in *Praise House* (1990). Theresa Cousar is seen holding Viola Sheely in a protective embrace as (left to right) Grisha Coleman, Amy Pivar, Christine King, and Marlies Yearby surround them with warning gestures. (Photograph © by Cylla von Tiedemann; used by permission.)

Ailey American Dance Theater; *Praise House* (1990), a historical odyssey of the life of African-American painter Minnie Evans that was adapted for film and commissioned for the Public Broadcasting Service (PBS) series *Alive from Off Center;* and *Bones and Ash* (1995), based on the *Gilda Stories,* a novel by Jewelle Gomez.

Urban Bush Women has toured widely in the United States and abroad and has presented major seasons in New York at The Kitchen, the Joyce Theater, and the Brooklyn Academy of Music, and the ensemble has appeared at major festivals, such as Jacob's Pillow, Spoleto U.S.A., and the National Black Arts Festival. In 1992 Zollar and the company received the New York Dance and Performance Award (called the Bessie award) and the 1994 Capezio Award.

BIBLIOGRAPHY

Lewis-Ferguson, Julinda. "Reviews/Eye on Performance: New York City." *Dance Magazine* (October 1994): 78–79.

Osumare, Halifu. "The New Moderns: The Paradox of Eclecticism and Singularity." In *African American Genius in Modern Dance,* edited by Gerald Myers. Durham, N.C., 1993.

Shange, Ntozake. "Urban Bush Women: Dances for the Voiceless." *New York Times* (8 September 1991).

Smalls, Linda. "Blacks Enrich Modern Dance." *American Visions* (June 1989): 24–29.

Zollar, Jawole Willa Jo. "A Self-Study." In *Black Choreographers Moving: A National Dialogue,* edited by Julinda Lewis-Ferguson. Berkeley, 1991.

MELANYE WHITE-DIXON

ZORINA, VERA (Eva Brigitta Hartwig; born 2 January 1917 in Berlin), dancer and actress. The only child of a German father and a Norwegian mother, Brigitta Hartwig began her formal ballet training in Berlin at age six, studying first with Evgenia Eduardova, then with Victor Gsovsky. At age fourteen, she made her debut as the First Fairy in Max Reinhardt's production of *A Midsummer Night's Dream* (1930) and, the following year, performed in his production of *Tales of Hoffmann* (1931). Only two years later, having moved to London and continued her dance studies with Nikolai Legat and Marie Rambert, she had achieved stardom and was appearing on a West End stage with Anton Dolin in *Ballerina* (1933), a play with ballet interludes.

In 1934 she was invited by Colonel de Basil to join the Ballets Russes de Monte Carlo and thereafter was known as Vera Zorina (the easiest to pronounce of several Russianized stage names from which she had to choose). As a soloist with the Ballets Russes, she performed the Can-Can in *La Boutique Fantasque,* the Street Dancer in *Le Beau Danube,* and Action in *Les Présages,* all under the direction of Léonide Massine, with whom, offstage, she shared a brief but torrid love affair. In 1936 she left the Ballets Russes to play the temperamental Russian ballerina Vera Barnova in the London production of the Rodgers and Hart musical *On Your Toes* (1937). This production was received with great critical fanfare, and Zorina was soon being courted by film and stage producers from both sides of the Atlantic.

It was just at this time that Samuel Goldwyn, with the intention of showcasing ballet in his musical pictures, enlisted then rising star George Balanchine to choreograph a ballet sequence for his film *The Goldwyn Follies* (1938). Enticed by the prospect of working with Balanchine, Zorina signed a seven-year contract with Metro-Goldwyn-Mayer (MGM). With the combination of Zorina's grace and stylistic skill and Balanchine's ingenious choreography, Goldwyn's effort to integrate ballet into musicals proved instrumental in the popularization of ballet. In the process, Zorina—a stunning blond with a fabulous figure and a husky Germanic accent reminiscent of Greta Garbo and Marlene Dietrich—was thrust into Hollywood's glittering spotlight. She is perhaps most famous for her artful performance of the "Water Nymph Ballet" in *The Goldwyn Follies,* where she emerges from a pool of lilies, clad in a shift of clinging gold lamé. During the course of their work together Zorina and Balanchine became romantically involved, and they married on Christmas Eve 1938, shortly after the film was released.

ZORINA. *Louisiana Purchase,* a musical comedy with music and lyrics by Irving Berlin, opened on Broadway in May 1940. Its stars were Vera Zorina, William Gaxton, and Victor Moore. Ballet choreography was by George Balanchine; "modern dances" were created by Carl Randall. In the Paramount Pictures film released in 1941, Zorina shared top billing with Bob Hope and Victor Moore. The film included Balanchine's ballet "Tonight at the Mardi Gras," in which Zorina is pictured here, but did not credit the choreographer. Zorina's appearances in film musicals of the early 1940s did much to popularize dance and to bring ballet, in particular, to audiences who might have otherwise never been able to see it. (Photograph from the Dance Collection, New York Public Library for the Performing Arts.)

From 1938 to 1944, Zorina performed in many film musicals, including *On Your Toes* (1939), *I Was an Adventuress* (1940), *Star Spangled Rhythm* (1942), and *Follow the Boys* (1944); she also appeared in several Broadway musicals, including *I Married an Angel* (1938) and *Louisiana Purchase* (1940). The majority of these productions were choreographed by Balanchine, who meanwhile had begun to secure his position in the dance world. After the term of her MGM contract expired, Zorina attempted to refocus and reinvigorate her dance career. She performed as guest ballerina in several Ballet Theatre productions, including Fokine's *Helen of Troy* and *Petrouchka* (both 1943), and on the Broadway stage she had the speaking and dancing role of Ariel in a production of *The Tempest* (1945). She came to believe, however, that her glamorous image as a Hollywood star had obscured the public's perception of her as a serious dancer.

In 1946, after long separations due to both of their work schedules, Zorina and Balanchine were divorced, and she next married Goddard Lieberson, who went on to become president of Columbia Records. She subsequently enjoyed a career as a narrator–performer of such dramatic oratorios as Honegger's *Jeanne de'Arc au Bucher,* Stravinsky's *Perséphone,* and Debussy's *Le Martyre de Saint-Sébastien.* During the 1960s and 1970s, she worked as a director of opera productions for the Santa Fe Opera, the New York City Opera, and the Norwegian Opera.

BIBLIOGRAPHY

Berg, A. Scott. *Goldwyn: A Biography.* New York, 1989.
García-Márquez, Vicente. *Massine: A Biography.* New York, 1995.
Gruen, John. "Vera Zorina." In *The Private World of Ballet.* New York, 1975.
Taper, Bernard. *Balanchine: A Biography.* Rev. ed. New York, 1984.
Zorina, Vera. "The Inward and the Outward Eye." *Dance Magazine* (December 1959).
Zorina, Vera. *Zorina.* New York, 1986.

LIZA EWELL

ZORN NOTATION. Friedrich Albert Zorn (1815–c.1900), the inventor of the system of dance notation that bears his name, was a studious and highly regarded German dance master who settled in Odessa, Ukraine. Fascinated by the subject of dance notation, he entered into an extensive correspondence with Arthur Saint-Léon. He adopted Saint-Léon's system, which he subsequently am-

ZORN NOTATION. Like many systems for recording dance steps, Zorn notation is written to correspond to a musical staff. The symbols seen here beneath the treble clef denote a combination of *chassés, jetés, assemblés,* and *glissades.* (Reprinted from Zorn, 1905, p. 168.)

plified, perfected, and published in 1887 in *Grammatik der Tanzkunst,* in Leipzig. This book is concerned fundamentally with the correct performance of dance positions and steps and reveals the terminology and execution of mid-nineteenth-century ballet. Careful verbal descriptions accompany the notated sequences.

Zorn's drawings are much more pictorial than Saint-Léon's. Instead of a staff, he used only a base line: markings on the line indicate supporting legs and those above the line indicate legs in the air. In most instances, only legwork is shown; when arm and body position are needed, the full figure is drawn. Arrows to show the direction faced, or traveling, and indications for turning, details of foot positions, and so on, are placed under the base line. Specific movement signs, such as for lifting or putting down, are added to the figure drawings. Abbreviated forms are given for commonly used steps. Timing is indicated by figure drawings placed under the appropriate note of the music's melody line.

In addition to the contradance, quadrille, minuet, and the "Gavotte de Vestris," Zorn recorded *La Cachucha,* made famous by Fanny Elssler. Reconstructions of this work reveal weaknesses in the notation: certain steps, transitions, and rhythms are not clear, perhaps because of lack of notating experience or of adequate proofreading before printing.

Zorn's book, translated into Russian and English, received wide acclaim. Recommendations by more than one dance congress that Zorn's terminology and notation should be universally adopted were never implemented, however. In his advertisements, Zorn refers to publications of notated dances, but none has yet come to light.

[*See also* Notation.]

BIBLIOGRAPHY

Amer, Rita F. "Zorn's La Gavotte de G. Vestris." *Dance Notation Journal* 5 (Spring 1987): 25–28.

Guest, Ann Hutchinson. *Fanny Elssler's Cachucha.* New York, 1981.

Guest, Ann Hutchinson. *Choreo-Graphics: A Comparison of Dance Notation Systems from the Fifteenth Century to the Present.* New York, 1989.

Vacano, E. M. "Eine Grammatik der Tanzkunst (1888)." *Das Tanzarchiv* 23 (September 1975): 289–293.

Zorn, Friedrich Albert. *Grammatik der Tanzkunst.* Leipzig, 1887. Translated by Benjamin P. Coates as *Grammar of the Art of Dancing* (Boston, 1905).

ANN HUTCHINSON GUEST

ZOTOV, RAFAIL (Rafail Mikhailovich Zotov; born 1796, died 1871), Russian ballet critic and writer. The major chronicler of ballet events during the Romantic era in Russia, Zotov was a critic for *Severnaia pchela.* His writings also appeared in *Repertuar Russkogo teatr* and in *Panteon russkikh i vsiekh evropeiskikh teatrov.* His comprehensive, detailed accounts of theater and ballet events in Saint Petersburg were complemented by a broad view of the development of ballet in Russia and a perspicacious evaluation of European influences.

Zotov's articles in *Severnaia pchela* encompassed both the development of the Russian school and the Russian tours of European dancers and choreographers. Zotov's evaluation of the Russian school focused on performances of such dancers as Elena Andreanova (1819–1857), Avdotia Istomina (1799–1848), Anastasia Novitskaya (1790–1822), and Tatiana Smirnova (1821–1871). Regarding the Russian school, Zotov noted in 1847 that although Russia had talented dancers and an excellent corps de ballet, the public's interest could be revived only by developments in choreography, specifically by the arrival of "a Didelot, a new Prometheus, a brilliant new choreographer." Despite the impoverished state of choreography, however, Zotov wrote extensively about developments in ballet technique, noting that its advances constituted a synthesis of the old and the new, as was the case in contemporary music. Zotov also wrote about the performances in Russia of Marie Taglioni, Fanny Elssler, Carlotta Grisi, and Lucile Grahn, and he chronicled Jules Perrot's career in Russia.

In addition to his "Theater Chronicle" in *Severnaia pchela,* Zotov wrote two longer works. The first of these, "I moi vospominaniia o teatre" (My Theater Recollections), appeared in *Repertuar Russkogo teatr* in 1840. This work constituted a twenty-five-year account of performances in

Saint Petersburg with particular references to Didelot's work both in Russia and in Europe, to a comparative study of Istomina and Novitskaya, and to a discussion of Taglioni. Zotov's other longer article, "O nyneshem sostoianii Sankt-Petersburgskikh teatrov" (The Contemporary State of Saint Petersburg Theaters), was published the following year in *Panteon russkikh i vsekh evropeiskikh teatrov.* This work addressed such topics in theory and perception as form versus content, audience evaluation, and the role of the critic.

[*For similar discussion, see the entries on Koni, Levinson, Svetlov, and Volynsky.*]

BIBLIOGRAPHY

Guest, Ivor. *Jules Perrot: Master of the Romantic Ballet.* London, 1984.

Swift, Mary Grace. *A Loftier Flight: The Life and Accomplishments of Charles Louis Didelot.* Middletown, Conn., 1974. Includes a complete list of Didelot's productions.

Wiley, Roland John, trans. and ed. *A Century of Russian Ballet: Documents and Accounts, 1810–1910.* Oxford, 1990.

Zotov, Rafail. "I moi vospominaniia o teatre." In *Repertuar Russkogo teatr.* Saint Petersburg, 1840.

Zotov, Rafail. "O nyneshem sostoianii Sankt-Petersburgskikh teatrov." In *Panteon russkikh i vsiekh evropeiskikh teatrov,* edited by Fedor Koni. Saint Petersburg, 1841.

SUSAN COOK SUMMER

ZOTTO, MIGUEL ANGEL. *See* Plebs and Zotto. *See also* Tango.

ZUCCHI. A studio portrait, probably taken in the early 1880s in Italy. This likeness hardly does justice to the reputation of "the divine Virginia," noted for her sensual allure as much as for the artistry of her dancing. (Photograph by Schemboche; from the Dance Collection, New York Public Library for the Performing Arts.)

ZUCCHI, VIRGINIA (Virginia Eurosia Teresa Zucchi; born 10 February 1849 in Parma, died 9 October 1930 in Nice, France), Italian dancer. Renowned for the intensity of her acting and her feminine allure, Virginia Zucchi made her greatest impact in Russia, where she almost singlehandedly revived the public's flagging interest in ballet. Although few ballets were created for her, her dramatic gifts enabled her to make certain roles her own, notably the title role of Jules Perrot's *Esmeralda* and Padmana in Hippolyte Monplaisir's *Brahma.*

Zucchi studied with various teachers in Milan, though she was never admitted to the prestigious ballet school of the Teatro alla Scala. Following her debut in Varese in 1864, she began to make a name for herself in Italy. She essayed her two most famous roles early in her career—Esmeralda in Turin in 1869 and Padmana in Padua in 1873.

Zucchi first danced at La Scala in 1874 in Monplaisir's revival of *Estella,* a light ballet about a girl abducted by a rake. Despite a disappointing reception, she was invited to return the following year. From 1876 to 1878 she danced in Berlin in Paul Taglioni's *Flick und Flocks Abenteuer, Santanella,* and other ballets. The role of Lise in *La Fille Mal Gardée,* which Taglioni staged for her, became one of her favorites, as did Swanilda in *Coppélia,* for she had equal facility in comic and serious roles. In 1877 she danced Lise and Swanilda in Warsaw. She danced the role of Civilization in a revival of Luigi Manzotti's *Excelsior* at La Scala in 1883 and the title role in Manzotti's *Sieba* at the Eden-Théâtre in Paris later that year.

In 1885 Zucchi was engaged by Mikhail Lentovsky to appear at a minor theater, Kin Grust, in Saint Petersburg. Her overwhelming success led to an engagement with the Imperial Theaters that lasted for three seasons. During that time she danced in Marius Petipa's *La Fille du Pharaon* and *The King's Command;* he also choreographed a new pas de six for her standard, *Esmeralda.* Another triumph was *Fenella* (from Daniel Auber's opera *La Muette de Portici*), a favorite vehicle of actress-dancers.

The rabid excitement engendered by Zucchi's appearances in Russia was comparable to that evoked by Marie Taglioni and Fanny Elssler in an earlier day. Although Zucchi's detractors claimed that her realistic style of acting was inappropriate to the ballet, most viewers responded to her magnetism. Among her admirers were Ivan Vsevolozhsky, the powerful director of the Imperial Theaters, the future ballerina Matilda Kshessinska, and Alexandre Benois, later a key figure in the Ballets Russes. Zucchi was primarily a *terre à terre* dancer, possessed of phenomenally strong pointes; she tended to eschew steps of elevation and *batterie.* She knew how to exploit her great beauty and introduced to Russia the shorter skirts fashionable in Italy.

After her contract with the Imperial Theaters ended, Zucchi danced in smaller theaters in Saint Petersburg and Moscow. Konstantin Stanislavsky, who partnered her in an amateur production of *Esmeralda,* said that her muscular relaxation while acting taught him to eliminate his own physical and spiritual strain.

Toward the end of her career Zucchi staged and danced in the Venusberg scene of Richard Wagner's *Tannhäuser,* first in Bayreuth and then at the Paris Opera, where she appeared for the first time in 1895. She gave her final performances as a dancer in Milan in 1898. After her retirement she served on the juries of the annual examinations at La Scala's ballet school. Her niece, also called Virginia Zucchi, enjoyed a brief career at La Scala and the Teatro Colón in Buenos Aires.

BIBLIOGRAPHY

Benois, Alexandre. *Reminiscences of the Russian Ballet.* Translated by Mary Britnieva. London, 1941.

Guest, Ivor. *The Divine Virginia: A Biography of Virginia Zucchi.* New York, 1977.

Krasovskaya, Vera. "A Look at Virginia Zucchi." *Dance Chronicle* 1.1 (1977): 63–69.

Lo Iacono, Concetta. "La carne, la vita e il diavolo: I libretti dei balli di Virginia Zucchi." *La Danza Italiana* 4 (Spring 1986): 59–83.

Lo Iacono, Concetta. "Virginia Zucchi ed il teatro di danza de secondo ottocento." In *Incontri con la Danza 1993,* edited by Elena Grillo (1994): 47–57.

Wiley, Roland John, trans. and ed. *A Century of Russian Ballet: Documents and Accounts, 1810–1910.* Oxford, 1990.

ALBERTO TESTA
Translated from Italian

ZÜLLIG, HANS (born 1 February 1914 in Rorschach, Switzerland, died 8 November 1992 in Essen, Germany), Swiss ballet dancer, choreographer, and teacher. In the early 1930s, Züllig's decision to become a dancer defied common sense, as it violated social expectations for men in tradition-bound Switzerland. Consciously or not, his decision required great inner strength on the part of a youth in his teens. Züllig went to Essen, in Germany, to study with Sigurd Leeder and Kurt Jooss, whose connection with the principles of the Laban school and classical academic dance was of great importance to the young dancer.

So rapid was his progress that by 1935 Züllig had been appointed a soloist in Les Ballets Jooss, and over the next twelve years, until 1947, he danced with the troupe in its extended tours in the United States and South America. One of his most important roles was that of the Young Soldier in Jooss's *The Green Table.* Züllig also tried his hand at choreography, creating *Le Bosquet* in 1945. In 1948–1949 he danced as a soloist with the Sadler's Wells Theatre Ballet in London, and from 1949 to 1952 he was a soloist with the Folkwang Tanztheater in Essen.

In 1954, having ceased performing but still residing in Essen, Züllig began teaching at the Folkwang Schule, which was directed by Jooss. In 1956 he was engaged as teacher, dancer, and choreographer at the Universidad de Santiago de Chile, where Ernst Uthoff had been promoting the technique and work of Jooss for more than a decade. After several years in South America, Züllig returned to Europe in 1961 and resumed teaching at the Folkwang Schule, where in 1969 he was offered the post of director.

Züllig's path as a dancer was perhaps unusual for a Swiss, but his activity as a teacher of dance was in accord with a fundamental Swiss tradition, that of human development as defined by the great Swiss educator Heinrich Pestalozzi. Contrary to the Swiss impulse toward conformity, Pestalozzi sought to shape students by discovering and developing their inner strengths and abilities rather than by pressing them into an externally imposed mold. As a teacher of dance, Züllig always sought to awaken and release the inner impulses of his students, although he demanded—persistently, rigorously, and critically—that such impulses be shaped and directed with precision and not merely be allowed to burst forth haphazardly. Thus, his system of training was not aimed primarily at developing a specific style but rather at mastering body movement that, corresponding to anatomy, was functionally correct and harmoniously free. The results of his theories of teaching can be seen in the work of his students, such as Pina Bausch and Susanne Linke, who became professional dancers and choreographers.

BIBLIOGRAPHY

Barker, J. Stuart. "Ballets Jooss, 1953." *Dance and Dancers* (April 1953): 8–9.

Bartelt, Martin. "Hans Züllig." *Tanz International* 4 (February 1993): 12–15.

Pastori, Jean-Pierre. *Dance and Ballet in Switzerland.* Translated by Jacqueline Gartmann. 2d ed., rev. and enl. Zurich, 1989.

Schmülling, Friedhelm. "Stil in der Sackgasse? Mit einter Uraufführung in der Folkwang-Hochschule." *Das Tanzarchiv* 17 (June 1969): 20–21.

RICHARD MERZ
Translated from German

ZULU DANCE. *See* South Africa, *article on* Indigenous Dance.

ZURICH BALLET. The Zurich Ballet is part of the artistic ensemble of the Zurich Opera House, the cultural center of Switzerland's largest city. For the past several decades, the company has often shown promise of establishing itself as a company of international stature, but it has consistently failed to fulfill that promise. Given the sound financial resources of the opera house, this failure has been all the more frustrating, as the management of the Opera has often seemed to hinder rather than to encourage development of the ballet company, through hasty and inappropriate decisions not governed by the needs of the Zurich dance scene. In 1996, however, with the appointment of Heinz Spoerli as artistic director of the company, the outlook for the future became much brighter.

The history of the Zurich Ballet seems to reflect the sin-obsessed, anti-dance spirit of the city, as if it were haunted by the gloomy ghost of the sixteenth-century Swiss reformer Huldrych Zwingli. From 1834 to 1890, the year the old municipal theater burned down, only sixty-nine ballet performances were staged, and most of these where guest performances by outside troupes. During the first fifty years of the new municipal theater, which was dedicated in 1891, there were only a few performances of a small number of ballets, among them the biblically based *Die Josephslegende,* the most frequently performed work of all. Given a strait-laced public, it is hardly surprising that the popularity of dance was slow to develop in Zurich.

Because of the presence of the school of Rudolf Laban, Zurich became a center of the European modern dance movement in the years just before and during World War I, but the municipal theater continued to present mainly operas and operettas. Ballet was hardly ever seen. From 1934 to 1938, Pino and Pia Mlakar, both of whom were students of Laban, served as ballet directors at the Zurich Opera, and they did some significant work, including *The Devil in the Village* (1935) and *The Ballad of Medieval Love* (1937), both set to the music of the Yugoslav composer Fran Lhotka. Thereafter, during the years of World War II, ballet activity virtually ceased.

ZURICH BALLET. Using music by Giselher Klebe and a libretto by Tatjana Gsovsky, Jaroslav Berger staged *Menagerie* for the company in the early 1950s. Scenery and costumes were designed by Max Rothlisberger. (Photograph by Marka; reprinted from Horst Koegler, *Ballett International,* Berlin, 1960.)

A series of ballet masters after World War II included Hans Macke, Jaroslav Berger, and Robert Mayer, but none of them made the Zurich Ballet a major part of the cultural life of the city. Zurich enjoyed its first full flowering of ballet under Nicholas Beriozoff, who was appointed artistic director in 1964. With a well-trained troupe led by the English ballerina Gaye Fulton, Beriozoff gradually built up an impressive repertory including classical and Romantic ballets as well as modern full-length works of his own choreography. After Beriozoff's departure in 1971, a lack of direction led the Opera management to engage Rudolf Nureyev to mount an expensive production of *Raymonda* (1972), in which the company's internal crisis of purposelessness was only too apparent. The next few years saw a return to instability, as another series of ballet masters—Michel Descombey (1971–1973), Geoffrey Cauley (1973–1975), and Hans Meister and Jürg Burth (1975–1978)—assumed the directorship of the company.

In 1978, the Zurich Ballet entered a new, fruitful phase when the American dancer and ballet mistress Patricia Neary assumed direction of the company. She quickly began to build a repertory of neoclassical ballets by George Balanchine, many of which had never before been danced in Europe, in addition to well-known, evening-length story ballets. Of the former, Balanchine's *Stravinsky Violin Concerto* was a notable success; of the latter, the most popular was Heinz Spoerli's production of *Giselle,* staged in 1980 with Birgit Keil and Jonas Kåge in the leading roles. Together with her sister Coleen, who served as the company's ballet mistress, Patricia Neary helped the troupe achieve a new technical standard, which was evident in its performances of Nureyev's *Manfred* and *Don Quixote* while on tour in the United States in 1985. But apparently the Zurich Opera administration wanted something different. While Neary was still in the United States, she received word that her contract would not be extended.

Uwe Scholz, a young and inexperienced choreographer from Stuttgart, assumed the post of ballet director in the fall of 1985. This meant yet one more change for a troupe that for almost a decade before Neary's arrival had experienced many changes of leadership. Thus, another line of artistic development of the Zurich Ballet was interrupted, and the company once again faced an uncertain future.

Under Scholz, the repertory consisted largely of his own works, which displayed his skill for external brilliance, for glossy, virtuoso dancing, and for overwhelming scenic effects. Although these qualities were achieved at the cost of true artistic design and inner substance, Scholz's works found favor with the Zurich public. He remained in the post until the end of the 1990/91 season.

In 1991, Bernd Roger Bienert was appointed director of the company, and with him the Zurich Ballet once again found itself being led by a young artist with little experience in choreographing for a large troupe of dancers and no experience at all in directing a ballet company. For five years, the situation of the Zurich Ballet was difficult, both onstage and offstage. Binert's chief achievement was to bring Millicent Hodson and Kenneth Archer to Zurich to stage their brilliant reconstructions of Vaslav Nijinsky's *Le Sacre du Printemps* and Jean Börlin's *Skating Rink.* Binert left his post at the end of the 1995/96 season.

The current director of the Zurich Ballet is Heinz Spoerli, who is without question Switzerland's leading choreographer and ballet master. Soon after assuming his post in the fall of 1996 he staged his *Goldberg Variations* and then his fourth version of *A Midsummer Night's Dream,* which were both critical and popular successes. These works, one hopes, signal the beginning of a new era of high artistic achievement for the Zurich Ballet.

[*See also* Switzerland *and the entries on the principal figures mentioned herein.*]

BIBLIOGRAPHY

Bickel, Wilhelm. *100 Jahre Zürcher Stadttheater.* Zurich, 1934.

Pastori, Jean-Pierre. "The Emancipation of Dance in the Municipal Theatres." *Ballett International* 10 (June 1987): 12–18.

Pastori, Jean-Pierre. *Dance and Ballet in Switzerland.* Translated by Jacqueline Gartmann. 2d ed., rev. and enl. Zurich, 1989.

Rüegg, Reinhold. *Die Ersten fünfzig Jahre Zürcher Stadttheater, 1834–1884.* Zurich, 1925.

Scheier, Helmut. "Architecture and Choreography." *Ballett International / Tanz Aktuell* (May 1995): 32–37.

Sorell, Walter. "Watershedding the Arts." *Dance Magazine* (December 1986): 48–53.

Vollmer, Horst. "Direktorenkarussell." *Tanz und Gymnastik* 51.3 (1995): 42–46.

Whyte, Sally. "Towards a Company Style." *Dance and Dancers* (October 1987): 29–30.

Richard Merz
Translated from German

ALPHABETICAL LIST OF ENTRIES

Baylis, Nadine
Susan Au

Beaton, Cecil
Susan Au

Beatty, Talley
Melanye White-Dixon

Beauchamps, Pierre
Régine Astier

Beaujoyeulx, Balthazar de
Margaret M. McGowan

Beaumont, Cyril W.
Katherine M. Adelman

Beck, Hans
Allan Fridericia

Beck-Friis, Regina
Anna Greta Ståhle

Bedells, Phyllis
Beth Eliot Genné

Bedouin Dance
Ammon Shiloah

Beethoven, Ludwig van
Horst Koegler

Behle, Anna
Anna Greta Ståhle

Béjart, Maurice
Marie-Françoise Christout

Belarus
Yulia M. Churko

Belgium
Theatrical Dance
Luc Vervaeke
Dance Education
Luc Vervaeke

Belize
Carol Jenkins

Bellona
Jane Mink Rossen

Belsky, Igor
Arkady A. Sokolov-Kaminsky

Benesh Movement Notation
Tania Inman

Bennett, Michael
Camille Hardy

Bennington School of the Dance
Sali Ann Kiregsman

Benois, Alexandre
John E. Bowlt

Benserade, Isaac de
Marie-Françoise Christout

Berain, Jean
Jérôme de La Groce

Bérard, Christian
Peter Williams

Beretta, Caterina
Claudia Celi

Bergamasque
Emma Lewis Thomas

Berger, Augustin
Vladimír Vašut

Beriosova, Svetlana
Mary Clarke

Beriozoff, Nicholas
Horst Koegler

Berk, Fred
Judith Brin Ingber

Berkeley, Busby
Nancy Becker Schwartz

Berlin Opera Ballet
Horst Koegler

Berman, Eugene
John E. Bowlt

Berners, Lord
Noël Goodwin

Bernstein, Leonard
George Dorris,
Kenneth LaFave

Berry Brothers
Rusty E. Frank

Bessmertnova, Natalia
Alexander P. Demidov

Bettis, Valerie
Thomas Connors

Bey, Hannelore
Hartmut Regitz

Bharata Nāṭyam
Ritha Devi

Bhutan
Lin Lerner

Biagi, Vittorio
Monique Babsky

Bias, Fanny
Monique Babsky

Bibiena Family
Gerald L. Carr

Bible, Dance in the
Mayer I. Gruber

Biches, Les
Gunhild Oberzaucher-Schüller

Big Apple
Cynthia R. Millman

Bigottini, Émilie
Monique Babsky

Billy the Kid
Reba Ann Adler

Bintley, David
Cormac Rigby

Bjørnsson, Fredbjørn
Erik Aschengreen

Blache Family
Monique Babsky

Blacher, Boris
Horst Koegler

Black Crook, The
Camille Hardy

Black Hat Dance
Lin Lerner

Blair, David
Barbara Newman

Blangy, Hermine
Mary Grace Swift

Blank, Gustav
Horst Koegler

Blasis, Carlo
Alberto Testa

Blaska, Félix
Monique Babsky

Bliss, Arthur
Noël Goodwin

Blok, Lubov
Tim Scholl

Blondy, Michel
Régine Astier

Bluebell, Miss
George Perry

Blum, René
Kathrine Sorley Walker

Bodenwieser, Gertrud
Gabriele Schacherl

Bodenwieser Technique
Denise Puttock

Bodin, Louise
Gunhild Oberzaucher-Schüller

Body Therapies
An Overview
Margaret Pierpont
Alexander Technique
Lucy Venable
Bartenieff Fundamentals
Peggy Hackney
Feldenkrais Method
Norma Leistiko
Ideokinesis
Irene Dowd

Skinner Releasing Technique
Robert W. Davidson

Bogdanov Family
Valelry A. Kulakov

Bolender, Todd
William James Lawson

Bolero
Javier Suárez-Pajares

Bolger, Ray
Dawn Lille Horwitz

Bolm, Adolph
Lynn Garafola

Bolshoi Ballet
Elizabeth Souritz

Bonfanti, Marie
Barbara Barker

Bon Odori
Judy Van Zile

Boquet, Louis
Jérôme de La Gorce

Borchsenius, Valborg
Erik Aschengreen

Boris, Ruthanna
Leland Windreich

Borovansky, Edouard
Geoffrey William Hutton

Borri, Pasquale
Claudia Celi

Bosl, Heinz
Horst Koegler

Boston Ballet
Doris Hering

Bourdelle, Émile-Antoine
Susan Au

Bournonville, Antoine
Alan Fridericia

Bournonville, August
Patricia McAndrew

Bournonville Composers
Knud Arne Jürgensen

Bourrée
Meredith Ellis Little

Bovt, Violetta
Galina V. Inozemtseva

Bowman, Patricia
Ann Barzel

Boyarchikov, Nikolai
Natalia Y. Chernova

Brabants, Jeanne
Luc Vervaeke

Bradley, Buddy
Brenda Dixon Gottschild

Branle
Julia Sutton

Bravo, Guillermina
Alberto Dallal

Brazil
Ritual and Popular Dance
Morton Marks
Ballet
Katia Canton,
Marilía de Andrade
Modern Dance
Katia Canton
Dance Research and Publication
Katia Canton,
Marília de Andrade

Break Dancing
Sally Banes

Brenaa, Hans
Ebbe Mørk

Briantzev, Dmitri
Elizabeth Souritz

Brianza, Carlotta
Debra Hickenlooper Sowell

Brinson, Peter
Selma Jeanne Cohen

Brno Ballet
Vladimír Vašut

Brown, Carolyn
David Vaughan

Brown, Trisha
Sally Banes

Bruce, Christopher
Stephanie A. Jordan,
Bonnie Rowell

Bruhn, Erik
Erik Aschengreen

Bubbles, John W.
Jane Goldberg

Bugaku
William P. Malm

Bulgaria
Folk and Traditional Dance
Anna Ilieva
Theatrical Dance
Violetta Konsulova

Bunraku
Samuel L. Leiter

Burgmüller, Friedrich
Ole Nørlyng

Burmeister, Vladimir
Nikolai I. Elyash

Butler, John
Kitty Cunningham

Butō
Hasegawa Roku

Butsova, Hilda
Katy Matheson

Byrd, Donald
Robert Greskovic

Cage, John
Roy M. Close

Cajun Dance Traditions
Jerry C. Duke

Cakewalk
Brenda Dixon Gottschild

Callot, Jacques
Jeffrey Blanchard

Camargo, Marie
Régine Astier

Cambodia
Amy Catlin

Cameroon
Hansel Ndumbe Eyoh

Campra, André
Jérôme de La Gorce

Canada
Folk and Traditional Dance in French Canada
Ellen Shifrin
Theatrical Dance
Max Wyman
Contemporary Theatrical Dance
Iro Valaskakis Tembek
Dance Education
MaryJane Warner
Dance Research and Publication
Evan Alderson

Canary
Julia Sutton

Can-Can
Marie-Françoise Christout

Canfield
Carolyn Brown

Cannabich, Christian
Ole Nørlyng

Canziani, Guiseppe
Caludia Celi

CAPAB Ballet
Marina Grut

Capoeira
Iria d'Aquino

Caractères de la Danse, Les
Jeannine Dorvane

Carey Family
Susan Au

Caribbean Region
Jan Michael Hanvik

Caricature and Comic Art
Susan Au

Carmagnole, La
Jeannine Dorvane

Carnaval, Le
Suzanne Carbonneau

Caroso, Fabritio
Julia Sutton

Cascarda
Julia Sutton

Castanets
Matteo

Castle, Irene and Vernon
Iris M. Fanger

Catarina
Susan Au

Caverley, Thomas
Richard Ralph

Cébron, Jean
Horst Koegler

Cecchetti, Enrico
Claudia Celi

Céleste, Madame
Nancy Reynolds

Central and East Africa
Andrée Grau

Cerrito, Fanny
Susan Au

Chabukiani, Vakhtang
Éteri A. Dumbadze

Chaconne and Passacaille
Rebecca Harris-Warrick

Chain and Round Dances
Lisbet Torp

Chaki-Sircar, Manjusri
Sunil Kothari

Chalon, Alfred
Susan Au

Chandralekha
Sunil Kothari

Chandrashekhar, C. V.
Sunil Kothari

Chappell, William
Peter Williams

Character Dancing
Susan Au

Charisse, Cyd
Larry Billman

Charleroi/Danses
Luc Vervaeke

Charlip, Remy
Christopher Caines

Charrat, Janine
Irène Lidova

Chase, Lucia
Thomas Connors

Chauviré, Yvette
Irène Lidova

Checkmate
David Vaughan

Cheironomia
Libby Smigel

Chen Weiya
Ou Jian-ping

Chhau
Farley Richmond

Childs, Lucinda
Sally Banes

Chile
Folk and Traditional Dance
Raquel Barros Aldunate
Theatrical Dance
Luz Marmentini
Dance Research and Publication
Hans Ehrmann

China
An Overview
A. C. Scott
Folk and Minority Dance
Xu Suyin
Dance in Opera
Sophia Delza
Classical Dance
Lu Wenjian
Contemporary Theatrical Dance
Ou Jian-ping
Dance Research and Publication
Ou Jian-ping, Zhu Liren

Chiriaeff, Ludmilla
Claude Conyers

Chladek, Rosalia
Alfred Oberzaucher

Chladek Technique
Eva Selzer

Ch'oi Seung-hee
Alan C. Heyman

Choral Dancing
William Mullen

Cho T'aek-won
Alan C. Heyman

Sardana
PHILIPPA HEALE

Sardono
EDWARD HERBST

Sarukkai, Malavika
SUNIL KOTHARI

Satie, Erik
ROGER SHATTUCK

Sauguet, Henri
BAIRD HASTINGS

Savignano, Luciana
VITTORIA OTTOLENGHI

Scala Ballet
LUIGI ROSSI

Scapino Rotterdam
INE RIETSTAP

Scènes de Ballet
ALASTAIR MACAULAY

Scenic Design
ARNOLD ARONSON

Schall, Claus
OLE NØRLYNG

Schanne, Margrethe
HENRIK LUNDGREN

Schaufuss Family
ERIK ASCHENGREEN

Schayk, Toer van
LUUK UTRECHT

Schéhérazade
SUZANNE CARBONNEAU

Schēma
LIBBY SMIGEL

Schilling, Tom
HARTMUT REGITZ

Schneitzhoeffer, Jean
OLE NØRLYNG

Schollar, Ludmilla
LYNN GARAFOLA

Schönberg, Bessie
DEBORAH JOWITT

Schooling, Elisabeth
BARBARA NEWMAN

Schoop, Trudi
RICHARD MERZ

Schuman, William
GEORGE DORRIS

Schwarz Family
MONIQUE BABSKY

Scott, Margaret
GEOFFREY WILLIAM HUTTON

Scottish Ballet
GEOFFREY WEST

Seguidillas
PHILIPPA HEALE

Semenova, Marina
VALERIA I. URALSKAYA

Sen, Saswati
SUNIL KOTHARI

Seraphic Dialogue
DEBORAH JOWITT

Seregi, Lázló
GÉZA KÖRTVÉYLES

Serenade
REBA ANN ADLER

Sergeyev, Konstantin
VALENTINA V. PROKHOROVA

Serrano, Lupe
PATRICIA BARNES

Setterfield, Valda
AMANDA SMITH

Seymour, Lynn
CLEMENT CRISP

Shaker Dance
SUZANNE YOUNGERMAN

Shakers, The
MARCIA B. SIEGEL

Shamanism
THERESA KI-JA KIM

Shangana-Tsonga Dance
THOMAS F. JOHNSTON

Shankar, Uday
JOAN L. ERDMAN

Sharma, Uma
SUNIL KOTHARI

Sharp, Cecil
URSULA VAUGHAN WILLIAMS

Shawn, Ted
CHRISTENA L. SCHLUNDT

Shchedrin, Rodion
ELENA N. KURILENKO

Shearer, Moira
BARBARA NEWMAN

Shearer, Sybil
ANN BARZEL

Shigeyama Family
JONAH SALZ

Shimai
CARL WOLZ

Shishimai
SAMUEL L. LEITER

Shostakovich, Dmitri
MICHAEL OLIVER

Shurale
GALINA A. GULAYAEVA

Sibley, Antoinette
BARBARA NEWMAN

Siddiqui, Nahid
SHAYMA SAIYID

Sikinnis
LIBBY SMIGEL

Sikkim
ELIZABETH GOLDBLATT

Simone, Kirsten
CLAUDE CONYERS

Sims, Sandman
SALLY R. SOMMER

Singh, Bipin
SUNIL KOTHARI

Siretta, Dan
DAVID VAUGHAN

Sitara Devi
SUNIL KOTHARI

Skeaping, Mary
PETER BRINSON

Skibine, George
IRÈNE LIDOVA

Skirt Dance
MARTIE FELLOM

Slavenska, Mia
GEORGE JACKSON

Sleeping Beauty, The
Petipa Production
VERA M. KRASOVSKAYA
Later Productions
SUSAN AU

Slonimsky, Yuri
OLEG A. PETROV

Slovak National Theater Ballet
VLADIMÍR VAŠUT

Smith, George Washington
SUSAN AU

Smith, Oliver
CLAUDIA ROTH PIERPONT

Šmok, Pavel
VLADIMÍR VAŠUT

Snoek, Hans
INE RIETSTAP

Social Dance
Court and Social Dance before 1800
INGRID BRAINARD
Nineteenth-Century Social Dance
GRETCHEN SCHNEIDER
Twentieth-Century Social Dance to 1960
DON MCDONAGH
Twentieth-Century Social Dance since 1960
SALLY R. SOMMER

Sokolova, Lydia
JOAN ACOCELLA

Sokolow, Anna
DARCY HALL

Soloviev, Yuri
ARKADY A. SOKOLOV-KAMINSKY

Somes, Michael
BARBARA NEWMAN

Somnambule, La
SUSAN AU

Sonnambula, La
SUSAN AU

Soudeikine, Serge
JOHN E. BOWLT

Souritz, Elizabeth
SELMA JEANNE COHEN

South Africa
Indigenous Dance
ANDRÉE GRAU
Ballet
MARINA GRUT
Contemporary Theatrical Dance
ADRIENNE SICHEL

Southern Africa
JOHN BLACKING

Spagnoletta
JULIA SUTTON

Spain
Dance Traditions before 1700
LYNN MATLUCK BROOKS
Social and Theatrical Dance, 1700–1862
PHILIPPA HEALE
Theatrical Dance since 1862
LAURA KUMIN
Dance Research and Publication
NÈLIDA MONÉS I MESTRE, MARTA CARRASCO BENÍTEZ

Šparemblek, Milko
PIA MLAKAR

Spartacus
VICTOR V. VANSLOV

Spessivtseva, Olga
JEANNINE DORVANE

Spindrift
ANGELA KANE

Spoerli, Heinz
RICHARD MERZ

SYNOPTIC OUTLINE OF CONTENTS

[The outline presented on the following pages is intended to provide a general view of the conceptual scheme of this encyclopedia. Entries are arranged into nine major conceptual categories. To show the various components of the encyclopedia's coverage, each of these major categories is subdivided into a variety of sections. Because the headings for each category are not necessarily mutually exclusive, some entries in the encyclopedia are listed more than once. In general, biographical entries have been excluded because they are so numerous, except where a particular group is worthy of special mention.]

I LANDS AND PEOPLES

[*Part I of the outline is divided into two sections by broad geographical locations:* Lands *and* Peoples. *The first section presents a geographical listing of country articles; the second section focuses on the encyclopedia's coverage of specific cultural groups.*]

LANDS

Europe

Albania
Austria
- Theatrical Dance

Belarus
Belgium
- Theatrical Dance

Bulgaria
- Folk and Traditional Dance
- Theatrical Dance

Crete
- Dance in Ancient Crete
- Dance in Modern Crete

Czech Republic and Slovak Republic
- Folk and Traditional Dance
- Theatrical Dance

Denmark
- Traditional and Social Dance
- Dance in the Faeroe Islands
- Theatrical Dance

Estonia
Finland
- Traditional Dance
- Theatrical Dance
- Dance Research and Publication

France
- Recreational Dance
- Theatrical Dance, 1581–1789
- Theatrical Dance, 1789–1914
- Ballet since 1914
- Modern Dance before 1970
- Modern Dance since 1970

Germany
- Traditional and Social Dance
- Theatrical Dance, 1600–1945
- Theatrical Dance since 1945

Great Britain
- English Traditional Dance
- Scottish Folk and Traditional Dance
- Welsh Folk and Traditional Dance
- Manx Folk and Traditional Dance
- Theatrical Dance, 1560–1660
- Theatrical Dance, 1660–1772
- Theatrical Dance, 1772–1850
- Theatrical Dance since 1850
- Modern Dance

Greece
- Dance in Ancient Greece
- Dance in the Roman and Byzantine Period
- Dance in Modern Greece
- Ritual and Carnival Dance Traditions

Hungary
- Traditional and Popular Dance
- Theatrical Dance before World War II
- Theatrical Dance since World War II
- Modern Dance

Iceland
- Traditional Dance
- Theatrical Dance

Ireland
- Traditional Dance
- Theatrical Dance

Italy
- Dance Traditions before 1800
- Theatrical Dance, 1801–1940
- Theatrical Dance since 1940

Latvia
Lithuania
- Traditional Dance
- Theatrical Dance

Moldova
Netherlands
- Folk and Traditional Dance
- Social Dance
- Theatrical Dance before 1900
- Theatrical Dance, 1900–1945
- Theatrical Dance since 1945

Norway
- Folk, Traditional, and Social Dance
- Theatrical Dance before 1919
- Theatrical Dance, 1920–1958
- Theatrical Dance since 1958

Portugal
- Traditional Dance
- Theatrical Dance

Roman Empire
Romania
- Folk Dance
- Theatrical Dance

Russia
- Traditional Dance
- Theatrical Dance before 1917
- Theatrical Dance since 1917
- Secondary and Provincial Dance Companies
- Twentieth-Century Plastique

Spain
- Theatrical Dance before 1700
- Theatrical Dance, 1700–1862

Sweden
- Traditional Dance
- Theatrical Dance before 1771
- Theatrical Dance, 1771–1900
- Theatrical Dance since 1900
- Court Theaters

Switzerland
Ukraine
- Traditional Dance
- Theatrical Dance

Yugoslavia
- Traditional Dance
- Ballet
- Modern Dance
- Theatrical Dance since 1991

North Africa and Middle East

PRINCIPAL ARTICLES

Arabian Peninsula
Middle East
- An Overview

North Africa

SUPPORTING ARTICLES

Algeria
Egypt
- Dance in Ancient Egypt
- Traditional Dance
- Contemporary Dance Companies

Iran
Israel
- An Overview
- Ethnic Dance

Lebanon
Mesopotamia
Morocco
Turkey
Yemen

Sub-Saharan Africa

PRINCIPAL ARTICLES

Sub-Saharan Africa
- An Overview
- Popular Dance

West Africa
Central and East Africa
Southern Africa

SUPPORTING ARTICLES

Cameroon
Ethiopia
Ghana
- An Overview

II RITUAL AND RELIGION

[*Part II of the outline focuses on the role of religion and ritual in dance. The* Lands *and* Peoples *listed here are particularly rich in ritual dance traditions. It is important to note that some forms originated as rituals and over time became secularized; other forms began as celebrations and festivals that in turn became expressions of popular culture. Therefore, for additional discussion, see the* Folk and Traditional Dance *articles as well as the entries under* Festivals and Masquerades *listed in part III of this outline; and the* Dance Drama, Mask Dance Theater, and Puppetry *entries listed in part V. For related information, see* Aesthetics; Costume in African Traditions; Costume in Asian Traditions; European Traditional Dance; Mask and Makeup, *articles on* African Traditions *and* Asian Traditions.]

III FOLK, TRADITIONAL, AND POPULAR DANCE, FESTIVALS AND MASQUERADES

[*To describe the myriad ways people gather to dance and celebrate, part III of this outline is divided into three sections. The first section presents the encyclopedia's coverage of the rich diversity of world folk and traditional dance; the second section focuses on popular dance; the third section outlines a variety of celebrations that involve dance.*]

FOLK AND TRADITIONAL DANCE

SOCIAL AND POPULAR DANCE

FESTIVALS AND MASQUERADES

IV HISTORY OF WESTERN DANCE TO 1800

[*Part IV of the synoptic outline is divided into three sections to describe the history of dance in the ancient Mediterranean world and the development of Western court, social, and theatrical forms. For historical information on dance in non-western regions, see individual country entries.*]

ANCIENT MEDITERRANEAN WORLD

PRINCIPAL ARTICLES

SUPPORTING ARTICLES

EUROPE: MIDDLE AGES AND RENAISSANCE

PRINCIPAL ARTICLES

LANDS

[*Virtually every European country entry contains discussion on dance in the Middle Ages and Renaissance.*]

SUPPORTING ARTICLES

L'Abbé, Anthony
La Fontaine, Mademoiselle de
Lany Family
Lauchery, Étienne
Laval, Antoine Bandieri de
Le Picq, Charles
Lestang, Anne-Louis
Louis XIV
Lully, Jean-Baptiste
Lyonnois, Marie-Françoise
Marcel, François
Milon, Louis
Molière
Mouret, Jean-Joseph
Noverre, Jean-Georges
Pecour, Guillaume-Louis
Pirot, Antoine-Bonaventure
Placide, Alexandre
Playford, John
Prévost, Françoise
Price Family
Priest, Josiah
Purcell, Henry
Rameau, Jean-Philippe
Rameau, Pierre
Rich, John
Rinaldi, Antonio
Rodolphe, Jean-Joseph
Saint-André, Adrien Merger de
Sallé, Marie
Santlow, Hester
Subligny, Marie-Thérèse
Starzer, Joseph
Taglioni Family
Tomlinson, Kellom
Valberkh, Ivan
Vestris Family
Viganò, Salvatore
Violette, Eva Maria
Weaver, John

V THEATRICAL DANCE

[Part V of this outline presents the encyclopedia's coverage of the diversity of theatrical dance found throughout the world. It is arranged in two broad sections. The first section outlines ballet and contemporary theatrical dance; the second section focuses on non-western dance drama, mask dance theater, and puppetry. For further discussion of theatrical dance on a country-by-country basis, see the Lands section in part I of this synoptic outline. For related information on dance dramas and mask dance theater, see also Ritual and Religion *in part II of the outline and the entries under* Festivals and Masquerades *in part III. See also the encyclopedia's index for extensive coverage of dance companies, theatrical dance works, and entries on performers and choreographers.]*

BALLET AND CONTEMPORARY THEATRICAL DANCE

PRINCIPAL ARTICLES

Ballet Technique
- Major Schools
- Feet Positions
- Body Positions
- Directions
- Turning Movements
- Linking Movements
- Jumping Movements

Ballet Technique, History of
- French Court Dance
- Ballet in the Late Eighteenth- and Early-Nineteenth Centuries
- Ballet from the Mid-Nineteenth Century

Modern Dance Technique

SUPPORTING ARTICLES

Adage
Allegro
American Dance Festival
Arabesque
Attitude
Avant-garde Dance
Ausdruckstanz
Ballet Competitions
Battement
Batterie
Bauhaus, Dance and the
Bennington School of Dance
Bodenwieser Technique
Butō
Character Dancing
Chladek Technique
Costume in Western Traditions
- Modern Dance

Delsarte System of Expression
Folkwang Tanzstudio
Genres of Western Theatrical Dance
Grand Union
Jacob's Pillow
Judson Dance Theater
Mazurka
Movement Choir
New Dance Group
Partnering
Pas de Deux
Plié
Pointe Work
Rond de Jambe
Technical Manuals
- Publications, 1765–1859
- Publications since 1887

Travesty
Turnout
- Physical Mechanics
- History and Aesthetics

Wiesenthal Technique

DANCE DRAMA, MASK DANCE THEATER, AND PUPPETRY

PRINCIPAL ARTICLES

Asian Dance Traditions
- An Overview
- The Influence of Puppetry

China
- Dance in Opera

Indonesia
- Balinese Dance Theater
- Balinese Mask Dance Theater

Japan
- An Overview

India
- An Overview

Korea
- Masked Dance Theater

Mask and Makeup
- Asian Traditions

SUPPORTING ARTICLES

Baris
Bharata Nāṭyam
Black Hat Dance, The
Bugaku
Bunraku
Chhau
Geisha Dance
Gigaku
Hōshō School

Japanese Traditional Schools
Kabuki Theater
Kanze School
Kathak
Kathakaḷi
Kita School
Khōn
Kongō School
Konparu School
Kuchipudi
Kyōgen
Kuchipudi
Kūtiyāṭṭam
Kṛṣṇāṭṭam
Lakhǫn
Légong
Manōhrā
Mayong
Monhiniāṭṭam
Mudrā
Music For Dance
Asian Traditions
Nō
Oḍissi
Onnagata
Pencak
Shimai
Shishimai
Tinikling
Ves Dance
Wayang
Yakṣagāna
Williams, Petr
Worsaae, Jens-Jacob

VI ELEMENTS OF THEATRICAL DANCE

[*Part VI of this outline focuses on the encyclopedia's entries describing some of the basic components that go into the presentation of dance in a theatrical context. It is arranged in five sections:*
Costume Design
Theater, Stage, Scenery, and Lighting Design
Texts for Dance
Documenting Dance
Impresarios, Patrons, and Producers
See also the encyclopedia's index for extensive coverage of individual choreographers and performers.]

COSTUME DESIGN

PRINCIPAL ARTICLES
Costume in Asian Traditions
Costume in Western Traditions
An Overview
Modern Dance
Film and Popular Dance

SUPPORTING ARTICLES
Artists and Dance
Artists and Dance, 1760–1929
Artists and Dance, 1930–1945
Artists and Dance since 1945
Collaboration
Bauhaus, Dance and the
Designing for Dance
Footwear
Mask and Makeup
Asian Traditions
Western Traditions
Practice Clothes
Tutu

DESIGNERS
Bakst, Léon
Baylis, Nadine
Benois, Alexandre
Berain, Jean
Boquet, Louis
Charlip, Remy
Cocteau, Jean
Dmitriev, Vladimir
Edel, Alfredo
Fedorovitch, Sophie
Georgiadis, Nicholas
Gissey, Henry
Golovin, Aleksandr
Goncharova, Natalia
Jones, Inigo
Karinska, Barbara
Lami, Eugène Louis
Larionov, Mikhail
Lecomte, Hippolyte
Loquasto, Santo
Messel, Oliver
Picasso, Pablo
Rose, Jürgen
Soudeikine, Serge
Virsaladze, Simon
Wilhelm, C.

THEATER, STAGE, SCENERY, AND LIGHTING DESIGN

SUPPORTING ARTICLES
Artists and Dance
Artists and Dance, 1760–1929
Artists and Dance, 1930–1945
Artists and Dance since 1945
Collaboration
Designing for Dance
Hanamichi
Lighting for Dance
Historical Overview
Theory and Practice
Orchestra
Scenic Design
Theaters for Dance

DESIGNERS
Appia, Adolphe
Bakst, Léon
Baylis, Nadine
Beaton, Cecil
Benois, Alexandre
Berain, Jean
Bérard, Christian
Berman, Eugene
Bibiena Family
Boquet, Louis
Chappell, William
Charlip, Remy
Ciceri, Pierre
Cocteau, Jean
Craig, Gordon
Dmitriev, Vladimir
Dobujinsky, Mstislav
Edel, Alredo
Fedorovitch, Sophie
Georgiadis, Nicholas
Golovin, Aleksandr
Goncharova, Natalia
Hugo, Jean
Johns, Jasper
Jones, Inigo
Korovin, Konstantin
Larionov, Mikhail
Lauterer, Arch
Leventhal, Valery
Loquasto, Santo
Messel, Oliver
Noguchi, Isamu
Picasso, Pablo
Rauschenberg, Robert

Roerich, Nikolai
Rose, Jürgen
Rosenthal, Jean
Sanquirico, Alessandro
Schayk, Toer van
Smith, Oliver
Soudeikine, Serge
Tchelitchev, Pavel
Ter-Arutunian, Rouben
Virsaladze, Simon
Wilhelm, C.
Williams, Petr
Wilson, Robert
Worsaae, Jens-Jacob

TEXTS FOR DANCE

LIBRETTI

Jidaimono
Libretti for Dance
- Sixteenth- and Seventeenth-Century Libretti
- Eighteenth-Century Libretti
- Nineteenth- and Twentieth-Century Libretti

Nātyaśāstra

BIOGRAPHIES

Arnould-Mussot, Jean-François
Cocteau, Jean
Gautier, Théophile
Leventhal, Valery

DOCUMENTING DANCE

Benesh Movement Notation
Feuillet Notation
Film and Video
- Documenting Dance
- Ethnographic Studies
- Choreography for Camera

Guest, Ann Hutchinson
Kunst, Albrecht
Laban, Rudolf
Labanotation
Laban Principles of Movement Analysis
Loring, Eugene
Notation
Photography
Reconstruction
- Use of Historical Notations
- Use of Modern Scores
- Beyond Notation

Saint-Léon Notation
Stepanov Notation
Television
- Dance on Television in Canada
- Dance on Television in Europe
- Dance on Television in the United States

Zorn Notation

IMPRESARIOS, PATRONS, AND PRODUCERS

Berk, Fred
Blum, René
Chappell, William
Craig, Gordon
Diaghilev, Serge
Dmitriev, Vladimir
Gallini, Giovanni
Hilverding, Franz
Hurok, Sol
Kiralfy Family
Kronstam, Henning
Louis XIV
Rubinstein, Ida
Saddler, Donald
Shankar, Uday
Slonimsky, Yuri
Smith, Oliver
Wilson, Robert
Wright, Peter

VII POPULAR ENTERTAINMENT

[*Part VII of this outline presents the encyclopedia's coverage of dance and Western media and popular entertainment. For discussion of specific forms of non-Western popular culture, see* Film Musicals, *article on* Bollywood; Tamasha; Takarazuka; *the entries found in part V of this outline,* Dance Drama, Mask Dance Theater, and Puppetry; *and the articles on other non-Western forms of dance. The line between art and popular entertainment is often hard to draw and many of the articles in the encyclopedia have broad appeal to the general public.*]

GENERAL ARTICLES

American Bandstand
Ballroom Dance Competition
Circus
Commedia dell'Arte
Costume in Western Traditions
- Film and Popular Dance

Dance Marathons
Dance as Sport
Film Musicals
- Hollywood Film Musicals

Ice Dancing
Mime
Music Hall
- British Traditions
- French Traditions

Pantomime
Radio City Music Hall
Red Shoes, The
Television
- Dance on Television in Canada
- Dance on Television in Europe
- Dance on Television in the United States

United States of America
- Musical Theater

Vaudeville

SUPPORTING ARTICLES

Aerobic Dance
Apache Dance
Attitude and Shawl Dance
Big Apple
Black Crook
Break Dancing
Cakewalk
Can-Can
Capoeira
Danse du Ventre
Fan Dancing
Flamenco Dance
Jazz Dance
Lindy Hop
Orientalism
Precision Dancing
Red Shoes
Samba
Skirt Dance
Tango
Tap Dance

BIOGRAPHIES

Amaya, Carmen
Antonio and Rosario
Argentina, La
Argentinita, La

VIII DANCE AND OTHER DISCIPLINES

[Part VIII of this outline presents the encyclopedia's coverage of the influence of dance on ancillary disciplines as well as how scholars and practioners have, in turn, been inspired by various forms of human movement. It is arranged in five sections:

Aesthetics, Philosophy, and Theory in Dance
Visual arts
Training and Education
Science and Health
Music

[For related discussion on dance theory, see Technical Manuals, *and for related discussion on visual arts, see* Designing for Dance.]

AESTHETICS, PHILOSOPHY, AND THEORY IN DANCE

PRINCIPAL ARTICLES

THEORISTS

VISUAL ARTS

GENERAL ARTICLES

ARTISTS AND DESIGNERS

TRAINING AND EDUCATION

LANDS

SUPPORTING ARTICLES

BIOGRAPHIES

IX DANCE RESEARCH AND PUBLICATION

[*Part IX of this outline is divided into two sections. The first section presents the encyclopedia's coverage of the history of research, writing, and publication; the second section focuses on the role of criticism in understanding dance.*]

DANCE CRITICISM

INDEX

Note: Volume numbers are printed in boldface type, followed by a colon and relevant page numbers. Page numbers printed in boldface indicate a major discussion; those in italics refer to illustrations.